Major Problems
in American History
Since 1945

MAJOR PROBLEMS IN AMERICAN HISTORY SERIES

GENERAL EDITOR

THOMAS G. PATERSON

Major Problems
in American History
Since 1945

DOCUMENTS AND ESSAYS

EDITED BY
ROBERT GRIFFITH
UNIVERSITY OF MARYLAND, COLLEGE PARK

D. C. HEATH AND COMPANY
Lexington, Massachusetts   Toronto

Address editorial correspondence to:

D. C. Heath
125 Spring Street
Lexington, MA 02173

For Matthew and Jonathan
and all the others like them
who will inherit the world their parents have created

Preface

We live at the end of an era in U.S. and world history. The "postwar era," the forty-five years bounded on one end by the atomic bombing of Hiroshima and Nagasaki in 1945 and on the other by the dismantling of the Berlin Wall in 1989, is over, and we have entered a new age. Yet the history of the recent past continues to influence our lives in ways both obvious and subtle. Only by understanding the recent past can we free ourselves from its burdens and become fully self-conscious actors in shaping our future. I hope that the documents and essays in this volume will contribute in some small measure to such an understanding.

The first five chapters of this book examine the origins and character of the early postwar era. The next eight chapters explore the series of crises that challenged the nation and its leaders during the 1960s and 1970s. The final two chapters focus on the 1980s and early 1990s—on the end of the postwar period and the beginning of a new historical era. The documents introduce the historical problem and highlight key issues, while the essays, by historians, economists, and other commentators, reveal how different interpretations can result from reading the same documents or observing the same phenomena. The chapter introductions and the headnotes to the documents and the essays place the readings in historical and interpretive perspective.

Because I have taught courses on the recent history of the United States for more than two decades, I was delighted to have this opportunity to prepare a collection of documents and essays that could be used in classes such as my own. The task proved both more fascinating and more challenging than I had anticipated. To begin with, it was difficult to decide which "problems" to highlight. While some topics in the recent era have attracted much attention from historians—the origins of the Cold War, for example—many others have not. At one point I thought, only half-jokingly, that the real "problems" of the recent era were War, Peace, Justice, Equality, Love, Beauty, Community, and so on, and that these should perhaps be the volume's principal subjects. In the end, I settled on somewhat more conventionally defined topics. But other questions arose. Which topics, essays, and documents should be included, and which left out? The contemporary character of so many of the topics also posed considerable difficulty. For example, coherent or settled "schools of thought" do not exist among historians for a number of the featured issues. In these cases, debates often reflect little more than current political opinion. Moreover, it is at times quite difficult, especially when dealing with the very recent past, to distinguish clearly between a document and an essay. In the end, I sought to include as many "voices" as possible in my choices of documents and essays, trusting to the reader to test them one against the other. I look forward to hearing suggestions as to what I should or should not include in future editions, and so I invite students and teachers alike to write me, care of the Office of the Dean, College of Arts and Humanities, University of Maryland at College Park.

Many people have helped in the preparation of this volume. When I began to work on it, I wrote to historians throughout the country, seeking their suggestions and advice. Many responded generously, among them John D. Bennett, David Bernstein, Roger Biles, Scott L. Bills, Thomas E. Blantz, William L. Burton, Robert Collins, David Conrad, John D'Emilio, John Dittmer, Timothy Donovan, David Farber, Henry Feneu, George Q. Flynn, Mary E. Frederickson, Richard M. Fried, Mark T. Gilderhus, Charles H. Glatfelter, Ross Gregory, Michael J. Hogan, Richard Immerman, Maurice Isserman, John W. Jeffries, Harold Josephson, Burton I. Kaufman, Warren F. Kimball, Walter LaFeber, R. Alton Lee, Nelson Lichtenstein, Arthur F. McClure, Robert J. McMahon, Kim McQuaid, Carl H. Marlow, William Howard Moore, J. R. Morice, Arnold Offner, Kenneth O'Reilly, James R. Parker, James T. Patterson, William E. Pemberton, Linda Reed, Gary W. Reichard, Howard Schonberger, Michael S. Sherry, Ellen W. Shrecker, Marcia G. Synott, Eugene M. Tobin, William Tuttle, R. E. Welch, Jr., Allan M. Winkler, Larry Wittner, and Howard Zinn. As the volume took shape, detailed written reviews were provided by Numan V. Bartley, University of Georgia; Roger Biles, Oklahoma State University; William Brinker, Tennessee Technological University; Rodney Carlisle, Rutgers University, Camden; John D'Emilio, University of North Carolina at Greensboro; Samuel Hand, University of Vermont; Susan Hartmann, Ohio State University; Gary May, University of Delaware; Philip I. Mitterling, University of Colorado, Boulder; Mary Beth Norton, Cornell University; Thomas G. Ryan, University of Northern Iowa; John Sharpless, University of Wisconsin, Madison; Philip W. Warken, United States Naval Academy; Theodore A. Wilson, University of Kansas.

I owe a special debt to old friends and colleagues at the University of Massachusetts at Amherst, among them Paula Baker, Joyce Berkman, David Glassberg, Bruce Laurie, Stephen Nissenbaum, Dick Minear, Larry Owens, Kathy Peiss, Ronald Story, and Jack Tager, as well as to new friends and colleagues at the University of Maryland at College Park, including James Gilbert, Donna Hamilton, Keith Olson, and Charles Rutherford. I want to thank Jon Griffith, Dan Nissenbaum, and Molly Rutherford for their assistance. I am especially grateful to Margaret Orelup, Gregory Field, and David Murphy, without whose dedicated efforts this project would never have been finished. I also wish to thank Diane West, Joan Wood, and all the others with whom I work, for their patience and forbearance during the final months of the project. Finally, I thank Thomas G. Paterson of the University of Connecticut, general editor of the Major Problems in American History series, and the editors at D. C. Heath who helped bring this project to completion: managing editor Sylvia Mallory, senior history editor James Miller, permissions editor Margaret Roll, and production editor Sarah Doyle.

R. G.

Contents

CHAPTER 1
World War II and the Origins of Postwar America
Page 1

ESSAYS

Thomas G. Paterson • The Origins of the Postwar International System   **3**

Alan Wolfe • The Roots of Postwar Politics   **20**

William H. Chafe • The Social Politics of Race and Gender   **31**

CHAPTER 2
The Decision to Drop the Atomic Bomb on Japan
Page 49

DOCUMENTS

President Harry S Truman's Advisers Discuss the Atomic Bomb, May 1945   **50**

Atomic Scientists Urge an Alternative Course, June 1945   **51**

U.S. Science Advisers Endorse Dropping the Bomb, June 1945   **53**

General Leslie Groves Reports on a Successful Test, July 1945   **54**

President Truman Discusses the Bomb at Potsdam, July 1945   **55**

A Japanese Student Recalls the Moment the Bomb Exploded, August 1945   **57**

The U.S. Strategic Bombing Survey Concludes That the Bomb Was Unnecessary, 1946   **61**

ESSAYS

Herbert Feis • Shortening the War and Saving Lives   **66**

Martin J. Sherwin • The Bomb as a Weapon of Diplomacy   **75**

Michael S. Sherry • The Bomb as a Technology of Death   **87**

CHAPTER 3
The Cold War Begins
Page 99

DOCUMENTS

President Harry S Truman and His Advisers Debate U.S. Policy Toward the U.S.S.R., 1945   **100**

Russian Premier Joseph Stalin Defends Soviet Policy in Eastern Europe, 1945   **103**

Secretary of Commerce Henry A. Wallace Urges a Conciliatory Approach,
1946   **104**

White House Aide Clark M. Clifford Summarizes the Case for the Hard Line,
1946   **105**

The Truman Doctrine, 1947   **111**

Under Secretary of State Dean Acheson Calls for Economic Aid to Europe,
1947   **114**

The President's Advisers Urge Military Expansion, 1950   **115**

E S S A Y S

Joyce and Gabriel Kolko • Making the World Safe for American
Capitalism   **120**

John Lewis Gaddis • Soviet Unilateralism and the Origins of the Cold
War   **124**

Melvyn P. Leffler • The Truman Doctrine and the Rise of American
Globalism   **139**

C H A P T E R 4
*Truman, Eisenhower, and the Transformation of American Politics,
1945–1960*
Page 146

D O C U M E N T S

White House Aide Clark M. Clifford Advises President Harry S Truman,
1947   **147**

President Truman Campaigns for the Presidency, 1948   **153**

A Left-Wing Critic Assesses the Fair Deal, 1949   **155**

The American Medical Association Plans an Attack on "Socialized Medicine,"
1949   **157**

Governor Thomas E. Dewey and Dwight D. Eisenhower Discuss Presidential
Politics, 1949   **161**

Senator Joseph McCarthy Denounces the Democrats, 1950   **162**

Television and the Selling of the President, 1956   **164**

President Eisenhower Warns of the Military-Industrial Complex,
1961   **166**

E S S A Y S

Alonzo L. Hamby • Harry Truman and the New Cold War Liberalism   **168**

Robert Griffith • Dwight D. Eisenhower and the Corporate
Commonwealth   **177**

C H A P T E R 5
American Society in the 1950s
Page 199

D O C U M E N T S

U.S. Business Celebrates the "Miracle of America," 1948   **200**

A Report on the Baby Boom, 1954   **202**

Life Magazine Identifies the New Teen-age Market, 1959   **203**

Governor Adlai Stevenson Describes a Woman's Place, 1955   **204**

Economist John Kenneth Galbraith Examines Poverty in the "Affluent Society," 1958   **207**

A Beat Poet Waits for the Real America, 1958   **209**

E S S A Y S

John Patrick Diggins • The Proud Decade   **227**

Douglas T. Miller and Marion Nowak • The Precarious Prosperity of People's Capitalism   **213**

C H A P T E R 6
John F. Kennedy, the Cuban Revolution, and the Cold War
Page 235

D O C U M E N T S

Fidel Castro Denounces U.S. Policy Toward Cuba, 1960   **237**

President John F. Kennedy Calls for an Alliance for Progress, 1961   **240**

A Board of Inquiry Reports on the Bay of Pigs, 1961   **242**

A Senate Committee Investigates U.S. Plots to Assassinate Castro, 1960–1965   **247**

President Kennedy and His Advisers Debate Options in the Missile Crisis, 1962   **252**

President Kennedy Addresses the Nation on the Missile Crisis, 1962   **259**

Soviet Premier Nikita Khrushchev Appeals to President Kennedy, 1962   **263**

E S S A Y S

Thomas G. Paterson • Kennedy's Fixation with Cuba   **268**

Raymond L. Garthoff • Kennedy's Triumph at the Brink   **288**

C H A P T E R 7
Lyndon B. Johnson, the Great Society, and the Welfare State
Page 304

D O C U M E N T S

Michael Harrington Describes the "Other America," 1962   **306**

President Lyndon B. Johnson Declares War on Poverty, 1964   **309**

A Conservative Extols Work, Family, and Faith, 1981   **311**

Living in Poverty, 1959–1989: A Graphic   **314**

Homeless Children Speak, 1986, 1987   **315**

E S S A Y S

Sar A. Levitan and Robert Taggart • In the Defense of the Great Society   **317**

Charles Murray • The Poverty of the Great Society   **325**

Frances Fox Piven and Richard A. Cloward • Challenging the Great Society's Conservative Critics   **340**

CHAPTER 8
Martin Luther King, Jr., and the Struggle for African-American Equality
Page 353

D O C U M E N T S

The *New York Times* Records a Murder in Georgia, 1946   **354**

Malcom X Recalls Getting a "Conk," 1964   **355**

Brown v. *Board of Education*, 1954   **356**

Franklin McCain Remembers the First Sit-ins, 1960   **358**

Martin Luther King, Jr., "I Have a Dream," 1963   **361**

Stokely Carmichael Explains "Black Power," 1967   **364**

A Senate Committee Reports on the FBI's Campaign Against Martin Luther King, Jr., 1976   **368**

Police and Fire Department Logs Record an Urban Riot, 1967   **371**

E S S A Y S

Vincent Gordon Harding • King as Disturber of the Peace   **377**

William H. Chafe • The African-American Struggle as an Unfinished Revolution   **384**

CHAPTER 9
Vietnam and the Crisis of American Empire
Page 399

D O C U M E N T S

The Vietnamese Declare Their Independence, 1945   **400**

State Department Advisers Debate U.S. Support for the French in Vietnam, 1949   **402**

The Geneva Agreements, 1954   **404**

The Gulf of Tonkin Resolution, 1964   **406**

President Lyndon Johnson's Advisers Debate Expanding the War, 1965   **407**

War Stories as Told by the Combatants, Collected 1981   **413**

Wrong, Rambo! A Vietnam Veteran Looks Back, 1985   **420**

E S S A Y S

George McT. Kahin • The Cold War and American Intervention in Vietnam   **422**

George Herring • The Meaning of Vietnam   **434**

C H A P T E R 10
The New Left and the Politics of the 1960s
Page 446

D O C U M E N T S

The Port Huron Statement, 1963   **447**

Jerry Rubin: Self-Portrait of a Child of "Amerika," 1970   **452**

The Weathermen's Call for Revolution: "You Don't Need a Weatherman to Know Which Way the Wind Blows," 1969   **453**

A Senate Committee Probes the FBI's Secret Campaign Against the New Left, 1976   **455**

A Student Survivor Recalls the Tragedy at Kent State, 1970   **459**

Raymond Mungo Searches for a New Age at Total Loss Farm, 1970   **463**

E S S A Y S

Peter Collier and David Horowitz • The Sixties: Goodbye to All That   **467**

Tom Hayden • The Sixties: Times of Greatness and Wonder   **474**

Maurice Isserman and Michael Kazin • The Contradictory Legacy of the Sixties   **479**

C H A P T E R 11
From the Feminine Mystique to the New Feminism
Page 502

D O C U M E N T S

Betty Friedan on the Problem That Has No Name, 1963   **503**

NOW Statement of Purpose, 1966   **507**

Two Women Activists Consider Women's Role in the Civil-Rights Movement and the New Left, 1965   **510**

Feminists Affirm Women's Right to Control Their Own Bodies, 1973   **512**

The Supreme Court Rules on Abortion: *Roe* v. *Wade,* 1973   **517**

Jerry Falwell Sees a Threat to the American Family, 1980   **520**

Ellen Goodman Contrasts Two Generations of Women's Lives, 1989   **522**

E S S A Y S

Elaine Tyler May • The Origins of the New Feminism   **524**

John D'Emilio and Estelle Freedman • Sexual Liberalism and the New Feminism   **538**

C H A P T E R 12
Richard M. Nixon, Watergate, and the Crisis of the "Imperial" Presidency
Page 556

D O C U M E N T S

Richard M. Nixon on Being President, 1972   **557**

White House Counsel John W. Dean III Presents the "Enemies List,"
1971   **560**

President Richard M. Nixon Discusses the Watergate Break-in with Aide H. R.
Haldeman, 1972   **561**

Senator Sam J. Ervin on Watergate, 1974   **564**

President Nixon's Farewell, 1974   **568**

E S S A Y S

James A. Neuchterlein • Escaping Watergate: A Revisionist View of the Nixon
Presidency   **571**

Stanley I. Kutler • The Inescapability of Watergate   **584**

C H A P T E R 13
Growth, Technology, and the Fate of the Earth
Page 594

D O C U M E N T S

Rachel Carson Warns of a Silent Spring, 1962   **595**

An Environmental Activist Foresees Ecological Catastrophe, 1970   **596**

Barry Commoner Outlines the Four Laws of Ecology, 1971   **598**

Secretary of the Interior James G. Watt on Economic Development and the
Environment, 1981   **607**

A Worst-Case Forecast for the Greenhouse Effect, 1988   **611**

E S S A Y S

Samuel P. Hays • From Conservation to the New Environmentalism   **613**

Barry Commoner • Environmental Politics and the Fate of the Earth   **621**

C H A P T E R 14
Politics and Society in the Reagan Era
Page 639

D O C U M E N T S

President Jimmy Carter and the Crisis of the American Spirit, 1979   **641**

Presidential Candidate Ronald Reagan Calls for New Economic Policies,
1980   **644**

A New Right Activist Explains Conservative Successes, 1980   **647**

President Reagan on America's Spiritual Reawakening, 1983   **651**

Jesse Jackson Celebrates Common Ground and the Rainbow Coalition,
1988   **655**

President George Bush Seeks a Kinder, Gentler Nation, 1989   **657**

E S S A Y S

Thomas Byrne Edsall • The "Reagan Revolution" as a Revolution from
Above   **660**

Bennett Harrison and Barry Bluestone • Reaganomics and the Great
U-Turn   **676**

CHAPTER 15
Beyond the Cold War: American Foreign Policy in the Reagan-Bush Era
Page 689

D O C U M E N T S

President Ronald Reagan on Russia as an "Evil Empire," 1983 **690**

A Congressional Committee Reports on "Irangate," 1987 **693**

U.S. Military Spending, 1980–1990: A Graphic **694**

Soviet Leader Mikhail Gorbachev Charts a New Direction for the U.S.S.R., 1988 **699**

The *New York Times* Announces the End of the Cold War, 1989 **701**

President George Bush Proclaims a New World Order, 1990 **703**

E S S A Y S

John Lewis Gaddis • Ronald Reagan's Cold War Victory **705**

Richard J. Barnet • After the Cold War **710**

Major Problems
in American History
Since 1945

CHAPTER
1

World War II and the Origins of Postwar America

XXX

In the spring of 1945, the new president of the United States, Harry S Truman, anxiously surveyed a world in turmoil and transition. In Europe more than three decades of economic crisis and violent upheaval not only had inflicted an enormous toll in lives and material but had irreparably weakened the old, European-led world system that had organized international affairs for more than a century. Germany, which had dominated the continent economically and militarily during much of the twentieth century, now faced virtual annihilation as Allied armies closed in on Berlin from east and west. France and Great Britain, once mighty imperial nations and now ostensibly victorious, were only little better off than the vanquished. By contrast, the Soviet Union had emerged from the war a battered but nevertheless major new world power. In Asia the imminent defeat of Japan promised to alter the balance of power in the Pacific radically. Throughout the colonial world of Asia, Africa, and the Middle East, the collapse of imperial Europe released powerful revolutionary stirrings among peoples seeking self-determination and economic development.

The United States, which alone of the great powers had escaped the war's physical destruction, was now the strongest nation in the world. In victory, however, Americans and their leaders confronted many difficult questions involving how, toward what ends, and in whose interest their enormous resources would be deployed. What would be the character of America's postwar relations with its allies, especially the Soviet Union; with its vanquished enemies, Germany and Japan; with the war-devastated nations of Europe; and with the peoples of Latin America, Africa, Asia, and the Middle East? What role would the United States play in the recovery of shattered foreign nations and in the reconstruction of a stable postwar system of international relations? How would the costs and burdens of that role be distributed, and with what consequences at home and abroad?

In domestic affairs, President Truman and other Americans faced a second, equally daunting set of problems. The depression decade that had preceded World War II had produced enormous, if piecemeal and at times contradictory,

1

changes in U.S. politics and the American political economy. The New Deal had sought to impose social discipline on American capitalism, to protect individuals from arbitrary and impersonally inflicted deprivation, and to mobilize ordinary men and women in pursuit of a more democratic social and economic order. But the New Deal at the same time had aroused fierce opposition from U.S. business leaders, who were determined if not to destroy reform, then at least to turn it to their own purposes. The power and reach of the federal government had grown enormously during the depression and war, but the question of how and in whose interest that power would be used remained largely unanswered. Could the American economy be harnessed to democratic and egalitarian goals, or would it serve as a great engine of inequality and special privilege? Would the New Deal's supporters succeed in constraining the autonomy of private property through progressive taxation, vigorous proconsumer regulation, and public ownership? Or would government be used instead to secure and defend patterns of privilege? Would the federal government seek to redistribute power by encouraging the organization of the powerless, or would its authority now be used to restrain organized workers, farmers, and urban minorities?

A third set of postwar issues concerned the day-to-day lives of ordinary citizens. In 1945 a great metamorphosis in American society was under way as the continued spread of industrial organization, mass consumption, mass communication, and secular values transformed the nation from a patchwork of local village cultures into an increasingly interdependent, national culture. Both the Great Depression and the Second World War, moreover, powerfully reshaped American lives. "The great knife of the depression . . . cut down through the entire population, cleaving open the lives of rich as well as poor," wrote Robert and Helen Lynd upon their return in the 1930s to "Middletown," the midwestern city of Muncie, Indiana, which they had studied a decade earlier. "The experience has been more nearly universal than any prolonged recent emotional experience in the city's history; it has approached in its elemental shock the primary experiences of birth and death." The impact of war was even more profound and far-reaching. More than 12 million men and women had entered the armed forces, nearly a million of whom had been killed or wounded. More than 15 million others had taken work in the humming defense industries. In 1945, as the war drew to a close and the nation began its conversion to peacetime, Americans anxiously faced a future over which they had only partial control. Would they secure jobs in the transformed postwar society, and if so, on what terms? Would they find decent housing, and if so, where and at what costs? How would Americans confront the deep and potentially explosive divisions of race, class, and gender? What would be the character of relationships between husbands and wives, parents and children, friends and neighbors? How would balances be struck between private and public consumption, between development and preservation, between competition and community?

The way in which all these questions—foreign and domestic, political and economic, social and cultural—were answered; the way in which the conflicts of nations and classes and interests were resolved or institutionalized; the myriad compromises, arrangements, accommodations, bargains, and truces that were struck; the balances of power that resulted; all would mark the emergence in the late 1940s of a fundamentally new era in American and world history. The essays that follow explore the origins of this new postwar era.

XX *E S S A Y S*

In the first essay, excerpted from *On Every Front: The Making of the Cold War* (1979), diplomatic historian Thomas G. Paterson of the University of Connecticut examines the impact of World War II on world politics and the early efforts of U.S. leaders to shape the emerging new international system. In the second essay, political sociologist Alan Wolfe of the New School for Social Research argues that in the 1940s the older, conflict-ridden and redistributionist politics of the New Deal era gave way to a new politics of growth and social consensus. The subsequent collapse of this politics of growth in the 1970s, he argues, would usher in the changes of the Reagan era. The final essay, by historian William H. Chafe of Duke University, considers the wartime origins of the civil-rights movement and the modern women's movement, examining how the similar wartime experiences of African-Americans and women helped generate the new social politics of the postwar era.

The Origins of the Postwar International System

THOMAS G. PATERSON

Winston S. Churchill wore his usual bulldog visage. The ever-present cigar and hunched gait, other familiar trademarks of the British prime minister, also drew the crowd's attention on that very hot day of July 16, 1945. He was surveying the dusty remains of the Nazi capital—"that rubble heap near Potsdam," murmured one Berliner. This time a preoccupied Churchill evinced little interest in his curious onlookers. What captured Churchill's regard was the grisly aftermath in Berlin of heavy Allied bombing and artillery fire and stout German resistance. He and the passengers in his motorcade grew sick, utterly stunned by the stark display of carnage in the German city.

"There is nothing to do here," sighed a dispirited Berliner. Old men, women, and children trudged along, aimlessly pushing wheelbarrows. Over a million people lived in cellars, ruins, and makeshift suburban shacks, trading what they could for precious scraps of food to support their meager diet. Sixty-five to 75 percent of the city was levelled or damaged. The once-prized chariot of victory on the Brandenb[u]rg Gate had been reduced to a gnarled mass of molten metal. The Reichstag was a hollow shell. Some *"Nicht für Juden"* signs were still posted, ugly reminders of the German extermination of European Jews. Industrial equipment which survived the bombings had been torn from its foundations by the Russians as war booty, leaving stripped, hull-like factories. Partially buried corpses lay rotting in the sun. Visitors and citizens alike recoiled from the stench of death that hung everywhere. Lord Moran, who accompanied Churchill in Berlin, "felt a sense of nausea." Worse, "it was like the first time I saw a surgeon open a belly and the intestines gushed out."

The curious prime minister entered what was left of Adolf Hitler's Chancellery. The Führer's marble-topped desk lay in a thousand pieces. Iron Crosses, military ribbons, and papers littered the floor. Uncharacteristically, Churchill said little as the descent into Hitler's damp hideaway apparently induced quiet reflection. Members of the prime minister's party picked up souvenirs; one pocketed a fragment of Hitler's world map. Depressed by what he saw, General H. L. Ismay hurried away to his villa to take a hot bath and a strong drink. That night Churchill finally talked about his visit to the Chancellery. "It was from there that Hitler planned to govern the world," he mused. "A good many have tried that; all failed." Savoring the Allied victory, the prime minister smiled contentedly and went to bed.

The president of the United States, Harry S. Truman, surveyed Berlin that same day. After reviewing the American 2nd Armored Division, the president led his entourage down the Wilhelmstrasse to the Chancellery of the Third Reich, all the while growing more awestruck by the destruction of the city. "That's what happens," he remarked, "when a man overreaches himself." For two hours Truman rode through Berlin's streets. "I was thankful," he noted later, "that the United States had been spared the unbelievable devastation of this war." Berlin had actually appeared worse a month earlier, before Berliners, under the stern guidance of Russian and other Allied soldiers, began to stack bricks and shovel ashes. American diplomat Robert Murphy found that "the odor of death was everywhere." Indeed, "the canals were choked with bodies and refuse." General Lucius Clay, who would soon become the military governor of the American zone, was also stunned. "The streets were piled high with debris which left in many places only a narrow one-way passage between mounds of rubble, and frequent detours had to be made where bridges and viaducts were destroyed. . . . It was like a city of the dead."

From urban center to rural village, Germany looked charred and ravaged. Bomb-gutted Cologne and Nuremberg were hardly recognizable. Ninety-three percent of the houses in Düsseldorf were totally destroyed. Hamburg, Stuttgart, and Dresden had been laid waste by firebombs and firestorms. In Dresden mounds of bodies had to be bulldozed into mass graves or burned on huge makeshift grills, so great was the toll and the fear of epidemic disease. An American Army Air Corpsman flying low over the country at the end of the war could not spot streets or homes in Mannheim— only tossed dirt. "Aachen," he observed, "lay bleaching in the sun like bones on a desert." A disbelieving companion gazed at the pulverized land below and asked, "Where do the people live?"

Hospitals, schools, and churches throughout Germany felt the war's fury. Fourteen of the nation's twenty-three universities were severely damaged. Transportation and communication systems were disrupted. Untreated sewage flowed into waterways, spreading disease. Water traffic on the Rhine River, which before the war had been greater than that of the Suez or Panama Canals, was now negligible; demolished bridges and sunken vessels

blocked the artery. Industrial plants, once the marvel of Europe, lay prostrate. The Ruhr, which had produced 400,000 tons of coal a day, could
manage only a paltry 25,000 in 1945. "If we had then realized the confusion
and chaos which existed," General Clay wrote five years after the war, "we
would indeed have thought ours a hopeless task."

In Churchill's country, the war claimed a frightful toll. Some observers
after V-E Day made the grim observation that the Germans looked better
fed and less ragged than the British. The air blitz which struck London,
Coventry, and other cities in 1940–41, and then subsided somewhat, began
anew in 1944 with German V-1 and V-2 rockets which indiscriminately
pounded buildings and people. Major sections of London were badly mangled, turning that regal city into a shabby, battered replica of itself. The
Foreign Office building lost most of its windows and doors, and No. 10
Downing Street had no windows and few tiles in place. After one attack,
it took workmen six hours to free a woman from a tumbled row house on
Stepney High Street. She was asked if she had a husband. "Yes," she
snapped. "He's at the front, the dirty coward."

The "front" constantly shifted with the fortunes of war, and few European nations were spared from marauding armies and death-dealing bombers. In Greece in 1945 a million people were homeless. About one-quarter
of the nation's buildings were damaged or destroyed, and farm yields were
down by 50 percent. One-third of all cattle were lost. Eighty percent of
railway rolling stock and three-quarters of the ocean shipping fleet were
incapacitated. Before leaving Greece the Germans blasted the walls of the
Corinth Canal, filling it with 900,000 cubic yards of earth. The modern port
facilities of Piraeus lay in ruins. Gravely undernourished people found hospitals overcrowded. Five hundred thousand registered cases of tuberculosis
spelled epidemic. An American doctor who tried to work at the Athens
Red Cross Hospital in early 1945, during an outbreak of civil war, found
that the "operating room had been blown up with all the glass gone and
even the surgical instruments had been melted by the magnesium bombs
and were lying around in heaps of molten metal."

In neighboring Yugoslavia the retreating Germans had devastated the
countryside, causing starvation in some regions. Upon liberation only one
of Yugoslavia's seven large power stations was operating, and the rails running through the Danube valley, which linked the nation to other European
states, were rendered useless. In the Hungarian capital of Budapest, the
splendor of the Hap[s]burgs had given way inelegantly to the specter of
death. All the bridges over the Danube were demolished, houses were
flattened, and the 860-room royal palace of Maria Theresa and Franz Josef
stood only as a maze of walls. In Austria German fires and Allied bombs
had gutted 70 percent of the center of Vienna, not even sparing the seven-
hundred-year-old St. Stephen's Cathedral. Women searched for sticks in the
Vienna Woods, there being no coal for fuel. Elderly Viennese men and
women looked pallid; young people were listless as they begged for GI
rations. In Czechoslovakia and Italy, Prague and Rome had mercifully escaped large-scale devastation, but such blessings were rare. Italian agricul-

tural production was down 50 percent. People in Naples clawed like cats through garbage cans for tidbits of food. Before abandoning that city, the Germans had wrecked the gas, electric, and water systems and put the torch to the university. In the Netherlands, 540,000 acres were flooded and Rotterdam was battered. As for France, Paris had largely been spared, but almost 20 percent of the buildings in the entire country were destroyed— twice the number demolished in World War I. Ninety percent of French trucks were out of action, and much of the French fleet rested on the bottom of the harbor at Toulon.

John Hersey, whose book *Hiroshima* was to expose the ghastly details of the Asian atomic holocaust, also witnessed the tragedy of Warsaw, Poland—"destroyed, systematically, street by street, alley by alley, house by house. . . . Nothing is left except a mockery of architecture." Travelling with a Polish officer who was returning from battle to his native city, Hersey watched as desperate Poles scratched at the flesh of a fallen army horse, quickly leaving a steaming skeleton. "God, my God, God," whispered the horrified officer. Almost six million Poles died in World War II. Polish Jews had been deliberately exterminated, with the Auschwitz concentration camp setting barbaric records in human cremation. The cities of Gdynia, Danzig, and Stettin were mauled. In this predominantly agricultural nation, one-sixth of the farms were inoperable, 70 percent of the horses gone, and one-third of the cattle dead. American ambassador Arthur Bliss Lane flew into Warsaw on an Army C-47 in July 1945. The seven-mile trip from the airport to the center of the city gave him the "chill of deep depression:"

> I could see only a handful of houses left unharmed; all others were bombed or gutted by fire. The smoky smell of long-dead fires hung in the air. The sickening sweet odor of burned human flesh was a grim warning that we were entering a city of the dead. . . . The scene was depressingly lacking in the normal bustle and movement of a city. . . . But the most terrible sight of all was that of the one-legged children.

To the east the Ukraine ranked high in the gruesome tally of war losses. This area of 181,000 square miles, before the war a mainstay of the Soviet economy, with its large production of coal, pig iron, steel, and manganese, as well as farm goods, now lay denuded by the Soviet scorched-earth policy and the German rampage. Mines were blown up and flooded, the Dnieper Dam blasted, whole farm villages razed, tractors wrecked, and livestock massacred or driven off. The modern Zaporozhal steel plant near the Dnieper Dam was reduced to acres and acres of tangled debris. In the Brovary district alone, 12,099 out of 16,000 prewar farm buildings were destroyed. Famine and starvation were widespread in this drought-stricken region. The Soviet Socialist Republic of Byelorussia fared no better. Minsk looked like Warsaw. Five miles beyond that city, thirty-four pits held the corpses of 150,000 people murdered and buried by the Germans. The much fought-over province of Vitebsk counted 300,000 dead.

Correspondent Harrison Salisbury called Sevastopol "a city of the dead." Of the city's 15,000 houses, only 500 remained standing after the German retreat. "If a room has three walls and a ceiling," the mayor told Salisbury, "we count it in good shape." Another reporter, Alexander Werth, passed through Istra, west of Moscow, and saw nothing but a "forest of chimney-stacks." As for Stalingrad, American ambassador W. Averell Harriman viewed "a desert of broken brick and rubble, the survivors huddling in cellars or tar-paper shanties." The people of Moscow looked haggard as they piled rubble. The domes of the Kremlin, blackened with war paint, still cut the skyline, but its occupants now governed a Russia which had suffered the awesome wartime loss of 15 to 20 million dead. Visiting Russia less than a year after the close of the war, the Secretary General of the United Nations found "the chaos of charred and twisted villages and cities . . . the most complete exhibit of destruction I have ever witnessed."

Europe lost more than 30 million people in the Second World War. The grisly statistical gallery ranked Russia an uncontested first. Then came Poland with 5.8 million dead; Germany, with 4.5 million; Yugoslavia, 1.5 million; France, 600,000; Rumania, 460,000; Hungary, 430,000; Czechoslovakia, 415,000; Italy, 410,000; Britain, 400,000; and the Netherlands, 210,000. C. Day Lewis's "War Poem" read:

> They lie in the Sunday Street
> Like effigies thrown down after a fête
> Among the bare-faced houses frankly yawning revulsion,
> Fag ends of fires, litter of rubble, stale
> Confetti sprinkle of blood. . . .

As for the living, they had to endure food shortages, closed factories, idle fields, cold stoves, currency inflation, festering wounds. In West Germany alone, two million cripples hobbled about. Thirty-four percent of the Germans born in 1924 were badly mutilated in some way by 1945. The sad photographs of ill-clad, skeletal bodies struggling for life in Germany's concentration camps provided evidence enough of the human depredation. Displaced persons (DPs) provided another picture. "The wind will tell you what has come to us, /It rolls our brittle bones from pole to pole," went "The Refugees' Testament." Many dazed refugees wandered helplessly through Europe, searching for relatives, for friends, for a livelihood, for a ride home. The words of British writer Richard Mayne have poignantly depicted the lives of Europe's survivors:

> To many of the troops who first encountered them, the people in parts of Europe seemed a population of cripples, of women and children and the very old. Some were starving; some were sick with typhus or dysentery. . . . The survivors, gray-faced ghosts in parodies of clothing, trundled their salvaged belongings in homemade handcarts—rugs, threadbare overcoats, a kettle, an alarm clock, a battered toy. They waited at stand-pipes for a dribble of brown water; they queued for bread and potatoes; they rummaged for sticks and scraps. For them, this waste land of rubble, rags, and hunger was a prison without privacy or dignity; and like all prisons, it smelled. It smelled of dust, oil, gunpowder, and greasy metal; of drains and vermin; of decay and burning and the unburied dead.

So it was in parts of Asia as well, where Japanese forces had been beaten back to their small imperial islands and finally battered with fire-bombs and two monumental atomic blasts. The lush vegetation of the Philippines and numerous Pacific islands was singed and burned, whole jungles disappearing. A British official who stopped at Okinawa remarked that it looked like the Somme after World War I. China had known population pressure, famine, and epidemics before the war. But Japanese plunder, the destruction of cities, disruption of vital agricultural production, and the displacement of its people increased the burdens that the Chinese had to bear in the postwar period. Hunan and Kwangsi were devastated. Along with Kwangtung, these provinces were visited by famine; millions suffered malnutrition and outright starvation. Cholera, plague, tuberculosis, smallpox, and malaria struck a population which had only 12,000 physicians—one for every 40,000 people. In 1938 the key dikes along the Yellow River—"China's Sorrow"—were blown up, killing thousands and flooding three million acres of fertile land. China's rivers now rampaged in the Spring and Summer through vulnerable villages. Manchuria's industrial plants were destroyed or dismantled, and China's small railroad network was a shambles. Some 1.32 million Chinese soldiers died; incalculable civilian losses were greater. Kiang Ling's "The Chinese Refugee" captured the times:

> Weeping I left my loved hills;
> Now by this flat long river
> Wandering, homeless, fleeing, fearing . . .
> Wandering till what time?
> Fleeing to what clime?
> Today's riches are ashes tomorrow;
> In a moment joy turns into sorrow.
> How call this yours or mine,
> How rich and poor define?
> In the eyes of death and flame
> Rich and poor are all the same.

For defeated Japan, the bitter results of imperial dreams could be measured in the loss of 2 million lives. Tokyo's population was reduced from 6.5 million to 3 million by war's end, and 700,000 of the city's buildings were destroyed. American planes had dropped napalm-filled bombs, engulfing the city in chemically induced firestorms which generated temperatures of up to 1,800°F. The odor of burning flesh drifted upwards, sickening the pilots who delivered the horrible punishment. In one savage attack alone, on May 23, 1945, 83,000 people died in what observers described as a mass burning. The fifteen-mile stretch between Yokohama and Tokyo, said an American officer who accompanied American general Douglas MacArthur to Japan, had become a "wilderness of rubble." A light dust hung in the air, staining visitors' clothing. Wood-and-paper houses had been reduced to powdered ashes, factories to twisted metal. A shanty town of rusted, corrugated sheets and other junk ringed the capital city, its inhabitants reminding some observers of the Okies who trekked to California during the

Great Depression—except that the Japanese scene was more emotionally debilitating. Only the downtown commercial district was free from the mounds of debris. One of the first American naval officers to arrive in the humbled Japanese city wrote to a friend that "I feel like a tramp who has become used to sleeping in a graveyard." A British visitor, Lord Alanbrooke, also visited Tokyo: "Everywhere the same desolation; it must be seen to be believed."

Hiroshima and Nagasaki were special cases, sharing and suffering a special fate. Hiroshima had been Japan's eighth largest city. A residential, commercial center of 250,000 people, it was singled out by American officials because it also housed regional military headquarters. Until August 6, 1945, a cloudless, warm day, Hiroshima had not had to endure large-scale American bombing raids. But at 8:15 AM the crew of the *Enola Gay,* a specially outfitted B-29, unleashed "Little Boy," an atomic device packing the power of 20,000 tons of TNT. The bomb fell for fifty seconds and exploded about 2,000 feet above ground. A blinding streak of light raced across the sky; a tremendous boom punctuated the air. A huge, purplish cloud of dust, smoke, and debris shot 40,000 feet into the atmosphere. At ground level the heat became suffocating, the winds violent. Buildings instantly disintegrated. Shadows were etched in stone. Trees were stripped of their leaves. Fires erupted everywhere, and the sky grew dark. Survivors staggered toward water to quench their intense thirst. Skin peeled from burned bodies. A maimed resident, Dr. Michihiko Hachiya, noted that "no one talked, and the ominous silence was relieved only by a subdued rustle among so many people, restless, in pain, anxious, and afraid, waiting for something else to happen." The toll: seventy to eighty thousand dead, an equal number wounded, and 81 percent of the city's buildings destroyed. Three days later the nightmare was repeated in Nagasaki, where at least 35,000 died. Upon hearing of the success of the world's first nuclear destruction of a city, President Truman remarked, "this is the greatest thing in history."

Whether this historical judgment was accurate or not, the tragedy at Hiroshima was but one chapter in the story of massive, war-induced destruction. This story, with all its horrid details, must be catalogued not for its shock value but for its illustration of how large were the problems of the postwar world, how shaky the scaffolding of the international order. Hitler once said about his warmongering pursuits that "we may be destroyed, but if we are, we shall drag a world with us—a world in flames." He partially succeeded, and World War II, like any war of substantial duration, served as an agent of conspicuous change, of revolution. The conflagration of 1939–45 was so wrenching, so total, so profound, that a world was overturned—not simply a material world of crops, buildings, and rails, not simply a human world of healthy and productive laborers, farmers, businessmen, and intellectuals, not simply a secure world of close-knit families and communities, not simply a military world of Nazi stormtroopers and Japanese kamikazis, but all that and more. The war also unhinged the world of stable politics, inherited wisdom, traditions, institutions, alliances, loyalties, commerce, and classes. When Acting Secretary of State Dean Acheson surveyed the problems facing American foreign policy in the postwar era, he saw as uppermost "social *disintegration,* political *disintegration,* the loss of faith by people in leaders who have led them in the past, and a great deal of economic *disintegration.*"

Leaders of all political persuasions, as they witnessed the immensity of the destruction, spoke of a new age without knowing its dimensions. The normal way of doing things now seemed inappropriate, although as creatures of the past, the survivors remained attached to ideas and institutions which seemed to provide security through familiarity. They sensed the seriousness and the enormity of the tasks of cleaning up the rubble, of putting the broken world back together again, of shaping an orderly international system. Yet it was evident, too, that few nations or individuals had the material resources, talent, and desire—the sheer energy, guts, and money—to mold a brave new world out of the discredited and crumbled old. If the reconstruction tasks seemed herculean, however, the opportunities appeared boundless for the ambitious, the hearty, and the caring. One vigorous, optimistic, well-intentioned, competitive voice sounded above the rubble that constituted London, Berlin, Warsaw, Minsk and Tokyo. That voice echoed with power from the United States, the wartime "arsenal of democracy."

At war's end President Truman declared a two-day national holiday. Horns, bells, and makeshift noisemakers sounded across the nation. Paraders in Los Angeles played leapfrog on Hollywood Boulevard; farther north, jubilant sailors broke windows along San Francisco's Market Street. In New York City tons of litter were tossed from the windows of skyscrapers on cheering crowds below. Stock market prices shot up. A five-year-old boy recorded the August 1945 moment: "This is the best year. The war is over. Two wars are over. Everyone is happy. Tins cans are rolling. Everything is confused. And little pieces of paper." It was truly a happy time. Not only was the dying over, but the United States had emerged from the global conflict in the unique position of an unscathed belligerent. No bombs fell on American cities. No armies ravaged the countryside. No American boundaries were redrawn. Factories stood in place, producing goods at an impressive rate. In August, at the General Motors plant in Moraine, Ohio, shiny new Frigidaire refrigerators and airplane propeller blades moved along parallel assembly lines. Farms were rich in crops, and full employment during the war years had buoyed family savings. "The American people," remarked the director of the Office of War Mobilization and Reconversion, "are in the pleasant predicament of having to learn to live 50 percent better than they have ever lived before."

Whereas much of Europe and Asia faced the massive task of "reconstruction," the United States faced "reconversion"—adjusting the huge war machine to peacetime purposes. Automobile plants had to convert production from tanks to cars, a delightful prospect for auto manufacturers, who knew that Americans were eager to spend their wartime earnings on consumer goods once again. With great pride Americans applauded their good fortune. They were different. They had no rubble to clear. "The Russians knew," said Joseph Stalin in a grand understatement, that "things are not bad in the United States."

Americans had worries. Some feared that the sparkling prosperity of the war years would dissipate in a postwar economic disaster. They remembered that military production, not Roosevelt's New Deal reform program, had pulled the United States out of the Great Depression of the 1930s. Would there be enough jobs for the returning GIs? They also suffered temporary shortages of many goods, sugar and gasoline among them, and resented the rationing which limited their economic freedom. "Hey, don'tche know there's a war on?" said clerks to anxious consumers. There were not enough houses to meet the needs of an expanding and mobile American population, which grew from 131 million to 140 million during the war years. The national debt skyrock[et]ed from $37 billion to $269 billion. The war cost the federal government $664 billion. Inflation threatened economic stability. At least 10 million American families lived in poverty. Still, these national pains, although arousing grumbles, seemed bearable or were played down. As *Fortune* magazine commented two months after V-J Day: "August 14, 1945, marked not only the war's end but the beginning of the greatest peacetime industrial boom in the world's history."

Cold data justified *Fortune's* enthusiasm. The Gross National Product of the United States expanded from $90.5 billion (1939) to $211.9 billion (1945). Steel production jumped from 53 million tons in 1939 to 80 million tons at the close of the war. American businessmen, cut off from rubber imports from the Dutch East Indies during the war, developed synthetic rubber, launching a new industry. New aluminum plants went up, and the aircraft industry, in infancy when Germany attacked Poland, became a major new business as well. In 1939 only 5,856 military and civil airplanes were turned out; but in 1945 the figure reached 48,912, a decline from the peak of over 95,000 in 1944. All told, over 300,000 aircraft rolled from American factories during the war—a figure far surpassing that of any other nation, including Germany and Japan combined. Employment in the aircraft industry swelled 1,600 percent. With its numerous aircraft factories, Southern California bustled, becoming a mecca for dreamers of wealth and adventure. Four hundred forty-four thousand people moved toLos Angeles during the war.

Workers' wages kept up with inflation during the war years. Women took jobs once held by men who were called to military duty. Unable to spend their abundant incomes on the shrinking supply of consumer items during the war, many Americans visited their banks. Total personal savings increased from $6.85 billion to $36.41 billion. Americans continued to spend for pleasure as well. The World Series of baseball played on, and films whirred at local theaters. Beaches beckoned vacationers. In the summer of 1944, as Europe and Asia reeled from the blasts of war, Americans flocked to resorts and racetracks. Betting in horse racing totalled a record-breaking $1.4 billion in 1945, even though the tracks were closed from January to May. Farmers enjoyed some of their best years of the twentieth century. Whereas in 1939 they counted 66 million head of cattle, by 1945 that figure reached 83 million. Agricultural output increased 15 percent. American universities also enjoyed improvements. Government contracts for scientific research went to the California Institute for Technology for rocket studies; Princeton received grants for ballistics research. In mid-1945 the Massachusetts Institute for Technology held government contracts worth $117 million. The GI Bill, which offered money to veterans for their college educations, promised higher enrollments. Despite uncertainties about the future, life looked good to Americans and after the hardships and setbacks of the depression decade, "the old self-confident America was coming into its stride again." Wartime musicals like *Carousel* and *Oklahoma* caught the optimistic mood, and sluggers Joe DiMaggio and Ted Williams were heading home to reclaim their baseball fame.

When foreign delegates journeyed to San Francisco for the United Nations Conference in April of 1945, many crossed the territorial United States and could not help but notice the stark contrast with war-torn Europe and Asia. Soviet Foreign Minister V. M. Molotov once referred to statistics in the *World Almanac* to remind Americans about their uniqueness as prosperous survivors of the Second World War. During a conversation with Stalin in 1944, the President of the United States Chamber of Commerce, Eric A. Johnston, citing the American example, lectured the Soviet leader about the need for a better distribution of goods in Russia. Stalin replied, ". . . but in order to distribute, there must be something to distribute." Months before, at the Teheran Conference, Stalin had toasted the United States as a "country of machines," applauding its great productive capacity for delivering victory to the Allies. Truman's words also bear repeating: "I was thankful that the United States had been spared the unbelievable devastation of this war." Even the death count for American servicemen, about 400,000, appeared merciful when compared to staggering figures elsewhere. Indeed, the *Saturday Evening Post* editorialized in 1945 that "we Americans can boast that we are not as other men are." The war had overturned a world, and many Americans believed that they were now on top of it. A new international system for the postwar era was in the making. . . .

In the rubble-strewn postwar world, international relations changed markedly from prewar interactions. Any historical period, such as the Cold War, is identified by a particular structure of relationships among the world's leading nations—by, in short, the international "system." Thus, the Napoleonic era of the late eighteenth and early nineteenth centuries was characterized by bipolarism, wherein France and Britain vied for world mastery, established alliances with lesser powers, frequently clashed in war, and managed far-flung empires. The period between the Congress of Vienna in 1815 and the outbreak of World War I in 1914, often called the era of Pax Britannica, was multipolar, with a number of leading actors on the international stage who preferred diplomatic negotiations to military combat and who deliberately set about to create a balance of power for the maintenance of a conservative, imperial, antirevolutionary world.

Any international system is conflict-ridden. "Peace," after all, is a very abstract term, difficult to employ as a description of any era. "Anarchy" probably more aptly approximates historical reality. The attempts nations make to reduce the anarchy constitute our diplomatic history. Conflict is inherent in any international system simply because countries seldom share common goals, interests, or ideologies. Some nations are more powerful or influential than others and flaunt their superiority. Others may resist. Some countries are dependent upon others. Some have what others want—territory, food, water, minerals, labor, and a multitude of things over which peoples have squabbled for centuries. Great nations are always looking for friends who will join them in formal or informal alliances to check the growth of those states they consider unfriendly or potentially so. Small nations have to be wary of the major actors, who may cast longing eyes on them and exploit their vulnerability. Nations which may wish to remain "neutral" or unaligned are wooed or cajoled.

The leading powers, whether aligned or at loggerheads, watch one another suspiciously, on the assumption that in international politics, as in business, one can supposedly trust friends seldom, enemies never. Slight shifts in the distribution of power—of resources—arouse concern. What one government considers "defense," another labels "offense." The construction of a military base, the testing of a new weapon, a request to alter a boundary, the signing of a treaty—all can be defined as both defensive or offensive, depending upon one's point of view. A rifle is a defensive weapon if seen from the butt, but it is a weapon of attack if one is staring into the muzzle. Suspicion and fear, those ancient diseases, undermine trust and prompt countermeasures. Leaders may assume evil intentions on the part of other nations and plan for the worst. Governments feel compelled to match the decisions of those whom they assume to be adversaries. Failure to develop a new weapon, for example, might entail extreme risk, for an enemy might gain advantage by producing it. Hence, leaders often escalate the level of conflict and chances for war through exaggerated perceptions of danger. In short, there is always an expanding nation, and there are countries reacting to that expansion. Differences in goals among the several parties of the international system feed instability. The degree of conflict may vary, but there is always conflict. "This is a lawless world," University of Chicago Professor Herman Finer told a radio audience in 1947, "because it is a world without a common morality or a common superior. Nationalisms and moralities collide."

Higher degrees of conflict are reached when the international system undergoes significant change, when it metamorphoses into a new or revised system. Such was the case after World War II. Change, by definition, is destabilizing. Some postwar leaders, even though immersed in day-to-day decisionmaking, pondered the general characteristics of the international system. They knew that significant changes had altered the configuration of power. As participants in and shapers of a new age, they were "present at the creation." But the outline of the new system was only vaguely evident. With the historian's advantage of hindsight, however, we can delineate the peculiar properties of the postwar world and suggest that the process of creating a new system out of the ashes of the discredited prewar system intensified the conflict inherent in any international structure.

Yet this view of systemic conflict cannot serve as a comprehensive explanation for the origins of the Cold War. For if the Soviet–American confrontation was simply the inevitable product of the conflict-ridden international system, there would be little purpose in studying the leaders, ideas, policies, or needs of individual nations, because events would be largely beyond their control. Under this interpretation the system would dictate antagonistic relations. It would not matter whether different personalities or different national policies existed. Few scholars, however, subscribe to this restricted analysis of history. We know that leaders made choices, even if they only dimly understood their consequences. Harry S. Truman, Winston Churchill, and Joseph Stalin helped to create the international system to which they had to react. A complete history of the beginnings of the Cold War, then, must include not only the traits of the international system but also the dynamics of particular nations and individuals. . . . [A] macroanalytic view will enable us to identify the opportunities and constraints which faced the major actors. Or, as Professor Bruce M. Russett has suggested, this level of analysis outlines the "menu" of world affairs—the choices available, as well as the limits of choice. It sketches the "big picture," so that the disparate components of the postwar system can be examined in proper relationship. It helps us to determine which nations held real or potential power and why, ultimately, they moved toward restrictive spheres of influence and away from a community of interest and international cooperation.

Conflict in the postwar years was accentuated by wrenching changes in the international system—a redistribution of power and a departure from a Europe-centered world. Two nations emerged from the rubble of World War II to claim first rank. The competitive interaction between the United States and the Soviet Union—"like two big dogs chewing on a bone," said Senator J. William Fulbright—contributed to the bipolarism of the immediate postwar years. "Not since Rome and Carthage," Dean Acheson observed, "had there been such a polarization of power on this earth." This new bipolar structure replaced the multipolar system of the 1930s, wherein at least six nations were active, influential participants. By the late 1940s, decisions made in Washington, D.C. and Moscow often determined whether people in other nations voted, where they lived, and how much they ate. The nations which had tried to wield such authority in the 1930s had fallen from their elevated status. Japan, Italy, and Germany were defeated and occupied; England, nearly bankrupt, dependent, and unable to police its empire, was reduced to a resentful second-rate power; France, much of whose territory had been held by the Germans during the war, was still suffering from unstable politics and no longer mustered international respect.

The abrupt removal of Germany and Japan from positions of high authority in international relations created power vacuums in Europe and Asia. The United States and Soviet Russia, eager to fulfill their visions of the postwar world and to seize opportunities for extending their respective influence, were attracted to these vacuums. With the old barriers to American and Soviet expansion gone, Russia and America clashed over occupation policies in Germany, Italy, Japan, Austria, and Korea. They squabbled over which political groups should replace the Nazi regimes in Eastern Europe. The filling of gaps or vacuums in any system is a natural process. In the postwar period the gaps were huge and worldwide, inviting a high degree of competition and conflict.

Another change wrought by World War II was the destruction of the economic world. The war cut an ugly scar across Europe and Asia, but bypassed one major nation, the United States. "If Hitler succeeds in nothing else," mused OSS officer Allen Dulles, "like Samson, he may pull down the pillars of the temple and leave a long and hard road of reconstruction." The postwar task was forbidding. Not only did cities have to be rebuilt, factories opened, people put back to work, rails repaired, rivers and roads made passable, and crop yields increased, but the flow of international commerce and finance had to be reestablished if nations were to raise through exports the revenue needed to buy the imports required for recovery. Many old commercial and financial patterns had been broken and, given the obstacle of economic wreckage, new exchanges were difficult to establish. Where would Germany's vital coal and steel go? Would industrial Western Europe and agricultural Eastern Europe recreate old commercial ties? Would the restrictive trade practices of the 1930s, especially the tariff barriers, continue into the 1940s? Would subservient colonies continue to serve as sources of rich raw materials? Could international agreements and organizations curb economic nationalism? Would trade be conducted on a multilateral, "open door" basis, as the United States preferred, or by bilateral or preferential methods, as many others, such as Britain and Russia, practiced? The answers helped to define the international system of the post-1945 era. These issues held more importance than simple economics, for leaders recognized that the economic disorders of the 1930s and the far-reaching impact of the Great Depression contributed to political chaos, aggression, and war. The new international system, it was hoped, would create stable economic conditions which would facilitate the development of pacific international relations. Yet the very efforts to realize these hopes engendered conflict.

World War II also bequeathed domestic political turmoil to its survivors. The regimes of the 1930s, now discredited, vied with insurgent groups for the governing power in many states. Socialists, Communists, and other varieties of the political left, many of whom had fought in the underground resistance movements and had thus earned some popular respect, challenged the more entrenched, conservative elites, many of whom had escaped into exile when the German armies rolled into their countries. In Poland, the Communist, Soviet-endorsed Lublin Poles challenged the political standing of the Poles who had fled to London. The conservative Dutch government-in-exile watched warily as leftist resistance groups gradually built a popular following. Political confusion in the Netherlands was heightened by the wartime loss of voting lists. In Greece a coalition of leftists in the National

Liberation Front (EAM) vigorously resisted the return to power of a British-created government and the unpopular Greek monarchy of King George. In France Charles de Gaulle vied for power with the Communists. In China the civil war, which had raged for years between the Communists of Mao Tse-tung and the Nationalists of Chiang Kai-shek, flared up again at the close of the war. Yugoslavia was the scene of political battle between Josip Broz Tito's Partisans and a group headed by Dr. Ivan Subasic of the London emigré government, which in turn suffered strained ties with King Peter. Moreover, in the occupied nations of Germany, Austria, and Korea, the victors created competitive zones, postponing the creation of central governments. In the defeated countries of Japan and Italy, American officials decided who would rule, whereas in parts of Eastern Europe, Soviet officials placed Communists in positions of authority.

The major powers, in short, intervened abroad to exploit the political opportunities created by the destructive scythe of World War II. The stakes seemed high. A change in a nation's political orientation might presage a change in its international alignment. The great powers tended to ignore local conditions which might mitigate against alignment with an outside power. Americans feared that a leftist or Communist Greece would look to the East and permit menacing Soviet bases on Greek territory or open the door to a Soviet naval presence in the Mediterranean. The Russians dreaded a conservative anti-Soviet Polish government led by the London faction, for it might prove so weak and so hostile to Moscow as to permit a revived Germany to send stormtroopers once again through the Polish corridor into the heart of Russia. A Communist China, thought Americans, might align with Russia; a Nationalist China would remain in the American camp. All in all, the rearranging of political structures *within* nations drew the major powers into competition, accentuating the conflict inherent in the postwar international system.

If the war threw politics into chaos, it also hastened the disintegration of colonial and informal empires. The Japanese movement into French Indochina and their drive for Dutch East Indies oil had led to Pearl Harbor in 1941. The initially successful Japanese expansion had the effect of demonstrating to many Asian nationalists that their white imperial masters could be defeated. Some nationalists collaborated during the war with their Asian brethren from Tokyo, and the Japanese, in need of administrators to manage occupied areas, trained and armed some native leaders. Japan granted Burma considerable autonomy in 1942, for example, and after the war the Burmese were determined not to return to a position of subservience to Great Britain. At the end of the war, the European powers, exhausted and financially hobbled, had to struggle to reestablish mastery over rebellious colonies. The appeal of the principle of self-determination, still echoing from the days of Woodrow Wilson and given new emphasis by the Atlantic Charter of 1941, was far-reaching.

No empire seemed immune to disintegration. The United States granted the Philippines independence in 1946. The British, worn low by the war and by the challenges of nationalist groups demanding independence, retreated from India (and Pakistan) in 1947 and from Burma and Ceylon in 1948. Israel, carved out of British-governed Palestine, became a new independent state in 1948. The British also found it difficult to maintain their sphere of influence in Iran, Greece, and Egypt and began retreats from those politically unsteady states. The French attempted to hold on to Indochina, where nationalist forces led by Ho Chi Minh had declared an independent Vietnam. Bloody battle ensued, leading ultimately to French withdrawal in 1954. The Dutch also decided to fight, but after four debilitating years of combat, they pulled out of Indonesia in 1949. The defeated Japanese were forced to give up their claims to Formosa and Korea, as well as Pacific island groups. Italy departed from Ethiopia and lost its African colonies of Tripolitania (Libya) and Eritrea. Lebanon, Syria, and Jordan, areas once managed by Europeans, gained independence in 1943, 1944, and 1946, respectively.

The world map, as after World War I, was redrawn. The emergence of so many new states, and the instability associated with the transfer of authority, shook the very foundations of the international system. Power was being redistributed. In varying degrees, Russia and America competed for the allegiance of the new governments, meddled in colonial rebellions, and generally sought to exploit opportunities for an extension of their influence. Again, the stakes seemed high. The new nations could serve as strategic bases, markets for exports, sources of vital raw materials, sites for investments, and votes in international organizations. States such as India, which chose nonalignment in the developing Cold War, were wooed with foreign aid and ideological appeals. In the case of Indochina, the powers supported different sides: Washington backed the ruling French, and Moscow endorsed Ho and his insurgents.

As one United States government study noted, the disintegration of empires, especially the withdrawal of the British from their once vast domain, created an "over-all situation of near chaos" in the international system. In some areas, such as Southeast Asia, it meant a "new balance of power." The upheaval was fundamental: "Old values are being changed and new ones sought. New friendships are being formed." The international system creaked and swayed under this unsettled burden.

Conflict also sprang from efforts to launch a new international organization to replace the defunct League of Nations. At the Dumbarton Oaks Conference in 1944, the Allies initiated plans for a United Nations Organization. The United States, Britain, and Russia were its chief architects, and the institution they created at the San Francisco Conference from April to June of 1945 reflected their insistence on big-power domination. They agreed upon a veto power for the five "permanent members" of the Security Council (Britain, Russia, United States, France, and China) and assigned the General Assembly, the forum for smaller nations, a subordinate status. Nevertheless, because each of the Allies recognized that the new international body was potentially an instrument, through bloc voting, of one nation's foreign policy, they argued. Churchill crudely complained that China, hardly a "great" power, would be a "faggot vote on the side of the United States," and Russia protested that France would simply represent a British vote. "China was a joke," remarked State Department veteran John Hickerson, "a FDR joke." Because Britain could marshall the votes of several of its Commonwealth countries and the United States could count on most of the Latin American nations in the General Assembly, the conferees at the Yalta Conference of early 1945 granted Russia three votes, in order to alter somewhat the glaring imbalance.

Such compromise, however, broke down at the San Francisco Conference. Membership applications from Argentina and Poland produced heated differences. Against vehement Soviet objections Argentina, which had declared war against Germany at the last minute and which some critics considered a "fascist" nation, gained membership after the United States backed its application and the nations of the Western Hemisphere voted "yes" as a bloc. Yet when Lublin-led Poland, not yet reorganized according to the American interpretation of the Yalta accords, applied for entry, the United States voted "no," and the conference denied Poland a seat. Moscow railed at this, charging a double standard. The United Nations Organization, which held its first session in January of 1946, thus began amidst controversy. Rather than serving as a stabilizing force in the postwar international system, the United Nations early became a source of conflict, a verbal battleground for the allegiance of world opinion, a vehicle for condemnatory resolutions, a largely United States–dominated institution, and a graveyard for idealistic hopes—in short, part of a "masquerade peace."

The postwar international system suffered, too, from the destabilizing effect of the new atomic bomb. The "most terrible weapon ever known in human history," Secretary of War Henry L. Stimson quietly told the President, unsettled the world community, for it was an agent of massive human destruction, and "in a world atmosphere already extremely sensitive to power, the introduction of this weapon has profoundly affected political considerations in all sections of the globe." Nations which possessed "the bomb" seemed to hold an advantage in international politics, for it could serve as a deterrent against an adversary as well as a means to annihilate an enemy. When combined with air power and a long-range delivery capability, it also hurdled geographical boundaries, rendering them useless as protective elements in a nation's security shield. With the perfecting of air war in World War II, "the roof blew off the territorial state." As General Douglas MacArthur remarked after the atomic explosions: "Well, this changes warfare!" The prospect of nuclear annihilation bothered everybody, but the United States was especially concerned about nuclear proliferation, which meant the loss of its atomic monopoly.

A question dogged the peacemakers: How were they to control the development, spread, and use of atomic energy? There had been arms races before, and ineffective disarmament conferences in the 1920s and 1930s, but the postwar nuclear race was conducted at a far different and more dangerous level. The atomic bomb was the "absolute weapon," not only more violent but also capable of speedy delivery, rapid retaliation, and immediate cataclysm. Challenging the American monopoly, the Soviet Union successfully produced its own bomb in 1949. As the two bickering major powers groped for ways in which to deal with "the bomb" and undertook their atomic development programs, others held their breath. One observer suggested that a Soviet–American war "might not end with *one* Rome but with *two* Carthages." The atomic bomb, uncontrolled, envied, copied, and brandished, became a major obstacle to a peaceful, orderly postwar international system.

The shrinkage of the world and the growth of a global outlook must be included in any estimation of the impact of World War II on the international system. Geography had not changed, but ways of moving across it and of thinking about it had. Improvements in transportation, especially in aviation, brought nations closer to one another. The world seemed more compact and accessible. People had to think now not only in traditional land miles but also in flying hours. In a popularization for school children, N. L. Englehardt, Jr. urged his young readers to think "air thoughts" and titled one of his chapters "How the World Has Shrunk." Because the Atlantic Ocean could be traversed easily and quickly, that once-prominent barrier between the Old and New Worlds disappeared. As America was brought closer to Europe and the world, American strategic thinking expanded as well. In the world contracted by science, events in Greece or Iran or China held greater significance than ever before for American security. The Japanese attack upon Pearl Harbor, accomplished after crossing 3,500 miles of the Pacific Ocean, had proved that great distances no longer served as protectors of security. "If you imagine two or three hundred Pearl Harbors occurring all over the United States," prophesied Assistant Secretary of State A. A. Berle, "you will have a rough picture of what the next war might look like. . . ." Observers began to speak not only of an "atomic age," but of an "air age" and a "global age." The global war of 1939–45 had helped spawn a postwar globalism—an international interdependence. "The entire relations of the United States with the world," declared Dean Acheson, "are a seamless web. . . ." Geographical isolation was gone with the past. Stimson perceived that the United States could never again "be an island to herself. No private program and no public policy, in any sector of our national life can now escape from the compelling fact that if it is not framed with reference to the world, it is framed with perfect futility."

United States Chief of Staff General George C. Marshall typified strategic reconsiderations. "For probably the last time in the history of warfare those ocean distances were a vital factor in our defense. We may elect again to depend on others and the whim and error of potential enemies, but if we do we will be carrying the treasure and freedom of this great Nation in a paper bag." Because frontiers had been extended, because nations were brought nearer one another, and because the world had shrunk, the major powers coveted bases far from home, much as the United States had sought and acquired bases in the Caribbean in the early twentieth century to protect the Panama Canal. "We are now concerned with the peace of the entire world," said Marshall. Two years later President Truman described a "much smaller earth—an earth whose broad oceans have shrunk and whose national protections have been taken away by new weapons of destruction." In a similar vein, a joint Chiefs of Staff report of late 1947 looked ten years into the future and predicted a "continuing shrinkage of the world from the accelerated pace of technological progress." In short, a new aspect of the postwar international system was the interdependence or intertwining of events in all parts of the world, thereby drawing great powers into confrontations as never before. Globalism insured conflict.

The Roots of Postwar Politics

ALAN WOLFE

The United States came out of World War II facing extremely important decisions about how it would organize its government and how it would relate to the world. For a variety of reasons, . . . neither the policies nor the constituencies of the New Deal were appropriate to the economic and political realities that faced Harry Truman. The conditions that had called for the New Deal having changed, the question facing postwar America was how to develop a new political formula for the organization and use of power.

Two possible courses seemed likely as the war came to an end. From the right end of the political spectrum, an anguished and bitter cry for a return to "normalcy" could be heard. Reflected in the Congress elected in 1946, conservative sentiment called for a return to business civilization; a holy, if inexpensive, crusade against communism; and a reassertion of once popular isolationist values. From the left a call was issued to carry the New Deal forward to its logical conclusion in some form of democratic socialism, American style (though, given the vocabulary of American politics, it could never be called that). Full employment, economic planning, national health insurance, and a commitment to peace organized through the United Nations—these would be the planks of a progressive program for America.

Whatever the differences between them, the right and left courses were both *political* options. Because neither was consensual, either would have required a popular mobilization and the building of new constituencies to support it. There was a sense of movement to both programs, one forward, the other back. Both implied struggle, dissent, controversy. Both were organized around an assertion of a particular vision and a sense of the means to achieve it. The key to understanding the formation of America's impasse, and the inability of both the Democrats and the Republicans to work their way out of it, lies in the fact that neither of these courses was chosen in 1946. Instead of making a political choice, America opted for an economic surrogate. A bipartisan coalition was formed to pursue economic expansion, at home through growth and overseas through empire. Once the rationale of the political system became the enhancement of growth, everything changed, including the role of political parties, the structure of political ideology, the nature of public policy, and the meaning of dissent. America embarked on a massive experiment. Politics would concern itself with the means—growth—and the ends, or purpose, of social life would take care of themselves.

Unlike political choice, economic growth offered a smooth and potentially harmonious future—instead of divisive, possibly ugly, and certainly disruptive struggles over redistributional issues. Rapid economic growth, it was felt, could expand the pie sufficiently so that it would not have to be cut in a different way. And expansion overseas could create an imperial dividend, a periodic bounty from empire that would augment the sugar in the pie in the first place. Between them, economic growth and the imperial dividend created a whole new approach to government, one that would not so much exercise political power to make choices as it would manage expansion and empire to avoid choice. Growth, in other words, was transpolitical. While liberals blame conservatives for America's impasse and conservatives say that the fault lies with liberals, the truth is that growth allowed policies that substituted economic performance for political ideology. America sought, not what would create the best, but what would work the best. United behind a growth strategy, America expanded enormously in the postwar period, witnessing, some say, the greatest economic miracle in the modern world. So overwhelming was this growth that it created its own brand of politics, a compromise over policy so pleasing and rewarding that it would continue with unstoppable force long after the growth came to a halt, thereby worsening America's economic performance with the same determination with which it had once enhanced it.

The political costs of economic growth were not calculated for some time, and many refuse to examine them even now. Yet in retrospect it seems clear what happened. In the late 1940s, advocates of growth were believers in liberal ideals like economic planning, social welfare, international idealism, and foreign aid. But once the quest for growth became an all-consuming passion, those liberal objectives became dependent on conservative instruments. Growth at home could not take place without business confidence, and so liberals set out to win business support with favorable policies. Overseas expansion, to be made palatable to a generally isolationist America, had to be rationalized in terms of national security, encouraging a dependence on the military. With liberal objectives tied so firmly to conservative means, America developed a postwar political formula filled with contradictory language. Social justice would be pursued with all the vigor of profit maximization, while America would export to the world both humanitarianism and military power. Liberalism, in short, was submerged into the quest for growth; when its head popped up again, it was no longer liberalism. Without growth, the Democratic party, as Carter's presidency demonstrated, was a political organization without a political vision, something clearly recognized by the voters in 1980.

But if liberalism was seduced by its devotion to growth, so was conservatism. In the late 1940s, there was a genuine conservative tradition in the United States. Its faith was in economic competition, its roots in the farmers and small businessmen of the Middle West, its vision isolationist and even pacifist, and its conception of trade protectionist. An expanding economy at home, pushed forward by increasingly concentrated corporations and the benefits of overseas trade, dominated by multinational corporations and protected by a flourishing defense industry located in the South and West, transformed American conservatism as thoroughly as it did New Deal liberalism. Ronald Reagan bears as much resemblance to Robert Taft as Jimmy Carter does to Franklin Roosevelt. In the 1980s, the Republican party . . . has become what the Democrats have rejected: the party of domestic economic growth and imperial expansion.

In their quest for respectability among business and the military, postwar liberals lost faith in their own objectives. Conservatives, whose links to business and some sectors of the military were strong, were incapable of becoming the majority party because they had given the world Herbert Hoover. For liberals, growth was a substitute for the respectability they lacked. For conservatives, growth became the key to the popularity they sought to gain. Just as liberals sublimated objectives like social justice into a quest for business and overseas expansion, conservatives would come to seek a balanced budget and stable prices through expanded profits and higher military spending. American liberalism lost its sense of purpose as it sought in expansion the resolution to its internal contradictions. With the arrival of the Reagan presidency, American conservatism promises to do exactly the same thing. . . .

America was fundamentally changed by World War II, in every conceivable way. Economically, the war had a wondrous impact upon the gross national product (GNP). In 1929, the GNP stood at $103.4 billion, which then fell to $55.8 billion by 1933. Six years of New Deal policies saw the figure rise to $90.8 billion in 1939, still below the peak of ten years earlier. During the war, however, economic activity grew by leaps and bounds. The GNP reached $100 billion by 1940, $129.9 in 1941, $158.3 in 1942, $192 in 1943, and $210 in 1944. At least this much can be said: war enabled production to take place once again.

But the need to turn out as many weapons as the economy was capable of generating was only a quantitative change, and there were important qualitative ones as well. Most noticeable was the growing role played by government. Public spending, $9 billion in 1940, increased tenfold to $98 billion in 1945. The government offered the staggering sum of $175 billion in prime contracts between June 1940 and September 1944. Over one-third of all manufacturing structures and equipment existing in the United States during this period was constructed through the $17 billion worth of new plants financed by government to speed the war effort. There could no longer be any doubt that government was capable of playing a positive role in economic stimulation.

In 1945, *Fortune* carried a Roper poll showing that only 41 percent of the American population thought that a postwar recession could be avoided. It was generally assumed in America that periods of bust would follow periods of boom the way that thunder follows lightning. Yet the conditions of wartime production augured a transformation in the cyclical nature of American capitalism. First, the sheer size of the mobilization involved, much greater than in World War I, ensured that prewar conditions would not return in the same form; the sharply reduced military budget for fiscal year (FY) 1947, for example, was still $13 billion *higher* than the last prewar budget of 1940. Similarly, the number of civilian workers on federal payrolls after the war, and the number of women and men in uniform, was much higher than a decade earlier. Second, vast savings by consumers, not spendable during the war, kept the economy afloat after the war had ended. Third, the Federal Reserve Board made a decision during the war to support the price of government securities at a predetermined rate, and this prevented tight-money advocates from constricting the economy in the late 1940s. Finally, the war had created an effective system of wage-and-price controls, enabling expansion to take place without rapidly rising prices. Policymakers were thus able to prove that full employment and stable prices could coexist, so long as a political authority with appropriate power existed to ensure it.

Yet another qualitative change in the American economy brought about by the war was the freedom given to the United States by its strength in the world economy. Most countries at most times worry that trading rivals will increase their share of the world's output and threaten the advantages of domestic manufacturers. For the United States in the postwar period, the problem was the exact opposite of this. The U.S. economy was so much richer than those of war-devastated Europe that the latter were unable to absorb American surplus production; domestic unemployment would result unless the United States worked to *improve* the relative economic standing of its rivals. Some sense of the American advantage in the world economy is given by the fact that almost half of the world's manufactured goods in 1947 were made in the United States. The dollar was far and away the world's strongest currency, especially since the collapse of the pound sterling. When the near U.S. monopoly on gold is considered—one estimate placed it as high as 72 percent of the world's supply in 1949—America seemed in a position to benefit from economic changes in the world, not to be held down by them as it was during the Great Depression.

Nor was any other country in the world powerful enough to challenge the United States militarily. Germany and Japan, having been defeated, became the objects of an American effort to increase their productivity while keeping them under American political protection. The so-called underdeveloped countries were as poor after the war as they had been before it, so there was no need to worry about them. Only from the Soviet Union could any possible challenge be forthcoming, and the Soviet Union had been an American ally during the war. In the late 1940s, and to the present day, there would be those who talked of a Soviet military threat to the United States, often with cataclysmic imagery. Certainly in the immediate postwar period these fears proved to be exaggerated. The Soviet Union had left its troops behind in Europe, but it had neither the weaponry nor the sophistication to challenge the United States at a time when policymakers allowed themselves to become haunted by a Soviet "threat."

Between them, domestic economic expansion, measured in the growth of the GNP, and the benefits to be obtained from unchallenged economic and military power combined to make the New Deal inappropriate to the situation of the late 1940s. New Deal measures had often been geared to doing—anything to get the economy out of its doldrums. But the postwar situation, with stimulation already in place, demanded something different. Two dominant points of view existed. There were a number of articulate economic activists who argued a fundamental restructuring of the economy in order to plan and direct the changes taking place. Domestic economic management, they claimed, must ensure full employment and the adequate use of all other resources, while America would join with the rest of the world in sponsoring global economic reforms to ensure greater prosperity. Opposed to these activists were businessmen and more orthodox economists, who held that, with the Depression over, the time had come to return to business as usual: a greater reliance on the private sector and international economic practices that increased American wealth, not the world's liquidity. In short, the fact that the economic situation of the late 1940s was different from that of the mid-1930s seemed to foreshadow a direction distinct from the ad hoc character of New Deal emergency measures.

Such a direction could only come from the political system, yet the politics of the late 1940s were as stagnant as the economy was dynamic. Shortly before America entered World War II, a political stalemate had emerged in the United States. The New Deal ran out of energy when its last major reform, a Wages and Hours Law, was passed in 1938. Conservative Democrats from the South and Republican isolationists from the West formed a coalition in Congress that was able to block Roosevelt from developing either a global foreign policy or a far-sighted domestic policy, yet the conservative bloc was still not strong enough to create an alternative government strategy of its own. National unity produced by war overshadowed this deadlock for five years, but it would emerge again when the war was over. And when the war did end, Americans discovered that the conditions of wartime production, the rise in influence of the military, and the creation of a new political mood all deepened the political stalemate by strengthening the veto power of the conservative bloc.

Relations between business and government—touchy and suspicious during the Great Depression—went through two major changes during World War II. First, business began a political offensive designed to regain a positive image and to absolve itself as much as possible from any blame for the Depression. This offensive has to be rated a success. The large number of business executives who came to Washington "without compensation" to direct the war effort extracted major political concessions for their economic experience. The National Resources Planning Board, an agency that some New Dealers hoped to use to guide the economy in the postwar period, was abolished. Jesse Jones, Roosevelt's secretary of commerce, led the campaign from within to restore business influence. No-strike pledges kept labor subservient. In the guise of defeating Germany, businessmen were also defeating the New Deal, and they were determined to preserve their victory once the war ended. The more liberal New Dealers were in dismay. "I don't like to overuse the word 'fascist,'" Chester Bowles, head of the Office of Price Administration, wrote to Vice-President Henry Wallace in 1944, "but it does seem to me the only phrase that can be applied to the kind of thinking which I ran into among some groups in business."

The political offensive of business during the war was facilitated by a second change in its relationship with government: business had, under the exigencies of wartime planning, become more monopolistic. The American economy in the twentieth century has been divided into a competitive and a monopolistic sector, the former dependent on the market, the latter trying to control the market. With government assuming the risks of entrepreneurship through cost-plus contracting, the monopoly sector of the economy was strengthened during the war. Thirty-three corporations received over one-half of the total prime contracts, while ten alone received over 30 percent. Before the war there had been a significant element of antitrust sentiment in New Deal philosophy: Thurman Arnold, in charge of the antitrust division of the Justice Department, had tried to keep alive Louis Brandeis's faith in competition. This philosophy all but disappeared among liberals as the war brought concentration to a new peak and made competition seem somehow unpatriotic. With their power over markets more secure, monopoly-sector businessmen would be able to defeat, or at least to control, attempts to regulate them in the public interest. Indeed, a substantial portion of government intervention would become devoted to strengthening monopolization, not to curtailing it.

Besides a strengthened and revitalized business class, the war, not unexpectedly, had given rise to a powerful military apparatus, one closely connected to conservative Southern Democrats and Western Republicans. Before World War II, America had been an isolationist power, without a permanent standing army and without a substantial infrastructure in defense production. The creation of precisely such an infrastructure during the war raised the question of what would happen when peace returned. One does not need a conspiracy theory of history to suggest that military leaders and their supporters in the new defense industries would fight to preserve the privileges they had gained during the war. Spokesmen for the military sector were guilty of nothing more than the typically American pursuit of self-interest when they exaggerated military threats to the United States in order to enhance their economic and political power. The permanence of the new military sector, powerful in Congress due to the overrepresentation of the South, was a fact of life that made the political situation of the 1940s quite different from that of the 1930s.

Finally, war changed the nature of demagoguery in the United States. There has never been a time when America was without its advocates of simple-minded scapegoatism, but during the Depression the targets of the attack were often respectable elements, especially Wall Street. Even when anti-Semitic in nature, the demagoguery of the 1930s had a populistic tinge, enough to make established powers squirm. But if economic slowdowns unleash populistic themes, wars often give rise to reactionary ones. As early as the elections of 1944, the political coloration of the United States turned conservative. Right-wing appeals—anticommunism, racism, fear of modernity, antiurbanism—were gaining in strength day by day. Whoever could control the anger and frustration sparked by the war could ride to political power, and it became clear early on that business and the military were in a better position to channel this sentiment against the New Deal than the New Dealers were to use it to their own advantage. The objects of popular fury in the 1930s would become the beneficiaries of that fury in the 1940s.

As a result of these changes, the overwhelming political need to give direction to a set of economic transformations could not be met. Indeed, directions of all sorts seemed suspect. "A nation accustomed to the categorical yes or no, to war or peace and prosperity or depression," Eric Goldman wrote, "found itself in the nagging realm of the maybe. The liberals worried over the conservatives and the conservatives watched the liberals with an uneasiness akin to dread." The stalemate that had been foreshadowed in 1938 returned, and with a vengeance. Conservatives had become a major force in Congress, but liberals still held the executive. . . . [The deadlock was resolved by the emergence during the Truman years of a new politics of growth.] [R]apid economic growth could work to expand the federal budget, rewarding voters without offending vested interests. Economic growth would become the invisible glue that would hold [Truman's] strategy together. And since growth can only be obtained by offering concessions to businessmen in order to induce them to invest, [Truman's] popular electoral base could be held together only by following policies advantageous to big business. Domestic policy under the Democrats in the postwar years would become a search for the proper way to win business confidence.

The foreign policy consequences implicit in [Truman's] strategy were similarly unanticipated. Without a reform tradition to hold it together, the electoral coalition of the Democratic party could be unified around anticommunism. Furthermore, the creation of a *Pax Americana* rationalized through cold war policies would provide economic benefits in the form of an imperial dividend, just as a domestic growth strategy would expand the size of the pie. Finally, a move toward a global foreign policy and a domestic emphasis on anticommunism would, in Truman's words, "take the ball away from the right." For all these reasons, the Democrats were forced, by the logic of a growth imperative, toward an anticommunist foreign policy, one that would provide immediate political rewards in the 1948 election. There were, however, long-term consequences. For one thing, the more Truman tried to steal the ball from the right, the stronger the right seemed to become. Moreover, just as a domestic growth strategy produced dependence on winning business confidence, an imperial foreign policy produced dependence on the military and its eventual industrial complex. Foreign policy under the Democrats in the postwar years would become a search for the proper way to win the confidence of the guardians of national security.

[It thus] followed [that] the pursuit of economic growth and the expansion of empire [were] the two directions that could solve the problems of the political stalemate. Growth, both in the economy and in the empire, would get around the logjam by widening the river. To pursue that growth, a new coalition came to power in American politics. This coalition advocated an overall expansion of the economy through macroeconomic policies made acceptable to the monopoly sector of the economy. From the surplus generated through growth, it offered domestic policies to the poor and the minorities that would, it was hoped, enable them to take part in the reshaping of the cities and countryside that would follow from growth priorities. Based upon the rapid expansion of the economy, it developed a foreign policy that combined a reorganization of the world under American economic hegemony with military power to ensure American influence. Finally, it offered to incorporate the world's poor into the growth machine through foreign aid and developmental assistance. The tasks established by the growth coalition were herculean, but anything seemed possible in an expanding economy. America had never before seen anything like this coalition, and it may never see anything like it again. The uniqueness of the growth coalition can be established by ascertaining what it was not.

While Truman kept alive the spirit of the New Deal in his Fair Deal rhetoric, the growth coalition that stirred during his presidency was *not* the same as the domestic coalition organized by Franklin Delano Roosevelt to support the New Deal. There was little room on ship for liberal politicians who kept alive an aggressive and articulate concern with income redistribution, economic planning, or international idealism. Radicals who had risen to power in the 1930s based upon their ability to mobilize discontent from below were replaced by "pragmatic" liberals who were sympathetic to monopoly power and anticommunism. Those liberal politicians who could not forget the New Deal but did join the growth coalition, like Chester Bowles of Connecticut or Wilson Wyatt of Kentucky, would always be somewhat out of place. The growth-oriented liberalism of the times was determined to exclude, in Arthur Schlesinger, Jr.'s, marvelous phrase, the "Dough-faced," those who were not hard-headed or realistic enough to understand that growth and empire, unlike dissent and reform, meant concessions to established sources of power.

But if the coalition lopped off the left end of opinion, it also isolated itself from the right. Mr. Republican, Senator Robert Taft of Ohio, was the *bête noire* of the new coalition, for his tight-money financial policies and his isolationism had no place in a world oriented to expansion. Growth policies presupposed the use of government at home to enlarge the economy and the use of government abroad to enhance the empire. The whole venture would be expensive (though its advocates claimed that it would pay for itself). It would mean a confrontation with traditional American values of localism and private virtue. Looking backward to Lockean liberalism and nativistic isolationism was as ideologically repugnant to the growth coalition as looking forward to social democracy and economic planning.

The rise of the growth coalition was facilitated—some would say mandated—by the economic transformations taking place in America. The three most important were economic concentration, growing state intervention, and expansion overseas. All three created a new economic basis that became the core turf of the growth coalition.

Robert Taft's Republicanism had been based on an alliance between competitive-sector businessmen operating close to the margin and small-scale farmers concentrated in the Midwest. Both forces were becoming anachronistic in the economic atmosphere of the late 1940s. Monopoly-sector businessmen, protected by their control over prices from labor costs and overseas competition, could afford to be more liberal toward domestic innovations like the welfare state and toward free trade. The growth of monopolization, linked to multinational expansion and to the debt-encouraging practices of Wall Street banks and investment houses, made the rise of the growth coalition possible.

But growth also changed the traditional basis of New Deal support. Roosevelt's electoral majorities had been formed by mobilizing sentiment among the dispossessed, from tenant farmers to the working class. Growth politics, however, implied organized interest groups, not mobilization from below. The crucial constituencies of growth politics were unions not workers, civil rights organizations not blacks. The growth coalition could be held together so long as liberal monopoly-sector businessmen were willing to engage in an informal alliance with similarly monopolistic unions, together expanding productivity so that both could benefit. In that way, labor's almost instinctive protectionism could be modified to support free-trade policies, while the threat that labor posed by its reformism could be channeled instead into cooperation with management. In other words, the social and economic basis of the growth coalition was an East Coast-based, European-oriented, financial and industrial elite located in large monopolistic corporations that had made its peace with conservative, anticommunist labor leaders and Democratic party interest groups that wanted urban growth and development.

The emergence of the growth coalition, then, was something new. Unlike conservative Republicanism, it favored state intervention at home and was opposed to isolationism abroad. But unlike the New Deal, it was not a reformist, mobilizing movement, and it sought free-trade policies toward the rest of the world. Sometimes called the "vital center" and other times designated "cold war liberalism," the growth coalition should properly be characterized by its dominant belief: the idea that growth at home and expansion abroad could unify the interests of the dominant sectors of the economy with an electoral base that would keep it in power so long as growth continued. . . .

By 1950, the growth coalition had defeated any serious opposition to its left. Henry Wallace and the Progressive party had been disgraced, and anticommunism had established itself as a permanent feature in American political life. There was still, however, a major problem on the right. The growth coalition was only half formed; it required a Republican administration to complete it. . . .

[The] Eisenhower administration actually solidified the triumph of growth politics. After eight years of Republican rule, the old-fashioned Republican notions of laissez-faire monetarism and overseas isolationism could barely be heard. (Indeed, when the Republican right would make itself visible again, in 1964, it would bear little relationship to Taftism; from this time forward, the "right" would advocate more extreme cold war policies than the center and would base itself on a military sector that was heavily dependent on government spending.) Eisenhower legitimated growth by not abandoning it. His main domestic advisers . . . were hardly economic activists, . . . but nor were they monetarists. The administration's specialists on defense and foreign policy . . . were holding down the military budget, but they surely were not isolationists. With Eisenhower, ideas about growth did not rush forward into the future, but neither did they slip backwards into the past.

During the 1950s, the political vocabulary of the United States underwent a major transformation. When the New Deal was the decisive frame of reference, debate was divided into two camps called liberal and conservative. Liberals were those who believed that the government should play a positive role in correcting the abuses of capitalism by promoting a concern with equality and social justice. Conservatives argued that business had made America great and that therefore as few reforms as possible should be passed that would undermine its privileges. While the terms liberal and conservative were retained in America, their meaning shifted as growth priorities were accepted by both parties. From now on, a liberal was one who believed that growth should happen rapidly and a conservative, one who believed that growth should happen in a more tempered fashion. There were other differences, of course. Liberals were willing to use government to bring about more rapid growth, and they also argued that growth could create a fiscal dividend out of which more welfare benefits could be financed. In addition, liberals combined their notions of economic expansion at home with a call for imperial expansion overseas; the creation of the national security state and an aggressive foreign policy were basically liberal inventions. Similarly, conservatives, though committed to growth, wished to see it occur through the private sector, with Washington acting like a rabid fan, cheering business on. Moreover, conservatives did not want growth to occur at such a fast pace that it would cause inflation; and, tied more closely to the protectionist and competitive sector of the economy, they were dubious about a zealous pursuit of overseas empire. But these were differences in emphasis, not in basic outlook. By the end of the Eisenhower period, words like liberal and conservative no longer meant what they did during the New Deal. A senator like Paul Douglas and a Republican like Nelson Rockefeller agreed on little else but spending huge sums to promote economic expansion, making them both "liberals." Arthur Burns had little in common with Everett Dirksen or Richard Russell, but they all urged caution in too rapid a commitment to expansion, making them all "conservatives."

Growth created its own particular politics. Liberal notions of growth were embodied in a constellation of forces: the executive branch of the Democratic party; Eastern Republicanism; unions, particularly in the monopoly sector; constituents of the New Deal voting coalition; the free-trade, monopolistic, financial wing of business; universities; and downtown redevelopment interests in the major cities. Conservative growth advocates settled in the Southern and congressional wing of the Democratic party, the Western wing of the Republican party, the military–industrial complex, the water–public works–Army Corps of Engineers network, agribusiness, protectionist and isolationist business concerns, and, ultimately, the aerospace, high technology industries of the 1960s. Neither wing of the growth network could govern by itself. Liberals, with a built-in electoral majority, needed to make their policies acceptable to business and the military in order to pass legislation. Conservatives, secure among the powerful, needed to liberalize their programs in order to win national elections. As each wing of the growth network lurched toward the center in search of what it did not have, a pattern of politics was created that would last for a generation. Here are the main features of what I will call *growth politics:*

1. Liberal advocates of growth would, in general, dominate the executive branch, while Congress would institutionalize the power of conservative ideas about growth. Thus, the passage of legislation in the postwar years often represented uneasy compromises between contrasting conceptions of growth. . . .
2. Despite a later cynicism about the political parties, there were real differences between them, but the differences were not ideological ones. Democrats, at least most of them, saw domestic and overseas growth as a means of solving problems, while Republicans saw problems with domestic and overseas growth. The debates between the parties were real, but they concerned how fast and at what cost growth should be achieved.
3. In spite of these differences in approach, the parties often became indistinguishable in practice. For in order to carry out their notions, liberals had to win the confidence of business and the military and therefore they made their notions more conservative, while conservatives, distrusted by the voters, expanded their ideas to make them more liberal.
4. Since growth was the agreed-upon goal, politics in America would no longer be divided along even minimal class lines, as it was becoming during the New Deal, and would no longer be encumbered by discussions of "issues." Debates would concern means, not ends. Major questions of public policy were simply removed from debate. Growth, in short, presupposed the suppression of fundamental political choice. The purpose of campaigns and elections was to ratify technical decisions about how expeditiously growth was occurring, not to mandate radical departures in policy.
5. As a result of all the preceding, neither wing of the growth coalition would seek to mobilize discontent from below, to tap new sources of support among underrepresented groups, or to encourage whatever popular protest existed in society. Liberal growth advocates connected themselves to interests like unions, not to passions like the labor movement.

Conservatives needed popular support to come to power, but discovered a preference for demagogic themes ("Had enough?" "law and order") as an alternative to building a mass base. There would be few new sources of political energy forthcoming. "Politics" would come to mean a discussion among interest groups, not an attempt to develop a vision of a better society.

6. Finally, each wing of the growth coalition would discover, over time, that it had more in common with the other than it did with the base out of which it had emerged. Liberal growth advocates found themselves to be more comfortable with the conservative wing of the growth coalition than they did with old-fashioned progressives and unreconstructed New Dealers, while conservative growth advocates could talk more easily to hard-headed economic activists than they could to extremists on the radical right. The two wings of the growth coalition deeply needed each other, and while they would engage in political combat in public, they would often arrange harmonious compromises in private.

The consolidation of this growth-oriented pattern of politics under Eisenhower was the most important consequence of the Republican interregnum of the 1950s. Not only did it imply a containment of the isolationist and laissez-faire right, it also curtailed the last stirrings of the New Deal left. . . .

By 1960, expectations of growth had become such an institutionalized feature of American politics that, the next time the liberal wing of the coalition came to power, it would not find itself hampered as it was under Truman. The transformation that had come over the American political system was apparent within a year after John F. Kennedy assumed office.

The Social Politics of Race and Gender

WILLIAM H. CHAFE

Until the beginning of World War II, a combination of economic, political, and social intimidation successfully undercut the possibility of a concerted drive among black Americans for racial equality. Although protest organizations such as the NAACP worked effectively within the court system for legal change, the vast majority of black people lived in circumstances that precluded social protest. Three out of four blacks lived in the South, where the crop lien system operated to keep both white and black tenant farmers in a state of perpetual economic bondage. A pervasive etiquette of race, reinforced wherever necessary by terrorism, prevented even minor challenges to the status quo. During the New Deal a number of Roosevelt Administration officials supported changes to help blacks, including fair allocation of relief money in many places and a larger recognition of blacks in political appointments. Still, the first to suffer from the Depression had been those

From *Women and Equality: Changing Patterns in American Culture* by William H. Chafe, pp. 84–106. Copyright © 1977 by Oxford University Press, Inc. Reprinted by permission.

at the bottom, and even the supposedly friendly Roosevelt Administration failed to put its weight behind legislation to abolish lynching or outlaw the poll tax. At the end of the 1930's the masses of black people were still oppressed, politically and economically, and protest organizations voiced anger at the failure of New Deal leaders to act on even the most clear-cut issues of civil rights.

World War II brought a significant departure from past patterns—in the behavior of blacks if not in the dominant culture's attitudes. The urgency of meeting the defense crisis made it imperative for the government to recruit into industry and the armed forces millions of people who previously had been excluded from significant positions in society. Black leaders, recognizing an unparalleled opportunity, used the lever of the crisis to drive home a series of demands for reform which, if put into effect, would bring greater civil rights for blacks in return for loyal support of the war effort. The most notable example of this strategy was the March on Washington Movement (MOW) led by labor organizer A. Philip Randolph in 1941. Threatening to bring as many as 50,000 black protestors to Washington in the midst of Congressional debate on military preparedness bills, Randolph and his coalition of black leaders successfully extracted from the Administration a pledge to secure equal opportunity for blacks in all defense-related industries. The MOW Movement, composed exclusively of blacks, represented a daring departure and forced the national Administration to acknowledge, at least formally, black complaints.

On a deeper level, however, the war itself proved more decisive to the long-term history of change in race relations. By causing a massive dislocation of population and forcing millions of people into new experiences, the war created a context in which some people both perceived and responded to the issue of race in a different way. The vicious cycle of social control which had compelled obedience to traditional patterns as the price for survival was at least partially broken by the massive jolt of full-scale war. Although little was accomplished in the way of permanent progress toward equality, the changes which did occur laid the foundations for the development of mass protest activity in subsequent years.

The first great impact of the war was an accelerated migration of blacks from the South, and within the South from farm to city. Whether lured by a specific job in a munitions plant, ordered by a directive from the Selective Service, or simply beckoned by the prospect of a better life elsewhere, millions of black Southerners boarded trains and buses and headed north and west. When they arrived at their destinations, they frequently found living situations less attractive than they had expected. The urban ghetto, with its overcrowded housing, hard-pressed social facilities, and oppressive discrimination, seemed to many not much better than what they had left behind. Yet there was a difference as well. The Northern urban political machine sought votes and offered some political recognition in return. The community was new, the imminent tyranny of small-town authorities was removed, and psychological freedom was greater. The very act of physical mobility brought independence from the overwhelming constraints of social control in small Southern communities. If the controls existed in different forms in the new community, there was at least the possibility of different perspectives and a heightened sense of what might be done to achieve a better life.

The second major effect of the war was a limited amount of economic mobility. The lure of jobs in the North and in urban areas of the South was not totally without substance. Some 2,000,000 blacks were employed in defense plants during the war and another 200,000 joined the federal civil service. Most of these jobs were at low levels. Blacks continued to be hired as janitors or as scrub-women rather than as technicians or secretaries. Still, as the war progressed, there was more chance of better positions. In 1940 the number of blacks employed in professional, white-collar, skilled or semi-skilled jobs had been less than 20 per cent. A decade later the figure had climbed to 33 per cent, largely as a result of wartime changes. The number of blacks in labor unions doubled to 1,250,000 during the war years. The end result was thus a confused picture: enough upward mobility had occurred to spur hope, but constant discrimination reinforced a sense of how much needed to be done.

The third great impact came in the armed forces. When the war began, blacks protested vigorously that they were not drafted in proportion to their numbers in the population. They insisted on being trained alongside whites and given the same opportunity to fight in combat units. Although some progress occurred on these issues, persistent maltreatment of black soldiers made a mockery of the government's claim to be fighting a war against racism. While President Roosevelt repeatedly told the world that the country was fighting for freedom and democracy, training camps were torn by prejudice and discrimination, Red Cross blood supplies were segregated into "white" and "colored," and blacks frequently were the victims of violence from whites in local communities where they were stationed.

Significantly, each of the major shifts initiated by World War II exhibited a common theme: the interaction of some change for the better with pervasive reminders of ongoing racism. The chemistry of the process was crucial. At the same time that new exposure to travel, jobs, and higher expectations exerted an emancipating effect on people's perception of the world, day-to-day contact with discrimination in the armed forces, poor housing in the urban ghetto, and blatant prejudice on the job had an embittering effect. The juxtaposition could not help but spawn anger and frustration. The experience of some improvement generated the expectation for still more, and, when those expectations were dashed, a rising tide of frustration and protest resulted.

In this sense, the experience of black Americans during World War II provided a paradigm for race relations over the ensuing three decades. The major theme of black history from the 40's through the 70's has been of promises made and then betrayed, creating a framework for ever growing disillusionment among blacks and an increasing insistence among them on direct action to secure their rights.

The promise of effective progress on civil rights through a biracial coalition of liberals took specific form in the mid-40's. During the war itself, crowded living conditions, racial conflict over jobs, and the resentment of angry whites led to numerous race riots. The frightening example of racial turmoil caused many white leaders to pledge support for change in race relations. During the Truman Administration especially, the record of verbal support for civil rights seemed strong. Truman appointed a special Committee on Civil Rights with enough liberals on it to guarantee that the subsequent report would spell out in detail the measures needed to correct discrimination. Truman enthusiastically endorsed the report early in 1948 and later became the first President to take his political campaign to Harlem. The subsequent outpouring of black votes for Truman—the margin of victory in some states—caused many observers to see the President's statements on civil rights as the key to his re-election.

Verbal support rarely translated into action, however. Fearful of alienating his political constituency in the white South, Truman never pushed hard for implementation of his civil rights recommendations, nor did he take decisive executive action to deliver on the promises he had made. Although the order to desegregate the armed forces was issued in 1948, the majority of military units remained segregated until after the Korean War. From the perspective of the President, of course, more had been done to legitimize the issue of civil rights and educate the public than ever before. But from the point of view of many blacks, the words had accomplished little for the people being talked about. Truman's symbolic political action during the campaign had continued to encourage hope, but when it came to substance, the record was skimpy.

In some ways the most decisive embodiment of the theme of promise and betrayal came with the Supreme Court's 1954 ruling in *Brown* v. *Board of Education* declaring that segregated schools were unconstitutional. The black press responded to the decision with universal acclaim, voicing the conviction of most black people that the Court's action meant an end forthwith to all the evils of segregation. Much of the white press expressed the same expectation of rapid change, and even some Southern governors appeared resigned to major shifts. Yet the practical response once again fell drastically short of the mark. President Eisenhower consistently refused to lend moral support for the decision; the courts themselves backed off from requiring immediate enforcement; and almost every Southern state—tacitly encouraged by Washington's inaction—successfully avoided even minimal steps toward desegregation.

Bitter disappointment over the failure to enforce the *Brown* decision took place in the context of continued frustration in other areas as well. The fact that black people remained poor at a time when the rest of the nation seemed to be making giant strides toward affluence only accentuated discontent. In 1959 a black college graduate could expect to earn in a lifetime less than a white person with an eighth grade education. Nearly half of all black citizens fell below the poverty line. While blacks watched the same tantalizing television ads as whites and shared the same desire for a decent house and adequate schooling for their children, they were consistently denied the chance to acquire good housing or hold the jobs which would give them access to the "affluent" society.

It was against this background of rising expectations and continuing disillusionment that black Americans took matters into their own hands. The emergence of the modern civil rights movement can be traced to the December day in 1955 when Rosa Parks refused to move to the back of a Montgomery bus and was arrested as a result. The next day the black community of Montgomery responded with a total boycott of the city's bus lines. The year-long siege that followed was notable for three primary reasons: first, it showed that virtually 100 per cent of the black population was willing to stand up for its rights regardless of intimidation, thereby shattering the tired cliché that local blacks were satisfied; second, it illustrated the way in which a movement once under way generates its own momentum and vision, as the boycott committee's demands changed from greater courtesy toward blacks within a segregated bus system to a demand for complete desegregation of the buses; and third, it brought to the fore a young black minister who preached a philosophy of non-violent resistance as a means of overcoming racial injustice. Under Martin Luther King, Jr.'s, leadership, the church—the foremost institution within the black community and in the past frequently an instrument of social control—became at once the center of a mass movement for social change. Four years later, the same spirit that had motivated the Montgomery movement led black students in Greensboro, North Carolina, to sit in at the local Woolworth's lunch counter and demand equal service. Within days, their example was emulated by other black students throughout the South, as sit-ins erupted in nearly every state below the Mason-Dixon line. As one demonstration led to another, protest became a national by-word, and the era of modern-day social activism was begun.

Even in the halcyon days of the civil rights movement, however, the theme of promises betrayed continued to shape the history of race relations. Although white students from the North and some from the South joined blacks in sit-ins and kneel-ins and pray-ins, politicians in Washington failed to respond with decisive actions. John F. Kennedy promised to sign an executive order barring discrimination in federally financed housing, then waited two years before putting pen to paper. The Justice Department pledged protection for travelers seeking to desegregate interstate buses and for voter registration workers, but in far too many cases FBI agents stood by as local white sheriffs beat up peaceful demonstrators. In addition, the conquest of some barriers to equality simply disclosed the presence of others, and as more and more young people joined the movement, impatience over government inaction outpaced the slow rate of progress. As civil rights leaders pointed out, it was one thing to have the right to eat at the Holiday Inn and another to have the money to buy decent food. As the problem of racism was probed deeper and deeper, confidence in the willingness of the government to respond adequately diminished even further.

Tensions within the movement itself highlighted the ongoing conflict over the value of looking to whites for support. Martin Luther King, Jr., headed an informal national coalition of church leaders, labor representatives, liberal politicians, Northern white financial supporters, and blacks. The fact that he was forced to be responsive to all elements of the coalition in order to achieve his legislative goals irritated younger and more radical activists. From the perspective of some members of the Student Non-violent Coordinating Committee (SNCC), it sometimes seemed that King cared more about cultivating the media and his Northern liberal constituency than about blacks working in the rural counties of Alabama, Georgia, and Mississippi. To young militants the white establishment had done nothing to earn consideration from the civil rights movement. When the March on Washington took place in the summer of 1963, influential white liberals had urged SNCC leader John Lewis to tone down his speech because it was too radical. And when the Mississippi Freedom Democratic Party went to the Democratic National Convention in 1964 with damning evidence of fraud and intimidation on the part of Mississippi's white Democrats, it was Northern white liberals who were responsible for forcing through a compromise which gave blacks only two seats instead of the twenty they sought and could have won.

As a result there developed within the movement itself a growing demand for blacks to be in complete control, even if that meant the exclusion of whites. The slogan "black and white together" had appealed to the deepest idealism of many young Americans, white and black, who wished to eliminate the tensions born of centuries of racism and create a "beloved community." But to many members of SNCC, working with whites became synonymous with continued paternalism and white domination. Black leaders like Stokely Carmichael and Rap Brown asked whether integration was not, in its own way, another form of subjugation, with blacks accepting white norms, white habits, and white souls. If integration meant assimilation, what would happen to the black past, the distinctive characteristics of black culture, and above all the right of black people to define and carve out their own destiny?

It was within the context of these tensions that the issue of racial pride and identity came to the fore in the summer of 1966 with Stokely Carmichael's call for "Black Power." Quickly the new slogan came to symbolize the determination of blacks to define themselves and control their own communities. Coinciding with the growing interest in African dress, hairstyles, language, and culture, the phrase "Black Power" represented a conscious proclamation that many blacks were no longer willing to accept white promises or white standards. In the years prior to the 1960's blacks had been petitioners, seeking their rights within the established order and appealing to the historic American Creed of equal opportunity and brotherhood. The Negro Dream, Martin Luther King, Jr., had said in the 1963 March on Washington, was rooted "in the American dream." Now many blacks were demanding instead of petitioning, and stating to the wider society that they would determine the scope of their own destiny. Whatever the final consequences of the shift in strategy and symbols, it was clear that a new era had dawned. No longer would many blacks accept the definition of their place—psychological, political or economic—as dictated by whites. No longer would they subscribe to the "rules of the game" established by the dominant culture—at least not unless they chose to do so.

For women as well, the period beginning in 1940 marked a time of change. Although enactment of the Nineteenth Amendment represented an important achievement on the road to equality, it did not . . . generate significant change in how sex roles were defined and allocated. Overt discrimination, together with traditional patterns of socialization, combined to discourage most women from departing from their prescribed sphere. There were few role models to emulate, little possibility of social approval, and the pervasive pressure of the culture to marry and conform to the ideal of homemaker. In such a situation most women did not question the boundaries set for them by their parents, peers, and schools.

World War II provided the occasion for at least a temporary change in this pattern. The desperate need for workers to produce munitions as well as take the jobs of men gone off to fight led to a massive public relations campaign designed to recruit women into the labor force. "YOU'RE GOING TO EMPLOY WOMEN," a War Department pamphlet stated. Almost overnight, the labor force was transformed by an influx of female workers. In one California aircraft plant, 13,000 men and no women had been employed in the fall of 1941. A year later there were 13,000 women and 11,000 men. More than six and a half million women joined the work force in the four years of war, a 57 per cent increase in the number of women workers. Women performed almost every job imaginable, from running huge cranes to repairing aircraft engines to driving taxi cabs. More important, most of the workers came from the home and previously had been occupied exclusively as homemakers. Nearly 75 per cent of the new workers were married, and 60 per cent were over thirty-five.

Despite these vast statistical changes, however, little progress took place on issues of equality between the sexes. The National War Labor Board issued orders calling for equal pay for equal work, but the government's anti-inflation policy, together with loopholes in the directive, made it possible for most employers to continue discriminating in the wages they paid men and women simply by changing job labels from "female" to "worker-trainee." Women for the most part were excluded from major policy-making decisions within business and government. In addition, public officials were slow to respond to the urgent need for community services to help women workers. This was particularly true in the case of day-care centers. Absenteeism in order to take care of children was a primary cause of lost work hours among women, yet until the last eighteen months of the war little was done to provide public facilities to deal with the problem.

Although government agencies like the Labor Department's Women's Bureau and private organizations such as the National Business and Professional Women's Clubs pressed for greater government action, the vast majority of women workers did not engage in militant protest about their working conditions or subscribe to any feminist cause. Most came to work in the first place out of patriotism or a desire to keep the family together economically in the midst of wartime. Most found that they enjoyed their work, welcomed the challenge, were grateful for the camaraderie of fellow workers, and could use the money. At the same time there was little evidence of feminist consciousness or commitment to the notion of equal rights and opportunities between the sexes. Wages were higher than before, better jobs were available, and concerted protest was minimal.

Nevertheless, expectations among women about their own social and economic roles changed drastically during the war. In 1942 very few of those women who took jobs indicated that they planned to stay once the fighting was over. A return to home and children seemed nearly a universal expectation. By 1945, in contrast, approximately 75 to 80 per cent of women war workers indicated that they intended, or at least desired, to remain on the job. Such women enjoyed the social and economic advantages of working and saw no reason why they should give up their positions. As one worker commented, "War jobs have uncovered unsuspected abilities in American women. Why lose all these abilities because of a belief that a woman's place is in the home. For some it is, for others not."

Within this context, the major theme in the experience of women during the postwar years was a gap between the behavior of women in the labor force and the resurgence of traditional attitudes toward woman's "place" in the home. Almost immediately after the war ended, a concerted campaign developed among political leaders, the media, and employers to persuade women to return to the home. The war had been an unsettling experience, uprooting millions of people from home and family. Since women were seen as the anchor of the family, it seemed to many observers imperative that they return to the home lest the entire society be thrown out of kilter. As one sociologist wrote, "Women must bear and rear children. Husbands must support them." Throughout the late 1940's and 1950's, what Betty Friedan would later call the "feminine mystique" became a ubiquitous force in the popular culture. Any mother who worked, one psychiatrist wrote, was "stimulated by neurotic competition." Magazines featured spreads of three- and four-children families, praised women who became professionals at home-making, and glorified family togetherness.

Even as the campaign to bring women back to the kitchen flourished, however, the percentage of women in the labor force continued to spiral. Inflation, a rising standard of living, and the desire to share the benefits of consumerism all encouraged the growth of the two-income family. In the 1950's women in the labor force were increasing at a rate four times faster than men, and by 1960 40 per cent of all women over sixteen were in the labor force compared with 25 per cent in 1940. More important, most of the new workers were married and many had young children. By the end of the 1960's nearly 45 per cent of all married women were employed compared with 15 per cent in 1940, and the figure included more than half of all mothers with children aged six to seventeen. Ironically, the same women who were described in the *Ladies' Home Journal* and *McCall's* as thriving on housework were spending an increasing amount of their time in gainful employment. The contradiction between cultural norms and actual behavior could hardly have been more pronounced.

Still, most women appeared able to live with the contradiction, or at least were not sufficiently disturbed by it to challenge traditional attitudes.

Throughout most of the late 1940's and 1950's, feminism remained a marginal movement with little popular support. Popular attitudes were reflected in a Women's Bureau memorandum, which described feminists as "a small but militant group of leisure class women [giving vent] to their resentment at not having been born men." Most women workers had not taken their jobs out of a desire to compete with men but rather to help the family—a traditional role—so that children could go to college, a new addition could be built on the house, or the family could have a longer and better vacation. The vast majority of female workers were employed in traditional "woman's work," which featured almost total occupational segregation and little if any possibility of upward mobility. In short, women had expanded their sphere outside of the home, but without altering either the assumptions about their "place" or the actual pattern of discrimination which kept them in sex-typed jobs. To work was one thing; to call into question traditional attitudes toward sex roles was another. For the latter to happen, new perceptions had to evolve and a new frame of reference had to develop.

If feminist consciousness itself was slow to develop, however, a process of change was under way which helped prepare the ground for action later on. The very fact of massive increases in female employment destroyed the reality of traditional notions of woman's "place" in the home. No longer did conventional stereotypes correspond to women's experience. Moreover, some changes within the family occurred as a result of women's employment. Children of parents who both worked grew up with substantially different ideas of what was permissible for men and women to do. Daughters of working mothers indicated that they, too, planned to work after marriage, and numerous studies showed that young girls were more likely to name their mother as the person they most admired if she worked than if she did not work. None of these changes signified progress toward equality, but they did help provide a basis for a challenge to traditional attitudes.

The event which more than any other crystallized a sense of grievance among later women activists was the emergence of the civil rights movement. Because women did not live together in a ghetto or share a common political and economic experience on a continuing basis, they had tended to view their problems as individual rather than social. As Betty Friedan observed in *The Feminine Mystique,* many discontented women talked about "a problem that has no name," convinced that their own unhappiness was something personal. The civil rights movement, however, focused attention on the extent to which groups of people were oppressed on the basis of cultural and physical characteristics. As women saw and participated in demonstrations demanding freedom and personal dignity, they perceived, like their abolitionist forerunners, a connection to their own lives and hence the possibility of acting for themselves as a group.

The civil rights movement proved significant on one level as a model for political activity and a vehicle for legislative reform. When the 1964 Civil Rights Act was passed, Title VII included a ban on discrimination in employment on the basis of sex as well as race. Older women activists—particularly business and professional women, and veterans of national and state Commissions on the Status of Women—seized on Title VII as an instrument for change. When the government failed to act on complaints of sex discrimination, these activists formed the National Organization of Women (NOW) in 1966 to mobilize pressure on behalf of women's rights. Other groups quickly followed. The Women's Equity Action League organized in 1970 to press court actions for women's civil rights, and in one of the most notable events of the legal battle, instituted a class action complaint against every university in the country for the practice of sex discrimination. The National Women's Political Caucus, in turn, developed to push the nation's political parties toward recognition of women's rights. At each step along the way, black organizations and political strategy provided a model.

Just as important, the civil rights movement itself spurred younger women participants to take action against the discrimination which they experienced from their colleagues in the movement. Repeatedly, young women in SNCC (and later SDS) found that they were either excluded from policy-making positions or treated as servants. On the basis of heightened consciousness about sex discrimination in their own immediate lives, as well as participation in a movement designed to eliminate inequality wherever it existed, young women in the movement organized themselves to seek change. Mobilized into action by personal experience, they took the organizing skills and ideological lessons which they had learned in the civil rights movement and became the initiators of the women's liberation movement. Together with the founders of NOW and the discontented middle-class women who had been galvanized by the message of Betty Friedan, these young women provided the core around which a revived woman's movement developed.

The principal organizing tactic of the new feminism was the "consciousness raising" session where women gathered to reveal and discuss in a supportive atmosphere the problems they had encountered on the basis of their sex. Such sessions provided the energy for the entire movement, transforming the perceptions of the participants about their own lives and leading to activity designed to overcome discrimination. As movement women talked about their experiences and came to the realization that they shared a common grievance, they also grew in the conviction that their grievances could be redressed only by acting together.

The consciousness raising session addressed a primary obstacle to political effectiveness: the lack of sex solidarity. If women were to wage an effective struggle, it was reasoned, they needed to forge bonds of togetherness that would transcend their isolation in individual families and foster the same sense of collective experience which blacks or Chicanos derived from living together in a ghetto. A community of support was needed, and the women's liberation group provided such a community for its members. Though a wife might be unable to express dissatisfaction to her husband on her own, the existence of an intimate circle of associates sharing a common purpose offered reinforcement and an incentive for action. Similarly, community institutions such as schools and hospitals were likely to prove more responsive to the organized effort of a woman's group than to the request of a single individual. The consciousness raising group thus served as a departure point for the principal strategy of women's liberation: to use sex solidarity as a means of breaking down sex barriers and sex stereotypes.

By 1970 the woman's movement had itself become a major force for change within the society. Treated as a joke by some, it provoked profound and energetic resistance from others. Yet the drive for new attitudes and new patterns of behavior continued and grew. A legal suit which described the American Telephone and Telegraph Company as "the largest oppressor of women workers in the United States" produced an out of court settlement of back pay to women workers and more important, a plan to change hiring and promotion practices so that men would be placed in formerly all "female" jobs and women would be assigned to previously all "male" positions. Charges of discrimination within colleges and universities led to government investigation, and an order for educational institutions to provide affirmative action plans for hiring and promoting women and blacks. And women in politics secured the pledge of major parties and candidates to guarantee women an important voice in party councils. The biggest change of all, however, was the fact that a growing minority of women insisted on finding a new definition of their identity—one which would no longer rely on cultural preconceptions of masculinity and femininity. In so doing, they rejected the cultural norms of the past and attempted to create new ground rules for relations between the sexes in the future.

Clearly, important differences separate the experience of blacks and women during the last three decades. To begin with, blacks exhibited a much greater readiness to protest than women. A full-scale civil rights movement emerged in the black population by the end of the 1950's and would have been supported prior to that time had the context been right. In contrast, it took until the late 1960's before a strong women's movement developed. Similarly, it would be foolish to underestimate the conflicts which have existed between women and blacks. As we have seen, black men and most black women have viewed the women's movement as a diversionary struggle that constitutes a potential threat to the primary goal of racial freedom and strength. On the other side, many white women have shown indifference, or at least insensitivity, to the issue of racism.

Nevertheless, the parallels that emerge from comparing the two case studies are striking, particularly if one looks at the components contributing to change. The similarity lies not in the substantive identity of female and black response (although there were substantive connections), but in the process by which change occurred, and the progression of both groups through comparable layers of change, culminating in a remarkably similar effort by black and female activists to define their own goals and identity. Thus, despite the disparity of experience in the two groups, similar variables have been involved in the process of change through which each moved.

The first parallel consists of the impact of World War II on the status quo as it existed for both groups. The war intervened in the prevailing pattern of daily life to create what the sociologist Neil Smelser [in his *Theory of Collective Behavior* (1965)] has called the "structural conduciveness" for change. Indeed, it took an event of the magnitude of world war to disrupt the cycle of economic, political, psychological, and internal controls that previously had maintained women and blacks in their assigned "place." World War II accomplished this by reordering, for the moment at least, the priorities of the society, making possible the entry of women and blacks into roles and activities hitherto considered inappropriate. Like an electric shock, the war jarred the social system and prompted a rearranging of roles, perceptions, and responsibilities.

Significantly, the war crisis called forth character traits radically different from those that had been emphasized before, thereby helping to pave the way for longer lasting change. As a result of the manpower emergency, the government and other institutions encouraged people who previously had been taught to be docile—i.e., "well adjusted" to their condition—to become instead aggressive, self-sufficient, and confident. Those who had been warned to stay in their place now were told it was a matter of patriotic duty to leave that place and assert themselves in new roles. The war thus placed a premium on personality attributes most psychologists would view as healthy (even if deviant by previous standards), as opposed to a pattern of pathological adjustment to a situation of discrimination. In short, for the first time in the lives of many people character traits necessary to freedom and independence were encouraged; once given the possibility for expression, it was not likely such attributes would quickly disappear.

The second major parallel was a pattern of glaring contradiction between norms and reality that developed for both groups after the war. The nature of the contradictions differed significantly for blacks as opposed to women. In the one instance, norms of equality and non-discrimination received an infusion of vitality during and after World War II, and the contradiction consisted of a failure by the government and others to enforce the renewed verbal commitment to equality and justice. The disparity between promise and reality helped to accentuate black anger and frustration. In the case of women, on the other hand, norms remained constant, while behavior deviated more and more from traditional ideas. The central concept of the "feminine mystique"—the all-consuming glory of domesticity—was at odds with the rapidly rising number of women who were employed and who seemed to enjoy working outside the home.

Regardless of the nature of the contradiction, the core point was the significance of such stress for social change. Traditional cultural norms remain unchallenged as long as people's behavior is perceived as either consistent with the norms or irrelevant to them. Thus when the "place" of most American women was in fact in the home, there was no frame of reference in reality from which to attack the conventional norm. Conversely, as long as the values of equal opportunity and justice were not viewed as applicable to blacks, there was little basis for the dominant culture to support civil rights activity. The emergence of glaring inconsistencies, in contrast, highlights the presence of a problem requiring action. In the case of both women and blacks, the existence of contradictions between norms and behavior in the postwar period did not automatically mean the start of a collective protest movement; but building upon the changes of World War II, the contradictions provided one more ingredient to the foundation necessary for social movements to develop.

The third element common to the process of change was the presence of a catalyst that galvanized already existing elements and helped forge them into a social movement. The role of a catalyst, or a "precipitating event" as Smelser calls it, is to provide the final connection that in turn brings different ingredients together and transforms what was previously diffuse and passive into something focused and active. The catalytic event is not itself sufficient to generate collective behavior, but it is the indispensable factor that helps give form and direction to the otherwise unrelated components of change.

In the case of the civil rights movement, the 1954 *Brown* decision and the failure to implement it provided such a catalyst. The *Brown* decision itself, of course, represented in its purest form the promise of equal rights which had been held forth to black Americans. The aftermath, in turn, exemplified, in stark terms, the gap between promise and performance. In the face of such high expectations, the absence of any meaningful progress spurred the direct action which took place, first in Montgomery, then throughout the South. The convergence of hope and disillusionment around a simple yet powerfully symbolic event brought energy and focus to civil rights protest.

In a similar fashion, the civil rights movement itself served as a catalytic event for the women's movement. Up until the early 1960's, those who had consistently advocated a feminist position, or suggested in less explicit ways the need for a change in women's status, had been unable to find a vehicle to communicate their message, or a way to connect their views to the existing social environment. The civil rights movement both provided a dramatic example of the point which women activists were trying to communicate, and it provided a model of protest which helped bring a women's movement to life. It thereby gave women a profoundly political picture of their society and underlined the significance of sex consciousness as an organizing principle. Just as the *Brown* decision had crystallized the issue of protest for blacks, the civil rights movement illustrated with unmistakable clarity to women the possibility of people uniting on the basis of sex identity to preserve their dignity and secure equal treatment.

The fourth common element was the development of an innovative tactic which in the case of both women and blacks served as a rallying point for activists and a symbol of protest. In the postwar history of race relations, the discovery of the sit-in tactic by four black college students in Greensboro, North Carolina, provided such a rallying point. The nonviolent sit-ins served an astonishing variety of purposes: they gave blacks an opportunity to assert their rights in a manner which most Northerners could not construe as threatening or violent; they dramatized the brutality of a system which would not give basic human respect to black Americans; they demanded incredible discipline, sacrifice, and mutual confidence from the demonstrators, thereby forging a human bond indispensable to a movement; and they provided an ideal vehicle for broadcasting to the nation the message of the movement and its quest for support. Perhaps most important, the sit-ins embodied in action the new vision of community that was the movement's essence— people coming together out of mutual conviction to express their belief in themselves, their rejection of an older way of doing things, and their affirmation of a fundamentally different perception of how life could be.

For women activists the consciousness-raising session served a similar purpose. Begun in the civil rights and student movements as a means for women to express to each other their common sense of grievance, the consciousness-raising group quickly became the principal means for giving women a sense of solidarity and a vehicle for probing their common experience of sex discrimination. The result was the development in a supportive atmosphere of a profound feeling of grievance and commitment to change. Whether in a radical commune, a university community, or a corporation where women simply chose to get together to talk (never using the words consciousness-raising), the women's group helped to address the major problem faced by women in the past—the absence of an institution for expressing both solidarity and concern. As Gerda Lerner has observed, within a woman's group "reticence and the inability to speak out soon vanish in a supportive atmosphere. Members freely share their experiences and thoughts with one another, learn to reveal themselves, and develop feelings of solidarity and love for women. . . . the effect of the group is to free the energy of its members and channel them into action." For women throughout the country who became active in one form or another of the women's movement, the discussion group served as the basic forum for developing a sense of strength, solidarity, and commitment. It thereby provided the "social space" for women to grow into a new perception of themselves, and move on to activities devoted to eliminating sex discrimination.

Perhaps the most compelling parallel, however, is the extent to which activism brought growing numbers of blacks and women to reject the norms of the dominant culture and embark on a course of self-definition and determination. Throughout American history, both black and female protestors have been torn between strategies of identifying with the dominant values of the culture or rejecting them. For the most part, dissidents from both groups have taken the opportunities available to white males as the standard of what should be open to everyone. Thus black integrationists announced as their goal full participation in all segments of the society, including joint access to and involvement in the major institutions of white America. Similarly, women protestors have demanded that they be treated in the same way as men in seeking jobs and political influence. There have always been members of both groups, of course, who advocated either separatism or the development of a distinctive set of values, but overall, emulation of the dominant culture has been a primary theme of protest groups.

One of the consequences of this strategy, however, has been a tendency to accept the opposition's ground rules and premises. Those wishing access to the "system" frequently have absorbed the values, customs, and language of those in power. Hence, upwardly mobile blacks have tried to "make it" on the white man's terms, dressing and acting by white middle-class standards and even adopting similar political and social views. Aspiring career women, in turn, frequently have accepted general cultural views of female character traits as a means of solidifying their own acceptance, rather than endanger their status by demanding a revision of cultural norms. Thus, for example, Frances Perkins, the first woman Cabinet member and Secretary of Labor under Franklin Roosevelt, often endorsed the notion that woman's "place" was in the home and that married women in particular should not abandon their responsibilities there for the sake of making money.

As both black protest and women's liberation developed during the 1960's, a growing number of more militant activists started to question this strategy of accepting the dominant culture's standards. Despite the major changes accomplished through remedial legislation, many of the less obvious means of social control, such as the socialization process and psychological manipulation, remained intact. Statutes which outlawed economic discrimination or attempted to ensure equal opportunity could not eradicate the subtle cultural and social pressures to conform to one's "place." In addition, as Cynthia Fuchs Epstein has shown in her study of prospective career women, one of the most effective forms of sex discrimination has been to exclude women from the interpersonal and informal networks where the "bright young men" are chosen. Thus, some of the more radical proponents of change in both movements emphasized the need to reassess the strategy of reform legislation and working within the values of the existing system. They directed their energies, instead, toward breaking the bonds of socialization and shifting the cultural ground rules.

One manifestation of this development was the revival in both groups of a demand for a study of their respective pasts. Richard Wright had observed in *Black Boy* that "nothing about the problems of Negroes was ever taught in the classrooms at school; and whenever I would raise those questions with the boys, they would either remain silent or turn the subject into a joke. They were vocal about the petty individual wrongs they suffered, but they possessed no desire for a knowledge of the picture as a whole." In the 1960's the creation of women's studies and black studies programs seemed part of a common effort to recover an independent heritage within which to define one's self and develop a basis for relating to the dominant culture. Since women and blacks in the past had been alienated from their own history (and, some thought, intentionally taught to devalue themselves), they needed to recover a positive sense of self as a means of combating the control of the dominant cultural system. Though many criticized the academic justification and merits of such programs, activists in both movements saw them as central to declaring independence from those in the society who in the past had defined black and female history *for* those groups.

The same theme was manifested in the attention activists of both groups paid to common language usage. Words like "chick" or "girl" were only the most obvious examples of language that communicated the powerful social message that women were to be dealt with as sex objects and not quite adult people. The daily vocabulary of the society was full of even more subtle references, including the use of Mrs. and Miss as a means of defining women by their relationship to men—hence, not allowing women to be defined on their own terms. Black activists insisted on a similar control over the words used to describe them. The term "Negro," though still used by many, came to be viewed as a white label rather than a term growing out of the black community itself. Attention to Africanisms grew stronger as black Americans sought to re-establish links with their past. New styles of dress, more frequent usage of African words (*uhuru*, for example, as a synonym for freedom), and reliance on external signs of cultural distinctiveness such as an "Afro" hair style or African jewelry became badges of a new independence from the dominant white culture. Women activists, with their conscious rejection of the ornaments of consumer costuming such as makeup, girdles, and dresses, engaged in the same kind of rebellion against how others had defined them.

Not surprisingly, dissidents from both groups insisted also on changing the etiquettes of race and sex. Supporters of women's liberation refused to be treated as delicate or helpless creatures who needed doors opened for them or special assistance to sit down at a table. Such treatment, they reasoned, was only the benevolent side of a process, the malevolent side of which involved exclusion from important decisions, the best jobs, and equal rights of sex and self-assertion. Militant blacks, in turn, pointed out the paternalism of whites who wished to do "for" them those things that, by implication, they could not do themselves. Blacks who accepted white sponsorship for membership in private clubs were denounced by militants as "Toms" whose support of tokenism was aiding the enemy. Instead, reliance on members of one's own group for intellectual, emotional, and social support became the norm for the more angry members of both the women's movement and the black movement.

Perhaps the most radical manifestation of the new trend was the insistence of some members of both groups on total separatism. The evolution of black nationalism as a political strategy and a cultural way of life had as one of its purposes the announcement to white America that blacks would set their own standards, determine their own values, and establish their own institutions, no longer permitting whites to dictate the rules of the game. Some radical women set out to accomplish the same goal. Emphasizing the need of women to be "woman-identified" and not to take any portion of their self-image from dependence on men, they worked to build a network of institutions from printing presses to credit unions to feminist communes and health clinics as a means of declaring independence from the institutions and mores of the dominant culture.

Whatever the efficacy or validity of these individual efforts at cultural revolt, there seemed to be an underlying parallel implicit in the activities of both women and black protestors. Some members of both groups believed that the possibilities for further change depended at least in part on *who* defined the problems, *how* the problems were perceived, and what range of options was considered. According to this reasoning, as long as the rules were set by those who held power, there could only be as much substantive improvement as was consistent with the perpetuation of the society as it existed. Clearly, most Wall Street brokers would define the problem of poverty differently than would a welfare mother from Harlem. Reflecting this belief, both black and female activists asserted the need to reject the traditional view of their problems offered by the dominant society. Unless people defined themselves and determined their own agenda, they argued, those in power would set the ground rules and thus control the outcome of the game. In this sense, more militant female and black activists argued that separatism was a basic step toward making it possible for each group to interact with the dominant culture on its own terms. Although theoretically a sound strategy, as evidenced by the success of ethnic groups with strong separate institutions, this approach also presumed a willingness to use one's independent base as a departure point for coalition and interaction with groups inside of the dominant culture—an element of the strategy largely missing in the discussions of the late 60's and the 70's.

The ultimate irony of the separatist parallel, of course, was that precisely because dissident women and blacks insisted on cultural autonomy and self-determination, the possibilities for working together within a unified alliance became less and less. As Catharine Stimpson observed, "blacks must liberate themselves from whites, including white women; women must liberate themselves from men, including black men. Everyone's liberation must be self-won." If such a conclusion made less than likely a coalition of diverse groups, it also illustrated how closely black and women activists shared certain processes of development as they approached the question of how to bring about change in their own lives.

⋙ *F U R T H E R   R E A D I N G*

Karen Tucker Anderson, *Wartime Women: Sex Roles, Family Relations, and the Status of Women During World War II* (1981)

Robert Beitzell, *The Uneasy Alliance* (1972)

John Morton Blum, *V Was for Victory: Politics and American Culture During World War II* (1976)

A. Russell Buchanan, *The United States and World War II* (1964)

James M. Burns, *Roosevelt: The Soldier of Freedom* (1970)

D'Ann Mae Campbell, *Women at War with America: Private Lives in a Patriotic America* (1984)

Bruce Catton, *The War Lords of Washington* (1948)

Alan Clive, *State of War* (1979)

Richard M. Dalfiume, *Desegregation in the United States Armed Forces; Fighting on Two Fronts: 1939–1953* (1969)

Robert Dallek, *Franklin D. Roosevelt and American Foreign Policy, 1933–1945* (1979)

Roger Daniels, *Concentration Camps USA: Japanese Americans and World War II* (1971)

Robert A. Divine, *Roosevelt and World War II* (1969)

N. F. Dreisziger, ed., *Mobilization for Total War: The Canadian, American, and British Experience, 1914–1918, 1937–1945* (1981)

Peter B. Evans, Dietrich Rueschemeyer, and Theda Skocpol, eds., *Bringing the State Back In* (1985)

Otis L. Graham, Jr., *Toward a Planned Society: From Roosevelt to Nixon* (1976)

Mark Jonathan Harris, Franklin D. Mitchell, and Stephen Schecter, eds., *Homefront: America During World War II* (1984)

Susan Hartmann, *The Home Front and Beyond* (1982)

Maureen Honey, *Creating Rosie the Riveter: Class, Gender and Propaganda During World War II* (1984)

Barry D. Karl, *The Uneasy State: The United States from 1915 to 1945* (1983)

Michael Leigh, *Mobilizing Consent: Public Opinion and American Foreign Policy, 1937–1947* (1986)

Nelson Lichtenstein, *Labor's War at Home: The CIO in World War II* (1982)

Richard R. Lingeman, *Don't You Know There's a War On?* (1970)

William H. McNeill, *America, Britain, and Russia* (1953)

Dean L. May, *From New Deal to New Economics: The American Liberal Response to the Recession of 1937* (1981)

Ruth Milkman, *Gender at Work: The Dynamics of Job Segregation by Sex During World War II* (1988)

Alan S. Milward, *War, Economy, and Society: 1939–1945* (1977)

Geoffrey Perrett, *Days of Sadness, Years of Triumph: The American People, 1939–1945* (1973)

Richard Polenberg, *War and Society: The United States, 1941–1945* (1972)

Theodore Rosenof, *Patterns of Political Economy in America: The Failure to Develop a Democratic Left Synthesis, 1933–1950* (1983)

Leila Rupp, *Mobilizing Women for War* (1978)

Studs Terkel, *"The Good War": An Oral History of World War II* (1984)

Christopher Thorne, *Allies of a Kind* (1978)

———, *The Issue of War* (1985)

James Titus, ed., *The Home Front and War in the Twentieth Century* (1984)

Philip W. Warken, *A History of the National Resources Planning Board, 1933–1943* (1979)

David S. Wyman, *The Abandonment of the Jews: America and the Holocaust, 1941–1945* (1984)

CHAPTER
2

The Decision to Drop
the Atomic Bomb on Japan

✕✕✕

The United States' decision to drop atomic bombs on the Japanese cities of Hiro-shima and Nagasaki on August 6 and 9, 1945, was a pivotal event in world history. Rooted in the twentieth-century revolution in physics, the bombing opened a radically new chapter in the application of science and engineering, one that would threaten not just to transform the world but to destroy it. It signaled, too, a revolution in the nature of warfare, a marriage of the tradi-tional rivalries of nation-states with an awesome new technology of unprece-dented destructiveness. It brought to an end the most destructive war in human history and foreshadowed a new Cold War that would shape international af-fairs for the next forty years.

Not surprisingly, the decision to unleash the bombs has provoked continuing historical debate. Was their use necessary, as President Harry S Truman argued at the time, to bring the war to a close and to save both American and Japa-nese lives? Or would the Japanese soon have been defeated anyway by the U.S. naval blockade and aerial bombardment? What would have been the impact on the Japanese of the planned declaration of war by the Soviet Union? To what degree was Truman's resort to the bombing influenced by growing conflict be-tween the United States and the Soviet Union: did the administration hope to intimidate the Russians in Eastern Europe or finish the war in the Pacific before they could enter the fighting and thus demand a voice in the postwar settlement?

Debate has raged, too, over other possible reasons (beyond strategic objec-tives) for the United States' decision and has at the same time raised chilling moral questions. For example, to what extent was the decision influenced by ra-cial prejudice and by the institutionalized wartime depiction of the Japanese as evil and inhuman? Before using the bomb, should the United States have dem-onstrated its terrible destructiveness—perhaps in Tokyo harbor, as some scientists suggested at the time—or at least have provided an explicit warning? Was the use of atomic bombs, weapons that in a blinding instant killed tens of thousands of men, women, and children, immoral? Was the bombing any more immoral than the reliance on weapons that produced the millions of other deaths during World War II, than the aerial assaults on London and Dresden, or than the awful firebombing of Tokyo? What is one to say of a weapon that not only kills but, through radiation and the resulting genetic damage, continues to kill long after the debris settles? Does the bomb's immorality lie in more than the holocaust unleashed over Hiroshima and Nagasaki on those August days of 1945; does it further rest on the potential of atomic warfare to wreak destruction on a scale that would make even those horrors seem small by comparison?

Still other questions haunt those who have debated the bombing of Hiroshima and Nagasaki. For example, how does one assess the ultimate costs of the new age of atomic warfare that followed the fateful event—costs measured not only by the taxes necessary to sustain new nuclear technologies but by the resultant delays in or denials of productive social investments? Have atomic weapons, by their very destructiveness, made war so terrible as to be unthinkable, and the world hence more peaceful? Or has the proliferation of atomic technology, especially in an international system no longer dominated by the bipolar struggle of the United States and the U.S.S.R., made our world unimaginably dangerous?

⋙ D O C U M E N T S

As the top-secret Manhattan Project neared completion, U.S. leaders debated the use of the new weapon that the scientists and engineers were to produce. In the first document, the Interim Committee appointed by President Truman recommends the bomb's immediate use. In the second document a group of scientists engaged in work on the bomb at the University of Chicago urge a demonstration of the bomb's destructiveness on some uninhabited target. Their proposal was rejected, however, by the government's own scientific advisory committee, as the third selection reveals. "Because of the urgency of this matter," J. Robert Oppenheimer, the director of the Manhattan Project laboratory at Los Alamos, New Mexico, wrote in a covering memorandum, "the panel was not able to devote as extended a collective deliberation to the problem as it undoubtedly warrants."
The initial successful test of the bomb on July 16, 1945, is described in the fourth document by Major General Leslie R. Groves, the commanding general of the Manhattan Project. As the excerpt from the president's diary (document five) reveals, the bomb was much on Truman's mind as he met with Soviet premier Joseph Stalin and British prime minister Winston Churchill at Potsdam. The horror and devastation wrought by the bomb is painfully recalled in the sixth document, by Atsuko Tsujioka, a young student who was living in Hiroshima on the day the bomb fell. The final selection, drawn from a report by the U.S. Strategic Bombing Survey, is based on captured Japanese documents and interviews with Japanese military and political leaders conducted during the fall of 1945.

President Harry S Truman's Advisers Discuss the Atomic Bomb, May 1945

Secretary [of War Henry L.] Stimson explained that the Interim Committee had been appointed by him, with the approval of the President, to make recommendations on temporary war-time controls, public announcement, legislation and post-war organization. The Secretary gave high praise to the brilliant and effective assistance rendered to the project by the scientists of the country and expressed great appreciation to the four scientists present for their great contributions to the work and their willingness to advise on the many complex problems that the Interim Committee had to face. He expressed the hope that the scientists would feel completely free to express their views on any phase of the subject.

The Committee had been termed an "Interim Committee" because it was expected that when the project became more widely known a permanent organization established by Congressional action or by treaty arrangements would be necessary.

The Secretary explained that General Marshall shared responsibility with him for making recommendations to the President on this project with particular reference to its military aspects; therefore, it was considered highly desirable that General Marshall be present at this meeting to secure at first hand the views of the scientists.

The Secretary expressed the view, a view shared by [Army Chief of Staff] General [George C.] Marshall, that this project should not be considered simply in terms of military weapons, but as a new relationship of man to the universe. This discovery might be compared to the discoveries of the Copernican theory and of the laws of gravity, but far more important than these in its effect on the lives of men. While the advances in the field to date had been fostered by the needs of war, it was important to realize that the implications of the project went far beyond the needs of the present war. It must be controlled if possible to make it an assurance of future peace rather than a menace to civilization.

It was pointed out that one atomic bomb on [an] arsenal would not be much different from the effect caused by any Air Corps strike of present dimensions. However, Dr. [J. Robert] Oppenheimer [Director of the Manhattan Project's Los Alamos Research Laboratory] stated that the visual effect of an atomic bombing would be tremendous. It would be accompanied by a brilliant luminescence which would rise to a height of 10,000 to 20,000 feet. The neutron effect of the explosion would be dangerous to life for a radius of at least two-thirds of a mile.

After much discussion concerning various types of targets and the effects to be produced, *the Secretary expressed the conclusion, on which there was general agreement, that we could not give the Japanese any warning; that we could not concentrate on a civilian area; but that we should seek to make a profound psychological impression on as many of the inhabitants as possible. At the suggestion of Dr. [James B.] Conant [President of Harvard University and Chairman of the National Defense Research Committee] the Secretary agreed that the most desirable target would be a vital war plant employing a large number of workers and closely surrounded by workers' houses.*

Atomic Scientists Urge an Alternative Course, June 1945

The only reason to treat nuclear power differently from all the other developments in the field of physics is its staggering possibilities as a means of political pressure in peace and sudden destruction in war. All present plans for the organization of research, scientific and industrial development, and publication in the field of nucleonics are conditioned by the political and military climate in which one expects those plans to be carried out. Therefore, in making suggestions for the postwar organization of nucleonics, a discussion of political problems cannot be avoided. The scientists on this Project do not presume to speak authoritatively on problems of national and international policy. However, we found ourselves, by the force of events, the last five years in the position of a small group of citizens cognizant of a grave danger for the safety of this country as well as for the future of all the other nations, of which the rest of mankind is unaware. We therefore felt it our duty to urge that the political problems, arising from the mastering of nuclear power, be recognized in all their gravity, and that appropriate steps be taken for their study and the preparation of necessary decisions. We hope that the creation of the Committee by the Secretary of War [Henry L. Stimson] to deal with all aspects of nucleonics, indicates that these implications have been recognized by the government. We feel that our acquaintance with the scientific elements of the situation and prolonged preoccupation with its world-wide political implications, imposes on us the obligation to offer to the Committee some suggestions as to the possible solution of these grave problems.

The development of nuclear power not only constitutes an important addition to the technological and military power of the United States, but also creates grave political and economic problems for the future of this country.

Nuclear bombs cannot possibly remain a "secret weapon" at the exclusive disposal of this country, for more than a few years. The scientific facts on which their construction is based are well known to scientists of other countries. Unless an effective international control of nuclear explosives is instituted, a race of nuclear armaments is certain to ensue following the first revelation of our possession of nuclear weapons to the world. Within ten years other countries may have nuclear bombs, each of which, weighing less than a ton, could destroy an urban area of more than five square miles. In the war to which such an armaments race is likely to lead, the United States, with its agglomeration of population and industry in comparatively few metropolitan districts, will be at a disadvantage compared to the nations whose population and industry are scattered over large areas.

We believe that these considerations make the use of nuclear bombs for an early, unannounced attack against Japan inadvisable. If the United States would be the first to release this new means of indiscriminate destruction upon mankind, she would sacrifice public support throughout the world, precipitate the race of armaments, and prejudice the possibility of reaching an international agreement on the future control of such weapons.

Much more favorable conditions for the eventual achievement of such an agreement could be created if nuclear bombs were first revealed to the world by a demonstration in an appropriately selected uninhabited area.

If chances for the establishment of an effective international control of nuclear weapons will have to be considered slight at the present time, then not only the use of these weapons against Japan, but even their early demonstration may be contrary to the interests of this country. A postponement of such a demonstration will have in this case the advantage of delaying the beginning of the nuclear armaments race as long as possible. If, during the time gained, ample support could be made available for further development of the field in this country, the postponement would substantially increase the lead which we have established during the present war, and our position in an armament race or in any later attempt at international agreement will thus be strengthened.

On the other hand, if no adequate public support for the development of nucleonics will be available without a demonstration, the postponement of the latter may be deemed inadvisable, because enough information might leak out to cause other nations to start the armament race, in which we will then be at a disadvantage. At the same time, the distrust of other nations may be aroused by a confirmed development under cover of secrecy, making it more difficult eventually to reach an agreement with them.

If the government should decide in favor of an early demonstration of nuclear weapons it will then have the possibility to take into account the public opinion of this country and of the other nations before deciding whether these weapons should be used in the war against Japan. In this way, other nations may assume a share of responsibility for such a fateful decision.

To sum up, we urge that the use of nuclear bombs in this war be considered as a problem of long-range national policy rather than military expediency, and that this policy be directed primarily to the achievement of an agreement permitting an effective international control of the means of nuclear warfare.

U.S. Science Advisers Endorse Dropping the Bomb, June 1945

You have asked us to comment on the initial use of the new weapon. This use, in our opinion, should be such as to promote a satisfactory adjustment of our international relations. At the same time, we recognize our obligation to our nation to use the weapons to help save American lives in the Japanese war.

(1) To accomplish these ends we recommend that before the weapons are used not only Britain, but also Russia, France, and China be advised that we have made considerable progress in our work on atomic weapons, that these may be ready to use during the present war, and that we would welcome suggestions as to how we can cooperate in making this development contribute to improved international relations.

(2) The opinions of our scientific colleagues on the initial use of these weapons are not unanimous: they range from the proposal of a purely technical demonstration to that of the military application best designed to induce surrender. Those who advocate a purely technical demonstration would wish to outlaw the use of atomic weapons, and have

feared that if we use the weapons now our position in future negotiations will be prejudiced. Others emphasize the opportunity of saving American lives by immediate military use, and believe that such use will improve the international prospects, in that they are more concerned with the prevention of war than with the elimination of this specific weapon. We find ourselves closer to these latter views; we can propose no technical demonstration likely to bring an end to the war; we see no acceptable alternative to direct military use.

(3) With regard to these general aspects of the use of atomic energy, it is clear that we, as scientific men, have no proprietary rights. It is true that we are among the few citizens who have had occasion to give thoughtful consideration to these problems during the past few years. We have, however, no claim to special competence in solving the po-litical, social, and military problems which are presented by the advent of atomic power.

General Leslie Groves Reports on a Successful Test, July 1945

1. This is not a concise, formal military report but an attempt to recite what I would have told you if you had been here on my return from New Mexico.

2. At 0530, 16 July 1945, in a remote section of the Alamogordo Air Base, New Mexico, the first full scale test was made of the implosion type atomic fission bomb. For the first time in history there was a nuclear explosion. And what an explosion! . . . The bomb was not dropped from an airplane but was exploded on a platform on top of a 100-foot high steel tower.

3. The test was successful beyond the most optimistic expectations of any-one. Based on the data which it has been possible to work up to date, I estimate the energy generated to be in excess of the equivalent of 15,000 to 20,000 tons of TNT; and this is a conservative estimate. Data based on measurements which we have not yet been able to reconcile would make the energy release several times the conservative figure. There were tremendous blast effects. For a brief period there was a lighting effect within a radius of 20 miles equal to several suns in midday; a huge ball of fire was formed which lasted for several seconds. This ball mushroomed and rose to a height of over ten thousand feet before it dimmed. The light from the explosion was seen clearly at Albuquerque, Sante Fe, Silver City, El Paso and other points generally to about 180 miles away. The sound was heard to the same distance in a few instances but generally to about 100 miles. Only a few windows were broken although one was some 125 miles away. A massive cloud was formed which surged and billowed upward with tremendous power, reaching the substratosphere at an elevation of 41,000 feet, 36,000 feet above the ground, in about five minutes, breaking without interruption through a temperature inversion at 17,000 feet which most of the scientists thought

would stop it. Two supplementary explosions occurred in the cloud shortly after the main explosion. The cloud contained several thousand tons of dust picked up from the ground and a considerable amount of iron in the gaseous form. Our present thought is that this iron ignited when it mixed with the oxygen in the air to cause these supplementary explosions. Huge concentrations of highly radioactive materials resulted from the fission and were contained in this cloud.

4.   A crater from which all vegetation had vanished, with a diameter of 1200 feet and a slight slope toward the center, was formed. In the center was a shallow bowl 130 feet in diameter and 6 feet in depth. The material within the crater was deeply pulverized dirt. The material within the outer circle is greenish and can be distinctly seen from as much as 5 miles away. The steel from the tower was evaporated. 1500 feet away there was a four-inch iron pipe 16 feet high set in concrete and strongly guyed. It disappeared completely.

5.   One-half mile from the explosion there was a massive steel test cylinder weighing 220 tons. The base of the cylinder was solidly encased in concrete. Surrounding the cylinder was a strong steel tower 70 feet high, firmly anchored to concrete foundations. This tower is comparable to a steel building bay that would be found in typical 15 or 20 story skyscraper or in warehouse construction. Forty tons of steel were used to fabricate the tower which was 70 feet high, the height of a six story building. The cross bracing was much stronger than that normally used in ordinary steel construction. The absence of the solid walls of a building gave the blast a much less effective surface to push against. The blast tore the tower from its foundations, twisted it, ripped it apart and left it flat on the ground. The effects on the tower indicate that, at that distance, unshielded permanent steel and masonry buildings would have been destroyed. I no longer consider the Pentagon a safe shelter from such a bomb. Enclosed are a sketch showing the tower before the explosion and a telephotograph showing what it looked like afterwards. None of us had expected it to be damaged.

6.   The cloud traveled to a great height first in the form of a ball, then mushroomed, then changed into a long trailing chimney-shaped column and finally was sent in several directions by the variable winds at the different elevations. It deposited its dust and radioactive materials over a wide area.

President Truman Discusses the Bomb at Potsdam, July 1945

[Potsdam]
July 17, [19]45

Just spent a couple of hours with Stalin. Joe Davies called on Maiski and made the date last night for noon today. Promptly a few minutes before twelve I looked up from the desk and there stood Stalin in the doorway. I got to my feet and advanced to meet him. He put out his hand and smiled. I did the same[,] we shook[,] I greeted Molotov and the interpreter and we sat down. After the usual polite remarks we got down to business. I told Stalin that I am no diplomat but usually said yes & no to questions after hearing all the argument [sic]. It pleased him. I asked him if he had the agenda for the meeting. He said he had and that he had some more questions to present. I told him to fire away. He did and it is dynamite—but I have some dynamite too which I am not exploding now. He wants to fire [Generalissimo Francisco] Franco [the Spanish fascist dictator], to which I wouldn't object and divide up the Italian colonies, and other mandates, some no doubt that the British have. Then he got on the Chinese situation[,] told us what agreements had been reached and what was in abeyance. Most of the big points are settled. He'll be in the Jap War on August 15th. Fini Japs when that comes about. We had lunch[,] talked socially[,] put on a real show drinking toasts to everyone then had pictures made in the back yard. I can deal with Stalin. He's honest—but smart as hell.

[Potsdam]
July 18, [19]45

At breakfast with nephew Harry, a sergeant in the Field Artillery [in which Truman had served as a Captain during World War I]. He is a good soldier and a nice boy. They took him off [the troopship] Queen Elizabeth at Glasco [Glasgow] and flew him here. Sending him home Friday. Went to lunch with P.M. [British Prime Minister Winston Churchill] at 1:30 walked around to British Hqrs [Headquarters]. Met at the gate by Mr. Churchill. Guard of honor drawn up. Fine body of men Scottish Guards Band played the Star Spangled Banner. Inspected Guard and went in for lunch. P.M. & I ate alone. Discussed Manhattan [Project] (it is a success). Decided to tell Stalin about it. Stalin had told P.M. of telegram from Jap Emperor asking for peace. Stalin also read his answer to me. It was satisfactory. Believe Japs will fold up before Russia comes in.

I am sure they will when Manhattan appears over their homeland. I shall inform Stalin about it at an opportune time. Stalin's luncheon was a most satisfactory meeting. I invited him to come to the U.S. Told him I'd send the Battleship Missouri for him if he'd come. He said he wanted to cooperate with U.S. in peace as we had cooperated in War but it would be harder. Said he was grossly misunderstood in the U.S. and I was misunderstood in Russia. I told him that we each could help to remedy that situation in our home countries and that I intended to try with all I had to do my part at home. He gave me a most cordial smile and said he would do as much in Russia.

We then went to the conference and it was my job to present the Ministers' proposed agenda. There were three proposals and I banged them through in short order, much to the surprise of Mr. Churchill. Stalin was very much pleased. Churchill was too after he had recovered. I'm not going to stay around this terrible place all summer just to listen to speeches. I'll go home to the Senate for that.

[Potsdam]
July 25, 1945

We met at 11 A.M. today. That is Stalin, Churchill and the U.S. President. But I had a most important session with Lord Mountbatten & General Marshall before that. We have discovered the most terrible bomb in the history of the world. It may be the fire destruction prophesied in the Euphrates Valley Era, after Noah and his fabulous Ark.

Anyway we "think" we have found the way to cause a disintegration of the atom. An experiment in the New Mexico desert was startling—to put it mildly. Thirteen pounds of the explosive caused the complete disintegration of a steel tower 60 feet high, created a crater 6 feet deep and 1200 feet in diameter, knocked over a steel tower 1/2 mile away and knocked men down 10,000 yards away. The explosion was visible for more than 200 miles and audible for 40 miles and more.

This weapon is to be used against Japan between now and August 10th. I have told the Sec[retary]. of War, Mr. [Henry] Stimson to use so that military objectives and soldiers and sailors are the target and not women and children. Even if the Japs are savages, ruthless, merciless and fanatic, we as the leader of the world for the common welfare cannot drop this terrible bomb on the old Capitol [Kyoto] or the new [Tokyo].

He & I are in accord. The target will be a purely military one and we will issue a warning statement asking the Japs to surrender and save lives. I'm sure they will not do that, but we will have given them the chance. It is certainly a good thing for the world that Hitler's crowd or Stalin's did not discover this atomic bomb. It seems to me to be the most terrible thing ever discovered, but it can be made the most useful.

A Japanese Student Recalls the Moment the Bomb Exploded, August 1945

Ah, that instant! I felt as though I had been struck on the back with something like a big hammer, and thrown into boiling oil. For some time I was unconscious. When I abruptly came to again, everything around me was smothered in black smoke; it was all like a dream or something that didn't make sense. My chest hurt, I could barely breathe, and I thought 'This is the end!' I pressed my chest tightly and lay face down on the ground, and ever so many times I called for help:

"Mother!" "Mother!" "Father!" but of course in that place there was no answer from Mother, no answer from Father.

This time I was really resigned to the thought that I was done for, but

From Dr. Arata Osada, ed., *Children of the A-Bomb* (1959).

as I lay quietly face down on the ground, suddenly there drifted into my mind the smiling face of my littlest sister who is dead now. Oh! I recovered my senses. Through a darkness like the bottom of Hell I could hear the voices of the other students calling for their mothers. I could barely sense the fact that the students seemed to be running away from that place. I immediately got up, and without any definite idea of escaping I just frantically ran in the direction they were all taking. As we came close to Tsurumi Bridge a red hot electric wire wrapped itself around both my ankles. I don't know how but I managed to pull it off, and as though I were moving in a dream I reached the end of the bridge. By this time everything had long since changed to white smoke. The place where I had been working was Tanaka-cho, a little more than 600 yards from the center of the explosion. Although I should have been at a place straight in from Tsurumi Bridge, I seem to have been blown a good way to the north, and I felt as though the directions were all changed around.

At the base of the bridge, inside a big cistern that had been dug out there, was a mother weeping and holding above her head a naked baby that was burned bright red all over its body, and another mother was crying and sobbing as she gave her burned breast to her baby. In the cistern the students stood with only their heads above the water and their two hands, which they clasped as they imploringly cried and screamed, calling their parents. But every single person who passed was wounded, all of them, and there was no one to turn to for help. The singed hair on people's heads was frizzled up and whitish, and covered with dust—from their appearance you couldn't believe that they were human creatures of this world. Looking at these people made me think suddenly 'It can't be possible that I—.' I looked at my two hands and found them covered with blood, and from my arms something that looked like rags was hanging and inside I could see the healthy-looking flesh with its mingled colors of white, red and black. Shocked, I put my hand into my *mompei* pocket to get out my handkerchief, but there was no handkerchief, nor pocket either. And my *mompei* were also burned off below my hips. I could feel my face gradually swelling up, but there was nothing I could do about it, and when some of my friends suggested that we try to return to our homes in the suburbs, I set out with them. As we walked along, fires were blazing high on both sides of us, and my back was painfully hot. From inside the wreckage of the houses we would hear screaming voices calling "Help!" and then the flames would swallow up everything. A child of about six, all covered with blood, holding a kitchen pot in his arms, was facing a burning house, stamping his feet and screaming something. I was in such a state that I didn't even know what to do about myself, so I could hardly attempt to be much help to him, and there was nothing to do but let him go. I wonder what happened to those people? Those people trapped under the houses? The four of us, simply obsessed with the idea of reaching home at the earliest possible minute, hurried long in just the opposite direction from that of the fleeing townspeople—straight toward the center of the blast area. However when we came to Inarimachi, we found that the iron bridge had collapsed and we could not go any farther.

We turned about there and ran toward Futaba Hill. When we were close to the foot of the hill I simply couldn't make my legs carry me another step.

"Wait for me. Please wait for me," I said, and practically crawling, I finally reached the foot of the hill. Luckily there were some kind soldiers from a medical unit there, and they carried me up the hill to a place where I could lie down. There they gave me first aid treatment right away. It seemed that I had received a terrific blow on the back of my head, and there were fragments of roof tile left there. They pulled these out and bandaged the wound for me.

"You just lie there quietly. Your teacher will surely be along any minute now to take care of you," they said to comfort me.

But no matter how long I waited, my teacher didn't come. (Our teachers themselves were severely wounded; some of them died on the afternoon of the sixth, and all of them were dead by the next day.)

Finally the soldiers couldn't wait any longer, and they carried us one by one on their backs down to the barracks at the foot of the hill. A Red Cross flag was waving there. They carried us inside and asked the doctors to take care of us right away. But there were so many wounded people that we had to wait a very long time for our turn to come. In the meantime my strength was exhausted and I couldn't even keep myself standing up. At last they gave us treatment, and we spent the night there. The big buildings in the city were burning steadily, bright red against the dark sky. As the night wore on, the barracks gradually filled to overflowing with moaning voices—over in one corner someone shrieking "Bring me a straw mat if there's nothing better," and here a patient rolling about even on top of people too badly burned to move.

The first night came to an end. From earliest morning voices calling "Water, water," came from every side. I too was so thirsty I could hardly bear it. Inside the barracks there was a sink with water in it. Even though I knew that all sorts of things drained into it and the water was dirty, I scooped up some of that milk-coffee-colored water with my shoe and drank it. Maybe it is because I was normally healthy—anyway my mind was perfectly clear even though I had that severe wound, and since I knew there was a stream running right behind the barracks, I got up and took that shoe and went and drank and drank. And after that any number of times I brought water and gave it to the people who were lying near me and to the soldiers who were wounded. My drawers got soaking wet every time but they soon dried in the blazing hot sun. I had only had my burns painted once with mercurochrome, and they had turned black and were all wet. I was trying to get them dried by the sun so they would harden up. My friends, and the other people too, could not move after they once lay down. Their backs and arms and legs were all slippery where the skin had peeled off, and even if I wanted to raise them up, there was no place I could take hold of them. From about noon of the second day people began to come in a few at a time. I got a white rice-ball from those people, but since my whole face was burned and I couldn't open my mouth very well, I spilled the grains of rice all around when I tried to eat, and only a little bit of it finally ended up in my mouth. By the third day I too was all swollen up, even around my eyes, and I had to lie there beside my friends unable to move at all. And drawn on by the delirious ravings of my friends, I was talking away at random in a dreamy state between sleeping and waking. All at once—was it a dream?—I had a feeling that my father and big sister had come from the foot of the hill to take me away. I was awfully happy, and I forced my eyes open with my hands and looked all around, but I couldn't see anything in the dim light. All the people who came always kept calling the names of the streets and their family names. My father and four or five of our neighbors were searching around for me day after day and finally on the evening of the third day they discovered me in one corner of the barracks at the foot of Futaba Hill. On my blouse there was sewn a name-tag that my father had written for me; the letters had been burned out just as though that part of the cloth had been eaten away by moths, and it was by this that they were able to find me.

"Atchan. This is Father."

When he said that, I was so happy that I couldn't say a word—I could only nod my head. My swollen eyes wouldn't open, so I couldn't see my father's face. This is how I was rescued.

Even now the scars of those wounds remain over my whole body. On my head, my face, my arms, my legs and my chest. As I stroke these blackish-red raised scars on my arms, and every time I look in a mirror at this face of mine which is not like my face, and think that never again will I be able to see my former face and that I have to live my life forever in this condition, it becomes too sad to bear. At the time I lost hope for the future. And not for a single moment could I get rid of the feeling that I had become a cripple. And naturally, for that reason I hated to meet people. And along with that, I couldn't get out of my mind the thought that so many of my good friends, and the teachers who had taken care of me so lovingly, had died under such pitiable circumstances, and I was continually choked with tears. No matter what I thought about, I was likely to be suspicious, and I took a pessimistic attitude toward everything. And my voice, which until now had been a pleasant one that all my friends liked, was lost all at once and became a hoarse voice without any volume. Every time I think about these things, my chest feels as though a terribly tight band is closing around it. But with human beings, it isn't only a beautiful outward appearance that is good. True beauty, worthy of a human being, takes away an ugly appearance and makes it into a splendid one. When I first realized that, my spirit softened somewhat. At the present time, with a fresh hope for life, and studying earnestly to discipline both my body and spirit, I cannot help seeking the inner sort of beauty which comes from a cultivated mind.

Science—what in the world is this science? Such an atom bomb is undoubtedly a crystal of scientific progress. But can it really be said that a thing which takes several hundred thousand human lives at one time is true scientific development? No, science ought to be something that to the very last stimulates those advancements of civilization which are beneficial to mankind. Moreover, the mission of science is to raise the standard of living of mankind. It ought never to be such a thing as would annihilate the life of mankind. It is also obvious that the power of the atom, instead of being thus used as a means of making human beings lose their lives, ought to be turned to the advancement of human civilization. It is my hope that in the future such a tragic event as this will never make a second appearance in this world. And I want things to work out so that atomic energy will be the power which will give birth to a peaceful world. I believe there is no necessity for mankind to experience directly such suffering.

The U.S. Strategic Bombing Survey Concludes That the Bomb Was Unnecessary, 1946

1. Blockade of Japan's sea communications exploited the basic vulnerability of an island enemy which, with inherently second-power resources, was struggling to enlarge its capabilities by milking the raw materials of a rich conquered area. Acute dependence upon imports of such basic items as oil, iron ore, coal, bauxite, food, etc., caused Japan's shipping position even in the fall of 1941 to appear deficient to several members of the Jushin [an informal group of elder statesmen] whose opinions were declared to [then prime minister, General Hideki] Tojo before the Pearl Harbor attack. These fears were well-founded, at least for long-term fighting, since Japan began the war with 6,000,000 tons of merchant shipping, which were barely sufficient for estimated minimum requirements. Her capacity to build was quickly exceeded by losses. Eighty-eight percent of Japan's total merchant shipping available during the war was sunk. United States submarines sank 55 percent of the total lost. Our Navy and Army air forces made important contributions by sinking 40 percent of Japan's total shipping lost, by interdiction of sea routes, and by an aerial mining program carried out by B–29s in the last months of the war which sealed off the vital Inland Sea and disrupted every major home island port. The blockade prevented exploitation of conquered resources, kept Japan's economy off balance, created shortages of materials which in turn limited war production, and deprived her of oil in amounts sufficient to immobilize fleet and air units and to impair training. These effects were intimately associated with the political conditions culminating in the fall of Tojo and [former premier, General Kunikai] Koiso. The direct military and economic limitations imposed by shortages created virtually insoluble political as well as economic problems in attempting to achieve war production adequate for the defense of Japan. The special feeling of vulnerability to blockade, to which a dependent island people are ever subject, increased and dramatized, especially to the leaders, the hopelessness of their position and favored the growing conviction that the defeat was inevitable.

2. While the blockade was definitive in strangling Japan's war mobilization and production, it cannot be considered separately from the pressure of our concurrent military operations, with which it formed a shears that scissored Japan's military potential into an ineffectual remnant. In the early engagements that stemmed the Japanese advance and in the subsequent

battle for bases, the application of our air power against vital forces which Japan committed piecemeal in defense of these perimeter positions enabled us largely to destroy her navy and reduce her air forces to impotence before the home islands could be brought under direct air attack. Throughout these operations we were employing air power effectively and potently in ways the Japanese leaders understood and feared, and had no adequate defense to withstand. Although a core of bitter-end resistance lay in Japan's army and navy until the Imperial rescript was signed, it should be noted that Tojo's collapse and the introduction of peace-making factions into the succeeding Koiso government quickly followed the loss of Saipan in July 1944. Also, after the costly and vitiating defeats in the Palaus, Philippines, and at Iwo Jima, Koiso was in turn succeeded shortly after our Okinawa landings of 1 April 1945 by the [Admiral Baron Kantaro] Suzuki cabinet, which was formed with the specific mandate to terminate the war. In these campaigns, dictated by our need for air mastery and won by immediate air control, while Japan's loss of effective naval and land-based air forces was overwhelming, her military attrition was not complete, since our operations used up by no means all of her ground and Kamikaze forces. Japan's principal land armies were in fact never defeated, a consideration which also supported the military's continued last-ditch resistance to the surrender decision. It nevertheless appears that after the loss of the Marianas in July–August 1944, the military commands, though unconvinced of final victory, viewed defense against our subsequent operations as affording an opportunity for only a limited success, a tactical victory which might, so they hoped, have created a purchase from which to try for a negotiated peace under terms more favorable than unconditional surrender.

3. Fear of home island bombing was persuasive to the political leaders even before its direct effects could be felt. News of the B–29 and its intended capabilities reached Japan in 1943. B–29 raids on Kyushu [with Shikoku, Hokkaido, and Honshu, the Japanese home islands] and southern Honshu [the main home island] targets began from China bases on 15 June 1944. With the loss of Saipan in early July 1944, many leaders became wholly convinced of Japan's eventual defeat, one factor being that from Marianas bases the homeland would be brought under the kind of intensive, shattering air assault even then being administered to their German partner. The timing of the strategic bombing attack affected its role in the surrender decision. After the Marianas were lost but before the first attacks were flown in November 1944, Tojo had been unseated and peacemakers introduced into the Government as prominent elements. The war economy had already passed its peak, fleet and air forces had been critically weakened, confidence of the "intelligentsia" in the Government and the military had been deflated, and confidence of the people in eventual victory was weakening. By mid-1944 shortages of food and civilian supplies were reflected in reduced living standards. Therefore the actual physical destruction wrought by strategic bombing assumed the role of an accelerator, to assist and expedite forces already in motion. It added a tremendous quantitative weight to those forces. Since the means of resisting direct air attacks had already been largely

destroyed, it represented the full exploitation of air control by an air weapon. These attacks became definitive in the surrender decision because they broadened the realization of defeat by bringing it home to the people and dramatized to the whole nation what the small peace party already knew. They proved day in and day out, and night after night, that the United States did control the air and could exploit it. They lowered morale by demonstrating the disadvantages of total war directly, added a vital increment of both actual and clearly foreseeable future production loss by both precision and area attacks, and applied pressure on the surrender decision by eliminating the hope of successful final resistance.

4. When Japan was defeated without invasion, a recurrent question arose as to what effect the threat of a home-island invasion had had upon the surrender decision. It was contended that the threat of invasion, if not the actual operation, was a requirement to induce acceptance of the surrender terms. On this tangled issue the evidence and hindsight are clear. The fact is, of course, that Japan did surrender without invasion, and with its principal armies intact. Testimony before the Survey shows that the expected "violation of the sacred homeland" raised few fears which expedited the decision to surrender beforehand. Government and Imperial household leaders felt some concern for the "destruction of the Japanese people", but the people were already being shattered by direct air attacks. Anticipated landings were even viewed by the military with hope that they would afford a means of inflicting casualties sufficiently high to improve their chances of a negotiated peace. Preparation of defenses against landings diverted certain resources from dispersal and cushioning moves which might have partially mitigated our air blows. But in Japan's then depleted state, the diversion was not significant. The responsible leaders in power read correctly the true situation and embraced surrender well before invasion was expected.

5. So long as Germany remained in the war that fact contributed to the core of Japanese resistance. Slight evidence exists that some hope was held for a long-promised German miracle weapon. A telegram received on 6 May in the German embassy at Tokyo revealed that Hitler was dead, the promised new weapon had failed to materialize and that Germany would surrender within a matter of hours. [Lord Keeper of the Privy Seal, Marquis Koichi] Kido believed, presumably on Japanese Army representations, that the Army would not countenance peace moves so long as Germany continued to fight. It is not clear whether this was a face-saving position, designed to avoid a prior Japanese surrender. In any case on 9 May 1945, immediately after the Nazi capitulation, General [Korechika] Anami, the War Minister, asked the Cabinet for an Imperial conference to reconsider the war situation. The significant fact, however, is that Japan was pursuing peace before the Nazis collapsed, and the impoverishment and fragmentation of the German people had already afforded a portent of similar consequences for an intransigent Japan.

6. The Hiroshima and Nagasaki atomic bombs did not defeat Japan, nor by the testimony of the enemy leaders who ended the war did they persuade Japan to accept unconditional surrender. The Emperor [Hirohito],

the Lord Privy Seal, the Prime Minister, the Foreign Minister [Shigenori Toga], and the Navy Minister [Admiral Mitsumara Yonai] had decided as early as May of 1945 that the war should be ended even if it meant acceptance of defeat on allied terms. The War Minister and the two chiefs of staff opposed unconditional surrender. The impact of the Hiroshima attack was to bring further urgency and lubrication to the machinery of achieving peace, primarily by contributing to a situation which permitted the Prime Minister to bring the Emperor overtly and directly into a position where his decision for immediate acceptance of the Potsdam Declaration could be used to override the remaining objectors. Thus, although the atomic bombs changed no votes of the Supreme War Direction Council concerning the Potsdam terms, they did foreshorten the war and expedite the peace.

Events and testimony which support these conclusions are blue-printed from the chronology established in the first sections of this report:

(*a*) The mission of the Suzuki government, appointed 7 April 1945, was to make peace. An appearance of negotiating for terms less onerous than unconditional surrender was maintained in order to contain the military and bureaucratic elements still determined on a final Bushido ["The Way of the Warrior," the pre-1868-Samurais' code of honor, which advocated fighting to the death] defense, and perhaps even more importantly to obtain freedom to create peace with a minimum of personal danger and internal obstruction. It seems clear however that in extremis the peace-makers would have peace, and peace on any terms. This was the gist of advice given to Hirohito by the Jushin in February, the declared conclusion of Kido in April, the underlying reason for Koiso's fall in April, the specific injunction of the Emperor to Suzuki on becoming premier which was known to all members of his cabinet.

(*b*) A series of conferences of the Supreme War Direction Council before Hirohito on the subject of continuing or terminating the war began on 8 June and continued through 14 August. At the 8 June meeting the war situation was reviewed. On 20 June the Emperor, supported by the Premier, Foreign Minister, and Navy Minister, declared for peace; the Army Minister and the two chiefs of staff did not concur. On 10 July the Emperor again urged haste in the moves to mediate through Russia, but Potsdam intervened. While the Government still awaited a Russian answer, the Hiroshima bomb was dropped on 6 August.

(*c*) Consideration of the Potsdam terms within the Supreme War Direction Council revealed the same three-to-three cleavage which first appeared at the Imperial conference on 20 June. On the morning of 9 August Premier Suzuki and Hirohito decided at once to accept the Potsdam terms; meetings and moves thereafter were designed to legalize the decision and prepare the Imperial rescript. At the conclusive Imperial conference, on the night of 9–10 August, the Supreme War Direction Council still split three-to-three. It was necessary for the Emperor finally to repeat his desire for acceptance of the Potsdam terms.

(*d*) Indubitably the Hiroshima bomb and the rumor derived from interrogation of an American prisoner (B–29 pilot) who stated that an atom bomb attack on Tokyo was scheduled for 12 August introduced urgency in the minds of the Government and magnified the pressure behind its moves to end the war.

7. The sequence of events just recited also defines the effect of Russia's entry into the Pacific war on 8 August 1945. Coming 2 days after the Hiroshima bomb, the move neither defeated Japan nor materially hastened the acceptance of surrender nor changed the votes of the Supreme War Direction Council. Negotiation for Russia to intercede began the forepart of May 1945 in both Tokyo and Moscow. [Prince Funimaro] Konoye, the intended emissary to the Soviets, stated to the Survey that while ostensibly he was to negotiate, he received direct and secret instructions from the Emperor to secure peace at any price, notwithstanding its severity. [Hisatsune] Sakomizu, the chief cabinet secretary, alleged that while awaiting the Russian answer on mediation, Suzuki and Togo decided that were it negative direct overtures would be made to the United States. Efforts toward peace through the Russians, forestalled by the imminent departure of Stalin and Molotov for Potsdam, were answered by the Red Army's advance into Manchuria. The Kwantung army [the Japanese army in China], already weakened by diversion of its units and logistics to bolster island defenses in the South and written off for the defense of Japan proper, faced inescapable defeat.

There is little point in attempting more precisely to impute Japan's unconditional surrender to any one of the numerous causes which jointly and cumulatively were responsible for Japan's disaster. Concerning the absoluteness of her defeat there can be no doubt. The time lapse between military impotence and political acceptance of the inevitable might have been shorter had the political structure of Japan permitted a more rapid and decisive determination of national policies. It seems clear, however, that air supremacy and its later exploitation over Japan proper was the major factor which determined the timing of Japan's surrender and obviated any need for invasion.

Based on a detailed investigation of all the facts and supported by the testimony of the surviving Japanese leaders involved, it is the Survey's opinion that certainly prior to 31 December 1945, and in all probability prior to 1 November 1945, Japan would have surrendered even if the atomic bombs had not been dropped, even if Russia had not entered the war, and even if no invasion had been planned or contemplated.

🎌 *E S S A Y S*

In *The Atomic Bomb and the End of World War II* (1966), former State Department adviser and diplomatic historian Herbert Feis concluded, as had Henry Stimson and other U.S. leaders at the time, that the bomb was used to bring the war to a speedy conclusion. Although in retrospect it no longer appeared that the bomb had been essential to ending the war, the decision to use it was nevertheless justified, in Feis's view. In the late sixties and early seventies, revisionist historians of the Cold War argued that the bomb's use was dictated less by military necessity than by a desire to intimidate the Russians and to end the war in the Pacific before their entry. Historian Martin J. Sherwin of Tufts University explores these and related issues in the second essay, an excerpt drawn from his book *A World Destroyed: The Atomic Bomb and the Grand Alliance* (1975). In the final essay, from his book *The Rise of American Air Power: The Creation of Armageddon* (1987), historian Michael S. Sherry of Northwestern University traces the emergence of new concepts of aerial warfare that accompanied changing military technologies and that made the bombing of civilian populations acceptable, whether by atomic or by "conventional" means.

Shortening the War and Saving Lives

HERBERT FEIS

At the time of the event, only some contributing scientists protested the use of the atomic bomb against a vulnerable live target. The peoples fighting Japan looked upon its employment against the enemy as a natural act of war, and rejoiced at the swift ending it brought about. Any qualms they might have had over the cruel suffering of the victims were routed by the thought that if Germans or Japanese had developed this weapon they would surely have used it. Subsequently, however, as the blast and radiation effects of this new projectile were more fully appreciated, and as more and more powerful kinds were spawned, the precedent act has been regarded by many with rue.

Whether, if the United States had pledged itself as soon as the war ended to destroy the other bombs it had and dismantle the factories in which they were made other countries would have been willing to join with it in a trustworthy system of control of atomic energy, must remain forever a provocation to the speculative historian. But most probably the dismal failure to reach any restraining agreement was an inexpugnable accompaniment to the suspicions, animosities, fears and hatred that have been so rampant after the war. Unable to arrive at genuine peace with each other through mutual good will, respect and understanding, they live under the common canopy of mutual terror. Little wonder then that foreboding dominates the memory of the laboratory triumphs of the physicists, the achievements of the engineers, the test at Alamogordo and the display at Hiroshima.

In the evolving discussion about the decision to use the bomb, several related but separable questions have been commingled. One of these, and by far the easiest to answer conclusively, is whether it was *essential* to do so in order to compel Japan to surrender on our terms before it was invaded.

Some of the decision-makers were confident that the invasion of the main islands of Japan would not be necessary to compel surrender quickly and unconditionally. Japan's ability to fend off our tremendous naval and air assaults was shattered. It seemed to them that the Japanese people, crowded in their small islands, with insufficient and destructible supplies of food and oil, would have to give in soon—unless bent on national suicide. Among those were Secretary of the Navy Forrestal and Under Secretary Bard and Admiral Leahy and General Spaatz, the Commander of our Strategic Air Force.

But others, especially those in the Army, remained convinced that final victory on our own terms could only be achieved on land, as it had been in the Philippines, Iwo Jima, Okinawa. Had not their military histories taught them that a hopelessly beaten Confederate Army had battled on? Had they not witnessed the refusal of the Germans under the fanatic Hitler to give up long after any chance of winning was gone, and how that people rallied from the shattering air attacks on their cities? Would the war in Europe continue many months longer, they argued, except for the combined crushing assaults of large land armies from the East, the West, the South?

To the historian, taught by the accumulated records and testimony, the answer is obvious. There cannot be a well-grounded dissent from the conclusion reached as early as 1945 by members of the U.S. Strategic Bombing Survey. After inspection of the condition to which Japan was reduced, by studies of the military position and the trend of Japanese popular and official opinion, they estimated ". . . that certainly prior to 31 December 1945, and in all probability prior to 1 November 1945, Japan would have surrendered even if the atomic bombs had not been dropped, even if Russia had not entered the war, and even if no invasion had been planned or contemplated."

If then the use of the bomb was not essential, was it justified—justified, that is, as the surest way in combination with other measures to bring about the earliest surrender? That is a harder question to answer, and a more troubling one than it was thought to be at the time of decision.

It may be contended with the grim support by history that no exceptional justification for the use of the bomb need be sought or given. For the prevalent rule of nations—except when "knighthood was in flower"—has allowed the use of any and all weapons in war except any banned by explicit agreement; and this was the prevailing view at the time, qualified only by revulsion againt use of weapons and methods deemed needlessly inhumane such as poisoning of wells and torture. Did not, it should be borne in mind, every one of the contending nations strive its utmost to invent and produce more deadly weapons, faster planes of greater bomb capacity, new types of mines, rockets and buzz-bombs? And was not each and every improved sort of killing weapon brought into action without ado or reproach? For this reason alone, almost all professional military men, and those in uniform in 1945, would then have denied that any special justification for the use of the bomb was needed, and would still dispose of the subject in this way.

The more thoughtful might add that the decision to use the bomb was not really important; that the measures of permanent significance to mankind had been taken when physicists learned how to split the atom, and when scientists and engineers and builders succeeded in encasing the energy of the fissured atom in a bomb; and that after these were achieved, it made little or no difference if this novel weapon was used against Japan, since it would certainly be used in the future time unless nations renounced war.

Or if it were not, other equally dreadful threats would remain; chemical and biological ways of bringing death; and these were already in the secret arsenals of nations.

The source of restraint lies in fear of consequences; fear of the fact that the enemy will use the same terrible weapon. This was, for example, why neither side used poison gas in the war. When humane feeling is allied to such fear, it may command respect, and even those striving to win a war may recognize that "virtue it is to abstain even from that which is lawful."

These considerations seem to me conclusive defenses of our right, legal and historical, for the use of the atomic bomb against Japan. Those who made the decision took them for granted. They thus felt free to make it without scruples on these scores.

Their reckoning, I believe the record clearly indicates, was governed by one reason deemed paramount: that by using the bomb the agony of war might be ended most quickly and lives be saved. It was believed with deep apprehension that many thousands, probably tens of thousands, of lives of Allied combatants would have to be spent in the continuation of our air and sea bombardment and blockade, victims mainly of Japanese suicide planes. In spite of its confidence in ultimate success, our assailant naval force felt vulnerable, because of grim and agonizing experience. Since the desperate kamikaze attacks began, suicide planes had sunk 34 American ships, including 3 aircraft carriers, and damaged 285 (including 36 carriers of all sizes and sorts, 15 battleships, 15 cruisers and 87 destroyers). During the Okinawa campaign alone, 16 of our ships had been sunk and 185 damaged (including 7 carriers, 10 battleships and 5 cruisers).

It was reliably known that the Japanese were assembling thousands of planes, of all kinds and conditions, to fling against the invasion fleet and the troop-carrying ships. Thus, should it prove necessary to carry out the plans for invasion, not only of Kyushu but also of the Tokyo Plain, it was feared by Stimson and Marshall that the American casualties alone might mount to hundreds of thousands. Our allies, it was reckoned, would suffer corresponding losses.

But the people who would have suffered most, had the war gone on much longer and their country been invaded, were the Japanese. One American incendiary air raid on the Tokyo area in March 1945 did more damage and killed and injured more Japanese than the bomb on Hiroshima. Even greater groups of American bombing planes would have hovered over Japan, consuming the land, its people and its food, with blast and fire, leaving them no place to hide, no chance to rest, no hope of reprieve. A glance at the chart kept in the Headquarters of the U.S. Strategic Air Force at Guam, with its steeply ascending record of bombing flights during the summer of 1945 and scheduled for the next month or two, leaves visions of horror of which Hiroshima is only a local illustration. Observation of the plight of the country and its people made soon after the war ended left me appalled at what those would have had to endure had the war gone on.

But the same official forecasts of what it was thought would occur if we had to fight on, gave sharper shape to the impelling reason for the development of the bomb—to end the war victoriously. Thus the decision to use the bomb seemed to be the natural culminating act for the achievement of a settled purpose as attested by its leading sponsors:

General Groves: "My mission as given to me by Secretary of War Stimson [in October 1942] was to produce this [the atomic bomb] at the earliest possible date so as to bring the war to a conclusion."

Truman: "I regarded the bomb as a military weapon and never had any doubt that it should be used."

Churchill: "The historic fact remains . . . that the decision whether or not to use the atomic bomb to compel the surrender of Japan was never even an issue. There was unanimous, automatic, unquestioned agreement around our table; nor did I ever hear the slightest suggestion that we should do otherwise."

Stimson: "Stimson believed, both at the time and later, that the dominant fact of 1945 was war, and that therefore, necessarily, the dominant objective was victory. If victory could be speeded by using the bomb, it should be used; if victory must be delayed in order to use the bomb, it should *not* be used. So far as he knew, this general view was fully shared by the President and all his associates."

Some of those men who concurred in the decision to use the bomb discerned other advantages and justifications. It is likely that Churchill, and probably also Truman, conceived that besides bringing the war to a quick end, it would improve the chances of arranging a satisfactory peace both in Europe and in the Far East. Stimson and [Secretary of State James F.] Byrnes certainly had that thought in mind. For would not the same dramatic proof of western power that shocked Japan into surrender impress the Russians also? Might it not influence them to be more restrained? Might it not make more effective the resistance of the western allies to excessive Soviet pretensions and ventures, such as the Soviet bid for a military base in the Black Sea Straits, and a foreseen demand for a part in the occupation and control of Japan akin to that which it had in Germany? In short, the bomb, it may have been thought or hoped, would not only subdue the Japanese aggressors, but perhaps also monitor Russian behavior.

Recognition of this element in official thinking must not be distorted into an accusation that the American government engaged in what Soviet propagandists and historians have called "atomic blackmail." To the contrary, even after the American government knew that it would have the supreme weapon, it keenly sought to preserve the friendly connection with the Soviet Union. It rebuffed Churchill's proposals that the Western allies face down the Soviet government in some climactic confrontation over the outward thrust of Soviet power. After the testing of the bomb, at the Potsdam Conference, it patiently sought compromise solutions for situations in dispute. While knowledge of the successful test may have somewhat stiffened Truman's resistance to some of the furthest-reaching Soviet wishes, it did not cause him to alter American aims or terms as previously defined. In brief, and obviously, the men who determined American policy strove to achieve a stable international order by peaceful ways. They were not swayed by an excited wish to impose our will on the rest of the world by keeping atomic bombs poised over their lives. Even as the American government proceeded to use the bomb against Japan, it was brewing proposals for controlling its production and banning its use, except possibly as an international measure to enforce peace.

Had—the query continues to haunt the historian—the American government, *before* using the bomb, informed Stalin candidly of its nature and potential, and solicited his cooperation in some system of international control, might the Soviet government have reacted differently? Might it have been deflected from making the utmost effort to master the task of producing like weapons and accumulating them as a national atomic force? It is highly improbable, I think, considering Stalin's determination, as evidenced at Potsdam, to wear down Western resistance to Soviet claims, his suspicions and soaring assurance, and his belief that nations respected only strength. It would have been like him, in fact, to regard our confidential briefing as a subtle way of threatening the Soviet government, of trying to frighten it to accede to our wishes.

My best surmise is that while openness would have disarmed some foreign critics and improved the reception abroad of our later proposals for control, it would not really have influenced the Soviet policy. Nevertheless, it is regrettable that we did not take Stalin into at least the outer regions of our confidence, thereby indicating to the world that we were not intent on keeping unto ourselves a secret means of domination. After all, our secrecy and our elaborate security measures in the end were ineffectual and suffused the atmosphere with the scent of enmity.

This train of inference about other reasons for using the bomb—confluent with the wish to end the war quickly and with minimum loss of life— that may also have figured in the minds of those who made the decision, can be carried further. The scientists who served on the Scientific Panel, as the narrative has told, were gravely aware of the lasting and supreme significance of the achievement. Stimson, sharing their perception of its bearing upon human destiny, was impelled, despite age and fatigue, to write memo after memo expounding his conviction that every effort must be exerted to get the nations to cooperate to prevent impending mutual destruction.

These official parents of this new form of force verged toward the conclusion that it would confront the whole world with a crucial and ultimate choice: to renounce war or perish. But would the nations defer to that reality unless the horrifying power of this new weapon to destroy human life was proven by human sacrifice? Would they realize otherwise that it was imperative that they subordinate themselves to the new international security organization that had just been created in San Francisco? Would they submit to the necessary restraints unless convinced that if they did not, they would all be consumed together in the vengeful bursts of atomic explosions? Thus, even men genuinely regretful about the deaths and suffering that would be caused by the use of the bomb, could think of the act as an essential step toward the creation of a peaceful political order. And connectedly, that undeniable proof of the destructive power of atomic energy would foster a willingness to subject its development to the collectivity of nations; for unless it was so controlled, any one country with a great atomic force could defy the rest.

As recounted, there were those who believed all these purposes would be better served if the bomb was introduced in some other way. They urged that before using it against Japan its immense destructive power should be displayed to the world by dropping it in some remote, uninhabited or emptied spot—an isolated island perhaps, or over a dense forest area, or on a mountain top, or in the sea near land. All suggestions of this sort were judged impractical, ineffective and/or risky.

A genuine fear of failure persisted despite accumulated evidence that the weapon was going to bear out the scientists' prediction. It will be remembered that as early as December 1944, Groves had been sure enough that one of the two types of bomb being produced (the type that was dropped on Hiroshima) would work satisfactorily, to report to Stimson that he and presumably his technical advisers did not think a preliminary full test essential. This confidence mounted as the effort neared fruition. The physicist, [Henry D.] Smyth, who wrote up the authorized explanation of the undertaking, entered in his notes that "the end of June [1945] finds us expecting from day to day to hear of the explosion of the first atomic bomb devised by man. All the problems are believed to have been solved at least well enough to make a bomb practicable. A sustained neutron chain reaction resulting from nuclear fission has been demonstrated; the conditions necessary to cause such a reaction to occur explosively have been established and can be achieved. . . ."

But the responsible officials and military men still had nervous fears of failure. As recalled summarily by Stimson, in explanation of the decision not to warn Japan in advance of the nature and destructive power of the weapon, "Even the New Mexico test would not give final proof that any given bomb was certain to explode when dropped from an airplane. Quite apart from the generally unfamiliar nature of atomic explosives, there was the whole problem of exploding a bomb at a predetermined height in the air by a complicated mechanism which could not be tested in the static test of New Mexico."

This uncertainty remained despite the numerous varied trials that had been made in flight with a simulated bomb casing and components. For many precautions had been conceived and taken against each and every one of these hazards; many rehearsals to enable trained mechanics and bombing crews to detect any causes of failure beforehand and to correct them.

Then there were chances of human error or accident. What if the heavily laden plane carrying the bomb and fuel needed for the long flight to the point selected for the demonstration crashed? What if the individuals entrusted with the task of turning the containing tube (in the U-235 gun type bomb that was first available for use in Japan) into an atomic weapon, faulted?

Then, also, there were chances of physical defects. Some part of the mechanism of any single specimen might turn out to be defective and malfunction.

Still another opposed reason was that the American government had so few of the new bombs. One would be consumed by the New Mexico test; another (of a different type) was promised in time for use after July 31; and it was reckoned a third by August 6th; and no others according to the schedule given to the decision-makers in June, until about August 20th. By using all—two or three—with utmost effectiveness, the desired quick end of the war might well be brought about. If one of these was misspent in a demonstration that went awry for any reason, could the trial be justified to the men in uniform whose lives were in hazard every day the war went on?

Suppose an announced demonstration had failed. Would the consequences have been serious? Stimson, and even more decidedly Byrnes and Groves, thought so. They believed that if it did not come off "as advertised," the Japanese would take fresh heart and fight on harder and longer. They feared, also, that an uproar would ensue in Congress if the demonstration fizzled or failed to budge the Japanese. They had accepted the unavoidable risks of condemnation if the project on which such vast sums had been spent turned out to be a mistaken venture. But they were not willing to widen the margin of exposure for any other purpose. They tried to dismiss their worries as did the experienced construction engineer whom Robert Patterson, the Under Secretary of War, asked to size up the operation at Oak Ridge. On his return he assured Patterson, "You have really nothing to worry about. If the project succeeds, no one will investigate what was done, and if it does not succeed, every one will investigate nothing else the rest of your life."

Such were the grave apprehensions of the decision-makers of the consequences of a failure in an attempted demonstration. I cannot refrain from remarking that I do not think they would have been as upsetting or harmful as imagined. The stimulant to Japanese military morale would have been very brief. In the United States, criticism would have faded as soon as the bomb was successfully proven—leaving admiration for a noble purpose.

However, speculation on this subject may be regarded as a professional indulgence. For, in fact, even if the decision-makers had not feared a possible failure in demonstration, they would not have tried it. For they deemed it most unlikely that a demonstration could end the war as quickly and surely as hurling the bomb on Japan; and that was their duty as they saw it. No matter what the place and setting for the demonstration, they were sure it would not give an adequate impression of its appalling destructive power, would not register its full meaning in human lives. The desired explosive impression on the Japanese, it was concluded, could be produced only by the actual awful experience. Such precursory opinion was in accord with Stimson's subsequent interpretation of why its use was so effective.

"But the atomic bomb was more than a weapon of terrible destruction; it was a psychological weapon. In March, 1945, our Air Force had launched the first incendiary raid on the Tokyo area. In this raid more damage was done and more casualties were inflicted than was the case at Hiroshima. Hundreds of bombers took part and hundreds of tons of incendiaries were dropped. Similar successive raids burned out a great part of the urban areas of Japan, but the Japanese fought on. On August 6th a B-29 dropped a single atomic bomb on Hiroshima. Three days later a second bomb was dropped on Nagasaki and the war was over.''

It has since been contended, and with perseverance, that even if the drop on Hiroshima was justified by its purpose and results, that the second drop on Nagasaki was not. For the exponents of this opinion think that if right after Hiroshima the American government had made it clear, as they did later, that the Japanese authorities could retain the Emperor, they would have surrendered; and hence the destruction of Nagasaki was unnecessary.

This is a tenable judgment. But the records of happenings within Japanese ruling circles during the few days between Hiroshima and Nagasaki foster the impression that if the second bomb had not been dropped, the Japanese rulers would have delayed, perhaps for some weeks, the response which was preliminary to capitulation. The military heads would have been so firm in opposition that the Emperor would probably have waited until the situation became more hopeless before overruling them.

The first reports which the military investigating group that the Japanese Chief of Staff hurried to Hiroshima gave out minimized the awfulness of the effects of the bomb, describing the burns suffered from the blast by persons clothed in white and those in shelters as relatively light. Military headquarters started to issue announcements of counter measures which could be effective against the new bomb. The truth about its nature and effects, as estimated by a group of physicists after their inspection, was only made known to the Cabinet on the morning of the 9th while the mushroom cloud was over Nagasaki. Even thereafter, the Army heads accepted the decision to surrender only because the Emperor's openly declared conclusion relieved them of shame and humiliation, and lessened their fear of disobedience by their subordinates.

Thus, to repeat, it is probable that by intensifying the dread of the new weapon—of which, so far as the Japanese knew, we might have many more—the strike against Nagasaki hastened the surrender. But whether merely by a few days or few weeks is not to be known.

In summary it can be concluded that the decision to drop the bombs upon Hiroshima and Nagasaki ought not to be censured. The reasons were—under the circumstances of the time—weighty and valid enough. But a cluster of worrisome queries remain which the passage of time has coated with greater political, ethical and historical interest.

One of these [is] whether or not the desired quick surrender could have been induced if the American government had been more explicit in its explanations of how the Japanese people and Emperor would fare after surrender. . . .

Another, which has often been asked, is why ten days were allowed to pass between the receipt of information regarding the results of the test of the bomb and the issuance of our final warning. I think the delay was due to an intent to be sure that if the warning was at first unheeded, it could be driven quickly and deeply home by the bombs. Thus we waited until we knew all was in readiness to drop them. These tactics worked. But I wonder whether it might not have been wiser to issue the warning sooner, and thus to have allowed the Japanese authorities more time to ponder its meaning and acceptability. I think it not out of the question that if allowed, say, another fortnight, the Emperor might have imposed his final decision before the bomb was set for use. However, because of the blinding fury and pride of the fighting men, it is unlikely. He hardly would have dared to do so until the explosion of the atomic bomb destroyed the argument that Japan could secure a better peace if it continued to refuse to surrender unconditionally.

But what if the American government had fully revealed the results of the New Mexico test to the Japanese (and the whole world)? Could that have induced the desired quick surrender? The most promising time for such revelations would have been in connection with the issuance of the Potsdam Declaration; for by then the American air assaults and naval bombardments were spreading havoc everywhere, and most Japanese were aware they had no way of countering them, no good idea of how to survive them. Suppose, to be more precise, the American government had published the reports on the test which were sent by General Groves to Potsdam for Stimson and the President, such photographs of the explosion and of the mushroom cloud and the testimony of scientists about the destructive power of the weapon that were available. Might not that broadcast knowledge, prefaced by an explanation that one of our purposes was to spare the Japanese, have had enough shock effect to cause the Emperor to overrule the resistant Japanese military leaders?

Perhaps. But in order to make the disclosure as impressive as possible, it might have been necessary to postpone the issuance of the final warning— perhaps until the end of the Potsdam Conference. The test was July 16th; it would have taken time to assemble convincing accounts and photographs, and explanation. This postponement might have prolonged slightly the period of combat.

However, in retrospect, I believe that the risk should have been taken and the cost endured; for by so doing this we might have been spared the need to introduce atomic weapons into war. In the likely event that the Japanese would not have been swayed by this explicit warning of what would happen to them if they rejected our ultimatum, we as a people would be freer of any regret—I will not say remorse—at the necessity of enrolling Hiroshima and Nagasaki in the annals of history.

But the mind, circling upon itself, returns to the point of wondering whether, if the exterminating power of the bomb had not been actually displayed, the nations would have been impelled to make even as faltering an effort as they have to agree on measures to save themselves from mutual extinction by this ultimate weapon. In a novel published in 1914, H. G. Wells prophesied that nations would not recognize the impossibility of war "until the atomic bomb burst in their fumbling hands." Now, two great wars later, it remains entirely uncertain whether they will bow before its imperative.

The Bomb as a Weapon of Diplomacy

MARTIN J. SHERWIN

On the eve of the Potsdam Conference the most widely accepted attitude toward the atomic bomb was an extension of how it was seen and valued earlier—a potential instrument of military and diplomatic policy. Caught between the remnants of war and the uncertainties of peace, policymakers and scientists were trapped by their own unquestioned assumptions. Not only the conclusion of the war but the organization of an acceptable peace seemed to depend—for [Secretary of State James F.] Byrnes, [Secretary of War Henry L.] Stimson, and [President Harry S] Truman as well as for [Director of the Manhattan Project's Los Alamos Research Laboratory J. Robert] Oppenheimer, and [physicist Edward] Teller—upon the success of the atomic attacks against Japan. The secret development of this terrible weapon, during a war fought for total victory, created a logic of its own: a quest for a total solution to a set of related problems that appeared incapable of being resolved incrementally. As [physicist Leo] Szilard first suggested in January 1944, the bomb might provide its own solution—a military demonstration held out the possibility of literally blasting old diplomatic calculations out of existence.

The senior American policymakers who traveled to Potsdam were imbued with this hope. Fervent believers in the rightness of their course, convinced that world peace depended upon Soviet acceptance of their views, they waited for the results from Alamogordo to learn whether they had the means at their disposal to ensure Soviet compliance with their plans for the postwar world. "The bomb as a merely probable weapon had seemed a weak reed on which to rely, but the bomb as a colossal reality was very different," Stimson wrote, recalling his own reaction to news of the flawless test. American diplomacy had gained "a badly needed 'equalizer,' " and further diplomatic efforts to bring the Russians into the war against Japan suddenly appeared "largely pointless." The decision to use the bomb to end the war could no longer be distinguished from the desire to use it to stabilize the peace.

The news from Alamogordo instilled a new sense of confidence in the American delegation. Arguments that the Japanese should be offered specific inducements to surrender, or that the negotiators should compromise with the Soviets, disappeared. Within weeks this new power would be demonstrated to the world under combat conditions. Then Tokyo and Moscow would surely reconsider their stubborn policies; America's sole possession of this extraordinary weapon promised their acquiescence. Having invested so much in the performance of the bomb, it is perhaps not surprising that Truman, upon learning of the outcome of the raid against Hiroshima, made the vile remark: "This is the greatest thing in history."

I *"A Blind Woman Who Saw the Light"*

Truman carried a heavy burden of anticipation to Potsdam. This first major test of his diplomatic skills promised to engage some of the most difficult issues of the war. Did Stalin intend to join the final assault against Japan in time to save a significant number of American lives? If he did, would he expand his territorial demands in the Far East? Could American-Soviet differences over Eastern Europe be resolved harmoniously? Would Stalin compromise in exchange for American economic assistance? How was Germany to be ruled? Finally, beyond these issues of policy, Truman faced a question more personally pressing: how well would he measure up against Stalin and Churchill at the negotiating table?

As late as July 3, the unfamiliar formalities of international diplomacy and the uncertainties of the outcome of the conference found him less than enthusiastic about the challenge. "Wish I didn't have to go," he wrote his mother and sister, "but I do and it can't be stopped now." Coating a hard grain of truth with a soft Midwestern colloquialism, several aides described the political environment to the President on the day of his departure: "We think that as a well known Missouri horse trader, the American people expect you to bring something home to them." It was an expectation he needed to fulfill. By the early morning hours of July 7, when he departed for Potsdam from Newport News, Virginia, aboard the U.S.S. *Augusta,* he had come to believe that the results of the test at Alamogordo would determine to a large measure how well he could accomplish that goal. He had no intention of employing the bomb explicitly as an instrument of diplomacy during the conference, but a successful test would assure him at the very least that he need make no politically embarrassing concessions there.

Truman and his closest advisers therefore placed a high value on knowing with complete certainty that they possessed the bomb as a backstop for their diplomatic policies—a value underlined by their efforts to have the test conducted prior to the opening of the conference. When Oppenheimer reported to Groves on July 2 that the preferred date, July 14, entailed unacceptable risks and a "frantic" situation, and therefore could not safely be met, his request for a mere three-day delay was denied. There were other reasons why it was extremely important that the test be performed by the earlier date, Groves informed him that morning. And again at 5:45 in the evening, after discussing the situation with Harrison and Bundy, Groves called Los Alamos to confirm his earlier decision. The "upper crust want[s] it as soon as possible," he said. Although he was not in agreement with their decision, he had to "stress the urgency of having it done the 14th."

Despite Oppenheimer's best efforts to comply, the bomb was not ready for testing until the early morning hours of July 16. News from Alamogordo reached Potsdam in stages between July 16 and 21. The reports came to

Stimson, who passed them on to Truman, Byrnes, and Churchill. As each document filled in more details of the extraordinary, successful performance of the first atomic bomb, the spirits of the Anglo-American leaders rose. Churchill was "intensely interested and greatly cheered up" by the first reports, while Truman was "evidently very greatly reenforced," Stimson wrote in his diary. The full impact of the historic explosion on the Potsdam negotiators was delayed, however, until the sixth day of the conference, July 21, when a complete report from Groves arrived by courier. Stimson was deeply impressed: "It was an immensely powerful document, clearly and well written and with supporting documents of the highest importance." Eschewing formal military language, Groves described the event in vivid detail:

> At 0530, 16 July 1945, in a remote section of the Alamogordo Air Base, New Mexico, the first full scale test was made of the implosion type atomic fission bomb. . . . The test was successful beyond the most optimistic expectations of anyone. Based on the data which it has been possible to work up to date, I estimate the energy generated to be in excess of the equivalent of 15,000 to 20,000 tons of TNT; and this is a conservative estimate.

Groves then reviewed the bomb blast's effects: an incredible fire ball as bright as several midday suns; a mushroom cloud that shot 41,000 feet into the substratosphere; a tremendous crash that broke a window 125 miles away; a crater 1,200 feet in diameter; a forty-ton steel tower one-half mile from the explosion destroyed. The Pentagon (whose construction Groves had directed) was not a safe shelter from such a bomb, he concluded. "With the assistance of the Office of Censorship we were able to limit the news stories to the approved release supplemented in the local papers by brief stories from the many eyewitnesses not connected with our project. One of these was a blind woman who saw the light."

At 3:30 that afternoon at the President's quarters in Potsdam, "the Little White House," Stimson reviewed Groves's report with Truman and Byrnes. "They were immensely pleased," he recalled. "The President was tremendously pepped up by it and spoke to me of it again and again when I saw him. He said it gave him an entirely new feeling of confidence and he thanked me for having come to the Conference and being present to help him in this way."

Fortified by this news, the President left at 5 P.M. for the fifth plenary session, where he took command of the debate with a vigor he had not displayed at previous meetings. "I shall state frankly what I think," he told Stalin. "He stood up to the Russians in a most emphatic and decisive manner," Churchill observed, "telling them as to certain demands that they absolutely could not have and that the United States was entirely against them." "Now I know what happened to Truman yesterday," the Prime Minister remarked after reading Groves's report. "I couldn't understand it. When he got to the meeting after having read this report he was a changed man. He told the Russians [and the British, he should have added] just where they got on and off and generally bossed the whole meeting." [U.S.

Ambassador to the Soviet Union W. Averell] Harriman perceived the change in attitude too. Despite a general feeling among the American delegation that the Russians were recklessly expanding their demands, he commented to Stimson on July 23 about "the increasing cheerfulness evidently caused by the news from us [about Alamogordo]." Truman directly confirmed the influence of the bomb on his attitude and his negotiating position that same day when he discussed the situation with Stimson. The President assured him that despite Soviet demands he was standing firm and "he was apparently relying greatly upon the information as to S-1." It appeared to Stimson that the "program for S-1 is tying in what we are doing in all fields."

Several days later Byrnes explained to Special Ambassador Joseph Davies, who had been invited to the conference by Truman, how important the bomb had become to him. Byrnes "was having a hard time with reparations," Davies wrote, but the "details as to the success of the atomic bomb, which he had just received, gave him confidence that the Soviets would agree as to these difficulties." Davies was deeply disturbed. "Byrnes' attitude that the atomic bomb assured ultimate success in negotiations disturbed me more than his description of its success amazed me," he wrote in his diary. "I told him the threat wouldn't work, and might do irreparable harm."

But Davies did not make policy, and to remain faithful to the historical record the views of those who did need to be taken seriously. To recognize that the President and his advisers weighed the implications of the successful test in relation to all aspects of American policy does not *ipso facto* justify ascribing diabolical motivations to them. Historians who have chosen to ignore, or more recently those who have sought to explain away, the effect of Alamogordo on the Potsdam negotiators have not succeeded in correcting the exaggerated influence of the bomb described by others. Under the circumstances, how could American policymakers have failed to be affected by Groves's description of that historic explosion? The experience of war at once blinded them to any moral constraints against using the new weapon and encouraged them to seek whatever military or diplomatic advantages its use might incur. The United States was in control of a "final arbiter of force." At the crossroads of war and diplomacy the temptation to seize this advantage was irresistible.

Truman's decision to reopen the question of whether the Soviets were needed to conclude the war against Japan provides the clearest example of the bomb's influence on American policy. As early as May 1945, Acting Secretary of State (and former ambassador to Japan) Joseph C. Grew had urged the President, the Secretaries of War and the Navy, and high State Department officials to modify the insistence on "unconditional surrender." The Japanese would never give up, he argued, without assurances that the present dynasty and the institution of the Emperor would not be destroyed. Without such a guarantee, even members of Japan's peace faction were powerless before the weight of national tradition and the determination of the armed forces to continue the struggle. Unconditional surrender, however, had become a political shibboleth by the time Truman took office, a slogan that embodied for the American public what the sacrifices of war seemed to be all about. Neither Truman nor Byrnes, consummate politicians to the core, was ready to retreat publicly from this path that Roosevelt had blazed. Grew's suggestion was therefore set aside, and Truman came to Potsdam hoping to secure a Soviet declaration of war against Japan. With the invasion of the Japanese mainland scheduled for November 1945, there was still time for the Soviets to divert the powerful Japanese Manchurian Army.

By the end of the first week of the Potsdam Conference, however, the negotiating position assumed by the Soviets created second thoughts about the consequences of their assistance. Considering the generally hostile attitude toward the Russians pervading the American delegation, those second thoughts are not surprising. Even before the conference opened, Davies found Special Ambassador Edwin Pauley and his reparations negotiators determined to "out-trade the so and so's—or else." He was told by Byrnes that the Russians could only be dealt with in a tough manner, and that Truman was "constantly being hammered on the idea that this was the only way to handle them." [Senior Military Advisor to the President Admiral William D.] Leahy and Harriman were forcefully advocating the idea that it was essential to be tough with the Russians. "The fact is," Davies commented on July 15, "that the anti-Soviet prejudices in the [State] Department and in other departments has [sic] surrounded the President to a degree where it makes the situation very dangerous."

Dangerous indeed, for the inevitable tough bargaining at Potsdam led the American delegates quickly to the conclusion that the Soviets were living up to their worst expectations (while the Soviet delegates no doubt reached the same conclusions about the Americans). They were "throwing aside all their previous restraint as to being a continental power . . . seeking to branch in all directions," Stimson wrote in his diary. Although Truman considered many of their new demands a bluff, the feeling grew among senior American officials that the Russians were out to absorb as much as they could get. They were trying to extend their influence in Eastern Europe, Stimson reported, in Turkey, in the Italian Mediterranean colonies, and elsewhere. Even an effort to obtain solitary control over Korea seemed possible.

What could be done? Truman instructed Stimson to find out whether [U.S. Army Chief of Staff General George] "Marshall felt that we needed the Russians in the war or whether we could get along without them." The answer, that they were not needed, was relayed to the President as follows: The massing of Soviet troops along the Chinese border was already tying up Japan's forces in Manchuria, and now that the atomic bomb was a reality the value of Soviet assistance had declined. Moreover, if the Soviets intended to enter the war they could not in any case be stopped. Truman decided not to request their help. The conference notes of Walter Brown, press secretary to Byrnes, explain his motives in advocating that decision: the Secretary was "still hoping for time, believing after atomic bomb [sic] Japan will surrender and Russia will not get in so much on the kill, thereby being in a position to press for claims against China."

Although the combination of news of the successful test and the expansion of Soviet territorial demands changed the attitude of American policymakers toward Soviet participation in the Far Eastern war, it did not incline them to lay the bomb on the negotiating table. Their policy of letting the weapon speak for itself in the next week or two remained unaltered. Only Churchill, who had earlier opposed any revelation about the bomb to Stalin, changed his mind. Not only did he agree after reading Groves's report that the Russians should be informed about the existence of the project as the Interim Committee had recommended, but he was "inclined to use it as an argument in our favor in the negotiations." But Truman was not. Following the letter of the Committee's recommendation rather than its spirit, which embodied the hope that an overture to Stalin would initiate the process toward international control, Truman "casually mentioned to Stalin, after the plenary session on July 24, "that we had a new weapon of unusual destructive force." Stalin's reply was unexpectedly brief: "He was glad to hear it and hoped we would make 'good use of it against the Japanese,' " Truman reported. A letter from [Special Assistant to the Secretary of State] Charles Bohlen confirms the President's description of this colloquy: "My recollection and impression . . . is that he [Truman] wished to make his statement as casual as possible and for this reason without taking me, his interpreter, with him he strolled over to Stalin. . . ."

The steady course toward a postwar atomic armaments race that [Danish physicist Niels] Bohr had sought to alter passed several important markers at Potsdam. Not only were Soviet fears about the consequences of an American atomic bomb heightened, but on the American side, what little commitment there was among high officials for the international control of atomic energy all but vanished. Stimson, the most determined advocate of international control within the Truman administration in June, had executed a complete *volte face* on the issue by July 26. In a long memorandum to the President, "Reflections on the Basic Problems Which Confront Us," he outlined a new position and the considerations that brought it about. The nature of the Soviet government—a police state—precluded the possibility of effective international control. He was unwilling to abandon hope altogether, but the atmosphere the Soviets had created at Potsdam led him to believe that, at the present juncture, even "with the best of efforts we cannot understand each other." Fearing that a new war and the destruction of civilization would result if a hostile relationship became permanent, he urged that his government direct its thoughts "constantly to the time and the method of attacking the basic difficulty and the means we may have in hand to produce results." How, in other words, could Soviet society be liberalized? Until free speech was granted, it was necessary to proceed along the path toward international control slowly "and constantly explore the question how our headstart in X [the atomic bomb] and the Russian desire to participate can be used to bring us nearer to the removal of the basic difficulties. . . ." The Secretary was still thinking in terms of the *quid pro quo* he had first advocated in December 1944; but the terms of the trade had now escalated from geography to ideology, from the modification of Soviet foreign policy to the reconstruction of Soviet society.

II "A Graveyard with Not a Tombstone Standing"

A similar purpose guided American policy toward Japan. The democratization of Japanese society remained an undisputed goal throughout the war, though there existed strong differences of opinion over how to achieve it. While Grew and Stimson argued in the spring and summer of 1945 that the Emperor's remaining was a necessary corollary to the process, Assistant Secretaries of State Dean Acheson and Archibald MacLeish insisted that the institution itself was fundamentally antidemocratic and had to be eliminated. This debate—which bore closely on the question of whether or not to modify the demand for unconditional surrender—was temporarily settled by Byrnes, who sided with Acheson and MacLeish on the advice of the ailing former Secretary of State, Cordell Hull. Having blocked what appeared under the circumstances to be Japan's last viable exit from the war, U.S. policymakers concentrated on ways to open another: a severe psychological shock inflicted by successive atomic bombings held out the possibility of altering the Japanese government's determination to continue the hopeless struggle. The selection of targets reflected this intention, which had been guiding the Air Force's bombing strategy since March; the central purpose of the terrible fire bomb raids on Tokyo was not so much to destroy Japanese fighting capability as to weaken the will of the people and government to continue the war.

Guided by instructions from Groves, a Target Committee composed of Manhattan Project scientists and ordnance specialists studied the available options, and developed criteria for their selection. The report of the Committee's second and third meetings, held in Oppenheimer's office at Los Alamos on May 10 and 11, provides a straightforward summary of its orientation. The minutes record their conclusion that any small, strictly military target should be located in a much larger area subject to blast damage "to avoid undue risks of the weapon being lost due to bad placing of the bomb." The members of the Committee agreed, too, that psychological factors in the target selection were of great importance. "Two aspects of this," the report states, "are (1) obtaining the greatest psychological effect against Japan and (2) making the initial use sufficiently spectacular *for the importance of the weapon to be internationally recognized* when publicity on it is released."

One city stood out above all others in light of the Committee's criteria—Kyoto, the ancient capital of Japan and the center of her civilization for more than a thousand years. Located 300 miles southwest of Tokyo, part of the Osaka-Kobe industrial complex, its numerous shrines, palaces, temples, and universities were surrounded on three sides by ranges of high hills, at the northern end of a plain. "Kyoto has the advantage," the Committee observed in terms that utterly defy logic, "of the people being more highly intelligent and hence better able to appreciate the significance of the weapon."

The Target Committee's concern that the full implications of the bomb be recognized reflected a pervasive anxiety among all who worried about the role of the bomb in the postwar world. As an instrument of peace based upon the international control of atomic energy, or as an instrument of diplomacy to be used in postwar negotiations, the influence of the weapon depended upon a general recognition that pre-atomic age calculations had to give way to new realities. If the Japanese did not accept this view, the war would continue; if the Russians ignored it, the peace would be lost. In this sense the bomb became its own message, and within the context of the war those who participated in the decisionmaking process were consumed by a single objective—to transmit the message in the most dramatic fashion possible.

Here Stimson dissented. The residents of Kyoto were spared their assigned role because he refused to accept this last assumption. "This is one time I'm going to be the final deciding authority. Nobody's going to tell me what to do on this. On this matter I am the kingpin," he told Groves as he struck Kyoto from the list. After explaining the city's history to the startled and disappointed general, he rejected Groves's argument that Kyoto's large industrial area and geographic layout dictated its selection.

Almost six weeks later, Harrison wired Stimson at Potsdam that his military advisers wanted his "pet city" reinstated as a target. But the old man stood firm. "Aware of no factors to change my decision," he wired back. "On the contrary new factors here tend to confirm it." Already planning to groom Japan as an outpost for American interests in the Far East, he feared that the "bitterness which would be caused by such a wanton act might make it impossible during the long postwar period to reconcile the Japanese to us in that area rather than to the Russians." He pointed out to Truman, who agreed with him, that "it might thus be the means of preventing what our policy demanded, namely a sympathetic Japan to the United States in case there should be any aggression by Russia in Manchuria." That he failed to question as well *any* use of the bomb indicates how deeply rooted were his assumptions about the appropriateness of that decision, and how firmly he had integrated them into the context of the war. It never occurred to Stimson that the destruction of any city, or two cities, might be considered "wanton."

By July 23 the schedule for the atomic attack was settled. Stimson was notified that a uranium bomb would be available soon after August 1. The first plutonium bomb, the type tested at Trinity (Alamogordo), would be ready for delivery about August 6, and a second plutonium bomb was expected by August 24. Additional ones would be produced at an accelerating rate from possibly three in September to perhaps seven or more in December. The specially trained B-29 crews of the 509th Composite Group were to deliver the first bomb as soon as weather permitted visual bombing after August 3. The targets were: Hiroshima, Kokura, Niigata, and Nagasaki.

On July 23, Oppenheimer informed General Thomas Farrell, Groves's executive officer, and [Navy] Captain William S. Parsons, the Manhattan Project's ordnance specialist who would arm both bombs aboard the attacking aircraft, that the bombs were expected to perform well. "As a result of the Trinity shot we are led to expect a very similar performance from the first Little Boy [uranium bomb] and the first plutonium Fat Man." Oppenheimer predicted that the energy release of either bomb would fall between 12,000 to 20,000 tons, and that the blast effect would be equivalent to from 8,000 to 15,000 tons of TNT. The fireball would be of greater brilliance and longer duration than that of the Trinity shot, since no dust would be mixed with it at the detonation altitude of 2,000 feet. Yet lethal radiation from the bomb would reach the ground. "The possibilities of a less than optimal performance of the Little Boy are quite small and should be ignored," he noted, while the possibility that the plutonium bomb would give a less than optimal performance was about twelve percent. While there was about a six percent chance that the energy release would be under five thousand tons TNT equivalent, he did not expect it to be less than one thousand tons unless a component actually malfunctioned.

Two weeks later Hiroshima was destroyed: "The gun type [uranium] bomb was ready at Tinian on 31 July awaiting the first favourable weather," Groves reported to General Marshall on August 6, 1945. "The daily 24 hour advance forecasts kept indicating unsatisfactory conditions until 3 August when there was a prediction of possible good weather over the targets for 4 August at 2200Z (5 August 0700 Tinian or 4 August 1800 EWT). Later predictions delayed this a day. At 5 August 0415Z General [Curtis E.] LeMay finalized the take-off time, final assembly of the bomb proceeded and take-off actually occurred on schedule at 1645Z 5 August. Two B-29's with recording instruments and special scientific observers accompanied the vital plane. The anticipated weather over the targets was not certain to be good but only fair."

The initial report from the attack plane was succinct and unambiguous. "Target at Hiroshima attacked visually ⅒th cloud at 052315Z. No fighters no flak." The results were clear-cut. The visible effects were greater than in the New Mexico test, the crew reported. The city was totally destroyed. Perhaps 100,000 of its citizens were killed immediately, and tens of thousands more left dying of radiation poisoning—among them, two U.S. Navy fliers imprisoned in the city jail.

Two days later, as the radioactive dust settled over Hiroshima, Ambassador Naotake Sato entered Foreign Minister Molotov's study in the Kremlin at 5 P.M. Moscow time. Having arrived hoping to enlist the Soviets as mediators between the Anglo-American and Japanese governments, he was unprepared for the message he received: a state of war would exist between the Soviet Union and Japan on the following day. Two hours later (1 A.M. August 9, Tokyo time), Soviet forces crossed the Manchurian border driving back the depleted forces of Japan's once powerful Kwantung army. Japan's moment of decision had arrived, but before it was recognized and acted on, a second city was to be destroyed.

The rationale that had loosed the first atomic attack was about to unleash the second one too—unconditional surrender had to be accepted immediately or, as Truman announced, the Japanese "may expect a rain of ruin from the air, the like of which has never been seen on this earth. . . ." Yet the first atomic attack together with the Soviet declaration of war had marshaled the end-the-war advocates within the Japanese government to action despite the danger of assassination these advocates faced. "In short," the leading student of Japan's decision to surrender has written, the peace advocates "recognized in the atomic bomb and the Soviet entry into the war not just an imperative need to give in but actually a supreme opportunity to turn the tide against the die-hards and to shake the government loose from the yoke of military oppression under which it had been laboring so long." By August 9 the decision to sue for surrender had become inevitable, though the tragedy's Japanese protagonists needed time to recite their lines. If Washington had maintained closer control over the scheduling of the atomic bomb raids, the annihilation of Nagasaki could have been avoided. But as it happened, the initiative had been left with the bomber command on the island of Tinian. Norman Ramsey, the leading physicist on the island, described to Oppenheimer the sequence of events that led to the second atomic attack before the Japanese government had absorbed the shock and implications of the first:

> Our original schedule called for take off on the morning of 11 August local time (10 August Washington time). However, on the evening of 7 August we concluded that we could safely advance the date to August 10. When we proposed this to [Colonel Paul W.] Tibbets [commander of the 509th Composite Group] he said it was too bad we could not advance the date still another day since good weather was forecast for 9 August with at least five days of bad weather forecast to follow. We agreed to try with the understanding we might miss our schedule since we were unwilling to speed any operation which might conceivably affect either safety or reliability. Finally at 11 P.M. on 8 August the unit was in the plane and completely and thoroughly checked out. Take off was at about 3 A.M. We all aged ten years until the plane cleared the island. We were scheduled to receive a strike report at 10:30 A.M. 9 August, but all we heard until 12:30 was the very worried query from the fastax ship, "Did the strike plane abort?" Finally we received the message from Ashworth that the secondary target had been bombed largely by radar and that at least technically the unit functioned even better than Hiroshima although there was some doubt as to the location of the bomb.

There was some doubt too about its victims—the likelihood that, here again, among the tens of thousands in this "graveyard with not a tombstone standing" were American prisoners of war. This is suggested by a message from Headquarters, U.S. Army Strategic Air Forces, Guam, to the War Department on July 31: "Reports prisoner of war sources, not verified by photos, give location of Allied prisoner of war camp one mile north of center of city of Nagasaki. Does this influence the choice of this target for initial Centerboard operation? Request immediate reply." The reply came quickly: "Targets previously assigned for Centerboard remain unchanged."

What effect did this second holocaust delivered only three days after the first have on the decision of the Japanese to surrender? The fact that Nagasaki was destroyed before Japan's leaders had absorbed the shock of

Hiroshima, or the shock and implications of the Soviet declaration of war, precludes an accurate assessment. The rapid succession of crises blurred the significance of each. "The machinery of [the Japanese] government," Professor [Robert J. C.] Butow has observed, "had ground to a halt [on August 9] not because it had been damaged but because it had been thrown off balance. The factors which should have urged speedy and smooth operation had engendered exactly the opposite results." Yet the argument that the second bombing gave the Emperor the opportunity to convince the military that Allied surrender terms had to be accepted is not convincing; it assumes that until the Emperor was informed about Nagasaki he was not inclined either to accept or to advocate surrender. Nothing could be further from the truth. The surrender movement began soon after the fall of Saipan in July 1944, and as early as June 22, 1945, the day Okinawa was wrenched from Japanese control, the Emperor took his first cautious step toward undermining those committed to continue the useless struggle. At an Imperial Conference called to discuss the course of events and their implications, he requested the Cabinet or the Supreme Command to consider alternatives to the decision to fight to the end. Ambassador Sato's mission to Moscow was a direct response to that request, and by July 13 Japan's willingness to capitulate became clear: "Unconditional surrender is the only obstacle to peace . . . ," Foreign Minister Shigenori Togo wired Sato.

Having broken the Japanese code before the war, American Intelligence was able to—and did—relay this message to the President, but it had no effect whatever on efforts to bring the war to a conclusion. The need to provide the Japanese with a positive, specific commitment preserving the throne paralyzed any further American initiative, and the anticipated effect of the atomic bombs made an American compromise appear unnecessary, or even undesirable. The Potsdam Declaration of July 26 calling for the surrender of Japan was decidedly unhelpful to those Japanese who were searching for a means of bringing the war to a conclusion. "Following are our terms. We will not deviate from them. There are no alternatives. We shall brook no delay," it firmly stated. Calling for the elimination of the authority and influence "of those who have deceived and misled the people of Japan into embarking on world conquest" and warning that "stern justice shall be meted out to all war criminals, including those who have visited cruelties upon our prisoners," the proclamation offered the military diehards in the Japanese government more ammunition to continue the war than it offered their opponents to end it. Was there any evidence here that the leaders of the United States, Great Britain, and China did not consider the Emperor one of those who had "deceived and misled the people of Japan"? Was there any guarantee that the Emperor would not be considered a war criminal? The statements that a new government would be formed "in accordance with the freely expressed will of the Japanese people," and the call for the unconditional surrender of "all Japanese armed forces" (rather than the government of Japan or the Japanese people) offered scant support for those who wanted peace without sacrificing the throne. The Japanese government's response to the Potsdam Declaration was to "mokusatsu" it—literally "to kill with silence," or, more idiomatically, "to take no notice of," "to treat with silent contempt," or "to ignore." It was an unfortunate reply, for the Americans concluded that the Japanese were determined to fight on. "In the face of this rejection," Stimson wrote in his autobiography, "we could only proceed to demonstrate that the ultimatum had meant exactly what it said when it stated that if the Japanese continued the war, 'the full application of our military power, backed by our resolve, will mean the inevitable and complete destruction of the Japanese armed forces and just as inevitably the utter devastation of the Japanese homeland.' For such a purpose," the Secretary continued, "the atomic bomb was an eminently suitable weapon."

Yet a painful question remains even for those who accept the exigencies of war as the terrible rationalization for the first atomic bomb: Did the destruction of Nagasaki significantly hasten Japan's decision to surrender?

In the early morning hours of August 10, in the Emperor's bomb shelter adjoining the imperial library, Premier Kantaro Suzuki startled his divided colleagues on the Supreme Council with the announcement, "Your Imperial Majesty's decision is requested. . . ." That decision, "to accept the Allied proclamation on the basis outlined by the Foreign Minister," brought the war to its conclusion—on the condition that the United States guarantee the survival of dynasty and Emperor. That unconditional surrender remained an obstacle to peace in the wake of Hiroshima, Nagasaki, and the Soviet declaration of war—until the government of the United States offered the necessary (albeit veiled) assurance that neither Emperor nor throne would be destroyed—suggests the possibility, which even Stimson later recognized, that *neither* bomb may have been necessary; and certainly that the second one was not.

What effect did the atomic bomb have on American wartime diplomacy?

The diplomacy of atomic energy came to rest during the war on a simple and dangerous assumption: that the Soviet government would surrender important geographical, political, and ideological objectives in exchange for the neutralization of the new weapon. Warnings from [President of the Carnegie Institute and Chairman of the Office of Scientific Research and Development Vannevar] Bush and [President of Harvard University and Chairman of the National Defense Research Committee Dr. James B.] Conant that the Russians might be able to reach atomic parity within three to five years were ignored in favor of Groves's estimate that it would take the Soviet Union twenty to fifty years to catch up. Even if the Russians had the scientific talent, Groves argued, they could not possibly possess the necessary industrial capability. Although Groves and those who heeded his advice were aware that a similar kind of arrogance had led atomic scientists in Germany to underestimate American potential during the war, their low opinion of the Soviets blinded them to the validity of such an analogy. As a result, those who conducted the foreign policy of the United States became too confident, too certain, that through the accomplishments of American science, technology, and industry they could alone make the "new world" into one better than the old. American diplomacy and prestige suffered grievously in the process: an opportunity was missed during the war to gauge the extent of Soviet interest in the international control of atomic energy, and the need for a comprehensive postwar policy on atomic energy was ignored. No one thought to consider how the bomb would be used to restructure international relations if the Soviets did not choose to "cooperate."

And they did not cooperate. At the London Foreign Minister's Conference in September, Molotov engaged in a strategy of "reverse atomic diplomacy," joking about the bomb and underplaying its value. Byrnes, who had gone to the conference expecting that "the presence of the bomb in his pocket" (as he told Stimson) would "get [him] through," was thrown completely off balance. Three months and a day after Hiroshima was bombed, on the eve of the Anglo-American-Canadian atomic energy conference in Washington[,] Bush wrote that the whole matter of international relations relating to atomic energy "is in a thoroughly chaotic condition." The technology of war was already being hailed as the symbol of peace, and it was becoming increasingly clear that instead of promoting American postwar aims, wartime atomic energy policies had made them more difficult to achieve. As American-Soviet relations deteriorated, Hiroshima and Nagasaki rose as symbols of a new American barbarism, and as explanations for the origins of the cold war. A century before, Henry Adams had tersely phrased the truth that had now received a final, unequivocal confirmation: "Man has mounted science, and is now run away with."

The Bomb as a Technology of Death

MICHAEL S. SHERRY

Ever since the telegraph was invented, and doubtless long before, field generals have complained of interference from superiors safe in capitals and insensitive to war's realities. Oversight—watchful, suspicious, domineering—was not new to warfare in 1944. The novelty lay partly in the technology of control. Through radio and teletype and through the rapid courier service and the personal visits made possible by air transport, Washington's contact with its far-flung Asian bomber commands was even more exacting than it was with the strategic air forces in Europe. The sheer volume of communications—ranging from [Commander of the U.S. Army Air Forces, Lieutenant General Henry H.] Arnold's chatty but pointed personal letters to reams of target information and the trivial detritus of military bureaucracy—was also novel. [Major General Haywood] Hansell had earlier presided over the creation of this communications net during organization of the Twentieth's headquarters, but he quickly became "sick of it" when he began commanding bomber missions from the Marianas in November: "The machine worked 24 hours a day all right, without stopping. Most of the messages seemed to consist of questions that I couldn't answer. I began to understand the meaning of the remark ascribed to Lord Palmerston to the effect that

Excerpts from Michael S. Sherry, *The Rise of American Air Power: The Creation of Armageddon.* Copyright © 1987. Reprinted by permission of Yale University Press.

the disintegration of the British Empire had begun with the invention of the telegraph." In Hansell's case, it was his own command that was soon to disintegrate.

More important was the organizational novelty involved. It was one thing for a capital to keep close tabs on what its commanders were doing, another to plan in great detail what they would do, as Washington headquarters did in 1944. To be sure, the long line of communications to Saipan, Guam, and Kharagpur sometimes stretched thin, no flood of directives from on high could entirely substitute for judgment on the spot, the field commander with suitable drive could adapt orders to his purposes, and Arnold's volatile temperament undercut any tendencies to settle into bureaucratic routine.

Nonetheless, the supervision from Washington was at times remarkable. "General Arnold's control of the U.S. Air Force is as complete, virtually, as is Hitler's control of Germany," observed an English officer with pardonable exaggeration. "He is a complete dictator. . . . Be discovered doing something Arnold does not like and Arnold sacks you—like that." No more than [Army Chief of Staff George C.] Marshall and [Chief of Naval Operations Admiral Ernest J.] King could Arnold always play such an imperial role: in an air force huge by 1944, he was more than ever dependent on a growing headquarters staff and on a heart whose failings repeatedly removed him from day-to-day control of the air force. Yet if not always wielded personally by Arnold, power usually remained in his headquarters. "It is a current saying that you cannot run a war from Washington," [General Lauris] Norstad commented in September. "The fact is, however, that all of this war has been run to a larger degree than most people realized from Washington." If anything, Washington's grip tightened late in the war, for the completion of the tedious business of mobilizing men and planes by 1944 left headquarters free to exercise the "very real prerogatives of command over world-wide operations."

Officers at headquarters regarded such centralized control as another operational imperative. To weave bomber operations into the broader fabric of strategy, informed judgments had to be made from Washington, by men who had a global perspective on strategy, not by the theater commander who saw "the general situation through glasses prescribed by the local optician," as Arnold pointedly put it to [General Claire] Chennault. In particular, coordination of the widely separated bomber commands of the Twentieth Air Force seemed impossible from any other vantage point, all the more so since the Pacific theater had no unified command. As usual, operational necessities were only part of the story, however. Centralized command also satisfied air force ambitions. Only with it could the airmen prevent theater commanders from seizing control of the bombers in pursuit of "tempting local plums"; only with it could they cultivate the image of a global air force with revolutionary consequences for world geopolitics; only with it could Arnold have the operational command he had never before enjoyed. And only centralization permitted maximum use of the techniques of operations research and bureaucratic management enjoying favor in Washington—the full employment of the forces of civilian militarism.

One result of this centralization was the physical distance it interposed between decision makers on the one hand and the conveyers and victims of destruction on the other. Modern communications and transportation, far from facilitating the close witness of war, impeded it by allowing decision-making to take place far away. In such circumstances, William Blanchard speculates, "Man no longer feels his aggressive impulses with the same intensity. Aggression is viewed more with the intellect," through the "*symbolic representation* of events rather than his own awareness." To the authorities in the Pentagon, what the bombers did was represented by strike photos, telegraphed reports, and statistical summaries. They enlivened symbols and abstractions with an occasional visit to the field, but even then they were hundreds of miles away from the action.

Operational commanders also experienced war secondhand, for the notion that the practice of war could be separated from its management was also applied to them. When [General Curtis] LeMay insisted that he fly missions with the 21st Bomber Command he headed up in the fall of 1944, he found the "people upstairs were yipping shrilly at the idea." They included "those misguided souls in Washington [who] had the notion that a commanding officer didn't need to be qualified as an Aircraft Commander. He had a lot of *those* folks under him. . . . *His* job was to proceed in his own echelon and on his own exalted level." For LeMay, command meant the sharing of danger, the knowledge derived from firsthand experience, not the bureaucrat's management of men. But his victory in this skirmish was token—permission to fly one mission. The more cerebral Hansell was equally determined to fly but found that his slight familiarity with the atomic bomb (about which LeMay then knew nothing) and Allied code-breaking prohibited his participation in combat missions as well.

Whether Arnold did not feel "his aggressive impulses with the same intensity" because of his distance from the war is difficult to prove. But the difference made by his remote position is suggested by comparing his recollections of the war with those of LeMay, so direct a participant in combat and destruction before he reached India, who portrayed much more frankly and fully the destructive fury of American bombers. Even Marshall, another and more preeminent organizer of victory, seemed more sensitive to the nature and magnitude of death in war, in part because it became more personal with the death in battle of his stepson. For the air force commanding general who never served in combat or overseas, war's remoteness took several forms.

More than most military operations, the Twentieth Air Force waged war by assembly-line procedures that divided tasks and fractionated responsibilities. The end product of its efforts—the target folder, and then the destruction—emerged from a long planning process in which the designers rarely saw their creation, and the operators had little to do with the design. Acting on the broad directives coming from the JCS [Joint Chiefs of Staff] and Arnold, civilian and military experts examined data on the enemy's military and economic systems and drew conclusions about which target systems would be the most vulnerable to destruction. Much of that work took place outside regular military channels altogether, in the work of the Committee of Operations Analysts, men who had almost no firsthand contact with war. The task of translating those conclusions into specific targets and priorities fell to other men, in the plans and operations staffs of the air force and the Joint Target Group. Staff for the Headquarters Twentieth Air Force also helped to choose the timing and order of attacks on targets. At the bomber commands, LeMay and Hansell then conducted photographic surveillance and analysis, compiled the glossy target folders used by airmen, factored in operational considerations—weather patterns, available strengths, estimates of enemy reactions, and so forth—and, usually, chose the specific days and force assignments for attack. Once a mission was carried out, the whole process was reversed, as streams of information flowed back to Washington for evaluation. . . .

Washington waged the air war by remote control, thereby reducing a sense of responsibility for the destruction that war entailed. Nor did distance from the enemy and bureaucratic methods of waging war against him create a less vindictive approach to war than that favored by men in the field with more direct contact with the enemy. There was no demonstrable correlation between vindictiveness toward the enemy and proximity to him: Washington, far from acting to curb the excesses of a Hansell or LeMay, often prodded them into more destructive action. Besides, vindictiveness was not a prerequisite to pursuing the most destructive course with the enemy: insofar as airmen viewed their war as the task of applying the proper technique, the motives and rewards for intensifying its fury had little to do with satisfying their visceral hostilities toward the enemy. Washington's distance from the consequences of what it planned and ordered allowed the destruction to go forward smoothly, without engaging emotions and moral questions about its consequences. Nor was physical and bureaucratic remoteness from war the only kind of distance the men in Washington maintained.

Air force planners employed methods of analysis and styles of language that also distanced them from war's realities. In one way, this was hardly their intention. "It is not sufficient merely to bomb Japan," Norstad reminded an audience. "The targets selected, the timing, the weight must be chosen with surgical skill." It was the planners' job to help connect means and ends, to show how the force available could be used to secure victory. Often enough, the connection was hard to maintain, either affectively or conceptually, as designs for incendiary war showed.

Though central to Marshall's scheme for intimidating Japan on the eve of Pearl Harbor, firebombing as a large-scale practicality became possible only after American entry into the war, when the technical work was carried out by the Army Chemical Warfare Service, the National Defense Research Committee, and the petrochemical industry. Much of their experimental work, presided over by the Harvard chemist Louis Fieser, concerned tactical weapons—flamethrowers and the jellied gasoline that Fieser's scientists produced by adding extracts from aluminum naphthanate and aluminum palmitate (from which Fieser drew the name *napalm*). Fieser, although he regarded use of poison gas as "inhumane," relished development of incendiary bombs for strategic use, some of his experiments taking bizarre form. In 1943, he launched a project to release captive bats carrying tiny incendiaries from American bombers. These creatures, given to roosting in dark attics and cellars, would ignite thousands of fires in the highly flammable buildings of Japan's cities. Fieser imagined "a surprise attack on Tokyo" with fires "popping all over the city at 4 A.M." Tests continued for many months until "a number of bat bombs, blown out of the target area by high winds, burned down a theater, the officers' club, and a general's sedan at Carlsbad [New Mexico] Army Air Field." Other impractical but prophetic ideas flowed from the Chemical Warfare Service—experiments in showering incendiary "leaves" over forests and grainfields, an early exercise in the arts of defoliation. In the bizarre, Japan sometimes matched the United States, as in its hapless effort to rain balloon-bombs on the United States.

The major preoccupation of the American chemists was the development of reliable incendiaries to be dropped by aircraft against enemy cities. Much effort was necessary to produce bombs which did not disintegrate under field conditions and which penetrated rooftops and zeroed in on targets without being blown off course. The Chemical Warfare Service was up to the task. Model enemy towns were constructed at proving grounds in the United States, the effort at authenticity measured by the employment of German Jewish architects to design the German towns and by the attention to detail down to "the curtains, children's toys, and clothing hanging in the closets." In testing incendiary attacks on mock Japanese workers' districts, teams of firefighters were brought in to quell the blaze with methods the Japanese would use. The tests against "Little Tokios" inspired confidence that "fires would sweep an entire community" and cause "tremendous casualties. . . ."

Interest in firebombing Japanese cities crystallized earlier and more intensely. Initial studies by the air force staff had emphasized the classic precepts of high-explosive bombing of precision targets, but by 1943 incendiary war attracted sustained approval. It was supported by British planners and by the prime minister himself, who in May spoke to the American Congress of "the process, so necessary and desirable, of laying the cities and other munitions centres of Japan in ashes, for in ashes they must surely lie before peace comes back to the world." In Arnold's Committee of Operations Analysts (COA), military members compromised long-standing air force doctrine to press for incendiary bombing, while Guido Perera, the lawyer and leading civilian member, "felt it was wrong for the Air Force to turn from precision bombing to area attacks." As "a cynic might add— it is worse than immoral because it is ineffective." So he recalled in his memoirs at least, but little trace of his doubts or of any discernible difference between civilians and professional officers on firebombing survived among contemporary records. . . .

Staff officers and operations researchers continued to press the case for incendiary attacks, first experimental, then comprehensive. A September 4

[1944] report by a COA subcommittee acknowledged that full-scale attacks on six large urban areas would not likely "affect front line strength." But there was satisfaction in another projected measurement: the attacks "will produce very great economic loss, measured in man months of industrial labor—probably greater loss per ton of bombs despatched than attacks on any other target system." Damage to industry would merely be a welcome side effect of the general dislocation caused by the "dehousing" of some 7,750,000 workers and the evacuation of many more. The report was a rarity in that it explicitly made an estimate of probable enemy casualties, extrapolating its figures from the great Tokyo fire of 1923: some 560,000 Japanese, almost half in Tokyo, would be killed, missing, or seriously wounded. Otherwise, in applying their skills as economists and lawyers, the experts usually measured the effects of bombing by the statistics and language of cost-benefit analysis.

When the full committee issued revised guidelines in October (omitting any mention of casualties), it recommended an incendiary assault on Japan's cities to come after a precision campaign, when a sufficiently large force of bombers had been assembled to permit highly concentrated fire raids. As usual, the analysts made no attempt to project how such raids would help secure final victory, simply implying their relationship to victory. Shortly thereafter the newly formed Joint Target Group, a Joint Chiefs of Staff agency, gave qualified approval to the COA report.

At the same time, in another indication of civilian interest in incendiary war, Vannevar Bush forwarded to Arnold the recommendations of an operations researcher on his staff at the Office of Scientific Research and Development. Incendiary bombing, it was argued,

> may be the golden opportunity of strategic bombardment in this war—and possibly one of the outstanding opportunities in all history to do the greatest damage . . . for a minimum of effort. Estimates of economic danage expected indicate that incendiary attack of Japanese cities may be at least five times as effective, ton for ton, as precision bombing of selected strategic targets as practiced in the European theater. However, the dry economic statistics, impressive as they may be, still do not take account of the further and unpredictable effect on the Japanese war effort of a national catastrophe of such magnitude—entirely unprecedented in history.

Still, "dry economic statistics" were what the analyst had to offer, again leaving the impression that "the greatest damage to the enemy for a minimum of effort" had become a goal apart from victory, in part because it was more easily measurable. Bush recognized that the issue of incendiary bombing involved "humanitarian aspects" for which a decision "will have to be made at a high level if it has not been done already." Nothing came of his recommendation, no doubt because the air force believed it had already received sufficient sanction from the president. . . .

In November, as pressure to conduct further incendiary tests mounted, air officers increasingly mimicked the language of the civilian analysts: "Dehousing industrial workers causes a greater loss of man hours per ton of bombs dropped than can be accomplished by any other method." "De-housing" was becoming the favorite euphemism for a variety of virtues perceived in an incendiary assault, some spelled out—workers' absenteeism, lower morale, paralyzed systems—some usually left unspoken: the maimed bodies and bewildering toll of the dead. Target analysts recognized that such assault would inflict scant damage on primary military and industrial establishments. But few questioned the moral or strategic wisdom of the planned campaign. Some worked very hard to make the enemy population the objective of the bombers. Helmut E. Landsberg, a German meteorologist advising the Twentieth Air Force staff, produced a report entitled "Disease Rates after Tokyo Earthquake of 1923" and concluded that "if an influenza epidemic is started as a result of a saturation attack upon the big cities, absenteeism in industrial plants can be expected to soar." Better yet, he suggested, "the casualty rate will be increased if the attacks are made during the cold season," when survivors crowded into public buildings and hospitals would spread "serious epidemics. . . ."

The rhetoric and methodology of civilian expertise also defined goals by the distance they interposed between the designers and victims of destruction. The more sophisticated the methods of destruction became, the less language and methods of measurement allowed men to acknowledge the nature of that destruction. A dehumanized rhetoric of technique reduced the enemy to quantifiable abstractions. Statistics of man-hours lost and workers dehoused objectified many of the enemy's experiences and banished almost altogether one category, his death. Certainly Arnold, LeMay, and [Arthur] Harris [head of the Royal Air Force Bomber Command] were brutally frank in their vocabulary on occasion; dehumanized language alone did not compel men to kill and destroy on the scale they did. But, reinforced by other forms of distance characteristic of the air war, it did allow them to do so while insulating their consciences and souls. And by doing so, it helped to push victory from view and to elevate destruction into a goal. "To all sides in a conflict," [Lord Solly] Zuckerman [director of the British Bombing Survey Unit] has commented, "the goal of war must always be victory, but victory has over the course of history almost always been associated with destruction, so much so that destruction has become a kind of vested characteristic of war." The application of operations research to war, at least as practiced in 1944, was one source of that tendency. . . .

The leaders and technicians of the American air force were driven by technological fanaticism—a pursuit of destructive ends expressed, sanctioned, and disguised by the organization and application of technological means. Destruction was rarely the acknowledged final purpose for the men who made air war possible. Rather, they declared that it served the purpose of securing victory and that its forms were dictated by technological, organizational, and strategic imperatives. In practice, they often waged destruction as a functional end in itself, without a clear comprehension of its relationship to stated purposes.

To label these men fanatics or their mentality and behavior as fanatical may defy the usual understanding of the terms, which sees in fanaticism the workings of a single-minded, frenzied emotional devotion to a cause. Intensity of emotion hardly seemed to characterize men whose virtue was their capacity for rational examination of problems. "The fanatic cannot tolerate scientific thought," it has been said. Moreover, "fanaticism is a megalomaniacal condition," one notable for "a jealous, vindictive and monomaniacal faith," usually in a party, an organization, or a leader in which is invested a "unique saving function." The air force certainly inspired among its professional officers an intense loyalty but rarely a monomaniacal allegiance. While some wartime scientists maintained an unquestioning faith in their methodology and its beneficence, by no means did all. Nor was faith in the American or the Allied cause always intense or evenly shared. What characterized the experts in air war was their flexibility and control, the ease with which they worked among a variety of organizations serving many purposes, and the skill with which they balanced personal, professional, bureaucratic, and ideological goals. Indeed, the practice of air war grew out of a convergence of diverse appeals, needs, and opportunities, diversity imparting to the bombing much of its momentum.

Fanaticism in the context of World War II usually refers to America's enemies—the Nazis, genocidal in ideology and practice, and the Japanese, whose cult of spiritual strength sent thousands of men to their deaths in kamikaze attacks. In more recent expressions of fanaticism—the acts of terrorism carried out by shadowy religious organizations from the Middle East, for example—self-destructiveness seems the salient characteristic, indeed the hidden desire of the fanatic. In contrast, if anything seemed to bind Americans together during World War II, it was self-preservation, the lowest common denominator of support for the war effort.

Why, then, call the practitioners of air war fanatics, and what shared mentality constituted their fanaticism? For one thing, fanatical acts are not always the product of frenzied or hateful individuals, as Hannah Arendt has shown in capturing the banality of Adolf Eichmann. For another, there was a suggestion of the megalomaniacal among the practitioners of air war in their aspirations for technological omnipotence: over the natural universe for some of the scientists, over the geographic and political world for the airmen striving to achieve a "global" air force, with men like John von Neumann embracing both aspirations. For sure, these aspirations did not often appear suicidal or self-destructive to the men who held them. Yet the technology they created or promoted—finally the atomic bomb but to some degree the apparatus of "conventional" air war as well—carried that self-destructive potential for the nation and the world, and not simply in retrospect inasmuch as the world-ending potential of aerial warfare had been recognized before the war by writers like H. G. Wells and during the war by some atomic scientists and policymakers.

The shared mentality of the fanatics of air war was their dedication to assembling and perfecting their methods of destruction, and the way that doing so overshadowed the original purposes justifying destruction. Their coolness, their faith in rational problem-solving, did not easily appear fanatical because its language was the language of rationality and technique.

It apparently expressed the triumph of a new set of values, ones often called modern or bureaucratic, which displaced more traditional ones by which people were defined according to racial, ethnic, religious, and national differences. Yet it is by no means clear that such values had entirely displaced more traditional ones. For one thing, whatever their individual value system, those who waged air war served as the instrument of national passions that were often decidedly racist in character. For another, their rhetoric, as in the use of the term "dehousing," allowed them to express aggressive and destructive impulses in other terms, impulses that did not necessarily disappear from motivation, simply from view.

It was easier to regard the decisions that took lives as the products of technological, strategic, and bureaucratic imperatives. In the face of these imperatives, men felt a helplessness that allowed them to escape responsibility or fulfilled a wish to do so. Actions ceased to be recognized as the product of aggressive wills and became foreordained, irresistible. Certainly, the complexities of modern technology, bureaucracy, and war-making were real enough. The American political system had built-in impediments to accountability because of its diffuse nature, aggravated by the division of responsibilities among the three services. The functional distribution of power along the chain of command and the compartmentalization that accompanied it had much the same effect. Efforts to centralize power, as with Arnold's command of the Twentieth Air Force, did not necessarily enhance accountability at the top because leaders were so remote from war's realities. Rarely were these arrangements designed deliberately to negate accountability—as usual, they were a response to perceived necessities. Yet, for a nation with a benign image of its role in the world, eager to mete out punishment to its enemies but reluctant to proclaim its intent to do so, these arrangements were also attractive, desirable.

The lack of a proclaimed intent to destroy, the sense of being driven by the twin demands of bureaucracy and technology, distinguished America's technological fanaticism from its enemies' ideological fanaticism. That both were fanatical was not easily recognizable at the time because the forms were so different. The enemy, particularly the Japanese, had little choice but to be profligate in the expenditure of manpower and therefore in the fervid exhortation of men to hatred and sacrifice—they were not, and knew they were not, a match in economic and technological terms for the Allies. The United States had different resources with which to be fanatical: resources allowing it to take the lives of others more than its own, ones whose accompanying rhetoric of technique disguised the will to destroy. As lavish with machines as the enemy was with men, Americans appeared to themselves to practice restraint, to be immune from the passion to destroy that characterized their enemies and from the urge to self-destruction as well.

The distinction between technological and ideological fanaticism was not absolute. It could not be, given how war often elicits similar behavior from disparate combatants. On occasion, particularly when their backs were to the wall early in the war, Americans celebrated the suicidal defense of hopeless positions, and if the rhetoric of technique dominated official expression, a rhetoric of racial and martial passion often dominated the larger culture. Allies like the Soviet Union, although zealous in pursuing technological advantage when possible, also could be profligate indeed in the expenditure of manpower. When conditions were favorable, the Japanese relied on technical superiority; it was not suicidal tactics that destroyed the American fleet at Pearl Harbor. Even when frankly suicidal tactics were employed, they had a military rationale, for the intent was to take the enemy along.

Likewise, the fact that both the United States and its enemies were fanatical did not mean that the differences between them in the forms of fanaticism were inconsequential. Destruction disguised as technique carried the gravest implications for the fate of enemy civilians. At the same time, it had inherent limits because it had little sanction apart from the prosecution of war. Since destruction was felt, but rarely proclaimed officially, as a good in itself, its sanction continued only as long as the war and the mobilization of technique that went with it continued. It made all the difference in the world to the Japanese—if we are to contrast their fate to that of the Jews— that however much vengeance may have motivated Americans, it did not become official policy and remained fulfilled by policies undertaken for other stated reasons.

Technological fanaticism had many sources: in the nature of strategic air power, whose benefits promised to be so large yet whose consequences were so hard to observe; in its demands for technique that distanced men from its consequences; in war's powerful emotions, difficult to recognize given America's strategic position and its own self-image. At bottom, technological fanaticism was the product of two distinct but related phenomena: one—the will to destroy—ancient and recurrent; the other—the technical means of destruction—modern. Their convergence resulted in the evil of American bombing. But it was sin of a peculiarly modern kind because it seemed so inadvertent, seemed to involve so little choice. Illusions about modern technology had made aerial holocaust seem unthinkable before it occurred and simply imperative once it began. It was the product of a slow accretion of large fears, thoughtless assumptions, and at best discrete decisions.

In one sense, the disjunction between means and ends that characterized the bombing seems at odds with the tenor of wartime political culture in the United States. The very vagueness of American purposes and the difficulty of achieving consensus about them in a diverse nation immune to immediate destruction led American leaders to define purposes by the lowest common denominators of survival and victory. If victory was a dominant, rationalizing value, was not a premium placed on how destruction would contribute to it? In practice, the focus on victory tended to validate any form of destruction that vaguely promised to secure it. Since political authority defined the path to victory as lying so substantially through production and technological effort, the focus tended to remain on means rather than ends. And progress by the preferred method of victory, war by war, could be measured most easily in terms of the destruction it wrought; the connection of that destruction to the end of victory was as easily presumed as it was hard to prove.

In their long journey from Pearl Harbor to the enemy's surrender on the decks of the *Missouri,* Americans might be likened to a man forced to set out on a cross-country car trip. As he drives along, the trip gathers its own interest, momentum, and challenge. He finds himself diverting to places he had not imagined; he tinkers with his car and enjoys feeling it run faster and smoother and discovers a power and mastery in manipulating it. Perhaps he did not choose this mode of travel conscious of the pleasures it would bring; he thought it necessary because of the baggage he wanted to bring along and because it was cheaper to travel this way, and after all, he already knew how to drive. Nor does he forget what his destination is, but as he travels he does not dwell on its importance; it will take care of itself if he makes the trip properly. Once the trip is done, it rapidly fades from memory, its pleasures and challenges now comfortably tucked away in his mind as necessities imposed on him in order to enable him to reach his destination, not as choices he had the freedom to make.

By December 1944, Americans were close to their destination, closer than most of them realized. Proximity was not evident, not with one more range of mountains to cross, not with the trip itself generating such excitement and anxiety, not with the machine built to make the trip yet to be fully tested. There was perhaps even a hope that the mountains would stand tall, to provide full measure for the test. "To test the [atomic] bomb's real destructiveness," Arnold later wrote about his concerns near the end of the war, "three or four cities must be saved intact from the B-29's regular operations as unspoiled targets for the new weapon. Which cities should be spared was a problem," he added. To Arnold, it seems, the test was as important as the destination. It lay ahead, with not only the atomic bomb but the "regular" forms of fire his bombers could hurl at Japanese cities. Technological fanaticism, long developing, could now be fully expressed.

⋈ *F U R T H E R   R E A D I N G*

Gar Alperovitz, *Atomic Diplomacy: Hiroshima and Potsdam* (1965)

Paul J. Baker, ed., *The Atomic Bomb: The Great Decision* (1968)

Robert C. Batchelder, *The Irreversible Decision* (1962)

Barton J. Bernstein, ed., *The Atomic Bomb: The Critical Issues* (1976)

———, "The Perils and Politics of Surrender: Ending the War with Japan and Avoiding the Third Atomic Bomb," *Pacific Historical Review* (February 1977), 1–27

P. M. S. Blackett, *Fear, War, and the Bomb: Military and Political Consequences of Atomic Energy* (1949)

Paul Boyer, *By the Bomb's Early Light: American Thought and Culture at the Dawn of the Atomic Age* (1985)

Robert J. C. Butow, *Japan's Decision to Surrender* (1954)

Otis Cary, "Atomic Bomb Targeting: Myths and Realities," *Japan Quarterly* 26:4 (1979), 506–514

John W. Dower, *War Without Mercy: Race and Power in the Pacific War* (1986)

Herbert Feis, *The Atomic Bomb and the End of World War II* (1966)

Edwin Fogelman, ed., *Hiroshima: The Decision to Use the A-Bomb* (1964)

Gregg Herken, *The Winning Weapon: The Atomic Bomb in the Cold War* (1981)

John Hersey, *Hiroshima* (1946)

Richard G. Hewlett and Oscar G. Anderson, *The New World, 1939–1946: A History of the United States Atomic Energy Commission* (1962)

George E. Hopkins, "Bombing and the American Conscience During World War II," *The Historian* 28:451 (1966), 451–473

Masuji Ibuse, *Black Rain* (1969)

Fletcher Knebel and Charles W. Bailey II, *No High Ground* (1960)

Robert Jay Lifton, *Death in Life: Survivors of Hiroshima* (1967)

Richard Rhodes, *The Making of the Atomic Bomb* (1986)

Lisle A. Rose, *Dubious Victory: The United States and the End of World War II* (1973)

Michael S. Sherry, *The Rise of American Air Power: The Creation of Armageddon* (1987)

Martin J. Sherwin, *A World Destroyed: The Atomic Bomb and the Grand Alliance* (1975)

Spencer R. Weart, *Nuclear Fear: A History of Images* (1988)

Peter Wyden, *Day One: Before Hiroshima and After* (1985)

CHAPTER
3

The Cold War Begins

✗✗✗

Germany's final defeat in the spring of 1945 ended an era in which European nations had dominated world politics through their vast colonial empires and commercial networks. The United States and the Soviet Union would take the lead in the new era. The United States, which alone among the great powers had escaped the devastation of war on its own soil, was in 1945 unquestionably the most powerful nation in the world, and the prospect of a new American-led world—what magazine publisher Henry Luce had called an American century—seemed realistic. The U.S.S.R., although it had suffered enormous losses during the war, remained the most powerful military presence on the European continent, and propelled by its own history and ideology, soon challenged American leadership. The conflict between these two powerful nations, what came to be called the Cold War, not only would shape international relations for the next forty-five years but would deeply affect both nations' political, economic, and cultural life.

The Cold War would ultimately embrace much of the Third World (comprising Africa, Asia, Latin America, and the Middle East), where it often transformed local struggles into ''hot'' proxy wars between the superpowers. Yet the Cold War began in Europe, just as, forty-five years later, it would come to an end on that continent. It was here that the U.S. vision of a postwar world of American-led liberal democracies ran up against the Soviet Union's fears for its own security and its determination to refashion much of Eastern Europe in its own image.

There is an enormous historical literature on the Cold War, filled with conflicting interpretations. Was conflict precipitated by an aggressive and expansionist U.S.S.R., as most early, ''orthodox'' interpretations of the Cold War insisted? Or, as later generations of ''revisionist'' historians have argued, was the United States, in its efforts to create a postwar world that reflected its own interests, also responsible? What were the sources of U.S. policy: domestic politics? A need to secure foreign markets? Strategic and geopolitical considerations? What role did misperception play in shaping U.S. and Soviet responses? To what extent did allies and clients successfully maneuver the great powers? Could the Cold War have been avoided, or its enormous costs in lost lives, distorted priorities, and political repression somehow minimized? Or will the disorder that is likely to accompany the dissolution of the Cold War make some now yearn for the lost stability of the ''long peace''?

99

✕✕ D O C U M E N T S

One of the first issues to divide the United States and the Soviet Union was the future of postwar Poland. In the first document, President Harry S Truman, who had only recently acceded to the presidency following the death of Franklin D. Roosevelt, agrees with hard-line advisers who argue that Soviet actions in Poland are part of a larger pattern of communist expansion that ought to be resisted. Russian fears that a truly independent Poland would threaten the security of their borders are voiced in the second document by Soviet leader Joseph Stalin, who insists that the United States is going back on assurances made by Roosevelt at the February 1945 Big Three meeting at Yalta in the Crimea.

By July 1946 conflict with the Soviet Union had grown to the point that Secretary of Commerce and former Vice President Henry A. Wallace would appeal to Truman (the third document) to reverse what he believed was the warlike drift of U.S. policy. Most of Truman's advisers took a very different view, however, which White House aide Clark M. Clifford and his assistant, George M. Elsey, summarized in the conclusion of his September 1946 report to the president, reprinted here as the fourth document. Yet not until 1947 would Truman publicly embrace the new diplomacy of "containment," in calling for economic and military assistance to suppress a rebellion against the Greek government and announcing the Truman Doctrine (selection five), a broad new policy of support for "free peoples" throughout the world. The implementation of such a policy quickly led American leaders such as Under Secretary of State Dean Acheson to appeal for economic aid to Europe (document six), in what would eventually become the Marshall Plan. The new diplomacy would also require a massive expansion of U.S. military programs, as the president's national security advisers would argue in NSC-68, an April 1950 report to the president, the conclusions of which are reproduced here as the final document.

President Harry S Truman and His Advisers
Debate U.S. Policy
Toward the U.S.S.R., 1945

The Secretary of State [Edward R. Stettinius, Jr.] told the meeting that Mr. [V. M.] Molotov [Soviet Union's foreign minister] had arrived in good spirits yesterday and had had a good talk with the President [Harry S Truman] yesterday evening but that at the Foreign Ministers meeting later great difficulties had developed over the Polish question. The continuance of the meeting this morning had produced no improvement and a complete deadlock had been reached on the subject of the carrying out of the Yalta agreement on Poland. The Secretary said that the truth of the matter was the Lublin or Warsaw Government was not representative of the Polish people and that it was now clear that the Soviet Government intended to try to enforce upon the United States and British Governments this puppet government of Poland and obtain its acceptance as the legal government of Poland. He said that as they all recalled at Yalta an agreement had been reached regarding the formation of a new Polish Government representative of the people by means of the reorganization of the present provisional government in consultation with other Polish democratic leaders. He said it had been made plain to Mr. Molotov how seriously the United States Government regarded this matter and how much public confidence would be shaken by our failure to carry out the Crimean [Yalta] decision.

The President said that he had told Mr. Molotov last night that he intended fully to carry out all the agreements reached by President Roosevelt at the Crimea. He added that he felt our agreements with the Soviet Union so far had been a one way street and that could not continue; it was now or never. He intended to go on with the plans for San Francisco [the organizing meeting of the United Nations] and if the Russians did not wish to join us they could go to hell. The President then asked in rotation the officials present for their view.

[Secretary of War Henry L.] Stimson said that this whole difficulty with the Russians over Poland was new to him and he felt it was important to find out what the Russians were driving at. He said in the big military matters the Soviet Government had kept their word and that the military authorities of the United States had come to count on it. In fact he said that they had often been better than their promise. He said it was important to find out what motives they had in mind in regard to these border countries and that their ideas of independence and democracy in areas that they regarded as vital to the Soviet Union are different from ours. Mr. Stimson remarked that they had a good deal of trouble on minor military matters and it was necessary in these cases to teach them manners. In this case he said that without fully understanding how seriously the Russians took this Polish question we might be heading into very dangerous water. He remarked that 25 years ago virtually all of Poland had been Russian.

[Secretary of the Navy James V.] Forrestal said that he felt that this difficulty over Poland could not be treated as an isolated incident, that there had been many evidences of the Soviet desire to dominate adjacent countries and to disregard the wishes of her allies. He said he had felt that for some time the Russians had considered that we would not object if they took over all of Eastern Europe into their power. He said it was his profound conviction that if the Russians were to be rigid in their attitude we had better have a show down with them now than later.

Ambassador [to the Soviet Union W. Averell] Harriman said that in regard to Mr. Stimson's question as to the issues and the motives he felt that when [Soviet leader Josef] Stalin and Molotov had returned to Moscow after Yalta they had been informed by Bierut (the present head of the provisional government) concerning the situation in Poland and had realized that the provisional government was in a shaky condition and that the introduction of any genuine Polish leader such as Mikolajczyk would probably mean the elimination of the Soviet hand-picked group. He remarked that the real issue was whether we were to be a party to a program of Soviet domination of Poland. He said obviously we were faced with a possibility of a real break with the Russians but he felt that if properly handled it might be avoided. The President said that he had no intention of delivering an ultimatum to Mr. Molotov but merely to make clear the position of this Government.

Mr. Stimson observed that he would like to know how far the Russian reaction to a strong position on Poland would go. He said he thought that the Russians perhaps were being more realistic than we were in regard to their own security.

Admiral [William D.] Leahy [senior military advisor to the president] said that he had left Yalta with the impression that the Soviet Government had no intention of permitting a free government to operate in Poland and that he would have been surprised had the Soviet Government behaved any differently than it had. In his opinion the Yalta agreement was susceptible to two interpretations. He added that he felt that it was a serious matter to break with the Russians but that we should tell them that we stood for a free and independent Poland.

The Secretary of State then read the part of the Yalta decision relating to the formation of the new Government and the holding of free elections and said he felt that this was susceptible of only one interpretation.

General [George C.] Marshall [Army Chief of Staff] said he was not familiar with the Polish issue and its political aspects. He said from the military point of view the situation in Europe was secure but that they hoped for Soviet participation in the war against Japan at a time when it would be useful to us. The Russians had it within their power to delay their entry into the Far Eastern war until we had done all the dirty work. He said the difficulties with the Russians such as in the case of Crossword usually straightened out. He was inclined to agree with Mr. Stimson that possibility of a break with Russia was very serious.

Mr. Stimson observed that he agreed with General Marshall and that he felt that the Russians would not yield on the Polish question. He said we must understand that outside the United States with the exception of Great Britain there was no country that understood free elections; that the party in power always ran the election as he well knew from his experience in Nicaragua. [In 1927 Stimson served as President Coolidge's special emissary to Nicaragua.]

Admiral [Ernest J.] King [Chief of Naval Operations] inquired whether the issue was the invitation to the Lublin Government to San Francisco. The President informed him that that was a settled matter and not the issue. The issue was the execution of agreements entered into between this Government and the Soviet Union. He said he intended to tell Mr. Molotov that we expected Russia to carry out the Yalta decision as we were prepared to do for our part.

Ambassador Harriman then remarked that while it was true that the Soviet Union had kept its big agreements on military matters that those were decisions which it had already reached by itself but that on other military matters it was impossible to say they had lived up to their commitments. He said for example over a year ago they had agreed to start on preparations for collaboration in the Far Eastern war but that none of these had been carried out. He asked General Deane to express his opinion.

General [John R.] Deane [commander of the U.S. military mission in the Soviet Union] said that he felt that the Soviet Union would enter the Pacific war as soon as it was able irrespective of what happened in other fields. He felt that the Russians must do this because they could not afford too long a period of let down for their people who were tired, there was only a short season in which offensive action against Manchuria was possible and that they would not dare attempt a Bulgarian gambit in the Far East. He said he was convinced after his experiences in Moscow that if we were afraid of the Russians we would get nowhere and he felt that we should be firm when we were right.

The President then thanked the military representation and said that he felt that he had their point of view well in mind and would ask the Secretary of State and his advisers to stay behind to work out the details of his forthcoming talk with Mr. Molotov.

The President then said that he was satisfied that from a military point of view there was no reason why we should fail to stand up to our understanding of the Crimean agreements and he requested the Secretary of State to prepare for him (1) a statement to be handed to Mr. Molotov for communication to Marshal Stalin, (2) a list of points he might mention orally to Mr. Molotov and (3) a draft of a statement to the press. He said he would be prepared to receive the Secretary of State and his advisers just as soon as this could be done and afterwards he would see Mr. Molotov. The Secretary agreed and said he would have the drafts in the President's hands by 5:00 o'clock.

Russian Premier Joseph Stalin Defends Soviet Policy in Eastern Europe, 1945

The Chairman of the Council of People's Commissars of the Soviet Union (Stalin) to President Truman

[Moscow,] 24 April 1945.

I have received your joint with Prime Minister Churchill message of April 18, and have also received on April 24 the message transmitted to me through V. M. Molotov.

1. From these messages it is clear that you continue to consider the Provisional Polish Government not as a kernel for the future government of national unity, but just like one of the groups equal to any other group of Poles.

Such an understanding of the position of the Polish Government and such an attitude towards it is very difficult to reconcile with the decisions of the Crimea Conference on Poland. At the Crimea Conference all three of us, including also President Roosevelt, proceeded from the fact that the Provisional Polish Government, as the one now operating in Poland and enjoying the confidence and support of the majority of the Polish people, should be the kernel, i.e. the main part of the new reorganized government of nation unity. You, evidently, do not agree to such an understanding of the matter. Declining the Yugoslav example as a pattern for Poland, you thereby confirm that the Provisional Polish Government cannot be considered as a basis and kernel for the future government of national unity.

2. It is also necessary to take into account the fact that Poland borders with the Soviet Union, what cannot be said of Great Britain and the United States.

The question on Poland has the same meaning for the security of the Soviet Union as the question on Belgium and Greece for the security of Great Britain.

You, apparently, do not agree that the Soviet Union has a right to make efforts that there should exist in Poland a government friendly toward the Soviet Union, and that the Soviet government cannot agree to existence in Poland of a government hostile toward it. Besides everything else, this is demanded by the blood of the Soviet people abundantly shed on the field of Poland in the name of liberation of Poland. I do not know whether there has been established in Greece a really representative government, and whether the government in Belgium is really democratic. The Soviet Union was not consulted when these governments were being established there. The Soviet Government did not lay claim to interference in these affairs as it understands the whole importance of Belgium and Greece for the security of Great Britain.

It is not clear why, while the question on Poland is discussed it is not wanted to take into consideration the interests of the Soviet Union from the point of view of its security.

3. Such conditions must be recognized [as] unusual when two governments—those of the United States and Great Britain—beforehand settle with the Polish question in which the Soviet Union is first of all and most of all interested and put the government of the USSR in an unbearable position trying to dictate to it their demands.

I have to state that such a situation cannot favor a harmonious solution of the question on Poland.

4. I am ready to fulfill your request and do everything possible to reach a harmonious solution, but you demand too much of me. In other words, you demand that I renounce the interests of security of the Soviet Union, but I cannot turn against my country.

In my opinion there is one way out of this situation; to adopt the Yugoslav example as a pattern for Poland. I believe this would allow [us] to come to a harmonious solution.

Secretary of Commerce Henry A. Wallace
Urges a Conciliatory Approach, 1946

My dear Mr. President:

I hope you will excuse this long letter. Personally I hate to write long letters, and I hate to receive them.

My only excuse is that this subject is a very important one—probably the most important in the world today. I checked with you about this last

Thursday and you suggested after Cabinet meeting on Friday that you would like to have my views.

I have been increasingly disturbed about the trend of international affairs since the end of the war, and I am even more troubled by the apparently growing feeling among the American people that another war is coming and the only way that we can head it off is to arm ourselves to the teeth. Yet all of past history indicates that an armaments race does not lead to peace but to war. The months just ahead may well be the crucial period which will decide whether the civilized world will go down in destruction after the five or ten years needed for several nations to arm themselves with atomic bombs. Therefore I want to give you my views on how the present trend toward conflict might be averted.

How do American actions since V-J Day appear to other nations? I mean by actions the concrete things like $13 billion for the War and Navy Departments, the Bikini tests of the atomic bomb and continued production of bombs, the plan to arm Latin America with our weapons, production of B-29s and planned production of B-36s, and the effort to secure air bases spread over half the globe from which the other half of the globe can be bombed. I cannot but feel that these actions must make it look to the rest of the world as if we were only paying lip service to peace at the conference table. These facts rather make it appear either (1) that we are preparing ourselves to win the war which we regard as inevitable or (2) that we are trying to build up a predominance of force to intimidate the rest of mankind. How would it look to us if Russia had the atomic bomb and we did not, if Russia had 10,000-mile bombers and air bases within a thousand miles of our coast lines and we did not? . . .

Other Problems of American-Russian Relationships

I believe that for the United States and Russia to live together in peace is the most important single problem facing the world today. Many people, in view of the relatively satisfactory outcome of the recent Paris Conference, feel that good progress is being made on the problem of working out relations between the Anglo-Saxon powers and Russia. This feeling seems to me to be resting on superficial appearances more productive of a temporary truce than of final peace. On the whole, as we look beneath the surface in late July of 1946, our actions and those of the western powers in general carry with them the ultimate danger of a third world war—this time an atomic world war. As the strongest single nation, and the nation whose leadership is followed by the entire world with the exception of Russia and a few weak neighboring countries in Eastern Europe, I believe that we have the opportunity to lead the world to peace.

White House Aide Clark M. Clifford Summarizes the Case for the Hard Line, 1946

The primary objective of United States policy toward the Soviet Union is to convince Soviet leaders that it is in their interest to participate in a system of world cooperation, that there are no fundamental causes for war between our two nations, and that the security and prosperity of the Soviet Union, and that of the rest of the world as well, is being jeopardized by aggressive militaristic imperialism such as that in which the Soviet Union is now engaged.

However, these same leaders with whom we hope to achieve an understanding on the principles of international peace appear to believe that a war with the United States and the other leading capitalistic nations is inevitable. They are increasing their military power and the sphere of Soviet influence in preparation for the "inevitable" conflict, and they are trying to weaken and subvert their potential opponents by every means at their disposal. So long as these men adhere to these beliefs, it is highly dangerous to conclude that hope of international peace lies only in "accord," "mutual understanding," or "solidarity" with the Soviet Union.

Adoption of such a policy would impel the United States to make sacrifices for the sake of Soviet–U.S. relations, which would only have the effect of raising Soviet hopes and increasing Soviet demands, and to ignore alternative lines of policy, which might be much more compatible with our own national and international interests.

The Soviet Government will never be easy to "get along with." The American people must accustom themselves to this thought, not as a cause for despair, but as a fact to be faced objectively and courageously. If we find it impossible to enlist Soviet cooperation in the solution of world problems, we should be prepared to join with the British and other Western countries in an attempt to build up a world of our own which will pursue its own objectives and will recognize the Soviet orbit as a distinct entity with which conflict is not predestined but with which we cannot pursue common aims.

As long as the Soviet Government maintains its present foreign policy, based upon the theory of an ultimate struggle between Communism and Capitalism, the United States must assume that the U.S.S.R. might fight at any time for the twofold purpose of expanding the territory under communist control and weakening its potential capitalist opponents. The Soviet Union was able to flow into the political vacuum of the Balkans, Eastern Europe, the Near East, Manchuria and Korea because no other nation was both willing and able to prevent it. Soviet leaders were encouraged by easy success and they are now preparing to take over new areas in the same way. The Soviet Union, as Stalin euphemistically phrased it, is preparing "for any eventuality."

Unless the United States is willing to sacrifice its future security for the sake of "accord" with the U.S.S.R. now, this government must, as a first step toward world stabilization, seek to prevent additional Soviet aggression. The greater the area controlled by the Soviet Union, the greater the military requirements of this country will be. Our present military plans are based on the assumption that, for the next few years at least, Western Europe, the Middle East, China and Japan will remain outside the Soviet sphere. If the Soviet Union acquires control of one or more of these areas, the military forces required to hold in check those of the U.S.S.R. and prevent still further acquisitions will be substantially enlarged. That will also be true if any of the naval and air bases in the Atlantic and Pacific, upon which our present plans rest, are given up. This government should be prepared, while scrupulously avoiding any act which would be an excuse for the Soviets to begin a war, to resist vigorously and successfully any efforts of the U.S.S.R. to expand into areas vital to American security.

The language of military power is the only language which disciples of power politics understand. The United States must use that language in order that Soviet leaders will realize that our government is determined to uphold the interests of its citizens and the rights of small nations. Compromise and concessions are considered, by the Soviets, to be evidences of weakness and they are encouraged by our "retreats" to make new and greater demands.

The main deterrent to Soviet attack on the United States, or to attack on areas of the world which are vital to our security, will be the military power of this country. It must be made apparent to the Soviet Government that our strength will be sufficient to repel any attack and sufficient to defeat the U.S.S.R. decisively if a war should start. The prospect of defeat is the only sure means of deterring the Soviet Union.

The Soviet Union's vulnerability is limited due to the vast area over which its key industries and natural resources are widely dispersed, but it is vulnerable to atomic weapons, biological warfare, and long-range air power. Therefore, in order to maintain our strength at a level which will be effective in restraining the Soviet Union, the United States must be prepared to wage atomic and biological warfare. A highly mechanized army, which can be moved either by sea or by air, capable of seizing and holding strategic areas, must be supported by powerful naval and air forces. A war with the U.S.S.R. would be "total" in a more horrible sense than any previous war and there must be constant research for both offensive and defensive weapons.

Whether it would actually be in this country's interest to employ atomic and biological weapons against the Soviet Union in the event of hostilities is a question which would require careful consideration in the light of the circumstances prevailing at the time. The decision would probably be influenced by a number of factors, such as the Soviet Union's capacity to employ similar weapons, which can not now be estimated. But the important point is that the United States must be prepared to wage atomic and biological warfare if necessary. The mere fact of preparedness may be the only powerful deterrent to Soviet aggressive action and in this sense the only sure guaranty of peace.

The United States, with a military potential composed primarily of highly effective technical weapons, should entertain no proposal for disarmament or limitation of armament as long as the possibility of Soviet aggression exists. Any discussion on the limitation of armaments should be pursued slowly and carefully with the knowledge constantly in mind that proposals on outlawing atomic warfare and long-range offensive weapons would greatly limit United States strength, while only moderately affecting the Soviet Union. The Soviet Union relies primarily on a large infantry and artillery force and the result of such arms limitation would be to deprive the United States of its most effective weapons without impairing the Soviet Union's ability to wage a quick war of aggression in Western Europe, the Middle East or the Far East.

The Soviet Government's rigid controls on travellers, and its internal security measures, enable it to develop military weapons and build up military forces without our knowledge. The United States should not agree to arms limitations until adequate intelligence of events in the U.S.S.R. is available and, as long as this situation prevails, no effort should be spared to make our forces adequate and strong. Unification of the services and the adoption of universal military training would be strong aids in carrying out a forthright United States policy. In addition to increasing the efficiency of our armed forces, this program would have a salutary psychological effect upon Soviet ambitions.

Comparable to our caution in agreeing to arms limitation, the United States should avoid premature disclosure of scientific and technological information relating to war materiel until we are assured of either a change in Soviet policies or workable international controls. Any disclosure would decrease the advantage the United States now has in technological fields and diminish our strength in relation to that of the U.S.S.R.

In addition to maintaining our own strength, the United States should support and assist all democratic countries which are in any way menaced or endangered by the U.S.S.R. Providing military support in case of attack is a last resort; a more effective barrier to communism is strong economic support. Trade agreements, loans and technical missions strengthen our ties with friendly nations and are effective demonstrations that capitalism is at least the equal of communism. The United States can do much to ensure that economic opportunities, personal freedom and social equality are made possible in countries outside the Soviet sphere by generous financial assistance. Our policy on reparations should be directed toward strengthening the areas we are endeavoring to keep outside the Soviet sphere. Our efforts to break down trade barriers, open up rivers and international waterways, and bring about economic unification of countries, now divided by occupation armies, are also directed toward the re-establishment of vigorous and healthy noncommunist economies.

The Soviet Union recognizes the effectiveness of American economic assistance to small nations and denounces it bitterly by constant propaganda. The United States should realize that Soviet propaganda is dangerous (especially when American "imperialism" is emphasized) and should avoid any actions which give an appearance of truth to the Soviet charges. A determined effort should be made to expose the fallacies of such propaganda.

There are some trouble-spots which will require diligent and considered effort on the part of the United States if Soviet penetration and eventual domination is to be prevented. In the Far East, for example, this country should continue to strive for a unified and economically stable China, a reconstructed and democratic Japan, and a unified and independent Korea. We must ensure Philippine prosperity and we should assist in the peaceful solution, along noncommunistic lines, of the political problems of Southeast Asia and India.

With respect to the United Nations, we are faced with the fact that the U.S.S.R. uses the United Nations as a means of achieving its own ends. We should support the United Nations and all other organizations contributing to international understanding, but if the Soviet Union should threaten to resign at any time because it fails to have its own way, the United States should not oppose Soviet departure. It would be better to continue the United Nations as an association of democratic states than to sacrifice our principles to Soviet threats.

Since our difficulties with the Soviet Union are due primarily to the doctrines and actions of a small ruling clique and not the Soviet people, the United States should strive energetically to bring about a better understanding of the United States among influential Soviets and to counteract the anti-American propaganda which the Kremlin feeds to the Soviet people. To the greatest extent tolerated by the Soviet Government, we should distribute books, magazines, newspapers and movies among the Soviets, beam radio broadcasts to the U.S.S.R., and press for an exchange of tourists, students and educators. We should aim, through intellectual and cultural contacts, to convince Soviet leaders that the United States has no aggressive intentions and that the nature of our society is such that peaceful coexistence of capitalistic and communistic states is possible.

A long-range program of this sort may succeed where individual high-level conversations and negotiations between American and Soviet diplomats may fail in bringing about any basic change in the Soviet outlook. The general pattern of the Soviet system is too firmly established to be altered suddenly by any individual—even Stalin. Conferences and negotiations may continue to attain individual objectives but it appears highly improbable that we can persuade the Soviets, by conferences alone, to change the character of their philosophy and society. If they can be influenced in ways beneficial to our interests, it will be primarily by what we do rather than by what we say, and it is likely to be a slow and laborious process.

Our best chances of influencing Soviet leaders consist in making it unmistakably clear that action contrary to our conception of a decent world order will redound to the disadvantage of the Soviet regime whereas friendly and cooperative action will pay dividends. If this position can be maintained firmly enough and long enough, the logic of it must permeate eventually into the Soviet system.

Cooperation by the Soviets can result in increased trade. The United States Government must always bear in mind, however, that questions as to the extent and nature of American trade should be determined by the overall interests of this country. It should also bear in mind that, while Soviet policy can conceivably be influenced by the hope of obtaining greater economic assistance from this country, it is unlikely that the Soviet Government will entertain sentiments of gratitude for aid once it has been granted and it is unlikely to be induced by goodwill gifts to modify its general policies. For the time being, economic aid granted to the Soviet Government or other governments within its sphere, and the fruits of private trade with persons inside these countries, will go to strengthen the entire world program of the Kremlin. This is also true of the proposals to send American engineers, scientists and technicians to share the benefits of their education and experience with Soviet counterparts. So long as Soviet industry is devoted to building up the Soviet military potential, such proposals have a direct bearing on American security.

Within the United States, communist penetration should be exposed and eliminated whenever the national security is endangered. The armed forces, government agencies and heavy industries are the principal targets for communistic infiltration at present.

Because the Soviet Union is a highly-centralized state, whose leaders exercise rigid discipline and control of all governmental functions, its government acts with speed, consistency, and boldness. Democratic governments are usually loosely organized, with a high degree of autonomy in government departments and agencies. Government policies at times are confused, misunderstood, or disregarded by subordinate officials. The United States can not afford to be uncertain of its policies toward the Soviet Union. There must be such effective coordination within the government that our military and civil policies concerning the U.S.S.R., her satellites, and our Allies are consistent and forceful. Any uncertainty or discrepancy will be seized immediately by the Soviets and exploited at our cost.

Our policies must also be global in scope. By time-honored custom, we have regarded "European Policy," "Near Eastern Policy," "Indian Policy" and "Chinese Policy" as separate problems to be handled by experts in each field. But the areas involved, far removed from each other by our conventional standards, all border on the Soviet Union and our actions with respect to each must be considered in the light of overall Soviet objectives.

Only a well-informed public will support the stern policies which Soviet activities make imperative and which the United States Government must adopt. The American people should be fully informed about the difficulties in getting along with the Soviet Union, and the record of Soviet evasion, misrepresentation, aggression and militarism should be made public.

In conclusion, as long as the Soviet Government adheres to its present policy, the United States should maintain military forces powerful enough to restrain the Soviet Union and to confine Soviet influence to its present area. All nations not now within the Soviet sphere should be given generous economic assistance and political support in their opposition to Soviet penetration. Economic aid may also be given to the Soviet Government and private trade with the U.S.S.R. permitted provided the results are beneficial to our interests and do not simply strengthen the Soviet program. We should continue to work for cultural and intellectual understanding between the United States and the Soviet Union but that does not mean that, under the guise of an exchange program, communist subversion and infiltration in the United States will be tolerated. In order to carry out an effective policy

world get on their feet and become self-supporting there c₁
or economic stability in the world and no lasting peace or p
of us. Without outside aid, the process of recovery in many
take so long as to give rise to hopelessness and despair. In
freedom and democracy and the independence of nations
survive, for hopeless and hungry people often resort to desp
The war will not be over until the people of the world can
clothe themselves and face the future with some degree of ₍

Since world demand exceeds our ability to supply, we ar
to concentrate our emergency assistance in areas where i
effective in building world political and economic stability,
human freedom and democratic institutions, in fostering libeɪ
icies, and in strengthening the authority of the United Natio

This is merely common sense and sound practice. It is iɪ
the policy announced by President Truman in his special messaȝ
on March 12 on aid to Greece and Turkey. Free peoples wh
to preserve their independence and democratic institutions anɗ
doms against totalitarian pressures, either internal or external
top priority for American reconstruction aid. This is no moɪ
recognition, as President Truman said, "that totalitarian regiɪ
on free peoples, by direct or indirect aggression, undermine the
of international peace and hence the security of the United Stₐ

The President's Advisers
Urge Military Expansion, 1950

Within the past thirty-five years the world has experienced two g
of tremendous violence. It has witnessed two revolutions—the Rₗ ____ aɪɪɗ
the Chinese—of extreme scope and intensity. It has also seen the collapse
of five empires—the Ottoman, the Austro-Hungarian, German, Italian and
Japanese—and the drastic decline of two major imperial systems, the British
and the French. During the span of one generation, the international distribution of power has been fundamentally altered. For several centuries it
had proved impossible for any one nation to gain such preponderant strength
that a coalition of other nations could not in time face it with greater strength.
The international scene was marked by recurring periods of violence and
war, but a system of sovereign and independent states was maintained, over
which no state was able to achieve hegemony.

Two complex sets of factors have now basically altered this historical
distribution of power. First, the defeat of Germany and Japan and the decline
of the British and French Empires have interacted with the development of
the United States and the Soviet Union in such a way that power has
increasingly gravitated to these two centers. Second, the Soviet Union, unlike

Excerpts from "NSC-68: A Report to the National Security Council," April 14, 1950, from
The Naval War College Review 27/6, May/June 1975, pp. 51–108. Reprinted by permission of
the Naval War College Review.

previous aspirants to hegemony, is animated by a new fanatic faith, antithetical to our own, and seeks to impose its absolute authority over the rest of the world. Conflict has, therefore, become endemic and is waged, on the part of the Soviet Union, by violent or non-violent methods in accordance with the dictates of expediency. With the development of increasingly terrifying weapons of mass destruction, every individual faces the ever-present possibility of annihilation should the conflict enter the phase of total war.

On the one hand, the people of the world yearn for relief from the anxiety arising from the risk of atomic war. On the other hand, any substantial further extension of the area under the domination of the Kremlin would raise the possibility that no coalition adequate to confront the Kremlin with greater strength could be assembled. It is in this context that this Republic and its citizens in the ascendancy of their strength stand in their deepest peril.

The issues that face us are momentous, involving the fulfillment or destruction not only of this Republic but of civilization itself. They are issues which will not await our deliberations. With conscience and resolution this Government and the people it represents must now take new and fateful decisions. . . .

Our overall policy at the present time may be described as one designed to foster a world environment in which the American system can survive and flourish. It therefore rejects the concept of isolation and affirms the necessity of our positive participation in the world community.

This broad intention embraces two subsidiary policies. One is a policy which we would probably pursue even if there were no Soviet threat. It is a policy of attempting to develop a healthy international community. The other is the policy of "containing" the Soviet system. These two policies are closely interrelated and interact on one another. Nevertheless, the distinction between them is basically valid and contributes to a clearer understanding of what we are trying to do.

The policy of striving to develop a healthy international community is the long-term constructive effort which we are engaged in. It was this policy which gave rise to our vigorous sponsorship of the United Nations. It is of course the principal reason for our long continuing endeavors to create and now develop the Inter-American system. It, as much as containment, underlay our efforts to rehabilitate Western Europe. Most of our international economic activities can likewise be explained in terms of this policy.

In a world of polarized power, the policies designed to develop a healthy international community are more than ever necessary to our own strength. . . .

A comprehensive and decisive program to win the peace and frustrate the Kremlin design should be so designed that it can be sustained for as long as necessary to achieve our national objectives. It would probably involve:

1. The development of an adequate political and economic framework for the achievement of our long-range objectives.

2. A substantial increase in expenditures for military purposes adequate to meet the requirements for the tasks listed in Section D-1.
3. A substantial increase in military assistance programs, designed to foster cooperative efforts, which will adequately and efficiently meet the requirements of our allies for the tasks referred to in Section D-1-*e*.
4. Some increase in economic assistance programs and recognition of the need to continue these programs until their purposes have been accomplished.
5. A concerted attack on the problem of the United States balance of payments, along the lines already approved by the President.
6. Development of programs designed to build and maintain confidence among other peoples in our strength and resolution, and to wage overt psychological warfare calculated to encourage mass defections from Soviet allegiance and to frustrate the Kremlin design in other ways.
7. Intensification of affirmative and timely measures and operations by covert means in the fields of economic warfare and political and psychological warfare with a view to fomenting and supporting unrest and revolt in selected strategic satellite countries.
8. Development of internal security and civilian defense programs.
9. Improvement and intensification of intelligence activities.
10. Reduction of Federal expenditures for purposes other than defense and foreign assistance, if necessary by the deferment of certain desirable programs.
11. Increased taxes. . . .

Conclusions and Recommendations

The foregoing analysis indicates that the probable fission bomb capability and possible thermonuclear bomb capability of the Soviet Union have greatly intensified the Soviet threat to the security of the United States. This threat is of the same character as that described in NSC 20/4 (approved by the President on November 24, 1948) but is more immediate than had previously been estimated. In particular, the United States now faces the contingency that within the next four or five years the Soviet Union will possess the military capability of delivering a surprise atomic attack of such weight that the United States must have substantially increased general air, ground, and sea strength, atomic capabilities, and air and civilian defenses to deter war and to provide reasonable assurance, in the event of war, that it could survive the initial blow and go on to the eventual attainment of its objectives. In turn, this contingency requires the intensification of our efforts in the fields of intelligence and research and development. . . .

In the light of present and prospective Soviet atomic capabilities, the action which can be taken under present programs and plans, however, becomes dangerously inadequate, in both timing and scope, to accomplish the rapid progress toward the attainment of the United States political, economic, and military objectives which is now imperative.

A continuation of present trends would result in a serious decline in the strength of the free world relative to the Soviet Union and its satellites. This unfavorable trend arises from the inadequacy of current programs and plans rather than from any error in our objectives and aims. These trends lead in the direction of isolation, not by deliberate decision but by lack of the necessary basis for a vigorous initiative in the conflict with the Soviet Union.

Our position as the center of power in the free world places a heavy responsibility upon the United States for leadership. We must organize and enlist the energies and resources of the free world in a positive program for peace which will frustrate the Kremlin design for world domination by creating a situation in the free world to which the Kremlin will be compelled to adjust. Without such a cooperative effort, led by the United States, we will have to make gradual withdrawals under pressure until we discover one day that we have sacrificed positions of vital interest.

It is imperative that this trend be reversed by a much more rapid and concerted build-up of the actual strength of both the United States and the other nations of the free world. The analysis shows that this will be costly and will involve significant domestic financial and economic adjustments.

The execution of such a build-up, however, requires that the United States have an affirmative program beyond the solely defensive one of countering the threat posed by the Soviet Union. This program must light the path to peace and order among nations in a system based on freedom and justice, as contemplated in the Charter of the United Nations. Further, it must envisage the political and economic measures with which and the military shield behind which the free world can work to frustrate the Kremlin design by the strategy of the cold war; for every consideration of devotion to our fundamental values and to our national security demands that we achieve our objectives by the strategy of the cold war, building up our military strength in order that it may not have to be used. The only sure victory lies in the frustration of the Kremlin design by the steady development of the moral and material strength of the free world and its projection into the Soviet world in such a way as to bring about an internal change in the Soviet system. Such a positive program—harmonious with our fundamental national purpose and our objectives—is necessary if we are to regain and retain the initiative and to win and hold the necessary popular support and cooperation in the United States and the rest of the free world.

This program should include a plan for negotiation with the Soviet Union, developed and agreed with our allies and which is consonant with our objectives. The United States and its allies, particularly the United Kingdom and France, should always be ready to negotiate with the Soviet Union on terms consistent with our objectives. The present world situation, however, is one which militates against successful negotiations with the Kremlin—for the terms of agreements on important pending issues would reflect present realities and would therefore be unacceptable, if not disastrous, to the United States and the rest of the free world. After a decision and a start on building up the strength of the free world has been made, it might then be desirable for the United States to take an initiative in seeking negotiations in the hope that it might facilitate the process of accommodation by the Kremlin to the new situation. Failing that, the unwillingness of the Kremlin to accept equitable terms or its bad faith in observing them would assist in consolidating popular opinion in the free world in support of the measures necessary to sustain the build-up.

In summary, we must, by means of a rapid and sustained build-up of the political, economic, and military strength of the free world, and by means of an affirmative program intended to wrest the initiative from the Soviet Union, confront it with convincing evidence of the determination and ability of the free world to frustrate the Kremlin design of a world dominated by its will. Such evidence is the only means short of war which eventually may force the Kremlin to abandon its present course of action and to negotiate acceptable agreements on issues of major importance.

The whole success of the proposed program hangs ultimately on recognition by this Government, the American people, and all free peoples, that the cold war is in fact a real war in which the survival of the free world is at stake. Essential prerequisites to success are consultations with Congressional leaders designed to make the program the object of non-partisan legislative support, and a presentation to the public of a full explanation of the facts and implications of the present international situation. The prosecution of the program will require of us all the ingenuity, sacrifice, and unity demanded by the vital importance of the issue and the tenacity to persevere until our national objectives have been attained.

ѫ *E S S A Y S*

Historians Joyce and Gabriel Kolko have written extensively on the foreign policies of modern America. In the first essay, from the introduction to their 1972 revisionist study of postwar U.S. foreign policy, *The Limits of Power: The World and United States Foreign Policy, 1945–1954,* they argue that the Cold War was rooted not in the containment of communism, as most earlier historians had maintained, but in the powerful and expanding requirements of American capitalism. Joyce Kolko is also the author of *America and the Crisis of World Capitalism* (1974) and *Restructuring the World Economy* (1988). Gabriel Kolko, author of a number of books, is Distinguished Research Professor of History at York University in Toronto. In the second selection, from *The Long Peace: Inquiries into the History of the Cold War* (1987), diplomatic historian John Lewis Gaddis of Ohio University argues by contrast that the Cold War was the product of what he calls Soviet unilateralism and that President Truman's response to the Russians was at least initially cautious and defensive. The Russians' behavior, Gaddis concludes, "alarmed not just Americans but a good portion of the rest of the world as well." In the final essay, diplomatic historian Melvyn P. Leffler of the University of Virginia examines the broad, global definition that American leaders gave to U.S. interests and the way in which this perspective affected their reactions to Soviet policies and their growing disinclination to bargain or compromise. The goal of U.S. policy, Leffler observes, was "to contain Soviet/Communist power and create a stable international order conducive to U.S. economic and political interests."

Making the World Safe for American Capitalism

JOYCE AND GABRIEL KOLKO

The United States' ultimate objective at the end of World War II was both to sustain and to reform world capitalism. The tension between doing both eventually prevented America from accomplishing either in a shape fully satisfactory to itself. The task confronting Washington was to dissolve the impact not merely of World War II on the structure of the world economy but of the depression of 1929 and World War I as well—to reverse, in brief, most of the consequences of twentieth-century history. "The main prize of the victory of the United Nations," the State Department summed up the United States' vision in November 1945, "is a limited and temporary power to establish the kind of world we want to live in." That was the prodigious task before it.

The goal was monumental, and always beyond attainment. The clarity with which the men in power perceived it, however, reflected the intensely sophisticated wartime discussions of economic peace aims that had especially preoccupied the State Department. What they could not overcome was the direct contradictions between the various instrumentalities and policies with which the United States hoped to achieve its goals, the incompatibility between reforming world capitalism and stemming the seemingly no less imminent threat of the Left and Communism, and the fact that the other non-Communist states were always to retain a very different conception of their national interest from the one that Washington advanced for them.

In essence, during and immediately after World War II the key American leaders articulated an economic interpretation of the sources of world conflict that usefully complemented their vision of the United States' postwar global needs. With or without such a rationale, the structural problems and goals of the American economy would have persisted, but the fact remains that the conjunction between an American-sponsored internationalist ideology and objective national necessity was made, and it was to grow with time. [Secretary of State] Cordell Hull, who assumed major responsibility for the United States' wartime definition of its economic goals, was completely devoted to the premise that economic rivalry was the primary cause of world military conflict and that if one could remove barriers to freer trade and the exchange of raw materials and goods, universal harmony would follow. "International monetary and financial problems have been a source of conflict for a generation," Secretary of the Treasury Henry Morgenthau, Jr., typically explained to the Senate in June 1945. "We must see that after this war they do not become the basis for new conflicts." The danger was that as a result of wartime exchange and trade controls, all the prewar impediments to trade were emerging ". . . with greater ingenuity and with greater effectiveness than ever before."

In the name of future peace, therefore, the United States committed itself to the reconstruction of prewar world capitalism—to the elimination of trade and financial barriers, exclusive trading blocs, and restrictive policies of every sort. It more frequently advanced this solution, however, on behalf of long-term American prosperity, and it was this motive that the rest of the world—capitalist and noncapitalist alike—most fully appreciated. This purpose, too, shaped the contours of functional United States trade and financial policies and convinced the remainder of the world that in the name of universal welfare the United States was actually advancing its own self-interest. For when American leaders referred to multilateral trade or the "open door," not for a moment did they conceive of the emergence of a situation in which United States businessmen were naturally excluded from some central, even dominant role in a region because of superior competition from other countries. Virtually synonymous with multilateral trade, in Washington's definition, was greater American economic activity and expansion.

"[T]he establishment of a liberal trading system and the attainment of an expanding world economy," to cite Secretary of State James F. Byrnes's well-worn phrase taken from Hull, was one of the most frequent themes in the policy statements of key American leaders in the years following the war. Unless it were attained, "American exports will face new and greater obstacles in various foreign markets . . . ," the tireless State Department trade specialist, Willard L. Thorp, warned in November 1945. His superior, Assistant Secretary William L. Clayton, was always candid about the goals of this policy: "So, let us admit right off that our objective has as its background the needs and interests of the people of the United States. . . . We need markets—big markets—around the world in which to buy and sell. We ask no special privileges in any of these markets." Men such as Clayton were aware of the critical weight which a relatively small increase in American exports or investments overseas might have in sharply increasing net profits of United States firms, but above all they were concerned with the nation's shifting position and dependence on foreign raw materials. "Due to the serious depletion of our natural resources during the war, we must now import many metals and minerals. . . . Indeed we are today net importers of practically all the important metals and minerals except two—coal and oil. Who knows how long we can go without importing oil?" Given this vital dependence, which extended well beyond principle but had far-reaching implications to the economic sinews of national power, ". . . what happens to American-owned reserves of such materials abroad is a matter of national concern." There was a point, in brief, at which the question of nominal ideology would prove secondary to that of "national security and interest." In the area of petroleum, preeminently, this consideration was repeatedly to justify American efforts to create dominant and exclusive positions in various countries.

The necessary conclusion of this vision, as we shall see again and again, was the belief that socialism, state ownership, and Third World economic development were fundamentally inimical to American global objectives. Decision-makers articulated this assumption both privately and publicly, with sophistication or at times rather baldly. "The selective processes of society's evolution through the ages have proved that the institution of private property ranks with those of religion and the family as a bulwark of civilization," Assistant Secretary of State Spruille Braden declared in September 1946. "To tamper with private enterprise, except to apply well-conceived, legal, and essential controls, will precipitate a disintegration of life and liberty as we conceive and treasure them." Key American leaders who were not, as in Braden's case, also personally major overseas investors fully shared such premises. ". . . [O]ur foreign trade, export and import, must in the long run be privately handled and privately financed if it is to serve well this country and world economy," Truman stated in June 1946; "[o]ur common aim is the return of our foreign commerce and investments to private channels as soon as possible." Even when temporarily unattainable, these values and objectives helped to reorient the goals and tools of American foreign economic policy after periods of enforced compromises.

What was clear from such premises was that the American vision of the new world economy it was seeking to recast from the materials of the old had no place in it for socialism or for the exclusion, for whatever the reason, of American investment. "We believe that the best way to get oil and develop it," Thorp phrased it in a variation of this theme in February 1948, "is through the operation of private oil companies. . . . We are trying in general and in particular to convince these other countries that it is very much in their own interest to let down the barriers and permit foreign capital to come in and help develop their reserves and their resources." Certain it was that such "freedom" was deemed essential to American economic and strategic interests.

The historian will search in vain for any dissenting analyses in Washington of the causes of the world's economic malaise, alternative responses to it, and other less self-serving goals the United States might seek to attain in the ideal world system the American leaders were to articulate so clearly. Key leaders readily confronted the operational disparity between the loftier justifications for American objectives and crass self-interest. What the United States would not consider, however, was that the problem facing the world was not simply the maladjustment of the trade and financial structure, which was to prove but a reflection of much deeper ills, but the beginning of a vast, slowly evolving shift in the control of world power and the purposes and actions of the larger bulk of mankind. For the Americans based their definition of the global situation on their evaluation of European events, first and foremost, and on power-in-hand or as it had been in the past when England or Germany defined the course of world affairs. They did not estimate the potential of Asia, Latin America, or Africa as being of central importance. And they saw even the current economic problems of Europe, ultimately, as something superficial and short-lived.

Given the disparity between its articulated goals and the realities of both Europe and the world, and the fact that the political and social preconditions for the attainment of its economic ends scarcely prevailed, the basis for subsequent American interventionism was further intensified. By 1946, only the United States was strong enough to attempt to reform world capitalism and to define ambitious goals that by necessity were to lay down major obstacles to the revolutionary social, political, and economic patterns already evolving throughout the world. Washington was almost immediately to learn that to reform and integrate the remaining capitalist nations, it would first have to preserve them. Such a policy was to involve gains, and losses too. Its success was ultimately to prove partial and temporary.

In its role as a reformer of the world economy in order to achieve its own national interest and expand, the United States was able to evoke liberal rhetoric even as it sought to penetrate and assimilate Britain's former economic power. And in its function as a preserver of the vestiges of capitalism and moribund social classes and systems, it was also to call upon its power and conservative sense of order. There was no contradiction in this seeming duality; they are simply the two sides of what was ultimately to prove a remarkably consistent and clear national policy throughout the postwar era and down to this very day. . . .

The United States entered the postwar world circumscribed by itself, by the heritage of the depression, the limitations and logic of its domestically oriented capitalism, and the structural conditions the war created and thrust upon it. These factors would have existed regardless of the status of the Left in the world, the problem of the Soviet Union, the disintegration of the colonial systems, and the like, but they only helped to color the specific nature of America's response to a complicated world it was determined, in any event, to reform and guide in ways compatible with American requirements and interests. That the United States would have thrust outward after the war, with something like its poorly fitting synthesis of moralism, charity, calculation, and need, was certain.

The real question was less America's postwar role, destined to be active under any circumstance, than how it would respond to the prospect of failure on its own terms. Its ultimate policy would be expressed in the consistency with which it, too, practiced its standard of economic conduct for other states, and also whether the logic of its goals required domination or true internationalism in the sense of a community of interests that were compatible. But nothing in the history of the twentieth century justified the belief that a nation can attain great economic power without profoundly serious conflicts with other states. Wartime economic experience with England had shown how deeply inconsistent American ideals became in practice. Ultimately, the question of the logic of successful economic expansion and transformation raised the fateful issue, which all imperialist powers had confronted in preceding decades, of the political and military preconditions of American economic hegemony requiring physical intervention into any corner of the globe that might demand it.

If what the United States proposed as a doctrine for the rest of the world proved irrelevant, the question would reduce itself to the control of power, returning world affairs to the conflict between states within parameters and assumptions well known to the bloodied world by 1946. If England would not conform, how then to relate to it, in terms of both the future of its sphere of influence and its economic role? If Western Europe should go its way, what then? If Eastern Europe were divorced from the world economy, how might this affect relations with the responsible culprits? If change in the colonial world threatened to produce a vacuum or, even worse, new societies inimical to long-term American interests and needs, what response did the great stakes warrant? And, should the most optimistic assumptions fail, and the American fear of the Left, in both its Communist and its socialist forms, prove well founded, would the United States prefer the natural and only allies it might find in the opposition to profound social changes in the world that threatened their common interests? What role would the classic Right and forces of counterrevolution, and the entities of Germany and Japan, play in the fulfillment of America's goals? What, ultimately, would be the compromises between the abstract, often incompatible ideals of American economic postwar goals and the realities of a war-wracked world moving to heal itself in its own way? At the end of World War II, as the American leaders considered such dilemmas as they then comprehended, and went ahead without consciousness of the ultimate significance of not a few of their acts, the United States' economic goals and needs provided the foundations for their responses to the dominant problems of our era.

Soviet Unilateralism and the Origins of the Cold War

JOHN LEWIS GADDIS

Wartime lack of concern over the powerful position the Soviet Union would occupy in the postwar world had been predicated upon the assumption that the Russians would continue to act in concert with their American and British allies. So long as the Grand Alliance remained intact, Western statesmen could assure each other, Moscow's emergence as the dominant Eurasian power would pose no threat. But during the final months of the war, there began to appear unsettling indications of a determination on Stalin's part to secure postwar interests without reference to the corresponding interests of his wartime associates. It was these manifestations of unilateralism that first set off alarm bells in the West about Russian intentions; the resulting uneasiness in turn stimulated deeper and more profound anxieties.

"I am becoming increasingly concerned," Secretary of State [Cordell] Hull warned Ambassador W. Averell Harriman early in 1944, "over the . . . successive moves of the Soviet Government in the field of foreign relations." Hull went on to observe in this message, drafted by Soviet specialist Charles E. Bohlen, that whatever the legitimacy of Moscow's security interests in Eastern Europe—"and as you know we have carefully avoided and shall continue to avoid any disruption with the Soviet Government on the merits of such questions"—unilateral actions to secure those interests "cannot fail to do irreparable harm to the whole cause of international collaboration." The American people would not be disposed to participate in any postwar scheme of world organization which would be seen "as a cover for another great power to pursue a course of unilateral action in the international sphere based on superior force." It was "of the utmost importance that the principle of consultation and cooperation with the Soviet Union be kept alive at all costs, but some measures of cooperation in relation to world public opinion must be forthcoming from the Soviet Government."

This document reflects as well as any other the point from which American statesmen began to develop concerns about the postwar intentions of the Soviet Union. The United States had not challenged Moscow's determination to retain the boundaries it had secured as a result of Stalin's unsavory pact with Hitler in 1939, nor had it questioned the Russians' right to a postwar sphere of influence in what remained of Eastern Europe. It was prepared to grant similar concessions in East Asia in return for eventual U.S.S.R. participation in the war against Japan. But because the Roosevelt administration had justified American entry into the war as a defense of self-determination, and because it had committed the nation to participation in a postwar world collective security organization as a means of implementing that principle, it required from the Soviet Union a measure of discretion and restraint in consolidating these areas of control. Unilateral action seemed likely to endanger the balance of power, not by allowing the Russians to dominate areas beyond their borders—that domination was assumed—but rather by weakening the American capacity for countervailing action in the postwar world by provoking, first, public disillusionment and then, as a consequence, a revival of the isolationism the President and his advisers had fought so long and so hard to overcome.

The Russians, to put it mildly, were less than sensitive to these concerns. As their armies moved into Eastern Europe in 1944 they immediately set out to undermine potential sources of opposition, not just in the former enemy countries of Rumania, Bulgaria, and Hungary, but most conspicuously of all in Poland, which had been, after all, an ally. The callousness with which the Red Army allowed the Germans to decimate the anti-communist resistance in Warsaw late that summer shocked Western statesmen; meanwhile British and American representatives on Allied Control Commissions in the Balkans found themselves denied any significant influence in shaping occupation policies there as well. Moscow had interpreted Western restraint as a sign of weakness, Harrison reported in September: "Unless we take issue with the present policy there is every indication that the Soviet Union will become a world bully wherever their interests are involved. . . . No written agreements can be of any value unless they are carried out in a spirit of give and take and recognition of the interests of other people."

Franklin Roosevelt made valiant efforts at Yalta to make Stalin aware of the need to observe the proprieties in Eastern Europe, but these proved unsuccessful almost at once when the Soviet leader interpreted agreements made to hold free elections there as in fact license to impose still tighter control on Poland and Rumania. "Averell is right," Roosevelt complained three weeks before his death. "We can't do business with Stalin. He has broken every one of the promises he made at Yalta." F.D.R. had not been prepared, on the basis of these difficulties, to write off all possibilities of postwar cooperation with the Russians. But Soviet unilateralism does appear to have convinced him, by the time of his death, that efforts to win Stalin's trust had not worked; and that future policy toward the Soviet Union would have to be based on a strict *quid pro quo* basis.

Harry S Truman emphatically agreed. Although the new Chief Executive had had no direct experience in the conduct of foreign affairs, he could have hardly believed more firmly in the importance of keeping one's word. "When I say I'm going to do something, I do it," he once wrote, "or [I] bust my insides trying to do it." It was characteristic of him that he did not believe in divorce because "when you make a contract you should keep it." Convinced that the Yalta agreements on free elections in Eastern Europe were in fact contracts, determined to demonstrate decisiveness in an awesome and unexpected position of responsibility, Truman resolved—probably more categorically than Roosevelt would have done—to hold the Russians to what they had agreed to. It was this determination that occasioned the new President's sharp rejoinder to Soviet Foreign Minister V. M. Molotov after less than two weeks in office: "Carry out your agreements and you won't get talked to like that." A month later he complained again that the Russians were not honoring their agreements: they were, he told Henry Wallace, "like people from across the tracks whose manners were very bad."

The experience of meeting Stalin personally at Potsdam seems to have modified the President's attitude somewhat. The Soviet autocrat evoked memories of the Kansas City political boss Tom Pendergast, a man with whom deals could be made because he had always kept his word. "I can deal with Stalin," Truman noted in his diary at Potsdam. "He is honest— but smart as hell." Disturbed by rumors of the dictator's ill health, the President worried about what would happen "if Joe suddenly passed out" because his potential successors lacked sincerity. For several years afterward, there persisted in Truman's mind the notion that difficulties with the Russians reflected Stalin's internal political problems—interference from a recalcitrant Politburo was the most frequent explanation—rather than any personal desire on the Soviet leader's part to violate his word.

But deals had to be honored if they were to work, and with the return of peace instances of Soviet unilateralism began to proliferate. Reasonably free elections took place in Hungary and Czechoslovakia, but only in those countries: Moscow's grip on Poland, Rumania, and Bulgaria remained as tight as ever. The Russians joined the French in resisting central economic administration of occupied Germany; they also arbitrarily transferred a substantial portion of that country's eastern territory to Poland. Attempts to reunify another divided nation, Korea, came to naught as the Russians refused to tolerate anything other than a satellite government there. The Soviet Union rejected participation in the World Bank and the International Monetary Fund, institutions American planners regarded as critical for postwar economic recovery. And Stalin was showing strong signs, as 1945 ended, of exploiting the presence of Soviet troops in northern Iran to carve out yet another sphere of influence there. He was "trying to find a basis for an understanding which would give him confidence that an agreement reached with the Russians would be lived up to," Truman told his advisers in December, 1945. He had such confidence in dealing with the British, the Dutch, and the Chinese (though not the French), "but there is no evidence yet that the Russians intend to change their habits so far as honoring contracts is concerned."

The Chief Executive's initial inclination had been to regard these difficulties simply as failures of communication; with that explanation in mind, he had authorized Secretary of State [James F.] Byrnes to make one more effort to settle them at a hastily called meeting of foreign ministers in Moscow in December. By that time, though, public and Congressional impatience with Soviet unilateralism had considerably intensified. Sensitive to these pressures, irritated by Byrnes' eagerness to reach agreements without consulting him, Truman early in 1946 proclaimed to himself—if not directly to Byrnes, as he later claimed—his intention to stop "babying" the Soviets: "Unless Russia is faced with an iron fist and strong language another war is in the making. Only one language do they understand—'how many divisions have you?' I do not think we should play at compromise any longer."

There was, in fact, no compromise when the Russians failed to meet their agreed-upon deadline for removing their troops from Iran: instead the administration confronted Moscow publicly in the United Nations Security Council and forced a humiliating withdrawal. Truman drew the appropriate conclusions: "Told him to tell Stalin I held him to be a man to keep his word," he noted in his appointment book after a meeting with the newly designated ambassador to the Soviet Union, Walter Bedell Smith, on March 23. "Troops in Iran after March 2 upset that theory." By June, he was writing to the author Pearl Buck that "the United States has performed no unfriendly act nor made a single unfriendly gesture toward the great Russian nation. . . . How has Russia met our friendly overtures?" The following month, after *New York Times* correspondent Brooks Atkinson had published a series of articles highly critical of the Russians, Truman pointedly invited him to the White House. That same day he told his advisers that he was "tired of our being pushed around," that "here a little, there a little, they are chiseling from us," and that "now is [the] time to take [a] stand on Russia."

It was in this spirit that the President authorized the first comprehensive study of Soviet-American relations to be carried out within the government. Compiled under the direction of his Special Counsel, Clark M. Clifford, and written after consultations with the Departments of State, War, Navy, the Joint Chiefs of Staff and the Director of Central Intelligence, the report acknowledged that agreements between nations were at times susceptible to differing interpretations. Nonetheless, it argued, there existed a persistent pattern on Moscow's part of either unilaterally implementing such agreements in such a way as to serve Soviet interest, or encouraging satellites to do so. "[T]here is no question," the report emphasized, "where the primary responsibility lies."

The implications could only be that the Soviet Union had no intention of cooperating with the West to maintain the existing balance of power; that it sought to expand its own influence as widely as possible without regard for the security requirements of its former allies; and that, when circumstances were right, it would be prepared to risk war to attain that objective. American policy could no longer be based upon the assumption of shared interests, therefore; priorities henceforth would have to be directed toward the accumulation of sufficient military strength to deter war if possible and to win it if necessary, while at the same time keeping open possibilities for dealing with the Russians should a change of heart in the Kremlin eventually occur. "[I]t is our hope," the report concluded, "that they will eventually change their minds and work out with us a fair and equitable settlement when they realize that we are too strong to be beaten and too determined to be frightened."

President Truman received the Clifford report on September 24, four days after he had fired Henry Wallace from the Cabinet for publicly advocating a more conciliatory policy toward the Soviet Union. There is no question that he agreed with its general conclusions: on the day before he dismissed Wallace he had complained in his diary about

> Reds, phonies, and . . . parlor pinks [who] can see no wrong in Russia's four and one half million armed forces, in Russia's loot of Poland, Austria, Hungary, Rumania, Manchuria. . . . But when we help our friends in China who fought on our side it is terrible. When Russia loots the industrial plant of those same friends it is all right. When Russia occupies Persia for oil that is heavenly.

But Truman chose not to use the Clifford report, as he might have, to justify increased military appropriations; instead he ordered all copies to be locked in the White House safe, where they remained for the duration of the administration. "There is too much loose talk about the Russian situation," he had written former Vice President John Nance Garner on the day after Wallace's dismissal. "We are not going to have any shooting trouble with them but they are tough bargainers and always ask for the whole earth, expecting maybe to get an acre."

The President's cautious reaction to the manifestations of Soviet unilateralism catalogued in the Clifford report reflected a desire to avoid hasty and ill-considered action, but certainly no continuing assumption of common interest. Repeated demonstrations of Moscow's callousness to the priorities and sensibilities of its former allies had by this time virtually drained the reservoir of good will toward the Russians that had built up during the war. American leaders had been inclined, for many months, to give the Kremlin the benefit of the doubt: to assume, despite accumulating evidence to the contrary, that difficulties with Moscow had arisen out of misunderstandings rather than fundamental conflicts of interest. But such charitableness could not continue indefinitely, as Winston Churchill pointed out in the summer of 1946: "The American eagle sits on his perch, a large strong bird with formidable beak and claws. . . . Mr. Gromyko [Soviet ambassador] is sent every day to prod him with a sharp sickle, now on his beak, now under his wing, now in his tail feathers. All the time the eagle keeps quite still, but it would be a great mistake to suppose that nothing is going on inside the breast of the eagle."

In fact, a good deal was going on inside the breast of the eagle, all of it related in one way or another to attempting to explain the motivation for Moscow's puzzling behavior. Throughout the period of wartime cooperation there had lingered in the minds of most Americans latent but persistent suspicions about Russia, suspicions that extended back to, and even beyond, the Bolshevik Revolution. These grew out of the fact that the Soviet Union combined—as no other country in the world at that time did—two characteristics that Americans found particularly objectionable: arbitrary rule and ideological militancy. As long as the direct Axis threat remained, Americans had been willing to overlook these shortcomings, even to hope that in time they would disappear. But after 1945, with no common foe to compel unity, with ample evidence that the Russians intended to proceed on their own rather than in concert with their former allies to consolidate postwar interests, the predisposition to assume the worst about Moscow's intentions came out into the open once again.

Americans had not always found cooperation with authoritarian regimes to be impossible: the Russian-American relationship itself had been friendly throughout most of its early history, despite the vast cultural and political differences that separated the two countries. But toward the end of the 19th century a combination of circumstances—increasing repression within Russia, a keener American sensitivity to conditions inside other countries, growing rivalries between Washington and St. Petersburg over spheres of influence in East Asia—had produced in the United States the suspicion that a connection existed between autocratic rule at home and aggressiveness in foreign affairs. Parallel concerns had accompanied the deterioration of relations with imperial Germany prior to World War I; certainly participation in that conflict, which Woodrow Wilson justified by stressing the linkage between autocracy and aggression, served powerfully to reinforce this idea. Determination to remain aloof from European involvements caused Americans to worry less about such matters during the 1920's and early 1930's—indeed, the economic distress of the latter decade even produced in some circles a grudging respect for dictatorships—but the experience of fighting Germany and Japan during World War II brought back repugnance for arbitrary rule with a vengeance. It would not take very many signs of aggressiveness on the part of totalitarian regimes in the postwar world—even totalitarian former allies—to convince Americans that the connection between domestic despotism and international expansionism still prevailed.

"If we fought Germany because of our belief that a police state and a democratic state could not exist in the same world," Rear Admiral Ellery W. Stone told Secretary of the Navy James Forrestal in July, 1946, then "it must necessarily follow that we could not afford to lie down before Russia." The simple fact that the Soviet Union was a totalitarian state raised suspicions that its foreign policy would proceed from priorities incompatible with those of the democracies—priorities now elaborately enshrined in the procedures the United Nations had established for settling international disputes. Totalitarian states, Americans assumed, relied upon force or the threat of force to secure their interests; such nations could hardly be expected to share Washington's aspiration to see the rule of law ultimately govern relations between nations. "[I]t is not Communism but Totalitarianism which is the potential threat," publisher Arthur Hays Sulzberger pointed out. ". . . [O]nly people who have a Bill of Rights are not the potential enemies of other people."

The point, for Truman, was fundamental. "Really there is no difference between the government which Mr. Molotov represents and the one the Czar represented—or the one Hitler spoke for," he privately wrote in November, 1946. And, again, informally, in May, 1947: "There isn't any difference in totalitarian states. . . . Nazi, Communist or Fascist, or Franco, or anything else—they are all alike. . . . The police state is a police state; I don't care what you call it." The President's public speeches during 1947 provided virtually a running commentary on the dangers of totalitarianism: "Freedom has flourished where power has been dispersed. It has languished where power has been too highly centralized." More than that, excessive concentrations of power produced temptations to use them. "The stronger the voice of a people in the formulation of national policies, the less the danger of aggression. When all governments derive their just powers from the consent of the governed, there will be enduring peace." There was no conflict between the requirements of justice and order: "The attainment of worldwide respect for essential human rights is synonymous with the attainment of world peace."

It was no accident, then, that when the President in the most famous speech of his career characterized the world as divided between two ways of life, one reflecting "the will of the majority," the other based "upon the will of a minority forcibly imposed upon the majority," it was the distinction between democracy and totalitarianism to which he referred. By so doing, he implicitly linked his own justification of American action to restore the balance of power in Europe to those advanced by Franklin Roosevelt in the Atlantic Charter and by Woodrow Wilson in the Fourteen Points: in each case the assumption was the ultimate incompatibility of autocratic and democratic institutions. The fact that this particular autocracy also embraced the ideology of communism was, for Truman, relatively insignificant.

That certainly was not the case for most Americans, though. Nothing— not even totalitarianism—did more to arouse suspicion about the Soviet Union's behavior than that country's long-standing and self-proclaimed intention to seek the overthrow of capitalist governments throughout the world. American hostility toward communism went back to the earliest days of the Bolshevik Revolution: to Russia's abandonment of the Allied cause in World War I; to the terror, expropriations, and executions that soon followed; to the postwar Red Scare, with its suggestion that even the United States might not be immune from the bacillus of revolution. The Soviet Union's commitment to communism had been the primary justification for Washington's refusal to recognize that country until 1933; and even after that date Moscow's claim to be the vanguard of world revolution had continued to plague relations with Washington. Stalin implicitly acknowledged the corrosive effects of ideology upon his dealings with the West in 1943 when, eager for an Anglo-American commitment to establish a Second Front, he abolished the Comintern, Lenin's designated instrument for bringing about the world proletarian revolution. But there could be no guarantee that such restraint would continue once Moscow's enemies had been defeated. As a Department of State memorandum put it in 1944, it was necessary to keep in mind the Soviet conviction that "there is an irreconcilable chasm between 'socialism' and 'capitalism' and that any temporary association in a common interest [is] an association of expediency for a specific purpose but with no underlying affinity of fundamental interest, civilization, or tradition."

"I expressed it as my view that it would not be difficult to work with Russia provided we were dealing with her only as a national entity," James Forrestal noted in his diary during the summer of 1945. "[T]he real problem was whether or not Russian policy called for a continuation of the Third International's objectives, namely, world revolution and the application of the political principles of the dialectical materialists for the entire world." Evidence that the Kremlin still harbored such ambitions arose from two sets of circumstances: the Russians' use of communist parties in Eastern Europe as instruments with which to create their sphere of influence there; and the increasing success of communist parties in Western Europe, the Eastern Mediterranean, and China. In restrospect, it is not at all clear that these phenomena were related: the popularity of communist parties outside the Soviet sphere grew primarily out of their effectiveness as resistance fighters against the Axis; in Eastern Europe the communists owed their prominence chiefly to Moscow's reliance on them to consolidate its control. Nor was it obvious that the Soviet Union's use of foreign communist parties to promote its interests necessarily proved an ideological motivation for its policies.

But these fine points were difficult to keep in mind as the end of the war brought increases in the militancy—and anti-American rhetoric—of all communist parties, not least that of the Soviet Union itself. When combined with the indisputable evidence of Moscow's unilateral expansionism, when considered against the record of how Nazi Germany had used "fifth columns" before the war, it is not surprising that concern about the ideological dimension of the Soviet challenge should have surfaced as well. "The tendency is increasingly marked," the British Embassy in Washington reported in August, 1946, "to detect the Soviet mind or hand behind every move which seems to threaten or embarrass the United States or its friends, and to link events in one part of the world with those in another." The editors of *Newsweek* put it more bluntly: "U.S. officials in the best position to judge fear they have confirmation that the Soviet Government has made up its mind that capitalism must be destroyed if Communism is to live."

Both the "totalitarian" and the "ideological" explanations of Soviet behavior had in common the assumption that one was dealing with a compulsive internally driven process, unresponsive to gestures of restraint or goodwill from the outside. There had been yet a third interpretation of Moscow's unilateralism, popular during the war, that had seen it as growing out of a quite understandable preoccupation with security capable of being alleviated by patient Western efforts to win the Russians' trust. President Roosevelt himself had made this "insecurity" theory the basis of his policy toward the Soviet Union, and it had remained very much alive—though under increasing challenge—during the first months of the Truman administration. But theories require validation if they are to be sustained: however persuasive the "insecurity" model of Soviet behavior may be in retrospect, what struck most observers at the time was the utter imperviousness of Stalin's regime to the gestures of restraint and goodwill that emanated from the West during and immediately after the war. Moscow's perceived failure to reciprocate these initiatives made it more and more difficult to sustain an interpretation of Soviet actions based on "insecurity," as Henry Wallace found out when he attempted during the spring and summer of 1946, to revive it within the inner councils of the government. The "totalitarian" and "ideological" models were the obvious alternatives.

It is ironic that the individual most influential in discrediting "insecurity" as an explanation of Soviet unilateralism shared many of its basic assumptions. George F. Kennan had never been inclined to interpret Soviet behavior in either strictly totalitarian or ideological terms. As a keen student of Russian history and culture, he was fully aware of the lack of self-confidence that plagued the Stalinist government, and of the extent to which its unilateralism was defensively motivated. But he emphatically did not share the view of Wallace and others that these attitudes could be modified from the outside. It was in an effort to bring official Washington to see that point that Kennan crafted the February, 1946, "long telegram," to this day the single most influential explanation of postwar Soviet behavior, and one which powerfully reinforced the growing tendency within the United States to interpret Moscow's actions in a sinister light.

The "long telegram" had the great influence that it did because it provided a way to fuse concerns about totalitarianism and communism in dealing with the Soviet Union. It portrayed that state as one in which an autocratic tradition had become incorporated within an ideological compulsion to treat the outside world as hostile. The conclusion was clear: no actions the United States or its Western allies could take would alleviate Stalin's suspicion; the best one could do was to look to one's own defenses—and to the strength and self-confidence of one's own society—and wait for the internal forces of change within the Soviet system to have their effect.

There is a definite psychological satisfaction, when confronted with a phenomenon one does not understand, in finding a simple but persuasive explanation. Whatever the actual intentions of its author, the "long telegram" performed that function within the government in 1946; a similar analysis would find a wider audience the following year in the form of the famous "X" article in *Foreign Affairs*. The "totalitarian-ideological" model of Soviet behavior provided a clear, plausible, and in many ways, gratifying explanation of the Russians' failure to cooperate with their former allies in building a lasting peace: it absolved the United States of responsibility for the breakdown of wartime cooperation; it made any future relaxation of tensions dependent upon changes of heart in Moscow, not Washington. Americans did not welcome the onset of the Cold War. But the rationale they worked out to account for its appearance at least had the advantage of allowing them to approach the coming contest with a reasonably clear conscience.

The Soviet Union's emergence as a potential adversary closed an obvious gap in Washington's thinking about the postwar world. A generalized sense of vulnerability, related both to historical experience and to technological change, had caused United States officials to regard preservation of a global balance of power as a vital interest even before specific challenges to that balance had manifested themselves. This situation of perceived vulnerability in the absence of apparent threat accounts for the failure of the United States to deploy forces and establish bases in the way one might have expected had the Russians been seen as the enemy from the beginning. But Soviet unilateralism, together with the conclusions about the roots of Soviet behavior that unilateralism provoked, had by 1947 created a credible source of danger, with the result that American strategy now took on a clearer and more purposeful aspect.

Central to it was the defense of Western Europe, a priority so basic that it was more often assumed than articulated. "[I]t is not a question of what men think now," the Joint Chiefs of Staff noted in the spring of 1947; "[it] is something that has been demonstrated by what we have had to do, though tardily, and therefore at greater risk and cost, in actual warfare in the past. . . . The entire area of Western Europe is in first place as an area of strategic importance to the United States." And yet, American planners had given remarkably little thought to the means by which that part of the world might be secured against Soviet expansionism. Their assumption— again mostly unstated—had been that Great Britain would provide the necessary counter presence, and that the United States could concern itself with other matters. It had done just that throughout 1946, concentrating on resisting Soviet pressures aimed at Iran and Turkey, consolidating its position in Japan and southern Korea, mediating the Chinese civil war, and attempting to resolve the diplomatic stalemate over Germany.

The British decision to withdraw military assistance from Greece and Turkey in February, 1947, forced a reconsideration of these priorities, not because two countries were of critical importance in and of themselves, but because of the way in which London's action dramatized the failure of Western Europe as a whole to recover from the war. A major consequence of that conflict had been, in [British geopolitician Sir Halford] Mackinder's terminology, a severe weakening of the "rimland" states surrounding the Soviet "heartland," leaving only the "world island"—effectively the United States—as a countervailing balance. But it was not until 1947 that Washington officials realized the full implications of that fact and set about taking corrective action.

At no point—despite references to the possibility of war in the 1946 Clifford report—did these officials seriously anticipate a Soviet military attack in Europe. Estimates of Moscow's intentions, whether from the Pentagon, the State Department, or the intelligence community, consistently discounted the possibility that the Russians might risk a direct military confrontation within the foreseeable future. Several considerations contributed to that judgment, not least of which was the damage the Soviet Union itself had suffered during the war and the still relatively primitive character of its air and naval forces. But these estimates also suggested that the Russians would not need to use force to gain their objectives, because of the ease with which war-weakened neighbors could be psychologically intimidated. "[I]f the countries of the world lose confidence in us," General George A. Lincoln of the War Department General Staff told the Senate Foreign Relations Committee early in April, 1947, "they may in effect pass under the Iron Curtain without any pressure other than the subversive pressure being put on them."

American planners assumed a direct correlation between economic health, psychological self-confidence, and the capacity for defense. As a State-War-Navy Coordinating Committee report noted that same month: "[E]conomic weaknesses may give rise to instability and subsequently to political shifts which adversely affect the security of the U.S." This could happen through "boring from within" tactics or the threat of overwhelming external force, but in either event the outcome from the standpoint of American interests would be grim. "Without further prompt and substantial aid from the United States," Under Secretary William Clayton argued, "economic, social and political disintegration will overwhelm Europe."

A Soviet-dominated Europe would pose obvious military dangers, even if military means were not used to secure it. In a clear echo of the wartime Mackinder-Spykman analysis [Professor Nicholas John Spykman, author of *America's Strategy in World Politics* (1942)], the Joint Chiefs of Staff pointed out that the Western hemisphere contained 40 percent of the earth's land surface but only 25 percent of its population. "The potential military strength of the Old World in terms of manpower . . . and war-making capacity is enormously greater than that of our area of defense commitments, in which the United States is the only arsenal nation." It was obvious, therefore, that in case of war "we must have the support of some of the countries of the Old World unless our military strength is to be overshadowed by that of our enemies." Western Europe was particularly important, not just because that region contained "almost all potentially strong nations who can reasonably be expected to ally themselves with the United States," but also because without access to the eastern shore of the Atlantic, "the shortest and most direct avenue of attack against our enemies will almost certainly be denied us."

The economic consequences of a European collapse were less clear. The

Truman administration found it convenient to argue publicly that the effect on the American domestic economy, in terms of lost exports, would be little short of disastrous. What strikes one in retrospect, though, is how self-sufficient that economy actually was. Exports as a percentage of gross national product did not rise above 6.5 percent between 1945 and 1950, a figure lower than had normally been the case before the Great Depression, when the government had adamantly resisted any kind of official aid for European reconstruction. American investment in Western Europe in the early postwar years was actually less than European investment in the United States. It seems likely that administration officials stressed the economic implications of the crisis not because these stood out above others, but because Washington had chosen economic assistance as the quickest and most effective way to respond to it. It was easier to sell an unprecedented foreign-aid package as a program to ensure American prosperity than as a strategy for redressing the balance of power.

But it was the psychological implications of an extension of Soviet influence over Europe that probably most concerned American leaders. Although the term "domino theory" would not come into currency for another decade, administration officials worried deeply about the "bandwagon" effect that might ensue if the perception became widespread that the momentum in world affairs was on the Russians' side. And despite the United States' own history of isolationism, despite its relative self-sufficiency, there was a very real fear of what might happen if the nation were left without friends in the world. In one sense, this fear grew out of the tradition of American exceptionalism: the United States had always viewed itself as both apart from and a model for the rest of the world; it could hardly have regarded with equanimity evidence that its example was no longer relevant. But, in another sense, it was precisely the unexceptional character of Americans in relation to the rest of the world that was at issue here: who was to say that, buoyed by success in Europe, the totalitarian instinct might not take hold in the United States as well? "There is a little bit of the totalitarian buried somewhere, way down deep, in each and every one of us," George Kennan reminded students at the National War College in the spring of 1947. "It is only the cheerful light of confidence and security which keeps this evil genius down. . . . If confidence and security were to disappear, don't think that he would not be waiting to take their place."

The strategy of containment brought together the new American interest in maintaining a global balance of power with the perceived Muscovite challenge to that equilibrium in a part of the world that could hardly have been more pivotal—Western Europe. It sought to deal with that danger primarily by economic rather than military means; its goal was not so much the creation of an American hegemony as it was a re-creation of independent centers of power capable of balancing each other as well as the Russians. This is hardly the place to evaluate the success of that strategy or to trace its subsequent mutations and incarnations: these subjects have received excessively lengthy treatment elsewhere. Suffice it to say that the strategy could not have evolved without the perception of vulnerability brought about by the war, and the all-too-successful—if inadvertent—efforts of the Russians to give that abstraction an alarming reality.

Soviet historians have argued with unsurprising consistency through the years that the United States over-reacted to the "threat" posed by the U.S.S.R. in the wake of World War II. During the late 1960's and early 1970's, a number of American students of the early Cold War expressed agreement with that conclusion, though not with the methods that had been used to arrive at it. In an interesting inversion of Kennan's theory regarding Russian behavior, these accounts portrayed official Washington as having in one way or another fabricated the myth of a hostile Soviet Union in order to justify its own internally motivated drive for international hegemony. The difficulty with this argument was the impossibility of verifying it, for without access to Soviet sources there could be no definite conclusions regarding its accuracy: one cannot credibly assess responsibility when one can confirm the motives of only one side. The intervening years have brought us no nearer to a resolution of that problem, but they have witnessed the emergence of several new lines of historical interpretation that appear to call into question the thesis of American "over-reaction."

One of these involves a reconsideration of Stalin's policy by a new generation of scholars equally conversant, not only with the very limited number of Soviet and Eastern European sources that are available, but with the overwhelming array of recently declassified American and British documents as well. The effect of this work is to confirm neither the "totalitarian" nor the "ideological" explanations of Stalin's actions that were popular during the early Cold War years, but rather to see that dictator as having followed an "imperial" model of expansion: a pattern of behavior motivated by insecurity and characterized by caution, to be sure, but one that was also incapable of defining the limits of security requirements and that sought, as a result, to fill power vacuums where this could be done without encountering resistance. The effect of this policy was twofold: to incorporate within the Soviet sphere what Vojtech Mastny has called "a cluster of sullen dependencies" that probably contributed to more than they subtracted from Moscow's nervousness; and to alarm, and ultimately alienate, the United States and its Western European allies, who saw Stalin's inability to define the full extent of his security requirements as likely to undermine their own.

It may well be, as William Taubman has argued, that the West gave up on the possibility of cooperation with the West. But Taubman points out that any such cooperation would have been on the Kremlin leader's terms and for his purposes; it would have been designed "to foster Soviet control of Eastern Europe whether directly (in the case of Poland, Rumania, and Bulgaria) or indirectly (in Hungary and Czechoslovakia); to expand Soviet influence in Western Europe, the Near East and Asia; to position the USSR for even greater gains when the next Western economic crisis struck; and to achieve all this while subsidized to the tune of at least six billion dollars in American credits." Western statesmen may perhaps be pardoned for not having shared this particular vision of the postwar world.

Nor are they condemned, in the new historiography, for having resorted to a strategy of containment; indeed Mastny goes so far as to suggest that the West's responsibility for the coming of the Cold War lies more in the passive and dilatory character of its response than in its aggressiveness; "any Western policy likely to restrain [Stalin] would have had to follow a harder rather than a softer line; it would also have had a better chance to succeed if applied sooner rather than later." Containment no doubt reinforced Stalin's suspicion of the West, but it can hardly be said to have created it; without containment, according to this new line of interpretation, the fears Western statesmen held at the time regarding Soviet expansionism might well have become reality.

Historians are also beginning to study the involvement of third parties in the early Cold War; this work sheds new light on the question of who saw whom as a threat. What emerges from it so far is the extent to which states along the periphery of the U.S.S.R. tended to share Washington's concern about Soviet intentions, and indeed to welcome American intervention in their affairs as a counterweight. The Norwegian historian Geir Lundestad has pointed out that Washington's influence actually expanded more rapidly than did that of the Russians in the postwar world, but he argues that this happened because the United States was *encouraged* to assert its power in order to balance that of the Russians. Bruce Kuniholm has documented a similar pattern in the Near East: in 1946 the Iranian government was demanding not less but greater American interference in its internal affairs on the grounds, as the U.S. ambassador put it, that "[t]he only way they can think of to counteract one influence is to invite another." But the clearest case of all is the policy of Great Britain, which as Terry Anderson and Robert Hathaway have demonstrated, amounted almost to a conspiracy to involve the United States more actively in world affairs.

"If we cannot have a world community with the Russians as a constructive member," a British Foreign Office official minuted early in 1946, "it seems clear that the next best hope for peace and stability is that the rest of the world, including the vital North American arsenal, should be united in defense of whatever degree of stability we can attain." This is as good a summary of London's early Cold War policy, under both the Churchill and Attlee governments, as one is apt to find. The British had come earlier than their American allies to the conclusion that cooperation with the Russians was not going to be possible; certainly they welcomed—and, at times, sought to reinforce—the increasing indications from Washington throughout 1946 and early 1947 that the Truman administration had come to share that view. Their analysis of the reasons for Soviet unilateralism roughly paralleled that of the Americans; nor were they inclined to find fault—apart from some wincing at the rhetorical excesses involved—with the strategies Washington proposed to deal with that problem. Indeed, if anything, London's attitude was that the Americans were not doing enough; it was this conviction that led Foreign Secretary Ernest Bevin late in 1947 to propose to the United States a formal and permanent peacetime military alliance with Western Europe.

It is, of course, easy to see self-serving motivations at work in the invitations the British government and its counterparts in Western Europe and the Near East extended to the United States to expand its influence in their parts of the world. It could be argued that had that desire for an American presence not existed, these "third party" assessments of Russian intentions might have been considerably less alarmist than they were. But that is missing the point, for it is also the case that had a credible Soviet threat not presented itself, these countries would not have been seeking the expansion of American power in the first place. "It has really become a matter of the defence of western civilisation," the British Foreign Office concluded early in 1948:

> [N]ot only is the Soviet government not prepared at the present state to co-operate in any real sense with any non-Communist . . . Government, but it is actively preparing to extend its hold over the remaining portion of continental Europe and, subsequently, over the Middle East and no doubt the bulk of the Far East as well. . . . [P]hysical control of the Eurasian land mass and eventual control of the whole World Island is what the Politburo is aiming at—no less a thing than that. The immensity of the aim should not betray us into believing in its impracticality. Indeed, unless positive and vigorous steps are shortly taken by those other states who are in a position to take them . . . the Soviet Union will gain political and strategical advantages which will set the great Communist machine in action, leading either to the establishment of a World Dictatorship or (more probably) to the collapse of organised society over great stretches of the globe.

It is significant that this top-secret Foreign Office document, circulated only within the highest levels of the British government and declassified only after the passage of more than three decades, should have revealed an assessment of the Soviet threat more sweeping in character and apocalyptic in tone than anything in the record of private or public statements by major American officials at the time. The progression from Mackinder to [author of *The Decline of the West* Oswald] Spengler, it appears, was easier than one might think.

History, inescapably, involves viewing distant pasts through the prism of more recent ones. The incontestable fact that the United States overreacted more than once during the subsequent history of the Cold War to the perceived threat of Soviet and/or "communist" expansionism has, to an extent, blinded us to the equally demonstrable fact that in the immediate postwar years the behavior of the Russians alarmed not just Americans but a good portion of the rest of the world as well. How well-founded that alarm was—how accurately it reflected the realities that shaped Soviet policy— are issues upon which there are legitimate grounds for disagreement. But to deny that the alarm itself was sincere, or that Americans were not alone in perceiving it, is to distort the view through the prism more than is necessary. Fear, after all, can be genuine without being rational. And, as Sigmund Freud once pointed out, even paranoids can have real enemies.

The Truman Doctrine
and the Rise of American Globalism

MELVYN P. LEFFLER

Challenged with the greatest public relations task ever faced by a president, Truman and his advisers could not resist the temptation to simplify Soviet intentions. Throughout 1945 and early 1946 serious efforts had been made to appraise the relative importance of the strategic, economic, political, and ideological factors shaping Soviet policy. After the spring of 1946, however, these efforts ceased. George F. Kennan's assessment in the "long" telegram became the established verity, and a new prominence was given to the ideological and totalitarian character of Soviet foreign policy. This was dramatically evident in James V. Forrestal's fixation with Marxist-Leninist doctrine, in the State Department's March 1946 estimate of Soviet policy which served as a framework for military studies, and in the lengthy memorandum on U.S.–Soviet relations prepared by Clark Clifford and George Elsey for President Truman in the summer of 1946. While detailed and thoughtful assessments of Soviet short-term intentions persisted, almost always emphasizing the Kremlin's desire to avoid war, the notion that the Soviet Union sought world domination became the fundamental postulate of American national security doctrine.

Yet recent studies of Soviet foreign policy underscore the importance of examining the Kremlin's intentions and objectives with rigor, subtlety, and sophistication. The closer historians and political scientists scrutinize Soviet foreign policy in the immediate postwar era, the more difficult it becomes to generalize and simplify. Vojtech Mastny has emphasized Stalin's opportunism; Adam Ulam and William Taubman have portrayed his caution, apprehension, and circumspection; William O. McCagg has imaginatively suggested the host of institutional, economic, personal, and ideological impulses that engulfed Soviet foreign policy; and Werner G. Hahn has argued that the postwar revival of ideology within the Soviet Union had little to do with foreign policy. We now have reason to believe that Stalin was treading warily lest he provoke the West. During 1946 and early 1947 the Soviet leader probably discouraged revolutionary activity abroad. Notwithstanding his determination to dominate the Eastern European periphery, to seek opportunities in Iran and Turkey, and to orient Germany and Austria toward the East, he seemed to prefer an overall policy of détente, to use Taubman's phrase. Only after the proclamation of the Truman Doctrine, the announcement of the Marshall Plan, and the merger of the three western zones in Germany did Stalin accept the reality of the Cold War, encourage revolutionary action in Western Europe, establish the Cominform, and consolidate Soviet domination in the areas occupied at the end of World War II, particularly Hungary, Czechoslovakia, and East Germany.

Text from "From the Truman Doctrine to the Carter Doctrine: Lessons and Dilemmas of the Cold War," from *Diplomatic History*, vol. 7, no. 4. Copyright 1983 by Scholarly Resources Inc. Reprinted by permission of Scholarly Resources Inc.

If it is important to probe more deeply into Soviet intentions, it is equally imperative to develop a correct appreciation of Soviet military strength. At the time of the Truman Doctrine, American analysts recognized two critical features about Soviet military capabilities. First, the Soviet Union, because of prevailing power vacuums, could overrun in a few months all of Western Europe, much of the Middle East, and sizable chunks of Manchuria and North China. Second, the Soviet Union could not inflict serious damage on the American homeland, could not compete with a mobilized American economy, and, therefore, could not wage war successfully against the United States. Because American analysts and policymakers appreciated Soviet military weaknesses vis-à-vis the United States, they remained confident that Soviet leaders would avoid war, back down in a crisis, and succumb to demonstrations of American diplomatic determination. Kennan predicted this in his "long" telegram, and the Soviets behaved, as predicted, when they withdrew from Iran, refrained from intervention in Greece, and avoided military conflict over Berlin.

The disparity in capabilities to wage war against one another, the fundamental economic strength of the United States, and the strategic weaknesses of the Soviet Union allowed American officials to develop and implement a broad conception of national security. The overriding U.S. national security imperative, as revealed in scores of military planning documents, intelligence reports, and interagency papers, was to prevent Soviet control of the raw materials and manpower of Europe and Asia lest the Soviet Union use these resources to enhance its long-term capabilities to wage war against the United States. In other words, American officials perceived the Soviet Union as a hostile ideological foe, feared the appeal of communism, believed that Communist parties everywhere were subservient to the Kremlin, and assumed that if Communists took control anywhere in Eurasia, the latent military power of the Soviet Union would be enhanced and the economic vitality of the West would be diminished.

In early 1947 to contain Soviet/Communist power and create a stable international order conducive to U.S. economic and political interests, the Truman administration prepared to rehabilitate German industry, rebuild Western Europe, revive Japan, and implant American power on the very borders of the Soviet Union. Containment along the so-called northern tier (Greece, Turkey, and Iran) also was essential to preserve Western access to Middle East oil in peacetime and to fight more effectively in wartime should conflict unexpectedly erupt.

From the American perspective, these initiatives appeared prudent, just, and urgent; they were not designed to threaten the Soviet Union. With all sincerity Ambassador Walter Bedell Smith told Stalin in April 1946 that it was impossible for Americans to envisage any threat to the Soviet Union. Approximately one year later Secretary of State George C. Marshall expressed much the same thought to the Soviet dictator. Kennan, Clifford, and Elsey were absolutely certain that Soviet suspicions and anxieties were simply a ruse to justify the Kremlin's totalitarian control at home and/or ruthless conquest abroad.

A key lesson of the Truman Doctrine era, therefore, is for Americans to develop a better grasp of how their actions impinge upon the interests of potential adversaries and of how their own concept of security may endanger the perceived security of other powers. By mid-1947 the American security frontier stretched to the Elbe, the Dardanelles, and the Sea of Japan. More significantly, the American conception of security encompassed, among other things, the economic rebuilding of the Soviet Union's traditional enemies, Germany and Japan, and the assumption of British strategic interests in areas of long-standing Anglo-Soviet rivalry in the Middle East and Southwest Asia. If Stalin's fears of latent American power were as great as Ulam has suggested, American actions in 1947 were certain to intensify those apprehensions because these initiatives directly and indirectly influenced power relationships in areas of historic and vital interest to the Soviet Union.

There is then an enduring paradox: the policies that rehabilitated the industrial heartlands of Europe and Asia, that revitalized Western European liberalism and capitalism, and that safeguarded the petroleum resources of the Middle East were the same policies that culminated in the division of Europe, the elimination of the last vestiges of democracy in Hungary and Czechoslovakia, and the institutionalization of the Cold War. Only the disparity in the overall Soviet-American power relationship permitted the United States to exclude the Soviets from Japan, bar them from bases in the Dardanelles, and shut them out of the Ruhr-Rhineland industrial complex. Likewise, Soviet power enabled Stalin to consolidate a sphere of terror and repression in Eastern Europe.

So it might seem that Kennan's view of holding four of the five major power centers came to dominate the foreign policy of the Truman administration. Yet this was not the case. In the aftermath of World War II, vacuums of powers existed throughout Eurasia, and interest and apprehension impelled the United States to fill these vacuums. During the summer of 1946, Clifford and Elsey emphasized, with Kennan's endorsement, the need "to support and assist *all* democratic countries which are *in any way* menaced or endangered by the U.S.S.R." They specifically named China, Korea, India, the Philippines, and Southeast Asia. In preparing their studies for the Truman Doctrine, State Department officials were fully cognizant, in Joseph Jones's words, that "not just the fate of Greece was at stake. Greece was the key to a much wider situation: the freedom and security of a large part of the world." The Marshall Plan, then, accentuated the West's interest in Middle East oil. The decision to revive Japan, as Michael Schaller has shown, generated even greater concern with preserving access to the markets and raw materials of Southeast Asia.

Apprehension reinforced interest; that is, the fear that these resources might be controlled by the Kremlin reinforced U.S. determination to combat Communist efforts, particularly in Asia. This was true even in China, where, despite all the agonizing reappraisals and pervasive doubts, the United States provided almost $3 billion in aid to the Chinese nationalists from 1945 to 1949. And in mid-1949, when salvaging China was recognized as hopeless, Secretary of State Acheson instructed his trusted aide Philip Jessup to draw up programs for non-Communist Asia on the assumption that it was "a fundamental decision of American policy that the United States does not intend to permit any further communist domination on the continent of Asia or in Southeast Asia."

The definition of American interests as global was apparent in almost every important document of the Truman Doctrine era (1946–50). The Clifford/Elsey report of September 1946, Acheson and Clayton's testimony on the Truman Doctrine, NSC 7, NSC 20/4, and NSC 68 all projected American interests everywhere as did Kennan's "long" telegram and "X" article. If no financial or military commitments to Southeast Asia were made in the initial postwar years, it was not because American officials foreswore an interest in that part of the world but because they perceived no immediate threat and recognized that American resources were circumscribed. Once they perceived a threat, U.S. officials mobilized the resources to become involved. While Truman's advisers did seek to set priorities among different geographic areas, their explicit goal always was to contain Soviet/Communist influence throughout Eurasia. Hence, the prospects for American commitment, even in areas of peripheral interest, were high from the onset.

An important lesson to be learned from the Truman Doctrine era is the need to differentiate among interests, carefully identify vital interests, refrain from ideological crusades, and avoid the temptation to define all major interests as national security imperatives justifying the use of force. Once interests are defined and commitments are incurred, there is almost irresistible pressure to build up commensurate military capabilities. Truman initially hoped to limit defense expenditures. Yet once American interests were defined in global terms, an enormous gap emerged between interests and commitments on the one hand and capabilities on the other. As global instability persisted, nationalist unrest mounted, Soviet military capabilities grew, and as American prestige became vested in the maintenance of a non-Communist world order, the entire national security bureaucracy came to support a massive military buildup at home and abroad.

The accretion of American power was justified, at least in part, on the need to negotiate from strength. Presumably the failure to resolve differences was the result of Soviet negotiating intransigence and insufficient American leverage. Yet it is apparent that the stalemate in negotiations was as much the result of unreasonable American expectations as of Soviet obstinacy. Truman accepted Averell Harriman's advice that negotiations entail mutual concessions, but he expected to get his way 85 percent of the time. Stalin, Truman wrote his wife from Potsdam, "seems to like it when I hit him with a hammer." While tough, Truman's attitude was a lot more flexible than the one expressed by Acheson in March 1947 when he insisted in executive session hearings that "it is a mistake to believe that you can, at any time, sit down with the Russians and solve questions. . . ."

It was not the absence of American strength that precluded constructive negotiations; it was the inflexibility of the Soviet and U.S. negotiating positions. The Soviets were obdurate on Eastern European questions. On most other matters the United States was equally intractable. Recent books by

Patricia Dawson Ward and Robert L. Messer illuminate the negotiating box in which even the malleable James F. Byrnes found himself. Gregg Herken and Larry G. Gerber demonstrate how the Baruch Plan was framed to safeguard all American interests and to place upon the Soviet Union all the initial risks of an agreement on the control of atomic energy. J. Samuel Walker has portrayed the unreceptive attitude of American officials toward negotiations in early 1948, and Ulam has lamented the unwillingness of American officials to discuss a resolution of the German problem. Conversely, throughout these years American negotiators often privately acknowledged that the Soviet position on many matters was not intransigent. Not only was this the view of Byrnes but also that of such disparate negotiators as George A. Lincoln, Lucius Clay, Ferdinand Eberstadt, and Warren Austin. But Americans did not have the patience to negotiate because European economic dislocation threatened indigenous revolution or Communist electoral victories. Either possibility seemed to portend an aggrandizement of Soviet power which American officials could no longer accept.

The foregoing is not intended to suggest that flexible negotiators could easily have resolved the momentous and contentious issues that divided Soviet and American officials. It is still not clear whether any way could have been found to safeguard legitimate American security imperatives without arousing Soviet apprehensions, jeopardizing vital Soviet interests, and eliciting Soviet countermeasures. What is clear is that by 1947 American policymakers no longer wanted to negotiate and compromise. They simplified Soviet intentions, subordinated Soviet strategic and economic concerns, focused on the ideological roots and totalitarian character of the Soviet system, and ignored the possible repercussions of their own policies on Soviet behavior. In the midst of the feverish efforts to build up situations of strength, even those officials like Kennan who sometimes preached the efficacy of nonmilitary and "asymmetrical" containment, gradually lost their influence. Any appraisal of postwar U.S. policy that seeks to establish the Truman Doctrine era as a model of successful policymaking must take note of these developments.

✕ *F U R T H E R   R E A D I N G*

Stephen Ambrose, *Rise to Globalism: American Foreign Policy, 1938–1980s* (1976)

Terry H. Anderson, *The United States, Great Britain, and the Cold War, 1944–1947* (1981)

Robert M. Blum, *Drawing the Line: The Origins of American Containment Policy in East Asia* (1982)

Michael Boll, *Cold War in the Balkans* (1984)

Lynn Etheridge Davis, *The Cold War Begins: Soviet-American Conflict over Eastern Europe* (1974)

Hugh DeSantis, *The Diplomacy of Silence: The American Foreign Service, the Soviet Union, and the Cold War, 1933–1947* (1980)

Robert J. Donovan, *Conflict and Crisis: The Presidency of Harry S. Truman, 1945–1948* (1977)

————, *The Tumultuous Years: The Presidency of Harry S. Truman, 1949–1953* (1982)

Herbert Feis, *From Trust to Terror* (1970)

Richard Freeland, *The Truman Doctrine and the Origins of McCarthyism* (1973)

John Lewis Gaddis, *Russia, the Soviet Union, and the United States* (1978)

————, *The Long Peace: Inquiries into the History of the Cold War* (1987)

————, *Strategies of Containment* (1982)

————, *The United States and the Origins of the Cold War, 1941–1947* (1972)

Lloyd C. Gardner, *Architects of Illusion: Men and Ideas in American Foreign Policy, 1941–1949* (1970)

Lloyd C. Gardner, Arthur M. Schlesinger, Jr., and Hans J. Morgenthau, *Origins of the Cold War* (1970)

John Gimbel, *The American Occupation of Germany* (1968)

————, *The Origins of the Marshall Plan* (1976)

James L. Gormly, *The Collapse of the Grand Alliance, 1945–1948* (1987)

Norman Graebner, ed., *The National Security: Its Theory and Practice, 1945–1960* (1986)

John L. Harper, *America and the Reconstruction of Italy* (1986)

George C. Herring, *Aid to Russia, 1941–46: Strategy, Diplomacy, the Origins of the Cold War* (1973)

Michael J. Hogan, *The Marshall Plan: America, Britain, and the Reconstruction of Western Europe, 1947–1952* (1987)

Walter Isaacson and Evan Thomas, *The Wise Men, Six Friends and the World They Made: Acheson, Bohlen, Harriman, Kennan, Lovett, McCloy* (1986)

Gabriel Kolko, *The Politics of War: The World and United States Foreign Policy, 1943–1945* (1968)

Joyce Kolko and Gabriel Kolko, *The Limits of Power: The World and United States Foreign Policy, 1945–1954* (1972)

Bruce Kuklick, *American Policy and the Division of Germany* (1972)

Bruce R. Kuniholm, *The Origins of the Cold War in the Near East: Great Power Conflict and Diplomacy in Iran, Turkey, and Greece* (1980)

Walter LaFeber, *America, Russia and the Cold War* (1980)

Deborah Larson, *Origins of Containment* (1985)

Melvyn P. Leffler, "The American Conception of National Security and the Beginnings of the Cold War, 1945–1948," *American Historical Review*, 89 (1984), 346–381

Ralph Levering, *The Cold War* (1988)

Geir Lundestad, *The American Non-Policy Towards Eastern Europe, 1943–1947* (1975)

David McLellan, *Dean Acheson* (1976)

Robert J. Maddox, *From War to Cold War: The Education of Harry S. Truman* (1988)

————, *The New Left and the Origins of the Cold War* (1973)

Vojtech Mastny, *Russia's Road to the Cold War: Diplomacy, Warfare, and the Politics of Communism, 1941–1945* (1979)

David Allan Mayers, *Cracking the Monolith: U.S. Policy Against the Sino-Soviet Alliance, 1949–1955* (1986)

Robert L. Messer, *The End of an Alliance: James F. Byrnes, Roosevelt, Truman, and the Origins of the Cold War* (1982)

James E. Miller, *The United States and Italy, 1940–1950* (1986)

Alan Milward, *The Reconstruction of Western Europe, 1945–51* (1984)

David S. Painter, *Oil and the American Century* (1986)

Thomas G. Paterson, *Meeting the Communist Threat: Truman to Reagan* (1988)

————, *On Every Front: The Making of the Cold War* (1979)

————, *The Origins of the Cold War* (1984)

————, *Soviet-American Confrontation* (1973)

Robert A. Pollard, *Economic Security and the Origins of the Cold War* (1985)

Michael Schaller, *The American Occupation of Japan: The Origins of the Cold War in Asia* (1985)

Gaddis Smith, *Dean Acheson* (1972)

William Taubman, *Stalin's American Policy: From Entente to Détente to Cold War* (1982)

Athan G. Theoharis, *The Yalta Myths* (1970)

Hugh Thomas, *Armed Truce: The Beginnings of the Cold War, 1945–46* (1987)

Kenneth W. Thompson, *Cold War Theories* (1981)

Robert W. Tucker, *The Radical Left and American Foreign Policy* (1971)

Adam Ulam, *The Rivals: America and Russia Since World War II* (1972)

J. Samuel Walter, *Henry A. Wallace and American Foreign Policy* (1976)

Samuel F. Wells, Jr., "Sounding the Tocsin: NSC-68 and the Soviet Threat," *International Security,* 4 (1979), 116–158

William A. Williams, *The Tragedy of American Foreign Policy* (1962)

Lawrence Wittner, *American Intervention in Greece, 1943–1949* (1982)

Daniel Yergin, *Shattered Peace: The Origins of the Cold War and the National Security State* (1977)

CHAPTER
4

Truman, Eisenhower, and the Transformation of American Politics, 1945–1960

※

American politics had been refashioned during the upheavals of the 1930s by the emergence of a new Democratic majority of workers, farmers, and ethnic minorities and by the rise of the modern New Deal state. Following World War II, American politics would be transformed in very different ways by the Cold War and the resurgence of conservatism. The Cold War reorganized the nation's political priorities around issues of foreign policy and national security. This transformation was accompanied, moreover, by a strident anticommunism that strengthened the influence of conservatives, whose earlier attacks on New Deal domestic programs had gone largely unheeded. Disagreements among Americans over U.S. policy toward the Soviet Union (and over the role of communists in American life) shattered the American Left, divided and weakened the Democratic party, and shifted the nation's political center of gravity decisively toward the right. In its most extreme manifestation—what came to be called McCarthyism—the new anticommunist politics virtually dominated the country's attention from the late forties to the mid-fifties. The political mobilization of American business, which had begun in the late 1930s in response to the New Deal, played an equally important, if less prominent, role in transforming postwar politics. Deeply disturbed by developments in the thirties, business leaders sought to arrest the continued momentum of New Deal liberalism and to refashion the New Deal state in their own interests. They deployed their enormous political resources in many arenas: in Congress and the courts, in the halls of state and local governments, in the workplace and in local communities, in the press, radio, and television; and they employed a wide variety of both traditional and new techniques: campaign financing, litigation, philanthropy, the sponsorship of research, institutional advertising, and public relations. The goal of these efforts, at least partially realized, was to change not just the nation's politics but its political culture; to win not only elections but also the hearts and minds of the American people. The election of Harry S Truman in 1948 marked the last hurrah of the sometimes raw, class-conscious politics of the New Deal. The election of Dwight D. Eisenhower only four years later symbolized the advent of the new, more conservative consensus of the 1950s.

ⅩⅩ DOCUMENTS

In the first document, White House aide Clark M. Clifford shrewdly analyzes the "politics of 1948" and advises incumbent president Harry S Truman on how to win election. In many of his campaign speeches, some of which are excerpted in document two, Truman seemed to heed Clifford's advice, excoriating the Republicans and attempting to rally the many disparate elements of the Democratic New Deal coalition. Following his upset victory, Truman proposed a series of reforms in labor, agriculture, health care, housing, and civil rights that he called the Fair Deal. As the third selection reveals, some left-wing critics, among them Leo J. Linder of the National Lawyer's Guild, complained that Truman's commitment to progressive reform, as measured by his FY 1950 budget proposal, did not go nearly far enough. Many presidential proposals were blocked, moreover, by powerful interest groups such as the American Medical Association, the American Federation of Farm Bureaus, and the National Association of Manufacturers. The fourth document outlines the massive public-relations campaign launched by the AMA against national health insurance. Meanwhile, Republican leaders such as New York governor Thomas E. Dewey, the party's unsuccessful candidate for president in both 1944 and 1948, sought to enlist the enormously popular Dwight D. Eisenhower in the GOP cause (the fifth document). What remained of Truman's legislative program was soon overtaken by the rising tide of anticommunism, symbolized by Senator Joseph R. McCarthy's demagogic attacks on the Democrats (document six) and by the outbreak of the Korean War in June 1950. The seventh selection, the script of an Eisenhower campaign advertisement, suggests the new, growing role of television in marketing presidential candidates. Like Truman, Eisenhower led a nation wherein politics and economics had been transformed by the Cold War. In the final selection, excerpted from his farewell address, Eisenhower warns of the dangers of the "military-industrial complex."

White House Aide Clark M. Clifford
Advises President Harry S Truman, 1947

The title of this memorandum might well be "The Politics of 1948." The aim of the memorandum is to outline a course of political conduct for the Administration extending from November, 1947 to November, 1948. . . .

The basic premise of this memorandum—that the Democratic Party is an unhappy alliance of Southern conservatives, Western progressives and Big City labor—is very trite, but it is also very true. And it is equally true that the success or failure of the Democratic leadership can be precisely measured by its ability to lead enough members of these three misfit groups to the polls on the first Tuesday after the first Monday of November, 1948. . . .

1. . . . It should be assumed . . . that the [Republican] candidate is [Thomas E.] Dewey (the only man to lead the President in the *Fortune* Poll); and that, because of his 1944 experience and because of the extremely efficient group of men he has drawn around him, he will be a resourceful, intelligent and highly dangerous candidate, even more difficult to defeat than in 1944.

2. *President Truman will be elected if the Administration will successfully concentrate on the traditional Democratic alliance between the South and West.* . . .

If the Democrats carry the solid South and also those Western states carried in 1944, they will have 216 of the required 266 electoral votes. And if the Democratic Party is powerful enough to capture the West, it will almost certainly pick up enough of the doubtful Middlewestern and Eastern states to get 50 more votes (e.g. Missouri's 14 votes). We could lose New York, Pennsylvania, Illinois, New Jersey, Ohio, Massachusetts—all the "big" states—and still win.

Therefore, political and program planning demands concentration upon the West and its problems, including reclamation, floods, and agriculture. It is the Number One Priority for the 1948 campaign. The Republican Congress has already done its share to give the West to the Administration.

3. *Henry Wallace will be the candidate of a third party.* . . . Wallace is gambling for high stakes. He hopes to defeat President Truman by splitting the Democratic Party and then inherit its leadership so he can be the candidate of 1952. . . .

It is also very dangerous to assume that the only supporters of Wallace are the Communists. True enough, they give him a disciplined hard-working organization and collect the money to run his campaign. But he also has a large following throughout the country, particularly of the young voters who are attracted by the idealism that he—and he alone—is talking and who regard war as the one evil greater than any other. He will also derive support from the pacifists, which means a great number of organized women and from whatever irreconcilable and die-hard isolationists remain. He will attract votes—and money—from the "lunatic fringe." The California Townsendites are already pledged to him.

In a close election, no votes can be ignored. The only safe working hypothesis is to assume *now* that Wallace will run on a third party ticket. Every effort must be made *now* jointly and at one and the same time— although, of course, by different groups—to dissuade him and also to identify him and isolate him in the public mind with the Communists.

4. *The independent and progressive voter will hold the balance of power in 1948; he will not actively support President Truman unless a great effort is made.* The Democratic and Republican Parties each have a minimum, a residue, of voters whose loyalty almost nothing can shake. The independent voter who shifts on the issues comprises a group which today is probably larger than both.

The truth is that the old "party organization" control is gone forever.

Better education, the rise of the mass pressure group, the economic depression of the 30's, the growth of government functions—all these have contributed to the downfall of "the organization." Tammany, Hague, Kelley and the rest of the straight party leaders, while still important, are no longer omnipotent, no longer able to determine the issues. For practical political purposes, they are moribund; they cannot be relied on to do the job alone.

They have been supplanted in large measure by the pressure groups. In these pressure groups are the farmers, still traditionally Republican, and organized labor which became "traditionally Democratic" under Roosevelt. Another loosely organized group are the progressives who followed Roosevelt for four elections but are increasingly restive under President Truman, mostly because of the reactionary domination exercised over the Democratic Party by the Congressional Southerners who, although a minority of the Democratic Party, are a majority of the Party-in-Congress and are assuming control of the Party organization councils. And also among these groups are the racial groups who have learned to use the vote as an economic weapon and who can no longer be satisfied with a Tammany turkey on Thanksgiving.

a. *The Farmer.* The farm vote is in most ways identical with the Winning of the West—the Number One Priority. The farmer is at least at present favorably inclined toward the Truman Administration. His crops are good. However the high prices may be affecting the rest of the people, they help him more than hurt him. Parity will protect him—and the Marshall Plan will aid him. The economic and political trend of the Administration (except its tax program) is going his way. Whether prosperity makes him the conservative he usually becomes in good times remains to be seen—but, if it does, nothing much can be done about it in terms of more political or economic favors to woo him back to the Democratic banner.

b. *Labor.* President Truman and the Democratic Party cannot win without the *active* support of organized labor. It is dangerous to assume that labor now has nowhere else to go in 1948. *Labor can stay home.*

The rank and file of the workers are not yet politically minded; they will not, therefore, vote or work actively unless they are inspired to do so. They were so inspired by Roosevelt. They were *not* so inspired in the 1946 Congressional elections. In those elections they did not vote Republican but they *did stay home.* The labor group has always been politically inactive during prosperity. When they are well fed they are not interested. They will probably be well fed in 1948. The effort to get out the labor vote will thus have to be even more strenuous than in 1944.

The President's veto of the Taft-Hartley Bill, coupled with vehement dislike of the Republicans because they passed it over his veto does indicate that as of today Labor is friendly to the President. . . .

c. *The "Liberals."* The liberal and progressive leaders are not overly enthusiastic about the Administration. Foreign policy has forced the large bulk to break sharply with Wallace and the fellow-travelers. And, of course, they find no hope in Republican activities as evidenced by the recent Congress. Fear of the Republicans may drive them to activity for President

Truman, but at present there is no disposition to do much more than stay home on election day. Whether their reasons are valid or otherwise, many of them feel that the progressive wing has been cut off by the Southerners and the "organization" leaders from any say in the Democratic Party. This is particularly true of such organizations as *Americans for Democratic Action* where most of the Roosevelt New Dealers have found haven. . . .

The liberals are numerically small. But, similar to manufacturers and financiers of the Republican Party, they are far more influential than mere numbers entitle them to be. The businessman has influence because he contributes his money. The liberal exerts unusual influence because he is articulate. The "right" may have the money, but the "left" has always had the pen. If the "intellectual" can be induced to back the President, he will do so in the press, on the radio, and in the movies. He is the artist of propaganda. He is the "idea man" for the people. Since the rise of the pressure groups, the men of ideas who can appeal to them on their own ground, in their own words, have become an essential ally to the alert candidate in modern American politics.

d. *The Negro.* Since 1932 when, after intensive work by President Roosevelt, their leaders swung the Pennsylvania Negro bloc into the Democratic column with the classic remark, "Turn your picture of Abraham Lincoln to the wall—we have paid that debt," the northern Negro has voted Democratic (with the exception of 1946 in New York). A theory of many professional politicians is that the northern Negro voter today holds the balance of power in Presidential elections for the simple arithmetical reason that the Negroes not only vote in a bloc but are geographically concentrated in the pivotal, large and closely contested electoral states such as New York, Illinois, Pennsylvania, Ohio and Michigan. This theory may or may not be absolutely true, but it is certainly close enough to the truth to be extremely arguable.

In great measure, this explains the assiduous and continuous cultivation of the New York Negro vote by Governor Dewey and his insistence that his controllable legislature pass a state anti-discrimination act. No less an authority than Ed Flynn has said privately that Dewey will take New York from President Truman in 1948 because he controls the Negro and Italian blocs. . . .

Unless there are new and real efforts (as distinguished from mere political gestures which are today thoroughly understood and strongly resented by sophisticated Negro leaders), the Negro bloc, which, certainly in Illinois and probably in New York and Ohio, *does* hold the balance of power, will go Republican.

e. *The Jew.* The Jewish vote, insofar as it can be thought of as a bloc, is important only in New York. But (except for Wilson in 1916) no candidate since 1876 has lost New York and won the Presidency, and its 47 votes are naturally the first prize in any election. Centered in New York City, that vote is normally Democratic and, if large enough, is sufficient to counteract the upstate vote and deliver the state to President Truman. Today the Jewish bloc is interested primarily in Palestine and will continue to be an uncertain quantity right up to the time of election. Even though there is general approval among the Jewish people regarding the United Nations report on Palestine, the group is still torn with conflicting views and dissension. It will be extremely difficult to decide some of the vexing questions which will arise in the months to come on the basis of political expediency. In the long run, there is likely to be greater gain if the Palestine problem is approached on the basis of reaching decisions founded upon intrinsic merit.

f. *The Catholic.* The Catholic vote is traditionally Democratic. The controlling element in this group today from a political standpoint is the distrust and fear of Communism. It is reported that Senator Mead, in his candidacy for Governor of New York, lost Catholic votes because he tolerated a loose alliance with the American Labor Party which is controlled by the Communists. The attitude of the President and the Administration toward Communism should exert a definite appeal to this group but it is entirely possible that closer liaison should be established. . . .

5. *The foreign policy issues of the 1948 campaign will be our relations with the USSR and the Administration's handling of foreign reconstruction and relief.* The probability that the foreign affairs of the United States will remain on a basis of "bi-partisan cooperation" is unfortunately remote. The stakes in a Presidential contest are so huge that the temptation to make an issue of anything on which there is any segment or group of dissatisfied voters is too irresistible.

There is considerable political advantage to the Administration in its battle with the Kremlin. The best guess today is that our poor relations with Russia will intensify. The nation is already united behind the President on this issue. The worse matters get, up to a fairly certain point—real danger of imminent war—the more is there a sense of crisis. In times of crisis the American citizen tends to back up his President. And on the issue of policy toward Russia, President Truman is comparatively invulnerable to attack because of his brilliant appointment of General Marshall who has convinced the public that as Secretary of State he is nonpartisan and above politics.

In a flank attack tied up with foreign policy, the Republicans have tried to identify the Administration with the domestic Communists. The President adroitly stole their thunder by initiating his own Government employee loyalty investigation procedure and the more frank Republicans admit it. But their efforts will intensify as the election approaches, particularly when the meagre results of the civil service investigations are made public by the Republican Congress. . . .

Insofar as it has control of the situation, the Administration should select the issues upon which there will be conflict with the majority in Congress. It can assume it will get no major part of its own program approved. Its tactics must, therefore, be entirely different than if there were any real point to bargaining and compromise. Its recommendations—in the State of the Union message and elsewhere—must be tailored for the voter, not the Congressman; they must display a label which reads "no compromises." The strategy on the Taft-Hartley Bill—refusal to bargain with the Republicans and to accept any compromises—paid big political dividends. That strategy should be expanded in the next session to include all the *domestic* issues. . . .

c. *The Insulation of Henry Wallace*. Wallace should be put under attack whenever the moment is psychologically correct. . . .

But there is only futility in the delusion that Wallace can be insulated merely by yelling at him. As his own lieutenants say, and accurately, in their private conversation, "Henry can be stopped quite easily; all President Truman has to do is move to the left and our ground is cut out from under us; but we are quite sure he won't do it." . . .

The September 11th speech by Wallace . . . appealed to the atavistic fear of all progressives—the fear of "Wall Street." This fear is not the sole property of the progressives. It belongs traditionally to the Democratic Party. It began with the agrarian Jefferson's battle against Hamilton, it continued with Jackson's fight against Nicholas Biddle's bank, it found its silver tongue in the crusades of William Jennings Bryan, and it came to full flower under Wilson and Franklin Roosevelt. In a very important sense, it is the reason for the Democratic Party—because the only way to explain the lasting alliance between the South and the West is their mutual fear of domination by the industrial East. Today the South can agree on no issue with the West—except "Wall Street." . . .

President Truman must carry the West to win. To carry the West, he must be "liberal"; he cannot afford to be shackled with the Wall Street label by any so-called progressive movement. . . .

Having performed yeoman service for those interests (e.g., the "Real Estate Lobby") which provide the financial sinews for political warfare, the Republican strategists proclaimed their intentions to swing "left" in the next session.

Senator Taft, their leader on domestic policy, has three strings to his bow: Housing, Education (relief for teachers) and Health. The people, including the veterans, are stirred up about housing and rents, and the teachers have votes. The Republicans plan to raise the minimum wage level, do what they can for the DP's [Displaced Persons, WWII refugees], and give the Negro his FEPC and civil rights legislation, or try to.

All this means they are chasing votes in earnest. And it emphasizes the only tenable Democratic strategy, which is to continue to stay to the "left" of them.

The Democrats hold the Presidency. The Presidency is vastly more flexible than the Congress, which means merely that a President can always act much faster—and more often—than can any group of Senators or Congressmen.

The President has a great opportunity of presenting his program to the American people in his message on the State of the Union. He can present his recommendations simply and clearly to the Congress so that the people will know what the President is asking the Congress to do. There is little possibility that he will get much cooperation from the Congress but we want the President to be in position to receive the credit for whatever they do accomplish while also being in position to criticize the Congress for being obstructionists in failing to comply with other recommendations. This will be a fertile field for the development of campaign issues.

President Truman Campaigns for the Presidency, 1948

In Detroit, September 6 (Labor Day): Truman declared that the new Taft-Hartley law was "only a foretaste of what you will get if the Republican reaction is allowed to grow." That the old cycle of "boom and bust" would be renewed. In fact: "The 'boom' is on for them, and the 'bust' has begun for you." "The reactionary of today is a shrewd man," he declared. "He is in many ways much shrewder than the reactionaries of the twenties. He is a man with a calculating machine where his heart ought to be. He has learned a great deal about how to get his way by observing demagogues and reactionaries in other countries." "Labor has always had to fight for its gains. Now you are fighting for the whole future of the labor movement."

At Dexter, Iowa, September 18: "You remember the big boom and the great crash of 1929. You remember that in 1932 the position of the farmer had become so desperate that there was actual violence in many farming communities. You remember that insurance companies and banks took over much of the land of small independent farmers—223,000 farmers lost their farms." New Deal had rescued the nation's farmers, Truman continued, and they would continue to enjoy high prices unless "the Wall Street reactionaries . . . these gluttons of privilege" won back control of government. "The Republican Congress has already stuck a pitchfork in the farmer's back. . . . The Republican reactionaries . . . are attacking the whole structure of price supports for farm products. . . . These Republican gluttons of privilege are cold men. They are cunning men. . . . What they have taken away from you thus far would be only an appetizer for the economic tapeworm of big business."

At Denver, Colo., September 20: The Republicans were beginning "to tear down the whole western development program." "Ask yourself a question. Who benefits from the building of dams if the government does not also build transmission lines to carry the power from the dams to the people? Who benefits? The private power interests benefit, of course—at your expense."

At Roseville, Calif., Sept. 22: That the Republican Congress "tried to choke you to death in this valley" by cutting off appropriations for publicly owned electric power lines.

At Fresno, Calif., September 23: "You have got a terrible Congressman here in this district. . . . He is one of the worst obstructionists in the Congress. He has done everything he possibly could to cut the throats of the farmer and the laboring man. If you send him back, that will be your fault if you get your throats cut."

At Merced, Calif., September 23: "Republican policy is to let the big fellows get the big incomes, and let a little of it trickle down off the table like the crumbs [that] fell to Lazarus."

At Colton, Calif., September 24: "Republicans are just simply tools of big business. They believe that there is a top strata in the country that ought to run the government and that ought to profit from the government. . . ."

In Texas, September 27: "Republican candidates are apparently trying to sing the American voters to sleep with a lullaby about unity in domestic affairs. . . . They want the kind of unity that benefits the National Association of Manufacturers. . . . They don't want unity. They want surrender."

In Carbondale, Ill., October 1: The Republicans "have begun to nail the American consumer to the wall with spikes of greed."

In Louisville, Ky., October 1: "Some of you may think I'm exaggerating when I say that the Republican party is the party of special privilege. Some of you may think I am exaggerating when I say I've watched big business using its lobbies and spending its millions in Washington to turn the Congress away from its duty to serve the people."

"You don't have to take my word for it. Look at the record. Look at the record on inflation.

"Right after the end of the war, big business in this country set out to destroy the laws which were protecting the consumer against exploitation.

"This drive was spearheaded by the National Association of Manufacturers, the most powerful organization of big business in this country. . . .

"In 1946, the NAM set out on a well-planned and well-financed campaign to destroy price control. . . .

"[T]he director of public relations of the National Association of Manufacturers told how his organization spent $3,000,000 in 1946 to destroy OPA [the Office of Price Administration, the wartime agency charged with maintaining prices]. The NAM spent $1,500,000 on newspaper advertising. They set their own speakers to make a thousand talks before women's clubs, civic organizations and college students.

"A specially designed publication went to 37,000 school teachers, another one to 15,000 clergymen, another one to 35,000 farm leaders, and still another to 40,000 leaders of women's clubs. A special clip sheet went to 7,500 weekly newspapers and to 2,500 columnists and editorial writers.

"There never was a more vicious or a better organized campaign to mislead and deceive the American people. . . .

"Their own publicity director said that when NAM started the campaign against OPA a survey showed that 85 per cent of the people believed that OPA was absolutely necessary. In November, 1946, after the NAM campaign, only 26 per cent of the people believed that OPA was vital. . . .

"Well, prices adjusted themselves all right. They adjusted themselves the NAM way—the big business way—they went up and up."

Wilmington, Del., Oct. 6: Truman charged that whereas Herbert Hoover had once promised to put two cars in every garage, that Republican housing policy now sought to "put two families in every garage."

Philadelphia, Oct. 6: Truman declared that the Republicans wanted to roll up all the people in the country "into one big company union and run it for the benefit of the National Association of Manufacturers."

Chicago, Ill., October 25: "The real danger to our democracy . . . comes mainly from the powerful reactionary forces which are silently undermining our democratic institutions. . . . When a few men get control of the economy of a nation, they find a 'front man' to run the country for them." In Germany "they put money and influence behind Adolph Hitler. We know the rest of the story. We also know that in Italy, in the 1920s, powerful Italian businessmen backed Mussolini, and that in the 1930s Japanese financiers helped Tojo's military clique take over Japan."

HST warned against "a new outcropping of demogogues among us. Dangerous men, who are trying to win followers for their war on democracy, are attacking Catholics and Jews and Negroes and other minority races and religions."

New York, October 28: "It is my desire to help build in Palestine a strong, prosperous, free and independent state. It must be large enough, free enough, and strong enough to make its people self-supporting and secure."

Harlem, October 29: "Our determination to attain the goal of equal rights and equal opportunity must be resolute and unswerving."

A Left-Wing Critic Assesses the Fair Deal, 1949

The Fair Deal Budget and the Nation's Social Welfare Needs

The State of the Union Message, the Economic Report of the President, and the Federal Budget presented by the President in January, 1949, constitute a statement of our national goals and policies, a survey of our economic situation, and a program of government income and expenditures designed to carry into effect our national policies and achieve our national goals. While the State of the Union Message indicates in broad outline the Fair Deal program upon which the President was elected, it is to the Budget we must look for the clearest statement of how the President proposes to translate his Fair Deal promises into life.

In his State of the Union Message to Congress, President Truman enunciated these guiding principles of the Fair Deal: "We have rejected the discredited theory that the fortunes of the Nation should be in the hands of a privileged few. . . . We have abandoned the 'trickle down' concept of national prosperity. . . . Instead, we believe that our economic system should rest on a democratic foundation and that wealth should be created for the benefit of all."

Since it is the Budget for the coming fiscal year which translates the President's program into the arithmetic of income and expenditures, it is to the Budget that we must look for the dimensions of the "Fair Deal" which will actually be given to the American people by its government. We therefore begin this paper with an analysis of the President's Budget.

I. *The Budget*

The Budget states the expectation of receipts of $41 billion and of expenditures of $41.9 billion.

The total Budget expenditures involve an increase of $1.7 billion over

A. *Expenditures*
1. *Budget Expenditures*

The Budget expenditures are itemized as follows:

National Defense	$14.3 Billion
International Affairs and Finance	6.7
Veterans' Services and Benefits	5.5
Interest on Public Debt	5.5
General Government	1.2
National Resources	1.9
Agriculture and Agricultural Resources	1.7
Transportation and Communication	1.6
Labor	.2
Finance, Commerce & Industry	.1
Total Budget Expenditures Outside of Social Welfare	$38.7 Billion
Social Welfare, Health & Security	2.4
Housing & Community Facilities	.4
Education and General Research	.4
Total Social Welfare Expenditures	$ 3.2
Total Budget Expenditures	$41.9 Billion

estimated Budget expenditures for the previous fiscal year 1949. The net increase is largely due to an increase of $2.6 billion in national defense expenditures. Budget expenditures for social welfare, health and security, housing and community facilities, and education and research are to increase by $764 million. The major decrease is in expenditures for veterans' services and benefits, which are to be cut $1.3 billion.

A breakdown of the Budget reveals that 52¢ out of every dollar of expenditures will go for national defense, international affairs and atomic energy (some 90% of atomic energy expenditures being for military purposes). Veterans' services and benefits and the interest on the national debt will take 26¢. Thus, 78¢ out of every Budget dollar will be used to pay for armaments and the costs of World War I and World War II.

By contrast, expenditures for social welfare, health and security, housing and community facilities, and education and general research will amount to only 7.6¢. Less than 14.5¢ will be spent for all other government activities. The civilian side of the Budget is actually smaller than the 22% indicated here. Expenditures for aviation, mineral exploration, synthetic fuel production, etc. are included in the civilian Budget by the President, although a considerable portion of those appropriations are directly allocated for military purposes.

Budget expenditures under the new "Fair Deal" legislation proposed by the President will amount to no more than $529 million, or 1.3¢ of every Budget dollar. Thus, for social welfare, health and security, the President recommends an increase of $65 million in public assistance expenditures and $15 million to launch a system of medical care insurance. Under housing and community facilities, the President lists expenditures of $10 million for slum clearance, $129 million for low-rent housing and $20 million for farm housing. Under education and general research, the President proposes expenditures of $290 million for Federal aid to education.

Distribution of the Tax Load

If we break down the proposed tax load that the President wants the American people to assume, adding in the $4 billion in new taxes and the $2 billion in new payroll taxes, we find the following distribution:

Direct Taxes on Individuals	39.6%
Corporate Taxes	29.2%
Excise Taxes	16.0%
Federal Payroll Taxes	10.7%
Customs and Miscellaneous	4.5%
Total	100.0%

President Truman does not redistribute the Federal tax load in accordance with the democratic principle of taxation according to ability to pay. The Budget merely continues and aggravates the existing maldistribution of tax burdens. Since consumers bear the cost of excise taxes and payroll taxes, in addition to direct individual taxes, 66.3% of the total burden is carried directly and indirectly by individuals.

It should be noted that payroll and excise taxes, which have no relationship to the ability to pay and which bear most heavily upon the great mass of low income people in the country, constitute a total of $13.2 billion. Excise and payroll taxes, in fact, will contribute 26.7% of the government's tax revenues, approximately the same as contributed by corporations even after the proposed increase recommended by the President. Corporations actually will carry only 29.2% of the load. The remaining 4.5% of tax receipts will come from customs and miscellaneous taxes.

With two-thirds of the tax burden placed on the shoulders of the people, the Budget hardly approximates the Truman promise to abandon the 'trickle down' concept of national prosperity. His tax program does not cut a single cent from excise taxes; it does not lighten the tax burden of the low income groups. It proposes merely to increase corporate taxes by about $2.5 billion (assuming that the tax rate on corporations will be increased from 38% to 45%), when raising corporate taxes by $12 billion would still leave corporations with profits after taxes of $10 billion, twice as much as in 1939.

The American Medical Association
Plans an Attack on
"Socialized Medicine," 1949

To State Campaign Chairmen and State Medical Society Secretaries

Dear Fellow Workers:

The skeletonized Plan of Campaign presented in this booklet is designed to list, in simple steps, the basic responsibilities and activities of the *National, State* and *County* organizations.

Many States, we know, already have their projects well under way, and some of the States have budgeted activities (such as radio, newspaper and moving picture advertising) not covered in our simplified blueprint. Some of the States already have sent us outlines of their programs and others have plans which soon will reach us. So that there can be a helpful exchange of ideas between the States, we plan to make the most practical and helpful of these programs available to all of the State Societies.

Our State Plan of Campaign is intended as an outline of *basic activities,* which are essential to a successful campaign, and which can be carried on at little cost to the individual States, except for publicity, special mailings, distribution of campaign materials, etc.

Under this simplified program, the main expense to the States will be in time and energy. The A.M.A.'s National Campaign Headquarters will carry the bulk of the money cost, furnishing the States with all pamphlets, posters, reprint material, form speeches, resolutions and letters, cartoons, mats and other materials. The individual States can then amplify this basic program as local conditions may require, or as their funds permit.

Sincerely

WHITAKER & BAXTER

A Simplified Blueprint of the Campaign Against Compulsory Health Insurance

(Prepared by Clem Whitaker & Leone Baxter, directors of the National Education Campaign of the American Medical Association, for the information of State and County Medical Societies; February 21, 1949)

The general strategy, major issues and fundamental procedures of the campaign were fully outlined during the meeting of State Medical Society leaders with A.M.A. representatives and the campaign management in Chicago, February 12.

This skeletonized Plan of Campaign is simply a working blueprint, designed to define the separate responsibilities of the National, State and County organizations—and to outline the basic steps in getting the job in operation.

There is no need to review the general program, except to underline two major objectives:

First, this is *an affirmative campaign.* Defeating compulsory health insurance is the immediate job, but stopping the agitation for compulsory health insurance, by enrolling the people in sound voluntary health insurance systems, is our most important objective. That's the only way to resolve this problem.

Second, this must be *a broad, public campaign*—with leaders in every walk of life participating—not just a doctors' campaign. But the work of getting the people alerted and recruited for the battle, that's the responsibility of doctors and their lay representatives.

In setting up State and County campaigns, this basic precept of sound campaigning should be kept in mind:

A simple campaign program, vigorously and carefully carried out, is much more effective than an ambitious, complicated program, with some of the bases left uncovered.

Start with a program you know you can handle with the money and manpower available. Then amplify it later. Tireless personal work and unbounded enthusiasm for your cause are the most important factors in successful campaigning.

The National Campaign Structure

The Coordinating Committee of the American Medical Association, headed by Dr. Elmer L. Henderson, Chairman of the Board of Trustees, is charged with overall responsibility for the conduct of the campaign and is *the policy-making board of the campaign.*

The Campaign Directors are responsible to The Coordinating Committee.

The Coordinating Committee, in turn, is responsible to The House of Delegates.

The Job at National Headquarters

The job at National Campaign Headquarters, eliminating activities which cannot be covered in a thumb-nail sketch of operations, breaks down as follows:

1. Development and direction of *national planning and campaign strategy.*

2. Direction of *the National publicity campaign,* utilizing, largely, the existing, normal channels—the press associations, major newspapers, radio networks and television, the great national magazines, trade publications, newsletters, et cetera. *The first objective in this phase of the National campaign will be to get medicine off the defensive, and to conduct an affirmative program of education.* An intensive campaign *for* voluntary health insurance will be conducted concurrently with the drive *against* compulsory health insurance.

3. Direction of *the National-organization-endorsement drive,* designed to mobilize hundreds of the great National organizations in support of medicine's cause. This is a vital step in broadening the campaign into a public crusade. The National Headquarters will need constant aid from the State Societies in carrying out this part of the program. (Kansas spearheaded the work which brought an endorsement from the American Farm Bureau Federation; California first initiated the drive which brought favorable action from the American Legion National Convention.)

4. National *coordination of the work in the 48 States,* the District of Columbia and the several Territories. There will be a constant flow of in-

formation between National and State headquarters, with reports of changing conditions and vital developments in the campaign. Programs and ideas which have worked successfully in some of the States will be made available, through a National exchange service, to the others.

5. *Production of all basic campaign literature and* materials, including posters, pamphlets, leaflets, reprints, form resolutions and form speeches, cartoons and mats, publicity which can be adapted for State use, lists of organizations, conventions, etc. This is one of the biggest and most urgent jobs in National Headquarters—and the materials will start to flow to the States just as fast as copy-writers, artists, engravers and printers can turn out finished products. As an indication of the tremendous production problems involved, in carrying our story direct to the American people, press runs of pamphlets and other materials are expected to total 100 million copies during the first twelve months of the campaign. About one-third of that stockpile of "ammunition" will be released directly through National facilities, with the remaining two-thirds destined for distribution through the States.

6. Organization and direction of *a National Speakers Bureau* to cover top-assignment speaking engagements. State Medical Societies are urgently requested to send in the names of dynamic speakers (either doctors or laymen) who are *qualified* and *willing* to take out-of-State assignments. Our immediate goal: *Two top men from each State!*

7. Direction of *a National Women's Campaign,* geared to bring the support of the major women's organizations, and to arouse women throughout the Nation to the threat of socialized medicine.

8. Active *cooperation with the pre-paid medical and hospital plans and the accident and health insurance companies in an all-out drive to provide the American people with voluntary health insurance coverage.* Special literature will be produced for use of the voluntary systems—and the A.M.A. campaign will be closely meshed with the promotional work of the Blue Shield, Blue Cross and private indemnity companies.

The State Medical Societies' Job

One of the first jobs of every State Medical Society (where it hasn't already been done) will be to organize every County Society into a hard-driving campaign organization.

Due to varying local conditions, each State, of course, will work out its own campaign structure—and the relationship between the State and County Societies in the conduct of the campaign. Many of the States already have scheduled meetings of County representatives, patterned somewhat after the National meeting of State leaders in Chicago on February 12. In other States, battle orders are going out by letter, telegraph and telephone.

Auxiliaries

Above all, don't overlook or discount the Auxiliaries in setting up your State-County campaign organization. The women may be one of the answers to your problem of literature distribution; they certainly should be of positive assistance in getting endorsements from women's clubs, in talking to club editors on the newspapers, in helping to build an effective Speakers' Bureau. A doctor's wife usually has more time than a busy doctor—and she has a personal stake in this campaign!

Governor Thomas E. Dewey and Dwight D. Eisenhower Discuss Presidential Politics, 1949

July 7 [1949]

Gov[ernor]. [Thomas] Dewey [Republican-New York] visited by yesterday. He stayed at my house for 2 hours. He say's he's worried about the country's future—& that *I* am the only one who can do anything about it.

The Gov. says that I am a public possession—that such standing as I have in the affections or respect of our citizenry is like[-]wise public property. All of this, though, must be carefully guarded to use in the service of all the people.

(Although I'm merely repeating some one else's exposition, the mere writing of such things almost makes me dive under the table.)

He feels that N.Y. [New York] State is vital to any Republican Aspirant to Presidency.

He assumes I am a Republican & would like to be President. (When this last came out I was flabbergasted. I must have had a funny look on my face, because he said, "I know you disclaimed political ambition in a verbose, wordy document but that was when you were just a soldier."

(This reaffirms a conviction I have formed, which is that no denial of political ambition will ever be believed by a politician—unless the disclaimer is so old he is tottering rapidly to the grave. In this case the refusal would not be a denial of ambition—merely an expression of regret.)

The Governor then gave me the reasons he believed that only I (if I should carefully preserve my assets) can save this country from going to hades in the handbasket of paternalism—socialism,—dictatorship. He knows that I consider our greatest danger the unawareness of our majorities while aggregated minorities work their hands into our pockets and their seats to the places of the mighty! So he dwelt at length on the preservation of freedom—my favorite subject!!!!

The Gov. Next outlined a political career for me—starting very soon.

a. Declare my Republicanism
b. Run for Governor of N.Y. State & be elected.
c. Accept nomination for Presidency—but always keep fairly still as to my political views.

His reasoning is as follows:

All middle class citizens of education have a common belief that tendencies toward centralization & paternalism must be halted & reversed. No

one who voices these views can be elected. He quotes efforts of Hoover—
Landon, Wilkie, [and] Himself.

Consequently, we must look around for someone of great popularity &
who has not frittered away his political assets by taking positive stands against
national planning, etc., etc.

Elect such a man to Presidency, *after which* he must lead it back to safe
channels & paths.

Senator Joseph McCarthy
Denounces the Democrats, 1950

The great difference between our western Christian world and the atheistic
Communist world is not political, gentlemen, it is moral. For instance, the
Marxian idea of confiscating the land and factories and running the entire
economy as a single enterprise is momentous. Likewise, Lenin's invention
of the one-party police state as a way to make Marx's idea work is hardly
less momentous.

Stalin's resolute putting across of these two ideas, of course, did much
to divide the world. With only these differences, however, the east and west
could most certainly still live in peace.

The real, basic difference, however, lies in the religion of immoralism—
invented by Marx, preached feverishly by Lenin, and carried to unimaginable
extremes by Stalin. This religion of immoralism, if the Red half of the world
triumphs—and well it may, gentlemen—this religion of immoralism will
more deeply wound and damage mankind than any conceivable economic
or political system.

Karl Marx dismissed God as a hoax, and Lenin and Stalin have added
in clear-cut, unmistakable language their resolve that no nation, no people
who believe in a god, can exist side by side with their communistic state.

Karl Marx, for example, expelled people from his Communist Party for
mentioning such things as love, justice, humanity [,] or morality. He called
this "soulful ravings" and "sloppy sentimentality."

While Lincoln was a relatively young man in his late thirties, Karl Marx
boasted that the Communist specter was haunting Europe. Since that time,
hundreds of millions of people and vast areas of the world have come under
Communist domination. Today, less than 100 years after Lincoln's death,
Stalin brags that this Communist specter is not only haunting the world, but
is about to completely subjugate it.

Today we are engaged in a final all-out battle between communistic
atheism and Christianity. The modern champions of communism have selected this as the time, and ladies and gentlemen, the chips are down—they
are truly down.

Lest there be any doubt that the time has been chosen, let us go directly
to the leader of communism today—Joseph Stalin. Here is what he said—
not back in 1928, not before the war, not during the war—but 2 years after
the last war was ended: "To think that the Communist revolution can be
carried out peacefully, within the framework of a Christian democracy,

means one has either gone out of one's mind and lost all normal understanding, or has grossly and openly repudiated the Communist revolution."

This is what was said by Lenin in 1919—and quoted with approval by Stalin in 1947:

"We are living," says Lenin, "not merely in a state, but in a system of states, and the existence of the Soviet Republic side by side with Christian states for a long time is unthinkable—one or the other must triumph in the end. And that before that end supervenes, a series of frightful collisions between the Soviet Republic and the bourgeois states will be inevitable."

Ladies and gentlemen, can there be anyone tonight who is so blind as to say that the war is not on? Can there be anyone who fails to realize that the Communist world has said the time is now—that this is the time for the showdown between the democratic Christian world and the communistic atheistic world?

Unless we face this fact, we shall pay the price that must be paid by those who wait too long.

Six years ago, at the time of the first conference to map out the peace, there was within the Soviet orbit, 180,000,000 people. Lined up on the anti-totalitarian side there were in the world at that time, roughly 1,625,000,000 people. Today, only 6 years later, there are 80,000,000,000 [*sic*] people under the absolute domination of Soviet Russia—an increase of over 400 percent. On our side, the figure has shrunk to around 500,000 [*sic*]. In other words, in less than 6 years the odds have changed from 9 to 1 in our favor to 8 to 1 against us.

This indicates the swiftness of the tempo of Communist victories and American defeats in the cold war. As one of our outstanding historical figures once said, "When a great democracy is destroyed, it will not be from enemies without, but rather because of enemies within."

The truth of this statement is becoming terrifyingly clear as we see this country each day losing on every front.

At war's end we were physically the strongest nation on earth—and at least potentially the most powerful intellectually and morally. Ours could have been the honor of being a beacon in the desert of destruction—shining proof that civilization was not yet ready to destroy itself. Unfortunately, we have failed miserably and tragically to arise to the opportunity.

The reason why we find ourselves in a position of impotency is not because our only powerful potential enemy has sent men to invade our shores—but rather because of the traitorous actions of those who have been treated so well by this Nation. It has not been the less fortunate, or members of minority groups who have been traitorous to this Nation—but rather those who have had all the benefits that the wealthiest Nation on earth has had to offer—the finest homes, the finest college education and the finest jobs in government we can give.

This is glaringly true in the State Department. There the bright young men who are born with silver spoons in their mouths are the ones who have been most traitorous. . . . And, ladies and gentlemen, while I cannot take the time to name all the men in the State Department who have been named as active members of the Communist Party and members of a spy ring, I have here in my hand a list of 205—a list of names that were made known to the Secretary of State [Dean Acheson] as being members of the Communist Party and who nevertheless are still working and shaping policy in the State Department.

One thing to remember in discussing the Communists in our Government is that we are not dealing with spies who get 30 pieces of silver to steal the blueprints of a new weapon. We are dealing with a far more sinister type of activity because it permits the enemy to guide and shape our policy.

Television and the Selling of the President, 1956

1. (OPEN ON)
CU [close-up] of Eisenhower's face grinning.
A CU of him on speaker's platform preferably
at convention, waving to roaring crowds.

NARRATOR: This is the most famous grin in the world.

2. (CUT TO)
Longer shot of above to include crowd.

NARRATOR: This is probably the best loved man in all the world. A man elected President of the United States by the largest majority in history.

3. (CUT TO)
Shot of "Eisenhower" banner being brought down convention aisle.

NARRATOR: People in America . . . people all over the world . . . look to this one man with their hopes for the future.

4. (CUT TO)
ECU [Extreme close-up] of "I like Ike" button.

NARRATOR: *Everybody* seems to "like Ike"

5. (CUT BACK TO)
Long shot of Ike waving on platform.

NARRATOR: Why do people "like Ike"? The experts say it's because of his integrity . . . his basic humility. But it's also because . . . people seem to know . . . what Ike thinks of *them.*

6. (CUT TO)
Shot of Eisenhower on platform waving. This is shot from behind the president, looking out on the convention floor.

The Selling of the President, 1956. Citizens for Eisenhower–Nixon, 1956, box 6, Young and Rubicam Papers, Dwight D. Eisenhower Library.

NARRATOR: What does President Eisenhower think of all the people in the world who look to him for hope? What does he think of America and its future?

7. (DISSOLVE TO BLACK)

NARRATOR: What does President Eisenhower think of *you?*

8. (DISSOLVE UP)
Average looking man in front lawn of average looking house.

NARRATOR: Well, first he thinks you're an *individual.* There's no such thing as a "common" man to President Eisenhower. You're an individual with rights, privileges . . . and responsibilities. And one of your basic rights is the security that your national government is sincerely and honestly working for your best interests.

9. Wife and children come out of door to man.

NARRATOR: It is your right to bring children into the world [in] the secure knowledge that their future is clear and uncluttered by staggering debt . . . overwhelming inflation.

10. (CUT TO)
Group of school children running up school steps. A couple are colored.

NARRATOR: President Eisenhower believes that it is your privilege to send your children to the school of their choice.

11. (CUT TO)
CU of face of colored child.

12. (CUT TO)
Guided missile launching.

NARRATOR: President Eisenhower believes that you're willing to assume the responsibility of *strength* . . . that prevents wars from happening.

13. (CUT TO)
Factory workers.

NARRATOR: He thinks that you're entitled to a steady job . . . and that you shouldn't have to surrender the major part of your earnings back to the government in taxes.

14. (CUT TO)
Farmer driving home down road on tractor.

NARRATOR: President Eisenhower thinks that *you* have integrity . . . basic humility . . . and honesty. That *you* as an individual want only the right to make your own way in the world with decency and dignity.

15.   (CUT TO)
Shot of mammoth utilities project (St. Lawrence Seaway).

NARRATOR: And what does Ike think of your *future?* Well, he's a man who looks toward tomorrow with confidence and excitement. And under Ike, America has begun more projects for tomorrow than ever before. Projects that will make America stronger and greater every single day of *your* lifetime . . . and your children's.

16.   (CUT BACK TO)
Ike at convention.

NARRATOR: President Eisenhower is an optimist. He believes that all of us can meet the challenges of today and tomorrow with confidence.

17.   (CUT TO)
CU of smiling Ike's face.

NARRATOR: And maybe that's part of the reason so many of us like *Ike.* Ike likes *us.*

President Eisenhower Warns of the Military-Industrial Complex, 1961

A vital element in keeping the peace is our military establishment. Our arms must be mighty, ready for instant action, so that no potential aggressor may be tempted to risk his own destruction.

Our military organization today bears little relation to that known by any of my predecessors in peacetime, or indeed by the fighting men of World War II or Korea.

Until the latest of our world conflicts, the United States had no armaments industry. American makers of plowshares could, with time and as required, make swords as well. But now we can no longer risk emergency improvisation of national defense; we have been compelled to create a permanent armaments industry of vast proportions. Added to this, three and a half million men and women are directly engaged in the defense establishment. We annually spend on military security more than the net income of all United States corporations.

This conjunction of an immense military establishment and a large arms industry is new in the American experience. The total influence—economic, political, even spiritual—is felt in every city, every State house, every office of the Federal government. We recognize the imperative need for this development. Yet we must not fail to comprehend its grave implications. Our toil, resources and livelihood are all involved; so is the very structure of our society.

In the councils of government, we must guard against the acquisition of unwarranted influence, whether sought or unsought, by the military-industrial complex. The potential for the disastrous rise of misplaced power exists and will persist.

We must never let the weight of this combination endanger our liberties or democratic processes. We should take nothing for granted. Only an alert and knowledgeable citizenry can compel the proper meshing of the huge industrial and military machinery of defense with our peaceful methods and goals, so that security and liberty may prosper together.

Akin to, and largely responsible for the sweeping changes in our industrial-military posture, has been the technological revolution during recent decades.

In this revolution, research has become central; it also becomes more formalized, complex, and costly. A steadily increasing share is conducted for, by, or at the direction of, the Federal government.

Today, the solitary inventor, tinkering in his shop, has been overshadowed by task forces of scientists in laboratories and testing fields. In the same fashion, the free university, historically the fountainhead of free ideas and scientific discovery, has experienced a revolution in the conduct of research. Partly because of the huge costs involved, a government contract becomes virtually a substitute for intellectual curiosity. For every old blackboard there are now hundreds of new electronic computers.

The prospect of domination of the nation's scholars by Federal employment, project allocations, and the power of money is ever present— and is gravely to be regarded.

Yet, in holding scientific research and discovery in respect, as we should, we must also be alert to the equal and opposite danger that public policy could itself become the captive of a scientific-technological elite.

It is the task of statesmanship to mold, to balance, and to integrate these and other forces, new and old, within the principles of our democratic system—ever aiming toward the supreme goals of our free society.

☒ E S S A Y S

In the first essay, historian Alonzo L. Hamby of Ohio University, who has written extensively on the Truman presidency, argues that Truman played a key role in the transformation of New Deal liberalism and the emergence of a new, more moderate "Cold War" liberalism. He praises Truman and the new liberals for what he views as their constructive adaptation to the new foreign and domestic circumstances of the postwar era. In the second essay, Robert Griffith of the University of Maryland at College Park argues that the Eisenhower presidency marked an important, though not entirely successful, effort to forge a new conservative politics and political economy that would adapt traditional conservative concerns to the new postwar world of large-scale organization and global diplomacy.

Harry Truman and the New Cold War Liberalism

ALONZO L. HAMBY

"Every segment of our population and every individual has a right to expect from our Government a fair deal," declared Harry S. Truman in early 1949. In 1945 and 1946 the Truman administration had almost crumbled under the stresses of postwar reconversion; in 1947 and 1948 it had fought a frustrating, if politically rewarding, battle with the Republican Eightieth Congress. Buoyed by his remarkable victory of 1948 and given Democratic majorities in both houses of Congress, Truman hoped to achieve an impressive record of domestic reform. The president systematized his past proposals, added some new ones, and gave his program a name that would both connect his administration with the legacy of the New Deal and give it a distinct identity. The Fair Deal, while based solidly upon the New Deal tradition, differed from its predecessor in significant aspects of mood and detail. It reflected not only Truman's own aspirations but also a style of liberalism that had begun to move beyond the New Deal during World War II and had come to maturity during the early years of the cold war—"the vital center."

Throughout the history of the United States the main stream of reform has been within the broad Lockean-capitalist consensus to which most Americans subscribe. The Great Depression, however, had caused liberal reformers to question capitalism as never before; mass unemployment at home and the rise of an aggressive fascism out of the ruins of capitalism abroad seemed to provide proof that the old system had failed beyond repair. One logical response with appeal to many reform thinkers and leaders was the movement for a popular front of all reform and radical forces, most strongly united by a determination to stop the spread of fascism but also seeking newer and better socioeconomic arrangements, even "revolutionary" ones. The New Deal itself, faced with the actual responsibility of governing, took a far more moderate course, searching for a viable middle way that would preserve capitalism; yet even the New Dealers, unable to overcome the depression, were increasingly driven to the conclusion that capitalism had become incapable of the growth needed to provide reasonably full employment.

The thirties did not exactly constitute the fabled "Red Decade" of right-wing mythologists. Most liberals who worked within the government sought American solutions to American problems and appear to have been only marginally influenced by foreign examples. Those outside the government were more likely to look toward European patterns. The most enduring appeal they found was in Scandinavian welfarism, but many were at least provisionally drawn to Soviet communism. A liberal of the thirties, quite in line with the popular-front mood, was more likely to think of himself as part of an undifferentiated Left and more prone to consider substitutes for capitalism than were earlier progressives. The failure of capitalism at home

---

"The Vital Center, the Fair Deal, and the Quest for a Liberal Political Economy" by Alonzo L. Hamby, from *American Historical Review*, June 1972, pp. 653–678. © Alonzo L. Hamby.

and abroad did not throw the liberals en masse into the Communist party, but it shook old assumptions to an extent that left few unaffected.

Temporarily shattered by the Nazi-Soviet Pact of 1939, popular-front foreign policy staged a resurgence during World War II and received an aura of legitimacy from President Roosevelt's effort to forge a lasting alliance with the Soviet Union. During the war and the years immediately following, advocates of Soviet-American friendship could use the Roosevelt name and symbolism as a potent appeal. Yet at the same time World War II eroded the domestic side of popular frontism. The war eliminated the depression— as the New Deal had not—and demonstrated the potential of American industry. To a large extent, moreover, businessmen managed the economic war effort, and, while the liberals frequently criticized them on matters of detail, it was hard to refute the statistics of success. One result was a wide-spread repudiation of the psychology of scarcity, which had grown out of the long years of the depression. Leading progressives popularized the vision of an ever-expanding capitalist economy balanced by Keynesian fiscal meth-ods and buffered by extensive social welfare programs. Their intellectual leader was the eminent economist Alvin H. Hansen and their political leader was Vice-President Henry A. Wallace, who demonstrated that it had become possible, even natural, to be a popular fronter in foreign policy and an advocate of "progressive capitalism" at home. The liberal mission was no longer to achieve a new socioeconomic system or even to prop up a "mature," worn-out economy; it was to realize capitalism's capacity for endless growth.

The cold war completed the demise of the popular-front mood. Groups and individuals that thought of themselves as liberal came increasingly to perceive the Soviet Union as an expansionist, totalitarian force and the American Communist party as the slavish, antiliberal representative of Soviet despotism. In 1947 an influential group of liberals established Americans for Democratic Action (ADA) with the express purpose of isolating Communists and pro-Communists from the main stream of liberal politics. Key foreign policy events that followed—the Russian rejection of the Marshall Plan, the Czech coup, and the Berlin Blockade—inclined most progressives toward the ADA position. In 1948 the *New Republic,* probably the most sensitive barometer of progressive opinion, rejected the popular-front style of Henry Wallace's presidential candidacy and endorsed Truman. Wallace's weak showing on election day demonstrated a massive liberal repudiation of the Soviet Union and the Communist party. . . .

Arthur M. Schlesinger, Jr. gave the new liberalism a name with the publication of *The Vital Center.* An exercise in political philosophy and an exhortation to American progressives, the volume won an impressive re-ception. "It seemed to me one of those books which may suddenly and clearly announce the spirit of an age to itself," wrote Jonathan Daniels. Deeply influenced personally and intellectually by Reinhold Niebuhr, Schles-inger castigated the popular-front liberals as sentimental believers in progress and human perfectionism who, yearning for utopias, had been seduced by the surface idealism of communism and the Soviet experiment. Awake only to the evils of fascism, they had sympathized with at least some aspects of the Soviet experience and had accepted the Communists as allies in a common struggle, not understanding that such a tactic could lead only to self-destruction. The "restoration of radical nerve" had come with the rise of a non-Communist Left in Europe and the United States, largely through the efforts of younger liberals whose impressions of the Soviet Union stemmed from the Stalinist purges of the 1930s rather than the idealism of the Russian Revolution. The new liberalism—or "radicalism" as Schlesinger preferred to call it—unconditionally rejected all varieties of totalitarianism. Applied to foreign affairs it stood for a dual policy of vigilantly containing communism and encouraging the democratic Left abroad. Believing "in the integrity of the individual, in the limited state, in due process of law, in empiricism and gradualism," it was acutely aware of the weaknesses of human nature and of the dangers of excessive concentration of power. Devoted to the furtherance of individual liberty, it stood for a mixed economy, featuring partial government planning and ownership, antitrust action to discipline private big business, and welfare programs to provide a minimum of security and subsistence to all. The conception of liberalism as a sort of centrism had its liabilities. Schlesinger found it natural to identify with "responsible conservatives" such as Charles Evans Hughes and Henry I. Stimson; liberals, he suggested, might find common cause with this group, especially on matters of civil rights and civil liberties. Doubtless he was correct, and it was tempting, after militantly rejecting the revolutionary totalitarian ideology of communism, to conceive of the liberal effort to preserve humane, democratic values as akin to an intelligent conservatism; yet even the creed of a Hughes or a Stimson provided few answers for the problems that preoccupied the liberals. Unfortunately it was but a short step from the vital center to the superficialities of the "New Conservatism" of the 1950s.

Whatever its inner weaknesses, the vital-center approach gave the liberal movement a moral integrity and consistency that had been absent during the popular-front era. Its implications, moreover, went beyond the affairs of diplomacy or the tactical wisdom of a liberal-Communist alliance: its approach to political economy rejected what remained of domestic popular frontism and idealized the New Deal as an effort to establish a mixed economy that would preserve the essentials of capitalism while mitigating its abuses. Even the business community was recognized as a potentially constructive, if frequently wrongheaded, force in American life. The vital-center liberals looked to Niebuhr for a sociopolitical theory and to Keynes for an approach to economics, convinced that this combination provided the best possible foundation for human freedom. In 1948 a group of Keynesians published the major liberal economic manifesto of the Truman era, *Saving American Capitalism*. The title accurately represented the way in which vital-center liberalism was a return to the traditional American progressive impulse.

The legislative goals Truman announced for his administration, while not devised to meet the needs of an abstract theory, were well in tune with the vital-center approach: anti-inflation measures, a more progressive tax structure, repeal of the Taft-Hartley Act, a higher minimum wage, a farm program based on the concepts of abundant production and parity income [the Brannan Plan], resource development and public power programs, expansion of social security, national medical insurance, federal aid to education, extensive housing legislation, and civil rights bills. The president's most controversial request was for authority to increase plant facilities in such basic industries as steel, preferably through federal financing of private enterprise but through outright government construction if necessary. Roundly condemned by right-wing opponents as "socialistic" and soon dropped by the administration, the proposal was actually intended to meet the demands of a prosperous, growing capitalist economy and emerged from the Fair Deal's search for the proper degree of government intervention to preserve the established American economic structure. "Between the reactionaries of the extreme left with their talk about revolution and class warfare, and the reactionaries of the extreme right with their hysterical cries of bankruptcy and despair, lies the way of progress," Truman declared in November 1949.

The Fair Deal was a conscious effort to continue the purpose of the New Deal but not necessarily its methods. Not forced to meet the emergencies of economic depression, given a solid point of departure by their predecessors, and led by a president more prone than FDR to demand programmatic coherence, the Fair Dealers made a systematic effort to discover techniques that would be at once more equitable and more practical in alleviating the problems of unequal wealth and opportunity. Thinking in terms of abundance rather than scarcity, they attempted to adapt the New Deal tradition to postwar prosperity. Seeking to go beyond the New Deal while preserving its objectives, the Truman administration advocated a more sweeping and better-ordered reform agenda. Yet in the quest for political means, Truman and the vital-center liberals could only fall back upon one of the oldest dreams of American reform—the Jacksonian-Populist vision of a union of producing classes, an invincible farmer-labor coalition. While superficially plausible, the Fair Deal's political strategy proved too weak to handle the burden thrust upon it.

The Fair Deal seemed to oscillate between militancy and moderation. New Dealers had frequently gloried in accusations of "liberalism" or "radicalism"; Fair Dealers tended to shrink from such labels. The New Dealers had often lusted for political combat; the Fair Dealers were generally more low keyed. Election campaigns demanded an aggressiveness that would arouse the Democratic presidential party, but the continued strength of the conservative coalition in Congress dictated accommodation in the postelection efforts to secure passage of legislative proposals. Such tactics reflected Truman's personal political experience and instincts, but they also developed naturally out of the climate of postwar America. The crisis of economic depression had produced one style of political rhetoric; the problems of prosperity and inflation brought forth another. . . .

During 1949 and early 1950 the Truman administration managed a record of substantial legislative accomplishment, but it consisted almost entirely of additions to such New Deal programs as the minimum wage, social security, and public power. The Housing Act of 1949, with its provisions for large-scale public housing, appeared to be a breakthrough, but weak administration, local opposition, and inadequate financing subsequently vitiated hopes that it would help the poor. Acting on his executive authority, Truman took an important step by forcing the army to agree to a policy of desegregation. The heart of the Fair Deal, however—repeal of the Taft-Hartley Act, civil rights legislation, aid to education, national medical insurance, and the Brannan Plan—failed in Congress. Given the power of the well-entrenched conservative coalition and a widespread mood of public apathy about big new reforms, Truman could only enlarge upon the record of his predecessor.

Democratic strategists hoped for a mandate in the congressional elections of 1950. In the spring Truman made a successful whistle-stop tour of the West and Midwest, rousing party enthusiasm and apparently demonstrating a solid personal popularity. Loveland's victory provided further encouragement, and in California the aggressive Fair Dealer Helen Gahagan Douglas won the Democratic nomination for the Senate by a thumping margin. Two incumbent Fair Deal supporters—Frank Graham of North Carolina and Claude Pepper of Florida—lost their senatorial primaries, but, as Southerners who had run afoul of the race issue, they did not seem to be indicators of national trends. Nevertheless, the hope of cutting into the strength of the conservative opposition ran counter to the historical pattern of mid-term elections. The beginning of the Korean War at the end of June destroyed any chances of success.

The most immediate impact of Korea was to refuel an anti-Communist extremism that might otherwise have sputtered out. Senator Joseph R. McCarthy had begun his rise to prominence in February 1950, but he had failed to prove any of his multiple allegations and seemed definitively discredited by the investigations of a special Senate committee headed by Millard Tydings. McCarthy, it is true, was a talented demagogue who should have been taken more seriously by the liberals and the Truman administration in early 1950, but it seems probable that his appeal would have waned more quickly if the cold war with communism had not suddenly become hot. As it was, many of his Senate colleagues rushed to emulate him. In September 1950 Congress passed the McCarran Internal Security Act; only a handful of congressional liberals dared dissent from the overwhelming vote in favor. Truman's subsequent veto was intelligent and courageous, but was issued more for the history books than with any real hope of success. In the subsequent campaign, liberal Democrats, whether they had voted for the McCarran Act or not, found themselves facing charges of softness toward communism.

The war hurt the administration in other ways. It touched off a brief but serious inflation, which caused widespread consumer irritation. By stimulating demand for agricultural products it brought most farm prices up to parity levels and thereby undercut whatever attractiveness the Brannan Plan had developed in rural areas. Finally it removed the Democratic party's most effective spokesman—the president—from active participation in the campaign. Forced to play the role of war leader, Truman allowed himself only one major partisan speech, delivered in St. Louis on the eve of the balloting.

The Fair Deal might have been a winning issue in a nation oriented toward domestic concerns and recovering from an economic recession; it had much less appeal in a country obsessed with Communist aggression and experiencing an inflationary war boom. The reaction against the administration was especially strong in the Midwest. Indiana's Democratic aspirant for the Senate asked Oscar Ewing to stay out of the state. In Iowa, Loveland desperately attempted to reverse his identification with the Brannan Plan. In Missouri the managers of senatorial candidate Thomas C. Hennings, Jr. privately asked White House aides to make Truman's St. Louis speech a foreign policy address that would skip lightly over Fair Deal issues. A few days before the election the columnist Stewart Alsop returned from a Midwestern trip convinced that the region had never been more conservative. Nevertheless, Truman's political advisers, and probably Truman himself, felt that the Fair Deal still had appeal. Given the basic strength of the economy and the victories in Korea that followed the Inchon landing, the White House believed that the Democrats could easily rebut generalized charges of fumbling or softness toward communism. In mid-October the Democratic National Committee and many local leaders were so confident of success that their main concern was simply to get out the vote.

The November results, however, showed a Democratic loss of twenty-eight seats in the House of Representatives and five seats in the Senate. Truman seized every opportunity to remind all who would listen that the numbers were small by traditional mid-term standards. Liberal political analysts, including Kenneth Hechler, a White House staffer, and Gus Tyler of the International Ladies Garment Workers Union, subjected the returns to close scrutiny and all but pronounced a Democratic victory. All the same, most of the Democrats who went under had been staunch Fair Dealers. Republican candidates, including John Marshall Butler in Maryland, Richard M. Nixon in California, Everett McKinley Dirksen in Illinois, and Robert A. Taft in Ohio, scored some of the most spectacular GOP victories by blending right-wing conservatism with McCarthyism. The Midwestern losses were especially disappointing. Hechler argued that the corn-belt vote primarily reflected urban defections and that the Democrats had done comparatively well among farmers. Perhaps so, but for all practical purposes the results put an end to the Brannan strategy of constructing a farmer-labor coalition. Truman was probably more accurate than Hechler when, with characteristic overstatement, he privately expressed his disappointment: "The main trouble with the farmers is that they hate labor so badly that they will not vote for their own interests."

Thereafter, with the Chinese intervention transforming the Korean War into a more serious conflict and with the dismissal of General Douglas MacArthur in April 1951, Truman faced a tough attack from a Republican opposition determined to capitalize upon the frustrations of Korea. Finding it necessary to place party unity above all else, he quietly shelved most of his domestic legislative program and sought to bring the conservative wing of his party behind his military and defense policies. He secretly asked Richard B. Russell of Georgia, the kingpin of the Southern conservatives, to assume the Democratic leadership in the Senate. Russell, content with the substance of power, declined and gave his nod to Ernest W. McFarland of Arizona, an amiable tool of the Southern bloc; Truman made no effort to prevent McFarland's selection as Senate majority leader. The president's State of the Union message was devoted almost entirely to foreign policy and defense mobilization and mentioned social welfare programs only as an afterthought. Subsequently Truman told a press conference that while he supported the Fair Deal as much as ever, "first things come first, and our defense programs must have top priority."

Truman's success in achieving a minimum degree of party unity became apparent in the weeks of investigation and accusation that followed General MacArthur's return to America. Russell, playing the role of parliamentarian-statesman to the hilt and cashing in on his great prestige with senators of both parties, chaired the Senate committee that looked into the MacArthur incident, and he saw to it that the administration was able to deliver a thorough rebuttal to the general. The Northern liberal, Brien McMahon of Connecticut, relentlessly grilled hostile witnesses. The Western representative of oil and gas interests, Robert S. Kerr of Oklahoma, lashed out at MacArthur himself with a vehemence and effectiveness that no other Democrat could match. The tandem efforts of Russell, McMahon, and Kerr demonstrated the new party solidarity, but in terms of the Fair Deal the price was high.

In July 1951 the Federal Power Commission renounced the authority to regulate "independent" (non-pipeline-owning) natural gas producers. The ruling amounted to an administrative enactment of a bill, sponsored by Kerr, which Truman had vetoed a year earlier; Truman's close friend and most recent appointee to the Federal Power Commission, Mon Wallgren, cast the deciding vote. Although he talked like a militant liberal in a private conversation with ADA leaders, the president stalled throughout 1951 on repeated demands for the establishment of a Korean War Fair Employment Practices Committee. In December the administration established an ineffective Committee on Government Contract Compliance. Other domestic programs were soft-pedaled to near-invisibility.

Yet even the Korean War was not entirely inimical to reform. Its exigencies forced the army to transform its policy of integration into practice. Korea also provided a test for one of the basic underpinnings of the Fair Deal—Leon Keyserling's philosophy of economic expansion. Truman did not in the end fully embrace Keyserling's policies, but in the main he followed the guidance of his chief economic adviser. The Korean War years demonstrated the extent to which Keyserling's economics diverged from conventional New Deal–World War II Keynesianism and revealed both the strengths and weaknesses of his approach.

From the outbreak of the fighting, most liberals favored either immediate strong economic controls akin to those that had held down inflation in World War II or at least the establishment of stand-by machinery that could impose them rapidly. Truman disliked such measures on the basis of both principle and politics. He and his diplomatic advisers also wanted to signal the Soviet Union that the United States regarded the North Korean attack as a limited challenge meriting a limited response. Keyserling's expansionary economics provided an attractive alternative to the liberal clamor for controls. Convinced that extensive controls would put the economy in a strait jacket and retard the expansion necessary to meet both consumer and defense needs and assuming a North Korean defeat in a few months, the administration decided to accept a short-term, war-scare inflation (probably unavoidable in any case) and concentrate on economic growth, which would be underwritten in large measure by tax incentives for business. An expanding economy would be the best long-term answer to inflation: growth policies could fit a small war into the economy, avoid the social and political strains accompanying wartime controls, and reduce inflationary pressures to a level at which fiscal and monetary policies could contain them. Liberals outside the administration watched with alarm as prices went up, but Truman and Keyserling continued to gamble on a quick end to the war and the development of an economy capable of producing both guns and butter.

Their plan might have worked fairly well had the United States not overreached itself militarily in Korea. The Chinese intervention of November 1950 wrecked hopes of a quick recovery, set off another round of scare buying, and intensified war demands upon the economy. The administration quickly threw up a price-wage control structure, but by the end of February 1951, eight months after the beginning of the Korean conflict, the consumer price index had risen eight per cent (an annual rate of twelve per cent). Keyserling agreed that the new situation necessitated controls, but he accepted them with reluctance and sought to keep them as simple as possible, even at the risk of benefiting profiteers. "We'll never be able to out-control the Russians," he told a Senate committee, "but we can out-produce them." Speaking to an ADA economic conference, he asserted that many liberals, in their opposition to tax breaks for large business and in their demands for stronger controls, were confusing the Korean War with World War II and "engaging merely in hackneyed slogans out of the past."

Most liberals disagreed with Keyserling's emphases. As production was his first imperative, an end to the wage-price spiral was theirs. "Unless we are willing seriously to endanger the basis of existence of the American middle class, we must stop prices from rising," wrote Hans Landsberg in the *Reporter*. The liberals assumed that economic expansion was possible within a framework of rigid, tightly administered controls. Chester Bowles observed that the controlled economy of World War II had turned out a twofold increase in industrial production. John Kenneth Galbraith rejected the idea that Keyserling's expansionary policies could outrun the inflationary pressures they themselves created. The bulk of liberals regarded the administration approach as dangerous, the product of political expediency rather than sound economic analysis.

Neither Keyserling nor the more conventional liberals won a complete victory. Truman, who understood all too well the political dangers of a prolonged inflation, made substantial concessions to the controllers, led by Michael V. DiSalle, head of the Office of Price Stabilization. In the interest of fairness Truman approved a more complex system of price controls than

Keyserling thought desirable, giving DiSalle considerable leeway to roll back some prices while approving advances in other areas. By March 1951 inflation was under control; during the final ten months of the year the cost-of-living index increased by less than two and one-half per cent. The waves of scare buying that followed the North Korean attack and the Chinese intervention had subsided. Higher taxes and restraints on credit were beginning to affect consumer buying. The Federal Reserve System, despite opposition from the administration, initiated a stringent monetary policy. Tax breaks for businesses expanding plant facilities presaged increased productive capacity. All these factors, along with the government stabilization program, discouraged an inflationary psychology.

At the time, however, it appeared to most economic observers that the lull was only temporary. Many of the administration's liberal critics refused even to admit the existence of a lull and called for tougher controls as if prices were still skyrocketing. More moderate analysts feared that the impact of large government defense orders would set off another inflationary spiral in the fall. Influenced by such expectations, Truman ostentatiously mounted an anti-inflation crusade, demanding that Congress not only extend his control authority, due to expire on June 30, but actually strengthen it. In fact the Defense Production Act of 1951 weakened the president's powers considerably. Truman signed it reluctantly, comparing it to "a bulldozer, crashing aimlessly through existing pricing formulas, leaving havoc in its wake." A subsequent tax bill failed to meet administration revenue requests and increased the danger of serious inflation.

Yet price stability persisted through 1952, in large measure because defense production, hampered by multiple shortages and bottlenecks, lagged far behind its timetable. In late 1951 these problems and the fear of renewed inflation led Truman to decide in favor of a "stretch-out" of defense production schedules; in doing so he overrode Keyserling's urgings for an all-out effort to break the bottlenecks and concentrate relentlessly upon expansion. Given the serious problems in defense industry, the stretch-out decision may have seemed necessary to Truman, but it also carried the dividend of economic stability.

The president had steered a course between the orthodox liberal obsession with inflation and Keyserling's easy disregard of its perils; perhaps as a result the economy failed to expand at the rate Keyserling had hoped. On balance, however, Truman's approach to the political economy of the Korean War was closer to Keyserling's, and the conflict produced a dramatic economic growth. Before the war the peak gross national product had been $285 billion in 1948; by the end of 1952 the GNP (measured in constant dollar values) had reached a rate of $350 billion. The production index of durable manufactured goods had averaged 237 in 1950; by the last quarter of 1952 it had reached 313. The expansion, even if less than Keyserling had wanted, was breathtaking. Moreover, aside from the probably unavoidable inflation that accompanied the early months of the war, this remarkable growth had occurred in a climate of economic stability. Using a somewhat more orthodox approach than Keyserling preferred, the administration had achieved one of the central goals of the Fair Deal.

In its effort to carry on with the reforming impulse of the New Deal the Truman administration faced nearly insuperable obstacles. A loosely knit but nonetheless effective conservative coalition had controlled Congress since 1939, successfully defying Franklin Roosevelt long before it had to deal with Truman. Postwar prosperity muted economic liberalism and encouraged a mood of apathy toward new reform breakthroughs, although Truman's victory in 1948 indicated that most of the elements of the old Roosevelt coalition were determined to preserve the gains of the New Deal. The cold war probably made it more difficult to focus public attention upon reform and dealt severe blows to civil liberties. It did, however, give impetus to the movement for Negro equality.

The Fair Deal attempted to adapt liberalism to the new conditions. Under the intellectual leadership of Leon Keyserling it formulated policies that sought to transcend the conflicts of the New Deal era by encouraging an economic growth that could provide abundance for all Americans. With Charles Brannan pointing the way, the Truman administration tried to translate abundance into a political coalition that could provide the votes for its social welfare policies. The political strategy, ambitious but unrealistic, collapsed under the weight of the Korean War. Keyserling's economics, on the other hand, received a lift from Korea; in a period of adversity the Fair Deal was able to achieve at least one of its objectives.

Dwight D. Eisenhower and the Corporate Commonwealth

ROBERT GRIFFITH

At the heart of [President Dwight David] Eisenhower's thinking was a struggle to reconcile and resolve the most fundamental conflicts of modern society. Industrialization, mass production and distribution, and the growth of urban populations had, he believed, all combined to create a complex, interdependent social system—a system that possessed the potential for the production of great wealth and material abundance but that was also precariously vulnerable to destruction through the selfish antagonisms of class conflict. In the nineteenth century, as he traced America's recent past, the power of "concentrated wealth" had become "a menace to the self-respect, opportunities, and livelihood of great groups of ordinary citizens" and had "compelled drastic action for the preservation of the laborer's dignity—for the welfare of himself and his family." Although the legislative reforms of the Progressive and New Deal eras had, in his view, largely ameliorated such dangers, the threat of class conflict remained. The single most important source of "all our problems," he wrote a prominent business leader in early 1952, was the disunity born of "the great chasms separating economic group-

"Dwight D. Eisenhower and the Corporate Commonwealth" by Robert Griffith, from *American Historical Review*, February 1982, pp. 87–122. Reprinted by permission.

ings." Not only did capital, labor, agriculture, and other interests contend among themselves, but each also sought to bend public policy to its own selfish ends: "such divisions, even though economic in origin, inevitably become so clearly reflected in political organization and doctrine that they damage both our political and economic structures, thus enlarging and perpetuating initial effects." In his diary, he posed the question in terms of Lenin's analysis of the contradictions within capitalism and of the conflict between capital and labor, between antagonistic capitalistic states, and between capitalist and underdeveloped nations. Although he did not accept the inevitability of such conflicts, he did recognize that "the principal contradiction in the whole system comes about because of the inability of men to forego immediate gain for a long time good," and he worried that "we do not yet have a sufficient number of people who are ready to make the immediate sacrifice in favor of a long-term investment."

Modern organization proved an especially difficult dilemma for Eisenhower. He extolled the new forms of corporate organization, the purpose of which, as he saw it, was "to produce orderliness, which means restriction upon irresponsible human action," but he feared that organization also posed grave dangers for traditional economic and political liberties. If organization was necessary for the orderly conduct of human affairs, it was nevertheless "difficult to define the exact line of demarcation between rules of conduct on the one hand, and unjustifiable seizure of power on the other." Even more threatening was the prospect that organized interests—"pressure groups," he usually called them—would impose their narrow ends upon the state or that the state itself would become little more than a battleground for class conflict. As he told a Columbia University audience in 1948, "danger arises from too great a concentration of power in the hands of any individual or group: The power of concentrated finance, the power of selfish pressure groups, the power of any class organized in opposition to the whole—any one of these, when allowed to dominate is fully capable of destroying individual freedom."

For Eisenhower, as for other postwar conservatives, the dangers of such politicized conflict were all too readily apparent. Indeed, the Democratic party of the New and Fair Deals, built through appeals to selfish class interest, seemed to embody all of the most threatening tendencies of American democracy. In his inaugural address as president of Columbia in 1948, Eisenhower decried "demogogic appeals to class selfishness, greed, and hate" and warned against what he called "a regimented statism." Six months later, in a commencement address, he attacked "pressure groups" and politicians who appealed "to all that was selfish in humankind." Speaking to the American Bar Association in September 1949—an address to which he returned in later years as the touchstone of his political philosophy—he denounced Marxian concepts of class conflict and called for the defense of freedom from "the unbearable selfishness of vested interest" and from "the blindness of those who, protesting devotion to the public welfare, falsely declare that only government can bring us happiness, security and opportunity."

Eisenhower nevertheless believed that the clash of classes was neither necessary nor inexorable. Indeed, the great lesson of the twentieth century was, for him at least, the interdependence of class interests, not their irreconcilability. "In our tightly knit economy, all professions and callings—no matter how widely separated they may be in purpose and technique—all have points of contact and areas of common interest," he declared in 1947. "Banker or housewife, farmer, carpenter, soldier—no one of us can live and act without effect on all the others." In early 1952 he suggested to businessman George Sloan "that agriculture, labor, management and capital frequently speak of themselves as if each were a separate and self-sufficient enterprise or community. Yet the simple fact is that each is helpless without the others; only as an effective member of an integrated team can any one of them prosper." Maximum production was possible "only when management, labor and capital work in harmony . . . ; no prosperity for one economic group is permanently possible except as all groups prosper." Drawing heavily, though perhaps unconsciously, on the social thought of Herbert Hoover, Eisenhower repeatedly called for voluntary cooperation among America's diverse economic interests. Competition and self-interest, he insisted, must be "accompanied by a readiness to cooperate wholeheartedly for the performance of community and national functions." Indeed, the secret of American success in World War II, he declared on another occasion, was that "Americans welded into a cooperative unit the enterprise, initiative, spirit and will of many million free men and women." As William E. Robinson, a close friend, noted in 1948, Eisenhower believed not in "rugged individualism in the old-fashioned Republican sense of the word" but in "freedom and independence for the individual with its collateral responsibility for cooperation." At Columbia, one of his proudest achievements was the creation of the American Assembly, in which he hoped the leaders of business, labor, government, and the professions would meet to study and plan cooperatively for the future. "We must find a way," he told the American Academy of Political Science in 1950, "to bring big business, labor, professions and government officials together with . . . experts and . . . study and work out these problems in the calmness of a nonpartisan . . . atmosphere."

From his fears of class conflict and from his vision of a mutually cooperative, voluntarist society came Eisenhower's commitment to what he called "the middle way," a phrase that dominated almost all of his thinking after 1948. The "middle way" was not just a political platitude but rather signified his struggle to resolve the fundamental tensions of the modern state. The term defined not only a political position—between capital and labor, between entrepreneurial liberalism and socialism, between the Republican Right and the Democratic Left—but also a series of programmatic commitments and a style of leadership. Initially, the "middle way" entailed arresting the momentum of New Deal liberalism and ensuring, as he wrote a prominent business supporter, that "our economy . . . remain, to the greatest possible extent, in private hands." In his diary, and in conversations and correspondence with friends, he worried about the dangerous "drift toward statism," a trend that, he declared, "must be halted in its tracks."

Yet he was also cautious enough and realistic enough to realize that this could not be done abruptly. He agreed with former president Hoover, who warned him in early 1953 that it would be impossible to accomplish a dramatic reversal and that the best that the new administration could hope to achieve would be a gradual "flattening of the curve of this particular trend." He believed, moreover, that at least some forms of state action were not only expedient but necessary. Government must, he argued, "prevent or correct abuses springing from the unregulated practice of a private economy" and must provide laws "necessary to an orderly and a measurably free life." The complexities of modern economic life "require the application to all of us of commonly agreed-upon rules and regulations in order that the accidents of mass production will not defeat or destroy the right of the individual to political and economic freedom." More importantly, he believed that government should actively promote social harmony and encourage those mutually beneficial, voluntary, and cooperative activities that lay at the center of his vision of the good society; the essence of citizenship entailed "blend[ing], without coercion, the individual good and the common good." Above all, he told the American Bar Association, "we need more economic understanding and working arrangements that will bind labor and management . . . into a far tighter voluntary cooperative unit than we now have." The task of leadership, he wrote, was to bring "diversities together in a common purpose."

The greatest obstacle to this corporatist commonwealth, in Eisenhower's view, was politics, a word he almost always used pejoratively to signify the selfish actions of special interests and classes. "Pressure groups," he warned a Columbia audience, "often pretend to a moral purpose that examination proves to be false. The vote-seeker rarely hesitates to appeal to all that is selfish in humankind." "When politicians begin to talk about *issues*," he wrote a friend, "they are often talking about those things on which they feel it expedient to make extravagant promises to various pressure groups." He distrusted popular opinion, which he believed was both uninformed and short-sighted, and he complained to friends that congressmen were oversensitive "to even transitory resentments in their several districts." The political game, he wrote his brother Edgar, was "a combination of gossip, innuendo, sly character assassination, and outright lies" in which "the demagogue tries to develop a saleable list of items to hold before the public." Disturbed by the bitter rhetoric of the 1948 election, with its fiery appeals to class interest, he confided to his diary the wish that both Democrats and Republicans would embrace the middle of the road and "choose some issues outside the nation's economy on which to fight out elections."

Eisenhower believed that the inevitable conflicts produced by the short-sighted and self-interested actions of classes and interest groups could be resolved only through the leadership of public-spirited and professionally skilled managers such as himself, who could exercise the disinterested judgment necessary to avoid calamities such as war or depression and achieve long-range goals such as peace and high productivity. The task of such leadership was to quell the passion of the masses, to encourage self-discipline on the part of business, labor, and agriculture, and to promote the pursuit of long-term, enlightened self-interest rather than immediate gain. "To induce people to do more," he wrote his close friend and former aide General Alfred M. Gruenther in May 1953, "leadership has the chore of informing people and attempting to inspire them to real sacrifice." Both at home and abroad people had to be prepared to endure hardship and discipline. The real question, as he wrote to a prominent Wall Street banker, was "whether national leaders here and abroad have the courage and strength to stand up and tell the truth and to keep repeating the truth regardless of vilification and abuse, until people at large will accept and act upon the clear facts."

Eisenhower's commitment to social harmony, self-discipline, limited government, and a depoliticized, administrative state all dictated, in turn, an approach to leadership that stressed restraint, patience, moderation, and flexibility. "I am convinced," he wrote his friend Everett ("Swede") Hazlett in 1952, "that leadership in the political as well as in other spheres consists largely in making progress through compromise." He deplored "the table-pounding, name-calling methods that columnists so much love," not so much because he feared "a good fight" but because he thought that "such methods are normally futile." In a letter to a friend, he praised Lincoln as "the greatest compromiser and astute master of expediency that we have known" and confessed that he, too, was "a bit on the pragmatic side by inclination." His belief in the mediatory role of government and his fear of popular politics was also reflected in his intense concern with public relations, which he saw not just as a means of political or personal aggrandizement but as a technique for defusing political conflict, limiting the role of the state, engineering support for administrative decisions, and forging consensus. He told the leaders of the Advertising Council in early 1953 that "the only way to avoid centralized domination" was "through an increased readiness to cooperate in the solution of group problems. As problems become more complex, we must find new ways to achieve cooperation—new mechanisms for discovering our problems and getting them over to the American people." The Advertising Council, whose conservative messages were carried annually in hundreds of thousands of so-called public service advertisements, was just such a mechanism, Eisenhower declared, "one of our great agencies for the preservation of freedom."

Eisenhower's belief in an American commonwealth was paralleled by a Wilsonian faith in a world order through which, as he told a London Guildhall audience in 1945, "all nations can enjoy the fruitfulness of the earth." Like most other Wilsonians, he accompanied this idealistic vision with a fairly hard-headed grasp of America's postwar needs. Foreign policy, he wrote a friend in late 1951, should be based primarily on "the need for the United States to obtain certain raw materials to sustain its economy, and, when possible, to preserve profitable foreign markets for our surpluses." There is, he wrote John Foster Dulles in 1953, a "direct connection between a prosperous and happy America and the execution of an intelligent foreign policy." Like other prominent American leaders, he feared communism not only as a military menace but also as an economic threat that would close off to America "the great industrial complex of Western Europe" and the raw material–producing nations of Africa and Asia. "Where [then] would we get the materials needed for our existence," he asked a friend in 1951. Here too, he wrote in his diary in the summer of 1953, America confronted what Marxists called the "contradictions of capitalism," both the conflict among "capitalist states for the domination of the world's surface" and the conflict "between the advanced, industrialized nations of the world and the dependent masses of backward peoples." Here too, in Eisenhower's view, the conflict, though real, was necessary and inexorable *only* if nations could not abandon their immediate selfish interests for mutual cooperation. As in domestic affairs he believed that politics was principally the expression of selfish interests and that the task of leadership was "to bring men and nations to the point where they will give to the long-term promise the same value that they give to immediate and individual gains." If we could resolve the issues of world trade and cooperation on the basis of the "long-term good of all," he concluded, "we could laugh at the other so-called 'contradictions' in our system, and . . . be so secure against the Communist menace that it would gradually dry up and wither away."

Like most prominent internationalists, Eisenhower generally supported the foreign and military policies of the Truman administration, yet here, too, his thinking was characterized by balance, moderation, and concern for long-term consequences. Thus, in endorsing the diplomacy of containment, he nevertheless remained more pacific than most of his military and civilian contemporaries. America must not seek "to preserve order in the sense of the Roman Peace, where one nation, due to its dominant position in the world, rules all others," he warned newspaper columnist Dorothy Thompson. To his father-in-law, he wrote, "We are traveling a long and rocky road toward a satisfactory world order but the big thing is that we never give up for an instant. No war can be anything else but a grave setback to such progress. The one thing that disturbs me is the readiness of people to discuss war as a means of advancing peace. To me this is a contradiction in terms." Eisenhower did not share the feeling of vulnerability that pervaded so much of the military during the early postwar era. "It is a grievous error to forget for one second the might and power of this great Republic," he cautioned Walter Bedell Smith in late 1947. He believed that both Soviet power and intent were limited and that in dealing with the Russians the United States ought to employ "patience, tolerance and a spirit of understanding." Following the Berlin blockade and Korea, he adopted a more hardline attitude toward the Russians, but he refused even then to be stampeded by those who believed that Armageddon was just around the corner.

He believed in military preparedness, but only in moderation. As army chief of staff he had worked on behalf of military unification and universal military training and had attempted, without success, to restrain the abrupt contraction of defense budgets that followed the end of the war. He nevertheless believed that resources were limited and that armed forces were, as he put it, "nonproductive, sterile organizations whose purposes are, at the best, largely negative." By early 1952, following the rapid military expansion that accompanied the Korean War, he was worried over the expenditure of "unconscionable sums" for an indefinite duration. As in foreign and domestic affairs, concern for the enduring integrity of the system was the controlling issue. Every expenditure, he insisted, "must be weighed and gauged in the light of probable long-term *internal* effect." Here again, however, selfish interests often threatened the collective good. The danger arose not just from the short-sighted partisanship of congressional budget-cutters but often-times from the service bureaucracies themselves. During World War II and again during the battles over unification and joint strategic planning, Eisenhower struggled to strike a balance among the competing claims of the services, and his letters and diaries are filled with angry denunciations of military self-interest. Here too, reconciliation of conflict and pursuit of the national interest rested with disinterested professional leadership and with the self-discipline and commitment to long-term goals of competing parties.

For Eisenhower, then, the corporate commonwealth was not just a series of vague generalities, but a broad, internally consistent, social philosophy that brought together an interpretation of America's recent past, a vision of the good society both at home and abroad, and a style of leadership through which such an order might be obtained.

Eisenhower's vision of a corporate commonwealth did not, of course, originate with him. Indeed, variations of this concept—with its emphasis on organization, cooperation, and social harmony—go back at least to the Progressive era and the National Civic Federation, to the businessmen such as Bernard M. Baruch and Gerard Swope who served on the War Industries Board during the First World War, to Herbert Hoover and his advocacy of the "associative state," to Edward Filene, Henry S. Dennison, and other apostles of welfare capitalism in the 1920s, and to the big businessmen who during the New Deal joined the Department of Commerce's Business Advisory Council (BAC) and helped shape the structure and operation of the National Recovery Administration. Common to all of these activities was an attempt to fashion a new corporative economy that would avoid both the destructive disorder of unregulated capitalism and the threat to business autonomy posed by socialism.

In spite of their considerable power and prestige, "corporate liberals" remained a minority voice in national politics and even within the business community itself. By the mid-1930s, moreover, the depression and the some-time radicalism of the New Deal had disrupted their attempts to forge an alliance between business and government. After 1934 all but a handful of business leaders abandoned efforts at collaboration with the Roosevelt administration, while the president, in turn, now excoriated the "economic royalists." World War II, however, served to reinvigorate corporate liberalism. Mobilization brought thousands of executives into government, effectively dampened New Deal criticism, and created, at least temporarily, the kind of partnership between business and government that corporate liberals had long extolled. In addition, the wartime revival of corporate liberalism gave birth to important new organizations, such as the Committee for Economic Development (CED) and the Advertising Council.

The relationship of corporate liberals to the Roosevelt and Truman administrations, however, remained uneasy. On the one hand, they welcomed cooperation between business and government and recognized that the state could serve as a powerful positive instrument for moderating economic conflict, regulating domestic markets, promoting international trade, and sustaining economic growth. On the other, they feared that the popularity of the New Deal and the power of its progressive constituencies might lead, piecemeal, to a semisocialist state whose fiscal and regulatory policies would ultimately destroy private enterprise. As William Benton, one of the founders of the Committee for Economic Development, wrote in 1944, the leaders of government ought to "rid the economy of injurious or unnecessary regulation, as well as administration that is hostile or harmful," and pursue "constructive fiscal, monetary and other policies that provide a climate in which a private enterprise system can flourish." Businessmen, for their part, he continued, must learn to cooperate with government in the exercise of those powers that had become clearly necessary in a modern economy and display a "high degree of imagination, goodwill and inventiveness" in order to work out "improved rules of the game." If business failed to plan for the postwar, warned Paul G. Hoffman, another CED founder, "the Government will be forced to step in, and collectivism will come to postwar America—by default rather than design." "We must plan carefully and strike hard," one of Hoffman's business correspondents bluntly wrote. "Otherwise the new dealers will plan for all of us." The strategic problem faced by corporate liberals in the postwar era was, thus, how to obtain the benefits of state intervention, while avoiding its dangers. Their immediate, tactical problem was how to win political power in an era still dominated by the passionate and well-remembered struggles of the 1930s. Not surprisingly, they quickly discovered in Eisenhower the solution to both dilemmas. As a widely admired war hero, he was pre-eminently electable. More importantly, as they were soon to discover, his political and economic views in many ways closely approximated their own. . . .

These influential business and political leaders were convinced, out of both ideology and expedience, that the election of Eisenhower was a necessity. On the one hand, they greatly feared the implications of continued Democratic rule; on the other, they distrusted the views of Republican Senator Robert A. Taft of Ohio, especially on foreign policy. More importantly, they were certain he could not win. As Eisenhower later recalled in a letter to his brother Edgar,

> In 1948, '49, '50, '51 and early '52, many hundreds of people were urging me to go into politics. Scores of different reasons were advanced as to why I should do so, but in general they all boiled down to something as follows: "The country is going socialistic so rapidly that, unless Republicans can get in immediately and defeat this trend, our country is gone. Four more years of New Dealism and there will be no turning back. This is our last chance."

No one put it more bluntly than Thomas E. Dewey, who in 1949 told Eisenhower that only he could "save this country from going to Hades in the handbasket of paternalism-socialism-dictatorship." The problem, declared the twice-defeated presidential aspirant, was that, although "all middle-class citizens of education have a common belief that tendencies toward centralization and paternalism must be halted and reversed, no one who voices these views can be elected." This meant, Dewey continued, that "we must look around for someone of great popularity and who has not frittered away his political assets by taking positive stands against national planning, etc., etc. Elect such a man to the Presidency, *after which* he must lead us back to safe channels and paths."

The support of business men such as Robinson and Hoffman, publishers such as Helen Rogers Reid and Henry Luce, and politicians such as Dewey and Henry Cabot Lodge became absolutely critical to the Eisenhower campaign. These men and women not only convinced Eisenhower that he had a duty to run for the presidency but also reinforced his views on political economy, marshalled enormous financial and editorial support for his candidacy, and managed to force his nomination upon the reluctant regulars of the Republican party. Taft was more correct than not when he bitterly complained in the wake of the Republican convention that Eisenhower had been installed by "the power of the New York financial interests and a large number of businessmen subject to New York influence" and by the nation's great newspapers, many of which "turned themselves into propaganda sheets." The concept of a corporate commonwealth was, then, not just an exercise in political platitude but an ideology that rationalized a critically important development in American economic life and mobilized a powerful constituency behind the election of Eisenhower as president of the United States.

The vision of a corporate commonwealth, which was the touchstone of Eisenhower's political philosophy and which drew to his support so many progressive capitalists, also shaped the policies and politics of his administration. As president, Eisenhower sought to create a noncoercive, self-disciplined, and harmonious corporate society by limiting the New Deal state, forging cooperative relations between business and government, promoting social harmony and consensus at home, and maintaining a stable and Western-oriented international order abroad. These efforts represented a serious, in many ways even sophisticated, attempt to escape the dilemmas created by modern economic organization. They also revealed the sharp limitations of such an ideology, its class bias, and its profoundly antidemocratic character.

Eisenhower believed that the federal state posed a dangerous threat to economic liberties, and he was determined to arrest the growth of government and slowly but firmly to "bend the curve" away from public enterprise. He lifted wage-price controls, initiated new policies to prevent government competition with business, reduced the federal budget and lowered taxes on industry and capital. He signed legislation turning over oil-rich "submerged lands" to the states and strongly supported deregulation of natural gas. He withdrew federal opposition to private hydroelectric development in Idaho and California and sought to prevent further expansion of the Tennessee

Valley Authority. In the critical new field of nuclear energy, he sponsored legislation that ended exclusive federal control of development.

Eisenhower was not, however, a conservative ideologue, intent on returning the nation's economic relations to those of 1900. He clearly recognized that the state must play an active role in sustaining high productivity and employment. As he wrote his brother Milton in early 1954, "Maintenance of prosperity is one field of governmental concern that interests me mightily and one on which I have talked incessantly to associates, advisers, and assistants ever since last January. In these days I am sure that government has to be the principal coordinator and, in many cases, the actual operator for the many things that the approach of depression would demand." Like most conservatives, however, he feared inflation more than unemployment and was willing to accept slower growth and higher joblessness in return for wage and price stability. He preferred to act cautiously and often indirectly, avoiding a highly visible or intrusive federal presence. He believed strongly, moreover, in the necessity for self-discipline on the part of both business and labor. As he declared in 1957, the national interest must take precedence over the temporary advantages that might be secured by particular groups at the expense of all the people. "Should we persistently fail to discipline ourselves," he warned, there would be inexorable pressure for government to intervene and "freedom will step by step disappear." . . .

Eisenhower combined his attempt to limit the role of the federal state with a strong and pervasive emphasis on cooperation between business and government. He drew about him a cabinet whose members he hoped would share his own faith in partnership and corporate self-government; he appointed representatives of business and industry to important regulatory boards and commissions; and he greatly expanded the government's already elaborate network of industrial advisory committees. The influence of existing groups such as the Business Advisory Council (BAC) and the National Petroleum Council was increased, while many new advisory committees were created. At the Department of Commerce, for example, Secretary Sinclair Weeks announced, following wide consultation with industry and trade association leaders, the creation of a new Business and Services Administration, which would preside over an extensive network of advisory committees designed to help allocate materials required by defense and atomic energy programs and make recommendations on applications for accelerated tax amortization, federal loan assistance, stockpiling, and other matters. Every department, Eisenhower assured the BAC in early 1953, was engaged in organizing similar bodies on a more or less formal or informal basis. Similarly, the famous stag dinners to which he invited the leaders of America's great corporations were not just ritual celebrations of success but meetings at which Eisenhower hoped to exchange views with men whose opinions he respected and whose support was indispensable to his broader purposes. He hoped, it seems clear, that such gatherings would also stimulate business leaders to think in broad, cooperative terms and not just according to their more immediate and parochial interests.

Eisenhower's stress on cooperation and industrial self-government was nowhere better revealed than in his approach to fiscal and monetary policy. Although he believed that the state should play an important role in maintaining prosperity, he also believed in what he called "shared responsibility" between business and government. During the recession of 1954 he privately urged bankers to lower interest rates and make credit more easily available; in 1955 he attempted, unsuccessfully, to persuade auto industry leaders to restrain prices and production; during the recession years of 1954 and 1958 he enlisted the services of the Advertising Council, which launched massive advertising campaigns designed to promote "Confidence in a Growing America," and, though never explicitly stated, confidence in the administration as well; and in 1958–59 he quietly sought to organize corporate leaders behind his wage and price stabilization policies.

The administration of antitrust policy under Eisenhower was characterized, similarly, by the widespread use of prefiling conferences, consent decrees, and premerger clearances, all of which emphasized cooperation and quiet negotiation. When business complaints of harassment reached the president, moreover, he admonished Attorney General Herbert Brownell, Jr., to reassure the business community as to "the true attitude of this Administration," which was that "continued prosperity and growth of the economy" could come "only through the cooperation of labor, management and government, and that such cooperation requires a readiness of all parties to observe the law (or to seek legislative changes in it) but the avoidance on the part of government of all kinds of petty annoyances brought about merely by personal bias."

The very success of such strategies, of course, depended on the ability and willingness of business leaders to exercise restraint and discipline. Eisenhower fully understood the enormous power of modern business and how decisions made by corporate boards could affect "the whole life of the United States." He understood also, as he told economic adviser Gabriel Hauge, how such a situation "could be very dangerous unless people act with the greatest wisdom and concert for the nation." His speeches, his conversations, and his private correspondence are literally filled with appeals for corporate "statesmanship" and responsibility. Nothing so angered him, moreover, as what he considered corporate shortsightedness—the demand by some business groups for tax reduction regardless of the fiscal consequences, the pressure for tariff protection from inefficient producers, the refusal of steel and auto industry leaders to hold down prices, the unwillingness of the automakers to smooth out production and help stabilize the business cycle. When in mid-1955 steel companies announced an increase in steel prices of seven dollars per ton, he told Ann Whitman that he was "pretty disgusted with businessmen and didn't know when he would get over it." He was outraged by the heavy-handed lobbying and even bribery that accompanied the drive for deregulation of natural gas and that compelled him to veto a bill he otherwise favored. "I want to give business a honorable place," he angrily declared, "but they make crooks out of themselves." To the cabinet he worried aloud about "the contradiction that existed when the greatest exponents of a free economy failed to exercise the restraint necessary to a free economy. . . ."

The search for stability and social harmony underlying Eisenhower's vision of a corporate commonwealth also shaped his style of presidential leadership. This style was quite obviously a product of his experience as a military leader and of his conviction that modern government was so large and complex that no individual could master all of its intricacies. It was clearly reinforced by the practical necessity of working for the most part with a Congress organized by the opposing party. It was also shaped, however, by the conservative and consensual goals of his presidency and by his belief in the limited role of the political state, in the dangers of popular politics, in the importance of persuasion rather than coercion, and in the necessity for voluntary discipline, restraint, and cooperation among America's powerful economic groupings. Its purpose was to deflect attention not only from himself but also from the national government itself, to deflate and depoliticize expectations raised by two decades of Democratic rule. Thus, he sought to govern by indirection, delegating authority to those he trusted and with whom he was in basic agreement, but insulating himself from the controversy and criticism their actions might provoke. He tried quite deliberately to appear above partisan politics, refused to be drawn into personal confrontations, and almost never displayed in public his legendary temper. To those around him, he repeatedly counseled moderation and restraint. The task of the political leader, he wrote in a long letter to Nelson Rockefeller, was "to devise plans along which humans [can] make constructive progress. This means that the plan or program itself tends to fall in the 'gray' category even though an earnest attempt is made to apply the black and white values of moral truths. . . . Perfection is not quickly reached; the plan is therefore 'gray' or 'middle-of-the-road.' "

His experience as president also reinforced his distrust of popular democracy. People in the aggregate, he seemed to believe, were all too prone to self-seeking and all too vulnerable to the blandishments of demagogues. Congress was a warren of greedy special interests (an "occupational hazard," one aide quipped), while the press was little more than an endless source of "distortion and gross error." Mistrustful of democracy, he opposed most efforts to modify the nation's constitutional arrangements. He believed that the Bricker Amendment would undermine the foundations of presidential authority in foreign affairs, and that attempts by Henry Cabot Lodge and others to change the electoral system by introducing proportional voting would make the American system "closer to a democracy, less of a republic." "We can't let just a popular majority sweep us in one direction," he told Vice President Nixon, "because then you can't recover." He defended the Supreme Court not because he always agreed with its decisions, but because he believed that "one of the great functions of the Supreme Court was to provide needed stability in a form of government where political expediency might at times carry parties and political leaders to extremes."

Fear of popular politics and a commitment to voluntarism and corporate self-government also shaped Eisenhower's preoccupation with public relations: if he hoped to avoid coercive state intervention and to encourage the resolution of conflict among powerful interests, his chief techniques had to be persuasive; and if the principle [*sic*] threat to this process arose from lack of discipline among the masses and the demagogic promises of politicians, then public relations must play an even more important role in encouraging restraint, defusing dangerous issues, dampening protest and legitimizing corporate rule. The administration faced problems "not unlike the advertising and sales activity of a great industrial organization," he noted in 1953; and, while it was necessary to have "a good product to sell," it was also necessary "to have an effective and persuasive way of informing the public of the excellence of that product." He established a standing committee on public relations within the White House, followed closely the public relations efforts of the Republican national committee, and maintained a steady correspondence with friends and advisors from the world of corporate public relations. He directed the organization of special campaigns on agriculture, highways, public power, labor relations, and economic policy, and he enlisted the support of powerful private groups such as the Advertising Council in publicizing his policies. He was exceptionally skillful in his press relations. He maintained a wide correspondence with many publishers and editors, invited them frequently to his stag dinners, and even employed them on occasion to conduct confidential surveys on his behalf. He was extremely sensitive to adverse comment in the press and frequently sought to counter such criticism, though almost always obliquely.

Eisenhower did not, however, limit these efforts, which he frequently referred to as "selling the American people," to advertising his highly marketable personality or even to promoting the specific programs of the administration but directed them as well toward the broader, long-term goals of his presidency—winning popular acceptance of the discipline and self-restraint necessary to the corporate commonwealth and helping "our people understand that they must avoid extremes in reaching solutions to the social, economic and political problems that are constantly with us." His approach to these broad aims was nowhere better illustrated than in the creation, near the end of his second term, of a commission to identify and publicize national goals for the 1960s. Chief among these goals, Eisenhower made clear in advance, was the "American aspiration . . . to develop a world in which all peoples will be living at peace under cooperative policies with maximum standards of living and opportunity for all." The most important purpose of the study, he noted privately, "was to outline for the American people problems involved in mobilizing public opinion in a democracy in order to make the hard decisions that would be needed to successfully compete in an indefinite cold war."

Eisenhower's deep concern for public order and consensus influenced his response to [Senator] Joseph R. McCarthy and the discordant Cold War politics of anticommunism. While he repeatedly insisted on the importance of justice and fair play, he tended, almost without exception, to resolve conflicts between security and civil liberties in favor of the state. He supported legislation to strip citizenship from those convicted under the Smith Act of conspiring to advocate the violent overthrow of the government, to compel witnesses to testify in national security investigations, to legalize the use of wiretap information in internal security cases, and to broaden and redefine espionage and sabotage laws. One of his earliest actions as president was to institute a drastic new internal security program that broadened the criteria for federal employment to include not only loyalty and security but also "suitability," abolished the hearing and review procedures established by the Truman administration, and extended the power of summary dismissal, previously reserved to heads of sensitive departments such as state and defense, to all federal agencies and departments. He continued the Truman administration's prosecution of Communist leaders under the Smith Act and approved, in outline at least, the FBI's covert and extralegal COIN-TELPRO efforts "to promote disruption within the ranks of the Communist Party." He was well aware, moreover, of the FBI's euphemistically labeled "custodial detention" program and was prepared to order suspected subversives rounded up in time of national emergency. Although he believed that little new evidence had been produced to implicate J. Robert Oppenheimer [the physicist who headed the team that developed the atomic bomb] and that the case had been "constantly reviewed and reexamined over a number of years," Eisenhower nevertheless quickly ordered the famous physicist's security clearance lifted and later defended the AEC's finding that Oppenheimer was a security risk. And, although he considered commuting the sentences of Julius and Ethel Rosenberg [executed as spies for the Soviet Union], he finally decided, as he wrote his son, that "the exemplary feature of the punishment, the hope that it would deter others, is something that cannot be ignored."

Although Eisenhower had himself on occasion employed the communist issue for political purposes, he nevertheless loathed McCarthy and was sharply critical of the highly publicized investigations in Congress. What he objected to most strenuously in the Congressional proceedings, however, was not so much their arbitrary violation of individual liberties but rather the disorderly and partisan atmosphere in which they were conducted. The job of routing subversives, he believed, was primarily administrative, not legislative—a task for orderly and bureaucratic resolution, not partisan debate. His strongest and most direct stand against the Congressional inquisitors came in the spring of of 1954, when he invoked the doctrine of executive privilege in order to protect the privacy of advice offered within the executive branch. He bluntly told Congressional leaders, "Any man who testified as to the advice he gave me won't be working for me that night. . . . I will not allow people around me to be subpoenaed and you might just as well know it now."

He refused to be drawn into a direct confrontation with McCarthy, however, despite repeated entreaties from friends and advisors who feared that the senator's continued depredations would undermine the president's leadership. This reluctance arose in part from his realistic, if cynical, respect for McCarthy's support among Senate Republicans, in part from his personal dislike for the philippic mode. It also derived, however, from his sophisticated analysis of the relationships between McCarthy, the media, and the presidency. McCarthy, he wrote, owed "his entire prominence and influence . . . to the publicity media of the nation." The president, on the other hand, also possessed a "terrific headline value." He noted to his friend Hazlett that, "whenever the President takes part in a newspaper trial of some individual of whom he disapproves, one thing is automatically accomplished. This is an increase in the headline value of the individual attacked." He chose instead to combat McCarthy through indirection: he urged Republican senators to attack him, ordered a reluctant Richard M. Nixon into combat in order to prevent McCarthy from monopolizing network television, encouraged Paul Hoffman and others to organize an anti-McCarthy movement, prevented McCarthy from addressing party gatherings, and suggested, with great circumspection, that publishers and media executives resist the senator's demands for time and space. He even suggested—only half jokingly— that since McCarthy had been built up by the press, the press should "develop a collusion to ignore him." In the end, of course, the Senate did act, however reluctantly, in censuring the senator from Wisconsin. Eisenhower remained publicly aloof from the controversy, the press began to ignore McCarthy, and a measure of tranquility returned to American politics. By his own terms, if not by those of liberals or civil libertarians, the president had succeeded in bringing an era to an end.

The sharpest challenge to Eisenhower's quest for consensus, however, and the one that revealed most clearly the class and racial bias of his ideology, was the struggle by black Americans for civil rights and economic justice. Like most men of power, Eisenhower fully subscribed to the hierarchical values of corporate America. Though he believed in the principle of equality of opportunity, he also subscribed to its less frequently stated corollary— that such opportunity inevitably created inequality of condition. He shared many of the conventional prejudices common among upper-middle class white Americans toward blacks and other minorities. He believed in equality before the law but not in "social equality." He did not think, he told Arthur Larson, that everyone had to mingle socially "or that a Negro should court my daughter." These attitudes shaped his response to the emerging racial crisis of the 1950s and reinforced the fundamentally conservative elements of his political philosophy: his narrow construction of what was permissible and desirable for the national government to do, his fear of popular passion and his distrust of politics, his preference for cooperation over coercion, and his tendency to insulate the presidency from controversial issues. As president, he opposed the establishment of a Federal Fair Employment Practices Commission as well as any efforts that might project the national government any deeper into the school desegregation controversy opened up by the Brown decision in 1954. Not until 1956 did he call for civil rights legislation, and then only at the insistence of Attorney General Brownell. His support was limited, moreover, to the area of voting rights, where federal responsibility seemed clear, and to the creation of a bipartisan commission to study the problem. The proposed legislation, he assured Senate Majority Leader

Lyndon B. Johnson, represented "the mildest civil rights bill possible"; even so, the measure was drastically weakened before enactment in 1957. Three years later, prodded by his own Civil Rights Commission, he again called for legislation, this time an extremely modest proposal that became the Civil Rights Act of 1960.

In civil rights, as in other areas, he preferred to act administratively, without widespread publicity, and where federal jurisdiction was uncontested—for example, in the desegregation of navy yards and the integration of public facilities in the District of Columbia. He also sought, privately, to persuade prominent Southerners to embrace his own goals of moderation and gradual progress. He feared the passions aroused by civil rights, both among blacks and Southern whites, and repeatedly preached patience, calmness, and forbearance. As he told Booker T. Washington's daughter, "I like to feel that where we have to change the hearts of men, we cannot do it by cold lawmaking, but must make these changes by appealing to reason, by prayer, and by constantly working at it through our own efforts." He insisted, moreover, on insulating himself from the actions of the Supreme Court, the Civil Rights Commission, and even his own attorney general. Thus, in the school desegregation cases he carefully avoided identification with Attorney General Brownell, whose *amicus curiae* brief had drawn sharp criticism from Southern conservatives. He repeatedly refused to endorse the Brown decision or to identify himself publicly with the goal of desegregation. Privately, he thought the decision a mistake that would set back racial progress throughout the South. Desegregation, he believed, would require over thirty to forty years to complete. When efforts at conciliation failed and he was compelled, however reluctantly, to dispatch federal troops to Little Rock, Arkansas, he carefully couched his actions in terms of defending civil order, not civil rights. As he explained to his friend Hazlett, "My biggest problem has been to make people see . . . that my main interest is not in the integration or segregation question. My opinion as to the wisdom or timeliness of the Supreme Court's decision has nothing to do with the case. . . . If the day comes when we can obey the orders of our Courts only when we personally approve of them, the end of the American system . . . will not be far off." In civil rights, as in other areas, a concern for order and stability predominated; and it was the president's firm intention, as he told South Carolina Governor James F. Byrnes, "to make haste slowly."

Eisenhower's quest for a corporate commonwealth at home was paralleled and inextricably bound to the struggle to create, at least among the so-called free nations, an interdependent and cooperative world order. Like other American leaders he believed that freedom, security, and prosperity were indivisible and that little domestic progress was possible in the absence of an international "atmosphere in which America can be safe and prosperous." The challenge to such a system, he believed, was threefold: most obviously from the Soviet Union and other Communist nations but also from the Western nations, which might unthinkingly allow the world to fall victim to communism because each was "too preoccupied with its own local and selfish interests," and from within the United States itself, where greedy pressure groups might undermine long-run national and international interests. If, on the one hand, a disorderly and dangerous world could disrupt America's future progress and prosperity, so, on the other hand, greed and shortsightedness at home could undermine American goals abroad. The purpose of foreign policy therefore lay in the mastery of these contradictions. This meant, to begin with, convincing Western nations that their (and America's) long-run interests demanded cooperation and mutual restraint. Too often, he believed, such cooperation was sacrificed to what he considered parochial interests and loyalties: the Arab-Israeli conflict in the Middle East, the Indian-Pakistani struggle over Kashmir, Korean antagonism toward Japan, and the unwillingness of European colonial powers to yield their prewar empires, to cite some of the examples he most frequently used in his private correspondence.

Sound foreign policy and broad, long-term national interests also meant that it was often necessary to restrain domestic interests. Expanded international trade, for example, which he considered absolutely vital to American and world prosperity, demanded a willingness to lower barriers to foreign imports, even at the expense of domestic producers; and nothing so irritated him as the clamor of businessmen for protection. "Daily I am impressed by the short-sightedness bordering upon tragic stupidity of many who fancy themselves to be the greatest believers in and supporters of capitalism . . . but who blindly support measures and conditions that cannot fail in the long run to destroy any free economic system," he angrily wrote in his diary. Many businessmen, he complained, were "so concerned for their own particular immediate market and prosperity that they utterly fail to see that the United States cannot continue to live in a world where it must, for the disposal of its products, export vast portions of its industrial and agricultural products unless it also imports a sufficiently great amount of foreign products to allow countries to pay for the surpluses they receive from us." Similarly, Americans had to be willing to bear the costs of collective security, if for no other reason than to avoid what he believed would be the far greater costs of military and economic isolation. To his friend Hazlett he wrote that "we must pursue a broad and intelligent program of loans, trade, technical assistance and, under current conditions, mutual guarantees of security. We must stop talking about 'give aways.' We must understand that our foreign expenditures are investments in America's future." He gave what he called a "simple example: No other nation is exhausting its irreplaceable resources so rapidly as is ours. Unless we are careful to build up and maintain a great group of international friends ready to trade with us, where do we hope to get all the materials that we will one day need as our rate of consumption continues and accelerates." He bluntly told a group of prominent businessmen at a White House dinner that "we cannot have prosperity without security and we must have friends with whom to trade."

Eisenhower shared the conservative, anticommunist premises that animated both earlier and subsequent administrations, and he could act with ruthless efficiency when he believed that risks were limited and important national interests at stake. In Iran, where he had directed the overthrow of

Muhammad Mossadegh and the return of young Shah Muhammad Reza Pahlevi, he believed that "we were in imminent danger of losing Iran, and sixty percent of the known oil reserves of the world," and he boasted privately that through his actions "that threat had been largely, if not totally, removed." In Guatemala, he ordered a highly secret CIA operation that overturned the moderately leftist government of Jacobo Arbenz Guzman and replaced it with the reactionary, but pro-American, dictatorship of Carlos Castillo Armas. In the Far East he was even willing to threaten nuclear war, especially against the Chinese, who had no capacity to retaliate in kind. Yet for the most part his conduct of foreign affairs was distinguished by restraint, especially when the risks seemed high and the dangers of miscalculation great—he understood that the refusal to act was often the wisest course of action. As Robert Divine recently concluded, "Almost all of Eisenhower's foreign policy achievements were negative in nature. He ended the Korean war, he refused to intervene militarily in Indochina, he refrained from involving the United States in the Suez crisis, he avoided war with China over Quemoy and Matsu, he resisted the temptation to force a showdown over Berlin, he stopped exploding nuclear weapons in the atmosphere."

Yet Eisenhower could never quite transcend the logic of his premises, as his response to revolutionary nationalism clearly revealed. Like many sophisticated conservatives, he opposed traditional European colonialism as costly, impractical, and ultimately self-defeating. From his experience in the Philippines, moreover, he knew firsthand of "the intensity and force of the spirit of nationalism that is gripping all peoples of the world today." He believed, as he wrote George Humphrey, that the "*protection of our own interests and our own system* demands . . . that we . . . understand that the spirit of nationalism, coupled with a deep hunger for some betterment in physical conditions and living standards, creates a critical situation in the under-developed areas of the world." He had at first believed that the free flow of goods and capital would in itself sustain economic development and that cooperation among nations and a friendly door to private investment would promote growth throughout the world. He later came to believe that enlightened self-interest required that the operation of the international market be supplemented by public capital. He expected, however, that new nations would follow the American model of capitalist growth. Self-determination did not include the right to choose a radical road to development. Nor could he ever disentangle his response to social revolutions from his reaction to the foreign and military policies of the Soviet Union and China, as in the case of Indochina. If Eisenhower displayed restraint by refusing to intervene on behalf of the French in Indochina, it was a restraint produced more by France's refusal to grant its colonies full independence and permit the United States a decisive role in the military conduct of the war than by any particular reluctance on Eisenhower's part to employ force against social revolutions. The president wrote Hazlett in October 1954 that he had been unable to obtain "the conditions under which I felt the United States could properly intervene to protect its own interests." Eisenhower was determined, moreover, to draw the line in Southeast Asia—"we have got to keep the Pacific an American lake," he told his advisors. Following the French collapse he committed the United States to the support of a client state south of the seventeenth parallel and to the undermining of the agreements reached at Geneva in 1954. These actions, as much as any, led to the expanded American involvement in Vietnam in the decade that followed.

Nor, finally, could Eisenhower escape the costly and destructive momentum of the warfare state. He believed that the Soviet challenge to the United States was indefinite, not immediate, and that it posed an economic and political threat as well as a military one. He was convinced that high levels of defense spending, such as those that had accompanied World War II and Korea, could not be indefinitely sustained without producing economic disorder and a resort to pervasive state intervention. As president he sought to reduce the level of America's defense effort, the so-called New Look, and was willing to permit by the end of the decade a relative increase in Soviet power. He embraced the concept of deterrent sufficiency rather than superiority—"why have more when we have as much destructive power as we do now," he asked Congressional leaders. Although he understood the problems posed by limited wars—"the enemy's political and military nibbling," he called it in a letter to Winston Churchill—he remained reluctant to "deploy and tie down our forces around the Soviet periphery in small wars." His efforts to hold down military spending drew sharp criticism from within the armed services and Congress, however, and during his second administration the struggle to maintain what he believed was an appropriate balance between the nation's military and economic requirements consumed much of his energy.

The battle to hold down defense spending also forced Eisenhower to confront some of the dilemmas raised by his reliance on partnership and professionalism. He had deliberately chosen an industrialist to head the defense department—"We have earlier tried two investment bankers, a lawyer and a soldier," he observed—in the hope of imposing discipline and order on the services and strengthening cooperative relations with business. Many of his other defense appointments were also drawn from industry and finance, and the industrial advisory system begun during earlier administrations was expanded and strengthened. Similarly, Eisenhower hoped to recruit disinterested and expert military advisors, especially for the Joint Chiefs of Staff, who could rise above the petty loyalties of the services and, together with the civilian leadership, help promote broad national goals. He was, in all of this, disappointed. Wilson and the other businessmen who staffed defense failed to impose order, and, although Eisenhower succeeded in reorganizing the department in 1958, he increasingly came to believe that its problems were systemic. Service rivalry continued almost unabated, with each branch seeming to believe that it was "exclusively responsible for the defense of the United States." The Joint Chiefs of Staff failed to provide "disinterested, competent advice," and instead in many instances they became special pleaders for their services. Most importantly, Eisenhower came to believe that defense contractors themselves were exercising far too much influence over military budgets, and he expressed a keen interest in John J. McCloy's observation that "the inter-service game extends right down through the corporations, depending upon which branch their contracts flow from and it even goes into the academic institutions depending from where their research grants flow." In his farewell address Eisenhower noted the "conjunction of an immense military establishment and a large arms industry" and warned against "the acquisition of unwarranted influence . . . by the military industrial complex."

The Eisenhower presidency was thus shaped by the self-conscious quest for a corporate commonwealth in which the contradictions of modern capitalism would be resolved through cooperation, self-restraint, discipline, and disinterested public service. The power of the state would be carefully limited, budgets prudently managed, cooperative arrangements forged between business and government, and conflicts defused through skillful governance and public relations. Enlightened diplomacy would similarly resolve potential conflicts among both developed and developing states and ensure a stable and harmonious world order. Only by understanding the centrality of this quest can we begin to grasp the inner coherence of the Eisenhower presidency and, more importantly, its relationship to the twentieth-century search for a new political economy. Indeed, the struggle to define the character of that new system has been the most important issue in modern American politics, from Populism and Progressivism through Hoover and the New Deal to the contemporary debate over "reindustrialization" and the proper relationship between government and economic life. In understanding Eisenhower we begin to understand our past, our present, and—at least in part—the alternatives before us. It is precisely because of this resonance, however, that we must be careful to avoid facile and misleading analogies and to label any conclusions provisional.

Eisenhower's quest for a new order was, on one level at least, an enormous success. The years of his presidency were among the most prosperous, peaceful, and politically tranquil in this century, and he left office one of the most popular chief executives in American history. But this was, as he himself would have been quick to note, a calculus of only short-term results. He had succeeded in slowing the growth of the federal state and, as in the case of the highway program, insulating its operations from popular politics. He had also succeeded in expanding cooperative arrangements between government and business and in accelerating the interpenetration of public and private sectors. In all of this, of course, his presidency served to rationalize the efforts of American business to refashion the New Deal state. But he did not succeed in securing that concert of private interests that would insure stable and orderly growth and on which his vision of a corporate commonwealth depended. Indeed, before his presidency had ended there was already widespread evidence of disorder and dysfunction: business leaders had repeatedly failed to exercise the restraint and self-discipline that such a system demanded, the problems of agriculture had proven politically irresolvable, and employers and labor unions were increasingly "tending to settle their differences without regard to the impact on the economy." Nor did he succeed in surmounting the tensions of class, race, and sex that surged like powerful undercurrents just beneath the surface of American culture. The tendency, encouraged during his presidency, to substitute private consumption for public politics laid a heavy—if then still invisible—tax on limited resources, increased political alienation, and undercut his own emphasis on sacrifice and discipline. Revolutions throughout the Third World created growing international tension and heightened the conflict between his tactical emphasis on the limits of American power and the globalism to which he and other American leaders continued to subscribe. Critics, including some former supporters, now began to accuse the president of lack of leadership, demanding not only a more activist foreign policy but also a level of military spending that he clearly feared would produce disastrous consequences. By 1958 he was wondering plaintively "whether immediate greed would ever surrender to the long-term good of the whole world." His attempt to fashion a corporate commonwealth foundered, finally, on the problem of succession and on the inability of the Republican party to generate a disinterested leadership capable of sustaining his vision. His deep ambivalence over Nixon turned on precisely this point—"it is terrible," he pointedly told Ann Whitman, "when people get politically ambitious."

Within a decade the fragile consensus of the 1950s shattered on the hard realities of war and revolution, of class and racial conflict, of repression and indulgence. Such a failure was probably inevitable; for despite his pragmatism and lucid intelligence Eisenhower was at heart a visionary. Alarmed by the self-interested destructiveness of contemporary economic life, he had fashioned a deeply conservative image of a good society in which conflict would yield to cooperation, greed to discipline, coercion to self-government. Such a vision was no match for the vast and powerful forces of modern America.

﷼ *F U R T H E R   R E A D I N G*

Charles C. Alexander, *Holding the Line: The Eisenhower Era, 1952–1961* (1975)
Stephen E. Ambrose, *Eisenhower* (2 vols., 1983, 1985)
William C. Berman, *The Politics of Civil Rights in the Truman Administration* (1970)
Barton J. Bernstein, ed., *Politics and Policies of the Truman Administration* (1970)
Michael R. Beschloss, *Mayday: The U-2 Affair* (1986)
Robert F. Burk, *Dwight D. Eisenhower: Hero & Politician* (1986)
————, *The Eisenhower Administration and Black Civil Rights* (1984)
Richard Dean Burns, *Harry S. Truman: A Bibliography of His Times and Presidency* (1984)
David Caute, *The Great Fear: The Anti-Communist Purge Under Truman and Eisenhower* (1978)
Burt Cochran, *Harry Truman and the Crisis Presidency* (1973)
Blanche Wiesen Cook, *The Declassified Eisenhower: A Divided Legacy* (1981)
Robert Divine, *Eisenhower and the Cold War* (1981)
Robert J. Donovan, *Conflict and Crisis: The Presidency of Harry S. Truman, 1945–1948* (1977)
————, *Tumultuous Years: The Presidency of Harry S. Truman, 1949–1953* (1982)
Robert H. Ferrell, *Harry S. Truman and the Modern American Presidency* (1983)
Richard Freeland, *The Truman Doctrine and the Origins of McCarthyism* (1972)

Richard M. Fried, *Nightmare in Red* (1990)

Eric Goldman, *The Crucial Decade and After: America, 1945–1960* (1960)

Fred I. Greenstein, *The Hidden Hand Presidency: Eisenhower as Leader* (1982)

Robert Griffith, *The Politics of Fear: Joseph R. McCarthy and the Senate* (1970, 1987)

—— and Athan Theoharis, eds., *The Spector: Original Essays on the Cold War and the Origins of McCarthyism* (1974)

Alonzo Hamby, *Beyond the New Deal: Harry S Truman and American Liberalism* (1973)

Richard F. Haynes, *The Awesome Power: Harry S. Truman as Commander in Chief* (1973)

Burton I. Kaufman, *Trade and Aid: Eisenhower's Foreign Economic Policy* (1982)

Richard S. Kirkendall, ed., *The Truman Period as a Research Field* (1967)

——, *The Truman Period as a Research Field: A Reappraisal, 1972* (1973)

Michael J. Lacey, ed., *The Truman Presidency* (1989)

Everett Ladd, Jr., and Charles Hadley, *Transformations in the American Party System: Political Coalitions from the New Deal to the 1970s* (1978)

Peter Lyon, *Eisenhower: Portrait of the Hero* (1974)

Mary S. McAuliffe, *Crisis on the Left: Cold War Politics and American Liberals, 1947–1954* (1978)

Arthur F. McClure, *The Truman Administration and the Problems of Postwar Labor, 1945–1946* (1969)

Donald R. McCoy, *The Presidency of Harry S. Truman* (1984)

——, and Richard Ruetten, *Quest and Response: Minority Rights and the Truman Administration* (1973)

Norman Markowitz, *The Rise and Fall of the People's Century: Henry A. Wallace and American Liberalism, 1941–1948* (1973)

Richard A. Melanson and David Mayers, eds., *Reevaluating Eisenhower: American Foreign Policy in the Fifties* (1987)

Merle Miller, *Plain Speaking: An Oral Biography of Harry S. Truman* (1974)

Richard L. Miller, *Truman: The Rise to Power* (1986)

Kenneth O'Reilly, *Hoover and the Un-Americans: The FBI, HUAC, and the Red Menace* (1983)

David M. Oshinsky, *A Conspiracy So Immense: The World of Joe McCarthy* (1983)

Herbert S. Parmet, *Eisenhower and the American Crusades* (1972)

William E. Pemberton, *Harry S. Truman: Fair Dealer and Cold Warrior* (1989)

Gale E. Peterson, *President Harry S. Truman and the Independent Regulatory Commissions* (1973)

Cabell Phillips, *The Truman Presidency: The History of a Triumphant Succession* (1966)

Monte S. Poen, *Harry S Truman Versus the Medical Lobby* (1979)

Ronald Radosh and Joyce Milton, *The Rosenberg File: A Search for the Truth* (1983)

Thomas C. Reeves, *The Life and Times of Joe McCarthy* (1983)

Gary W. Reichard, *The Reaffirmation of Republicanism* (1975)

——, *Politics as Usual: The Age of Truman and Eisenhower* (1988)

Elmo Richardson, *The Eisenhower Presidency* (1979)

Athan Theoharis, ed., *The Truman Presidency: The Origins of the Imperial Presidency and the National Security State* (1979)

——, *Spying on Americans* (1978)

——, *Seeds of Repression: Harry S. Truman and the Origins of McCarthyism* (1970)

J. Samuel Walker, *Henry A. Wallace and American Foreign Policy* (1976)

Richard Walton, *Henry Wallace, Harry Truman, and the Cold War* (1976)

Martin P. Wattenberg, *The Decline of American Political Parties, 1952–1980* (1984)

Allen Weinstein, *Perjury: The Hiss-Chambers Case* (1978)

CHAPTER
5

American Society
in the 1950s

XX

For most Americans, the 1950s were a decade of unprecedented prosperity, economic growth, high employment, and the rapid if uneven spread of homesteads
in suburbia. It was a decade marked not only by the mass production of consumer goods and services, but by the increasingly important role of advertising
and mass communication in organizing consumption—in ensuring that what
was produced was in fact consumed. It was a decade, finally, in which the
dominant cultural imagery surrounded Americans in all walks of life with a se-
lectively distorted vision of America as a dynamic, classless, and benignly consensual society.

This vision contained enough truth to make it credible to many Americans,
who in fact were doing far better than they had during the fifteen years of war
and depression that had immediately preceded the postwar era. But if the 1950s
was an age of affluence, it was also an age of anxiety—anxiety over the Cold
War, Korea, and McCarthyism; over the threat of nuclear war; and over the
growing bureaucratization and impersonality of the new mass society. Moreover,
the experiences of countless people clashed with the decade's dominant imagery:
for example, the millions of Americans who remained mired in poverty, in what
Michael Harrington would later call "the other America"; the millions of African-Americans whose struggle against segregation would soon ignite the civil-
rights movement; the educated, middle-class women whose quiet desperation
Betty Friedan would later explore in The Feminine Mystique; even young people, in many ways the decade's principal beneficiaries, who, like Philip Caputo
in A Rumor of War, came to wonder if there was more to life than "sleek,
new schools smelling of fresh plaster and floor wax; supermarkets full of Wonder
Bread and Bird's Eye frozen peas; rows of centrally heated split-levels that lined
dirtless streets on which nothing ever happened." For these and others like
them, the 1950s would be marked by a struggle, often unequal and often unsuccessful, to create alternative values and understandings that would validate
their own feelings and experiences.

✕ *D O C U M E N T S*

During the late 1940s and early 1950s, U.S. business spent millions of dollars on campaigns to convince Americans of the benefits of the American economic system. The first document, an excerpt from a pamphlet entitled "The Miracle of America," was part of a multimillion-dollar effort launched in 1948 by the Advertising Council, a trade association of advertising agencies, media, and large corporate advertisers. Fueling the rapid economic growth of the 1950s was a sharp increase in the birthrate, a demographic phenomenon considered in the second document, a report on the so-called baby boom. This population spurt would influence social trends for the next four decades as the "baby boomers" successively entered schools, colleges, and the workplace; had children of their own; and assumed positions of economic and cultural power. As the third document, an article from *Life* magazine, suggests, by the late 1950s American business and advertising had identified a growing "teen market."

Most cultural authorities of the fifties insisted that women's place was in the home and that women could find fulfillment only as wives and mothers, a message that Democratic presidential candidate Governor Adlai Stevenson carried to the 1955 graduating class of Smith College, as the fourth selection reveals. One of the most incisive critiques of the 1950s was economist John Kenneth Galbraith's *The Affluent Society* (1958), from which the fifth document is excerpted. While most of the decade's cultural authorities celebrated the "miracle of America" in one fashion or another, a few voices were raised in dissent, among them that of "beat" poet Lawrence Ferlinghetti, whose poem "I Am Waiting" is reprinted as the final document.

U.S. Business Celebrates the "Miracle of America," 1948

It all started . . . when Junior looked up from his homework:

"It says here America is great and powerful on account of the American economic system. What's our economic system, Dad?"

Dad put his paper down and appeared to be thinking hard.

"I'd like to know, too," Mother put in. "I think in these times *every* American ought to be informed about what makes up the American way of life."

"So do I," Sis added.

"Well, I could give you all sorts of answers," Dad said. "But maybe we ought to get the story straight from the one who knows it best."

"Who's that?" asked Junior.

"You'll recognize him all right," Dad said. "Let's go!"

So they did . . .

Junior gasped. "Gee whiz—I know *him!*"

"Uncle Sam," Dad began, "my boy here wants to know what makes America great. You know—our economic system and all that. Fact is, I guess we all do." . . .

"In the early days, men and animals did most of our work.

"The Miracle of America," a pamphlet prepared for The Advertising Council, Inc. (1948). Excerpts.

"We even used the wind to run our machines.

"Then we began to use water power to turn millstones and run looms. But in some places no water power was to be had.

"We needed something better. Our inventors and business men kept testing and trying. There would be big rewards in our free market for reliable power that could be used *anywhere.*

"At last we had it—thanks to an ingenious Scotsman—James Watt. He invented an engine driven by steam made from coal!

"Later still Americans developed engines run by gasoline and electricity.

"Now we're looking for ways to use atomic power. . . .

"Americans are known as inventive people. Why? Because we have had the incentive to profit by making improvements—and backing them with our savings.

"When our people realized that they were free to shape their own destinies, they began to devise machines which multiplied each man's work power.

"In 1799, Eli Whitney, inventor of the cotton gin that did 50 men's work, made history with an order for muskets awarded by the U.S. Army. Instead of building each gun separately, he turned out standard parts which could be used interchangeably on *any* gun.

"Hearing of this, the clocksmith Eli Terry started to make clocks on the same principle. With all the laborious fitting eliminated, he found that he could sell clocks for $10 apiece instead of the regular $25. In three years, he and his partner, Seth Thomas sold 5,000.

"Eli Terry saw that if he cut his costs by mass production, and distributed a bigger volume more widely, he would benefit more people and make more money. And it worked out exactly that way!

"Pins had long been made by hand, selling as high as 20 cents each. Then a Connecticut man perfected machines to make *two million pins a week!*

"Down through the years, Americans invented hundreds of thousands of work-saving machines.

"Of course, it takes money to make and install those new, labor-saving machines in factories—more money than any one man could afford. A machine for one worker often costs thousands of dollars. So the owner took in many *partners*—thrifty men and women who received *stock* in exchange for their money. All these *partners* joined to form a *company* which they owned together. In order to make a profit in competition with other companies, they had to turn out better and less expensive products.

"The same new freedoms that made Americans ingenious and inventive made us better and better workers—no matter what our jobs.

"The planners and managers of industry found new and improved ways of designing factories and work flow—so that goods were turned out more quickly and cheaply.

"They found new and better ways to get those goods from the factories to the stores and into the homes. Advertising and selling opened up bigger markets by telling the story to millions.

"And the individual worker became steadily more skillful at his job. He realized that the more he could produce during the hours he worked, the more he would increase his own value. When many workers did that, it added up to national prosperity!

"Labor unions and collective bargaining strengthened the worker's sense of security and improved working conditions. The result is that America gradually developed the greatest group of skilled workers and technicians the world has ever seen. . . .

"It is because we Americans *produce* so much better for every hour we work that we *earn* more and can *buy* more. . . .

". . . and the end is not yet. We have learned that *in the long run*

"When output per hour goes up, prices drop, so more people can buy and all of us gain.

"But when output per hour goes down, prices rise, so fewer people can buy and all of us lose.

"Of course, there are unusual periods when these principles don't seem to work—times when business is far above or far below normal. But over the long pull you'll find that these rules of productivity *do* apply.

"On the average, productivity has increased in the United States almost one-fifth every 10 years since 1850. We topped this in the 20 years 1920–1940, and we can do it again!"

"Can we keep right on doing it?" Dad asked.

"We certainly can!" Uncle Sam replied. "If everybody who plays a part in making things will team up to do it, we can raise productivity so far and so fast that we can share the benefits and have real security for *all* our people."

A Report on the Baby Boom, 1954

The trend toward larger families among married college graduates is still continuing, the Population Reference Bureau reports.

For the last eight years, since 1946, the number of babies per graduate has been going up. The increase is greater for men graduates than for women.

"There is even a possibility," says a report in the Population Bulletin, "that members of the class of 1944 will replace themselves in the new generation." Statisticians figure that each graduate must have an average of 2.1 children to be sure that one will live to grow up, marry and have children to carry on the chain unbroken.

The low was reached by men graduates in the class of 1922 with 1.70 children per graduate; by women in the class of 1926 with 1.18.

For many years in the United States the tendency among white women of child-bearing age has been for those with the most education to have the fewest children. The figure in 1940 was 1.23 for college graduates as compared with 4.33 for women who had not gone beyond fourth grade.

The institution leading in number of children per graduate, for men of both the class 1944 and the class 1929 and women for the class 1929, is

---

"Baby Boom Continues Among College Grads," *Science News Letter*, June 19, 1954.

Brigham Young University in Utah. But this university is outdistanced by the 1944 women graduates of St. Mary's College in Indiana.

The increasing fertility of recent college graduates is attributed to an improvement in economic conditions and to changing attitudes toward marriage. In the 20's and early 30's, marriage and birth rates were both low. People were marrying later in life.

Now that it is easier for young couples to set up their home and start families, they are marrying younger. Births are not deferred as often nor as long as they were 15 years ago.

Life Magazine Identifies
the New Teen-age Market, 1959

To some people the vision of a leggy adolescent happily squealing over the latest fancy present from Daddy is just another example of the way teen-agers are spoiled to death these days. But to a growing number of businessmen the picture spells out the profitable fact that the American teen-agers have emerged as a big-time consumer in the U.S. economy. They are multiplying in numbers. They spend more and have more spent on them. And they have minds of their own about what they want.

The time is past when a boy's chief possession was his bike and a girl's party wardrobe consisted of a fancy dress worn with a string of dime-store pearls. What Depression-bred parents may still think of as luxuries are looked on as necessities by their offspring. Today teen-agers surround themselves with a fantastic array of garish and often expensive baubles and amusements. They own 10 million phonographs, over a million TV sets, 13 million cameras. Nobody knows how much parents spend on them for actual necessities nor to what extent teen-agers act as hidden persuaders on their parents' other buying habits. Counting only what is spent to satisfy their special teen-age demands, the youngsters and their parents will shell out about $10 billion this year, a billion more than the total sales of GM.

Until recently businessmen have largely ignored the teen-age market. But now they are spending millions on advertising and razzle-dazzle promotional stunts. Their efforts so far seem only to have scratched the surface of a rich lode. In 1970, when the teen-age population expands from its present 18 million to 28 million, the market may be worth $20 billion. If parents have any idea of organized revolt, it is already too late. Teen-age spending is so important that such action would send quivers through the entire national economy. . . .

At 17 Suzie Slattery of Van Nuys, Calif. fits any businessman's dream of the ideal teen-age consumer. The daughter of a reasonably well-to-do TV announcer, Suzie costs her parents close to $4,000 a year, far more than average for the country but not much more than many of the upper middle income families of her town. In an expanding economy more and more teen-

"A Young $10 Billion Power: The US Teen-age Consumer Has Become a Major Factor in the Nation's Economy" from *LIFE* (August 31, 1959), pp. 78–84. Courtesy of *LIFE* MAGAZINE. Reprinted with permission.

agers will be moving up into Suzie's bracket or be influenced as consumers by her example.

Last year $1,500 was spent on Suzie's clothes and $550 for her entertainment. Her annual food bill comes to $900. She pays $4 every two weeks at the beauty parlor. She has her own telephone and even has her own soda fountain in the house. On summer vacation days she loves to wander with her mother through fashionable department stores, picking out frocks or furnishings for her room or silver and expensive crockery for the hope chest she has already started.

As a high school graduation present, Suzie was given a holiday cruise to Hawaii and is now in the midst of a new clothes-buying spree for college. Her parents' constant indulgence has not spoiled Suzie. She takes for granted all the luxuries that surround her because she has had them all her life. But she also has a good mind and some serious interests. A top student in her school, she is entering Occidental College this fall and will major in political science. . . .

Some Fascinating Facts About a Booming Market

FOOD: Teen-agers eat 20% more than adults. They down 3½ billion quarts of milk every year, almost four times as much as is drunk by infant population under 1. Teen-agers are a main prop of the ice cream industry, gobble 145 million gallons a year.

BEAUTY CARE: Teen-agers spent $20 million on lipstick last year, $25 million on deodorants (a fifth of total sold), $9 million on home permanents. Male teen-agers own 2 million electric razors.

ENTERTAINMENT: Teen-agers lay out more than $1.5 billion a year for entertainment. They spend about $75 million on single pop records. Although they create new musical idols, they are staunchly faithful to the old. Elvis Presley, still their favorite, has sold 25 million copies of single records in four years, an all-time high.

HOMEMAKERS: Major items like furniture and silver are moving into the teen-age market because of growing number of teen-age marriages. One third of all 18- and 19-year-old girls are already married. More than 600,000 teen-agers will be married this year. Teen-agers are now starting hope chests at 15.

CREDIT RISKS: Some 800,000 teen-agers work at full-time jobs and can buy major items on credit.

Governor Adlai Stevenson
Describes a Woman's Place, 1955

I think there is much you can do about our crisis in the humble role of housewife.

The peoples of the West are still struggling with the problems of a free

---

Adlai Stevenson, "A Purpose for Modern Woman," excerpted from a Commencement Address, Smith College, 1955, in *Women's Home Companion* (September 1955).

society and just now are in dire trouble. For to create a free society is at all times a precarious and audacious experiment. Its bedrock is the concept of man as an end in himself. But violent pressures are constantly battering away at this concept, reducing man once again to subordinate status, limiting his range of choice, abrogating his responsibility and returning him to his primitive status of anonymity in the social group. I think you can be more helpful in identifying, isolating and combatting these pressures, this virus, than you perhaps realize.

Let me put it this way: individualism has promoted technological advance, technology promoted increased specialization, and specialization promoted an ever closer economic interdependence between specialties.

As the old order disintegrated into this confederation of narrow specialties, each pulling in the direction of its particular interest, the individual person tended to become absorbed literally by his particular function in society. Having sacrificed wholeness of mind and breadth of outlook to the demands of their specialties, individuals no longer responded to social stimuli as total human beings; rather they reacted in partial ways as members of an economic class or industry or profession whose concern was with some limited self-interest.

Thus this typical Western man, or typical Western husband, operates well in the realm of means, as the Romans did before him. But outside his specialty, in the realm of ends, he is apt to operate poorly or not at all. And this neglect of the cultivation of more mature values can only mean that his life, and the life of the society he determines, will lack valid purpose, however busy and even profitable it may be.

And here's where you come in: to restore valid, meaningful purpose to life in your home; to beware of instinctive group reaction to the forces which play upon you and yours, to watch for and arrest the constant gravitational pulls to which we are all exposed—your workaday husband especially—in our specialized, fragmented society, that tend to widen the breach between reason and emotion, between means and ends.

And let me also remind you that you will live, most of you, in an environment in which "facts," the data of the senses, are glorified, and values—judgments—are assigned inferior status as mere "matters of opinion." It is an environment in which art is often regarded as an adornment of civilization rather than a vital element of it, while philosophy is not only neglected but deemed faintly disreputable because "it never gets you anywhere." Even religion, you will find, commands a lot of earnest allegiance that is more verbal than real, more formal than felt.

You may be hitched to one of these creatures we call "Western man" and I think part of your job is to keep him Western, to keep him truly purposeful, to keep him whole. In short—while I have had very little experience as a wife or mother—I think one of the biggest jobs for many of you will be to frustrate the crushing and corrupting effects of specialization, to integrate means and ends, to develop that balanced tension of mind and spirit which can be properly called "integrity."

This assignment for you, as wives and mothers, has great advantages.

In the first place, it is home work—you can do it in the living-room with a baby in your lap or in the kitchen with a can opener in your hand. If you're really clever, maybe you can even practice your saving arts on that unsuspecting man while he's watching television!

And, secondly, it is important work worthy of you, whoever you are, or your education, whatever it is, because we will defeat totalitarian, authoritarian ideas only by better ideas; we will frustrate the evils of vocational specialization only by the virtues of intellectual generalization. Since Western rationalism and Eastern spiritualism met in Athens and that mighty creative fire broke out, collectivism in various forms has collided with individualism time and again. This twentieth-century collision, this "crisis" we are forever talking about, will be won at last not on the battlefield but in the head and heart.

So you see, I have some rather large notions about you and what you have to do to rescue us wretched slaves of specialization and group thinking from further shrinkage and contraction of mind and spirit. But you will have to be alert or you may get caught yourself—even in the kitchen or the nursery—by the steady pressures with which you will be surrounded. . . .

Women, especially educated women, have a unique opportunity to influence us, man and boy, and to play a direct part in the unfolding drama of our free society. But I am told that nowadays the young wife or mother is short of time for such subtle arts, that things are not what they used to be; that once immersed in the very pressing and particular problems of domesticity, many women feel frustrated and far apart from the great issues and stirring debates for which their education has given them understanding and relish. Once they read Baudelaire. Now it is the Consumers' Guide. Once they wrote poetry. Now it's the laundry list. Once they discussed art and philosophy until late in the night. Now they are so tired they fall asleep as soon as the dishes are finished. There is, often, a sense of contraction, of closing horizons and lost opportunities. They had hoped to play their part in the crisis of the age. But what they do is wash the diapers. (Or do they any longer?)

Now I hope I have not painted too depressing a view of your future, for the fact is that Western marriage and motherhood are yet another instance of the emergence of individual freedom in our Western society. Their basis is the recognition in women as well as men of the primacy of personality and individuality. I have just returned from sub-Sahara Africa where the illiteracy of the African mother is a formidable obstacle to the education and advancement of her child and where polygamy and female labor are still the dominant system.

The point is that whether we talk of Africa, Islam or Asia, women "never had it so good" as you do. And in spite of the difficulties of domesticity, you have a way to participate actively in the crisis in addition to keeping yourself and those about you straight on the difference between means and ends, mind and spirit, reason and emotion—not to mention keeping your man straight on the differences between Botticelli and Chianti. . . .

In modern America the home is not the boundary of a woman's life. There are outside activities aplenty. But even more important is the fact, surely, that what you have learned and can learn will fit you for the primary task of making homes and whole human beings in whom the rational values of freedom, tolerance, charity and free inquiry can take root.

Economist John Kenneth Galbraith Examines Poverty in the "Affluent Society," 1958

The final problem of the productive society is what it produces. This manifests itself in an implacable tendency to provide an opulent supply of some things and a niggardly yield of others. This disparity carries to the point where it is a cause of social discomfort and social unhealth. The line which divides our area of wealth from our area of poverty is roughly that which divides privately produced and marketed goods and services from publicly rendered services. Our wealth in the first is not only in startling contrast with the meagerness of the latter, but our wealth in privately produced goods is, to a marked degree, the cause of crisis in the supply of public services. For we have failed to see the importance, indeed the urgent need, of maintaining a balance between the two.

This disparity between our flow of private and public goods and services is no matter of subjective judgment. On the contrary, it is the source of the most extensive comment which only stops short of the direct contrast being made here. In the years following World War II, the papers of any major city—those of New York were an excellent example—told daily of the shortages and shortcomings in the elementary municipal and metropolitan services. The schools were old and overcrowded. The police force was under strength and underpaid. The parks and playgrounds were insufficient. Streets and empty lots were filthy, and the sanitation staff was underequipped and in need of men. Access to the city by those who work there was uncertain and painful and becoming more so. Internal transportation was overcrowded, unhealthful, and dirty. So was the air. Parking on the streets had to be prohibited, and there was no space elsewhere. These deficiencies were not in new and novel services but in old and established ones. Cities have long swept their streets, helped their people move around, educated them, kept order, and provided horse rails for vehicles which sought to pause. That their residents should have a nontoxic supply of air suggests no revolutionary dalliance with socialism.

The discussion of this public poverty competed, on the whole successfully, with the stories of ever-increasing opulence in privately produced goods. The Gross National Product was rising. So were retail sales. So was personal income. Labor productivity had also advanced. The automobiles that could not be parked were being produced at an expanded rate. The

children, though without schools, subject in the playgrounds to the affec-
tionate interest of adults with odd tastes, and disposed to increasingly imaginative forms of delinquency, were admirably equipped with television
sets. We had difficulty finding storage space for the great surpluses of food
despite a national disposition to obesity. Food was grown and packaged
under private auspices. The care and refreshment of the mind, in contrast
with the stomach, was principally in the public domain. Our colleges and
universities were severely overcrowded and underprovided, and the same
was true of the mental hospitals.

The contrast was and remains evident not alone to those who read. The
family which takes its mauve and cerise, air-conditioned, power-steered, and
power-braked automobile out for a tour passes through cities that are badly
paved, made hideous by litter, blighted buildings, billboards, and posts for
wires that should long since have been put underground. They pass on into
a countryside that has been rendered largely invisible by commercial art.
(The goods which the latter advertise have an absolute priority in our value
system. Such aesthetic considerations as a view of the countryside accordingly
come second. On such matters we are consistent.) They picnic on exquisitely
packaged food from a portable icebox by a polluted stream and go on to
spend the night at a park which is a menace to public health and morals.
Just before dozing off on an air mattress, beneath a nylon tent, amid the
stench of decaying refuse, they may reflect vaguely on the curious unevenness
of their blessings. Is this, indeed, the American genius? . . .

A feature of the years immediately following World War II was a remarkable attack on the notion of expanding and improving public services.
During the depression years such services had been elaborated and improved
partly in order to fill some small part of the vacuum left by the shrinkage
of private production. During the war years the role of government was
vastly expanded. After that came the reaction. Much of it, unquestionably,
was motivated by a desire to rehabilitate the prestige of private production
and therewith of producers. No doubt some who joined the attack hoped,
at least tacitly, that it might be possible to sidestep the truce on taxation
vis-à-vis equality by having less taxation of all kinds. For a time the notion
that our public services had somehow become inflated and excessive was all
but axiomatic. Even liberal politicians did not seriously protest. They found
it necessary to aver that they were in favor of public economy too.

In this discussion a certain mystique was attributed to the satisfaction
of privately supplied wants. A community decision to have a new school
means that the individual surrenders the necessary amount, willy-nilly, in
his taxes. But if he is left with that income, he is a free man. He can decide
between a better car or a television set. This was advanced with some
solemnity as an argument for the TV set. The difficulty is that this argument
leaves the community with no way of preferring the school. All private
wants, where the individual can choose, are inherently superior to all public
desires which must be paid for by taxation and with an inevitable component
of compulsion.

The cost of public services was also held to be a desolating burden on private production, although this was at a time when the private production was burgeoning. Urgent warnings were issued of the unfavorable effects of taxation on investment—"I don't know of a surer way of killing off the incentive to invest than by imposing taxes which are regarded by people as punitive." This was at a time when the inflationary effect of a very high level of investment was causing concern. The same individuals who were warning about the inimical effects of taxes were strongly advocating a monetary policy designed to reduce investment. However, an understanding of our economic discourse requires an appreciation of one of its basic rules: men of high position are allowed, by a special act of grace, to accommodate their reasoning to the answer they need. Logic is only required in those of lesser rank.

Finally it was argued, with no little vigor, that expanding government posed a grave threat to individual liberties. "Where distinction and rank is achieved almost exclusively by becoming a civil servant of the state . . . it is too much to expect that many will long prefer freedom to security."

With time this attack on public services has somewhat subsided. The disorder associated with social imbalance has become visible even if the need for balance between private and public services is still imperfectly appreciated.

Freedom also seemed to be surviving. Perhaps it was realized that all organized activity requires concessions by the individual to the group. This is true of the policeman who joins the police force, the teacher who gets a job at the high school, and the executive who makes his way up the hierarchy of Du Pont. If there are differences between public and private organization, they are of kind rather than of degree. As this is written the pendulum has in fact swung back. Our liberties are now menaced by the conformity exacted by the large corporation and its impulse to create, for its own purposes, the organization man. This danger we may also survive.

Nonetheless, the postwar onslaught on the public services left a lasting imprint. To suggest that we canvass our public wants to see where happiness can be improved by more and better services has a sharply radical tone. Even public services to avoid disorder must be defended. By contrast the man who devises a nostrum for a nonexistent need and then successfully promotes both remains one of nature's noblemen.

A Beat Poet Waits for the Real America, 1958

I Am Waiting

> I am waiting for my case to come up
> and I am waiting
> for a rebirth of wonder
> and I am waiting for someone
> to really discover America

and wail
and I am waiting
for the discovery
of a new symbolic western frontier
and I am waiting
for the American Eagle
to really spread its wings
and straighten up and fly right
and I am waiting
for the Age of Anxiety
to drop dead
and I am waiting
for the war to be fought
which will make the world safe
for anarchy
and I am waiting
for the final withering away
of all governments
and I am perpetually awaiting
a rebirth of wonder

I am waiting for the Second Coming
and I am waiting
for a religious revival
to sweep thru the state of Arizona
and I am waiting
for the Grapes of Wrath to be stored
and I am waiting
for them to prove
that God is really American
and I am seriously waiting
for Billy Graham and Elvis Presley
to exchange roles seriously
and I am waiting
to see God on television
piped onto church altars
if only they can find
the right channel
to tune in on
and I am waiting
for the Last Supper to be served again
with a strange new appetizer
and I am perpetually awaiting
a rebirth of wonder

I am waiting for my number to be called
and I am waiting
for the living end
and I am waiting
for dad to come home
his pockets full
of irradiated silver dollars

and I am waiting
for the atomic tests to end
and I am waiting happily
for things to get much worse
before they improve
and I am waiting
for the Salvation Army to take over
and I am waiting
for the human crowd
to wander off a cliff somewhere
clutching its atomic umbrella
and I am waiting
for Ike to act
and I am waiting
for the meek to be blessed
and inherit the earth
without taxes
and I am waiting
for forests and animals
to reclaim the earth as theirs
and I am waiting
for a way to be devised
to destroy all nationalisms
without killing anybody
and I am waiting
for linnets and planets to fall like rain
and I am waiting for lovers and weepers
to lie down together again
in a new rebirth of wonder

I am waiting for the Great Divide to be crossed
and I am anxiously waiting
for the secret of eternal life to be discovered
by an obscure general practitioner
and save me forever from certain death
and I am waiting
for life to begin
and I am waiting
for the storms of life
to be over
and I am waiting
to set sail for happiness
and I am waiting
for a reconstructed Mayflower
to reach America
with its picture story and tv rights
sold in advance to the natives
and I am waiting
for the lost music to sound again
in the Lost Continent
in a new rebirth of wonder

I am waiting for the day
that maketh all things clear
and I am waiting
for Ole Man River
to just stop rolling along
past the country club
and I am waiting
for the deepest South
to just stop Reconstructing itself
in its own image
and I am waiting
for a sweet desegregated chariot
to swing low
and carry me back to Ole Virginie
and I am waiting
for Ole Virginie to discover
just why Darkies are born
and I am waiting
for God to lookout
from Lookout Mountain
and see the Ode to the Confederate Dead
as a real farce
and I am awaiting retribution
for what America did
to Tom Sawyer
and I am perpetually awaiting
a rebirth of wonder

I am waiting for Tom Swift to grow up
and I am waiting
for the American Boy
to take off Beauty's clothes
and get on top of her
and I am waiting
for Alice in Wonderland
to retransmit to me
her total dream of innocence
and I am waiting
for Childe Roland to come
to the final darkest tower
and I am waiting
for Aphrodite
to grow live arms
at a final disarmament conference
in a new rebirth of wonder

I am waiting
to get some intimations
of immortality
by recollecting my early childhood
and I am waiting
for the green mornings to come again
youth's dumb green fields come back again

and I am waiting
for some strains of unpremeditated art
to shake my typewriter
and I am waiting to write
the great indelible poem
and I am waiting
for the last long careless rapture
and I am perpetually waiting
for the fleeing lovers on the Grecian Urn
to catch each other up at last
and embrace
and I am awaiting
perpetually and forever
a renaissance of wonder

⋈ *E S S A Y S*

Historians have often disagreed in their assessments of the 1950s. Most early books on the postwar years, like Eric Goldman's widely read *The Crucial Decade* (1955), shared the era's commitment to the Cold War and the mixed economy of the New Deal state but sharply criticized its political conservatism and cultural blandness. During the 1960s and early 1970s, by contrast, new "revisionist" historians painted a far more critical portrait of the decade. "If Fortune smiled on the postwar United States," concluded Lawrence S. Wittner in *Cold War America* (1974), "she reserved her keenest delights for the forces of privilege." By the end of the 1980s, more conservative historians such as John Patrick Diggins in *The Proud Decades* (1989) and William O'Neill in *American High* (1989) were recalling the decade more fondly as a time of relative peace and prosperity.

In the first essay, Michigan State University historian Douglas T. Miller and journalist Marion Nowak, in a chapter from their book *The Fifties: The Way We Really Were* (1977), describe a "precarious prosperity" plagued by waste, pollution, poverty, and the threat of nuclear annihilation. In the second essay, excerpted from his book *The Proud Decade*, Diggins, a historian at the University of California, Irvine, concludes that the fifties were a time of "unbounded possibility" during which most Americans not only survived but prospered.

How does one account for these two sharply differing interpretations? To what extent do they merely reflect the times in which they are written? How different is the evidence offered in each of them? Is one more persuasive than the other? Can both be right? Are there other ways of sorting out the complex meanings of the decade?

The Precarious Prosperity of People's Capitalism

DOUGLAS T. MILLER and MARION NOWAK

The American economic system, according to most fifties observers, was a pretty wonderful thing. But what to call it? Surely "capitalism" was an inadequate label, conveying, as it did, a world of sweatshop laborers ruled by ruthless robber barons. Many people wondered if a more accurate descriptive phrase could not be found. William Nichols, the editor of *This Week,* the magazine supplement stuffed into many Sunday newspapers, decided to see. On March 4, 1951, he authored an article (later reprinted in *Reader's Digest*) entitled "Wanted: A New Name for Capitalism." "How shall we describe this system," Nichols asked, "imperfect, but always improving, and always capable of further improvement—where men move forward together, working together, building together, producing always more and more, and sharing together the rewards of their increased production?" He proposed a few possible choices: "the new capitalism," "democratic capitalism," "economic democracy," "productivism." But, not entirely satisfied with any of those, he asked readers to submit their own suggestions and included a handy coupon for that purpose. A surprising 15,000 coupons came back. "Never in my whole editorial experience," Nichols later recalled, "have I touched so live a nerve."

At about the same time that Nichols was attempting to rename capitalism, three very popular books appeared offering explanations of the new economic system. The editors of *Fortune* wrote of *U.S.A.: The Permanent Revolution;* Peter Drucker told of *The New Society,* Frederick Lewis Allen of *The Big Change.* Each study related a similar story: In the United States we have never had it so good. Our industrial society, in Drucker's words, was *"beyond Capitalism and Socialism. It is a new society transcending both."* Not since the precrash days of Hoover and Calvin Coolidge was such lavish praise bestowed on the business community. "It is not the capitalists who are using the people," claimed the Luce men at *Fortune,* "but the people who are using the capitalists. Capital has become, not the master of this society, but its servant." "U.S. capitalism," they continued, "is *popular* capitalism, not only in the sense that it has popular support, but in the deeper sense that the people as a whole participate in it and use it."

Like most books of the early fifties, there was a sense of cold war urgency to these studies. The United States, the bastion of freedom and capitalism, was being derided, not just by our communist enemies but even by many of our European friends whom we were generously helping back on their feet. These people did not understand—capitalism was fine here. Maybe not perfect, but damn good, and, even more important, it was self-correcting. "Karl Marx," asserted the *Fortune* editors, "based his philosophy on the fatalistic assumption that what he described as the inherent defects of capitalism are above the will of men to affect them. It has remained for the history of U.S. Capitalism, beginning as early as the 1870s, to show that the moral convictions of men can change the course of capitalist development."

Allen's book, the most popular of the three, while not quite so naive as the *Fortune* study (at least he implied that the New Deal had something to do with making capitalists responsible), told a similar success story. *The Big Change* is subtitled "America Transforms Itself 1900–1950." Allen chose as his theme "the changes which have taken place in the character and quality of American life by reason of what might be called the democratization of our economic system, or the adjustment of capitalism to democratic ends." From the days of the Carnegies, Rockefellers, and Morgans when "America seemed in danger of becoming a land in which the millionaires had more and more and the rest less and less," Allen unfolded a tale of unrevolutionary but steady change leading to the nearly classless utopia of mid-century. By his own figures over a quarter of all American families had to subsist on less than $2,000 a year and nearly half on less than $3,000. Nevertheless, he went on to paint a picture of one big happy middle class. "We had brought about a virtually automatic redistribution of income from the well-to-do to the less well-to-do."

Even more impressive "than the narrowing of the gap in *income* between rich and poor has been the narrowing of the gap between them in their ways of living." To prove this he gave two memorable examples. First he noted that in 1949 some 543 million pairs of nylon stockings were sold—enough to provide every woman over 14 with nine or ten pairs. This led him to exclaim: "How is that for an example of the dynamic logic of mass production producing luxury for all?" His second example of the "convergence between the ways of living of rich and poor" involved workmen standing about a New York City street excavation. Allen noticed that one of the men held an iron rod "presumably used for prying off manhole covers. . . . I looked twice to see what he was doing with that rod. He was practicing a graceful golf stroke."

None of these three studies denied that big business dominated American life. But that was fine because big business was benevolent. "When I was growing up," Allen approvingly quoted Ralph Coghlan of the St. Louis *Post-Dispatch*, "the word 'soulless' corporation was a very common term. . . . Well, in my lifetime I have seen a remarkable change in this. I don't know whether it could be said that corporations have obtained souls, but at least they have obtained intelligence." "Modern management exhibits," the *Fortune* editors lyricized, "a sense of responsibility toward its employees, not only to prevent or anticipate the demands of labor unions . . . but for the simple, obvious, and honest reason that a satisfied loyal group of employees is at least as much of an asset as a modern plant or a vital piece of machinery." These editors actually believed that "the problem, indeed, may be to prevent management from becoming overgenerous."

Under such a benevolent system these prophets foresaw the dawning of an era of harmony between labor and management. Strikes, claimed Allen, were no longer regarded "as class warfare but as a sort of game played between two teams, one of which has numbers on its side while the other has authority and money." The *Fortune* editors concurred: "Never have left-wing ideologies had so little influence on the American labor movement as they have today." The difference between European workers and American, they all asserted, was that here laborers had a personal stake in the general economy. "In this country," Drucker proclaimed, *"one out of every eight workers—other than farm hands—has a direct investment in industrial securities."* Even the American Federation of Labor house organ *Labor's Monthly Survey,* noted the *Fortune* writers, "ran an admirable treatise on investment and small estate management." They were all pleased that, as Allen stated, "very few Americans seriously propose any *really wholesale* change in our evolving system."

Numerous other observers of the mid-century American scene agreed— capitalism had united with democracy in what had to be at least the second greatest story ever told. "Easy Street," puffed *Time* correspondent Thomas Griffith, "now stretches from coast to coast." Adlai Stevenson, during his 1952 campaign, joined the chorus: "The United States at mid-century stands on the threshold of abundance for all." To Republican Henry Luce that threshold was already crossed: "In mid-twentieth-century America, bread is a drug on the market. Our problem is not to get bread, but to get rid of bread." Even visiting French neo-Thomist Jacques Maritain chimed in about our "economic humanism":

> The vital, pragmatic, completely unsystematic pressure exercised by the American people and the American soul on the structures of our modern industrial civilization is transforming from within the inner dynamism and historical trends of the industrial regime. It is causing this regime to pass beyond capitalism. The people have thus vanquished the inner logic of the industrial regime considered in its first historical phase, and have, almost without knowing it, inaugurated a really new phase in modern civilization.

Businessmen themselves, however, seemed somewhat reluctant to bask in the praise or to share the optimism. The era of the Great Depression with its dual horrors of economic collapse and government intervention was still too vivid a memory. Though prosperity was in evidence, many business leaders had come to accept the inevitability of another crash. If by some miracle a crash could be averted, what was to prevent the entire system from being sapped by "creeping socialism?" Although "that man in Washington" was dead, his Missouri running mate remained in the White House as the fifties opened. Business laments were frequent. The American economic system, claimed the president of United States Steel at an April 21, 1950, luncheon meeting in Baltimore, was "in deadlier peril than it has been in my lifetime." Even after Eisenhower and the Republicans presumably ended the "twenty years of treason," business leaders were not entirely happy. As late as 1955 the newly elected president of the National Association of Manufacturers announced "creeping socialism is now walking," and concluded "we're already well on our way to the achievement of the Communist State as blueprinted by Marx."

But such rhetoric was less common by the mid-fifties, and one suspects that it continued only as a kind of ritual. Most businessmen by that time had come to believe they really were the good guys. Not only did numerous social observers tell them this, but the Eisenhower administration as well. Ike's first cabinet reflected the probusiness views, consisting of, as TRB [Richard L. Strout] of *The New Republic* quipped, "eight millionaires and a plumber." The plumber, Secretary of Labor Martin Durkin (he had been president of the plumber's union), resigned a few months later. Other cabinet members quickly let business know where the administration stood. Even before taking office as Secretary of Defense, Charles Wilson, then president of General Motors, told the Senate Armed Services Committee that "what was good for our country was good for General Motors and vice versa." In 1953, Secretary of Commerce Sinclair Weeks assured the annual gathering of the National Association of Manufacturers that "a climate favorable to business has most definitely been substituted for the socialism of recent years." Even our foreign policy, Eisenhower promised, would "be based on the need for America to obtain profitable foreign markets and raw materials to sustain her economy." Industrial leaders breathed a sigh of relief. "The United States has had a close call," U.S. Steel president Clifford Hood noted soon after Ike was safely ensconced in Washington. "It was taken on a long detour toward Socialism. . . . We have turned and now face toward private capitalism."

In such a climate businessmen could not help but feel good. They too began telling the world of the glories of American capitalism. Public relations people became a permanent part of large corporations and helped spread the word about industrial altruism. In the 20 years from 1944 to 1964 the number of public relation firms jumped from 100 to 1,500. Corporate-made movies and corporate-employed speakers told schoolchildren and Rotary clubbers about America's great manufacturing enterprises. Boy and Girl Scouts, little leaguers, and other wholesome youth groups became the beneficiaries of local corporate charity, and in many communities new symphony orchestras, art museums, and civic centers publicly proclaimed the spirit of philanthropic business. In case the message was not clear, some companies spelled it out more bluntly. "General Electric," read the bold headlines of a two-page *Harper's* ad (January 1956), "has a billion-dollar belief in U.S. progress."

The annual company reports to stockholders became glossier, artier, more dazzling. No longer were they filled with just dry statistics. Companies began including big colored pictures, cartoons, comic strips, phonograph records, even sample merchandise. One corporation, Charles Pfizer and Company, had their annual report reprinted in the New York *Times,* the Chicago *Tribune,* and the Los Angeles *Times* "for [in their words] the many thousands of newspaper readers who may not have had an opportunity to see just how a typical American corporation reports to its owners." The report filled an entire section of the Sunday *Times.* In the early fifties, Standard Oil of New Jersey and General Electric pioneered in encouraging large attendance at annual stockholders' meetings. Other companies followed suit and soon these annual gatherings, complete with fried-chicken boxed lunches, looked more like family reunions or pep rallies than serious business affairs.

The apotheosis of the probusiness mentality emerged as one of the great myths of the fifties—"People's Capitalism." The expression came into vogue in 1956, though the ideas behind it were implicit in the early fifties capitalist eulogies of Allen, Drucker, and the *Fortune* editors. In another two-page General Electric ad picturing a happy gathering of stockholders (*Harper's,* August 1956), the headline read: "PEOPLE'S CAPITALISM—What makes it work for you?" It announced: "Our American brand of capitalism is distinctive and unusually successful because it is 'people's capitalism': all the people share in its responsibilities and benefits." The ad went on to list the eight characteristics of people's capitalism: 1) opportunity for each individual to develop to his highest potential; 2) high volume at prices within reach of all; 3) high wages, high productivity, high purchasing power; 4) constant innovation combined with the scrapping of the obsolete; 5) consumer credit and installment sales; 6) leisure through a short "highly productive" work week; 7) a "broad share ownership of American business"; 8) competition as the spark of our economy.

The term "people's capitalism" was coined by the Advertising Council. Early in 1956 the Council prepared an exhibit under that title to be shown internationally under the auspices of the United States Information Agency. The exhibit was first set up in February 1956 at Union Station in Washington, D.C., where Eisenhower and other dignitaries viewed it. Later the program toured Latin America, Europe, Africa, and Asia. It contrasted America of 1776 with 1956 by showing a crude log cabin alongside "a modern steel prefabricated five-room house, including all the modern labor-saving appliances." Display cards in the exhibit made the point that 60 per cent of American families owned their own homes and 75 per cent of American farmers owned their own land. Cards further asserted that 70 million Americans had savings accounts; 115 million had life insurance policies; 10 million owned shares in American companies. In other words the USIA announced: "in the United States almost everybody is a 'capitalist.'"

The major emphasis of the people's capitalism propagandists was on the wide distribution of stock ownership. "The economy of the United States," claimed M. Nadler in a 1956 pamphlet, "is rapidly assuming the character of what may be termed 'People's Capitalism,' under which the production facilities of the nation—notably manufacturing—have come to be increasingly owned by people in the middle and lower income brackets." Big businesses like United States Steel, certified the president of that company, Roger Blough, in a January 1957 speech, "are owned by millions of people in all walks of life." Marx's ideal is realized in America, affirmed the author of an Esso corporation pamphlet, *The Story of Creative Capital.* "Yes, the people own the tools of production. . . . How odd to find that it is here, in the capitalism he reviled, that the promise of the tools has been fulfilled." Edward Maher, writing for *Reader's Digest,* agreed. "This is a new kind of capitalism for the world to contemplate—capitalism for the many, not for the few. Communism or socialism will have a hard time matching it."

Most of these assertions, of course, were advertising and public relations fantasies. Actually the percentage of the population owning stock was lower in 1956 than in 1930. Only 3.5 per cent of employed persons were stock owners (about the same percentage as in the twenties and thirties). Among industrial workers fewer than 1.5 per cent held securities and few of them owned as much as $1,000 worth. According to Victor Perlo, an economist who investigated the people's capitalism claims, any one of several rich families—Rockefellers, du Ponts, Mellons—owned much more stock than "all the wage earners in the U.S." In fact "the market value of Rockefeller holdings in a single corporation, Standard Oil of New Jersey, was twice the market value of all the holdings of all American wage earners." There was no evidence of any significant widening of the concentrated ownership and control of the corporate structure. As the Senate Committee on Banking and Currency reported in 1955, "less than one per cent of all American families owned over four-fifths of all publicly held stocks owned by individuals." With power so imbalanced, even those small investors who did exist had no influence whatever in corporate affairs. Perlo correctly concluded in regard to people's capitalism that "the widespread diffusion of this theory signifies only the effectiveness of organized propaganda."

Perlo's refutation of people's capitalism claims, published in a scholarly journal in 1958, in no way dampened the ardor of the public love affair with big business. It's ironic, a *Life* reporter mused, that "of all the great industrial nations, the one that clings most tenaciously to private capitalism has come closest to the socialist goal of providing abundance for all in a classless society." To Peter Drucker it did not even make sense to talk of this country as a middle-class society since "a middle class has to have a class on either side to be in the middle." The admen agreed. "Gimbel's takes note of a new trend in American living," headlined a big ad for that department store in the New York *Times*, January 10, 1954: "The 'Booming Middle Class' is taking over—and no longer are we living up to the Joneses (Chauncy Montague Jones et familia)—we're living down to the Joneses (Charlie Jones and the wife and kids). It's bye-bye, upstairs chambermaid—ta, ta liveried chauffeur—good riddance to the lorgnette, limousine, and solid-gold lavatory. The new Good Life is casual, de-frilled, comfortable, fun—and isn't it marvelous. Gimbel's is all for the bright, young, can't-be-fooled Charlie Joneses."

Even liberal intellectuals not easily taken in by the ads or the people's capitalism propaganda developed positive theories regarding the American economy. Former New Dealers Adolf Berle and David Lilienthal, noted critics of big business in the thirties, became staunch defenders of the corporate giants in the fifties. Berle wrote positively of what he termed *The 20th Century Capitalist Revolution*, claiming among other things that "the corporations have a conscience." "Bigness," argued Lilienthal, once the controversial head of TVA, was wonderful. "In U.S.A. 1952, Bigness in industry is itself one of the most effective ways—sometimes the only effective way—to maintain competition." In fact, he concluded, "bigness can be an expression of the heroic size of man himself as he comes to a new-found greatness."

Historians, who had attacked the robber barons so mercilessly in the thirties, now elevated those same nabobs to the role of industrial statesmen. Allan Nevins' biography of John D. Rockefeller made even that crotchety and crooked magnate into an American savior.

But the most influential of the liberal intellectuals when it came to explaining the marvels of capitalism was John Kenneth Galbraith. Here was a realist. He did not celebrate people's capitalism. Nor did he accept the idea that competition kept business in line—the most basic assumption of economists and corporate executives alike. In 1952 Galbraith published *American Capitalism*, putting forth his theory of "countervailing power."

American Capitalism tried to show why the economic system worked so well even though it fit no traditional theories. Galbraith admitted that most major industries were dominated by a few giant companies—oligopoly. But like Lilienthal and Berle he welcomed bigness; it was more efficient, more productive, and provided more funds for research. Unlike most others, however, Galbraith was willing to admit that an oligopolistic economy was not a competitive one. The price differential between Camels, Luckies, and Chesterfields, or between Chevrolets, Fords, and Plymouths, was minimal and was far more the result of collusion than of free competition. How then was the power of big business kept in check? Galbraith's answer was simple. If put in Newtonian terms it might read: "original power begets an equal and opposite countervailing power." In Galbraith's own words: "Private economic power is held in check by the countervailing power of those who are subject to it. The first begets the second." That is, power was inevitably checked by a corresponding power, and these powers working at cross purposes made the system function for the common good. Best of all this was a "self-generating" phenomenon. Thus "in the ultimate sense it was the power of the steel industry, not the organizing abilities of John L. Lewis and Philip Murray, that brought the United Steel Workers into being."

Galbraith's examples of actual working countervailing powers were few, but he repeated them often. There was, of course, organized labor to protect workers in major industries. There also existed the buying power of large retailers—A&P, Sears Roebuck, and so on—acting as a check on high prices for the consumer. Finally, there was the power of the farmer who with the aid of government price supports was able to counter the power of the giant food producers.

Galbraith's theory of the role of government was interesting. Like the two Roosevelts, he saw the state as a referee stepping in to protect those unable to protect themselves with minimum wage and maximum hour laws, social security, farm price supports. And like the classical economists and Marxian communists, he ultimately saw the state as at least shrinking if not entirely withering away. This would take place once sufficient countervailing powers were operative. As Galbraith wrote: "Given the existence of private market power in the economy, the growth of countervailing power strengthens the capacity of the economy for autonomous self-regulation and thereby lessens the amount of over-all government control or planning that is required or sought." This was a reassuring theory. Liberals and conservatives alike loved it. Like the Constitution itself, or Madison's famed Federalist ten, the countervailing power thesis conjured up an image of self-interested factions checking and balancing one another and in so doing producing an ideal economy where all benefit.

Galbraith's assessment of the economic system, recognizing as it did both the dominance of the giant corporations and the absence of competition, was more realistic than those of Allen, Drucker, Berle, or other business apologists. Yet it was basically flawed. He either ignored or minimized many things. For instance, Galbraith overlooked the fact that there could be collusion between supposedly countervailing powers; the fact that big business maintained a disproportionate amount of power; the fact that under this supposedly benign system millions lived in utter poverty; the fact that in-flation wiped out savings and lowered the living standards of millons; the fact that millions of able-bodied persons remained unemployed; the fact that the whole system was subject to periodic declines in the business cycle; the fact that waste and environmental exploitation were basic to the prosperity; and, most basic, the fact that the prosperity of the era rested primarily on cold war military spending.

When one examines the actual workings of the American economic system in the 1950s, a quite different picture emerges from that painted by either Galbraith or the people's capitalism celebrants. To be sure, talk of prosperity was not altogether a fiction. The massive military spending of World War II ended the depression as no New Deal measures had come close to doing. Economists and business leaders feared a slump after 1945. But the spending of vast amounts by consumers, who had saved over $150 billion during the war, combined with the increasingly heavy outlays for defense led instead to continued economic growth. Per capita disposable consumption measured in 1960 dollars increased from $1,274 in the depression year 1940 to $1,824 by 1960. During those same years the Gross National Product (GNP) grew from about $100 billion annually to over $500 billion. By 1955, the United States, with but six per cent of the world's population, was producing nearly 50 per cent of the world's goods. Personal consumption reached record heights. In 1952 the Department of Commerce listed such consumption at $218 billion, including such items as $255 million spent on chewing gum, $235 million on greeting cards, $130 million on laxatives and cathartics, $38 million on stomach sweeteners, and $23 million on mouthwash.

Big business was dominant and grew more so in the fifties. Between 1940 and 1960 the percentage of the total labor force classified as self-employed dropped from 26 to 11 per cent. Most people worked for giant corporations. In major industries a few huge firms controlled most business. In the manufacture of automobiles, agricultural machinery, tires, cigarettes, aluminum, liquor, meat products, copper, tin cans, and office machinery, three companies prevailed. In steel, chemicals, and dairy products, about six did. These corporate giants were well entrenched. Out of 1,001 largest manufacturing firms in 1951, all but nine were in existence at the end of the decade. Smaller companies merged with larger ones at the rate of about 800 a year. By the late fifties the top five per cent of American corporations received 87.7 per cent of all corporate net income. The big companies desiring stability tended to cooperatively manage such things as prices and markets. A *New Republic* reporter, for example, discovered that on three different occasions TVA received exactly identical bids on equipment from competitive firms. On one such bid for electrical cable, seven different com-panies listed the same price: $198,438.24.

The major facet of the fifties economy disregarded by most of its de-fenders was the utter dependence on defense spending. War had ended the depression. War preparation, the Korean conflict, and more war preparation sustained prosperity in the postwar era. Government budgets for arms yearly ran to 15 or 20 per cent of the entire Gross National Product. Between 1947 and 1957, defense expenditures, exclusive of veterans' payments, totaled over $325 billion.

It was not that economists totally overlooked this single most important economic expenditure. Rather they made two questionable assumptions: first, that if a more peaceful period came, much of the defense spending could be channeled into highways, housing, health, and welfare; second, that such expenditures were essential for national security and therefore not a proper area for economic debate. On this latter point, Galbraith stated quite typically that the United States "is being forced to spend for military purposes" and "obviously cannot [or should not] reduce these expenditures for reasons of fiscal policy." Such thinking ignored the tremendously powerful military-industrial complex's vested interest in an arms economy. It also overlooked the fact that while the generally conservative Congress almost never balked at bills labeled defense, that body was not about to pump billions into welfare and public services. Thus it remained that the basic bulwark of the nation's much-vaunted prosperity was destructive weaponry. Hydrogen bombs, B-52 bombers, a nuclear navy, guided missiles—America the beautiful rested firmly on the potential Armageddon: death supporting life.

Another basic problem with the American economy was that it depended on an ever-accelerating volume of consumer spending, much of it for luxuries. Three questionable tactics were employed to assure high levels of product consumption: massive advertising, credit buying, and planned obsolescence.

With price competition virtually eliminated, competitive activities took the form of salesmanship and advertising. Advertisers tried to convince the public that their product was of higher quality, finer style, better for you: "Be Happy Go Lucky"—"LSMFT—Lucky Strike Means Fine Tobacco," "Call for Phillip Morris," "I'd Walk a Mile for a Camel"—"Test Camels in your T-zone." Of all American businesses, tobacco companies devoted the highest percentage of their $4 billion earnings to advertising. In 1953–54, medical reports linked smoking to lung cancer and heart disease. Throughout the remainder of the fifties, companies bragged endlessly about how low in tar and how mild their brands were ("Pall Malls are longer, filters your smoke further and makes it mild.") Cancer which had been rare in the early twentieth century claimed 255,000 lives in 1957; lung cancer ranked first among types of cancer killers.

Advertising was big business and grew during the fifties at a faster rate than did the GNP. In 1955 some $8 billion was spent stimulating consumers to buy. By the end of the decade this rose to nearly $12 billion. Admen toyed with all kinds of motivational research. Subliminal ads, flashed so briefly on the screen they could only be perceived subconsciously, were also first explored at this time. The package often became more important than the product packaged.

One side effect of massive advertising expenditures was that it led to business control of the content on radio, TV, and to a slightly lesser extent in newspapers and magazines. These media became primarily vehicles for advertiser messages. But ads worked. As Robert Sarnoff, president of the National Broadcasting Company, claimed in 1956: "The reason we have such a high standard of living is because advertising has created an American frame of mind that makes people want more things, better things and newer things."

To make certain that people could purchase the products that advertising convinced them they needed, credit was vastly extended in the fifties. Poverty, Henry Luce assured Americans in 1956, was merely the "habit of thinking poorly." There was no need to think poorly in the fifties. Even without the money you could have the goods. It was of course necessary to convince people that the old American habit of thrift was no longer a sacred virtue. Motivational researcher Dr. Ernest Dichter, in a bulletin to businessmen, described the problem of changing people's values from thrift to spending: "We are now confronted with the problem of permitting the average American to feel moral . . . even when he is spending, even when he is not saving, even when he is taking two vacations a year and buying a second or third car. One of the basic problems of prosperity, then, is to demonstrate that the hedonistic approach to his life is a moral, not an immoral one." In preaching an ethic of consumption and impulse-release, Madison Avenue unwittingly played a role similar to that of Henry Miller and the Beats—proclaiming the virtues of the uninhibited life. J. Walter Thompson, the nation's largest ad agency, even found a way to put old Ben Franklin to use in the battle against thrift by quoting Ben as having said: "Is not the hope of being one day able to purchase and enjoy luxuries a great spur to labor and industry?" This thought of Franklin's, the agency asserted, "appears to be a mature afterthought, qualifying his earlier more familiar writings on the importance of thrift."

The admen were mostly successful in the battle against thrift. Installment purchases caused consumer indebtedness to soar during the fifties from $73 billion to $196 billion. Charge cards multiplied. By 1960, Sears Roebuck alone had over ten million credit accounts, one for every five American families. Revolving credit whereby one could remain indefinitely in debt up to a certain amount—say $500—became very popular. The special credit card was born in the fifties, beginning with the Diners Club founded in 1950. Though initiated to provide credit to a select few at a handful of New York's finest restaurants, the Diners Club proved so popular that its uses and membership were quickly extended. By 1958 it was billing over $90 million annually to some 750,000 members. The all-purpose American Express card was launched in the mid-fifties. Hotel chains, oil companies, car rental services, the phone company, and thousands of other businesses issued their own credit cards. Such cards stimulated buying. *U.S. News & World Report* noted that "the credit-card agencies believe a person is likely to spend more money if he buys with a credit card. One of the companies that issues the cards says that, on the average, people who charge purchases spend about 35 per cent more than those who pay cash." The apparent bountifulness provided by credit obscured its essential function: creating affluence where none existed.

The third factor necessary to sustain consumer spending was planned obsolescence. "Just past the midmark of the 20th century," noted a 1956 *Business Week,* and "it looks as though all of our business forces are bent on getting every one to Borrow. Spend. Buy. Waste. Want." In Aldous Huxley's *Brave New World* sleeping children were indoctrinated with the message: "I do love having new clothes. But old clothes are beastly. . . . Ending is better than mending." The fifties fashion industry agreed. Addressing 400 fashion experts at a Fashion Group luncheon in 1950, B. Earl Puckett of Allied Stores insisted that "basic utility cannot be the foundation of a prosperous apparel industry. We must accelerate obsolescence." General Motors was credited by the *Business Week* article quoted above with having "adopted the annual model change, helping to establish the auto industry's renowned principle of 'planned obsolescence.' " Henry Ford, after all, had been a production man aiming to produce the same simple black car year after year. But Ford Motors had long since overthrown his ideas and joined the waste race of numerous poorly put together yearly models.

Obtrusive advertising, massive personal indebtedness, mountains of junked cars, millions in military spending—a nice basis on which to build a lasting prosperity. Or was it? By the late fifties some former believers began to have their doubts. John Kenneth Galbraith was one. In 1958 he published *The Affluent Society.* The title suggested yet another paean to American prosperity such as his earlier *American Capitalism* had been. Indeed many superficial readers accepted it as such, and the term "affluent society" took its place beside "people's capitalism" in the lexicon of national self-congratulation. But a close reading of *Affluent Society* conveys a very different picture. At one point in the book, Galbraith described a typical family out for a drive in their "mauve and cerise, air-conditioned, power-steered, and power-braked automobile." They pass "through cities that are badly paved, made hideous by litter, blighted buildings, billboards, and posts for wires that should long since have been put underground." Finally reaching the country they find a roadside landscape "rendered largely invisible by commercial art." Undissuaded, they stop to picnic "on exquisitely packaged food from a portable icebox by a polluted stream and go on to spend the night at a park which is a menace to public health and morals. Just before dozing off on an air mattress, beneath a nylon tent, amid the stench of decaying refuse, they may reflect vaguely on the curious unevenness of their blessings. Is this, indeed, the American genius?"

Well, was it? Galbraith's answers were hard to swallow for those who had already swallowed the whole people's capitalism dream. His thesis was that, despite the plethora of privately produced consumer goods, the public sector of the economy was impoverished, causing the country to wallow in "an atmosphere of private opulence and public squalor." Schools suffered from crowding, inadequate facilities, and poorly paid teachers. Hospitals, mental institutions, clinics, and prisons were inadequate, understaffed, and overfilled. The air was becoming unbearable. Rivers already were open sewers. Natural resources were rapidly being exhausted. All this resulted from the concentration on producing goods for profit. With profit as the dominant value, desperately needed public services which brought no profit naturally lagged. Thus, we could produce endless numbers of cars, ever bigger, gaudier, more powerful. But we neglected the public services required by increased consumption of automobiles: safe highways, parking facilities, traffic controls, traffic police, hospitals, and numerous related needs. Galbraith summed this up well with another example: "The more goods people procure, the more packages they discard and the more trash that must be carried away. If the appropriate sanitation services are not provided, the counterpart of increasing opulence will be deepening filth. The greater the wealth the thicker will be the dirt. This indubitably describes a tendency of our time."

The solution Galbraith recommended for solving this problem of socio-economic imbalance between the private and public sectors was for the government greatly to increase expenditures for public needs even if this meant higher taxes. The result, he predicted, would be a restoration of balance and an end to the related problems of unemployment and poverty. Actually there was little new in these proposals. Galbraith was really calling for a revived New Deal, only this time as a cure to the ills of affluence, not depression. But the book did much to stir the complacency of late-fifties economic thinking. Galbraith became an advisor to John F. Kennedy and helped plan some of the liberal reforms of the early sixties.

Another factor rippling the calm surface of the economic consensus in the late fifties was the rediscovery of poverty. Early in the decade observers outdid one another in proclaiming all Americans to be prosperous, upwardly mobile middle class. *Esquire* even ran a chart, only half in jest, on "How to Tell a Rich Girl" from the rich-looking secretary. (The real rich girl wears plain pumps, goes to Europe with her real daddy, and wears white underwear.) When poverty was noticed at all it was generally assumed to be a temporary aberration; a few more years of an upswinging GNP and it would be eliminated. Thus David Riesman and Nathan Glazer in a 1955 essay related how "15 years of prosperity" had caused the "mass of underprivileged people" to "virtually disappear," though they did add as an afterthought (tucked in a footnote at the end): "To be sure, there are enclaves where the underprivileged can still be found as in the Southern Alleghenies or the rural Deep South."

But by the late fifties, radical observers such as Michael Harrington and Harvey Swados began pointing out an entire culture of poverty amid America's plenty. In 1957 (a prosperous year), a study by Robert Lampmann of the University of Wisconsin revealed 32.2 million persons, nearly a quarter of the population, had incomes below government-proclaimed poverty levels. Millions more, while not starving, had minimal comforts. In the fifties only six in ten dwelling units had the basic plumbing facilities of private flush toilet, private bath, and hot running water; 50 per cent of the houses lacked central heating. In 1959, a quarter of the population had *no* liquid assets; over half the population had no savings accounts.

Like "people's capitalism," "we're all middle class" was mythic. Not only did poverty persist, but the gap between rich and poor, if anything, increased in the decade. The top 0.5 per cent of individuals had 25 per cent of all personal wealth by 1955; this was up from 19.3 per cent in 1949. The top group owned 80 per cent of the corporate stock held by individuals and well over 90 per cent of corporate bonds. Harvard studies during the fifties found that upward mobility in the Soviet Union was as great as that in the United States. Even a *Fortune* investigation indicated that economic opportunities for workingmen were declining. Added to this was an average annual unemployment rate of nearly five per cent throughout the fifties, reaching as high as 6.8 per cent or 4.7 million people in 1958.

Few persons read writers like Harrington and Swados. But Galbraith's best-selling *Affluent Society* also included a chapter on "The New Position of Poverty" which aimed to shatter the myth that "with increasing output poverty must disappear." And myth it was. As Galbraith stated, "the most certain thing about modern poverty is that it is not efficiently remedied by a general and tolerably well-distributed advance in income." Unfortunately, however, it was not until the 1962 publication of Harrington's very influential *The Other America* that any sizable segment of the populace became at all concerned about poverty. For most people, poverty remained invisible.

The most commonly heard economic criticism in the late fifties did not concern poverty, unemployment, waste, environmental pollution, or dependence on armaments. It was that the GNP was not growing at a fast enough rate. Growth became the great panacea. Special, costly commissions of experts would huddle and issue wordy tomes calling for faster growth. The four per cent growth rate of the GNP must be raised to five per cent, claimed the 1958 report of the prestigious group funded by the Rockefellers. Perhaps there was a sense in the fifties that history was finally closing in on America; growth might stave off this process. Certainly there was a belief that the United States was in a growth race with the Soviet Union and that the fate of the free world depended on its outcome. Some government officials spoke of the need to step up the rate of growth to six or seven per cent. To continue our present laggard growth, asserted CIA head Allen Dulles at decade's end, was "virtually to commit economic suicide."

And so, despite a growing national doubt, the decade ended economically as it began—spewing forth an ever-increasing volume of bombs, bazookas, bubble gum, cars and tanks, deodorants, crying dolls, hula hoops, pillows, and pollution. They called it people's capitalism. In reality it was a precarious prosperity maintained by cold war spending, highway and automobile building, sprawling suburbias, overeating, overbuying, forced premature obsolescence—always plagued by waste, unemployment, poverty, inequality, misuse of the environment, lack of public services, and the threat of annihilation.

The Proud Decade

JOHN PATRICK DIGGINS

Although McCarthyism, the cold war, Korea and politics dominated front pages in the fifties, opinion polls profiled the American people as preoccupied with their own lives and largely nonpolitical. To most white, middle-class Americans the fifties meant television; bobby sox and the bunny hop; bermuda shorts and gray flannel suits; "I Love Lucy"; Marlon Brando astride a motorcycle and Elvis belting out "Hound Dog"; Lolita the nymphet; crew cut and duck's ass hairstyles; Marilyn Monroe; James Dean; cruising and panty raids; preppies and their cashmeres and two-toned saddle shoes; Willie Mays; Rocky Graziano; drive-in movies and restaurants; diners with chrome-leg tables and backless stools; suburbia; barbecued steaks; Billy Graham and the way to God without sacrifice; the Kinsey Report and the way to sex without sin. Few items in this list would strike one as serious, but many of them have proved durable. Indeed, such subjects fascinate even members of the post-fifties generation. In the seventies and eighties mass magazines like *Newsweek* and *Life* devoted special issues to the fifties as "The Good Old Days" and Hollywood produced *The Last Picture Show*, *American Graffiti,* and *The Way We Were.* Nostalgia even succeeded in trivializing the Korean War, as with the immensely popular "M*A*S*H."

Nostalgia is one way to ease the pain of the present. Those who survived the sixties, a decade that witnessed the turmoils of the Vietnam War and the tragedies of political assassination, looked back wistfully on the fifties as a period of peace and prosperity. Many of those who survived the fifties, however, particularly writers and professors, passed a different verdict. "Good-by to the fifties—and good riddance," wrote the historian Eric Goldman, "the dullest and dreariest in all our history." "The Eisenhower years," judged columnist William Shannon, "have been years of flabbiness and self-satisfaction and gross materialism. . . . The loudest sound in the land has been the oink-and-grunt of private hoggishness. . . . It has been the age of the slob." The socialist Michael Harrington called the decade "a moral disaster, an amusing waste of time," and the novelist Norman Mailer derided it as "one of the worst decades in the history of man." The poet Robert Lowell summed up his impatience in two lines: "These are the tranquil Fifties, and I am forty./Ought I to regret my seedtime?"

On the other side of the political spectrum, conservative writers tended to praise the fifties as "the happiest, most stable, most rational period the western world has ever known since 1914." They point to the seemingly pleasant fact that in the fifties, in contrast to the sixties, many nations like India and Burma achieved independence without resorting to armed force. The same era enjoyed a postwar prosperity and overcame a massive unemployment that had haunted the depression generation, and did it without

Reprinted from *The Proud Decades, America in War and Peace, 1941–1960,* by John Patrick Diggins, pp. 177–178, 348–350. By permission of W.W. Norton & Company, Inc. Copyright © 1988 by John Patrick Diggins.

raising inflation. Yet even conservatives conceded that the fifties were not a "creative time" in the realm of high culture. This was all right for many of them since "creative periods have too often a way of coinciding with periods of death and destruction."

Whatever the retrospective of writers and intellectuals, those who lived through the fifties looked upon them as a period of unbounded possibility. This was especially true of the beginning of the decade when the lure and novelty of material comforts seemed irresistible. Toward the end of the decade a barely noticeable undercurrent of dissatisfaction emerged and by the early sixties a minority of women and men would rebel against the conditions of the fifties and wonder what had gone wrong with their lives. A sweet decade for the many, it became a sour experience for the few who would go on to question not only the feminine mystique but the masculine as well. In dealing with the fifties one must deal with its contented and its discontents. . . .

The economic context is crucial. Between 1950 and 1958, the economy expanded enormously. A steady high growth rate of 4.7 percent heralded remarkable increases in living standards and other conditions of life. This prosperity derived from a combination of factors: (a) the lingering postwar back-up demand for consumer goods together with increased purchasing power as a result of savings; (b) the expansion of plant and machine tool capacity, and other technological advances left by the war and revived by the cold war and Korean conflict; (c) the appearance of new and modernized industries ranging from electronics to plastics; (d) population growth and the expansion of large cities; (e) increases in the productivity, or output per man-hour, of the working force; and (f) the commitment to foreign aid, which made possible overseas credits and American exports.

America experienced three mild recessions in the fifties, but through them all the rate of personal income grew and reached a record high of a 3.9 percent rise in 1960. If few became rich, the great majority lived more comfortably than ever before and enjoyed shorter hours on the job, as America moved to the five-day work week. Prior to the Second World War only 25 percent of the farming population had electricity. By the end of the fifties more than 80 percent had not only lighting but telephones, refrigerators, and televisions.

The generation that had borne the depression and the war was now eager to put politics behind and move into a bountiful new world. One strong indicator of confidence in the future was a sudden baby boom. Demographers had been predicting a postwar relative decline in fertility rates and no expansion of immigration quotas. Instead, population leaped from 130 million in 1940 to 165 million by the mid-fifties, the biggest increase in the history of the Republic. Population migrated as well as grew, spreading into the region that came to be called "the sun belt," states like Florida, Texas, Arizona, and California. Farms and small towns lost population. Many big cities, while still growing with lower-class and minority inhabitants, witnessed the flight of the middle class to the periphery. The massive phenomenon of suburbia would rip apart and remake the texture of social life in America.

Suburbia met a need and fulfilled a dream. During the depression and the war most Americans lived in apartments, flats, or small houses within an inner city. After the war, with GIs returning and the marriage rate doubling, as many as two million young couples had to share a dwelling with their relatives. Some settled for a cot in the living room, while married college students often had to live in off-campus quonset huts. Their immediate need for space in which to raise a family was answered by the almost overnight appearance of tracts, subdivisions, and other developments that sprawled across the landscape. Ironically, while suburban growth cut into the natural environment, felling trees and turning fields into asphalt streets, the emotional appeal of suburbia lay in a desire to recapture the greenness and calm of rural life. Thus eastern tracts featured such names as "Crystal Stream," "Robin Meadows," and "Stonybrook," while in the West the Spanish motif of "Villa Serena" and "Tierra Vista" conveyed the ambience of old, preindustrial California. In California the tracts were developed by Henry J. Kaiser and Henry Doelger, who drew on their war-time skills for mass production to provide ranch-style homes complete with backyards and front lawns. In the Northeast William Levitt offered New Yorkers and Pennsylvanians houses with shuttered windows and steep pitched roofs to mimic the cozy Cape Cod look. Levitt had never liked cities. Having no patience with people who did, he saw his opportunity after the war when the government agreed to guarantee to banks the entire amount of a veteran's mortgage, making it possible for him to move in with no down payment, depending on the Veteran Administration's assessment of the value of the specific property. To keep building costs down, Levitt transformed the housing industry by using prefabricated walls and frames assembled on the site. In an effort to foster community spirit, he and other builders added schools, swimming pools, tennis courts, and athletic fields with Little League diamonds. For young members of the aspiring middle class, suburbia was a paradise of comfort and convenience.

Others were not so sure. "Is this the American dream, or is it a nightmare?" asked *House Beautiful*. Architectural and cultural critics complained of the monotony of house after house with the same facade, paint, and lawn inhabited by people willing to sign an agreement to keep them the same. One song writer would call them "little boxes made of ticky-tacky." Some children who grew up in them would agree, rebelling in the following decade against all that was sterile and standardized. The most angry critic was the cultural historian Lewis Mumford, author of *The City in History*. Mumford feared that Levitt was doing more to destroy the modern city than did the World War II aerial bombings. He also feared that suburbia was transforming the American character, rendering it dreary and conformist when it should be daring and courageous. "In the mass movement into suburban areas a new kind of community was produced, which caricatured both the historic city and the archetypal suburban refuge, a multitude of uniform, unidentifiable houses, lined up inflexibly at uniform distances, on uniform roads, in a treeless communal waste, inhabited by people in the same class, the same income, the same age group, witnessing the same television performances, eating the same tasteless pre-fabricated foods from the same freezers, conforming in every outward and inward respect to a common mold."

Admonishments aside, Americans were falling in love with suburbia—at least at first; some would have second thoughts and later wonder what they had bought, the theme of the cheerless film *No Down Payment* (1957). By the end of the fifties one-fourth of the population had moved to such areas. If not beautiful, suburbia was affordable, and thousands of homeless veterans were grateful to have their place in the sun for $65 per month on a full purchase price of $6,990 that included separate bedrooms for the children and a kitchen full of glittering gadgets. Such amenities also enabled housewives to be free of some domestic chores as they became involved in community affairs while their husbands commuted to work in the cities. A frequent event was the Tupperware party, arranged by wives ostensibly to sell household conveniences but also to overcome isolation and boredom. The most serious drawback of suburbia was that its planners envisaged no need for public transportation. As a result, suburbanites became forever dependent upon the automobile. When their children reached driving age, some households became three- or even four-car families. But in the fifties, when gasoline was relatively cheap and the promising new freeways wide and uncongested, the car was seen as a solution, not a problem. Indeed, for proud teenagers it was the supreme status symbol, the one possession that with its "souped-up" carburetors and lowered chassis and various metallic colors, answered the need for freedom and diversity in a community of flatness and conformity.

In the fifties, car was king. Freeways, multilevel parking lots, shopping centers, motels, and drive-in restaurants and theaters all catered to the person behind the wheel. By 1956 an estimated seventy-five million cars and trucks were on American roads. One out of every seven workers held a job connected to the automobile industry. In suburbia the station wagon became a common sight. But really to fulfill the American dream one needed a Cadillac, or so advertisers informed the arriviste of new wealth with such effectiveness that one had to wait a year for delivery. Almost all American automobiles grew longer and wider. Their supersize and horsepower, together with more chrome and bigger tailfins, served no useful transportation purpose but were powerful enhancers of self-esteem. At the end of the decade, when many rich Texans, some country-western singers, salesmen, and even gangsters and pimps owned a Cadillac, it became what it always was, gauche, and its image declined from the sublime to the ridiculous.

In the fifties the spectacle of waste, once regarded by the older morality as a sign of sin, had become a sign of status. It was no coincidence that Americans junked almost as many cars as Detroit manufactured, thereby fulfilling Thorstein Veblen's earlier prediction that modern man would be more interested in displaying and destroying goods than in producing them. Veblen's insight into "conspicuous consumption" also took on real meaning in this era as Americans rushed out to buy the latest novelty, whether it was a convertible, TV set, deep-freeze, electric carving knife, or the "New Look" Christian Dior evening dress. The postwar splurge of consumption had been made possible by the $100 billion of savings Americans had banked during the war. Immediately after the war, household appliances were in demand, then luxuries like fashionable clothes and imported wines. For those who bought homes for $8,000 or more, luxuries were seen as necessities. The middle-class suburbanite looked out his window and "needed" what his neighbor had—a white Corvette or a swimming pool. Travel to Europe, once regarded as the "Grand Tour" only for the rich and famous, became accessible to millions of Americans in the fifties. For the masses who remained at home and took to the road, new tourist attractions sprang up, like Disneyland. Mass recreational mobility changed the nation's eating habits. In 1954 in San Bernardino, California, Ray Kroc, a high-school dropout, devised a precision stand for turning out french fries, beverages, and fifteen-cent hamburgers that grew rapidly into a fast-food empire: McDonald's.

Spending less time cooking and eating, Americans had more time for shopping. Discount houses such as Korvette's and Grant's opened up for the lower-middle class while the prestigious Neiman-Marcus catered to the needs of oil-rich Texans. Parents raised in the depression naturally felt that more was better, not only for themselves but particularly for their children. Teenagers splurged on phonograph records, bedroom decorations, cashmere sweaters, trips to Hawaii, motor-scooters, and hot rods. The seemingly infinite indulgence of the young worried many parents even as they contributed to it. In a survey 94 percent of the mothers interviewed reported that their children had asked them to buy various goods they had seen on television.

Television in America, unlike in England and much of Western Europe, was supported by the advertising industry, which did more than any other institution to fill the viewer's eyes with images of abundance. Advertisers spent $10 billion a year to persuade, not to say manipulate, the people into buying products that promised to improve their lives, whether frozen peas or French perfume. Professional football, the prime target for beer ads, invented the "two-minute warning" in the last quarter to accommodate commercials. Confronted by a medical report linking smoking to lung cancer, tobacco companies increased their ad campaigns with jingles like "Be Happy Go Lucky!" Television bloomed with romantic scenes of a dashing young man offering a cigarette to a seductively beautiful woman under a full moon. As violins rose, the match was lit, and her face turned into that of a goddess— young, eager, divine. Partial take-offs from the Bogart-Bacall films of the early forties, Madison Avenue could readily exploit such scenes, perhaps realizing that desire can always be tempted precisely because it can never be completely fulfilled.

What facilitated the illusion of fulfillment was a little rectangle of plastic dubbed the credit card. In 1950 Diner's Club distributed credit cards to select wealthy New Yorkers to give them the privilege of eating at swank restaurants without fumbling for money. By the end of the decade Sears Roebuck alone had more than ten million accounts for those who chose to live on credit or, more bluntly, to be in debt. Installment buying shot consumer indebtedness up to $196 billion, so high that certain department stores offered "debt counselors" for worried customers. One soothing nostrum was a good stiff martini, the favorite drink of suburbia and the commuters' circle. Drinking rose sharply in the fifties. So did prescription-drugs use. Sales of "tranquilizers" soared; by 1959, 1,159,000 pounds had been consumed. The following decade the Food and Drug Administration discovered that the once-popular pill "miltown" had no medicinal value. But for the fifties generation, coping with the boss's demands at work and the children's at home, popping tranquilizing drugs became a respectable adult addiction. That mental anxiety should accompany material abundance is no surprise. For centuries moralists had warned that people become unhappy when they get what they want—or think they want. Suburbia offered Americans the cleanliness and safety of a planned community, but nothing is more hopeless than planned happiness.

The Truman and Eisenhower years gave Americans a sense of pride in themselves and confidence in the future. It is questionable whether either sentiment survived the fifties intact. The America that emerged victorious from World War II was not the same America fifteen years later. The decline of confidence resulted in part from the changing nature of warfare brought by modern technology. After the Second World War Americans could take pride in the performance of their soldiers. With the increasing complexity of the cold war, which offered the possibility of either covert CIA operations or nuclear attack and retaliation, warfare seemed more and more a choice between the dishonorable and the suicidal; and if new inventions in sophisticated missile weaponry would make some Americans feel proud of their technological achievements, it was a pride born of fear.

The cold war itself, however, is not the only explanation for the decline of self-assurance that came to be felt at the end of the Eisenhower years. Equally troubling was the sense of unease and discontent. No one had predicted it. In 1950, for example, *Fortune* published a book with the curious title, *U.S.A., the Permanent Revolution*. The title, taken from Leon Trotsky, was meant to depict a new way of life founded on unlimited prosperity, active citizen participation, winning friends aboard with generous foreign aid and free-trade policies, and proudly accepting the burdens of history as a great world power. America must be understood not as a nation of definite goals but of indefinite growth. "Americans wish that other people could see their country as it really is: not as an achievement but as a *process*—a process of becoming." But can there be growth without conscious direction and meaning? "Why should we assume that America has *any* meaning?" the editors asked. "Rightly understood, the principles that embody the meaning of America are the very forces that have done most to change America."

By 1960, all confidence that America could simply be accepted as a process of continual growth and change came to be questioned and in many instances rejected. "What is wrong with America?" queried the *U.S. News and World Report*. "What shall we do with our greatness?" asked the editors of *Life*. President Eisenhower set up a "Commission on National Goals" and Walter Lippmann analyzed the "Anatomy of Discontent," which he specified as a willingness to fulfill them. The Reverend Billy Graham thought Americans overextended themselves in more concrete ways. "We overeat, overdrink, oversex, and overplay. . . . We have tried to fill ourselves with science and education, with better living and pleasure . . . but we are still empty and bored." Adlai Stevenson doubted that America's "permanent revolution" would have any impact on the rest of the world. "With the supermarket as our temple and the singing commercial as our litany, are we likely to fire the world with an irresistible vision of America's exalted purpose and inspiring way of life?" "Something has gone wrong in America," complained the novelist John Steinbeck of his fellow people. "Having too many things, they spend their hours and money on the couch searching for a soul." Everywhere Americans were engaged in the "great debate" about "the national purpose." Americans have become worried, journalists concluded, because they feel they lack inspiring ideals and because they have been led to believe that they do not need them. "The case of the missing purpose," wrote a philosopher in *The Nation,* "is a case of human beings missing the purpose of life." The proud decades were over.

Or were they? Several months before Eisenhower's farewell and Kennedy's inauguration, things were changing. Within a few years America would be addressing problems it never knew existed and some people would be singing "We Shall Overcome!" Yet even before the sixties ended America would be more divided than ever, the two Kennedys and King dead, and the Republicans back in office. Now it was Nixon who promised to bring Americans "back together again." Henceforth, the period of the fifties, once regarded as a dreadful aberration standing between the more compassionate thirties and activist sixties, would seem more and more the steady norm of America's political temper. The generation of the sixties experienced the previous decade as a burden that had to be radically transformed, and some of its worst aspects were confronted and eradicated. But as the radical sixties petered out, it became all the more clear that the two decades beginning with the Second World War shaped the nation's environment and consciousness in more enduring ways than had once been expected. The forties and perhaps especially the fifties are still living in the present, and the assumptions and values of the two decades have become ingrained in our habits and institutions. "What is the national purpose?" asked Dean Acheson in response to the great debate of the late fifties. "To survive and, perchance, to prosper." In doing both well, America still had good reason to be proud of itself.

▓ *F U R T H E R   R E A D I N G*

Eric Barnouw, *Tube of Plenty: The Evolution of American Television* (1975)
John Brooks, *The Great Leap: The Past Twenty-five Years in America* (1966)
Paul A. Carter, *Another Part of the Fifties* (1983)
Bruce Cook, *The Beat Generation* (1971)
John Patrick Diggins, *The Proud Decades: America in War and Peace, 1941–1960* (1988)
Barbara Ehrenreich, *The Hearts of Men: American Dreams and the Flight from Commitment* (1983)

Benita Eisler, *Private Lives: Men and Women of the Fifties* (1986)

James J. Flink, *The Car Culture* (1975)

John K. Galbraith, *The Affluent Society* (1958)

——, *American Capitalism: The Concept of Countervailing Power* (1956)

Herbert Gans, *The Levittowners* (1982)

——, *Popular Culture and High Culture* (1975)

James B. Gilbert, *A Cycle of Outrage: Juvenile Delinquency and the Mass Media in the 1950s* (1986)

——, *Another Chance: Postwar America, 1945–1968* (rev. ed., 1986)

Jeffrey Hart, *When the Going Was Good: American Life in the Fifties* (1982)

Kenneth T. Jackson, *Crabgrass Frontier: The Suburbanization of America* (1985)

Marty Jezer, *The Dark Ages: Life in the United States, 1945–1960* (1982)

Landon Y. Jones, *Great Expectations: America and the Baby Boom Generation* (1980)

George Lipsitz, *Class and Culture in Cold War America* (1982)

Dennis McNally, *Desolate Angel: Jack Kerouac, the Beat Generation, and America* (1978)

David Mark, *Democratic Vistas: Television in American Culture* (1984)

Elaine Tyler May, *Homeward Bound: American Families in the Cold War Era* (1988)

Larry May, ed., *Recasting America: Culture and Politics in the Age of Cold War America* (1989)

Donald B. Meyers, *The Positive Thinkers* (1965)

Douglas T. Miller and Marion Nowak, *The Fifties* (1977)

Herman Philip Miller, *Rich Man, Poor Man* (1964)

C. Wright Mills, *White Collar: The American Middle Classes* (1951)

George H. Nash, *The Conservative Intellectual Movement in America Since 1945* (1976)

William O'Neill, *American High* (1989)

Vance Packard, *The Hidden Persuaders* (1957)

Richard Parker, *The Myth of the Middle Class* (1972)

Richard H. Pells, *The Liberal Mind in a Conservative Age: American Intellectuals in the 1940s and 1950s* (1985)

Benjamin Rader, *In Its Own Image: How Television Has Transformed Sports* (1985)

David Riesman, *The Lonely Crowd: A Study of the Changing American Character* (1950)

Joseph Satin, ed., *The 1950s: America's "Placid" Decade* (1960)

William H. Whyte, *The Organization Man* (1956)

John F. Kennedy, the Cuban Revolution, and the Cold War

XXX

To comprehend the nature of the United States' troubled relations with Cuba during the 1960s requires an understanding of at least three separate but inter-related topics: the history of U.S. relations with Latin America, especially the Caribbean; the response of the United States to social revolutions both in Latin America and throughout the Third World; and the United States' Cold War struggle with the Soviet Union. The history of relations between the United States and Cuba serves in turn to highlight patterns that were common to post-war U.S. policy throughout the Third World, including Southeast Asia and the Middle East.

Throughout the early twentieth century, the United States had exercised a dominant influence in Latin America and particularly in the Caribbean, featur-ing armed interventions in Cuba, Colombia (Panama), the Dominican Republic, Haiti, Nicaragua, and Mexico. The United States forswore such military actions in 1933 with Franklin D. Roosevelt's Good Neighbor Policy; but following World War II that policy was increasingly honored in the breach as the United States intervened directly or indirectly in Guatemala (under Eisenhower), Cuba (Kennedy), the Dominican Republic (Johnson), Chile (Nixon), Nicaragua (Reagan), Grenada (Reagan), and Panama (Bush). Seen from this perspective, Kennedy's ''fixation'' with Cuba was simply part of a deeply rooted historical pattern.

U.S. leaders were especially troubled by the growth of social revolutions throughout Latin America, revolutions that they feared would threaten the na-tion's economic interests—property, investments, and markets—as well as its strategic control of the region. Cuban revolutionary Fidel Castro, whose forces overthrew the dictatorship of Juan Batista in 1959, posed a special threat as a result of his seizure of industries owned by U.S. investors and by his rapid rise as a popular symbol of resistance to the United States.

It was the Cold War with the Soviet Union, however, that helped revive *historic patterns of U.S. intervention and served to heighten and rationalize growing fears of social revolution. In Latin America as in Asia, the United States identified most revolutions with the foreign policies of the Soviet Union— in part because many Latin American revolutions were led by men and women who were socialists, if not communists; in part because the Soviet Union often supported such revolutions when it was in its interests to do so; but also because American leaders themselves seemed unable or unwilling to distinguish between indigenous social change and foreign subversion. Reflexive opposition to social revolutions thus became a cardinal theme of the Cold War era.*

    In 1954, for example, the United States engineered the overthrow of the democratically elected, reformist government of Guatemala. Established in 1944 following decades of dictatorship, the new Guatemalan government had introduced various reforms, including the nationalization of lands belonging to the powerful United Fruit Company. The protests of United Fruit, combined with (largely groundless) fears that Guatemala might become a beachhead of Soviet influence in the region, led the Eisenhower administration to launch a CIA-led coup that resulted in the overthrow of the Guatemalan government and the installation of a right-wing, pro-U.S. dictatorship. The success of the Guatemalan intervention served, in turn, as a model for the U.S. officials who planned the abortive 1961 Bay of Pigs landing in Cuba.

    U.S.–Cuban relations were thus shaped by a long history of U.S. involvement in Cuban affairs, by strong opposition to the new economic programs of the Cuban revolution, and by a growing fear on the part of U.S. leaders that the victory of the Cuban revolutionaries would also become a Cold War victory for the Soviet Union. The process was dialectic: Castro was a dedicated revolutionary. Given the history of U.S.–Cuban relations, given also the extent of U.S. property and investments in the island, it was altogether likely that the revolution would evolve in ways antagonistic to American interests. U.S. opposition, and especially its failed attempt to overthrow the new Cuban government, strongly reinforced the direction and pace of that evolution, helping to propel Castro and the Cubans into an ever tighter embrace of the Soviet Union. This development, in turn, tempted the Soviets to introduce nuclear weapons into Cuba, thus setting the stage for the Cuban missile crisis.

✗✗ D O C U M E N T S

By October 1960, relations between the United States and the new Cuban government had already badly deteriorated. In the first document, a 1960 speech before the United Nations, the new Cuban leader Fidel Castro traces the history of U.S. relations with his nation, defends the Cuban revolution, denounces U.S. efforts to overthrow his government, and praises the Soviet Union. Castro's speech, which is excerpted from the *United Nations Review*, follows the UN practice of paraphrasing the speaker's remarks, rather than reporting them directly. On March 13, 1961, Kennedy announced the Alliance for Progress (see the second selection), a boldly ambitious plan to stimulate economic development and democracy throughout Latin America while avoiding radical social revolutions of the Cuban variety. The alliance failed, partly because the Kennedy administration remained divided over the degree of support for social and economic reform versus military aid to right-wing (but pro-American) dictators, partly because Kennedy's successors weakened the program, and partly, too, because many of Latin America's economic and political problems were simply beyond the ability of the United States to solve.

During the same month in which Kennedy introduced the Alliance for Progress, he and his advisers put the finishing touches on their plan for a CIA-backed invasion of Cuba by Cuban exiles. In the wake of its failure, Kennedy appointed a top-secret board of inquiry under General Maxwell Taylor. The third document is excerpted from the board's report, dated June 13, 1961. U.S. efforts to overthrow Castro included numerous plots to assassinate the Cuban leader. In 1975, following Watergate, a Select Committee of the U.S. Senate chaired by Senator Frank Church of Idaho opened an investigation of these and other covert activities by U.S. intelligence agencies. The fourth document is excerpted from the Senate committee's report on *Alleged Assassination Plots Involving Foreign Leaders* (1975).

During the summer of 1962, the Soviet Union began to ship nuclear missiles to Cuba. The discovery of these missiles in October 1962 precipitated the Cuban missile crisis. The fifth document is taken from the transcripts of two meetings on October 16, 1962, in which Kennedy and his top advisers first discussed possible responses to the crisis. The sixth selection is the president's public address to the nation on October 22. Soviet premier Nikita Khrushchev's initial, private response to Kennedy's action, dated October 26, 1962, is reprinted as the seventh document. The following day, Khrushchev wrote again, adopting a more formal, hardline stance. One of the Kennedy administration's most critical decisions was to ignore the second letter and respond instead to the first.

Fidel Castro Denounces U.S. Policy Toward Cuba, 1960

The Prime Minister of Cuba recalled to the Assembly that many speakers who had preceded him on the rostrum had quite correctly referred to the problem of Cuba as one of the problems facing the world. As far as the world is concerned, he said, the problem of Cuba had come to a head in the last two years, and as such it was a new problem. Before that, the world had few reasons for knowing that his country existed; for many it was an offshoot—in reality, a colony—of the United States.

He traced the history of Cuba and referred to the law passed by the United States Congress at the time of the American military occupation of Cuba during the war with Spain, which, he claimed, said that the Constitution of Cuba—which was then being drafted—must have a rider under which the United States would be granted the right to intervene in Cuba's political affairs and to lease certain parts of the country for naval bases or for their coal deposits. In other words, the right to intervene and to lease naval bases was imposed by force by the legislative body of another country, since Cuban senators were clearly told that if they did not accept, the occupation forces would not be withdrawn.

The colonization of Cuba, he asserted, began with the acquisition of the best land by United States firms, concessions of Cuban natural resources and public services—concessions of all kinds. Cuba eventually had to fight to attain its independence, which was finally achieved after seven bloody years of tyranny "of those in our country who were nothing but the cat's-paws of those who dominated the country economically." The Batista Government of Cuba was appropriate for the United States monopolies, but not for the Cuban people.

How could any system inimical to the interests of the people stay in power unless by force? These were the governments that the guiding circles of United States policy preferred, he said, and that was why governments of force still ruled in Latin America.

Of course circumstances changed, and the United States Government was now said to oppose that of [Dominican Generalissimo Rafael] Trujillo, but not that of Paraguay or of Nicaragua. The latter was no longer a government of force, but "a monarchy that is as constitutional almost as that of the United Kingdom."

Mr. Castro traced some of the conditions which he said the successful revolution in Cuba had uncovered. Public services, he alleged, all belonged to United States monopolies and a major portion of the banking business, importing business, oil refineries, sugar production, the lion's share of arable land and the most important industries in all fields in Cuba belonged to North American companies. The balance of payments from 1950 to 1960 was favorable to the United States by one billion dollars.

What the Revolutionary Government had wanted to do was to devote itself to the settling of its own problems at home; to carry out a program for the betterment of its people. But when the Revolutionary Government began to pass laws to overcome the advantages obtained by the monopolies, difficulties arose. Then "we began to be called communists; then we began to be painted red," he said.

The first unfriendly act perpetrated by the Government of the United States, he said, was to throw open its doors to a gang of murderers, bloodthirsty criminals who had murdered hundreds of defenceless peasants, who had never tired of torturing prisoners for many, many years, who had killed right and left. These hordes were received by the United States with open arms. Why this unfriendly act on the part of the Government of the United States toward Cuba? At the time Cuba could not understand, but now saw the reason clearly. The policy was part of an attitude of the United States.

He also criticized and blamed the United States Government for the fact that bombs were dropped on the sugar fields of Cuba before the harvest was in, and he accused the United States Government for allowing the planes which dropped the bombs to leave United States territory.

But, he said, aerial incursions finally stopped. Then came economic aggression. It was said that agrarian reform would cause chaos in agricultural production. That was not the case. Had it been so, the United States would not have had to carry on its economic aggression. They could have trusted in the Revolutionary Government's ruining the country. Fortunately that did not happen. Cuba needed new markets for its products. Therefore it signed a trade treaty with the Soviet Union to sell it a million tons of sugar and to purchase a certain amount of Russian products. Surely no one could say that was incorrect.

What could Cuba do? Go to the United Nations and denounce this economic aggression? The United Nations has power to deal with these matters; but it sought an investigation to be carried out by the Organization of American States. As a result, the United States was not condemned. No, the Soviet Union was condemned. All the Soviet Union had said was that if there was military aggression against Cuba, it would support the victims with rockets. Since when was the support of a weak country, conditioned on attack by a powerful country, regarded as interference. If there were no possibility that Cuba would be attacked, then there was no possibility that there would be Soviet support.

"We, the small countries," he added, "do not as yet feel too secure about the preservation of our rights. That is why, when we decide to be free, we know full well that we become free at our own risk."

The Cuban revolution, he continued, was changing. What was yesterday a land [of] misery, a land of illiterates, was gradually becoming one of the most enlightened, advanced and developed lands of the continent. Developing this theme, he gave figures about the building of schools, housing, and industries, told of the success of plans for conservation of natural resources, medical plans and other advances since the revolution.

In view of the tremendous reality of underdevelopment, the United States Government, at Bogotá, had come out with a plan for economic development, but he criticized it, saying that the governments of Latin America were being offered not the resources for economic development but resources for social development: houses for people who have no work, schools to which children could not go, and hospitals that would be unnecessary if there were enough food to eat. Cuba was not included in this proposed assistance, but they were not going to get angry about that because the Cubans were solving their own problems.

The Government of Cuba, he said, had always been ready to discuss its problems with the Government of the United States, but the latter had not been willing to do so. He quoted notes which had been addressed to the United States in January and February last, and a reply which said that the United States could not accept the conditions for negotiation laid down in those notes. The Government and the people of Cuba, he said, were much concerned "at the aggressive turn in American policy regarding Cuba" and denounced the efforts of the United States to promote "the organization of subversive movements against the Revolutionary Government of Cuba."

He also said the United States had taken over "in a military manner" Honduran territory—*Islas Cisnes* (Swan Islands)—in violation of treaties, set up a powerful broadcasting station for subversive groups and was promoting subversion and the landing of armed forces in Cuba.

Turning to the subject of the United States leased naval base in Cuba, Mr. Castro said there was fear and concern in Cuba "of a country that has followed an aggressive and warlike policy possessing a base in the very heart of our island, that turns our island into the possible victim of any international conflict. It forces us to run the risk of any atomic conflict without us having even the slightest intervention in the problem." . . .

The case of Cuba, continued Mr. Castro, was the case of all the underdeveloped colonial countries and the problems he had described in relation to Cuba applied perfectly well to the whole of Latin America, where, he alleged, the economic resources were controlled by the North American monopolies. There is a United Nations report, he said, which explains how even private capital, instead of going to the countries which need it most for setting up basic industries, is preferably being channelled to the more industrialized countries. The development of Latin America, he added, would have to be achieved through public investment, planned and granted unconditionally without any political strings attached. In this, the problems of Latin America were like the problems of Africa and Asia.

"The world," he declared, "has been divided among the monopolistic interests, which do not wish to see the development of peoples but to exploit the natural resources of the countries and to exploit the people."

President John F. Kennedy Calls for an Alliance for Progress, 1961

One hundred and thirty-nine years ago this week the United States, stirred by the heroic struggles of its fellow Americans, urged the independence and recognition of the new Latin American Republics. It was then, at the dawn of freedom throughout this hemisphere, that [Simon] Bolívar spoke of his desire to see the Americas fashioned into the greatest region in the world, "greatest," he said, "not so much by virtue of her area and her wealth, as by her freedom and her glory."

Never, in the long history of our hemisphere, has this dream been nearer to fulfillment, and never has it been in greater danger.

The genius of our scientists has given us the tools to bring abundance to our land, strength to our industry, and knowledge to our people. For the first time we have the capacity to strike off the remaining bonds of poverty and ignorance—to free our people for the spiritual and intellectual fulfillment which has always been the goal of our civilization.

Yet at this very moment of maximum opportunity, we confront the same forces which have imperiled America throughout its history—the alien forces which once again seek to impose the despotisms of the Old World on the people of the New.

I have asked you to come here today so that I might discuss these challenges and these dangers.

Common Ties Uniting the Republics

We meet together as firm and ancient friends, united by history and experience and by our determination to advance the values of American civilization. For this new world of ours is not merely an accident of geography. Our continents are bound together by a common history—the endless exploration of new frontiers. Our nations are the product of a common struggle—the revolt from colonial rule. And our people share a common heritage—the quest for the dignity and the freedom of man.

The revolutions which gave us birth ignited, in the words of Thomas

Paine, "a spark never to be extinguished." And across vast, turbulent continents these American ideals still stir man's struggle for national independence and individual freedom. But as we welcome the spread of the American Revolution to other lands, we must also remember that our own struggle—the revolution which began in Philadelphia in 1776 and in Caracas in 1811—is not yet finished. Our hemisphere's mission is not yet completed. *For our unfulfilled task is to demonstrate to the entire world that man's unsatisfied aspiration for economic progress and social justice can best be achieved by free men working within a framework of democratic institutions.* If we can do this in our own hemisphere, and for our own people, we may yet realize the prophecy of the great Mexican patriot, Benito Juarez, that "democracy is the destiny of future humanity."

As a citizen of the United States let me be the first to admit that we North Americans have not always grasped the significance of this common mission, just as it is also true that many in your own countries have not fully understood the urgency of the need to lift people from poverty and ignorance and despair. But we must turn from these mistakes—from the failures and the misunderstandings of the past—to a future full of peril but bright with hope.

Throughout Latin America—a continent rich in resources and in the spiritual and cultural achievements of its people—millions of men and women suffer the daily degradations of hunger and poverty. They lack decent shelter or protection from disease. Their children are deprived of the education or the jobs which are the gateway to a better life. And each day the problems grow more urgent. Population growth is outpacing economic growth, low living standards are even further endangered, and discontent— the discontent of a people who know that abundance and the tools of progress are at last within their reach—that discontent is growing. In the words of José Figueres, "once dormant peoples are struggling upward toward the sun, toward a better life."

If we are to meet a problem so staggering in its dimensions, our approach must itself be equally bold, an approach consistent with the majestic concept of Operation Pan America. Therefore I have called on all the people of the hemisphere to join in a new Alliance for Progress—*Alianza para Progreso*— a vast cooperative effort, unparalleled in magnitude and nobility of purpose, to satisfy the basic needs of the American people for homes, work and land, health and schools—*techo, trabajo y tierra, salud y escuela. . . .*

To achieve this goal political freedom must accompany material progress. Our Alliance for Progress is an alliance of free governments—and it must work to eliminate tyranny from a hemisphere in which it has no rightful place. Therefore let us express our special friendship to the people of Cuba and the Dominican Republic—and the hope they will soon rejoin the society of free men, uniting with us in our common effort.

This political freedom must be accompanied by social change. For unless necessary social reforms, including land and tax reform, are freely made, unless we broaden the opportunity of all of our people, unless the great mass of Americans share in increasing prosperity, then our alliance, our revolution, our dream, and our freedom will fail. But we call for social change by free men—change in the spirit of Washington and Jefferson, of Bolívar and San Martín and Martí—not change which seeks to impose on men tyrannies which we cast out a century and a half ago. Our motto is what it has always been—progress yes, tyranny no—*progreso sí, tiranía no!*

But our greatest challenge comes from within—the task of creating an American civilization where spiritual and cultural values are strengthened by an ever-broadening base of material advance, where, within the rich diversity of its own traditions, each nation is free to follow its own path toward progress.

The completion of our task will, of course, require the efforts of all the governments of our hemisphere. But the efforts of governments alone will never be enough. In the end the people must choose and the people must help themselves.

And so I say to the men and women of the Americas—to the *campesino* in the fields, to the *obrero* in the cities, to the *estudiante* in the schools— prepare your mind and heart for the task ahead, call forth your strength, and let each devote his energies to the betterment of all so that your children and our children in this hemisphere can find an ever richer and a freer life.

Let us once again transform the American Continent into a vast crucible of revolutionary ideas and efforts, a tribute to the power of the creative energies of free men and women, an example to all the world that liberty and progress walk hand in hand. Let us once again awaken our American revolution until it guides the struggles of people everywhere—not with an imperialism of force or fear but the rule of courage and freedom and hope for the future of man.

A Board of Inquiry Reports on the Bay of Pigs, 1961

1. Although the Cuban situation had been the subject of serious study in the Special Group [a senior oversight committee], Central Intelligence Agency [CIA] and other government agencies since 1958, this study takes as its point of departure the basic policy paper, "A Program of Covert Action Against the Castro Regime," approved by the President on 17 March 1960. This document, developed by the Central Intelligence Agency and indorsed by the Special Group, provided a program divided into four parts to bring about the replacement of the Castro regime by covert means:

   a. The creation of a responsible and unified Cuban opposition to the Castro regime located outside of Cuba.

   b. The development of means for mass communication to the Cuban people as a part of a powerful propaganda offensive.

   c. The creation and development of a covert intelligence and action

Operation Zapata: The "Ultrasensitive" Report and Testimony of the Board of Inquiry on the Bay of Pigs (Frederick, Md., 1981). Pp. 3–9, 11–15, excerpts.

organization within Cuba which would be responsive to the orders and directions of the exile opposition.

    d. The development of a paramilitary force outside of Cuba for future guerrilla action.

2. Since the primary purpose of this study is to examine the paramilitary actions growing out of this program and its successive modifications, the paragraph referring to the paramilitary aspects of the plan is quoted in its entirety:

    d. Preparations have already been made for the development of an adequate paramilitary force outside of Cuba, together with mechanisms for the necessary logistics support of covert military operations on the island. Initially a cadre of leaders will be recruited after careful screening and trained as paramilitary instructors. In a second phase a number of paramilitary cadres will be trained at secure locations outside of the United States so as to be available for immediate deployment into Cuba to organize, train and lead resistance forces recruited there both before and after the establishment of one or more active centers of resistance. The creation of this capability will require a minimum of six months and probably closer to eight. In the meanwhile, a limited air capability for resupply and for infiltration and exfiltration already exists under CIA control and can be rather easily expanded if and when the situation requires. Within two months it is hoped to parallel this with a small air supply capability under deep cover as a commercial operation in another country.

3. It is apparent from the above excerpt that at the time of approval of this document the concept of paramilitary action was limited to the recruitment of a cadre of leaders and the training of a number of paramilitary cadres for subsequent use as guerrillas in Cuba.

4. The CIA began at once to implement the decisions contained in the policy paper on 17 March 1960. A target of 300 men was set for the recruitment of guerrillas to be trained covertly outside the United States. "Radio Swan" was installed on Swan Island and ready for broadcasting on 17 May 1960. Steps were taken to develop the FRD (*Frente Revolucionario Democrático*) as the Cuban front organization composed of a broad spectrum of Cuban political elements other than Communists and Batistianos. On August 18th, a progress report was given to the President and the Cabinet, at which time a budget of some $13 million was approved, as well as the use of Department of Defense personnel and equipment. However, it was specified at this time that no United States military personnel were to be used in a combat status.

5. Sometime in the summer of 1960 the paramilitary concept for the operation began to change. It appears that leaders in the CIA Task Force set up in January 1960 to direct the project were the first to entertain the thought of a Cuban strike force to land on the Cuban coast in

supplementation of the guerrilla action contemplated under the March 17, 1960 paper. These CIA officers began to consider the formation of a small force of infantry (200–300 men) for contingency employment in conjunction with other paramilitary operations, and in June began to form a small Cuban tactical air force. Eventually it was decided to equip this force with B-26 aircraft which had been widely distributed to foreign countries including countries in Latin America.

6. There were ample reasons for this new trend of thought. The air drops into Cuba were not proving effective. There were increasingly heavy shipments of Communist arms to Cuba, accompanied by evidence of increasingly effective control of the civilian population by Castro. The Special Group became aware of these adverse factors which were discussed repeatedly in the Committee meetings during the fall of 1960. The minutes of the conferences indicate a declining confidence in the effectiveness of guerrilla efforts alone to overthrow Castro.

7. In this atmosphere the CIA began to implement the new concept, increasing the size of the Cuban force in training and reorienting the training toward preparation for its use as an assault force on the Cuban coast. On November 4th, CIA in Washington dispatched a cable to the project officer in Guatemala describing what was wanted. The cable directed a reduction of the guerrilla teams in training to 60 men and the introduction of conventional training for the remainder as an amphibious and airborne assault force. From that time on, the training emphasis was placed on the assault mission and there is no evidence that the members of the assault force received any further preparation for guerrilla-type operations. The men became deeply imbued with the importance of the landing operation and its superiority over any form of guerrilla action to the point that it would have been difficult later to persuade them to return to a guerrilla-type mission. The final training of the Cubans was done by

1½ lines deleted

in Guatemala where 400–500 Cubans had been assembled. . . .

10. The Director of Central Intelligence [Allen Dulles] briefed the President [Eisenhower] on the new paramilitary concept on 29 November 1960 and received the indication that the President wished the project expedited. The concept was formally presented to the Special Group on December 8, 1960. At this meeting, [   ] in charge of the paramilitary section for the Cuba project, described the new concept as one consisting of an amphibious landing on the Cuban coast of 600–750 men equipped with weapons of extraordinarily heavy fire power. The landing would be preceded by preliminary air strikes launched from Nicaragua against military targets. Air strikes as well as supply flights would continue after the landing. The objective would be to seize, hold a limited area in Cuba, maintain a visible presence, and then to draw dissident elements to the landing force, which hopefully would trigger a general uprising. This amphibious landing would not

entirely eliminate the previous concept for infiltrating guerrilla teams. It was expected that some 60–80 men would be infiltrated prior to the amphibious landing. . . .

16. On November 18, 1960, President-elect [John F.] Kennedy had first learned of the existence of a plan for the overthrow of Castro through a call on him at Palm Beach by Mr. [Allen] Dulles and Mr. [Richard] Bissell [Deputy Director of Central Intelligence for Plans]. He received his first briefing on the developing plan as President on January 28 at a meeting which included the Vice President [Lyndon B. Johnson], Secretary of State [Dean Rusk], Secretary of Defense [Robert McNamara], the Director of Central Intelligence [John McCone], the Chairman of the Joint Chiefs of Staff [General Maxwell Taylor], Assistant Secretary [of State Thomas] Mann, Assistant Secretary [of Defense Paul] Nitze, Mr. Tracy Barnes [Bissell's assistant], and Mr. McGeorge Bundy [the National Security Adviser].

After considerable discussion, the President authorized the following:

   a. A continuation and accentuation of current activities of the CIA, including increased propaganda, increased political action, and increased sabotage. Continued overflights of Cuba were specifically authorized.
   b. The Defense Department was to review CIA proposals for the active deployment of anti-Castro Cuban forces on Cuban territory and the results of this analysis were to be promptly reported to the CIA.
   c. The State Department was to prepare a concrete proposal for action with other Latin American countries to isolate the Castro regime and to bring against it the judgment of the Organization of American States. It was expected that this proposal

2½ lines deleted

19. While the Joint Chiefs of Staff [JCS] supported the Trinidad Plan as one having "a fair chance of success" the plan encountered difficulties in other quarters. From its inception the plan had been developed under the ground rule that it must retain a covert character, that is, it should include no action which, if revealed, could not be plausibly denied by the United States and should look to the world as an operation exclusively conducted by Cubans. This ground rule meant, among other things, that no U.S. military forces or individuals could take part in combat operations. In due course it was extended to exclude pre-D-Day air strikes in support of the landing since such strikes could not have the appearance of being launched from Cuban soil before an airstrip had been seized by the landing force. This effort to treat as covert an operation which in reality could not be concealed or shielded from the presumption of U.S. involvement raised in due course many serious obstacles to the successful conduct of the operation which will be the subject of subsequent comment.

20. The President and his advisors were thoroughly aware of the difficulties of preserving the covert character of an operation as visible as a landing on a hostile shore and from the outset viewed the Trinidad Plan with caution. In particular, the State Department representatives opposed features of the plan because of the difficulty of concealing U.S. participation and also because of their fear of adverse reactions to the United States in Latin American countries and in the United Nations. They objected in particular to the conduct of any tactical air operations unless these aircraft were either actually or ostensibly based on Cuban soil.

21. On the other hand, working to overcome this reluctance to approve the Trinidad Plan was the need to decide quickly what to do with the Cuban Expeditionary Force. The President was informed that this force must leave Guatemala within a limited time and that, further, it could not be held together long in the United States if it were moved there. If the decision were taken to disband the force, that fact would soon become known and would be interpreted as a renunciation by the U.S. of the effort to free Cuba from Castro. Faced with two unattractive alternatives, the President and his advisors asked the CIA to come up with various proposals for the use of this force as alternatives to Trinidad.

22. These proposals were the subject of detailed consideration on March 11th when the President and the National Security Council met to consider the various plans then being entertained for Cuba. Mr. Bissell of CIA presented a paper entitled, "Proposed Operation Against Cuba" which summarized the action to date and presented four alternative courses of action. It concluded by recommending the Trinidad Plan which he described to be an operation in the form of an assault in force preceded by a diversionary landing as the action having the best chance of achieving the desired result. The assault in force was to consist of an amphibious/airborne assault with concurrent (but no prior) tactical air support, to seize a beachhead contiguous to terrain suitable for guerrilla operations. The provisional government would land as soon as the beachhead had been secured. If initial military operations were successful and especially if there were evidence of spreading disaffection against the Castro regime, the provisional government could be recognized and a legal basis provided for U.S. logistic support.

23. The military plan contemplated the holding of a perimeter around a beachhead area. It was believed that initial attacks by the Castro militia, even if conducted in considerable force, could be successfully resisted. The scale of the operation, a display of professional competence and determination on the part of the assault force would, it was hoped, demoralize the Castro militia, cause defections therefrom, impair the morale of the Castro regime and induce widespread rebellion.

24. After full discussion of this plan the President indicated that he was willing to go ahead with the overall project, but that he could not endorse a plan so "spectacular" as Trinidad. He directed that the CIA planners come up with other alternative methods of employing the Cuban forces. An acceptable plan should provide for a "quiet" landing, preferably at

night, without having the appearance of a World War II-type amphibious assault. The State Department requested that any beachhead seized should include an airfield capable of supporting B-26 operations, to which any tactical air operations could be attributed.

25. During the period 13–15 March the paramilitary staff of CIA worked intensively to devise a plan or plans having the desired characteristics, and presented a briefing to the JCS Working Group late in the morning of March 14. They produced for consideration three such alternatives as general concepts. They were based on three possible landing areas: (1) the Preston area on the north coast of Oriente Province; (2) the south coast of Las Villas between Trinidad and Cienfuegos; and (3) the eastern Zapata area near Cochinos Bay.

26. On March 14th these three alternatives were referred to the Joint Chiefs of Staff for their evaluation. The Joint Staff prepared this evaluation, the results of which the respective service action officers presented to their respective Chiefs prior to the JCS meeting on 15 March. At this meeting, following a briefing by the Joint Staff Working Group, the Joint Chiefs approved the evaluation and reported to the Secretary of Defense that of the three, the Zapata concept was considered the most feasible and the most likely to accomplish the objective. They added that none of the alternative concepts were considered as feasible and likely to accomplish the objective as the Trinidad Plan. . . .

28. On the same day as the Chiefs' action, March 15th, the President was briefed at the White House on the three alternative courses of action which the Chiefs had considered. After full discussion, the President again withheld approval of the plan and directed certain modifications to be considered. The CIA returned on the following day, March 16th, and presented a modification for the landing at Zapata which Mr. Bissell considered on balance more advantageous than the Trinidad Plan, wherein there would be airdrops at first light instead of the previous day in the late afternoon, with the landing in the night and all the ships withdrawn from the objective area by dawn without completing the unloading at that time. The President authorized them to proceed with the plan, but still without giving it his formal approval.

A Senate Committee Investigates U.S. Plots to Assassinate Castro, 1960–1965

We have found concrete evidence of at least eight plots involving the CIA to assassinate Fidel Castro from 1960 to 1965. Although some of the assassination plots did not advance beyond the stage of planning and preparation, one plot, involving the use of underworld figures, reportedly twice progressed to the point of sending poison pills to Cuba and dispatching teams to commit the deed. Another plot involved furnishing weapons and other assassination devices to a Cuban dissident. The proposed assassination devices ran the gamut from high-powered rifles to poison pills, poison pens, deadly bacterial powders, and other devices which strain the imagination.

The most ironic of these plots took place on November 22, 1963—the very day that President [John F.] Kennedy was shot in Dallas—when a CIA official offered a poison pen to a Cuban for use against Castro while at the same time an emissary from President Kennedy was meeting with Castro to explore the possibility of improved relations.

The following narrative sets forth the facts of assassination plots against Castro as established before the Committee by witnesses and documentary evidence. . . .

(a) Plots: Early 1960

(i) Plots to Destroy Castro's Public Image.   Efforts against Castro did not begin with assassination attempts.

From March through August 1960, during the last year of the Eisenhower Administration, the CIA considered plans to undermine Castro's charismatic appeal by sabotaging his speeches. According to the 1967 Report of the CIA's Inspector General, an official in the Technical Services Division (TSD) recalled discussing a scheme to spray Castro's broadcasting studio with a chemical which produced effects similar to LSD, but the scheme was rejected because the chemical was unreliable. During this period, TSD impregnated a box of cigars with a chemical which produced temporary disorientation, hoping to induce Castro to smoke one of the cigars before delivering a speech. The Inspector General also reported a plan to destroy Castro's image as "The Beard" by dusting his shoes with thallium salts, a strong depilatory that would cause his beard to fall out. The depilatory was to be administered during a trip outside Cuba, when it was anticipated Castro would leave his shoes outside the door of his hotel room to be shined. TSD procured the chemical and tested it on animals, but apparently abandoned the scheme because Castro cancelled his trip.

(ii) Accident Plot.   The first action against the life of a Cuban leader sponsored by the CIA of which the Committee is aware took place in 1960. A Cuban who had volunteered to assist the CIA in gathering intelligence informed his case officer in Havana that he would probably be in contact with Raul Castro [Fidel Castro's brother and Minister of Defense]. CIA Headquarters and field stations were requested to inform the Havana Station of any intelligence needs that the Cuban might fulfill. The case officer testified that he and the Cuban contemplated only acquiring intelligence information and that assassination was not proposed by them.

The cable from the Havana Station was received at Headquarters on the night of July 20. The duty officer, who was summoned to Headquarters from his home, contacted Tracy Barnes, Deputy to Richard Bissell, CIA's Deputy Director for Plans and the man in charge of CIA's covert action directorate. The duty officer also contacted J. C. King, Chief of the Western Hemisphere Division within the Directorate for Plans.

Following their instructions, he sent a cable to the Havana Station early in the morning of July 21, stating: "Possible removal top three leaders is receiving serious consideration at HQS." The cable inquired whether the Cuban was sufficiently motivated to risk "arranging an accident" involving Raul Castro and advised that the station could "at discretion contact subject to determine willingness to cooperate and his suggestions on details." Ten thousand dollars was authorized as payment "after successful completion," but no advance payment was permitted because of the possibility that the Cuban was a double agent. According to the case officer, this cable represented "quite a departure from the conventional activities we'd been asked to handle."

The case officer contacted the Cuban and told him of the proposal. The case officer avoided the word "assassinate" but made it clear that the CIA contemplated an "accident to neutralize this leader's [Raul's] influence." After being assured that his sons would be given a college education in the event of his death, the Cuban agreed to take a "calculated risk," limited to possibilities that might pass as accidental.

Immediately after returning to the station the case officer was told that a cable had just arrived stating: "Do not pursue ref. Would like to drop matter." This cable was signed by Tracy Barnes.

It was, of course, too late to "drop the matter" since the Cuban had already left to contact Raul Castro. When the Cuban returned, he told the case officer that he had not had an opportunity to arrange an accident.

(iii) Poison Cigars.   A notation in the records of the Operations Division, CIA's Office of Medical Services, indicates that on August 16, 1960, an official was given a box of Castro's favorite cigars with instructions to treat them with lethal poison. The cigars were contaminated with a botulinum toxin so potent that a person would die after putting one in his mouth. The official reported that the cigars were ready on October 7, 1960; TSD notes indicate that they were delivered to an unidentified person on February 13, 1961. The record does not disclose whether an attempt was made to pass the cigars to Castro.

(b) Use of Underworld Figures—Phase I (Pre-Bay of Pigs)

(i) The Initial Plan.   In August 1960, the CIA took steps to enlist members of the criminal underworld with gambling syndicate contacts to aid in assassinating Castro. The origin of the plot is uncertain. According to the 1967 Inspector General's Report,

> Bissell recalls that the idea originated with J. C. King, then Chief of W. H. Division, although King now recalls having only had limited knowledge of such a plan and at a much later date—about mid-1962.

Bissell testified that:

> I remember a conversation which I would have put in early autumn or late summer between myself and Colonel Edwards [Director of the Office of Security], and I have some dim recollection of some earlier conversation I

had had with Colonel J. C. King, Chief of the Western Hemisphere Division, and the subject matter of both of those conversations was a capability to eliminate Castro if such action should be decided upon.

The earliest concrete evidence of the operation is a conversation between DDP Bissell and Colonel Sheffield Edwards, Director of the Office of Security. Edwards recalled that Bissell asked him to locate someone who could assassinate Castro. Bissell confirmed that he requested Edwards to find someone to assassinate Castro and believed that Edwards raised the idea of contacting members of a gambling syndicate operating in Cuba.

Edwards assigned the mission to the Chief of the Operational Support Division of the Office of Security. The Support Chief recalled that Edwards had said that he and Bissell were looking for someone to "eliminate" or "assassinate" Castro.

Edwards and the Support Chief decided to rely on Robert A. Maheu to recruit someone "tough enough" to handle the job. Maheu was an ex-FBI agent who had entered into a career as a private investigator in 1954. A former FBI associate of Maheu's was employed in the CIA's Office of Security and had arranged for the CIA to use Maheu in several sensitive covert operations in which "he didn't want to have an Agency person or a government person get caught." Maheu was initially paid a monthly retainer by the CIA of $500, but it was terminated after his detective agency became more lucrative. The Operational Support Chief had served as Maheu's case officer since the Agency first began using Maheu's services, and by 1960 they had become close personal friends.

Sometime in late August or early September 1960, the Support Chief approached Maheu about the proposed operation. As Maheu recalls the conversation, the Support Chief asked him to contact John Rosselli, an underworld figure with possible gambling contacts in Las Vegas, to determine if he would participate in a plan to "dispose" of Castro. Maheu handled the details of setting up the operation and keeping the Support Chief informed of developments. After Rosselli and Maheu had been in Miami for a short time, and certainly prior to October 18, Rosselli introduced Maheu to two individuals on whom Rosselli intended to rely: "Sam Gold," who would serve as a "back-up man," or "key" man and "Joe," whom "Gold" said would serve as a courier to Cuba and make arrangements there. The Support Chief, who was using the name "Jim Olds," said he had met "Sam" and "Joe" once, and then only briefly.

The Support Chief testified that he learned the true identities of his associates one morning when Maheu called and asked him to examine the "Parade" supplement to the *Miami Times*. An article on the Attorney General's ten-most-wanted criminals list revealed that "Sam Gold" was Momo Salvatore Giancana, a Chicago-based gangster, and "Joe" was Santos Trafficante, the Cosa Nostra chieftain in Cuba. The Support Chief reported his discovery to Edwards, but did not know whether Edwards reported this fact to his superiors. The Support Chief testified that this incident occurred after "we were up to our ears in it," a month or so after Giancana had been brought into the operation, but prior to giving the poison pills to Rosselli.

Maheu recalled that it was Giancana's job to locate someone in Castro's entourage who could accomplish the assassination, and that he met almost daily with Giancana over a substantial period of time. Although Maheu described Giancana as playing a "key role," Rosselli claimed that none of the Cubans eventually used in the operation were acquired through Giancana's contacts. . . .

Rosselli told the Support Chief that Trafficante believed a certain leading figure in the Cuban exile movement might be able to accomplish the assassination. The Inspector General's Report suggests that this Cuban may have been receiving funds from Trafficante and other racketeers interested in securing "gambling, prostitution, and dope monopolies" in Cuba after the overthrow of Castro. The Report speculated that the Cuban was interested in the assassination scheme as a means of financing the purchase of arms and communications equipment.

The Cuban claimed to have a contact inside a restaurant frequented by Castro. As a prerequisite to the deal, he demanded cash and $1,000 worth of communications equipment. The Support Chief recalled that Colonel J. C. King, head of the Western Hemisphere Division, gave him $50,000 in Bissell's office to pay the Cuban if he successfully assassinated Castro. The Support Chief stated that Bissell also authorized him to give the Cuban the requested electronics equipment.

Bissell testified that he did not doubt that some cash was given to the Support Chief, and that he was aware that the poison pills had been prepared. Bissell did not recall the meeting described above, and considered it unlikely that the Support Chief would have been given the money in his office. The Inspector General's Report, relying on an Office of Security memorandum to the DDCI dated June 24, 1966, as well as on an interview with the person who signed the voucher for the funds, placed the amount passed at $10,000. If the Inspector General's conclusions were correct, the funds which Bissell allegedly authorized were probably the advance payment to the Cuban, and not the $150,000 that was to be paid to him after Castro's death.

The record does clearly reflect, however, that communications equipment was delivered to the Cuban and that he was paid advance money to cover his expenses, probably in the amount of $10,000. The money and pills were delivered at a meeting between Maheu, Rosselli, Trafficante, and the Cuban at the Fountainebleau Hotel in Miami. As Rosselli recalled, Maheu:

> opened his briefcase and dumped a whole lot of money on his lap . . . and also came up with the capsules and he explained how they were going to be used. As far as I remember, they couldn't be used in boiling soups and things like that, but they could be used in water or otherwise, but they couldn't last forever. . . . It had to be done as quickly as possible.

The attempt met with failure. According to the Inspector General's Report, Edwards believed the scheme failed because Castro stopped visiting the restaurant where the "asset" was employed. Maheu suggested an alternative reason. He recalled being informed that after the pills had been delivered to Cuba, "the go signal still had to be received before in fact they were administered." He testified that he was informed by the Support Chief sometime after the operation that the Cubans had an opportunity to administer the pills to Fidel Castro and either Che Guevarra or Raul Castro, but that the "go signal" never came. Maheu did not know who was responsible for giving the signal. The Cuban subsequently returned the cash and the pills.

President Kennedy and His Advisers Debate Options in the Missile Crisis, 1962

Meeting of 11:50 A.M.–12:57 P.M.

LUNDAHL [Art Lundahl, National Photographic Interpretation Center]: This is a result of the photography taken Sunday, sir.

JFK: Yeah.

LUNDAHL: There's a medium-range ballistic missile launch site and two new military encampments on the southern edge of Sierra del Rosario in west central Cuba.

JFK: Where would that be?

LUNDAHL: Uh, west central, sir. That. . . .

JFK: Yeah. . . .

LUNDAHL: Well, on site on one of the encampments contains a total of at least fourteen canvas-covered missile trailers measuring 67 feet in length, 9 feet in width. The overall length of the trailers plus the tow-bars is approximately 80 feet. The other encampment contains vehicles and tents but with no missile trailers. . . .

JFK: How far advanced is this? . . . How do you know this is a medium-range ballistic missile?

LUNDAHL: The length, sir.

JFK: The what? The length?

LUNDAHL: The length of it. Yes.

JFK: The length of the missile? Which part? I mean which . . .

LUNDAHL: . . . the missile [word unintelligible] indicates which one is [words unintelligible]. . . .

JFK: Is this ready to be fired?

GRAYBEAL [Sidney Graybeal]: No, sir.

JFK: How long have we got. . . . We can't tell, I take it . . .

GRAYBEAL: No, sir.

JFK: . . . how long before it can be fired?

GRAYBEAL: That depends on how ready the . . .

JFK: But, what does it have to be fired from?

GRAYBEAL: It would have to be fired from a stable hard surface. This could be packed dirt; it could be concrete or, or asphalt. The surface has to be hard, then you put a flame deflect-, a deflector plate on there to direct the missile.

McNAMARA [Robert McNamara, secretary of defense]: Would you care to comment on the position of nuclear warheads—this is in relation to the question from the president—explain when these can be fired?

GRAYBEAL: Sir, we've looked very hard. We can find nothing that would spell nuclear warhead in term [*sic*] of any isolated area or unique security in this particular area. The mating of the nuclear warhead to the missile from some of the other short range missiles there would take about, uh, a couple of hours to do this.

McNAMARA: This is not defensed, I believe, at the moment?

LUNDAHL: Not yet, sir. . . .

RUSK [Dean Rusk, secretary of state]: Don't you have to assume these are nuclear? . . .

McNAMARA: There's no question about that. The question is one of readiness of the, to fire and—and this is highly critical in forming our plans— that the time between today and the time when the readiness to fire capability develops is a very important thing. To estimate that we need to know where these warheads are, and we have not yet found any probable storage of warheads and hence it seems extremely unlikely that they are now ready to fire or may be ready to fire within a matter of hours or even a day or two. . . .

JFK: Secretary Rusk?

RUSK: Yes. [Well?], Mr. President, this is a, of course, a [widely?] serious development. It's one that we, all of us, had not really believed the Soviets could, uh, carry this far. Uh, they, uh, seemed to be denying that they were going to establish bases of their own [in the same?] [words unintelligible] with a Soviet base, thus making it [essential to or essentially?] Cuban point of view. The Cubans couldn't [word unintelligible] with it anyhow, so. . . . Now, uhm, I do think we have to set in motion a chain of events that will eliminate this base. I don't think we [can?] sit still. The questioning becomes whether we do it by sudden, unannounced strike of some sort, or we, uh, build up the crisis to the point where the other side has to consider very seriously about giving in, or, or even the Cubans themselves, uh, take some, take some action on this. The thing that I'm, of course, very conscious of is that there is no such thing, I think, as unilateral action by the United States. It's so [eminently or heavily?] involved with 2 allies and confrontation in many places, that any action that we take, uh, will greatly increase the risks of direct action involving, uh, our other alliances and our other forces in other parts of the world. Uhm, so I think we, we have to think very hard about two major, uh, courses of action as alternatives. One is the quick strike. The point where we [make or think?], that is the, uh, overwhelming, overriding necessity to take all the risks that are involved doing that. I don't think this in itself would require an invasion of Cuba. I think that with or without such an invasion, in other words if we make it clear that, uh, what we're doing is eliminating this particular base or any other such base that is established. We ourselves are not moved to general war, we're simply doing what we said we would do if they took certain action. Uh, or we're going to decide that this is the time to eliminate the Cuban problem by actual eliminate the island.

The other would be, if we have a few days—from the military point of view, if we have the whole time—uh, then I would think that, uh, there would be another course of action, a combination of things that, uh, we might wish to consider. Uhm, first, uh, that we, uh, stimulate the OAS procedure immediately for prompt action to make it quite clear that the entire hemisphere considers that the Rio Pact has been violated [and actually?] what acts should [we take or be taken?] in, under the terms of the Rio Pact. . . .

I think also that we ought to consider getting some word to Castro, perhaps through the Canadian ambassador in Havana or through, uh, his representative at the U.N. Uh, I think perhaps the Canadian ambassador would be best, the better channel to get to Castro [apart?] privately and tell him that, uh, this is no longer support for Cuba, that Cuba is being victimized here, and that, uh, the Soviets are preparing Cuba for destruction or betrayal.

You saw the [*New York*] *Times* story yesterday morning that high Soviet officials were saying, "We'll trade Cuba for Berlin." This ought to be brought to Castro's attention. It ought to be said to Castro that, uh, uh, this kind of a base is intolerable and not acceptable. The time has now come when he must take the interests of the Cuban people, must now break clearly with the Soviet Union, prevent this missile base from becoming operational.

And I think there are certain military, uhm, uh, actions that we could, we might well want to take straight away. First, to, uh, to call up, uh, highly selective units [no more than?] 150,000. Unless we feel that it's better, more desirable to go to a general national emergency so that we have complete freedom of action. If we announce, at the time that we announce this development—and I think we do have to announce this development some time this week—uh, we announce that, uh, we are conducting a surveillance of Cuba, over Cuba, and we will enforce our right to do so. We reject the mission of secrecy in this hemisphere in any matters of this sort. We, we reinforce our forces in Guantanamo. We reinforce our forces in the southeastern part of the United States—whatever is necessary from the military point of view to be able to give, to deliver an overwhelming strike at any of these installations, including the SAM sites. And, uh, also, to take care of any, uh, MIGs or bombers that might make a pass at Miami or at the United States. Build up heavy forces, uh, if those are not already in position. . . .

I think also that we need a few days, uhm, to alert our other allies, for consultation with NATO. I'll assume that we can move on this line at the same time to interrupt all air traffic from free world countries going into Cuba, insist to the Mexicans, the Dutch, that they stop their planes from coming in. Tell the British, who, and anyone else who's involved at this point, that, uh, if they're interested in peace, that they've got to stop their ships from Cuban trade at this point. Uh, in other words, isolate Cuba completely without at this particular moment a, uh, a forceful blockade. . . .

But I think that, by large, there are, there are these two broad alternatives: one, the quick strike; the other, to alert our allies and Mr. Khrushchev that there is utterly serious crisis in the making here, and that, uh. . . . Mr. Khrushchev may not himself really understand that or believe that at this point. I think we'll be facing a situation that could well lead to general war. . . .

McNAMARA: Mr. President, there are a number of unknowns in this situation I want to comment upon, and, in relation to them, I would like to outline very briefly some possible military alternatives and ask General Taylor to expand upon them.

But before commenting on either the unknowns or outlining some military alternatives, there are two propositions I would suggest that we ought to accept as, uh, foundations for our further thinking. My first is that if we are to conduct an air strike against these installations, or against any part of Cuba, we must agree now that we will schedule that prior to the time these missile sites become operational. I'm not prepared to say when that will be, but I think it is extremely important that our talk and our discussion be founded on this premise: that any air strike will be planned to take place prior to the time they become operational. Because, if they become operational before the air strike, I do not believe we can state we can knock them out before they can be launched; and if they're launched there is almost certain to be, uh, chaos in part of the east coast or the area, uh, in a radius of six hundred to a thousand miles from Cuba.

Uh, secondly, I, I would submit the proposition that any air strike must be directed not solely against the missile sites, but against the missile sites plus the airfields plus the aircraft which may not be on the airfields but hidden by that time plus all potential nuclear storage sites. Now, this is a fairly extensive air strike. It is not just a strike against the missile sites; and there would be associated with it potential casualties of Cubans, not of U.S. citizens, but potential casualties of Cubans in, at least in the hundreds, more likely in the low thousands, say two or three thousand. It seems to me these two propositions, uh, should underlie our, our discussion.

Now, what kinds of military action are we capable of carrying out and what may be some of the consequences? Uh, we could carry out an air strike within a matter of days. We would be ready for the start of such an air strike within, within a matter of days. If it were absolutely essential, it could be done almost literally within a matter of hours. I believe the chiefs would prefer that it be deferred for a matter of days, but we are prepared for that quickly. The air strike could continue for a matter of days following the initial day, if necessary. Uh, presumably there would be some political discussions taking place either just before the air strike or both before and during. In any event, we would be prepared, following the air strike, for an air, invasion, both by air and by sea. . . . Associated with this air strike undoubtedly should be some degree of mobilization. Uh, I would think of the mobilization coming not before the air strike but either concurrently with or somewhat following, say possibly five days afterwards, depending upon the possible invasion requirements. The character of the mobilization would be such that it could be carried out in its first phase at least within the limits of the authority granted by Congress. There might have to be a second phase, and then it would require a declaration of a national emergency.

Now, this is very sketchily the military, uh, capabilities, and I think you may wish to hear General Taylor, uh, outline his choice. . . .

TAYLOR [General Maxwell Taylor, chairman of the Joint Chiefs of Staff]: Uh, we're impressed, Mr. President, with the great importance of getting a, a strike with all the benefits of surprise, uh, which would mean *ideally* that we would have all the missiles that are in Cuba above ground where we can take them out. Uh, that, that desire runs counter to the strong point the secretary made if the other optimum would be to get every missile before it could, becomes operational. Uh, practically, I think the, our knowledge of the timing of the readiness is going to be so, so, uh, difficult that we'll never have the, the exact permanent, uh, the perfect timing. . . . It's a little hard to say in terms of time how much I'm discussing. But we must do a good job the first time we go in there, uh, pushing a 100 percent just as far, as closely as we can with our, with our strike. . . .

I would also mention among the, the military actions we should take that once we have destroyed as many of these offensive weapons as possible, we should, should prevent any more coming in, which means a naval blockade. . . .

JFK: What is the, uh, advant-. . . . Must be some major reason for the Russians to, uh, set this up as a. . . . Must be that they're not satisfied with their ICBMs. What'd be the reason that they would, uh. . . .

TAYLOR: What it'd give 'em is primary, it makes the launching base, uh, for short range missiles against the United States to supplement their rather [deceptive?] ICBM system, for example. There's one reason. . . .

RUSK: Still, about why the Soviets are doing this, uhm, Mr. McCone [John A. McCone, director of the Central Intelligence Agency] suggested some weeks ago that one thing Mr. Khrushchev may have in mind is that, uh, uh, he knows that we have a substantial nuclear superiority, but he also knows that we don't really live under fear of his nuclear weapons to the extent that, uh, he has to live under fear of ours. Also we have nuclear weapons nearby, in Turkey and places like that.

JFK: How many weapons do we have in Turkey?

TAYLOR?: We have Jupiter missiles. . . .

McNAMARA?: About fifteen, I believe it is. . . .

RUSK: Uhm, and that Mr. McCone expresses the view that Khrushchev may feel that it's important for us to learn about living under medium-range missiles, and he's doing that to sort of balance that, uh, that political, psychological [plank?]. I think also that, uh, Berlin is, uh, very much involved in this. Uhm, for the first time, I'm beginning really to wonder whether maybe Mr. Khrushchev is entirely rational about Berlin. We've [hardly?] talked about his obsession with it. And I think we have to, uh, keep our eye on that element. But, uh, they may be thinking that they can either bargain Berlin and Cuba against each other, or that they could provoke us into a kind of action in Cuba which would give an umbrella for them to take action with respect to Berlin. In other words like the Suez-Hungary combination. If they could provoke us into taking the first overt action, then the world would be confused and they would have, uh, what they would consider to be justification for making a move somewhere else. But, uh, I must say I don't really see the rationality of, uh, the Soviets' pushing it this far unless they grossly misunderstand the importance of Cuba to this country.

JFK: Uh, eh, well, this, which . . . What you're really talking about are two or three different, uh, [tense?] operations. One is the strike just on this, these three bases. One, the second is the broader one that Secretary McNamara was talking about, which is on the airfields and on the SAM sites and on anything else connected with, uh, missiles. Third is doing both of those things and also at the same time launching a blockade, which requires really the, uh, the, uh, third and which is a larger step. And then, as I take it, the fourth question is the, uh, degree of consultation.

RFK [Robert F. Kennedy]: Mr. President.

JFK: Yes.

RFK: We have the fifth one, really, which is the invasion. I would say that, uh, you're dropping bombs all over Cuba if you do the second, uh, air, the airports, knocking out their planes, dropping it on all their missiles. You're covering most of Cuba. You're going to kill an awful lot of people, and, uh, we're going to take an awful lot of heat on it . . .

JFK: I don't believe it takes us, at least, uh. . . . How long did it take to get in a position where we can invade Cuba? Almost a month? Two months?

McNamara: No, sir. . . .

JFK: I think we ought to, what we ought to do is, is, uh, after this meeting this afternoon, we ought to meet tonight again at six, consider these various, uh, proposals. In the meanwhile, we'll go ahead with this maximum, whatever is needed from the flights, and, in addition, we will. . . . I don't think we got much time on these missiles. They may be. . . . So it may be that we just have to, we can't wait two weeks while we're getting ready to, to roll. Maybe just have to just take *them out,* and continue our other preparations if we decide to do that. That may be where we end up. I think we ought to, beginning right now, be preparing to. . . . Because that's what we're going to do *anyway.* We're certainly going to do number one; we're going to take out these, uh, missiles. Uh, the questions will be whether, which, what I would describe as number two, which would be a general air strike. That we're not ready to say, but we should be in preparation for it. The third is the, is the, uh, the general invasion. At least we're going to do number one, so it seems to me that we don't have to wait very long. We, we ought to be making *those* preparations.

BUNDY [McGeorge Bundy, assistant for national security affairs]: You want to be clear, Mr. President, whether we have *definitely* decided *against* a political track. I, myself, think we ought . . .

TAYLOR?: Well, we'll have . . .

BUNDY: . . . to work out a contingency on that.

TAYLOR?: We, we'll develop both tracks.

Meeting of 6:30–7:55 P.M.

MCNAMARA: Mr. President, could I outline three courses of action we have considered and speak very briefly on each one? The first is what I would call the political course of action, in which we, uh, follow some of the possibilities that Secretary Rusk mentioned this morning by approaching Castro, by approaching Khrushchev, by discussing with our allies. An overt and open approach politically to the problem [attempting, or in order?] to solve it. This seemed to me likely to lead to no satisfactory result, and it almost stops subsequent military action. . . .

A second course of action we haven't discussed but lies in between the military course we began discussing a moment ago and the political course of action is a course of action that would involve declaration of open surveillance; a statement that we would immediately impose an, uh, a blockade against *offensive* weapons entering Cuba in the future; and an indication that with our open-surveillance reconnaissance which we would plan to maintain indefinitely for the future. . . .

But the third course of action is any one of these variants of military action directed against Cuba, starting with an air attack against the missiles. The Chiefs are strongly opposed to so limited an air attack. But even so limited an air attack is a very extensive air attack. It's not twenty sorties or fifty sorties or a hundred sorties, but probably several hundred sorties. Uh, we haven't worked out the details. It's very difficult to do so when we lack certain intelligence that we hope to have tomorrow or the next day. But it's a substantial air attack. . . . I don't believe we have considered the consequences of any of these actions satisfactorily, and because we haven't considered the consequences, I'm not sure we're taking all the action we ought to take now to minimize those. I, I don't know quite what kind of a world we live in after we've struck Cuba, and we, we've started it. . . .

TAYLOR: And you'll miss some [missiles].

MCNAMARA: And you'll miss some. That's right. Now after we've launched sorties, what kind of a world do we live in? How, how do we stop at that point? I don't know the answer to this. I think tonight State and we ought to work on the consequences of any one of these courses of actions, consequences which I don't believe are entirely clear. . . .

JFK: If the, uh, it doesn't increase very much their strategic, uh, strength, why is it, uh, can any Russian expert tell us why they. . . . After all Khrushchev demonstrated a sense of caution [thousands?]. . .

SPEAKER?: Well, there are several, several possible . . .

JFK: . . . Berlin, he's been cautious, I mean, he hasn't been, uh . . .

BALL [George W. Ball, under secretary of state]: Several possibilities, Mr. President. One of them is that he has given us word now that he's coming over in November to, to the UN. If, he may be proceeding on the assumption, and this lack of a sense of *apparent* urgency would seem to, to support this, that this *isn't* going to be discovered at the moment and that, uh, when he comes over this is something he can do, a ploy. That here is Cuba armed against the United States, or possibly use it to try to trade something in Berlin, saying he'll disarm Cuba, if, uh, if we'll yield some of our interests in Berlin and some arrangement for it. I mean, that this is a, it's a trading ploy.

BUNDY: I would think one thing that I would still cling to is that he's not likely to give Fidel Castro nuclear warheads. I don't believe that has happened or is likely to happen.

JFK: Why does he put these in there though?

BUNDY: Soviet-controlled nuclear warheads [of the kind?] . . .

JFK: That's right, but what is the advantage of that? It's just as if we suddenly began to put a major number of MRBMs [Medium-Range Ballistic Missiles] in Turkey. Now that'd be goddam dangerous, I would think.

BUNDY: Well, we *did*, Mr. President. . . .

JFK: Yeah, but that was five years ago. . . .

BALL: Yes, I think, I think you, you look at this possibility that this is an attempt to, to add to his strategic capabilities. A second consideration is that it is simply a trading ploy, that he, he wants this in so that he could, he could [words unintelligible]. . . .

SPEAKER?: Isn't it puzzling, also, there are no evidence of any troops protecting the sites?

TAYLOR: Well, there're troops there. At least there're tents. . . .

McNAMARA: But they look like [words unintelligible]. It's as if you could walk over the fields into those vans.

JFK: Well, it's a goddam mystery to me. I don't know enough about the Soviet Union, but if anybody can tell me any other time since the Berlin blockade where the Russians have given us so clear provocation, I don't know when it's been, because they've been awfully cautious really. The Russians, I never. . . . Now, maybe our mistake was in not saying some time *before* this summer that if they do this we're [word unintelligible] to act. . . .

President Kennedy Addresses the Nation on the Missile Crisis, 1962

Good evening, my fellow citizens:

This Government, as promised, has maintained the closest surveillance of the Soviet military buildup on the island of Cuba. Within the past week, unmistakable evidence has established the fact that a series of offensive missile sites is now in preparation on that imprisoned island. The purpose of these bases can be none other than to provide a nuclear strike capability against the Western Hemisphere.

Upon receiving the first preliminary hard information of this nature last Tuesday morning at 9 a.m., I directed that our surveillance be stepped up. And having now confirmed and completed our evaluation of the evidence and our decision on a course of action, this Government feels obliged to report this new crisis to you in fullest detail.

The characteristics of these new missile sites indicate two distinct types of installations. Several of them include medium range ballistic missiles, capable of carrying a nuclear warhead for a distance of more than 1,000 nautical miles. Each of these missiles, in short, is capable of striking Washington, D.C., the Panama Canal, Cape Canaveral, Mexico City, or any other city in the southeastern part of the United States, in Central America, or in the Caribbean area.

Additional sites not yet completed appear to be designed for intermediate range ballistic missiles—capable of traveling more than twice as far—and thus capable of striking most of the major cities in the Western Hemisphere, ranging as far north as Hudson Bay, Canada, and as far south as Lima, Peru. In addition, jet bombers, capable of carrying nuclear weapons, are now being uncrated and assembled in Cuba, while the necessary air bases are being prepared.

This urgent transformation of Cuba into an important strategic base— by the presence of these large, long-range, and clearly offensive weapons of sudden mass destruction—constitutes an explicit threat to the peace and security of all the Americas, in flagrant and deliberate defiance of the Rio Pact of 1947, the traditions of this Nation and hemisphere, the joint resolution of the 87th Congress, the Charter of the United Nations, and my own public warnings to the Soviets on September 4 and 13. This action also contradicts the repeated assurances of Soviet spokesmen, both publicly and privately delivered, that the arms buildup in Cuba would retain its original defensive character, and that the Soviet Union had no need or desire to station strategic missiles on the territory of any other nation.

The size of this undertaking makes clear that it has been planned for some months. Yet only last month, after I had made clear the distinction between any introduction of ground-to-ground missiles and the existence of defensive antiaircraft missiles, the Soviet Government publicly stated on September 11 that, and I quote, "the armaments and military equipment sent to Cuba are designed exclusively for defensive purposes," that, and I quote the Soviet Government, "there is no need for the Soviet Government to shift its weapons . . . for a retaliatory blow to any other country, for instance Cuba," and that, and I quote their government, "the Soviet Union has so powerful rockets to carry these nuclear warheads that there is no need to search for sites for them beyond the boundaries of the Soviet Union." That statement was false.

Only last Thursday, as evidence of this rapid offensive buildup was already in my hand, Soviet Foreign Minister Gromyko told me in my office that he was instructed to make it clear once again, as he said his government had already done, that Soviet assistance to Cuba, and I quote, "pursued solely the purpose of contributing to the defense capabilities of Cuba," that, and I quote him, "training by Soviet specialists of Cuban nationals in handling defensive armaments was by no means offensive, and if it were otherwise," Mr. Gromyko went on, "the Soviet Government would never become involved in rendering such assistance." That statement also was false.

Neither the United States of America nor the world community of nations can tolerate deliberate deception and offensive threats on the part of any nation, large or small. We no longer live in a world where only the actual firing of weapons represents a sufficient challenge to a nation's security to constitute maximum peril. Nuclear weapons are so destructive and ballistic missiles are so swift, that any substantially increased possibility of their use or any sudden change in their deployment may well be regarded as a definite threat to peace.

For many years, both the Soviet Union and the United States, recognizing this fact, have deployed strategic nuclear weapons with great care, never upsetting the precarious status quo which insured that these weapons would not be used in the absence of some vital challenge. Our own strategic missiles have never been transferred to the territory of any other nation under a cloak of secrecy and deception; and our history—unlike that of the Soviets since the end of World War II—demonstrates that we have no desire to dominate or conquer any other nation or impose our system upon its people. Nevertheless, American citizens have become adjusted to living daily on the bull's-eye of Soviet missiles located inside the U.S.S.R. or in submarines.

In that sense, missiles in Cuba add to an already clear and present danger—although it should be noted the nations of Latin America have never previously been subjected to a potential nuclear threat.

But this secret, swift, and extraordinary buildup of Communist missiles—in an area well known to have a special and historical relationship to the United States and the nations of the Western Hemisphere, in violation of Soviet assurances, and in defiance of American and hemispheric policy—this sudden, clandestine decision to station strategic weapons for the first time outside of Soviet soil—is a deliberately provocative and unjustified change in the status quo which cannot be accepted by this country, if our courage and our commitments are ever to be trusted again by either friend or foe.

The 1930's taught us a clear lesson: aggressive conduct, if allowed to go unchecked and unchallenged, ultimately leads to war. This nation is opposed to war. We are also true to our word. Our unswerving objective, therefore, must be to prevent the use of these missiles against this or any other country, and to secure their withdrawal or elimination from the Western Hemisphere.

Our policy has been one of patience and restraint, as befits a peaceful and powerful nation, which leads a worldwide alliance. We have been determined not to be diverted from our central concerns by mere irritants and fanatics. But now further action is required—and it is under way; and these actions may only be the beginning. We will not prematurely or unnecessarily risk the costs of worldwide nuclear war in which even the fruits of victory would be ashes in our mouth—but neither will we shrink from that risk at any time it must be faced.

Acting, therefore, in the defense of our own security and of the entire Western Hemisphere, and under the authority entrusted to me by the Constitution as endorsed by the resolution of the Congress, I have directed that the following *initial* steps be taken immediately:

First: To halt this offensive buildup, a strict quarantine on all offensive military equipment under shipment to Cuba is being initiated. All ships of any kind bound for Cuba from whatever nation or port will, if found to contain cargoes of offensive weapons, be turned back. This quarantine will be extended, if needed, to other types of cargo and carriers. We are not at this time, however, denying the necessities of life as the Soviets attempted to do in their Berlin blockade of 1948.

Second: I have directed the continued and increased close surveillance of Cuba and its military buildup. The foreign ministers of the OAS, in their communique of October 6, rejected secrecy on such matters in this hemisphere. Should these offensive military preparations continue, thus increasing the threat to the hemisphere, further action will be justified. I have directed the Armed Forces to prepare for any eventualities; and I trust that in the interest of both the Cuban people and the Soviet technicians at the sites, the hazards to all concerned of continuing this threat will be recognized.

Third: It shall be the policy of this Nation to regard any nuclear missile launched from Cuba against any nation in the Western Hemisphere as an attack by the Soviet Union on the United States, requiring a full retaliatory response upon the Soviet Union.

Fourth: As a necessary military precaution, I have reinforced our base at Guantanamo, evacuated today the dependents of our personnel there, and ordered additional military units to be on a standby alert basis.

Fifth: We are calling tonight for an immediate meeting of the Organ of Consultation under the Organization of American States, to consider this threat to hemispheric security and to invoke articles 6 and 8 of the Rio Treaty in support of all necessary action. The United Nations Charter allows for regional security arrangements—and the nations of this hemisphere decided long ago against the military presence of outside powers. Our other allies around the world have also been alerted.

Sixth: Under the Charter of the United Nations, we are asking tonight that an emergency meeting of the Security Council be convoked without delay to take action against this latest Soviet threat to world peace. Our resolution will call for the prompt dismantling and withdrawal of all offensive weapons in Cuba, under the supervision of U.N. observers, before the quarantine can be lifted.

Seventh and finally: I call upon Chairman Khrushchev to halt and eliminate this clandestine, reckless, and provocative threat to world peace and to stable relations between our two nations. I call upon him further to abandon this course of world domination, and to join in an historic effort to end the perilous arms race and to transform the history of man. He has an opportunity now to move the world back from the abyss of destruction—by returning to his government's own words that it had no need to station missiles outside its own territory, and withdrawing these weapons from Cuba—by refraining from any action which will widen or deepen the present crisis—and then by participating in a search for peaceful and permanent solutions.

Soviet Premier Nikita Khrushchev Appeals to President Kennedy, 1962

[Moscow,] *October 26, 1962.*

Dear Mr. President:

I have received your letter of October 25. From your letter, I got the feeling that you have some understanding of the situation which has developed and (some) sense of responsibility. I value this.

Now we have already publicly exchanged our evaluations of the events around Cuba and each of us has set forth his explanation and his understanding of these events. Consequently, I would judge that, apparently, a continuation of an exchange of opinions at such a distance, even in the form of secret letters, will hardly add anything to that which one side has already said to the other.

I think you will understand me correctly if you are really concerned about the welfare of the world. Everyone needs peace: both capitalists, if they have not lost their reason, and, still more, communists, people who know how to value not only their own lives but, more than anything, the lives of the peoples. We, communists, are against all wars between states in general and have been defending the cause of peace since we came into the world. We have always regarded war as a calamity, and not as a game nor as a means of the attainment of definite goals, nor, all the more, as a goal in itself. Our goals are clear, and the means to attain them is labor. War is our enemy and a calamity for all the peoples.

It is thus that we, Soviet people, and, together with us, other peoples as well, understand the questions of war and peace. I can, in any case, firmly say this for the peoples of the socialist countries, as well as for all progressive people who want peace, happiness, and friendship among peoples.

I see, Mr. President, that you too are not devoid of a sense of anxiety for the fate of the world, of understanding, and of what war entails. What would a war give you? You are threatening us with war. But you well know that the very least which you would receive in reply would be that you would experience the same consequences as those which you sent us. And that must be clear to us, people invested with authority, trust, and responsibility. We must not succumb to intoxication and petty passions, regardless of whether elections are impending in this or that country, or not impending. These are all transient things, but if indeed war should break out, then it would not be in our power to stop it, for such is the logic of war. I have participated in two wars and know that war ends when it has rolled through cities and villages, everywhere sowing death and destruction.

In the name of the Soviet Government and the Soviet people, I assure you that your conclusions regarding offensive weapons on Cuba are groundless. It is apparent from what you have written me that our conceptions are different on this score, or rather, we have different estimates of these or those military means. Indeed, in reality, the same forms of weapons can have different interpretations.

You are a military man and, I hope, will understand me. Let us take for example a simple cannon. What sort of means is this: offensive or defensive? A cannon is a defensive means if it is set up to defend boundaries or a fortified area. But if one concentrates artillery, and adds to it the necessary number of troops, then the same cannons do become an offensive means, because they prepare and clear the way for infantry to attack. The same happens with missile-nuclear weapons as well, with any type of this weapon.

You are mistaken if you think that any of our means on Cuba are offensive. However, let us not quarrel now. It is apparent that I will not be able to convince you of this. But I say to you: you, Mr. President, are a military man and should understand: can one attack, if one has on one's territory even an enormous quantity of missiles of various effective radiuses and various power, but using only these means. These missiles are a means of extermination and destruction. But one cannot attack with these missiles, even nuclear missiles of a power of 100 megatons because only people, troops, can attack. Without people, any means however powerful cannot be offensive.

How can one, consequently, give such a completely incorrect interpretation as you are now giving, to the effect that some sort of means on Cuba are offensive. All the means located there, and I assure you of this, have a defensive character, are on Cuba solely for the purposes of defense, and we have sent them to Cuba at the request of the Cuban Government. You, however, say that these are offensive means.

But, Mr. President, do you really seriously think that Cuba can attack the United States and that even we together with Cuba can attack you from the territory of Cuba? Can you really think that way? How is it possible? We do not understand this. Has something so new appeared in military strategy that one can think that it is possible to attack thus. I say precisely attack, and not destroy, since barbarians, people who have lost their sense, destroy.

I believe that you have no basis to think this way. You can regard us with distrust, but, in any case, you can be calm in this regard, that we are of sound mind and understand perfectly well that if we attack you, you will respond the same way. But you too will receive the same that you hurl against us. And I think that you also understand this. My conversation with you in Vienna gives me the right to talk to you this way.

This indicates that we are normal people, that we correctly understand and correctly evaluate the situation. Consequently, how can we permit the incorrect actions which you ascribe to us? Only lunatics or suicides, who themselves want to perish and to destroy the whole world before they die, could do this. We, however, want to live and do not at all want to destroy your country. We want something quite different: to compete with your country on a peaceful basis. We quarrel with you, we have differences on ideological questions. But our view of the world consists in this, that ideological questions, as well as economic problems, should be solved not by military means, they must be solved on the basis of peaceful competition, i.e., as this is understood in capitalist society, on the basis of competition. We have proceeded and are proceeding from the fact that the peaceful coexistence of the two different social-political systems, now existing in the world, is necessary, that it is necessary to assure a stable peace. That is the sort of principle we hold.

You have now proclaimed piratical measures, which were employed in the Middle Ages, when ships proceeding in international waters were attacked, and you have called this "a quarantine" around Cuba. Our vessels, apparently, will soon enter the zone which your Navy is patrolling. I assure you that these vessels, now bound for Cuba, are carrying the most innocent peaceful cargoes. Do you really think that we only occupy ourselves with the carriage of so-called offensive weapons, atomic and hydrogen bombs? Although perhaps your military people imagine that these (cargoes) are some sort of special type of weapon, I assure you that they are the most ordinary peaceful products.

Consequently, Mr. President, let us show good sense. I assure you that on those ships, which are bound for Cuba, there are no weapons at all. The weapons which were necessary for the defense of Cuba are already there. I do not want to say that there were not any shipments of weapons at all. No, there were such shipments. But now Cuba has already received the necessary means of defense.

I don't know whether you can understand me and believe me. But I should like to have you believe in yourself and to agree that one cannot give way to passions; it is necessary to control them. And in what direction are events now developing? If you stop the vessels, then, as you yourself know, that would be piracy. If we started to do that with regard to your ships, then you would also be as indignant as we and the whole world now are. One cannot give another interpretation to such actions, because one cannot legalize lawlessness. If this were permitted, then there would be no peace, there would also be no peaceful coexistence. We should then be forced to put into effect the necessary measures of a defensive character to protect our interests in accordance with international law. Why should this be done? To what would all this lead?

Let us normalize relations. We have received an appeal from the Acting Secretary General of the UN, U Thant, with his proposals. I have already answered him. His proposals come to this, that our side should not transport armaments of any kind to Cuba during a certain period of time, while negotiations are being conducted—and we are ready to enter such negotiations—and the other side should not undertake any sort of piratical actions against vessels engaged in navigation on the high seas. I consider these proposals reasonable. This would be a way out of the situation which has been created, which would give the peoples the possibility of breathing calmly. You have asked what happened, what evoked the delivery of weapons to Cuba? You have spoken about this to our Minister of Foreign Affairs. I will tell you frankly, Mr. President, what evoked it.

We were very grieved by the fact—I spoke about it in Vienna—that a landing took place, that an attack on Cuba was committed, as a result of which many Cubans perished. You yourself told me then that this had been a mistake. I respected that explanation. You repeated it to me several times, pointing out that not everybody occupying a high position would acknowledge his mistakes as you had done. I value such frankness. For my part, I told you that we too possess no less courage; we also acknowledged those mistakes which had been committed during the history of our state, and not only acknowledged, but sharply condemned them.

If you are really concerned about the peace and welfare of your people, and this is your responsibility as President, then I, as the Chairman of the Council of Ministers, am concerned for my people. Moreover, the preservation of world peace should be our joint concern, since if, under contemporary conditions, war should break out, it would be a war not only between the reciprocal claims, but a worldwide cruel and destructive war.

Why have we proceeded to assist Cuba with military and economic aid? The answer is: we have proceeded to do so only for reasons of humanitarianism. At one time, our people itself had a revolution, when Russia was still a backward country. We were attacked then. We were the target of attack by many countries. The USA participated in that adventure. This has been recorded by participants in the aggression against our country. A whole book has been written about this by General [William Sidney] Graves, who, at that time, commanded the US expeditionary corps. Graves called it "The American Adventure in Siberia."

We know how difficult it is to accomplish a revolution and how difficult it is to reconstruct a country on new foundations. We sincerely sympathize with Cuba and the Cuban people, but we are not interfering in questions of domestic structure, we are not interfering in their affairs. The Soviet Union desires to help the Cubans build their life as they themselves wish and that others should not hinder them.

You once said that the United States was not preparing an invasion. But you also declared that you sympathized with the Cuban counterrevolutionary emigrants, that you support them and would help them to realize their plans against the present government of Cuba. It is also not a secret to anyone that the threat of armed attack, aggression, has constantly hung, and continues to hang over Cuba. It was only this which impelled us to respond to the request of the Cuban government to furnish it aid for the strengthening of the defensive capacity of this country.

If assurances were given by the President and the government of the United States that the USA itself would not participate in an attack on Cuba and would restrain others from actions of this sort, if you would recall your fleet, this would immediately change everything. I am not speaking for Fidel Castro, but I think that he and the government of Cuba, evidently, would declare demobilization and would appeal to the people to get down to peaceful labor. Then, too, the question of armaments would disappear, since, if there is no threat, then armaments are a burden for every people. Then, too, the question of the destruction, not only of the armaments which you call offensive, but of all other armaments as well, would look different.

I spoke in the name of the Soviet government in the United Nations and introduced a proposal for the disbandment of all armies and for the destruction of all armaments. How then can I now count on those armaments?

Armaments bring only disasters. When one accumulates them, this damages the economy, and if one puts them to use, then they destroy people on both sides. Consequently, only a madman can believe that armaments are the principal means in the life of society. No, they are an enforced loss of human energy, and what is more are for the destruction of man himself. If people do not show wisdom, then in the final analysis they will come to a clash, like blind moles, and then reciprocal extermination will begin.

Let us therefore show statesmanlike wisdom. I propose: we, for our part, will declare that our ships, bound for Cuba, will not carry any kind of armaments. You would declare that the United States will not invade Cuba with its forces and will not support any sort of forces which might intend to carry out an invasion of Cuba. Then the necessity for the presence of our military specialists in Cuba would disappear.

Mr. President, I appeal to you to weigh well what the aggressive, piratical actions, which you have declared the USA intends to carry out in international waters, would lead to. You yourself know that any sensible man simply cannot agree with this, cannot recognize your right to such actions.

If you did this as the first step towards the unleashing of war, well then, it is evident that nothing else is left to us but to accept this challenge of yours. If, however, you have not lost your self-control and sensibly conceive what this might lead to, then, Mr. President, we and you ought not now to pull on the ends of the rope in which you have tied the knot of war, because the more the two of us pull, the tighter that knot will be tied. And a moment may come when that knot will be tied so tight that even he who tied it will not have the strength to untie it, and then it will be necessary to cut that knot. And what that would mean is not for me to explain to you, because you yourself understand perfectly of what terrible forces our countries dispose.

Consequently, if there is no intention to tighten that knot and thereby to doom the world to the catastrophe of thermonuclear war, then let us not only relax the forces pulling on the ends of the rope, let us take measures to untie that knot. We are ready for this.

We welcome all forces which stand on positions of peace. Consequently, I expressed gratitude to Mr. Bertrand Russell, too, who manifests alarm and concern for the fate of the world, and I readily responded to the appeal of the Acting Secretary General of the UN, U Thant.

There, Mr. President, are my thoughts, which, if you agreed with them, could put an end to that tense situation which is disturbing all peoples.

These thoughts are dictated by a sincere desire to relieve the situation, to remove the threat of war.

Respectfully yours,

N. Khrushchev.

✖ *E S S A Y S*

In the first essay, diplomatic historian Thomas G. Paterson of the University of Connecticut places John F. Kennedy's policies toward Cuba in a broad perspective, linking U.S. attempts to overthrow the Castro government with the subsequent missile crisis. A prominent critic of U.S. Cold War policies, Paterson suggests that Kennedy was responsible for the failure of U.S. policy toward Cuba, a program that posed a real risk of nuclear war and left as its legacy a bitter hostility that continues even today to shape U.S.–Cuban relations. The second essay, by Raymond L. Garthoff, focuses on the Cuban missile crisis and on the confrontation between the United States and the Soviet Union. Garthoff was a staff-level State Department adviser who was deeply involved in the deliberations over the U.S. response to the Soviet missiles. In this essay he draws on his own recollections as well as interviews and documents from U.S. and Soviet sources. Garthoff concludes that the Kennedy administration acted in a statesmanlike fashion, seeking a middle ground that avoided both a preemptive first strike, which had been urged by some military and CIA officials, and purely diplomatic approaches, which he believes would have been ineffective and unwise.

Kennedy's Fixation with Cuba

THOMAS G. PATERSON

"My God," muttered Richard Helms of the Central Intelligence Agency, "these Kennedys keep the pressure on about Castro." Another CIA officer heard it straight from the Kennedy brothers: "Get off your ass about Cuba." Defense Secretary Robert McNamara remembered that "we were hysterical about Castro at the time of the Bay of Pigs and thereafter." As someone said, Cuba was one of the four-letter words of the 1960s.

President John F. Kennedy spent as much or more time on Cuba as on any other foreign policy issue. Cuba stood at the center of his administration's admitted greatest failure, the Bay of Pigs, and its alleged greatest success, the missile crisis. Contrary to some Kennedy memoirists and scholars who have claimed that Kennedy was often trapped by a bureaucracy he could not control and distracted by other time-consuming issues, the President was knowledgeable, engaged, and influential on matters Cuban.

Why did President Kennedy and his chief advisers indulge such a fixation

Abridged from *Kennedy's Quest for Victory: American Foreign Policy, 1961–1963*, edited by Thomas G. Paterson, 1989, pp. 123–155. Copyright © 1989 by Oxford University Press, Inc. Reprinted by permission.

with Cuba and direct so many United States resources to an unrelenting campaign to monitor, harass, isolate, and ultimately destroy Havana's radical regime? One answer springs from a candid remark by Robert F. Kennedy. Looking back at the early 1960s, he wondered "if we did not pay a very great price for being more energetic than wise about a lot of things, especially Cuba." The Kennedys' famed eagerness for action became exaggerated in the case of Cuba. They always wanted to get moving on Cuba, and Castro dared them to try. The popular, intelligent, but erratic Cuban leader, who came down from the Sierra Maestra Mountains in January 1959 to overthrow the United States ally Fulgencio Batista, hurled harsh words at Washington and defiantly challenged the Kennedy model of evolutionary, capitalist development so evident in the Alliance for Progress. As charismatic figures charting new frontiers, the President and *Jefe Máximo* often personalized the Cuban-American contest. Kennedy harbored a "deep feeling against Castro," as one White House aide noted, and the Cuban thought the American "an intelligent and able leader of American imperialism." After the Bay of Pigs invasion, Castro branded Kennedy a new Hitler. To Kennedy's great annoyance, Castro could not be wheedled or beaten.

Kennedy's ardent war against *Fidelismo* may also have stemmed from his feeling that Castro had double-crossed him. As a senator, Kennedy had initially joined many Americans in welcoming the Cuban Revolution as a decided advancement over the "oppressive" Batista dictatorship. Linking Castro to the legacy of Bolívar, Kennedy urged a "patient attitude" toward the new government, which he did not see as Communist. Denying repeatedly that he was a Communist, Castro had in fact proclaimed his allegiance to democracy and private property. But in the process of legitimizing his revolution and resisting United States pressure, Castro became increasingly radical. Americans grew impatient with the regime's highly charged anti-Yankeeism, postponement of elections, jailing of critics, and nationalization of property. The President rejected the idea that intense United States hostility to the Cuban Revolution may have contributed to Castro's tightening political grip and flirtation with the Soviet Union. Nor did Kennedy and other Americans wish to acknowledge the measurable benefits of the revolution—improvements in education, medical care, and housing and the elimination of the island's infamous corruption that once had been the American mafia's domain. Instead, Kennedy officials concluded that Cuba's was a "betrayed revolution."

Richard N. Goodwin, the young White House and State Department official with responsibilities for Latin America, provided another explanation for the Kennedy fixation with Cuba. He remarked that "the entire history of the Cold War, its positions and assumption, converged upon the 'problem of Cuba.'" Indeed, the Cold War dominated international politics, and in the zero-sum accounting of the time, a loss for "us" meant a gain for "them." As Cuban-American relations steadily deteriorated, Cuban-Soviet relations gradually improved. Not only did Americans come to believe that a once-loyal ally had jilted them for the tawdry embrace of the Soviets; they also grew alarmed that Castro sneered at the Monroe Doctrine by inviting the

Soviet military to the island. When Castro in late 1961 declared himself a Marxist-Leninist, Americans who had long denounced him as a Communist then felt vindicated. American leaders began to speak of Cuban membership in the "Sino-Soviet bloc," thus providing Communists with a "spearhead" to penetrate the Western Hemisphere. From the moment of victory, Castro had called for Cuban-style revolutions throughout Latin America, and Havana had sent agents and arms to other nations to kindle radical fires. Castro's revolutionary mission happened to coincide with Nikita Khrushchev's alarming statement that the Soviet Union supported wars of national liberation worldwide. It mattered little to Americans that the two appeals appeared independently or that Havana and Moscow differed markedly over the best method for promoting revolutionary change—the Soviets insisted on utilizing Communist parties within political systems, whereas the Cubans espoused peoples' rebellions. Cuba came to represent the Cold War in the United States' backyard.

Besides the Kennedy style and the Cold War, American politics influenced the administration's Cuba policy. In the 1960 presidential campaign, Kennedy had seized the Cuban issue to counter Richard Nixon's charge that the inexperienced Democratic candidate would abandon Quemoy and Matsu to Communism and prove no match for the hard-nosed Khrushchev. "In 1952 the Republicans ran on a program of rolling back the Iron Curtain in Eastern Europe," Kennedy jabbed. "Today the Iron Curtain is 90 miles off the coast of the United States." Privately he asked, "How would *we* have saved Cuba if we had [had] the power?" but he nonetheless valued the political payback from his attack. "What the hell," he informed his aides, "they never told us how they would have saved China [in 1949]." He did recommend a controversial method to reclaim Cuba for the American system. Apparently unaware that President Dwight D. Eisenhower had initiated a clandestine CIA program to train Cuban exiles for an invasion of the island, candidate Kennedy bluntly called for just such a project. After exploiting the Cuban issue, Kennedy, upon becoming President, could not easily have retreated. Partisan politics kept his gaze fixed on the defiant Caribbean leader. Everyone seemed eager to know when Kennedy would knock Castro off his perch, and many expected the President to act before the next election.

Overarching all explanations for Kennedy's obsession with Cuba is a major phenomenon of twentieth-century world history: the steady erosion of the authority of imperial powers, which had built systems of dependent, client, and colonial governments. The strong currents of decolonization, anti-imperialism, revolutionary nationalism, and social revolution, sometimes in combination, undermined the instruments the imperial nations had used to maintain control and order.

The Cuban revolution constituted an example of this process of breaking up and breaking away. American leaders reacted so hostilely to this revolution not simply because Castro and his 26th of July Movement taunted them or because domestic politics and the Cold War swayed them, but because Cuba, as symbol and reality, challenged United States hegemony in Latin America. The specter of "another Cuba" haunted President Kennedy, not just because it would hurt him politically but because, as George W. Ball put it, "the game would be up through a good deal of Latin America." Americans refused to accept a revolution that not only targeted Batista and their island assets but also the Monroe Doctrine and the United States' claim to political, economic, and military leadership in the hemisphere. Given this fundamental conflict, a breakdown in Cuban-American relations seemed inevitable: Cuba sought independence and radical social change, which would necessarily come at the expense of the United States, and the latter, not unexpectedly, defended its interests against revolutionary nationalism. As Castro once remarked, "The United States *had* to fight his revolution." Khrushchev, in pondering the American campaign against Cuba, once asked: "Why should an elephant be afraid of a mouse?" The Soviet leader, who certainly knew his own nation's imperial record in suppressing its neighbors when they became too independent-minded, surely knew that the answer to his question could be found in the intense American fear that the Cuban Revolution would become contagious and further diminish United States hegemony in the Western Hemisphere.

After the United States helped expel Spain from Cuba in 1898 and imposed the Platt Amendment on the island in 1903, Americans gained influence through military interventions, occupations, threats, economic penetration, and political manipulation. By 1959 Americans dominated Cuba's oil, telephone, mining, and electric industries and produced more than a third of its sugar. That year, too, the United States bought 74 percent of Cuba's exports and supplied 65 percent of the island's imports. Because the United States had such tremendous economic favors to dispense (especially a quota system that guaranteed Cuba sugar sales in the American market), Washington wielded political influence in Havana. The United States also stationed a military mission in Cuba and sent arms to Batista's forces. The CIA infiltrated political groups and helped Batista organize an anti-Communist police unit.

After having underestimated Castro's 26th of July Movement and the depth of unrest on the island, the Eisenhower Administration tried to manipulate Cuba on the very eve of Castro's victory. With the President's blessing and CIA instructions, William D. Pawley, owner of Cuban lands and former Ambassador to Brazil, traveled to Havana to press Batista to resign in favor of a military junta in order to prevent the 26th of July Movement's imminent triumph. The Cuban President balked, and Pawley's mission aborted. Even after this setback, the United States' continued sense of its strength in Cuba appeared in a CIA report: it concluded that "no sane man undertaking to govern and reform Cuba would have chosen to pick a fight with the US." Because Castro did not honor traditional United States power in his nation, he must have possessed a "psychotic personality," argued CIA officers. Americans, unable or unwilling to acknowledge that the Cuban Revolution tapped deep nationalistic feelings and that their own repeated interventionism and island interests made the United States a primary target, preferred to depict Fidel Castro as a crazed *guerrillero* whose temporarily frenzied people would toss him out when their rationality returned.

The Eisenhower Administration bequeathed to its successor an unproductive tit-for-tat process of confrontation with Cuba and a legacy of failure. In 1959–1960, with Ambassador Philip Bonsal thinking that Castro suffered "mental unbalance at times" and Eisenhower concluding that the Cuban leader "begins to look like a madman," Havana and Washington traded punch for punch. In November 1959 the President decided to encourage anti-Castro groups within Cuba to "check" or "replace" the revolutionary regime, and thus end an anti-Americanism that was "having serious adverse effects on the United States position in Latin America and corresponding advantages for international Communism." In March of the next year Eisenhower ordered the CIA to train Cuban exiles for an invasion of their homeland—this shortly after Cuba signed a trade treaty with the Soviet Union. The CIA, as well, hatched assassination plots against Castro and staged hit-and-run attacks along the Cuban coast. As Cuba undertook land reform that struck at American interests and nationalized American-owned industries, the United States in 1960 suspended Cuba's sugar quota and forbade American exports to the island, drastically cutting a once-flourishing commerce. On January 3, 1961, fearing an invasion and certain that the American embassy was a "nest of spies" aligned with counterrevolutionaries who were burning cane fields and sabotaging buildings, Castro heatedly demanded that the embassy staff be reduced to the small size of the Cuban delegation in Washington. The United States promptly broke diplomatic relations with Cuba.

Eisenhower failed to topple Castro, but American pressure accelerated the radicalization of the revolution and helped open the door to the Soviets. Moscow bought sugar, supplied technicians, armed the militia, and offered generous trade terms. Although the revolution's radicalization was probably inevitable, it was not inexorable that Cuba would end up in the Soviet camp. Hostile United States policies ensured that outcome. Revolutionary Cuba needed outside assistance to survive. "Russia came to Castro's rescue," as Bonsal himself has concluded, "only after the United States had taken steps designed to overthrow him."

Kennedy's foreign policy troubles have sometimes been explained as inheritances from Eisenhower that shackled the new president with problems not of his own making. To be sure, Kennedy inherited the Cuban problem from Eisenhower. But he did not simply continue his predecessor's anti-Castro policies. Kennedy greatly exaggerated the Cuban threat, attributing to Castro a capability to export revolution that the Cuban leader never had and lavishing on him an attention he did not deserve. Castro was "an affront to our pride" and a "mischief maker," Walter Lippmann wisely wrote, but he was not a "mortal threat" to the United States. Because of his obsession with Cuba, Kennedy significantly increased the pressures against the upstart island. He thus helped generate major crises, including the October 1962 missile crisis. Kennedy inherited the Cuban problem—and he made it worse.

The questions of whether and under what conditions to approve an exile expedition dominated the President's discussion of Cuba in his first few months in office. Although Kennedy always reserved the authority to cancel the operation right up to the moment of departure, his choices, made after much deliberation, pointed in one direction: Go. National security adviser McGeorge Bundy later said that the president "really was looking for ways to make it work . . . and allowed himself to be persuaded it would work and the risks were acceptable." Not simply a prisoner of events or of the Eisenhower legacy, Kennedy associated so closely with the covert operation that it became identified as *his*. He listened to but rejected the counsel of doubting advisers, and he never revealed moral or legal qualms about violently overthrowing a sovereign government. He never requested a contingency plan to disband the exile brigade. In questioning aides, the President worried most about which methods would deliver success and whether the guiding hand of the United States could be concealed. Kennedy sought deniability of an American role but never the demise of the project.

The Bay of Pigs plan began to unravel from the start. As the brigade's old, slow freighters plowed their way to Cuba, B-26 airplanes took to the skies from Nicaragua. On April 15, D-Day-minus-2, the brigade pilots destroyed several parked planes of Castro's meager air force. That same day, as part of a preinvasion ploy, a lone, artificially damaged B-26 flew directly to Miami, where its pilot claimed that he had defected from the Cuban military and had just bombed his country's airfields. But the cover story soon cracked. Snooping journalists noticed that the nose cone of the B-26 was metal; Cuban planes had plastic noses. They observed too that the aircraft's guns had not been fired. The American hand was being exposed. The President, still insistent upon hiding American complicity, decided to cancel a D-Day (or second) air strike against the remnants of the Cuban air force. CIA officials protested, because they believed the invasion force could not succeed unless Castro's few planes were knocked out. After conferring with Secretary Dean Rusk, Kennedy stuck with his decision.

Shortly after midnight on April 17, more than 1,400 commandos motored in small boats to the beaches at Bahía de Cochinos. The invaders immediately tangled with Castro's militia. Some commandos never made it because their boats broke apart on razor-sharp coral reefs. Castro's marauding airplanes shot down two brigade B-26s and sank ships carrying essential communications equipment and ammunition. The brigade fought ferociously but nonetheless failed to establish a beachhead. Would Washington try to salvage the mission? Kennedy turned down CIA appeals to dispatch planes from the nearby USS *Essex*, but he did permit some jets to provide air cover for a new B-26 attack from Nicaragua. Manned this time by American CIA pilots, the B-26s arrived an hour after the jets had come and gone. Cuban aircraft downed the B-26s, killing four Americans. With Castro's boasting that the *mercenarios* had been foiled, the final toll was grim: 114 of the exile brigade dead and 1,189 captured. A pall settled over the White House.

"How could I have been so stupid, to let them go ahead?" Kennedy asked an assistant. Stupid or not, Kennedy knew the answers to his own question. First, he dearly sought to oust Castro and score a victory in the

Cold War. Second, his personality and style encouraged action. Always driven to win, Kennedy believed, as one aide said, "that his disapproval of the plan would be a show of weakness inconsistent with his general stance." One foreign policy observer explained "how the President got such bad advice from such good advisers":

> The discussion on which they were asked to advise was presented as a choice between action and inaction. . . . None of the President's advisers wants it said of him by his colleagues . . . that he . . . loses his nerve when the going gets hot. The Harvard intellectuals are especially vulnerable, the more so from being new on the scene. They are conscious of the fact that the tough-minded military suspect them of being soft-headed. They have to show that they are he-men too, that they can act as well as lecture.

Third, fear of nasty political repercussions influenced the President. Told to disband, brigade members might have refused to give up their arms or even have mutinied. In any case, Republicans would have scorned a weak-kneed administration. Kennedy approved the operation, finally, because he felt a sense of urgency. CIA analysts advised that time was on Castro's side. Delay would permit the Soviets to strengthen the Cuban military, perhaps with MiG fighters, and the rainy season was about to begin, making military maneuver difficult. As well, the Guatemalan president, facing awkward questions about Cuban trainees in his country, beseeched Washington to move the exiles out by late April.

Failures in intelligence, operations, decision-making, and judgment doomed the Bay of Pigs undertaking. The most controversial operational question remains the cancelled second D-Day air strike. Postcrisis critics have complained that the President lost his nerve and made a decision that condemned the expedition to disaster. Castro and Bissell have agreed that Cuban air supremacy was important to Cuba's triumph. But was it decisive? A preemptive strike on D-Day against the Cuban air force would not have delivered victory to the invaders. After the first air attack, Castro had dispersed his planes; the brigade's B-26s would have encountered considerable difficulty in locating and destroying them. And even if a D-Day assault had disabled all of Castro's planes, then what? *La brigada*'s 1,400 men would have had to face Castro's army of 25,000 and the nation's 200,000 militia. The commandos most likely would not have survived the overwhelming power of the Cuban military.

Kennedy and his advisers believed that the invasion would ignite a popular revolt against an unpopular government. No rebellion erupted. Kennedy also assumed that should the brigade prove incapable of taking territory, it could melt into the mountains and become a guerrilla army. But the mountains lay 80 miles away, with impassable swamps between. The guerrilla option, which like the belief in a rebellion, probably led Kennedy to suppress doubts about the operation, was actually impossible. As well, Kennedy officials nurtured the fiction that American participation could be hidden and plausibly denied. "Trying to mount an operation of this magnitude from the United States," a CIA official later wrote, "is about as covert as walking nude across Times Square without attracting attention." Nonetheless, until his decision to cancel the second strike, Kennedy clung to his wishful thinking about deniability.

"Mr. President, it could have been worse," remarked an assistant to Ambassador to the United Nations Adlai Stevenson. How? asked Kennedy. "It might have succeeded." Had all gone well with the chain reaction of beachhead, rebellion, and Castro's death (the CIA planned to kill him before the invasion) or departure, the victory, observed one diplomat, would have "exchanged a Castro pesthouse for a post-Castro asylum." Tainted as an American stooge, the head of the new government would have struggled to win public favor. Castro and his many well-armed followers would probably have initiated a protracted guerrilla war against the American-created regime. The Soviets might have helped Castro's forces, and volunteers from around the world might have swelled the resistance—like the Spanish Civil War of the 1930s, as historian-turned-presidential-adviser Arthur M. Schlesinger, Jr., had warned at the time. The United States would have had to save its puppet government through military aid, advisers, and maybe even troops. To have sustained a successful Bay of Pigs invasion, then, the Kennedy Administration probably would have had to undertake a prolonged and expensive occupation of the island.

As it was, defeat did not chasten the administration. While a secret presidential panel investigated the disaster, Kennedy and his advisers huddled. At the April 20 Cabinet meeting, Under Secretary of State Chester Bowles, who had opposed the operation, found his colleagues "almost savage." Robert Kennedy became especially agitated, Bowles told his diary, and "there was an almost frantic reaction for an action program which people would grab onto." Under Secretary Bowles was "yellowed-bellied," press secretary Pierre Salinger snorted, and "we're going to get him." White House aide Harris Wofford shot back: "Why don't you get those who got us into this mess?" Kennedy pushed Bowles out of the State Department later in the year.

On April 20 the beleaguered President spoke out. "Let the record show," he boomed, "that our restraint is not inexhaustible." Indeed, the United States intended to carry on a "relentless" struggle with Communism in "every corner of the globe." In familiar words, Kennedy declared that "the complacent, the self-indulgent, the soft societies are about to be swept away with the debris of history. Only the strong . . . can possibly survive." That day, too, Kennedy ordered American military advisers in Laos to put on their uniforms to show United States resolution in the face of defeat. "A new urgency" was injected into "Kennedy's concern for counterinsurgency," recalled General Maxwell Taylor.

Robert Kennedy told counterinsurgency specialist Colonel Edward Lansdale that the Bay of Pigs "insult needed to be redressed rather quickly." But that redressing faced some heady obstacles. The anti-Castro underground lay shattered. Cuban security forces, before and after the landing, rounded up, jailed, killed, or converted thousands of anti-regime subversives, most of whom were surprised because the CIA had not forewarned them about

D-Day. In the United States the Cuban Revolutionary Council splintered as the demoralized and angry Cuban community descended once again into fierce factionalism. Castro triumphantly exploited patriotic nationalism to strengthen his regime. Instead of driving the Soviets out of Cuba, the botched Bay of Pigs operation drew Havana and Moscow closer together. Understandably fearing another invasion, perhaps with American troops, Castro sought Soviet military assistance. The Soviets shipped small arms, machine guns, howitzers, armored personnel carriers, patrol boats, tanks, surface-to-air missiles, and, ultimately, nuclear missiles that could reach into the United States itself.

Persuaded that "there can be no long-term living with Castro as a neighbor," Kennedy officials launched a multitrack program of covert, economic, diplomatic, and propagandistic elements. Encouraged by the White House, the CIA created a huge operations station in Miami called JMWAVE to recruit and organize Cuban exiles. In Washington, Robert Kennedy became a ramrod for action. At a November 4 White House meeting, the Attorney General made his pitch: "stir things up on the island with espionage, sabotage, general disorder." The President himself asked Colonel Lansdale to direct Operation Mongoose—"to use our available assets . . . to help Cuba overthrow the Communist regime."

Operation Mongoose and JMWAVE, although failing to unseat Castro, punished Cubans. CIA-handled saboteurs burned cane fields and blew up factories and oil storage tanks. In a December 1961 raid, for example, a seven-man team blasted a railroad bridge, derailed an approaching train, and torched a sugar warehouse. Myriad exile groups, from Alpha 66 to the Revolutionary Student Directorate, left the Florida Keys to stage hit-and-run attacks along Cuba's coast. CIA agents contaminated goods leaving European ports for Cuba, and they bribed European manufacturers to produce faulty equipment for Cuba—as when a German industrialist shipped off-center ball bearings. British-made Leland buses were sabotaged too. These spoiling operations compelled the Castro government to divert scarce resources from economic and social programs to coastal defense and internal surveillance. They also pushed Cuba toward greater dependence upon the Soviet Union.

The CIA devised new plots to kill Castro. Poisonous cigars, pills, and needles were directed Castro's way, but to no avail. Did the Kennedys know about these death schemes? Robert Kennedy learned about them in mid-1962, and his biographer Arthur M. Schlesinger, Jr., claims that the Attorney General ordered an end to assassination projects—but they did not end. John Kennedy said at the time that in general he disapproved the killing of foreign leaders. The President apparently never directly ordered the assassination of Castro; at least no trail of documents leads to the Kennedy White House. But, of course, the word *assassination* was never uttered in the presence of the President or committed to paper so that he could be protected by the principle of plausible deniability. What was always mentioned was the need to remove Castro. "And if killing him was one of the things that was to be done in this connection," assassination was attempted because "we felt we were acting within the guidelines." So bespoke Bissell's replacement, Richard Helms. President Kennedy may or may not have known about the assassination plots, but he did set the general guidelines.

Intensified economic coercion joined assassination and sabotage as methods to undermine the Castro government. American officials did not expect the economic denial program alone to force Castro's fall. But they did seek to inhibit the island's economic development, thereby decelerating socialization, spurring Cuban discontent, and diminishing Cuba's appeal as a model for Latin America. In February 1962 Kennedy further tightened the economic screws by banning most imports of Cuban products (especially tobacco). *El bloqueo*, as the Cubans called the embargo, hurt. Cuba was forced to pay higher freight costs, enlarge its foreign debt, and suffer innumerable factory shutdowns due to the lack of spare parts once bought in the United States. Cuba's economic woes also stemmed from the flight of technicians and managers, a decline in tourism, high workers' absenteeism rates, the drying up of foreign capital investment, hastily conceived policies to diversify the economy, and suffocating government controls. The overall effect on Cuba of American economic measures was not what Washington intended: greater political centralization, more state management, closer ties to the Soviet Union. By 1962, 82 percent of Cuba's exports flowed to Communist countries, and 85 percent of its imports came from them. As with military defense, so with the economy: the Soviet Union became Cuba's lifeline.

The Kennedy Administration also lobbied the OAS (Organization of American States) to isolate Cuba. Eisenhower had grown frustrated with the regional organization's refusal to "do something about Castro." But after Castro declared himself a Marxist-Leninist in late 1961, the United States managed to obtain the votes to oust Cuba from the OAS, even though Mexico voted "nay" and Argentina, Brazil, Chile, Bolivia, and Ecuador abstained. The expulsion registered loudly in Havana, which interpreted it as "political preparation for an invasion." By early 1962, moreover, fifteen Latin American states had answered Washington's call to break relations with Cuba.

By the spring of 1962, then, Cuba was losing on several fronts in its contest with the United States: diplomatic isolation in the hemisphere, ouster from the OAS, economic embargo, CIA assistance to anti-Castro rebels in Cuba, exile raids and sabotage, assassination plots, Operation Mongoose, and the successful launching of the anti-Cuban Alliance for Progress. After the American failure at the Bay of Pigs and in the face of the studied American effort to cripple the Cuban Revolution, "Were we right or wrong to fear direct invasion [next]?" Fidel Castro later asked. Although Kennedy had actually ruled out invasion as a method to overthrow Castro, in large part because Latin American opinion would have been so negative and American casualties would have been so staggering, Castro could think only the worst in 1962. After all, some Washington politicians were shouting for invasion, and Kennedy officials spoke frankly about getting rid of Castro.

It may be plausibly argued, then, that had there been no exile expedition, no destructive covert activities, and no economic and diplomatic boycott—

had there been no concerted United States vendetta to quash the Cuban Revolution—there would not have been an October missile crisis. The principal source for that frightening crisis lay in Kennedy's unvarnished hostility toward Cuba and in Castro's understandable apprehension that an invasion by the United States was inevitable.

The origins of the missile crisis, in other words, derived largely from United States–Cuban tensions. To stress only the global dimension of Soviet-American competition, as is commonly done, is like saying that a basketball game can be played without a court. Cuba was the court. To slight the local or regional sources of the conflict is to miss a central point: Nikita Khrushchev would never have had the opportunity to begin his dangerous missile game if Kennedy had not been attempting to expunge Castro and his revolution from the hemisphere. This interpretation does not dismiss but incorporates the view, predominant in the scholarly literature, that the emplacement of nuclear missiles in Cuba served the Soviet strategic goal of catching up in the nuclear arms race. Rather, this interpretation emphasizes that both Cuba and the Soviet Union calculated that their interests would be served by putting medium- and intermediate-range rockets on the island. Havana hoped to gain deterrent power to thwart an expected American invasion and Moscow hoped to enhance its deterrent power in the Cold War and save a new ally. From Castro's perspective, the United States would not start a local, conventional war out of fear that it would then have to risk a nuclear war. "We'd carried out the Bay of Pigs operation, never intending to use American military force—but the Kremlin didn't know that," Defense Secretary Robert McNamara recalled. "We were running covert operations against Castro [and] people in the Pentagon were even talking about a first strike [nuclear policy]. . . . So the Soviets may well have believed we were seeking Castro's overthrow *plus* a first strike capability. This may have led them to do what they did in Cuba."

Cuba's eagerness for Soviet military assistance is well documented in the contemporary record. Castro and other Cuban officials made repeated, consistent, and compelling statements that their nation faced an American onslaught. "Cuba took measures to defend its security against a systematic policy of hostility and aggression," Castro privately explained to United Nations Secretary General U Thant during the October crisis. Contemporary, secret, now declassified United States documents also reveal that American decision-makers knew that the Cuban-Soviet military linkage, which included the June 1962 agreement on nuclear missiles, grew from Cuba's fear of invasion. They did not say so publicly, of course, for such would have acknowledged their own responsibility for generating what the CIA called "invasion scares." In early October, for example, the Department of State cabled its diplomatic posts that Castro feared an American invasion and that "the available evidence suggests strongly that this crash build-up of military and economic assistance did not represent a Soviet initiative but rather a response to insistent demands from Castro for help."

On October 14 an American U-2 plane photographed missile sites in Cuba, providing the first "hard" evidence, as distinct from the "soft" reports of exiles, that the island was becoming a nuclear base. "He can't do that to me!" snapped Kennedy when he saw the pictures on October 16. He had warned the Soviets that the United States would not suffer "offensive" weapons in Cuba, although the warnings had come after the Cuban-Soviet decision of early summer. The President convened his top advisers on October 16. His first questions focused on the firing readiness of the missiles and the probability that they carried nuclear warheads. The tentative answers were negative, although he was advised that the missiles could become operational in a brief time. Discussion of military options (invasion? air strike?) dominated this first meeting. Kennedy's immediate preference became clear: "We're certainly going . . . to take out these . . . missiles." McGeorge Bundy urged consideration not only of military plans but of a "political track" or diplomacy. But Kennedy showed little interest in negotiations. When McNamara mentioned that diplomacy might precede military action, the President immediately switched the discussion to another question: How long would it take to get air strikes organized?

At a second meeting on October 16, Rusk argued against the surprise air strike that General Maxwell Taylor had bluntly advocated. The Secretary of State recommended instead "a direct message to Castro." At the close of Rusk's remarks, Kennedy immediately asked: "Can we get a little idea about what the military thing *is*?" Bundy then posed a question now central to the history of the missile crisis: "How gravely does this change the strategic balance?" McNamara thought "not at all," but Taylor disputed him. Kennedy himself was uncertain, but he did complain that the missile emplacement in Cuba "makes them look like they're co-equal with us." And, added Treasury Secretary C. Douglas Dillon, who obviously knew the President's competitive personality, the presence of the missiles made it appear that "we're scared of the Cubans."

Then the rambling discussion turned to Khrushchev's motivation. The Russian leader had been cautious on Berlin, Kennedy said. "It's just as if we suddenly began to put a major number of MRBMs in Turkey," the President went on. "Now that'd be goddam dangerous." Bundy jumped in: "Well, we *did*, Mr. President." Not liking the sound of a double standard, Kennedy lamely answered, "Yeah, but that was five years ago." Actually, the American Jupiter missiles in Turkey, under a 1959 agreement with Ankara, were put into launch position in mid-1961—during the Kennedy Administration—and not turned over to Turkish forces until October 22, 1962, the very day Kennedy informed Moscow that it must withdraw its SS-4 or medium-range (1,020 miles) missiles from Cuba.

For the next several days, Kennedy's group of advisers, named the Executive Committee or Ex Comm, met frequently in tight secrecy. Taylor later summarized policy options: "talk them out," "squeeze them out," or "shoot them out." In exhausting sessions marked by frank disagreement and changing minds, Ex Comm members weighed the advantages and disadvantages of invasion, bombing, quarantine, and diplomacy. The President gradually moved with a majority of Ex Comm advisers toward a quarantine or blockade of Cuba: incoming ships would be stopped and inspected for military cargo. McNamara persistently argued this alternative against the generals, Dillon, CIA Director John McCone, and Dean Acheson, all of whom urged an air strike. When queried if an air strike would knock out all of the known missiles, Taylor replied: "The best we can offer you is to destroy 90 percent. . . ." In other words, some missiles in Cuba would remain in place for firing against the United States. Robert Kennedy also worried that the Soviets might react unpredictably with military force, "which could be so serious as to lead to general nuclear war." In any case, the Attorney General insisted, there would be no "Pearl Harbor type of attack" on *his* brother's record.

By October 22 the President had made two decisions. The chief decision was to quarantine Cuba to prevent further military shipments and to impress the Soviets with American resolve to force the missiles out. If the Soviets balked, more drastic measures would be undertaken. The second decision was to inform the Soviets of United States policy through a television address rather than through diplomatic channels. Ex Comm advisers have dubiously argued that a surprise public speech was necessary to rally world opinion behind United States policy and to prevent Khrushchev from issuing a "blustering ultimatum." At least two Ex Comm participants recommended that negotiations be tried first. Former Ambassador to the Soviet Union Charles Bohlen advised that Moscow would have to retaliate against the United States if its technicians were killed by American bombs. As an alternative, a stern letter to Khrushchev should be "tested" as a method to gain withdrawal of the missiles. "I don't see the urgency of military action," Bohlen told the President. And a grim Ambassador to the United Nations Adlai Stevenson appealed to an unreceptive Kennedy: "The existence of nuclear missile bases anywhere is negotiable before we start anything." Going into the crisis, Kennedy refused to negotiate with either Khrushchev or Castro.

In his evening television speech on October 22, Kennedy recalled the special United States relationship with the Western Hemisphere, and he reminded Americans that the lessons of the 1930s taught them to resist aggression and surrender. The President lectured the Soviets to reverse their "deliberately provocative" decision by dismantling their "strategic" missiles in Cuba, and he announced the Caribbean quarantine as an "initial" step. The missile crisis soon became an international war of nerves. More than sixty American ships went on patrol to enforce the blockade. The Strategic Air Command went on nuclear alert, moving upward to Defense Condition (DEFCON 2) for the first time ever (the next level is deployment for combat). B-52 bombers, loaded with nuclear weapons, stood ready, and men and equipment moved to the southeastern United States to prepare for an invasion (thousands of road maps of Cuba were distributed). American diplomats hastened to inform NATO allies; the OAS voted to endorse United States policy. Strangely, the Soviets did not mobilize or redeploy their huge military, nor did they take measures to make their strategic forces less vulnerable. The Soviets also refrained from testing the quarantine: their ships turned around and went home. But what next? On October 26, Kennedy and some Ex Comm members, thinking that the Soviets were stalling, soured on the quarantine. Sentiment for military action strengthened.

The "first real blink" in the crisis came in the afternoon of the twenty-sixth. A Soviet embassy officer, Aleksander Fomin, called ABC correspondent John Scali and asked for a meeting. They talked in a Washington restaurant, where Scali was surprised to hear Fomin urge him to carry a message to the television journalist's high-level friends in the State Department: the Soviet Union would withdraw the missiles if the United States would promise not to invade Cuba. Scali scurried to Rusk, who sent the unusual emissary back to Fomin with the reply that American leaders were interested in discussing the proposal. In the meantime, a private Khrushchev letter arrived with the same offer, as well as with a pointed reminder for Kennedy: the missiles were in Cuba only because the United States had been threatening the island.

The next morning, another letter came. Khrushchev now upped the stakes: he would trade the missiles in Cuba for the American missiles in Turkey. An angry Kennedy felt boxed because "we are now in the position of risking war in Cuba and in Berlin over missiles in Turkey which are of little military value." Indeed, the President in early 1961 had expressed doubts about the military efficacy of the Jupiters in Turkey and had later directed the Defense Department to prepare a study for phasing them out. But he had not ordered their removal. Now they seemed to stand in the way of settling the October crisis, for Kennedy hesitated to accept a swap—first, because he did not want to appear to be giving up anything in the face of Soviet provocation; second, because he knew the proud Turks would be upset with the appearance of being "traded off in order to appease an enemy"; and third, because acceptance of a missile trade would lend credence to charges that the United States all along had been applying a double standard. Kennedy told his Ex Comm advisers that Khrushchev's offer caused "embarrassment," for most people would think it "a very fair trade." Indeed, Moscow had played "a very good card." Some of Kennedy's advisers had explored the issue days before Khrushchev's second letter. Stevenson had recommended a horse trade, and Ambassador W. Averell Harriman counseled that America's "ring of bases" around the Soviet Union had proved "counter-productive." The way out of the crisis, Harriman said, was to let Khrushchev save face through an agreement to withdraw the Jupiters. Such a bargain would also permit Khrushchev to gain politically on his tough-minded military and "swing" toward improved relations with the United States.

This discussion raises another question: What if the Soviets and Cubans had *announced* in the summer of 1962 that they were deploying a limited number of missiles—the same number as Americans had stationed in Turkey (and Italy)? Would the United States have been able to compel reversal of a publicly announced decision and prevent emplacement without having to abandon the Jupiters in Turkey in a negotiated deal? Some Ex Comm advisers later suggested that, in such a case, Washington might not even have sought to force withdrawal of the SS-4s from Cuba. Many people abroad, including some European allies, would have asked if the USSR had any less right than the United States to practice deterrence. Moscow no doubt calculated differently—that Washington would attempt to halt shipments of missiles—and thus tried to sneak them in.

In the afternoon of October 27, more bad news rocked the White House: an American U-2 plane had overflown the eastern part of the Soviet Union, probably because its equipment malfunctioned. Soviet fighters scrambled to intercept it, and American jets from Alaska took flight to rescue the errant aircraft. Although the spy plane flew home without having sparked a dog fight, Moscow might have read the incident as provocative. Worse still, a U-2 was shot down over Cuba by a surface-to-air missile (SAM). *Cubans*, after having fought Soviet soldiers for control of the SAM sites, may have brought down the U-2. American decision-makers assumed at the time that the Soviets manned the SAM batteries; thus the shoot-down seemed to constitute a dangerous escalation. A distressed McNamara now thought "invasion had become almost inevitable." But Kennedy hesitated to retaliate, surely scared about taking a step in the direction of nuclear war. Upon brother Robert's advice, the President decided to ignore Khrushchev's second letter and answer the first. And he dispatched the Attorney General to deliver an ultimatum to Soviet Ambassador Anatoly Dobrynin: start pulling out the missiles within forty-eight hours or "we would remove them." After Dobrynin asked about the Jupiters in Turkey, Robert Kennedy presented an important American concession: they would be dismantled if the problem in Cuba were resolved. As the President had said in an Ex Comm meeting, "We can't very well invade Cuba with all its toil . . . when we could have gotten them out by making a deal on the same missiles in Turkey." But should the Soviets leak word of a "deal," Robert Kennedy told the Soviet ambassador, the United States would disavow the offer. Just in case this unusual style of diplomacy failed, the President ordered the calling up of Air Force reservists. In the last Ex Comm meeting on October 27, McNamara reminded his colleagues that the United States had to have two contingencies ready if a diplomatic settlement could not be reached: a response to expected Soviet action in Europe and a government to take power in Cuba after an American invasion. Someone remarked: "Suppose we make Bobby mayor of Havana."

On October 28, faced with an ultimatum, a concession, and the possibility that the Cubans would shoot down another U-2 and precipitate a Soviet-American conflagration, Khrushchev retreated. An agreement, although not written, was struck: the Soviet Union agreed to dismantle the MRBMs under United Nations supervision, and the United States pledged not to invade Cuba. In April 1963 the Jupiter missiles came down in Turkey. Castro remained skeptical of the no-invasion pledge. As he once remarked to U Thant, it was difficult for Cubans to believe a simple American "promise not to commit a crime."

John F. Kennedy's handling of the Cuban missile crisis has received high grades as a success story and model for crisis management. But it was a near miss. "We were in luck," Ambassador John Kenneth Galbraith ruminated, "but success in a lottery is no argument for lotteries." Many close calls threatened to send the crisis to greater levels of danger. Besides the two U-2 incidents, there was the serious possibility that a "crackpot" exile group would attempt to assassinate Castro or raid the island during the crisis. As well, Operation Mongoose sabotage teams were inside Cuba during the crisis and could not be reached by their CIA handlers. What if this "half-assed operation," Robert Kennedy worried, ignited trouble? One of these teams actually did blow up a Cuban factory on November 8. To cite another mishap: not until October 27 did the administration think to inform the Soviets that the quarantine line was an arc measured at 500 nautical miles from Cape Maisi, Cuba. What if a Soviet captain inadvertently piloted his ship into the blockade zone? When the commander of the Strategic Air Command issued DEFCON 2 alert instructions, he did so in the clear instead of in code because he wanted to impress the Soviets. Alerts serve to prepare American forces for war, but they also carry the danger of escalation, because movement to a higher category might be read by an adversary as American planning for a first strike. Under such circumstances, the adversary might be tempted to strike first. Finally, the Navy's antisubmarine warfare activities carried the potential of escalating the crisis. Soviet submarines prowled near the quarantine line, and, following standing orders, Navy ships forced several of them to surface. In one case, a Navy commander exercised the high-risk option of dropping a depth charge on a Soviet submarine. As in so many of these examples, decision-makers in Washington actually lost some control of the crisis to personnel at the operational level.

Ex Comm members represented considerable intellectual talent and experience, and the policy they urged upon the President ultimately forced the Soviets to back down. But a mythology of grandeur, illusion of control, and embellishment of performance have obscured the history of the committee. The group never functioned independently of the President. In an example of what scholar Richard Ned Lebow has called "promotional leadership," Kennedy picked his advisers, directed them to drive the missiles out, and used his brother as a "policeman" at meetings. Ex Comm debated alternatives under "intense strain," often in a "state of anxiety and emotional exhaustion." Apparently two advisers suffered such stress that they became passive and unable to perform their responsibilities. An assistant to Adlai Stevenson recalled that he had had to become an Ex Comm "back-up" for the ambassador because, "while he could speak clearly, his memory wasn't very clear." Asked if failing health produced this condition, Vice-Admiral Charles Wellborn answered that the "emotional state and nervous tension that was involved in it [missile crisis] had this effect." Stevenson was feeling "pretty frightened." So apparently was Dean Rusk. Robert Kennedy remembered that the Secretary of State "frequently could not attend our meetings" because "he had a virtually complete breakdown mentally and physically." We cannot determine how stress affected the advice Ex Comm gave Kennedy, but we know that the crisis managers struggled against time, sleep, exhaustion, and themselves, and they did not always think clearheadedly at a time when the stakes were very high. Had Stevenson and Rusk, both of whom recommended diplomacy and compromise, been steadier, the option of negotiations *at the start* might have received a better hearing and the world might have been spared the grueling confrontation.

Contemporaries and scholars have debated Kennedy's shunning of formal, private negotiations and traditional, diplomatic channels and his opting instead for a public showdown through a surprise television speech. It does not appear that he acted this way because he thought the Soviets would protract talks until the missiles had become fully operational. Even before his television address, he knew that many of the missiles were ready to fire, and Ex Comm worked under the assumption that the SS-4s were armed with nuclear warheads. Nor did Kennedy initially stiff-arm negotiations in order to score a foreign policy victory just before the November congressional elections. Politics does not explain his decisions; indeed, the most popular political position most likely would have been an air strike and invasion to rid the island of both the missiles and Castro. Did Kennedy initially reject diplomacy because the Soviet missiles intolerably altered the strategic balance? Kennedy seems to have leaned toward McNamara's argument that the missiles in Cuba did not make a difference, given the fact that the Soviets already possessed enough capability to inflict unacceptable damage on some American cities.

President Kennedy eschewed diplomatic talks before October 22 because his strong Cold War views, drawing of lessons from the past, and personal hostility toward Castro's Cuba recommended confrontation. His conspicuous style of boldness, toughness, and craving for victory also influenced him, and he resented that Khrushchev had tried to trick him by stating that no offensive weapons would be placed in Cuba and then clandestinely sending them. Kennedy had warned Moscow not to station such weapons on the island; if he did not force the Soviets to back down, he worried, his personal credibility would have been undermined. And even if the missiles did not markedly change the strategic balance, the new missiles in Cuba gave the appearance of doing so. One Ex Comm member remarked that the question is "psychological," and Kennedy agreed that the matter was as much "political" as "military." Kennedy acted so boldly, too, because the Soviet missile deployment challenged the Monroe Doctrine and United States hegemony in Latin America. Finally, with other tests in Berlin and Southeast Asia looming, the United States believed it had to make emphatic its determination to stand firm in the Cold War. Remember, Rusk has said, "aggression feeds upon success."

President Kennedy helped precipitate the missile crisis by harassing Cuba through his multitrack program. Then he reacted to the crisis by suspending diplomacy in favor of public confrontation. In the end, he frightened himself. In order to postpone doomsday, or at least to prevent a high-casualty invasion of Cuba, he moderated the American response and compromised. Khrushchev withdrew his mistake while gaining what Ambassador Llewellyn Thompson thought was the "important thing" for the Soviet leader: being able to say, "I saved Cuba. I stopped an invasion."

Kennedy may have missed an opportunity to negotiate a more comprehensive settlement: he did not give serious attention to a Brazilian proposal, offered in the United Nations on October 25, to denuclearize Latin America. This proposal also sought to guarantee the territorial integrity of each nation in the region. Harriman recommended a day later that the United States accept the Brazilian plan but enlarge it: the United States and the Soviet Union would agree not to place nuclear weapons in any nation in the world other than in nuclear powers. Thus Great Britain could hold American missiles, but Turkey and Italy could not. Nor could Soviet missiles be deployed in Cuba or Eastern Europe. Looking beyond the crisis, Harriman presented his scheme "as a first and important step towards disarmament." Perhaps there could have been another aspect of a far-reaching agreement: the United States would turn Guantánamo over to Cuba in exchange for a Cuban pledge to end the Soviets' military presence on the island. In short, under these provisions, both American and Soviet militaries would leave Cuba, Latin America would become off-limits to nuclear weapons, Cuba's territorial integrity would be guaranteed, and Moscow and Washington would make a modest nod toward arms control. Would the Cubans have accepted such a deal? Given his extreme anger with Moscow after the Soviets disengaged the missiles, Castro may well have grasped an opportunity to begin a process toward improved relations with Washington. Such a bargain, of course, would have required *Cuban-American* discussions. Yet Kennedy never seemed open to such talks. Why? Because they would have legitimized the Castro-Communist government and signified a Cold War defeat.

In the end, Castro remained in power, the Soviets continued to garrison troops on the island and subsidize the Cuban economy, the United States persisted in its campaign of harassment, and new Soviet-American contests over Cuba erupted (1970 and 1979). The Soviets, exposed as nuclear inferiors, vowed to catch up in the arms race. At the same time, perhaps the "jagged edges" of Kennedy's Cold Warriorism were smoothed. In the aftermath of the missile crisis, Moscow and Washington installed a teletype "hot line" to facilitate communication. The nuclear war scare during the missile crisis also nudged the superpowers to conclude the long-standing talks on a test ban treaty. Negotiated by Harriman in Moscow, the treaty, signed on July 25, 1963, was limited, not comprehensive (banning only tests in the atmosphere, outer space, and beneath the surface of the oceans). Although some analysts have trumpeted the treaty as a major accomplishment because it started the superpowers on a path toward arms control, the agreement did not prevent a plethora of underground nuclear detonations or slow the cascading arms race. It nonetheless stands as one of just a few successes in the diplomatic record of the Kennedy Administration.

After the missile crisis, Cubans complained, Kennedy played a "double game." The President showed some interest in accommodation at the same time that he reinvigorated anti-Cuban programs. Washington intended by early 1963 to "tighten the noose" around Cuba. Operation Mongoose had been put on hold during the October crisis, but raids by exiles, some of them no doubt perpetrated with CIA collaboration, and most of them monitored but not stopped by American authorities, remained a menace. In March 1963, after an exile "action group" attacked a Soviet ship in Cuban waters, Kennedy speculated that such freelance raids no longer served a "useful purpose." Did they not strengthen the "Russian position in Cuba and the Communist control of Cuba and justify repressive measures within Cuba . . . ?" The President ordered restrictions on unauthorized exile activities because they had failed to deliver "any real blow at Castro." Raiding parties still managed to slip out of the Florida Keys to sabotage and kill in Cuba, and the administration itself, to mollify the more than 500 anti-Castro groups, may have "backed away" from enforcing its own restrictions.

After the missile crisis, Castro sought better relations with Washington, and he made gestures toward détente. He sent home thousands of Soviet military personnel and released some political prisoners, including a few Americans. He remarked in April 1963 that the prisoner release could mark a beginning toward rapprochement. But then the mercurial leader departed for a four-week trip to the Soviet Union, where he patched up relations with Khrushchev and won promises of more foreign aid. Washington stirred against Moscow's "grandiose" reception of Castro, his "tone of defiance rather than conciliation," and the refurbished Soviet-Cuban alliance. Soon Robert Kennedy asked the CIA to "develop a list of possible actions which might be undertaken against Cuba." In mid-June the National Security Council approved a new sabotage program. The CIA quickly cranked up new dirty tricks and revitalized its assassination option by making contact with a traitorous Cuban official, Rolando Cubela Secades. Code-named AM/LASH, he plotted with the CIA to kill Fidel Castro. In Florida, American officials intercepted and arrested saboteurs heading for Cuba, but they usually released them and seldom prosecuted. Alpha 66 and Commando L raiders hit oil facilities, sugar mills, and industrial plants.

In the fall of 1963 Cuba continued to seek an accommodation. Through contact with a member of Stevenson's United Nations staff, William Attwood, the Cuban government signaled once again its interest in improving relations. The President authorized an eager Attwood to work up an agenda with the Cubans. Yet on November 18, Kennedy sounded less the conciliator and more the warrior. In a tough-minded speech, he reiterated the familiar charges against Castro's "small band of conspirators." The President, Bundy privately reported, sought to "encourage anti-Castro elements within Cuba to revolt" and to "indicate that we would not permit another Cuba in the hemisphere."

On November 22, while Castro was discussing chances for Cuban-American détente with French journalist Jean Daniel, the news of the assassination in Dallas arrived. "This is bad news," the stunned Cuban mumbled repeatedly. What would become of his overture? Castro wondered. In Washington, the new Lyndon B. Johnson Administration decided to put the "tenuous" and "marginal" contacts "on ice." Castro also worried that he would be held personally responsible for Kennedy's death because assassin Lee Harvey Oswald had professed to be pro-Castro (he may actually have been leading a covert life as an anti-Castro agitator). Some Americans did blame the Cuban regime. And although several official investigations have concluded that Cuban officials played no part in the assassination, conspiracy theories persist. One theory actually points an accusing finger at disgruntled anti-Castro Cuban exiles in the United States.

At the time of his death, Kennedy's Cuba policy was moving in opposite directions—probing for talks but sustaining multitrack pressures. "How can you figure him out?" Castro had asked in late October 1963. On the day that Kennedy died, AM/LASH rendezvoused with CIA agents in Paris, where the Cuban spy received a ballpoint pen rigged with a poisonous hypodermic needle intended to produce Castro's death instantly. But AM/LASH was but one obstacle to improved Cuban-American relations. For Kennedy and Castro to have reached détente, each would have had to suppress strong views and national interests as they defined them at the time. Would Castro have risked a cooling of his close relationship with the Soviet Union and Cuban Communists at a time when Washington still worked for his ouster, some Americans yelped constantly for a United States invasion, and the next presidential election might send a conservative Republican to the White House or keep the hawkish Johnson there? Would Castro have been willing to sever his lifeline? Would Castro have abandoned his bonds with Latin American revolutionaries in order to win a lifting of American economic sanctions?

From the Kennedy 1960s to the Reagan 1980s, United States policy has consistently demanded two Cuban concessions: an end to support for revolutions in the hemisphere and an end to the Soviet military presence on the island. Havana has just as consistently refused to budge on either point before seeing United States concessions: abolition of the economic embargo and American respect for Cuban sovereignty. As for Kennedy, could he have quieted the Cuban exile community, disciplined the CIA, and persuaded hard-line State Department officials? Would he have been willing to withstand the political backlash from his dealing with "Communist Cuba"? More important, did he want to improve relations with Cuba? Would he have shelved his intense, sometimes personal, three-year war against Cuba and disbanded the myriad spoiling operations? Would he ever have accepted the legitimacy of a radical revolution in the United States sphere of influence? It does not seem likely that either Kennedy, had he lived, or Castro could have overcome the roadblocks that they and their national interests had erected.

The Cuban-American confrontation was and is a question of the Cold War, domestic American politics, and personalities. Above all else, it has been primarily a question of faltering United States hegemony in the hemisphere. Kennedy struggled to preserve that hegemony. In the end, he failed because he could not achieve his well-defined and ardently pursued goals for Cuba. His administration bequeathed to successors an impressive fixation both resistant to diplomatic opportunity and attractive to political demagoguery.

Kennedy's Triumph at the Brink

RAYMOND L. GARTHOFF

The U.S. Decision

On the morning of October 16 President Kennedy was shown photographs of Soviet SS-4 launching installations under construction in Cuba, taken two days earlier by a U-2 reconnaissance airplane. He held two long meetings that day, beginning an intensive series of meetings by the group of senior government officials later (from October 23) officially termed the "Ex Comm" (Executive Committee of the National Security Council, or NSC).

A great deal has been written about these seven days of meetings culminating in President Kennedy's public address of October 22. Several of the participants have written accounts or provided information to journalists who soon wrote books on the crisis. There was never any doubt or debate about the U.S. objective. From the first day, the president never wavered from one basic decision: the Soviet missiles must be removed. There were differing views on the *military* significance of the missiles (Secretary of Defense Robert McNamara downplayed their significance to the strategic balance, while Assistant Secretary of Defense Paul Nitze and the chairman of the Joint Chiefs of Staff, General Maxwell Taylor, stressed their military significance). But more basic was the common judgment that the secret, surreptitious Soviet attempt to install the missiles despite the president's clear warnings could not be accepted. There was little consideration of the fact that the Soviet decision must have been made at least four or five months earlier and could not have been easily reversed in September. But that would not have changed the basic decision.

The key issue for decision, then, over that week was not what the U.S. objective should be, but how to attain it. There were three basic paths: (1) *destroy* the missiles by attacking them; (2) *compel* the Soviet leaders to remove the missiles by pressure; and (3) *induce* the Soviets to remove the missiles by negotiation, probably involving a trade for American concessions. The latter two were not entirely exclusive; there could be pressure *and* negotiation, but there was a clear difference. As General Taylor later characterized the three alternatives, we could "take them out" by our own military action; "squeeze them out" by pressure; or "buy them out" by counterconcessions. That the Soviet action was seen as a political challenge and as the result of duplicity strengthened inclinations not to choose the third alternative.

Underlying these deliberations was another significant fact virtually never addressed in American discussions. It had to do with the perceived Soviet motivation. *No one* in the U.S. government believed that the deployment of Soviet missiles was intended to deter a U.S. invasion of Cuba. This was true of all those of us whose task was to estimate Soviet intentions and advise the leadership: the intelligence community, led by the CIA; Ambas-

Text from *Reflections on the Cuban Missile Crisis* by Raymond L. Garthoff, 1989, pp. 43–54, 73–74, 80–96. Reprinted with permission of The Brookings Institution.

sador-at-Large Llewellyn E. ("Tommy") Thompson, Jr., personally advising the president and the Ex Comm; and several senior specialists in the Department of State, including myself. Most important, it was also the belief of President Kennedy, Secretary of State Dean Rusk, Secretary of Defense McNamara, national security adviser McGeorge Bundy, and other government leaders. Political and expert judgments coincided on this point.

We saw the principal Soviet objective as redressing a strategic inferiority, publicly revealed and growing in disparity. There was no possibility for an early change in this strategic imbalance through building up intercontinental forces—ICBMs, submarine-launched ballistic missiles (SLBMs), or strategic bombers. While Soviet strategic weapons deployment programs then under way (the SS-7 and SS-8 ICBMs) could help, it would be several years before really satisfactory systems then under development would be ready for deployment (the SS-9 and SS-11 ICBMs, and the SS-N-6, the Soviet equivalent of the Polaris SLBM system). Soviet SS-4 MRBM and SS-5 IRBM missiles in Cuba could, however, provide an interim substitute, ersatz ICBMs, so to speak.

Beyond that basic agreement as to the strategic rationale underlying the Soviet decision, there was some divergence of views on whether this was more a defensive political-military measure, or an offensive one. All agreed that the Soviet leaders wanted in general to strengthen their standing in the correlation of forces; most analysts—and political leaders—believed that Khrushchev and the Soviet leadership intended to renew pressures over the Berlin issue from a position of greater strength. Many also believed that the Soviet leaders would use their missiles in Cuba as leverage to place pressure on American military bases around the Soviet Union. As noted earlier, it remains the judgment of most American analysts and historians today that the main Soviet aim in deploying the missiles in Cuba was to bolster Soviet strategic military power and diplomatic-political strength, and that deterrence of an American attack on Cuba was at most a secondary objective.

Notwithstanding the assessment of Soviet strategic inferiority, and the incentive or temptation for Soviet leaders to deploy intermediate-range missiles in Cuba, it was also the unanimous consensus of Soviet affairs experts in the intelligence community and elsewhere in the government that the Soviets would *not* attempt to deploy missiles in Cuba. It was reasoned that while Soviet strategic inferiority gave them an incentive to place missiles in Cuba, it also made that action too risky. In addition, the Soviets had never deployed nuclear weapons outside their own territory (except on naval ships), and exercised very strict controls. Risks even apart from the American reaction were deemed to make such a deployment unlikely. A special national intelligence estimate prepared in mid-September reaffirmed that judgment. There was one notable exception: Director of Central Intelligence McCone, a conservative Republican, believed the Soviets were planning to deploy offensive missiles in Cuba, and so advised the president. During the critical last weeks of September and early October he repeatedly sent such warnings from his honeymoon trip to Europe. But his judgment on this matter was discounted.

Minister of Foreign Affairs Andrei Gromyko visited Washington and met with President Kennedy on October 18. This meeting was important in several respects. Kennedy repeated his warnings of September 4 and 13, but did not ask Gromyko outright whether there were Soviet missiles in Cuba. Gromyko said the Soviet Union would not introduce "offensive arms," but did not say what the Soviet government meant by that term. Kennedy and his advisers considered Gromyko's position to have been duplicitous. They also, after October 16, regarded as disinformation the many assurances that the Soviet Union would not put offensive missiles into Cuba that had earlier been conveyed, including further assurances by Ambassador Dobrynin, most recently on October 13 to former Under Secretary of State Chester Bowles. The most rankling, with the possible exception of Gromyko's evasion, was an assurance through an established and trusted informal channel from Khrushchev personally to the president received by Robert Kennedy on October 22, several days after American discovery of the missiles. At that time, Robert Kennedy had been told by Soviet Embassy counselor Georgi Bol'shakov, after the latter's return from Moscow, that he had been summoned to meet with Khrushchev and Mikoyan and instructed to convey an assurance to the president that "no missile capable of reaching the United States will be placed in Cuba."

The second aspect of Gromyko's visit was a proposal to the president for a summit meeting of the two leaders, some time following the American congressional elections in November. Although Kennedy made a vaguely positive response, he instructed Ambassador Thompson to tell Ambassador Dobrynin that same night at dinner that a summit would not be appropriate under current conditions and would require proper preparations. U.S. advisers and political leaders saw the Soviet proposal for a summit, and the earlier assurances that the Soviet Union would not cause any problems for the Kennedy administration before the November 7 elections, as signs that by the time of a summit meeting in late November or December, Khrushchev planned to make publicly known that the Soviet missiles were already deployed and operational in Cuba, and buttressed by this new position of strength, to make new demands, probably on the status of Berlin.

Later critics of the president's handling of the crisis have asked why he did not tell Gromyko about the missiles, or send a private message to Khrushchev, and give the Soviet leader an opportunity to save face by withdrawing the missiles quietly. Ambassador Charles E. ("Chip") Bohlen had suggested a letter to Khrushchev on October 18. Kennedy and several of his close advisers did try for two days, October 18 to 20, to draft such a letter. But they were unable to find a formula that would be sufficiently persuasive without itself precipitating a crisis. Moreover, there was a consensus that it would be undesirable to let the Soviets take the initiative. I believe the decision not to do so was sound. In any case, the decision not to raise the matter privately with Khrushchev (and still less with Gromyko) was deliberate and considered.

Within several days the members of the Ex Comm and the president himself decided on what they regarded as the middle course: a blockade (termed a "quarantine" to avoid the status of belligerency entailed under international law by imposing a naval blockade) to interdict any further shipment of Soviet offensive arms to Cuba. Advocates of an American air attack on the missile facilities (and Cuban air force bases and other large airfields, also considered militarily necessary) were not helped in their case by the U.S. Air Force judgment that this would require 500 sorties—and that even then there could be no guarantee that all the missiles would be destroyed, or civilians spared.

Some revisionist historical analyses of the crisis have stressed American concern with urgency before the Soviet missiles would become "operational," and the fact that the United States continued to press its position even after most of the missile facilities were deemed operational as meaning that a sense of urgency was maintained for ulterior purposes and that diplomacy could have proceeded at less than crisis pressure. It is true that on the first day or two some, in particular Secretary McNamara, stressed urgency of decision before the missiles should become operational. In fact on the first day he argued that an air strike should only be considered "on the assumption that we can carry it off before these [missiles] become operational." But this did not drive a decision for early attack, and by the end of the first week the concern was less over the current status of the missile sites—by then estimated and assumed, for reasons of prudence, to be operational— than over the possibility that with time they would become accepted as a new status quo.

Contrary to Soviet and Cuban claims, no U.S. plan for an invasion of Cuba was under way. Nonetheless, while those who have most stressed the fact that the United States had not made a decision to attack Cuba are correct, they have sometimes leaned too far toward dismissing the relevance of this contingency planning to the history of the times. As earlier noted, contingency plans existed, and indeed as a conventional arms buildup in Cuba proceeded in the summer and fall, steps were taken to enhance U.S. readiness to carry out those plans. A series of measures were taken in September and the first half of October. In particular, on October 1, two weeks before discovery of the missiles, Secretary McNamara met with the Joint Chiefs of Staff and directed that readiness for possible implementation of the contingency plans be raised. For example, U.S. Air Force tactical air units designated to meet the contingency war plan for an air strike (Oplan 312) were put under the operational control of CINCSTRIKE (Commander-in-Chief, Strike Command); U.S. Navy forces were earmarked for 6-hour, 12-hour, and 24-hour reaction times, and the war plan was revised to put the base at Mariel for Soviet Komar missile patrol boats on the air-strike priority target list. On October 6 increased readiness was also directed for forces earmarked for Oplan 314 and 316, the two war plan variants for invasion of Cuba.

Most important, on October 8 the Joint Chiefs referred to CINCLANT a memorandum from Secretary of Defense McNamara listing the "contingencies under which military action against Cuba may be necessary and toward which our military planning should be oriented." One of these, to be sure, was "evidence that the Castro regime has permitted the positioning of [Soviet] bloc offensive weapons on Cuban soil or in Cuban harbors," but this was only one of six, and listed second. First remained "Soviet action against Western rights in Berlin calling for a Western response including among other actions a blockade of Communist or other shipping enroute to Cuba." Also included were "an attack against the Guantanamo Naval Base or against U.S. planes or vessels outside Cuban territorial air space or waters"; "a substantial popular uprising in Cuba, the leaders of which request assistance in recovering Cuban independence from the Castro Soviet puppet regime"; "Cuban armed assistance to subversion in other parts of the Western Hemisphere"; and, finally, a very open "contingency" indeed: "a decision by the President that affairs in Cuba have reached a point inconsistent with continuing U.S. national security." But no decision had been made to attack Cuba, and the intensified contingency planning from late August to mid-October was a preliminary response to the Cuban arms buildup.

During the crisis deliberations after October 16, however, there was some significant military and political sentiment that following an air strike it would probably be necessary to mount an invasion of the island to destroy Cuban military power, and that it would be desirable at the same time to end Castro's rule. An air strike remained a possible recourse if the quarantine was not successful in inducing the Soviet leaders to agree to remove the missiles, but it seemed better to begin with more limited actions and then, if necessary, escalate. Also, the third alternative, a diplomatic negotiating path, was in fact expected to develop. There was, however, reluctance to think in terms of American concessions in general, as well as any specific terms. The only top adviser who did so with any passion, Adlai Stevenson, was as a result considered too much a "dove." The leading "hawk," calling for an immediate air strike and defeat of Castro's rule, was former Secretary of State Dean Acheson, called upon for advice in the first days of the crisis. But others also held this view, especially in the first few days, when it was the majority view. Fortunately, there was a full week for deliberation.

It should be stressed, as many have observed, that the ability to devote an entire week to deliberation and decision free of public pressure, and free of Soviet action or interaction, was crucial. It was also unique; no other past crisis has had, and none in the future can be expected to have, such a lengthy period for decision free from external and domestic political pressures.

The overriding issue in the first phase was to decide on the precise objective and course of action to deal with the surreptitious Soviet deployment of medium- and intermediate-range missiles in Cuba. This stage was marked by secret meetings, most held in Under Secretary of State Ball's office in the State Department to avoid the attention that arrivals for meetings at the White House would entail. "Scenarios" providing action-response sequences were developed for three major alternative courses of action: a "political path," for a diplomatic deal with the Soviet Union, probably through a summit meeting with Khrushchev; a "blockade" (later termed a "quarantine"), a selective and possibly gradual tightening naval cordon to prevent the arrival of more missiles and to compel Soviet withdrawal of those already in Cuba; and an "air-strike option," to destroy the missiles and launch facilities, probably with land invasion to follow to ensure no reconstitution of a military threat to the United States—also, of course, disposing of Castro once and for all. Some members of the Ex Comm sought limited advice from their own staffs as the week progressed, and assistance was discreetly provided for some scenario writing. But by and large the order of the day was to limit participation to the select senior officials in frequent and often lengthy meetings. By the end of the week a great deal of staff support for certain key diplomatic actions was required: preparations for rallying the support of the Organization of American States for the quarantine; preparations for last-hour consultations with key allies; preparations to call a UN Security Council meeting; preparations for key congressional consultations; and the like. Military contingency planning was under way, and preparations were made for implementing a blockade.

During the first stage, one key element was predicting the Soviet response or, more accurately, estimating the range of possible Soviet responses, and the American actions that could help to channel such responses in desired directions and away from the most dangerous and undesired ones. The analyses and estimates of Soviet responses were all keyed to the alternative U.S. actions and related scenarios.

Once the president had spoken, American attention shifted from our decision to the Soviet response. And the Soviet leadership suddenly realized it was in a first-class crisis. . . .

The Confrontation

Preparations for an invasion, as well as an air strike, continued to be made as a possible recourse, if necessary, to resolve the problem. Besides military preparations (including mobilization of military civil government teams for occupation tasks), on October 25 President Kennedy authorized a program, christened "Bugle Call," to prepare leaflets to drop over Cuba, in anticipation of an invasion. By the 27th some five million leaflets had been printed in Spanish, and the U.S. Air Force was ready to drop them whenever ordered. The order was, of course, never given.

The American military buildup for a possible invasion of Cuba was impressive. At the height of preparations the invasion force included one Marine and five U.S. Army (two airborne) divisions (with another Marine brigade and one and one-third more Army divisions as a follow-on reserve if needed): more than 100,000 Army and 40,000 Marine combat troops. The Air Force and Navy tactical air forces had 579 combat aircraft ready; the Navy had 183 ships, including 8 aircraft carriers, on station. The air-strike plan called for 1,190 strike sorties on the first day. The airborne paratroop force, 14,500 strong, to be dropped on the first day was comparable to the force dropped during the invasion of Normandy. Potential casualties were estimated at some 18,500 in ten days of combat. The buildup continued even after agreement on Soviet withdrawal of the missiles, peaking on November 15, and for most of the forces "standing down" began only late in November.

Some covert CIA "assets" may have been introduced into Cuba during the crisis as part of the preparations for possible American invasion, although available declassified documents do not provide confirmation. Those assets were separate from the teams assigned sabotage and subversive missions under the Mongoose program. Rather, they were to serve as "pathfinders" for local reconnaissance, carrying out preparations to facilitate safe landings for later American Special Forces and regular airborne and perhaps also amphibious assault forces. Apart from the above-noted regular forces amassed for an invasion, U.S. Army Special Forces (Green Beret) troops were also ready for special operations (and, at a later stage, possibly counterinsurgency actions) against Cuban forces, and an interservice Joint Unconventional Warfare Task Force was established and set up two operating bases. . . .

At midday on Friday, October 26, a breakthrough was seen when Aleksandr Fomin, officially the Soviet Embassy public affairs counselor in Washington (but believed to be the KGB *resident*, or station chief), insisted on urgently arranging a meeting with ABC News correspondent John Scali. It seemed clear that the Soviets had sought to use a deniable and dispensable but trusted Soviet intelligence contact out of official channels to take a sounding and float a trial balloon. The Soviets—or, more precisely, whomever Fomin was representing, presumably Khrushchev—sounded out a potential deal: Soviet removal of the missiles from Cuba, under UN inspection, in exchange for a U.S. public commitment not to invade Cuba. Scali reported the conversation and was taken to Secretary Rusk. Rusk's reply, cleared with the president, was that the United States saw "real possibilities" along the lines suggested, but that "time is very urgent."

New information requires modifying two important elements of this traditional account. First, contrary to the American assumptions in October 1962 and since, Fomin was apparently *not* instructed or authorized by Moscow to propose terms for a possible settlement; his probe was strictly his own. The Ex Comm assumption that Fomin's more precise offer represented a filling in of Khrushchev's proposal and that the two were "really a single package" was not warranted. Moreover, his report on the American reaction was not received in Moscow in time to inspire or even influence Khrushchev's message.

On October 26 also UN Secretary General U Thant suggested to Ambassador Adlai Stevenson and John J. McCloy that an American assurance that it would not attack Cuba might be an appropriate quid pro quo for a Soviet withdrawal of its missiles. That suggestion was also thought to have been discreetly planted by the Soviets.

Hours later, between 6:00 and 9:00 p.m., a message from Chairman Khrushchev to the president was received piecemeal. It bore all the marks of Khrushchev's personal style and raised speculation in Washington that it might have been sent without clearance by the Presidium. Khrushchev proposed that, if the United States would undertake not to invade Cuba (with its own or proxy forces), the reason for the Soviet stationing of missiles there would be eliminated, and implied that the missiles could then be withdrawn. While the potential deal was not fully explicit, in the light of the Fomin message it seemed clear and to provide the basis for an agreement.

As the president and his Ex Comm advisers were preparing on the morning of the 27th to respond favorably, a second message was received at about 10 o'clock, this time adding a demand for the withdrawal of the American missiles in Turkey. The new message caused great concern. The mood became even more grim when, minutes later, word was received that a U-2 reconnaissance plane had been shot down over Cuba and the pilot killed. Moreover, in the next few hours, for the first time two low-level reconnaissance flights were also fired upon. Meanwhile, one of the Soviet ships, the tanker *Grozny*, had resumed movement toward the quarantine line. Some speculated that Khrushchev might no longer be in control or able to agree to a deal on the basis of the first message.

New light has recently been thrown on the question of the hardening of terms in the second Khrushchev message, the one received on October 27. A senior Soviet source explained that the first letter, with its vague but attractive offer, written in haste early on October 26, was sent after Soviet intelligence had reported an American attack on Cuba was possibly imminent. The Soviet leaders believed time had run out. When later intelligence modified that estimate and time seemed to be available for some diplomatic bargaining, the second letter with its stiffer demands was sent.

The full story behind the shooting down of the U-2 by an SA-2 surface-to-air missile (SAM) has also lately emerged. None of our speculations at the time were correct: it was not an action taken by Khrushchev (under pressure or otherwise), nor by a more hard-line element in the leadership in Moscow, nor under standing instructions, nor by the Cubans.

That someone in the Soviet leadership, necessarily high in the military or able to give an order to the military, had created the incident in an unsuccessful attempt to forestall Khrushchev's efforts to arrange a compromise was seriously considered as a possible explanation.

Another possibility given some credence in the Washington intelligence community during the crisis was that the air defense system radars had simply been unable to engage the high-flying U-2s earlier. A deficiency in Cuban high-altitude radar capability had delayed activation of the SAM system; October 27 might just have been the first time it was able to intercept.

The possibility that the Cubans had shot down the U-2 was rejected by U.S. intelligence analysts at the time because they believed, correctly, that the SAM system was entirely under Soviet manning and control. Nonetheless, years later a former aide to Castro, Carlos Franqui, held that Fidel Castro himself, while on an inspection visit to a Soviet SAM site, asked how the system operated and how to fire the missiles. When shown, he suddenly fired the missile. This story, for a number of reasons, including the improbability that the Castro inspection would have coincided with a U-2 flight within range, can be dismissed. Castro himself denied that he fired the missile and has stated that, although he had ordered the antiaircraft gunfire, the

Soviets had shot down the U-2 with a SAM missile without clearing it (although, he added, he would not have objected).

Most intriguing was the suggestion, advanced in 1987 in an article based on leaked National Security Agency (NSA) intercepts of Soviet military communications in Cuba, that Cuban forces had overrun a Soviet SAM site and shot down the U-2. The NSA intercepts did not cover the actual shoot-down but disclosed Soviet casualties and dispatch of a Soviet military security detachment on the night of October 26 from another post in the general area of the SAM site. Authoritative Soviet and Cuban sources have since revealed that an accidental explosion at a munitions dump caused the casualties and triggered dispatch of a security detachment as well as medical personnel before the possibility of an attack had been dispelled. The Cubans probably could not have fired a SAM missile even if they had seized the site; no Cubans had yet begun training with the SAM system.

An even more bizarre explanation had surfaced briefly soon after the crisis. The *New York Times* reported rumors circulating among Communist diplomats that *Chinese* military personnel had manned the site and shot down the American plane. Actually, this public rumor was grounded in a secret report by a senior Polish general to a military audience in Warsaw on November 12, 1962, on what he had been told in Moscow. It was transparently a disinformation attempt by Soviet intelligence to fan anti-Chinese sentiment in response to the sharp Chinese attacks on the Soviet handling of the crisis.

In fact, the plane was shot down as the result of a decision taken by two local Soviet air defense commanders in Cuba, without authorization from Moscow and contravening at least the intent of their standing orders. In explanation of this action, some Soviet sources, in particular Ambassador Alekseyev, say they were influenced by Castro's orders to his forces on October 27 to shoot down the U.S. reconnaissance aircraft, and when a U-2 was in range decided out of solidarity to interpret their orders as allowing them to fire. The local commander for the SAM units in the eastern part of the island, Major General Igor Statsenko, made the decision, cleared with Lieutenant General Stepan Grechko in Havana. Time did not permit clearance even with General Davidkov or General Pliyev, the air defense and overall commanders of Soviet forces in Cuba. Their standing air defense instructions had been to fire in the event of an American attack on Cuba; they interpreted this to allow firing at an American aircraft violating Cuban sovereign airspace, even though that had not been the interpretation earlier placed on the instructions. General Volkogonov has disclosed that Marshal Malinovsky promptly dispatched to the Soviet forces command in Cuba a mild reprimand and firm restatement of orders not to fire on U.S. reconnaissance aircraft, explaining that they had fired "prematurely," and that efforts were under way to resolve the conflict through political means.

General Statsenko, one of the two officers responsible, in an article written just before his death in October 1987, while not acknowledging his role in the incident, sought to defend his action, referring to it as a "justified rebuff" to the "American air pirates" and claiming that it "strengthened the faith of Cuban workers in a capability to defend their independence."

It is disturbing that this kind of initiative by subordinate field officers was not treated more severely. General Volkogonov, and other responsible Soviet officials, state that the standing orders of the Soviet command in Cuba concerning the medium-range surface-to-surface missile forces were far more restrictive and clear than for the surface-to-air missiles: the medium-range missiles were not to be made capable of firing or placed in firing position, much less fired, without explicit instructions from Moscow.

In Washington, the conjunction of the second, tougher, Khrushchev message with the shootdown of the U-2 intensified differences within the Ex Comm over what course of action to take, as well as underlining the urgency of decision. The Joint Chiefs recommended an air strike and invasion. The State Department proposed a draft message flatly rejecting the Turkish missile trade demanded in the second letter. Others objected that it would be difficult for the administration to persuade world opinion, and perhaps opinion at home as well, that prolonging or intensifying the crisis was preferable to withdrawing obsolete missiles from Turkey. In the end, on the basis of suggestions by Thompson, Sorensen, and Robert Kennedy, the president decided to respond positively to the first message and simply to ignore the second.

On October 27 the president sent a message to Khrushchev in effect accepting his proposal of October 26. The president had his brother Robert, known to all as his close confidant, deliver the message through Ambassador Dobrynin also and orally give him several additional points. In conveying the message to Dobrynin, Robert Kennedy stressed both the president's readiness to give assurances against an invasion of Cuba and the urgency of a prompt Soviet acceptance. If the *Soviets* did not promptly agree to remove the missiles, "*we* [the United States] would remove them." This was not a bluff. Plans had been set for a possible air strike on Monday or Tuesday morning (October 29 or 30), although the president had *not* made any final decision, even contingently.

Only six years later did it become known that Robert Kennedy had also informed Dobrynin that the president had long been thinking of phasing out the missiles from Turkey and Italy. With an improvement in relations after a resolution of the crisis, the president expected that "within a short time after this crisis was over, those missiles would be gone." He noted, however, that the stationing of the missiles in Turkey had been a NATO decision, and that the United States could not unilaterally decide to remove them. Disposition of the missiles in Turkey could therefore not be part of a U.S.-Soviet agreement on the missiles in Cuba.

The essential elements of the American proposal of October 27 were an *ultimatum* (although Kennedy's published account does not indicate so precisely, the Soviets understood they had only some forty-eight hours), *coupled with a way out,* the noninvasion undertaking in exchange for removal of the missiles, *and accompanied by the additional sweetener* of the private assurance of an American intention to remove the missiles from Turkey and Italy. The prospect of a reciprocal American action, even if not as an integral or public quid pro quo, certainly made it easier for Khrushchev to accept the basic over-the-table settlement.

A new page in the crisis history is emerging from several recent Soviet disclosures. It now appears that there was a previously unreported earlier meeting of Robert Kennedy with Ambassador Dobrynin at the Soviet Embassy on October 26. In this meeting, after Dobrynin had argued against a double standard in considering American missile and other bases around the Soviet Union legitimate while denying the legitimacy of Soviet missiles in Cuba, Robert Kennedy reportedly asked if the missiles in Turkey were really that important, and took the initiative in informing Dobrynin that his brother had been planning to phase out the missiles in Turkey. He then left the room to talk with the president, and upon his return confirmed the president's intention to remove the missiles from Turkey if the overall situation was normalized. Dobrynin then reported this possibility to Moscow. It thus now seems likely that this indication of American intention to remove the Jupiters from Turkey, in conjunction with the revised intelligence estimate on the imminence of American action against Cuba, prompted introduction of the proposal for removal of the missiles from Turkey in the second message received on October 27.

Another recent revelation throws additional light on the situation. McGeorge Bundy has disclosed that the decision to have Robert Kennedy add the "sweetener" on the Jupiter missiles was made by the president in a small group of Ex Comm members in the Oval Office after the Ex Comm meeting on the 27th, and that it was Dean Rusk who proposed it. As Bundy notes, the fact that Rusk, stalwart on interests of the NATO alliance, made the proposal encouraged rapid consensus and presidential decision. Whether Rusk was aware of the earlier Robert Kennedy–Dobrynin discussion of this matter is not clear, but he was aware of the president's own favorable inclination and saw it as appropriate to assist the president in using this diplomatic asset. This is the newly revealed background to Robert Kennedy's conversation with Dobryn'n late on October 27 when he confirmed the president's intention to remove the Jupiter missiles from Turkey and Italy.

The hours between the president's message of October 27 and the Soviet reply the next morning were extremely tense in Washington (and no doubt in Moscow too). This was the day called "Black Saturday" because of the disappointment and deep concern after the second Khrushchev message. There was an FBI report that the Soviet Mission in New York was preparing to destroy its records, a precautionary measure if diplomatic relations were going to be suddenly severed. And in Moscow for the first time "popular" demonstrations were mounted in front of the U.S. Embassay. Was Khrushchev still in charge, and could he now accept the deal he himself had proposed? Also on October 27–28 communists in Venezuela, heeding a public call from Castro, bombed four U.S. oil company power stations in the Lake Maracaibo region. While not controlled by Moscow, and probably not by Havana either, this action added to the sense of tension in the Ex Comm.

Another incident that contributed to the tension was an unintended American military action. On October 27 a U-2 reconnaissance plane, apparently on a routine air-sampling nuclear detection mission, strayed over the Chukhotsk peninsula in northeastern Siberia and caused a local Soviet air defense reaction. The pilot had made a navigational error and returned to Alaska under U.S. fighter escort without incident. President Kennedy, when told of it, broke the tension with a harsh laugh and comment, "There is always some so-and-so [sonofabitch] who doesn't get the word."

Moscow probably saw the U-2 intrusion as yet another crass American reminder of its strategic superiority. The location of the incident argued against its being taken as a serious military reconnaissance mission of the type that might be made on the eve of hostilities, if it was soberly evaluated. But it undoubtedly contributed to the rising tension.

Khrushchev complained about the overflight in his next message, asking if it were a "provocation," happening "at a time as troubled as the one through which we are passing, when everything has been put into combat readiness." Kennedy expressed regret for the intrusion by the unarmed plane, attributed it to a serious navigational error by the pilot, and said he would "see to it that every precaution is taken to prevent recurrence." The next day a standdown of all U-2 flights around the Soviet Union was ordered.

Rusk arranged for Scali to contact Fomin again and give him hell for the "double cross" of the Soviet step back in the second message, which threatened to drive the crisis again to a dangerous point. Scali, without instructions to do so, even overstated by saying that "an invasion of Cuba is only a matter of hours away." Fomin's message to Moscow after this second conversation may well have reinforced Khrushchev's determination and strengthened arguments to accept the American proposal, as Fomin later told Scali.

Soviet sources, including Gromyko at the Moscow conference, despite many disclosures concerning the crisis, have been unwilling or unable to provide information on the deliberations of Khrushchev and his "Ex Comm" in those critical days of the crisis. Nonetheless, we now know a good deal about the considerations in the forefront of Khrushchev's thinking at that time, in particular on the crucial day, October 27.

Above all, President Kennedy had offered to accept a commitment not to invade Cuba. Whatever Khrushchev's own view of that possibility—and as we have seen there are signs he took it seriously—an American commitment not to attack Cuba met three basic needs: it would justify both the deployment of Soviet missiles in Cuba and their withdrawal; it would assuage Castro; and it would remove the imminent dangers of more serious Soviet defeats in losing Cuba or risking war with the United States.

But beyond these were other considerations. One was a real danger that the situation would slip out of control. This risk was not merely in some unanticipated or even uncontrolled American action, but also in some uncontrolled Soviet or Cuban action. Several knowledgeable Soviet officials have emphasized that the unauthorized Soviet shootdown of an American U-2 came as a surprise and shock to Khrushchev. This uncontrolled local

Soviet action, plus coincidental Cuban initiation of antiaircraft firing on low-flying reconnaissance aircraft, almost certainly contributed to Khrushchev's determination on October 28 to end the confrontation quickly, without bargaining for better terms, before it could slip out of control.

Of particular importance was a message from Castro that Khrushchev received on the morning of October 27. Castro, while long convinced that the United States was determined to overthrow the Cuban Revolution, had been confident during the crisis that the United States would back down, assuming (as he did) that the Soviet Union stood firm. On October 26, he received convincing intelligence that American military preparations were keyed to launching an air attack and invasion on October 29 or 30, and for the first time became alarmed at this situation. In fact, he became so alarmed that he went to the Soviet Embassy in Havana and spent the night of October 26 in a bomb-shelter there, during which time he wrote a message to Khrushchev (with, according to Ambassador Alekseyev, that envoy's assistance), which was urgently cabled to Moscow. Authoritative Cuban and Soviet sources are agreed on the above facts. There is, however, some uncertainty over what action (if any) Castro asked Khrushchev to take. My own reconstruction from several conflicting accounts is that Castro heatedly asked Khrushchev what he was going to do about the situation, which was supposed to have been dealt with by putting the missiles in Cuba.

Khrushchev himself, in his speech to the Supreme Soviet in December 1962 in which he detailed (and sought to justify) Soviet actions in the crisis, while not of course referring to Castro's letter or any recommendations in it, cited information from Cuba as well as from Soviet intelligence as indicating the imminence of an American attack. Castro's warning, and his alarm (however expressed), undoubtedly had a different effect than he had intended or expected. On top of Castro's order to his antiaircraft guns to fire, the unauthorized Soviet shootdown, the American U-2 intrusion over the USSR, and the reports of U.S. preparations for an imminent attack, the warning could only have encouraged Khrushchev to accept the deal Kennedy was offering. And he promptly did.

According to a senior Soviet diplomat, Khrushchev personally told him that the United States was ready on October 27 to invade Cuba, and that he decided to pull the missiles out because a communist Cuba without missiles was better for Soviet interests than a U.S.-occupied Cuba. While not confirmed, this account is very plausible. It also accords with other information as to the Soviet decision.

The United States later received information from a reliable Soviet source that the Soviet leadership had by then decided not to go to war over Cuba even if America invaded, and formalized that decision in a signed top secret Central Committee directive.

The Soviet leaders promptly agreed to the president's proposal, which is to say his recasting of the first Khrushchev proposal, on October 28 and publicly broadcast the fact. President Kennedy in turn issued a statement welcoming Khrushchev's "statesmanlike" decision to withdraw the missiles (omitting to mention that part of the deal was an American pledge of noninvasion of Cuba). Thus the crisis was essentially resolved that day.

From the Soviet (and Cuban) standpoint, the United States had made a major concession. If one believed that the United States had been intending to invade Cuba, an American pledge under the circumstances was an important step. On the other hand, if the U.S. leadership was not planning an invasion, a pledge of restraint was no real sacrifice, while obtaining the removal of the Soviet missiles *was* important, for domestic political, international political, and military reasons. Within the U.S. leadership, there was no real debate over acceptance of a noninvasion commitment. There had been those who favored an air strike and invasion in order to remove both the missiles and Castro, but once the alternative of removing the missiles without resort to force was a real choice, *no one* in the Ex Comm argued for invading or even keeping an invasion option.

What would have happened if the Soviet government had not agreed on October 28? If it had narrowed the possibilities for negotiation and insisted that the missiles would stay, the United States might well eventually have attacked the missile bases, followed by an invasion. If it had agreed to remove its missiles from Cuba, but insisted on a formal U.S. pledge to remove American missiles from Turkey, a diplomatic solution could probably have been found. But the risks were high.

No one can be absolutely certain what President Kennedy would have done if Khrushchev had rejected his proposal of October 27 and defied his tacit ultimatum. At the time, I and many others on the Ex Comm or working closely with it believed he would have ordered an air strike. Others, however, including Robert McNamara and McGeorge Bundy, believed he would have tightened the quarantine by including petroleum, and perhaps taken other steps short of direct military action, while continuing to negotiate. Some of his closest advisers, Theodore Sorensen and Arthur Schlesinger, believed he would have made further concessions, including if necessary an outright deal trading our missiles in Turkey for the Soviet missiles in Cuba. It should be recalled that in 1962, and indeed until 1969, most members of the Ex Comm and all others except a handful of close advisers of the president knew nothing of the unilateral "sweetener" in Robert Kennedy's statement to Dobrynin of American intentions to phase out the missiles in Turkey and Italy.

Only in 1987 did Dean Rusk disclose information that makes it appear highly likely that President Kennedy would not have launched an air strike but instead continued negotiations. Rusk revealed that on October 27, after sending Robert Kennedy to deliver the key message to Dobrynin, President Kennedy privately asked Rusk to call the late Andrew Cordier, the former deputy UN secretary general then at Columbia University, and ask him to be prepared to suggest to Secretary General U Thant that he propose to both the Soviet Union and the United States that they remove their missiles respectively from Cuba and Turkey. Cordier was given a precise message to this effect, but told not to actually make the suggestion until receiving a signal from Rusk. Thus President Kennedy wanted to have in ready reserve a neutral request to which he could respond favorably much more easily than he could to a Soviet demand. While the whole question was rendered moot by Khrushchev's acceptance of the president's October 27 proposal, it is clear that Kennedy was more inclined to pursue additional negotiations and even to accept a compromise involving an explicit commitment to withdrawing U.S. missiles rather than attack Cuba.

Nonetheless, the situation was fraught with dangers of slipping out of control. I believe that both the U.S. and Soviet leaderships reached a sensible and statesmanlike compromise resolution of the problem.

₩₩ *F U R T H E R   R E A D I N G*

Elie Abel, *The Missile Crisis* (1966)
Graham T. Allison, *Essence of Decision: Explaining the Cuban Missile Crisis* (1971)
William Attwood, *The Twilight Struggle: Tales of the Cold War* (1987)
Richard J. Barnet, *Intervention and Revolution* (1972)
Barton J. Bernstein, "The Cuban Missile Crisis: Trading the Jupiters in Turkey?"
     Political Science Quarterly, 95 (1980), 97–125
———, "The Week We Almost Went to War," *Bulletin of the Atomic Scientists*, 32
     (1976), 12–21
Richard K. Betts, *Nuclear Blackmail and Nuclear Balance* (1987)
Cole Blaisier, *The Hovering Giant: U.S. Responses to Revolutionary Change in Latin
     America* (1975)
James G. Blight and David A. Welch, *On the Brink: Americans and Soviets Reex-
     amine the Cuban Missile Crisis* (1989)
David Burner, *John F. Kennedy and a New Generation* (1988)
David Detzer, *The Brink: Cuban Missile Crisis, 1962* (1979)
Herbert S. Dinerstein, *The Making of the Cuban Missile Crisis* (1976)
Robert A. Divine, ed., *The Cuban Missile Crisis* (1971)
Jorge I. Dominguez, *Cuba: Order and Revolution* (1978)
Raymond L. Garthoff, *Reflections on the Cuban Missile Crisis* (1987, 1989)
Alexander M. George and Richard Smoke, *Deterrence in American Foreign Policy*
     (1964)
Richard N. Goodwin, *The American Condition* (1974)
Maurice Halperin, *The Rise and Decline of Fidel Castro* (1972)
———, *The Taming of Fidel Castro* (1981)
Jim Heath, *Decade of Disillusionment* (1975)
Trumbull Higgins, *The Perfect Failure* (1987)
Roger Hillsman, *To Move a Nation: The Politics of Foreign Policy in the Admin-
     istration of John F. Kennedy* (1967)
Haynes B. Johnson et al., *The Bay of Pigs* (1964)
Robert F. Kennedy, *Thirteen Days: A Memoir of the Cuban Missile Crisis* (1969)
Montague Kern, Patricia W. Levering, and Ralph B. Levering, *The Kennedy Crises:
     The Press, the Presidency, and Foreign Policy* (1983)
Walter LaFeber, *Inevitable Revolutions: The United States in Central America* (1983)
David A. Larson, ed., *The "Cuban Crisis" of 1962: Selected Documents, Chronology,
     and Bibliography* (2nd ed., 1986)
Richard Ned Lebow, *Between Peace and War* (1981)
Lee Lockwood, *Castro's Cuba, Cuba's Fidel* (1967)
Morris Morley, *Imperial State and Revolution: The United States and Cuba, 1952–
     1987* (1987)

Operation ZAPATA: The "Ultrasensitive" Report and Testimony of the Board of Inquiry on the Bay of Pigs (1981)

Henry M. Pachter, *Collision Course: The Cuban Missile Crisis and Coexistence* (1963)

Herbert S. Parmet, *JFK: The Presidency of John F. Kennedy* (1983)

Ronald R. Pope, ed., *Soviet Views on the Cuban Missile Crisis: Myth and Reality in Foreign Policy Analysis* (1982)

Thomas Powers, *The Man Who Kept the Secrets* (1981)

Stephen G. Rabe, *Eisenhower and Latin America: The Foreign Policy of Anti-Communism* (1988)

Arthur Schlesinger, Jr., *A Thousand Days* (1977)

———, *Robert F. Kennedy and His Times* (1978)

Glenn T. Seaborg and Benjamin J. Loeb, *Kennedy, Khrushchev, and the Test Ban* (1981)

Theodore C. Sorensen, *Kennedy* (1965)

Tad Szulc, *Fidel* (1986)

Kenneth W. Thompson, ed., *The Kennedy Presidency* (1985)

Richard J. Walton, *The Cold War and Counterrevolution* (1972)

David A. Welch, ed., *Proceedings of the Hawk's Cay Conference on the Cuban Missile Crisis, March 5–8, 1987* (1987)

Richard E. Welch, Jr., *Response to Revolution: The United States and Cuba, 1959–1961* (1985)

Garry Wills, *The Kennedy Imprisonment* (1983)

Peter Wyden, *Bay of Pigs* (1980)

Lyndon B. Johnson, the Great Society, and the Welfare State

XXX

The Great Society, as President Lyndon B. Johnson and others called the flood of social-welfare legislation enacted between 1964 and 1968, marked a watershed in the evolution of the American welfare state. Like the New Deal of the 1930s, to which it has often been compared, it profoundly altered the scope and character of the federal government and profoundly affected the daily lives of millions of ordinary Americans.

During the Great Depression of the 1930s, the federal government had assumed some measure of new responsibilities toward the unemployed, the elderly, and the poor. The Social Security Act of 1935, with its provisions for unemployment insurance, old-age pensions, and support for dependent children, laid the foundation for the modern welfare state. More important, many Americans altered their basic assumptions about the proper role of government. By 1944 Roosevelt could speak confidently of an ''economic bill of rights'' that promised food, housing, jobs, and education for every American. Neither Roosevelt nor his immediate successors delivered on those promises, however, with the result that in the following two decades, little growth or innovation could be measured in the programs established during the New Deal.

All this changed in the mid-1960s when President Johnson, with the aid of an expanding U.S. economy and pliant Democratic majorities in Congress, won passage of a host of new laws on health, housing, education, and poverty. Although modest by comparison with the welfare state of most Western European countries, the new and expanded programs of the Great Society were nevertheless among the most important changes in American government in the postwar era. They touched the lives of ordinary Americans in a myriad of both obvious and subtle ways, from diminishing the fears with which older people faced the prospect of costly medical expenses to increasing the share of the gross national product assigned to this and other ''entitlement'' programs. By the early 1970s the poverty rate had fallen to 11 percent, and even moderate conservatives like Presi-

dent Richard Nixon were considering broad, income-support programs that were designed to reduce it even more. Nothing came of these efforts, however, and as the economy foundered in the mid-1970s, the rate of poverty leveled off and then began to rise, especially during the deep recession that accompanied the first two years of the Reagan administration.

During the 1980s, President Ronald Reagan and other conservatives launched major, if selective, attacks on the welfare state and other New Deal and Great Society programs. Some programs were eliminated, others sharply reduced; but many, especially broad-based entitlement programs such as Medicare and social security, proved highly impervious to conservative (or liberal, for that matter) change. Reagan's fiscal and other policies reduced support for the poorest while benefiting the very rich, but the welfare state itself proved remarkably durable. After a quarter of a century, poverty continued to mark the lives of many Americans and the debate over how best to address it remained unresolved.

𝗫 D O C U M E N T S

Despite rapid economic growth and widespread prosperity in the 1950s, at the decade's end as many as 50 million Americans remained impoverished. Michael Harrington's 1962 book *The Other America,* from which the first document is excerpted, was part of a "rediscovery" of poverty during the early 1960s. In his first annual message to Congress on January 8, 1964 (the second document), President Johnson called for an "unconditional war on poverty." Although the rate of poverty declined during the late 1960s and early 1970s, the accompanying expansion of the nation's welfare system sparked sharp debate among both liberals and conservatives about the nature of poverty and public policy. Conservatives such as George Gilder, whose book *Wealth and Poverty* (1981) was frequently cited by members of the Reagan administration, argued that welfare, far from helping to alleviate poverty, actually contributed to it (document three). One could overcome poverty, Gilder maintained, only through hard work, strong family bonds, and faith in the future. Liberals, of course, continued to argue that poverty was rooted more in broad economic and social changes than in the character of poor people themselves, and continued to insist on the necessity for governmental action.

Poverty rose steeply during the deep recession of the early Reagan administration (document four); and despite the economic recovery that began in 1984, the plight of the poorest Americans continued to deteriorate. Nowhere was this fact more true than in large cities, where growing numbers of displaced homeless people congregated. The final document is drawn from the testimony of homeless children before two congressional committees in 1986 and 1987.

Michael Harrington Describes the "Other America," 1962

There is a familiar America. It is celebrated in speeches and advertised on television and in the magazines. It has the highest mass standard of living the world has ever known.

In the 1950's this America worried about itself, yet even its anxieties were products of abundance. The title of a brilliant book was widely misinterpreted, and the familiar America began to call itself "the affluent society." There was introspection about Madison Avenue and tail fins; there was discussion of the emotional suffering taking place in the suburbs. In all this, there was an implicit assumption that the basic grinding economic problems had been solved in the United States. In this theory the nation's problems were no longer a matter of basic human needs, of food, shelter, and clothing. Now they were seen as qualitative, a question of learning to live decently amid luxury.

While this discussion was carried on, there existed another America. In it dwelt somewhere between 40,000,000 and 50,000,000 citizens of this land. They were poor. They still are.

To be sure, the other America is not impoverished in the same sense as those poor nations where millions cling to hunger as a defense against starvation. This country has escaped such extremes. That does not change the fact that tens of millions of Americans are, at this very moment, maimed in body and spirit, existing at levels beneath those necessary for human decency. If these people are not starving, they are hungry, and sometimes fat with hunger, for that is what cheap foods do. They are without adequate housing and education and medical care.

The Government has documented what this means to the bodies of the poor, and the figures will be cited throughout this book. But even more basic, this poverty twists and deforms the spirit. The American poor are pessimistic and defeated, and they are victimized by mental suffering to a degree unknown in Suburbia.

This book is a description of the world in which these people live; it is about the other America. Here are the unskilled workers, the migrant farm workers, the aged, the minorities, and all the others who live in the economic underworld of American life. In all this, there will be statistics, and that offers the opportunity for disagreement among honest and sincere men. I would ask the reader to respond critically to every assertion, but not to allow statistical quibbling to obscure the huge, enormous, and intolerable fact of poverty in America. For, when all is said and done, that fact is unmistakable, whatever its exact dimensions, and the truly human reaction can only be outrage. As W. H. Auden wrote:

> Hunger allows no choice
> To the citizen or the police;
> We must love one another or die.

The millions who are poor in the United States tend to become increasingly invisible. Here is a great mass of people, yet it takes an effort of the intellect and will even to see them.

I discovered this personally in a curious way. After I wrote my first article on poverty in America, I had all the statistics down on paper. I had proved to my satisfaction that there were around 50,000,000 poor in this country. Yet, I realized I did not believe my own figures. The poor existed in the Government reports; they were percentages and numbers in long, close columns, but they were not part of my experience. I could prove that the other America existed, but I had never been there.

My response was not accidental. It was typical of what is happening to an entire society, and it reflects profound social changes in this nation. The other America, the America of poverty, is hidden today in a way that it never was before. Its millions are socially invisible to the rest of us. No wonder that so many misinterpreted [John K.] Galbraith's title and assumed that "the affluent society" meant that everyone had a decent standard of life. The misinterpretation was true as far as the actual day-to-day lives of two-thirds of the nation were concerned. Thus, one must begin a description of the other America by understanding why we do not see it.

There are perennial reasons that make the other America an invisible land.

Poverty is often off the beaten track. It always has been. The ordinary tourist never left the main highway, and today he rides interstate turnpikes. He does not go into the valleys of Pennsylvania where the towns look like movie sets of Wales in the thirties. He does not see the company houses in rows, the rutted roads (the poor always have bad roads whether they live in the city, in towns, or on farms), and everything is black and dirty. And even if he were to pass through such a place by accident, the tourist would not meet the unemployed men in the bar or the women coming home from a runaway sweatshop.

Then, too, beauty and myths are perennial masks of poverty. The traveler comes to the Appalachians in the lovely season. He sees the hills, the streams, the foliage—but not the poor. Or perhaps he looks at a run-down mountain house and, remembering [French Enlightenment philosopher Jean-Jacques] Rousseau rather than seeing with his eyes, decides that "those people" are truly fortunate to be living the way they are and that they are lucky to be exempt from the strains and tensions of the middle class. The only problem is that "those people," the quaint inhabitants of those hills, are undereducated, underprivileged, lack medical care, and are in the process of being forced from the land into a life in the cities, where they are misfits.

These are normal and obvious causes of the invisibility of the poor. They operated a generation ago; they will be functioning a generation hence. It is more important to understand that the very development of American society is creating a new kind of blindness about poverty. The poor are increasingly slipping out of the very experience and consciousness of the nation.

If the middle class never did like ugliness and poverty, it was at least aware of them. "Across the tracks" was not a very long way to go. There were forays into the slums at Christmas time; there were charitable organizations that brought contact with the poor. Occasionally, almost everyone passed through the Negro ghetto or the blocks of tenements, if only to get downtown to work or to entertainment.

Now the American city has been transformed. The poor still inhabit the miserable housing in the central area, but they are increasingly isolated from contact with, or sight of, anybody else. Middle-class women coming in from Suburbia on a rare trip may catch the merest glimpse of the other America on the way to an evening at the theater, but their children are segregated in suburban schools. The business or professional man may drive along the fringes of slums in a car or bus, but it is not an important experience to him. The failures, the unskilled, the disabled, the aged, and the minorities are right there, across the tracks, where they have always been. But hardly anyone else is.

In short, the very development of the American city has removed poverty from the living, emotional experience of millions upon millions of middle-class Americans. Living out in the suburbs, it is easy to assume that ours is, indeed, an affluent society.

This new segregation of poverty is compounded by a well-meaning ignorance. A good many concerned and sympathetic Americans are aware that there is much discussion of urban renewal. Suddenly, driving through the city, they notice that a familiar slum has been torn down and that there are towering, modern buildings where once there had been tenements or hovels. There is a warm feeling of satisfaction, of pride in the way things are working out: the poor, it is obvious, are being taken care of.

The irony in this . . . is that the truth is nearly the exact opposite to the impression. The total impact of the various housing programs in postwar America has been to squeeze more and more people into existing slums. More often than not, the modern apartment in a towering building rents at $40 a room or more. For, during the past decade and a half, there has been more subsidization of middle- and upper-income housing than there has been for the poor.

Clothes make the poor invisible too: America has the best-dressed poverty the world has ever known. For a variety of reasons, the benefits of mass production have been spread much more evenly in this area than in many others. It is much easier in the United States to be decently dressed than it is to be decently housed, fed, or doctored. Even people with terribly depressed incomes can look prosperous.

This is an extremely important factor in defining our emotional and existential ignorance of poverty. In Detroit the existence of social classes became much more difficult to discern the day the companies put lockers in the plants. From that moment on, one did not see men in work clothes on the way to the factory, but citizens in slacks and white shirts. This process has been magnified with the poor throughout the country. There are tens of thousands of Americans in the big cities who are wearing shoes, perhaps even a stylishly cut suit or dress, and yet are hungry. It is not a matter of planning, though it almost seems as if the affluent society had given out costumes to the poor so that they would not offend the rest of society with the sight of rags.

Then, many of the poor are the wrong age to be seen. A good number of them (over 8,000,000) are sixty-five years of age or better; an even larger number are under eighteen. The aged members of the other America are often sick, and they cannot move. Another group of them live out their lives in loneliness and frustration: they sit in rented rooms, or else they stay close to a house in a neighborhood that has completely changed from the old days. Indeed, one of the worst aspects of poverty among the aged is that these people are out of sight and out of mind, and alone.

The young are somewhat more visible, yet they too stay close to their neighborhoods. Sometimes they advertise their poverty through a lurid tabloid story about a gang killing. But generally they do not disturb the quiet streets of the middle class.

And finally, the poor are politically invisible. It is one of the cruelest ironies of social life in advanced countries that the dispossessed at the bottom of society are unable to speak for themselves. The people of the other America do not, by far and large, belong to unions, to fraternal organizations, or to political parties. They are without lobbies of their own; they put forward no legislative program. As a group, they are atomized. They have no face; they have no voice.

Thus, there is not even a cynical political motive for caring about the poor, as in the old days. Because the slums are no longer centers of powerful political organizations, the politicians need not really care about their inhabitants. The slums are no longer visible to the middle class, so much of the idealistic urge to fight for those who need help is gone. Only the social agencies have a really direct involvement with the other America, and they are without any great political power.

To the extent that the poor have a spokesman in American life, that role is played by the labor movement. The unions have their own particular idealism, an ideology of concern. More than that, they realize that the existence of a reservoir of cheap, unorganized labor is a menace to wages and working conditions throughout the entire economy. Thus, many union legislative proposals—to extend the coverage of minimum wage and social security, to organize migrant farm laborers—articulate the needs of the poor.

That the poor are invisible is one of the most important things about them. They are not simply neglected and forgotten as in the old rhetoric of reform; what is much worse, they are not seen.

President Lyndon B. Johnson
Declares War on Poverty, 1964

Let this session of Congress be known as the session which did more for civil rights than the last hundred sessions combined; as the session which enacted the most far-reaching tax cut of our time; as the session which declared all-out war on human poverty and unemployment in these United States; as the session which finally recognized the health needs of all our older citizens; as the session which reformed our tangled transportation and transit policies; as the session which achieved the most effective, efficient foreign aid program ever; and as the session which helped to build more homes, more schools, more libraries, and more hospitals than any single session of Congress in the history of our Republic. . . .

This budget, and this year's legislative program, are designed to help each and every American citizen fulfill his basic hopes—his hopes for a fair chance to make good; his hopes for fair play from the law; his hopes for a full-time job on full-time pay, his hopes for a decent home for his family in a decent community; his hopes for a good school for his children with good teachers; and his hopes for security when faced with sickness or unemployment or old age.

Unfortunately, many Americans live on the outskirts of hope—some because of their poverty, and some because of their color, and all too many because of both. Our task is to help replace their despair with opportunity.

This administration today, here and now, declares unconditional war on poverty in America. I urge this Congress and all Americans to join with me in that effort.

It will not be a short or easy struggle, no single weapon or strategy will suffice, but we shall not rest until that was is won. The richest Nation on earth can afford to win it. We cannot afford to lose it. One thousand dollars invested in salvaging an unemployable youth today can return $40,000 or more in his lifetime.

Poverty is a national problem, requiring improved national organization and support. But this attack, to be effective, must also be organized at the State and the local level and must be supported and directed by State and local efforts.

For the war against poverty will not be won here in Washington. It must be won in the field, in every private home, in every public office, from the courthouse to the White House.

The program I shall propose will emphasize this cooperative approach to help that one-fifth of all American families with incomes too small to even meet their basic needs.

Our chief weapons in a more pinpointed attack will be better schools, and better health, and better homes, and better training, and better job opportunities to help more Americans, especially young Americans, escape from squalor and misery and unemployment rolls where other citizens help to carry them.

Very often a lack of jobs and money is not the cause of poverty, but the symptom. The cause may lie deeper—in our failure to give our fellow citizens a fair chance to develop their own capacities, in a lack of education and training, in a lack of medical care and housing, in a lack of decent communities in which to live and bring up their children.

But whatever the cause, our joint Federal-local effort must pursue poverty, pursue it wherever it exists—in city slums and small towns, in sharecropper shacks or in migrant worker camps, on Indian Reservations, among whites as well as Negroes, among the young as well as the aged, in the boom towns and in the depressed areas.

Our aim is not only to relieve the symptom of poverty, but to cure it and, above all, to prevent it. No single piece of legislation, however, is going to suffice.

We will launch a special effort in the chronically distressed areas of Appalachia.

We must expand our small but our successful area redevelopment program.

We must enact youth employment legislation to put jobless, aimless, hopeless youngsters to work on useful projects.

We must distribute more food to the needy through a broader food stamp program.

We must create a National Service Corps to help the economically handicapped of our own country as the Peace Corps now helps those abroad.

We must modernize our unemployment insurance and establish a high-level commission on automation. If we have the brain power to invent these machines, we have the brain power to make certain that they are a boon and not a bane to humanity.

We must extend the coverage of our minimum wage laws to more than 2 million workers now lacking this basic protection of purchasing power.

We must, by including special school aid funds as part of our education program, improve the quality of teaching, training, and counseling in our hardest hit areas.

We must build more libraries in every area and more hospitals and nursing homes under the Hill-Burton Act, and train more nurses to staff them.

We must provide hospital insurance for our older citizens financed by every worker and his employer under Social Security, contributing no more than $1 a month during the employee's working career to protect him in his old age in a dignified manner without cost to the Treasury, against the devastating hardship of prolonged or repeated illness.

We must, as a part of a revised housing and urban renewal program, give more help to those displaced by slum clearance, provide more housing for our poor and our elderly, and seek as our ultimate goal in our free enterprise system a decent home for every American family.

We must help obtain more modern mass transit within our communities as well as low-cost transportation between them.

Above all, we must release $11 billion of tax reduction into the private spending stream to create new jobs and new markets in every area of this land.

A Conservative Extols
Work, Family, and Faith, 1981

The only dependable route from poverty is always work, family, and faith. The first principle is that in order to move up, the poor must not only work, they must work harder than the classes above them. Every previous generation of the lower class has made such efforts. But the current poor, white even more than black, are refusing to work hard. Irwin Garfinkel and Robert Haveman, authors of an ingenious and sophisticated study of what they call *Earnings Capacity Utilization Rates,* have calculated the degree to which various income groups use their opportunities—how hard they work outside the home. This study shows that, for several understandable reasons, the current poor work substantially less, for fewer hours and weeks a year, and earn less in proportion to their age, education, and other credentials (even *after* correcting the figures for unemployment, disability, and presumed discrimination) than either their predecessors in American cities or those now above them on the income scale. (The study was made at the federally funded Institute for Research on Poverty at the University of Wisconsin and used data from the census and the Michigan longitudinal survey.) The findings lend important confirmation to the growing body of evidence that work effort is the crucial unmeasured variable in American productivity and income distribution, and that current welfare and other subsidy programs substantially reduce work. The poor choose leisure not because of moral weakness, but because they are paid to do so.

A program to lift by transfers and preferences the incomes of less diligent groups is politically divisive—and very unlikely—because it incurs the bitter resistance of the real working class. In addition, such an effort breaks the psychological link between effort and reward, which is crucial to long-run upward mobility. Because effective work consists not in merely fulfilling the requirements of labor contracts, but in "putting out" with alertness and emotional commitment, workers have to understand and feel deeply that what they are given depends on what they give—that they must supply work in order to demand goods. Parents and schools must inculcate this idea in their children both by instruction and example. Nothing is more deadly to achievement than the belief that effort will not be rewarded, that the world is a bleak and discriminatory place in which only the predatory and the specially preferred can get ahead. Such a view in the home discourages the work effort in school that shapes earnings capacity afterward. As with so many aspects of human performance, work effort begins in family experiences, and its sources can be best explored through an examination of family structure.

Indeed, after work the second principle of upward mobility is the maintenance of monogamous marriage and family. Adjusting for discrimination against women and for child-care responsibilities, the Wisconsin study indicates that married men work between two and one-third and four times harder than married women, and more than twice as hard as female family heads. The work effort of married men increases with their age, credentials, education, job experience, and birth of children, while the work effort of married women steadily declines. Most important in judging the impact of marriage, husbands work 50 percent harder than bachelors of comparable age, education, and skills.

The effect of marriage, thus, is to increase the work effort of men by about half. Since men have higher earnings capacity to begin with, and since the female capacity-utilization figures would be even lower without an adjustment for discrimination, it is manifest that the maintenance of families is the key factor in reducing poverty.

Once a family is headed by a woman, it is almost impossible for it to greatly raise its income even if the woman is highly educated and trained and she hires day-care or domestic help. Her family responsibilities and distractions tend to prevent her from the kind of all-out commitment that is necessary for the full use of earning power. Few women with children make earning money the top priority in their lives.

A married man, on the other hand, is spurred by the claims of family to channel his otherwise disruptive male aggressions into his performance as a provider for a wife and children. These sexual differences alone, which manifest themselves in all societies known to anthropology, dictate that the first priority of any serious program against poverty is to strengthen the male role in poor families.

These narrow measures of work effort touch on just part of the manifold interplay between family and poverty. Edward Banfield's *The Unheavenly City* defines the lower class largely by its lack of an orientation to the future. Living from day to day and from hand to mouth, lower class individuals are unable to plan or save or keep a job. Banfield gives the impression that short-time horizons are a deep-seated psychological defect afflicting hundreds of thousands of the poor.

There is no question that Banfield puts his finger on a crucial problem of the poor and that he develops and documents his theme in an unrivaled classic of disciplined social science. But he fails to show how millions of men, equally present oriented, equally buffeted by impulse and blind to the future, have managed to become far-seeing members of the middle classes. He also fails to explain how millions of apparently future-oriented men can become dissolute followers of the sensuous moment, neglecting their jobs, dissipating their income and wealth, pursuing a horizon no longer than the most time-bound of the poor.

What Banfield is in fact describing in his lower-class category is largely the temperament of single, divorced, and separated men. The key to lower-class life in contemporary America is that unrelated individuals, as the census calls them, are so numerous and conspicuous that they set the tone for the entire community. Their congregation in ghettos, moreover, magnifies greatly their impact on the black poor, male and female (though, as Banfield rightly observes, this style of instant gratification is chiefly a male trait).

The short-sighted outlook of poverty stems largely from the breakdown of family responsibilities among fathers. The lives of the poor, all too often, are governed by the rhythms of tension and release that characterize the sexual experience of young single men. Because female sexuality, as it evolved over the millennia, is psychologically rooted in the bearing and nurturing of children, women have long horizons within their very bodies, glimpses of eternity within their wombs. Civilized society is dependent upon the submission of the short-term sexuality of young men to the extended maternal horizons of women. This is what happens in monogamous marriage; the man disciplines his sexuality and extends it into the future through the womb of a woman. The woman gives him access to his children, otherwise forever denied him; and he gives her the product of his labor, otherwise dissipated on temporary pleasures. The woman gives him a unique link to the future and a vision of it; he gives her faithfulness and a commitment to a lifetime of hard work. If work effort is the first principle of overcoming poverty, marriage is the prime source of upwardly mobile work.

It is love that changes the short horizons of youth and poverty into the long horizons of marriage and career. When marriages fail, the man often returns to the more primitive rhythms of singleness. On the average, his income drops by one-third and he shows a far higher propensity for drink, drugs, and crime. But when marriages in general hold firm and men in general love and support their children, Banfield's lower-class style changes into middle-class futurity.

The key to the intractable poverty of the hardcore American poor is the dominance of single and separated men in poor communities. Black "unrelated individuals" are not much more likely to be in poverty than white ones. The problem is neither race nor matriarchy in any meaningful sense. It is familial anarchy among the concentrated poor of the inner city, in which flamboyant and impulsive youths rather than responsible men provide the themes of aspiration. The result is that male sexual rhythms tend to prevail, and boys are brought up without authoritative fathers in the home to instill in them the values of responsible paternity: the discipline and love of children and the dependable performance of the provider role.

Living in Poverty, 1959–1989: A Graphic

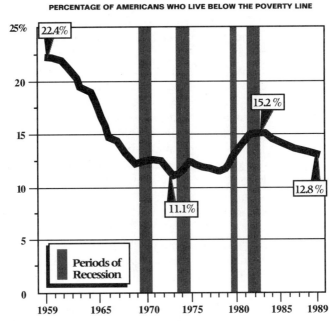

PERCENTAGE OF AMERICANS WHO LIVE BELOW THE POVERTY LINE

Graphic "Living in Poverty, 1959–1989." *The Washington Post,* September 27, 1990. © 1991 by The Washington Post Company. Reprinted with permission.

Homeless Children Speak, 1986, 1987

My name is Yvette Diaz. I am 12 years old. I live in the Martinique Hotel, 49 West 32nd Street, New York City. I live in rooms 1107 to 1108. There are two rooms. I live here with my mother, two sisters, 9 and 7, and my three-year-old brother. We have lived in the Martinique Hotel for almost two years now. I am living at the Martinique Hotel because my aunt's house burned down, and we didn't have any place to live.

We were living in my aunt's house in Brooklyn because my father was discharged from the United States Air Force in the State of Washington, and the family came back to New York where we originally came from. We couldn't find an apartment right away, so we stayed with my aunt. Then, the house burned down, and we went to the Martinique Hotel.

Since we are living in New York at the Martinique, I have been going to P.S. 64, which is on East 6th Street in Manhattan. When I first started school here, I was absent a lot, because the bus that took us to school in the mornings was late a lot of times, and other times I didn't get up on time. We didn't have an alarm clock. Finally, my mother saved up enough to buy one. This year I have not been absent many times because the bus is on time, and we have an alarm clock.

I don't like the hotel, because there is always a lot of trouble there. Many things happen that make me afraid. I don't go down into the street to play, because there is no place to play on the streets. The streets are dangerous, with all kinds of sick people who are on drugs or crazy. My mother is afraid to let me go downstairs. Only this Saturday, my friend, the security guard at the hotel, Mr. Santiago, was killed on my floor. He was shot by another man and killed. The blood is still on the walls and on the floor. Anyway, people are afraid to open the door to even look out. There are a lot of people on drugs in the hotel. Sometimes you can find needles and other things that drugs come in, all over the hallways.

Our apartment was broken into when we were out. They stole the radio and our telephone alarm clock. We have a TV but they didn't get that, because we hid it in the closet under other things every time we leave the rooms.

We can't cook in the apartment. My mother sneaked a hot plate in, because we don't have enough money to eat out every night. They, the hotel, warned us that if we are caught cooking in the rooms, we could be sent to a shelter.

I play in the hallways with my friends from other rooms on my floor. Sometimes, even that isn't safe. A boy, about 15 or 16, came over to me and wanted to take me up to the 16th floor. I got frightened and ran into my room and told my mother. She went to the Police and she was told this same boy was showing his private parts to girls before, and that it was reported to them. If he bothered me again, I was to tell the Police.

The five of us live in two rooms at this hotel. There is only one bathroom. We don't have mice or rats like some of the other people who live in the hotel, because we have a cat.

I go to the extended day program at my school, P.S. 64. We go from 3:00 to 6:00 every weekday except Friday. I get help with my homework for 45 minutes every day and then we have computer, arts and crafts, dancing, gym and game room. I like it and we also get a hot dinner every night before we go home on the bus. I finish all my homework here as the teacher helps me and it is quiet so I can really understand what I am doing.

If I could have anything that I want, I wish that we had our own apartment in a nice, clean building and a place that I could go outside to play in that is safe. I want that most of all for me and my family.

My name is David Bright. I am ten years old. I am homeless. I am often hungry. Right now I live in the Martinique Hotel. The Martinique is a mad house. The hallways are dangerous. Many things could happen to you while you're in the hallways. Like you could be shot or raped. The roaches and rats are a big problem too. But being raped is worse. There are people who rape little boys in the hallways.

I am often hungry because I don't get enough to eat. Homeless kids are taken to schools far away. When the bus comes late I can't even get breakfast at school. When I arrive the bell rings, then breakfast just stops. I just can't think in school when I'm hungry. My mind just stops thinking and this can't go on forever. That's because I want to learn. I want to get a good education. Learning is fun for me.

There are too many little kids in the hotel who never go to school. There just is not enough room in the schools for them. Just like there's not enough homes for poor children and not enough food.

When I grow up I will be the President of the United States. When I am the President every American will have a home. Every American will have something to eat every day. Everyone in America will have a little money in his pocket. When I am President no ten year old boy like me will have to put his head down on the desk at school because it hurts to be hungry.

My name is Liberty Eggink. I'm eleven years old and live in the Martinique Hotel, one of the many shelters for homeless kids in New York City. I feel, well sort of angry about it. It seems like more and more people are homeless and nobody is being helped. It also is a very sad thing that little babies have to suffer the way they are in these homeless families. There is a baby on the fourth floor that has scabies on her body. The baby is only five months old. I don't think any one is really trying to help. We have no place to cook which is hard on the mothers, trying to cook a decent meal for a family with no kitchen, just a hot plate and washing the dishes in the bathroom. Some people hate doing dishes but I like doing dishes in a proper kitchen. Here there is no place to put clean or dirty dishes.

There is no place for kids to play, so they play in the halls. Sunday is the worst because garbage overflows everywhere!!

I feel scared at night when I hear a little kid scream!! It is too dangerous so, I really hate being homeless. I wish we had a home.

I'm Jewel Eggink. I am nine years old and I live in the Martinique Hotel. Being homeless is terrible. You can't relax. You're always hiked up and scared. In a real house everything smells nice. I think that things can be better. I just think things can be better.

My name is David. I am eighteen years old. I am homeless. While people sit at home and wonder, over a good dinner, or during the commercial break, what should be done about the plight of the homeless in America, children are dying of malnutrition, hunger and despair.

Homelessness is not G rated material. Little children should not be exposed to it. What kind of future does a child have who knows no other life, outside that of a welfare hotel?

There is no future for a homeless child, only the death of childhood.

XX *E S S A Y S*

The debate over the welfare state among contemporary scholars echoes the deep divisions among Americans over the nature of poverty and government's appropriate response. The first essay, by liberal social scientists Sar A. Levitan and Robert Taggart, is excerpted from their book *The Promise of Greatness: The Social Programs of the Last Decade and Their Major Achievements* (1976). Levitan is Research Professor of Economics and Director of the Center for Social Policy Studies at George Washington University; Taggart, former director of the National Manpower Policy Task Force, is President of the Remediation and Training Institute. Theirs is the voice of Democratic liberalism, defending the vision and accomplishments of the Great Society. The second essay, by Charles Murray, is taken from *Losing Ground* (1984), the most important conservative critique of the welfare policies of the Johnson years. Murray is a sociologist at the American Enterprise Institute, a conservative "think tank." Focusing on the able-bodied poor—single women with children, and men who have dropped out of the work force, perhaps a third of all poor people—Murray argues that the War on Poverty not only failed to lift such people out of poverty but actually contributed to their remaining poor. In the final essay, which appears in Fred Block et al., *The Mean Season: The Attack on the Welfare State* (1987), radical social scientists Frances Fox Piven and Richard A. Cloward of Columbia University challenge both the methods and the conclusions of Murray and other conservatives.

In Defense of the Great Society

SAR A. LEVITAN and ROBERT TAGGART

President [Lyndon B.] Johnson's vision of a Great Society, contrasting so markedly with the phlegmatic ideology of the preceding decade, stirred the nation. Under the banner of the Great Society, there was a dramatic acceleration of governmental efforts to insure the well-being of all citizens, to equalize opportunity for minorities and the disadvantaged, to eliminate, or at least mitigate, the social, economic, and legal foundations of inequality and deprivation. Congress moved ahead on a vast range of long-debated social welfare measures and pushed on into uncharted seas. In its 1,866 days the Johnson administration moved vigorously to implement these new laws and to fully utilize existing authority. The Warren Court [after its Chief Justice, Earl Warren] aided this dynamism with sweeping, precedent-setting decisions on a number of critical issues. The public supported this activism, giving Lyndon Johnson the largest plurality in history, his Democratic party an overwhelming majority in both Houses of Congress, and his administration high public approval ratings as action got underway.

Just four years later, a very different mood prevailed in the nation— one of fear, distrust, anger, and alienation. Presidential nominee Richard Nixon, claiming to speak for the "forgotten American," put it succinctly: "For the past five years we have been deluged by government programs for the unemployed, programs for cities, programs for the poor, and we have reaped from these programs an ugly harvest of frustration, violence and failure across the land." Urging return to normalcy and promising to correct the many mistakes of the Great Society but also bolstered by discontent with the Vietnam war, President Nixon eked out a narrow victory. But four years later with essentially the same platform he almost matched the Johnson landslide, garnering more than three of every five ballots. While voters returned a Democratic Congress, the 1972 victory was interpreted, at least by the administration, as a repudiation of the Great Society and its vision.

Within another three years, there was a new President and an embittered nation had substantially increased the Democratic majority in Congress. Yet this represented more an indictment of President Nixon's leadership than a negation of his philosophy. The criticism of the Great Society had become firmly rooted, and if anything, the distressing economic, political, and international events of the 1970s intensified the general sense of dissatisfaction.

Economic traumas, the Vietnam war, urban unrest, and Watergate had had a major impact on social philosophy and policy. The war undermined the moral authority of the Great Society and drained the resources needed for the full implementation of its agenda. Even more fundamentally, the activism of the 1960s was nurtured by a booming economy providing the resources for expanded governmental efforts. As growth slowed and then reversed in the 1970s, the price tag of previous commitments became more onerous and opposition more strident. Yet throughout our nation's history, military, political, and economic changes have resulted in sweeping turns in philosophy and policy. Values and hopes tend to move dialectically; institutions and groups threatened by change gradually reassert themselves while the have-nots are coopted. That the Great Society's vision was subsequently rejected was neither a historically unique nor an unexpected pattern. . . .

The essence of the Great Society was increased federal intervention to assist the disadvantaged and disenfranchised by providing needed goods, services, and income and by changing the socioeconomic system. Government action begins with legislation. Perhaps the most characteristic scene of the Great Society years was President Lyndon B. Johnson signing important new laws and with rhetorical flourish promising to wipe out poverty, urban and rural blights, and age-old inequities in education, civil rights, health, and housing. Whatever the effectiveness of the legislation, there is no debate about its scale and scope. In almost every area of social welfare policy, the federal government shouldered new responsibilities.

Poverty and Income Support Initiatives

In his first State of the Union message, President Johnson declared an unconditional war on poverty. The Economic Opportunity Act, passed in 1964, was the first offensive, spawning a wide array of programs to mitigate the consequences and to eliminate the causes of poverty. The Community Action Program established community based agencies to mobilize the poor and to give them a voice in decision making. Legal services, adult education, neighborhood health centers, and a number of other approaches were developed under this umbrella. The Job Corps sought to alter the lives of disadvantaged youths through intensive training and education in a residential setting away from their poverty environments. The Neighborhood Youth Corps was to provide work experience and needed income to teenagers in and out of school. VISTA sought to mobilize volunteer workers to go out among the poor and help them. Head Start aimed to equalize opportunity at the starting gate through improved early education, while Upward Bound was to provide talented but disadvantaged students a chance for higher education. The Office of Economic Opportunity was created to administer these diverse efforts, to represent the interests of the poor in the federal establishment, and to serve as a catalyst for mobilizing government and private resources. While the commitments never matched the promise, the war on poverty was significant in moving beyond simple care for the poor in an attempt to alter the economic and social causes of poverty.

If the antipoverty effort was the favorite child of the Great Society, it was the whipping boy of the Nixon administration. One by one, poverty programs were transferred from the Office of Economic Opportunity to other agencies until only the umbrella was left; and in 1974 it was closed. Yet the poverty activities themselves took root, gaining a firm foothold in the galaxy of federal responsibilities.

When it came to caring for the needy, as opposed to alleviating the causes of need, the contrasts between the Johnson and Nixon legislative records were not as marked. The Great Society is frequently blamed or credited for the welfare explosion which occurred in the late 1960s and continued through the early 1970s, but this development was not the direct product of federal legislative initiatives. The only major changes in the welfare system were the 1967 Social Security amendments, which sought to halt expansion by providing incentives for recipients of Aid to Families with Dependent Children to work their way off relief. The welfare reforms proposed by the Nixon administration also sought to slow growth but were, in some ways, more liberal than previous policies in that they would have guaranteed an income for all poor families.

Health Programs

The passage of Medicare and Medicaid in 1965 was probably the foremost legislative achievement of the Johnson administration. Federally operated health insurance for the aged had first been proposed and actively pushed by President Truman. Vehemently opposed by the American Medical Association as a step on the road to socialized medicine, the issue was debated for the next two decades. President Kennedy advocated a modest system covering hospital costs, but President Johnson was firmly committed to a more ambitious measure. His first special message to Congress in 1965 dealt with health. What resulted was not only a comprehensive insurance program for the aged but a major expansion of previous aid programs for public assistance recipients. These two programs went far toward delivering health care as a right and a reality for the aged and poor.

More health care resources were needed to meet this expanded demand, and the Johnson administration followed through with a number of legislative measures to expand supply. In 1964 a nurses' training program was initiated, and in 1965 and 1968 aid was increased for medical schools and needy medical students. In 1966 and 1968 similar assistance was given for the training of allied health manpower. Funds were provided for the staffing of mental retardation facilities, for the expansion of birth control programs, and for the establishment of treatment facilities for narcotics addicts and alcoholics. The Partnership for Health program, launched in 1966, was aimed at rationalizing the delivery system through better areawide planning, as well as improving public health, migrant, and immigrant programs.

One of the six great goals of the Nixon administration was to improve and increase the availability of health care, but its approach was markedly different. "We must recognize," President Nixon said, "that we cannot simply buy our way to better medicine. We have already been trying that too long . . . It must be our goal not merely to finance a more expensive medical system, but to organize a more efficient one." The major aim was thus to cut back and reform the Great Society initiatives. Besides vetoing three HEW [Department of Health, Education, and Welfare] appropriations bills in his first term, in part because of excess health funding, the President vetoed an extension of the longstanding grant program for hospital construction and modernization and sought to reduce maternal and child health programs. In 1971 the administration effectively stalled a $60 billion proposal for a comprehensive health insurance program with a counterproposal involving annual federal outlays one twentieth as great. The only other legislation pushed by the Nixon administration (other than a $100 million fight against cancer and heart disease) was reform of the medical delivery system to establish prepaid group practices as well as professional standards review organizations to monitor doctors serving Medicare and Medicaid patients.

Medicare and Medicaid were also amended in hopes of cutting down on their rapid growth.

Federal Aid for Education

There were no general federal programs of aid for elementary, secondary, or higher education before the 1960s. While the needs of the expanding public schools were apparent, action had stalled for more than two decades over the school segregation and church-state questions. Federal aid was opposed by segregationists who saw it as an instrument to force integration and inhibited by clashes between opponents and advocates of aid to parochial schools. The Civil Rights Act of 1964 reduced the first roadblock, while the second was circumvented by emphasizing aid to needy children regardless of the school in which they were located. The result was the swift passage in 1965 of the Elementary and Secondary Education Act, which provided funds to support programs "designed to meet the special educational needs of educationally deprived children," including experimentation with new teaching methods, bilingual instruction, and special offerings for the mentally and physically handicapped.

The Higher Education Act of 1965 was equally significant. It authorized scholarships and low interest loans for undergraduate students based only on need, and it expanded the work-study program begun the year before under the Economic Opportunity Act. In addition, the antipoverty law initiated the Upward Bound program aimed to help talented disadvantaged youth to prepare for college.

The education record of the Nixon administration paled in comparison. Four vetoes in the first term involved "excessive" congressional appropriations for education. The President was in office more than three years before he proposed his first major education legislation to expand grants for needy college students. As it turned out, however, this program was funded at modest levels and did not much increase education financing for students from poor families. The Nixon administration favored federal aid for desegregating school districts and a moratorium on busing. The latter was enacted but ruled unconstitutional by the Supreme Court.

Shelter and Subsidies

The Johnson administration initiated the first major low-income housing programs since the New Deal. The longstanding public housing program had promised "a decent home and suitable living environment for every American family," but its performance fell far short of the rhetoric, and construction was relatively dormant over the 1950s and early 1960s. The Great Society, therefore, introduced a whole range of new tools to stimulate production and to subsidize the costs of housing for the needy.

The Housing and Urban Development Act of 1965 reduced interest rates on loans for rental units built for the poor and the elderly. Public housing agencies were authorized to lease private dwellings. Rent supplements were introduced for low-income tenants in specified units. The Housing and Urban Development Act of 1968 established programs to subsidize interest rates on private loans for units renting or being sold to low-income families.

The Nixon administration actively applied these new tools in its first few years. Production of assisted units reached an all-time high. But there were no new legislative initiatives other than some minor reforms to correct observed deficiencies. As costs mounted, administrative support wavered and in 1973 all construction was halted in order to study alternatives to the Great Society programs that were pronounced failures.

Employment and Training

Until the 1960s little was done to help the millions of Americans failing in or being failed by the labor market. This was changed under the Johnson administration. The Manpower Development and Training Act, passed in 1962 to train the technologically displaced, was expanded and redirected to the hard core unemployed. The Economic Opportunity Act of 1964 created the Neighborhood Youth Corps and the Job Corps, as well as Work Experience and Training to help public assistance recipients and other needy persons, Operation Mainstream to employ primarily older workers in rural settings, and New Careers to fund paraprofessional training and employment opportunities for the disadvantaged. The 1967 Concentrated Employment Program provided block grants to community groups for comprehensive attacks on employment problems, and in the same year the Work Incentive program was implemented to train and place welfare recipients. Private firms were subsidized to hire and train the disadvantaged the next year, and vocational rehabilitation was extended to the socioeconomically handicapped.

There were also some important legislative initiatives in the 1970s. The Emergency Employment Act of 1971, providing funds to state and local governments to hire the unemployed, was the first general public employment effort since the New Deal. Congress passed this legislation over the President's opposition and despite a veto of a similar bill in 1970. On the other hand, the administration favored the Comprehensive Employment and Training Act of 1973, which combined many of the Great Society's categorical programs into a block grant to state and local governments. Public employment programs were expanded somewhat under the Ford administration to deal with the massive joblessness in 1974 and 1975, but endorsement was far from enthusiastic and a large job creation bill was vetoed in 1975.

Civil Rights

The civil rights record of the Johnson administration was certainly one of its greatest achievements, and some have characterized the 1960s as a Second Reconstruction. There was no general civil rights legislation in the twentieth century until 1957 when a limited measure was passed to protect registered voters from threats and intimidation. In rapid succession during the Johnson years, laws were passed to make discrimination illegal in almost all public realms. The Civil Rights Act of 1964 was the cornerstone, guaranteeing voting rights, access to public accommodations, equal employment, and educational opportunity. The Voting Rights Act of 1965 strengthened the federal government's hand in registering minorities. Housing discrimination was barred three years later. . . .

New laws inevitably require new outlays, and the legislative activism of the Great Society was reflected in the rapid growth of federal social welfare expenditures which continued through the Nixon years. Many undertakings begun with relatively small initial expenditures for research, planning, and experimentation developed into massive obligations as more eligible persons participated. Reorganization and reform usually increased rather than reduced outlays. Once begun, spending was difficult to stop as recipients and beneficiaries defended their newly acquired benefits. The expansionary process begun by the Johnson administration continued under its successors despite their aim of restraint and retrenchment. Measured by spending, the contrasts between the Johnson and the Nixon–Ford administrations are far less significant than the differences between the entire 1965–75 decade and the two preceding ones. . . .

The Johnson administration pressed Congress to enact measures in health care, civil rights, and education which were debated for years without result. Legislation dealing with poverty, manpower training, and housing pushed into new areas or ventured totally new approaches. The first half of the 1970s was mostly spent digesting these measures, with no legislative initiatives of comparable scale or scope.

New and expanded social welfare efforts required dramatically increased spending and the growth momentum begun in the Great Society continued through the early 1970s. From a historical perspective, the entire decade beginning in 1965 represented an acceleration of the long-run trend toward greater federal responsibilities. There was, however, a leveling off in the later years and this would have been more marked if two recessions had not intensified needs.

The response to the active braking efforts by the Nixon administration was sluggish. Through vetoes, impoundment, and zealous interpretations of executive privilege, the momentum of the Great Society was gradually dissipated. In the absence of new laws and initiatives, which the Nixon and Ford administrations tried to avoid, the impetus for future social welfare expansion was also reduced.

The laws, expenditures, and administrative actions were only the outward manifestations of an underlying set of aims, assumptions, and approaches. While the underlying philosophies can only be inferred, the following generalizations seem to square with the facts and give some better understanding of the essence of the Great Society.

First, its fundamental aim was to use the federal government's power to correct societal inequities as well as to guarantee a minimal standard of welfare for every citizen. While the term welfare state has a pejorative connotation to many—and President Johnson was no more in favor of handouts than President Nixon—the Great Society's activism clearly expanded the jurisdiction of the government in protecting the welfare of its citizens. The alternative was to rely on market processes to improve the welfare of all citizens on the assumption that tampering with the engines of economic betterment would be self-defeating. As society and the economy have grown more complex, government intervention has necessarily increased. The Great Society's thrust was to speed up this trend to achieve goals immediately rather than waiting for slower, more conventional processes. The Nixon and Ford administrations sought to "leave well enough alone" or even to try to reverse the momentum of governmental growth.

Second, the Johnson administration was willing, and indeed tried, to commit the nation to future actions. The rapid growth of the AFDC caseload and some other developments were not engineered and came as unpleasant surprises to policy makers, but in most other instances the clear intent was to build a groundwork and to generate momentum for change. The mortgages came due in the Nixon administration, and there was less latitude for new initiatives. But potentials for action were not realized. The preoccupation with retrenchment and reform in the 1970s laid the groundwork for future inaction.

Third, the Great Society was posited on the assumption that the nation's resources would be constantly expanding and that by redirecting a portion of this growth, social problems could be overcome while still allowing for expanded private activity and consumption. The anticipation of a fiscal dividend was basic to the Great Society architects, who, while firm believers in the private enterprise system, felt that government activities could be expanded out of growth. It is ironic that a less optimistic view was held by those claiming to defend the "great motor" of progress—the free market economy—by reducing government activity. Just as it is possible to overestimate the resource dividend and to overcommit the nation, it is equally possible to underestimate and to undercommit. The problem is to reach a balanced appraisal of the long term, not to get overly enthusiastic about rapid growth nor overly disturbed by temporary stagnation.

Fourth, the Great Society viewed the federal government as a lever of institutional change. Its power in the product and labor markets as a buyer and employer was used to alter private sector practices and to compensate for their effects. There was no hesitancy to push forward with new regulations such as civil rights laws to alter private sector institutions. Federal grants to state and local governments were given with many strings attached, and even more, state and local agencies were bypassed in order to create competing delivery systems and to test alternative approaches. In contrast, the subsequent administrations have relied upon established institutions to achieve social goals and emphasized the direct impacts of government programs.

Fifth, the Great Society relied on the categorical approach, specifying exactly how funds were to be spent and initiating separate programs for separate problems. The result was an active, federal, centralized system of government. The next two administrations challenged the categorical programs as duplicative, wasteful, and ill-considered, preferring revenue sharing as an alternative, "comprehensive" solution. Implicit was a decentralization of authority to the state and local level under the auspices of elected officials.

Sixth, the Great Society believed in compensatory efforts to alter the lives of disadvantaged individuals. Human resources development programs from preschool education to vocational training were emphasized. The paradigm was the Job Corps, which created a completely structured environment with the aim of dramatically changing the future of disadvantaged youth. The subsequent attack on the Job Corps was symbolic of the administration's opposition to "meddling" with individual lives and its belief that it was enough to open doors without helping people through.

Seventh, the Great Society was willing to take bold steps to experiment with different approaches on a large scale. Efforts to change institutions and individuals are inherently uncertain, high risk ventures. It would have been much safer and much less wasteful to use tried and true approaches, but change may be good for its own sake and new approaches may work more efficiently after the learning curve period. The Johnson administration, influenced by social thinkers and tinkerers, was willing to take the risks, hoping for the best. It refused to neglect needs or to rely on the "filtering-down" of overall gains. President Johnson's view was, in his own words, that "We have the power to shape the civilization that we want."

The Poverty of the Great Society

CHARLES MURRAY

The increases in federal expenditures for social-welfare programs between 1950 and 1980 were extraordinary. Using constant dollars as the basis for comparison, spending for health and medical programs in 1980 was six times greater than in 1950; public assistance costs, 13 times greater; education costs, 24 times greater; social insurance costs, 27 times greater; housing costs, 129 times greater. Overall, civilian social-welfare costs increased 20-fold from 1950 to 1980. During the same period, the U.S. population increased by half.

The revolution began, as so many revolutions begin, with reform. It sprang from the simplest, most benign of objectives. President John F. Kennedy wanted the federal welfare effort to be a force for social progress. In his welfare message to Congress in 1962, he wrote: "The goals of our public welfare program must be positive and constructive . . . . [The welfare program] must stress the integrity and preservation of the family unit. It must contribute to the attack on dependency, juvenile delinquency, family breakdown, illegitimacy, ill health, and disability. It must reduce the incidence of these problems, prevent their occurrence and recurrence, and strengthen and protect the vulnerable in a highly competitive world."

Innocuous as his words sound today, Kennedy was engaged in a major departure from precedent. No president—not Dwight D. Eisenhower, nor Harry S Truman, nor Franklin D. Roosevelt, nor any of their predecessors— had seen the federal role in this light. This was something new.

The 1950s saw the last years of a popular consensus about the purpose of welfare that had survived, with remarkably little alteration, since the Republic was founded and, for that matter, could trace its roots to the Poor Laws of Elizabethan England. Its premise was elemental: A civilized society does not let its people starve in the streets. It makes "a decent provision," as Samuel Johnson put it, for those who would otherwise be destitute.

This decent provision was hedged with qualifications, for while some people could be considered the "deserving" poor (the involuntarily unemployed and the helpless) others were undeserving indeed and merely sought to take advantage of the community's generosity. Everyone, including many of the poor, agreed that this was so. Thus the dilemma: How is a civilized society to take care of the deserving without encouraging people to become undeserving? How does it do good without also doing harm?

By the late 1950s, there was widespread dissatisfaction with the American system's failure to resolve the dilemma. Care for the elderly and the disabled was not at issue. Social Security and other measures to help them were generally accepted as appropriate steps for the federal government to take. The problem—and, it should be emphasized, the one that will be addressed throughout this discussion—was what to do for the able-bodied of working age. On this score, two broad, very different, perceptions of the current state of affairs had fed the dissatisfaction.

On the Right and among large numbers of blue-collar Democrats, there was increasing resentment at the *permanence* of welfare. It was acceptable for a worker to receive unemployment checks while looking for a job. But it was quite another thing for society to be supporting a healthy adult year after year.

Although it accounted for only one percent of the federal budget in 1958, AFDC was the focal point for the resentment. The New Deal sponsors of AFDC had intended to help the widow with small children—to tide her over between the loss of her husband and the day when the children were old enough to take over her support.

By the 1950s, however, it had become embarrassingly clear that most of the women receiving AFDC were not widows. Many of them had not even been married. Worst of all, they did not stop having babies after the first lapse. They kept having more. This had not been part of the plan.

The most flagrantly unrepentant, to judge from media portrayals, seemed to be black. The statistics show, in fact, that whites have always been the largest single group of AFDC recipients, but the stereotype that stirred the critics was the family of four, five, six, and more children reared at government expense, and somehow the stories published about such families always seemed to talk about black families.

Thus the *Atlantic Monthly,* a sober-minded and liberally oriented magazine, ran a story in its April 1960 issue describing, in muckraking detail, the cases of "Charlotte," with 14 children, "Maude," with nine (several of whom were fathered, it was reported, by an illiterate mental defective), and others who were portrayed as mindlessly accumulating children, neglecting them, and producing generations that would come back to haunt America in the decades to come. All of the examples were black, lending a troubling overtone to the closing paragraph. "What is particularly disturbing to social workers, judges, and other public officials," the author concluded, "is not simply the failure of these people to support themselves but the complete breakdown of moral values. . . ."

Meanwhile, as many politicians, writers, and middle Americans were inveighing against the welfare mother, leaders of the Left and of minorities of all political persuasions were beginning to express their outrage at what they saw as pervasive injustice in the American system. The statistics on unemployment and wages, on infant mortality and life expectancy, on education and voter registration—the open, sanctioned discrimination in everything from union membership, to access to lunch counters, to admission to universities—all were counterpoint to articles in the news media about welfare mothers. Yes, the critics of the system agreed, welfare was too often permanent, but thanks to opportunity denied rather than opportunity spurned.

White indignation at the deplorable morals of the welfare recipients and white guilt over who was responsible collided, and at just about the same time that a new political center was evolving. During the 1950s, the Right had, in effect, accepted the New Deal and made it respectable. The Left, for its part, was now less dogmatic, more wary of ideologues. *New York Times* columnist Arthur Krock commented in 1960 that "when the national platforms and candidates of 1960 have been chosen, the American voters will find it difficult to detect a major ideological difference between the two major parties." The "New Center" was not only a matter of issues; perhaps more importantly, it reflected a new frame of mind.

John F. Kennedy exploited this frame of mind and found support for an entirely new approach to the welfare mess. In substance, the program President Kennedy proposed in his 1962 message to Congress was modest. It consisted of a few training programs and other rehabilitative efforts amounting to only $59 million in the 1963 budget. But by shifting the focus of welfare policy away from the dole and toward *escape* from the dole, Kennedy gave the federal government a continuing responsibility for helping Americans to help themselves. The essence of the approach was expressed in the slogan that later became a rallying cry for the War on Poverty, "Give a hand, not a handout."

Editorialists took up the theme. The time was right: The country was at peace, the economy was healthy, and the cause was worthy. In the "can-do," sleeves-rolled-up spirit of the since-maligned Best and Brightest, the domestic policy-makers of the Kennedy administration and, later, the managers of Lyndon Johnson's War on Poverty saw themselves as hard-nosed idealists who would be able to get results where the social workers had failed. Their premise: Most of the able-bodied folk on welfare would work if only given the opportunity. Their program: Train the chronically unemployed, train the youngsters growing up without skills or resources, help them get that first job. Their promise: The able-bodied would soon be on their way to permanent self-sufficiency.

The ultimate test of a new welfare program, Charles Frankel wrote at the time, "will be the effect it will have on producing individuals who, like Eliza Doolittle at the conclusion of *Pygmalion,* are prepared to walk out on those who have helped them and to open competitive enterprises of their own."

Kennedy implemented fragments of his program—the Public Welfare Amendments of 1962, the first Manpower Development and Training Act, for example. But, taken as a whole, he did not preside over costly social innovations. Social-welfare outlays under Kennedy rose less rapidly than they had under Eisenhower. Kennedy's legacy to Lyndon Johnson was not a new system but a new tone, new expectations, and a new consensus that the federal government had a continuing responsibility to help poor Americans help themselves.

Johnson lost no time in giving substance to Kennedy's rhetoric. The initial antipoverty bill, the Economic Opportunity Act, was written, debated, passed, and signed (in August of 1964) within Johnson's first nine months in the Oval Office. The bill was a faithful attempt to follow the "hand, not a handout" script. It provided for job training; part-time jobs for teen-agers and college students; community antipoverty programs; loans to low-income farmers and businessmen; and establishment of a domestic Peace Corps, later to become part of ACTION. There was not a handout in the lot. Johnson was careful to point this out at the signing ceremony, incorporating into his remarks the cheerful prediction that "the days of the dole in this country are numbered."

President Johnson waged war on poverty enthusiastically. In rapid order, he and Congress gave the nation food stamps, Medicare, Medicaid, a vastly expanded public housing program, and other subsidies. But in the process, he also worked the revolution. In only three years, from 1964 to 1967, social-welfare policy switched from the intention of ending the dole to the institution of permanent income transfers. These transfers embraced not only the traditionally eligible recipients of the dole but large new segments of the American population who are best described as the "working poor." It was a polar change in policy that went almost entirely unrecognized as such while it was happening.

Four major forces impelled this fundamental shift:

1. *The triumph of the economy.* One explanation for the reforms of the 1964–67 period, and why they came then rather than earlier, is so simple that it is sometimes overlooked: 1964–67 was the first time that we thought we could afford them. The nation was extremely rich and extremely confident of its ability to keep getting richer. Economists believed that in Keynesian

economics they had found the key to perpetual prosperity. Judicious use of public spending to revive consumer buying power seemed as if it would preclude any repetition of the Great Depression. John Maynard Keynes graced *Time*'s cover in 1965, and the magazine quoted President Johnson's economic adviser, Charles Schultze: "We can't prevent every little wiggle in the economic cycle, [but] we now can prevent a major slide."

2. *The discovery of "structural" poverty.* As previously indicated, from the end of World War II until the early 1960s, little in the popular press, in political rhetoric, or in the published work of American scholars focused on poverty in America. Then, in 1962, came Michael Harrington's *The Other America.* His thesis was that a huge population of poor people—50 million by his count—was living in our midst, ignored. "To be poor," Harrington wrote, "is not simply to be deprived of the material things of this world. It is to enter a fatal, futile universe, an America within America with a twisted spirit." The ranks of the poor consisted of the aged, the unskilled, women heading households with small children, and others who were bound to be bypassed, no matter how much economic growth occurred, because of the way that the capitalist economy distributed income. Poverty was not just a matter of isolated "pockets"; it was built into the American system. Within a few years, an almost unbroken intellectual consensus had formed behind the structuralists' underlying premise: Poverty is not a consequence of indolence or vice. The system is to blame.

3. *The long, hot summers.* This perception of the "system" as the problem and of the individual as a victim was obliquely reinforced by the racial violence of the mid-1960s. The first phase of the civil-rights movement had culminated in the signing of a sweeping Civil Rights Act by Lyndon Johnson in July of 1964; for all practical purposes, the national legislative struggle for equality was over. A voting-rights bill remained to be enacted a year later, but the generalized legal clout granted in the 1964 act was enormous. Yet 13 days after the Civil Rights Act became law, bloody race riots erupted in Harlem. More riots followed that summer in Rochester, Paterson, Philadelphia, and Dixmoor, a suburb of Chicago. In 1965, came the week of Watts. In 1967, rioting in Detroit claimed 43 lives.

Why did these and scores of other cities explore in racial violence? High expectations had gone unfulfilled. Long-delayed equality of rights under the law had not quickly been translated into equality of condition. Blacks blamed this situation on an entrenched pattern of Northern racism, and whites who saw themselves as friends of the civil-rights movement tended to agree. White confusion and guilt created what Daniel Patrick Moynihan has called "a near-obsessive concern to locate the 'blame' for poverty, especially Negro poverty, on forces and institutions outside the community concerned." If American society were to blame for the riots, for the economic discrepancies between whites and blacks, for poverty among all races; and if society's responsibilities were not fulfilled simply by enforcing *legal* equality, then a social-welfare program would have to be devised to go beyond equality of opportunity. It would have to promise equality of *outcome.* A "hand" was no longer enough.

4. *The failed experiment.* Riots and black militancy constituted one of

the two real-world developments that made the structural view of poverty attractive. The second was the early realization, within the senior ranks of the Johnson administration as well as among its critics, that the much-publicized bootstrapping programs were not working as expected. Scores of case studies of Community Action programs showed projects that either had never gotten beyond the planning stage or were bogged down in bureaucratic infighting. Job-training programs produced disappointing results.

It soon became clear that the Eliza Doolittle model was not going to end poverty. In April of 1967, Joseph Califano, a principal aide to President Johnson, called reporters into his office to tell them that a government analysis had shown that only 50,000 persons, or fewer than one percent of the 7.3 million people then on welfare, were capable of being given skills and training to make them self-sufficient. The repudiation of the dream—to end the dole once and for all—was complete.

Later that year, in a column that ran on Christmas Eve, *New York Times* columnist Tom Wicker summed up the implications for policy toward the poor: "Really compassionate and effective reforms to do something about poverty in America," he wrote, "would have to recognize, first, that large numbers of the poor are always going to have to be helped. Whether for physical or mental reasons, or whatever, they cannot keep pace. . . . Thus the aim of getting everyone off welfare and into 'participation in our affluent society' is unreal and a pipe dream. . . . [A] decent standard of living ought to be made available not just to an eligible few but to everyone, and without degrading restrictions and police-like investigations."

Once it was accepted in Washington that the American system was to blame for able-bodied people being poor, principles that had largely gone unchallenged since the Republic's early days became hoary and obsolete. A new wisdom took over. . . .

The shift in assumptions about welfare policy occurred among a group that was small relative to the entire population but of enormous influence. It is perhaps best labeled the "intelligentsia"—a broad and diffuse group in late 20th-century America. It includes the upper echelons of (in no particular order of importance) academia, journalism, publishing, and the vast network of foundations, institutes, and research centers that has been woven into partnership with government during the last 30 years. It also includes congressional staffers as well as many civil servants in key positions just below the presidential appointment level, where so much of policy formation goes on.

The salient feature of the intelligentsia is that, at any given moment, it is the custodian of the received wisdom. It originates most of the ideas in the dialogue about policy, writes about them, embeds them in memoranda for presidential aides. Most of all, it confers respectability on ideas. The process is akin to fashion. Ideas are "in" and ideas are "out" for reasons having something to do with their merit but also with their being new.

The last half of the 1960s saw remarkably broad agreement among the various sectors of the intelligentsia on the directions in which a just and effective federal social policy must move, and this agreement, this "elite wisdom," represented an abrupt shift from the past. By the end of 1967, the nature of the political dialogue had been altered beyond recognition. It was not just that certain types of legislation had more support than before, but that the premises themselves—the "everybody-knows-that" premises— had shifted in the minds of the people who were instrumental in making policy. The most important of these changed premises was the one that I have described: the belief that, left alone, the system would perpetuate unacceptable inequalities. The system itself was flawed.

The policy ramifications of the new wisdom were labyrinthine. Eligibility requirements were loosened for welfare of all kinds. New "in-kind" transfer programs, such as food stamps and Medicaid, were set into place and gradually expanded. And for the first time, provision was made for the *working* poor.

In the fiscal 1964 federal budget, the last of the pre-Johnson budgets, public-assistance funds for working people had been essentially nil. The major programs for people of working age—AFDC and unemployment compensation—were for the jobless.

The exclusion of working people (no matter how small their incomes) was not accidental, but neither was it much talked about. A citizen in good standing was self-supporting. To have a job was *ipso facto* to be self-supporting. If the income from that job was less than one liked, it was up to one to do something about it. This was not the opinion only of middle America; it was the old elite wisdom as well. Certainly, it did not seem to occur to leaders of either political party prior to 1964 that people who had jobs ought to get welfare assistance.

At bottom, however, the consensus about no welfare for working people rested on a fragile assumption—that adults are responsible for the state in which they find themselves. The assumption required a certain suspension of disbelief. (Most people had recognized for years that one's inheritance mattered, circumstances mattered, luck mattered.) Because this assumption was not absolutely true, a second assumption was needed to buttress it: All things considered, the "system" was doing all that it *properly* could do by trying to provide equal opportunity.

Once the second assumption had been toppled—once it was accepted that the system itself was to blame for people being poor—policy principles that had gone unargued were instantaneously outdated. Among these was the principle that government should not support employed people. If the system were to blame for a person's entrapment in a job that paid too little money for a decent existence, then the principle was palpably unfair—so unfair that, like the principle that it replaced, it did not need to be debated.

Richard Nixon exemplified the breadth of the new consensus. Nixon lambasted the Great Society during the 1968 campaign. In office, he set about dismantling its symbolic appurtenances (including the OEO). But it was Nixon who, in 1969, proposed the Family Assistance Plan, a form of negative income tax that would have guaranteed every American family of four a "floor" income of $1,500 to $1,800. He argued that Washington must "recognize that it has not less of an obligation to the working poor than to the nonworking poor."

Congress rejected the Family Assistance Plan. But the same legislators authorized the creation of a new category of welfare assistance (Supplemental Security Income) and voted large increases in funding for food stamps, public housing, Social Security, and other forms of welfare for which working people were eligible. The number of participants in the Food Stamp Program, for example, grew from 424,000 in 1965 to 11.6 million by the end of President Nixon's first term. In constant dollars, Washington during the five Johnson years spent some $57 billion on the category the Census Bureau calls "public aid" (*not* including pensions, Social Security, education or housing programs); during the first five Nixon years, the government spent more than twice that amount on these same public-aid programs.

Hardly anyone except the most obdurate reactionaries opposed such efforts in principle, and once the principle was established, the scope and cost of the programs continued to escalate. Hardly anyone now argued that it was fundamentally *wrong* to take tax dollars from one worker, whose paycheck the government had decided was too large, and give the dollars to another worker, whose paycheck the government had decided was too small. Ten years earlier, hardly anyone, in or out of Congress, would have argued the opposite.

Other changes in the nature of the rapidly expanding welfare system were wrought less by legislation than by administrative fiat. As Nathan Glazer has written, "Today, crucial documents in American history are not necessarily to be found in legislation, executive action, or even the court orders of our powerful judiciary. The modest reporting forms issued by regulatory agencies may be as consequential as any of these." The enforcement of eligibility rules for unemployment insurance, disability compensation, AFDC, and other welfare programs was relaxed considerably during the 1960s, occasionally by means of explicit directives but often through a generally understood but hard-to-document change in the "way of doing business." From time to time, the judicial branch mandated its own procedural refinements, such as when the Supreme Court, in 1968, struck down the "man-in-the-house" rule, declaring that a woman is entitled to receive AFDC benefits even if she is cohabiting with a man.

Underlying all of these developments was the assumption that the distinction between the deserving and the undeserving poor was no longer relevant. That assumption, plus the companion federal commitment to assisting both the working and the nonworking poor, animated the changes in the rules that took place beginning in the mid-1960s. By the mid-1970s, a sizable welfare complex had been built on the foundation laid during the Johnson administration. It consisted of a broad range of job-training programs, "entitlements," and noncash transfers of goods and services. In 1980, it cost the taxpayer some $64 billion. This figure does *not* count Social

Security or Medicare, which are for the elderly; does *not* count unemployment insurance, which is for the temporarily out-of-work; and does *not* count Workman's Compensation, which is for those who have suffered work-related disabilities.

During an average month in that year of 1980, some 21.1 million Americans were participating in the Food Stamp Program, 10.6 million were recipients of AFDC, 4.2 million received Supplemental Security Income, and 21.6 million availed themselves of health care under Medicaid. All of these programs were "means-tested," meaning that one's eligibility depended essentially on the level of one's income. In this manner did the social system identify its victims and offer redress.

Policy-makers and legislators hoped for a variety of good things from the War on Poverty, from the creation of entitlements, the expansion of benefits, and the widening population of eligible recipients. Perhaps some of the poor might even "escape" from the dole. But escaping the dole was no longer as important as escaping poverty. Whatever else they did, the new programs were to increase the *material well-being* of the poor. They were now meant to reduce poverty, not dependency.

The story of what happened to poverty in the years after the reforms took effect, when compared to the situation *before* they were enacted, does not appear to make sense. The numbers go the wrong way at the wrong time.

Yes, the proportion of the population living in poverty did fall during the five Johnson years, from 18 percent in 1964 to 13 percent in 1968. But it is difficult to argue that the Great Society programs were primarily responsible. Not only was the funding for these programs still small during that period, the drop in poverty was not any greater than past experience would have led policy-makers to expect.

In 1950, as noted above, approximately 30 percent of the population would be considered poor. From that level, the number of people living in poverty dropped by 17 percentage points over the next 18 years. The Johnson administration, with a spectacular economy at work, presided over a five-percentage-point drop in five years—its fair share. Then, during the late 1960s, improvement slowed. During the 1970s, it stopped altogether. A higher proportion of the American population was officially poor in 1980 than at any time since 1967. This proportion hit a low point, 11 percent, in 1973. By 1980, it stood at 13 percent and was heading up. The number of people living in poverty stopped declining just as the public assistance program budgets and the rate of increase in those budgets were highest.

This perverse result was vividly apparent, for example, in the federally funded job training and employment programs. During the early years of the Great Society, it was thought that making enough jobs available would win the War on Poverty. To be sure, some poor people—the disabled, some of the elderly, perhaps single-parent mothers of young children—would have to be given other kinds of help as well; but for most of the working-age population, making a job available was believed to be the answer.

Between 1950 and 1960, the Department of Labor did virtually nothing to help poor people train for, or find, jobs. During the first half of the 1960s, it spent a comparatively trivial $500 million (in 1980 dollars) on jobs programs. Between 1965 and 1969, as the Johnson initiatives got under way, a more substantial $8.8 billion (in 1980 dollars) was spent. During the 1970s, through fiscal year 1980, expenditures totaled a whopping $76.7 billion.

The number of persons involved is even more impressive than the money. From the time that the first Manpower Development and Training Act trainees were cycled through the program (in 1962–63) through fiscal year 1980, some 32.6 *million* persons were reported to have enrolled in one or another of the Department of Labor's jobs programs. The total number cannot, of course, be taken at face value. Many of the programs were short-lived or badly run, many participants dropped out before they finished, and many individuals counted in that 32.6 million figure were repeaters. But the training and employment programs constituted an enormous national effort nonetheless.

Furthermore, the effort was concentrated on a relatively small portion of the population. From the beginning, the focus of the government jobs programs was on disadvantaged youths in their late teens and early twenties. These young people had reached the most critical time in their job development. They were supposed to be the most trainable. And they had the longest time to reap the benefits of outside help.

The contrast between the government's hands-off policy during the 1950s and its massive intervention during the 1970s is so great that it seems inconceivable that we should not be able to observe positive changes in the employment statistics. And yet the statistics went in exactly the wrong direction for the group that was at the top of the priority target list—black youths in the 16-to-24 age bracket.

During the early 1950s, black youths had an unemployment rate almost identical to that of whites. (For 16-to-17-year-olds, in 1951, it was 9.5 percent for whites, 8.7 percent for blacks.) During the last half of the 1950s, the rate of unemployment among young blacks increased, largely because of the loss of agricultural jobs for black teen-agers, especially in the South. The rate stabilized during the early 1960s at the unacceptably high rate of roughly one-quarter of the black labor force in this age group. It appeared to observers at the time that a large segment of black youth was being frozen out of the job market, and this concern motivated congressional support for the early jobs programs.

Black unemployment among the older of the job entrants improved somewhat during the Vietnam War years, although the figures remained higher than one might have predicted from the Korean War experience. But during the late 1960s—at the very moment when the jobs programs began their unprecedented expansion—the black youth unemployment rate began to rise again, steeply, and it continued to do so throughout the 1970s. In

1980, for example, it stood at 33 percent for black males aged 18 to 19, and 38 percent for those aged 16 to 17.

If young whites had been doing as badly as young blacks, we could ascribe the trends to economic factors that affected everybody, educated or not, rich or poor, discriminated against or not. But young blacks lost ground to whites. This is apparent when we examine the ratio of black unemployment to white unemployment—the measure of the racial differential—for new job entrants. From 1961 to 1965, for example, when there were virtually no jobs programs, the black-to-white ratio for 18-to-19-year-olds averaged 1.7 to 1. From 1966 to 1970, with a much stronger economy *plus* the many new jobs programs, the ratio averaged 2.2 to 1. From 1970 to 1980, when the jobs programs were enrolling millions annually, the ratio averaged 2.3 to 1.

Something was happening to depress employment among young blacks. The easy explanation—that job opportunities for young blacks were just not there no matter how hard people searched—runs into trouble when statistics on labor-force participation (LFP) are considered.

A "participant" in the labor force is one who either is working or is actively looking for work. The statistics on LFP are as informative in their own way as the statistics on unemployment. In the long run, they may be even more important. While the unemployment rate measures current economic conditions, participation in the labor force measures an individual's fundamental economic stance: Does he have an active intention of working, given the opportunity?

In 1954, fully 85 percent of black males aged 16 and older were in the labor force, a rate essentially comparable to that of white males. This was nothing new. Black males had been participating in the labor force at equal or higher rates than white males since the turn of the century.

Beginning in 1966, black-male LFP started to fall substantially faster than white-male LFP. Between 1954 and 1965, the black reduction in LFP was 17 percent greater than that for whites. Between 1965 and 1980, it was 252 percent greater. The divergence that occurred was not a minor statistical blip but a change of astounding magnitude. America had seen large-scale *entry* into the labor force before, but never had it witnessed large-scale voluntary *withdrawal* from (or failure to enlist in) the labor force by able-bodied males. The sharpest slide occurred not during the 1970s, when the economy was troubled, but during the 1965–69 period, when unemployment was at historic lows.

As in the case of unemployment, age is at the center of the explanation. The younger the age group, it turns out, the greater the decline in black LFP, the greater the divergence with whites, and the sooner "dropping out" began. The phenomenon, in other words, was generational. For whatever reasons, black males born during the early 1950s and thereafter shared an attitude toward the labor market different from that of black males born earlier. If one looks at three different age "cohorts"—say, black males born in 1938, 1944, and 1952—one discovers that, as far as labor-force participation is concerned, members of the two older black groups behaved much like each other and much like their white contemporaries. The younger group, the cohort of 1952, was far less fortunate.

What was different about being born in 1952? Nothing, necessarily. The difference lay in the environments in which the three age cohorts came of age in the labor market. The members of the 1938 cohort turned 16 in 1954, when the world was not different *in the rules governing the job market* from the world of 1960, the year that the youths born in 1944 turned 16. The cohort born in 1952, on the other hand, reached the age of 16 in 1968; by then the rules had been changed radically.

As far as the labor market was concerned, the changes were surely all for the best—more training programs for poor and minority youth, better regulations on equal opportunity and widespread social support for their enforcement, higher minimum wages, a red-hot economy—and still the cohort of 1952 youngsters fared far worse than their older brothers and their white counterparts.

They behaved in ways that, for many, forfeited their futures as economically independent adults. They behaved in those ways because, under the new rules, it seemed both profitable and rational to do so. For the new rules pandered to that most human of impulses, the pursuit of one's short-term advantage.

There is bitter irony in the fact that poverty stopped dropping as spending on poverty increased, that labor-force participation decreased as the economy boomed, and that unemployment increased as the jobs programs reached their height. And yet, throughout the 1970s, mainstream politicians, academics, journalists, and bureaucrats remained committed to a way of thinking about poor people and social policy that manifestly failed to produce results. There seemed little to be done except sweat it out. The budgets for job training, food stamps, and the various social-action programs continued to grow almost by inertia.

There had been an alternative set of ideas all along, of course. If, during the 1960s and 1970s, there was an elite wisdom that shaped the directions of social policy, there was also a popular wisdom that explained why things were falling apart.

The popular wisdom is just that—the views to be heard in blue-collar bars or country-club lounges in most parts of the United States. It is the inarticulate constellation of worries and suspicions that helped elect Ronald Reagan in 1980. It is perhaps more precisely called a white popular wisdom, but some of its major themes are also voiced quietly by a conservative black working class, and by many among the poor of both races.

The popular wisdom is characterized by hostility toward welfare (it makes people lazy), toward lenient judges (they encourage crime), and toward socially conscious schools (too busy busing kids to teach them how to read). The popular wisdom disapproves of favoritism for blacks and of too many written-in rights for minorities of all sorts. It says that the government is meddling far too much in things that are none of its business.

The hostility one hears in the *vox populi* accounts, perhaps, for the reluctance of more intellectually sophisticated people to consider whether it might not be right. To listen carefully to the popular wisdom is also to hear a good deal of mean-spirited (often racist) invective. Acknowledging the merits of its insights is seen by many well-meaning Americans as approving of the invective as well. And one might add that, to the minds of many professional social analysts, the explanations of the popular wisdom are too *simple,* too unsubtle, to be true. . . .

Beginning in the mid-1960s, it was easier to get along without a job. It was easier to have a baby without being responsible for it (for a man) and without having to have a husband (for a woman). It was easier to get away with crime. Because it was easier to get away with crime, it was easier to support a drug habit. Because it was easier to get along without a job, it was easier to ignore education. Because it was easier to get along without a job, it was easier to walk away from a job—and thereby accumulate a record as an unreliable employee which, in turn, made it more difficult to get any but the least important, most dispensable kinds of work. . . .

The second too-typical reaction is to ask, usually in a tone of heavy disbelief: "Do you seriously think that these girls are deciding to have babies so that they can get on welfare?" To which the answer is, of course, No—in the sense that (presumably) few calculate the decision so deliberately. But if the question is changed slightly, to be: "Are decisions about marriage and children and work affected by economic considerations?" the answer is, of course, Yes—throughout history, and in every social class. During the 1960s and 1970s, the nature of these considerations was decisively altered for one set of Americans and one only: poor people. And millions of poor people, especially the young, began to behave much differently from before.

Changes in the tangible incentives and disincentives are only part of the story. Another equally important tool that society uses (consciously or not) to manage behavior is status, which serves as both a goad to ambition and a reward for certain types of behavior. Beginning in the 1960s, changes in social policy withdrew status from the low-income, independent working family, with disastrous consequences for the quality of life of such families. Status was withdrawn from the very kinds of behavior that help poor people escape from poverty.

Historically, poor people in America have been a variegated group with complex status distinctions. There were the genteel poor, who had lost their money but not their manners. There were the poor people who were called "trash"—not just without money but also uncouth and generally unpleasant company. There were the immigrant poor who, even as they were climbing out of poverty, maintained elaborate status structures, even in the most crowded tenements. And there were the farmers, most of whom were cash-poor but, nevertheless, were widely believed to be the backbone of the nation and on a considerably higher moral plane than the effete rich.

The status distinctions were based on the assumption that people were responsible for their actions and, specifically, responsible for taking care of

themselves and their families as best they could. A person who was chronically unable to hold a job, who neglected children and spouse, was a bum
and a no good, and was consigned by his neighbors to the lowest circle of
status. This held true in most communities, regardless of race.

But once it was assumed by policy-makers or their intellectual advisers
that the system was to blame when a person was chronically out of work
and that the system was even to blame when a person neglected spouse and
family, then the moral distinctions eroded. It was no longer deemed proper
among mainstream writers, politicians, and rule-makers to draw a distinction
between the deserving and the undeserving poor. The very term "deserving
poor" was laughed out of use—witness the reaction of political columnists
and cartoonists to the use of "truly needy" by officials of the Reagan administration. The poor were simply poor: None were permitted to be superior
to others, all were victims.

Viewing the poor as victims prompted several new departures. One was
the drive to rid welfare of its stigma. Welfare had heretofore been a blot
on the recipient's reputation. Now, because it was no longer deemed the
recipient's fault that welfare aid was needed, the stigma had to be removed.
To this end, the portrayal and administration of the welfare system was
changed dramatically. In addition to changing practices that stigmatized
recipients (by discouraging at-home eligibility investigations, for example),
the government deliberately mounted a propaganda effort. As early as 1965,
the OEO began sending out emissaries to spread the word that it was morally
permissible to be on welfare. Federal Community Action grants provided
the wherewithal for booklets, speeches, and one-on-one evangelizing by staff
workers. Welfare was to be considered a right, not charity.

The government's efforts were reinforced by the National Welfare Rights
Organization (NWRO), founded in 1966 and led by George Wiley. The
innovative aspect of the welfare-rights movement was not that poor people
were organizing. It was that their focus had shifted. No longer did the
protestors proclaim, "We don't want charity, we want jobs." During the
last half of the 1960s, the NWRO demonstrators were agitating not so much
for jobs as for the right to long-term, unfettered, generous charity. Without
stigma attached to being on welfare, how was one to take pride in *not* being
on welfare?

Arguably, the most insidious single change affecting status relationships
within the poor community was the introduction of "means-tested" welfare
benefits, benefits available to anyone whose income fell below a certain
threshold.

One of the insights of game theory involves the psychological importance
of natural boundaries—What makes it easier to quit smoking than to cut
down? What leads bargainers to compromise on a round number or to "split
the difference"? With poor people, the traditional boundary was accepting
no charity at all from anyone outside the family.

Means-tested programs effectively ended such useful taboos. One may
approve or disapprove of food stamps, Medicaid, and housing assistance,
but one result was unavoidable: In time, virtually all low-income persons

became recipients of federal charity. Pride in independence was further compromised, and so was a certain degree of pressure on the younger generation to make good on the family tradition of never accepting charity. The notion that there is an intrinsic good in working, even if one does not *have* to, may have impressive philosophical credentials, but it is not very convincing, at least to many young people whose values are still being formed.

In the end, post-1964 social policy robbed the responsible and deserving poor of neighborhood status even as it eroded their incentive to make investments—in time, energy, psychic commitment, and money—that might pay off in upward mobility for themselves, or for their children, over the long-term. Over a period of years, the changes in the rules of the economic game caused status conventions to flip completely in some communities. To someone who is not yet persuaded of the satisfactions of making one's own way, there is something truly laughable about an individual who doggedly keeps working at a lousy, "dead-end" job for no tangible reason at all. The man who keeps working is a chump.

Realistically, it makes little sense to suppose that anything actually *can* be done, or in any event will be. Significant reform of social policy in the United States does not seem likely in the near future. Ours is, after all, a system that, faced with bankruptcy of Social Security during the early 1980's, went into paroxysms of anxiety at the prospect of delaying the recipients' cost-of-living increase for six months.

But the cautiousness of the system is not in itself worrisome. Reform is often inappropriate, and it should always be undertaken carefully and slowly. What *should* worry us is a peculiar escapism that has for two decades gripped the consideration of social policy in America. It seems that those who legislate, administer, and write about social policy can tolerate any increase in actual suffering or demoralization so long as the system in place does not explicitly permit it. It is better, by the logic we have been living with, that we *try* to take care of 100 percent of the problem and make matters worse than that we solve 75 percent of the problem with a solution that does not try to do anything about the rest.

Escapism is a natural response. Most Americans want to help. It makes us feel bad to think of neglected children and rat-infested slums, and we are happy to pay for the thought that people who are good at taking care of such things are out there. If the number of neglected children and the number of rats seem to be going up instead of down, it is understandable that we choose to focus on how much we put into the effort instead of what comes out. The tax checks we write buy us, for relatively little money and no effort at all, a quieted conscience. The more we pay, the more certain we can be that we have done our part. A solution—say, scrapping much of the modern welfare edifice—that would have us pay less, accomplish more, *and* acknowledge that some would go unhelped, is unacceptable.

As a result, the barrier to radical reform of social policy is not the pain that it would cause the intended beneficiaries of the present system, but the pain that it would cause the donors. The real contest over the direction of social policy in America is not between people who want to cut budgets and people who want to help. When reforms finally do occur, they will happen not because stingy people have won but because generous people have stopped kidding themselves.

Challenging the Great Society's Conservative Critics

FRANCES FOX PIVEN and RICHARD A. CLOWARD

The intellectual foundation for a major attack on the AFDC [Aid to Families with Dependent Children] program has been built over the past two decades. Edward Banfield's book *The Unheavenly City* (1970) helped put the cornerstone in place with the argument that the poor were doomed to poverty by their inability to defer gratification, and that interventions by "do-gooders" were therefore useless. The conservative thesis began to take fuller form in Nathan Glazer's 1971 article "The Limits of Social Policy" and in Susan Sheehan's 1976 depiction of the life of a Puerto Rican AFDC mother and family. Martin Anderson's *Welfare* (1978) was extremely influential, especially his general conclusion the welfare system has "created a new caste of Americans—perhaps as much as one-tenth of this nation—a caste of people almost totally dependent on the state, with little hope or prospect of breaking free. Perhaps we should call them the Dependent Americans." And after Reagan launched the attack on the relief programs in 1981, four additional works appeared which extended and consolidated the rationale for the conservative mobilization: George Gilder's *Wealth and Poverty* (1981), Ken Auletta's 1982 book *The Underclass,* Charles Murray's *Losing Ground* (1984), and Lawrence M. Mead's *Beyond Entitlement: The Social Obligations of Citizenship* (1986).

These works fit the pattern of antiwelfare rhetoric laid out centuries ago. Increases in the types and amounts of social spending in the late 1960s and early 1970s are summed up. Then the point is made that conditions among the poor deteriorated: family breakdown, out-of-wedlock births, weakened attachments to the labor force, crime and delinquency, poor school performance, and deeper poverty. With this correlation established, it is "obvious" that welfare is the cause of disorganization and poverty. So many more dollars spent in one year, so much more disorganization and poverty in the next. The remedies, too, run true to the classical formulae. Slash or dismantle the programs; or at the least, orient them more strictly to the market—for example, by requiring recipients to "work off" relief payments.

This period of relief conflict has some distinctive features, however. Nothing has been so striking as the steadfast popular support of the social programs. Public opinion surveys show that a large majority of Americans approve of the social programs; in fact, approval has been growing during the Reagan years. Programs for the aged enjoy virtually unanimous favor, partly because the elderly themselves constitute a significant fraction of national opinion polls, and because they are organized to protect their interests. Furthermore, these programs substantially relieve adult children of responsibility for their aging parents, so the nonelderly also have a major stake in them. And despite anxieties about the future solvency of the Social Security system, working-age people hope these benefits will be available to them at retirement.

Americans also believe in the fairness of providing the unemployed and disabled with financial assistance. And there is even considerable support for the poor-serving programs, such as AFDC, which were generally scorned in the past. To be sure, since the Great Depression the polls have consistently shown that about three in four favor the *idea* of helping the poor. But there was also strong public antipathy to the particular government programs for the poor, especially to AFDC. That has changed. Most people agree that the Reagan administration's cuts have hurt the poor, and they have become more supportive of the means-tested programs as efforts to cut them continue. The Heritage Foundation, for example, reported poll findings in 1985 showing that "three in four Americans think that poor people who receive welfare and food stamps need the assistance," they are more positive toward these programs than three years earlier, and "fewer people criticized government aid for fostering dependence among the poor." The Federal Advisory Commission on InterGovernmental Relations reported 1982 poll results showing that "the public, if faced with necessity to accept cutbacks in state and local government services, would prefer cuts in assistance to parks and recreation, colleges and universities, and streets and highways over aid to the needy. Only 7 percent favored cuts in services to the needy." None of this is to say that these preferences are necessarily salient. The way most people vote, for example, is determined mainly by the state of the economy, not by the state of the social programs. But if the Reagan administration had actually succeeded in making Social Security voluntary, or in eliminating or substantially slashing the major programs for the poor, disabled, and unemployed, there might well have been a reaction in the election of 1984.

Even with these qualifications, popular support constitutes a major obstacle to the success of the attack on the welfare state, as we predicted it would at the outset of the Reagan era. Despite some administrative restructuring and budget cuts, the income-maintenance programs remain basically intact. We thought the current campaign would fail mainly because of changes in American political culture associated with the political economy of an advanced industrial society. In particular, beginning with the Great Depression, the enlarging role of government in the economy has undermined the legitimacy of traditional *laissez-faire* ideas and given rise to a greatly strengthened popular belief that the state is responsible for economic well-being. It is this popular economic conviction which poses the main political obstacle to the business community's determination to slash social provision.

Public opinion presents a similar challenge to intellectuals allied with the attack. This is probably the main reason why so much of their writing about social provision has veered away from programs where the idea of economic rights is most firmly established, as is true of Social Security and, to a lesser extent, of the unemployment and disability programs. The main attack has narrowed down to welfare and the nutritional subsidies for the poor, programs about which the public is more ambivalent. Despite the sympathy for the impoverished expressed in the public opinion polls, the AFDC program and its beneficiaries remain vulnerable to the classical stereotypes associated with pauperism, and it is these stereotypes that conservatives are attempting to revitalize. Moreover, unlike elderly or disability claimants, AFDC recipients are unorganized and are therefore unable to respond to charges effectively. The narrowing of the debate over the welfare state to AFDC is obscured by the sweeping titles or subtitles of the conservative literature, such as Glazer's "Limits of Social Policy" or Murray's "Social Policy 1950–1980." But it is the AFDC and the nutritional programs with which these works largely deal. In effect, the propaganda mobilization against the welfare state is based on a strategy of tarring it with the AFDC brush.

Whether the critics intend it or not, singling out AFDC inevitably becomes an attack on minorities. A majority of the women and children on AFDC are blacks and Hispanics; the charges are not so much against "dependent Americans" as against "dependent minority Americans." Race is a deep and fiercely divisive factor in American political culture. The attack on the welfare state reflects this division and draws strength from it. In this sense, the AFDC brush being used to tar the welfare state is indeed black. . . .

One main charge by the critics is that social spending has generated a virtual epidemic of poor families headed by women. The evidence they cite in support of this charge is mainly about black families. By 1983, the proportion of single-parent families among whites had moved up to 12 percent, and that among Hispanics to 23 percent. For blacks, however, the figure was 42 percent. In all of the data describing the range of processes leading to female headship, blacks stood out. In 1980, one-third of all live births among white teenagers were outside marriage, but 85 percent of black births were. Compared to white women, black women have higher rates of separation, and lower rates of remarriage following divorce. Finally, there has been a sharp fall in the rates of marriage among younger black women as compared to younger white women. For all these reasons, families with female heads are becoming predominant among the black poor.

The main case against AFDC is based on the apparent correlation between the growth of black families headed by women and the growth in the AFDC rolls. The rise in this family form is alleged to have occurred in the late 1960s and early 1970s, and it was in those same years that the AFDC rolls rose rapidly. In both 1940 and 1950, the proportion of black families headed by women was 18 percent, and it rose modestly to 22 percent by 1960. But then the proportion shot upward, reaching 28 percent in 1970 and 35 percent in 1975. Consistently, the AFDC rolls in 1960 included only about 750,000 families, and then they too shot upward, reaching 2.5 million in 1970 and 3.5 million in 1975.

To the critics, these parallel trends make for an inescapable conclusion. The expanded availability of AFDC after the mid-1960s caused female-headed families to form on an unprecedented scale by encouraging illegitimacy, separation, and divorce. However, this explanation leaves two large questions unanswered.

First, is it credible to think that the family system of the poor was transformed from a two-parent to a one-parent system in less than a decade? The AFDC rise was extremely precipitous. Between 1960 and the early 1970s, the rolls rose from 750,000 to more than 3 million, and about 75 percent of that increase took place *after* 1965. If AFDC was responsible for the rapid growth in female headship, then it produced that effect in little more than five years, and that is not a reasonable conclusion. More likely, as we will argue, *a large reservoir of poor families headed by women had already formed, and unprecedented numbers of them applied for AFDC in the 1960s because they came to think of welfare as a right.*

Second, if AFDC was responsible for the growth of families with female heads, as the critics charge, why should that effect have been so much greater for blacks than for other groups? This question has not even been raised, much less answered. Just to raise it makes clear that the availability of AFDC did not uniquely affect blacks, although other forces did. *We will maintain that the growth of black single-parent families had been set in motion by a series of social and economic upheavals that did in fact specifically affect blacks, and that these upheavals were under way long before the AFDC rise.*

One of the striking characteristics of the present debate is the extent to which the social and economic antecedents of the rises in *both* black single-parent families and the AFDC rolls have been ignored. The tendency is to treat social spending as if it were the only influence on the lives of the poor. The 1940s and 1950s were years of a mass exodus by blacks from the rural South, and migration has always been associated with the weakening of family life. Moreover, even though the black middle class expanded during these decades, many newly urban blacks were in severe economic straits. Between 1954 and 1964, the national nonwhite unemployment rate ranged between 10 and 13 percent. Subemployment rates, which count the number unemployed for 15 weeks during the year as well as those working at extremely low wages, were first calculated in 1966, and showed a nonwhite rate of 22 percent compared to a white rate of 8 percent. In nine of the major central-city ghettos to which blacks had migrated, the nonwhite subemployment rate averaged 33 percent in 1966. Had this measure been calculated during the recessions of the late 1950s, the rate would have been much higher. Furthermore, black migrants concentrated in urban areas that experienced little or no economic growth in the early 1960s. For example,

New York, Chicago, Philadelphia, Baltimore, Newark, and Los Angeles all showed less employment gain than the national average of 7 percent between 1963 and 1965. New York and Los Angeles showed no gain at all.

The combined impact of migration and these urban economic conditions on family structure was plain enough. Between 1940 and 1965, the rate of live illegitimate births among unmarried black women between the ages of fifteen and forty-four rose from 3.6 to 9.8 percent; for whites, the illegitimacy rates were only 0.4 percent and 1.2 percent in these two years. Furthermore, the ratio of these illegitimate births to all live births also began to rise, although the reasons were complex, such as a rise in the proportion of young people, a falling fertility rate among the married, and a falling rate of marriage. Consequently, between 1940 and 1965 the ratio of illegitimate births to all live births for blacks rose from 17 to 26 percent, but the illegitimacy ratio for whites only moved up from 2 to 4 percent. By 1966, just as the AFDC explosion was about to occur, 42 percent of black families with incomes under $3,000 had come to be headed by females, compared to 23 percent of white families. In other words, by the mid-1960s huge pools of impoverished families headed by women had built up in the cities. *However, the full extent of this buildup was not noticed.*

In earlier decades, it had been common for single mothers and their children to live with their parent or parents in three-generation families with the result that the census undercounted them. Family members were typically described by their relationship to the extended-family head—single mothers were described as daughters, for example. Many single-parent subunits thus remained unidentified, and therefore uncounted. This measurement problem was recognized only recently. As we noted [earlier] when Census coding procedures were changed between 1981 and 1983, *the number of subunits identified actually doubled. . . .*

The AFDC explosion did in fact produce an explosion in the number of families headed by females, but not at all in the sense that it provided incentives for such families to form. What it did instead was to make *visible* hundreds of thousands of families that had previously not been counted because they were subunits of larger families. The liberalization of AFDC in the late 1960s—especially the raising of grant levels in northern states— made it financially possible for these single mothers and their children to establish independent households. And that is exactly what a great many of them did.

It has been estimated that more than one-third of the officially recorded growth of female-headed families between 1940 and 1970 resulted from an increase in independent living arrangements. Recent studies show that this tendency accelerated rapidly in the 1970s. Of black children born into single-parent families during the 1969–1973 period, 60 percent lived in households headed mainly by a grandparent or grandparents, as did 56 percent of white children born into single-parent families; in the 1974–1979 period, however, those proportions fell to 37 percent of black children and 24 percent of white children. And the process is continuing.

Indeed, for all the considerable research that is now available on the question whether AFDC causes changes in family structure—including more illegitimacy, separation, and divorce and less frequent remarriage—AFDC has been shown to have had only one definitive effect. In states with higher benefit levels, AFDC provided female family heads with the resources to live separately from their parent or parents. And once they established independent living arrangements, *the Census identified them,* thus making it appear that the rate of formation of these families was far greater beginning in the late sixties than in earlier periods. In this sense, the expansion of the AFDC rolls created the "facts" that made it possible for critics such as Murray to claim that the black family system in particular had collapsed all of a sudden, and that AFDC was responsible.

To sum up, migration and urban unemployment and subemployment put the black family under intense stress after 1940, and the proportion of single-parent families began to climb. The full extent of this growth was not recorded officially, however, until a pattern of independent living was set in motion by mass protest and the rise in the welfare rolls that followed in the late 1960s. In other words, *single-parent families were much less likely to be counted before the AFDC rolls expanded, and they were much more likely to be counted thereafter.* Consequently, the correlation between the growth of the AFDC rolls and black female headship is spurious; it is an artifact of official recording procedures. . . .

We have yet to discuss what we consider the most serious intellectual constriction that results from ceding the research agenda to the critics. It is the ubiquitous acceptance of the premise that the impact of welfare on work and family patterns ought properly be the main criterion for evaluating the programs. If the availability of welfare benefits reduces work effort among recipients, and if the availability of benefits increases the rate of marital dissolution, then *ipso facto* the programs are to be condemned. With this assumption, the welfare state researchers are unwittingly lending support to a class and gender mobilization that can only worsen welfare state programs and worsen the condition of the poor, especially poor women.

The ideological basis of this premise is deeply rooted: it is the contemporary representation of the nineteenth-century idea that the giving of relief is a violation of natural law. Then and now, natural law did not actually refer to nature, but to a socially constructed system of economic relations called capitalism (and to a socially constructed system of family relations called patriarchy, which we will discuss in a moment). The argument is that welfare programs must not be allowed to interfere in any way with the operations of capitalist markets. The Commissioners who designed the New Poor Law of 1834 captured this understanding of the proper relation of social provision to the market in the principle of "less eligibility," which meant that those who receive relief must always be worse off than the lowest-paid worker.

> The first and most essential of all conditions, a principle which we find universally admitted, even by those whose practice is at variance with it, is, that his [the relief recipient's] situation on the whole shall not be made really or apparently so eligible [desirable] as the situation of the independent laborer of the lowest class.

Undergirding the assumption that social provision must not be allowed to interfere with wage labor—an assumption which, if not "universally admitted," is surely shared by both critics and defenders of the American welfare state—is the deep and long-standing conviction that the "self-regulating" market is and should be the pre-eminent social institution. The market does and must organize society, dictating what government can and should do, and in this sense, it sets the limits of political possibility. The market does and should determine where people live and how their communities ought to be organized, and in this sense, it shapes our collective life. The market does and should mold us as individuals by inculcating the personality traits that lead us to work hard and consume even harder.

The idea that the self-regulating market must necessarily be pre-eminent in political, social, and individual life is capitalism's central myth. In the nineteenth century, this idea was so unquestioned that social commentators treated the inevitable hegemony of the market as a natural law. The myth gained its force, not because it accurately described reality—capitalist markets in fact always depended on state policies, and collective and individual life never was shaped solely by economic forces—but because it captured the broad sweep of the historical process through which the spread of markets smashed traditional economic arrangements fixed by law and custom. In this sense, the myth served in the construction of a new social order, and it served the interests of the bourgeoisie that rose with the new social order.

In reality, of course, modern capitalism has become progressively more deeply and intricately dependent on state policies: for regulating and stabilizing the pace and direction of economic activity, and for providing necessary economic infrastructure; for the conduct of foreign and defense policy on which overseas markets depend; and for the huge military and aerospace contracts that now sustain whole sectors of the economy. All of these policies can be understood as at least partly the result of the political efforts of businessmen to limit their exposure to the instability and insecurity of the self-regulating market. In this large sense, it is capitalists themselves, by their demands for state intervention, who have given the lie to the myth that powered their ascendancy.

The myth of the self-regulating market has outlived the conditions that gave rise to it. Nevertheless, the myth remains part of our cultural repertoire, and is regularly hauled out in political combat over the welfare state. The myth of the self-regulating market thus continues to set the parameters of debate on social welfare programs. Neither the antagonists nor the protagonists in the current debate over welfare state programs challenge the premise of the inviolability of the market. If welfare state programs are defended, it is presumably because they have few or no labor-market effects.

The force of this assumption and the ideological conviction that animates it are suggested by the unthinking use of the term "dependency" to characterize the condition of people who receive welfare benefits. The term is charged with connotations of psychological ineptitude associated with welfare receipt, connotations embroidered by journalistic accounts of the lives of welfare recipients. By contrast, those who work for wages, no matter the kind of work they do, or the conditions under which they work, or the wages they receive, are presumably "independent," with the associated psychological traits of personal discipline and self-reliance. This language and these connotations reflect the myth of the self-regulating market, which depicts the buying and selling of labor as the interplay of free actors, all vigorously pursuing their own advantage on more or less equal terms. But this language and its connotations do not match the reality of participation in the labor market for most people, and they certainly do not match the experience of wage workers at the bottom of the labor market. They do not describe labor-market participation in the fast-food industry, or in retailing, or in office-cleaning companies, or in hospitals. In these jobs, low wages and insecure employment make workers vulnerable and *dependent*—vulnerable to the vagaries of market conditions, and dependent on the whims and interests of particular employers.

If anything, given the realities of the labor market, and especially the nonunion and low-wage sectors of the labor market, it is the availability of welfare benefits that introduces a measure of independence into the circumstances of workers. Knowing they can turn to unemployment benefits or welfare benefits if they are fired probably makes workers a little more secure in their dealings with employers and therefore a little more "independent." The evidence reported earlier . . . suggests that many people do use welfare in just this way. Contrary to the stereotype of a large permanent underclass created by welfare usage, many people move on and off the welfare rolls, and a majority stay on rolls for relatively short periods of less than two years. Moreover, until legislation introduced by the Reagan administration terminated supplementary benefits to women who were working but whose earnings were low, many people used welfare income in combination with other sources of income, primarily wage income. These facts suggest that, rather than miring them in dependency, welfare benefits help people cope with unsettled and difficult life circumstances, including unsettled and difficult employment circumstances. It is not farfetched to say that income-protection programs make many people a little more self-reliant.

Welfare state programs protect people from the vagaries of the labor market and the power of particular employers by providing income that is not conditional on market performance. That is their great accomplishment, for it not only eases the worst poverty but brings a small measure of security into the lives of people who are otherwise very insecure. But that accomplishment has its price. The income supports that reduce insecurity and make people more independent also blunt the force of market incentives and disincentives. After all, desperate people without any protections at all will work at any job, no matter how harsh the terms. This is the heart of what the conflict over the welfare state is about, and it is what conflicts over relief have always been about.

No contrivance of policy can break this tension between the welfare state and the market. To the extent that people are given some economic protection and are not stripped of social respect by the conditions attached to that protection, there must be some work-disincentive effects. More humane programs, which permit people to live in physical decency and do not stigmatize them, will have larger disincentive effects. Of course, these disincentives can always be outweighed by improvements in working conditions. But by the same reasoning, contracting welfare state benefits and making the treatment of beneficiaries more onerous allows employers to degrade working conditions further. Researchers who treat the avoidance of disincentive effects as a policy imperative rule out the possibility of a more humane welfare state, and even lend tacit support to efforts to make existing programs more restrictive. In the process, they smooth the way for further assaults on the conditions of work at the bottom of the American economy.

Discussions of welfare "dependency" and family life are just as much marked by inconsistency. Thus women raising their children by themselves who rely on welfare programs for income are considered dependent, and therefore they and their children are supposedly susceptible to all of the demoralizing consequences associated with "dependency." But women in traditional two-parent households who rely on men for their income are not labeled dependent, or at least no one worries that dependency disables them and makes them incapable of socializing their children adequately for future labor-force participation and marriage. Nor does anyone worry over the effects of dependency on women who rely on alimony or child-support payments or on other "unearned" assets.

In fact, just as the availability of income supports helps people (mainly women) cope with the vagaries of the labor market, so does it reduce the helplessness of women and children in the face of the weakening of the traditional family. Whatever the causes of rising rates of divorce and separation and out-of-wedlock births, these patterns are spreading in all sectors of American society, and indeed in all Western societies. This erosion of the traditional family form makes all women acutely vulnerable economically, including those still living with men and sharing in a family wage. For many women, marital breakup means that after contributing years of unpaid household labor in exchange for a share of the wages earned by men, they and their children confront the threat or the reality of being cut off, in most cases with only negligible alimony or child-support payments, if any at all. The NOW Legal Defense and Education Fund estimates that only one in four of the families with children headed by women receive child-support payments regularly. And as Weitzman documents, in California the average woman's standard of living drops by 73 percent in the first year of divorce, while the average man's improves by 42 percent. At the same time, women confront a labor market in which they are still largely segregated in low-wage occupations, an arrangement justified historically by the idea that women were only secondary earners. Welfare payments provide some security for women and their children in the face of the upheaval in traditional family arrangements. The data show that "family events" are even more important than unemployment in explaining why women turn to AFDC.

The availability of welfare benefits is almost surely not the fundamental cause of changing family patterns, just as welfare benefits are not an important cause of unemployment. Nevertheless, while it is clear that these changes in the family have roots in society-wide changes, it also seems reasonable to surmise that the availability of welfare has some influence on the way women (and the men with whom they are associated) respond to these changes. If income supports reduce the vulnerability of women, then the absence or reduction of such supports might well make them more fearful of the prospect of raising children without men, and more willing therefore to bend to the demands men make. In this sense, access to income independent of the whim or will of male breadwinners is similar in its effects to access to income independent of the whim or will of employers. By providing a measure of security to women and children, the social programs make women a little less vulnerable and a little more independent in the face of a male power that, at least in the short run, actually increases as traditional family norms that previously constrained the behavior of men weaken and the threat of breakup becomes more acute. In other words, it may well be that the availability of welfare weakens the element of economic compulsion in traditional family relations, and in that limited sense may contribute to marital breakup or to the failure of women to marry in the first place. But preserving traditional families by preserving the economic power of men is a policy objective which at the very least demands public scrutiny and discussion.

In sum, very large choices about our institutional life, choices with profound moral consequences, are dictated by the assumption that welfare policies must not be allowed to intrude on the labor market or on the traditional family. These choices have not been examined in the debate over the welfare state. Instead, work and family are treated by all sides as inviolable. But since there is an inherent and ineradicable tension between the welfare state and the unfettered market, and between the welfare state and the patriarchal family, and because these tensions increase as the welfare state is liberalized, the effect of that assumption is to greatly weaken the defense of the welfare state.

Indeed, the only defense that remains possible is to acquiesce in efforts to mold social programs according to the old principle of "less eligibility." Welfare programs are in effect defended only insofar as the circumstances of recipients remain "less eligible" or less desirable than even those of the lowest-paid worker, and less eligible than even the circumstances of women and children in the poorest two-parent family or in the most abusive male-headed households. Consistently, so long as the imperative of work on any terms is assumed, there is no persuasive basis for enjoining against measures to make welfare programs more restrictive, such as the coercive workfare programs that are spreading across the country under the Reagan administration's prodding, except perhaps to argue that these programs have been shown to be ineffective.

Just as the defense of the welfare state is weakened when the primacy of the market and the traditional family are treated as axiomatic, so is the contemplation of more generous and less punitive welfare state programs precluded. Even the imagination of authentic reforms is stifled because a more generous and humane welfare state would almost surely increase work-disincentive and family-disincentive effects. As a consequence, there is little public discussion of raising social welfare benefits to levels that would permit a living standard that does not mire people in poverty and marginalize them from the larger culture. There is little discussion of the consolidation of programs so that people are not shuffled among a rat's maze of different programs designed to specify exactly the various circumstances that do or do not entitle people to benefits, and to precisely what benefits, in a restrictive and work-conforming welfare state. Elaborate and arcane categories such as AFDC, SSI, and UI make it far more difficult for people to understand their entitlements, and also divide people whose circumstances are otherwise similar, thus weakening them as political constituencies. Similarly, so long as the imperatives of market and family are assumed, there can be no thought of the possibility of simplifying eligibility criteria so that people can effectively exercise *rights* in dealing with welfare state bureaucracies. And we cannot even imagine the possibilities for innovative forms of social provision that might encourage the development of a sense of community, a spirit of democracy, and an appreciation of diversity within the terrain of the welfare state. All of these possibilities are categorically eliminated by the assumption that the market and the traditional family must at all costs remain pre-eminent.

In other words, so long as work and family are assumed to be inviolable, the central moral choices that we as a society in fact make through our welfare policies remain concealed, the options defined away by ideological fiat. These choices are enormous in their scope. They include the relative power we think workers and employers should have in labor market relations, and husbands and wives in family relations. Our welfare policies also bear directly on the question whether the work women do in rearing children and caring for families is to be regarded as a legitimate contribution to our society. Current policies that are contorted by mechanisms intended to force mothers into the labor market obviously deny that contribution. Welfare policies are also choices through which we create and recreate the culture of class and race in our society, both through the impoverishment and ritual degradation of recipients and as a result of the material and social crippling of the children who will be tomorrow's adult poor. These policies are also choices about the question, so profoundly important to us collectively, of how much we want to tolerate the widespread insecurities and inequalities considered necessary for the optimal functioning of labor markets. And the scale and organization of our welfare state programs also bears importantly on the great classical question of the appropriate relationship of government, markets, and families. These are all moral choices of profound importance, and they ought not to be buried in the unthinking assumption that wage work and the traditional family must be considered sacred, no matter the costs.

Finally, these moral dilemmas have become more acute, and the political stakes in how they are resolved have grown, as a result of the major transformations occurring in the American economy and family. By invoking the myth of the pre-eminence of the market during a period of economic transition and uncertainty, the vulnerability of people at the bottom is increased. In the name of "natural law" we take sides in the contemporary class conflict whose repercussions could be awesome. The current efforts of employers to reduce wages and increase work discipline are in part a response to economic instability, and particularly to heightened international competition and sagging profits. But the conditions that prompted this employer mobilization to force working people to absorb the costs of a restructured economic order have also become a weapon in the campaign. The threat of disinvestment or offshore production or roboticization is regularly used to beat down worker demands, for increased economic flux makes working people more fearful and quicker to concede to employer demands. Similarly, increased family instability makes women more fearful, and therefore heightens the power of men. It is because the protections provided by the welfare state bear on the power relations of the market and the traditional family that these policies have come under attack. But that is also the reason that the conflict over the welfare state is a conflict about the future shape of American society.

⋙ F U R T H E R   R E A D I N G

Henry J. Aaron, *Politics and the Professors: The Great Society in Perspective* (1978)

Martin Anderson, *Welfare: The Political Economy of Welfare Reform in the United States* (1978)

Ken Auletta, *The Underclass* (1982)

June Axinn and Mark J. Stern, *Dependency and Poverty: Old Problems in a New World* (1988)

Richard D. Bingham et al., *The Homeless in Contemporary Society* (1987)

Fred Block et al., *The Mean Season: The Attack on the Welfare State* (1987)

Vincent J. Burke and Lee Burke, *Nixon's Good Deed: Welfare Reform* (1974)

Committee on Health Care for Homeless People (CHCHP), *Homelessness, Health, and Human Needs* (1988)

Sheldon H. Danziger and Daniel H. Weinberger, eds., *Fighting Poverty* (1986)

Greg Duncan, *Years of Poverty, Years of Plenty* (1984)

Marian Wright Edelman, *Families in Peril: An Agenda for Social Change* (1987)

David T. Ellwood, *Poor Support: Poverty in the American Family* (1988)

John Erickson and Charles Wilhelm, eds., *Housing the Homeless* (1986)

Marvin E. Gettleman and David Mermelstein, eds., *The Great Society Reader: The Failure of American Liberalism* (1967)

George Gilder, *Wealth and Poverty* (1981)

Eli Ginzberg and Robert M. Solow, eds., *The Great Society* (1974)

Douglas G. Glasgow, *The Black Underclass: Poverty, Unemployment, and Entrapment of Ghetto Youth* (1980)

Eric Goldman, *The Tragedy of Lyndon Johnson* (1968)

Amy Gutman, ed., *Democracy and the Welfare State* (1988)

Michael Harrington, *The New American Poverty* (1984)

——, *The Other America* (1962)

Robert H. Haveman, *Poverty Policy and Poverty Research: The Great Society and the Social Sciences* (1987)

Jim F. Heath, *Decade of Disillusionment* (1976)

Barbara C. Jordan and Elspeth D. Rostow, eds., *The Great Society: A Twenty Year Critique* (1986)

Michael B. Katz, *In the Shadow of the Poorhouse* (1986)

——, *The Undeserving Poor: From the War on Poverty to the War on Welfare* (1989)

Doris Kearns, *Lyndon Johnson and the American Dream* (1976)

Daniel Knapp and Kenneth Polk, *Scouting the War on Poverty* (1971)

Robert Kuttner, *The Economic Illusion: The False Choice Between Prosperity and Social Justice* (1984)

Sar Levitan, *The Great Society's Poor Law: A New Approach to Poverty* (1969)

—— and Isaac Shapiro, *Working But Poor: America's Contradiction* (1987)

—— and Robert Taggert, *The Promise of Greatness* (1976)

Frank Levy, *Dollars and Dreams: The Changing American Income Distribution* (1987)

Michael G. H. McGeary and Laurence E. Lynn, eds., *Urban Change and Poverty* (1988)

Allen Matusow, *The Unraveling of America: A History of Liberalism in the 1960s* (1984)

Lawrence M. Meade, *Beyond Entitlement: The Social Obligations of Citizenship* (1986)

Ramesh Mishra, *The Welfare State in Crisis: Social Thought and Social Change* (1984)

J. Donald Moon, ed., *Responsibility, Rights and Welfare: The Theory of the Welfare State* (1988)

Daniel P. Moynihan, *Maximum Feasible Misunderstanding* (1969)

——, *Family and Nation* (1986)

Charles Murray, *Losing Ground: American Social Policy, 1950–1980* (1984)

National Conference of Catholic Bishops, *Economic Justice for All* (1986)

James T. Patterson, *America's Struggle Against Poverty* (1981)

Paul Peterson, ed., *The New Urban Reality* (1985)

Frances Fox Piven and Richard A. Cloward, *Regulating the Poor: The Functions of Public Welfare* (1971)

——, *The New Class War: Reagan's Attack on the Welfare State and Its Consequences* (1982)

Harell R. Rodgers, Jr., *Poor Women, Poor Families: The Economic Plight of America's Female-Headed Households* (1986)

William P. Ryan, *Equality* (1982)

John E. Schwarz, *America's Hidden Success: A Reassessment of Twenty Years of Public Policy* (1983)

James L. Sundquist, *Politics and Policy: The Eisenhower, Kennedy, and Johnson Years* (1968)

David C. Warner, ed., *Toward New Human Rights: The Social Policies of the Kennedy and Johnson Administrations* (1977)

William Julius Wilson, *The Truly Disadvantaged: The Inner City, the Underclass, and Public Policy* (1987)

David Zarefsky, *President Johnson's War on Poverty: Rhetoric and History* (1986)

Martin Luther King, Jr., and the Struggle for African-American Equality

XX

As historian William Chafe suggests in his essay beginning on p. 384, the drive for freedom and equality by African-Americans was one of the most important developments in postwar America. The struggle played out not only in the courts and in the halls of Congress but in the streets, in churches, and at lunchroom counters throughout the nation. It was a struggle not just of individual leaders, however charismatic, but of ordinary men and women who found the courage and dignity to demand change. The changes they demanded, as the following documents and essays suggest, raise questions, many of them yet unresolved, that go to the heart of the American experience. For example, what do Americans mean when they profess to believe in equality? Do we believe in equality of condition or only in equality of opportunity? How has race (or gender or class) limited the application of such beliefs? What actions are appropriate for government and other institutions to take in the pursuit of equality, and which are inappropriate?

XX *D O C U M E N T S*

World War II marked a watershed in the history of civil rights as many African-Americans served in the armed forces, albeit in segregated units; as other blacks found work in defense plants; and as wartime rhetoric about freedom and democracy raised expectations of expanded civil rights. Most important, African-Americans themselves displayed a new confidence and determination. The return of African-American soldiers was nevertheless greeted by violence in parts of the South, as a *New York Times* report of February 27, 1946, reprinted as the first selection, reveals. At the core of the struggle for equality were issues of pride and self-esteem. In the second document, an excerpt from *The Autobiography of*

Malcolm X, the radical Muslim activist Malcolm recalls the painful process of "conking" his hair to make it look like a white man's. In the third document, Chief Justice Earl Warren delivers the Supreme Court's unanimous opinion in the historic case of *Brown* v. *the Board of Education of Topeka, Kansas,* which declared separate educational facilities to be inherently unequal.

Beginning with the Montgomery bus boycott of 1955–1956, the history of the civil-rights movement was increasingly shaped by courageous men and women who directly challenged the Jim Crow system of segregation and discrimination. In the fourth selection, an interview with reporter Howell Raines, participant Franklin McCain recalls the first sit-in of the 1960s. Only twenty-six years old when he helped lead the Montgomery boycott, Martin Luther King, Jr., quickly became the movement's most charismatic leader. His address before the Lincoln Memorial during the March on Washington in August 1963 (the fifth document) is one of the most famous speeches in American history. By the mid-1960s, however, King's leadership was increasingly challenged by younger, more radical activists such as Stokely Carmichael, a leader of the Student Non-violent Coordinating Committee (SNCC), who in the sixth document defends the new call for "black power." Resistance to the civil-rights movement occurred not just in the South, where beatings and even murder were not infrequent, but throughout the nation, including even federal law enforcement agencies such as the Federal Bureau of Investigation, which carried out an elaborate secret campaign to discredit King. The seventh document is excerpted from a 1976 investigation of the FBI by a U.S. Senate Committee chaired by Democratic senator Frank Church of Idaho.

As the focus of the struggle for equality shifted from the South to the North and from civil rights to economic justice, the level of anger and frustration steadily mounted, exploding in the mid-1960s in a series of riots that convulsed almost every major city in the United States. The eighth document, reprinted from the *Milwaukee Journal,* logs the reports by police and fire fighters in Milwaukee, Wisconsin, during a riot that erupted late at night on July 30, 1967.

The *New York Times* Records a Murder in Georgia, 1946

Monroe, Ga., July 26—Two young Negroes, one a veteran just returned from the war, and their wives were lined up last night near a secluded road and shot dead by an unmasked band of twenty white men.

The ghastly details of the multiple lynching were told today by Loy Harrison, a well-to-do white farmer who had just hired the Negroes to work on his farm. Harrison was bringing the Negroes to his farm when his car was waylaid by the mob eight miles from Monroe. Questioning of one of the Negroes by the mob indicated, Harrison said, that he was suspected of having stabbed his former employer, a white man. The Negroes, Roger Malcolm and George Dorsey, both 27, were removed from the car and led down a side road.

The women, who were sisters and who had just recently married Malcolm and Dorsey, began to scream. Then a mob member said that one of the women had recognized him.

"Get those damned women, too," the mob leader shouted.

Several of the men then came back and dragged the shrieking women from the automobile. A few moments later Mr. Harrison heard the shots— many of them and the mob dispersed.

The grotesquely sprawled bodies were found in a clump of bushes beside a little-used sideroad, the upper parts of the bodies scarcely recognizable from the mass of bullet holes.

Dorsey's mother, Monia Williams, said that her son had just been discharged after five years in the Army and that she had received his discharge button in the mail just this week.

The lynching was the first in the nation in nearly a year and was the first multiple lynching since two 14-year-old Negro boys were hanged by a Mississippi mob in October, 1942. For Georgia it was the first lynching of more than one person since 1918 when ten Negroes were lynched in Brooks County.

Malcolm X Recalls Getting a "Conk," 1964

Shorty soon decided that my hair was finally long enough to be conked. He had promised to school me in how to beat the barbershops' three- and four-dollar price by making up congolene, and then conking ourselves.

I took the little list of ingredients he had printed out for me, and went to a grocery store, where I got a can of Red Devil lye, two eggs, and two medium-sized white potatoes. Then at the drugstore near the poolroom, I asked for a large jar of vaseline, a large bar of soap, a large-toothed comb and a fine-toothed comb, one of those rubber hoses with a metal spray-head, a rubber apron and a pair of gloves.

"Going to lay on that first conk?" the drugstore man asked me. I proudly told him, grinning, "Right!"

Shorty paid six dollars a week for a room in his cousin's shabby apartment. His cousin wasn't at home. "It's like the pad's mine, he spends so much time with his woman," Shorty said. "Now, you watch me—"

He peeled the potatoes and thin-sliced them into a quart-sized Mason fruit jar, then started stirring them with a wooden spoon as he gradually poured in a little over half the can of lye. "Never use a metal spoon; the lye will turn it black," he told me.

A jelly-like, starchy-looking glop resulted from the lye and potatoes, and Shorty broke in the two eggs, stirring real fast—his own conk and dark face bent down close. The congolene turned pale-yellowish. "Feel the jar," Shorty said. I cupped my hand against the outside, and snatched it away. "Damn right, it's hot, that's the lye," he said. "So you know it's going to burn when I comb it in—it burns *bad*. But the longer you can stand it, the straighter the hair."

He made me sit down, and he tied the string of the new rubber apron tightly around my neck, and combed up my bush of hair. Then, from the

The Autobiography of Malcolm X (1964; Grove Paperback Edition, 1966), pp. 52–55.

big vaseline jar, he took a handful and massaged it hard all through my hair and into the scalp. He also thickly vaselined my neck, ears and forehead. "When I get to washing out your head, be sure to tell me anywhere you feel any little stinging," Shorty warned me, washing his hands, then pulling on the rubber gloves, and tying on his own rubber apron. "You always got to remember that any congolene left in burns a sore into your head."

The congolene just felt warm when Shorty started combing it in. But then my head caught fire.

I gritted my teeth and tried to pull the sides of the kitchen table together. The comb felt as if it was raking my skin off.

My eyes watered, my nose was running. I couldn't stand it any longer; I bolted to the washbasin. I was cursing Shorty with every name I could think of when he got the spray going and started soap-lathering my head.

He lathered and spray-rinsed, lathered and spray-rinsed, maybe ten or twelve times, each time gradually closing the hot-water faucet, until the rinse was cold, and that helped some.

"You feel any stinging spots?"

"No," I managed to say. My knees were trembling.

"Sit back down, then. I think we got it all out okay."

The flame came back as Shorty, with a thick towel, started drying my head, rubbing hard. *"Easy, man, easy!"* I kept shouting.

"The first time's always worst. You get used to it better before long. You took it real good, homeboy. You got a good conk."

When Shorty let me stand up and see in the mirror, my hair hung down in limp, damp strings. My scalp still flamed, but not as badly; I could bear it. He draped the towel around my shoulders, over my rubber apron, and began again vaselining my hair.

I could feel him combing, straight back, first the big comb, then the fine-tooth one.

Then, he was using a razor, very delicately, on the back of my neck. Then, finally, shaping the sideburns.

My first view in the mirror blotted out the hurting. I'd seen some pretty conks, but when it's the first time, on your *own* head, the transformation, after the lifetime of kinks, is staggering.

The mirror reflected Shorty behind me. We both were grinning and sweating. And on top of my head was this thick, smooth sheen of shining red hair—real red—as straight as any white man's.

Brown v. Board of Education, 1954

These cases come to us from the States of Kansas, South Carolina, Virginia, and Delaware. They are premised on different facts and different local conditions, but a common legal question justifies their consideration together in this consolidated opinion.

In each of the cases, minors of the Negro race, through their legal representatives, seek the aid of the courts in obtaining admission to the public schools of their community on a nonsegregated basis. In each instance, they had been denied admission to schools attended by white children under laws requiring or permitting segregation according to race. This segregation was alleged to deprive the plaintiffs of the equal protection of the laws under the Fourteenth Amendment. In each of the cases other than the Delaware case, a three-judge federal district court denied relief to the plaintiffs on the so-called "separate but equal" doctrine announced by this Court in *Plessy* v. *Ferguson*, 163 U.S. 537. Under that doctrine, equality of treatment is accorded when the races are provided substantially equal facilities, even though these facilities be separate. . . .

The plaintiffs contend that segregated public schools are not "equal" and cannot be made "equal," and that hence they are deprived of the equal protection of the laws. . . .

In approaching this problem, we cannot turn the clock back to 1868 when the Amendment was adopted, or even to 1896 when *Plessy* v. *Ferguson* was written. We must consider public education in the light of its full development and its present place in American life throughout the Nation. Only in this way can it be determined if segregation in public schools deprives these plaintiffs of the equal protection of the laws.

Today, education is perhaps the most important function of state and local governments. Compulsory school attendance laws and the great expenditures for education both demonstrate our recognition of the importance of education to our democratic society. It is required in the performance of our most basic public responsibilities, even service in the armed forces. It is the very foundation of good citizenship. Today it is a principal instrument in awakening the child to cultural values, in preparing him for later professional training, and in helping him to adjust normally to his environment. In these days, it is doubtful that any child may reasonably be expected to succeed in life if he is denied the opportunity of an education. Such an opportunity, when the state has undertaken to provide it, is a right which must be made available to all on equal terms.

We come then to the question presented: Does segregation of children in public schools solely on the basis of race, even though the physical facilities and other "tangible" factors may be equal, deprive the children of the minority group of equal educational opportunities? We believe that it does.

In *Sweatt* v. *Painter, supra,* in finding that a segregated law school for Negroes could not provide them equal educational opportunities, this Court relied in large part on "those qualities which are incapable of objective measurement but which make for greatness in a law school." In *McLaurin* v. *Oklahoma State Regents, supra,* the Court, in requiring that a Negro admitted to a white graduate school be treated like all other students, again resorted to intangible considerations: ". . . his ability to study, to engage in discussions and exchange views with other students, and in general, to learn his profession." Such considerations apply with added force to children in grade and high schools. To separate them from others of similar age and qualifications solely because of their race generates a feeling of inferiority as to their status in the community that may affect their hearts and minds in a way unlikely ever to be undone. The effect of this separation on their educational opportunities was well stated by a finding in the Kansas case by a court which nevertheless felt compelled to rule against the Negro plaintiffs:

> "Segregation of white and colored children in public schools has a detrimental effect upon the colored children. The impact is greater when it has the sanction of the law; for the policy of separating the races is usually interpreted as denoting the inferiority of the negro group. A sense of inferiority affects the motivation of a child to learn. Segregation with the sanction of law, therefore, has a tendency to [retard] the educational and mental development of negro children and to deprive them of some of the benefits they would receive in a racial[ly] integrated school system."

Whatever may have been the extent of psychological knowledge at the time of *Plessy* v. *Ferguson,* this finding is amply supported by modern authority. Any language in *Plessy* v. *Ferguson* contrary to this finding is rejected.

We conclude that in the field of public education the doctrine of "separate but equal" has no place. Separate educational facilities are inherently unequal. Therefore, we hold that the plaintiffs and others similarly situated for whom the actions have been brought are, by reason of the segregation complained of, deprived of the equal protection of the laws guaranteed by the Fourteenth Amendment.

Franklin McCain Remembers the First Sit-ins, 1960

[Howell Raines:] It was one of those group friendships that spring up among college freshmen. In their first semester at all-black North Carolina A&T College in Greensboro, he [Franklin McCain] and Ezell Blair, Jr., David Richmond, and Joseph McNeil became inseparable. They would study together, eat together, and "as young freshmen often do in college dormitories late at night, when they finish studying or when they want to cop out from studying . . . resort to the old-fashion type bull session."

Through the fall, their talks continued. He remembers them as "elementary philosophers," young idealists talking about justice and injustice, hypocrisy, how imperfectly their society embodied its own ideals. Slowly their talks swung to a debate as old as philosophy itself: at what point does the moral man act against injustice? ". . . I think the thing that precipitated the sit-in, the idea of the sit-in, more than anything else, was that little bit of incentive and that little bit of courage that each of us instilled within each other."

[McCain:] The planning process was on a Sunday night, I remember it quite well. I think it was Joseph who said, "It's time that we take some action now. We've been getting together, and we've been, up to this point, still like most people we've talked about for the past few weeks or so—that is, people who talk a lot but, in fact, make very little action." After selecting the technique, then we said, "Let's go down and just ask for service." It certainly wasn't titled a "sit-in" or "sit-down" at that time. "Let's just go down to Woolworth's tomorrow and ask for service, and the tactic is going to be simply this: we'll just stay there." We never anticipated being served, certainly, the first day anyway. "We'll stay until we get served." And I think Ezell said, "Well, you know that might be weeks, that might be months, that might be never." And I think it was the consensus of the group, we said, "Well, that's just the chance we'll have to take."

What's likely to happen? Now, I think that that was a question that all of us asked ourselves. . . . What's going to happen once we sit down? Of course, nobody had the answers. Even your wildest imagination couldn't lead you to believe what would, in fact, happen.

[Raines:] Why Woolworth's?

[McCain:] They advertise in public media, newspapers, radios, television, that sort of thing. They tell you to come in: "Yes, buy the toothpaste; yes, come in and buy the notebook paper. . . . No, we don't separate your money in this cash register; but, no, please don't step down to the hot dog stand. . . ." The whole system, of course, was unjust, but that just seemed like insult added to injury. That was just like pouring salt into an open wound. That's inviting you to do something. . . .

Once getting there . . . we did make purchases of school supplies and took the patience and time to get receipts for our purchases, and Joseph and myself went over to the counter and asked to be served coffee and doughnuts. As anticipated, the reply was "I'm sorry, we don't serve you here." And of course we said, "We just beg to disagree with you. We've in fact already been served; you've served us already and that's just not quite true." The attendant or waitress was a little bit dumbfounded, just didn't know what to say under circumstances like that. And we said, "We wonder why you'd invite us in to serve us at one counter and deny service at another. If this is a private club or private concern, then we believe you ought to sell membership cards and sell only to persons who have a membership card. If we don't have a card, then we'd know pretty well that we shouldn't come in or even attempt to come in." That didn't go over too well, simply because I don't really think she understood what we were talking about, and for the second reason, she had no logical response to a statement like that. And the only thing that an individual in her case or position could do is, of course, call the manager. [Laughs] Well, at this time, I think we were joined by Dave Richmond and Ezell Blair at the counter with us, after that dialogue.

[Raines:] Were you afraid at this point?

[McCain:] Oh, hell yes, no question about that. [Laughs] At that point there was a policeman who had walked in off the street, who was pacing the aisle . . . behind us, where we were seated, with his club in his hand, just sort of knocking it in his hand, and just looking mean and red and a little bit upset and a little bit disgusted. And you had the feeling that he didn't know what the hell to do. You had the feeling that this is the first time that this big bad man with the gun and the club has been pushed in a corner, and he's got absolutely no defense, and the thing that's killing him more than anything else—he doesn't know what he can or what he cannot do. He's defenseless. Usually his defense is offense, and we've provoked him, yes, but we haven't provoked him outwardly enough for him to resort to violence. And I think this is just killing him; you can see it all over him.

People in the store were—we got mixed reactions from people in the store. A couple of old ladies . . . came up to pat us on the back sort of and say, "Ah, you should have done it ten years ago. It's a good thing I think you're doing."

[Raines:] These were black ladies.

[McCain:] No, these are white ladies.

[Raines:] Really?

[McCain:] Yes, and by the same token, we had some white ladies and white men come up and say to us, "Nasty, dirty niggers, you know you don't belong here at the lunch counter. There's a counter—" There was, in fact, a counter downstairs in the Woolworth store, a stand-up type counter where they sold hot dogs. . . .

[Raines:] But at any rate, there were expressions of support from white people that day?

[McCain:] Absolutely right. Absolutely. And I think probably that was certainly one incentive for additional courage on the part of us. And the other thing that helped us psychologically quite a lot was seeing the policeman pace the aisle and not be able to do anything. I think that this probably gave us more strength, more encouragement, than anything else on that particular day, on day one.

[Raines:] Unexpected as it was, the well-wishing from the elderly white women was hardly more surprising than the scorn of a middle-aged black dishwasher behind the counter. She said, "That's why we can't get anyplace today, because of people like you, rabble-rousers, troublemakers. . . . this counter is reserved for white people, it always has been, and you are all aware of that. So why don't you go on out and stop making trouble?"

He has since seen the woman at, of all places, a reunion commemorating the event in which she played so unsupportive a role.

[McCain:] [She said] "Yes, I did say it and I said it because, first of all, I was afraid for what would happen to you as young black boys. Secondly, I was afraid of what would happen to me as an individual who had a job at the Woolworth store. I might have been fired and that's my livelihood. . . ."

It took me a long time to really understand that statement . . . but I know why she said it. She said it out of fear more than anything else. I've come to understand that, and my elders say to me that it's maturity that makes me understand why she said that some fifteen years ago.

[Raines:] But, moved by neither praise nor scorn, he and the others waited for the waitress to return with the manager, a career Woolworth's employee named C. L. Harris.

[McCain:] That was real amusin' as well [laughing] because by then we had the confidence, my goodness, of a Mack truck. And there was virtually nothing that could move us, there was virtually nothing probably at that point that could really frighten us off. . . . If it's possible to know what it means to have your soul cleansed—I felt pretty clean at that time. I probably felt better on that day than I've ever felt in my life. Seems like a lot of feelings of guilt or what-have-you suddenly left me, and I felt as though I had gained my manhood, so to speak, and not only gained it, but had developed quite a lot of respect for it. Not Franklin McCain only as an individual, but I felt as though the manhood of a number of other black persons had been restored and had gotten some respect from just that one day.

Martin Luther King, Jr., "I Have a Dream," 1963

I am happy to join with you today in what will go down in history as the greatest demonstration for freedom in the history of our nation.

Fivescore years ago, a great American, in whose symbolic shadow we stand today, signed the Emancipation Proclamation. This momentous decree came as a great beacon light of hope to millions of Negro slaves who had been seared in the flames of withering injustice. It came as a joyous daybreak to end the long night of their captivity.

But one hundred years later, the Negro still is not free; one hundred years later, the life of the Negro is still sadly crippled by the manacles of segregation and the chains of discrimination; one hundred years later, the Negro lives on a lonely island of poverty in the midst of a vast ocean of material prosperity; one hundred years later, the Negro is still languished in the corners of American society and finds himself in exile in his own land.

So we've come here today to dramatize a shameful condition. In a sense we've come to our nation's capital to cash a check. When the architects of our republic wrote the magnificent words of the Constitution and the Declaration of Independence, they were signing a promissory note to which every American was to fall heir. This note was the promise that all men, yes, black men as well as white men, would be guaranteed the unalienable rights of life, liberty, and the pursuit of happiness.

It is obvious today that America has defaulted on this promissory note in so far as her citizens of color are concerned. Instead of honoring this sacred obligation, America has given the Negro people a bad check; a check which has come back marked "insufficient funds." We refuse to believe that there are insufficient funds in the great vaults of opportunity of this nation. And so we've come to cash this check, a check that will give us upon demand the riches of freedom and the security of justice.

We have also come to this hallowed spot to remind America of the fierce urgency of now. This is no time to engage in the luxury of cooling off or to take the tranquilizing drug of gradualism. Now is the time to make real the promises of democracy; now is the time to rise from the dark and desolate valley of segregation to the sunlit path of racial justice; now is the

Dr. Martin Luther King, Jr., "I Have a Dream" from James Melvin Washington, ed., *A Testament of Hope: The Essential Writings of Martin Luther King, Jr.,* pp. 217–220. Copyright © 1963 by Martin Luther King, Jr. Reprinted by permission of Joan Daves Agency.

time to lift our nation from the quicksands of racial injustice to the solid rock of brotherhood; now is the time to make justice a reality for all God's children. It would be fatal for the nation to overlook the urgency of the moment. This sweltering summer of the Negro's legitimate discontent will not pass until there is an invigorating autumn of freedom and equality.

Nineteen sixty-three is not an end, but a beginning. And those who hope that the Negro needed to blow off steam and will now be content, will have a rude awakening if the nation returns to business as usual.

There will be neither rest nor tranquility in America until the Negro is granted his citizenship rights. The whirlwinds of revolt will continue to shake the foundations of our nation until the bright day of justice emerges.

But there is something that I must say to my people who stand on the warm threshold which leads into the palace of justice. In the process of gaining our rightful place we must not be guilty of wrongful deeds.

Let us not seek to satisfy our thirst for freedom by drinking from the cup of bitterness and hatred. We must forever conduct our struggle on the high plane of dignity and discipline. We must not allow our creative protest to degenerate into physical violence. Again and again we must rise to the majestic heights of meeting physical force with soul force.

The marvelous new militancy which has engulfed the Negro community must not lead us to a distrust of all white people, for many of our white brothers, as evidenced by their presence here today, have come to realize that their destiny is tied up with our destiny and they have come to realize that their freedom is inextricably bound to our freedom. This offense we share mounted to storm the battlements of injustice must be carried forth by a biracial army. We cannot walk alone.

And as we walk, we must make the pledge that we shall always march ahead. We cannot turn back. There are those who are asking the devotees of civil rights, "When will you be satisfied?" We can never be satisfied as long as the Negro is the victim of the unspeakable horrors of police brutality.

We can never be satisfied as long as our bodies, heavy with fatigue of travel, cannot gain lodging in the motels of the highways and the hotels of the cities. We cannot be satisfied as long as the Negro's basic mobility is from a smaller ghetto to a larger one.

We can never be satisfied as long as our children are stripped of their selfhood and robbed of their dignity by signs stating "for whites only." We cannot be satisfied as long as a Negro in Mississippi cannot vote and a Negro in New York believes he has nothing for which to vote. No, we are not satisfied, and we will not be satisfied until justice rolls down like waters and righteousness like a mighty stream.

I am not unmindful that some of you have come here out of excessive trials and tribulation. Some of you have come fresh from narrow jail cells. Some of you have come from areas where your quest for freedom left you battered by the storms of persecution and staggered by the winds of police brutality. You have been the veterans of creative suffering. Continue to work with the faith that unearned suffering is redemptive.

Go back to Mississippi; go back to Alabama; go back to South Carolina;

go back to Georgia; go back to Louisiana; go back to the slums and ghettos of the northern cities, knowing that somehow this situation can, and will be changed. Let us not wallow in the valley of despair.

So I say to you, my friends, that even though we must face the difficulties of today and tomorrow, I still have a dream. It is a dream deeply rooted in the American dream that one day this nation will rise up and live out the true meaning of its creed—we hold these truths to be self-evident, that all men are created equal.

I have a dream that one day on the red hills of Georgia, sons of former slaves and sons of former slave-owners will be able to sit down together at the table of brotherhood.

I have a dream that one day, even the state of Mississippi, a state sweltering with the heat of injustice, sweltering with the heat of oppression, will be transformed into an oasis of freedom and justice.

I have a dream my four little children will one day live in a nation where they will not be judged by the color of their skin but by content of their character. I have a dream today!

I have a dream that one day, down in Alabama, with its vicious racists, with its governor having his lips dripping with the words of interposition and nullification, that one day, right there in Alabama, little black boys and black girls will be able to join hands with little white boys and white girls as sisters and brothers. I have a dream today!

I have a dream that one day every valley shall be exalted, every hill and mountain shall be made low, the rough places shall be made plain, and the crooked places shall be made straight and the glory of the Lord will be revealed and all flesh shall see it together.

This is our hope. This is the faith that I go back to the South with.

With this faith we will be able to hear out of the mountain of despair a stone of hope. With this faith we will be able to transform the jangling discords of our nation into a beautiful symphony of brotherhood.

With this faith we will be able to work together, to pray together, to struggle together, to go to jail together, to stand up for freedom together, knowing that we will be free one day. This will be the day when all of God's children will be able to sing with new meaning—"my country 'tis of thee; sweet land of liberty; of thee I sing; land where my fathers died, land of the pilgrim's pride; from every mountain side, let freedom ring"—and if America is to be a great nation, this must become true.

So let freedom ring from the prodigious hilltops of New Hampshire.

Let freedom ring from the mighty mountains of New York.

Let freedom ring from the heightening Alleghenies of Pennsylvania.

Let freedom ring from the snow-capped Rockies of Colorado.

Let freedom ring from the curvaceous slopes of California.

But not only that.

Let freedom ring from Stone Mountain of Georgia.

Let freedom ring from Lookout Mountain of Tennessee.

Let freedom ring from every hill and molehill of Mississippi, from every mountainside, let freedom ring.

And when we allow freedom to ring, when we let it ring from every village and hamlet, from every state and city, we will be able to speed up that day when all of God's children—black men and white men, Jews and Gentiles, Catholics and Protestants—will be able to join hands and to sing in the words of the old Negro spiritual, "Free at last, free at last; thank God Almighty, we are free at last."

Stokely Carmichael Explains "Black Power," 1967

One of the tragedies of the struggle against racism is that up to now there has been no national organization which could speak to the growing militancy of young black people in the urban ghetto. There has been only a civil rights movement, whose tone of voice was adapted to an audience of liberal whites. It served as a sort of buffer zone between them and angry young blacks. None of its so-called leaders could go into a rioting community and be listened to. In a sense, I blame ourselves—together with the mass media— for what has happened in Watts, Harlem, Chicago, Cleveland, Omaha. Each time the people in those cities saw Martin Luther King get slapped, they became angry; when they saw four little black girls bombed to death, they were angrier; and when nothing happened, they were steaming. We had nothing to offer that they could see, except to go out and be beaten again. We helped to build their frustration.

For too many years, black Americans marched and had their heads broken and got shot. They were saying to the country, "Look, you guys are supposed to be nice guys and we are only going to do what we are supposed to do—why do you beat us up, why don't you give us what we ask, why don't you straighten yourselves out?" After years of this, we are at almost the same point—because we demonstrated from a position of weakness. We cannot be expected any longer to march and have our heads broken in order to say to whites: come on, you're nice guys. For you are not nice guys. We have found you out.

An organization which claims to speak for the needs of a community— as does the Student Nonviolent Coordinating Committee—must speak in the tone of that community, not as somebody else's buffer zone. This is the significance of black power as a slogan. For once, black people are going to use the words they want to use—not just the words whites want to hear. And they will do this no matter how often the press tries to stop the use of the slogan by equating it with racism or separatism.

An organization which claims to be working for the needs of a community—as SNCC does—must work to provide that community with a position of strength from which to make its voice heard. This is the significance of black power beyond the slogan.

Black power can be clearly defined for those who do not attach the fears of white America to their questions about it. We should begin with the basic

"What We Want" by Stokely Carmichael explaining "Black Power" from *The New York Review of Books,* Vol. 7 (September 22, 1966), pp. 5–6, 8. Reprinted by permission of Kwame Ture (Stokely Carmichael).

fact that black Americans have two problems: they are poor and they are black. All other problems arise from this two-sided reality: lack of education, the so-called apathy of black men. Any program to end racism must address itself to that double reality.

Almost from its beginning, SNCC sought to address itself to both conditions with a program aimed at winning political power for impoverished Southern blacks. We had to begin with politics because black Americans are a propertyless people in a country where property is valued above all. We had to work for power, because this country does not function by morality, love, and nonviolence, but by power. Thus we determined to win political power, with the idea of moving on from there into activity that would have economic effects. With power, the masses could *make or participate in making* the decisions which govern their destinies, and thus create basic change in their day-to-day lives.

But if political power seemed to be the key to self-determination, it was also obvious that the key had been thrown down a deep well many years earlier. Disenfranchisement, maintained by racist terror, made it impossible to talk about organizing for political power in 1960. The right to vote had to be won, and SNCC workers devoted their energies to this from 1961 to 1965. They set up voter registration drives in the Deep South. They created pressure for the vote by holding mock elections in Mississippi in 1963 and by helping to establish the Mississippi Freedom Democratic Party (MFDP) in 1964. That struggle was eased, though not won, with the passage of the 1965 Voting Rights Act. SNCC workers could then address themselves to the question: "Who can we vote for, to have our needs met—how do we make our vote meaningful? . . ."

SNCC today is working in both North and South on programs of voter registration and independent political organizing. In some places, such as Alabama, Los Angeles, New York, Philadelphia, and New Jersey, independent organizing under the black panther symbol is in progress. The creation of a national "black panther party" must come about; it will take time to build, and it is much too early to predict its success. We have no infallible master plan and we make no claim to exclusive knowledge of how to end racism; different groups will work in their own different ways. SNCC cannot spell out the full logistics of self-determination but it can address itself to the problem by helping black communities define their needs, realize their strength, and go into action along a variety of lines which they must choose for themselves. Without knowing all the answers, It can address itself to the basic problem of poverty; to the fact that in Lowndes County, 86 white families own 90 percent of the land. What are black people in that county going to do for jobs, where are they going to get money? There must be reallocation of land, of money.

Ultimately, the economic foundations of this country must be shaken if black people are to control their lives. The colonies of the United States— and this includes the black ghettoes within its borders, north and south— must be liberated. For a century, this nation has been like an octopus of exploitation, its tentacles stretching from Mississippi and Harlem to South

America, the Middle East, southern Africa, and Vietnam; the form of exploitation varies from area to area but the essential result has been the same—a powerful few have been maintained and enriched at the expense of the poor and voiceless colored masses. This pattern must be broken. As its grip loosens here and there around the world, the hopes of black Americans become more realistic. For racism to die, a totally different America must be born.

This is what the white society does not wish to face; this is why that society prefers to talk about integration. But integration speaks not at all to the problem of poverty, only to the problem of blackness. Integration today means the man who "makes it," leaving his black brothers behind in the ghetto as fast as his new sports car will take him. It has no relevance to the Harlem wino or to the cottonpicker making three dollars a day. As a lady I know in Alabama once said, "the food that Ralph Bunche eats doesn't fill my stomach."

Integration, moreover, speaks to the problem of blackness in a despicable way. As a goal, it has been based on complete acceptance of the fact that *in order to have* a decent house or education, blacks must move into a white neighborhood or send their children to a white school. This reinforces, among both black and white, the idea that "white" is automatically better and "black" is by definition inferior. This is why integration is a subterfuge for the maintenance of white supremacy. It allows the nation to focus on a handful of Southern children who get into white schools, at great price, and to ignore the 94 percent who are left behind in unimproved all-black schools. Such situations will not change until black people have power—to control their own school boards, in this case. Then Negroes become equal in a way that means something, and integration ceases to be a one-way street. Then integration doesn't mean draining skills and energies from the ghetto into white neighborhoods; then it can mean white people moving from Beverly Hills into Watts, white people joining the Lowndes County Freedom Organization. Then integration becomes relevant. . . .

White America will not face the problem of color, the reality of it. The well-intended say: "We're all human, everybody is really decent, we must forget color." But color cannot be "forgotten" until its weight is recognized and dealt with. White America will not acknowledge that the ways in which this country sees itself are contradicted by being black—and always have been. Whereas most of the people who settled this country came here for freedom or for economic opportunity, blacks were brought here to be slaves. When the Lowndes County Freedom Organization chose the black panther as its symbol, it was christened by the press "the Black Panther Party"— but the Alabama Democratic Party, whose symbol is a rooster, has never been called the White Cock Party. No one ever talked about "white power" because power in this country *is* white. All this adds up to more than merely identifying a group phenomenon by some catchy name or adjective. The furor over that black panther reveals the problems that white America has with color and sex; the furor over "black power" reveals how deep racism runs and the great fear which is attached to it.

Whites will not see that I, for example, as a person oppressed because of my blackness, have common cause with other blacks who are oppressed because of blackness. This is not to say that there are no white people who see things as I do, but that it is black people I must speak to first. It must be the oppressed to whom SNCC addresses itself primarily, not to friends from the oppressing group.

From birth, black people are told a set of lies about themselves. We are told that we are lazy—yet I drive through the Delta area of Mississippi and watch black people picking cotton in the hot sun for fourteen hours. We are told, "If you work hard, you'll succeed"—but if that were true, black people would own this country. We are oppressed because we are black—not because we are ignorant, not because we are lazy, not because we're stupid (and got good rhythm), but because we're black.

I remember that when I was a boy, I used to go to see Tarzan movies on Saturday. White Tarzan used to beat up the black natives. I would sit there yelling, "Kill the beasts, kill the savages, kill 'em!" I was saying: Kill *me*. It was as if a Jewish boy watched Nazis taking Jews off to concentration camps and cheered them on. Today, I want the chief to beat hell out of Tarzan and send him back to Europe. But it takes time to become free of the lies and their shaming effect on black minds. It takes time to reject the most important lie; that black people inherently can't do the same things white people can do, unless white people help them.

The need for psychological equality is the reason why SNCC today believes that blacks must organize in the black community. Only black people can convey the revolutionary idea that black people are able to do things themselves. Only they can help create in the community an aroused and continuing black consciousness that will provide the basis for political strength. In the past, white allies have furthered white supremacy without the whites involved realizing it—or wanting it, I think. Black people must do things for themselves; they must get poverty money they will control and spend themselves, they must conduct tutorial programs themselves so that black children can identify with black people. This is one reason Africa has such importance: The reality of black men ruling their own nations gives blacks elsewhere a sense of possibility, of power, which they do not now have.

This does not mean we don't welcome help, or friends. But we want the right to decide whether anyone is, in fact, our friend. In the past, black Americans have been almost the only people whom everybody and his momma could jump up and call their friends. We have been tokens, symbols, objects—as I was in high school to many young whites, who liked having "a Negro friend." We want to decide who is our friend, and we will not accept someone who comes to us and says: "If you do X, Y, and Z, then I'll help you." We will not be told whom we should choose as allies. We will not be isolated from any group or nation except by our own choice. We cannot have the oppressors telling the oppressed how to rid themselves of the oppressor. . . .

Black people do not want to "take over" this country. They don't want to "get whitey"; they just want to get him off their backs, as the saying goes. It was for example the exploitation by Jewish landlords and merchants which first created black resentment toward Jews—not Judaism. The white man is irrelevant to blacks, except as an oppressive force. Blacks want to be in his place, yes, but not in order to terrorize and lynch and starve him. They want to be in his place because that is where a decent life can be had.

But our vision is not merely of a society in which all black men have enough to buy the good things of life. When we urge that black money go into black pockets, we mean the communal pocket. We want to see money go back into the community and used to benefit it. We want to see the cooperative concept applied in business and banking. We want to see black ghetto residents demand that an exploiting landlord or storekeeper sell them, at minimal cost, a building or a shop that they will own and improve co-operatively; they can back their demand with a rent strike, or a boycott, and a community so unified behind them that no one else will move into the building or buy at the store. The society we seek to build among black people, then, is not a capitalist one. It is a society in which the spirit of community and humanistic love prevail. The word love is suspect; black expectations of what it might produce have been betrayed too often. But those were expectations of a response from the white community, which failed us. The love we seek to encourage is within the black community, the only American community where men call each other "brother" when they meet. We can build a community of love only where we have the ability and power to do so: among blacks.

As for white America, perhaps it can stop crying out against "black supremacy," "black nationalism," "racism in reverse," and begin facing reality. The reality is that this nation, from top to bottom, is racist; that racism is not primarily a problem of "human relations" but of an exploitation maintained—either actively or through silence—by the society as a whole. Camus and Sartre have asked, can a man condemn himself? Can whites, particularly liberal whites, condemn themselves? Can they stop blaming us, and blame their own system? Are they capable of the shame which might become a revolutionary emotion?

We have found that they usually cannot condemn themselves, and so we have done it. But the rebuilding of this society, if at all possible, is basically the responsibility of whites—not blacks. We won't fight to save the present society, in Vietnam or anywhere else. We are just going to work, in the way *we* see fit, and on our goals *we* define, not for civil rights but for all our human rights.

A Senate Committee Reports on the FBI's Campaign Against Martin Luther King, Jr., 1976

From December 1963 until his death in 1968, Martin Luther King, Jr. was the target of an intensive campaign by the Federal Bureau of Investigation to "neutralize" him as an effective civil rights leader. In the words of the man in charge of the FBI's "war" against Dr. King:

No holds barred. We have used [similar] techniques against Soviet agents. [The same methods were] brought home against any organization against which we were targeted. We did not differentiate. This is a rough, tough business.

The FBI collected information about Dr. King's plans and activities through an extensive surveillance program, employing nearly every intelligence-gathering technique at the Bureau's disposal. Wiretaps, which were initially approved by Attorney General Robert F. Kennedy, were maintained on Dr. King's home telephone from October 1963 until mid-1965; the SCLC headquarter's telephones were covered by wiretaps for an even longer period. Phones in the homes and offices of some of Dr. King's close advisers were also wiretapped. The FBI has acknowledged 16 occasions on which microphones were hidden in Dr. King's hotel and motel rooms in an "attempt" to obtain information about the "private activities of King and his advisers" for use to "completely discredit" them.

FBI informants in the civil rights movement and reports from field offices kept the Bureau's headquarters informed of developments in the civil rights field. The FBI's presence was so intrusive that one major figure in the civil rights movement testified that his colleagues referred to themselves as members of "the FBI's golden record club."

The FBI's formal program to discredit Dr. King with Government officials began with the distribution of a "monograph" which the FBI realized could "be regarded as a personal attack on Martin Luther King," and which was subsequently described by a Justice Department official as "a personal diatribe . . . a personal attack without evidentiary support."

Congressional leaders were warned "off the record" about alleged dangers posed by Reverend King. The FBI responded to Dr. King's receipt of the Nobel Peace Prize by attempting to undermine his reception by foreign heads of state and American ambassadors in the countries that he planned to visit. When Dr. King returned to the United States, steps were taken to reduce support for a huge banquet and a special "day" that were being planned in his honor.

The FBI's program to destroy Dr. King as the leader of the civil rights movement entailed attempts to discredit him with churches, universities, and the press. Steps were taken to attempt to convince the National Council of Churches, the Baptist World Alliance, and leading Protestant ministers to halt financial support of the Southern Christian Leadership Conference (SCLC), and to persuade them that "Negro leaders should completely isolate King and remove him from the role he is now occupying in civil rights activities." When the FBI learned that Dr. King intended to visit the Pope, an agent was dispatched to persuade Francis Cardinal Spellman to warn the Pope about "the likely embarrassment that may result to the Pope should he grant King an audience." The FBI sought to influence universities to withhold honorary degrees from Dr. King. Attempts were made to prevent the publication of articles favorable to Dr. King and to find "friendly" news sources that would print unfavorable articles. The FBI offered to play for reporters tape recordings allegedly made from microphone surveillance of Dr. King's hotel rooms.

The FBI mailed Dr. King a tape recording made from its microphone coverage. According to the Chief of the FBI's Domestic Intelligence Division, the tape was intended to precipitate a separation between Dr. King and his wife in the belief that the separation would reduce Dr. King's stature. The tape recording was accompanied by a note which Dr. King and his advisers interpreted as a threat to release the tape recording unless Dr. King committed suicide. The FBI also made preparations to promote someone "to assume the role of leadership of the Negro people when King has been completely discredited."

The campaign against Dr. King included attempts to destroy the Southern Christian Leadership Conference by cutting off its sources of funds. The FBI considered, and on some occasions executed, plans to cut off the support of some of the SCLC's major contributors, including religious organizations, a labor union, and donors of grants such as the Ford Foundation. One FBI field office recommended that the FBI send letters to the SCLC's donors over Dr. King's forged signature warning them that the SCLC was under investigation by the Internal Revenue Service. The IRS files on Dr. King and the SCLC were carefully scrutinized for financial irregularities. For over a year, the FBI unsuccessfully attempted to establish that Dr. King had a secret foreign bank account in which he was sequestering funds.

The FBI campaign to discredit and destroy Dr. King was marked by extreme personal vindictiveness. As early as 1962, Director Hoover penned on an FBI memorandum, "King is no good." At the August 1963 March on Washington, Dr. King told the country of his dream that "all of God's children, black men and white men, Jews and Gentiles, Protestants and Catholics, will be able to join hands and sing in the words of the old Negro spiritual, 'Free at last, free at last. Thank God, almighty, I'm free at last.'" The FBI's Domestic Intelligence Division described this "demagogic speech" as yet more evidence that Dr. King was "the most dangerous and effective Negro leader in the country." Shortly afterward, *Time* magazine chose Dr. King as the "Man of the Year," an honor which elicited Director Hoover's comment that "they had to dig deep in the garbage to come up with this one." Hoover wrote "astounding" across the memorandum informing him that Dr. King had been granted an audience with the Pope despite the FBI's efforts to prevent such a meeting. The depth of Director Hoover's bitterness toward Dr. King, a bitterness which he had effectively communicated to his subordinates in the FBI, was apparent from the FBI's attempts to sully Dr. King's reputation long after his death. Plans were made to "brief" congressional leaders in 1969 to prevent the passage of a "Martin Luther King Day." In 1970, Director Hoover told reporters that Dr. King was the "last one in the world who should ever have received" the Nobel Peace Prize.

Police and Fire Department Logs
Record an Urban Riot, 1967

Police and fire department radios blared out the urgent messages as the tempo of the riot built up Sunday night and Monday. The radios of the two departments were the only sure way to keep track of the riot's size and the direction it moved.

Not all of the calls could be heard because of different frequencies used to broadcast. Two that could be heard indicated the scope of the rioting.

The radio calls were monitored from 11:35 p.m. Sunday to 5:15 a.m. Monday, the time of the most intense activity. The messages recorded were reports by police and firemen on the street, the police command center at N. 4th st. and W. Garfield av., and dispatchers in city hall and the safety building. The log:

11:35 p.m.—Looters entering a Goodyear store at 1815 W. Fond du Lac.

11:42—Rubbish fire 2400 N. 3d st.

11:45—Get some help at 3rd and Lloyd; the fire's out of control.

11:45—Rubbish fire extinguished at 3rd and McKinley.

11:46—Garage fire at 21st and Concordia.

11:50—They're beginning to loot at 3rd and Brown.

11:51—We're pulling the beat man out at 3rd and Wright. We're getting nailed pretty hard. Watch out!

11:51—Unconfirmed report of squad car tipped over.

11:52—Have Chief Breier call the mayor or his administrator.

11:54—Kids throwing stones at passing cars on foot bridge over 6th st., just south of North av.

11:54—Notify owner show window broken at appliance store 3356 N. Green Bay.

11:56—Man shot at 3rd and Vine. Send ambulance. (Believed to be a looter.)

11:56—Battalion 2 reported from a fire scene that it needed protection.

11:57—Crowds out of control at Meinecke and Wright. Looting going on.

11:58—Businessman trapped in building at 2555 N. 3rd st. Being pummeled by rocks.

12:02 a.m.—All shotguns being brought down from headquarters and training school. Taken to command post at 4th and Garfield.

12:03—Fire 3rd and Meinecke, Martin service station.

12:05—Fires in alley 2300 block of N. 3rd.

12:08—See if you can raise some ministers.

12:09—Group breaking into convalescent home at 107 E. Garfield.

12:10—Box alarm of fire N. 5th and Vliet sts.

12:11—Sheriff's department advises 50 men standing by waiting for chief's order.

Diary of an Urban Riot, 1967, *The Milwaukee Journal*, July 31, 1967.

12:15—No. 5 captain advises that four reverends are on the way to the command post.

12:16—Burglary in progress at 13th and Burleigh.

12:16—Merchants police alarm at 2741 N. Teutonia.

12:17—Halyard and Lloyd, about 50 youths stoning automobiles.

12:20—Burglary in progress at 2401 N. 3rd st.

12:24—Wagonload of patrolmen need helmets.

12:25—Call for fire department, rear of 2300 N. 3rd st. Also need additional officers.

12:26—Group going toward Wisconsin av.

12:28—1900 N. Buffum, another fire set.

12:28—Gang beating a white man at 4th and Wright.

12:28—Fire at National Food store, 2354 N. 3rd st.

12:28—2741 N. Teutonia. They've smashed windows wide open. Notify the owner.

12:30—Request Mount Sinai hospital remain open. Keep emergency personnel on.

12:31—3rd and Highland. Eight police confronting a crowd of 50 marching toward Wisconsin av.

12:32—Get hold of sheriff's department hard helmets and bring them to command post.

12:32—Cars being set on fire 16th and Vliet.

12:33—Fifth Dist. police station being attacked. (The message was garbled.)

12:35—They're breaking into Badger Plating. 1300 N. Water.

12:36—Telephone alarm of fire at N. 16th and W. Vliet.

12:37—Brink's called. They want to move their trucks from 431 W. Galena at 1 a.m.

12:40—Report from citizen that they've broken windows at Kaufman Motors at 3rd and Burleigh and they're stealing motorcycles.

12:40—Firemen report that they are being stoned at 3rd and Clark.

12:40—About 25 persons are attacking a service station at 3rd and Burleigh.

12:42—Request for more squads at 15th and Vliet. A crowd is gathering.

12:44—We need more squads at 3200 N. Green Bay.

12:44—3rd and Burleigh at the motorcycle shop. We've got motorcycles lying in the street.

12:46—We've got a large group of punks who need some attention at 1301 N. Center.

12:48—Squad is stuck in sand at 2nd and Meinecke.

12:49—Check bank at 27th and Vliet. Auto seen fleeing the scene.

12:50—We have a report of looters in a tavern. 3rd and Green Bay.

12:51—More looting at Woolworth's, 13th and Vliet.

12:52—Large group at 12th and Galena with guns and golf clubs.

12:53—Check injured man at 24th and Lisbon.

12:53—Large group breaking windows at 13th and Vliet.

12:58—Telephone alarm of fire, 3rd and Clark.

12:58—Breaking into Kellers, beer depot, 5th and Center.

12:59—Injured man, 12th and Lloyd.

12:59—Plankinton and Michigan; numerous lootings in area.

12:59—Box alarm, 2nd and Chambers.

1:00—Telephone alarm of fire, 2018 N. 5th st.

1:00—Looting reported at 21st and Walnut.

1:00—Group in white Cadillac throwing bricks and rocks at homes in the 2300 block of N. 20th.

1:00—Pedestrian struck, 24th and Lisbon.

1:03—Large group congregating at Teutonia and Center.

1:04—Auto accident, 12th and Lloyd. Passenger injured pretty badly.

1:04—Burglar alarm, Sangor Drugs, 800 W. North av.

1:05—Reports of shooting at 2nd and Clark.

1:05—Autos being tipped at 3rd and Meinecke.

1:05—Two white males with rifles in the 2900 block of N. 3rd.

1:06—Check 2nd and Wright. Report of woman being beaten.

1:07—Pedestrian struck 24th pl. and Lisbon.

1:08—Report of gas pump burning, 16th and Highland.

1:08—Report of looting, 12th and Cherry.

1:09—We have report of looting at 5th and North.

1:13—Large group in parking lot with weapons at 2nd and Michigan.

1:13—Looting at Super America station, 17th and Atkinson.

1:14—Groups throwing rocks at 6th and Cherry.

1:14—Ambulance sent. 2nd and Meinecke.

1:15—Box alarm of fire, 16th and Juneau.

1:16—They are entering grocery stores at 15th and Vliet and 16th and Cherry.

1:17—One reduced line (fire hose) working on buildings at 16th and Juneau.

1:22—Burglar alarm at Palay's Men's shop, 1200 W. Walnut st.

1:25—Looting at store at 11th and Center.

1:27—Group of 20 to 30 walking east on Meinecke armed with bottles, bricks and weapons.

1:28—Looting, Royal Cleaners, 5th and North.

1:30—Accident, 10th and Ring.

1:31—Sergeant reports that his group has no shotguns.

1:31—Large group approaching Teutonia and Center.

1:33—Fifteen cars loaded with Negroes going west on North av.

1:37—Group of 40 Negroes at 29th and Vliet.

1:38—Squad at 14th and Walnut has prisoners.

1:39—They're looting the Kohl's Beverage Center, 3700 N. Teutonia av.

1:40—They're beating a woman at 5th and Wright.

1:41—Large group of Negroes at jewelry store at 37th and North.

1:42—Large group of Negroes leaving 37th and North. We have just moved them.

1:43—Two burglar alarms, 925 W. North and 1400 W. North. av.

1:44—People buying cans of gasoline at 35th and Meinecke.

1:45—Accident at 1st and Meinecke, large group gathering, send help.

1:46—We're closing down all service stations in the 3rd police district.

1:46—Box alarm fire, 12th and Garfield.

1:48—Broken window at 928 W. North, nobody around.

1:48—Box alarm fire at 2nd and Hadley.

1:49—We're standing by at Ken's Gun shop, 48th and North. Everything is OK here.

1:49—Check 15th and McKinley. People trapped in an auto.

1:50—Check a large group armed with bottles at 27th and Wells.

1:51—Bus driver reports rocks being thrown at busses at 14th and Fond du Lac.

1:51—Man being beaten at 1st and Meinecke.

1:56—Officer needs assistance, 15th and Center.

1:58—Send a couple of squads to 3rd and Hadley. They're looting up here.

1:59—We have shooting from an automobile in the vicinity of Buffum and Center.

2:00—Large fight at 12th and Reservoir.

2:01—Check for windows being broken, 2500 block of N. Downer.

2:02—We have 25 people following three patrolmen at 4th and Walnut.

2:02—We need a wagon at 6th and North. We've got a couple of stone throwers.

2:03—Send ambulance. One dead already. Send ambulance, 134 W. Center. Man shot in head by sniper.

2:05—Four cars of Negroes at 2nd and Vliet.

2:06—Truck on fire, 12th and Galena.

2:06—Another ambulance, 2nd and Center.

2:10—Window smashed at television store, 27th and Atkinson.

2:10—2nd and Center. Tear gas and ambulance, We're shooting at house.

2:12—Another ambulance, 2nd and Center.

2:12—Sound of gunshots, 12th and Walnut.

2:12—Get some tear gas here, 2nd and Center. We have at least one policeman shot.

2:12—We need shotguns here at 2nd and Center.

2:13—We're sending help.

2:13—2nd and Center. Two coppers shot. We're requesting help immediately. Two coppers shot.

2:15—Request for ambulances to stand by, 4th and Garfield. Ambulance, 2nd and Center, hurry, hurry.

2:16—Disregard the ambulance. We're taking the wounded officer ourselves.

2:17—1000 N. 3rd st. Camera shop broken into. We've got the guys.

2:18—Large fire at 3rd and Center.

2:19—Notify fire department, fire bomb at 3rd and Center.

2:20—Check for five carloads of Negroes at 3rd and Morgan.

2:20—Large crowd of juveniles gathering at 1st and Wright. Cars are burning.

2:22—Meet squad at 3rd and State. They are going in after looters.

2:22—Meet squad at 3rd and Cherry. We've got looters.

2:23—Negro juveniles with guns at 32nd and McKinley.

2:24—Negroes just broke into service station at 31st and Capitol.

2:24—Looting at beer depot at 23rd and Burleigh.

2:25—Looting at drugstore at 13th and Burleigh.

2:25—Looting at liquor store, 8th and North.

2:25—All squads—close up service stations for the night.

2:29—Supermarket on fire, 10th and Burleigh.

2:29—We're pinned down at 2nd and Center (by sniper).

2:38—Send fire department, 3rd and Center, big blaze.

2:40—Tell No. 3 squads to stop any roving cars with Negro males. Stop them and check the trunks for guns and contraband.

2:41—Large fire at 3rd and Center. Fire department unable to get into area.

2:42—We've got the prisoner. He has been shot.

2:43—People in house at 130 Center st.

2:45—Officer shot in chest or stomach. Taking him to county general hospital. Notify Dr. Worman to be in surgery.

2:47—Wagon, 130 W. Concordia for looters.

2:47—People at 130 W. Center st. refuse to answer door.

2:47—Another fire at 130 W. Center. Can you see it?

2:50—Battalion 2 reported. We've got two police officers up here. We're not going in until we get an all clear from them.

2:51—Fire at 1st and Center. Firemen are pinned down by sniper fire.

2:57—How about the searchlights at 2nd and Center? We're still waiting.

3:02—Firemen are pinned down by sniper fire at 1st and Center. Searchlights are needed.

3:06—We need rifle ammo at 2nd and Center.

3:06—Looting jewelry store at 35th and Lisbon.

3:07—Advise, where is sniper? (Answer partly blurred) at 134 W. Center. He may be in there. The whole front of the house is on fire.

3:10—Large, group of Negro males, 26th and Vliet. One is injured.

3:13—Report of a man shot at 2664-A N. 1st st.

3:16—Fire department still being held down by snipers at 2nd and Center. Can't get in.

3:20—Need an ambulance at 1st and Center.

3:21—Conveying officer to County general hospital from 2nd and Center.

3:23—Ten additional men to 1st and Center.

3:30—Turn in a second alarm at fire, 2nd and Center.

3:34—Stealing cars from a dealer at 3rd and Hadley.

3:35—We are making numerous arrests of prisoners in cars with guns and contraband.

3:35—They're looting; gunshots heard, 5th and Center.

3:35—Fire in the middle of the street, 1st and Wright.

3:36—Looting, 3501 N. Holton.

3:38—Small fire extinguished at 2841 N. 5th st.

3:41—Men with guns, 27th and Teutonia.

3:43—We have an automobile fire, 1st and Wright.

3:47—Need an ambulance at 2nd and Center, injured fireman.

3:48—Someone is shooting at 6th and North.

3:49—Check an ambulance request at 2629 N. 3rd st. Possible gunshot wound.

3:50—Looting at drugstore, 13th and Burleigh.

3:52—Sniper has men pinned down, 2300 block N. 3rd.

3:53—Sgt. Lanza is pinned down. We're sending help.

3:56—Sgt. Lanza, are you pinned down?

3:56—Sgt. Lanza replied: "We heard two shots, we're afraid to move."

3:58—Subject is on roof on National Food store (at 2354 N. 3rd, Lanza's location). He has a red shirt on.

3:59—I'm in the National Food store parking store. We've seen the guy move. We need a high powered rifle.

3:59—They are shooting tear gas over the building (the National food store). They are shooting too far.

3:59—They're still shooting too far. If they keep overshooting, we are going to need gas masks here.

4:00—2500 block of N. 3rd. fire department reports their men are pinned down (by the sniper on National Food store building).

4:00—Burglar running east from 3rd and Atkinson.

4:00—Tell men in rear (of National Food store) to hold their fire. We're going in.

4:00—Hold your fire, men going in from front of store.

4:01—Shooting in alley, 1204 W. Wright.

4:03—All units, do not enter 3rd street in 2500 block because of sniper fire.

4:04—Engine 29 from 3rd and Hadley fighting an auto fire, plenty of protection here.

4:04—Check for large group of Negroes starting fires going west from Lloyd.

4:05—Box alarm fire at 9th and Meinecke.

4:06—Send some gas masks, 2300 block N. 3rd st.

4:07—Battalion chief suggested fire engines stop using sirens. Respond to alarms without sirens. People are coming out to see what is happening.

4:11—Tell fire department to stop at 3rd and North. We'll pick up ladders there. (Police wanted the ladders to get to roof of National Food store building.)

4:12—Send a man with a shotgun. We do not have one.

4:13—Check for crowd gathered at 7th and Center.

4:14—Sgt. Lanza, they can put men on discount store at rear. Building is higher up; you can cover the whole area.

4:18—Several drunken Negroes went into Keller's (a liquor store).

4:22—Sgt. Lanza needs lights in the 2300 block of N. 3rd st.

4:25—Men are going up on ladders at the National food store. They are on the roof now.

4:28—Sgt. Fender says 2300 block of N. 3rd is clear. (No sniper was found on the roof of the National Food store.)

4:30—Caution, all squads using call boxes. Possible booby traps.

4:32—County general hospital advises they now have room for more patients.

4:32—No room in city jail. Take all prisoners to outlying districts.

4:34—Check for subjects trying to break in homes vicinity 15th and Center.

4:35—Sgt. Lanza: Any blankets available for officers? They're wet and freezing over here. (It had rained.)

4:37—Obtain about 100 blankets and take them to the command post.

4:40—Check for looting on Wisconsin av. between 10th and 11th.

4:44—The fire at 2nd and Center is under control. Just smoldering embers. (Three homes had burned.)

4:45—Have you contacted the chief about calling the mayor? The mayor is still waiting.

4:47—First floor fire at 11th and Concordia being extinguished with a hand pump.

✖ E S S A Y S

As the 1980s drew to a close, historians debated both the successes and the failures of the civil-rights movement. The many laws, court decisions, and public policies that had sustained racial segregation since the 19th century had been swept aside, but much of their legacy still remained deeply embedded in the nation's social structure. Although some mostly middle-class African-Americans had profited from new economic opportunities created by the civil-rights movement, the plight of poor African-Americans had actually deteriorated. The growing opposition to affirmative action and other minority programs by the White House, moreover, threatened to further slow the pace of change. This is the context for the two essays that follow. Vincent Gordon Harding, a friend of King and the former director of the Martin Luther King, Jr., Center for Nonviolent Social Change in Atlanta, challenges the bland, unthreatening image of King that increasingly dominates public celebrations of his life. In the second essay, historian William H. Chafe of Duke University assesses both the triumphs and the limitations of the civil-rights revolution.

King as Disturber of the Peace

VINCENT GORDON HARDING

In the 1970s, as a fascinating variety of voices began to press the nation to decide where it stood concerning the memory and meaning of Martin Luther

"Beyond Amnesia: Martin Luther King, Jr., and the Future of America" by Vincent G. Harding from *Journal of American History* 74 (September 1987), pp. 468–476. Reprinted by permission of the Journal of American History.

King, Jr., and as we instinctively sought an easy way to deal with the unrelenting power of this disturber of all unjust peace, a black poet perhaps best reflected our ambivalence. Carl Wendell Hines wrote:

> Now that he is safely dead
> let us praise him
>   build monuments to his glory
>   sing hosannas to his name.
>   Dead men make
> such convenient heroes; They
>   cannot rise
> To challenge the images
>   we would fashion from their lives.
>   And besides,
> it is easier to build monuments
>   than to make a better world.

Then as the voices of artists and family and millions of black people (and their votes, and their nonblack allies) began to build, the sad wisdom of Hines's words seemed to sharpen and to cut deeper at every moment. For it became increasingly clear that most of those who were leading the campaign for the national holiday had chosen, consciously or unconsciously, to allow King to become a convenient hero, to try to tailor him to the shape and mood of mainstream, liberal/moderate America.

Symbolic of the direction given the campaign has been the unremitting focus on the 1963 March on Washington, the never-ending repetition of the great speech and its dream metaphor, the sometimes innocent and sometimes manipulative boxing of King into the relatively safe categories of "civil rights leader," "great orator," harmless dreamer of black and white children on the hillside. And surely nothing could be more ironic or amnesiac than having Vice-President George Bush, the former head of the Central Intelligence Agency, the probable White House overseer of Contra actions, speaking words in King's honor. Or was it more ironic to watch the representatives of the Marine Corps, carrying fresh memories from the invasion of Grenada and from their training for Libya and for Nicaragua, playing "We Shall Overcome," while the bust of the prince of nonviolence was placed in the Capitol rotunda, without a word being spoken about nonviolence?

It appears as if the price for the first national holiday honoring a black man is the development of a massive case of national amnesia concerning who that black man really was. At both personal and collective levels, of course, it is often the case that amnesia is not ultimately harmful to the patient. However, in this case it is very dangerous, for the things we have chosen to forget about King (and about ourselves) constitute some of the most hopeful possibilities and resources for our magnificent and very needy nation. Indeed, I would suggest that we Americans have chosen amnesia rather than continue King's painful, uncharted, and often disruptive struggle toward a more perfect union. I would also suggest that those of us who are historians and citizens have a special responsibility to challenge the loss of memory, in ourselves and others, to allow our skills in probing the past to become resources for healing and for hope, not simply sources of pages in books or of steps in careers. In other words, if as Hines wrote, Martin King "cannot rise to challenge" those who would make him a harmless black icon, then *we* surely can—assuming that we are still alive.

Although there are many points at which our challenge to the comfortable images might be raised, I believe that the central encounters with King that begin to take us beyond the static March-on-Washington, "integrationist," "civil rights leader" image are located in Chicago and Mississippi in 1966. During the winter of that year King moved North. He was driven by the fires of Watts and the early hot summers of 1964 and 1965. Challenged and nurtured by the powerful commitment of Malcolm X to the black street forces, he was also compelled by his own deep compassion for the urban black community—whose peculiar problems were not fundamentally addressed by the civil rights laws so early won in the South. Under such urgent compulsion, King left his familiar southern base and stepped out on very unfamiliar turf. For Hamlin Avenue on Chicago's blighted West Side was a long way from the marvelous, costly victories of Selma, St. Augustine, and Birmingham, and Mayor Richard Daley was a consummate professional compared to the sheriffs, mayors, and police commissioners of the South. But King had made his choice, and it is one that we dare not forget.

By 1966 King had made an essentially religious commitment to the poor, and he was prepared to say:

> I choose to identify with the underprivileged. I choose to identify with the poor. I choose to give my life for the hungry. I choose to give my life for those who have been left out of the sunlight of opportunity. I choose to live for and with those who find themselves seeing life as a long and desolate corridor with no exit sign. This is the way I'm going. If it means suffering a little bit, I'm going that way. If it means sacrificing, I'm going that way. If it means dying for them, I'm going that way, because I heard a voice saying, "Do something for others."

We understand nothing about the King whose life ended in the midst of a struggle for garbage workers if we miss that earlier offering of himself to the struggle against poverty in America, to the continuing battle for the empowerment of the powerless—in this nation, in Vietnam, in South Africa, in Central America, and beyond.

In a sense, it was that commitment that took him from Chicago to Mississippi in the late spring of 1966, as he responded to the attempted assassination of James Meredith, taking up with others that enigmatic hero's "march against fear." There on the highways of the Magnolia State we have a second crucial encounter with the forgotten King. He was an embattled leader, the King who was challenged, chastened, and inspired by the courageous, foolhardy Young Turks of the Student Nonviolent Coordinating Committee. He was attentive to those veterans of the struggle who raised the cry for "Black Power," who made public the long simmering challenge to King's leadership, who increasingly voiced their doubts about the primacy of nonviolence as a way of struggle, and who seemed prepared to read whites out of the movement. Perhaps the most important aspect of the Meredith March for King's development was the question the young people raised in many forms: "Dr. King, why do you want us to love white folks before we even love ourselves?" From then on the issues of black self-love, of black and white power, and of the need to develop a more militant form of nonviolence that could challenge and enlist the rising rage of urban black youth were never far from King's consciousness. Along with his deepening commitment to the poor, those were the subjects and questions that did much to shape the hero we have forgotten.

One of the reasons for our amnesia, of course, is the fact that the forgotten King is not easy to handle now. Indeed, he never was. In 1967, after spending two hectic weeks traveling with the impassioned black prophet, David Halberstam, a perceptive journalist, reported that

> King has decided to represent the ghettos; he will work in them and speak for them. But their voice is harsh and alienated. If King is to speak for them truly, then his voice must reflect theirs; it too must be alienated, and it is likely to be increasingly at odds with the rest of American society.

Halberstam was right, but only partly so. After the Selma marches of 1965, King's voice did sound harsher in its criticism of the mainstream American way of life and its dominant values—including the assumption that the United States had the right to police the world for "free enterprise." Not only did the white mainstream object to such uncompromising criticism from a "civil rights leader" who was supposed to know his place, but respectable black people were increasingly uncomfortable as well. For some of them were making use of the fragile doorways that the freedom movement had helped open. Others, after years of frustration, were finally being promoted into the positions of responsibility and higher earnings that their skills and experience should have earlier made available. Too often, King was considered a threat to them as well, especially as his commitment to the poor drove him to increasingly radical assessments of the systemic flaws in the American economic order, an order they had finally begun to enjoy.

But Halberstam, a man of words, saw only part of the picture. King did more than *speak* for the ghettos. He was committed to mobilizing and organizing them for self-liberating action. That was his deeper threat to the status quo, beyond words, beyond alienation. That was what King's friend Rabbi Abraham Heschel surely understood when he introduced King to an assembly of rabbis in these words: "Martin Luther King is a voice, a vision and a way. I call upon every Jew to harken to his voice, to share his vision, to follow in his way. The whole future of America will depend on the impact and influence of Dr. King."

Part of what we have forgotten, then, is King's vision, beyond the appealing dream of black and white children holding hands, beyond the necessary goal of "civil rights." From the outset, he held a vision for all America, often calling the black movement more than a quest for rights— a struggle "to redeem the soul of America." By the end of his life, no one who paid attention could mistake the depth and meaning of that vision. At the convention of the Southern Christian Leadership Conference (SCLC) in 1967, King announced, "We must go from this convention and say, 'America, you must be born again . . . your whole structure must be changed.' " He insisted that "the problem of racism, the problem of economic exploitation, and the problem of war are all tied together." These, King said, were "the triple evils" that the freedom movement must address as it set itself to the challenge of "restructuring the whole of American society." This was the vision behind the call he issued in his final public speech in Memphis on April 3, 1968: "Let us move on in these powerful days, these days of challenge to make America what it ought to be. We have an opportunity to make America a better nation."

That final speech was delivered to a crowd of some two thousand persons, mostly black residents of Memphis who had come out in a soaking rain to hear King and to support the garbage workers' union in its struggle for justice. King's challenge to his last movement audience reminds us that he also carried a large and powerful vision concerning the role of black people and others of the "disinherited" in American society. His vision always included more than "rights" or "equal opportunity." On December 5, 1955, at the public meeting that launched the Montgomery bus boycott and Martin Luther King, Jr., into the heart of twentieth century history, King had announced,

> We, the disinherited of this land, we who have been oppressed so long, are tired of going through the long night of captivity. And now we are reaching out for the daybreak of freedom and justice and equality.

As a result of that decision and that movement, King said,

> when the history books are written in the future somebody will have to say "There lived a race of people, of black people, fleecy locks and black complexion, a people who had the moral courage to stand up for their rights, and thereby they injected a new meaning into the veins of history and of civilization." And we're gonna do that. God grant that we will do it before it's too late.

From beginning to end, the grand vision, the magnificent obsession never left him, the audacious hope for America and its disinherited. Only in the light of that dual vision can we understand his voice, especially in its increasing alienation from the mainstream, in its urgent movement beyond the black and white civil rights establishment. In his last years, the vision led him to call repeatedly for "a reconstruction of the entire society, a revolution of values." Only as we recapture the wholeness of King's vision can we understand his conclusion in 1967 that "something is wrong with capitalism as it now stands in the United States." Only then can we grasp his word to his co-workers in SCLC: "We are not interested in being integrated into *this* value structure. Power must be relocated." The vision leads directly to the voice, calling for "a radical redistribution of economic and political power" as the only way to meet the real needs of the poor in America.

When our memories allow us to absorb King's vision of a transformed America and a transforming force of black people and their allies, then we understand his powerful critique of the American war in Vietnam. After he struggled with his conscience about how open to make his opposition, after he endured intense pressure to be quiet from Washington and from the civil rights establishment, King's social vision and his religious faith stood him in good stead. He spoke out in a stirring series of statements and actions and declared:

> Never again will I be silent on an issue that is destroying the soul of our nation and destroying thousands and thousands of little children in Vietnam.
> . . . the time has come for a real prophecy, and I'm willing to go that road.

Of course, King knew the costly way of prophets—as did the rabbi who called us "to follow in his way." We must assume that neither the black prophet nor his Jewish brother was speaking idle words, opening up frivolous ways. Rather those were visions, voices, and ways not meant to be forgotten.

Indeed, in a nation where the gap between rich and poor continues to expand with cruel regularity, where the numbers of black and Hispanic poor vie with each other for supremacy, where farmers and industrial workers are in profound crisis, where racism continues to proclaim its ruthless American presence, who can afford to forget King's compassionate and courageous movement toward justice? When the leaders of the country spew reams of lies to Congress and the people alike, in public and private statements, when the official keepers of the nation's best hopes seem locked in what King called "paranoid anti-communism," when we make cynical mercenaries out of jobless young people, sacrificing them to a rigid militarism that threatens the future of the world, do we dare repress the memory of a man who called us to struggle bravely toward "the daybreak of freedom and justice and equality"? Dare we forget a man who told us that "a nation that continues year after year to spend more money on military defense than on programs of social uplift is approaching spiritual death"?

Clearly, we serve our scholarship and our citizenship most faithfully when we move ourselves and others beyond amnesia toward encounters with the jagged leading edges of King's prophetic vision. When we do that we recognize that Martin King himself was unclear about many aspects of the "way" he had chosen. In his commitment to the poor, in his search for the redistribution of wealth and power in America, in his relentless stand against war, in his determination to help America "repent of her modern economic imperialism," he set out on a largely uncharted way. Still, several polestars pointed the way for him, and they may suggest creative directions for our personal and collective lives.

As King searched for a way for Americans to press the nation toward its best possibilities, toward its next birth of freedom and justice, he held fast to several basic assumptions. Perhaps it will help to remember them:

1. He seemed convinced that in the last part of the twentieth century, anyone who still held a vision of "a more perfect union" and worked toward that goal had to be prepared to move toward fundamental, structural changes in the mainstream values, economic and political structures, and traditional leadership of American society.

2. King believed that those who are committed to a real, renewed war against poverty in America must recognize the connections between our domestic economic and political problems and the unhealthy position that we occupy in the military, economic, and political wards of the global community. In other words, what King called "the triple evils of racism, extreme materialism and militarism" could be effectively fought only by addressing their reality and relationships in our life at home and abroad.

3. Unlike many participants in current discussions of poverty and "the underclass" in American society, King assumed that his ultimate commitment was to help find the ways by which the full energies and angers of the poor could be challenged, organized, and engaged in a revolutionary process that confronted the status quo and opened creative new possibilities for them and for the nation. Surely this was what he meant when he said,

   > the dispossessed of this nation—the poor, both white and Negro—live in a cruelly unjust society. They must organize a revolution against that injustice, not against the lives of . . . their fellow citizens, but against the structures through which the society is refusing to lift . . . the load of poverty

4. By the last months of his life, as King reflected on the developments in the freedom movement since its energies had turned northward and since some of its participants had begun to offer more radical challenges to the policies of the federal government at home and abroad, he reached an inescapable conclusion. The next stages of the struggle for a just American order could no longer expect even the reluctant support from the national government that the movement had received since Montgomery. Now, he said, "We must formulate a program and we must fashion the new tactics which do not count on government good will, but instead serve to compel unwilling authorities to yield to the mandates of justice."

5. Defying most of the conventional wisdom of black and white America, King determined to hold fast to both of his fundamental, religiously based commitments: to the humanizing empowerment and transformation of the poor and of the nation and to the way of nonviolence and creative peace making. His attempt to create a Poor People's Campaign to challenge—and, if necessary, to disrupt—the federal government on its home ground was an expression of this wild and beautiful experiment in creating nonviolent revolution. Planning for a massive campaign of civil disobedience carried on by poor people of all races, aided by their un-poor allies, King announced, "We've got to make it known that until our problem is solved, America may have many, many days, but they

will be full of trouble. There will be no rest, there will be no tranquility in this country until the nation comes to terms with [that problem]."

For those who seek a gentle, non-abrasive hero whose recorded speeches can be used as inspirational resources for rocking our memories to sleep, Martin Luther King, Jr., is surely the wrong man. However, if there is even a chance that Rabbi Heschel was correct, that the untranquil King and his peace-disturbing vision, words, and deeds hold the key to the future of America, then another story unfolds, another search begins. We who are scholars and citizens then owe ourselves, our children, and our nation a far more serious exploration and comprehension of the man and the widespread movement with which he was identified.

Recently, the Afro-American liberation theologian Cornel West said of King, "As a proponent of nonviolent resistance, he holds out the only slim hope for social sanity in a violence-prone world." What if both the black theologian and the Jewish scholar-mystic are correct? What if the way that King was exploring is indeed vital to the future of our nation and our world? For scholars, citizens, or celebrants to forget the real man and his deepest implications would be not only faithless, but also suicidal. For in the light of the news that inundates us every day, where else do we go from here to make a better world?

The African-American Struggle as an Unfinished Revolution

WILLIAM H. CHAFE

Without question, the movement for black freedom and equality constituted the most important domestic development of post-war America—arguably, the most important domestic event in the 20th century. The civil rights movement provided the energy, the inspiration, and the model for virtually every effort of social reform that emerged in the remarkable decade of the 1960s. The women's movement, the anti-war movement, the student movement, the movement to end poverty, the struggle for Indian rights, Chicano rights, and gay rights—none of these would have been conceivable were it not for the driving force of the civil rights movement. If the movement achieved nothing more than to provide the leadership for other social activists in the 1960s and 70s, this alone would be sufficient.

But the civil rights movement was much more. It toppled segregation, destroyed discrimination within the law against the blacks and members of other minority groups, led to the massive increase in the franchise accomplished by the Voting Rights Act of 1965, paved the way for countless legal and political battles to abolish economic discrimination under the 1964 Civil Rights Act, and achieved—albeit a hundred years late—the legal rights to full citizenship deferred at the end of the First Reconstruction. In addition, during the course of achieving these victories, the civil rights movement laid bare the political, cultural, and structural barriers to complete equality that persist with enormous power to this day, in American society.

It is now known that race is only one of the vehicles for denying people autonomy and freedom. In a different form, but with almost equal devastation, gender and class function in a similar way. From the beginnings of our country, the three forces together—gender, class, and race—have largely shaped a person's life chances. Whether one was born male or female, rich or poor, black or white, determine the power one could exercise, the opportunities available for a career, the emotions it was deemed appropriate to express, the rights one could lay claim to. But for most of this period, attention focused on one or the other of the three. Despite occasional alliances of workers with civil rights advocates, or of feminists with immigrant garment workers and black sharecroppers, the emphasis of social activists seeking freedom for one group tended to be on their own specific objectives rather than on the interlocking way in which the different forms of oppression reinforced each other. Thus women suffragists in the 19th century disassociated themselves from the 14th and 15th amendments, and trade union leaders eschewed the recruitment of women or blacks. The result was that whenever movements for social change came too close to success, opponents could use the strategy of divide and conquer to pit against each other those who were the greatest victims of inequality. Today, we understand the intersection of gender, class, and race better than we ever have before, and in large part the reason for this is the way in which the civil rights movement has helped to highlight that intersection through both its victories and its defeats.

Secondly, the history of the civil rights movement illuminates the ongoing conflict within American culture between the values associated with individual freedom and those associated with collective advancement. If in fact the goal of the freedom movement was to achieve a situation in which each individual could stand alone to compete as best he or she could, despite the residual and collective impact of gender, class, and race, then it must be said that the freedom movement of the 1960s achieved, at least in the law, the substance of its aims. But if the goal was rather to assure equality as a result, not just as an idea, then collective measures are essential—measures that specifically address the ways in which class, gender, and race have functioned in the past, and function today, to deny freedom and opportunity. Both in the history of its own goals, and the history of its efforts to implement those goals, therefore, the civil rights movement provides a case study of both the limitations and possibilities of reform in our society.

Perhaps the most important place to start in an effort to understand the civil rights movement is to recognize that its strength was rooted in the collective solidarity and vitality of black institutions. To this day, many whites tend—mistakenly—to identify the 1960s civil rights movement as a band of integrated marchers proceeding to the Lincoln Memorial. In fact, the movement to destroy segregation drew its inspiration from all-black segregated institutions. The young people who led the sit-in movement in Greensboro went to Shiloh Baptist Church, an all-black congregation. The minister of that church had taken part in civil rights demonstrations while a student at Shaw, an all-black college in Raleigh. Many of the protestors had received their introduction to civil rights in the all-black NAACP [National Association for the Advancement of Colored People] Youth group in Greensboro. They were graduates of all-black Dudley High School, where they had encountered teachers who used the classroom to exhort them to be the best students they could be, and who used the homeroom period to have them address voter registration envelopes. Although there were certainly class differences in the black community in Greensboro and elsewhere, all black citizens lived in the same area of town, prevented from moving by housing segregation. When the demonstrations began, they were supported by the entire community—old people, skilled workers, service workers, the employed, and the unemployed. It was a movement that, whatever its goals, spoke for a united community.

In Mississippi as well, black institutions provided the home-base for the drive to end Jim Crow. Occasionally ministers and school principals opposed the efforts of Robert Moses and others to recruit participants in the struggle. But when the students walked out, they walked out of all-black high schools, and when they met together with SNCC [Student Non-violent Co-ordinating Committee] workers, they met in black churches. While class may have been on some people's minds, it was not a critical issue for people like Amzie Moore, Hazel Palmer, Hartman Turnbow, or Fannie Lou Hamer.

Despite that collective base, the goals of the movement seemed very much within the tradition of individual reform movements in American history. With an optimism about the responsiveness of American institutions that seems naive in today's world, the student protestors in Greensboro and the civil rights workers in Mississippi believed that they could achieve "Freedom Now." If only the laws that sanctioned racial discrimination and the signs which said "white only" were abolished, they believed, black Americans could achieve equal opportunity and secure their place in the sun. The goal, as conservatives . . . enjoy telling us [today], was to forget about race, to have color blind admissions to jobs and schools, to have black Americans treated as individuals, with the color of their skin forgotten.

But even as the nation focused on the rhetoric that celebrated individual freedom and integration, there were others in the movement who sustained a vision of larger, more collective, more structural change. Nationalism and collective race advancement, of course, had always been part of the dialectic of black reform efforts. But in the early 1960s as well, there was an emphasis upon the economic sources of oppression and the need for more than just freedom as a right. "The current sit-ins and other demonstrations," Ella Baker told the first SNCC Conference, "are concerned with something much bigger than a hamburger or even a giant sized coke." The students, she insisted, were looking for "a group centered leadership, rather than a leader-centered pattern of organization." Similarly, they sought the collective goals of abolishing economic squalor and educational deprivation. When the SNCC workers who heard Baker went to Mississippi and Alabama and Georgia, they quickly discovered that poverty was as much a source of oppression as racism and that the two were intertwined. Teachers were fired from schools if they advocated racial freedom, sharecroppers were evicted from their land, credit was cancelled. More to the point, poor housing, disease, and depression were part of the daily life of civil rights workers who came to understand that the vote—even the law—offered only a partial answer to the quest for freedom, because, in the end, far-reaching structural change in wealth and income and power were central to achieving equality.

The same sub-theme of economic change was articulated by Bayard Rustin, a close associate of Martin Luther King, Jr., and A. Philip Randolph. Significantly, the goal of the March on Washington in 1963—a march which Rustin coordinated and suggested—was jobs as well as freedom. His own call for a domestic Marshall Plan emphasized the inextricable connection of racial equality and economic equality. While downplaying his own socialist past, Rustin kept in the forefront of the civil right agenda the need to seek systemic change within America.

In some ways, of course, the war on poverty was a consequence of the civil rights movement's emphasis on economic reform. The civil rights movement brought home to many privileged Americans a new awareness of the connection between racial and economic inequality. Largely as a result of the ethical thrust of the civil rights movement, John Kennedy authorized the campaign to abolish poverty, ordering his aides to draft legislation for the program just two days after his June 8, 1963, speech in which, for the first time, he forcefully identified himself with the struggle for civil rights. Lyndon Johnson continued that effort, eloquently telling Congress in 1965:

> Somehow you never forget what poverty and hatred can do when you see its scars on the hopeful face of a young child . . . It never occurred to me in my fondest dreams that I might have the chance to help the sons and daughters of those students and to help people like them all over the country. But now I do have that chance—[and] I mean to use it . . . I want to be the president who educated young children . . . who helped to feed the hungry . . . to help the poor to find their own way.

That year, 43 per cent of all black families were poor, earning under $3,000 per year. Black unemployment was twice that of white unemployment, with black teenage unemployment 100 per cent higher than black adult unemployment. Fewer than 40 per cent of black teenagers finished high school. Now, with Johnson's commitment, it appeared for a moment at least that there would be a possibility of achieving the economic component of the vision for social change articulated by Ella Baker and Bayard Rustin.

But it was not to be. There were, in effect, three approaches to combatting poverty. The most radical involved a conscious effort to redistribute wealth and income through creating new jobs, building new houses, revitalizing cities, creating a new infrastructure of social welfare institutions, and enacting massive tax reform. But such an approach presumed a collective conflict between those who had power and those who did not, implicitly setting one group against another. Such an approach totally violated Lyndon

Johnson's commitment to consensus. The second approach was more quantitative in nature, simply using income transfers such as food stamps and health care to provide enough of a margin for poor people so that they could rise above the level of poverty. The third approach, and the one eventually chosen, was more consistent with traditional American values of individualism. By this strategy, individual poor people would be given a chance to overcome the disabilities that surrounded them, and enabled to "earn" a higher standard of living. Here the emphasis was on eliminating, in the Administration's words, "the handicaps that now deny the poor *fair access* to the expanding incomes of a growing economy." In this scenario, an unequal distribution of power and wealth was not the problem. Rather, it was inadequate availability of opportunity.

In the end, the war on poverty included a combination of transfer payments, educational efforts, and psychological incentives. But basically, it involved an effort to change the *attitudes* of the poor, in Sargent Shriver's words, "to move those in poverty from indifference to interest, ignorance to awareness, resignation to ambition, and an attitude of withdrawal to one of participation."

Even with this approach, it is important to acknowledge that the war on poverty did make a difference. Black family income had risen to 60 percent of white family income by the end of 1968, compared to only 54 per cent in 1965. The percentage of black families earning under $3,000 fell from 41 per cent in 1960 to 23 per cent in 1968. Nevertheless, the war on poverty remained a disappointment overall, with blacks who were concentrated in the poorest neighborhoods in the nation actually seeing their condition deteriorate rather than improve. Instead of being an unconditional war, the anti-poverty effort, historian Mark Gelfand has observed, represents "a classic incident of the American habit of substituting good intentions for cold hard cash." The war on poverty fell victim to another war nine thousand miles away in Southeast Asia. When the anti-poverty program started officials anticipated the expenditures would exceed $10.4 billion per year by 1970. In fact, OEO [Office of Economic Opportunity] appropriations never exceeded more than $2 billion per year under Lyndon Johnson.

In the meantime, many SNCC workers who had begun in 1960 and 1961 full of confidence about America's capacity for reform had begun to alter radically their understanding of the issues, rejecting the individualist and integrationist approach associated with the early movement and opting instead for a collectivist strategy based on racial solidarity. Although Black Power had many definitions, its origins were embedded in the political and economic experiences encountered by SNCC workers during the mid-1960s. Not only did daily contact with malnutrition, disease, and economic intimidation convince SNCC workers that systemic change in the economy was essential for racial equality; the same workers had also become convinced that the only way to achieve such change was by establishing an independent political base through which blacks could define their own agenda, shape their own strategy, and control their own lives.

Repeatedly, white Americans, however liberal, had defaulted on promises made. It was not just the FBI agents who stood by taking notes while black demonstrators were beaten, nor a Justice Department that refused to file suits in most places where black rights were systematically denied. It was also "friends" who seemed to insist on the necessity of deferring to those in power on issues that seemed fundamental to civil rights workers. Thus, when Hubert Humphrey, Joseph Rauh and others urged the Mississippi Freedom Democratic Party (MFDP) to accept a hollow compromise at the Atlantic City Democratic Convention in 1964 rather than engage in a floor fight that might bring the victory they deserved, SNCC workers balked. As one Mississippi black woman declared, "to compromise would let Jim Crow be . . . ain't no Democratic Party worth that. We've been treated like beasts in Mississippi. They shot us down like animals. We risked our lives coming here. . . . Politics must be corrupt if it don't care none about people down there."

Ultimately, the Black Power movement represented an affirmation that "race" could not be abolished as a reality in America. It was a source of pride and strength, as well as of discrimination, in American society. To many white Americans, Martin Luther King, Jr., held forth the possibility that 300 years of history could be erased, that through Christian faith, mutual commitment, and idealistic love, Americans could put behind them the legacy of slavery and Jim Crow and walk together to the promised land. King's message had been instrumental in securing support for the legislative objectives of the civil rights movement, helping to forge the national coalition that resulted in enactment of the Civil Rights Act of 1964 and the Voting Rights Act of 1965. But for many SNCC workers, the utopian vision that had attracted white support represented a delusion that promised to subvert their own changing vision of what was necessary. And so, at the moment when the civil rights movement achieved its greatest success, the movement itself was fragmenting, torn deeply by conflict over both its goals and strategy.

The election year of 1968 represented perhaps the last opportunity to put together a program that would address the issues of class as well as race. Beginning in 1965, Martin Luther King, Jr., had become a leading spokesman for the anti-war movement in the United States, convinced that events in Vietnam were inextricably tied to racial justice in America. Simultaneously, he articulated a far broader vision of the connection between racial justice and economic democracy. More and more convinced the legislation which barred discrimination meant little without redistribution of wealth and power, King directly linked economic and racial issues. "We must recognize," he told his staff in 1967, "that we can't solve our problems now until there is a radical distribution of economic and political power." Class, he said, was as important as race.

> The black revolution is much more than struggle for the rights of Negroes. It is forcing America to face all its inter-related flaws—racism, poverty, militarism, and materialism. It is exposing evils that are rooted deeply in the whole structure of our society. It reveals systemic rather than superficial flaws and suggests that radical reconstruction of society itself is the real issue to be faced.

Instead of reform, King declared, blacks had to move toward revolution, to an era that would "raise certain basic questions about the whole society. . . . We are engaged in a class struggle . . . dealing with the problem of the gulf between the haves and the haves-nots."

At the same time, Robert F. Kennedy was emphasizing similar themes. In the years after his brother's death, he had become more and more engaged—emotionally—in the struggles of the poor. "Perhaps we cannot prevent this world from being a world in which children are tortured," Kennedy quoted in his journal from Camus, "but we can reduce the number of tortured children."

Abroad, he identified himself with workers in Chile, protestors in South Africa, anti-war demonstrators at home. He had become, Murray Kempton wrote, "our first politician for the pariahs, our great national outsider, our lonely reproach, the natural standard held out to all rebels." While never embracing black power, Kennedy did devote more and more attention to the issues of unemployment, disease, and health in northern ghettos. "He did things that I wouldn't do," Marian Wright Edelman said, "he went into the dirtiest, filthiest, poorest homes . . . and he would sit with a baby with open sores whose belly was bloated from malnutrition and he'd sit and touch and hold those babies . . . I wouldn't do that." Kennedy too talked about the "gulf between the haves and the have nots," expressed his outrage at the institutional violence of poverty and malnutrition, and proclaimed his commitment to dramatic change.

Through parallel paths, both Kennedy and King had come to new understandings of what was necessary in American society to achieve racial justice, and each, in his own way, reached out to forge coalitions that might provide a vehicle for achieving their mutual vision. To many, their efforts represented the last hope for peaceful change using existing political means. With the assassination of both men within two months of each other in the spring of 1968, those hopes crumpled. Perhaps they were doomed from the beginning. Perhaps the notion of transforming America was romantic and utopian. Perhaps those who believed in the goals that Kennedy and King espoused should have found a way to continue.

But instead, those who *opposed* the goals of Kennedy and King—and who in a larger sense opposed the collectivist ideas associated with economic equality and black power—appealed successfully to traditional American values and assumed power. Richard Nixon was now President, the Southern strategy reigned supreme in the White House, and American society and politics took a new direction. In the history of the civil rights movement and the movements it spawned for social and economic equality, 1968 represented a critical turning point away from the possibility of collective solutions to structural inequality.

Instead, supporters of the civil rights movement found the years after 1968 relatively bleak. To be sure, school desegregation advanced more rapidly than at any time since the *Brown* decision, and with the Supreme Court's ruling in *Swan* v. *Mecklenburg,* formal resistance by school systems to desegration finally collapsed. There were gains as well in affirmative action, and even the Nixon administration supported the "Philadelphia plan" which mandated a quota of minority employees in construction projects funded by federal dollars. Counter-balancing these policies, however, was a systematic campaign by Republicans—subsequently brought to culmination under Ronald Reagan—to recruit white southerners to their party, using pronouncements against civil rights organizations as a primary recruitment tool. Nixon denounced busing, sought judicial appointments that would please conservative white southerners, and mobilized a political constituency based upon loyalty to traditional values of law and order, often seen as code words for racism. Government programs of infiltration and subversion divided militant black groups, with agent provocateurs providing the occasion for deploying police power to intimidate or destroy militant groups. In one year alone, twenty-eight Black Panthers fell victim to police bullets.

Disorganized and divided, civil rights groups lost a sense of coherence and direction. No one took the place of Dr. King as a national black spokesman, or leader of a potentially united movement. SNCC and CORE [Congress of Racial Equality] fell apart before the divisive politics of Black Power: SCLC [Southern Christian Leadership Conference] floundered without clear direction; and the NAACP and Urban League struggled just to retain their traditional constituencies. Among other things, the fate of these civil rights organizations reflected their own success. There was no longer a visible, dramatic, clear-cut enemy. It was hard to mobilize a march when there was no theatre to desegregate, no county courthouse to picket over disenfranchisement. The profound problems which remained—institutional racism, unemployment, absence of capital—did not lend themselves to simple slogans or easy solutions. To the extent that a social movement requires transcendent symbols around which to organize, the early 1970s offered few vehicles for collective mobilization. On top of everything else there developed a widespread revulsion against the activism of the 1960s, especially its more militant form, as though someone had administered a massive anti-activism inoculation to the nation. Even Watergate worked to the disadvantage of civil rights groups, focusing the nation's attention on preserving the constitutional processes of government, and thereby helping to divert attention from agendas for further social and economic change.

Significantly, the major movement to retain vitality and direction in the new era of conservatism—feminism—was the last movement to grow out of the civil rights struggle. As it evolved, the women's movement in many ways paralleled the civil rights struggle. The National Organization for Women was started in 1966 in order to secure compliance with the provisions of the 1964 Civil Rights Act which prohibited discrimination on the basis of sex as well as race in employment practices. Like the NAACP, NOW worked within existing political and economic structures to seek reform, using litigation, lobbying, and legislation to counter discrimination against women and to broaden access to equal opportunity. The women's liberation movement, the more radical wing of feminism, grew out of SNCC and SDS [Students for a Democratic Society]. Composed primarily of younger women, supporters of women's liberation had encountered traditional attitudes of male dominance and exploitation within the civil rights struggle. Initially, black women and white women within SNCC cooperated to protest their treatment as second-class citizens, but as black power became more and more a salient force within SNCC, white women began to organize their own movement, both within SDS, and in university communities throughout the nation. Supporters of women's liberation challenged every dimension of the social, economic, and cultural barriers that existed against women. In many ways paralleling SNCC, they frequently endorsed radical economic programs, as well as a strategy of separatism and self-help. On occasion, members of the women's liberation movement attempted to strike alliances with civil rights groups and workers groups, but for the most part, feminism was perceived by both working women and blacks as a primarily white middle class movement. Black women responded more favorably to "feminist" issues like equal pay, child care, and abortion rights than any other group in the population, but most felt that race was the primary issue in their lives, and that joining the struggle to abolish gender discrimination must take second place to the central question of abolishing racial discrimination.

In this context, the primary feature of the 1970s and early 1980s has been an almost schizophrenic pattern of progress and decline for former victims of discrimination, with those who are above a certain economic level able to take advantage of the triumphs of the 1960s, while those below a certain economic level have found the texture of their lives deteriorating to the point of resignation and defeat. Hundreds of thousands of black Americans were able to take advantage of the gains of the 1960s to progress swiftly into the mainstream of American economic life. With the Civil Rights Act of 1964, the Voting Rights Act of 1965, and the Housing Act of 1968 removing legal obstacles to employment, political participation, and dreams of moving into a house of one's choice, many blacks were able to claim the benefits of complete participation in a way of life previously limited to those with a white skin. Those in a position to do so moved ahead to maximize the opportunity available, and in the process helped to transform their lives.

Economic statistics offer one barometer of some of the gains made possible by the civil rights movement. The number of blacks living in poverty, for example, declined from over 40 per cent in 1959 to nearly 20 per cent in 1968. In the meantime the proportion of black families earning more than $10,000 a year leaped from 13 per cent in 1960 to 31 per cent in 1971. Although, overall, black incomes still averaged only 59 or 60 per cent of white income, that was still an increase over the 48 per cent of 1959. In many areas of the country the gap was still narrower. Outside of the South, husband and wife two-income families earned 88 per cent of what white two-income families received. In 1977, twenty-five to twenty-nine year old black males who graduated from high school earned 75 per cent of what their white peers earned, and black men with college degrees earned 93 per cent as much as their white counterparts. Among employed black women, 34 per cent were in the technical, sales, and administrative support categories by 1980—more than double the percentage of a decade earlier—and only 2 per cent less than the figure for white women. The Voting Rights Act, meanwhile, led to substantial gains in political representation, with black mayors elected in such large cities as Los Angeles, Detroit, Oakland, Atlanta, and Cleveland, and Congressional representation increasing from 4 in 1959 to 18 by 1980.

In the educational arena as well, dramatic changes occurred. The median number of school years for black citizens increased from 10.7 in 1960 to 12.2 in 1970, the latter only .5 per cent less than that for whites. In 1960 only a quarter of a million black Americans were enrolled in the nation's colleges. Seventeen years later, that figure had increased by 500 per cent to 1.1 million, with the U.S. Census Bureau concluding that "among high school graduates, blacks and whites are attending colleges at about the same rate." The average number of visits from corporate recruiters to black colleges soared from 4 in 1960 to 297 in the 1970s, with the increase partly reflected in the rise of black male workers in white collar positions from 16 per cent in 1964 to 24 per cent in 1974 (compared to 40 per cent for whites). In the north, at least, black college graduates could even expect to earn slightly more than whites at entry level positions.

Not surprisingly, some observers described the results as a "story of massive black success." Ben Wattenberg and Richard Scammon concluded that as many as half of all black families had joined the middle class, and even those skeptical of such figures acknowledged that the number of blacks in the middle class occupations had increased dramatically. Clearly, the civil rights movement had made a difference.

How then to explain the other side of the coin, the massive decline in life possibilities and economic status for millions of American blacks. In 1954, the unemployment rate among black teenagers was only slightly higher than that for white teenagers. Today [1986] it is more than twice as high, and throughout the 1970s, exceeded 40 per cent. Black adult unemployment is twice as high as white adult unemployment, and black teenage unemployment is five times as high as black adult employment. As more and more whites have left America's urban areas, they have been replaced by blacks, but urban dwellers more often than not work in low level service jobs. In 1970, 60 per cent of black men in our central cities occupied such positions in contrast to only 33 per cent of white men. While the percentage of black high school graduates to go onto college is coming closer to that of white high school graduates, the percentage of blacks who *graduate* from high school is falling behind, with only 68 per cent of black males receiving high school diplomas compared to 85 per cent of whites. While some college-educated blacks are enjoying significant success in finding white collar and managerial positions in the suburbs and in corporate America, the number of decent manufacturing jobs and service jobs is declining, leaving thousands of blacks in central cities without employment. New York City experienced a 100 per cent increase in its welfare rolls from 1965 to 1975, and Chicago welfare rolls doubled from 1970 to 1975. By the mid-80s, more than half of all black children under six were living in poverty.

Thus, black America appears to be moving more and more toward a class differentiated social structure. Income differentials among blacks were widening, according to black economist Andrew Brimmer. Indeed, the black sociologist William J. Wilson concluded that divisions among blacks had deepened so much that "now the life chances of individual blacks have more to do with their economic class position than with their day-to-day encounters with whites."

Significantly, a parallel pattern emerged in the status of American women. If college educated and middle-class women proved most receptive to the ideology of feminism, they also appeared to have benefited most significantly from the new ideology. During the 1970s the number of women in college who anticipated entering traditionally "feminine" professions such as elementary and secondary school teaching plummeted from 31 per cent to 10 per cent, while the proportion of women entering law school and medical school mushroomed by 500 per cent. Today most law schools boast entering classes that are at least 40 per cent women. (The figures had been 5 to 8 per cent during the years 1940 to 1960). According to public opinion surveys, growing numbers of college women declared that a career was just as important as marriage in achieving a sense of personal fulfillment, and projections for labor market participation anticipated a job curve for college women that by year 2000 would parallel that for college men. Although some of the optimism associated with such projections may be suspect, it is undeniable that for some women—especially the college-educated young—changes have occurred in the areas of economic opportunity and personal self-fulfillment that would have been unheard of thirty years ago. It also seems clear that these gains are directly connected to the women's movement and to the civil rights struggle.

But in the case of women as well as of black Americans, the success stories of those who are bright, talented, and from economically secure backgrounds stand in stark contrast to the experience of millions who either live in poverty or whose participation in the labor force consists of dead-end sex-segregated and low paying jobs. Over 80 per cent of all women workers are clustered in just 20 out of the 420 occupations listed by the Census Bureau. Most of these are in the area of service work. Even women who are able to work frequently earn incomes that place them below the poverty level. Approximately 25 per cent of all working women who were head of households with children in 1983 received incomes beneath poverty level.

Experts predict that if present trends continue, by the year 2000 all poor people in America will either be women or children. This startling assessment correlates directly with the massive increase in recent years of female-headed households—a 72 per cent increase during the 1970s alone. A few simple figures tell the impact of that increase. A child born into a family with no father present has one chance in three of being poor; if the family is headed by a man alone the chances of a child being poor are one in ten; and if both parents are present the chances of being poor are only in nineteen. This "feminization of poverty" reflects not only structural changes in the job market, with a decrease in skills and decent paying jobs, but also inadequate training for better jobs among those caught in the spiral of downward mobility. More than half of all single-parent families are headed by people who have never completed high school. Many of the children who are now poor as the result of teenage pregnancies, with one out of every six children in the 1970s being born to a teenage mother. Most frequently these mothers are not married, have dropped out of school and thus become even more deeply trapped by poverty.

It is at this point that the intersection of gender, class and race becomes most clear. While the number of white families headed by women increased by more than 50 per cent in the 1970s (from 9 to 14 per cent) the number of black families headed by women now amounts to almost half of all black families. In some inner city ghettos nearly 70 per cent of all black children are born to single mothers. As Eleanor Holmes Norton has noted, "you can't underestimate the stress of raising a child in the ghetto by yourself, without a grandmother, without an aunt, with no one you can turn to." In 1978, a female-headed black family earned a median income of less than $6,000—compared to $16,000 earned by two-parent black families. Yet one of the reasons black women were living alone was because there were no jobs for black men. Unemployment rates for black male teenagers of more than 50 per cent help to explain why black female teenagers bear children out of wedlock and without financial support from the father, particularly in a society where, in many states, welfare payments are contingent upon there being no male present in the home.

Thus it all becomes a vicious cycle. Young men in the ghetto cannot find jobs. Young women in the ghetto need welfare to support their children. Welfare rules discriminate against those who have a husband present. The end result is that black women become heads of families descending further into poverty. Welfare becomes a way of life because there is no alternative. In 1980, 40,000 youngsters in New York City dropped out of high school, but of the 105,000 annual job openings in New York, only 9,000 were for messengers, janitors, bus boys, or maids—those occupations available for people without skill or education. The result is an ever-growing group called by some the "underclass," virtually none of whom have completed high school, most of whom are now locked into a cycle of permanent poverty. As a result, even while 35 to 45 per cent of black families have succeeded in achieving a middle class lifestyle, another 30 per cent have experienced a steady decline into ever deeper poverty, totally bereft of gains from the civil rights struggle of the 1960s, captured by the triple burden of gender, class, and race.

Ironically, the gains of desegregation have made even less likely the opportunity to forge a united campaign for improvement based upon racial identity alone. The well-educated, upwardly mobile beneficiaries of changes in the 1960s tend to move out of economically deprived neighborhoods. The home base of church, school, and community organizations that had existed during the era of segregation is gone. And there is an increasing distance between those who are able to take advantage of the opportunities in the mainstream society, and those who are increasingly pressed to the margins of that society, living a life of misery, no longer linked to those better-off than themselves by neighborhood bonds, common institutions, and the shared commitment to racial advancement.

Significantly those who are the chief victims of this new class bifurcation have also suffered a loss of political power. While commentators have widely discussed the decline in voter participation in American elections, the most striking fact of this decline is the class distribution of those who have stopped going to the polls. "When people ask where have all the voters gone," political scientist Walter Dean Burnham has noted, "they should really be asking 'where have all the working class Democrats gone." Nearly half of the congressional districts where voter participation declined more than twenty per cent in the 1960s and 70s were in the nation's three largest urban centers—precisely the areas most victimized by poverty, crime, and unemployment. The two congressional districts with the lowest turn out were Bedford Stuyvesant [in New York City], with an 18.8 per cent participation rate, and the South Bronx, with a 21.8 per cent rate. By contrast, Scarsdale [a wealthy New York suburb] had a turn out rate of more than 70 per cent. The people in these urban areas feel left out, with no stake in government, and no hope that their involvement can make a difference. For such people, the Voting Rights Act of 1965 and the Civil Rights Act of 1964 have little meaning except for the paper that they were written on. What makes this declining voter participation even more devastating is that it has occurred simultaneously with increased mobilization of conservative voters around social issues such as "law and order," "busing," "affirmative action," and welfare.

In the end, therefore, any overall assessment of the civil rights movement must reflect the growing split that has occurred between those able to take advantage of the gains made during the 1960s, and those for whom these gains mean little. Certainly, there can be no gainsaying the extraordinary triumphs recorded in the nation's laws as a result of the civil rights movement, nor the advances made in the aftermath of these laws by large numbers of blacks, women, and others who have individually been able to take advantage of the new opportunities that have developed. If the primary purpose of the civil rights movement is defined as individual freedom, and the opportunity to secure personal gains previously denied on the basis of race, then the movement would have to be described as a complete success. But the civil rights movement had more than the goal of individual freedom. From Ella Baker to Bayard Rustin to Martin Luther King, Jr., its leaders spoke of the collective goals of racial *and* economic equality, narrowing the gap between the haves and the have-nots, creating a situation where all black people, all poor people, all victims of discrimination, would have substantive access to new opportunity as well as simply the theoretical right to advance.

On this second criterion, the verdict must be primarily negative. When the civil rights movement was compatible with the traditional values of individualism and competitiveness in American society, its demands were granted, however reluctantly. But where the movement threatened structural change, questioned deep-seated cultural values, and entered areas that would require a redistribution of political and economic power, resistance set in.

Even those "collective gains" that were made, as in the area of affirmative action, now seem in doubt. Not only is the Supreme Court unclear about supporting affirmative action programs; the Reagan administration is adamantly opposed, with enforcement of affirmative action policies down by 75 per cent over the last four years. It would appear that as long as individual reforms do not threaten the basic structure of political and economic power in this society, they can be accepted, regardless of gender or race. But when substantial change of a collective nature is proposed, the going becomes much more difficult.

Unfortunately, while the nation may be arriving at a new understanding of how gender, race, and class intersect to create a two-tiered society, how it attacks this problem is still unclear. If the history of the civil rights movement teaches anything, it is the importance of linking programs for change to values that are widely shared in the dominant culture. Yet all must beware of the fate that occurred during the 1960s, when the collective goals of the movement were separated from the individual goals. In that direction lies a new divide and conquer strategy, with individual success stories used to obscure the massive social problems reflected in the feminization of poverty.

Thus, while acknowledging dramatic gains achieved as a consequence of the civil rights movement, it is necessary, in Vincent Harding's words, to recognize the evolving nature of the struggle, and be open to new alliances, new approaches, new understandings of the collective goals sought. And even though the nature of the movement changes, the fundamental tenet articulated by Frederick Douglass 100 years ago must be remembered: "Power concedes nothing without a demand. It never has and it never will."

₪ *F U R T H E R   R E A D I N G*

Numan V. Bartley, *The Rise of Massive Resistance: Race and Politics in the South During the 1950s* (1969)

William C. Berman, *The Politics of Civil Rights in the Truman Administration* (1970)

Rhoda Lois Blumberg, *Civil Rights: The 1960s Freedom Struggle* (1984)

Taylor Branch, *Parting the Waters: America in the King Years, 1954–1963* (1988)

Carl M. Brauer, *John F. Kennedy and the Second Reconstruction* (1977)

Robert F. Burk, *The Eisenhower Administration and Black Civil Rights* (1984)

Clayborne Carson, *In Struggle: SNCC and the Black Awakening of the 1960s* (1981)

William H. Chafe, *Civilities and Civil Rights: Greensboro, North Carolina, and the Black Struggle for Freedom* (1980)

Charles W. Eagles and David L. Lewis, eds., *The Civil Rights Movement in America* (1986)

James Farmer, *Lay Bare the Heart: An Autobiography of the Civil Rights Movement* (1985)

James Foreman, *The Making of Black Revolutionaries* (1985)

Tony Freyer, *Little Rock Crisis: A Constitutional Interpretation* (1984)

David J. Garrow, *Bearing the Cross: Martin Luther King, Jr., and the Southern Christian Leadership Conference* (1987)

———, *Protest at Selma: Martin Luther King, Jr., and the Voting Rights Act* (1978)

Peter Goldman, *The Death and Life of Malcolm X* (1979)

Hugh Davis Graham, *The Civil Rights Era: Origins and Development of National Policy, 1960–1972* (1990)

Alex Haley, comp., *The Autobiography of Malcolm X* (1965)

James C. Harvey, *Black Civil Rights During the Johnson Administration* (1973)

———, *Civil Rights During the Kennedy Administration* (1971)

Martin L. King, Jr., *Why We Can't Wait* (1964)

———, *Where Do We Go from Here: Chaos or Community?* (1968)

Mary King, *Freedom Song: A Personal Story of the 1960s Civil Rights Movement* (1987)

Richard Kluger, *Simple Justice* (1977)

Steven F. Lawson, *Black Ballots: Voting Rights in the South, 1944–1969* (1976)

———, *In Pursuit of Power* (1985)

David L. Lewis, *King: A Biography* (1978)

Doug McAdam, *Freedom Summer* (1988)

Neil R. McMillen, *The Citizens' Council: Organized Resistance to the Second Reconstruction, 1954–64* (1971)

Manning Marable, *Race, Reform and Rebellion: The Second Reconstruction in Black America, 1945–1982* (1984)

August Meier and Elliot Rudwick, *CORE: A Study in the Civil Rights Movement, 1942–1968* (1972)

Aldon D. Morris, *The Origins of the Civil Rights Movement: Black Communities Organizing* (1984)

Stephen B. Oates, *Let the Trumpet Sound: The Life of Martin Luther King, Jr.* (1982)

Howell Raines, ed., *My Soul Is Rested: Movement Days in the Deep South Remembered* (1982)

Cleveland Sellers with Robert Terrell, *The River of No Return* (1973)

Harvard Sitkoff, *The Struggle for Black Equality, 1954–1980* (1981)

Milton Viorst, *Fire in the Streets: America in the 1960's* (1979)

Pat Watters and Reese Cleghorn, *Climbing Jacob's Ladder: The Arrival of Negroes in Southern Politics* (1967)

Robert Weisbrot, *Freedom Bound: A History of the American Civil Rights Movement* (1990)

Roy Wilkins and Tom Matthews, *The Autobiography of Roy Wilkins* (1982)

J. Harvie Wilkinson III, *From Brown to Bakke: The Supreme Court and School Integration: 1954–1978* (1979)

Juan Williams, *Eyes on the Prize: America's Civil Rights Years, 1954–1965* (1965)

Harris Wofford, *Of Kennedys and Kings: Making Sense of the Sixties* (1980)

Raymond Wolters, *The Burden of Brown: Thirty Years of School Desegregation* (1984)

Howard Zinn, *SNCC: The New Abolitionists* (1965)

Vietnam and the Crisis
of American Empire

XXX

The Vietnam War was the most traumatic event in postwar American history. It cost the lives of more than 50,000 Americans and of hundreds of thousands of Vietnamese and other Southeast Asians. It shattered the presidency of Lyndon Johnson, dealt the Democratic party a defeat from which it still has not recovered, and divided the American people more deeply than at any other time since the Civil War.

On one level, the war in Vietnam was the product of the Cold War and the projection of the ideas, interests, and strategies associated with that struggle onto a postcolonial world of nationalism and social revolution. It was also the logical outgrowth of America's postwar effort to maintain what Truman adviser Clark M. Clifford had once described as "our conception of a decent world order" or what Henry Luce had earlier called "an American century." The U.S. defeat in Vietnam, combined with the growing economic ascendancy of Japan and Western Europe, would mark the beginning of the end of the postwar "American era."

Among the many questions that continue to preoccupy historians and other students of the Vietnamese War, three in particular stand out: How (and why) did the United States come to tie its own fate to the creation and maintenance of an American-dominated, anticommunist regime in Southeast Asia? Given that commitment, how (and with what consequences) did the United States conduct the war? And finally, what are the lessons of Vietnam, especially in a world no longer dominated by the Cold War but in which the forces of nationalism and social revolution remain very powerful?

XXX *D O C U M E N T S*

As World War II drew to a close and Japanese control over Vietnam waned, the Vietminh, whose forces represented a powerful fusion of communism and nationalism, seized power throughout much of the country. With an eye toward winning U.S. support, they issued a Declaration of Independence (the first document), which began with a familiar passage. The French effort to regain control of Vietnam and the resulting First Indochina War (1946–1954) posed a dilemma for U.S. policymakers: should the United States accept the victory of a movement that, like that in China, was both communist and nationalist, or should it support the French colonial regime led by Boa Dai? In the second document, State Department officials Raymond B. Fosdick and W. Walton Butterworth argue the two sides of the dilemma. The U.S. government, of course, followed the advice of the latter.

The French defeat was sealed on July 21, 1954, by the Geneva Agreements (the third document), which temporarily divided Vietnam along the 17th parallel, established procedures for the nation's reunification, and sought to insulate it from further outside intervention. Despite the Geneva Accords, the United States soon replaced France as the dominant Western power in Vietnam. Its efforts to create and sustain a new, anticommunist government, however, drew the United States deeper and deeper into conflict with the National Liberation Front (NLF, or Vietcong) in the South and with the Democratic Republic of Vietnam (North Vietnam). In 1964, when American warships were fired upon in the Gulf of Tonkin off the North Vietnam coast (where they had been conducting electronic surveillance and providing cover for South Vietnamese attacks), President Lyndon Johnson seized the opportunity to push through Congress the so-called Gulf of Tonkin Resolution (document four), which he would later use to justify the continuing U.S. war in Vietnam.

Although U.S. military advisers had been present in Vietnam since the 1950s, American combat troops did not arrive until early 1965. Not until July 28, 1965, moreover, did the Johnson administration decide to greatly expand the U.S. effort. The fifth document is composed of two memoranda, one by Secretary of Defense Robert S. McNamara urging escalation and one by Under Secretary of State George Ball arguing that the United States should seek a compromise solution. Despite superior weapons and resources, U.S. military forces could never fully subdue their Vietnamese enemies. American soldiers, unprepared to wage a guerrilla war in a foreign land amidst an unfamiliar people, and lacking the broad popular support that had sustained troops in earlier wars, became increasingly frustrated, angry, and disillusioned, as is revealed in interviews collected by Mark Baker in *NAM: The Vietnam War in the Words of the Men and Women Who Fought There*, excerpted as the sixth document. A decade after the fall of Vietnam, Americans continued to debate the war's legacy. The Reagan administration in particular sought to overcome what it called the Vietnam syndrome and to prove that "America was back." Thomas J. Vallely, a Marine Corps veteran who later campaigned against the war, strongly criticizes this approach in the final documentary selection.

The Vietnamese Declare Their Independence, 1945

"We hold truths that all men are created equal, that they are endowed by their Creator with certain unalienable Rights, among these are Life, Liberty and the pursuit of Happiness."

This immortal statement is extracted from the Declaration of Independence of the United States of America in 1776. Understood in the broader sense, this means: "All peoples on the earth are born equal; every person has the right to live to be happy and free."

The Declaration of Human and Civic Rights proclaimed by the French Revolution in 1791 likewise propounds: "Every man is born equal and enjoys free and equal rights."

These are undeniable truths.

Yet, during and throughout the last eighty years, the French imperialists, abusing the principles of "Freedom, equality and fraternity," have violated the integrity of our ancestral land and oppressed our countrymen. Their deeds run counter to the ideals of humanity and justice.

In the political field, they have denied us every freedom. They have enforced upon us inhuman laws. They have set up three different political regimes in Northern, Central and Southern Viet Nam (Tonkin, Annam, and Cochinchina) in an attempt to disrupt our national, historical and ethical unity.

They have built more prisons than schools. They have callously ill-treated our fellow-compatriots. They have drowned our revolutions in blood.

They have sought to stifle public opinion and pursued a policy of obscurantism on the largest scale; they have forced upon us alcohol and opium in order to weaken our race.

In the economic field, they have shamelessly exploited our people, driven them into the worst misery and mercilessly plundered our country.

They have ruthlessly appropriated our rice fields, mines, forests and raw materials. They have arrogated to themselves the privilege of issuing banknotes, and monopolised all our external commerce. They have imposed hundreds of unjustifiable taxes, and reduced our countrymen, especially the peasants and petty tradesmen, to extreme poverty.

They have prevented the development of native capital enterprises; they have exploited our workers in the most barbarous manner.

In the autumn of 1940, when the Japanese fascists, in order to fight the Allies, invaded Indochina and set up new bases of war, the French imperialists surrendered on bended knees and handed over our country to the invaders.

Subsequently, under the joint French and Japanese yoke, our people were literally bled white. The consequences were dire in the extreme. From Quang Tri up to the North, two millions of our countrymen died from starvation during the first months of this year.

On March 9th, 1945, the Japanese disarmed the French troops. Again the French either fled or surrendered unconditionally. Thus, in no way have they proved capable of "protecting" us; on the contrary, within five years they have twice sold our country to the Japanese.

Before March 9th, many a time did the Viet Minh League invite the French to join in the fight against the Japanese. Instead of accepting this offer, the French, on the contrary, let loose a wild reign of terror with rigour worse than ever before against Viet Minh's partisans. They even slaughtered a great number of our *"condamnés politiques"* imprisoned at Yen Bay and Cao Bang.

Despite all that, our countrymen went on maintaining, vis-a-vis the French, a humane and even indulgent attitude. After the events of March

9th, the Viet Minh League helped many French to cross the borders, rescued others from Japanese prisons and, in general, protected the lives and properties of all the French in their territory.

In fact, since the autumn of 1940, our country ceased to be a French colony and became a Japanese possession.

After the Japanese surrender, our people, as a whole, rose up and proclaimed their sovereignty and founded the Democratic Republic of Viet Nam.

The truth is that we have wrung back our independence from Japanese hands and not from the French.

The French fled, the Japanese surrendered. Emperor Bao Dai abdicated, our people smashed the yoke which pressed hard upon us for nearly one hundred years, and finally made our Viet Nam an independent country. Our people at the same time overthrew the monarchical regime established tens of centuries ago, and founded the Republic.

For these reasons, we the members of the Provisional Government representing the entire people of Viet Nam, declare that we shall from now on have no more connections with imperialist France; we consider null and void all the treaties France has signed concerning Viet Nam, and we hereby cancel all the privileges that the French arrogated to themselves on our territory.

The Vietnamese people, animated by the same common resolve, are determined to fight to the death against all attempts at aggression by the French imperialists.

We are convinced that the Allies who have recognized the principles of equality of peoples at the Conferences of Teheran and San Francisco cannot but recognize the independence of Viet Nam.

A people which has so stubbornly opposed the French domination for more than 80 years, a people who, during these last years, so doggedly ranged itself and fought on the Allied side against Fascism, such a people has the right to be free, such a people must be independent.

For these reasons, we, the members of the Provisional Government of the Democratic Republic of Viet Nam, solemnly declare to the world:

"Viet Nam has the right to be free and independent and, in fact, has become free and independent. The people of Viet Nam decide to mobilise all their spiritual and material forces and to sacrifice their lives and property in order to safeguard their right of Liberty and Independence."

State Department Advisers
Debate U.S. Support for the
French in Vietnam, 1949

[November 4, 1949]

SECRET

MEMORANDUM FOR: Mr. [Philip C.] Jessup [Ambassador-at-Large]

In his memorandum of November 1 on Indochina, Mr. [Charles] Yost argues that "a further major advance of Communism will be considered as, and will in fact be, a defeat for the United States, whether or not we are directly involved." He therefore recommends, among other steps, support of the Bao Dai government (after the March 8 agreements are ratified) economic assistance to Bao Dai, etc.

It seems to me this point of view fails to take into consideration the possible, and I think the probable, consequences of such a decision. In grasping one horn of the dilemma, it ignores the other. My belief is that the Bao Dai regime is doomed. The compromises which the French are so reluctantly making cannot possibly save it. The Indochinese are pressing toward complete nationalism and nothing is going to stop them. They see all too clearly that France is offering them a kind of semi-colonialism; and to think that they will be content to settle for less than Indonesia has gained from the Dutch or India from the British is to underestimate the power of the forces that are sweeping Asia today.

What kind of independence is France offering the Indochinese today in the March 8th agreements?

(1) The foreign policy of Indochina is to be under the final control of France.

(2) French military bases are to be established and the Indochinese Army in time of war is to be under French direction.

(3) France is to be in charge of the so-called General Services:
    (a) Control of immigration
    (b) Communications
    (c) Industrial development of Indochina

(4) Customs receipts are to be divided between France and Indochina in accordance with a formula to be agreed upon.

(5) Extraterritorial courts for French citizens are to be continued.

This shabby business is a mockery of all the professions we have made in the Indonesian case. It probably represents an improvement over the brutal colonialism of earlier years, but it is now too late in the history of the world to try to settle for the price of this cheap substitute. For the United States to support France in this attempt will cost us our standing and prestige in all of Southeast Asia. A lot of that prestige went down the drain with Chiang Kai-shek [President of the then-recently exiled Republic of China]; the rest of it will go down with the Bao Dai regime if we support it. Ambassador [to China, John] Stuart calls our relationship to this regime "shameful" and I am inclined to agree with him.

Ev[erett] Case argued yesterday that it is too late to do anything else except support Bao Dai. I disagree. It is never too late to change a mistaken policy, particularly when the policy involves the kind of damage that our adherence to the Generalissimo [Chiang Kai-shek] brought us. Why get our fingers burned twice?

Ho Chi Minh as an alternative is decidedly unpleasant, but as was pointed out at our meeting with FE yesterday, there may be unpredictable and unseen factors in this situation which in the end will be more favorable to us than now seems probable. The fundamental antipathy of the Indochinese to China is one of the factors. Faced with a dilemma like this the best possible course is to wait for the breaks. Certainly we should not play our cards in such a way that once again, as in China, we seem to be allied with reaction. Whether the French like it or not, independence is coming to Indochina. Why, therefore, do we tie ourselves to the tail of their battered kite?

RAYMOND B. FOSDICK
[Consultant to the State Department on *Far Eastern Affairs*]

[To:] Mr. [Raymond B.] Fosdick   November 17, 1949

[From:] Mr. [W. Walton] Butterworth [Assistant Secretary of State for Far Eastern Affairs]
    Your November 4 Memorandum to Ambassador Jessup Regarding Indochina.

    Mr. Jessup has referred to me your memorandum to him of November 4, 1949 regarding Indochina which I have read with much interest.
    In general, the considerations which you raise have been very much in the foreground of our thinking. I do not believe, however, that we can necessarily conclude, as you apparently have, that the Bao Dai regime is doomed. There is no doubt in my mind that Bao Dai's chances of establishing a viable non-Communist state are not brilliant, but I feel that under certain circumstances, which admittedly may never arise, he might be successful.
    I think I can make our position clear by the following analogy: Because the odds are heavily against a horse entered in a given race, is no reason to withdraw that horse from the race although I agree that there is likewise no reason in these circumstances to back that horse heavily.
    I agree that we should not support France in Indochina because such action will damage our standing and prestige in all of Southeast Asia, but I feel that without committing ourselves to another operation similar in some respects to that which took place in China, we must allow Bao Dai his opportunity to succeed and we must do nothing deliberately to eliminate his opportunity.

The Geneva Agreements, 1954

Final declaration, dated the 21st July, 1954, of the Geneva Conference on the problem of restoring peace in Indo-China, in which the representatives of Cambodia, the Democratic Republic of Viet-nam, France, Laos, the People's Republic of China, the State of Viet-nam, the Union of Soviet Socialist Republics, the United Kingdom, and the United States of America took part.

    1. The Conference takes note of the Agreements ending hostilities in Cambodia, Laos and Viet-nam and organizing international control and the supervision of the execution of the provisions of these agreements.
    2. The Conference expresses satisfaction at the ending of hostilities in Cambodia, Laos and Viet-nam; the Conference expresses its conviction that

the execution of the provisions set out in the present Declaration and in the Agreements on the cessation of hostilities will permit Cambodia, Laos [and] Viet-nam henceforth to play their part, in full independence and sovereignty, in the peaceful community of nations.

3. The Conference takes note of the declarations made by the Governments of Cambodia and of Laos of their intention to adopt measures permitting all citizens to take their place in the national community, in particular by participating in the next general elections, which, in conformity with the constitution of each of these countries, shall take place in the course of the year 1955, by secret ballot and in conditions of respect for fundamental freedoms.

4. The Conference takes note of the clauses in the Agreement on the cessation of hostilities in Viet-nam prohibiting the introduction into Viet-nam of foreign troops and military personnel as well as of all kinds of arms and munitions. The Conference also takes note of the declarations made by the Governments of Cambodia and Laos of their resolution not to request foreign aid, whether in war material, in personnel or in instructors except for the purpose of the effective defence of their territory and, in the case of Laos, to the extent defined by the Agreements on the cessation of hostilities in Laos.

5. The Conference takes note of the clauses in the Agreement on the cessation of hostilities in Viet-nam to the effect that no military base under the control of a foreign State may be established in the regrouping zones of the two parties, the latter having the obligation to see that the zones allotted to them shall not constitute part of any military alliance and shall not be utilized for the resumption of hostilities or in the service of an aggressive policy. The Conference also takes note of the declarations of the Governments of Cambodia and Laos to the effect that they will not join in any agreement with other States if this agreement includes the obligation to participate in a military alliance not in conformity with the principles of the Charter of the United Nations or, in the case of Laos, with the principles of the Agreement on the cessation of hostilities in Laos or, so long as their security is not threatened, the obligation to establish bases on Cambodian or Laotian territory for the military forces of foreign Powers.

6. The Conference recognizes that the essential purpose of the Agreement relating to Viet-nam is to settle military questions with a view to ending hostilities and that the military demarcation line is provisional and should not in any way be interpreted as constituting a political or territorial boundary. The Conference expresses its conviction that the execution of the provisions set out in the present Declaration and in the Agreement on the cessation of hostilities creates the necessary basis for the achievement in the near future of a political settlement in Viet-nam.

7. The Conference declares that, so far as Viet-nam is concerned, the settlement of political problems, effected on the basis of respect for the principles of independence, unity and territorial integrity, shall permit the Vietnamese people to enjoy the fundamental freedoms, guaranteed by democratic institutions established as a result of free general elections by secret

ballot. In order to ensure that sufficient progress in the restoration of peace has been made and that all the necessary conditions obtain for free expression of the national will, general elections shall be held in July 1956, under the supervision of an international commission composed of representatives of the Member States of the International Supervisory Commission, referred to in the Agreement on the cessation of hostilities. Consultations will be held on this subject between the competent representative authorities of the two zones from 20 July 1955 onwards.

8. The provisions of the Agreements on the cessation of hostilities intended to ensure the protection of individuals and of property must be most strictly applied and must, in particular, allow everyone in Viet-nam to decide freely in which zone he wishes to live.

9. The competent representative authorities of the Northern and Southern zones of Viet-nam, as well as the authorities of Laos and Cambodia, must not permit any individual or collective reprisals against persons who have collaborated in any way with one of the parties during the war, or against members of such persons' families.

10. The Conference takes note of the declaration of the Government of the French Republic to the effect that it is ready to withdraw its troops from the territory of Cambodia, Laos and Viet-nam, at the request of the governments concerned and within periods which shall be fixed by agreement between the parties except in the cases where, by agreement between the two parties, a certain number of French troops shall remain at specified points and for a specified time.

11. The Conference takes note of the declaration of the French Government to the effect that for the settlement of all the problems connected with the re-establishment and consolidation of peace in Cambodia, Laos and Viet-nam, the French Government will proceed from the principle of respect for the independence and sovereignty, unity and territorial integrity of Cambodia, Laos and Viet-nam.

12. In their relations with Cambodia, Laos and Viet-nam, each member of the Geneva Conference undertakes to respect the sovereignty, the independence, the unity and the territorial integrity of the above-mentioned States, and to refrain from any interference in their internal affairs.

13. The members of the Conference agree to consult one another on any question which may be referred to them by the International Supervisory Commission, in order to study such measures as may prove necessary to ensure that the Agreements on the cessation of hostilities in Cambodia, Laos and Viet-nam are respected.

The Gulf of Tonkin Resolution, 1964

Whereas naval units of the Communist regime in [North] Vietnam, in violation of the principles of the Charter of the United Nations and of international law, have deliberately and repeatedly attacked United States naval vessels lawfully present in international waters, and have thereby created a serious threat to international peace; and

Whereas these attacks are part of a deliberate and systematic campaign of aggression that the Communist regime in North Vietnam has been waging against its neighbors and the nations joined with them in the collective defense of their freedom; and

Whereas the United States is assisting the peoples of southeast Asia to protect their freedom and has no territorial, military or political ambitions in that area, but desires only that these peoples should be left in peace to work out their own destinies in their own way: Now, therefore, be it

Resolved by the Senate and House of Representatives of the United States of America in Congress assembled, That the Congress approves and supports the determination of the President, as Commander in Chief, to take all necessary measures to repel any armed attack against the forces of the United States and to prevent further aggression.

Sec. 2. The United States regards as vital to its national interest and to world peace the maintenance of international peace and security in southeast Asia. Consonant with the Constitution of the United States and the Charter of the United Nations and in accordance with its obligations under the Southeast Asia Collective Defense Treaty, the United States is, therefore, prepared, as the President determines, to take all necessary steps, including the use of armed force, to assist any member or protocol state of the Southeast Asia Collective Defense Treaty requesting assistance in defense of its freedom.

Sec. 3. This resolution shall expire when the President shall determine that the peace and security of the area is reasonably assured by international conditions created by action of the United Nations or otherwise, except that it may be terminated earlier by concurrent resolution of the Congress.

President Lyndon Johnson's Advisers
Debate Expanding the War, 1965

Robert S. McNamara

[26 June 1965; revised 1 July 1965]

Introduction

Our objective is to create conditions for a favorable settlement by demonstrating to the VC [Viet Cong]/DRV [Democratic Republic of Vietnam—North Vietnam] that the odds are against their winning. Under present conditions, however, the chances of achieving this objective are small—and the VC are winning now—largely because the ratio of guerrilla to anti-guerrilla forces is unfavorable to the government. With this in mind, we must choose among three courses of action with respect to South Vietnam: (1) Cut our losses and withdraw under the best conditions that can be arranged; (2) continue at about the present level, with US forces limited to say, 75,000, holding on and playing for the breaks while recognizing that our position will probably grow weaker; or (3) expand substantially the US military pressure against the Viet Cong in the South and the North Vietnamese in the North and at the same time launch a vigorous effort on the political side to get negotiations started. An outline of the third of these approaches follows.

I. Expanded Military Moves

The following military moves should be taken together with the political initiatives in Part II below.

A. Inside South Vietnam. Increase US/SVN military strength in SVN enough to prove to the VC that they cannot win and thus to turn the tide of the war. . . .

B. Against North Vietnam. While avoiding striking population and industrial targets not closely related to the DRV's supply of war material to the VC, we should announce to Hanoi and carry out actions to destroy such supplies and to interdict their flow into and out of North Vietnam. . . .

II. Expanded Political Moves

Together with the above military moves, we should take the following political initiatives in order (a) to open a dialogue with Hanoi, Peking, and the VC looking toward a settlement in Vietnam, (b) to keep the Soviet Union from deepening its military involvement and support of North Vietnam until the time when settlement can be achieved, and (c) to cement the support for US policy by the US public, allies and friends, and to keep international opposition at a manageable level. While our approaches may be rebuffed until the tide begins to turn, they nevertheless should be made. . . .

III. Evaluation of the Above Program

A. Domestic US Reaction. Even though casualties will increase and the war will continue for some time, the United States public will support this course of action because it is a combined military-political program designed and likely to bring about a favorable solution to the Vietnam problem.

B. Communist Reaction to the Expanded Programs.
    1. Soviet. The Soviets can be expected to continue to contribute materiel and advisors to the North Vietnamese. Increased US bombing of Vietnam, including targets in Hanoi and Haiphong, SAM [surface-to-air missile] sites and airfields, and mining of North Vietnamese harbors, might oblige the Soviet Union to enter the contest more actively with volunteers and aircraft. This might result in minor encounters between US and Soviet personnel.
    2. China. So long as no US or GVN [Government of Vietnam—South Vietnam] troops invade North Vietnam and so long as no US or GVN aircraft attack Chinese territory, the Chinese probably will not send regular

ground forces or aircraft into the war. However, the possibility of a more active Soviet involvement in North Vietnam might precipitate a Chinese introduction of land forces, probably dubbed volunteers, to preclude the Soviets' taking a pre-eminent position in North Vietnam.

3. North Vietnam. North Vietnam will not move towards the negotiating table until the tide begins to turn in the south. When that happens, they may seek to counter it by sending large numbers of men into South Vietnam.

4. Viet Cong. The VC, especially if they continue to take high losses, can be expected to depend increasingly upon the PAVN [People's Army of Vietnam, regular forces of North Vietnam] forces as the war moves into a more conventional phase; but they may find ways of continuing almost indefinitely their present intensive military, guerrilla and terror activities, particularly if reinforced with some regular PAVN units. A key question on the military side is whether POL [petroleum-oil-lubricants], ammunition, and cadres can be cut off and if they are cut off whether this really renders the Viet Cong impotent. A key question on the political side is whether any arrangement acceptable to us would be acceptable to the VC.

C. Estimate of Success.

1. Militarily. The success of the above program from a military point of view turns on whether the increased effort stems the tide in the South; that in turn depends on two things—on whether the South Vietnamese hold their own in terms of numbers and fighting spirit, and on whether the US forces can be effective in a quick-reaction reserve role, a role in which they have not been tested. The number of US troops is too small to make a significant difference in the traditional 10–1 government-guerrilla formula, but it is not too small to make a significant difference in the kind of war which seems to be evolving in Vietnam—a "Third Stage" or conventional war in which it is easier to identify, locate and attack the enemy. (South Vietnam has 141 battalions as compared with an estimated equivalent number of VC battalions. The 44 US/3d country battalions mentioned above are the equivalent of 100 South Vietnamese battalions.)

2. Politically. It is frequently alleged that such a large expansion of US military personnel, their expanded military role (which would put them in close contact and offer some degree of control over South Vietnamese citizens), and the inevitable expansion of US voice in the operation of the GVN economy and facilities, command and government services will be unpopular; it is said that they could lead to the rejection of the government which supported this American presence, to an irresistible pressure for expulsion of the Americans, and to the greatly increased saleability of Communist propaganda. Whether these allegations are true, we do not know.

The political initiatives are likely to be successful in the early stages only to demonstrate US good faith; they will pay off toward an actual settlement only after the tide begins to turn (unless we lower our sights substantially). The tide almost certainly cannot begin to turn in less than a few months, and may not for a year or more; the war is one of attrition and will be a long one. Since troops once committed as a practical matter cannot be removed, since US casualties will rise, since we should take call-up actions to support the additional forces in Vietnam, the test of endurance may be as much in the United States as in Vietnam.

3. Generally (CIA [Central Intelligence Agency] estimate). Over the longer term we doubt if the Communists are likely to change their basic strategy in Vietnam (i.e., aggressive and steadily mounting insurgency) unless and until two conditions prevail: (1) they are forced to accept a situation in the war in the South which offers them no prospect of an early victory and no grounds for hope that they can simply outlast the US and (2) North Vietnam itself is under continuing and increasingly damaging punitive attack. So long as the Communists think they scent the possibility of an early victory (which is probably now the case), we believe that they will persevere and accept extremely severe damage to the North. Conversely, if North Vietnam itself is not hurting, Hanoi's doctrinaire leaders will probably be ready to carry on the Southern struggle almost indefinitely. If, however, both of the conditions outlined above should be brought to pass, we believe Hanoi probably would, at least for a period of time, alter its basic strategy and course of action in South Vietnam.

Hanoi might do so in several ways. Going for a conference as a political way of gaining a respite from attack would be one. Alternatively it might reduce the level of insurgent activity in the hopes that this would force the US to stop its punishment of the North but not prevent the US and GVN from remaining subject to wearying harassment in the South. Or, Hanoi might order the VC to suspend operations in the hopes that in a period of temporary tranquility, domestic and international opinion would force the US to disengage without destroying the VC apparatus or the roots of VC strength. Finally, Hanoi might decide that the US/GVN will to fight could still be broken and the tide of war turned back in favor of the VC by launching a massive PAVN assault on the South. This is a less likely option in the cirumstances we have posited, but still a contingency for which the US must be prepared.

George W. Ball

[1 July 1965]

1. A Losing War: The South Vietnamese are losing the war to the Viet Cong [formally, the National Liberation Front]. No one can assure you that we can beat the Viet Cong or even force them to the conference table on our terms no matter how many hundred thousand *white foreign* (US) troops we deploy.

No one has demonstrated that a white ground force of whatever size can win a guerrilla war—which is at the same time a civil war between Asians—in jungle terrain in the midst of a population that refuses cooperation to the white forces (and the SVN [South Vietnam]) and thus provides a great intelligence advantage to the other side. Three recent incidents vividly illustrate this point:

(a) The sneak attack on the Danang Air Base which involved penetration of a defense perimeter guarded by 9,000 Marines. *This raid was possible only because of the cooperation of the local inhabitants.*

(b) The B-52 raid that failed to hit the Viet Cong *who had obviously been tipped off.*

(c) The search-and-destroy mission of the 173rd Airborne Brigade which spent three days looking for the Viet Cong, suffered 23 casualties, and never made contact with the enemy *who had obviously gotten advance word of their assignment.*

2. The Question to Decide: Should we limit our liabilities in South Viet-Nam and try to find a way out with minimal long-term cost?

The alternative—no matter what we may wish it to be—is almost certainly a protracted war involving an open-ended commitment of US forces, mounting US casualties, no assurance of a satisfactory solution, and a serious danger of escalation at the end of the road.

3. Need for a Decision Now: So long as our forces are restricted to advising and assisting the South Vietnamese, the struggle will remain a civil war between Asian peoples. Once we deploy substantial numbers of troops in combat it will become a war between the United States and a large part of the population of South Viet-Nam, organized and directed from North Viet-Nam and backed by the resources of both Moscow and Peiping.

The decision you face now, therefore, is crucial. Once large numbers of US troops are committed to direct combat they will begin to take heavy casualties in a war they are ill-equipped to fight in a non-cooperative if not downright hostile countryside.

Once we suffer large casualties we will have started a well-nigh irreversible process. Our involvement will be so great that we cannot—without national humiliation—stop short of achieving our complete objectives. *Of the two possibilities I think humiliation would be more likely than the achievement of our objectives—even after we had paid terrible costs.*

4. A Compromise Solution: Should we commit US manpower and prestige to a terrain so unfavorable as to give a very large advantage to the enemy—or should we seek a compromise settlement which achieves less than our stated objectives and thus cut our losses while we still have the freedom of maneuver to do so?

5. Costs of Compromise Solution: The answer involves a judgment as to the costs to the United States of such a compromise settlement in terms of our relations with the countries in the area of South Viet-Nam, the credibility of our commitments, and our prestige around the world. In my judgment, if we act before we commit substantial US forces to combat in South Viet-Nam we can, by accepting some short-term costs, avoid what may well be a long-term catastrophe. I believe we have tended greatly to exaggerate the costs involved in a compromise settlement. An appreciation of probable costs is contained in the attached memorandum.

6. With these considerations in mind, I strongly urge the following program:

A. Military Program

1. Complete all deployments already announced (15 battalions) but decide not to go beyond the total of 72,000 men represented by this figure.
2. Restrict the combat role of American forces to the June 9 announcement, making it clear to General Westmoreland that this announcement is to be strictly construed.
3. Continue bombing in the North but avoid the Hanoi-Haiphong area and any targets nearer to the Chinese border than those already struck.

B. Political Program

1. In any political approaches so far, we have been the prisoners of whatever South Vietnamese Government was momentarily in power. If we are ever to move toward a settlement it will probably be because the South Vietnamese Government pulls the rug out from under us and makes its own deal *or* because we go forward quietly without advance pre-arrangement with Saigon.
2. So far we have not given the other side a reason to believe that there is *any* flexibility in our negotiating approach. And the other side has been unwilling to accept what *in their terms* is complete capitulation.
3. Now is the time to start some serious diplomatic feelers, looking towards a solution based on some application of the self-determination principle.
4. I would recommend approaching Hanoi rather than any of the other probable parties (the National Liberation Front, Moscow or Peiping). Hanoi is the only one that has given any signs of interest in discussion. Peiping has been rigidly opposed. Moscow has recommended that we negotiate with Hanoi. The National Liberation Front has been silent.
5. There are several channels to the North Vietnamese but I think the best one is through their representative in Paris, Mai Van Bo. Initial feelers with Bo should be directed toward a discussion both of the four points we have put forward and the four points put forward by Hanoi as a basis for negotiation. We can accept all but one of Hanoi's four points and hopefully we should be able to agree on some ground rules for serious negotiation—including no pre-conditions.
6. If the initial feelers lead to further secret exploratory talks we can inject the concept of self-determination that would permit the Viet Cong some hope of achieving some of their political objectives through local elections or some other device.
7. The contact on our side should be handled through a non-governmental cutout (possibly a reliable newspaperman who can be repudiated.)
8. If progress can be made at this level the basis can be laid for a multi-national conference. At some point obviously the government of South Viet-Nam will have to be brought on board but I would postpone this step until after a substantial feeling out of Hanoi.
9. Before moving to any formal conference we should be prepared to agree that once the conference is started (a) the United States will stand down its bombing of the North, (b) the South Vietnamese will initiate no

offensive operations in the South, and (c) the DRV [Democratic Republic of Vietnam] will stop terrorism and other aggressive acts in the South.

10. Negotiations at the conference should aim at incorporating our understanding with Hanoi in the form of a multi-national agreement guaranteed by the United States, the Soviet Union and possibly other parties, and providing for an international mechanism to supervise its execution.

War Stories as Told by
the Combatants, Collected 1981

Boot Camp

The bus pulls into the receiving area. There's a guy with a Smokey Bear hat out there really looking lean and mean. He gets on the bus and starts reeling this shit off, "All right, you'll grab your bag. You'll get off the bus. You'll fall into the yellow footprints painted on the pavement . . ."

It was really funny, a take-off from *Gomer Pyle*. The guy within arm's reach of the Marine was laughing just like everybody else. Smokey Bear whipped around and smacked him right in the face, knocked him halfway through the window. His head bounced off the luggage rack and he reeled back out in the aisle.

Smiles froze on faces. My heart stopped. We realized, "Hey, this guy isn't fooling around. He's going to come through this bus and kick all our asses." People started flying out of the door.

I came down with a couple of guys who were Puerto Rican street gang material from the big city and they thought they were bad news. They fell down the steps on top of me. We all stumble into the right footprints on the ground and Smokey marches us into some barracks and stands us at attention. He's yelling and screaming, really intimidating. You dumped all of your stuff out on a table and he went by and just threw everything away. We were too scared to say anything to him.

I was next to this big Puerto Rican dude. Smokey catches the dude looking at him out of the corner of his eye. He says, "Are you eye-fucking me, boy? I don't want your scuzzy eyes looking at me. You think this is funny? I hope you fuck up. I hate you Puerto Rican cocksuckers."

Eyes in the back of his head, Smokey sees a guy's eyes flick and he's there to punch him in the chest, five feet to the wall and back again. My knees were shaking. "What the fuck have I gotten myself into?"

Then they march us into some barracks. Bare mattresses and springs. It's like a concentration camp. They turn the lights on and leave us there. My stomach is in a knot. I'm lying there thinking, "What happened to my world?" Reality has suddenly turned to liquid shit before my very eyes. Kids were crying, rolling in their bunks. I'm so depressed, I can't believe this is happening to me.

We're there for a couple of hours. You're in your civilian clothes and you've been in them for a couple of days. You feel like shit. When they march you out, all of a sudden it's by the numbers. All your hair's gone. You don't even know who you are. You get a duffel bag and they're dumping things in it. Everybody hates you and they're fucking with you left and right. You get your shots. You stand at attention. People are passing out on their feet. Going rigid and falling on their faces and the corpsmen are laughing at them. Nobody talks to you, they scream. Nothing they give you fits. You look like shit and you feel like shit. A bunch of drill instructors put you back in receiving and that's when the shit really hits the fan.

"Going Down South"

"Going down South" they called it in Okinawa. Braniff Airlines comes down all painted in their designer colors, puce and canary yellow. There were stewardesses on the plane, air conditioning. You would think we were going to Phoenix or something. But you know that you're going to Vietnam with a plane full of Marines.

It's about a two-and-a-half-hour flight down there. I was looking out the window as we were landing in Da Nang and there ain't nothing. It's just sticks, hovels with tin roofs. It's Dogpatch. That's what they called the area where we were.

The door opens and there's a blast of hot air that drops you to your knees. The head stewardess gets up and says, "Well, we're here in Da Nang. We hope you boys have a good tour. We'll see you one year from now." Those words kicked in an echo chamber in my mind—One Year From Now. Oh shit.

The First Guys I Saw Killed

I remember the first guys I saw killed. We were providing security for Army engineers on an island formed where two rivers split apart. The island was an R&R resort for the VC. The engineers were bulldozing it flat, making the whole place into a big parking lot to deny the VC that area. We'd go on sweeps and they would follow us in with the bulldozers. I was weapons platoon commander which meant I just sort of tagged along with one CO. It was all horseshit.

We were walking along and there was an explosion, we got popped. Then just dead silence.

"Corpsman up!" I was right next to the corpsman, so I went running with him. There was a guy up the trail who had been hit and a guy right next to us. The man closer to us was writhing on the ground, his back arching up. He was gasping, hoarse, dragging air into his lungs. There was a perfect round hole about the size of a pencil, right in the middle of his sternum.

Then he just stopped moving. The corpsman started giving him mouth-to-mouth resuscitation and I was giving him heart massage. No response. So the doc gave him a tracheotomy, opened his throat and stuck in a black tube. I started breathing through that and the corpsman gave him heart massage and we switched off.

We did it for about five minutes to no avail. The kid was gone, dead. Except for that little hole, there was no blood—just that little hole in his chest.

I looked at him—blond, All-American, crewcut with these pale ice-blue eyes. I stood up and looked back into those eyes. Those eyes looked right through me, right through my skull and out the back of my head. I turned around and looked at the sky in the direction that his eyes were looking to see what he was staring at. I though I was going to see something.

It ran through my mind for a moment, "Did his mother feel something, did his father feel something, did anybody? Was she reaching for a can of peas in the supermarket and feel a tug or a jolt and not know what it was? Does anybody close to him know that he just died?"

He Bought the Farm

I was following a blood trail. He was losing more and more blood. It was twenty minutes after the fire fight, so some of the blood was dry right by the first bushes I came to. The color really changes as you follow along. It gets more bubbly, frothy-looking and wetter. Which means that you're gaining on the guy.

The tension really increases. I'd seen all those stories of these fucking heroes who are badly wounded and stay behind to keep the heat off their buddies. American war movies are filled with those scenes. You figured the Vietnamese are about the same.

As the trail got fresher my steps got slower. In the beginning there was a lot of blood, but I guess he probably stemmed the flow. When I came to him, he had this tourniquet on his left leg. That's where he got shot pretty bad. He'd done a good job with the tourniquet. You would figure that—well, maybe not, I guess he was an ignorant North Vietnamese soldier—he could have just put up a white flag and I would have left him alone, you know just captured him. He could have surrendered or something. I wasn't out there to fuck with him at that point.

I heard a noise and me and a couple of guys nearby all fired at one time and put about 300 rounds in that one bush. That was it. He bought the farm. We were pretty upset when we saw the guy. He didn't have a piece in his hand, he didn't have a weapon on him. About fifteen feet from his body was an AK.

He had on black tennis shoes, black canvas with the ball on the ankles like you used to wear when you were a kid. I had seen the print of his sneakers every once in a while on the ground.

An American P.O.W.

They harped on this business of, "Cooperate and we'll let you go home. Know the truth and you'll know what you have to do. As soon as you demonstrate your good faith, we'll let you go home." Demonstrating good faith was doing whatever they told you to do. In this case, they wanted me to write a political statement and sign it, which I refused to do. Eventually they wrote one for me and I refused to sign it, too.

Then the really severe physical torture started. Initially they were kind of crude, just being beaten with a heavy stick. Later on they became more sophisticated with their torture, particularly after I was moved to North Vietnam. One of their most effective tortures is one we called the rope trick. They tie your body in an extremely uncomfortable position and leave you like that for a couple of days.

Pain is a natural defense mechanism of the body. You touch something that's hot and the signals go up to the brain. The brain sends a message back to the muscles to pull back within a split second. It's an electrical system. Just like any electrical system, the human nervous system has circuit breakers built into it, because the brain can stand just so much pain sensation before it causes damage. When the pain gets too great, these circuit breakers shut off any feeling of pain. I'm sure you've heard cases of people losing limbs in a car wreck or other accident and they say they feel nothing. Several days later when the pain begins to return, the doctor is pleased because that means they are getting better. The pain has actually subsided before they can feel it. That same principle applies to torture.

A beating is not effective torture because after the first few blows, you don't feel anything. To force a person into an extremely uncomfortable position and then make him stay that way causes excruciating pain—but not quite enough to activate the circuit breakers.

One time I was put into a cage that was about eighteen inches square and five feet long. I'm broader than that in the shoulders and well over five feet tall, so you can imagine the cramping effect that had. I was chained hand and foot with wrist locks jammed tightly together, crammed into this cage and left there for three months. I had refused to bow to them. After three months they took me out and beat the living hell out of me and eventually taught me to bow. But I made them work for it.

Interrogating a Captured Vietnamese

When we had to interrogate some of the prisoners, we used to take three gooks up in a helicopter about a thousand feet. We're with an intelligence officer, G2 section from the general staff. He's in civilian clothes. We got our Kit Carson up with us to do the translation.

He grabs the first one and says, "Talk." We say, *"Crackadill, sakmile, crackadill."* *Crackadill* was "to kill."

The first gook wouldn't talk, Intelligence give you the signal, thumb toward the door, and you push the guy out. The other two gooks look to see this guy going out the helicopter door.

If the second guy didn't look like he wants to say something or he's lying, the intelligence officer says, "This guy out the door." You'd kick him out, because you're supposed to do what these intelligence officers tell you to do. They're speaking for the Army. The last prisoner is crying and he's like a typewriter. He's talking Vietnamese like crazy. That's human nature. This guy is running his mouth. You can't keep him from talking. You'd have to gag him to make him shut up. The Kit Carson is translating all this thing.

Before we get back to the base camp, after this guy do all the talking and the intelligence officer document everything, they kick him out the door anyway. Even the good gook, they'd give the word on him and throw him out the door.

We went up with three prisoners and we come back with zero prisoners. Nobody looks around and asks, "You went up with three prisoners, what happened to them?" We come back, and the intelligence officer goes back to wherever they go back to and carry the information to the command.

We're Supposed to Be Saving These People

I know Marines that made more gooks than they killed, just by treating them bad. It's funny when you don't expect to get mercy from anyone, you're very reluctant to show it. So you really breed hideous people over there, for the cause of National Defense. If you sit down here on the couch, it seems ugly. At the time, they weren't ugly. They were the things to do. Considering what else is going on this was nothing.

I Blew Up a Village One Time

I blew up a village one time. It was a village outside of which my squad got ambushed. Myself and my three squad leaders went in with three demolition packs, twenty pounds of C4 apiece.

We crimped the blasting caps onto the time fuses with our teeth. Stick them in the C4, load up the hooch with whatever there was. Smoke a cigarette to light up the fuse. Time it.

"Okay, we're lighting now."

"Hey, mine's not lit."

"You better get it fast, man, 'cause mine's lit."

"You got about five or six seconds. Go." Then we hauled ass out of there and BLAM. That was fun.

All the people were gone by then, so it was nothing but pigs and chickens. We got in line and shot the shit out of the livestock, pigs squealing across in front of us. It was a way of blowing off steam. We did My Lai with farm animals.

They Got Pears

We were running security on a road in a free-fire zone. In Vietnam you had a friendly zone and you had a free-fire zone. Anything that crossed into the free-fire zone was fair game. Any gook—woman, man, boy, girl—it was game to you. Anybody come along with a cart or just walking and we would go through their stuff.

We was in the field twenty days or so. Up in the depots in the rear they got steaks. We didn't get steaks. We ate mainly C-rations, lousy C-rations and dry things that came out of cans.

These gooks are riding by in a Lambretta, which is like a motorbike except you sit people in the back. We say, "Hey, let's stop these gooks." So we came out of the bush and we pulled them over to the side.

"What you got there? Hey, you VC? What do you got?" It was a baby-san and a papa-san. I guess she was a teenager, maybe about fifteen or sixteen. The papa-san was forty, a mature man.

They had a can of pears! American pears in a big green can marked with a big U.S. on it in large print. We say, "Isn't this some shit. Here we are in the field, we don't know what pears is. They got pears! and *we* don't have pears." I'll never forget the guys' faces in the unit from the GIs up to the captain. We are shit in the field, and the guys in the rear have given these gooks pears, man.

Right away a guy took a bayonet and he opened up the pears. We're fighting, literally fighting, to eat pears. Food! It wasn't fresh, but it was something other than the shit they put together chemically and pressed into a can. It was like the man brought me steak and potatoes and I was back in my mother's house eating Sunday dinner.

Most of the guys didn't get any pears. I got a few pears and I got to drink the juice in the can. So we turned around and we said, "Hey, ain't this something? These gooks is riding around with pears. How did you get pears?"

"GI give them to me." He worked in a mess hall back in the rear somewhere.

"The GIs gave you pears? Oh, yeah? For that, we're going to screw your daughter." So we went running, taking the daughter. She was crying. I think she was a virgin. We pulled her pants down and put a gun to her head.

Guys are taking turns screwing her. It was like an animal pack. "Hey, he's taking too long to screw her." Nobody was turning their back or nothing. We just stood on line and we screwed her.

I was taking her body by force. Guys were standing over her with rifles, while I was screwing her. She says, "Why are you doing this to me? Why?" Some of the gooks could talk very good. "Hey, you're black, why are you doing this to me?"

We turned back to the father and we said, "So, you got pears. GIs are nice enough to give them to you." All the Vietnamese carried this ID card. Big old plastic ID card with a picture on it that says that they are okay in the Republic of Vietnam. So we ripped up the ID card. "Hey, we got a VC here, fellas. A VC stealing government stuff, huh? So you must be an infiltrator." We shot him.

As I said we was in that *free-fire zone*. We just started pumping rounds into him until the guy just busts open. He didn't have a face anymore.

Baby-san, she was crying. So a guy just put a rifle to her head and pulled the trigger just to put her out of the picture. Then we start pumping her with rounds. After we got finished shooting her, we start kicking them and stomping on them. That's what the hatred, the frustration was. After we raped her, took her cherry from her, after we shot her in the head, you understand what I'm saying, we literally start stomping her body.

And everybody was laughing about it. It's like seeing the lions around a just-killed zebra. You see them in these animal pictures, *Wild Kingdom* or something. The whole pride comes around and they start feasting on the body. We kicked the face in, kicked in the ribs and everything else.

Then we start cutting the ears off. We cut her nose off. The captain says, "Who's going to get the ears? Who's going to get the nose? So-and-so's turn to get the ears." A good friend of mine—a white guy from California—he flipped out in the Nam. The dude would fall down and cry, fall down and beg somebody to let him have the ears. Captain says, "Well, let So-and-so get the ears this time. You had the last kill. Let him get it this time." So we let this guy get the ears. We cut off one of her breasts and one guy got the breast. But the trophy was the ears. I had got a finger from the papa-san. That was about it, what I got from the incident. We let the bodies stay there mutilated.

Coming Home

I got back to the World, but this wasn't the World that I had left. I was born again. Like the Christians say, "Be born again." I did not fit into the real world anymore. For that twelve months in the Nam, I used to sit down and imagine what I would do in the World when I got back. I'll be with this woman, I'm going to do this and that. I came back to the World and I see people rioting about Nam. People hated GIs for being in the Nam. They was blaming us. I flipped out. I couldn't believe it.

I was in a VA hospital the first time I heard anybody saying, "Those fucking guys over in Vietnam. Look what they're doing." Man, it did something to me. Like I was guilty. I was a criminal. You had sentenced me to die. These are the same people from when I left the year before. I'm back but I don't belong. I wanted to go back to the Nam. I would have re-upped, but I was all wounded. This world was alienating, what people was talking about, what people was liking.

When my mom came to see me, she was a different person. I didn't hate her or nothing like that. But it was a different person. I couldn't communicate with her. I just looked at her. We talked and it was over.

I would just sit in the room in the hospital and my mind would flash back. I would have dreams about the Nam, the Nam and action. I could see myself fighting, when I'm actually sitting in a VA hospital on the bed. I could see myself back in the Nam.

This is not the World. Lord, how can they do this to me? How can they bring me back to a World where I don't know what they're talking about? The United States is saying one thing. The people are saying something else. President Nixon is talking about the Silent Majority. The people are in the streets protesting. Who are these people out here protesting while there are guys in the Nam going through psychological and physical hell? Walking in monsoon when it rains for months at a time. Being sniped at. Being killed. Stepping in booby traps. Catching jungle rot. Getting eaten up by leeches. How can they say the war is unjust? How can you walk out of Nam and leave guys out in the field or missing in action?

I wasn't thinking they were un-American, but man, somebody pulled the rug out from under us. Somebody stabbed us in the back. The average person in the peace struggle didn't understand. We got stabbed in the back by the Army, while we were in the Army. We got stabbed in the back when we got back to the United States by the Peace people. We got stabbed in the back by President Nixon. He's talking nonsense. Henry Kissinger is talking about peace and ending the war. All this is garbage.

Wrong, Rambo! A Vietnam Veteran Looks Back, 1985

August 13, 1969. I was a 19-year-old member of India Company, 3d Battalion, 5th Marines. As we moved through a strip of Vietnam known to the Americans as the Arizona Territory, we walked into an L-shaped ambush sprung by the North Vietnamese Army.

The enemy's opening fire instantly killed our battalion commander and his radio operator. Pinned to the ground in a rice paddy, the rest of us faced a choice: lie low and wait to be picked off one at a time, or charge the enemy guns, and, with luck, some of us would shoot our way to safety.

Our wounded captain gave the order to charge. Somehow we outfought the enemy and turned them back. But not without a heavy price: Half of India Company lay dead or wounded.

The next day, those of us who survived rested in the tranquil refuge of China Beach, just 23 miles from where the battle had taken place, and began to write letters to the families of those who didn't. Searching for reasons to explain their sons' sacrifice, I sat on China Beach and questioned why America had come to Vietnam. I didn't have the answers. I decided then that those who had died in Vietnam had died for nothing.

After my tour in Vietnam was up, I came back to the States and fought to end the war. There had to be another way to be for freedom in the world than through tragedies like Vietnam. By ending the war, we could bring the survivors home from a place where they never should have been.

On the 14th of August, 1985, however, 16 years to the day since my first time there, I returned to China Beach. I came not as a Marine in combat

---

Thomas J. Vallely, "Dishonoring the Vietnam Tragedy." *Boston Globe*, November 10, 1985.

gear, but as a civilian, a guest of the Vietnamese government, a member of the first group of American veterans to travel the land we fought upon with veterans of the Vietnamese army.

China Beach hadn't changed much. I thought again of those who had died. I thought of those who had come home wounded in body or spirit, many of them to die later in the States. I thought of how long it took our country to honor their service, finally on a black marble wall in Washington, on Veterans Day just three years ago tomorrow.

More than anything else, though, I no longer felt, as I had 16 years before, that my friends had died for nothing. For in their dying, we, as a nation, became wiser about ourselves, about the world and our role in it.

The members of India Company, and millions of other Americans, fought to change Vietnam. But, in the end, Vietnam changed little. What changed was America. Most Americans no longer accept the illusion that we can defy history, as we tried to in Vietnam. We should mourn the loss of American lives in Vietnam. We needn't mourn the loss of the illusions that brought us there.

Today, as a veteran, I am bothered that some would dishonor the memory of those who died in Vietnam by reviving America's shattered illusions. "Are you gonna let us win this time?" Rambo demands to know as impressionable kids watch in air-conditioned awe. As the Rambo illusion would have it, our gallant soldiers would've won in Vietnam if only they'd been turned loose by the bureaucratic wimps on the home front.

Wrong, Rambo, dead wrong. The bureaucrats didn't put us into a winnable war and then tie our hands. What they did was actually far worse. They put us into a war that was as unwinnable as it was immoral. They put us into a war that even they could not explain, and, so, young men died for old men's pride.

The fact is, the Vietnam War was probably settled long before we ever got there. Ho Chi Minh's forces gained dominance with their victory at Dien Bien Phu, a good decade before the first US Marine landed. And our ally, what we knew for 20 years as South Vietnam, wasn't a real nation but a make-believe government with little popular support. An illusion.

The illusion of American invincibility should have been left behind in Vietnam. But, then, there's Rambo, whose appeal, unfortunately, is not limited to youthful moviegoers alone. The Rambo mystique even invades Washington: While policy makers fall over themselves to flex American muscle in the world, macho journalists, from the safety of their typewriters, lob verbal grenades at tiny Third World countries.

The truth is, these veterans of tough-talk know as much about war as the gullible teen-agers flocking to suburban mall theaters for a glimpse of Rambo.

On China Beach this August, I wondered if we could have handled Vietnam differently. We tried to beat history—to stop the inevitable from happening, and we were wrong. We should learn from Vietnam that history can't be beaten.

But neither can history be ignored. We cannot allow the need to avoid another Vietnam let us selfishly retreat from the realistic problems of the world. America *does* have a role to play in the world, as a moral force, a beacon of hope, a model of democratic idealism. We cannot turn our backs to injustice, whatever its form, be it terrorism, tyranny, poverty, hunger or torture.

We will come closer to knowing how we should engage the world if we understand what happened to us in Vietnam. We entered that war in defiance of history, we stayed there in defiance of morality. If we, as a nation, are to live up to our moral responsibilities and stand up for freedom around the globe, we had better be able to answer the questions I asked myself as a Marine at China Beach.

✗✗✗ E S S A Y S

In the first selection, political scientist and Southeast Asia specialist George McT. Kahin of Cornell University describes the critical sequence of events by which the United States supplanted the French and established its own client regime in South Vietnam. In the second essay, U. S. diplomatic historian George Herring of the University of Kentucky describes the final collapse of South Vietnam and discusses the war's legacy in both Southeast Asia and the United States.

The Cold War and American Intervention in Vietnam

GEORGE McT. KAHIN

The middle months of 1954 marked a major turning point in the American relationship with Vietnam. It was during this period that the United States made the most fundamental decision of its thirty-year involvement—the critical prerequisite to the subsequent incremental steps that culminated in President [Lyndon] Johnson's famous escalation a decade later. Although this first major increase in American intervention was essentially political, it had important and clearly understood military implications. It was sustainable initially only by the threat of U.S. armed intervention and ultimately by its actual execution. So for the second time Washington attempted to establish an anticommunist government in Vietnam; but now it acted alone, no longer in association with France, and its effort was focused primarily on just the southern half of the country.

In this new departure the Eisenhower administration intervened directly in Vietnam, displacing France as the major external power. Rather than working through the French to support the Bao Dai regime, which claimed authority over all Vietnam, the United States took on the mission of establishing a separate noncommunist state in just the southern regroupment zone prescribed by the Geneva Agreements. The administration believed that, without the encumbrance of the old French colonial presence to undermine

From *Intervention: How America Became Involved in Vietnam* by George McT. Kahin. Copyright © 1986 by George McT. Kahin. Reprinted by permission of Alfred A. Knopf, Inc.

its nationalist legitimacy, a revamped Bao Dai regime, with Ngo Dinh Diem as its prime minister, could, if given sufficient American support, stand a good chance of competing effectively with the DRV [Democratic Republic of Vietnam, the government in the North led by Ho Chi Minh]. In addition, though their hopes on this score were apparently not so strong, senior U.S. officials thought it possible that this American-backed government would ultimately be able to absorb the North into a single anticommunist state. However unrealistic this second proposition, it was still the presidentially endorsed U.S. objective at least as late as 1958. In April of that year the National Security Council [NSC] reiterated its aim to "work toward the weakening of the Communists in the North and South Viet Nam in order to bring about the eventual peaceful reunification of a free and independent Viet Nam under anti-Communist leadership."

To understand this major shift in the United States' approach to Vietnam, one must assess the changed pattern of factors influencing American policy in the immediate post-Geneva period. The original, European-oriented calculations that had propelled the United States into its limited intervention in the early postwar years increasingly yielded place to considerations rooted primarily in the new ascendancy of communist power in China. Europe did still continue to exert an important influence on American Vietnam policy right through the Geneva Conference, however, because of the pivotal importance of the projected European Defense Community [EDC] to Washington's Soviet containment strategy. But when the French Parliament defeated EDC soon after the close of the conference, European objectives ceased to have a significant effect on American policy toward Vietnam.

Although the French rejection of EDC only temporarily delayed German rearmament, it entailed the loss of most of France's once-formidable leverage with the United States, which had derived from Washington's uncertainty regarding French domestic politics and the extent to which France could be counted on to cooperate with American economic and military objectives in Europe. The potential of communism in France had by now dramatically ebbed, and the balance of her internal politics no longer threatened her continued presence in an American-led military alignment aimed at containing Soviet power in Europe. Indeed, the large noncommunist majority in the Chamber of Deputies saw such an alignment as clearly in their country's self-interest. The shoe was now on the other foot, for, as France began to face mounting militant nationalist pressures in her North African colonies during the fall of 1954, she badly needed American backing to maintain her ascendancy there.

Other factors important to the previous American preoccupation with Vietnam were, however, still operative: the enduring myth that communism was global and monolithic; the conviction that China was expansionist; and American domestic political pressures centering on the "loss of China" syndrome, whereby all administrations feared being accused of losing additional territory to communist control. But it was, of course, against the Democrats—not [President Dwight D.] Eisenhower's Republicans—that the charge of China's "loss" had been leveled. Moreover, in contrast to the American involvement in China's civil war, the congressional and public perception was thus far of primarily French, not American, responsibility for developments in Vietnam, and France stood out clearly as a lightning rod to divert attacks from the administration's record there. At this stage, fear of domestic criticism, although a factor, was not fundamental to the administration's new decision for a major American involvement. It would only become an important consideration after the Eisenhower administration had publicly committed itself to sustaining a separate state free of communist control in the southern half of Vietnam.

What, then, explains the decision to intervene directly in Vietnam? To the three above-mentioned continuing determinants two new major factors had now been added. First was [Secretary of State] John Foster Dulles's retrospective analysis—subscribed to by Eisenhower—of the American failure in China, and the lessons he derived from this for policy toward Southeast Asia; and second was the inspiration he and Eisenhower drew from a set of analogies between conditions and the potential for American actions in Vietnam, and recent American and British experiences in other parts of the world.

Dulles approached the conflicts between Southeast Asian peoples and the colonial powers with certain strongly held views. Like his predecessor, Dean Acheson [Secretary of State for President Harry S Truman], he had little faith in the self-governing capacity of Southeast Asians who gained their independence from colonial powers through revolution. He was convinced that, without the involvement and guidance of the democratic West, nationalist movements in these countries would probably be drawn into communist-controlled political channels—and this, he believed, was likely even after they had attained full independence. With respect to the peoples of Indochina and Indonesia in particular, he felt that until they attained a greater degree of political maturity, the West had an ongoing obligation to help ensure that communists did not take over; and if the Western colonial powers withdrew, the United States had a responsibility to assume this burden.

From Chiang Kai-shek's defeat in China, Dulles drew a lesson that he regarded as applicable to Southeast Asian countries threatened by communist power. One of the main reasons he saw for the failure of American China policy was that "The territorial integrity of China became a shibboleth. We finally got a territorially integrated China—for whose benefit? The Communists." In other words, while certainly aware of the faults of the Kuomintang [Chiang Kai-shek's political party, which ruled the Republic of China] regime, Dulles saw its defeat by the Chinese communists as largely attributable to American acquiescence in Chiang's shortsighted attempt to win control over the whole of China concurrently. A more effective strategy would have been to accept temporarily a loss of the country's territorial integrity, yielding part of it to communist power, while concentrating Kuomintang and American resources in order to husband as much of the mainland as possible free of Mao's control [Mao Tse-tung led the Chinese Communist party]. Chiang's residual mainland territory would have provided a base for mounting a rollback of communist control.

Some nine months before the beginning of the Geneva Conference on Indochina, this lesson was being applied to the situation in Indonesia. In late 1953 President Eisenhower counseled Hugh S. Cumming, his administration's first ambassador to Indonesia, that "as against a unified Indonesia which would fall to the Communists and a break up of that country into smaller segments he would prefer the latter." Dulles was more explicit, stating to the ambassador, "As between a territorially united Indonesia which is leaning and progressing towards communism and a break up of that country into racial and geographical units, I would prefer the latter as furnishing a fulcrum from which the United States could work later to help them eliminate communism in one place or another, and then in the end, if they so wish arrive back again at a united Indonesia."

If Eisenhower and Dulles considered this lesson from China to have such validity for Indonesia, it must have seemed even more applicable to the situation in Vietnam. In any case, their approach to Vietnam both during and after the Geneva Conference was consistent with, and undoubtedly to a significant extent shaped by, their perception of the causes of the "failure" in China.

But why did Eisenhower and Dulles believe that the United States had the capacity to implement in Vietnam what they considered to be the logical propositions derived from their retrospective analysis of the "failure" in China? That question cannot be answered without reference to the administration's evaluation of earlier American experiences in Greece, Iran, Guatemala, and especially the Philippines, together with what was regarded as an equally relevant British experience in Malaya. Its assessment of recent developments in these countries tended to reinforce an already self-assured and assertive postwar American "can-do" hubris, inclining policymakers to believe that the success of the United States in meeting challenges from communists or other socioeconomic radicals in these other places demonstrated abilities that could be applied in Vietnam. These combined to encourage the Eisenhower administration to intervene directly in Vietnam in the belief that it could work its own political will there to achieve a solution more consistent with American interests than that provided by the Geneva Conference.

A minority of American officials perceived that conditions in Vietnam were in fact fundamentally different from these other situations. But senior policymakers continued to draw inspiration and self-assurance from these precedents until well after the Eisenhower administration had embarked on a much deeper political intervention and commitment of American prestige in Vietnam. The simplistic analogies, sometimes referred to as "models," provided by these experiences continued to inform U.S. policy throughout [President John F.] Kennedy's administration and during the first part of Johnson's.

In Greece, where the United States had taken over from the British in late 1947, Washington believed that the critical factor in turning the tide against a peasant-backed, communist-led insurrection had been the injection of a large amount of American money, weaponry, and a military mission incorporating some five hundred advisers. American officials thought that this intervention, which had relied heavily on forced relocation of peasants, had been decisive in shoring up a faltering anticommunist government and forcing the insurgents to abandon their struggle and fade away into the hills within two years. The belief that this American experience in Greece was pertinent to Vietnam outlasted the Eisenhower administration. It was revived repeatedly under Kennedy and Johnson, especially by Walt Rostow, but also, though less insistently, by William P. Bundy, assistant secretary of state for Far Eastern affairs under Johnson, who had been in Greece during the American campaign there and as late as 1967 was still talking about the possibility of "a Greek solution" in Vietnam.

In Iran in 1953—just a year before the Eisenhower administration's major decision on Vietnam—a covert U.S. program mounted primarily by the CIA [Central Intelligence Agency] had brought down a radical, albeit noncommunist, government led by Mohammed Mossadegh that had been bent on ending foreign domination of the country's oil production, and then returned the recently ousted shah to power. The administration also took great satisfaction in the outcome of its largely covert intervention during the spring of 1954 in Guatemala. This had successfully ousted a noncommunist but radical president who had been willing to accept the support of communists as well as other political groups and been regarded as a threat to American economic interests.

Britain's experience in Malaya was at least as important as the Greek precedent. By 1953 the British were finally beginning to gain the upper hand in their effort to subdue an insurgency of some Malayan Chinese that had broken out five years previously. They attributed their success primarily to an extensive program of forced resettlement of rural Chinese, on whom their enemy was or might be reliant for food and intelligence. After 1959, when a communist-led insurgency finally re-emerged in South Vietnam, Washington saw the presumed Malayan analogy as especially relevant, and commenced to emphasize a policy of population resettlement in rural areas. The Kennedy administration was equally insistent on seeing a Malayan analogy and even more attracted to a resettlement strategy, a predilection that continued under Johnson and Nixon.

But the most influential of all these precedents was the recent example of the Philippines. During 1953–54 American officials helped secure the position of secretary of defense in the Philippines for their own candidate, Ramon Magsaysay, and they then worked successfully to ensure his election as president. While he held these positions, they cooperated effectively with him to suppress a potent communist-led, agrarian-based insurgency, the Hukbalahap. The administration believed it could achieve similar results through its own chosen political instrument six hundred miles to the east in Vietnam. And if the CIA's Colonel Edward Lansdale had been so effective in helping to organize this effort in the Philippines, why should he not be equally successful in Vietnam? In January 1964 Assistant Secretary for East

Asian Affairs Roger Hilsman was still looking for "a Vietnamese Magsay-say," and well into that year Secretary of Defense McNamara and Secretary of State Rusk, along with several other senior officials, were still seeing pertinent precedents in the Philippine and Malayan experiences.

The truth was that in character and context the Vietnam insurgency was only superficially akin, at best, to those in the Philippines, Malaya, and Greece. Nevertheless, the defeats of these earlier communist-led insurgencies, in combination with the heady American "successes" in Guatemala and Iran, encouraged the Eisenhower administration in its conviction that it had the capacity to work its will in determining Vietnam's political future.

Shaped primarily by Dulles, but with full support from the president, the administration's new Vietnam policy from the outset involved repudiating the two key political features of the Geneva Agreements: the stipulation that the line separating the two military zones "should not in any way be interpreted as constituting a political or territorial boundary," and the reunification elections, which had been an even more central condition for the armistice. The new policy also entailed two major positive steps by the United States. First, a mutual defense pact between it and several allies in effect treated the seventeenth parallel as a political boundary and provided in advance a measure of protection to the southern regroupment zone against attack by forces based in the North or against "internal subversion." Second, the United States displaced France's political and military presence in this area, taking over as paymaster to the Vietnamese civil servants and soldiers who had collaborated with the French and providing American training and advisers to the previously French-officered Vietnamese auxiliary component of the French expeditionary force. Still headed by Bao Dai as "chief of state," the "State of Vietnam" retained its name but was now restricted to the territory south of the seventeenth parallel. Into this area the United States pumped a massive amount of financial support, dwarfing what France had managed to provide.

These twin American efforts at an end run around some of Geneva's central provisions did not emerge fresh and full-blown after the conference. In the months preceding and during it, American policymakers had laid much of the groundwork for the two interdependent policies of building up a separate southern-Vietnamese state and protecting it from external assault and internal political opposition.

The still-unconsummated process of organizing United Action, initiated by the United States during the conference, now merged into an American-sponsored regional defense organization which was finally embodied in the Manila Pact of September 8, 1954 (ratified by the U.S. Congress February 19, 1955). In effect, the threat of an American-led anticommunist military intervention that had provided France with such useful leverage in Geneva was now spelled out with greater precision and institutionalized into a loosely structured alliance. Popularly known as SEATO (Southeast Asia Treaty Organization), it included the United States, Britain, France, Australia, and New Zealand, together with the only three Asian states Washington could induce to join—the Philippines, Thailand, and Pakistan (the last-named expecting that membership would give it leverage against India). Initially, the French were sufficiently scrupulous about Geneva's provisions for the neutralization of Indochina to resist Dulles's attempt to include Cambodia, Laos, and especially South Vietnam (where the stipulation against adherence to any military alliance was explicit) as members of SEATO. But through the device of adding a protocol to the treaty projecting an "umbrella of protection" over these three areas, Dulles was able to circumvent the impediment. The protocol stipulated that the treaty's provisions extended to Cambodia, Laos, and "the free territory under the jurisdiction of the State of Vietnam," even though they were not signatories of the treaty. Prince Sihanouk [the Cambodian ruler] promptly repudiated Cambodia's inclusion, and with its neutralization in 1962 Laos was officially removed from jurisdiction of the protocol. Predictably, however, this protection was accepted by the French and Bao Dai for the temporary military regroupment zone south of the seventeenth parallel provided for at the Geneva Conference, now referred to as "the free territory of Vietnam." This was made explicit in a joint Eisenhower-Diem communiqué on May 11, 1957, after U.S. officials were satisfied that Ngo Dinh Diem's authority had been sufficiently established in this half of the country.

SEATO's members saw its main objective as being "to deter massive military aggression," the United States stipulating that its own involvement would be limited to cases where the aggressor was communist. Though all its signatories saw the alliance as a deterrent against a possible attack by China, the United States, France, and at least some other members regarded it as providing a similar deterrent against the possibility of an assault by Hanoi into the regroupment zone of French forces south of the seventeenth parallel.

SEATO's apparently broad international base disguised a decided lack of enthusiasm on the part of some of its participants, and it was never effective as a vehicle for collective action. The formula did, however, provide subsequent American administrations with the basis for inducing Americans to believe that U.S. military involvement in Indochina had international sanction. Much more important, it provided what the executive branch came to assert was congressional authority for direct military intervention there. Indeed, SEATO's significance ultimately lay more in what came to be construed as a congressional licensing of unilateral U.S. anticommunist military intervention in Southeast Asia than in its role as a collective defense organization. This was not what the Senate had had in mind when it approved the treaty, but what happened in practice.

Nevertheless, during the decade prior to the August 1964 Tonkin Gulf Resolution, SEATO provided the major rationale for a U.S. military role in Indochina. And when, within two years, the 1964 resolution had become discredited because of a crystallization of congressional suspicion as to the circumstances surrounding its passage, SEATO once more provided the president with what was asserted to be "the legal basis" for that involvement.

For two decades SEATO was referred to as an American "commitment." Having signed the treaty, the United States was indeed committed to it. But that treaty itself did not—as successive administrations encouraged the public to believe—commit the United States to defend South Vietnam. In fact, no such pledge was made either by the members of SEATO collectively or by the United States unilaterally. The *ex post facto* presidential interpretation of SEATO that alleged it did so departed widely from the mandate actually agreed to by the U.S. Senate and did violence to its intent. Yet this interpretation gradually became the accepted conventional public perception. It was strongly enough established in the Kennedy administration to be used as justification for escalating involvement beyond the largely political and economic dimension pursued by Eisenhower to the level of direct U.S. military intervention. . . . By granting protection in advance to Vietnam's southern regroupment zone against any attack by communist forces in the North, SEATO endowed the seventeenth parallel with the political character the Geneva Conference had prohibited and laid a foundation for recognizing a separate statehood for this southern area. This was, indeed, the administration's intention, and, five days before the conference concluded, Dulles informed an executive session of the Senate Foreign Relations Committee, "In fact the military regrouping [zones] will be apt to gradually become a live *de facto* political division. . . .

With SEATO providing the context for establishing an American-protected state in the southern half of Vietnam, the Eisenhower administration concurrently moved ahead with the second prong of its new Vietnam policy. This was the much more straightforward effort to endow that area with the attributes of governmental power, substituting a dependence on the United States for a previous dependence on France, and ensuring a leadership congenial to and shaped by the administration. This new American political venture retained the same name as its French-sponsored predecessor—the "State of Vietnam"—and Bao Dai stayed on as chief of state for some fifteen months after Geneva, thereby providing a transitional bridge. In this politically precarious period, while the French and Vietminh military forces regrouped and Paris incrementally transferred the fundamental attributes of government to the State of Vietnam, an American presence gradually replaced that of France. During this process Bao Dai, still comfortably ensconced on the French Riviera, progressively, albeit reluctantly, yielded more and more power to Ngo Dinh Diem, the Catholic leader and U.S. protégé whom he had appointed as prime minister in June 1954. . . .

By the beginning of May 1955, there was no longer any qualification in Washington's commitment to Diem. The remaining obstacle to the consolidation of a separate anticommunist southern state was the Geneva Conference's clear-cut stipulation that national reunification elections be held in mid-1956 and that consultations to prepare for them be conducted in mid-1955. Certainly some American officials acknowledged that the elections constituted a "binding commitment," and they, along with the French and British, were fearful that repudiating them would destroy the most important positive feature of the Geneva Conference—the military armistice. As the NSC reported, the French believed that "failure to hold elections would provoke a resumption of hostilities by the Vietminh in which France would be directly and involuntarily involved due to the probable presence at least of large numbers of the French Expeditionary Corps through 1955 and the first half of 1956." And American officials feared that, if a refusal to hold elections led to an end of the armistice and a renewal of Vietminh military activity, Britain and France might not support forceful U.S. action to counter it. At the SEATO meeting in February 1955, both allies made clear that this would indeed be the case.

A State Department intelligence report of September 15 expected that along with Canada and India of the International Control Commission, Britain and France would "continue to press for action in sufficient conformity with the agreements so that the Communists will have no excuse for breaking the cease-fire." It warned:

> If Diem is emboldened to reject or continue postponement of the elections stipulated in the Geneva Agreements, the DRV can be expected to seek its goal of unification (and control) through other means. Subject to calculation of what is feasible without stimulating U.S. military involvement the DRV would probably be prepared to use any methods necessary and would use pressures as strong as permitted by prevailing conditions in overall bloc relations with the non-communist world. . . . Should the DRV conclude that elections are unlikely in fact, it is probable that the communists will greatly increase their subversive as well as political pressures against the South. The DRV, however, would probably seek to avoid direct U.S. military intervention and would probably, therefore, choose a maximum guerrilla and subversive effort rather than direct aggression to obtain its objective of control over a unified Vietnam.

As late as the Kennedy administration it was acknowledged internally that, if Diem's government did not consider itself bound by the Geneva Agreements' provision for elections, then the legal basis of a demand for Vietminh compliance with features of the accords advantageous to the U.S. and Diem, "such as respect for [the] demarcation line and ceasefire," could be called into question. In short, one party to an agreement could not ignore a central provision it found unpalatable and expect the other party to adhere to provisions *it* disliked.

It was understood, then, that there were serious risks in supporting Diem's opposition to national elections, but the potential risks if they were held were regarded as even greater, for American intelligence sources were unanimous that Diem would lose any national election. Extensive studies by American intelligence bodies subsequent to the Geneva Conference all reinforced the conclusion that national elections could only lead to the DRV's victory. A report prepared by the State Department's Division of Research on February 1, 1955, considered that "Almost any type of election that could conceivably be held in Vietnam in 1956 would, on the basis of present trends, give the Communists a very significant if not decisive advantage." It went on to point out that the establishment of "conditions of electoral freedom . . . might operate to favor the Communists more than their opponents." Even in the South, it judged, "maximum conditions of freedom and the maximum degree of international supervision might well operate to Communist advantage and allow considerable Communist strength in the South to manifest itself at the polls." This analysis concluded that "It would appear on balance, therefore, seriously questionable whether the South should make a major issue of free political conditions in the period preceding and during whatever type of elections might finally be decided for Vietnam."

The Eisenhower administration could not afford to risk elections, and it encouraged Diem in his own, understandable disposition to avoid them. That the administration was aware of the implications of this decision is clear from a State Department assessment of September 1955: "Only if Diem were to feel sufficiently assured of direct U.S. support against Communist reprisals, and if the U.S. were prepared to accept the consequences of such a development including some degree of alienation of its Western allies and Asian neutrals, would Diem be likely to persist in a position directly opposed to eventual holding of elections."

The administration was prepared to give him those assurances and accept these consequences. The NSC Planning Board had concluded shortly before that, if denial of victory to Hanoi through prevention of all-Vietnam elections resulted in a renewal of hostilities, the United States had to be prepared to oppose the Vietminh "with U.S. armed forces if necessary, and feasible— consulting Congress in advance if the emergency permits—preferably in concert with the Manila Pact allies of the U.S., but if necessary alone." The United States then developed contingency plans for the immediate deployment of air and naval power in Vietnam in the event of "overt aggression by Vietminh forces." This would be followed by the "early movement of mobile U.S. [ground] forces for the purpose of conducting joint operations for tasks beyond the capabilities of South Vietnamese forces."

Sure of U.S. backing, Diem now assumed a bold and confident posture in opposition to the national elections that were so central to the Geneva Agreements (and indeed he now repudiated all of its political provisions that did not suit his interests). He and his American supporters insisted that, since the Bao Dai-Diem government had not itself agreed to the accords, it was not bound by them. Furthermore, they advanced the equally specious argument that the accords had stipulated "fundamental freedoms and democratic institutions" as prerequisites to any election (rather than as their anticipated consequences, as Article 14a actually posited) and that since these conditions did not yet exist it would be impossible for any meaningful voting to take place—even if by secret ballot under the aegis of the International Control Commission, as the agreements provided.

Initially American officials thought that, while avoiding the elections scheduled for mid-1956, Diem should at least make the gesture of participating in the preliminary consultations with representatives of the DRV on the plans for the conduct and supervision of the elections, which had been scheduled for mid-1955. On the basis of such consultation, it was argued, Diem's position that conditions for free elections and international supervision could not be met would appear more plausible. An unwillingness even to discuss the conditions for voting put him on weak ground for alleging in advance that it would not be fair. Moreover, the National Security Council concluded, "The over-all United States position in the world would be harmed by U.S. identification with a policy which appeared to be directed towards avoidance of elections," and "world opinion, and for that matter domestic U.S. opinion, would have difficulty in understanding why the U.S. should oppose in Vietnam the democratic procedures which the U.S. had advocated for Korea, Austria and Germany." Senior American officials, however, were not disposed to pressure Diem to participate even in such preliminary consultations, and by the time the meetings were scheduled, official U.S. policy had swung behind him in his refusal to do so.

The Hanoi government had clearly not anticipated Diem's ability to repudiate this key provision of the Geneva Agreements. Along with most of the Geneva participants, it had assumed that until mid-1956 France would still be exercising sufficient authority in the South to ensure holding both the consultations and the subsequent elections. By mid-1955, however, most French troops had been sent to North Africa and the French economic and political presence had become overshadowed by that of the United States; during the three-month period before the 1956 elections were to be held, the French High Command for Vietnam was dissolved and the last French combat units were withdrawn. As was later acknowledged by Secretary of Defense Robert McNamara in a memorandum to President Johnson, "Only the U.S. presence after 1954 held the south together . . . and enabled Diem to refuse to go through with the 1954 provision calling for nationwide free elections in 1956."

During 1955 and 1956 Ho and Prime Minister Pham Van Dong sent repeated requests to Diem for consultations on holding elections. But these were ignored, as were Hanoi's numerous appeals to Britain and the Soviet Union, co-chairmen of the Geneva Conference, who, Hanoi understood, shared an ongoing responsibility for seeing that the agreements were implemented. Neither Britain nor the Soviet Union and China—both of which were bent upon pursuing policies of détente with the United States—showed much interest in seeing that the political provisions of Geneva were carried out. Moscow tried to pass the buck to Paris, saying France was primarily responsible for seeing them implemented. But with the withdrawal of her troops from Vietnam, France now had little political leverage there, and she was too dependent on American economic support and political backing of her interests elsewhere in the world, particularly North Africa, to challenge the repudiation of the elections.

The Soviet Union's demeanor led the State Department to conclude that it was "disinclined to risk broad policy objectives elsewhere in the world for the sake of rigid support for DRV demands." The State Department believed that Hanoi's dependence upon China and the Soviet Union for military supplies and economic support was sufficient to ensure that without their backing it would be reluctant to attack South Vietnam militarily, since this would involve "a substantial risk of U.S. (or broader Western) counteraction." Now less than two years after Geneva, Washington saw little prospect that Moscow or Peking would be inclined to provide such support. Consequently, the department concluded that Hanoi recognized its "inability to achieve a military victory against Western arms through an 'adventurist' attack unsupported by the Bloc."

Moscow's unwillingness to shoulder responsibility for implementing Geneva's political provisions was evident in talks held in April-May 1956 between representatives of Britain and the Soviet Union in their capacity as ongoing co-chairmen of the conference. Soviet Foreign Minister Andrei Gromyko "did not press for either the holding of elections or the reconvening of the Geneva Conference to discuss elections within a stated period" and agreed with his British counterpart on simply "maintaining the cease-fire, and essentially the [political] status-quo for the time being." The Soviet Union demonstrated the full extent of its disengagement in January 1957, when the Eisenhower administration was attempting to line up international support in its abortive effort to secure Saigon's representation in the United Nations. It was then that Khrushchev went so far as to propose that, along with North and South Korea, Diem's State of South Vietnam and the DRV be represented in the United Nations as "two separate states," a proposal with which the Peking government concurred, even though acknowledging that it was unacceptable to Hanoi. Since the data stipulated for the national reunification elections had by then passed, this proposition appears to have signaled implicit acceptance by Moscow and Peking of Vietnam's ongoing partition. Understandably, Ho Chi Minh, "in evident surprise, violently dissented."

By the beginning of 1957, then, China and the Soviet Union, as well as France and Britain, appeared content to let Vietnam remain divided, thereby increasing the Eisenhower administration's confidence that it could build a viable separate state in the southern half of the country without its additional transgressions against the Geneva Agreements being seriously challenged.

If the two communist powers, the world at large, or the American public harbored any doubts as to the Eisenhower administration's commitment to its mission of building a new Vietnamese state, these were undoubtedly dispelled in May 1957, when the administration invited the man it had chosen to head this state, Ngo Dinh Diem, on a two-week state visit to the United States. Not only was he accorded the signal honor of addressing a joint session of the American Congress, but Eisenhower had him flown in the presidential plane to Washington and personally met him at the airport— an honor bestowed on only one other foreign leader in the first four years of Eisenhower's presidency.

The decisive change in American policy that unfolded during the years immediately following the Geneva Conference was by no means inevitable; certainly it was not something the Eisenhower administration unwittingly backed into. It was a positive, calculated step into a direct and much deeper involvement than the earlier attempts to work through France. Moreover, this step was taken at a time when the United States had a clear option to avoid any direct commitment. Indeed, the Geneva Agreements offered the United States a broad avenue leading away from even the limited and indirect intervention it had pursued during the previous decade. The capitulation recognized at Geneva was, after all, generally viewed as French, not American, entailing responsibilities that were basically French. Instead of seizing on this clear option, the administration had moved assertively into a much more fundamental phase of intervention, and in doing so staked American honor and prestige on a policy that, once undertaken, was difficult to reverse.

The Meaning of Vietnam

GEORGE HERRING

The "peace" agreements of January 1973 merely established a framework for continuing the war without direct American participation. North Vietnam still sought unification of the country on its terms; South Vietnam struggled to survive as an independent nation, and some U.S. officials, including President Nixon, continued to support its aspirations. The cease-fire thus existed only on paper. This last phase of the war was of remarkably short duration, however. Dependent on the United States from its birth, the Saigon government had great difficulty functioning on its own. Moreover, because of the Watergate scandals and American war-weariness, [President Richard M.] Nixon was not able to live up to the commitments he had made to [South Vietnamese President, Nguyen Van] Thieu, and indeed in August 1974 he was forced to resign. Congress drastically cut back aid to South Vietnam, further eroding the Saigon government's already faltering will to resist. When North Vietnam mounted a major offensive in the spring of 1975, South Vietnam collapsed with stunning rapidity, dramatically ending the thirty-year war and leaving the United States, on the eve of its third century, frustrated and bewildered. . . .

The fall of South Vietnam just fifty-five days after the onset of the North Vietnamese offensive was symptomatic of the malaise which had afflicted the nation since its birth. Political fragmentation, the lack of able far-sighted leaders, and a tired and corrupt elite which could not adjust to the revolution that swept Vietnam after 1945 afforded a perilously weak basis for nationhood. Given these harsh realities, the American effort to create a bastion of anti-Communism south of the seventeenth parallel was probably doomed from the start. The United States could not effect the needed changes in South Vietnamese society without jeopardizing the order it sought, and there was no long-range hope of stability without revolutionary change. The Americans could provide money and weapons, but they could not furnish the ingredients necessary for political stability and military success. Despairing of the capacity of the South Vietnamese to save themselves, the United States had assumed the burden in 1965, only to toss it back in the laps of its clients when the American people tired of the war. The dependency of the early years persisted long after the United States had shifted to Vietnamization, however. To the very end and despite overwhelming evidence

From *America's Longest War: The United States in Vietnam, 1950–1975* by George Herring, 1985, pp. 268–281. Reprinted by permission of McGraw-Hill Book Company.

to the contrary, Thieu and his cohorts clung desperately to the belief that the United States would not abandon them.

With the North Vietnamese victory, the "dominoes" in Indochina quickly toppled. Cambodia in fact fell before South Vietnam, ending a peculiarly brutal war and initiating a period of unprecedented cruelty. Between 1970 and 1972, the United States had spent over $400 million in support of Lon Nol's [Cambodian] government and army, and heavy bombing continued until Congress legislated its end in August 1973. In six months of 1973, the bombing exceeded 250,000 tons, more than was dropped on Japan in all of World War II. Lon Nol's government and army were ineffectual even by South Vietnamese standards, however, and with extensive support from North Vietnam and China, the Khmer Rouge pressed on toward Phnom Penh, using human-wave assaults in some areas. The government collapsed in mid-April, and the Khmer Rouge took over the capital on April 17. Thousands of lives were lost in the war, and over two million people were left refugees. The country as a whole faced starvation for the first time in its history. Upon taking over, the Khmer Rouge imposed the harshest form of totalitarianism and began the forced relocation of much of the population.

The end in Laos was less convulsive. The Laotian "settlement" of 1962 had been a dead letter from the start. A flimsy coalition government nominally upheld a precarious neutrality, while outsiders waged war up and down the land. The North Vietnamese used Laotian territory for their infiltration route into South Vietnam, and supported the insurgent Pathet Lao with supplies and as many as 20,000 "volunteers." While backing the "neutralist" government, the United States from 1962 to 1972 waged a "secret war" against North Vietnamese positions in Laos. When the bombing of North Vietnam was stopped at the end of 1968, Laos became the primary target. By 1973 the United States had dropped more than two million tons of bombs there, leaving many areas resembling a desert. At the same time, the CIA sponsored an army of Hmong or Meo tribesmen, led by General Vang Pao, which waged seasonal guerrilla warfare against the Ho Chi Minh Trail in Laos at enormous cost: more than 20,000 had been killed by the end of the war. The U.S. withdrawal from South Vietnam left the government without any chance of survival. An agreement of February 1973 created a coalition government in which the Pathet Lao held the upper hand. With the fall of Cambodia and South Vietnam, the Pathet Lao took over, making no effort to hide its subservience to North Vietnam.

The impact on world politics of America's failure in Vietnam was considerably less than U.S. policymakers had predicted. From Thailand to the Philippines, there was obvious nervousness, even demands for the removal of U.S. bases. Outside of Indochina, however, the dominoes did not fall. On the contrary, in the ten years after the end of the war, the non-Communist nations of Southeast Asia prospered and attained an unprecedented level of stability. The Soviet Union continued to build up its military arsenal. Along with Cuba, it intervened in civil wars in Angola, Zaire, and Ethiopia, and in 1979 it invaded neighboring Afghanistan. The Soviets soon bogged down in Afghanistan themselves, however, and one of the most significant and ironic effects of the end of the Vietnam War was to heighten tension among the various Communist nations, especially in Southeast Asia. The brutal Pol Pot [head of the Khmer Rouge] regime launched a grisly effort to rebuild Cambodia from the "Year Zero," resulting in the death of as many as two million people. More important from the Vietnamese standpoint, Cambodia established close ties with China. To preserve a "friendly" government next door, Vietnam invaded Cambodia in 1978, drove out Pol Pot and the Khmer Rouge, and established a puppet regime. China retaliated by invading Vietnam, provoking a short and inconclusive war. Sporadic border conflicts between Vietnam and China have persisted. The United States, which had gone to war in Vietnam in 1965 to contain China, found itself in the mid-1980s indirectly supporting China's efforts to contain Vietnam.

In Vietnam itself, the principal legacy of the war has been continued human suffering. The ultimate losers, of course, were the South Vietnamese. For those who remain in Vietnam there have been poverty, oppression, forced labor, and "reeducation" camps. More than 1.4 million South Vietnamese have fled the country since 1975. As many as 50,000 of these so-called boat people perished in flight, and some still languish in squalid refugee camps scattered throughout Southeast Asia. Nearly a million Vietnamese have resettled in other countries, over 725,000 of them in the United States. Most of them had to give up all their personal possessions merely to escape, and many left family behind.

Even for the ostensible winners, victory has been a bittersweet prize. The Hanoi regime has achieved what may have been its goal from the outset—hegemony in former French Indochina—but the cost has been enormous. An estimated 180,000 soldiers remain in Cambodia, facing stubborn resistance from a number of different guerrilla groups, a drain on an economy already strained to the breaking point. The task of maintaining hegemony in Laos and Cambodia and defending against a hostile China requires one of the world's twelve poorest countries to maintain the world's fourth largest army. Vietnam's postwar aggressiveness has cost it much of the international good will it earned in the war against the United States.

Moreover, Hanoi's long-standing objective of unifying Vietnam under its control appears still to have been achieved in name only. Historic differences between north and south were sharpened during the war, and even the brutal and heavy-handed methods employed by the Hanoi regime have not forced the south into a northern-made mold. Just as it resisted American influence in the 1960s, southern Vietnam continues to resist outside influence today, making the task of consolidation quite difficult. There are also signs that in the classic tradition of the Far East, the ways of the conquered are rubbing off on the conqueror. The corruption and Western consumer culture that epitomized Saigon during the American war have carried over to postwar Ho Chi Minh City, where the black market still flourishes and bribery is necessary to accomplish anything. More significant, Saigon's mores appear to have afflicted the northern officials sent south to enforce revolutionary purity and even to have filtered north to Hanoi.

For all Vietnamese, the most pressing legacy has been economic deprivation. Thirty years of war left the country in shambles, and the regime's ill-conceived postwar efforts to promote industry and collectivize agriculture made things worse. The economic growth rate has hovered around 2 percent instead of the 14 percent optimistically projected in the five-year plan of 1975. Per capita income has averaged around $100. Inflation has run as high as 50 percent and unemployment is chronic, especially in the cities. Record rice crops in recent years have eased a severe postwar food shortage, but the food supply remains far below the needs of the population and most foods are rationed and expensive. The postwar economic crisis has forced Hanoi to abandon its central goal of socialization of southern Vietnam. New economic policies have been designed to increase production by such capitalist gimmicks as bonuses, piecework rates, and limited managerial autonomy. The collectivization of agriculture has been scrapped, at least temporarily.

A central goal of the thirty-year war was to rid Vietnam of foreign domination, and here again victory has been less than complete. Because of its poverty and its forced isolation from the United States and China, Hanoi has been forced into a dependence on the Soviet Union that causes growing uneasiness and resentment. Some 6,000 Russians administer an aid program ranging between $1 and $2 billion per year. Russian aid bears a high price tag, moreover. To many Vietnamese, the Soviet presence is increasingly obnoxious, and some appear to regard their new ally as merely another in the long line of foreigners who have exploited their country. To a considerable degree, the legacy of victory for the Vietnamese has been one of disappointed dreams and continuing sacrifice and pain. The goals of the thirty-year war have been achieved only partially, if at all.

Ten years after the fall of Saigon, Vietnam appeared eager to break out of its diplomatic isolation from the West. Hanoi probably bungled an opportunity to establish relations with the United States in 1977 by demanding $3 billion in war reparations as a precondition. Relations between the two former enemies thereafter grew steadily worse. Vietnam's seeming indifference to the fate of some 2,500 U.S. servicemen still listed as missing in action in Southeast Asia deeply antagonized Americans. Its increasing closeness to the Soviet Union and its invasion of Cambodia widened an already large chasm. On the other side, Washington's reconciliation with China in 1979 reinforced Vietnam's already strong hostility toward the United States. The need for Western aid and technology and a wish to secure recognition of its position in Cambodia encouraged Hanoi in 1985 to seek an improvement of relations. It was more cooperative than at any time since the end of the war in dealing with MIA [Missing in Action, a term used to denote American servicemen not definitely known to have been Killed in Action (KIA) or taken prisoner] issues, and it eagerly sought a settlement on Cambodia. These approaches provided the United States an opportunity to wean Vietnam from its dependence on the Soviet Union and to resolve a number of issues left from the war, but lingering hostility toward the Vietnamese and fear of China's reaction posed major obstacles to an improvement in relations.

In the United States, the effects of the war have been more in the realm of the spirit than tangible. The fall of Saigon had a profound impact. Some Americans expressed hope that the nation could finally put aside a painful episode from its past and get on with the business of the future. Among a people accustomed to celebrating peace with ticker-tape parades, however, the end of the war left a deep residue of frustration, anger, and disillusionment. Americans generally agreed that the war had been a "senseless tragedy" and a "dark moment" in their nation's history. Some comforted themselves with the notion that the United States should never have become involved in Vietnam in the first place, but for others, particularly those who had lost loved ones, this was not enough. "Now it's all gone down the drain and it hurts. What did he die for?" asked a Pennsylvanian whose son had been killed in Vietnam. Many Americans expressed anger that the civilians did not permit the military to win the war. Others regarded the failure to win as a betrayal of American ideals and a sign of national weakness which boded poorly for the future. "It was the saddest day of my life when it sank in that we had lost the war," a Virginian lamented. The fall of Vietnam came at the very time the nation was preparing to celebrate the bicentennial of its birth, and the irony was painfully obvious. "The high hopes and wishful idealism with which the American nation had been born had not been destroyed," *Newsweek* observed, "but they had been chastened by the failure of America to work its will in Indochina."

In the immediate aftermath of the war, the nation experienced a self-conscious, collective amnesia. The angry debate over who lost Vietnam, so feared by Kennedy, Johnson, and Nixon, consisted of nothing more than a few sharp exchanges between the White House and Capitol Hill over responsibility for the April 1975 debacle. Perhaps because both parties were so deeply implicated in the war, Vietnam did not become a partisan political issue; because the memories were so painful, no one cared to dredge them up. On the contrary, many public figures called for restraint. "There is no profit at this time in hashing over the might-have-beens of the past," [Senator] Mike Mansfield states, "Nor is there any value in finger-pointing." Vietnam was all but ignored by the media. It was scarcely mentioned in the presidential campaign of 1976. "Today it is almost as though the war had never happened," the columnist Joseph C. Harsch noted in late 1975. "Americans have somehow blocked it out of their consciousness. They don't talk about it. They don't talk about its consequences."

Resentment and disillusionment nevertheless smoldered beneath the surface, provoking a sharp reaction against nearly three decades of crisis diplomacy and global intervention. Even before the war had ended, the traumatic experience of Vietnam, combined with the apparent improvement of relations with the Soviet Union and China and a growing preoccupation with domestic problems, produced a drastic reordering of national priorities. From the late 1940s to the 1960s, foreign policy had consistently headed the list of national concerns, but by the mid-1970s, it ranked well down the list. The public is "almost oblivious to foreign problems and foreign issues," opinion analyst Burns Roper remarked in late 1975. The Vietnam experience also provoked strong opposition to military intervention abroad, even in defense of America's oldest and staunchest allies. Polls taken shortly before the fall of Saigon indicated that only 36 percent of the American people felt it was important for the United States to make and keep commitments to other nations, and only 34 percent expressed willingness to send troops should the Russians attempt to take over West Berlin. A majority of Americans endorsed military intervention only in defense of Canada. "Vietnam has left a rancid aftertaste that clings to almost every mention of direct military intervention," the columnist David Broder observed. The cyclical theory of American foreign relations seemed confirmed. Having passed through a stormy period of global involvement, the United States appeared to be reverting to its more traditional role of abstention.

Those Americans who fought in the war were the primary victims of the nation's desire to forget. Younger on the average by seven years than their World War II counterparts, having endured a war far more complex and confusing, Vietnam veterans by the miracles of the jet age were whisked home virtually overnight to a nation that was hostile to the war or indifferent to their plight. Some were made to feel the guilt for the nation's moral transgressions; others, responsibility for its failure. Most simply met silence. Forced to turn inward, many veterans grew profoundly distrustful of the government that had sent them to war and deeply resentful of the nation's seeming ingratitude for their sacrifices. The great majority adjusted, although often with difficulty, but many veterans experienced problems with drugs and alcohol, joblessness, and broken homes. Many also suffered from post-traumatic stress disorder, the modern term for what had earlier been called shell shock or battle fatigue. The popular image of the Vietnam veteran in the immediate postwar years was that of a drug-crazed, gun-toting, and violence-prone individual unable to adjust to civilized society. When America in 1981 gave a lavish welcome home to a group of hostages returned from a long and much-publicized captivity in Iran, Vietnam veterans poured out the rage that had been bottled up for more than half a decade. They themselves constructed a memorial in Washington to honor the memory of the more than 58,000 comrades who did not return.

Within a short time after the end of the war, Vietnam's place in the national consciousness changed dramatically. The amnesia of the immediate postwar years proved no more than a passing phenomenon, and by the mid-1980s the war was being discussed to a degree and in ways that would have once seemed impossible. Vietnam produced a large and in some cases distinguished literature, much of it the work of veterans. Hollywood had all but ignored the war while it was going on, but in its aftermath filmmakers took up the subject in a large way, producing works ranging from the haunting *Deer Hunter*, to the surreal and spectacular *Apocalypse Now*, to a series of trashy films in which American superheroes returned to Vietnam to take care of unfinished business. No television leading man was worth his salt unless he had served in Vietnam. The Vietnam veteran, sometimes branded a war criminal in the 1960s, became a popular culture hero in the 1980s, the sturdy and self-sufficient warrior who had prevailed despite being let down by his government and nation. Two million Americans a year visited the stark but moving V-shaped memorial on Washington's mall, making it the second leading tourist attraction in the nation's capital. The hoopla that accompanied the tenth anniversary of the fall of Saigon made abundantly clear how deeply embedded Vietnam was in the national psyche.

If they were more willing to talk about Vietnam, Americans remained confused and divided about its meaning, particularly its implications for U.S. foreign policy. The indifference and tendency toward withdrawal so manifest in 1975 declined sharply over the next ten years. Bitter memories of Vietnam combined with the frustration of the Iranian hostage crisis to produce a growing assertiveness, a highly nationalistic impulse to defend perceived interests, even a yearning to restore the United States to its old position in the world. The breakdown of détente, the steady growth of Soviet military power, and the use of that power in Afghanistan produced a heightened concern for American security. The defense budget soared to record proportions in the early 1980s, and support for military intervention in defense of traditional allies increased significantly.

The new nationalism was tempered by lingering memories of Vietnam, however. Many Americans remained deeply skeptical of 1960s-style globalism and dubious of such internationalist mechanisms as foreign aid or even the United Nations. Ten years after the end of the war, a whopping majority still believed that intervention in Vietnam had been a mistake. Recollection of Vietnam produced strong opposition to intervention in third-world crises in Lebanon and Central America. Thus, in the aftermath of Vietnam, the public mood consisted of a strange amalgam of nostalgia and realism, assertiveness and caution.

The nation's foreign policy elite has been no more certain in its judgments on Vietnam than the mass public. Indeed, systematic polling of leadership groups makes clear that Vietnam was a "landmark event" that left "deep and profound" divisions. Americans agree that to construct a viable foreign policy they must learn from Vietnam. But they disagree sharply over what they should learn.

The basic issue remains the morality and wisdom of intervention in Vietnam. In the light of Hanoi's postwar actions, Americans are less likely to openly condemn their nation's intervention as immoral, an important sign of change in itself. Those who continue to feel that intervention was wrong argue that it was unnecessary or impractical or both, and most liberals still contend that at best it represented overcommitment in an area of peripheral national interest, at worst an act of questionable morality.

The conservative point of view has been more vocal in recent years and it takes two forms. Some, including President Ronald Reagan, have found in postwar events in Indochina reason to speak out anew on what they always felt was a fundamental reality—that, as Reagan has repeatedly stated, Vietnam was "in truth a noble war," a selfless attempt on the part of the United States to save a free nation from outside aggression. Others concede that the United States might have erred in getting involved in Vietnam in the first place, but they go on to insist that over time an important interest was established that had to be defended for the sake of U.S. credibility throughout the world.

The second great issue, on which Americans also sharply disagree, concerns the reasons for U.S. failure in Vietnam. Many of the leading participants in the war have concluded that America's failure was essentially instrumental, a result of the improper use of available tools. General Westmoreland and others blame the "ill-considered" policy of "graduated response" imposed on the military by civilian leaders, arguing that had the United States employed its military power quickly, decisively, and without limit, the war could have been won. Other critics view the fundamental mistakes as the choice of tools rather than how they were used, and they blame an unimaginative military as much as civilians. Instead of trying to fight World War II and Korea over in Vietnam, these critics argue, the military should have adapted to the unconventional war in which it found itself and shaped an appropriate counterinsurgency strategy to meet it. Still other commentators, including some military theorists, agree that military leaders were as responsible for the strategic failure as civilians. Critics such as Colonel Harry G. Summers, Jr., argue that instead of mounting costly and counterproductive search-and-destroy operations against guerrillas in South Vietnam, the United States should have used its own forces against North Vietnamese regulars along the seventeenth parallel to isolate the north from the south. Military leaders should also have insisted on a declaration of war to ensure that the war was not fought in "cold blood" and that popular support could be sustained.

The lessons drawn are as divergent as the arguments advanced. Those who feel that the United States lost because it did not act decisively conclude that if the nation becomes involved in war again, it must employ its military power with a view to winning quickly before public support erodes. Those who feel that the basic problem was the formulation rather than the execution of strategy insist that military and civilian leaders must think strategically, that they must examine more carefully the nature of the war and formulate more precisely the ways in which American power can best be used to attain clearly defined objectives.

Such lessons depend on the values and belief systems of those who pronounce them, of course, and those who opposed the war have reached quite different conclusions. To some former doves, the fundamental lesson is never to get involved in a land war in Asia; to others, it is to avoid intervention in international trouble spots unless the nation's vital interests are clearly at stake. Some commentators warn that policymakers must be wary of the sort of simplistic reasoning that produced the domino theory and the Munich analogy. Others point to the weaknesses of South Vietnam and admonish that "even a superpower can't save allies who are unable or unwilling to save themselves." For still others, the key lessons are that American power has distinct limits and that in order to be effective, American foreign policy must be true to the nation's historic ideals.

The ghost of Vietnam hovered over an increasingly divisive debate on the proper American response to revolutions in Central America. Shortly after taking office in 1981, President Reagan committed U.S. prestige to defending the government of El Salvador against a leftist-led insurgency, in part in the expectation that success there might exorcise the so-called Vietnam syndrome—the perceived reluctance of the American public in the wake of Vietnam to take on responsibilities in third-world countries. When the quick victory did not materialize, the administration expanded U.S. military aid to El Salvador, created a huge military base in Honduras, and launched a not-so-covert war to overthrow the Sandinista government of Nicaragua. The administration insisted that the United States must support non-Communist forces to avert in Central America the bloodshed and misery that followed the end of the war in Vietnam. At the same time, the military and the Defense Department have made clear that they will not go to war under the conditions that prevailed in Vietnam. On the other side, dovish critics ominously warn that U.S. intervention in Central America will lead straight into a quagmire like Vietnam.

The ongoing debate over U.S. involvement in Vietnam leaves many questions unanswered. Whether a more decisive use of military power could have brought a satisfactory conclusion to the war without causing even more disastrous consequences remains highly doubtful. Whether the adoption of a more vigorous and imaginative counterinsurgency program at an earlier stage could have wrested control of the countryside from the Vietcong can never be known, and the ability of the United States to develop such a program in an alien environment is dubious. That the United States exaggerated the importance of Vietnam, as the liberals suggest, seems clear. But their argument begs the question of how one determines the significance of a given area and the even more difficult question of assessing the ultimate costs of intervention at an early stage.

The fundamental weakness of many of the lessons learned thus far is that they assume the continued necessity and practicability of the containment policy, at least in modified form, thereby evading or ignoring altogether the central questions raised by the war. The United States intervened in Vietnam to block the apparent march of a Soviet-directed Communism across Asia, enlarged its commitment to halt a presumably expansionist Communist China, and eventually made Vietnam a test of its determination to uphold world order. By wrongly attributing the Vietnamese conflict to external sources, the United States drastically misjudged its internal dynamics. By intervening in what was essentially a local struggle, it placed itself at the mercy of local forces, a weak client, and a determined adversary. It elevated into a major international conflict what might have remained a localized struggle. By raising the stakes into a test of its own credibility, it perilously narrowed its options. A policy so flawed in its premises cannot help but fail, and in this case the results were disastrous.

Vietnam made clear the inherent unworkability of a policy of global containment. In the 1940s the world seemed dangerous but manageable. The United States enjoyed a position of unprecedented power and influence, and achieved some notable early successes in Europe. Much of America's power derived from the weakness of other nations rather than from its own intrinsic strength, however, and Vietnam demonstrated conclusively that its power, however great, had limits. The development of significant military capabilities by the Soviet Union and China made it extremely risky for the United States to use its military power in Vietnam on a scale necessary to achieve the desired results. Conditions in Vietnam itself and the constraints imposed by domestic opinion made it impossible to reach these goals with limited means. Vietnam makes clear that the United States cannot uphold its own concept of world order in the face of a stubborn and resolute, although much weaker, foe. The war did not bring about the decline of American power, as some have suggested, but was symptomatic of the limits of national power in an age of international diversity and nuclear weaponry.

To assume, therefore, that the United States can simply rouse itself from the nightmare of Vietnam and resume its accustomed role in a rapidly changing world would be to invite further disaster. The world of the 1980s is even more dangerous and much less manageable than that of the 1940s and 1950s. The proliferation of nuclear weapons, the emergence of a large number of new nations, the existence of a baffling array of regional and internal conflicts, have combined to produce a more confusing and disorderly world than at any time in the recent past. The ambiguous triangular relationship between the United States, the Soviet Union, and China has had a further destabilizing effect, creating enormous uncertainty and shifting tensions and giving lesser nations increased maneuverability and opportunity for mischief. A successful American adjustment to the new conditions requires the shedding of old approaches, most notably of the traditional oscillation between crusades to reform the world and angry withdrawal from it. To carry the "Never Again" syndrome to its logical conclusion and turn away from an ungrateful and hostile world could be calamitous. To regard Vietnam as an aberration, a unique experience from which nothing can be learned, would invite further frustration. To adapt to the new era, the United States must recognize its vulnerability, accept the limits to its power, and accommodate itself to many situations it does not like. Americans must understand that they will not be able to dictate solutions to world problems or to achieve all of their goals. Like it or not, Vietnam marked the end of an era in world history and of American foreign policy, an era marked by constructive achievements but blemished by ultimate, although not irreparable, failure.

☓☓ F U R T H E R   R E A D I N G

Mark Baker, *NAM: The Vietnam War in the Words of the Soldiers Who Fought There* (1981)

Loren Baritz, *Backfire: A History of How American Culture Led Us into Vietnam and Made Us Fight the Way We Did* (1985)

Larry Berman, *Planning a Tragedy* (1982)

William C. Berman, *William Fulbright and the Vietnam War: The Dissent of a Political Realist* (1988)

Melanie Billings-Yun, *Decision Against War: Eisenhower and Dien Bien Phu, 1954* (1988)

Peter Braestrup, *Big Story: How the American Press and Television Reported and Interpreted the Crisis of Tet, 1968, in Vietnam and Washington* (1983)

———, ed., *Vietnam as History* (1984)

C. D. B. Bryan, *Friendly Fire* (1976)

Joseph Buttinger, *Vietnam: A Political History* (1970)

Philip Caputo, *A Rumor of War* (1977)

Cincinnatus, *Self-Destruction: The Deterioration and Decay of the U.S. Army During the Vietnam Era* (1981)

Terry Deitz, *Republicans and Vietnam, 1961–1968* (1986)

Peter M. Dunn, *The First Vietnam War* (1985)

Gloria Emerson, *Winners and Losers: Battles, Retreats, Gains, Losses and Ruins from the Vietnam War* (1978)

Bernard B. Fall, *Street Without Joy* (1961)

Frances FitzGerald, *Fire in the Lake: The Vietnamese and the Americans in Vietnam* (1972)

Lloyd C. Gardner, *Approaching Vietnam: From World War II Through Dienbienphu* (1988)

Leslie H. Gelb with Richard K. Betts, *The Irony of Vietnam: The System Worked* (1979)

William C. Gibbons, *The U.S. Government and the Vietnam War* (1986–1987)

David Halberstam, *The Best and the Brightest* (1972)

David C. Hallin, *The "Uncensored War"* (1986)

John Hellman, *American Myth and the Legacy of Vietnam* (1986)

Herbert Hendin and Ann P. Haas, *Wounds of War: The Psychological Aftermath of Combat in Vietnam* (1985)

Michael Herr, *Dispatches* (1977)

George F. Herring, *America's Longest War: The United States and Vietnam, 1950–1975* (1985)

Stuart A. Herrington, *Silence Was a Weapon: The Vietnam War in the Villages* (1982)

Gary Hess, *The United States Emergence as a Southeast Asian Power* (1987)

Townsend Hoopes, *The Limits of Intervention* (1969, 1973)

Arnold R. Isaacs, *Without Honor: Defeat in Vietnam and Cambodia* (1983)

George McTurnan Kahin, *Intervention: How America Became Involved in Vietnam* (1987)

——— and John W. Lewis, *The United States in Vietnam* (1966)

Stanley Karnow, *Vietnam: A History* (1983)

Gabriel Kolko, *Anatomy of a War* (1985)

Andrew F. Krepinevich, Jr., *The Army and Vietnam* (1986)

Anthony Lake, ed., *The Vietnam Legacy* (1976)

Guenter Lewy, *America in Vietnam* (1978)

Kim McQuaid, *The Anxious Years: America in the Vietnam-Watergate Era* (1989)

Don Oberdorfer, *Tet!* (1971)

Bruce Palmer, Jr., *The 25 Year War* (1984)

Douglas Pike, *PAVN: People's Army of Vietnam* (1986)

———, *Vietnam and the Soviet Union* (1987)

Norman Podhoretz, *Why We Were in Vietnam* (1982)

John Prados, *The Sky Would Fall: Operation Vulture: The U.S. Bombing Mission in Indochina* (1982)

Andrew J. Rotter, *The Path to Vietnam: Origins of the American Commitment to Southeast Asia* (1987)

William J. Rust, *Kennedy in Vietnam* (1985)

Herbert Y. Schandler, *Lyndon Johnson and Vietnam: The Unmaking of a President* (1977)

Thomas J. Schoenbaum, *Waging Peace and War* (1988)

William Shawcross, *Sideshow: Kissinger, Nixon and the Destruction of Cambodia* (1979)

Neil Sheehan, *A Bright Shining Lie: John Paul Vann and America in Vietnam* (1988)

Melvin Small, *Johnson, Nixon, and the Doves* (1988)

Frank Snepp, *Decent Interval: An Insider's Account of Indecent Saigon's End* (1977)

Ronald Spector, *The United States Army in Vietnam, Advice and Support: The Early Years* (1983)

Shelby L. Stanton, *The Rise and Fall of an American Army* (1985)

Harry F. Summers, Jr., *On Strategy* (1982)

James C. Thompson, *Rolling Thunder* (1980)

Kathryn J. Turner, *Lyndon Johnson's Dual War: Vietnam and the Press* (1985)

Van Tieng Dung, *Our Great Spring Victory* (1980)

Vo Nguyen Giap and Van Tieng Dung, *How We Won the War* (1980)

John Wheeler, *Touched with Fire: The Future of the Vietnam Generation* (1984)

Nancy Zaroulis and Gerald Sullivan, *Who Spoke Up?* (1984)

The New Left and
the Politics of the 1960s

XXX

As the 1950s drew to a close and the chill of the McCarthy years faded and even Eisenhower's towering popularity waned, a new critical spirit quickened throughout much of America. It sprang from diverse sources: from the struggle against segregation that would soon become the modern civil-rights movement; from a growing awareness that despite wide prosperity, millions of Americans remained trapped in poverty; from escalating fears of nuclear war and increasing opposition to the Cold War; from a dawning realization of the social and environmental costs of the postwar system; and from the rising self-consciousness of the new postwar "baby boom" generation. It was this spirit of disquietude to which John F. Kennedy appealed in his promise to "get America moving again" along a "new frontier." And it was this same spirit that informed the early history of Students for a Democratic Society (SDS) and the New Left.

SDS represented a self-consciously new radicalism that, shunning the Marxist clichés of the thirties, called for "participatory democracy" and a reconstruction of American society that would replace "power rooted in possession, privilege, or circumstance [with] power and uniqueness rooted in love, reflectiveness, reason, and creativity." The new radicalism quickly divided into two powerful streams: one conventionally political, the other mainly cultural. SDS, which represented the first of these streams, would itself soon become radicalized and bitterly divided, though not before its critical spirit had deeply pervaded the era's thought and politics. The new cultural radicalism, meanwhile, swept up many young Americans in a tide of generational self-expression that featured bold new styles of music, dress, and behavior. After 1965, the New Left was increasingly defined by its opposition to the war in Vietnam, which brought thousands of new recruits into its ranks but which also contributed to its radicalization, repression, and eventual downfall.

Historians—many of whom were themselves deeply influenced by the new radicalism of the 1960s—have only begun to unpack the movement's meanings and significance. Not surprisingly, they have disagreed vigorously among themselves: some, echoing criticisms by the Old Left, fault the movement's lack of coherent ideology and disciplined organization; others, sympathetic to the move-

ment's origins, decry its disintegration into sectarian radicalism; still others, disillusioned or unsympathetic to begin with, view it as at best shallow and
ephemeral, at worst hypocritical and destructive. As the 1980s give way to the
1990s, how Americans reconstruct the history of the New Left becomes one of
the important ways in which they also chart their future.

※ D O C U M E N T S

The Port Huron Statement, excerpts from which are reprinted in the first document, was written by student activist Tom Hayden and others and adopted at the
annual convention of Students for a Democratic Society in 1962. It reflected the
early history of the New Left in its lack of doctrinaire ideology as well as in its
spirit of hope and optimism. SDS was nevertheless dedicated throughout its early
history to a more or less traditional politics of organization and struggle. Rebels
like Abbie Hoffman and Jerry Rubin, on the other hand, owed more to the new
cultural radicalism. The excerpt in the second document from Rubin's book *Do
It! Scenarios of the Revolution* (1970) captures the emphasis of the new "counterculture" on theatricality and self-expression. By the late 1960s, SDS was radicalized and bitterly divided. Among the most radical splinter factions were the
Weathermen, who took their name from Bob Dylan's "Subterranean Homesick
Blues." The Weathermen's 1969 call for revolution is reprinted from *New Left
Notes* (June 18, 1969) in the third document.

Opposition to the New Left was widespread among politicians, the press, and
the leaders of much of American business and industry. The Federal Bureau of
Investigation launched an illegal secret campaign to "expose, disrupt, and otherwise neutralize" the radical movement. This campaign is described in the fourth
document, an excerpt from a 1976 investigation of the FBI by a U.S. Senate
committee.

Many college students were caught up in the turmoil of the sixties, and most
dramatically so at Kent State University, where in 1970 four of them were killed
when Ohio National Guardsmen fired into a crowd of protesters. The recollections of one of the surviving students, Tom Grace, are reprinted in the fifth document. By the late 1960s, disillusionment had set in: SDS was deeply divided; the
war in Vietnam ground on; and the New Left had helped unseat Lyndon Johnson, only to get Richard Nixon as his successor. Many of the generation's new
radicals sought to restore their own lives—and perhaps in their own small way, to
work for the reform of the larger society—by fleeing to the rural countryside.
Among them was Raymond Mungo, an excerpt from whose book *Total Loss
Farm* (1970) is reprinted as the final document.

The Port Huron Statement, 1963

We are people of this generation, bred in at least modest comfort, housed
now in universities, looking uncomfortably to the world we inherit.

When we were kids the United States was the wealthiest and strongest
country in the world: the only one with the atom bomb, the least scarred
by modern war, an initiator of the United Nations that we thought would
distribute Western influence throughout the world. Freedom and equality
for each individual, government of, by, and for the people—these American

values we found good, principles by which we could live as men. Many of us began maturing in complacency.

As we grew, however, our comfort was penetrated by events too troubling to dismiss. First, the permeating and victimizing fact of human degradation, symbolized by the Southern struggle against racial bigotry, compelled most of us from silence to activism. Second, the enclosing fact of the Cold War, symbolized by the presence of the Bomb, brought awareness that we ourselves, and our friends, and millions of abstract "others" we knew more directly because of our common peril, might die at any time. We might deliberately ignore, or avoid, or fail to feel all other human problems, but not these two, for these were too immediate and crushing in their impact, too challenging in the demand that we as individuals take the responsibility for encounter and resolution.

While these and other problems either directly oppressed us or rankled our consciences and became our own subjective concerns, we began to see complicated and disturbing paradoxes in our surrounding America. The declaration "all men are created equal . . ." rang hollow before the facts of Negro life in the South and the big cities of the North. The proclaimed peaceful intentions of the United States contradicted its economic and military investments in the Cold War status quo.

We witnessed, and continue to witness, other paradoxes. With nuclear energy whole cities can easily be powered, yet the dominant nation-states seem more likely to unleash destruction greater than that incurred in all wars of human history. Although our own technology is destroying old and creating new forms of social organization, men still tolerate meaningless work and idleness. While two-thirds of mankind suffers undernourishment, our own upper classes revel amidst superfluous abundance. Although world population is expected to double in forty years, the nations still tolerate anarchy as a major principle of international conduct and uncontrolled exploitation governs the sapping of the earth's physical resources. Although mankind desperately needs revolutionary leadership, America rests in national stalemate, its goals ambiguous and tradition-bound instead of informed and clear, its democratic system apathetic and manipulated rather than "of, by, and for the people."

Not only did tarnish appear on our image of American virtue, not only did disillusion occur when the hypocrisy of American ideals was discovered, but we began to sense that what we had originally seen as the American Golden Age was actually the decline of an era. The worldwide outbreak of revolution against colonialism and imperialism, the entrenchment of totalitarian states, the menace of war, overpopulation, international disorder, supertechnology—these trends were testing the tenacity of our own commitment to democracy and freedom and our abilities to visualize their application to a world in upheaval.

Our work is guided by the sense that we may be the last generation in the experiment with living. But we are a minority—the vast majority of our people regard the temporary equilibriums of our society and world as eternally-functional parts. In this is perhaps the outstanding paradox: we ourselves are imbued with urgency, yet the message of our society is that there is no viable alternative to the present. Beneath the reassuring tones of the politicians, beneath the common opinion that America will "muddle through," beneath the stagnation of those who have closed their minds to the future, is the pervading feeling that there simply are no alternatives, that our times have witnessed the exhaustion not only of Utopias, but of any new departures as well. Feeling the press of complexity upon the emptiness of life, people are fearful of the thought that at any moment things might thrust out of control. They fear change itself, since change might smash whatever invisible framework seems to hold back chaos for them now. For most Americans, all crusades are suspect, threatening. The fact that each individual sees apathy in his fellows perpetuates the common reluctance to organize for change. The dominant institutions are complex enough to blunt the minds of their potential critics, and entrenched enough to swiftly dissipate or entirely repel the energies of protest and reform, thus limiting human expectancies. Then, too, we are a materially improved society, and by our own improvements we seem to have weakened the case for further change.

Some would have us believe that Americans feel contentment amidst prosperity—but might it not better be called a glaze above deeply-felt anxieties about their role in the new world? And if these anxieties produce a developed indifference to human affairs, do they not as well produce a yearning to believe there *is* an alternative to the present, that something *can* be done to change circumstances in the school, the workplaces, the bureaucracies, the government? It is to this latter yearning, at once the spark and engine of change, that we direct our present appeal. The search for truly democratic alternatives to the present, and a commitment to social experimentation with them, is a worthy and fulfilling human enterprise, one which moves us and, we hope, others today. On such a basis do we offer this document of our convictions and analysis: as an effort in understanding and changing the conditions of humanity in the late twentieth century, an effort rooted in the ancient, still unfulfilled conception of man attaining determining influence over his circumstances of life. . . .

Making values explicit—an initial task in establishing alternatives—is an activity that has been devalued and corrupted. The conventional moral terms of the age, the politician moralities—"free world," "people's democracies"—reflect realities poorly, if at all, and seem to function more as ruling myths than as descriptive principles. But neither has our experience in the universities brought us moral enlightenment. Our professors and administrators sacrifice controversy to public relations; their curriculums change more slowly than the living events of the world; their skills and silence are purchased by investors in the arms race; passion is called unscholastic. The questions we might want raised—what is really important? can we live in a different and better way? if we wanted to change society, how would we do it?—are not thought to be questions of a "fruitful, empirical nature," and thus are brushed aside.

Unlike youth in other countries we are used to moral leadership being exercised and moral dimensions being clarified by our elders. But today, for us, not even the liberal and socialist preachments of the past seem adequate to the forms of the present. Consider the old slogans: Capitalism Cannot Reform Itself, United Front Against Facism, General Strike, All Out on May Day. Or, more recently, No Cooperation with Commies and Fellow Travellers, Ideologies Are Exhausted, Bipartisanship, No Utopias. These are incomplete, and there are few new prophets. It has been said that our liberal and socialist predecessors were plagued by vision without program, while our own generation is plagued by program without vision. All around us there is astute grasp of method, technique—the committee, the ad hoc group, the lobbyist, the hard and soft sell, the make, the projected image— but, if pressed critically, such expertise is incompetent to explain its implicit ideals. It is highly fashionable to identify oneself by old categories, or by naming a respected political figure, or by explaining "how we would vote" on various issues.

Theoretic chaos has replaced the idealistic thinking of old—and, unable to reconstitute theoretic order, men have condemned idealism itself. Doubt has replaced hopefulness—and men act out a defeatism that is labelled realistic. The decline of utopia and hope is in fact one of the defining features of social life today. The reasons are various: the dreams of the older left were perverted by Stalinism and never recreated; the congressional stalemate makes men narrow their view of the possible; the specialization of human activity leaves little room for sweeping thought; the horrors of the twentieth century, symbolized in the gas-ovens and concentration camps and atom bombs, have blasted hopefulness. To be idealistic is to be considered apocalyptic, deluded. To have no serious aspirations, on the contrary, is to be "tough-minded."

In suggesting social goals and values, therefore, we are aware of entering a sphere of some disrepute. Perhaps matured by the past, we have no sure formulas, no closed theories—but that does not mean values are beyond discussion and tentative determination. A first task of any social movement is to convince people that the search for orienting theories and the creation of human values is complex but worthwhile. We are aware that to avoid platitudes we must analyze the concrete conditions of social order. But to direct such an analysis we must use the guideposts of basic principles. Our own social values involve conceptions of human beings, human relationships, and social systems.

We regard *men* as infinitely precious and possessed of unfulfilled capacities for reason, freedom, and love. In affirming these principles we are aware of countering perhaps the dominant conceptions of man in the twentieth century: that he is a thing to be manipulated, and that he is inherently incapable of directing his own affairs. We oppose the depersonalization that reduces human beings to the status of things—if anything, the brutalities of the twentieth century teach that means and ends are intimately related, that vague appeals to "posterity" cannot justify the mutilations of the present. We oppose, too, the doctrine of human incompetence because it rests essentially on the modern fact that men have been "competently" manipulated into incompetence—we see little reason why men cannot meet with increasing skill the complexities and responsibilities of their situation, if society is organized not for minority, but for majority, participation in decision-making.

Men have unrealized potential for self-cultivation, self-direction, self-understanding, and creativity. It is this potential that we regard as crucial and to which we appeal, not to the human potentiality for violence, unreason, and submission to authority. The goal of man and society should be human independence: a concern not with image of popularity but with finding a meaning in life that is personally authentic; a quality of mind not compulsively driven by a sense of powerlessness, nor one which unthinkingly adopts status values, nor one which represses all threats to its habits, but one which has full, spontaneous access to present and past experiences, one which easily unites the fragmented parts of personal history, one which openly faces problems which are troubling and unresolved; one with an intuitive awareness of possibilities, an active sense of curiosity, an ability and willingness to learn.

This kind of independence does not mean egoistic individualism—the object is not to have one's way so much as it is to have a way that is one's own. Nor do we deify man—we merely have faith in his potential.

Human relationships should involve fraternity and honesty. Human interdependence is contemporary fact; human brotherhood must be willed however, as a condition of future survival and as the most appropriate form of social relations. Personal links between man and man are needed, especially to go beyond the partial and fragmentary bonds of function that bind men only as worker to worker, employer to employee, teacher to student, American to Russian.

Loneliness, estrangement, isolation describe the vast distance between man and man today. These dominant tendencies cannot be overcome by better personnel management, nor by improved gadgets, but only when a love of man overcomes the idolotrous worship of things by man.

As the individualism we affirm is not egoism, the selflessness we affirm is not self-elimination. On the contrary, we believe in generosity of a kind that imprints one's unique individual qualities in the relation to other men, and to all human activity. Further, to dislike isolation is not to favor the abolition of privacy; the latter differs from isolation in that it occurs or is abolished according to individual will. Finally, we would replace power and personal uniqueness rooted in possession, privilege, or circumstance by power and uniqueness rooted in love, reflectiveness, reason, and creativity.

As a *social system* we seek the establishment of a democracy of individual participation, governed by two central aims: that the individual share in those social decisions determining the quality and direction of his life; that society be organized to encourage independence in men and provide the media for their common participation.

In a participatory democracy, the political life would be based in several root principles:

* that decision-making of basic social consequence be carried on by public groupings;

- that politics be seen positively, as the art of collectively creating an acceptable pattern of social relations;
- that politics has the function of bringing people out of isolation and into community, thus being a necessary, though not sufficient, means of finding meaning in personal life;
- that the political order should serve to clarify problems in a way instrumental to their solution; it should provide outlets for the expression of personal grievance and aspiration; opposing views should be organized so as to illuminate choices and facilitate the attainment of goals; channels should be commonly available to relate men to knowledge and to power so that private problems—from bad recreation facilities to personal alienation—are formulated as general issues.

The economic sphere would have as its basis the principles:
- that work should involve incentives worthier than money or survival. It should be educative, not stultifying; creative, not mechanical; self-direct, not manipulated, encouraging independence, a respect for others, a sense of dignity and a willingness to accept social responsibility, since it is this experience that has crucial influence on habits, perceptions and individual ethics;
- that the economic experience is so personally decisive that the individual must share in its full determination;
- that the economy itself is of such social importance that its major resources and means of production should be open to democratic participation and subject to democratic social regulation.

Like the political and economic ones, major social institutions—cultural, education, rehabilitative, and others—should be generally organized with the well-being and dignity of man as the essential measure of success.

In social change or interchange, we find violence to be abhorrent because it requires generally the transformation of the target, be it a human being or a community of people, into a depersonalized object of hate. It is imperative that the means of violence be abolished and the institutions—local, national, international—that encourage nonviolence as a condition of conflict be developed.

These are our central values, in skeletal form. It remains vital to understand their denial or attainment in the context of the modern world.

Jerry Rubin: Self-Portrait of a Child of "Amerika," 1970

I am a child of Amerika.

If I'm ever sent to Death Row for my revolutionary "crimes," I'll order as my last meal: a hamburger, french fries and a Coke.

I dig big cities.

I love to read the sports pages and gossip columns, listen to the radio and watch color TV.

I dig department stores, huge supermarkets and airports. I feel secure (though not necessarily hungry) when I see Howard Johnson's on the expressway.

I groove on Hollywood movies—even bad ones.

I speak only one language—English.

I love rock 'n' roll.

I collected baseball players' cards when I was a kid and wanted to play second base for the Cincinnati Reds, my home team.

I got a car when I was sixteen after flunking my first driver's test and crying for a week waiting to take it a second time.

I went to the kind of high school where you had to pass a test to get *in.*

I graduated in the bottom half of the class.

My classmates voted me the "busiest" senior in the school.

I had short, short, short hair.

I dug *Catcher in the Rye.*

I didn't have pimples.

I became an ace young reporter for the Cincinnati *Post and Times-Star.* *"Son,"* the managing editor said to me, *"someday you're going to be a helluva reporter, maybe the greatest reporter this city's ever seen."*

I loved Adlai Stevenson.

My father drove a truck delivering bread and later became an organizer in the Bakery Drivers' Union. He dug Jimmy Hoffa (so do I). He died of heart failure at fifty-two.

My mother had a college degree and played the piano. She died of cancer at the age of fifty-one.

I took care of my brother, Gil, from the time he was thirteen.

I dodged the draft.

I went to Oberlin College for a year, graduated from the University of Cincinnati, spent 1½ years in Israel and started graduate school at Berkeley.

I dropped out.

I dropped out of the White Race and the Amerikan nation.

I dig being free.

I like getting high.

I don't own a suit or tie.

I live for the revolution.

I'm a yippie!

I am an orphan of Amerika.

The Weathermen's Call
for Revolution: "You Don't Need a Weatherman
to Know Which Way the Wind Blows," 1969

People ask, what is the nature of the revolution that we talk about? Who will it be made by, and for, and what are its goals and strategy?

From *New Left Notes,* June 18, 1969. Reprinted with permission from WEATHERMAN by Harold Jacobs, © Ramparts Press, 1970, pp. 51–53.

The overriding consideration in answering these questions is that the main struggle going on in the world today is between US imperialism and the national liberation struggles against it. This is essential in defining political matters in the whole world: because it is by far the most powerful, every other empire and petty dictator is in the long run dependent on US imperialism, which has unified, allied with, and defended all of the reactionary forces of the whole world. Thus, in considering every other force or phenomenon, from Soviet imperialism or Israeli imperialism to "workers struggle" in France or Czechoslovakia, we determine who are our friends and who are our enemies according to whether they help US imperialism or fight to defeat it.

So the very first question people in this country must ask in considering the question of revolution is where they stand in relation to the United States as an oppressor nation, and where they stand in relation to the masses of people throughout the world whom US imperialism is oppressing.

The primary task of revolutionary struggle is to solve this principal contradiction on the side of the people of the world. It is the oppressed peoples of the world who have created the wealth of this empire and it is to them that it belongs; the goal of the revolutionary struggle must be the control and use of this wealth in the interests of the oppressed peoples of the world.

It is in this context that we must examine the revolutionary struggles in the United States. We are within the heartland of a world-wide monster, a country so rich from its world-wide plunder that even the crumbs doled out to the enslaved masses within its borders provide for material existence very much above the conditions of the masses of people of the world. The US empire, as a world-wide system, channels wealth, based upon the labor and resources of the rest of the world, into the United States. The relative affluence existing in the United States is directly dependent upon the labor and natural resources of the Vietnamese, the Angolans, the Bolivians and the rest of the peoples of the Third World. All of the United Airlines Astrojets, all of the Holiday Inns, all of Hertz's automobiles, your television set, car and wardrobe already belong, to a large degree to the people of the rest of the world.

Therefore, any conception of "socialist revolution" simply in terms of the working people of the United States, failing to recognize the full scope of interests of the most oppressed peoples of the world, is a conception of a fight for a particular privileged interest, and is a very dangerous ideology. While the control and use of the wealth of the Empire for the people of the whole world is also in the interests of the vast majority of the people in this country, if the goal is not clear from the start we will further the preservation of class society, oppression, war, genocide, and the complete emiseration of everyone, including the people of the US.

The goal is the destruction of US imperialism and the achievement of a classless world: world communism. Winning state power in the US will occur as a result of the military forces of the US overextending themselves around the world and being defeated piecemeal; struggle within the US will be a vital part of this process, but when the revolution triumphs in the US it will have been made by the people of the whole world. For socialism to be defined in national terms within so extreme and historical an oppressor nation as this is only imperialist national chauvinism on the part of the "movement."

A Senate Committee Probes the FBI's Secret Campaign Against the New Left, 1976

COINTELPRO is the FBI acronym for a series of covert action programs directed against domestic groups. In these programs, the Bureau went beyond the collection of intelligence to secret action designed to "disrupt" and "neutralize" target groups and individuals. The techniques were adopted wholesale from wartime counterintelligence, and ranged from the trivial (mailing reprints of *Reader's Digest* articles to college administrators) to the degrading (sending anonymous poison-pen letters intended to break up marriages) and the dangerous (encouraging gang warfare and falsely labeling members of a violent group as police informers).

This report is based on a staff study of more than 20,000 pages of Bureau documents, depositions of many of the Bureau agents involved in the programs, and interviews of several COINTELPRO targets. The examples selected for discussion necessarily represent a small percentage of the more than 2,000 approved COINTELPRO actions. Nevertheless, the cases demonstrate the consequences of a Government agency's decision to take the law into its own hands for the "greater good" of the country.

COINTELPRO began in 1956, in part because of frustration with Supreme Court rulings limiting the Government's power to proceed overtly against dissident groups; it ended in 1971 with the threat of public exposure. In the intervening 15 years, the Bureau conducted a sophisticated vigilante operation aimed squarely at preventing the exercise of First Amendment rights of speech and association, on the theory that preventing the growth of dangerous groups and the propagation of dangerous ideas would protect the national security and deter violence.

Many of the techniques used would be intolerable in a democratic society even if all of the targets had been involved in violent activity, but COINTELPRO went far beyond that. The unexpressed major premise of the programs was that a law enforcement agency has the duty to do whatever is necessary to combat perceived threats to the existing social and political order. . . .

7. New Left. The Internal Security Section had undergone a slow transition from concentrating on the "Old Left"—the CPUSA and SWP—to focusing primarily on the activities of the "New Left"—a term which had no precise definition within the Bureau. Some agents defined "New Left" functionally, by connection with protests. Others defined it by philosophy, particularly antiwar philosophy.

On October 28, 1968, the fifth and final COINTELPRO was started against this undefined group. The program was triggered in part by the Columbia campus disturbance. Once again, law enforcement methods had broken down, largely (in the Bureau's opinion) because college administrators refused to call the police on campus to deal with student demonstrations. The atmosphere at the time was described by the Headquarters agent who supervised the New Left COINTELPRO:

> During that particular time, there was considerable public, Administration— I mean governmental Administration—[and] news media interest in the protest movement to the extent that some groups, I don't recall any specifics, but some groups were calling for something to be done to blunt or reduce the protest movements that were disrupting campuses. I can't classify it as exactly an hysteria, but there was considerable interest [and concern]. That was the framework that we were working with. . . . It would be my impression that as a result of this hysteria, some governmental leaders were looking to the Bureau.

And, once again, the combination of perceived threat, public outcry, and law enforcement frustration produced a COINTELPRO.

According to the initiating letter, the counterintelligence program's purpose was to "expose, disrupt, and otherwise neutralize" the activities of the various New Left organizations, their leadership, and adherents, with particular attention to Key Activists, "the moving forces behind the New Left." The final paragraph contains an exhortation to a "forward look, enthusiasm, and interest" because of the Bureau's concern that "the anarchist activities of a few can paralyze institutions of learning, induction centers, cripple traffic, and tie the arms of law enforcement officials all to the detriment of our society." The internal memorandum recommending the program further sets forth the Bureau's concerns:

> Our Nation is undergoing an era of disruption and violence caused to a large extent by various individuals generally connected with the New Left. Some of these activists urge revolution in America and call for the defeat of the United States in Vietnam. They continually and falsely allege police brutality and do not hesitate to utilize unlawful acts to further their so-called causes.

The document continues:

> The New Left has on many occasions viciously and scurrilously attacked the Director and the Bureau in an attempt to hamper our investigation of it and to drive us off the college campuses.

Based on those factors, the Bureau decided to institute a new COINTELPRO.

8. New Left Directives. The Bureau's concern with "tying the hands of law enforcement officers," and with the perceived weakness of college administrators in refusing to call police onto the campus, led to a May 23, 1968, directive to all participating field offices to gather information on three categories of New Left activities:

> (1) false allegations of police brutality, to "counter the wide-spread charges of police brutality that invariably arise following student-police encounters";
> (2) immorality, depicting the "scurrilous and depraved nature of many of the characters, activities, habits, and living conditions representative of New Left adherents"; and
> (3) action by college administrators, "to show the value of college administrators and school officials taking a firm stand," and pointing out "whether and to what extent faculty members rendered aid and encouragement."

The letter continues, "Every avenue of possible embarrassment must be vigorously and enthusiastically explored. It cannot be expected that information of this type will be easily obtained, and an imaginative approach by your personnel is imperative to its success."

The order to furnish information on "immorality" was not carried out with sufficient enthusiasm. On October 9, 1968, headquarters sent another letter to all offices, taking them to task for their failure to "remain alert for and to seek specific data depicting the depraved nature and moral looseness of the New Left" and to "use this material in a vigorous and enthusiastic approach to neutralizing them." Recipient offices were again instructed to be "particularly alert for this type of data" and told:

> As the current school year commences, it can be expected that the New Left with its anti-war and anti-draft entourage will make every effort to confront college authorities, stifle military recruiting, and frustrate the Selective Service System. Each office will be expected, therefore, to afford this program continuous effective attention in order that no opportunity will be missed to destroy this insidious movement.

As to the police brutality and "college administrator" categories, the Bureau's belief that getting tough with students and demonstrators would solve the problem, and that any injuries which resulted were deserved, is reflected in the Bureau's reaction to allegations of police brutality following the Chicago Democratic Convention.

On August 28, 1968, a letter was sent to the Chicago field office instructing it to "obtain all possible evidence that would disprove these charges" [that the Chicago police used undue force] and to "consider measures by which cooperative news media may be used to counteract these allegations." The administrative "note" (for the file) states:

> Once again, the liberal press and the bleeding hearts and the forces on the left are taking advantage of the situation in Chicago surrounding the Democratic National Convention to attack the police and organized law enforcement agencies. . . . We should be mindful of this situation and develop all possible evidence to expose this activity and to refute these false allegations.

In the same vein, on September 9, 1968, an instruction was sent to all offices which had sent informants to the Chicago convention demonstrations, ordering them to debrief the informants for information "indicating incidents were staged to show police reacted with undue force and any information that authorities were baited by militants into using force." The offices were also to obtain evidence of possible violations of anti-riot laws.

The originating New Left letter had asked all recipient offices to respond with suggestions for counterintelligence action. Those responses were analyzed and a letter sent to all offices on July 6, 1968, setting forth twelve suggestions for counterintelligence action which could be utilized by all offices. Briefly the techniques are:

(1) preparing leaflets designed to discredit student demonstrators, using photographs of New Left leadership at the respective universities. "Naturally, the most obnoxious pictures should be used";

(2) instigating "personal conflicts or animosities" between New Left leaders;

(3) creating the impression that leaders are "informants for the Bureau or other law enforcement agencies";

(4) sending articles from student newspapers or the "underground press" which show the depravity of the New Left to university officials, donors, legislators, and parents. "Articles showing advocation of the use of narcotics and free sex are ideal";

(5) having members arrested on marijuana charges;

(6) sending anonymous letters about a student's activities to parents, neighbors, and the parents' employers. "This could have the effect of forcing the parents to take action";

(7) sending anonymous letters or leaflets describing the "activities and associations" of New Left faculty members and graduate assistants to university officials, legislators, Boards of Regents, and the press. "These letters should be signed 'A Concerned Alumni,' or 'A Concerned Taxpayer' ";

(8) using "cooperative press contacts" to emphasize that the "disruptive elements" constitute a "minority" of the students. "The press should demand an immediate referendum on the issue in question";

(9) exploiting the "hostility" among the SDS and other New Left groups toward the SWP, YSA, and Progressive Labor Party;

(10) using "friendly news media" and law enforcement officials to disrupt New Left coffeehouses near military bases which are attempting to "influence members of the Armed Forces";

(11) using cartoons, photographs, and anonymous letters to "ridicule" the New Left; and

(12) using "misinformation" to "confuse and disrupt" New Left activities, such as by notifying members that events have been cancelled.

As noted earlier, the lack of any Bureau definition of "New Left" resulted in targeting almost every anti-war group, and spread to students demonstrating against anything. One notable example is a proposal targeting a student who carried an "obscene" sign in a demonstration protesting administration censorship of the school newspaper, and another student who sent a letter to that paper defending the demonstration. In another[, an] article regarding "free love" on a university campus was anonymously mailed to college administrators and state officials since free love allows "an atmosphere to build up on campus that will be a fertile field for the New Left."

None of the Bureau witnesses deposed believes the New Left COINTELPRO was generally effective, in part because of the imprecise targeting.

A Student Survivor Recalls the Tragedy at Kent State, 1970

My first class of the day was at nine-fifty-five and my girlfriend was in the same class. Because of all the tumultuous disorder that had gone on for the preceding days, the professor, being an understanding man, gave people the option of leaving and taking the exam at another time if the events had interfered with their studying, or going ahead and taking the test. My girlfriend chose to make an exit; history was not her strong point. As far as I was concerned, I had no problem taking the test. So she left and I stayed. . . .

Toward the end of the class, I recall a student standing and saying that there was going to be a rally on the commons as soon as the class was over. I sat there for a few minutes deliberating as to whether I should go or not, and I remembered my earlier assurances to my girlfriend.

Then I thought to myself, This is too momentous; it's too important for me to stay away. Certainly I couldn't see any harm in my going over just to watch. So I went over there really with the intention of more or less surveying the scene, not knowing what I was going to find.

It was only a short five-minute walk to the commons. I found several hundred students, and some of my roommates, Alan Canfora and Jim Riggs, had flags, black flags, I believe. Alan had spray-painted "KENT" on it, and the other one was just a black flag, and they were waving these things about. So I was drawn to them right away. There was some chanting going on: "One, two, three, four, we don't want your fucking war" and "Pigs off campus."

The crowd had grouped around the victory bell, which had been historically used to signal victories in Kent State football games, and the bell was being sounded to signal students to congregate. There were at the very least another thousand or so observers and onlookers ringing the hills that surround this part of the commons.

At that point, a campus policeman in a National Guard jeep ordered the crowd, through the use of a bullhorn, to disperse and go to their homes. The policeman was riding shotgun, and I believe a National Guardsman was driving the jeep. "All you bystanders and innocent people go to your homes for your own safety," is what we heard. I think he had the best of intentions in terms of asking the crowd to disperse, but it did nothing but whip the crowd into a further frenzy.

We have to remember here the mind-set of people and everything that had gone on. A very adversarial atmosphere existed, and we felt that this was our campus, that we were doing nothing wrong, and that they had no right to order us to disperse. If anyone ought to leave, it's them, not us. That's how I felt.

I was standing there yelling and screaming along with everyone else, and then someone flung either a rock or a bottle at the jeep, which bounced harmlessly off the tire. I don't think it was necessarily meant to bounce off the tire; fortunately the person was not a very good shot. That, of course, alarmed the occupants of the jeep. I think they realized at that point—because of the crescendo the chants had reached, and also the fact that people were pitching objects in their direction—that we weren't going to leave.

So the jeep drove back to the National Guard lines which had formed on the other side of the commons in front of the remains of the burned ROTC building. Then the National Guardsmen leveled their bayonets at us and started to march across the commons in our direction, shooting tear gas as they came.

I was teargassed along with perhaps a thousand other people. Unlike some of the students, who delayed to throw rocks or tear-gas cannisters back in the direction of the National Guard, I chose to leave the area as fast as I could. I retreated to a girls' dormitory where there were some first-floor restrooms. The female students had opened up the windows and were passing out moistened paper towels so people could relieve the effects of the tear gas. So I went and I cleansed my eyes to the best of my ability, and that seemed to take care of me at the moment.

In the meantime, one group of National Guardsmen had advanced the same way that I had retreated, but they did not chase the students further. But another troop of the National Guard had gone right past and proceeded downhill onto the practice football field. There was a rather abrupt drop-off and a chain-link fence where some construction had been going on, and on the other three sides the National Guardsmen were ringed by students.

I cautiously moved a little closer and watched. Some students were throwing rocks at the National Guard, and some of the National Guard were picking up the rocks and throwing them back at the students. I didn't see any National Guardsmen hit by rocks. They seemed to be bouncing at their feet.

Then I remember that the National Guard troop seemed to get into a little huddle before leaving the practice football field. They reformed their lines and proceeded back up the hill. It was almost like the parting of the Red Sea. The students just moved to one side or the other to let the National Guardsmen pass, because no one in their right mind would have stood there as bayonets were coming.

A lot of people were screaming, "Get out of here, get off our campus," and in the midst of all this were some students, oddly enough, who were still wandering through the area with their textbooks, as if they were completely unaware of all that was taking place. I felt that I was still keeping a safe distance. I was 150, 165 feet away. I know that because it's since been paced off.

When the National Guardsmen got to the top of the hill, all of a sudden there was just a quick movement, a flurry of activity, and then a crack, or two cracks of rifle fire, and I thought, Oh, my God! I turned and started running as fast as I could. I don't think I got more than a step or two, and all of a sudden I was on the ground. It was just like somebody had come over and given me a body blow and knocked me right down.

The bullet had entered my left heel and had literally knocked me off my feet. I tried to raise myself, and I heard someone yelling, "Stay down, stay down! It's buckshot!" I looked up, and about five or ten feet away from me, behind a tree, was my roommate Alan Canfora. That was the first time I had seen him since we were down on the other side of the commons, chanting antiwar slogans.

So I threw myself back to the ground and lay as prone as possible to shield myself as much as I could, although like most people I was caught right in the open. I couldn't run, because I had already been hit. There was no cover. I just hugged the ground so as to expose as little of my body as possible to the gunfire.

It seemed like the bullets were going by within inches of my head. I can remember seeing people behind me, farther down the hill in the parking lot, dropping. I didn't know if they were being hit by bullets or they were just hugging the ground. We know today that it only lasted thirteen seconds, but it seemed like it kept going and going and going. And I remember thinking, When is this going to stop?

So I was lying there, and all of a sudden this real husky, well-built guy ran to me, picked me up like I was a sack of potatoes, and threw me over his shoulder. He carried me through the parking lot in the direction of a girls' dormitory. We went by one body, a huge puddle of blood. Head wounds always bleed very badly, and his was just awful.

The female students were screaming as I was carried into the dormitory and placed on a couch, bleeding all over the place. A nursing student applied a tourniquet to my leg. I never really felt that my life was in danger, but I could look down at my foot and I knew that I had one hell of a bad wound. The bullet blew the shoe right off my foot, and there was a bone sticking through my green sock. It looked like somebody had put my foot through a meatgrinder.

The ambulances came. Some attendants came in, put me on a stretcher, and carried me outside. The blood loss had lessened because of the tourniquet that was on my leg. I remember having my fist up in the air as a sign of defiance. They put me into the top tier in the ambulance rather than the lower one, which was already occupied. I remember my foot hitting the edge of the ambulance as I went in. From that moment on, until the time that I actually went under from the anesthesia at Robinson Memorial Hospital, I was probably in the most intense pain that I've ever experienced in my life.

They had the back doors closed by this time, and the ambulance was speeding away from the campus. I looked down and saw Sandy Scheuer. I had met Sandy about a week or two beforehand for the first and only time. She had been introduced to me by one of the guys who lived downstairs in my apartment complex. They were casual friends, and she struck me as being a very nice person.

She had a gaping bullet wound in the neck, and the ambulance attendants were tearing away the top two buttons of her blouse and then doing a heart massage. I remember their saying that it's no use, she's dead. And then they just pulled up the sheet over her head.

The ambulance got to the hospital, and it was a scene that's probably been played out any number of times when you have a big disaster. There were people running around, stretchers being wheeled in, and I was just put out in a hallway because the medical personnel were attending to the more severely wounded.

I had the tourniquet on my leg, so I wasn't bleeding all over the place, but the pain kept getting more excruciating. I was screaming by that time, "Get me something for this pain!" Then I was wheeled into an elevator and brought up to one of the other floors. I remember receiving some anesthesia and being told to count backward from ten. I didn't get very far, and then I was out.

The next thing I remember was waking up in a hospital bed. I looked up at the ceiling and then all of a sudden it came to me what had occurred. I didn't know how long I had been out, and I sat up as quickly as I could and looked down to see if my foot was still there. I could see the tips of my toes sticking out of a cast. I just lay back, and I breathed a big sigh of relief. . . .

Today, if I engage in any strenuous exercise, I'll have a noticeable limp for a couple of days afterward. But on the whole, I consider myself to be rather fortunate. I could have lost my foot; I could have been killed. Four people had been shot to death: Sandy Scheuer, Jeff Miller, Allison Krause, and Bill Schroeder. My roommate Alan Canfora was struck by gunfire. He was among the least injured of the thirteen people who were either mortally wounded or recovered.

Eventually federal indictments against enlisted men and noncommissioned officers in the Ohio National Guard were handed down. But, as it turned out, the judge ruled that the Justice Department failed to prove a case of conspiracy to violate our civil rights and dismissed the case before it was ever sent to the jury. That was the end of criminal proceedings against the Ohio National Guard. They got off scot-free.

But I think there are some guardsmen who are sorry for what happened. One guy in particular seemed to be genuinely remorseful. I remember his testimony. He has very poor eyesight, and on May 4 he couldn't get the gas mask on over his glasses, so he had to wear the gas mask without glasses. He was blind as a bat without them, and he admitted he just knew he was shooting in a certain direction. That was a startling admission. There was a guy out there who could hardly see, blasting away with an M-1.

. . . Every year from May 1971, which was the first anniversary of the killings, there has been a commemorative ceremony at Kent State that has attracted anywhere from one thousand students to eight thousand. So the issue has been kept alive there, and I'd say that the main focus now is to erect a proper and suitable memorial to the people who were killed there. The university has finally agreed to do that. They have commissioned a study as to what the memorial should look like, and what it should say.

I'm more concerned about what it says than what it looks like. Ever since I was young, I've been an avid reader of history, with a particular focus on the American Civil War, and for that reason I have more than the usual interest in the subject. When I go down to the Gettysburg battlefield or Antietam, I can read on those monuments about what took place there, what the casualty figures were, and I can try to envision what took place. Somebody should be able to do that at Kent State as well.

I think the memorial should state: "On May 4, 1970, units of the Ohio National Guard—Company H, 107th Armored Cavalry (Troop G) and Company A, 145th Infantry Regiment—shot and killed four student protesters and wounded nine others during a demonstration against the U.S. invasion of Cambodia." Straight-out, simple facts.

Raymond Mungo Searches for a New Age at Total Loss Farm, 1970

Friday: Portsmouth, N.H.

The farm in Vermont had fooled us, just as we hoped it would when we moved there in early '68; it had tricked even battle-scarred former youth militants into seeing the world as bright clusters of Day-Glo orange and red forest, rolling open meadows, sparkling brooks and streams. I had lived in industrial, eastern New England all my life, though, as well as worse places like New York and Washington, D.C., so I might have known better. But Vermont had blurred my memory, and when we finally left the farm for Portsmouth, I was all Thoreau and Frost, October up North, ain't life grand, all fresh and eager to begin rowing up the Concord and Merrimack rivers in the vanished footsteps of old Henry D. himself. Verandah Porche, queen of the Bay State Poets for Peace, packed the failing '59 VW and we went tearing down the mountain, kicking up good earth from the dirt road and barely slowing down for the 18th-century graveyard and all manner of wild animals now madly racing for shelter against the sharp winds of autumn in these hills. The frost was on the pumpkin, it was our second autumn together, and warm vibrations made the yellow farmhouse fairly glow in the dying daylight as we pointed east, over the Connecticut River, heading for our rendezvous with what *he* called "the placid current of our dreams." Knockout October day in 1969 in Vermont. All the trees had dropped acid.

The idea had come to me in a dream. It was one of those nights after Steve brought the Sunshine (wotta drug) when I'd wake up and sit bolt upright, alarmed at a sudden capacity, or *power,* I had acquired, to *see far.* I could see eternity in the vast darkness outside my window and inside my head, and I remembered feeling that way when but an infant. In my dream I was floating silently downstream in a birchbark canoe, speechless me watching vistas of bright New England autumn open up with each bend, slipping unnoticed between crimson mountains, blessing the warm sun by day and sleeping on beds of fresh leaves under a canary harvest moon by night. I was on the road to no special place, but no interstate highway with Savarinettes and Sunoco for this kid; in my dream, I was on a natural highway through the planet, the everlovin' me-sustainin' planet that never lets you down. Said Henry: "I have not yet put my foot through it."

It was the farm that had allowed me the luxury of this vision, for the farm had given me the insulation from America which the peace movement promised but cruelly denied. When we lived in Boston, Chicago, San Francisco, Washington (you name it, we lived there; some of us still live there), we dreamed of a New Age born of violent insurrection. We danced on the graves of war dead in Vietnam, every corpse was ammunition for Our Side; we set up a countergovernment down there in Washington, had marches, rallies and meetings; tried to fight fire with fire. Then Johnson resigned, yes, and the universities began to fall, the best and oldest ones first, and by God every 13-year-old in the suburbs was smoking dope and our numbers multiplying into the millions. But I woke up in the spring of 1968 and said, "This is not what I had in mind," because the movement had become my enemy; the movement was not flowers and doves and spontaneity, but another vicious system, the seed of a heartless bureaucracy, a minority Party vying for power rather than peace. It was then that we put away the schedule for the revolution, gathered together our dear ones and all our resources, and set off to Vermont in search of the New Age.

The New Age we were looking for proved to be very old indeed, and I've often wondered aloud at my luck for being 23 years old in a time and place in which only the past offers hope and inspiration; the future offers only artifice and blight. I travel now in a society of friends who heat their houses with hand-cut wood and eliminate in outhouses, who cut pine shingles with draw-knives and haul maple sugar sap on sleds, who weed potatoes with their university-trained hands, pushing long hair out of their way and thus marking their foreheads with beautiful penitent dust. We till the soil to atone for our fathers' destruction of it. We smell. We live far from the marketplaces in America by our own volition, and the powerful men left behind are happy to have us out of their way. They do not yet realize that their heirs will refuse to inhabit their hollow cities, will find them poisonous and lethal, will run back to the Stone Age if necessary for survival and peace.

Yet this canoe trip had to be made because there was adventure out there. We expected to find the Concord and Merrimack rivers polluted but still beautiful, and to witness firsthand the startling juxtaposition of old New England, land and water and mountains, and new America, factories and highways and dams; and to thus educate ourselves further in the works of God and man. We pushed on relentlessly, top speed 50 mph, in our eggshell Volkswagen (Hitler's manifestly correct conception of the common man's car), 100 miles to the sea. The week following, the week we'd spend in our canoe, was the very week when our countrymen would celebrate Columbus Day (anniversary of the European discovery of Americans), the New York Mets in the World (American) Series, and the National Moratorium to demand an "early end to the war." Since we mourn the ruthless extinction of the natives, have outgrown baseball, and long ago commenced our own total Moratorium on constructive participation in this society, our presence and support was irrelevant to all of these national pastimes. . . .

We *are* saving the world, of course, as the world for us extends to the boundaries of Total Loss Farm and the limits of our own experience; and Total Loss Farm is everywhere now, perhaps under your own rhubarb patch if you looked at it a little closer, and our experience all that anyone could hope to know of life. We were born and raised by parents who loved us at least until they lost us to a certain high-pitched whistle in the wind which they had gotten too old to hear; we work at maintaining ourselves, though our shared labor is seldom very taxing, for it takes little enough work to make plants grow, most of it is out of our hands, and our relationship to the work one of direct gratification and reward, as children insist on; we have children of our own, though they are fully peers by the time they've learned to eat and eliminate without physical help, and soon become more our masters than our students; and we die, sometimes in sulphurous flames, dramatic and shocking, other times silent and mysterious like the gone children wandering Europe with scenes of the parents engulfed in atrocity scrawled across their minds, but never to be spoken: "I come from Auschwitz, or Hué, or Boston, my father was shot for believing in God and hangs limp forever in front of our home as a reminder to the others; my mother was sold to the grim green soldiers for their sport, and my brother to be used as a woman; I escaped the country of the somnambulent and blind on the back of a wolf who prowled the ruins and took pity on me; I have come here to begin again."

Our parents must wonder where we are, this story is, as much as anything else, an attempt to fill them in, but it grows harder and harder to speak. Fortunately, it grows simultaneously less necessary. I have clothes on my back, though they are old, and a roof over my head and food for my belly. In this, I am luckier than many. I am surrounded by people who would give their own lives in defense of mine, for they know we will make it together or not at all. I wish to be reconciled with all of my enemies, and to live on the planet and glory in peaches to a ripe old age. I am willing to help you as much as I'm able, as a single person can help another, not as a movement or government can help a mass. I may ask for some help from you as well. If you come to my house with love in your heart and there's room for one more—for there isn't always—you may know I will feed you and house you for the night, if you need it. You may see me walking from town to town with my thumb outstretched to the highway, seeking a lift: don't pass me by.

You have seen me everywhere. I am not asking for the vote. I do not seek to be represented. I do not seek to tear down your buildings or march on your castle or sit at your desk. I am interested neither in destroying what you have put up nor in gaining control of your empire. I demand nothing, and nothing is my inheritance. I live in the world, in the woods, with my friends, where not many people come by and the planet is entire and friendly; we like to be left alone except by those who can help. You can help by giving the planet, and peace, a chance. I ask only that you treat yourself right, give yourself the best of everything; and in so doing, you will be acting for me as well. If you can't stop, at least wave as you go by. Slow down, perhaps stop working: you'll find the time for everything you really want to do.

Who am I? In the world of the farm, I am Grampaw, who still finds himself able to deliver of such bombastic lectures as this, thinks he has lived through such madness and chaos, such orgasm and ecstasy, that he has some lessons to give, sleeps with the dogs. I am a fool. I am also Pan, who does in Captain Hook with a sweep of his wooden sword: saying: I am youth! I am joy! I am freedom!

∭ E S S A Y S

Much recent historical work on the new radicalism of the 1960s has been written by men and women who themselves participated in the era's remarkable events. What is history and what is autobiography thus often becomes more a matter of narrative convention than of substantive difference. The first two essays in this chapter are technically memoirs, but they also express the sharply divergent interpretations of the decade that can be found in most conventional histories. Peter Collier and David Horowitz, former radicals who have penned successful popular biographies of the rich and powerful, recall a New Left of "self-aggrandising romance with corrupt Third Worldism; . . . casual indulgence of Soviet totalitarianism; [and] hypocritical and self-dramatizing anti-Americanism." By contrast, Tom Hayden, one of the founders of SDS and now a California state legislator, offers a catalogue of the decade's positive accomplishments in the second selection. The final selection was written by historians Maurice Isserman of Hamilton College and Michael Kazin of American University, former New Left activists. Their essay offers a sympathetic but balanced account of the movement's failures and successes.

The Sixties: Goodbye to All That

PETER COLLIER AND DAVID HOROWITZ

When we tell our old radical friends that we voted for Ronald Reagan last November, the response is usually one of annoyed incredulity. After making sure that we are not putting them on, our old friends make nervous jokes about Jerry Falwell and Phyllis Schlafly, about gods that have failed, about ageing yuppies ascending to consumer heaven in their BMWs. We remind them of an old adage: "Anyone under 40 who isn't a socialist has no heart—anyone over 40 who is a socialist has no brain."

Inevitably the talk becomes bitter. One old comrade, after a tirade in which she had denounced us as reactionaries and crypto-fascists, finally sputtered, "And the worst thing is that you've turned your back on the *Sixties*!" That was exactly right: casting our ballots for Ronald Reagan was indeed a way of finally saying goodbye to all that—to the self-aggrandising romance with corrupt Third Worldism; to the casual indulgence of Soviet totalitarianism; to the hypocritical and self-dramatising anti-Americanism which is the New Left's bequest to mainstream politics.

The instruments of popular culture may perhaps be forgiven for continuing to portray the '60s as a time of infectious idealism, but those of us who were active then have no excuse for abetting this banality. If in some ways it was the best of times, it was also the worst of times, an era of bloodthirsty fantasies as well as spiritual ones. We ourselves experienced both aspects, starting as civil-rights and anti-war activists and ending as co-editors of the New Left magazine *Ramparts*. The magazine post allowed us to write about the rough beast slouching through America and also to urge it on through non-editorial activities we thought of as clandestine until we later read about them in the FBI and CIA files we both accumulated.

Like other radicals in those early days, we were against electoral politics, regarding voting as one of those charades used by the ruling class to legitimate its power. We were even more against Reagan, then governor of California, having been roughed up by his troopers during the People's Park demonstrations in Berkeley and tear-gassed by his National Guard helicopters during the University of California's Third World Liberation Front Strike.

But neither elections nor elected officials seemed particularly important compared with the auguries of Revolution the Left saw everywhere by the end of the decade—in the way the nefarious Richard Nixon was widening the war in Indo-China; in the unprovoked attacks by paramilitary police against the Black Panther Party; in the formation of the "Weather Underground", a group willing to pick up the gun or the bomb. It was a time when the apocalypse struggling to be born seemed to need only the slightest assist from the radical midwife.

When we were in the voting booth this past November (in different

From "Who Killed the Spirit of '68: or, The Day the 'Ramparts' Fell" by Peter Collier and David Horowitz. *Encounter* (September/October 1985), 69–73.

precincts but of the same mind) we both thought back to the day in 1969 when Tom Hayden came by the office and, after getting a *Ramparts* donation to buy gas masks and other combat issue for Black Panther "guerrillas," announced portentously:

"Fascism is here, and we're all going to be in jail by the end of the year."

We agreed wholeheartedly with this apocalyptic vision and in fact had just written in an editorial:

"The system cannot be revitalised. It must be overthrown. As humanly as possible, but by any means necessary."

Every thought and perception in those days was filtered through the dark and distorting glass of the Viet Nam war.

The Left was hooked on Viet Nam. It was an addictive drug whose rush was a potent mix of melodrama, self-importance, and moral rectitude. Viet Nam was a universal solvent—the explanation for every evil we saw and the justification for every excess we committed. Trashing the windows of merchants on the main streets of America seemed warranted by the notion that these petty-bourgeois shopkeepers were cogs in the system of capitalist exploitation that was obliterating Viet Nam. Fantasising the death of local cops seemed warranted by the role they played as an occupying army in America's black ghettos, those mini-Viet Nams we yearned to see explode in domestic wars of liberation. Viet Nam caused us to acquire a new appreciation for foreign tyrants like Kim Il Sung of North Korea. Viet Nam also caused us to support the domestic extortionism and violence of groups like the Black Panthers, and to dismiss derisively Martin Luther King, Jr. as an "Uncle Tom." (The Left has conveniently forgotten this fact now that it finds it expedient to invoke King's name and reputation to further its domestic politics.)

How naive the New Left was can be debated, but by the end of the '60s we were not political novices. We knew that bad news from South-east Asia—the reports of bogged-down campaigns and the weekly body counts announced by Walter Cronkite—was good for the radical agenda. The more repressive our government in dealing with dissent at home, the more recruits for our cause and the sooner the appearance of the revolutionary Armageddon.

Our assumption that Viet Nam would be the political and moral fulcrum by which we would tip this country toward revolution foresaw every possibility except one: that the United States would pull out. Never had we thought that the US, the arch-imperial power, would of its own volition withdraw from Indo-China. This development violated a primary article of our hand-me-down Marxism: that political action through normal channels could not alter the course of the war. The system we had wanted to overthrow worked tardily and only at great cost, but it worked.

When American troops finally came home, some of us took the occasion to begin a long and painful re-examination of our political assumptions and beliefs. Others did not. For the diehards, there was a post-Viet Nam syndrome in its own way as debilitating as that suffered by people who had fought there—a sense of emptiness rather than exhilaration, a paradoxical desire to hold on to and breathe life back into the experience that had been their high for so many years.

As the post-Viet Nam decade progressed, the diehards on the left ignored conclusions about the viability of democratic traditions that might have been drawn from America's exit from Viet Nam and from the Watergate crisis that followed it, a time when the man whose ambitions they had feared most was removed from office by the Constitution rather than by a coup. The only "lessons" of Viet Nam the Left seemed interested in were those that emphasised the danger of American power abroad and the need to diminish it, a view that was injected into the Democratic party with the triumph of the McGovernite wing. The problem with this use of Viet Nam as a moral text for American policy, however, was that the pages following the fall of Saigon had been whited out.

No lesson, for instance, was seen in Hanoi's ruthless conquest of the South, the establishment of a police state in Saigon and the political oblivion of the National Liberation Front, whose struggle we on the Left had so passionately supported. It was not that credible information was lacking. Jean Lacouture wrote in 1976:

> "Never before have we had such proof of so many detained after a war. Not in Moscow in 1917. Not in Madrid in 1939, not in Paris and Rome in 1944, nor in Havana in 1959. . . ."

But this eminent French journalist, who had been regarded as something of an oracle when he was reporting America's derelictions during the war, was dismissed as a "sellout."

In 1977, when some former anti-war activists signed an "Appeal to the Conscience of Viet Nam" because of the more than 200,000 prisoners languishing in "Re-education Centres" and the new round of self-immolations by Buddhist monks, they were chastised by activist David Dellinger, Institute for Policy Studies fellow Richard Barnet, and other keepers of the flame in a *New York Times* advertisement that said in part:

> "The present government of Viet Nam should be hailed for its moderation and for its extraordinary effort to achieve reconciliation among all of its people."

When tens of thousands of unreconciled "Boat People" began to flee the repression of their Communist rulers, Joan Baez and others who spoke out in their behalf were attacked for breaking ranks with Hanoi.

Something might also have been learned from the fate of wretched Cambodia. But Leftists seemed so addicted to finding an American cause at the root of every problem that they couldn't recognise indigenous evils. As the Khmer Rouge were about to take over, Noam Chomsky wrote that their advent heralded a Cambodian liberation, "a new era of economic development and social justice." The new era turned out to be the killing fields that took the lives of two million Cambodians.

Finally, Viet Nam emerged as an imperialist power, taking control of Laos, invading Cambodia and threatening Thailand. But in a recent editorial, *The Nation* explains that the Vietnamese invaded Cambodia "to stop the killing and restore some semblance of civilised government to the devastated country." This bloody occupation is actually a "rescue mission," and should not "obscure the responsibility of the United States for the disasters in Indo-China," disasters that are being caused by playing the "China card" and refusing to normalise relations with Viet Nam. These acts on the part of the United States "make Vietnamese withdrawal from Cambodia unlikely"; only the White House can "remove the pressures on Viet Nam from all sides [that] would bring peace to a ravaged land." Such reasoning recalls the wonderful line from the Costa-Gavras film *Z*:

"Always blame the Americans. Even when you're wrong, you're right."

Another unacknowledged lesson from Indo-China involves the way in which Viet Nam has become a satellite of the Soviet Union (paying for foreign aid by sending labour brigades to its benefactor).

This development doesn't mesh well with the Left's ongoing romantic vision of Hanoi. It also threatens the Left's obstinate refusal to admit that during the mid-1970s—a time when American democracy was trying to heal itself from the twin traumas of the war and Watergate—the USSR was demonstrating that totalitarianism abhors a vacuum by moving into Africa, Central America, South-east Asia, and elsewhere. Instead of evaluating the Soviets because of the change in what we used to call "the objective conditions," the Left rationalises Soviet aggressions as the spasms of a petrified bureaucracy whose policies are annoying mainly because they distract attention from US malfeasance around the world.

If they were capable of looking intently at the Soviet Union, Leftists and Liberals alike would have to concur with Susan Sontag's contention (which many of them jeered at when she announced it) that Communism is simply left-wing fascism.

One of the reasons the Left has been so cautious in its reassessments of the Soviets is the fiction that the USSR is on the side of "history."

This assumption is echoed in Fred Halliday's euphoric claim, in a recent issue of *New Left Review,* that Soviet support was crucial to 14 Third-World revolutions during the era of *détente* (including such triumphs of human progress as Iran and South Yemen), and in Andrew Kopkind's fatuous observation that "the Soviet Union has almost always sided with the revolutionists, the liberationists, the insurgents." In Ethiopia?

Propped up by 200,000 Cuban legionnaires, the Marxist government of Mengistu Haile Mariam has as its main accomplishment a "Red Campaign of Terror" (its official designation) that killed thousands of people. Where were those who cheer the Soviets' work on behalf of the socialist *Zeitgeist* when this episode took place? Or this past fall when the Marxist liberator squandered more than $40 million on a party celebrating the 10th anniversary of his murderous rule while his people starved? Where were they to point out the moral when capitalist America rushed in 250 million metric tons of grain to help allay the Ethiopian starvation while the Soviets were managing to contribute only ten million metric tons? Where are they now that Mengistu withholds emergency food supplies from the starving provinces of Eritrea and Tigre because the people there are in rebellion against his tyranny?

Reagan is often upbraided for having described the Soviet Union as "an evil empire." Those opposed to this term seem to be offended aesthetically rather than politically. Just how wide of the mark is the President? Oppressing an array of nationalities whose populations far outnumber its own, Russia is the last of the old European empires, keeping in subjugation not only formerly independent states such as Estonia, Latvia, and Lithuania (Hitler's gift to Stalin), but also the nations of Eastern Europe. Every country "liberated" into the Soviet bloc has been transformed into a national prison, where the borders are guarded to keep the inmates in rather than the foreigners out.

The war in Afghanistan is much more a metaphor for the Soviets' view of the world than Viet Nam ever was for America's. Of the approximately 16 million people living in Afghanistan at the time of the Soviet invasion, an estimated one million have already been killed and wounded. There are now about four million refugees, a figure that does not include "internal" refugees—the hundreds of thousands of villagers forced to leave their scorched earth for the Soviet-controlled big cities, the only places where food is available. Or the thousands of Afghan children who have been taken to the Soviet Union to be "educated" and who will eventually be returned to their native land as spies and quislings.

Soviet strategy is based on a brutal rejoinder to Mao's poetic notion (which we old New Leftists used to enjoy citing) about guerrillas being like fish swimming in a sea of popular support. The Soviet solution is to boil the sea and ultimately drain it, leaving the fish exposed and gasping on barren land.

The Russian presence is characterised by systematic destruction of crops and medical facilities, indiscriminate terror against the civilian population, carpet bombings and the deadly "yellow rain" that even the Leftist Peoples Tribunal in Paris (successor to the Bertrand Russell War Crimes Tribunal) has said is being used in Afghanistan.

During each December anniversary of the Soviet invasion, when liberal politicians rediscover the *mujaheddin* guerrillas in the hills, after eleven months of moral amnesia, there are blithe references to Afghanistan as "Russia's Viet Nam."

Those who invoke the analogy seem to think that simply by doing so they have doomed the Russian storm-troopers to defeat. But this analogy is based on a misunderstanding of what Viet Nam was and what Afghanistan is. Unlike America's high-tech television war, Afghanistan is one of those old-fashioned encounters that take place in the dark. The Soviets make no attempt to win hearts and minds; the *"My Lais"* that are daily occurrences there cause no shock because they do not appear on Moscow TV. There are no scenes of the peasant children whose hands and faces have been destroyed by anti-personnel bombs in the shapes of toy trucks and butterflies a Los Angeles physician we know saw strewn over the Afghan countryside. There are no images of body-bags being offloaded from Soviet transports. Because there is no media coverage, there can be no growing revulsion on the home front, no protests on Soviet campuses and in Soviet streets, no clamour to bring the boys home.

Afghanistan is not "Russia's Viet Nam" not only because the nation committing the atrocities never sees them, but because the rest of the world is blacked out, too. At the height of the Viet Nam war there was a non-combatant army of foreign journalists to witness its conduct. In Afghanistan they are forbidden, as are the Red Cross and all other international relief agencies that were integral to what happened in Viet Nam. And without these witnesses, Afghanistan is a matter of "out of sight, out of mind."

In Viet Nam we waged a war against ourselves and lost. The Soviets will not let that happen to them. The truth of the Viet Nam analogy is not that guerrillas must inevitably bog down and defeat a superior force of invaders, but that war against indigenous forces by a superpower can be won if it is waged against a backdrop of international ignorance and apathy. The proper analogy for Afghanistan is not Viet Nam at all but rather Spain— not in the nature of the war, but in the symbolic value it has for our time— or should—in terms of democracy's will to resist aggression. Aid to the *mujaheddin* should not be a dirty little secret of the CIA, but a matter of public policy and national honour as well.

Perhaps the leading feature of the Left today is the moral selectivity that French social critic Jean-François Revel has identified as "the syndrome of the cross-eyed Left."

Leftists can describe Viet Nam's conquest and colonialisation of Cambodia as a "rescue mission," while reviling Ronald Reagan for applying the same term to the Grenada operation, although better than 90% of the island's population told independent pollsters they were grateful for the arrival of US troops. Forgetting for a moment that Afghanistan is "Russia's Viet Nam," Leftists call Grenada "America's Afghanistan," although people in Afghanistan (as one member of the resistance there told us) would literally die for the elections held in Grenada.

The Left's memory can be as selective as its morality. When it comes to past commitments that have failed, the Leftist mentality is utterly unable to produce a coherent balance sheet, let alone a profit-and-loss statement. The attitude toward Soviet penetration of the Americas is a good example. Current enthusiasm for the Sandinista régime in Nicaragua should recall to those of us old enough to remember a previous enthusiasm for Cuba 25 years ago. Many of us began our "New Leftism" with the "Fair Play for Cuba" demonstrations. We raised our voices and chanted, *"Cuba Si! Yanqui No!"* We embraced Fidel Castro not only because of the flamboyant personal style of the *barbudos* of his 26th of July Movement but also because Castro assured the world that his revolution belonged to neither Communists nor capitalists, that it was neither red nor black, but Cuban olive-green.

We attributed Castro's expanding links with Moscow to the US-sponsored invasion of the Bay of Pigs, and then to the "secret war" waged against

Cuba by US intelligence and paramilitary organisations. But while Castro's apologists in the United States may find it expedient to maintain these fictions, Carlos Franqui and other old Fidelistas now in exile have made it clear that Castro embraced the Soviets even before the US hostility became decisive, and that he steered his country into an alliance with the Soviets with considerable enthusiasm. Before the Bay of Pigs he put a Soviet general in charge of Cuban forces. Before the Bay of Pigs he destroyed Cuba's democratic trade-union movement, although its elected leadership was drawn from his own 26th of July Movement. He did so because he knew that the Stalinists of Cuba's Communist Party would be dependable cheerleaders and efficient policemen of his emerging dictatorship.

One symbolic event along the way that many of us missed was Castro's imprisonment of his old comrade Huber Matos, liberator of Matanzas Province, and one of the four key military leaders of the revolution. Matos's crime: criticising the growing influence of Cuban Communists (thereby jeopardising Castro's plans to use them as his palace guard). Matos's sentence: 20 years in a 4-by-11 concrete box. Given such a precedent, how can we fail to support Eden Pastora for taking up arms against early signs of similar totalitarianism in Nicaragua?

What has come of Cuba's revolution to break the chains of American imperialism? Soviets administer the still one-crop Cuban economy; Soviets train the Cuban army; and Soviet subsidies, fully one-quarter of Cuba's gross national product, prevent the Cuban treasury from going broke. Before the revolution, there were more than 35 independent newspapers and radio stations in Havana. Now, there is only the official voice of *Granma,* the Cuban *Pravda,* and a handful of other outlets spouting the same party line. Today Cuba is a more abject and deformed colony of the Soviet empire than it ever was of America. The arch-rebel of our youth, Fidel Castro, has become a party hack who cheerfully endorsed the rape of Czechoslovakia in 1968 and endorses the ongoing plunder of Afghanistan today, an ageing pimp who sells his young men to the Russians for use in their military adventures in return for $10 billion a year.

In Leftist circles, of course, such arguments are anathema, and no historical precedent, however daunting, can prevent outbreaks of radical chic.

Epidemics of radical chic cannot be prevented by referring to historical precedents. That perennial delinquent Abbie Hoffman will lead his Potemkin-village tours of Managua. The Hollywood stars will dish up Nicaraguan president Daniel Ortega as an exotic hors-d'oeuvre on the Beverly Hills cocktail circuit. In the self-righteous moral glow accompanying such gatherings, it will be forgotten that, through the offices of the US government, more economic and military aid was provided the Sandinistas in the first 18 months following their takeover than was given to Somoza in the previous 20 years, and that this aid was cut off primarily because of the clear signs that political pluralism in Nicaragua was being terminated.

Adherents of today's version of radical chic may never take seriously the words of Sandinista directorate member Bayardo Arce when he says that elections are a "hindrance" to the goal of "a dictatorship of the proletariat" and necessary only "as an expedient to deprive our enemies of an argument." They will ignore former Sandinista hero and now Contra leader Eden Pastora, who sees the Junta as traitors who have sold out the revolutionary dream. ("Now that we are occupied by foreign forces from Cuba and Russia, now that we are governed by a dictatorial government of nine men, now more than ever the Sandinista struggle is justified.") They will ignore opposition leader Arturo Cruz, an early supporter of the Sandinista revolution and previously critical of the Contras, when the worsening situation makes him change his mind and ask the Reagan administration to support them in a statement that should have the same weight as Andrei Sakharov's plea to the West to match the Soviet arms build-up.

American Leftists propose solutions for the people of Central America that they wouldn't dare propose for themselves. These armchair revolutionaries project their self-hatred and their contempt for the privileges of democracy—which allow them to live well and to think badly—on to people who would be only too grateful for the luxuries they disdain. Dismissing "bourgeois" rights as a decadent frill that the peoples of the Third World can't afford, Leftists spreadeagle the Central Americans between the dictators of the Right and the dictators of the Left. The latter, of course, are their chosen instruments for bringing social justice and economic well-being, although no Leftist revolution has yet provided impressive returns on either of these qualities and most have made the lives of their people considerably more wretched than they were before.

Voting is symbolic behaviour, a way of evaluating what one's country has been as well as what it might become. We do not accept Reagan's policies chapter and verse (especially in domestic policy, which we haven't discussed here), but we agree with his vision of the world as a place increasingly inhospitable to democracy and increasingly dangerous for America.

One of the few saving graces of age is a deeper perspective on the passions of youth. Looking back on the Left's revolutionary enthusiasms of the last 25 years, we have painfully learned what should have been obvious all along: that we live in an imperfect world that is bettered only with great difficulty and easily made worse—much worse. This is a conservative assessment, but on the basis of half a lifetime's experience, it seems about right.

The Sixties: Times of Greatness and Wonder

TOM HAYDEN

Looking back from life's mid-passage, what did the generation of the sixties achieve? What does it mean today?

By the most measurable standards, we accomplished more than we ex-

From *Reunion* by Tom Hayden. Copyright © 1988 by Tom Hayden. Reprinted by permission of Random House Inc.

pected, more than most generations ever accomplish. Consider the most obvious:

- Students led the civil rights movement, which destroyed a century-old segregation system and which politically enfranchised twenty million blacks.
- Students were the backbone of the antiwar movement, which forced our government to abandon its policies in Vietnam and the nation to reconsider the Cold War.
- Because of student criticism, most universities retreated from their traditional paternalism toward an acceptance of active student participation in decision making.
- Movement activists were the key factor in making Lyndon Johnson withdraw from the presidency in 1968 and in transforming the political rules that permitted reformers to prevail in the Democratic party, which then endorsed "participatory democracy" in its 1972 platform.
- The same movement was conceded the eighteen-year-old vote by the 1970s.
- These movements were direct catalysts for the reemergence of the women's movement, the birth of environmentalism, and other diverse causes.

In short, we opened up closed systems. From Georgia and Mississippi to the South as a whole, from Newark and Chicago to the cities of the North, from the 1965 Vietnam teach-ins to the 1973 War Powers Act, from the Democratic convention of 1968 to that of 1972, there was a steady evolution from patterns of exclusion toward greater citizen participation in basic decisions.

More generally, the New Left fostered a vision that gradually took hold throughout much of society. At the center of that vision was a moral view of human beings, "ordinary people" in the process of history, a view which held that systems should be designed for human beings and not the other way around. The dignity of the individual in this perspective could only be realized through active citizenship. That in turn required a society of citizens, or a democracy of participation, where individuals had a direct voice in the making of decisions about their own lives. We were expressing a rising dissatisfaction with all institutions, even liberal and expressly humane ones, that absorbed power into their hierarchies. Instead of "taking power," we imagined creating the new power out of the raw material of apathy. At the same time, new measurements of excellence, such as the quality of life and personal relationships, were to take on greater significance than external status symbols and material monuments, in both our lives and the existence of our country.

These perceptions and values are an ongoing legacy of our generation. They do not always prevail in our culture or politics today, nor are they always recognized as arising from the sixties. Yet their enduring and widening impact can be seen in a variety of ways. Enlightened business and labor viewpoints now concur that humane treatment of the worker, including participation in decision making, is not only an ethical good, but a plus for

productivity as well. More broadly, the survey researcher Daniel Yankelovich, in his book, *New Rules* concluded that

> the campus upheavals of the sixties gave us the first premonitory sign that
> the plates of American culture, after decades of stability, had begun to
> shift. . . . Then in the seventies the public as a whole began to experience
> them and the mass reappraisal of American life values was launched.

The Yankelovich study concluded that the mainstream American goal
is "to build a more productive economy and at the same time a society in
which the cravings of the spirit as well as material well-being can be satisfied."

These findings were also reflected in an extraordinary work of social
science, *Habits of the Heart,* published by a UC Berkeley team of researchers
in 1985. One of their purposes was to review and revive the nineteenth-
century French writer, Alexis de Toqueville, whose observations in *Democracy in America* in some ways foreshadowed the theme of participatory
democracy. De Toqueville celebrated the town meetings and voluntary associations that constituted the rich political core of early nineteenth-century
American society and warned of the dangers of rampant individualism, under
which participation could atrophy and be replaced by imperial forms of rule.
The authors of *Habits of the Heart,* responding to the resurgent individualism
of the religious right of the eighties, cited local chapters of the Campaign
for Economic Democracy among the many representative efforts at restoring
an emphasis on democracy at the community level, noting that "the morally
concerned social movement, informed by republican and biblical sentiments,
has stood us in good stead in the past and may still do so again."

These conclusions and many others like them represent nothing less than
the maturing of the awkward formulations of *The Port Huron Statement* into
the cultural vocabulary of the mainstream of American life.

The logical question then is why the New Left did not succeed in building
an organized and permanent leftist presence on the American political spectrum? Why did we produce so few political leaders? Why did we, who were
so able to shake existing institutions, leave so little behind? Part of me
inclines to the view of the New Left's better administrative leaders, like Paul
Booth and Richie Rothstein, that our profound distrust of leadership and
structure doomed us to failure on the level of political organization.

But the American political system is inhospitable to third parties, isolating them before gradually absorbing their ideas and activists into the two-
party system. The most that could have been organized out of the New Left
might have been an "adult" SDS, a kind of American Civil Liberties Union
for social justice. Of course, without the Kennedy assassinations the history
of our generation would have been different, and I believe most of the New
Left would have found itself politically involved as part of a new governing
coalition by the end of the sixties, just as Millie Jeffrey's generation became
linked with the politics of the New Deal. But it was not to be. Instead, in
Jack Newfield's summary phrase, we became "might have beens."

In the end, most of the sixties generation was not narrowly political.
Most were not interested in attaining office but in changing life-styles. They

were not so interested in being opinion makers as in changing the climate of opinion. Most felt personally ambiguous or distrustful of ambition and power and lacked the qualities that carried others into political careers. They were more likely to become professors (Todd Gitlin, Bill Ayers, Dick Flacks, John Froines, Bob Ross), labor leaders (Karen Nussbaum, Richie Rothstein, Paul Booth), social service advocates (Vivian Rothstein, Mary Varela, Casey Hayden), lawyers (Dan Siegel, Anne Weills, Bernardine Dohrn and six other former members of the Weather Underground), filmmakers (Bruce Gilbert, Paula Weinstein, Mark Rosenberg, Thom Mount), or therapists and counselors (Connie Brown, Andrea Cousins), than politicians. But if few of us went from protest marching to political office, the changes that the sixties generation made in public attitudes nevertheless became a factor that all politicians had to take seriously, including Ronald Reagan, who spent most of his presidency trying to reverse the legacy of the sixties.

There are such strong feelings of nostalgia on the one hand and loss on the other among so many who went through those times because the sixties were about more than practical reforms. It was a decade not focused simply on specific goals, like the organization of American workers in the thirties or the issue agendas of the Populist and Socialist parties at the century's beginning. The goal of the sixties was a larger transformation. Perhaps the only parallels might have been during the times of the American Revolution and Civil War, when individuals became caught up in remaking America itself. The goal of the sixties was, in a sense, the completion of the vision of the early revolutionaries and the abolitionists, for Tom Paine and Frederick Douglass wanted even more than the Bill of Rights or Emancipation Proclamation. True democrats, they wanted the fulfillment of the American promise through a different quality of relations between people, between government and governed, a participatory democracy within a genuinely human community. The sixties movements were inspired toward that loftier goal and were blocked in the quest by the intervention of fate.

Like the American revolutionary period, the awakening of the early sixties was a unique ingathering of young people—many of them potential leaders—to proclaim and then try to carry out a total redemptive vision. This visionary quest is what bound each of us together in a community, from Gandhian Freedom Riders to disillusioned Marxists. The gods of our parents had failed or become idols. Then a new spiritual force came in 1960, to move in the world. We felt ourselves to be the prophets of that force. When we first used the term *revolution,* it was not about overthrowing power but about overcoming hypocrisy, through a faithfulness to a democratic and spiritual heritage. Then came rejection and both physical and spiritual martyrdom, and later a discovery that we ourselves were not pure. We faltered, lost our way, became disoriented above all by death upon death. What began on a soaring spirit suddenly was over, perhaps to be finished permanently. We who claimed to be masters of our future discovered that we were not.

The sacrifices were many, and there were no distinguished service medals. In writing this book, I found it revealing that there is nowhere a factual summary of all the suffering that people went through—shootings, beatings, firings, expulsions, arrests, not to mention psychological pain—to achieve quite elementary goals in the sixties decade. It is as if the sacrifices were not worthy of record, but should be suppressed and forgotten. With the help of Eric Dey, a UCLA graduate student, I developed a minimal estimate of our untabulated sacrifices:

- During the southern civil rights movement (1960–68), at least 28 activists were killed, and 31,000 people were arrested. There is no calculating the numbers who were beaten, fired, or expelled from schools.
- In the black civil disorders of 1965–70, 188 people were killed, at least 7,612 were injured, and another 52,920 were arrested.
- In the campus and antiwar protests of 1965–71, for which data are woefully unrecorded, at least 14 were killed, thousands were injured or expelled from colleges, and at least 26,358 were arrested.
- It therefore would be safe to estimate that in a society priding itself on its openness, 100,000 arrests of protestors occurred in the decade of the sixties. They were prophets without honor in their time.

For all these reasons, the sixties leave a sense of troubling incompleteness and shortcoming alongside that of proud achievement. But if the time has remained difficult to capture, it is also possible that the sixties are not over. The decade itself was perhaps only the beginning of a time of vast change that is not yet fulfilled. Our generation, after all, has only lived into its middle years. Why conclude that life's most powerful moments already are behind us? If the sixties are not over, it is up to the sixties generation to continue trying to heal our wounds, find our truth, and apply our ideals with a new maturity to our nation's future.

Since 1980, however, the official mood of the nation has been contrary to a spirit of reconciliation. Rather, the tone has been one of escape from bitter realities toward an immortalizing vision of nostalgia proposed by President Reagan. There has been a strong pressure to wipe out the "Vietnam syndrome," which allegedly left us prostrate before our enemies. Thanks to greater military spending, we are told that America is "back," is "standing tall," that the "naysayers" have been vanquished. I find this stance to be an armed reminder of the most rigid view of my parents' generation when they wanted to impose the lessons of their experience on their children and grandchildren. But my personal experience gives me faith that this official obsession with restoring a mythic past will give way to wiser consciousness in the era ahead:

- An emerging generation of voters—about eighty million born since 1945—will seek newer philosophies than those which led to constant government scandal these past two decades.
- Those who experienced the inner reality of Vietnam—from the end of police clubs or in jungle darkness—will unite around a more mature foreign policy, based on the strength of democracy.
- Americans will increasingly look to human merits, rather than color, class, or gender, in choosing those who represent them, even for the presidency.

- The quality of life will replace the quantity of possessions as American's standard of excellence in our lifetime.
- A new generation of entrepreneurs will come to learn that human and natural resources require cultivation rather than depletion.
- Democracy and human rights will grow more powerfully contagious in a world linked by satellites and television.
- The assassinations of the sixties left a bleeding and broken connection in our personal lives and political culture; that connection must and will be restored by a new cycle of leadership.

Times filled with tragedy are also times of greatness and wonder, times that really matter, and times truly worth living through. Whatever the future holds, and as satisfying as my life is today, I miss the sixties and always will.

The Contradictory Legacy of the Sixties

MAURICE ISSERMAN AND MICHAEL KAZIN

As easy it was to tell black from white
It was all that easy to tell wrong from right
And our choices were few and the thought never hit
That the one road we travelled would ever shatter and split.

—"Bob Dylan's Dream,"
from *The Freewheelin' Bob Dylan*

I

So wrote Bob Dylan, not yet twenty-two years old, in what was in 1963 a prophetic—or at least prematurely nostalgic—elegy for the illusions of youthful commitment. Shatter and split the new radicalism certainly did, in the space of only a decade and in a way that left many of its adherents embittered and its historical reputation in tatters. After Ronald Reagan's two victories at the polls, the sixties, viewed at the time as the beginning of a new era of reform, seem instead a short interregnum amid the larger rightward shift in American politics that began during Franklin Roosevelt's troubled second term and continued through the 1980s. What difference, if any, did the decade of cultural and political upheaval encapsulated by the rise and fall of the New Left make?

Though the origins of the New Left can be traced back at least to the mid-1950s, radicalism only began to reemerge as a significant undercurrent on American campuses in 1960 when a heretofore obscure group called the Student League for Industrial Democracy (SLID) renamed itself Students for a Democratic Society (SDS). Under the leadership of two recent University of Michigan graduates, Al Haber and Tom Hayden, SDS became a small but increasingly influential network of campus activists. At its official

From Maurice Isserman and Michael Kazin, "The Failure and Success of the New Radicalism," in Steve Fraser and Gary Gerstle, *The Rise and Fall of the New Deal Order, 1930–1980.* Copyright © 1989 by Princeton University Press, pp. 212–242. Reprinted with permission.

founding convention, held in Port Huron, Michigan, in 1962, SDS adopted a manifesto declaring that the ideas and organizational forms familiar to earlier generations of Marxian radicals were outmoded. The "Port Huron Statement" dedicated SDS to the achievement of "participatory democracy" inside its own movement and within the larger society. Initially engaged on a wide variety of fronts, from civil rights to nuclear disarmament to university reform, by the mid-1960s, many SDS founders had left the campuses to concentrate on community organizing in the slums of northern cities. Ironically, just as SDS leaders began to forsake the campus, the Berkeley Free Speech Movement in the fall of 1964 and the Vietnam teach-in movement in the spring of 1965 signaled the growing responsiveness of college students to radical ideas.

The steady escalation of the war in Vietnam from the spring of 1965 up to the spring of 1968 spurred the growth of both a broadly based antiwar movement and of the campus New Left, and led the latter to adopt increasingly militant rhetoric and tactics. By the fall of 1967 the New Left had moved "from dissent to resistance." Teach-ins and silent vigils gave way to the seizure of campus buildings and disruptive street demonstrations. Under new and younger leadership SDS continued to grow, and eventually some of its original leaders, like Tom Hayden and Rennie Davis, were attracted back to antiwar organizing from the slums of Newark and Chicago.

In the aftermath of the bloody confrontations at the Chicago Democratic convention in the summer of 1968, and the indictment of Hayden, Davis, and six others for "conspiracy," most New Leftists abandoned whatever hopes they still cherished of reforming the existing political system. Declaring themselves allies and disciples of third-world Communist revolutionaries like Mao Zedong and Che Guevara, SDS leaders now conceived their principal role as one of "bringing the war home" to the "imperialist mother country." In 1969, SDS collapsed as small, self-proclaimed revolutionary vanguards squabbled over control of the organization, but the ranks of student radicals continued to increase through the 1969–70 school year. Polls showed that as many as three quarters of a million students identified themselves as adherents of the New Left. The national student strike that SDSers had long dreamed of but had never been able to pull off became a reality in the spring of 1970. Spontaneously organized in response to the invasion of Cambodia and the killing of four students at Kent State University, it effectively paralyzed the nation's university system.

The American writer John Dos Passos, describing the revolutionary exaltation and illusion of 1919 in his novel, *Three Soldiers,* declared: "Any spring is a time of overturn, but then Lenin was alive, the Seattle general strike had seemed the beginning of the flood instead of the beginning of the ebb." It soon became apparent to despairing New Leftists that the spring of 1970 marked a similar "beginning of the ebb." Former SDS president Carl Oglesby was one among many who took to the hills (literally, in his case) at the start of the new decade. As Oglesby would say in a bittersweet reflection years later: "There were a lot of good, righteous people showing up in places like Vermont and New Hampshire in those days. Lots of parties, great reefer, good acid. Lovely friends . . . I remember it with great fondness.

It was almost the best part of the struggle. The best part of the struggle was the surrender."

When the sixties were over, it seemed to many former activists that they had accomplished nothing. The "participatory democracy" the New Left sought in its early years remained a utopian dream; the "revolutionary youth movement" it built in its waning years had collapsed; the tiny "new communist parties" that one-time New Leftists tried to organize in the 1970s only illustrated once again the wisdom of Marx's comments in *The Eighteenth Brumaire* on the way history repeated turns tragedy into farce.

Yet in surveying the ruins of these successive political failures, it is striking that while "nothing" was accomplished by the New Left in its short life, everything was different afterward. If the years that followed the 1960s did not live up to the hopeful vision of the future sketched out in the Port Huron Statement, still they did not mark a return to the previous status quo. America certainly became a more politically and culturally contentious society because of what happened in the 1960s—and in some respects it also became a more just, open, and egalitarian one. On the coldest, darkest, and most reactionary days of the Reagan ascendancy, there was more radical belief and activity to be seen in the United States than was present anytime in the 1950s. As an organizational presence the New Left had vanished, but as a force in American political culture its impact continued to be felt.

The New Left was shaped by and came to embody a profound dislocation in American culture, and, in the end, it had more impact on the ideas that Americans had about themselves and their society than on structures of power that governed their lives. Young radicals articulated a critique of "everyday life" in the United States, which was, in time, taken up by millions of people who had little notion of where those ideas originated. In the course of the sixties and seventies, many Americans came to recognize and reject the prevalence of racial and sexual discrimination, to ask new questions about the legitimacy of established institutions and authority, and to oppose military adventures abroad. To understand the New Left's role in this transition, historians need both to explore the organizational dynamics of radical groups like SDS and to analyze the ways in which American culture shaped the young radicals who emerged to challenge the received wisdom of their society.

II

The late 1980s saw a revival of interest in both the ephemera and the history of the 1960s. Tie-dyed shirts, peace symbols, Beatles music, and one-time Yippie leader Abbie Hoffman all resurfaced on college campuses. Many students, while knowing little about the politics of the New Left, admired sixties protesters for being, as the credulous young character in a "Doonesbury" cartoon put it, "larger than life, bonded and driven by commitment, putting their lives on the line for a great cause."

Popular interest in and memories of the New Left often seem preoccupied with celebrities, fashion, and life-styles. The most accessible sources of information available on the sixties to young people in the eighties—

"classic rock" radio shows and Hollywood movies—were hardly designed to facilitate serious historical inquiry. In the 1983 film *The Big Chill,* director Lawrence Kasdan offered a vision of the sixties as a time of embarrassing idealism that produced enough good songs to fill out a sound track but otherwise bequeathed nothing of continuing relevance. The film depicted a group of supposed New Left veterans who gather to mourn the passing of one of their own. Although a brief reference is made to one of the characters having been seriously wounded in Vietnam, no one in the film seems at all interested in reflecting on the war or any of the other causes that moved them in their youth, let alone in making connections between their former beliefs and the world around them in the 1980s. Not once in a long, emotional weekend do any of them abandon their self-absorption long enough to mention the words "Ronald Reagan," "nuclear war," or "Central America."

The Big Chill did, however, contain a kernel of truth. "Politics," as conventionally defined, was only of secondary importance in the rise of the new radicalism of the 1960s. The emergence and celebration of generationally defined life-styles preceded the appearance of the New Left and, for most Americans throughout the 1960s, continued to overshadow the fate of organizations, candidates, and causes. As contemporary observers and historians have since agreed, the phenomenon of the "baby boom" determined the contours of the sixties' dizzying pace of change. Between 1945 and 1946, the birth rate in the United States leaped 20 percent. Thereafter, it continued to climb, peaking in 1957 when over four million babies were born in a single year. The impact of this unexpected development, which reversed a century-long decline in the birth rate, had effects everywhere—from the spread of suburbia to the transformation of the university system. At each stage of its life, the baby-boom generation has proven to be a voracious consumer of material goods, from diapers and cribs to microwave ovens and video cassette recorders. It has also shown an enormous capacity to absorb new forms of entertainment, new images, and new ideas about politics and society.

Starting with the Davy Crockett fad of the early 1950s, cultural entrepreneurs seeking to tap the disposable income controlled by the nation's young perfected their pitch and inadvertently helped shape a distinctive generational consciousness. Hollywood soon learned to gear its offerings to the tastes of the new generation. While ostensibly condemning juvenile delinquency, such movies as *The Wild One* and *Rebel without a Cause* in effect established actors like Marlon Brando and James Dean as icons of youthful rebellion. Elvis Presley's fusion of country music and rhythm and blues combined with the frank sensuality of his stage presence signaled the arrival of a new musical era; major record producers were quick to take note and seek imitators. To a far greater extent than their parents, baby boomers grew up surrounded by and at home in a world of mass culture and mass consumption. And it was precisely because they were so deeply imbued with the promise and assumptions of that world—believing the advertisers who told them that a time of unending affluence and total freedom of choice was at hand—that they were willing, at least for a few years, to forego the quest for economic security and its material tokens that obsessed the older generation. The purveyors of mass culture were thus unintentionally acting as the gravediggers of a depression-inspired and cold war–reinforced conservative cultural consensus.

As a college education became the norm rather than a privilege, millions of young people found themselves in a new socially determined developmental stage that extended adolescence into the middle twenties or even later. By the early 1960s, "youth communities" had sprung up on the outskirts of college campuses, often in the cheap housing available on the edge of black ghettos. There, surrounded by their peers, largely freed from adult supervision and spared for the time being the responsibilities of career, family, and mortgage, young people began to experiment with new manners, mores, stimulants, sexual behavior, and, in due time, forms of political expression.

"Beat" poets, artists, jazz musicians, and folksingers, though less commercially exploitable than Presley and his imitators, soon carved out their own niche on the margins of college communities as well as in such urban enclaves as New York's Greenwich Village and North Beach in San Francisco. Jack Kerouac's novel *On the Road,* a free-form chronicle of cultural alienation, became a best-seller when it appeared in 1957 and has never been out of print. Kerouac's protagonist, though displaying no discernible political sympathies, was thoroughly disenchanted with mainstream American values and sought refuge among and enlightenment from America's dispossessed and despised classes—tramps, winos, migrant farm laborers, black musicians. Norman Mailer's controversial essay "The White Negro," also published in 1957, celebrated white hipsters who "drifted out at night looking for action with a black man's code to fit their facts." Mailer predicted that "a time of violence, new hysteria, confusion and rebellion" would soon come along to "replace the time of conformity." The roots of the coming counterculture could be seen in the growing tendency among young whites to view black culture as a vibrant, sexually and emotionally honest alternative to what was regarded as the hypocrisy of the dominant culture. As Mailer noted, "in this wedding of the white and the black it was the Negro who brought the cultural dowry." Elvis Presley's first hit, "You Ain't Nothin' But a Hound Dog," was a "cover" version of a song first recorded by blues singer Willie Mae "Big Mama" Thornton. For some whites it would prove a short step from idolizing and imitating such black musicians as Thornton, Charlie Parker, and Chuck Berry, to doing the same with black civil rights activists like Robert Moses and Stokely Carmichael.

At precisely the moment when the first wave of the baby boom reached the college campuses, the southern civil rights movement exploded into newspaper headlines and the nation's consciousness through the use of an innovative strategy of mass, nonviolent civil disobedience. The 1960 southern sit-in movement, which attracted fifty thousand participants in the space of a few months, was sparked by four black college freshmen in Greensboro, North Carolina, who decided on their own to challenge the segregation of a Woolworth's lunch counter. Rennie Davis, a founder of SDS who was a sophomore at Oberlin College in 1960, recalled: "Here were four students from Greensboro who were suddenly all over *Life* magazine. There was a feeling that they were us and we were them, and a recognition that they were expressing something we were feeling as well and they'd won the attention of the country."

For sympathetic college students, the civil rights movement blended the appeal of "making history" with the potential for testing one's own sense of personal "authenticity" through an existential (and for those who joined the freedom rides or the voter registration campaigns in the South, quite genuine) brush with danger. In her book *Personal Politics,* historian Sara Evans described the compelling example set by the young black volunteers of the Student Non-Violent Coordinating Committee: "Eating, sleeping, working side by side day after day, SNCC activists created a way of life more than a set of ideas." Thus, in the early 1960s, the sort of quixotic identification with outcasts and outsiders offered by *On the Road* and "The White Negro" acquired a compelling moral and political relevance. A new style of bohemianism that embodied a cultural stance derived from the Beats, and a political critique inspired by the black freedom movement attracted a growing following among college-age white Americans.

The superheated ideological atmosphere of 1950s cold war America played an important role in shaping the political outlook of college students at the start of the new decade. They had grown up in a political culture that stressed the division of the world into absolute good and absolute evil, freedom versus totalitarianism. The cold war was justified in much the same terms that had been used in the recent victorious struggle against the Axis powers. Yet, beneath the surface agreement among conservatives and liberals on the need to contain the Soviet threat, certain ambiguities still lurked. For many Americans, the cold war summoned up an uncritical identification with the emerging national security state. But some others, loyal to the liberatory and antiracist beliefs that had fueled the war against fascism, tendered their support for the "free world" on a more conditional basis.

Consider the wide appeal that the classic World War II film *Casablanca* developed on college campuses by the early 1960s. *Casablanca* portrayed America as a redemptive force in a world too long dominated by brutal and amoral power relations, a beacon of light to refugees who had fled Nazi-occupied Europe and impatiently awaited the "plane to Lisbon" (and thence to New York). In the course of the film, Humphrey Bogart's character, saloonkeeper Rick Blaine, discards his cynical go-it-alone veneer to reveal his romantic idealism. Victor Laszlo, the European resistance leader, challenges Rick to recognize that "each of us has a destiny, for good or for evil." Rick responds by choosing to fight the good war (as would the United States days later, the film being set in early December 1941). But suppose the United States had chosen to back the likes of the sinister Nazi leader, Major Strasser, rather than Victor Laszlo? What would Rick's choice have been then? His conduct was the product of individual moral choice rather than unwavering patriotic allegiance—and what was freely given could, by implication, be just as freely withheld or withdrawn.

World War II also taught a lesson about the unspeakable horrors that could be committed by an advanced bureaucratic state that had lost its moral bearings. The Israeli capture and trial of former SS Obersturmbannführer

Adolf Eichmann in 1960–61 revived memories of the postwar Nuremburg trials; while Hannah Arendt's 1963 book *Eichmann in Jerusalem* made the "banality of evil" a commonplace of educated liberal discourse. Arendt argued that European Jews were the victims of a monstrous system that depended on the acquiescence of ordinary human beings. Eichmann had served so efficiently as a cog in the Nazi death machine not out of personal depravity or exceptional sadism but because of a lack of imagination: he proved incapable of comprehending the evil of his own actions. Among the conclusions Arendt drew from her meditation on the "banality of evil" was a surprisingly optimistic one. She no longer contended that totalitarianism was capable of stamping out every vestige of independent thought and resistance among its subject populations: "Under conditions of terror most people will comply but some people will not. . . . No more is required, and no more can reasonably be asked, for this planet to remain a place fit for human habitation."

Norman Mailer in his 1957 essay "The White Negro" had already begun to refer to American society as "totalitarian"; in the decade that followed, a lot of loose talk would be heard on the Left comparing Nazi Germany and the United States. But one need not have subscribed to such misleading analogies to be drawn to the moral imagery and lessons provided by the Nuremburg trials. In fact, if resisters to evil could be found even under the extreme conditions of Nazi oppression, could less be expected of those who enjoyed the protections of liberal democracy? Joan Libby, a Mount Holyoke College student and antiwar activist in the mid-1960s, became an organizer for the National Moratorium Committee in 1969. Her parents disapproved of her antiwar activities, and she found herself relying on the Nuremburg analogy in her arguments with them:

> Both my parents were Jewish, and one of the things I had had to learn about, of course, was the Holocaust, and one of the lessons in that always is that you shouldn't stand by and think somebody else is going to do it. That's a serious lesson, I think, for susceptible young people like myself— a powerful one. It becomes sort of an imperative. There's always a double-edged sword when you bring people up with the notion that you should take [moral] positions on things. You never know where they'll come out.

In 1961, John F. Kennedy had sounded the call for a selfless dedication to the (vaguely defined) national cause, significantly posed in terms of individual choice: "Ask not what your country can do for you, ask what you can do for your country." The same spirit of self-sacrificing idealism that led many students to volunteer for the Peace Corps led others to the civil rights movement. Many young white volunteers felt that their civil rights activism was sanctioned from on high (although SNCC's black field workers never shared that particular illusion, knowing how unresponsive the Justice Department was to their requests for protection against racist attacks). A succession of emotional and political blows followed, with the cumulative effect of redirecting the spirit of idealism away from the official agenda being set in Washington: there was fear of nuclear annihilation during the Cuban missile crisis in October 1962, indignation over the brutal treatment of civil rights demonstrators in Birmingham in the spring of 1963, shock at Kennedy's assassination that fall, distrust the following summer as a result of the Democratic convention's "compromise" that prevented the seating of Fannie Lou Hamer and other black delegates from the Mississippi Freedom Democratic Party, and dismay over the escalation of the war in Vietnam in the spring of 1965.

In the early-to-mid 1960s, an essential prop of the old order gave way in the minds of tens of thousands of young people. In more jaded times, like those which followed the Vietnam War and the Watergate scandal, disbelief in the official pronouncements of American foreign-policy makers would lead primarily to cynicism and apathy; but, in the 1960s, when the fervor of cold war liberalism was still a potent force, such disillusionment was often the prelude to an intensely moralistic conversion to political activism.

Bob Dylan's rapid rise to fame was emblematic of the newly emerging cultural and political sensibility. Dylan's first album, a combination of folk and blues interpretations and his own ironic ballads, was released in February 1962. It sold an unremarkable five thousand copies in its first year. But Dylan's second album, released in May of 1963, found a broad new audience. *The Freewheelin' Bob Dylan*, which featured protest songs like "Blowin' in the Wind," "Masters of War," and "A Hard Rain's A Gonna Fall," sold 200,000 copies by July 1963. The following month, Peter, Paul and Mary released a single of Dylan's "Blowin' in the Wind" that sold over 300,000 copies in less than two weeks, making it the first protest song ever to grace the hit parade.

Where were Dylan's new fans coming from, and what message did they seek in his music? "Blowin' in the Wind" was simultaneously a song about coming-of-age ("How many roads must a man walk down / Before you call him a man?") and about moral choice ("Yes, 'n' how many times can a man turn his head / Pretending he just doesn't see?"), as well as a promise that those who understood its message would soon help redeem the nation ("The answer, my friend, is blowin' in the wind / The answer is blowin' in the wind"). Young Americans in the 1960s were not the first generation to feel that they were more sensitive to hypocrisy and injustice than their elders. But due to the structural and ideological framework that had emerged in postwar America, they were primed for an opening to the Left in the early 1960s. The demographic bulge, the delayed entry into the adult world, the encouragement of generational consciousness by advertisers, the cultural identification with outsiders and marginal groups, the inspirational example of the civil rights movement, and the paradoxical influence of cold war liberalism were the raw materials from which a mass New Left would be fashioned over the next few years.

III

The chief organizational beneficiary of these trends would be SDS. As the war and the protests it inspired escalated in the mid-1960s, SDS grew rapidly. This occurred despite the fact that, after organizing the first antiwar march on Washington in April 1965, its leaders disdained sponsorship of any more such events because they did not address the root issue of an imperialist foreign policy—"stopping the seventh Vietnam from now," as one slogan put it. But the policies SDS leaders chose to embrace or reject had little to do with the organization's growth. As Steve Max, an early leader of the group, recalled in a recent interview: "The progression in SDS was to be more and more movement and less and less organization. It was a situation of a movement looking for a place to happen."

There were national headlines in the spring of 1965 when SDS's antiwar march attracted some twenty thousand participants. By the end of that school year, the SDS National Office (NO) was receiving a flood of letters from individuals and groups eager to affiliate, from places like Dodge City Community College in Kansas not previously known as loci of radical activity. It was no longer necessary for SDS to organize chapters: they organized themselves. Many recruits were members of preexisting local groups who sought access to the resources and prestige that only a national organization could provide.

A typical communication arrived at the NO in November 1965 from a student at Ventura College (near Los Angeles) inquiring about the possibility of affiliating his local "Free Students for America" (FSFA) with SDS:

> What I have read and heard of your group leads me to believe we think much in the same direction. The basic aims of the F.S.F.A. are the removal of all American troops from Viet Nam, the use of aid rather than soldiers to combat the growth of totalitarian governments throughout the world, the affirmation of the right of any individual not to kill and not to be forced to serve in any military organization.

The Ventura "Free Students" wanted to join SDS because "we feel there is considerably more creative power in the unity of many groups than there is in many separate groups." The NO's response was favorable, including only the proviso that if the "Free Students" became an official SDS chapter they would have to agree to admit nonpacifists.

The NO set up a system of campus "travelers" and regional offices, but these did little more than service existing chapters, distribute literature, and make an occasional statement to the media. New members were seldom "converted" to SDS ideology. If the SDS "old guard" had had its way, the organization would have functioned chiefly as a recruiting pool for future community organizers. Instead, reflecting the loosely formulated set of ideas, concerns, and political priorities that new members brought with them into the national organization, SDS chapters increasingly focused their efforts on resisting the war in Vietnam. Students did not become activists because they joined SDS; they joined SDS because they were already activists.

The SDS annual national conventions were important mainly as places where SDSers from around the country could make contacts and share experiences. Labored efforts to chart a coordinated national strategy (like an abortive "Ten Days to Shake the Empire" plan in 1968) were almost universally ignored by local chapters. To the extent that people in SDS chapters learned to speak a common language and pursue a common political agenda, they did so through a process of osmosis rather than central direction.

Just at the moment when it began to develop a significant national presence, SDS lost the ability to set its own agenda. Starting in 1965, SDS's concerns and the pace of its development were largely reactions to decisions being made in the White House and the Pentagon. The escalation of the Vietnam War thus simultaneously strengthened and weakened SDS. In the matter of a few months, it transformed the group from a small network of activists, most of whom knew one another, into a national movement with hundreds of chapters—and an organizational infrastructure that never managed to make the transition. And while the war galvanized protesters, it also bred frustration and extremism in their ranks. Vietnam was a particularly volatile issue around which to build a mass movement. No partial victories or breathing spaces could be won: the movement would either force the government to end the war, or it would fail. As a result the peace movement, with the New Left at its core, constantly swung back and forth between near-millennial expectations and dark and angry despair.

As the political climate changed after 1965, so did the New Left's cultural style. The new members who flooded into SDS (dubbed the "prairie power" contingent because so many of them came from places other than the usual urban centers of radical strength) were less likely to share the theoretical sophistication or intellectual ambitions of the group's founding generation. The new breed tended to be unschooled in and impatient with radical doctrine, intensely moralistic, suspicious of "elitism" and "bureaucracy," and immersed in the new cultural currents running through college towns.

In January 1966, three members of the newly organized SDS chapter at the University of Oklahoma were among those arrested in a marijuana raid on a private party in Norman. Newspapers throughout the country picked up the story, linking SDS with pot-smoking. The Norman police chief unabashedly revealed to local reporters that his suspicions of the students had been aroused by their politics as much as their alleged drug use: "Several of these people have been active in the Society [SDS]. . . . One of them had a receipt showing he had just joined the SDS." High bail was set for all the defendants, and two of them were locked up incommunicado in a state mental hospital for observation because of their long hair.

Jeff Shero, an SDS campus traveler and leading exponent of "prairie power" within the organization, visited Norman soon after the bust. He reported back to the NO that the police had assembled prescription drugs and antiwar literature for sensationalized photographs. Local newspapers reported that a book on "homosexuality" was found in the raided apartment. They neglected to mention the name of the book's author—Sigmund Freud. Shero was both indignant and amused at the crudity of the official antics, but he concluded that the affair had not done SDS any real political harm. "The chapter probably isn't irreparably damaged," he wrote to the NO. "Chapter people were mixed as to the effect of the raid, some actually thought it would be beneficial."

Steve Max and a few other "old guard" leaders of SDS had a different reaction. Speaking in a tone that reflected the assumptions of his earlier involvement with the Communist youth movement, Max regarded it a matter of "Socialist discipline" that "unless the organization votes to carry on a Legalize marijuana through a civil disobedience campaign, then our members ought not place themselves and the organization in a position where they can be put out of commission so easily." He wanted the Norman chapter suspended until it had, through some unspecified procedure, reformed itself. In a subsequent letter, he reiterated, "If we don't start to draw the line someplace we are going to wind up with a federation of dope rings instead of a national political organization."

But sentiment in the hinterland seemed to run in a completely opposite direction. One member from Ohio reported to the NO that news of the Norman arrests "strikes home in the Ohio area since a number of people including three friends have been arrested on charges involving pot." Although he realized that SDS might have good reasons to avoid involvement in a campaign to legalize pot-smoking, "nevertheless, I think this area is another expression of the lack of individual freedom in the society for an individual desiring to control his own life without interference."

The Norman SDS chapter was not suspended. Moreover, within a few years, SDS would not simply regard the use of drugs as a question of individual choice but would endorse it as yet another emblem of the revolutionary disaffection of the young. "Our whole life is a defiance of Amerika," the newspaper of the Weatherman SDS faction exulted in 1969. "It's moving in the streets, digging sounds, smoking dope . . . fighting pigs." By the late sixties, marijuana and LSD were circulating freely at national SDS conventions.

Underlying the ability and willingness of so many young radicals, along with others of their generation, to experiment with new "life-styles" (including drugs) was the economic prosperity of the postwar era. New Leftists took affluence for granted and despised its corrupting influence, unlike the Socialists and Communists of the 1930s who denounced capitalism for its inability to provide the minimum decencies of life to the poor. The great revolutionary drama of the New York theater in the 1930s had been Clifford Odets's *Waiting for Lefty,* which ended with the "workers" in the cast and the audience joining together in chanting "Strike, strike, strike!"

Perhaps the closest equivalent to Odets's work in the 1960s was the popular play by Peter Brooks, *The Persecution and Assassination of Jean Paul Marat as Performed by the Inmates of the Asylum of Charenton under the Direction of the Marquis de Sade* (or, as it was more commonly known, *Marat/Sade*), which suggested that conventional politics, even conventional revolutionary politics, was exhausted as a force for change. The final scene in *Marat/Sade* provoked the same kind of audience empathy as the climax of *Waiting for Lefty,* although this time the identification was not with striking workers but with rioting lunatics in an insane asylum, who sang "We want a revolution . . . NOW!" The song went on to become a kind of unofficial anthem of the Columbia strike in the spring of 1968.

Julian Beck's "Living Theater," which toured campuses during the late

1960s, went a step further than *Marat/Sade* by dispensing with scripts altogether. In a typical Living Theater production, the "actors" challenged the audience to join them on stage in disrobing, smoking marijuana, and milling around in a kind of pseudo-liberated confusion. A student who participated in a building seizure at the University of Chicago in 1969 saw a direct link between the decision by the local SDS chapter to take over the building and a visit shortly before by the Living Theater:

> The idea was to liberate yourself from the confining conventions of life, and to celebrate the irrational side of your nature, kind of let yourself go. . . At a place like the University of Chicago, this was really the opposite of every message that you'd been getting from the moment you stepped into the place. . . . This was the counterculture coming to us, and it stirred people up and made us feel like doing something dramatic.

Earlier generations of radicals had derided capitalism as an anarchic, irrational system; the new radicals scorned the system because it was *too* rational, based on a soul-destroying set of technological and bureaucratic imperatives that stifled individual expression. From university reform, where the slogan was "I am a human being, do not fold, spindle or mutilate," to draft resistance, where the buttons read "Not with my life, you don't," the New Left championed a form of radical individualism that was authentically American in derivation and flavor—ironically, all too "American" for the organizational well-being of the movement. For this deeply rooted individualism prepared the way for the development of a movement cult of "confrontation."

In the Communist, Socialist, and Trotskyist movements of the 1930s, young radicals had prided themselves on their analytic abilities, their skill in debate, their command of the intricacies of Marxist theory. In contrast, a kind of emotional and moral plain-speaking was the preferred rhetorical style among SDS leaders. Authenticity, usually described as "commitment," was the political and personal value New Leftists were most eager to display, a quality that could best be established by the willingness to "put your body on the line." Overcoming any lingering squeamishness about breaking the law (and plate-glass windows) was the ultimate "gut-check" that alone could establish whether you were "part of the problem or part of the solution."

The political deficiencies of this personal stance were not lost on some SDSers, though they found themselves powerless to correct the situation. As early as 1965, Lee Webb, former SDS national secretary, complained in an internal document that "SDS influences its membership to become more militant rather than more radical. . . . Calls to fight the draft, stop a troop train, burn a draft card, avoid all forms of liberalism, have become . . . the substitute for intellectual analysis and understanding." Late sixties SDS rhetoric, composed of equal parts Maoist jargon and black street rap, communicated little but the angry alienation of its practitioners. Nevertheless, it had a very potent appeal to the already-converted or would-be recruits in defining the cultural terrain of the movement—if you spoke the language, you were already a revolutionary. "Brothers," a high school student wrote to the NO in the late 1960s, "I sympathize with the movement and its goals. But information on what's going on is hard to come by in rural, conservative western Pennsylvania. Dig?"

By the late 1960s, SDS had grown to as many as a hundred thousand loosely affiliated members, while tens of thousands more could be counted as supporters of the movement. But off-campus, the New Left's activities, and the increasingly outrageous and opaque language in which they were justified, found few supporters. Ronald Reagan spoke for many Americans when he declared in the midst of the People's Park disorders in Berkeley in 1969 (which left one spectator dead from police buckshot), "If it's a blood bath they want, let it be now." The ferocity with which authorities sought to crack down on campus protest only exacerbated the appeal of extreme rhetoric and doctrines within SDS. In the summer of 1969 the organization splintered, with one small faction led by the Progressive Labor Party (PLP) heading for the factories, and another small faction led by Weatherman heading for the "underground." Neither the PLP nor Weatherman enlisted more than a tiny fraction of SDS members under their banners, but Weatherman's cultural style—which included a fervent if erratic promotion of drugs, sex, and rock and roll—gave it a measure of influence on campuses that the dour dogmatists in the PLP were never able to match. In the early 1970s underground newspapers gave extensive coverage to Weatherman's bombings and "communiqués"; posters in college dorms invited Bernardine Dohrn and other Weatherman fugitives to seek shelter.

IV

The demise of SDS did not retard the flowering of cultural radicalism. From campus towns to the "youth ghettos" of big cities and even to American military bases in Vietnam, a diffuse set of "countercultural" ideas, symbols, and behaviors circulated. "Liberation" was easy to achieve, since it was defined as the practice of a communal, playful, and sensual life-style. While they often ignored or explicitly rejected the politics advocated by "power-tripping" radicals, those immersed in the counterculture embraced beliefs the earlier New Left had first popularized. Alternative, participatory communities based on decentralized, small-scale technology and an ethic of loving mutuality had all been prefigured by the Port Huron Statement, the civil rights movement, and SDS's community-organizing projects. Garbed in apolitical dress, this vision continued to attract believers (many of them from working-class backgrounds) who never would have considered attending an SDS meeting. In the mid-1970s, pollster Daniel Yankelovich called attention to the ways in which new attitudes toward authority, sexual morality, and self-fulfillment had spread from elite college campuses to much of the younger population: "Indeed," he wrote, "we are amazed by the rapidity with which this process is now taking place."

As the sixties ended, some radical leaders withdrew from the increasingly fractious realm of left-wing politics to join rural communes or mystical cults, or to embrace various "new age" therapies. The well-publicized voyage of

Jerry Rubin from yippie revolutionary to yuppie networker is the best known, if not most representative, example of this process. Paul Potter, a former SDS president, was less self-serving and more reflective when he recorded his own painful withdrawal from the movement in his 1971 book *A Name for Ourselves*. Potter reaffirmed his belief in the values and concerns that had initially led him to the New Left, but rejected organized politics as a means of achieving a better world:

> I am less involved in changing America. . . . This does not mean that I am less angry or upset or horrified by this country than before. If anything, I am more profoundly and intuitively aware, day to day, of what an ugly society this is and how desperately it needs change. But my information comes less and less from the papers—more and more from my own experience with it.

Potter now sought to be "in touch with children," agonized about his lingering desire for power, and found solace in daily rituals. His lover Leni Wildflower (whose adopted surname represented a symbolic break with her Old Left parents) contributed an angry foreword to *A Name for Ourselves*:

> I am trying desperately to peel away the layers of lies—trying to pull back the skin of society, school, family. The expectations which somewhere along the line got internalized. The desire to "be something," the pretty deep conviction that I am *nothing* . . . And in the middle of my quest there are all these men laying their power-ego-identity trips on me.

The emergence of a new feminist movement had the paradoxical effect of drawing many New Left women into more active political participation while hastening the political withdrawal of many men. In the late 1960s and early 1970s few male leaders of the New Left escaped being taken to task for sexism by women in the movement. What more decisive step could men take to indicate repentance for past misdeeds than to abdicate any further claim to leadership? With the movement foundering, the "politically correct" decision often served to rationalize personal inclinations. Coinciding with the decline of the antiwar movement, a widespread and decentralized network of women's "consciousness raising" groups, health clinics, bookstores, newspapers, publishing houses, and similar enterprises emerged, giving new meaning to the original New Left call for a "beloved community."

V

"The sixties are over," literary critic Morris Dickstein wrote in 1977, "but they remain the watershed of our recent cultural history; they continue to affect the ambiance of our lives in innumerable ways." The passage of more than a decade and Ronald Reagan's two terms in office have not lessened the truth of that observation. In the 1980s, the conservative victors found it politically convenient to lump together the vestiges of New Deal–Great Society liberalism with the memory of the New Left to justify reversing both the social legislation and the "moral permissiveness" associated with the sixties. They were quite successful in cutting back or abolishing domestic programs that had no wealthy or powerful constituency. But as the New Right's plaintive refrain "Let Reagan be Reagan" indicated, conservatives did not have everything their own way in the 1980s. The right was forced to govern within a cultural environment that, in significant ways, limited what it could accomplish. Conservatives had to repackage many of their ideas and policies to appeal to a public that had caught a "democratic distemper" and was unwilling to defer automatically to its new governors.

The movements and events of the 1960s generated an attitudinal penumbra that glimmered long after SDS and SNCC had been eclipsed. Chastened by the collapse of "the movement," many pragmatic radicals entered the left wing of the Democratic party, helping transform its stance on foreign policy and producing at least a strong rhetorical commitment to equal rights for all disadvantaged groups. In the 1970s and 1980s, erstwhile New Leftists taking a few steps toward the center met and worked alongside liberals disenchanted with cold war shibboleths who were moving gradually to the Left. The activist Left largely shed traditional Marxist concerns for issues centering on the workplace and economic growth, groping instead for a new synthesis of environmentalism, feminism, antimilitarism, and interracial solidarity.

Right-wing movements also sought to exploit the mood of morally committed idealism that sixties radicals had done so much to create; in some instances, they proved more successful than their left-wing counterparts. The impulse to expose and attack illegitimate authority was turned against legislators who tried to "solve problems by throwing money at them," against a Democratic president who could neither free American hostages nor punish their captors, and against liberal judges perceived as protecting muggers, drug-pushers, or pornographers. At the same time, a vigorous libertarian spirit, itself a legacy of the sixties, acted as a countervailing force, preventing the New Right from imposing its version of morality on law and society. America's political culture in the 1980s thus contained enough contradictory impulses to baffle the pundits who assumed that Reagan's electoral victories represented a fundamental rightward shift.

American politics in the past decade has actually been characterized by the existence of a deep divide between two camps: one, a broad but disorganized Left, has attempted to defend and develop ideas, issues, and "lifestyles" that emerged in the sixties; the other, an equally diverse but far better organized Right, has built its own influence around popular revulsion from those same images and practices. New Leftists thus succeeded in transforming American politics—though not according to the sanguine script laid out at Port Huron. The continued influence of the movements of the 1960s has been most pronounced in five aspects of contemporary American society: intellectual life, perceptions of race and of gender, foreign policy, and the language of politics itself.

According to the mythology promoted by *The Big Chill*, sixties radicals had all "sold out" by the 1980s. The main characters in that film made their living by peddling running shoes or dope, writing trashy stories for *People* magazine, or starring in a trashy action series on television. In real life, no doubt, some came to such ends. But thousands of others took up jobs and professions that did not represent a break with their earlier political aspirations. They became social workers, union and community organizers, public school teachers, Legal Services lawyers, or doctors involved in occupational or neighborhood health programs. A recent study of the political attitudes held by aging "veterans of the protest movement" discovered that a majority retained the ideological predilections of their youth.

Significantly, many former radicals made careers in the "information industry," as academics, journalists, and media specialists. Conservative social scientists have done much viewing-with-alarm of this phenomenon. They blame a left-wing "new class" for undermining the public's faith in both domestic institutions and U.S. foreign policy. Opinion surveys of the "media elite" conducted by Robert Lichter and Stanley Rothman in the late 1970s found that print and electronic journalists and filmmakers overwhelmingly endorsed "strong affirmative action for blacks," as well as women's right to abortions; a near-majority agreed that the "U.S. exploits the Third World and causes poverty." Writing in *Partisan Review* in 1986, sociologist Paul Hollander condemned the Left's alleged "domination of the public political discourse" on campus, complaining that while its adherents may work "within the system," they are "without any sense of allegiance towards it." Prominent neoconservatives like Norman Podhoretz, Midge Decter, and Hilton Kramer sound similar alarms about the radical fifth columnists they believe have debauched American culture.

While these attacks on the "new class" suffer from hyperbole, they do gesture at a truth about contemporary thought. Radicals probably played a larger role in the universities and the media in the 1980s than at any previous time in American history. In the fields of history and literature, the most innovative scholars have been those who sympathetically illuminate the lives and thought of subaltern groups and "deconstruct" the works and reputations of famous writers and other authorities. Different schools of Marxism, feminism, and radical linguistic theory infuse this work, which, in the spirit of the New Left, questions not just established ideas (for that is the perpetual task of good scholarship) but the methods used to create them and the consequences that flow from their application in society. Far from having cloistered themselves, as some left-wing critics have charged, radical scholars have shown considerable concern for making their views available to a non-academic audience. Radical perspectives, albeit somewhat diluted ones, find their way into a surprising number of mainstream venues, from National Public Radio programming to the op-ed pages of the *New York Times* and the *Wall Street Journal,* to the Smithsonian's National Museum of American History, to historical sites like Harpers Ferry and Colonial Williamsburg (where blacksmiths in period dress pepper their narratives with insights culled from recent literature about slavery and abolitionism by such radical scholars as John Blassingame, Eugene Genovese, and Eric Foner).

None of this, to be sure, represents a left-wing cultural coup d'état. In the media, there is little evidence that the private views of reporters control the message being transmitted on the page and screen. In academia, radical assistant professors are as preoccupied with the scramble for tenure as colleagues on their right—and lack access to the patronage and sources of alternate employment that well-funded right-wing think tanks and the Reagan administration offered to a generation of young conservative intellectuals. Still, the contention in the media and the university over basic questions of ideology stands in sharp contrast with the intellectual scene of the 1950s when radical journalist I. F. Stone had to start his own shoestring newsletter to publish his acute exposés of government policies; while academic mavericks like Paul Baran and C. Wright Mills nurtured their ideas largely in isolation from their colleagues.

Since the 1960s, the politics of race has been a major battleground between Left and Right. On the one hand, "new class" individuals and institutions exhibit a heightened level of racial sensitivity. The study of the history and culture of minority groups is a staple of public education, at least in urban areas. Black history was the subject of the most popular television event of the 1970s ("Roots"), while a black family served as the model of domesticity on the most popular situation comedy of the 1980s ("The Cosby Show"), and Oprah Winfrey, black hostess of the most popular daytime television talk show, portrayed her own career as the product of struggles by Sojourner Truth, Harriet Tubman, and Fannie Lou Hamer.

Millions of middle-class whites have joined with blacks in establishing a firm line demarcating acceptable from unacceptable public conduct and expression regarding race. Together they have succeeded in delegitimating beliefs that were the norm among white Americans only a generation earlier. Since the mid-1970s, any nationally prominent public figure who has castigated blacks as a people, even with humorous intent, has quickly lost reputation, employment, or both. Consider the firings of agriculture secretary Earl Butz in 1975 for telling a racist joke; of baseball executive Al Campanis in 1987 for questioning, on a television show commemorating the anniversary of Jackie Robinson's major league debut, whether blacks had "the necessities" to make good managers; and of network football commentator Jimmy "the Greek" Snyder for claiming that blacks were bred by slaveholders to be faster and stronger than whites and for wanting to reserve front-office jobs for the latter. A record of hostility to the civil rights movement, even in the absence of evidence of personal racial prejudice, can also destroy careers. Judge Robert Bork's nomination to the Supreme Court was fatally damaged by the revelation that he had described the public accommodations section of the 1964 Civil Rights Act as embodying "a principle of unsurpassed ugliness," while Arizona governor Evan Meacham inspired a powerful impeachment movement when he refused to recognize Martin Luther King's birthday as a state holiday. The black leader, who, in his lifetime, was harassed by the FBI, mistrusted by the presidents he dealt with, and openly despised by millions of whites, is today a national icon.

But the new consensus on racial equality is far from universal. The Boston busing riots of the mid-1970s, the 1986 assault on three blacks who had the misfortune of having their car break down in the white Howard Beach neighborhood of New York City, and other events have revealed a bitter fraction of white working-class America that lashes out against those regarded as threats to its homes, jobs, and personal safety. Moreover, in the 1980s, students on major college campuses like Dartmouth, Penn State, and the University of Massachusetts (Amherst) engaged in racial slurs and, on a few occasions, even violence, demonstrating that segregation (albeit of an informal, interpersonal kind) still plagued these overwhelmingly white institutions. By opposing affirmative action (in the name of "equal opportunity") and welfare programs, conservative politicians have both contributed to and benefited from such conflicts.

Meanwhile, many middle-class whites share the perception that a black "underclass" has become fatally trapped within a nexus of family dissolution, drug abuse, and crime, past all reasonable hope of salvation. Radicals and liberals won an important victory when they transformed the public language and imagery of race. But at a time when racial inequality has become primarily a question of access to wealth and secure employment, they have, for the most part, fallen into a puzzled, if not indifferent, silence about issues more complicated than Jimmy the Greek's notions of slavery.

Attitudes about women and women's issues have undergone a similar change, taking a large cultural step forward while suffering a political step back, or at least sideward, in the struggle for equality of the sexes. The central ideological tenet of the new feminist movement was the idea that "the personal is political." The most intimate and seemingly mundane details of private life—housework and childcare, among many others—were seen as fundamentally linked to social power. In the late 1960s and early 1970s, feminists struck an enormously rich vein of anger and insight about personal issues that American radical movements had never systematically addressed before.

The mass media, initially inclined to dismiss the new feminists with the trivializing designation "bra-burners," by the mid-1970s made a dramatic about-face in their treatment of many of the movement's concerns. Notions like "equal pay for equal work" were easily assimilated into public discourse; today most young middle-class women routinely expect to have access to the same careers and to receive the same compensation as men. What is surprising, in retrospect, is how quickly other, more highly charged, issues— rape, abortion, family violence, incest—began to attract respectful coverage in the daily press and on television. Talk shows routinely broadcast heated discussions about sexuality, day care, and birth control. "Sexism" itself has become so common a concept that even so unreflective a Reaganite as Fawn Hall immediately made use of the phrase to respond to Senator Howell Heflin's accusation that she had stuffed classified documents into her underwear in order to smuggle them out of Oliver North's office.

Feminists have succeeded in establishing a new "common sense" about gender roles among the urban middle class—and beyond. By the mid-1980s, according to a synthesis of opinion polls, a majority of Americans agreed with positions that, at the end of the 1960s, were the province of radical feminists. They supported federally subsidized day-care centers, sex education for the young, and the idea that men and women should share house-

work and child rearing equally. Women from constituencies that the New
Left had tended to write off—the white working class, the Catholic church,
the suburbs—came to embrace feminist ideas and proposals in the course
of the 1970s even though many still feel constrained to preface their new
beliefs with the disclaimer, "I'm no women's libber, but . . ." It was as if
American society had been waiting for decades, with mounting nervousness
and impatience, for some group to have the courage to come along and
state the obvious about the problems between the sexes.

But, here too, not everyone was converted. The New Right accepted
the challenge of "personal politics" and responded by organizing its own
network of women activists. Phyllis Schlafly's Eagle Forum, the right-to-life
movement, and similar groups proved quite adept at stirring, articulating,
and channeling fears about the destruction of the male-headed "traditional
family." In tandem with rising conservative politicians, they were able to
block passage of the Equal Rights Amendment (despite the support the
ERA consistently received in national polls). As a result, organized feminism
stalled and began to be described, even by some Democrats, as merely
another "special interest."

The legacy of the sixties has continued to play an explicit role in framing
popular attitudes toward military intervention abroad. Despite the appeals
of President Reagan and other supporters of the Nicaraguan Contras, Americans have consistently opposed policies designed to overthrow the Sandinista
government by a margin of roughly 2 to 1. That sentiment is routinely
expressed as fear of stumbling into "another Vietnam"—a phrase worth
examining. Understandably, Americans remember the war as a time of futile
bloodletting. Many oppose U.S. intervention in Central America out of a
sense of pragmatic isolationism; if the conquest of Nicaragua looked to be
as effortless as that of Grenada, the public opinion polls would almost
certainly look different.

For many Americans, however, the lesson of Vietnam goes beyond the
need to avoid unwinnable wars. A plurality of Americans agrees retrospec-
tively with the judgment that the antiwar movement proclaimed in the 1960s.
In a May 1985 poll, taken at a moment when Reagan's popularity was as
yet untarnished by the Iran-Contra affair, 38 percent agreed that U.S. involvement in Vietnam had been both "wrong and immoral." Only 34 percent
concurred with the president's description of the war as a "noble cause."

Such an opinion, like that in any sphere of public controversy, reflects
both conclusions drawn from immediate experience and the cumulative influence of mass-mediated images and attitudes. The popularity, not to say
domination, of liberal, antiwar politics in Hollywood since the 1960s has
resulted in treatments of Vietnam that are harshly critical of the premises
that underlay U.S. policy. "MASH," the highest-rated television series of
the late 1970s, conveyed an implicitly pacifist message through characters
who mocked conventional military authority and held no particular grudge
against the Communist enemy. The 1978 film *Coming Home* depicted its
hero, a disabled antiwar veteran, besting his sexual and political rival, another veteran who had returned home with his body intact but his mind

mangled with militarist rage. The prize the two competed for was the love of a strong female character played by Jane Fonda. Oliver Stone's 1987 production *Platoon,* which won the Academy Award for Best Picture, portrayed the war as seen through the eyes of a young infantryman. Even as he fights a desperate battle for personal survival, the protagonist comes to reject the mindless brutality of the war as represented by a sinister, scar-faced sergeant (a rejection symbolized, according to the truest Hollywood convention, by the hero killing the bad guy).

But attitudes toward and images of the war remain a contested terrain in Hollywood, as they do for the larger public. Michael Cimino's *The Deer Hunter,* which won the Oscar for Best Picture the same year that *Coming Home* picked up the prizes for Best Actor and Actress, depicted Vietnamese culture as an evil, decadent force that bewildered and corrupted white ethnic GI's before killing them. Eight years later, Sylvester Stallone, in *Rambo: First Blood, Part II,* took revenge, like a bare-chested, overmuscled Western sheriff, on the Vietnamese outlaws who had once defeated him. By asking, "Do we get to win this time?" and then blasting away in the affirmative, Rambo was also attacking cowardly bureaucrats back home who had reputedly scuttled the patriotic cause. In the summer of 1987, Oliver North gained a brief but intense popularity when he enacted what might be called "Mr. Rambo Goes to Washington," in which yet another battle-hardened warrior stood up to a pack of pusillanimous civilians. Vietnam remains a nightmare legacy from the sixties that Americans repeatedly put behind them and yet obsessively continue to relive.

The politics of the two major parties also reflect the impact of sixties radicalism. The most direct influence appears within the Democratic party. In many areas, local Democratic activists began to move left during the 1968 presidential campaign and, in time, found their forces strengthened by an infusion of former New Leftists. By the 1980s, left Democrats represented a variety of "single-issue" movements—black, Chicano, feminist, environmentalist, peace, gay and lesbian, and elderly—as much as they did the party apparatus itself. Such organizations as the National Organization for Women, the Sierra Club, and SANE saw their memberships swell in the early 1980s and developed increasingly professional and intermittently powerful lobbies in Washington. Liberal and radical Democratic activists helped transform Jesse Jackson into a serious candidate for president, promoted Geraldine Ferraro's vice-presidential nomination in 1984, and set the anti-interventionist tenor of the party's foreign policy debates. To the dismay of many party officials in the South, and those elsewhere nostalgic for the days of Jim Farley and Richard Daley, "New Politics"–style Democrats increasingly supply the financial backing, political energy, and moral élan that keeps the party organization afloat.

Yet what gives life to one side also provides opportunity for the other. Since the 1960s, conservative Republicans have lured away traditional Democratic voters by portraying the GOP as the only safe haven for the white ethnic working class against the onslaught of the civil rights movement and the political and social insurgencies it spawned. After taking a Watergate-induced pause in the mid-1970s, this backlash intensified, as millions of white northern voters joined southerners in rejecting the presidential candidates of their own party whom they perceived as apostles of weakness abroad and captives of single-issue "special interests" at home. Meanwhile, the New Right was using the specter of a hedonistic, God-denying counterculture to raise funds and recruit activists. Thus both parties, each in its own way, still lived off energy generated in the 1960s.

Notions of "personal politics" took on a new meaning in the late 1980s as a series of prominent political figures fell victim to revelations about private moral transgressions. Circumstantial evidence of adultery derailed front-runner Gary Hart's 1988 presidential campaign, while the Supreme Court nomination of the conservative jurist Douglas Ginsburg collapsed amid reports that he had occasionally used marijuana. A libertarian impulse favoring open discussion of previously taboo subjects meshed with a lurid soap-opera-and-supermarket-tabloid-fed curiosity about the misdeeds of the highly placed. The unlucky offenders were punished not so much for having strayed from standards of behavior that relatively few American adults under the age of forty-five had themselves upheld, as for their lack of "authenticity": Hart's self-portrait of himself as a dedicated family man and Ginsburg's "law-and-order" stance were revealed as shams.

A final way in which the sixties have influenced American politics can be seen in the use of "populist" stances by politicians of all persuasions. The past quarter-century has been a fertile breeding ground for expressions of discontent that defy old categories of "liberal" and "conservative." Advocates of desegregation and all-white community schools, feminists and right-to-lifers, the New Left and the George Wallace presidential campaign, agreed on very little; but all railed against "the establishment" in the interests of the common folk. And from a disgruntled public, the majority of which, according to polls taken since the early 1970s, consistently feels "alienated from the power structure," come new waves of anti-elitist anger that invigorates such movements. In fact, the very language of these opinion surveys again demonstrates how conventional some New Left terminology has become.

Populism, of course, has long been a staple of American political discourse. Ignatius Donnelly, Huey Long, and Saul Alinsky were winning votes or building movements out of such material long before young radicals moved to urban slums in the early 1960s. The unique contribution of the new radicals was to broaden the scope of the populist critique, challenging the legitimacy of cultural as well as political and economic power structures.

In ways both trivial and serious, the example, language, and actions of sixties radicals offered millions of Americans a way to express the discontent generated by the triple debacle of Vietnam, Watergate, and seventies stagflation. Often it was the New Left's style rather than its politics that wound up being recycled in the 1970s and 1980s. Some otherwise law abiding "right-to-life" demonstrators risked arrest blockading abortion clinics while singing, in paraphrase of John Lennon, "All we are saying / is give life a chance." Campus conservatives distributed leaflets accusing Gulf Oil of "corporate murder" because the firm does business with the pro-Soviet government of Angola. New Leftists succeeded in exposing the bankrupt policies of the liberal state in the 1960s. But that very success activated right-wing critics of liberalism who championed a "counterculture" of their own, based on biblical injunctions, the patriarchal family, and the economic homilies of nineteenth-century capitalism.

The contradictory legacy of the sixties thus provides evidence of both the failures and successes of the new radicalism—"failures" that were sometimes unavoidable, and sometimes self-inflicted, and "successes" that usually were unrecognized and were often the opposite of what was intended. Richard Hofstadter wrote in *The Age of Reform* that while it may be "feasible and desirable to formulate ideal programs of reform, it is asking too much to expect that history will move . . . in a straight line to realize them." Despite the best efforts of the Reagan administration and the New Right, the 1980s did not represent a return to the "normalcy" of the 1950s. Young radicals never became serious contenders for state power, but the issues they raised and the language in which those issues were dramatized became the normal fare of American politics.

Whether scorned as pro-Communistic and nihilistic or smothered in bland nostalgia, the New Left's reputation in the late 1980s was not all that its founders might have hoped for. But the message of the young radicals had certainly been received.

✖ *F U R T H E R   R E A D I N G*

Ronald Berman, *America in the Sixties: An Intellectual History* (1978)
Winifred Breines, *Community and Organization in the New Left, 1962–1968* (1982)
David Caute, *The Year of the Barricades: A Journey Through 1968* (1988)
Peter Clecak, *Radical Paradoxes* (1973)
Dick Cluster, ed., *They Should Have Served That Cup of Coffee* (1979)
Joseph Conlin, *The Troubles: A Jaundiced Glance Back at the Movements of the Sixties* (1982)
Morris Dickstein, *Gates of Eden: American Culture in the Sixties* (1977)
Sara Evans, *Personal Politics: The Origins of Women's Liberation in the Civil Rights Movement and the New Left* (1979)
David Farber, *Chicago '68* (1988)
Ronald Fraser et al., *1968: A Student Generation in Revolt* (1988)
Todd Gitlin, *The Sixties: Years of Hope, Days of Rage* (1987)
———, *The Whole World Is Watching* (1980)
Fred Halstead, *Out There* (1978)
David Harris, *Dreams Die Hard: Three Men's Journey Through the Sixties* (1982)
Tom Hayden, *Reunion* (1988)
Maurice Isserman, *If I Had a Hammer . . . The Death of the Old Left and the Birth of the New Left* (1987)
George Katsiaficas, *The Imagination of the New Left: A Global Analysis of 1968* (1987)
Kenneth Keniston, *Young Radicals: Notes on Committed Youth* (1968)
———, *Youth and Dissent: The Rise of a New Opposition* (1971)
Cyril Levitt, *Children of Privilege: Student Revolt in the Sixties* (1984)
Guenter Lewy, *Peace and Revolution: The Moral Crisis of American Pacifism* (1988)

Allen J. Matusow, *The Unraveling of America: A History of Liberalism in the 1960s* (1984)

Michael W. Miles, *The Radical Probe: The Logic of Student Rebellion* (1971)

James Miller, *Democracy Is in the Streets* (1987)

Joan Morrison and Robert K. Morrison, eds., *From Camelot to Kent State: The Sixties Experience in the Words of Those Who Lived It* (1987)

William L. O'Neill, *Coming Apart: An Informal History of America in the 1960s* (1971)

Abe Peck, *Uncovering the Sixties* (1985)

Charles Perry, *Haight-Ashbury* (1985)

Thomas Powers, *Vietnam: The War at Home* (1973)

Charles Reich, *The Greening of America* (1970)

Theodore Roszak, *The Making of a Counter-Culture* (1969)

Kirkpatrick Sale, *SDS* (1973)

Sohnya Sayres et al. *The 60s Without Apology* (1984)

Irwin Unger, *The Movement: A History of the American New Left, 1959–1972* (1974)

Milton Viorst, *Fire in the Streets* (1981)

Tom Wolfe, *The Electric Kool-Aid Acid Test* (1969)

CHAPTER
11

From the Feminine Mystique
to the New Feminism

XXX

The publication in 1963 of Betty Friedan's The Feminine Mystique *opened a new chapter in American women's fight for equality, a struggle that in ensuing decades would transform American social relations. Like most revolutions, it was the product of a long historical gestation. Its roots lay in the broad social changes wrought by industrialization, urbanization, and the rise of a new economy based on mass consumption; the emergence of a more democratic and companionate family life; and the self-conscious strivings of nineteenth- and early-twentieth-century women for suffrage and sexual equality. The movement's immediate antecedents included the massive entry of women into the work force during World War II, a change only temporarily reversed during the late 1940s. But the postwar years were marked also by a powerful and pervasive ideology of domestic containment—the insistence by virtually all of the country's cultural authorities that women ought to seek fulfillment exclusively as wives and mothers. (Recall the speech in Chapter 5 by Democratic presidential candidate Adlai Stevenson to the 1955 graduating class of Smith College.) It was the tension between this powerful "feminine mystique" and the as yet largely unarticulated aspirations of women for freedom and equality that Betty Friedan would record in her influential book.*

Through The Feminine Mystique *women began to discover a common sense of frustration and even despair. Friedan, however, spoke for and to a largely middle-class audience of liberal women, some of whom would join her in 1966 in creating the National Organization of Women (NOW). Other, more radical voices were nurtured by the decade's civil-rights movement and potent New Left. Out of the crucible of these movements, women (mostly young women) would forge the social agenda of the new feminism, an agenda that included not only the political and economic opportunities stressed by NOW but also a more radical challenge to definitions of gender roles in American society.*

The transformation sought by the new feminists would encounter strong opposition: the resistance of men and of male-dominated institutions, the sharp limits to change imposed by class and race, and the mobilization of social conservatives by the New Right during the 1980s. Women's fight for equality never-

theless continues to shape the landscape of American society. Like the civil-rights movement, to which it has often been compared, it is an unfinished revolution whose final chapters will be written by Americans in the 1990s and beyond.

☒ D O C U M E N T S

The first document excerpts the opening chapter of Betty Friedan's *The Feminine Mystique* (1963). An analysis of the lives of college-educated, middle-class women in the 1950s, the book became an early classic of the new feminism. In 1966 Friedan would play a leading role in the creation of the National Organization of Women, whose statement of purpose is reprinted as the second selection. The third document, a 1965 memorandum by two young civil-rights workers, suggests important connections between civil rights and student radicalism on the one hand, and the origins of the new feminism on the other. The fourth document is excerpted from the preface to *Our Bodies, Ourselves* (1973), the best-selling manual on women's health care. It is a good account both of "consciousness-raising," as the process of collective intellectual liberation was sometimes called, and of the growing engagement of the women's movement with a broad range of gender-related issues.

In its landmark 1973 decision in the case of *Roe* v. *Wade* (the fifth document), the Supreme Court overturned a Texas law restricting women's right to abortion. The debate over abortion polarized Americans. Women's groups and most liberals defended the right of women to abortion on demand, while many Roman Catholics and conservatives sought to end legalized abortion. [In *Webster* v. *Reproductive Health Services* (1989), a more conservative Court limited the scope of the *Roe* decision by upholding portions of a restrictive Missouri law.] By the late 1970s, changes in U.S. society and family life had sparked a powerful conservative backlash, led by men like the Reverend Jerry Falwell, a television evangelist who in 1978 helped organize the Moral Majority, an organization of tradition-minded evangelical Christians. In the sixth document, Falwell warns of modern society's "vicious assault upon the American family." In the seventh document, newspaper columnist Ellen Goodman contrasts the lives of her own generation, which came of age in the 1950s and 1960s, with those of a younger generation growing up in the 1980s and 1990s.

Betty Friedan on the
Problem That Has No Name, 1963

The problem lay buried, unspoken, for many years in the minds of American women. It was a strange stirring, a sense of dissatisfaction, a yearning that women suffered in the middle of the twentieth century in the United States. Each suburban wife struggled with it alone. As she made the beds, shopped for groceries, matched slipcover material, ate peanut butter sandwiches with her children, chauffeured Cub Scouts and Brownies, lay beside her husband at night—she was afraid to ask even of herself the silent question—"Is this all?"

For over fifteen years there was no word of this yearning in the millions of words written about women, for women, in all the columns, books and articles by experts telling women their role was to seek fulfillment as wives and mothers. Over and over women heard in voices of tradition and of Freudian sophistication that they could desire no greater destiny than to glory in their own femininity. Experts told them how to catch a man and keep him, how to breastfeed children and handle their toilet training, how to cope with sibling rivalry and adolescent rebellion; how to buy a dishwasher, bake bread, cook gourmet snails, and build a swimming pool with their own hands; how to dress, look, and act more feminine and make marriage more exciting; how to keep their husbands from dying young and their sons from growing into delinquents. They were taught to pity the neurotic, unfeminine, unhappy women who wanted to be poets or physicists or presidents. They learned that truly feminine women do not want careers, higher education, political rights—the independence and the opportunities that the old-fashioned feminists fought for. Some women, in their forties and fifties, still remembered painfully giving up those dreams, but most of the younger women no longer even thought about them. A thousand expert voices applauded their femininity, their adjustment, their new maturity. All they had to do was devote their lives from earliest girlhood to finding a husband and bearing children.

By the end of the nineteen-fifties, the average marriage age of women in America dropped to 20, and was still dropping, into the teens. Fourteen million girls were engaged by 17. The proportion of women attending college in comparison with men dropped from 47 per cent in 1920 to 35 per cent in 1958. A century earlier, women had fought for higher education; now girls went to college to get a husband. By the mid-fifties, 60 per cent dropped out of college to marry, or because they were afraid too much education would be a marriage bar. Colleges built dormitories for "married students," but the students were almost always the husbands. A new degree was instituted for the wives—"Ph.T." (Putting Husband Through).

Then American girls began getting married in high school. And the women's magazines, deploring the unhappy statistics about these young marriages, urged that courses on marriage, and marriage counselors, be installed in the high schools. Girls started going steady at twelve and thirteen, in junior high. Manufacturers put out brassieres with false bosoms of foam rubber for little girls of ten. And an advertisement for a child's dress, sizes 3–6x, in the *New York Times* in the fall of 1960, said: "She Too Can Join the Man-Trap Set."

By the end of the fifties, the United States birthrate was overtaking India's. The birth-control movement, renamed Planned Parenthood, was asked to find a method whereby women who had been advised that a third or fourth baby would be born dead or defective might have it anyhow. Statisticians were especially astounded at the fantastic increase in the number of babies among college women. Where once they had two children, now they had four, five, six. Women who had once wanted careers were now making careers out of having babies. So rejoiced *Life* magazine in a 1956 paean to the movement of American women back to the home.

In a New York hospital, a woman had a nervous breakdown when she found she could not breastfeed her baby. In other hospitals, women dying of cancer refused a drug which research had proved might save their lives: its side effects were said to be unfeminine. "If I have only one life, let me live it as a blonde," a larger-than-life-sized picture of a pretty, vacuous woman proclaimed from newspaper, magazine, and drugstore ads. And across America, three out of every ten women dyed their hair blonde. They ate a chalk called Metrecal, instead of food, to shrink to the size of the thin young models. Department-store buyers reported that American women, since 1939, had become three and four sizes smaller. "Women are out to fit the clothes, instead of vice-versa," one buyer said.

Interior decorators were designing kitchens with mosaic murals and original paintings, for kitchens were once again the center of women's lives. Home sewing became a million-dollar industry. Many women no longer left their homes, except to shop, chauffeur their children, or attend a social engagement with their husbands. Girls were growing up in America without ever having jobs outside the home. In the late fifties, a sociological phenomenon was suddenly remarked: a third of American women now worked, but most were no longer young and very few were pursuing careers. They were married women who held part-time jobs, selling or secretarial, to put their husbands through school, their sons through college, or to help pay the mortgage. Or they were widows supporting families. Fewer and fewer women were entering professional work. The shortages in the nursing, social work, and teaching professions caused crises in almost every American city. Concerned over the Soviet Union's lead in the space race, scientists noted that America's greatest source of unused brainpower was women. But girls would not study physics: it was "unfeminine." A girl refused a science fellowship at Johns Hopkins to take a job in a real-estate office. All she wanted, she said, was what every other American girl wanted—to get married, have four children and live in a nice house in a nice suburb.

The suburban housewife—she was the dream image of the young American women and the envy, it was said, of women all over the world. The American housewife—freed by science and labor-saving appliances from the drudgery, the dangers of childbirth and the illnesses of her grandmother. She was healthy, beautiful, educated, concerned only about her husband, her children, her home. She had found true feminine fulfillment. As a housewife and mother, she was respected as a full and equal partner to man in his world. She was free to choose automobiles, clothes, appliances, supermarkets; she had everything that women ever dreamed of.

In the fifteen years after World War II, this mystique of feminine fulfillment became the cherished and self-perpetuating core of contemporary American culture. Millions of women lived their lives in the image of those pretty pictures of the American suburban housewife, kissing their husbands goodbye in front of the picture window, depositing their stationwagonsful of children at school, and smiling as they ran the new electric waxer over the spotless kitchen floor. They baked their own bread, sewed their own and their children's clothes, kept their new washing machines and dryers running all day. They changed the sheets on the beds twice a week instead of once, took the rug-hooking class in adult education, and pitied their poor frustrated mothers, who had dreamed of having a career. Their only dream was to be perfect wives and mothers; their highest ambition to have five children and a beautiful house, their only fight to get and keep their husbands. They had no thought for the unfeminine problems of the world outside the home; they wanted the men to make the major decisions. They gloried in their role as women, and wrote proudly on the census blank: "Occupation: housewife."

For over fifteen years, the words written for women, and the words women used when they talked to each other, while their husbands sat on the other side of the room and talked shop or politics or septic tanks, were about problems with their children, or how to keep their husbands happy, or improve their children's school, or cook chicken or make slipcovers. Nobody argued whether women were inferior or superior to men; they were simply different. Words like "emancipation" and "career" sounded strange and embarrassing; no one had used them for years. When a Frenchwoman named Simone de Beauvoir wrote a book called *The Second Sex,* an American critic commented that she obviously "didn't know what life was all about," and besides, she was talking about French women. The "woman problem" in America no longer existed.

If a woman had a problem in the 1950's and 1960's, she knew that something must be wrong with her marriage, or with herself. Other women were satisfied with their lives, she thought. What kind of a woman was she if she did not feel this mysterious fulfillment waxing the kitchen floor? She was so ashamed to admit her dissatisfaction that she never knew how many other women shared it. If she tried to tell her husband, he didn't understand what she was talking about. She did not really understand it herself. For over fifteen years women in America found it harder to talk about this problem than about sex. Even the psychoanalysts had no name for it. When a woman went to a psychiatrist for help, as many women did, she would say, "I'm so ashamed," or "I must be hopelessly neurotic." "I don't know what's wrong with women today," a suburban psychiatrist said uneasily. "I only know something is wrong because most of my patients happen to be women. And their problem isn't sexual." Most women with this problem did not go to see a psychoanalyst, however. "There's nothing wrong really," they kept telling themselves. "There isn't any problem."

But on an April morning in 1959, I heard a mother of four, having coffee with four other mothers in a suburban development fifteen miles from New York, say in a tone of quiet desperation, "the problem." And the others knew, without words, that she was not talking about a problem with her husband, or her children, or her home. Suddenly they realized they all shared the same problem, the problem that has no name. They began, hesitantly, to talk about it. Later, after they had picked up their children at nursery school and taken them home to nap, two of the women cried, in sheer relief, just to know they were not alone.

NOW Statement of Purpose, 1966

We, men and women who hereby constitute ourselves as the National Organization for Women, believe that the time has come for a new movement toward true equality for all women in America, and toward a fully equal partnership of the sexes, as part of the world-wide revolution of human rights now taking place within and beyond our national borders.

The purpose of NOW is to take action to bring women into full participation in the mainstream of American society now, exercising all the privileges and responsibilities thereof in truly equal partnership with men.

We believe the time has come to move beyond the abstract argument, discussion and symposia over the status and special nature of women which has raged in America in recent years; the time has come to confront, with concrete action, the conditions that now prevent women from enjoying the equality of opportunity and freedom of choice which is their right as individual Americans, and as human beings.

NOW is dedicated to the proposition that women first and foremost are human beings, who, like all other people in our society, must have the chance to develop their fullest human potential. We believe that women can achieve such equality only by accepting to the full the challenges and responsibilities they share with all other people in our society, as part of the decision-making mainstream of American political, economic and social life.

We organize to initiate or support action, nationally or in any part of this nation, by individuals or organizations, to break through the silken curtain of prejudice and discrimination against women in government, industry, the professions, the churches, the political parties, the judiciary, the labor unions, in education, science, medicine, law, religion and every other field of importance in American society. . . .

There is no civil rights movement to speak for women, as there has been for Negroes and other victims of discrimination. The National Organization for Women must therefore begin to speak.

WE BELIEVE that the power of American law, and the protection guaranteed by the U.S. Constitution to the civil rights of all individuals, must be effectively applied and enforced to isolate and remove patterns of sex discrimination, to ensure equality of opportunity in employment and education, and equality of civil and political rights and responsibilities on behalf of women, as well as for Negroes and other deprived groups.

We realize that women's problems are linked to many broader questions of social justice; their solution will require concerted action by many groups. Therefore, convinced that human rights for all are indivisible, we expect to give active support to the common cause of equal rights for all those who suffer discrimination and deprivation, and we call upon other organizations committed to such goals to support our efforts toward equality for women.

WE DO NOT ACCEPT the token appointment of a few women to high-level positions in government and industry as a substitute for a serious continuing effort to recruit and advance women according to their individual abilities. To this end, we urge American government and industry to mobilize the same resources of ingenuity and command with which they have solved problems of far greater difficulty than those now impeding the progress of women.

WE BELIEVE that this nation has a capacity at least as great as other nations, to innovate new social institutions which will enable women to enjoy true equality of opportunity and responsibility in society, without conflict with their responsibilities as mothers and homemakers. In such innovations, America does not lead the Western world, but lags by decades behind many European countries. We do not accept the traditional assumption that a woman has to choose between marriage and motherhood, on the one hand, and serious participation in industry or the professions on the other. We question the present expectation that all normal women will retire from job or profession for ten or fifteen years, to devote their full time to raising children, only to reenter the job market at a relatively minor level. This in itself is a deterrent to the aspirations of women, to their acceptance into management or professional training courses, and to the very possibility of equality of opportunity or real choice, for all but a few women. Above all, we reject the assumption that these problems are the unique responsibility of each individual woman, rather than a basic social dilemma which society must solve. True equality of opportunity and freedom of choice for women requires such practical and possible innovations as a nationwide network of child-care centers, which will make it unnecessary for women to retire completely from society until their children are grown, and national programs to provide retraining for women who have chosen to care for their own children full time.

WE BELIEVE that it is as essential for every girl to be educated to her full potential of human ability as it is for every boy—with the knowledge that such education is the key to effective participation in today's economy and that, for a girl as for a boy, education can only be serious where there is expectation that it will be used in society. We believe that American educators are capable of devising means of imparting such expectations to girl students. Moreover, we consider the decline in the proportion of women receiving higher and professional education to be evidence of discrimination. This discrimination may take the form of quotas against the admission of women to colleges and professional schools; lack of encouragement by parents, counselors and educators; denial of loans or fellowships; or the traditional or arbitrary procedures in graduate and professional training geared in terms of men, which inadvertently discriminate against women. We believe that the same serious attention must be given to high school dropouts who are girls as to boys.

WE REJECT the current assumptions that a man must carry the sole burden of supporting himself, his wife, and family, and that a woman is automatically entitled to lifelong support by a man upon her marriage, or that marriage, home and family are primarily woman's world and responsibility—hers, to dominate, his to support. We believe that a true partnership between the sexes demands a different concept of marriage, an equitable sharing of the responsibilities of home and children and of the economic burdens of their support. We believe that proper recognition should be given to the economic and social value of homemaking and child care. To these ends, we will seek to open a reexamination of laws and mores governing marriage and divorce, for we believe that the current state of "half-equality" between the sexes discriminates against both men and women, and is the cause of much unnecessary hostility between the sexes.

WE BELIEVE that women must now exercise their political rights and responsibilities as American citizens. They must refuse to be segregated on the basis of sex into separate-and-not-equal ladies' auxiliaries in the political parties, and they must demand representation according to their numbers in the regularly constituted party committees—at local, state, and national levels—and in the informal power structure, participating fully in the selection of candidates and political decision-making, and running for office themselves.

IN THE INTERESTS OF THE HUMAN DIGNITY OF WOMEN, we will protest and endeavor to change the false image of women now prevalent in the mass media, and in the texts, ceremonies, laws, and practices of our major social institutions. Such images perpetuate contempt for women by society and by women for themselves. We are similarly opposed to all policies and practices—in church, state, college, factory, or office—which, in the guise of protectiveness, not only deny opportunities but also foster in women self-denigration, dependence, and evasion of responsibility, undermine their confidence in their own abilities and foster contempt for women.

NOW WILL HOLD ITSELF INDEPENDENT OF ANY POLITICAL PARTY in order to mobilize the political power of all women and men intent on our goals. We will strive to ensure that no party, candidate, President, senator, governor, congressman, or any public official who betrays or ignores the principle of full equality between the sexes is elected or appointed to office. If it is necessary to mobilize the votes of men and women who believe in our cause, in order to win for women the final right to be fully free and equal human beings, we so commit ourselves.

WE BELIEVE THAT women will do most to create a new image of women by *acting* now, and by speaking out in behalf of their own equality, freedom, and human dignity—not in pleas for special privilege, nor in enmity toward men, who are also victims of the current half-equality between the sexes—but in an active, self-respecting partnership with men. By so doing, women will develop confidence in their own ability to determine actively, in partnership with men, the conditions of their life, their choices, their future and their society.

Two Women Activists Consider
Women's Role in the
Civil-Rights Movement and the New Left, 1965

We've talked a lot, to each other and to some of you, about our own and other women's problems in trying to live in our personal lives and in our work as independent and creative people. In these conversations we've found what seem to be recurrent ideas or themes. Maybe we can look at these things many of us perceive, often as a result of insights learned from the movement:

Sex and caste: There seem to be many parallels that can be drawn between treatment of Negroes and treatment of women in our society as a whole. But in particular, women we've talked to who work in the movement seem to be caught up in a common-law caste system that operates, sometimes subtly, forcing them to work around or outside hierarchical structures of power which may exclude them. Women seem to be placed in the same position of assumed subordination in personal situations too. It is a caste system which, at its worst, uses and exploits women.

This is complicated by several facts, among them: 1) The caste system is not institutionalized by law (women have the right to vote, to sue for divorce, etc.); 2) Women can't withdraw from the situation (a la nationalism) or overthrow it; 3) There are biological differences (even though those biological differences are usually discussed or accepted without taking present and future technology into account so we probably can't be sure what these differences mean). Many people who are very hip to the implications of the racial caste system, even people in the movement, don't seem to be able to see the sexual caste system and if the question is raised they respond with: "That's the way it's supposed to be. There are biological differences." Or with other statements which recall a white segregationist confronted with integration.

Women and problems of work: The caste system perspective dictates the roles assigned to women in the movement, and certainly even more to women outside the movement. Within the movement, questions arise in situations ranging from relationships of women organizers to men in the community, to who cleans the freedom house, to who holds leadership positions, to who does secretarial work, and who acts as spokesman for groups. Other problems arise between women with varying degrees of awareness of themselves as being as capable as men but held back from full participation, or between women who see themselves as needing more control of their work than other women demand. And there are problems with relationships between white women and black women.

"Sex and Caste: A Kind of Memo from Casey Hayden and Mary King to a number of other women in the peace and freedom movements," November 18, 1965, in *Personal Politics* by Sara Evans. Copyright © 1979 by Sara Evans. Reprinted by permission of Alfred A. Knopf, Inc.

Women and personal relations with men: Having learned from the movement to think radically about the personal worth and abilities of people
whose role in society had gone unchallenged before, a lot of women in the
movement have begun trying to apply those lessons to their own relations
with men. Each of us probably has her own story of the various results, and
of the internal struggle occasioned by trying to break out of very deeply
learned fears, needs, and self-perceptions, and of what happens when we
try to replace them with concepts of people and freedom learned from the
movement and organizing.

Institutions: Nearly everyone has real questions about those institutions
which shape perspectives on men and women: marriage, child rearing patterns, women's (and men's) magazines, etc. People are beginning to think
about and even to experiment with new forms in these areas.

Men's reactions to the questions raised here: A very few men seem to
feel, when they hear conversations involving these problems, that they have
a right to be present and participate in them, since they are so deeply
involved. At the same time, very few men can respond non-defensively,
since the whole idea is either beyond their comprehension or threatens and
exposes them. The usual response is laughter. That inability to see the whole
issue as serious, as the strait-jacketing of both sexes, and as societally determined often shapes our own response so that we learn to think in their
terms about ourselves and to feel silly rather than trust our inner feelings.
The problems we're listing here, and what others have said about them, are
therefore largely drawn from conversations among women only—and that
difficulty in establishing dialogue with men is a recurring theme among people
we've talked to.

Lack of community for discussion: Nobody is writing, or organizing or
talking publicly about women, in any way that reflects the problems that
various women in the movement come across and which we've tried to touch
above. Consider this quote from an article in the centennial issue of *The
Nation:*

> However equally we consider men and women, the work plans for husbands
> and wives cannot be given equal weight. A woman should not aim for "a
> second-level career" because she is a *woman;* from girlhood on she should
> recognize that, if she is also going to be a wife and mother, she will not
> be able to give as much to her work as she would if single. That is, she
> should not feel that she cannot aspire to directing the laboratory simply
> because she is a woman, but rather because she is also a wife and mother;
> as such, her work as a lab technician (or the equivalent in another field)
> should bring both satisfaction and the knowledge that, through it, she is
> fulfilling an additional role, making an additional contribution.

And that's about as deep as the analysis goes publicly, which is not
nearly so deep as we've heard many of you go in chance conversations.

The reason we want to try to open up dialogue is mostly subjective.
Working in the movement often intensifies personal problems, especially if

we start trying to apply things we're learning there to our personal lives. Perhaps we can start to talk with each other more openly than in the past and create a community of support for each other so we can deal with ourselves and others with integrity and can therefore keep working.

Objectively, the chances seem nil that we could start a movement based on anything as distant to general American thought as a sex-caste system. Therefore, most of us will probably want to work full time on problems such as war, poverty, race. The very fact that the country can't face, much less deal with, the questions we're raising means that the movement is one place to look for some relief. Real efforts at dialogue within the movement and with whatever liberal groups, community women, or students might listen are justified. That is, all the problems between men and women and all the problems of women functioning in society as equal human beings are among the most basic that people face. We've talked in the movement about trying to build a society which would see basic human problems (which are now seen as private troubles), as public problems and would try to shape institutions to meet human needs rather than shaping people to meet the needs of those with power. To raise questions like those above illustrates very directly that society hasn't dealt with some of its deepest problems and opens discussion of why that is so. (In one sense, it is a radicalizing question that can take people beyond legalistic solutions into areas of personal and institutional change.) The second objective reason we'd like to see discussion begin is that we've learned a great deal in the movement and perhaps this is one area where a determined attempt to apply ideas we've learned there can produce some new alternatives.

Feminists Affirm Women's Right to Control Their Own Bodies, 1973

The history of this book, *Our Bodies, Ourselves,* is lengthy and satisfying.

It began in a small discussion group on "women and their bodies" which was part of a women's conference held in Boston in the spring of 1969, one of the first gatherings of women meeting specifically to talk with other women. For many of us it was the very first time we had joined together with other women to talk and think about our lives and what we could do about them. Before the conference was over, some of us decided to keep on meeting as a group to continue the discussion, and so we did.

In the beginning we called ourselves "the doctors group." We had all experienced similar feelings of frustration and anger toward specific doctors and the medical maze in general, and initially we wanted to do something about those doctors who were condescending, paternalistic, judgmental and non-informative. As we talked and shared our experiences with one another, we realized just how much we had to learn about our bodies. So we decided on a summer project—to research those topics which we felt were particularly pertinent to learning about our bodies, to discuss in the group what we had learned, then to write papers individually or in groups of two or three, and finally to present the results in the fall as a course for women on women and their bodies.

As we developed the course we realized more and more that we really *were* capable of collecting, understanding, and evaluating medical information. Together we evaluated our reading of books and journals, our talks with doctors and friends who were medical students. We found we could discuss, question and argue with each other in a new spirit of cooperation rather than competition. We were equally struck by how important it was for us to be able to open up with one another and share our feelings about our bodies. The process of talking was as crucial as the facts themselves. Over time the facts and feelings melted together in ways that touched us very deeply and that is reflected in the changing titles of the course and then the book—from *Women and Their Bodies* to *Women and Our Bodies* to, finally, *Our Bodies, Ourselves.*

When we gave the course we met in any available free space we could get—in day schools, in nursery schools, in churches, in our homes. We wanted the course to stimulate the same kind of talking and sharing that we who had prepared the course had experienced. We had something to say, but we had a lot to learn as well; we did not want a traditional teacher-student relationship. At the end of ten to twelve sessions—which roughly covered the material in the current book—we found that many women felt both eager and competent to get together in small groups and share what they had learned with other women. We saw it as a never-ending process always involving more and more women.

After the first teaching of the course, we decided to revise our initial papers and mimeograph them so that other women could have copies as the course expanded. Eventually we got them printed and bound together in an inexpensive edition published by the New England Free Press. It was fascinating and very exciting for us to see what a constant demand there was for our book. It came out in several editions, a larger number being printed each time, and the time from one printing to the next becoming shorter. The growing volume of requests began to strain the staff of the New England Free Press. Since our book was clearly speaking to many people, we wanted to reach beyond the audience who lived in the area or who were acquainted with the New England Free Press. For wider distribution it made sense to publish our book commercially.

You may want to know who we are. Our ages range from twenty-five to forty-one, most of us are from middle-class backgrounds and have had at least some college education, and some of us have professional degrees. Some of us are married, some of us are separated, and some of us are single. Some of us have children of our own, some of us like spending time with children, and others of us are not sure we want to be with children.

In short, we are both a very ordinary and a very special group, as women are everywhere. We can describe only what life has been for us, though many of our experiences have been shared by other women. We realize that poor and nonwhite women have had greater difficulty in getting accurate information and adequate health care, and have most often been mistreated in the ways we describe in the book. Learning about our womanhood from the inside out has allowed us to cross over some of the socially created barriers of race, color, income and class, and to feel a sense of identity with all women in the experience of being female.

We are eleven individuals and we are a group. (The group has been ongoing for three years, and some of us have been together since the beginning. Others came in at later points. Our current collective has been together for one year.) We know each other well—our weaknesses as well as our strengths. We have learned through good times and bad how to work together (and how not to, as well). We recognize our similarities and differences and are learning to respect each person for her uniqueness. We love each other.

Many, many other women have worked with us on the book. A group of gay women got together specifically to do the chapter on lesbianism. Other chapters were done still differently. For instance, the mother of one woman in the group volunteered to work on menopause with some of us who have not gone through that experience ourselves. Other women contributed thoughts, feelings and comments as they passed through town or passed through our kitchens or workrooms. There are still other voices from letters, phone conversations, and a variety of discussions that are included in the chapters as excerpts of personal experiences. Many women have spoken for themselves in this book, though we in the collective do not agree with all that has been written. Some of us are even uncomfortable with part of the material. We have included it anyway, because we give more weight to accepting that we differ than to our uneasiness. We have been asked why this is exclusively a book about women, why we have restricted our course to women. Our answer is that we are women and, as women, do not consider ourselves experts on men (as men through the centuries have presumed to be experts on us). We are not implying that we think most twentieth-century men are much less alienated from their bodies than women are. But we know it is up to men to explore that for themselves, to come together and share their sense of themselves as we have done. We would like to read a book about men and their bodies.

We are offering a book that can be used in many different ways—individually, in a group, for a course. Our book contains real material about our bodies and ourselves that isn't available elsewhere, and we have tried to present it in a new way—an honest, humane and powerful way of thinking about ourselves and our lives. We want to share the knowledge and power that come with this way of thinking, and we want to share the feelings we have for each other—supportive and loving feelings that show we can indeed help one another grow.

From the very beginning of working together, first on the course that led to this book and then on the book itself, we have felt exhilarated and energized by our new knowledge. Finding out about our bodies and our bodies' needs, starting to take control over that area of our lives, has released for us an energy that has overflowed into our work, our friendships, our relationships with men and women, and for some of us, our marriages and our parenthood. In trying to figure out why this has had such a life-changing effect on us, we have come up with several important ways in which this kind of body education has been liberating for us and may be a starting point for the liberation of many other women.

First, we learned what we learned equally from professional sources—textbooks, medical journals, doctors, nurses—and from our own experiences. The facts were important, and we did careful research to get the information we had not had in the past. As we brought the facts to one another we learned a good deal, but in sharing our personal experiences relating to those facts we learned still more. Once we had learned what the "experts" had to tell us, we found we still had a lot to teach and to learn from one another. For instance, many of us had "learned" about the menstrual cycle in science or biology classes—we had perhaps even memorized the names of the menstrual hormones and what they did. But most of us did not remember much of what we had learned. This time when we read in a text that the onset of menstruation is a normal and universal occurrence in young girls from ages ten to eighteen, we started to talk about our first menstrual periods. We found that, for many of us, beginning to menstruate had not felt normal at all, but scary, embarrassing, mysterious. We realized that what we had been told about menstruation and what we had not been told—even the tone of voice it had been told in—had all had an effect on our feelings about being female. Similarly, the information from enlightened texts describing masturbation as a normal, common sexual activity did not really become our own until we began to pull up from inside ourselves and share what we had never before expressed—the confusion and shame we had been made to feel, and often still felt, about touching our bodies in a sexual way.

Learning about our bodies in this way is an exciting kind of learning, where information and feelings are allowed to interact. It makes the difference between rote memorization and relevant learning, between fragmented pieces of a puzzle and the integrated picture, between abstractions and real knowledge. We discovered that people don't learn very much when they are just passive recipients of information. We found that each individual's response to information was valid and useful, and that by sharing our responses we could develop a base on which to be critical of what the experts tell us. Whatever we need to learn now, in whatever area of our lives, we know more how to go about it.

A second important result of this kind of learning is that we are better prepared to evaluate the institutions that are supposed to meet our health needs—the hospitals, clinics, doctors, medical schools, nursing schools, public health departments, Medicaid bureaucracies and so on. For some of us it was the first time we had looked critically, and with strength, at the existing institutions serving us. The experience of learning just how little control we had over our lives and bodies, the coming together out of isolation to learn from each other in order to define what we needed, and the experience of supporting one another in demanding the changes that grew out of our developing critique—all were crucial and formative political experiences for us. We have felt our potential power as a force for political and social change.

The learning we have done while working on *Our Bodies, Ourselves* has been a good basis for growth in other areas of life for still another reason. For women throughout the centuries, ignorance about our bodies has had one major consequence—pregnancy. Until very recently pregnancies were all but inevitable, biology *was* our destiny—that is, because our bodies are designed to get pregnant and give birth and lactate, that is what all or most of us did. The courageous and dedicated work of people like Margaret Sanger started in the early twentieth century to spread and make available birth control methods that women could use, thereby freeing us from the traditional lifetime of pregnancies. But the societal expectation that a woman above all else will have babies does not die easily. When we first started talking to each other about this, we found that that old expectation had nudged most of us into a fairly rigid role of wife-and-motherhood from the moment we were born female. Even in 1969, when we first started the work that led to this book, we found that many of us were still getting pregnant when we didn't want to. It was not until we researched carefully and learned more about birth-control methods and abortion, about laws governing birth control and abortion, and not until we put all this information together with what it meant to us to be female, that we began to feel we could truly set out to control whether and when we would have babies.

This knowledge has freed us to a certain extent from the constant, energy-draining anxiety about becoming pregnant. It has made our pregnancies better because they no longer happen to us, but we actively choose them and enthusiastically participate in them. It has made our parenthood better because it is our choice rather than our destiny. This knowledge has freed us from playing the role of mother if it is not a role that fits us. It has given us a sense of a large life space to work in, an invigorating and challenging sense of time and room to discover the energies and talents that are in us, to do the work we want to do. And one of the things we most want to do is to help make this freedom of choice, this life span, available to every woman. This is why people in the women's movement have been so active in fighting against the inhumane legal restrictions, the imperfections of available contraceptives, the poor sex education, the highly priced and poorly administered health care that keep too many women from having this crucial control over their bodies.

There is a fourth reason why knowledge about our bodies has generated so much new energy. For us, body education is core education. Our bodies are the physical bases from which we move out into the world; ignorance, uncertainty—even, at worst, shame—about our physical selves create in us an alienation from ourselves that keeps us from being the whole people that we could be. Picture a woman trying to do work and to enter into equal and satisfying relationships with other people—when she feels physically weak because she has never tried to be strong; when she drains her energy trying to change her face, her figure, her hair, her smells, to match some ideal norm set by magazines, movies and TV; when she feels confused and ashamed of the menstrual blood that every month appears from some dark place in her body; when her internal body processes are a mystery to her and surface only to cause her trouble (an unplanned pregnancy, or cervical cancer); when she does not understand or enjoy sex and concentrates her sexual drives into aimless romantic fantasies, perverting and misusing a potential energy because she had been brought up to deny it. Learning to understand, accept, and be responsible for our physical selves, we are freed of some of these preoccupations and can start to use our untapped energies. Our image of ourselves is on a firmer base, we can be better friends and better lovers, better *people,* more self-confident, more autonomous, stronger and more whole.

The Supreme Court Rules on Abortion: *Roe* v. *Wade,* 1973

Mr. Justice [Harry A.] Blackmun delivered the opinion of the Court. . . .

We forthwith acknowledge our awareness of the sensitive and emotional nature of the abortion controversy, of the vigorous opposing views, even among physicians, and of the deep and seemingly absolute convictions that the subject inspires. One's philosophy, one's experiences, one's exposure to the raw edges of human existence, one's religious training, one's attitudes toward life and family and their values, and the moral standards one establishes and seeks to observe, are all likely to influence and to color one's thinking and conclusions about abortion. . . .

The Texas statutes that concern us here are Arts. 1191–1194 and 1196 of the State's Penal Code. These make it a crime to "procure an abortion," as therein defined, or to attempt one, except with respect to "an abortion procured or attempted by medical advice for the purpose of saving the life of the mother." Similar statutes are in existence in a majority of the States. . . .

Jane Roe, a single woman who was residing in Dallas County, Texas, instituted this federal action in March 1970 against the District Attorney of the county. She sought a declaratory judgment that the Texas criminal abortion statutes were unconstitutional on their face, and an injunction restraining the defendant from enforcing the statutes.

Roe alleged that she was unmarried and pregnant; that she wished to terminate her pregnancy by an abortion "performed by a competent, licensed physician, under safe, clinical conditions"; that she was unable to get a "legal" abortion in Texas because her life did not appear to be threatened by the continuation of her pregnancy; and that she could not afford to travel to another jurisdiction in order to secure a legal abortion under safe conditions. She claimed that the Texas statutes were unconstitutionally vague and that they abridged her right of personal privacy, protected by the First, Fourth, Fifth, Ninth, and Fourteenth Amendments. By an amendment to her complaint Roe purported to sue "on behalf of herself and all other women" similarly situated. . . .

The principal thrust of appellant's attack on the Texas statutes is that they improperly invade a right, said to be possessed by the pregnant woman, to choose to terminate her pregnancy. Appellant would discover this right in the concept of personal "liberty" embodied in the Fourteenth Amendment's Due Process Clause; or in personal, marital, familial, and sexual privacy said to be protected by the Bill of Rights . . . or among those rights reserved to the people by the Ninth Amendment, . . .

It perhaps is not generally appreciated that the restrictive criminal abortion laws in effect in a majority of States today are of relatively recent vintage. Those laws, generally proscribing abortion or its attempt at any time during pregnancy except when necessary to preserve the pregnant woman's life, are not of ancient or even of common-law origin. Instead, they derive from statutory changes effected, for the most part, in the latter half of the 19th century. . . . It is undisputed that at common law, abortion performed *before* "quickening"—the first recognizable movement of the fetus *in utero,* appearing usually from the 16th to the 18th week of pregnancy—was not an indictable offense. . . . In this country, the law in effect in all but a few States until mid-19th century was the pre-existing English common law. . . .

Gradually, in the middle and late 19th century the quickening distinction disappeared from the statutory law of most States and the degree of the offense and the penalties were increased. By the end of the 1950's, a large majority of the jurisdictions banned abortion, however and whenever performed, unless done to save or preserve the life of the mother. . . .

It is thus apparent that at common law, at the time of the adoption of our Constitution, and throughout the major portion of the 19th century, abortion was viewed with less disfavor than under most American statutes currently in effect. Phrasing it another way, a woman enjoyed a substantially broader right to terminate a pregnancy than she does in most States today. At least with respect to the early stage of pregnancy, and very possibly without such a limitation, the opportunity to make this choice was present in this country well into the 19th century. Even later, the law continued for some time to treat less punitively an abortion procured in early pregnancy. . . . When most criminal abortion laws were first enacted, the procedure was a hazardous one for the woman. . . . Modern medical techniques have altered this situation. . . . Mortality rates for women undergoing early abortions, where the procedure is legal, appear to be as low as or lower than the rates for normal childbirth. Consequently, any interest of the State in protecting the woman from an inherently hazardous procedure, except when it would be equally dangerous for her to forgo it, has largely disappeared.

Of course, important state interests in the areas of health and medical standards do remain. The State has a legitimate interest in seeing to it that abortion, like any other medical procedure, is performed under circumstances that insure maximum safety for the patient. . . .

The Constitution does not explicitly mention any right of privacy. In a line of decisions, however, . . . the Court has recognized that a right of personal privacy, or a guarantee of certain areas or zones of privacy, does exist under the Constitution. . . . This right of privacy, whether it be founded in the Fourteenth Amendment's concept of personal liberty and restrictions upon state action, as we feel it is, or, as the District Court determined, in the Ninth Amendment's reservation of rights to the people, is broad enough to encompass a woman's decision whether or not to terminate her pregnancy. . . .

We . . . conclude that the right of personal privacy includes the abortion decision, but that this right is not unqualified and must be considered against important state interests in regulation. . . .

In view of all this, we do not agree that, by adopting one theory of life, Texas may override the rights of the pregnant woman that are at stake. We repeat, however, that the State does have an important and legitimate interest in preserving and protecting the health of the pregnant woman, whether she be a resident of the State or a nonresident who seeks medical consultation and treatment there, and that it has still *another* important and legitimate interest in protecting the potentiality of human life. These interests are separate and distinct. Each grows in substantiality as the woman approaches term and, at a point during pregnancy, each becomes "compelling."

With respect to the State's important and legitimate interest in the health of the mother, the "compelling" point, in the light of present medical knowledge, is at approximately the end of the first trimester. This is so because of the now-established medical fact . . . that until the end of the first trimester mortality in abortion may be less than mortality in normal childbirth. It follows that, from and after this point, a State may regulate the abortion procedure to the extent that the regulation reasonably relates to the preservation and protection of maternal health. . . .

This means, on the other hand, that, for the period of pregnancy prior to this "compelling" point, the attending physician, in consultation with his patient, is free to determine, without regulation by the State, that, in his medical judgment, the patient's pregnancy should be terminated. If that decision is reached, the judgment may be effectuated by an abortion free of interference by the State.

With respect to the State's important and legitimate interest in potential life, the "compelling" point is at viability. This is so because the fetus then presumably has the capability of meaningful life outside the mother's womb. State regulation protective of fetal life after viability thus has both logical and biological justifications. If the State is interested in protecting fetal life after viability, it may go so far as to proscribe abortion during that period, except when it is necessary to preserve the life or health of the mother.

Measured against these standards, Art. 1196 of the Texas Penal Code, in restricting legal abortions to those "procured or attempted by medical advice for the purpose of saving the life of the mother," sweeps too broadly. The statute makes no distinction between abortions performed early in pregnancy and those performed later, and it limits to a single reason, "saving" the mother's life, the legal justification for the procedure. The statute, therefore, cannot survive the constitutional attack made upon it here.

Jerry Falwell Sees a
Threat to the American Family, 1980

There are only three institutions God ordained in the Bible: government, the church, and the family. The family is the God-ordained institution of the marriage of one man and one woman together for a lifetime with their biological or adopted children. The family is the fundamental building block and the basic unit of our society, and its continued health is a prerequisite for a healthy and prosperous nation. No nation has ever been stronger than the families within her. America's families are her strength and they symbolize the miracle of America.

Families in search of freedom to educate their children according to religious principles originally settled this land. Families in search of religious freedom, determined to work and enjoy the fruits of their labor, tamed this wild continent and built the highest living standard in the world. Families educating their children in moral principles have carried on the traditions of this free republic. Historically the greatness of America can be measured in the greatness of her families. But in the past twenty years a tremendous change has taken place.

There is a vicious assault upon the American family. More television programs depict homes of divorced or of single parents than depict the traditional family. Nearly every major family-theme TV program openly justifies divorce, homosexuality, and adultery. Some sociologists believe that the family unit, as we know it, could disappear by the year 2000. Increased divorce and remarriage have broken family loyalty, unity, and communications. We find increased insecurity in children who are the victims of divorced parents. Many of these children harden themselves to the possibility of genuine love, for fear that they will be hurt again. Their insulated lives make them poor future candidates for marriage, and many young people have no desire to marry whatsoever. But I believe that most Americans remain deeply committed to the idea of the family as a sacred institution. A minority of people in this country is trying to destroy what is most important to the majority, and the sad fact is that the majority is allowing it to happen. Americans must arise and accept the challenge of preserving our cherished family heritage. . . .

In the war against the family today, we find an arsenal of weapons. The first weapon is the cult of the playboy, the attitude that has permeated our society in these last twenty years. This playboy philosophy tells men that they do not have to be committed to their wife and to their children, but that they should be some kind of a "cool, free swinger." Sexual promiscuity has become the life style of America. The cult of the playboy is more than just a revolution of dirty magazines. It represents a life style that ultimately corrupts the family. Men are satisfying their lustful desires at the expense of family.

The second weapon against the family is the feminist revolution. This is the counterreaction to the cult of the playboy. Many women are saying, "Why should I be taken advantage of by chauvinists? I will get out and do my own thing. I will stand up for my rights. I will have my own dirty magazines." Feminists are saying that self-satisfaction is more important than the family. Most of the women who are leaders in the feminist movement promote an immoral life style.

In a drastic departure from the home, more than half of the women in our country are currently employed. Our nation is in serious danger when motherhood is considered a task that is "unrewarding, unfulfilling, and boring." I believe that a woman's call to be a wife and mother is the highest calling in the world. My wife is proud to be called a housewife. She is dedicated to making a happy and rich life for us and our three children. She does not consider her life work of making my life happy and that of loving and shaping the lives of our precious children inconsequential or demeaning. Women who choose to remain in the home should never feel inferior to those working outside, but should know they are fulfilling God's command for the home. . . .

Many women today say that they must work for economic reasons. Although inflation has placed a financial burden on the family, we are overly concerned about materialistic wealth. Many Americans consider it more important to have several cars in the driveway, a beautiful house, and two color television sets than to have a stable home environment for their children.

Men and women are seeking easy divorces. The October 15, 1979, *U.S. News & World Report* said that demographers estimate that 45 per cent of infants born in 1980 will live in one-parent families for at least part of their childhood. A person's character is determined by the pledges and promises he or she makes. A man or woman who does not keep his or her word can hardly be a good example to children, but thousands of men and women who have made a pledge of marriage, an eternal pledge of marriage, are breaking that promise in front of impressionable children.

Young people are living together today because they have observed parents who thought little of the eternal commitment they made to each other in their marriage vows. Couples living together cannot experience, however hard they try, the intimacy, security, and genuine love of a stable marriage in a relationship that is anything less than 100 per cent commitment. Parents are failing to teach their children a sense of commitment to relationships. Only marriage fulfills basic human needs for security and love. . . .

The answer to stable families with children who grow up to be great leaders in our society and who themselves have stable homes will not come from, as Judy Mann states, more part-time work for fathers and mothers, or parental leaves of absence, or thirty-hour weeks, or parental co-operatives and other forms of sharing childraising responsibilities. It will come only as men and women in America get in a right relationship to God and His principles for the home. . . .

Scripture declares that God has called the father to be the spiritual leader in his family. The husband is not to be the dictator of the family, but the spiritual leader. There is a great difference between a dictator and a leader. People follow dictators because they are forced to do so. They follow leaders because they want to. Good husbands who are godly men are good leaders. Their wives and children want to follow them and be under their protection. The husband is to be the decisionmaker and the one who motivates his family with love. The Bible says that husbands are to love their wives even as Christ also loved the church and gave Himself for it. A man is to be a servant to his family while at the same time being a leader. A husband and father is first of all to be a provider for his family. He is to take care of their physical needs and do this honestly by working and earning an income to meet those needs. Then he is to be a protector. He is to protect them not only from physical harm but from spiritual harm as well. He is to protect them from television programs and from magazines that would hurt them. Child abuse involves much more than physical abuse. We have little children today who are growing up in homes where mothers and fathers literally hate each other. Those children are living in a constant perpetual hate war that is destroying them. A father has a God-given responsibility to lead his family in their worship of God. A father is to be a godly example to his wife and children; he must be consistently living a good life style before his family. He is to pray with his family and read to them from the Word of God. A man cannot do these things if he does not know Jesus Christ as his Lord and Savior. The Bible says, "But as many as received him, to them gave he power to become the sons of God, even to them that believe on his name." (Jn. 1:12) The love of God is available to every man, and God has made an offer to us and asked us to receive the gift of salvation. Until men are in right relationship with God, there is no hope for righting our families of our nation. Because we have weak men we have weak homes, and children from these homes will probably grow up to become weak parents leading even weaker homes.

Ellen Goodman Contrasts
Two Generations of Women's Lives, 1989

The conversation began, as many of them do, with the following phrase: When we were your age . . . .

The group around the dinner table were women, two generations of them. The topic was relationships and pretty soon we came to the edge of the generation gap.

When we were your age, a single woman couldn't get birth control.

When we were your age, abortion was illegal.

When we were your age, sex was a very risky business.

When we were your age, all of our friends were thinking about marriage.

The four younger women in their college garb of sweaters and pants leaned forward to listen. It was late and we had met them in the city for wine and pasta. But suddenly, it was as if these young women were in nursery school and we were the adults who came to tell them a story they'd never heard.

One of the older women wondered gently if this was what the experts meant by cultural illiteracy. Her guests were women born during the years just before and after Bobby Kennedy was shot. On a pop quiz, they couldn't identify Da Nang, or name a member of the Nixon Cabinet, or define "Clean for Gene." All they knew of pre-sexual-revolution America was what they had seen in *Dirty Dancing*.

The other woman was sure her young dining companions had heard all this before, but it just hadn't registered. What is it that they say about sex talks between adults and children? Answer what is asked, no more, no less. The young will find out what they need to know. In their twenties, these young finally needed to know about then and now. When we were their age.

But as the evening wore on from wine to coffee, it became apparent to both of the delegates from the older generation that we were talking from one vantage point and they were listening from another. We were telling tales from the bad old days. They were listening with nostalgia. We were sure that they had much more freedom than we'd had. They were not.

I have thought about this exchange more than once since that dinner. Thought about the new realities of these young lives. About the brief blip of freedom—for better and worse—that can be seen receding. About what it's like to be twentysomething.

We were denied access to birth control by the law. Their access is now limited by anxiety. The pill that eased so many minds of short-term worries about pregnancy now comes with a set of long-term worries about breast cancer.

Legal abortion assured women that their lives would not be changed irrevocably by a single accident or error, one act of passion or victimization. Now that, too, is at risk. In the morning paper, there is a pro-choice ad that says: "After 16 years of safety, time is running out."

Sex and safety do not come in the same package. What does it mean to be twentysomething in the AIDS era? What does fear do to sexuality? Some women find it easier to say no than to say "condoms." Others wake up the morning after wondering not if they are pregnant, but if they are infected.

As for young marriages, it is an article of faith among my generation that it is better to wait than to end up, as we often did, divorced. It is an article of faith among mothers that their daughters should start careers first rather than wake up, as we did, unskilled.

But the pressure on the women to plan their lives with split-second timing and an eye on the biological clock begins younger and younger. At twentysomething, they look ahead, as we did not, and see their thirty-something sisters who are often stressed or lonely or in line at the fertility clinic.

From their vantage point, an early marriage may seem less like a risk than a shelter. Even in this age, they are the keepers of sexuality and fertility who feel many of these pressures more than the men in their lives.

Does this all sound too worrisome? If the quartet we dined with are any example, the younger generation of women is more self-confident, stronger, far more introspective than mine. They don't take much for granted. They don't live by a set program.

But it is not an easy time. Not at all. And sometimes I wonder how this generation, more pressured than you might imagine, will fill in the blanks as they tell their own children, "When I was your age . . ."

☒ E S S A Y S

In the first essay, the concluding chapter of her book *Homeward Bound: American Families in the Cold War Era* (1988), historian Elaine Tyler May of the University of Minnesota explores the ideology of postwar domesticity. Just as Cold War anticommunism sustained the new foreign policies of the 1940s and 1950s, she argues, so did an ideology of "domestic containment" mold American family life. The breakup of the Cold War consensus in the 1960s was similarly accompanied by the emergence of a new feminism. In the second article, excerpted from their book *Intimate Matters: A History of Sexuality in America* (1988), historians John D'Emilio of the University of North Carolina, Greensboro, and Estelle Freedman of Stanford University place more emphasis on the social and cultural context of the new feminism than on its political setting, and on its powerful role in reshaping the nation's understanding of sexuality.

The Origins of the New Feminism

ELAINE TYLER MAY

The thought of spending two weeks with two children in a close dark hole [family bomb shelter] was too horrible to think of and we knew we had to do something. Now that we women have started we will no longer be content to be dull uninformed housewives.

—Participant at a meeting of Women Strike for Peace, 1963

The politics of the cold war and the ideology and public policies that it spawned were crucial in shaping postwar family life and gender roles. As

Americans emerged from years of depression and war, they yearned for an abundant life freed from hardship. Yet they also worried about the very developments that promised to free them from the constraints of the past: consumerism, women's emancipation, and technological advances. Contained within the home, these liberating but also potentially dangerous trends might be tamed, where they could contribute to happiness. In private life as well as in foreign policy, containment seemed to offer the key to security.

With security as the common thread, the cold war ideology and the domestic revival reinforced each other. The powerful political consensus that supported cold war policies abroad and anticommunism at home fueled conformity to the suburban family ideal. In turn, the domestic ideology encouraged private solutions to social problems and further weakened the potential for challenges to the cold war consensus. Personal adaptation, rather than political resistance, characterized the era. But postwar domesticity never fully delivered on its promises. The baby-boom children who grew up in suburban homes abandoned the containment ethos when they came of age. As young adults in the 1960s, they challenged both the imperatives of the cold war and the domestic ideology that came with it. At the same time, they forged new paths to pursue the unfulfilled dreams of their parents.

When many baby boomers were still infants, however, domestic containment began to crumble under its own weight. Gradually, in the early 1960s, an increasing number of white middle-class Americans began to question the private therapeutic approach to solving social problems. Among the first to criticize the status quo were postwar parents themselves. In 1963, Betty Friedan published her exposé of domesticity, *The Feminine Mystique*. Friedan gave a name to the "problem that has no name" for career homemakers. A postwar wife and mother herself, Friedan spoke directly to women like those in the Kelly Longitudinal Study, who had lived according to the domestic containment ideology. She urged them to break away from their domestic confines, go back to school, pursue careers, and revive the vision of female independence that had been alive before World War II. *The Feminine Mystique* became an immediate bestseller and created a national sensation. The book enabled discontented women across the country to find their voices. It was as if someone was finally willing to say that the emperor had no clothes; soon a chorus joined in support. Hundreds of readers wrote to Friedan, telling their stories. These personal testimonies reveal the stated and unstated messages that this generation of parents gave their children.

The letters to Friedan reveal widespread disenchantment among women who had struggled to conform to the prevailing familial norm. Some of the writers were children of activist parents who had fought for equal rights in the early part of the century. Nearly all expressed the hope that their children would avoid the domestic trap in which they found themselves. One spoke harshly of herself and her peers, who embraced domestic containment:

My life spans the two eras—the ebb tide of feminism and the rise of the "mystique." My parents were products of the early twentieth century Liberalism and believed firmly that everyone—poor, Negroes, and women too—had a right to have a 'rendezvous with Destiny'. . . . My feeling of betrayal is not directed against society so much as at the women who beat the drums for the 'passionate journey' into darkness. . . . My undiluted wrath is expended on those of us who were educated, and therefore privileged, who put on our black organza nightgowns and went willingly, joyfully, without so much as a backward look at the hard-won freedoms handed down to us by the feminists (men and women). The men in my experience, were the interested by-standers, bewildered, amused, and maybe a bit joyful at having two mommies at home—one for the children and one for themselves."

She ended with a note that was echoed in many others: "My children grew up in the mystique jungle but somehow escaped it."

Another letter writer described herself as

. . . the mother of five and the wife of a successful partner in an investment banking firm. In seeking that something "more" out of life, I have tried large doses of everything from alcohol to religion, from a frenzy of sports activities to PTA . . . to every phase of church work . . . Each served its purpose at the time, but I suddenly realized that none had any real future. Our children are all in school except for the baby. . . . However, I felt that if I waited until she's in school I'll be too close to forty to learn any new tricks. I've seen too many women say they would "do something" when the last child went to school. The something has usually been bridge, bowling or drinking.

A Mount Holyoke graduate who joined the "stampede back to the nest" described her path into domesticity: "I entered graduate school at Yale, met a man, left school, and married in 1951. I have since then moved thirteen times, lived in eight states, had four miscarriages and produced two children." But she also struggled at home and alone to become a painter. So "finally, when I fill out the income tax now, it is occupation: Painter, not housewife." For this woman, the key was in her background: "My one advantage over the rest of my generation is, I suppose, the fact that I was raised in a family of feminists. . . . I still tend, belatedly and belligerently, to champion women's rights. The cloying and sentimental public effort of the last decade to raise the prestige of the home and represent it as demanding all that we have to give has more than once precipitated me into incoherent outrage." Nevertheless, it had also precipitated her out of graduate school and into domesticity.

Many of these educated women responded to Friedan's book by calling for a revival of political activism and lashing out at experts who promoted domesticity. Psychologists who endorsed the containment ideal were the targets of much of this wrath. In a six-page letter, a graduate of Cornell University with a master's degree—a mother of two married to a physician—complained, "Since scientific findings reveal the strong effect of the child's environment upon the child, the poor mother has been made to replace God in her omnipotence. It is the terror of this misinterpreted omnipotence that in many cases is keeping women home. I still remember the tear-stained face of a brilliant young woman economist who had earned a Ph.D. in her field when she had to give up a newly discovered exciting job because her pediatrician convinced her that her six- and three-year-old children would become social menaces without her presence 24 hours a day." She then quoted a school official who "politely drawled, 'Show me a delinquent child and I'll show you a working mother.' " A Vassar graduate also questioned the wisdom of experts. She wrote of going to an alumnae counselor who told her, "Go back to your kitchen and stay there and make jam!" Drawing on the language of the 1950s, she recalled, "I was a sissy—I paid attention to her! . . . I wonder how many other frustrated housewives have been similarly discouraged . . . by such lamentable suggestions?"

One of the most powerful indictments of the therapeutic model came from an occupant of a mental institution. She explained that she never married because, as a college sophomore, she "became interested in a great variety of things more important than electric waxers." Still, she felt she was affected by the domestic ideology in her "decision not to take fourth-year high school math for fear of being called a brain, and in a more important failure to ever make a real and substantial career choice. During college, I came close to marrying for security's sake, but at the last minute I called the wedding off; the world seemed so much bigger than split-level houses and I thought I had better start off to see it, which I did. . . . But when I began to think about marriage again at the ripe old age of 25, I found it was already too late: most of my contemporaries were already on the 3rd child and too busy mowing lawns and buying things to be much interested in existentialism or the political situation in Algeria."

Next she went to Europe where she had a series of love affairs with European men who were "much less fazed by my 'aggressive and competitive' personality than most of the American M.D.s and Ph.D.s that I had known." Finally, she returned home "to make the fatal mistake of embarking on psychoanalysis which . . . had the effect of landing me in my present residence: inside a mental hospital." She claimed that her "crackup" was due, in part, to her belief that "it was immoral not to be interested in matters such as poverty and the bomb." She believed that she had "wasted a life throwing tin spears at other people's electric dishwashers." At the end of her letter, she proposed some practical solutions to the problems that plagued her peers: later marriage, more sexual experimentation, divorce "as a reflection of the fact that some individuals do change over time" rather than "a sign of hopeless neuroticism or failure to adjust to one's sex role." She argued that "love and security are simply not the same thing. Security can come from many kinds of social relationships . . . among which marriage is only one, from continued contact with one's primary kin, from friendships, or from socially meaningful work." This nonconformist closed with a telling remark: "The price of deviating for me turned out to be an awfully high one but, nevertheless, the aim was real only because the bomb really does exist and hangs over the suburbs."

Other readers noticed other menaces hanging over the suburbs. One suburban housewife described ten of her neighbors whose problems ranged from hysteria to alcoholism. She wrote that "the only normal, happy one" was "a brilliant 46 year old teacher. . . . Her teenage daughter is a beautiful girl, a Merit scholarship finalist, who wants to be a mother!" As for herself, she claimed to be "a compulsive eater, have fits of extreme depression, once seriously considered suicide. I have an I.Q. in the 145–150 range." While an honors student in college, "I 'caught' a husband at 19, married him on my twentieth birthday, quit school pregnant, and now have six children! I am the typical stay-at-home, domineering mother and wife. I love my children yet I hate them, have actually wished them dead."

Not all the letters were so harsh, yet most agreed with Friedan that women suffered more than men from the effects of domesticity. Nevertheless, many readers thought that Friedan had slighted the oppressive nature of male gender roles. One wrote, "When I think of some of the problems the men students faced, I realize that they too suffer enormous stress and confusion. Don't both images have to be changed before a woman's situation truly improves?" Echoing similar sentiments, a writer from Far Rockaway, New York, recognized the connection between boredom at work and frustration at home: "What is wrong with the women trapped in the Feminine Mystique is what's wrong with men trapped in the Rat Race. . . . Isn't it true, that one of the problems, the biggest really, of our present day society is that there isn't enough meaningful creative work for *anyone* these days? Isn't that one of the reasons fathers are taking their parental role with the seriousness of a career?" Another chimed in, "I would very much like to see a book for the sons which does for them what yours does for the daughters." Added a 1951 college graduate who married in her senior year and ended up divorced with two children after six years, "How about the poor 'Male Mystique?' Seriously, they too have problems—'real men' so seldom match the popularly accepted image." An assistant professor of home economics argued, "The 'anomie' that you describe is not restricted to middle-class college-trained women. It is shared by middle-class men and women, but because the men are more absorbed in business and professions, they are less likely to find their way to the psychiatrist's couch."

Friedan's book sparked readers to comment not only on the connection between women's and men's fate, but between domesticity and cold war politics. One woman believed that political activism was the only way to bring women out of "their cozy cocoons in America," but she also perceived that challenges to women's roles would be seen as un-American. Women would need to "make determined efforts to free themselves," she noted, "and they may expect hostility from conservative elements politically as well as from their fellow timid sisters and timid men. I am not advocating that women become Communist sympathizers, but I am expecting that progressive women will be so labelled." One reader framed her response in a larger political context: "I should say that roots of *both* the Feminine Mystique *and* the tiresomeness of so many children could be traced to larger things like the cold war and the Bomb, and all the implications of same."

The common thread that linked those who responded to Friedan's book was their hope for their children. These postwar parents wanted to leave a different legacy to their children than the one provided by the model of their own lives. One wrote, "I want [my daughter] to grow up in a society where she will have a comfortable and important place." Another urged mothers "to help their daughters to avoid the traps into which they have already fallen." A housewife who was driven "very close to severe emotional illness" saved her sanity by going into business, but she had a "guilty feeling" for five years. She was one of many "parents who want to avoid these problems in their children. . . . It would be a crime to let another generation go as mine has; they would never know anything else! . . . I hope one day, when my daughter is older . . . perhaps she will understand enough that she will avoid becoming a miserable housewife!" One reader who described herself as "a drop-out from Oberlin College after two years to marry in 1947 . . . a victim of the Feminine Mystique . . . the mother of five" hoped that her daughter would avoid the "servile feeling" she experienced. "How can we help our daughters to avoid making the mistake of following the crowd into early marriage?"

Many of the daughters of these women got the message. Some of the early baby-boom children were already coming of age when Friedan's book appeared. They responded in ways that differed from the older readers. One young woman, reared during the era of domestic containment, resented the fact that her mother had not been a full-time homemaker. While her friends' mothers were home waiting for them after school with milk and cookies, her mother was completing her education. She decided that she would never deprive her own children that way. She was about to graduate from college when she suddenly began to question her goals. She confessed to Friedan that she had been desperate about marriage. "And, of course, my marriage would be ideal," she wrote. "Unlike my mother, who is back at school finishing her degree, I would be the *ideal* wife—unaggressive and feminine, subordinate—you know, a kind of nice ball of fluff for a rock of a man."

Gradually she came to a new realization: "These occasional thoughts, my love for my roommate entering medical school next fall, my confusion over Mom's 'home abandonment,' and my love for both books and children caused a kind of pervading uncertainty about my future that I could not shake. In the last few months, I found it hard to be patient, sympathetic, cheerful—hard to be anything but either grasping or weeping." Expressing remarkable insight into the sexual containment ethos, she continued, "And to top it off, my boyfriend and I nearly went too far (as they say) supported by *my* anxious feelings that he was all there was to hang on to, and the only future. I began to wonder, in light of my behavior, what was the matter with me anyway." She finally decided to go to graduate school, with the goal of teaching college English or editing children's books.

This college student shifted gears in time to avoid fulltime domesticity, but others were well along the path before they discovered that it did not lead to paradise. A 26-year-old mother of two sent Friedan the saga of her life:

> For the last few years, I have been on the "old housekeeping merry-go-round." . . . I cleaned and I cleaned . . . and then I cleaned some more! All day—every day. My mother had returned to teaching school when I was twelve, and I had resented it, and consequently vowed that when I

married and had children I would make it my vocation. I was quite convinced that I was very happy with my role in life as we had our own home and my husband is a good husband and father and a very sufficient provider. However, one night last November, all Hell broke loose in my psyche. I was sitting calmly reading when I became overwhelmed with waves of anxiety. I couldn't imagine what was happening. . . . I visited my family doctor. He put me on tranquilizers and diagnosed it as a mild state of anxiety. However there was no explanation. . . ."

She went on to relate her happy childhood, her college education that she ended to marry, and her job as a secretary that ended after eleven months when her first child was born. "I see now . . . I chose security over everything else." Finally, she went to see a psychiatrist. Like many other professionals at the time, his treatment was geared toward improving her mental state through drugs to help her better adapt to her situation. Rather than help her to alter the conditions that caused her emotional problems, the psychiatrist changed her tranquilizers. Four days later, she asked to go to the hospital and spent eleven days in a psychiatric ward.

Ultimately, it was not the medical experts but a friend who suggested what was causing "the nervousness and crying spells and sleeplessness" that had become "unbearable." Her friend "volunteered that the trouble was with my marriage." She and her husband began to see a marriage counselor who was a psychologist. She told him, "I felt I had something more to offer the world and wanted to do something about it." He suggested that she go back to school, which she did. "I now have a goal and no longer feel like a vegetable!" She discovered that the problem was not with her marriage; it was with her circumscribed life. But through it all, with the exception of the last psychologist she consulted, the experts were decidedly unhelpful.

Many of the women who wrote to Friedan were those who could respond to her call for self-realization through education and careers. They were affluent. If married, they had husbands who provided an income that was adequate enough to allow them to develop outside interests for self-fulfillment. But there were others who found Friedan's message troubling. It was fine to have ambitions, but it was another matter to work out of necessity, face a sex-segregated job market, and do double duty at home as well.

One woman expressed her irritation at "the false emphasis that is placed on the entire matter of women fulfilling themselves through a career. The vast majority of working women don't have careers. We have jobs, just like men. We work for money to buy things that our families need. If we're lucky, we like our jobs, and find some satisfaction in doing them well, but it is hard to hold a commercial job, raise a family and keep a house." Speaking for many of her peers, she continued:

> Most of us would be delighted to chuck the wage earning back in our husbands' laps and devote ourselves exclusively to homemaking and community projects. We worry about the children while we're at work. We don't really like to throw the last load of clothes in the washer at 11:30 P.M., and set the alarm for 6:00 so we can iron a blouse for a school age daughter, fix breakfast and school lunches all at the same time, do as much

housework as possible before bolting for the office, and face the rest of it, and the grocery shopping and preparing dinner when we get home. This isn't our idea of fulfillment. It doesn't make us more interesting people or more stimulating companions for our husbands. It just makes us very, very tired.

Describing the realities that prompted her to seek employment, this woman explained why employed wives were often "pretty good sports." She wrote, "Our husbands feel bad enough about not being able to handle the whole job without our financial help. Do you think we're going to say right out, 'My Joe just can't put five kids through college, and then Sue needed braces last year, and Johnny will need them, too, and the washer had to be replaced, and Ann was ashamed to bring friends home because the living room furniture was such a mess, so I went to work.' "

Another employed wife was not as good a sport. "Believe me," she wrote, "a modern woman of today would have to be *four* women to be everything that is expected of her." This 37-year-old mother of three had two years of college. She had held jobs on and off since her marriage. "My husband wants me to work not for the satisfaction I might get out of working, but for the extra money *he* will have for himself. . . . *But,* how about the extra burden it would put on me? I would go out to work if possible, but I cannot do that and come home to a house full of screaming kids, dishes piled in the sink, and mountains of laundry to do. It is no fun to come home and see the sweet, dear, lazy bum asleep on the couch after being on my feet all day. He still likes his home-made pies, cakes, and appetizing meals."

She continued with a history of her work roles: "I have worked in stores; the post-office; given dinners for a pot and pan outfit; minded children; and sold things door-to-door. At present, I take in sewing and ironing. . . . If I work, then my housework suffers and I get told about that. I would like nothing better than to just do my own work, have some time to myself once in a while so I could just go down-town once in a while without having someone else's work staring at me. I get very tired of reading about women working outside the home. . . . I cannot divide myself into more than one person. . . . I have plenty to occupy my time and I happen to enjoy being a house-wife."

This woman's bitterness against the demands of double duty was directed largely toward her husband. Her anger was intense: "My husband . . . thinks it's great for women to work, but until men get some of their Victorian ideas out of their heads then I am staying home. Unless he would be willing to help with the housework then I cannot go to work. He thinks he would lose some of his masculinity if anyone saw him hanging out the wash, or washing dishes. And if he *had* to give up any of his fishing or hunting or running around visiting his buddies to keep an eye on the kids, well, I'm not killing myself for the almighty dollar."

As these letters indicate, domestic containment was not going to die a quick or natural death. Yet it was clearly doomed from its own internal contradictions. Betty Friedan spoke for a generation whose children would later be credited with initiating a decade of political and social upheaval, but many of their parents had paved the way. Even those who thought that it was too late to change their own ways and routines knew it was not too late for their children. They encouraged their children—implicitly if not explicitly—to follow new paths. Frustrated women and exhausted men provided ambiguous role models for children hoping to avoid the discontent of their mothers and the pressure and ill health the stresses of the work place had inflicted on their fathers.

Still, change came slowly. In the early 1960s, it was not immediately obvious that a unique historical era was coming to an end. Signs that the postwar consensus was beginning to crack were hardly more visible than they had been in the fifties: a few voices of dissent from the intelligentsia, the growing popularity of counterculture heroes such as Elvis Presley and James Dean, and the spread of the civil rights movement from black activists in the South to northern whites. Oral contraceptives first became available in 1960, but they did not immediately bring about a change in behavior, even though years later, many would credit (or blame) "The Pill" for the "sexual revolution." Most cultural signs still pointed toward the cold war consensus at home and abroad, and the ideology of domesticity was still alive and well.

Although John F. Kennedy's election to the presidency in 1960 signalled the rise to power of a new, younger generation, Kennedy himself did little immediately to challenge the status quo after his close victory over Eisenhower's vice president, Richard M. Nixon. Aside from his youthful appearance and ethnic background, Kennedy represented cold war militance and masculine authority that was in tune with the American establishment. With his stylish wife at his side and his two small children, he seemed to embody the virtues of the American domestic ideal par excellence: the tough cold warrior who was also a warm family man.

Nevertheless, Kennedy's style and rhetoric, emphasizing vigor and the promise of change, encouraged Americans to embrace political activism and risk. Kennedy's famous inaugural challenge, "Ask not what your country can do for you; ask what you can do for your country," invited individual political engagement and implied that each person could make a difference in creating a better society. Shortly after Kennedy's election, the frustrations and resentments that had been expressed in the fifties not only publicly by black civil rights activists, artists, intellectuals, and the "beats," but privately by many members of the white middle class, began to surface.

On November 1, 1961, 50,000 American housewives walked out of their homes and jobs in a massive protest, "Women Strike for Peace." These activists were among the first postwar middle-class whites to organize against the social and political status quo. Several of the leaders of the strike were part of a small group of feminists who had worked on behalf of women's rights throughout the forties and the fifties. According to *Newsweek,* the strikers "were perfectly ordinary looking women. . . . They looked like the women you would see driving ranch wagons, or shopping at the village market, or attending PTA meetings . . . many [were] wheeling baby buggies or strollers." Within a year their numbers grew to several hundred thousand.

Anticommunists worried that Women Strike for Peace signaled that "the pro-Reds have moved in on our mothers and are using them for their own purposes," and the Federal Bureau of Investigation kept the group under surveillance from its inception in 1961. The following year, the leaders of Women Strike for Peace were called before the House Un-American Activities Committee. Under questioning, these women spoke as mothers, claiming that saving American children from nuclear extinction was the essence of "Americanism," thereby turning the ideology of domesticity against the assumptions of the cold war. These women carried the banner of motherhood into politics, much like their reformist Victorian sisters in the last century. But their ability to attack the cold war with domesticity as their tool and make a mockery of the congressional hearings indicates that the familial–cold war consensus was beginning to lose its grip.

Increasing political pressure resulted in several important new public policies that challenged the status quo. In 1961, President Kennedy established the President's Commission on the Status of Women, chaired appropriately by an activist from the 1930s, Eleanor Roosevelt. Within the next three years, Congress passed the Equal Pay Act and Title VII of the Civil Rights Act (which prohibited discrimination on the basis of sex, as well as race, color, religion, and national origin), and the United States and the Soviet Union signed the first treaty banning the atmospheric testing of nuclear weapons.

While these policies were taking shape, Students for a Democratic Society (SDS), inspired largely by the civil rights movement, gained thousands of members in chapters across the country. Out of the student movement came the antiwar movement and the new feminism. By the late sixties, hundreds of thousands of young activists mobilized against the gender assumptions as well as the cold war policies that had prevailed since World War II.

The simultaneous attack on domestic containment and the cold war ideology also found expression in the popular culture. Within a few months of the publication of *The Feminine Mystique* came Stanley Kubrick's film, *Dr. Strangelove: Or, How I Learned to Stop Worrying and Love the Bomb,* a biting satire that equated the madness of the cold war with Americans' unresolved sexual neuroses. Such attacks against the sanctity of the postwar domestic ideology and the politics of the cold war would have been risky endeavors ten years earlier. The film probably would have been suppressed and its creators called before the House Un-American Activities Committee. By the early sixties, however, although the cold war was still in full force, and some viewers found the film offensive and unAmerican, critics as well as audiences were, for the most part, wildly enthusiastic.

By the end of the decade, the new feminist movement had pushed beyond Betty Friedan's call for self-realization into a full-fledged assault on sexism in all its forms, organized by younger women who emerged from their activism in the civil rights movement and the New Left with newly discovered skills and strengths. The new feminists demanded access to professional occupations and skilled jobs, protested low wages, and worked for pay equity. They formed consciousness-raising groups all over the country, challenged the gender division of labor in the home, and railed against the sexual double standard. In a 1970 survey of women entering an open-admission, tuition-free public university, most saw their future role as "married career woman with children"—a vast change from the 1950s when most women of all classes saw their future career as homemaker. (By the 1980s, college women would be as career oriented as college men.) Young middle-class men also began to rebel. They reacted against the rigidity of male gender expectations by growing their hair long, rejecting the "grey flannel suit" for flowered shirts and beads, and resisting the draft that would force them to fight on behalf of cold war principles they did not endorse.

As these political movements gained momentum, public opinion remained resistant to change. Polls taken during the years that gave rise to widespread criticism of the status quo indicate that mainstream Americans continued to uphold the political consensus forged during the forties and fifties. In 1960, the majority of those polled were willing to pay higher taxes to keep the United States ahead in the arms race, and favored public funding for bomb shelters. Although atmospheric testing was banned in 1963 after a flurry of protest, testing continued underground, with little public resistance. Throughout most of the decade, the cold war continued to top the list of people's concerns.

Conservative attitudes toward sex and gender also prevailed. In 1965, 80 percent of those polled believed that schools should prohibit boys from wearing their hair long. A 1966 poll to determine the "ideal" family size yielded results that matched surveys taken in 1945 and 1957: the most common response was four or more children, given by 35 percent of those polled. It was not until 1971 that the figure dropped markedly, to 23 percent. In 1968, three out of four of those polled believed the nation's morals were getting worse, and as late as 1969, more than two-thirds believed that premarital sex was wrong.

Nevertheless, behavior was changing. 1960 signified a demographic watershed. The age at marriage began to rise after decades of decline. The birthrate began to dwindle as the first baby boomers reached childbearing age; within a decade, it was at an all-time low and still plummeting. The marriage rate also declined, as more people remained single or lived together as couples, families, and households without marriage. The divorce rate, after more than a decade of stability, began to rise gradually in the early sixties and then dramatically in the late sixties, skyrocketing to unprecedented heights in the early 1970s.

Critics of the youths of the 1960s complained that the family-centered ethic of "togetherness" gave way to the hedonistic celebration of "doing your own thing." But the moral distance between the baby boomers and their parents is a matter of some debate. The baby boomers continued to pursue the quest for meaning through intimacy that had been at the heart of the containment ethos, but they gave up on containment. Many abandoned the old containers: the traditional family, home-centered consumerism, marriage-centered sex, and cold-war centered politics. The youth culture, as well as the booming economy, encouraged them to be risk takers in ways that their security-oriented parents found unthinkable.

Spending became less home centered. Although some observers labeled the rebellious middle-class youths "antimaterialist," the younger generation did not give up on consumerism. They simply took it outside the home. Expenditures for housing and household operations, which had increased in the postwar years, leveled off in the 1960s, while recreational expenditures, which had been stable in the 1950s, accelerated in the 1960s. Spending was hardly out of fashion, but money was used for more individualistic, less familial, purposes.

Sexual containment also lost its power as a behavioral code, as intercourse outside marriage became the rule. Those who disapproved of premarital sex dropped from 68 percent in 1969 to 48 percent by 1973. The birth control pill undoubtedly made it easier and safer to have a sexual relationship without being married. Its availability was not the impetus for initiating those relationships, however, since most unmarried women did not use the Pill (or any form of birth control, for that matter) during their first intercourse experience. Time-honored sexual attitudes lingered long after behavior changed; as late as the 1970s, the majority of unmarried college students who had engaged in sexual intercourse disapproved of premarital sex. Although sexual containment may have disappeared, guilt and regret did not. Baby boomers did not abandon the quest for intimacy and sexual fulfillment; they simply abandoned the marital imperative.

Along with sex, living together no longer depended on marriage. In the late 1960s, the *New York Times* claimed that "cohabitation" (unmarried couples living together) was limited to a "tiny minority" within "the dissident youth subculture—the intellectual, politically liberal to radical, from middle- and upper-middle class backgrounds, anti-materialistic and anti-Establishment." The phenomenon became much more commonplace in the 1970s. During that decade, the number of unmarried couples who were living together tripled; among those aged 25 and under with no children, it increased eightfold. Although living together usually represented a postponement rather than a rejection of marriage, it changed the pattern of dating and mating that had characterized earlier decades. The marital-heterosexual imperative was further eroded by the increasing visibility and political activism of gay men and lesbians, who challenged prevailing definitions of sexual "normality" and called for the right of free choice in matters of sexual preference and behavior.

Marriage became much less "normative" than it had been. In the late 1970s, only 62 percent of all households included a married couple and only one-third contained two parents and children under age 18; 22 percent of all households consisted of people living alone. Compared to their parents, baby boomers were less inclined to scale down their expectations to sustain unsatisfying unions. As divorce became more common, the stigma surrounding it began to lift. Divorce did not mean a rejection of marriage, however;

four out of every five divorced persons remarried, half within three years. Divorced individuals at every age, in fact, were more likely to marry than those who had never married.

Marriage remained a popular institution, but it began to look different. As the birthrate declined, voluntary childlessness was on the rise. Women had their children later and held jobs outside the home to a greater extent than their mothers had, even when their children were small. In the early 1980s, half the married women with school-aged children held jobs, along with one-third of those with children under age 6. A solid majority of wives aged 20–24 were employed, compared to only 26 percent in 1950. The vast number of married women in the paid labor force called into question the assumption that they should be responsible for all household chores when they, like their husbands, came home after a hard day at work. According to polls taken in the late 1970s, a majority of young single men, as well as women, believed that when they married, both spouses would be employed and would share child care and housework equally. Nevertheless, domestic gender roles remained resistant to change. The evidence suggests that although men began to "help out" more with domestic chores, women still suffered from double duty and remained responsible for the lion's share of child care and housework.

In spite of all the challenges to the status quo, institutions were slow to change. As the baby boomers matured, many found that their aspirations had moved far beyond their opportunities. Young women still faced enormous difficulties if they hoped to combine a career with marriage. Problems surrounding child care, parental leaves, and the burdens of housework continued to plague employed mothers. Because of these persistent obstacles, female college students had high levels of anxiety and ambivalence toward the future. Political activism had done a great deal to improve opportunities for women and minorities, but only the very tip of the institutional iceberg had begun to melt. Sex segregation still prevailed in the work force. Although more women entered male-dominated professions, most working women still faced what their mothers had tried to avoid: overwork, inadequate pay, and extra burdens at home.

Women who took the risk of divorce may have escaped oppressive or even brutal marriages, but they also encountered what their security-oriented mothers had feared: poverty, loneliness, difficulties in caring for their children, and the exhausting life of a single parent. Divorced women often experienced an immediate and sharp decline in their standard of living. Since they usually gained custody of children and received less-than-adequate child support, the meagerness of their incomes made their lives even more difficult. Divorced women and their children were much more likely than men to fall into poverty; men generally experienced a higher standard of living after divorce. Even the legal triumphs that were hailed as harbingers of a more humane future often backfired, such as the no-fault divorce statutes. Because these new laws treated men and women "equally," they ignored the inequalities that marriage created and the lower earning power that left women with even more disadvantages after the dissolution of their marriages.

Married or divorced, professional as well as nonprofessional wage-earning women continued to face inequalities at work and at home. Nevertheless, political activism opened up new opportunities for women to achieve autonomy that had been unavailable to their mothers. Women of the fifties, constrained by tremendous cultural and economic pressures to conform to domestic containment, gave up their independence and personal ambitions. Once they made the choice to embrace domesticity, they did their best to thrive within it and claimed that their sacrifices were ultimately worthwhile. Many of their daughters abandoned security and material comfort to follow a more autonomous path that brought them face to face with economic hardship and pervasive discrimination. Yet, like their mothers, many would say that the struggles were worth it. Their mothers paid a price for security and dependence; the daughters paid a price for autonomy and independence. In both cases, the lack of equal opportunity for women limited their options. Yet there is no question that the daughters had more opportunities than their mothers as a result of the hard-won political achievements of the sixties and seventies: they were no longer bound to the home.

Political goals were only partially achieved, however. Even before the end of the 1960s, the "silent majority" rose up against the noisy, youthful minority. In 1968, the quintessential fifties politician, Richard Nixon, was back in the White House, this time as president. The ideology of the cold war, although dealt a serious blow by the disastrous war in Vietnam, remained a powerful force in national politics—and it continued to be tied to the ideology of domesticity. Those who claimed that South Vietnam fell as a result of softness against communism also blamed feminism for what they perceived as the destruction of the family.

It is no accident that in the wake of feminism, the sexual revolution, and the peace movement of the 1960s, the New Right emerged in the 1970s and 1980s as a powerful political force with the dual aims of reviving the cold war and reasserting the ideology of domesticity. It should not be surprising that the most vigorous opponent of the Equal Rights Amendment, Phyllis Schlafly, began her career as an avid Cold Warrior. Proponents of the New Right gained strength by calling for militance in foreign policy, opposing the Equal Rights Amendment, and condemning student radicalism, the counterculture, feminism, and the sexual revolution. They went on to triumph in 1980, with the election of Ronald Reagan to the presidency.

Reagan, like Nixon, received his political groundings in the late 1940s and 1950s as an anticommunist crusader in California. Appropriately, his media image was that of the family man par excellence, as he promoted home-centered consumerism as host of the General Electric Theater. The all-electric home that Reagan advertised (and also inhabited) was virtually identical to the "model home" Nixon praised in Moscow in 1959. In the 1960s, Reagan carried his image into California politics, where he promised to crack down on student protestors. With Reagan in the White House in the 1980s, the rhetoric of containment returned, with its support for cold-war militance and calls for a strengthened "traditional" family.

Although the cold war and the call for domesticity became fashionable once again, consensus no longer prevailed in the 1980s as it did in the years after World War II. The family landed squarely in the center of hotly contested politics. Insightful observers noted the continuing intersection of sexual and political ideology.

The New Right advocates of militance abroad also called for abolishing the feminist gains of the sixties and seventies, such as affirmative action and legalized abortion, while supporting "Star Wars" research and renewed civil defense strategies for a "winnable nuclear war." Those who favored arms control also called for equal opportunities for women. The political divide continued to separate cold warriors from those in favor of equality between the sexes. Meanwhile, personal lifestyles began to reflect a much wider range than they did in the 1940s and 1950s, when nearly everyone conformed to a pattern of early marriage and several children. With domestic containment virtually dismantled, no consensus prevailed in the familial realm.

It is clear that in recent decades, the domestic ideology and cold war militance have risen and fallen together. Immediately after World War II, stable family life seemed necessary for national security, civil defense, and the struggle for supremacy over the Soviet Union. For a generation of young adults who grew up amid depression and war, domestic containment was a logical response to specific historical circumstances. It allowed them to pursue, in the midst of a tense and precarious world situation, the quest for a sexually fulfilling, consumer-oriented personal life that was free from hardship. But the circumstances were different for their children, who broke the consensus surrounding the cold war and domestic containment. Whether the baby-boom children will ultimately be more successful than their parents in achieving fulfilling lives and a more just and tolerant world remains to be seen. But one thing is certain: gender, family, and national politics are still intertwined in the ongoing saga of postwar cultural change.

Sexual Liberalism and the New Feminism

JOHN D'EMILIO AND ESTELLE FREEDMAN

The year 1968 was a traumatic one for Americans. Mired in a seemingly endless war, the nation coped with the discontent that it provoked at home. A once popular president was driven from office, and two charismatic leaders, Martin Luther King and Robert F. Kennedy, were assassinated. The nation's black ghettos exploded with riots while white college students occupied campus buildings, marched in protest against the war, and rejected the values of middle America. In August, the whole world watched on television as Chicago police brutally attacked anti-war protesters outside the Democratic party's national convention.

In the midst of these conflicts, many Americans looked for reassuring signs of stability. If there was one cultural symbol of tranquil, happy times,

Excerpts from *Intimate Matters: A History of Sexuality in America* by John D'Emilio and Estelle Freedman, pp. 301–318. Copyright © 1988 by John D'Emilio and Estelle Freedman. Reprinted by permission of HarperCollins Publishers, Inc.

surely the Miss America pageant would qualify. Initiated in 1921 to bolster the Atlantic City tourist trade, it had over the years come to blend a variety of elements into a popular ritual of modern life. Young, attractive women displayed the curves of their bodies, but in modest, tasteful swimsuits that contained their erotic powers. They demonstrated appropriately feminine skills—hospitality, sociability, musical talent, poise—that marked them as future wives rather than loose women. Corporations scrambled to sponsor these events and, with the advent of television, spawned new contests to provide more opportunities for advertising their products alongside American beauties. By the mid-1960s, the Miss America pageant faced competition from Miss USA, Miss Universe, Miss Teen International pageant, and the Junior Miss pageant, among others. In an era when sex sold, the duties of a beauty queen might include perching for photographs on the fender of a new Oldsmobile, or presiding at the opening of a new soft-drink bottling plant. Meanwhile, millions of male television viewers enjoyed the parade of female bodies while women vicariously experienced the pain and happiness of contestants as the winner and runners-up were announced.

But by 1968 even the Miss America pageant had to contend with protest. Outside the convention hall in Atlantic City, over a hundred noisy demonstrators, all women, expressed their discontent with the "degrading mindless-boob girlie symbol" that the contest represented. They dumped objects of female "enslavement" into a giant "freedom trash can": girdles, bras, high-heeled shoes, false eyelashes, and hair curlers. Attacking the corporate commercialism as well as the sexual objectification that the contest endorsed, one poster announced, "Miss America Sells It." As a culmination of their action, these self-styled women's liberationists draped a sheep in yellow and blue ribbons, crowned it queen, and paraded it along the boardwalk while they sang, "There she is, Miss America!"

The Miss America protest helped put the women's liberation movement on the map. It also suggested that beneath the surface of a sexually liberal ethic lay serious discontent. By the end of the 1960s, young radical feminists and gay militants would be mounting political challenges to the liberal consensus on sex, while disaffected middle-class youth would simply turn away from it. In the process they initiated a new era of contention and change in the realm of sex.

Singles Life and Rebellious Youth

Paradoxically, the first major challenge to the marriage-oriented ethic of sexual liberalism came neither from political nor cultural radicals but rather from entrepreneurs who extended the logic of consumer capitalism to the realm of sex. In December 1953, Hugh Hefner published the first issue of *Playboy,* a glossy monthly which made its mark through color centerfolds of nude young women. Although other magazines aiming at a male audience had titillated readers with female flesh, the overtness of *Playboy,* according to one reviewer, "makes old issues of *Esquire,* in its most uninhibited days, look like trade bulletins from the W.C.T.U." [Women's Christian Temperance Union] Along with the pictures came an evolving philosophy that rejected any limits on sexual expression and reserved for marriage the harshest of criticism. *Playboy* encouraged its readers to "enjoy the pleasures the female has to offer without becoming emotionally involved." Appealing to men who were upwardly mobile, the magazine saw marriage as a financial trap. Better to spend one's money on self-indulgence and luxurious living, it proclaimed, than to become one of the "sorry, regimented husbands trudging down every woman-dominated street in this woman-dominated land."

Hefner parlayed his ability to arouse male fantasies into a financial and sexual empire. The circulation of his magazine rose rapidly, passing the million mark before the end of the 1950s, and peaking at six million in the early 1970s. Almost half the readers were single men. A quarter of the copies were sold on college campuses, suggesting a potentially affluent market with appeal for advertisers. By the mid-1960s, Hefner's personal fortune was estimated at $100 million. He had built a thirty-seven-story skyscraper in Chicago, owned a $6 million jet, and lived in a forty-eight-room mansion on Chicago's Gold Coast, along with thirty of his Playboy "bunnies."

In some ways, Hefner's style of actively propagating a philosophy of sexual libertinism seemed to confirm the worst predictions of nineteenth-century moralists who believed that sanctioning sex without marriage would lead to unbridled promiscuity. Hefner made himself available for magazine interviews and television appearances, where he attacked "our ferocious antisexuality, our dark antieroticism in America." The naked women of *Playboy,* he told his fascinated audiences, were "a symbol of disobedience, a triumph of sexuality, an end of Puritanism." The "Playmates of the Month" toured the country promoting the magazine, appearing at sporting events, business conventions, state fairs, and colleges. Dartmouth College hosted one as a weekend guest on the campus. To men skeptical of their ability to find such beauties for themselves, Hefner spoke in reassuring phrases:

> We suppose it's natural to think of the pulchritudinous Playmates as existing in a world apart. Actually, potential Playmates are all around you: the new secretary at your office, the doe-eyed beauty who sat opposite you at lunch yesterday, the girl who sells you shirts and ties at your favorite store. We found Miss July in our circulation department, processing subscriptions, renewals, and back copy orders.

For would-be imitators of Hefner, the *Playboy* approach to sex had one obvious flaw: where were the women who would cooperate? Hefner's assurances notwithstanding, most observers of the postwar sexual scene emphasized the relational aspects of female sexuality. Women's interest in the erotic appeared strongly attached to love and romance, to seriousness of purpose. Especially in an era that celebrated family domesticity, most young women might reasonably be assumed to see sex as a prelude to marriage.

Men in search of sex free of the obligations of matrimony found a welcome ally in Helen Gurley Brown. A career woman who would make her mark in publishing by transforming *Cosmopolitan* into a top-selling magazine, she initially won notoriety by writing *Sex and the Single Girl,* a runaway best-seller of the early 1960s. Intending it as a guidebook for the unwed working woman, Brown seemed to have as little use for marriage as Hefner did. Marriage, she wrote, "is insurance for the *worst* years of your life. During your best years you don't need a husband." Echoing *Playboy,* she told her readers that men were "cheaper emotionally and a lot more fun by the dozen." They were everywhere to be found, and easily obtainable. Since a wedding was not the object, Brown encouraged single women to play the field with married men. "It's a question of taking married men, but not taking them seriously," she wrote. "Use them in a perfectly nice way just as they use you. . . . One married man is dangerous. . . . A potpourri can be fun."

Brown was shrewd enough to recognize that many American women might harbor inhibitions about the cavalier sex life she was trumpeting. *Sex and the Single Girl* tackled the problem head-on. Brown urged her readers to "reconsider the idea that sex without marriage is dirty. . . . [S]ex was here a long time before marriage. You inherited your proclivity for it." Girls can say "yes," she suggested, even "nice, single girls." The pleasures were intoxicating: "an affair between a single woman and her lover can be un-adulterated, cliff-hanging sex." Brown advised women to enjoy the prop-ositions that would come their way and to use sex as the "powerful weapon" it was.

Brown's manifesto for the single woman shared more with *Playboy* than sexual libertinism. It, too, was premised on an ethic of success, prosperity, and consumption. The single woman was measured "by what she does rather than whom she belongs to." She had to live by her wits and sharpen her skills in order to make it in a competitive world. Brown offered pointers for "Squirming, Worming, Inching, and Pinching Your Way to the Top." Moreover, money was a prerequisite to the successful single life, and it would come not from the largess of a male admirer, but through hard work. Money bought the clothes, the cosmetics, the home furnishings, the catered parties, the vacations, and the other leisure activities that made the single girl attractive and envied.

Brown and Hefner, each in their own way, seemed to speak to the desires of at least some of America's unmarried. In the prosperous sixties, a portion of young urbanites participated in the creation of a new singles culture. Initially structured through informal institutions, singles life revolved around the parties and weekend clubs that energetic young men and women created in order to fill a social vacuum. Friday editions of city newspapers were sprinkled with classified ads announcing the upcoming events. But, before long, the market for heterosexual gathering places was invaded by enterprising businessmen. Throughout the country, singles bars began to populate the urban landscape, providing a setting for men and women to meet and form liaisons. Publishers threw together guidebooks for the un-attached, computer dating services sprang into existence, and builders con-structed youth-oriented apartment complexes so that the modern singles could party without the complaints of concerned parents or older Americans.

Although for some this new singles culture served to facilitate the quest for a spouse, its contours made it more of a sexual, than a marriage, market. As one young man described the New York scene, "New York is a single man's paradise. It doesn't pay to get married. . . . I am looking for a temporary companion, not a mate." The bars sustained casual contacts, not permanent relationships; the promise of excitement and adventure kept patrons returning. Women as well as men seemed to initiate encounters. One observer noted the "casual boy-meets-girl atmosphere" of singles meeting places. "A girl thinks nothing of dropping down at a table if she sees a man sitting alone—or of excusing herself if she spots someone more attractive." Having reached maturity in an era where sexual information and sexual experience were more easily accessible for the young, the singles generation of the 1960s pursued these paths into adulthood.

At first glance one might reasonably wonder what was new or distinctive about this world of urban nightlife and sexual encounters. After all, working-class youth at the turn of the century had sustained a sexual subculture rooted in commercialized amusements. But the unmarried youth of that era had elicited pity, scorn, or fear from the middle class who sought to control their behavior and made them the object of reformation efforts. Now, in the 1960s, young adults of the middle class were glamorized; they embodied the unspoken fantasies of a consumer society extended to the sphere of sex. These young singles very quickly became, in the opinion of one commentator, "a new, privileged, spotlighted, envied group." The singles label seemed to connote, "as in tennis, an endeavor more vigorous, more skilled, and more fun than mere doubles."

One reason, perhaps, for the shift in values was that the singles culture of the 1960s was moving with the stream of American life. In the Progressive era, the working girl raised the specter of social disorder and gender upheaval. In the postwar period, the single working woman was not only an accepted but also a necessary feature of economic life. The expansion of the retail and service sector of the labor force, the so-called pink-collar economy, drew women into the job market, married as well as single. Moreover, economic prosperity rested squarely upon an ethic of consumption, as business needed buyers for an endless array of consumer items. As one motivational psychologist told an audience of businessmen, "we are now confronted with the problem of permitting the average American to feel moral . . . even when he is spending, even when he is not saving. . . . One of the basic problems of prosperity, then, is to demonstrate that the hedonistic approach to his life is a moral, not an immoral one."

Sex and the single American offered one promising avenue for achieving this goal. Young, unmarried professionals had enormous discretionary buying power, comprising even in the 1960s a $60 billion market for sellers. As the barriers against sensual imagery fell, advertisers could shape their messages around appeals to the erotic and by glamorizing the lifestyles of the unmarried. In some instances, sexual meanings were not at all disguised. Mary Quant, the designer of the miniskirt, put bluntly the message behind her fashions. "Am I the only woman who has ever wanted to go to bed with a man in the afternoon?" she asked. "Any law-abiding female, it used to be thought, waits until dark. Well, there are lots of girls who don't want to wait. Mini-clothes are symbolic of them." Not only clothes and cosmetics, but cigarettes, soft drinks, cars, liquor, stereos, and a host of other unerotic products became vehicles for a sexual sell. The consumer economy of the sixties helps explain how the singles culture could emerge from a period seemingly rooted in a marital sexual ethic and why it won such ready acceptance.

While one segment of the middle-class young pursued sexual pleasure in the name of consumerist values, another broke with the tenets of sexual liberalism by rejecting the materialistic bias of modern capitalism. By the mid-1960s, white American college students were rousing themselves from a generation-long political stupor. Their numbers swelled by the first baby boomers, and inspired by the civil rights struggle of their black counterparts in the South, white students in growing numbers set themselves firmly against the "establishment." The Vietnam War, the draft, and charges of university complicity in the military effort propelled them to take political action on and off campus. With each passing year, the volume and intensity of youth protest escalated.

Part of what gave the rebellion of the sixties so much energy was its heady mix of politics and culture. More than a response to particular government policies, the student movement generated a complex critique of American social life. The acquiescence to racial inequality in a democracy, to poverty in the world's richest nation, and to a technologically sophisticated military struggle against a peasant population seemed a damning indictment of middle-class values. As Herbert Marcuse, the Marxist philosopher whose writings appealed to radical student leaders, put it,

> This society is obscene in producing and indecently exposing a stifling abundance of wares while depriving its victims abroad of the necessities of life; obscene in stuffing itself and its garbage cans while poisoning and burning the scarce foodstuffs in the fields of its aggression; obscene in the words and smiles of its politicians and entertainers. . . . Obscene is not the picture of a naked woman who exposes her pubic hair but that of a fully clad general who exposes his medals rewarded in a war of aggression; obscene is not the ritual of the Hippies but the declaration of a high dignitary of the Church that war is necessary for peace.

For some, protest against the war coincided with a rejection of the competitive values that bred success, and the materialism that sustained a consumer economy. Music, drugs, the symbolic adoption of different modes of dress and hairstyle, all combined to fuel the sense of breaking sharply from the culture in which the young had been reared.

Sexual issues were part and parcel of the decade's youth upheavals. On a number of campuses sexual freedom leagues shared attention with anti-war organizations. Students campaigned for an end to campus regulations governing visiting hours in the dorms. University health services found themselves targeted for denying oral contraceptives to the unmarried. Female students defied rules that prohibited them from living off-campus with their boyfriends. Some colleges broke sharply with tradition by acquiescing to demands for coed dorms. Alongside political buttons with the message "end the war" were those proclaiming "take it off" and "I'm willing if you are." By the end of the sixties, concerned parents and troubled administrators no doubt yearned for the days when students contented themselves with the ritualistic "panty raids" that marked the onset of spring.

Although cultural radicalism and political protest coincided for many college students, the hippie counterculture fully absorbed the energies of others. Surfacing in San Francisco, hippies first attracted media attention with their "Human Be-in" in Golden Gate Park in early 1967. Soon, hippie colonies were flourishing in most large cities and on the fringes of university towns. The "flower children," as the media dubbed them, ostentatiously mocked the values of the comfortable middle-class families from which they came. "Turn on, tune in, drop out," intoned by one of their gurus, Timothy Leary, symbolized the drug-oriented lifestyle and anti-materialistic ethic of the movement. To mainstream America, the hippies epitomized moral decay and sexual anarchy. Unlike nineteenth-century sex radicals who sought a sexual love based on spiritual values, hippie codes emphasized a freedom that was more overtly physical. As *Newsweek* reported:

> For the hippies, sex is not a matter of great debate, because as far as they are concerned the sexual revolution is accomplished. There are no hippies who believe in chastity, or look askance at marital infidelity, or see even marriage itself as a virtue. Physical love is a delight—to be chewed upon as often and as freely as a handful of sesame seeds.

Living in communes in the city and in rural areas, hippies allegedly abandoned, along with sexual restraint, allegiance to the nuclear family. The media reported children being raised in common, in an atmosphere of sexual freedom, in loose extended "families." Perhaps because they rejected so directly the institutions of family and marriage, the hippies elicited the strenuous condemnation of middle America.

By the late 1960s, the sexual iconoclasm of the counterculture appeared to reach beyond the confines of small enclaves of disaffected youth. In the summer of 1969, hundreds of thousands of the young converged on Woodstock, New York, for a rock festival in which drugs, nudity, and sexual encounters abounded. On Broadway, audiences gasped at the nudity displayed in the rock musical *Hair,* and at the defiance of taboos on sexually explicit language in *Oh! Calcutta!* whose title was a thinly veiled verbal play on the French "oh, quelle cunt tu as." Tabloids such as *Screw* began publication, devoting themselves entirely to sex and intent on shocking middle-class sensibilities. Clearly, the consensus that the tenets of sexual liberalism represented was shattering, as both the counterculture and the consumer culture broke with its emphasis on stable, marriage-centered sexual relationships. "The old taboos are dead or dying. A new, more permissive society is taking shape," one magazine observed. "The crucial question" was "where the new permissiveness is leading, whether the breakdown of the old order is going to lead to some new moral system, or whether it is simply going to lead to the progressive discarding of all social restraint."

The Second Wave of Feminism

Before that question could be answered, there arose challenges of a different sort to the sexual status quo. By the end of the 1960s the radicalism of American youth had given birth to two social movements which spoke directly to sexual matters. Women's liberation and gay liberation each presented a wide-ranging critique of deeply held assumptions about human sexual desire, its place in social life, and the hidden purposes it served. In particular, both movements analyzed the erotic as a vehicle for domination which, in complex ways, kept certain social groups in a subordinate place in society. No longer a natural "instinct" or "drive," sexuality emerged more clearly than ever as an issue of power and politics.

The postwar generation of American women had faced a set of conflicting role expectations that would have tested the sturdiest. On the one hand, a resurgence of domestic ideology exalted the roles of housewife and especially mother. "Anatomy decrees the life of a woman," one Harvard psychiatrist wrote, while Erik Erikson proclaimed that female "somatic design harbors an 'inner space' destined to bear the offspring of chosen men." Woman was defined by the man she married and the children she nurtured. In the baby-boom years of the late 1940s and 1950s, American women seemed to live out these expectations as many married at younger-than-ever ages and bore as many children as their grandmothers had. The accelerating migration of the white middle-class population away from the central city placed added demands upon the suburban housewife whose tasks grew to fill the expanded floor plan. Besides their domestic duties, many of these housewives had to seek employment outside the home to maintain the family's economic status. Between 1940 and 1960, the proportion of married women in the labor force doubled from fifteen to thirty percent. Forced to shape their employment experience around the demands of their domestic duties, many of these women labored part-time, left and reentered the labor market, and worked at jobs with little prospect of advancement. Small wonder, then, that when Betty Friedan published *The Feminine Mystique* in 1963, she reported deep reservoirs of discontent among American housewives, a predicament she labeled "the problem that has no name."

On the other hand, American women were also expected to be more than mothers and housekeepers. Marital ideals prescribed that she be an erotic companion to her husband, that the happiness of marriage would grow in proportion to the sexual magic generated between husband and wife. By the 1960s, Playboy Playmates and sexy single girls added another, more troubling ingredient to this sexual stew. Wives could look with concern at the sexual competition they faced from women who did not have to change diapers or cook for a family. For her part, the single woman might forever question her own femininity, lacking as she was the central attribute of motherhood. Whether dutiful wife or alluring single, the American woman was left to wonder whether she made the grade.

Some of the conflicts that American women faced were embedded within the system of sexual liberalism. Modern marriage was a sexual partnership, yet husbands and wives often approached the conjugal bed with widely divergent expectations about the meaning of sex. Many women hoped for love and affection; their partners sought orgasmic relief. The companionate ideal posited equality between spouses, yet wives remained economically dependent, aware that failure in marriage spelled disaster. As the birth control pill lessened the dangers of pregnancy, and the media portrayed the glamor of the single life, young women who had helped shape an ethic of "permissiveness with affection" found the rules suddenly altered. Placed on the defensive, they were rapidly losing the right to say no that nineteenth-century feminists had struggled to obtain.

Meanwhile, the conditions of life for American women were changing, promoting a rise in expectations. During the 1960s, the college population grew considerably and with it came a female cohort who might see work as more than a way station on the road to marriage. Problematic as the image of the single girl was, it did validate the choices of women who postponed marriage and sought fulfillment in a career. The birth control pill, too, though it magnified the sexual pressures that women faced, promised, in the words of one journalist, "a new kind of life," offering women "new freedom and new responsibilities." The proportion of women in the labor force continued to rise steadily during the 1960s, especially drawing in married women who had completed their families, whose children were in school, and who could look forward to uninterrupted employment. In 1964, Congress passed the Civil Rights Act, aimed at correcting racial inequality but including in its provisions gender-based discrimination. Soon, the federal government was flooded with complaints from women charging sex-bias in employment. By the mid-1960s one might almost say that American women were in search of a feminist movement.

Although women's rights advocates initiated the second wave of feminism when they founded the National Organization for Women in 1966, the energy that put feminism on the map came from another group of younger, radical women. Women's liberationists, as they labeled themselves, emerged from the ranks of the civil rights movement and the New Left. Motivated by lofty ideals of social equality, genuine democracy, and the dignity of the individual, they threw themselves into the struggle for social justice. Whether teaching in freedom schools in the South, organizing the poor in northern cities, or planning demonstrations against the war in Vietnam, these young women were taking their public roles seriously, acquiring leadership skills, and experiencing a sense of empowerment at odds with the prescriptive roles embodied in the feminine mystique.

The reality of life in "The Movement," however, departed dramatically from its rhetoric. Despite the nods in the direction of human liberation, male leaders in the New Left often exploited the labor of female members, devalued women's contributions to the cause, and kept leadership roles to themselves. All of this coexisted, moreover, in a climate hostile to middle-class notions of sexual morality. Women were expected to demonstrate their revolutionary fervor by breaking with conventional mores, yet sex became just another tool in the degradation of women. In an early feminist essay Marge Piercy, whose novels later chronicled the struggles of this generation, portrayed the dynamic:

> Fucking a staff into existence is only the extreme form of what passes for common practice in many places. A man can bring a woman into an organization by sleeping with her and remove her by ceasing to do so. A man can purge a woman for no other reason than that he has tired of her, knocked her up, or is after someone else. . . . There are cases of a woman excluded from a group for no other reason than that one of its leaders proved impotent with her.

For some male radicals, sex served as a vehicle to build solidarity with working-class youth. One leader of Students for a Democratic Society [SDS] at the University of Washington described how men would share time "balling a chick together" before going on a demonstration. Organizers against the war popularized the slogan "girls say yes to guys who say no" in their efforts to build resistance to the draft.

Such behavior and attitudes could not help but provoke a response. By the mid-1960s some movement women were beginning to speak out against the "gender caste system" that was developing. The reactions they elicited seemed to confirm their status as sexual objects. When the question of gender was raised in the Student Nonviolent Coordinating Committee [SNCC], Stokely Carmichael allegedly remarked that "the only position for women in SNCC is prone." Female SDSers fared no better. During a discussion of the "women's issue" at the organization's 1965 convention, a female speaker confronted catcalls from the audience. "She just needs a good screw," one male participant shouted. Similarly, at the counter-inaugural rally sponsored by a coalition of radical groups in January 1969, Shulamith Firestone, an early organizer of women's liberation, faced cries of "take her off the stage and fuck her!" as she tried to address the topic of women's oppression. Assaulted by such implacable hostility, women began abandoning New Left, gender-mixed organizations in droves, forming instead a loosely structured autonomous women's liberation movement. The first such group appeared in Chicago in 1967, but the network of relationships for sharing information among radicals was so elaborate that the impulse spread like wildfire. By the beginning of the 1970s, literally hundreds of local women's groups had taken root across the country.

The women who banded together moved quickly into the sphere of political action, but they also produced in short order a fairly elaborate body of theory that described and defined a system of gender oppression. Confronted with the paucity of radical analysis of woman's place in society, they relied on a process of "consciousness-raising" that generated both an individual understanding of their condition and the raw material from which to fashion a feminist world view. Exchanging experiences on a wide range of topics, these women discovered that their problems were not idiosyncratic, the peculiar outcome of unique relationships or family upbringing. Rather, their situations were widely shared. Out of this came the perception that "the personal is political," that the dilemmas women encountered came from a socially constructed and enforced system of gender roles that consigned women to an inferior position in society. In reaching these conclusions, radical women's liberationists laid the foundation for a vastly expanded terrain of politics. Marriage, the family, and motherhood were reinterpreted as institutions that maintained the oppression of women.

Although the women's liberation movement addressed a broad set of concerns, sexuality loomed especially large in its thinking. In their consciousness-raising groups, women discussed their feelings about their bodies and about sex, commenting on, "above all, the lack of ownership. . . . We realized," wrote one, that "married or not, our bodies had ownership by many: men, doctors, clothes and cosmetic manufacturers, advertisers, churches, schools—everyone but ourselves." Maturing as they had in the post-pill, sexually permissive climate of the 1960s, most had experienced firsthand the "sexual revolution" and found it wanting. For women, sexual freedom in contemporary America had become "the right that is a duty." As Dana Densmore described it in her "declaration of independence" from the sexual revolution:

> Under the banner of "not denying our sexuality" and pointing to repression in the past . . . many of us now embrace sexuality and its expression completely uncritically. As if present excess could make up for past deprivation. . . . Sexual relations in the world today are oppressive. . . . Sex is everywhere. It's forced down our throats. It's the great sop. . . . It makes us look as if we're free and active . . . and people seem to *believe* that sexual freedom is freedom.

"Everywhere," she wrote, women were seen as "sexual objects." Advertisers projected a sexual definition of the female, informing her that "blondes have more fun" or that a certain brand of toothpaste would give her mouth "sex appeal," advising her to "wear a Playtex bra if you have an average figure but don't want to look average." Bombarded with such messages, one feminist essay proclaimed, "ninety percent of the women in this country have an inferiority complex because they do not have turned-up noses, wear a size ten or under dress, have 'good legs,' flat stomachs, and fall within a certain age bracket." The reduction of women's bodies to erotic objects had debilitating effects. Women walking down the street were the targets of stares, catcalls, and whistles. Men would "use her body with their eyes," wrote Meredith Tax, a Boston feminist. "They will evaluate her market price. . . . They will make her a participant in their fantasies. . . . Any man has this power as *man,* the dominant sex, to dehumanize woman, even to herself. No woman can have an autonomous self unaffected by such encounters."

Theorists in the women's liberation movement cast a skeptical look at the sex act itself. A generation earlier, Kinsey had disputed the Freudian emphasis on the vaginal orgasm, but his argument was lost among the many other reactions his studies elicited. By the late 1960s, the social context had changed. The findings of William Masters and Virginia Johnson, sex researchers at Washington University in St. Louis, had received wide circulation. Although their conclusions could be shaped to various ends, the two sexologists had studied in detail the biological bases of human sexual responsiveness. Like Kinsey, they too broke sharply with Freudian theory by identifying stimulation of the clitoris, rather than the vagina, as the source of the female orgasm. But now, a nascent women's movement could take up the issue. Anne Koedt, in a classic and much reprinted essay, "The Myth of the Vaginal Orgasm" (1969), articulated the feminist implications of these findings. "Women have thus been defined sexually in terms of what pleases men," she wrote. The sexually mature female who reached orgasm through vaginal penetration was the creation of male sexual preferences. Women were kept in a state of sexual confusion, labeled frigid for failing to achieve "an orgasm which in fact does not exist," and led to feign sexual satisfaction in order to keep their partners content. Demolishing the myth had significance beyond the matter of erotic pleasure. "The recognition of clitoral orgasm," Koedt concluded, "would threaten the heterosexual *institution*. For it would indicate that sexual pleasure was obtainable from either men *or* women, thus making heterosexuality not an absolute, but an option. It would thus open up the whole question of *human* sexual relationships beyond the confines of the present male-female role system." Sex thus was reinterpreted as either a mechanism for maintaining female dependence or a vehicle for breaking free. Or, as Kate Millett, the author of a best-selling feminist manifesto, succinctly described it, the act of coitus was "a charged microcosm" of sexual politics.

The importance attached to sexual issues emerges most clearly when one looks at the early targets of feminist political energy. In an action that received widespread media coverage and brought women's liberation before the nation's eyes, radical feminists traveled to Atlantic City to protest the 1968 Miss America beauty pageant. In San Francisco, militant feminists disrupted the annual bridal fair sponsored by apparel manufacturers. Students at Grinnell College in Iowa staged a "nude-in" to protest the presence of a *Playboy* representative on campus. In New York City, women conducted a "whistle-in" on Wall Street during the lunch hour. Others leafleted the city's marriage bureau, informing women seeking licenses that "rape is legal in marriage," and that, "according to the United Nations, marriage is a 'slavery-like practice.' " Throughout the country, young feminists held speak-outs on rape, and invaded the hearings of state legislatures debating the reform of abortion laws. In Boston, one consciousness-raising group transformed itself into a publishing collective that wrote a feminist health and sex manual, *Our Bodies, Ourselves* (1973).

As the title of the popular volume suggested, this new generation of feminists, not unlike their nineteenth-century predecessors, saw control of their bodies as a key piece in their quest for liberation. Despite the negative sexual epithets that were often thrown at them—frigid, castrating, dyke, frustrated, or, simply, ugly—women's liberation was not "antisexual." Rather, the movement was attacking the sexual objectification of women, the reduction of women by the media and by men to little more than their sex appeal or their reproductive organs. Feminists disputed the possibility of equality in marriage or in other sexual relationships when women were economically dependent on men or had internalized values that made them doubt their self-worth. To them, the oppression of women had contaminated the sex act itself, while the sexual ideology of modern America reinforced female inequality. Women's liberationists expected that only a revolutionary transformation of society could remove the corruption that attached to sex. When women achieved full autonomy, then and only then would "sexual freedom" have real meaning.

Though the revolution did not come, this modern brand of feminism did make its mark upon the consciousness of America, affecting attitudes, custom, and law. In many ways, feminism initiated a reshaping of the nation's understanding of sexuality. For instance, when the movement began, the penal codes of most states demanded corroborating evidence in rape cases, permitted questions about the victim's sexual history, and required judges to repeat to the jury the seventeenth-century dictum that "rape is the easiest charge to make and the most difficult to prove." In North Carolina only a virgin could claim rape. The women's liberation movement popularized the idea that rape was not a crime of sexual passion. Rather, it was a case of violent assault, perpetrated not only by deranged strangers, but by male relatives, boyfriends, and husbands. In the course of the 1970s, most states rewrote their rape statutes, and in twenty-five of them a complete restructuring of the offense occurred along feminist lines, largely because of the lobbying of women's groups. Colleges instituted programs to advise female students about "acquaintance rape," and in some states husbands found themselves facing indictments for "marital rape." The women's movement also invented the phrase "sexual harassment" to describe the repeated and unwanted sexual advances that generations of female workers had faced on the job. Before long, judges were recognizing the problem as an illegal condition of employment prohibited by the Civil Rights Act of 1964, women were filing suits and winning, and major corporations were hiring feminists to run seminars designed to raise the consciousness of their employees. By no means did feminism effect an end either to sexual harassment or violent assault. But it did identify sexual violence as a key element maintaining the subordination of women, provided women with new ways of understanding their situation, and expanded the resources that women had for fighting back.

Perhaps the most dramatic change provoked by the women's movement came in the area of reproductive rights. Both the radicals in the women's liberation movement and more moderate feminists in organizations such as NOW recognized the pivotal position that woman's reproductive role occupied in the structure of gender oppression. Absolute control of fertility was critical if women were to attain full equality. Though advances in contraceptive technology and the removal of most barriers to access were sharply reducing the level of unwanted fertility, nineteenth-century statutes still criminalized abortion, thus placing a barrier between women and full control of their bodies. Meanwhile, the underground world of abortion, to which hundreds of thousands of women resorted every year, only reinforced a sense of helplessness and powerlessness before the workings of their own bodies. When feminism took root in the late sixties, a movement was already afoot in a number of states to reform abortion laws by giving doctors more room to recommend abortion. But feminists quickly transformed the debate, recasting the issue as one of "rights" over one's own body, and using militant tactics to achieve their goals. In New York City in 1969, radical feminists disrupted a state legislative hearing on abortion law reform; members of the Detroit Women's Liberation Coalition invaded the office of the county attorney who prosecuted abortionists; and Chicago feminists staged guerrilla theater performances at a convention of the American Medical Association. Responding to the pressure, a few states soon revised their statutes along lines closer to feminist models. Then, in January 1973, in the case of *Roe* v. *Wade,* the Supreme Court acted. Though it did not eliminate all restrictions on the performance of abortions, it declared unconstitutional any prohibitions on abortion in the first trimester, and made second-trimester abortions easily available. Feminists, caught unawares by this unexpected boon, hailed the decision as a major victory.

Although feminists made access to abortion a key measure of female autonomy, some women faced restrictions on their ability to have children. A few months after the *Roe* decision, the press focused national attention on the issue of sterilization abuse. In Alabama, Minnie Lee and Mary Alice Relf, two young black sisters aged twelve and fourteen, had been forcibly sterilized at a government-funded family planning clinic. Meanwhile, it came to light that in Aiken, South Carolina, the only doctor willing to deliver the babies of welfare recipients required that mothers of more than two children first agree to sterilization. In 1973, the National Abortion Action Coalition revealed that fourteen states were debating legislation designed to coerce women on welfare to undergo sterilization. As the sponsor of one such bill declared, "People who live like animals should be treated as such." It soon became clear that the forced sterilization of poor women of color was far more extensive than had previously been believed. One government official estimated that federal money funded between 100,000 and 200,000 operations per year. Reliable estimates of the sterilization rate among native American and Puerto Rican women ranged between one-quarter and two-fifths of the women of childbearing age. White feminists were slower to organize around the issue than were minority communities, which saw sterilization as a means of racial control. Though the federal government released stringent regulations in 1978 to limit the practice, the lack of effective enforcement mechanisms made it difficult to eliminate.

Feminists did not always find themselves in agreement over sexual matters, as their debates over lesbianism demonstrated. As militant feminists began attacking male supremacy, opponents countered by accusing feminists of sexual deviance. "Dyke-baiting" became a vehicle for impugning the

movement and trivializing female political grievances. Given the condemnation that attached to lesbianism, many feminists hastily denied the charges,
accepting the verdict that it was an issue of no significance. Betty Friedan
called it "a lavender herring." Yet lesbians were involved in building the
feminist movement from the outset and they responded to the hostility of
heterosexual feminists by constructing a sexual politics of their own.

With the revival of feminism in the late 1960s, lesbians flocked to the
cause of women's emancipation. In many ways they were a natural constituency for the movement. Closeted though they might be, they still had to
move in the public world of work to support themselves and thus encountered
directly the barriers women faced in the economic sphere. Without husbands
to provide them a legitimate status, and uninterested in playing the part of
the sexy single girl who chased men, lesbians confronted squarely the limited
options available to women. At the same time, the feminist movement was
offering a setting and a climate that encouraged previously heterosexual
women to come out, to explore the liberating possibilities of loving other
women. As Coletta Reid, an early recruit to women's liberation in Washington, D.C., explained it,

> Almost everything I was reading at the time led me toward lesbianism. If
> "The Myth of the Vaginal Orgasm" was true, then intercourse was not
> necessary or even relevant to *my* sexual satisfaction. If "Sexual Politics"
> was right that male sexuality was an expression of power and dominance,
> then I was choosing my own oppression to stay in a relationship with a
> man. If sex roles were an invention of society, then women—not just men—
> were possible people to love, in the fullest sense of that word. If I could
> hug and kiss a woman I loved, why couldn't I touch all of her body? Since
> my husband really thought men were superior, then wasn't my needing to
> be in a relationship with someone superior to me, self-hating and woman-
> hating? The conclusion seemed inescapable.

Reid was not the only one to pursue the logic of her intellectual environment.
The annals of the early women's movement were filled with the stories of
others who used it to move from a life as a heterosexual to lesbianism.

Their choices, and the presence of lesbians of long standing in women's
organizations, did not always please their compatriots. Products of their
culture, feminists were no less likely than other Americans to view lesbians
with disdain, to see their sexuality as a pathological aberration at worst, or
a private matter of no political consequence at best. Sensitive to the reaction
that the movement was eliciting in the minds of Americans, many feminists
sought to keep the issue quiet, to push lesbians out of sight. Sometimes,
the results were nasty. In the New York City chapter of NOW, the energy
and talent of Rita Mae Brown, a young lesbian soon to achieve fame as a
novelist, lifted her to a position of influence in the organization. Her insistence that lesbianism was a key feminist issue antagonized many of her
associates. Although Brown left NOW of her own choosing, others were
not so fortunate, as the chapter engaged in a purge of lesbian officers. Late
in 1970, the worst fears of some heterosexual feminists seemed confirmed

when the media picked up Kate Millett's acknowledgment of bisexuality. *Time,* hardly a friend of the movement, gave it prominent play. "Kate Millett herself contributed," the magazine commented,

> to the growing skepticism about the movement by acknowledging at a recent meeting that she is bisexual. The disclosure is bound to discredit her as a spokeswoman for her cause, cast further doubt on her theories, and reinforce the views of those skeptics who routinely dismiss all liberationists as lesbians.

Throughout the period from 1969 to 1971, women's organizations across the country were wracked by a "gay-straight" split, as tensions reached the boiling point.

Some lesbians responded to the antagonism of other feminists by leaving mixed organizations. Along with women from the nascent gay liberation movement, they formed lesbian-feminist groups of their own, fashioning in the process both a political agenda and a theory to sustain their efforts. During the early seventies, radicalized lesbians produced a body of writing that sought to reshape the contemporary understanding of same-sex relations between women and the larger issue of human sexual relations. "As the question of homosexuality has become public," wrote Charlotte Bunch, a member of the Furies collective in Washington, D.C., "reformists define it as a private question of who you sleep with in order to sidetrack our understanding of the politics of sex. For the Lesbian-Feminist, it is not private; it is a political matter of oppression, domination, and power." Heterosexuality was removed from the realm of the "natural," and reinterpreted as an ideology and an institution that kept women bound to men and blocked their struggle for full liberation. Seen from this vantage point, lesbianism became a form of political rebellion. "The Lesbian rejects male sexual/political domination; she defies his world, his social organization, his ideology, and his definition of her as inferior. Lesbianism puts women first while the society declares the male supreme. Lesbianism," Bunch continued, "threatens male supremacy at its core." Pushed to its logical conclusion this outlook implied that "feminists must become Lesbians if they hope to end male supremacy."

Not all feminists became lesbians, of course, and not all lesbians left the women's movement. Nor, for that matter, did all lesbians identify with feminism. But, as the political passions of the early seventies cooled, the goal of ending the oppression of lesbians became integrated into the agenda of mainstream feminism. Despite the resistance of liberals such as Friedan, organizations such as NOW eventually incorporated lesbian rights into their list of goals. As the gay movement of the 1970s grew and brought the issue of homosexuality into the open, a gradual healing of conflict allowed some lesbians and heterosexuals to work side by side, even as other lesbians continued to staff their own organizations and sustain an autonomous lesbian-feminist movement.

In the long run, perhaps the signal achievement of this first generation of self-conscious lesbian feminists was to put into bold relief the part that sexuality played in the subordination of women. In identifying female sexual expression so closely with the institution of marriage, modern sexual liberalism sustained an ideological construct that kept women in a domestic role, while reinforcing her inequality in the public sphere. To challenge the inevitability or naturalness of heterosexuality was to open new realms of freedom for females. As such, acceptance of lesbianism could serve as a benchmark for the whole panoply of sexual questions that the second wave of feminism raised. Whether the issue was reproductive control, rape, sexual harassment, medical authority, prostitutes' rights, or lesbianism, feminists sought an authentic autonomy in sexual matters and an end to the gender inequality that prevented its achievement.

XXX *F U R T H E R   R E A D I N G*

Karen T. Anderson, *Wartime Women: Sex Roles, Family Relations, and the Status of Women During World War II* (1981)
M. Joyce Baker, *Images of Women in Film: The War Years, 1941–1945* (1981)
Lois Banner, *Women in Modern America* (1984)
Mary Francis Berry, *Why the ERA Failed* (1986)
Janet Boles, *The Politics of the Equal Rights Amendment* (1979)
D'Ann Campbell, *Women at War with America* (1984)
Maren Lockwood Carden, *The New Feminist Movement* (1974)
William Chafe, *Women and Equality* (1977)
Robert Daniel, *American Women in the Twentieth Century* (1987)
Barbara Deckard, *The Women's Movement* (1983)
Jane DeHart-Mathews and Donald Mathews, *The Equal Rights Amendment and the Politics of Cultural Conflict* (1988)
John D'Emilio, *Sexual Politics, Sexual Communities: The Making of a Homosexual Minority in the United States, 1940–1970* (1983)
———and Estelle B. Freedman, *Intimate Matters: A History of Sexuality in America* (1988).
Barbara Ehrenreich, *The Hearts of Men* (1983)
Zilah Eisenstein, *The Radical Future of Liberal Feminism* (1983)
Sarah Evans, *Personal Politics: The Roots of Women's Liberation in the Civil Rights Movement and the New Left* (1979)
Carol Felsenthal, *Sweetheart of the Silent Majority: The Biography of Phyllis Schlafly* (1981)
Jo Freeman, *The Politics of Women's Liberation* (1975)
Betty Friedan, *The Feminine Mystique* (1963)
———, *It Changed My Life: Writings on the Women's Movement* (1976)
———, *The Second Stage* (1981)
Cynthia Harrison, *On Account of Sex: The Politics of Women's Issues, 1945–1968* (1988)
Susan Hartmann, *The Homefront and Beyond* (1982)
Joan Hoff-Wilson, *Rites of Passage: The Past and Future of the ERA* (1986)
Judith Hole and Ellen Levine, *Rebirth of Feminism* (1971)
Bell Hooks, *Ain't I a Woman? Black Women and Feminism* (1981)
Gloria Joseph and Jill Lewis, *Common Differences: Conflicts in Black and White Feminist Perspectives* (1981)
Ethel Klein, *Gender Politics* (1984)
Kristin Luker, *Abortion and the Politics of Motherhood* (1984)
Nancy McGlen and Karen O'Connor, *Women's Rights* (1983)
Jane Mansbridge, *Why We Lost the ERA* (1986)

Elaine Tyler May, *Homeward Bound: American Families in the Cold War Era* (1988)

Steven Mintz and Susan Kellogg, *Domestic Revolutions: A Social History of American Family Life* (1988)

James Mohr, *Abortion in America* (1980)

Rosalind Pollack Petchesky, *Abortion and Women's Choice* (1984)

Leila Rupp, *Mobilizing Women for War* (1978)

———and Verta Taylor, *Survival in the Doldrums: The American Women's Rights Movement, 1945 to 1960s* (1987)

Ann Snitow et al., eds., *Powers of Desire: The Politics of Sexuality* (1983)

Carol Vance, ed., *Pleasure and Danger: Exploring Female Sexuality* (1984)

Gayle Graham Yates, *What Women Want: The Ideas of the Movement* (1975)

CHAPTER
12

Richard M. Nixon, Watergate, and the Crisis of the ''Imperial'' Presidency

※

The arrest on June 17, 1972, of five men inside the headquarters of the Democratic National Committee in Washington's Watergate apartment complex began a dramatic episode in the history of the modern presidency. Before the scandal was over, President Richard Nixon would be forced to resign, many of his principal aides and advisers would be convicted of unlawful activities, and many of the heretofore secret workings of the government would be exposed for public inspection.

In the aftermath of the break-in, Nixon and his closest advisers had worked hard to cover up the involvement of White House aides and officials of the Committee to Re-Elect the President (CREEP). In the short run, they succeeded. The break-in did not become a major issue in the 1972 campaign, and Nixon won a resounding personal victory over his Democratic challenger, Senator George McGovern. But the cover-up came unraveled the following year, and along with it not just the role of the White House in the break-in but a whole chain of illegal and unethical activities on the part of Nixon's aides and campaign workers, ranging from spying on rival candidates to undertaking elaborate efforts to disrupt their campaigns. The investigation into the break-in and cover-up, moreover, spawned a series of subsidiary investigations into illegal activities on the part of the FBI, the CIA, the Internal Revenue Service, and other government agencies. Public reaction to Watergate became a major factor in the election of Democrat Jimmy Carter to the presidency in 1976.

In attempting to explain Watergate, most contemporary commentators stressed Nixon's personality and the venality of those around him. Others saw in the scandal symptoms not just of personal corruption but of a grave crisis in the postwar presidency. Since the administration of Franklin D. Roosevelt, presidential power had steadily grown. From the beginning of the Cold War, the U.S. government had become increasingly embroiled in covert and illegal activities abroad. It had also become more and more involved in the often illegal sur-

veillance of its own citizens and in the disruption of dissident political activity. Nixon's defenders correctly noted that many of the activities with which his administration was charged had precedents in the actions of previous presidents. Yet notable differences distinguished the Nixon White House's policies from those of his predecessors. Indeed, not only did Nixon and his supporters harass their political opponents with techniques previously reserved primarily for foreign foes or left-wing dissidents, but they did so on a scale that was without precedent in American history.

✖ D O C U M E N T S

Much of the discussion about Watergate has inevitably focused on Nixon's character and personality. The first document presents portions of a highly revealing interview with the president on December 20, 1972, shortly after the conclusion of his successful campaign for reelection. Among the activities unearthed during the Watergate investigation was an attempt by the Nixon White House to identify prominent critics and punish them by having the Internal Revenue Service audit their taxes, by denying them federal contracts or licenses, or by otherwise targeting them for harassment. In the second document, White House counsel John W. Dean III writes to aide John D. Ehrlichman on August 16, 1971, about "how we can use the available federal machinery to screw our political enemies." Lists of White House "enemies" would subsequently be compiled and discussed with the president. In the course of the Watergate investigation, Nixon was compelled to turn over the audiotapes of White House meetings that he had secretly recorded. In the third document, taped on the morning of June 23, 1972, Nixon and a top adviser, H. R. Haldeman, discuss the Watergate break-in and ways in which to prevent its investigation from implicating the White House.

The investigation of Watergate by the Select Committee of the U.S. Senate revealed not only the extent of the White House's involvement in the break-in and in other illegal activities but also its efforts to cover up that involvement. In the fourth document, the chair of the Select Committee, Democratic senator Sam J. Ervin, Jr., of North Carolina, summarizes the committee's findings. These conclusions in turn led to hearings before the House Judiciary Committee, which recommended that Nixon be impeached. Faced with the threat of impeachment, Nixon resigned. The final document records the president's farewell remarks to his cabinet and members of the White House staff. Vice President Gerald Ford, who became president upon Nixon's resignation, promptly pardoned the former president, thus sparing him from criminal proceedings.

Richard M. Nixon on Being President, 1972

I've been fortunate, I have not had to miss a day because of illness [in response to a question about his health]. I thought that was some kind of a record but I find that Truman beat it except he didn't do it in an elected four-year term. So, I'm the first four-year president who hasn't missed a day in office providing I make it to January 20. I've been blessed with a

"An Inverview with Richard Nixon," by Saul Pett from the *Boston Sunday Globe,* January 14, 1973. Reprinted with permission of the Associated Press.

strong physical makeup, probably as a result of inheritance. You know, I've never had a headache in my life and my stomach never bothers me. I believe in the battle, whether it's the battle of a campaign or the battle of this office, which is a continuing battle. It's always there wherever you go. I, perhaps, carry it more than others because that's my way.

It's important to live like a Spartan, . . . to have moderate eating and drinking habits. That's not to say I don't enjoy a good time. But the worst thing you can do in this job is to relax, to let up. One must have physical and mental discipline here. This office as presently furnished probably would drive President Johnson up the wall. He liked things going on. He kept three TV sets here. I have none here or in my bedroom. I find to handle crises the most important qualities one needs are balance, objectivity, an ability to act coolly. . . .

People probably think the President was jumping up and down, barking orders, at those times [referring to his decisions to invade Cambodia in 1970, and to bomb North Vietnam and mine Haiphong Harbor in 1972]. Actually, I have a reputation for being the coolest person in the room. In a way I am. I have trained myself to be that. The great decisions in this office require calm.

I could go up the wall watching TV commentators. I don't. I get my news from the news summary the staff prepares every day and it's great; it gives all sides. I never watch TV commentators or the news shows when they are about me. That's because I don't want decisions influenced by personal emotional reactions.

The major weakness of inexperienced people is that they take things personally, especially in politics and that can destroy you. . . . Years ago, when I was a young congressman, things got under my skin. Herblock the cartoonist got to me . . . But now when I walk into this office I am cool and calm. I read the news summary and get both sides. That's important because there are so many emotional issues these days, such as the war and busing and welfare. But I never allow myself to get emotional. Now, there are Congressmen and Senators who cut me up, Fulbright, for example. But when he comes here, we're the best of friends, at least, I feel I am.

Now, it's not true that I don't feel emotional or pay attention to what others feel. But the most important thing I can do is to make decisions for the long run. Vietnam, for example. Now, we're having a difficult time. Things don't seem as bright as they did. So, we've had to continue the May 8 policy to bomb the North. We will obtain the right kind of peace but we won't get it because of artificial deadlines, such as the election or Christmas or the inaugural.

Now when Henry Kissinger comes in here in the morning and brings up what Scotty Reston and the other columnists are saying, I tell him, "Henry, all that matters is that it comes out all right. Six months from now, nobody will remember what the columnists wrote." Decision makers can't be affected by current opinion, by TV barking at you and commentators banging away with the idea that World War III is coming because of the mining of Haiphong. Nor can decisions be affected by the demonstrators outside.

I find that getting away from the White House, from the Oval Office, from that 100 yards that one walks every day from the President's bedroom to the President's office or the extra 50 yards across to the EOB, getting away gives a sense of perspective which is very, very useful.

One constantly has the problem of either getting on top of the job or having the job get on top of you. I find that up here on top of a mountain it is easier for me to get on top of the job, to think in a more certainly relaxed way . . . also in a way in which one, if not interrupted either physically or personally or any other way, can think objectively with perception. . . .

I'll probably do better in the next four years having gone through a few crises in the White House, having weathered them and learned how to handle them coolly and not subjectively. I probably am more objective—I don't mean this as self-serving than most leaders . . . When you're too subjective, you tend to make mistakes.

In speeches or press conferences or interviews you have to be up and sharp. You can't be relaxed. The Redskins were relaxed in their last game of the regular season and they were flat and they got clobbered. You must be up for the great events. Up but not up tight. Having done it so often, I perhaps have a finer honed sense of this. But you can overdo it, overtrain and leave your fight in the dressing room.

When I came into office, I'd been through enough—those shattering defeats in 1960 and 1962, and then those eight years in the wilderness, the way DeGaulle and Churchill were. The result was I was able to confront tough problems without flapping. I don't flap easily. An individual tends to go to pieces when he's inexperienced. . . . Now, there are just not many kinds of tough problems I haven't had to face one way or another. In that respect, the fact that my political career required a comeback may have been a blessing.

Well, the greatest pleasure [in winning reelection to the presidency] was the kick the young people Tricia and Julie and Pat got out of it. Those defeats in 1960 and 1962 were so traumatic for them. To most women, things look black or white; a man tends to roll with events. Oh sure, I took it pretty hard myself. But then there was 1968 and 1972 capped it all, despite all that talk about a one-term presidency. After four years of the most devastating attacks on TV, in much of the media, in editorials and columns, and then all that talk in the last two or three weeks of the campaign of the gap narrowing . . . and then whap! A landslide, 49 states, 61 percent of the vote! You'd think I'd be elated then. But it has always been my experience that it doesn't really come to that. But the family—David and Eddie [sons-in-law] kept running to me in the Lincoln Sitting Room with the results. They were so excited they made me feel excited. Then, after my TV talk here and at the Shoreham Hotel and staying up for the California returns . . . Well, you're so drained emotionally at the end, you can't feel much.

You'd think that just when the time comes, you'd have your greatest day. But there is this letdown.

Now, there are some people leaving the administration and some staying. I try to recharge them. There can never be a letdown in this office. That's the danger of a landslide. I want everyone to have a new charge, a new sense of challenge. . . . There are those who say there are no restraints on a President if he doesn't have to run again. That is really a fatuous and superficial analysis of the presidency. . . . Individuals who serve here do not serve to get reelected but to do great things. And they could be even greater when you don't have to worry about reelection.

Now, what we want to do, we want everybody to think the challenge is just as great. The leader has to whip them up. The team goes just as far as the leader, as the quarterback and coach, and I am both.

White House Counsel John W. Dean III Presents the "Enemies List," 1971

[John W. Dean III to John D. Ehrlichman]   August 16, 1971

CONFIDENTIAL

MEMORANDUM

SUBJECT: *Dealing with our Political Enemies*

This memorandum addresses the matter of how we can maximize the fact of our incumbency in dealing with persons known to be active in their opposition to our Administration. Stated a bit more bluntly—how we can use the available federal machinery to screw our political enemies.

After reviewing this matter with a number of persons possessed of expertise in the field, I have concluded that we *do not* need an elaborate mechanism or game plan, rather we need a good project coordinator and full support for the project. In brief, the system would work as follows:

- Key members of the staff (e.g., [Charles] Colson, Dent Flanigan, [Patrick] Buchanan) should be requested to inform us as to who they feel we should be giving a hard time.
- The project coordinator should then determine what sorts of dealings these individuals have with the federal government and how we can best screw them (e.g., grant availability, federal contracts, litigation, prosecution, etc.).
- The project coordinator then should have access to and the full support of the top officials of the agency or department in proceeding to deal with the individual.

I have learned that there have been many efforts in the past to take such actions, but they have ultimately failed—in most cases—because of lack of support at the top. Of all those I have discussed this matter with, Lyn Nofziger appears the most knowledgeable and most interested. If Lyn had support he would enjoy undertaking this activity as the project coordinator. You are aware of some of Lyn's successes in the field, but he feels that he can only employ limited efforts because there is a lack of support.

As a next step, I would recommend that we develop a small list of names—not more than ten—as our targets for concentration. Request that Lyn "do a job" on them and if he finds he is getting cut off by a department or agency, that he inform us and we evaluate what is necessary to proceed. I feel it is important that we keep our targets limited for several reasons: (1) a low visibility of the project is imperative; (2) it will be easier to accomplish something real if we don't over expand our efforts; and (3) we can learn more about how to operate such an activity if we start small and build.

President Richard M. Nixon Discusses the Watergate Break-in with Aide H. R. Haldeman, 1972

June 23, 1972, from 10:04 to 11:39 AM

[Assistant to the President] *Haldeman:* Okay—that's fine. Now, on the investigation, you know, the Democratic break-in thing, we're back to the—in the, the problem area because the FBI is not under control, because [FBI Director L. Patrick] Gray doesn't exactly know how to control them, and they have, their investigation is now leading into some productive areas, because they've been able to trace the money, not through the money itself, but through the bank, you know, sources—the banker himself. And, and it goes in some directions we don't want it to go. Ah, also there have been some things, like an informant came in off the street to the FBI in Miami, who was a photographer or has a friend who is a photographer who developed some films through this guy, [Bernard L.] Barker [later convicted in the Watergate break-in], and the films had pictures of Democratic National Committee letter head documents and things. So I guess, so it's things like that that are gonna, that are filtering in. [Former Nixon Attorney-General and at the time head of Nixon's re-election effort, John N.] Mitchell came up with yesterday, and John Dean [Counsel to the President] analyzed very carefully last night and concludes, concurs now with Mitchell's recommendation that the only way to solve this, and we're set up beautifully to do it, ah, in that and that . . . the only network that paid any attention to it last night was NBC . . . they did a massive story on the Cuban [Barker and others of those caught at the Watergate were Cubans and had worked for the CIA in the 1960s]. . . .

Haldeman: That the way to handle this now is for us to have [Deputy Director, Central Intelligence, Vernon] Walters call Pat Gray and just say, "Stay the hell out of this . . . this is ah, business here we don't want you to go any further on it." That's not an unusual development, . . .

President: Um huh.

Haldeman: . . . And, uh, that would take care of it.

President: What about Pat Gray, ah, you mean he doesn't want to?

Haldeman: Pat does want to. He doesn't know how to, and he doesn't have, he doesn't have any basis for doing it. Given this, he will then have the basis. He'll call Mark Felt in, and the two of them . . . and Mark Felt wants to cooperate because . . .

President: Yeah.

Haldeman: He's ambitious . . .

President: Yeah.

Haldeman: Ah, he'll call him in and say, "We've got the signal from across the river to, to put the hold on this." And that will fit rather well because the FBI agents who are working the case, at this point, feel that's what it is. This is CIA.

President: But they've traced the money to 'em.

Haldeman: Well they have, they've traced to a name, but they haven't gotten to the guy yet.

President: Would it be somebody here?

Haldeman: Ken Dahlberg.

President: Who the hell is Ken Dahlberg?

Haldeman: He's ah, he gave $25,000 in Minnesota and ah, the check went directly in to this, to this guy Barker.

President: Maybe he's a . . . bum.

President: He didn't get this from the committee though, from [Nixon re-election committee's finance chief, Maurice] Stans.

Haldeman: Yeah. It is. It is. It's directly traceable and there's some more through some Texas people in—that went to the Mexican bank which they can also trace to the Mexican bank . . . they'll get their names today. And (pause)

President: Well, I mean, ah, there's no way . . . I'm just thinking if they don't cooperate, what do they say? They they, they were ap-proached by the Cubans. That's what Dahlberg has to say, the Texans too. Is that the idea?

Haldeman: Well, if they will. But then we're relying on more and more people all the time. That's the problem. And ah, they'll stop if we could, if we take this other step.

President: All right. Fine.

Haldeman: And, and they seem to feel the thing to do is get them to stop?

President: Right, fine.

Haldeman: They say the only way to do that is from White House instructions. And it's got to be to [Director of Central Intelligence, Richard] Helms and, ah, what's his name . . . ? Walters.

President: Walters.

Haldeman: And the proposal would be that [Assistant to the President for Domestic Affairs, John D.] Ehrlichman (coughs) and I call them in

President: All right, fine.

Haldeman: and say, ah . . .

President: How do you call him in, I mean you just, well, we protected Helms from one hell of a lot of things.

Haldeman: That's what Ehrlichman says.

President: Of course, this is a, this is a Hunt, you will—that will uncover a lot of things. You open that scab there's a hell of a lot of things and that we just feel that it would be very detrimental to have this thing go any further. This involves these Cubans, [E. Howard Hunt, a former CIA operative then working for Nixon's re-election campaign] Hunt, and a lot of hanky-panky that we have nothing to do with ourselves. Well what the hell, did Mitchell know about this thing to any much of a degree?

Haldeman: I think so. I don't think he knew the details, but I think he knew.

President: He didn't know how it was going to be handled though, with Dahlberg and the Texans and so forth? Well who was the asshole that did? (Unintelligible) Is it [G. Gordon Liddy, a former CIA agent employed by the Nixon White House and re-election committee] Liddy? Is that the fellow? He must be a little nuts.

Haldeman: He is.

President: I mean he just isn't well screwed on is he? Isn't that the problem?

Haldeman: No, but he was under pressure, apparently, to get more information, and as he got more pressure, he pushed the people harder to move harder on . . .

President: Pressure from Mitchell?

Haldeman: Apparently.

President: Oh, Mitchell, Mitchell was at the point that you made on this, that exactly what I need from you is on the—

Haldeman: Gemstone [an early plan for a "dirty-tricks" operation which evolved into the Watergate break-in operation], yeah.

President: All right, fine, I understand it all. We won't second-guess Mitchell and the rest. Thank God it wasn't [Special Assistant to the President, Charles] Colson.

Haldeman: The FBI interviewed Colson yesterday. They determined that would be a good thing to do.

President: Um hum. . . .

Haldeman: An interrogation, which he did, and that, the FBI guys working the case had concluded that there were one or two possibilities, one, that this was a White House, they don't think that there is anything at the Election Committee, they think it was either a White House operation and they had some obscure reasons for it, non political, . . .

President: Uh huh. . . .

Haldeman: Colson, yesterday, they concluded it was not the White House, but are now convinced it is a CIA thing, so the CIA turnoff would . . .

President: Well, not sure of their analysis, I'm not going to get that involved. I'm (unintelligible).

Haldeman: No, sir. We don't want you to.

President: You call them in. . . . Good. Good deal. Play it tough. That's the way they play it and that's the way we are going to play it.

Haldeman: O.K. We'll do it. . . .

President: When you get in these people . . . when you get these people in, say: "Look, the problem is that this will open the whole, the whole Bay of Pigs thing, and the President just feels that" ah, without going into the details . . . don't, don't lie to them to the extent to say there is no involvement, but just say this is sort of a comedy of errors, bizarre, without getting into it, "the President believes that it is going to open the whole Bay of Pigs thing up again. And, ah because these people are plugging for, for keeps and that they should call the FBI in and say that we wish for the country, don't go any further into this case," period!

Senator Sam J. Ervin on Watergate, 1974

President Nixon entrusted the management of his campaign for reelection and his campaign finances to the Committee for the Re-Election of the President, which was headed by former Attorney General John N. Mitchell, and the Finance Committee To Re-Elect the President, which was headed by former Secretary of Commerce, Maurice Stans. Since the two committees occupied offices in the same office building in Washington and worked in close conjunction, it seems proper to call them for ease of expression the Nixon reelection committees.

Watergate was a conglomerate of various illegal and unethical activities in which various officers and employees of the Nixon reelection committees and various White House aides of President Nixon participated in varying ways and degrees to accomplish these successive objectives:

1. To destroy, insofar as the Presidential election of 1972 was concerned, the integrity of the process by which the President of the United States is nominated and elected.

2. To hide from law enforcement officers, prosecutors, grand jurors, courts, the news media, and the American people the identities and wrongdoing of those officers and employees of the Nixon reelection committees, and those White House aides who had undertaken to destroy the integrity of the process by which the President of the United States is nominated and elected.

To accomplish the first of these objectives, the participating officers and employees of the reelection committees and the participating White House aides of President Nixon engaged in one or more of these things:

1. They exacted enormous contributions—usually in cash—from corporate executives by impliedly implanting in their minds the impressions that the making of the contributions was necessary to insure that the corporations would receive governmental favors, or avoid governmental disfavors, while President Nixon remained in the White House. A substantial portion of the contributions were made out of corporate funds in violation of a law enacted by Congress a generation ago.
2. They hid substantial parts of these contributions in cash in safes and secret deposits to conceal their sources and the identities of those who had made them.
3. They disbursed substantial portions of these hidden contributions in a surreptitious manner to finance the bugging and the burglary of the offices of the Democratic National Committee in the Watergate complex in Washington for the purpose of obtaining political intelligence; and to sabotage by dirty tricks, espionage, and scurrilous and false libels and slanders the campaigns and the reputations of honorable men, whose only offenses were that they sought the nomination of the Democratic Party for President and the opportunity to run against President Nixon for that office in the Presidential election of 1972.
4. They deemed the departments and agencies of the Federal Government to be the political playthings of the Nixon administration rather than impartial instruments for serving the people, and undertook to induce them to channel Federal contracts, grants, and loans to areas, groups, or individuals so as to promote the reelection of the President rather than to further the welfare of the people.
5. They branded as enemies of the President individuals and members of the news media who dissented from the President's policies and opposed his reelection, and conspired to urge the Department of Justice, the Federal Bureau of Investigation, the Internal Revenue Service, and the Federal Communications Commission to pervert the use of their legal powers to harass them for so doing.
6. They borrowed from the Central Intelligence Agency disguises which E. Howard Hunt used in political espionage operations, and photographic equipment which White House employees known as the "Plumbers" and their hired confederates used in connection with burglarizing the office of a psychiatrist which they believed contained information concerning Daniel Ellsberg which the White House was anxious to secure.
7. They assigned to E. Howard Hunt, who was at the time a White House consultant occupying an office in the Executive Office Building, the gruesome task of falsifying State Department documents which they contemplated using in their altered state to discredit the Democratic Party by defaming the memory of former President John Fitzgerald

Kennedy, who as the hapless victim of an assassin's bullet had been sleeping in the tongueless silence of the dreamless dust for 9 years.

8. They used campaign funds to hire saboteurs to forge and disseminate false and scurrilous libels of honorable men running for the Democratic Presidential nomination in Democratic Party primaries.

During the darkness of the early morning of June 17, 1972, James W. McCord, the security chief of the John Mitchell committee, and four residents of Miami, Fla., were arrested by Washington police while they were burglarizing the offices of the Democratic National Committee in the Watergate complex to obtain political intelligence. At the same time, the four residents of Miami had in their possession more than fifty $100 bills which were subsequently shown to be a part of campaign contributions made to the Nixon reelection committees.

On September 15, 1972, these five burglars, E. Howard Hunt, and Gordon Liddy, general counsel of the Stans committee, were indicted by the grand jury on charges arising out of the bugging and burglary of the Watergate.

They were placed on trial upon these charges before Judge John Sirica, and a petit jury in the U.S. District Court for the District of Columbia in January 1973. At that time, Hunt and the four residents of Miami pleaded guilty, and McCord and Liddy were found guilty by the petit jury. None of them took the witness stand during the trial.

The arrest of McCord and the four residents of Miami created consternation in the Nixon reelection committees and the White House. Thereupon, various officers and employees of the Nixon reelection committees and various White House aides undertook to conceal from law-enforcement officers, prosecutors, grand jurors, courts, the news media, and the American people the identities and activities of those officers and employees of the Nixon reelection committees and those White House aides who had participated in any way in the Watergate affair.

Various officers and employees of the Nixon reelection committees and various White House aides engaged in one or more of these acts to make the concealment effective and thus obstruct the due administration of justice:

1. They destroyed the records of the Nixon reelection committees antedating the bugging and the burglary.
2. They induced the Acting Director of the FBI, who was a Nixon appointee, to destroy the State Department documents which E. Howard Hunt had been falsifying.
3. They obtained from the Acting Director of the FBI copies of scores of interviews conducted by FBI agents in connection with their investigation of the bugging and the burglary, and were enabled thereby to coach their confederates to give false and misleading statements to the FBI.
4. They sought to persuade the FBI to refrain from investigating the sources of the campaign funds which were used to finance the bugging and the burglary.

5. They intimidated employees of the Nixon reelection committees and employees of the White House by having their lawyers present when these employees were being questioned by agents of the FBI, and thus deterred these employees from making full disclosures to the FBI.

6. They lied to agents of the FBI, prosecutors, and grand jurors who undertook to investigate the bugging and the burglary, and to Judge Sirica and the petit jurors who tried the seven original Watergate defendants in January 1973.

7. They persuaded the Department of Justice and the prosecutors to take out-of-court statements from Maurice Stans, President Nixon's chief campaign fundraiser, and Charles Colson, Egil Krogh, and David Young, White House aides, and Charles Colson's secretary, instead of requiring them to testify before the grand jury investigating the bugging and the burglary in conformity with the established procedures governing such matters, and thus denied the grand jurors the opportunity to question them.

8. They persuaded the Department of Justice and the prosecutors to refrain from asking Donald Segretti, their chief hired saboteur, any questions involving Herbert W. Kalmbach, the President's personal attorney, who was known by them to have paid Segretti for dirty tricks he perpetrated upon honorable men seeking the Democratic Presidential nomination, and who was subsequently identified before the Senate Select Committee as one who played a major role in the secret delivery of hush money to the seven original Watergate defendants.

9. They made cash payments totaling hundreds of thousands of dollars out of campaign funds in surreptitious ways to the seven original Watergate defendants as hush money to buy their silence and keep them from revealing their knowledge of the identities of the officers and employees of the Nixon reelection committees and the White House aides who had participated in the Watergate.

10. They gave assurances to some of the original seven defendants that they would receive Presidential clemency after serving short portions of their sentences if they refrained from divulging the identities and activities of the officers and employees of the Nixon reelection committees and the White House aides who had participated in the Watergate affair.

11. They made arrangements by which the attorneys who represented the seven original Watergate defendants received their fees in cash from moneys which had been collected to finance President Nixon's reelection campaign.

12. They induced the Department of Justice and the prosecutors of the seven original Watergate defendants to assure the news media and the general public that there was no evidence that any persons other than the seven original Watergate defendants were implicated in any way in any Watergate-related crimes.

13. They inspired massive efforts on the part of segments of the news media friendly to the administration to persuade the American people that most of the members of the Select Committee named by the Senate to

investigate the Watergate were biased and irresponsible men motivated solely by desires to exploit the matters they investigated for personal or partisan advantage, and that the allegations in the press that Presidential aides had been involved in the Watergate were venomous machinations of a hostile and unreliable press bent on destroying the country's confidence in a great and good President.

One shudders to think that the Watergate conspiracies might have been effectively concealed and their most dramatic episode might have been dismissed as a "third-rate" burglary conceived and committed solely by the seven original Watergate defendants had it not been for the courage and penetrating understanding of Judge Sirica, the thoroughness of the investigative reporting of Carl Bernstein, Bob Woodward, and other representatives of a free press, the labors of the Senate Select Committee and its excellent staff, and the dedication and diligence of Special Prosecutors Archibald Cox and Leon Jaworski and their associates.

President Nixon's Farewell, 1974

Members of the Cabinet, members of the White House Staff, all of our friends here:

I think the record should show that this is one of those spontaneous things that we always arrange whenever the President comes in to speak, and it will be so reported in the press, and we don't mind, because they have to call it as they see it.

But on our part, believe me, it is spontaneous.

You are here to say goodby to us, and we don't have a good word for it in English—the best is *au revoir*. We will see you again.

I just met with the members of the White House staff, you know, those who serve here in the White House day in and day out, and I asked them to do what I ask all of you to do to the extent that you can and, of course, are requested to do so: to serve our next President as you have served me and previous Presidents—because many of you have been here for many years—with devotion and dedication, because this office, great as it is, can only be as great as the men and women who work for and with the President.

This house, for example—I was thinking of it as we walked down this hall, and I was comparing it to some of the great houses of the world that I have been in. This isn't the biggest house. Many, and most, in even smaller countries, are much bigger. This isn't the finest house. Many in Europe, particularly, and in China, Asia, have paintings of great, great value, things that we just don't have here and, probably, will never have until we are 1,000 years old or older.

But this is the best house. It is the best house, because it has something far more important than numbers of people who serve, far more important than numbers of rooms or how big it is, far more important than numbers of magnificent pieces of art.

This house has a great heart, and that heart comes from those who serve. I was rather sorry they didn't come down. We said goodby to them upstairs. But they are really great. And I recall after so many times I have made speeches, and some of them pretty tough, yet, I always come back, or after a hard day—and my days usually have run rather long—I would always get a lift from them, because I might be a little down but they always smiled.

And so it is with you. I look around here, and I see so many on this staff that, you know, I should have been by your offices and shaken hands, and I would love to have talked to you and found out how to run the world—everybody wants to tell the President what to do, and boy, he needs to be told many times—but I just haven't had the time. But I want you to know that each and every one of you, I know, is indispensable to this Government.

I am proud of this Cabinet. I am proud of all the members who have served in our Cabinet. I am proud of our sub-Cabinet. I am proud of our White House Staff. As I pointed out last night, sure, we have done some things wrong in this Administration, and the top man always takes the responsibility, and I have never ducked it. But I want to say one thing: We can be proud of it—5½ years. No man or no woman came into this Administration and left it with more of this world's goods than when he came in. No man or no woman ever profited at the public expense or the public till. That tells something about you.

Mistakes, yes. But for personal gain, never. You did what you believed in. Sometimes right, sometimes wrong. And I only wish that I were a wealthy man—at the present time, I have got to find a way to pay my taxes—[*laughter*]—and if I were, I would like to recompense you for the sacrifices that all of you have made to serve in government.

But you are getting something in government—and I want you to tell this to your children, and I hope the Nation's children will hear it, too—something in government service that is far more important than money. It is a cause bigger than yourself. It is the cause of making this the greatest nation in the world, the leader of the world, because without our leadership, the world will know nothing but war, possibly starvation or worse, in the years ahead. With our leadership it will know peace, it will know plenty.

We have been generous, and we will be more generous in the future as we are able to. But most important, we must be strong here, strong in our hearts, strong in our souls, strong in our belief, and strong in our willingness to sacrifice, as you have been willing to sacrifice, in a pecuniary way, to serve in government.

There is something else I would like for you to tell your young people. You know, people often come in and say, "What will I tell my kids?" They look at government and say, sort of a rugged life, and they see the mistakes that are made. They get the impression that everybody is here for the purpose of feathering his nest. That is why I made this earlier point—not in this Administration, not one single man or woman.

And I say to them, there are many fine careers. This country needs good farmers, good businessmen, good plumbers, good carpenters.

I remember my old man. I think that they would have called him sort of a little man, common man. He didn't consider himself that way. You know what he was? He was a streetcar motorman first, and then he was a farmer, and then he had a lemon ranch. It was the poorest lemon ranch in California, I can assure you. He sold it before they found oil on it. [*Laughter*] And then he was a grocer. But he was a great man, because he did his job, and every job counts up to the hilt, regardless of what happens.

Nobody will ever write a book, probably, about my mother. Well, I guess all of you would say this about your mother—my mother was a saint. And I think of her, two boys dying of tuberculosis, nursing four others in order that she could take care of my older brother for 3 years in Arizona, and seeing each of them die, and when they died, it was like one of her own.

Yes, she will have no books written about her. But she was a saint.

Now, however, we look to the future. I had a little quote in the speech last night from T.R. [Theodore Roosevelt] As you know, I kind of like to read books. I am not educated, but I do read books—[*laughter*]—and the T.R. quote was a pretty good one.

Here is another one I found as I was reading, my last night in the White House, and this quote is about a young man. He was a young lawyer in New York. He had married a beautiful girl, and they had a lovely daughter, and then suddenly she died, and this is what he wrote. This was in his diary.

He said, "She was beautiful in face and form and lovelier still in spirit. As a flower she grew and as a fair young flower she died. Her life had been always in the sunshine. There had never come to her a single great sorrow. None ever knew her who did not love and revere her for her bright and sunny temper and her saintly unselfishness. Fair, pure and joyous as a maiden, loving, tender and happy as a young wife. When she had just become a mother, when her life seemed to be just begun and when the years seemed so bright before her, then by a strange and terrible fate death came to her. And when my heart's dearest died, the light went from my life forever."

That was T.R. in his twenties. He thought the light had gone from his life forever—but he went on. And he not only became President but, as an ex-President, he served his country, always in the arena, tempestuous, strong, sometimes wrong, sometimes right, but he was a man.

And as I leave, let me say, that is an example I think all of us should remember. We think sometimes when things happen that don't go the right way; we think that when you don't pass the bar exam the first time—I happened to, but I was just lucky; I mean, my writing was so poor the bar examiner said, "We have just got to let the guy through." We think that when someone dear to us dies, we think that when we lose an election, we think that when we suffer a defeat that all is ended. We think, as T.R. said, that the light had left his life forever.

Not true. It is only a beginning, always. The young must know it; the old must know it. It must always sustain us, because the greatness comes not when things go always good for you, but the greatness comes and you are really tested, when you take some knocks, some disappointments, when sadness comes, because only if you have been in the deepest valley can you ever know how magnificent it is to be on the highest mountain.

And so I say to you on this occasion, as we leave, we leave proud of the people who have stood by us and worked for us and served this country.

We want you to be proud of what you have done. We want you to continue to serve in government, if that is your wish. Always give your best, never get discouraged, never be petty; always remember, others may hate you, but those who hate you don't win unless you hate them, and then you destroy yourself.

And so, we leave with high hopes, in good spirit, and with deep humility, and with very much gratefulness in our hearts. I can only say to each and every one of you, we come from many faiths, we pray perhaps to different gods—but really the same God in a sense—but I want to say for each and every one of you, not only will we always remember you, not only will we always be grateful to you but always you will be in our hearts and you will be in our prayers.

Thank you very much.

⋈ E S S A Y S

Most early accounts of Watergate, such as Jonathan Schell's *Time of Illusion* (1976) and J. Anthony Lukas' *Nightmare: The Underside of the Nixon Years* (1976), were highly critical of Nixon and the many members of his administration who had participated in the Watergate break-in, the campaign of "dirty tricks" that preceded it, or the cover-up that followed. Watergate, they argued, was the product of both the swollen powers of a Cold War "imperial presidency" and of the criminal conduct of Nixon and his retainers. While many conservatives preferred to ignore Watergate, a few such as James A. Neuchterlein, the editor of the conservative journal, *First Things,* sought to defend the former president. In the first essay, Neuchterlein argues that Nixon's abuse of executive power had deep roots in the actions of his Democratic predecessors and that although Watergate was "an ugly and unforgivable business," it was used unfairly by partisan critics to tar "everything and everyone associated with the Nixon administration." In the second essay, historian Stanley I. Kutler of the University of Wisconsin notes that those who would minimize or dismiss the importance of Watergate have focused narrowly on the break-in itself, ignoring the many abuses of power that preceded it and the widespread and deliberate obstruction of justice that followed. Watergate remains, he concludes, the central drama of the Nixon presidency.

Escaping Watergate: A Revisionist View of the Nixon Presidency

JAMES A. NEUCHTERLEIN

Few of us by now can muster the will to wallow any further in Watergate. However we feel about Richard Nixon and the series of events that brought him down, we want above all to be done with both of them. Watergate has

---

"Watergate: Toward a Revisionist View" by James Neuchterlein. Reprinted from *Commentary,* August 1979, pp. 38–45, by permission; all rights reserved.

so overwhelmed contemporary political consciousness that we feel at once saturated with the lessons of the scandal and yet unsure precisely what they might mean for us. Our conceptual faculties benumbed under the continuing avalanche of Watergate literature—memoirs, recountings, analyses, and sermonizings—we feel it difficult to sort out what the event's significance finally consists in. In any case, we prefer to hear no more about it all just now.

Yet there are reasons for resisting the mood of stupefied exhaustion. There is still learning to be done from Watergate, and it may be, in fact, that we are only now getting far enough removed from the details of the scandal to begin to take proper measure of its meaning. Only as we begin to distance ourselves from the event can we get past the stage of conditioned response and automatic judgment in our reaction to accounts of it. Two recent memoirs by participants in the crisis—John J. Sirica and Maurice H. Stans—help us ponder aspects and nuances of Watergate that might previously have registered only partially or perhaps even not at all.

Before new lessons concerning Watergate can be absorbed, however, a number of old ones will first have to be unlearned. It is probably inevitable that any major event will occasion a good deal of earnest nonsense. Watergate certainly has.

There is, in the first instance, the matter of significance. Historians and political analysts have a natural inclination to assume that significant events must have significant meanings. Watergate suggests that this is not necessarily so. There was not more there than met the eye. The scandal had momentous political effects, but its circumstances were essentially banal, and it left little in the way of usable lessons or enduring implications. Watergate may by now be the most overinterpreted event of modern times; it simply will not bear the weight of the portentous meanings that have been attached to it. We have learned from it again the venerable lessons that politics should not be conducted as warfare and that we need to elect to high office those who understand that there are certain things that decent men simply do not do. Those are useful reminders, but they require us neither to reconstruct our political system nor to reorder our moral values.

It is perhaps most useful to view Watergate as constituting, in symbolic terms, the last act of the 60's. The scheme issued from an administration enveloped in a state-of-siege mentality, and that mentality grew out of the fevered and polarized political climate of the decade following the assassination of John F. Kennedy. By the end of Nixon's first term, the President and his advisers had become the victims of their ideological preconceptions. Convinced that the message of their accomplishments was being distorted or ignored by hostile media and agitated by left-wing approval of and even participation in leaks of national-security information—some important, some not—they conjured up from within their White House fortress a nightmare vision of a nation deceived and endangered by a radical minority. And they proceeded to act on the basis of that vision.

When politics is war, it is necessary, as in all combat situations, to gather intelligence on the enemy's strategy and tactics. There has never been any good evidence that Nixon knew in advance about the Watergate break-in, and there is probably no reason to doubt his continuing denials. But neither is there any reason to suppose that he would have objected if he had known, except possibly on grounds of prudence.

The cover-up—in which of course Nixon was involved, and virtually from the beginning—followed naturally from the failure of the break-in. There was no plot as such, simply the instinctive behavior of men caught in an incredible blunder, trying to extricate themselves in any way they could. The immediate and automatic decision to deny any higher authorization for the burglary led inexorably, one step after another, to the making of a quagmire. Nixon's own summary observation is self-serving but not inaccurate: "We . . . all simply wandered into a situation unthinkingly, trying to protect ourselves from what we saw as a political problem." The cover-up was sordid and inexcusable, but it was not—as it has been variously depicted—an inevitable product of the imperial Presidency, a function of some peculiarly American preoccupation with ambition, success, and power, or a grand conspiracy against constitutional government.

Much of the initial interpretative gas over Watergate is already dissipating. President Carter's inability to get much of anything at all that he wants from Congress, for example, makes it painfully obvious that we are in no present danger of a runaway Presidency. Carter's particular problems aside, it has been clear to most observers for a very long time that our constitutional arrangements are such that national leadership must come from the President. The Congress is simply not constructed to provide coherent direction to the nation in either foreign or domestic affairs. (A fascinating and relevant statistic: there are now, by recent count, 152 subcommittee chairmen among the members of the House of Representatives.) The Nixon White House undoubtedly misused its powers, but the primary lesson of Watergate remains that we need a vigilant public and honorable leaders, not a reshuffling of the constitutional division of powers.

If the imperial Presidency has lost currency as a Watergate theme, the idea of the scandal as a commentary on the decline of American morality seems still to have lingering attractions. From the very beginning, our public moralists seized on Watergate as a symbol of the nation's predilection for whoring after false gods. The first of the Watergate conspirators to break into print, Jeb Magruder, deputy director to John Mitchell on the Committee to Reelect the President (CRP), informed us in the title of his memoir that his had been *An American Life,* and he went on to wonder whether the Watergate crimes did not "somehow reflect larger failures in the values" of American society: "I think that I and many members of my generation placed far too much emphasis on our personal ambitions, on achieving success, as measured in materialistic terms, and far too little emphasis on moral and humanistic values." The Reverend William Sloane Coffin, Jr., summarized Magruder's involvement with Watergate as "an all-American experience." There was, we were meant to see, significance here.

Perhaps. Recognition of human frailty is always salutary in a society still resistant to notions of original sin. More particularly, it is difficult not to be appalled by the narcissistic preoccupation of a John Dean with vulgar success, particularly in his measuring of it: fast sports cars, lots of women, impressive office furnishings. (Dean, of course, like all the other born-again ex-Watergaters, assures us that "everything is different now.")

Nonetheless, we might well hesitate to blame Watergate on the traditional demons of personal ambition and desire for success. The old bitch goddess gets blamed for so much in general that one begins to wonder if she is responsible for anything in particular. We can safely assume that most major political figures in America—or anywhere else—are overachievers greatly attracted to power and success. Few such men, however, are normally implicated, at least to our knowledge, in criminal conspiracies. The men at the heart of the Watergate crimes—Nixon, Mitchell, H. R. Haldeman, John Ehrlichman—obviously wore ethical blinders, but the fundamental problem lay with their public political values, not their private moral ones. They had already achieved success and power, and neither materialism nor personal ambition had anything significant to do with their deliberations over Watergate.

Which brings us to the third of the conventional interpretations of Watergate: how close we all came to the loss of our constitutional liberties. There is, of course, considerable evidence that the Nixon administration frequently did step over the line of legitimate behavior: excessive wiretaps; the extra-legal plumbers unit; the Huston intelligence plan; the break-in at the office of Daniel Ellsberg's psychiatrist; attempts to manipulate the CIA and FBI; Watergate itself. Charles Colson at the height of his influence appears to have been a genuinely sinister figure, and too many other men in the Nixon White House, trembling under Haldeman's ultimate and recurring threat, "If you can't get the job done, we'll find someone who can," acted in ways that violated private and public decency. Moreover, the hardball politics was initiated and encouraged at the very top.

But this quite real problem of abuse of executive power has frequently been inflated out of reasonable proportion. One does not in any way have to accept Nixon's various *tu quoque* defenses as exculpation for his crimes to concede that in fact it did not all start with Watergate. It is an exaggeration to argue, as some have done, that the kind of constitutional improprieties Nixon indulged in had constituted standard operating procedure for most administrations since Franklin D. Roosevelt, but it cannot be denied that he was, in a number of areas, armed with considerable precedent. Nixon was chief of presidential sinners, but he was neither the first nor the only one. We have the Nixon tapes; it is probably just as well, from what we already know, that we don't have the Roosevelt, Kennedy, or Johnson ones.

Nor should it be forgotten that, as already noted, Nixon acted in part out of a genuine, if exaggerated, concern for national security. He cynically and egregiously invoked national-security concerns in the Watergate cover-up, where, of course, they were entirely irrelevant, but that was not always the case. Henry Kissinger and Nixon alike had become legitimately concerned over the effect of leaks of confidential information on the conduct of American foreign policy. Nixon's may have been the paranoid style, but, as the saying goes, paranoids do have enemies.

It is virtually impossible to raise these points without seeming to excuse or at least minimize Watergate. Yet it is worth taking that risk if only in an attempt to counter the still widespread assumption that the Nixon administration came close to undermining the American constitutional system. That assumption found its classic expression a few years back in the widely popular television mini-series, *Washington: Behind Closed Doors,* in which the Nixonesque President, along with all his other sins, contemplates the suspension of national elections. That particular piece of hysteria had originally arisen among the more febrile elements of the radical Left during Nixon's first term, and yet here it appeared again, only now blithely mingled in with all the things Nixon *had* done (or had ever been suspected of doing) in a program watched, and considered as truth, by millions of Americans. And the Nixon of that series, who is the Nixon large numbers of people have been led to believe is the genuine article, *could* have suspended national elections. What Nixon did was bad enough that we do not need to attribute to him intentions he never had, and Watergate by itself was bad enough— stupid, criminal, and inexcusable enough—that we do not need to make of it more than it was.

If many of the received lessons of Watergate appear on examination to be trivial, exaggerated, or even downright misleading, there are other aspects of the affair that deserve closer attention than they have so far attracted. The recent memoirs by Sirica and Stans help us to consider these less obvious lessons of the scandal, though not entirely in the ways that the authors intended.

When Maurice H. Stans summarizes his Watergate experience as *The Terrors of Justice,* we immediately suspect hyperbole, if not dissimulation. Yet looked at dispassionately—at least so far as the official record can establish it—his is a genuinely harrowing tale. Ponderously detailed, awkwardly written and organized, this book nonetheless largely persuades, so long, that is, as it sticks to the details of the author's experiences.

Prior to Watergate, Stans had one of those Horatio Alger careers so common in the catalogues of American experience that we forget how significant and impressive they are. Born to children of immigrants in very modest circumstances in Shakopee, Minnesota, in 1908, Stans rose, through ambition, talent, and hard work, to the very top of the accounting profession before entering public life. Having served in the Eisenhower administration, he developed a strong case of Potomac fever (his term) and decided by the mid-60's to attach himself to Richard Nixon's star as his most likely route back to Washington. His special talent was that of fund-raiser, and he took on that role for Nixon, first in the 1962 race for the governorship of California, and later and more enthusiastically in the 1968 campaign for presidential nomination and election. As with everything else that he took on in his career, Stans was good at his job (Dean has said that he was the only member of the administration "who could have tutored Bob Haldeman on efficiency") and Nixon rewarded him with the position of Secretary of Commerce. Indeed, Stans had been too good at his job, and when it came time for the bid for election to a second term, Nixon put such heavy pressure on him that Stans, against his own real wishes, resigned his cabinet position in early 1972 to become finance chairman of CRP.

There, of course, disaster struck. Since he was the man in charge of the money, it seemed obvious to investigators—and to the media—that Stans must have known something about the uses of the funds that were raised first to finance the Watergate break-in and later to aid in the cover-up. Yet the record seems clear that he did not. Stans insisted from the outset on a clear separation of duties within CRP between the finance and campaign committees: his committee would raise and disburse the funds, but it was not its job to judge or verify the uses to which the campaign committee felt the monies should be put. If expenditures were properly authorized by a member of the campaign committee, the finance committee would meet them. And within the finance operation, Stans put his own energies to raising money; he left it to the treasurer of his committee, Hugh Sloan, Jr., to pay it out.

Thus the money for Watergate was paid out by Sloan to G. Gordon Liddy on the authorization of Magruder, Mitchell's deputy director. Liddy was so secretive concerning the money's purposes that Sloan complained to Stans; Stans checked with Mitchell, who assured him, without going into detail, that the payment was legitimate; and Stans told Sloan to pay the money. Stans's only involvement with the cover-up was a payment of $75,000 on June 29, 1972 to Herbert Kalmbach for purposes that Kalmbach assured Stans were legitimate, but which turned out to be part of the payoffs to insure the silence of the Watergate burglars. On none of this are we required to accept Stans's word. The Watergate prosecutors never charged Stans with involvement in any aspect of Watergate, and none of the conspirators has ever suggested that he was part of their operations. We might wonder in a few instances why he did not raise more questions than he apparently did (it would seem naive to suppose that he did not harbor certain suspicions), but we have no good reason to doubt his absolute denial of criminal knowledge or action.

Even as the actual record began to emerge, however, the media continued to tell the story of Watergate as if Stans had somehow been at the center of things. Although he was never officially charged with involvement, there is still because of that coverage a widespread public assumption that Stans was in some vague manner part of the Watergate scandal.

That assumption blends into the wider and near universal belief that the entire Nixon fund-raising operation in 1972 was one great sinkhole of corruption. The range of corrupt practices charged against the operation Stans headed has been astonishingly broad: that the Nixon campaign received enormous illegal gifts from foreign sources, such as the Shah of Iran; that CRP fund-raisers, armed with lists of corporations in trouble with government agencies, went about exchanging promises of help for large contributions; that government contracts were promised in exchange for generous gifts to the campaign; that government jobs, especially ambassadorships, were in effect sold to the highest bidders (one potential contributor, assuming that was in fact the ways things operated, bluntly asked Stans, "How much for Luxembourg?"; Stans tells us he informed the man that Luxembourg was not for sale); that CRP urged contributors to pay in cash in order that *quid pro quo* dealings and other corrupt operations would be harder to trace; that a massive "laundering" operation was carried on by the committee to hide the sources of contributions; that an "enemy list" of those who had refused to contribute was kept for later retaliatory action by the administration.

All of these charges, Stans tells us, came under exhaustive scrutiny and investigation by the office of the Watergate special prosecutor. None of them, he insists, resulted in the laying of any criminal charges, much less the securing of any convictions:

> Insofar as the Nixon money-raising in 1972 was concerned, there were only a handful of nonwillful technical violations, and these were less significant individually and in the aggregate than similar oversights and violations by a number of other candidates who were not prosecuted.
>
> That was the surviving sum and substance of all of the alleged financial corruption in the 1972 Nixon campaign. Not a single proven case of corrupt action. No favors granted. No contracts awarded. No cases fixed. No ambassadorships sold. No illegal contributions from foreigners. No overseas laundries. No illegal solicitations. No list of companies in trouble with the government. No enemy lists. No fund-raising by government officials. No extortion or coercion. No intentional circumvention of the law in a single instance. That is precisely what the Department of Justice, the Special Prosecutor, and the courts found.

Stans seems justified in describing the five counts on which he was finally convicted—and fined $1,000 per count—as "technical violations." There were two charges of *non-willful* receipt of illegal corporate contributions and three charges of late reporting of contributions and payments. None of them, as described in detail by Stans, appears to have involved anything more than a minor and insignificant infraction of election-financing laws, and it seems clear that the violations would, under ordinary circumstances, simply have been ignored. Stans reluctantly pleaded guilty to these misdemeanors in 1975, he says, rather than face a protracted, expensive, and debilitating trial in a District of Columbia court which he feared would still be operating in an inflamed climate of opinion. One senses that a part of him now deeply regrets that decision.

Stans's reluctance to face a trial is easily understandable in the circumstances. He had already endured a trial in New York in 1974 in which he and Mitchell faced charges of conspiracy, obstruction of justice, and perjury in connection with receipt of a $200,000 campaign contribution in 1972 from financier Robert Vesco, supposedly in exchange for helping Vesco with an investigation of his activities by the Securities and Exchange Commission. The jury, faced with what Tom Wicker of the New York *Times* described as "clearly a weak case" for the prosecution, acquitted the defendants on all counts.

Stans cherishes that acquittal, but, as already noted, he knows that millions of Americans will remain forever persuaded that, if only in some indefinable way, he was nonetheless "mixed up in Watergate." That is his anguish, and it is impossible upon reading this memoir not in some measure to share it with him. It could be, of course, that he has not told us the full truth, that there are elements, of moral guilt especially, which he has not fully confronted. That, I must add, is not my reading of the book, and in any case—moral guilt or not—Stans does seem fully to have established that he was legally innocent of any significant wrongdoing in the variety of matters that have been gathered under the Watergate umbrella, and that he nonetheless became subject to an extraordinary and vicious campaign of smear and slander.

Stans lays out his case in excruciating and repetitive detail; he specifies what seem to him scores of instances of unfair treatment at the hands of investigators, prosecutors, district attorneys, politicians, public-interest groups, publishers, reporters, and editorialists. The massive misreporting of his situation by the media—some of it malicious, much of it simply ignorant and unprofessional—gets the most careful and, by any standard, devastating attention. Yet for all his sense of grievance and outrage, Stans maintains a restrained and dignified tone. Given all that he endured, he appears surprisingly free of bitterness and desire for vengeance. Moved at times to the edge of despair, he managed throughout his ordeal to hold on to his equanimity, largely through massive doses of old-fashioned American positive thinking. (During the Vesco trial, for example, Stans and his wife attended a variety of church services, "choosing among those listed in the Saturday papers the sermons with the most reassuring titles." By this process, the Stanses found themselves in frequent attendance at the Marble Collegiate Church listening to Dr. Norman Vincent Peale.)

Stans desires the exoneration of history, the reclaiming, as he told the Senate Watergate Committee, of "my good name." But that is not the limit of his intentions. He believes there are lessons in Watergate that transcend his own case. He wants, in fact, though he does not say so directly, to begin the process of Watergate revisionism.

Some of his arguments make good sense. He shows, for example, that much of the post-1972 passion for campaign reform, which climaxed in the passage of the Federal Election Campaign Act of 1974, stemmed from a misreading of the Watergate experience. He dismisses the argument that the break-in occurred because the Republicans had so much money lying around they could indulge nasty impulses that a tighter budget would have required them to resist: "Watergate happened because some persons in authority wanted it to happen; in one way or another they would have financed it, law or no law, surplus or no surplus."

More broadly, he argues that the 1974 law, which provided for government financing of presidential elections and which placed ceilings both on individual contributions and on campaign expenditures, swept through Congress on a wave of indignation over massive corruption in the financing of the 1972 Nixon campaign that, on this book's showing, never occurred. Those violations that did take place, Stans says, were covered under existing law, and he makes a persuasive case that the pre-Watergate campaign act of 1971, which did not limit expenditures but which did require disclosure of all contributions over $100, offered sufficient safeguards against improper financial influence on elections and on political behavior. He takes some consolation from the Supreme Court decision of 1975 which threw out the provisions of the new law limiting expenditures. As for the remaining limits on individual contributions, Stans's reminder that "special-interest money" is not restricted to large personal contributions should recommend itself to reformers currently exercised over the excessive influence of "single-interest" voting groups.

An ill-considered campaign reform law is not, however, in Stans's view, the worst of the results of the Watergate affair. For him, the great untold story of Watergate is that the "terrors of justice" descended not only on Maurice Stans but on countless others who became victims of the "hysteria" of the times. Stans does not deny that Watergate involved real crimes— though he thinks they have been "exaggerated"—but the whole weight of the book is to emphasize the wrongdoings not of the conspirators but of those who, in their eagerness to expose the crimes of Watergate, trampled on the rights and reputations of the innocent.

To Stans, the Watergate investigation stands in the tradition of Salem, frontier vigilante justice, racial lynchings, and the McCarthyism of the 50's; it was, he charges, a witch-hunt, "where accusation was taken for guilt and association with Richard Nixon's administration or reelection campaign was grounds for accusation." Watergate, in fact, "was in most respects a vastly greater and more far-reaching inquisition than anything that had gone before." These themes have eagerly been seized on by ideologues of the Right; the review in *Human Events,* for example, hailed the book for offering, at long last, the beginning of the "real history" of the scandal. This real history, the reviewer suggested, will expose the "official version" of Watergate as "a monstrous, unconscionable distortion of the truth" and reveal the actual record of "a reign of media and government terror unparalleled in American history."

Such a view of Watergate involves, of course, a monumental loss of proportion and lack of perspective. It is simply perverse to summarize the affair as an instance of the McCarthyism of the Left. There are witch-hunts and witch-hunts (as Stans rather lamely concedes at the end of his Salem/Watergate analogy) and we can distinguish among them only by asking certain necessary questions: Were there witches present? What was their nature? Were the weapons chosen to fight them appropriate to the occasion? It is in the face of such questions that an identification of Watergate with McCarthyism disintegrates.

In Watergate there were real witches; they had to be exorcised; and the weapons devised to combat them, while sometimes put to crude or illegitimate uses, were not fundamentally inappropriate. McCarthy had a real enemy (despite what many cold-war revisionists suggest), but he fought Communism largely in the wrong place and with weapons that disabled more innocent than guilty. The innocents of Watergate—and Stans has shown us that there were some—were not, as were the innocents of McCarthyism, the central element in the story. That they were incidental victims does not make their experience less tragic, but neither does that experience rightfully figure as the heart of the matter. In the end, of course, McCarthy's excesses badly discredited the anti-Communist cause. (He had considerable help, it should be noted, from those who, either out of willful ignorance or malicious intent, collapsed all anti-Communism into McCarthyism.) It is unlikely that Stans or anyone else will be able to persuade future generations that the pursuit of the truth of Watergate was so flawed in procedure as to suggest doubts concerning its purposes.

Keeping these distinctions in mind, we can nonetheless assess the *elements* of McCarthyism that did, in fact, creep into the Watergate investigations. One can fully believe that Richard Nixon and his associates deserved everything they got and still acknowledge that the investigation which brought them down included avoidable instances, official and unofficial, of false accusation, abuse and harassment, misrepresentation, and character assassination. There *were* occasions when the affair took on, as Stans says, a "Roman circus atmosphere" and there were too many assumptions of guilt by association. Genuinely innocent men suffered real injuries: loss of friends, loss of income, loss of reputation. Opportunistic politicians and social critics used the weapon of Watergate to settle old scores and to advance their ideological interests. Reporting and analysis by the media too often exceeded the bounds of fair comment. People who should have made it their business to discourage the populist fantasies concerning tyranny and corruption that Watergate inevitably bred instead fostered and nourished them. The Watergate investigation did what it had to do—uncover the crimes of the Nixon administration—but in the process it also did unnecessary damage to civil liberties and to political civility. It would be wrong to argue that partially discreditable means invalidated legitimate ends, but the cause neither of justice nor of historical accuracy would be served by denial of the tainted means.

The tangled conflict between means and ends presents itself in acute form in consideration of the role of Judge John J. Sirica in the Watergate affair. The advertising for *To Set the Record Straight* describes Sirica as the "one true hero" of Watergate. That view matches the popular perception, but careful analysis of the record suggests that Sirica was a more ambiguous sort of hero than his publishers imagine. Sirica did play a critical part in uncovering the facts of the scandal. The cover-up began to fall apart with James McCord's letter to the judge after the initial burglary trial indicating his willingness to break silence about the conspiracy (though there may well be exaggeration in Sirica's claim that without McCord's letter the case "would never have been broken"). Yet doubts arise concerning Sirica's actions during the first Watergate trial and its aftermath, doubts which his memoir does not dispel.

In the pages of this book, Sirica frequently comes across as a kind of Harry Truman of the judiciary. As Truman did, Sirica clearly thinks of himself as a plain man without supposing for a moment that he is only an ordinary one. Sensitive concerning his limited education (he finished high school at night, skipped college, and only got through law school on the third try after earlier dropping out twice), Sirica, like Truman, compensates for educational deficiencies with brisk decisiveness, firm self-confidence (perhaps not always fully felt), and an uncomplicated assurance that problems can be solved and moralities secured without excessive cerebration, equivocation, or concern with customary rules of procedure. Such a personality is not at home with intellectual uncertainty or moral ambiguity. It is qualities like these that helped Harry Truman make the most momentous political decisions without tortuous agonizing, but sometimes also without sufficient reflection. It is a similar cast of mind that allowed Sirica relentlessly to pursue the deeper truths of Watergate, with little apparent concern—then or now—that in so doing he occasionally bent the rules of judicial behavior.

Sirica's vigorous desire for natural justice and his untroubled sense of right and wrong persuaded him from the outset to use the burglary trial to get at the "truth" of Watergate hidden behind the simple facts of the break-in. His reputation in Washington legal circles as "Maximum John" did not at all hurt his efforts to find that truth. Sirica's reputation, combined with his clear indication of frustration and anger during the course of the trial that those behind the burglary were avoiding detection, no doubt inclined McCord to the view that honesty was, with this judge at least, a prudential policy. It was just four days before he was due to be sentenced that McCord decided to confide in Sirica.

Both before and after McCord broke, Sirica went to considerable lengths to bring the full story of Watergate to the surface. Unsatisfied with the prosecution's efforts to get at the higher-ups behind the burglary, he subjected Hugh Sloan, treasurer of CRP, to intense questioning concerning the origins and intended purposes of the money Sloan had handed over to Liddy. In the course of the questioning, Sirica made abundantly clear his suspicion that Sloan was telling less than the full truth. But Sirica's questioning of Sloan turns out to have added nothing substantial to what had already been revealed in the court record; its only significant effect was to impugn the honesty, before the court and the nation, of a man who, as Sirica himself now admits, had not lied. Yet Sirica feels no need in any way to apologize for his actions in the Sloan interrogation. He has, he says, "no regrets" over his action during the trial: "The more I think about it, the more I believe that it was the proper course to take and in fact the only course to take. . . . Simply stated, I had no intention of sitting on the bench like a nincompoop and watching the parade go by."

Sirica also used sentencing procedure both as a deterrent and as a method of getting behind the cover-up. Thus in March 1973 he sentenced Liddy to a $40,000 fine and up to 20 years in jail (at several points Sirica reveals the strong dislike he had developed for the "smart-alecky, cocky" Liddy); with the other break-in defendants, he issued "provisional" sentences of 35 to

40 years, on the understanding that those sentences would be reduced if the defendants cooperated with the continuing Watergate grand jury and with the Senate Watergate Committee. Again, Sirica appears entirely unable to understand the "great furor" created by his use of draconian discretionary sentencing in order to coerce testimony on the larger questions related to the case. Federal statutes allow for the provisional sentencing procedure, and Sirica does not find it necessary to meet objections that that procedure was inappropriate in these circumstances. He does insist that he at no time meant to follow through on the threat implicit in the provisional sentences: "I never had any intention whatsoever of putting those men in jail for thirty to forty years," he says. That is reassuring, but it still does not meet the question of the propriety of making the threat in the first place. (Eight months later, Sirica did issue final, lesser sentences to all the defendants except Liddy.)

In assessing the judge's actions in the break-in trial, it is necessary to keep in mind that the prosecutors had their own plans for breaking the cover-up. Sirica himself notes U.S. Attorney Earl Silbert's intention, once he had obtained convictions in the break-in, to give grants of immunity to the burglars and haul them all back before the Watergate grand jury "to give the full story behind the break-in."

One need not be in any measure an apologist for the Watergate criminals to raise questions over Sirica's behavior. Reviewing Sirica's memoir in the *New Republic,* Joseph L. Rauh, Jr., a former national chairman of Americans for Democratic Action and a prominent civil-rights, civil-liberties, and labor lawyer, pointedly notes the statement of the American Bar Association that "the only purpose of a criminal trial is to determine whether the prosecution has established the guilt of the accused as required by law, and the trial judge should not allow the proceedings to be used for any other purpose." Observing that Sirica not only allowed but himself used the proceedings for "other purposes," Rauh concludes that "there was no warrant for Sirica to go beyond his proper judicial role":

> And the statement of the Court of Appeals, in affirming the burglary con-
> victions, that Sirica's conduct of the trial "was in the highest tradition of
> his office as a federal judge," is more a commentary on anti-Watergate
> hysteria than a justification for Sirica's misuse of judicial power. This same
> hysteria brought spokesmen for the greatest civil-liberties organization in
> the history of the nation (American Civil Liberties Union) . . . to applaud
> Sirica's conduct. But all of this cannot alter the end-justifies-the-means
> philosophy that surrounded Sirica's actions.

In the course of his book, Sirica delivers himself of some gratuitous pronouncements on the character and fate of Richard Nixon that are worth noting. At one point, he discloses that had Nixon refused to turn over the tapes to the court, he would have found the President in contempt and forced compliance by levying large daily fines, because, he says, "I knew the President loved money." Sirica also announces that Nixon should not have been pardoned, but should have been indicted and tried, and had he been convicted in Sirica's court, "I would have sent him to jail." To the argument that Nixon could not have been tried because the proceedings would have dragged on for months or even years, disrupting the country, Sirica replies that any such delays would only have come from the defendant himself, and he proceeds to a truly bizarre comparison:

> Nixon's tactic was really the same as the tactic behind the behavior of the Black Panthers and others who in those years disrupted their trials by yelling and throwing things and screaming insults at the judge. Nixon's threatened uproar would have taken the more genteel form of legalistic objections and emotional appeals for sympathy, but that made him no different from the others. The only difference between them was that Nixon got away with it.

The argument here is doubly peculiar. In the first place, even granting that Nixon by his actions in Watergate invited a kind of permanent open season on himself, it still seems excessive to anticipate and criticize behavior on his part that never occurred. He surely has enough real sins to account for that it is not necessary to create imaginary ones for him. Beyond that, it seems incredible that a federal district judge could be so injudicious as to find no distinction between tearing up a courtroom and making "legalistic objections."

It is in connection with Richard Nixon that Watergate issues the greatest challenge to our capacity for reasonable judgment. The problem, of course, involves not Nixon's role in Watergate itself—judgments are all too easy to make there—but relating Watergate to our larger conclusions concerning the Nixon Presidency. It will always be impossible to think of Nixon without thinking of the scandal that drove him from office, but severe distortion results when, as is often currently the case, everything in the Nixon years is viewed *sub specie* Watergate. It is probably still too early to establish the necessary distinctions, but the process ought to start soon. (A good place to begin, incidentally, is with Nixon's own memoirs, which are considerably more useful and revealing than many critics have suggested.)

Those who hope to see Nixon given his due will do well to avoid the approach taken in *The Terrors of Justice*. Stans makes ritual concessions concerning the evils of Watergate, but he still finds it hard to take them all that seriously. The break-in was, he acknowledges, a crime, but it was only "a very minor one except for the political repercussions that followed it" (which is a little like saying that the striking of the iceberg by the *Titanic* was insignificant except for the sinking that followed it). In his handling of the affair, Nixon "stumbled over a molehill," and it still seems to Stans tragically unfair that because of Nixon's "clumsy handling of a small incident" it became possible for a coalition of "opportunistic politicians, an aggressive and hostile media, ambitious prosecutors, and organized 'public-interest' groups" to combine to bring down the administration. The worst that Stans can bring himself to say about Nixon and Watergate is that Nixon was a President "who tried too hard."

It is clearly unacceptable to plead for justice for the Nixon administration on the grounds that Watergate did not make any difference or that it was not the President's fault. Watergate was an ugly and unforgivable business, and Nixon's tragic destiny was of his own making. What the liberals, the commentators, and all the rest of his ancient enemies could not have done to him, Nixon did to himself—and to all of us (particularly those who shared, in varying degrees, in his administration's aims and purposes).

The only path to historical rehabilitation for Richard Nixon will be the recognition that there was more to his administration than Watergate. Stans is unconvincing as an apologist, but he becomes more persuasive when he suggests that there were a great many people who, because they lost their emotional and intellectual balance or because they harbored ideological purposes, unfairly decided after Watergate that everything and everyone associated with the Nixon administration were irredeemably corrupt. Watergate became a symbol of total depravity, and too many people who should have known better swept together under the Watergate umbrella, without discrimination, all that the Nixon people had ever touched. That was unfair; more important, it was historically inaccurate. It is at this point that historical revisionism on Watergate might fruitfully begin.

The Inescapability of Watergate

STANLEY I. KUTLER

"In the past few days," Richard Nixon told the nation on the evening of August 8, 1974, he had realized that he no longer had "a strong enough political base in the Congress" to maintain himself in office. The President's contention that he had to resign merely because he had lost his political base sounded the *leitmotif* for his last campaign—his struggle for the grace and favor of history. That political base was Nixon's to lose, yet his remarks implied that he had been the victim of a political conspiracy. He mentioned the Watergate "matter" only once.

Nixon's apologia alarmed his old nemesis Wright Patman, Chairman of the House Banking Committee. The morning after the speech, he wrote to House Judiciary Committee Chairman Peter Rodino, urging that the committee complete its investigation into Nixon's presidential conduct. Patman told Rodino it was imperative to preserve all the documents and tapes and to ensure that nothing was lost as a result of the presidential transition.

Patman understood the stakes. He suspected that "in the coming weeks and months, there will be some who will attempt to distort the record, [to] misconstrue events and to cloud the real issues." Watergate had been a "wrenching experience," he told Rodino, but nothing would be learned if the record were incomplete or distorted. He urged that the committee secure additional White House tapes and publish them. Patman had correctly complained on other occasions that the available tape transcripts revealed nothing of White House discussions between September 15, 1972, and February 28, 1973.

The thought of remaining in the limelight apparently was too much for Rodino. He had been a reluctant warrior from the outset. Now, with almost unseemly haste, he retreated to his familiar obscurity—and shut down the House impeachment inquiry. No one challenged him; Patman again found himself abandoned and isolated. Meanwhile, Rodino had given aid and comfort to Nixon's embarrassed supporters, one of whom had begged Leon Jaworski to put an "immediate end" to this "mess," and allow everyone to "quickly forget about it and go on about their business."

Nixon himself was more than ready to go about the business of refurbishing his historical reputation. What he said when he resigned, and what he did after that, signaled his campaign to capture the soul of history. Gerald Ford, never known for stern judgments of his contemporaries, remarked that Nixon's resignation-eve statement on his loss of political support dodged the real issue. Nixon, he complained, had failed to offer any note of contrition, refusing to "take that final step." Surely, Nixon had no desire for such finality. A contentious man, so self-consciously struggling to emulate Theodore Roosevelt's "man in the arena," Nixon simply could not couple the shame of resignation with the obscurity that public penance might bring. Wright Patman could but ponder the future implications of Rodino's decision to bow out. What, indeed, would history say?

Before and after his resignation, Nixon and his supporters either minimized Watergate or ignored it altogether. In May 1974 Nixon told Rabbi Baruch Korff that Watergate was the "thinnest scandal" in American history. Although embattled by that scandal near the end of his tenure, Nixon suggested to Alexander Haig that a failure to respond to a North Korean attack on an American reconnaissance plane in 1969 "was the most serious misjudgment of my Presidency, including Watergate." He assured his fallen aide, Charles Colson, that Colson's "dedicated service" to the nation would be remembered after Watergate had "become only a footnote in history." At an October 1973 press conference, Nixon anticipated his theme of victimization when he denounced his congressional and media opponents as spiteful enemies who sought to reverse "the mandate of 1972." Just after the resignation, David Eisenhower, the former President's son-in-law, said that in fifteen years, Watergate would "look pretty small." The President, Eisenhower said, had "simply acquiesced in the non-prosecution of aides who covered up a little operation into the opposition's political headquarters"—hardly something to be taken seriously. In an April 1988 television appearance, Nixon repeated the "footnote" thesis but added that his delay in bombing North Vietnam was the biggest mistake of his presidency.

If he could not reduce Watergate to banality, to something commonplace, Nixon's fallback position always was to insist that no wrong had occurred. "When the President does it, that means that it is not illegal," he told television interviewer David Frost in May 1977, in the first of many self-orchestrated "comebacks." He referred to the "political" (not criminal) activities that led to his resignation. Following the broadcast of the Frost interviews, a Gallup poll found that 44 percent of those who watched were more sympathetic toward Nixon than they had been, while 28 percent felt less so. Yet Nixon's early venture into revisionism and vindication failed dismally. Nearly three-quarters of the viewing audience believed he had been guilty of an obstruction of justice, and nearly as many thought he had lied during the Frost interviews themselves.

Fifteen years after the Watergate break-in, Nixon loyalists faithfully echoed their leader's interpretation. At a 1987 conference, H. R. Haldeman resurrected the "third-rate burglary" pronouncement of June 1972, calling it the work of "stupid" Nixon supporters. If the problem had been "handled within the White House staff structure from the outset," he said, the matter would have been contained—as if John Dean had ever worked for someone other than H. R. Haldeman. In a televised 1984 memoir, one which Nixon and his staff carefully controlled, the former President called the break-in a "botched" job, a "misdemeanor" that his enemies had turned into the "crime of the century." In 1988, Patrick Buchanan dismissed the Watergate events as "Mickey Mouse misdemeanors," evidently forgetting that felonies, as well as stupidity, followed the Watergate break-in. "A child of ten would have been able to figure out that it wasn't a sensible thing for [Nixon] to do, to try that cover-up," observed Richard Helms, no stranger to clandestine affairs. It was "one of the stupidest things that anybody could have done."

Those who would minimize or dismiss Watergate focused on the break-in of Democratic headquarters, an event of which the President and his closest staff members pled total ignorance, and at the same time avoided any discussion of the abuses of power that preceded the burglary and the obstruction of justice that followed it. Those acts, which are part of the Watergate story, run like a seamless web throughout the Nixon presidency, and while they constituted the focus of the impeachment proceedings, they were ignored in the interpretation imposed by the former President. William Ruckelshaus, a victim of the Saturday Night Massacre, had a different stake in the interpretation of Watergate, but one more in accord with the facts: "[T]he break-in was trivial but what happened afterwards was not trivial. It was profound." And Leon Jaworski, who perhaps understood Nixon's stonewalling better than anyone, brusquely noted: "To deny impeachable acts and criminal wrongdoing is untruthful. . . . They cannot be erased by the belated efforts of the man who created them." Jaworski had enthusiastically supported Nixon's re-election bid in 1972; his later judgment gave the lie to Nixon's bald claim that he had been undone by political enemies.

Revisionism perhaps is as inevitable as death and taxes, and the Watergate affair deserves some, to be sure. Contemporary commentator Nicholas von Hoffman, for example, shrewdly warned of the dangers of history written only from the perspective of the winners. The uncritical fascination with Judge John Sirica and his transformation into a neo-folk idol; the press's excessive claims for its role; the lynch-mob mentality of what von Hoffman called the "monotone" media; and some questionable prosecutorial tactics suggest topics that deserve more critical scrutiny. But that kind of revisionism is quite different from one that proceeds from the premise that "everyone" had engaged in abuses of power, that obstruction of justice was a matter of "national security," and that Nixon's actions pale into insignificance against the achievements of his Administration. Such attitudes come close to validating Voltaire's dictum that history is a pack of tricks the living play upon the dead.

How shall we remember Richard Nixon?

The movie is Woody Allen's *Sleeper* (1973); the scene is set in the year 2073; several people, apparently anthropologists, are watching old videotapes of Richard Nixon:

> *Doctor:* Some of us have a theory that he might once have been President of the United States, but that he did something horrendous. So that all records—everything was wiped out about him. There is nothing in the history books, there are no pictures on stamps, on money. . . .
>
> *Miles Monroe:* He actually was President of the United States but I know whenever he used to leave the White House, the Secret Service would count the silverware.

That, of course, was at the height of the Watergate affair. In the years that followed, Nixon regularly presented himself as an elder statesman and as a knowing political handicapper; still, for many, he remained a comic figure, a butt of derision, constantly forced back into private retreat as the barbs and jokes resonated. But the *Sleeper* lines about forgetting have a ring of painful reality. We are, to some extent, in danger of forgetting— not forgetting Richard Nixon, but forgetting what he did and what he symbolized to his contemporaries. History, after all, is not just what the present wishes to make of the past for its own purposes; present-mindedness has its own alphabet of sins. Historians are entitled to weigh the past by the measure of the evidence of long-term consequences, and they must weigh by the standards of that past, not those of their own time. Yet as Leon Jaworski cautioned, they must not uncritically accept the judgments of the actors themselves.

Memories proved short in some cases. The upper echelon of the so-called media "lynch mob," the American Society of Newspaper Editors, who had heard Nixon proclaim "I am not a crook" in 1973, welcomed him to their annual meeting in 1984 with a standing ovation. The former President expressed surprise that he had been asked so few Watergate questions. Two years later, *Newsweek* reported that when asked what he considered Watergate's greatest lesson, Nixon replied: "Just destroy all the tapes." Yet two weeks afterward, the same periodical proclaimed Nixon "rehabilitated," and featured him on its cover over the caption, "He's back." One scholar argued that Nixon might be the greatest domestic president of the twentieth century—a notion first advanced by John Ehrlichman—and described Watergate as only a "dim and distant curiosity" which eventually would be seen as "a relatively insignificant event." Worse yet, treatment of Watergate ran the danger of trivialization, as when the *Today* television show interviewed

Gordon Liddy for his views on the Soviet Union or when Jeb Magruder was selected to chair an ethics commission. Typically, media fascination with personality rather than with substance served to keep "the slippery former president" alive as a public figure, political writer David Broder noted, "when he ought to be living out his life in private and in disgrace."

The Nixon revisionism attempted to inflict a collective national amnesia on historians, the media, and our political leadership regarding Watergate. Watergate at times seemed lost in the mists of history, an odd fate for an event that consumed and convulsed the nation and tested the constitutional and political system as it had not been tested since the Civil War. But, in truth, once out of the White House, Richard Nixon commanded attention precisely because of his indissoluble links to Watergate, a connection indelibly engraved on our history. When asked in 1968 how he envisioned the first line of his *New York Times* obituary, Nixon replied: " 'He made a great contribution to the peace of the world.' " Twenty years later, he told reporters: "History will treat me fairly. Historians probably won't[,] because most historians are on the left, and I understand that"—resorting to a familiar refrain and technique. Then he asked that he be remembered most for his China initiative.

Nixon certainly will be remembered for his role in world affairs. He will receive heavy measures of both praise and criticism, and historians of both the Right and the Left probably will cross sides in unpredictable ways. It might never have occurred to Richard Nixon that so-called leftist historians helped rehabilitate Herbert Hoover. Whatever historians do, however, no "fair" history of the Nixon era can overlook the centrality of Watergate. Textbooks a century from now will inevitably speak of Richard Nixon as the first president to resign because of scandals. His achievements will get their due, as different generations weigh them, favorably or unfavorably, but they probably will not rival Watergate for historical attention.

Henry Kissinger contemptuously dismissed the political and media assault on the Nixon Administration as an "American extravaganza," something profoundly distasteful to him as a longtime admirer of the ordered past of nineteenth-century Europe. "Extravaganza," indeed; not every president has stood in danger of impeachment. Neither Nixon nor we can escape Watergate. Its history demands our serious attention; it was neither trivial nor insignificant. It raised important, painful questions about American political behavior and the American political system, questions that speak to the traditions and structure of American life. Whether the actors in the drama of Watergate confronted those questions successfully or unsuccessfully, directly or passively, honestly or conveniently, will be the subject for history. That is the significant, inescapable importance of Watergate.

The wars of Watergate are rooted in the lifelong political personality of Richard Nixon. His well-documented record of political paranoia, his determination to wreak vengeance on his enemies, and his overweening concern with winning his own elections, rather than with the fortunes of his colleagues or with the substance of policy, animated the thoughts and actions of his aides, who fulfilled his wishes.

The period is also bounded by much more than a burglary in 1972 and a resignation in 1974. The fall of Richard Nixon was the last act in a decade-long political melodrama that haunted the American stage, beginning with the civil rights movement and John F. Kennedy's assassination. War and unprecedented social protest about the war and other complex problems in American life followed and eventually culminated in Watergate. To that extent, Richard Nixon was the last casualty.

Richard Nixon cannot be separated from Watergate, however valiant his efforts. In time, Haldeman, Ehrlichman, Mitchell, Colson, Dean, Butterfield, Haig, and the other supporting players in the Watergate drama will fade into the same well-deserved obscurity as have their counterparts in other historical scandals. Ultimately, we leave behind the spear carriers, what the poet Coleridge called the Ancient Mariner's "strange and ghastly crew." But Nixon himself will remain as the one indisputably unforgettable and responsible actor.

President Nixon and his defenders have claimed that in the Watergate affair he behaved no differently from other presidents. Watergate emerged "exactly how the other side would have played it," Nixon said in 1977. It was all "politics pure and simple." With even less plausibility, he justified the crimes of Watergate as an outgrowth of the "end-justifies-the-means mentality of the 1960s." The long answer to all that is that *not* everyone did it. The short answer is that others' behavior is beside the point. Sam Ervin impatiently dismissed Nixon's plea: "Murder and theft have been committed since the earliest history of mankind, but that fact has not made murder meritorious or larceny legal." The Nixon rationalization rested on a claim that he was an unfortunate victim of time and place and deserves to be considered entirely apart from Watergate. Still, there is no dodging the fact that Watergate happened and he was found culpable.

Egil Krogh, who engineered an illegal break-in on Nixon's behalf, confessed that his work, "as official Government action, . . . struck at the heart of what the Government was established to protect, which is the . . . rights of each individual." His mission had not been designed to protect national security but to gain material to discredit Daniel Ellsburg (*sic*). Charles Colson similarly later admitted that "the official threats" to individual rights were wrong and had to be stopped. Yet the President himself repeatedly had initiated and encouraged those threats, and then had sacrificed his closest political subordinates to conceal his own involvement in their abuses of power and obstructions of justice. "I abdicated my moral judgments and turned them over to someone else," Ehrlichman confessed to Judge Sirica. Watergate gives us cause to ponder anew Alexander Hamilton's query in *Federalist I* whether in this nation, men would establish "good government from reflection and choice, or whether they are forever destined to depend for their political constitutions, on accident and force."

Richard Nixon discovered that the nation would tolerate an imperial president, but not an imperious one. Centuries of British and American constitutional experience have dictated limitations on executive power. However necessarily powerful the presidency may be in a fragile, dangerous world, however indispensable presidential action may seem for the nation's security and well-being, the practiced traditions of constitutionalism and the rule of law still count for much.

The Watergate wars offered eloquent testimony that the nation had a serious commitment to the rule of law. Our tradition has been that of a nation of laws, not of men only; a nation of orderly means and processes, not of burglars or imperious executives and their compliant servants. That tradition is the essence of American constitutionalism. John Ehrlichman— and Richard Nixon—suffered irreparable damage when Ehrlichman so cavalierly brushed aside Senator Herman Talmadge's concern for the security of home and person. Men are not angels, Madison said, and we wisely have fenced them in with constitutional prescriptions for the restraint of power. The legal order, as Alexander Bickel wrote at the time of Watergate, required "not a presumed, theoretical consent, but a continuous actual one, born of continuous responsibility." Rulers cannot legitimately impose a rule of law on the ruled unless they themselves will submit to it.

"[L]et us begin by committing ourselves to the truth, to see it like it is and tell it like it is, to find the truth, to speak the truth and to live the truth. That's what we will do," Richard Nixon told his fellow Republicans when they nominated him for the presidency in 1968. "Truth will become the hallmark of the Nixon Administration," Herbert Klein told reporters several weeks after the election. But lies became the quicksand that engulfed Nixon, estranged him from his natural political allies, and eventually snapped the fragile bond of trust between leaders and led that binds government and the people. Nixon's lies brought him to the dock and cost him his presidency. "I have impeached myself," he confessed in 1977.

Political language can conceal the truth, as George Orwell and others have noted. Often truth is concealed with a knowing wink between the political leader and his audience, and much of it is concealed in the language of symbolic politics. Richard Whalen, a one-time Nixon adviser and speechwriter, described how Nixon confined his conservative instincts to private company, while publicly positioning himself to the left—where, he believed, the votes were. "You don't know how to lie," Nixon told an early political associate. "If you can't lie, you'll never go anywhere." But for Nixon, lies led ultimately to a disgraceful resignation. At Republican leadership meetings throughout 1973 and 1974, Nixon's allies pleaded with him to "get it all out on the table." Nixon would say there was no more. But with repeated new disclosures, even those most steadfast among his supporters reached the point where, Congressman Barber Conable recalled, "you didn't believe anything." And still Nixon would insist, "it's all out there." The President informed Republican National Chairman George Bush, "George, I'm telling the truth." But the tape revelations reportedly devastated Bush; lying, a friend said, just was "not in George Bush's book."

Nixon confronted Democratic majorities in Congress throughout his presidency, a fact which doubtless contributed mightily to his sense of peril. But a numerical majority dictates organizational control, not necessarily ideological dominance. Friendly Southern Democrats and Republican loyalists regularly eased Nixon's path through his first term. Conflicts existed, to be sure, but he was not a President denied. The domestic achievements that Nixon and Ehrlichman claimed with such pride offer ample testimony to the President's success with Congress. The unfolding events in 1973 and 1974 weakened Nixon's support base in Congress, and the President's lies, deceit, "stonewalling"—to use the popular phrase of Watergate—eventually destroyed it.

The Saturday Night Massacre convinced many that Nixon had something to hide. The exposure of the taping system betrayed a sinister side to the White House. The 18½-minute tape gap, the incorrect transcripts, and the President's shifting explanations inexorably chipped away at his credibility. The Republican and Southern Democratic members of the House Judiciary Committee watched the President descend the slippery slope away from truth, convinced that he had lied. Repeated sentiments such as he expressed in August 1973—"That was and that is the simple truth"—were seen as hollow and perverse. The Republican loyalists on the House Judiciary Committee realized the irreparable damage of Nixon's lying. After the release of the "smoking gun" transcripts, they expressed amazement and dismay that for so long he had suppressed the truth about his role in Watergate; consequently, they sadly noted, the truth "could not be unleashed without destroying his presidency."

William Buckley thought that presidents must on occasion violate laws, but he judged that Nixon's denials of his actions magnified the violations. For Buckley, the denials, not Nixon's lawbreaking, constituted the President's "real" crimes. Nixon repeatedly promised the "truth," an old refrain that echoed the "Checkers" speech of 1952 when he said that the "best thing is to tell the truth." Barry Goldwater did not share Buckley's brief for moral relativism. "Truth is the foundation of a stable society," he insisted. "Its absence was the crux of Nixon's failure." With biting contempt, Goldwater read the indictment: Nixon had lied to his family, his friends, his political supporters in and out of Congress, the nation, and the world. "Tell the truth," Goldwater told Nixon when he visited the former President in his San Clemente exile in 1975. When he wrote his memoirs thirteen years later, Goldwater was still waiting for the truth from Richard Nixon.

Because he lied, Richard Nixon lost his political base. That deceit was intended to obscure the overwhelming evidence that he *had* abused power and he *had* obstructed justice. The actions of the President and his men were serious. More than seventy persons were convicted or offered guilty pleas as a consequence of the Age of Watergate. These included several Cabinet officers, two Oval Office aides, and numerous presidential assistants. Revisionism, to be whole, must produce more than pardons at the bar of history; it must produce the necessary exculpatory evidence.

Nixon's deeds as well as his own words, on tape, in public, and in his memoirs, convicted him. "I brought myself down. I gave them a sword. And they stuck it in," he bitterly observed. But he reminded us of what he was: "And, I guess, if I'd been in their position, I'd have done the same thing." Resignation, he once said, meant that he was guilty, and it would weaken the presidency he so cherished. For two years, he had resisted cooperation in the name of "preserving the presidency"—meaning, of course, himself. But in the end, he willingly sacrificed the presidency in order to save the President.

Political philosophers since the ancient Greeks have sought to understand the links between politics and ethical behavior—"virtue," as eighteenth-century men were fond of calling it. They agreed at least, Dwight Macdonald once wrote, "that there is some connection between ethics and politics and there is a problem involved." They all, he observed, rejected the "simplistic" view, so congenial to the "pragmatic" American mind, that there was no connection and no problem.

The eagerness of Nixon and his supporters to dismiss his misdeeds because "everyone does it" perversely twisted the conservative political tradition to which they subscribed, a tradition that rests upon virtue and morality. As the impeachment inquiry reached its climax, Congressman William Cohen recognized that perversion as he wondered how we had moved from the *Federalist Papers* of the 1780s to the Nixon tapes of the 1970s. Alexander Hamilton and James Madison, who had few illusions about human nature, nevertheless understood that leadership must rest on something other than covering up crimes or scheming to punish alleged enemies.

Americans idealize their presidents and hence expect them to meet the highest moral standards. People demand leaders better than themselves; such is the stuff of "heroes." Nixon's "tricky" image was one he never escaped. Watergate reinforced, and then confirmed, that image.

Competence and expertise were not enough to protect Richard Nixon. The President symbolizes "legitimacy, continuity, and morality"; Nixon tarnished the symbol, and it cost him dearly. What is clear, above all, is that the country had come together on the fundamental proposition that virtue mattered, that some ethical standard applied in political life. Thomas Jefferson once remarked that the whole art of government consists in being honest. George Washington, who gave a "Farewell Address" in 1796 far different from Nixon's, said that virtue and morality formed the "necessary spring of government" and were "indispensable supports" for political prosperity. "The mere politician," Washington insisted, "ought to respect and cherish them." Washington and the cherry tree myth are deeply ingrained in American civil religion. Richard Nixon never understood. Nearly a decade after he resigned, he wrote: "Virtue is not what lifts great leaders above others." But even those words of self-incrimination pale next to the most fateful ones he ever uttered: "I hereby resign."

✖ *F U R T H E R   R E A D I N G*

Stephen Ambrose, *Nixon: The Education of a Politician, 1913–1962* (1987)
Peri Arnold, *Making the Managerial Presidency* (1986)
Richard Ben-Veniste and George Frampton, Jr., *Stonewall: The Real Story of the Watergate Prosecution* (1977)
Carl Bernstein and Bob Woodward, *All the President's Men* (1974)
———, *The Final Days* (1976)

Fawn Brodie, *Richard Nixon: The Shaping of His Character* (1981)
Lewis Chester, Godfrey Hodgson, and Bruce Page, *An American Melodrama* (1969)
Samuel Dash, *Chief Counsel* (1976)
John Dean, *Blind Ambition* (1976)
———, *Lost Honor* (1982)
Harry Dent, *The Prodigal South Returns to Power* (1978)
John Ehrlichman, *Witness to Power: The Nixon Years* (1982)
Sam Ervin, *The Whole Truth: The Watergate Conspiracy* (1980)
Roland Evans, Jr., and Robert Novak, *Nixon in the White House* (1974)
Louis Fisher, *Constitutional Conflicts Between the President and Congress* (1985)
H. R. Haldeman, *The Ends of Power* (1978)
Paul J. Halpern, ed., *Why Watergate?* (1975)
Donald W. Harward, ed., *Crisis in Confidence: The Impact of Watergate* (1974)
Seymour Hersh, *The Price of Power: Kissinger in the Nixon White House* (1983)
Godfrey Hodgson, *All Things to All Men: The False Promise of the Modern American Presidency* (1980)
Jim Hougan, *Secret Agenda: Watergate, Deep Throat and the CIA* (1984)
Leon Jaworski, *Confession and Avoidance: A Memoir* (1979)
———, *The Right and the Power: The Prosecution of Watergate* (1976)
Clarence Kelley, *Kelley: The Story of an FBI Director* (1987)
Henry Kissinger, *White House Years* (1979)
———, *Years of Upheaval* (1982)
Herbert G. Klein, *Making It Perfectly Clear* (1980)
Richard Kleindienst, *Justice: The Memoirs of an Attorney General* (1985)
Stanley I. Kutler, *The Wars of Watergate: The Last Crisis of the Nixon Presidency* (1990)
Gladys Engel Lang and Kurt Lang, *The Battle for Public Opinion: The President, the Press, and the Polls During Watergate* (1983)
J. Anthony Lukas, *Nightmare: The Underside of the Nixon Years* (1976, 1988)
Theodore J. Lowi, *The Personal President: Power Invested, Promise Unfulfilled* (1985)
Joe McGinniss, *The Selling of the President* (1970)
Kim McQuaid, *The Anxious Years: America in the Vietnam-Watergate Era* (1989)
Jeb Stuart Magruder, *An American Life* (1974)
Earl Mazo, *Richard Nixon: A Political and Personal Portrait* (1959)
Roger Morris, *Uncertain Greatness: Henry Kissinger and American Foreign Policy* (1977)
Richard P. Nathan, *The Plot That Failed: Nixon and the Administrative Presidency* (1975)
Richard Nixon, *RN: The Memoirs of Richard Nixon* (1978)
Herbert Parmet, *Richard Nixon and His America* (1990)
Richard Gid Powers, *Secrecy and Power: The Life of J. Edgar Hoover* (1986)
Thomas Powers, *The Man Who Kept the Secrets: Richard Helms and the CIA* (1979)
William Safire, *Before the Fall* (1975)
Jonathan Schell, *The Time of Illusion* (1976)
Arthur Schlesinger, Jr., *The Imperial Presidency* (1973)
John J. Sirica, *To Set the Record Straight* (1979)
Joseph C. Spear, *Presidents and the Press: The Nixon Legacy* (1984)
Maurice Stans, *The Terrors of Justice* (1984)
James L. Sundquist, *The Decline and Resurgence of Congress* (1981)
Athan Theoharis and John Stuart Cox, *The Boss: J. Edgar Hoover and the Great American Inquisition* (1986)
Theodore H. White, *Breach of Faith: The Fall of Richard Nixon* (1975)
———, *The Making of the President, 1968* (1969)
Garry Wills, *Nixon Agonistes: The Crisis of the Self-Made Man* (1970)

CHAPTER
13

Growth, Technology, and the Fate of the Earth

⋈

What might be called technological progressivism has dominated much of U.S. history. Most Americans, or at least most powerful Americans, have believed deeply in progress through science, technology, and industrial development. Popular faith in technological progress was especially powerful during the years immediately following World War II, when untrammeled economic growth seemed the nation's highest priority.

By the late 1960s and early 1970s, however, growing numbers of Americans worried about the increasing pollution of the nation's air and water, the proliferation of toxic chemicals, and the accumulation of hazardous wastes. They began to demand more stringent regulation of industry and additional controls on growth and development. Many championed the creation of new, alternative technologies. Some called for a radical reorganization of American industry. A few even challenged the fundamental assumptions of technological progressivism: was continued economic growth compatible, they demanded to know, with the finite resources of a ''spaceship earth''?

The new environmentalism posed difficult questions for the United States and its leaders. Was there a trade-off between industrial growth and a healthy environment? If so, and if the cost of a better environment was slower growth, who would pay the price of fewer jobs or goods and services? Would it be possible to develop new and less polluting technologies? How would society assess the costs of these technologies? Were such radical changes possible in a political system dominated by interest-group government and in an economic system based on private capital? For that matter, given the increasing integration of the world economy, did not the solution of such problems also require new forms of international cooperation?

During the 1970s, the United States struggled with these problems with limited success. In the 1980s, however, the Reagan administration quickly abandoned the new environmentalism in the name of economic revival. By 1990 critics increasingly warned that future generations would pay the cost of such a policy in the form of a greatly degraded environment.

XX *D O C U M E N T S*

One of the first voices of the new environmentalism was that of Rachel Carson, whose book *Silent Spring* (1962) warned of the dangers of the insecticide DDT. The opening document is drawn from the book's introduction, entitled "A Fable for Tomorrow." The second document is by Dennis Hayes, the national coordinator of the new group Environmental Action and one of the organizers of Earth Day, a nationwide demonstration on April 22, 1970, to dramatize concern about the environment. Much of the scientific support for the new environmentalism came from the new science of ecology. In the third document, Washington University ecologist Barry Commoner outlines what he calls the four laws of ecology.

The new environmentalism evoked sharp criticism from business and industry and from the Republican administration of President Ronald Reagan. In the fourth document, Reagan's secretary of the interior James G. Watt defends the administration's new policies toward economic development and the environment. By the end of the 1980s, scientists and environmental activists had begun to identify new dangers, including those of environmental warming and the "greenhouse effect." The graphic and text reprinted in the closing document feature what the *New York Times* called "a worst-case forecast."

Rachel Carson Warns of a Silent Spring, 1962

A Fable for Tomorrow

There was once a town in the heart of America where all life seemed to live in harmony with its surroundings. The town lay in the midst of a checkerboard of prosperous farms, with fields of grain and hillsides of orchards where, in spring, white clouds of bloom drifted above the green fields. In autumn, oak and maple and birch set up a blaze of color that flamed and flickered across a backdrop of pines. Then foxes barked in the hills and deer silently crossed the fields, half hidden in the mists of the fall mornings.

Along the roads, laurel, viburnum and alder, great ferns and wildflowers delighted the traveler's eye through much of the year. Even in winter the roadsides were places of beauty, where countless birds came to feed on the berries and on the seed heads of the dried weeds rising above the snow. The countryside was, in fact, famous for the abundance and variety of its bird life, and when the flood of migrants was pouring through in spring and fall people traveled from great distances to observe them. Others came to fish the streams, which flowed clear and cold out of the hills and contained shady pools where trout lay. So it had been from the days many years ago when the first settlers raised their houses, sank their wells, and built their barns.

Then a strange blight crept over the area and everything began to change. Some evil spell had settled on the community: mysterious maladies swept the flocks of chickens; the cattle and sheep sickened and died. Everywhere was a shadow of death. The farmers spoke of much illness among their families. In the town the doctors had become more and more puzzled by new kinds of sickness appearing among their patients. There had been several sudden and unexplained deaths, not only among adults but even among children, who would be stricken suddenly while at play and die within a few hours.

There was a strange stillness. The birds, for example—where had they gone? Many people spoke of them, puzzled and disturbed. The feeding stations in the backyards were deserted. The few birds seen anywhere were moribund; they trembled violently and could not fly. It was a spring without voices. On the mornings that had once throbbed with the dawn chorus of robins, catbirds, doves, jays, wrens, and scores of other bird voices there was now no sound; only silence lay over the fields and woods and marsh.

On the farms the hens brooded, but no chicks hatched. The farmers complained that they were unable to raise any pigs—the litters were small and the young survived only a few days. The apple trees were coming into bloom but no bees droned among the blossoms, so there was no pollination and there would be no fruit.

The roadsides, once so attractive, were now lined with browned and withered vegetation as though swept by fire. These, too, were silent, deserted by all living things. Even the streams were now lifeless. Anglers no longer visited them, for all the fish had died.

In the gutters under the eaves and between the shingles of the roofs, a white granular powder still showed a few patches; some weeks before it had fallen like snow upon the roofs and the lawns, the fields and streams.

No witchcraft, no enemy action had silenced the rebirth of new life in this stricken world. The people had done it themselves.

An Environmental Activist Foresees Ecological Catastrophe, 1970

I suspect that the politicians and businessmen who are jumping on the environmental bandwagon don't have the slightest idea what they are getting into. They are talking about filters on smokestacks while we are challenging corporate irresponsibility. They are bursting with pride about plans for totally inadequate municipal sewage treatment plants; we are challenging the ethics of a society that, with only 6 percent of the world's population, accounts for more than half of the world's annual consumption of raw materials.

Our country is stealing from poorer nations and from generations yet unborn. We seem to have a reverse King Midas touch. Everything we touch turns to garbage—142 tons of smoke, 7 million junked cars, 30 million tons of paper, 28 billion bottles, 48 billion cans each year. We waste riches in planned obsolescence and invest the overwhelming bulk of our national budget in ABMs [Anti-Ballistic-Missiles] and MIRVs [Multiple Independently targeted Re-entry Vehicles]; ballistic missiles with multiple warheads

"The Beginning" by Dennis Hayes from *Earth Day—The Beginning, 1970,* pp. xiii–xv. Reprinted by permission of Dennis Hayes, Green Seal Inc.

each capable of guiding itself to its target] and other means of death. Russia can destroy every American twelve times; America can destroy every Russian forty times. I guess that is supposed to mean that we are ahead.

We're spending insanely large sums on military hardware instead of eliminating hunger and poverty. We squander our resources on moon dust while people live in wretched housing. We still waste lives and money on a war that we should never have entered and should get out of immediately.

We have made Vietnam an ecological catastrophe. Vietnam was once capable of producing a marketable surplus of grain. Now America must feed her. American bombs have pockmarked Vietnam with more than 2.6 million craters a year, some of them thirty feet deep. We spent $73 million on defoliation in Vietnam last year alone, much of it on 2,4,5–T, a herbicide [*Dioxin* or *Agent Orange*] we've now found causes birth defects. We dumped defoliants on Vietnam at the rate of 10,000 pounds a month, and in the last fiscal year alone we blackened 6,600 square miles. We cannot pretend to be concerned with the environment of this or any other country as long as we continue the war in Vietnam or wage war in Cambodia, Laos, or anywhere else.

But even if that war were over tomorrow, we would still be killing this planet. We are systematically destroying our land, our streams, and our seas. We foul our air, deaden our senses, and pollute our bodies. And it's getting worse.

America's political and business institutions don't seem yet to have realized that some of us want to live in this country thirty years from now. They had better come to recognize it soon. We don't have very much time. We cannot afford to give them very much time.

When it comes to salvaging the environment, the individual is almost powerless. You can pick up litter, and if you're diligent, you may be able to find some returnable bottles. But you are forced to breathe the lung-corroding poison which companies spew into the air. You cannot buy electricity from a power company which does not pollute. You cannot find products in biodegradable packages. You cannot even look to the manufacturer for reliable information on the ecological effects of a product.

You simply can't live an ecologically sound life in America. That is not one of the options open to you. Go shopping and you find dozens of laundry products; it seems like a tremendous array unless you know that most are made by three companies, and the differences in cleaning power are almost negligible. If you really want to be ecologically sound, you won't buy any detergents—just some old-fashioned laundry soap and a bit of soda. But there's nothing on those packages to tell you the phosphate content, and there's nothing in the supermarket to tell you, only meaningless advertising that keeps dunning you.

We are learning. In response, industry has turned the environmental problem over to its public relations men. We've been deluged with full-page ads about pollution problems and what's being done about them. It would appear from most of them that things are fine and will soon be perfect. But the people of America are still coughing. And our eyes are running, and our lungs are blackening, and our property is corroding, and we're getting angry. We're getting angry at half-truths, angry at semitruths, and angry at outright lies.

We are tired of being told that we are to blame for corporate depredations. Political and business leaders once hoped that they could turn the environmental movement into a massive antilitter campaign. They have failed. We have learned not to place our faith in regulatory agencies that are supposed to act in the public interest. We have learned not to believe the advertising that sells us presidents the way it sells us useless products.

We will not appeal any more to the conscience of institutions because institutions have no conscience. If we want them to do what is right, we must make them do what is right. We will use proxy fights, lawsuits, demonstrations, research, boycotts, ballots—whatever it takes. This may be our last chance. If environment is a fad, it's going to be our last fad.

Things as we know them are falling apart. There is an unease across this country today. People know that something is wrong. The war is part of it, but most critics of the war have, from the beginning, known that the war is only a symptom of something much deeper. Poor people have long known what is wrong. Now the alley garbage, the crowding and the unhappiness and the crime have spread beyond the ghetto and a whole society is coming to realize that it must drastically change course.

We are building a movement, a movement with a broad base, a movement which transcends traditional political boundaries. It is a movement that values people more than technology, people more than political boundaries and political ideologies, people more than profit. It will be a difficult fight. Earth Day is the beginning.

Barry Commoner Outlines
the Four Laws of Ecology, 1971

In broad outline, these are the environmental cycles which govern the behavior of the three great global systems: the air, the water, and the soil. Within each of them live many thousands of different species of living things. Each species is suited to its particular environmental niche, and each, through its life processes, affects the physical and chemical properties of its immediate environment.

Each living species is also linked to many others. These links are bewildering in their variety and marvelous in their intricate detail. An animal, such as a deer, may depend on plants for food; the plants depend on the action of soil bacteria for their nutrients; the bacteria in turn live on the organic wastes dropped by the animals on the soil. At the same time, the deer is food for the mountain lion. Insects may live on the juices of plants or gather pollen from their flowers. Other insects suck blood from animals. Bacteria may live on the internal tissues of animals and plants. Fungi degrade

From *The Closing Circle: Nature, Man & Technology* by Barry Commoner. Copyright © 1971 by Barry Commoner. Reprinted by permission of Alfred A. Knopf Inc.

the bodies of dead plants and animals. All this, many times multiplied and organized species by species in intricate, precise relationships, makes up the vast network of life on the earth.

The science that studies these relationships and the processes linking each living thing to the physical and chemical environment is *ecology*. It is the science of planetary housekeeping. For the environment is, so to speak, the house created on the earth *by* living things *for* living things. It is a young science and much of what it teaches has been learned from only small segments of the whole network of life on the earth. Ecology has not yet explicitly developed the kind of cohesive, simplifying generalizations exemplified by, say, the laws of physics. Nevertheless there are a number of generalizations that are already evident in what we now know about the ecosphere and that can be organized into a kind of informal set of "laws of ecology." These are described in what follows.

The First Law of Ecology:
Everything Is Connected to Everything Else

Some of the evidence that leads to this generalization has already been discussed. It reflects the existence of the elaborate network of interconnections in the ecosphere: among different living organisms, and between populations, species, and individual organisms and their physicochemical surroundings.

The single fact that an ecosystem consists of multiple interconnected parts, which act on one another, has some surprising consequences. Our ability to picture the behavior of such systems has been helped considerably by the development, even more recent than ecology, of the science of cybernetics. We owe the basic concept, and the word itself, to the inventive mind of the late Norbert Wiener.

The word "cybernetics" derives from the Greek word for helmsman; it is concerned with cycles of events that steer, or govern, the behavior of a system. The helmsman is part of a system that also includes the compass, the rudder, and the ship. If the ship veers off the chosen compass course, the change shows up in the movement of the compass needle. Observed and interpreted by the helmsman this event determines a subsequent one: the helmsman turns the rudder, which swings the ship back to its original course. When this happens, the compass needle returns to its original, on-course position and the cycle is complete. If the helmsman turns the rudder too far in response to a small deflection of the compass needle, the excess swing of the ship shows up in the compass—which signals the helmsman to correct his overreaction by an opposite movement. Thus the operation of this cycle stabilizes the course of the ship.

In quite a similar way, stabilizing cybernetic relations are built into an ecological cycle. Consider, for example, the fresh-water ecological cycle: fish—organic waste—bacteria of decay—inorganic products—algae—fish. Suppose that due to unusually warm summer weather there is a rapid growth of algae. This depletes the supply of inorganic nutrients so that two sectors of the cycle, algae and nutrients, are out of balance, but in opposite directions. The operation of the ecological cycle, like that of the ship, soon brings the situation back into balance. For the excess in algae increases the ease with which fish can feed on them; this reduces the algal population, increases fish waste production, and eventually leads to an increased level of nutrients when the waste decays. Thus, the levels of algae and nutrients tend to return to their original balanced position.

In such cybernetic systems the course is not maintained by rigid control, but flexibly. Thus the ship does not move unwaveringly on its path, but actually follows it in a wavelike motion that swings equally to both sides of the true course. The frequency of these swings depends on the relative speeds of the various steps in the cycle, such as the rate at which the ship responds to the rudder.

Ecological systems exhibit similar cycles, although these are often obscured by the effects of daily or seasonal variations in weather and environmental agents. The most famous examples of such ecological oscillations are the periodic fluctuations of the size of fur-bearing animal populations. For example, from trapping records in Canada it is known that the populations of rabbits and lynx follow ten-year fluctuations. When there are many rabbits the lynx prosper; the rising population of lynx increasingly ravages the rabbit population, reducing it; as the latter become scarce, there is insufficient food to support the now numerous lynx; as the lynx begin to die off, the rabbits are less fiercely hunted and increase in number. And so on. These oscillations are built into the operation of the simple cycle, in which the lynx population is positively related to the number of rabbits and the rabbit population is negatively related to the number of lynx.

In such an oscillating system there is always the danger that the whole system will collapse when an oscillation swings so wide of the balance point that the system can no longer compensate for it. Suppose, for example, in one particular swing of the rabbit-lynx cycle, the lynx manage to eat *all* the rabbits (or, for that matter, all but one). Now the rabbit population can no longer reproduce. As usual, the lynx begin to starve as the rabbits are consumed; but this time the drop in the lynx population is not followed by an increase in rabbits. The lynx then die off. The entire rabbit-lynx system collapses.

This is similar to the ecological collapse which accompanies what is called "eutrophication." If the nutrient level of the water becomes so high as to stimulate the rapid growth of algae, the dense algal population cannot be long sustained because of the intrinsic limitations of photosynthetic efficiency. As the thickness of the algal layer in the water increases, the light required for photosynthesis that can reach the lower parts of the algal layer becomes sharply diminished, so that any strong overgrowth of algae very quickly dies back, releasing organic debris. The organic matter level may then become so great that its decay totally depletes the oxygen content of the water. The bacteria of decay then die off, for they must have oxygen to survive. The entire aquatic cycle collapses.

The dynamic behavior of a cybernetic system—for example, the frequency of its natural oscillations, the speed with which it responds to external changes, and its over-all rate of operation—depends on the relative rates of its constituent steps. In the ship system, the compass needle swings in fractions of a second; the helmsman's reaction takes some seconds; the ship responds over a time of minutes. These different reaction times interact to produce, for example, the ship's characteristic oscillation frequency around its true course.

In the aquatic ecosystem, each biological step also has a characteristic reaction time, which depends on the metabolic and reproductive rates of the organisms involved. The time to produce a new generation of fish may be some months; of algae, a matter of days; decay bacteria can reproduce in a few hours. The metabolic rates of these organisms—that is, the rates at which they use nutrients, consume oxygen, or produce waste—is inversely related to their size. If the metabolic rate of a fish is 1, the algal rate is about 100, and the bacterial rate about 10,000.

If the entire cyclical system is to remain in balance, the over-all rate of turnover must be governed by the slowest step—in this case, the growth and metabolism of the fish. Any external effect that forces part of the cycle to operate faster than the over-all rate leads to trouble. So, for example, the rate of waste production by fish determines the rate of bacterial decay and the rate of oxygen consumption due to that decay. In a balanced situation, enough oxygen is produced by the algae and enters from the air to support the decay bacteria. Suppose that the rate at which organic waste enters the cycle is increased artificially, for example, by dumping sewage into the water. Now the decay bacteria are supplied with organic waste at a much higher level than usual; because of their rapid metabolism they are able to act quickly on the increased organic load. As a result, the rate of oxygen consumption by the decay bacteria can easily exceed the rate of oxygen production by the algae (and its rate of entry from the air) so that the oxygen level goes to zero and the system collapses. Thus, the rates of the separate processes in the cycle are in a natural state of balance which is maintained only so long as there are no external intrusions on the system. When such an effect originates outside the cycle, it is not controlled by the self-governing cyclical relations and is a threat to the stability of the whole system.

Ecosystems differ considerably in their rate characteristics and therefore vary a great deal in the speed with which they react to changed situations or approach the point of collapse. For example, aquatic ecosystems turn over much faster than soil ecosystems. Thus, an acre of richly populated marine shoreline or an acre of fish pond produces about seven times as much organic material as an acre of alfalfa annually. The slow turnover of the soil cycle is due to the rather low rate of one of its many steps—the release of nutrient from the soil's organic store, which is very much slower than the comparable step in aquatic systems.

The amount of stress which an ecosystem can absorb before it is driven to collapse is also a result of its various interconnections and their relative speeds of response. The more complex the ecosystem, the more successfully it can resist a stress. For example, in the rabbit-lynx system, if the lynx had an alternative source of food they might survive the sudden depletion of rabbits. In this way, branching—which establishes alternative pathways—increases the resistance of an ecosystem to stress. Most ecosystems are so complex that the cycles are not simple circular paths, but are crisscrossed with branches to form a network or a fabric of interconnections. Like a net, in which each knot is connected to others by several strands, such a fabric can resist collapse better than a simple, unbranched circle of threads—which if cut anywhere breaks down as a whole. Environmental pollution is often a sign that ecological links have been cut and that the ecosystem has been artificially simplified and made more vulnerable to stress and to final collapse.

The feedback characteristics of ecosystems result in amplification and intensification processes of considerable magnitude. For example, the fact that in food chains small organisms are eaten by bigger ones and the latter by still bigger ones inevitably results in the concentration of certain environmental constituents in the bodies of the largest organisms at the top of the food chain. Smaller organisms always exhibit much higher metabolic rates than larger ones, so that the amount of their food which is oxidized relative to the amount incorporated into the body of the organism is thereby greater. Consequently, an animal at the top of the food chain depends on the consumption of an enormously greater mass of the bodies of organisms lower down in the food chain. Therefore, any *non*metabolized material present in the lower organisms of this chain will become concentrated in the body of the top one. Thus, if the concentration of DDT [a highly effective pesticide with many dangerous side effects] (which is not readily metabolized) in the soil is 1 unit, earthworms living in the soil will achieve a concentration of from 10 to 40 units, and in woodcocks feeding on the earthworms the DDT level will rise to about 200 units.

All this results from a simple fact about ecosystems—everything is connected to everything else: the system is stabilized by its dynamic self-compensating properties; these same properties, if overstressed, can lead to a dramatic collapse; the complexity of the ecological network and its intrinsic rate of turnover determine how much it can be stressed, and for how long, without collapsing; the ecological network is an amplifier, so that a small perturbation in one place may have large, distant, long-delayed effects.

The Second Law of Ecology: Everything Must Go Somewhere

This is, of course, simply a somewhat informal restatement of a basic law of physics—that matter is indestructible. Applied to ecology, the law emphasizes that in nature there is no such thing as "waste." In every natural system, what is excreted by one organism as waste is taken up by another as food. Animals release carbon dioxide as a respiratory waste; this is an essential nutrient for green plants. Plants excrete oxygen, which is used by animals. Animal organic wastes nourish the bacteria of decay. Their wastes, inorganic materials such as nitrate, phosphate, and carbon dioxide, become algal nutrients.

A persistent effort to answer the question "Where does it go?" can yield a surprising amount of valuable information about an ecosystem. Consider, for example, the fate of a household item which contains mercury—a substance with environmental effects that have just recently surfaced. A dry-cell battery containing mercury is purchased, used to the point of exhaustion, and then "thrown out." But where does it really go? First it is placed in a container of rubbish; this is collected and taken to an incinerator. Here the mercury is heated; this produces mercury vapor which is emitted by the incinerator stack, and mercury *vapor* is toxic. Mercury vapor is carried by the wind, eventually brought to earth in rain or snow. Entering a mountain lake, let us say, the mercury condenses and sinks to the bottom. Here it is acted on by bacteria which convert it to methyl mercury. This is soluble and taken up by fish; since it is not metabolized, the mercury accumulates in the organs and flesh of the fish. The fish is caught and eaten by a man and the mercury becomes deposited in his organs, where it might be harmful. And so on.

This is an effective way to trace out an ecological path. It is also an excellent way to counteract the prevalent notion that something which is regarded as useless simply "goes away" when it is discarded. Nothing "goes away"; it is simply transferred from place to place, converted from one molecular form to another, acting on the life processes of any organism in which it becomes, for a time, lodged. One of the chief reasons for the present environmental crisis is that great amounts of materials have been extracted from the earth, converted into new forms, and discharged into the environment without taking into account that "everything has to go somewhere." The result, too often, is the accumulation of harmful amounts of material in places where, in nature, they do not belong.

The Third Law of Ecology: Nature Knows Best

In my experience this principle is likely to encounter considerable resistance, for it appears to contradict a deeply held idea about the unique competence of human beings. One of the most pervasive features of modern technology is the notion that it is intended to "improve on nature"—to provide food, clothing, shelter, and means of communication and expression which are superior to those available to man in nature. Stated baldly, the third law of ecology holds that any major man-made change in a natural system is likely to be *detrimental* to that system. This is a rather extreme claim; nevertheless I believe it has a good deal of merit if understood in a properly defined context.

I have found it useful to explain this principle by means of an analogy. Suppose you were to open the back of your watch, close your eyes, and poke a pencil into the exposed works. The almost certain result would be damage to the watch. Nevertheless, this result is not *absolutely* certain. There is some finite possibility that the watch was out of adjustment and that the random thrust of the pencil happened to make the precise change needed to improve it. However, this outcome is exceedingly improbable. The question at issue is: why? The answer is self-evident: there is a very considerable amount of what technologists now call "research and development" (or, more familiarly, "R & D") behind the watch. This means that over the years numerous watchmakers, each taught by a predecessor, have tried out a huge variety of detailed arrangements of watch works, have discarded those that are not compatible with the over-all operation of the system and retained the better features. In effect, the watch mechanism, as it now exists, represents a very restricted selection, from among an enormous variety of possible arrangements of component parts, of a singular organization of the watch works. Any random change made in the watch is likely to fall into the very large class of inconsistent, or harmful, arrangements which have been tried out in past watch-making experience and discarded. One might say, as a law of watches, that "the watchmaker knows best."

There is a close, and very meaningful, analogy in biological systems. It is possible to induce a certain range of random, inherited changes in a living thing by treating it with an agent, such as x-irradiation, that increases the frequency of mutations. Generally, exposure to x-rays increases the frequency of all mutations which have been observed, albeit very infrequently, in nature and can therefore be regarded as *possible* changes. What is significant, for our purpose, is the universal observation that when mutation frequency is enhanced by x-rays or other means, nearly all the mutations are harmful to the organisms and the great majority so damaging as to kill the organism before it is fully formed.

In other words, like the watch, a living organism that is forced to sustain a random change in its organization is almost certain to be damaged rather than improved. And in both cases, the explanation is the same—a great deal of "R & D." In effect there are some two to three billion years of "R & D" behind every living thing. In that time, a staggering number of new individual living things have been produced, affording in each case the opportunity to try out the suitability of some random genetic change. If the change damages the viability of the organism, it is likely to kill it before the change can be passed on to future generations. In this way, living things accumulate a complex organization of compatible parts; those possible arrangements that are not compatible with the whole are screened out over the long course of evolution. Thus, the structure of a present living thing or the organization of a current natural ecosystem is likely to be "best" in the sense that it has been so heavily screened for disadvantageous components that any new one is very likely to be worse than the present ones.

This principle is particularly relevant to the field of organic chemistry. Living things are composed of many thousands of different organic compounds, and it is sometimes imagined that at least some of these might be improved upon if they were replaced by some man-made variant of the natural substance. The third law of ecology suggests that the artificial introduction of an organic compound that does not occur in nature, but is man-made and is nevertheless active in a living system, is very likely to be harmful.

This is due to the fact that the varieties of chemical substances actually found in living things are vastly more restricted than the *possible* varieties.

A striking illustration is that if one molecule each of all the possible types of proteins were made, they would together weigh more than the observable universe. Obviously there are a fantastically large number of protein types that are *not* made by living cells. And on the basis of the foregoing, one would reason that many of these possible protein types were once formed in some particular living things, found to be harmful, and rejected through the death of the experiment. In the same way, living cells synthesize fatty acids (a type of organic molecule that contains carbon chains of various lengths) with even-numbered carbon chain lengths (i.e., 4, 6, 8, etc., carbons), but no fatty acids with odd-numbered carbon chain lengths. This suggests that the latter have once been tried out and found wanting. Similarly, organic compounds that contain attached nitrogen and oxygen atoms are singularly rare in living things. This should warn us that the artificial introduction of substances of this type would be dangerous. This is indeed the case, for such substances are usually toxic and frequently carcinogenic. And, I would suppose from the fact that DDT is nowhere found in nature, that somewhere, at some time in the past, some unfortunate cell synthesized this molecule—and died.

One of the striking facts about the chemistry of living systems is that for every organic substance produced by a living organism, there exists, somewhere in nature, an enzyme capable of breaking that substance down. In effect, no organic substance is synthesized unless there is provision for its degradation; recycling is thus enforced. Thus, when a new man-made organic substance is synthesized with a molecular structure that departs significantly from the types which occur in nature, it is probable that no degradative enzyme exists, and the material tends to accumulate.

Given these considerations, it would be prudent, I believe, to regard every man-made organic chemical *not* found in nature which has a strong action on any one organism as potentially dangerous to other forms of life. Operationally, this view means that all man-made organic compounds that are at all active biologically ought to be treated as we do drugs, or rather as we *should* treat them—prudently, cautiously. Such caution or prudence is, of course, impossible when billions of pounds of the substance are produced and broadly disseminated into the ecosystem where it can reach and affect numerous organisms not under our observation. Yet this is precisely what we have done with detergents, insecticides, and herbicides. The often catastrophic results lend considerable force to the view that "Nature knows best."

The Fourth Law of Ecology: There Is No Such Thing as a Free Lunch

In my experience, this idea has proven so illuminating for environmental problems that I have borrowed it from its original source, economics. The "law" derives from a story that economists like to tell about an oil-rich potentate who decided that his new wealth needed the guidance of economic science. Accordingly he ordered his advisers, on pain of death, to produce a set of volumes containing all the wisdom of economics. When the tomes arrived, the potentate was impatient and again issued an order—to reduce all the knowledge of economics to a single volume. The story goes on in this vein, as such stories will, until the advisers are required, if they are to survive, to reduce the totality of economic science to a single sentence. This is the origin of the "free lunch" law.

In ecology, as in economics, the law is intended to warn that every gain is won at some cost. In a way, this ecological law embodies the previous three laws. Because the global ecosystem is a connected whole, in which nothing can be gained or lost and which is not subject to over-all improvement, anything extracted from it by human effort must be replaced. Payment of this price cannot be avoided; it can only be delayed. The present environmental crisis is a warning that we have delayed nearly too long.

The preceding pages provide a view of the web of life on the earth. An effort has been made to develop this view from available facts, through logical relations, into a set of comprehensive generalizations. In other words, the effort has been scientific.

Nevertheless, it is difficult to ignore the embarrassing fact that the final generalizations which emerge from all this—the four laws of ecology—are ideas that have been widely held by many people without any scientific analysis or professional authorization. The complex web in which all life is enmeshed, and man's place in it, are clearly—and beautifully—described in the poems of Walt Whitman. A great deal about the interplay of the physical features of the environment and the creatures that inhabit it can be learned from *Moby Dick*. Mark Twain is not only a marvelous source of wisdom about the nature of the environment of the United States from the Mississippi westward, but also a rather incisive critic of the irrelevance of science which loses connection to the realities of life. As the critic Leo Marx reminds us, "Anyone familiar with the work of the classic American writers (I am thinking of men like Cooper, Emerson, Thoreau, Melville, Whitman, and Mark Twain) is likely to have developed an interest in what we recently have learned to call ecology."

Unfortunately, this literary heritage has not been enough to save us from ecological disaster. After all, every American technician, industrialist, agriculturist, or public official who has condoned or participated in the assault on the environment has read at least some of Cooper, Emerson, Thoreau, Melville, Whitman, and Mark Twain. Many of them are campers, bird-watchers, or avid fishermen, and therefore to some degree personally aware of the natural processes that the science of ecology hopes to elucidate. Nevertheless, most of them were taken unawares by the environmental crisis, failing to understand, apparently, that Thoreau's woods, Mark Twain's rivers, and Melville's oceans are *today* under attack.

The rising miasma of pollution has helped us to achieve this understanding. For, in Leo Marx's words, "The current environmental crisis has in a sense put a literal, factual, often quantifiable base under this poetic idea [i.e., the need for human harmony with nature]." This is perhaps the major value of the effort to show that the simple generalizations which have already emerged from perceptive human contact with the natural world have a valid base in the facts and principles of a science, ecology. Thus linked to science, these ideas become tools for restoring the damage inflicted on nature by the environmental crisis.

In the woods around Walden Pond or on the reaches of the Mississippi, most of the information needed to understand the natural world can be gained by personal experience. In the world of nuclear bombs, smog, and foul water, environmental understanding needs help from the scientist.

Secretary of the Interior James G. Watt on Economic Development and the Environment, 1981

Q Mr. Secretary, people are afraid that you are going to push for greater development of natural resources at the expense of the environment. How do you respond?

A With our technology, we can protect the environment and still bring on the development that is necessary for improving the quality of life and bolstering national defense. Environmental sensitivity requires a balance of economic development and environmental preservation.

In the last 10 years, we have not had proper energy and mineral development in America. If a crisis comes because of shortages and the political scene dictates a crash development program, I fear that it will be done without regard to the ecology. That's what we must avoid.

Q How much federally owned land will be leased for development and exploration?

A We will look at the resource base to determine what its best utilization will be. We're not going to try to determine that you ought to have *x* acres of wilderness and *x* acres dedicated to oil refineries, for example. What is important is finding out what is the best use for America of a particular piece of land.

Q Why do we need more development of federal lands?

A Because America needs more energy, more timber, more agricultural grazing. We have not had an oil-and-gas lease issued onshore Alaska since the mid-1960s. We have not had a major coal lease issued since the early 1970s. Applications have been pending for oil-and-gas leases in the overthrust belts of Wyoming, Montana and Idaho for 10 years. Our mining industry is in very bad shape. Yet we ask why there's an energy crisis.

Q What about mineral development and stockpiling?

A We need to build up a strategic-mineral reserve—a supply of minerals vital to the economy and to the nation's defense, such as cobalt, chromium and manganese.

Supplies of these strategic minerals have dropped dramatically because past administrations systematically closed America's public lands to mineral exploration and development. Two thirds to three quarters of America's public lands are closed to mineral development, even though a large share of these lands could, by law, be managed under multiple-use concepts.

We hope to change that by allowing more access to federal lands. In addition, the administration, in an effort to strengthen our defense posture, has authorized the purchase of cobalt—the first purchase of a strategic mineral in 20 years.

Q *Will that plan for mineral development clash with the interests of farmers and ranchers in the West?*

A The have-nots always battle the haves. If you dedicate a parcel of land to one use, others who would like to have that land will squabble. But we will aggressively pursue what we're calling a good-neighbor policy—to consult with land users, along with local and state-government officers. Amazing as it may seem, the federal government has made decisions on the use of those public lands without regard to local or state interests. That's really what has caused the sagebrush rebellion of Western farmers and business people.

Q *How do you avoid the social problems caused by rapid development in the Western states?*

A You've got to allow orderly development through time with proper environmental safeguards to avoid the crash expansion of a Gillette or Rock Springs, Wyo. These places were overrun with mobile homes and makeshift facilities because of surging growth brought on by energy exploration.

Instead, we must invite those who want to develop resources to come in and provide up-front money to build the schools and the sanitation facilities and the roads. They have to, in effect, prepay some of their taxes to take care of the social-economic pressures that are created. But it takes planning and a commitment to follow through.

Q *Can this country develop energy resources off its coasts without endangering fish and wildlife?*

A The marine scientists and the biologists tell us definitely that we can. The history of environmental protection from drilling on the outer continental shelf has been remarkably good. We have had only two spills of more than 1,000 barrels since 1970. Of course, a Mexican offshore well went out of control in 1979, causing damage to Padre Island, Tex., but I am advised that huge spill would not have happened under drilling procedures and environmental safeguards observed in U.S. waters.

A far bigger danger to the environment is the risk of spills from giant tankers carrying foreign oil to the U.S. If we could be fortunate enough to find a few more Prudhoe Bays off our coasts, we could lessen that dependence on foreign oil and the chances of environmental damages that go with it. But there's no way to tell for sure where and how much oil we have offshore unless we explore for it.

Q *How can the country increase the production and use of its huge coal resources?*

A Instead of having the Department of the Interior determine which tracts of federal land would best be mined, we want to rely more on the marketplace, which has more wisdom in allocating the resources than does the federal government. We want to allow the private sector to nominate the lands that are best for mining on the basis of accessibility to transportation and the quality of coal needed.

We also hope to rewrite regulations, as the law intends, to allow states more authority in determining how mined land is to be restored and reclaimed, instead of allowing Washington to dictate a uniform policy for all states. For example, instead of insisting that surface-mining firms restore lands to the original contour, states might decide to allow a tract to be set aside for a hospital, housing or some other pressing need.

Q *Why do you favor a moratorium on the creation of new national parks when so many are overcrowded?*

A There has been deterioration and degradation in almost every park because we have not been good stewards of what we have.

The emphasis in recent years has been on acquiring more and more lands while at the same time refusing to take care of the park lands we have.

We will reverse that. We have put a moratorium on the acquisition of additional lands until the economic situation changes. In the meantime, we have shifted substantial money to the National Park Service for restoration and improvement of these fragile lands.

Q *How can you make the most popular parks accessible to more people if you don't expand the parks?* A We need to provide proper access and development of facilities to handle people in the areas where they want to be. For example, they want to see Old Faithful. It doesn't help people to see that geyser if we buy another 100,000 acres outside the present boundaries of that park. So we're clearing up transportation bottlenecks and improving accommodations near popular attractions.

For our major parks—the "crown jewels"—people will be better served if we improve management techniques and give direction to the concessionaires to build the environmentally compatible facilities that allow people to enjoy the parks.

Q *Are more restrictions needed on park use?*

A In recent years, there's been a movement in the National Park Service to make parks available only to the select few. Attention needs to be given to all Americans—backpackers and people who go rafting on the rivers—as well as those who roll up to the park on a bus tour. We want parks to be attractive and accessible to people of all economic levels and not just to people who have lots of time and money.

A graphic illustration of this is the Colorado River in the Grand Canyon National Park. The purist wants that stretch of river to be available only to oar-powered rafts. But how many people can afford to get to Page, Ariz., and then commit lots of money and eight to 12 days to go down that river? People with less time available should also be allowed to use the river in motor-powered rafts. The only limitation should be to protect the resource base.

Q *How serious is the water-shortage problem in the West?*

A Very critical, this year especially. The most recent readings are that the snow pack this winter is about 60 percent of normal. That will probably cause some severe problems for all users—agriculture, industry and municipalities. The most pressing need in the West is for more water storage. That is desperately needed if we are going to meet the population pressures on the West and at the same time allow for development of resources.

But there really are no ideal locations left for huge facilities, such as the Grand Coulee Dam. We are talking about smaller reservoirs spread throughout the country. As with other issues, the best has already been taken, whether it is a site for a dam or for a new national park. The Eastern states need to rebuild their municipal water systems and provide more storage. The South still needs more flood control.

Q *Can't the government do a better job of regulating the use of water?*

A The federal government should not be involved in the regulation of water use. That is a state responsibility, and state laws are adequate. Our policy will be to work closely with the states and water users to see that the beneficiaries pay for future water-resource development. We will have to create innovative financing.

In the West, the government has a responsibility of ownership. The federal government owns roughly 50 percent of most of the West; in Nevada, it owns about 90 percent. There is a federal responsibility for developing water resources in that part of the country, and we will face up to that, along with users and resource owners who benefit from the water.

Q *Do you favor the breakup of large corporate farms that now get cheap, federally supplied water?*

A The administration will propose legislation that addresses the question of limiting the size of farms that can get federal water at low cost. We think we have worked out a formula that will be attractive in supporting the family-farm concept as well as introducing more-realistic market forces in pricing the delivery of water.

Q *You've been described as one who gets industry's advice on environmental matters. Are you listening to environmental groups as well?*

A We're getting some extremely good input from the environmental community out in the states—from people who live in communities to be affected by a change of direction by government. They love and understand the land. They speak with sincerity, address specific problems and offer concrete solutions. Candidly, we haven't received much constructive communication from the Washington, D.C., environmental community. Their agenda is a little different from that of the people really interested in what happens to the land and other resources.

Q *Should the Environmental Protection Agency be reduced in influence, say, by ending its broad rule-making authority?*
A Not at all. One purpose of government is to regulate where it is necessary that society be regulated. The challenge is to keep regulation from becoming so excessive that liberty is lost.

Q *Do you support the environmental movement?*
A Absolutely. This administration is in the mainstream of the environmental movement. In the late '60s, the environmental movement came on strong and, I think, with good purpose. Congress responded by passing a significant body of law to protect the environment. As someone charged with the task of being both the nation's chief environmentalist and its chief development advocate for public lands, I'm satisfied that we have adequate laws to protect the environment.

This administration will not have a legislative program with respect to natural-resource matters. Nor do our critics have a legislative program, because most of what they want already has been properly passed into law.

A Worst-Case Forecast for the Greenhouse Effect, 1988

Scientists disagree over just how bad the greenhouse effect will be. According to some of the most dire predictions, this is how bad a summer day might be in the year 2030:

The temperature in Washington, D.C., is over 100 degrees for the 10th straight day. Air conditioners are running at maximum around the clock, straining the generating capacity of electrical power plants and assuring another jump in already soaring utility rates.

In New York City, heat is not the only problem. Workers are raising levees to hold back the rising tidal waters of the Hudson and East Rivers.

In the South, another 100,000 acres of Louisiana wetland is being lost to the sea. But Chicago is suffering from another extreme. Evaporation has been causing Lake Michigan to recede from Lake Shore Drive, leaving behind an ever wider expanse of malodorous mud.

For the Midwest, drought has become a way of life. To adapt, Kansas farmers are experimenting with biologically engineered grains to see if they will yield a profitable crop in the increasingly dry and dusty heartland.

In Minnesota, Canada and Siberia, however, a longer and warmer growing season is producing bumper crops of corn and winter wheat. And residents of suburban and rural New England are fighting an infestation of insects caused by a mild winter.

Fire consumes a dying conifer forest in Yellowstone National Park.

Theory of the Greenhouse Effect

Factories and other sources of
pollution emit gases such as carbon
dioxide, nitrous oxides, chlorofluorocarbons and methane.

Accumulating in the
atmosphere, the gases
encircle the planet.

Pollution layer
works as an
insulating barrier,
retaining heat from
the earth.

As though surrounded
by the panels of a greenhouse, the
planet becomes hotter year by year.

Migration from the Southwest is increasing as high temperatures continue
and water supplies are becoming inadequate to sustain the population.

While North Americans and Europeans struggle with the effects of
changing weather patterns, people in some of the poorer countries of Africa
and Asia are being overwhelmed by the greenhouse effect.

Rising waters drive millions of farmers from their tiny plots in the Nile
Valley of Egypt and the Gangetic Delta of Bangladesh. The misery of the

hungry people of the Sahel region of Africa deepens as rising temperatures push the Sahara farther south.

狐 *E S S A Y S*

In the first essay, environmental historian Samuel P. Hays of the University of Pittsburgh traces the transition from conservation, with its emphasis on the careful management of resources for more effective production, to the new environmentalism, which he argues was the product of the post–World War II quest for a higher quality of living. In the second essay, ecologist Barry Commoner assesses both the successes and the failures of the new environmental politics.

From Conservation to the New Environmentalism

SAMUEL P. HAYS

Accounts of the rise of environmentalism frequently have emphasized its roots in the conservation movement of the early twentieth century. But environmental differed markedly from conservation affairs. The conservation movement was an effort on the part of leaders in science, technology, and government to bring about more efficient development of physical resources. The environmental movement, on the other hand, was far more widespread and popular, involving public values that stressed the quality of human experience and hence of the human environment. Conservation was an aspect of the history of production that stressed efficiency, whereas environment was a part of the history of consumption that stressed new aspects of the American standard of living.

Environmental objectives arose out of deep-seated changes in preferences and values associated with the massive social and economic transformation in the decades after 1945. Conservation had stirred technical and political leaders and then worked its way down from the top of the political order, but environmental concerns arose later from a broader base and worked their way from the middle levels of society outward, constantly to press upon a reluctant leadership. Many of the tendencies in efficient management of material resources originating in the conservation era came into sharp conflict with newer environmental objectives. The two sets of values were continually at loggerheads. . . .

From Conservation to Environment

In conservation, forests and waters were closely linked. As soil conservation and game management developed they became allied with both water and forest conservation in a shared set of attitudes. Together they emphasized

From *Beauty, Health, and Permanence: Environmental Politics in the United States, 1955–1985* by Samuel P. Hays, pp. 13–14, 21–32. Copyright © 1987. Reproduced with the permission of Cambridge University Press.

the scientific management of physical commodities and brought together technical specialists for a common purpose. Departments of state government dealing with such affairs were commonly called departments of natural resources. And professional training at academic institutions evolved from an initial interest in forestry to a larger set of natural resource or conservation matters.

The management of natural resources often displayed a close kinship with the entire movement for scientific management that evolved in the twentieth century and pervaded both industry and government. It emphasized large-scale systems of organization and control and increasing output through more intensive input. Professional expertise played an important role in all four facets of conservation, with strong links among them and a sense of kinship with the wider community of technical professions as a whole. Their self-respect came to be firmly connected to the desire to maintain high professional standards in resource management.

Equally important was the evolution of a common political outlook among resource specialists that professionals should be left free from "political influence" to determine how resources should be managed and for what purpose. This shared sense of professionalism was itself a political stance, an assertion that those with special training and expertise should determine the course of affairs. From the management of commodity resources in water, forests, soils, and wildlife emerged not just a sense of direction that stressed maximum output of physical resources but also a view about who should make decisions and how they should be made.

The coming conflicts between conservation and environment were rooted in different objectives: efficiency in the development of material commodities on amenities to enhance the quality of life. In these earlier years the national-parks movement and leaders such as John Muir had provided important beginnings for the latter. After World War II extensive changes in human values gave these intangible natural values far greater influence. To them now was added the growing view that air and water, as well as land, constituted a valuable human environment.

The early conservation movement had generated the first stages in shaping a "commons," a public domain of public ownership for public use and the public ownership of fish and wildlife as resources not subject to private appropriation. This sense of jointly held resources became extended in the later years to the concept of air, land, and water as an environment. Their significance as common resources shifted from a primary focus on commodities to become also meaningful as amenities that could enhance the quality of life.

The Search for Environmental Amenities

The most widespread source of emerging environmental interest was the search for a better life associated with home, community, and leisure. A new emphasis on smaller families developed, allowing parents to invest their limited time and income in fewer children. Child rearing was now oriented toward a more extended period of childhood in order to nurture abilities. Parents sought to provide creative-arts instructions, summer camps, and family vacations so as to foster self-development. Within this context the phrase "environmental quality" would have considerable personal meaning.

It also had meaning for place of residence. Millions of urban Americans desired to live on the fringe of the city where life was less congested, the air cleaner, noise reduced, and there was less concentrated waste from manifold human activities. In the nineteenth century only the well-to-do could afford to live some distance from work. Although streetcars enabled white-collar workers to live in the suburbs and work downtown, blue-collar employees still could not pay the cost of daily transportation. But the automobile largely lifted this limitation, and after World War II blue-collar workers were able to escape the industrial community as a place of residence. Still, by the 1970s as many as one-third of urban Americans wished they could live farther out in the countryside.

The search for a higher quality of living involved a desire for more space both inside and outside the home. Life in the city had been intensely crowded for urban dwellers. Often the street in front of the house had constituted the only available open space. Moving to the suburbs reflected a desire to enjoy a more natural setting, but it also evidenced the search for nature beyond the metropolitan area in the parks and woodlands of the countryside. This desire increased with the ease of access to rural areas by means of the automobile. The state-parks movement of the 1920s expressed the demand by city dwellers for places in which to enjoy the countryside on the weekend or during summer vacations.

There was also the desire to obtain private lands in the countryside so as to enjoy nature not found in the city. In the 1960s and 1970s the market for vacation homesites boomed. Newspaper advertisements abounded with phrases that signaled the important values: "by a sparkling stream," "abundant wildlife," "near the edge of a forest road," "200 feet of lakefront," "on the edge of a state forest."

This pursuit of natural values by city dwellers led to a remarkable turnabout in the attitudes of Americans toward natural environments. These had long been thought of as unused wastelands that could be made valuable only if developed. But after World War II many such areas came to be thought of as valuable only if left in their natural condition. Forested land, once thought of by many as dark, forbidding, and sinister, a place to be avoided because of the dangers lurking within, now was highly esteemed.

Wetlands, formerly known as swamplands, fit only for draining so that they could become productive agricultural land, were valued as natural systems, undisturbed and undeveloped. Similar positive attitudes were expressed for the prairies of the Midwest, the swamps of the South, and the pine barrens of the East. For many years wild animals had been seen as a threat to farmers and others. Little concern had been shown for the sharp decline even in the deer population, let alone among the bear and bobcat.

Yet by the 1960s and 1970s predators, as well as deer, small mammals, and wild turkey, had assumed a positive image for many Americans, and special measures were adopted to protect them and increase their numbers.

Close on the heels of these changes in attitude were new views about western deserts. The desert had long been thought of as a forbidding land where human habitation was impossible and travel was dangerous. The desert hardly figured in the debate over the Wilderness Act of 1964. But by the late 1970s this had changed. The increased popularity of nature photography had brought home the desert to the American people as a place of wonder and beauty. By 1976 western deserts had been explored and identified by many Americans as lands that should be protected in their natural condition.

Environmental Health and Well-being

The search for greater health and well-being constituted an equally significant element of the drive for environmental quality. Such concerns had firm roots in the earlier public-health movement, which emphasized the social conditions that gave rise to health problems. Improvements in water quality all but eliminated typhoid fever and other waterborne bacterial ailments while parasitic and viral diseases such as malaria and yellow fever were brought under control by sanitary measures. The discovery and widespread use of antibiotics after World War II limited the adverse effects of secondary infections. Such measures greatly reduced human suffering and prolonged life. But they also emphasized new causes of illness, many of them environmental.

As tuberculosis declined, other lung problems such as emphysema and cancer received more attention. The Tuberculosis Association changed its name to the American Lung Association to reflect the new emphasis; it became especially concerned with smoking as a cause of lung cancer and air pollution as a cause of pulmonary problems. Exposures formerly associated with infectious diseases now were found to be responsible for more deep-seated problems. Asbestos, for example, once had been thought of primarily as a cause of asbestosis, a pulmonary condition. Many lung problems arising from exposure to asbestos could not be treated with antibiotics and were found to be cancer.

Cancer received particular attention, as its incidence seemed to increase. By the late 1970s one-fourth of all living Americans would contract cancer during their lifetime, and two-thirds of these would die from it. The long latency period between exposure and the appearance of cancer created a sense of peril that made the disease more dramatic. At the same time, cancer was identified with either personal habits, such as smoking and diet, or environmental pollutants in air and water.

The new concerns for environmental health also focused on the workplace. Occupational dangers to workers had long been thought of mainly as posed by physical factors such as machinery. Increasingly the workplace was seen as an environment in which the air itself could transmit harmful substances to cause diseases in workers. Recognition of this danger came only slowly. Much of it awaited evidence accumulated from long-term studies of the relationship between occupational exposure and disease.

The concern for environmental health was primarily an urban phenomenon. The incidence of cancer was twice as high in cities as in the rural countryside, a difference attributed to the impact of urban pollution. The chemical products involved in manufacturing, increasing with each passing year after World War II, seemed especially to affect urban people adversely. The extensive use of the automobile in cities also posed continuing pollution threats. And studies of indoor air identified health hazards in offices and households.

Although older waterborne diseases had been controlled through chlorination and disinfection of drinking-water supplies, the rapid accumulation of newer chemical pollutants in the nation's rivers and its underground water generated new health concerns. Synthetic organic compounds, as well as heavy metals from industry, were discovered in many drinking-water sources. The disposal of industrial toxic wastes constituted an even more pervasive concern; they were often injected underground, but just as frequently they were disposed of in landfills from which they leaked into water supplies.

The increasing emphasis on environmental health arose from a rising level of expectations about health and well-being. As life expectancy increased, the average American could look forward to a decade or more of active life after retirement. As the threat of infectious disease decreased, fear of sudden death or disability from polio, secondary infections from simple surgical procedures such as appendectomies, or other dangers declined sharply. All this led to a new focus in health associated more with expectations of well-being than with fear of death. There was a special interest in the quality of life of elderly people. An increasing portion of the population became concerned about preventive health care, showing interest in physical fitness, food and diet, and protection from exposure to environmental pollutants. This marked innovation in ideas about personal health was an important element in the expanding concern for one's environment as a critical element in well-being.

The Ecological Perspective

Ecological objectives—an emphasis on the workings of natural biological and geological systems and the pressures human actions placed on them— were a third element of environmental concern. Whereas amenities involved an aesthetic response to the environment, and environmental health concerned a choice between cleaner and dirtier technologies within the built-up environment, ecological matters dealt with imbalances between developed and natural systems that had both current and long-term implications. These questions, therefore, involved ideas about permanence.

The term "ecology" had long referred to a branch of biology that emphasized study of the interaction of living organisms with their physical and biological environment. Popular ecology in the 1960s and 1970s went beyond that scientific meaning. One heard of the impact of people on "the ecology."

Professional ecologists disdained this corruption of the word as they had used it. Popular use involved both a broad meaning, the functioning of the biological and geological world, and a narrower one, the disruption of natural processes by human action, as well as the notion that the two, natural systems and human stress, needed to be brought into a better balance.

The popular ecological perspective was related in the ecology centers that arose in urban areas. Initially these grew out of the recycling move-ment—the collection of paper, glass, and tin cans for reprocessing. These centers drew together people who wished to help solve the litter problem and thus to enhance the aesthetic quality of their communities. But soon the concept of recycling seemed to spill over into larger ideas about natural cycles, a traditional ecological theme, and to human action to foster such processes. Ecology centers often expanded their activities into community organic gardens, nutrition and food for better health, and changing life-styles to reduce the human load on natural resources and natural systems.

An ecological perspective grew from the popularization of knowledge about natural processes. These were ideas significant to the study of ecology, but selected and modified by popular experience rather than as a result of formal study. An increasing number of personal or media encounters with the natural world gave rise to widely shared ideas about the functioning of biological and geological systems and the relationship of human beings to them.

Even before World War II, the problem of deer overpopulation on the north rim of the Grand Canyon, or imbalances between the numbers of deer and food in the cutover forestlands of Pennsylvania, Michigan, Wisconsin, and Minnesota, had popularized knowledge about predator-prey and food-population relationships. Overgrazing by cattle and sheep on the western range sparked discussions in the media of the problem of stress in plant communities in which, through overuse, the more vulnerable plants gave way to the hardier, reducing the variety of species. This conveyed the ideas that species diversity had evolved in the process of natural succession, that the number and diversity of species were reduced under population pressures, and that the capacity of ecological systems to sustain human use without major changes were limited.

The threat of toxic chemicals diffused throughout the biological world led to the spread of knowledge in the 1960s about biological and chemical cycles. Transported through the atmosphere, falling into water and on land, chemicals were absorbed by plants, eaten by animals and then by humans. With each step in that food chain they increased in concentration. Media coverage in the late 1950s and early 1960s of radioactive fallout from atomic testing increased awareness of these processes. The most dramatic example was radioactive cesium, which was absorbed by lichens in the Arctic, eaten by reindeer and in turn by Alaskan Eskimos and Laplanders, at each step increasing in concentration in fatty tissues.

The public encounter with pesticides drove home ideas about the ac-cumulation of toxic materials in the food chain. These persistent pesticides found their way into water to be taken up by small fish that were eaten by larger fish, and then by birds to produce weakened eggshells and reduced hatching. Rachel Carson's book *Silent Spring,* published in 1962, spread the word about the problem; even more influential was a widely reported administrative proceeding about DDT in Wisconsin in 1968 and 1969.

Experience with water pollution conveyed still further notions about ecological processes. If one lived in a coal-mining area one soon became aware that acid, formed from sulfur in coal, was toxic to aquatic life, leaving only those organisms that were adapted to stress. At a lake one learned of eutrophication, the way in which phosphates and nitrates from fertilizer and sewage provided nutrients that greatly increased the production of algae; these, in turn, decayed and used up the available oxygen required by fish. Eutrophic lakes with reduced fish life were widely known as dying lakes.

Water brought both ecological and biological phenomena closer together in the ecological perspective. The water cycle was pervasive; the natural cycle of rainfall, runoff, and percolation, flow to oceans and lakes, evaporation, and rainfall was readily understood. So also were malfunctions of this cycle as human activities diverted it into new physical channels, and these in turn generated adverse human consequences. In the nation's suburbs, for example, upstream construction of roads and shopping centers reduced land available for normal percolation of rainfall into soil and groundwater, increased runoff and caused flooding in downstream basements. Stream channelization deepened channels, destroyed the use of low-lying streamside areas as natural floodwater reservoirs, diverted water downstream to cause more flooding there, and lowered the water table. Near the seacoast it led to the intrusion of salt water in water supplies.

Such experiences as these led to an image of a web of life in which "everything was hitched to everything else." If human beings modified one part of that chain it could well have detrimental effects for them. And this realization led to the conviction that human action in relationship to the ecological world would have to be closely monitored and in many cases modified.

Ecological Life-Styles

The interest in natural processes led to criticism of life-styles that placed heavy loads on ecological systems. Many sought deliberately to change the houses in which they lived, the sources of their food, the approach to personal health, and their mode of work and leisure in order to "live more lightly on the earth."

These tendencies had some earlier roots. During the 1930s there were proposals for a more decentralized society, a technology of smaller scale, organic gardening and farming, and personal health care that emphasized preventive medicine. A few decades later the organic gardening and farming activities established by J. I. Rodale at Emmaus, Pennsylvania, became a creative center for such ventures. Its publication *Organic Gardening* was widely read; and its newsletter, the *Environmental Action Bulletin,* was an important source of information about environmental and ecological affairs.

In the 1970s a magazine from quite a different source, *Mother Earth News,* played a similar role; by 1977 its circulation had reached 550,000.

Ideas about ecological life-styles emphasized a personal responsibility for the impact of daily living on the wider natural world. Ways of working, living, and recreating should be changed so as to lower that pressure. This required individual commitment that brought into play a moral task: to conduct one's personal life so as to be consistent with the larger scheme of things.

Attention was focused on the enormous amounts of waste that people produced in their daily lives, the most dramatic example of which was the profusion of solid waste generated by advanced industrial societies. Was such elaborate packaging necessary? Another issue was wasteful use of energy— cars with low mileage per gallon, the use of mechanical gadgets powered with fossil fuel such as lawnmowers and off-road motorized vehicles, and more common energy-using household appliances. Ever changing styles, moreover, seemed to be altogether unnecessary. Such examples underlined the degree to which the American economy rested on excessive consumption that placed undue pressure on scarce resources.

These new life-styles revolved around three aspects of daily living: food, health, and shelter. The production and preparation of food could be carried out with far less input from intensive chemistry and technology and far more direct involvement with biological processes. Organic gardening, biological farming, and natural foods became increasingly popular. Natural-food stores arose first through mail-order houses that produced and sold organically grown food, then in cooperative retail outlets, and finally, as the demand grew, through franchise stores and natural food sections of supermarkets.

Health care seemed entirely too intensive in its scientific and technical context, too removed from personal relationships between individual and physician, too dependent on drugs and quick fixes. Increasing emphasis came to be placed on prevention, on habits of eating and exercise that could promote better health, rather than on cures. An intense debate, for example, persisted between those who sought to treat cancer after it was detected and those who stressed its prevention. The ecological approach was to remove the environmental cause and thus to attack illness at its origin. *Prevention,* published by the Rodale press, stressed these themes; it reached more than 2.5 million subscribers by the end of 1984.

The design and construction of houses, a part of the do-it-yourself move-ment, came to incorporate ecological perspectives. One could use natural materials, integrate internal and external space, and blend natural processes outside the building with internal arrangements. Building design had long insulated interior living from the elements, emphasizing protection from wind and rain, from cold in winter and heat in summer. Could houses not be designed to fit in with the slope of the land, perhaps be underground as well as aboveground, let in sunlight instead of keeping it out, bring the production of plants for both food and enjoyment into closer harmony with living quarters, and, through composting, for example, integrate waste dis-posal with the production of living things?

These emphases on food, health, and shelter were associated with themes of autonomy and self-help. The ecological perspective involved an affirmation of the capacity of individuals to take personal responsibility for their lives by designing with nature rather than with larger, remoter, and more centralized human institutions. There was a focus on natural materials, as contrasted with plastics, and especially those that were biologically generated, such as natural fibers. And there was interest in eliminating waste through reducing demands on one's environment, recycling, and natural processes. All these came to be summed up in the phrase the "conserver society."

These varied tendencies in thought and action that constituted the strands of environmental quality and ecology often came together. The most pervasive factor in this was the emphasis on the importance of a larger role for the natural world in the advanced industrial society. Aesthetic appreciation of nature often was closely connected with intellectual understanding as many people sought both to enjoy and to comprehend the natural settings around them. The adverse impacts of pollutants on human health and one's environment emphasized that the natural world was fragile and had to be cared for. Personal responsibility in life-style identified the natural world as a vantage point from which one tested appropriate human behavior. It was no wonder that ideas associated with biology, ecology, and geology came to be integral parts of popular thinking about the quality and permanence of life in modern society.

Environmental Politics and the Fate of the Earth

BARRY COMMONER

In the past few decades, the United States has witnessed a series of remarkable popular movements, the most prominent being the movements for civil rights, for the equality of women, for peace, and for the environment. People who have participated in these efforts are prone to reflect after a time on what has been accomplished. In the case of the civil-rights, women's, and peace movements, this is a subtle task, involving social processes that are not readily converted to "objective" numerical trends. To assess the impact of the environmental movement is easier, for the quality of the environment can be expressed in terms of generally unambiguous measurements: the changes, since the birth of the movement, in the amounts of harmful pollutants in the air or the water, or, for that matter, in our bodies; in the populations of fish or birds that have suffered environmental harm; in the efficacy of control measures.

The environmental movement is old enough now—its birth can be dated from the enthusiastic outburst of Earth Day, in April of 1970—to be held accountable for its successes and failures. Having made a serious claim on public attention and on the nation's resources, the movement's supporters cannot now evade the troublesome, potentially embarrassing question: What has been accomplished? Concern with the environment and efforts to improve it are today worldwide, but the United States is the place where the environmental movement first took hold, and where the earliest efforts were made, so it is a good place to look for answers. Since the early nineteen-seventies, the country has had basic laws that are intended to eliminate air and water pollution and to rid the environment of toxic chemicals and agricultural and urban wastes. National and state environmental agencies have been established; billions of dollars have been spent; powerful environmental lobbies have been created; local organizations have proliferated. Environmental issues have taken a permanent place in our political life.

In one respect, all this activity has clearly achieved an important success: we now know a good deal more about the state of the environment than we used to. In the last fifteen years, the United States has established monitoring systems that record the annual changes in environmental quality, and these give us an indication of what has happened in the environment since the effort to improve it began. The amounts of different pollutants that are emitted into the environment each year can be estimated fairly accurately for the nation as a whole from technical data on the behavior of cars, power plants, factories, and farms, though such measurements do not reveal the levels of pollutants that people actually encounter, which may differ a great deal, depending on how far they live from the pollutants' source. Local concentrations of some common pollutants—for example, the amount of dust or sulfur dioxide per cubic metre of air—are measured by a network of air-sampling devices that are stationed at fixed points, chiefly in cities, but the resultant information is spotty and not readily translatable into an average national trend. Water taken from rivers, lakes, underground sources, and wells is also analyzed from time to time for chemical and biological pollutants, but, again, the results are necessarily discrete and localized. Finally, there are less comprehensive measurements that determine the amounts of certain pollutants, such as pesticides, that have been taken up by wildlife, especially fish and birds, and there are also a few corresponding analyses of pollutants carried in the bodies of the human population.

The nation's basic environmental law, the National Environmental Policy Act of 1969, assigns to the federal Council on Environmental Quality the task of reporting these data. Unfortunately, among the first of the Reagan Administration's many cuts in domestic programs was a sixty-two-per-cent reduction in the C.E.Q. budget, which has diminished its reports, especially on water pollution. Nevertheless, by rounding out the C.E.Q. reports with special ones produced by various other government agencies it is possible to piece together a picture of how the environment has fared in the last ten or fifteen years.

Information about the trends in air pollution is available from annual reports published by the Environmental Protection Agency for the years between 1975 and 1985. (Data earlier than 1975 tend to be unreliable, because measurements were not standardized.) The E.P.A. reports describe changes in the emissions and local concentrations of the major airborne pollutants: particulates (dust), sulfur dioxide, lead, nitrogen oxides, volatile organic compounds, and ozone, a key ingredient of photochemical smog. One striking fact immediately emerges from the monitoring data: it is indeed possible to reduce the level of pollution sharply, for between 1975 and 1985 total annual lead emissions decreased by eighty-six per cent, and airborne concentrations of lead at national test sites have been correspondingly reduced. Lead, a notoriously toxic metal, has been responsible for serious health effects, such as mental retardation, especially among children living in heavily polluted areas. People have benefitted from the reduced emissions: the average lead levels in the blood of Americans decreased by thirty-seven per cent between 1976 and 1980.

The successful effort to reduce lead pollution only accentuates the failure to achieve a comparable reduction in the emissions of the other air pollutants, which, on the average, decreased by only thirteen and two-tenths per cent between 1975 and 1985. Of these pollutants, dust emissions have improved most—about thirty-two per cent—although actual concentrations in the air at some fifteen hundred test sites have improved somewhat less. But the annual improvements came to a halt in 1982, and since then emission levels of particulates have increased: they rose by more than four per cent between 1982 and 1985.

Sulfur dioxide is a particularly serious pollutant, for it diminishes the respiratory system's ability to deal with all other pollutants. It is also a major contributor to acid rain. Between 1975 and 1985, total sulfur-dioxide emissions declined by nineteen per cent, most of the change occurring between 1975 and 1981; since then, emissions have remained essentially constant. Average concentrations at national test sites improved somewhat more, in part because new power plants—a major source of sulfur dioxide—are being built outside urban areas, while most of the test sites are inside urban areas.

Carbon monoxide, a pollutant that causes respiratory problems, is produced chiefly by cars, trucks, and buses, and the effort to deal with it is based on control systems that reduce emissions from automobile exhausts. (The control devices also reduce waste-fuel emissions.) Total annual carbon-monoxide emissions decreased by fourteen per cent between 1975 and 1985, but between 1982 and 1985 they increased. In a number of cities, including New York, the levels of carbon monoxide still violate E.P.A. standards.

Photochemical smog, a complex mixture, is created when nitrogen oxides emitted from automobile exhausts and power plants are converted by sunlight into highly reactive molecules and these combine with waste fuel to form ozone and other noxious chemicals. The total emissions of nitrogen oxides *increased* by four per cent between 1975 and 1985. Ozone is not emitted as such but is formed in the air during smog reactions. Concentrations at national test sites decreased by fifteen per cent between 1975 and 1981, but have not changed since.

The noxious smog chemicals are responsible for serious health hazards; people with heart or respiratory problems are routinely warned to stay indoors during "smog alerts." This hazard is now more or less accepted as an unavoidable aspect of urban life. In some places, improvements in smog levels have been achieved by reducing traffic; yet smog continues to threaten health. For example, in Los Angeles, the worst-afflicted city, between 1973 and 1977 residents were subjected each year to at least two hundred and fifty days in which smog was at levels classified as "unhealthful," with more than a hundred and twenty-five of these classified as "very unhealthful." In most large American cities, residents are still exposed to unhealthful smog levels for fifty to a hundred and fifty days each year.

One consequence of air pollution is acid rain. In keeping with the ecological rule that everything has to go somewhere, sulfur dioxide and nitrogen oxides, once they have been emitted into the air, are picked up by rain and snow and brought down to earth in the form of sulfates and nitrates. Both these substances increase acidity, and in recent years many lakes—especially in the northeastern United States and Canada, but also in Europe—have become more acid. In some of these lakes, serious biological changes have occurred, often involving the virtual elimination of fish populations. In cities, acid rain erodes buildings and monuments.

Because scrubbers and the increased use of low-sulfur coal have reduced sulfur-dioxide emissions at coal-burning power plants, while emissions of nitrogen oxides from power plants and automotive vehicles have increased, there has been a noticeable shift in the relative contributions of these pollutants to acid rain. Reports from Hubbard Brook, a research station in New Hampshire, where acidity problems have been studied for a long time, show that as the sulfur content of precipitation declined by twenty-seven per cent between 1964 and 1981 the nitrate content increased by a hundred and thirty-seven per cent. Not much improvement can be expected in the acid-rain problem, given the negligible improvement in sulfur-dioxide emissions and the rising emissions of nitrogen oxides.

The ecological processes that govern the quality of surface waters are more complex than the chiefly chemical events that govern air pollution. A basic reason for the pollution of surface waters—rivers and lakes—as well as inshore marine waters is the stress placed on the natural ecological cycles that, if they are kept in balance, maintain water quality. If inadequate sewage-treatment systems dump excessive organic matter into a river or a lake, the accompanying fecal bacteria threaten health. As the excess organic matter is broken down by aquatic microorganisms, they may consume so much oxygen that fish begin to die. If urban and industrial waste and runoff from agricultural areas increase nitrate and phosphate concentrations beyond the levels maintained by a balanced cycle, eutrophication occurs. Heavy algal blooms are formed and soon die, burdening the system with excessive organic matter and reducing oxygen content. In addition, high nitrate levels in drinking water may create health problems such as methemoglobinemia (a condition that reduces the oxygen-carrying capacity of the blood, especially in infants) and may contribute to the formation of carcinogens. Toxic chemicals only add to these harmful effects.

In the last decade, particular rivers and lakes here and there have been cleaned up by closing sources of pollution and building new sewage-treatment plants. Yet in that period, nationally, there has been little or no over-all improvement in the levels of the five standard pollutants that determine water quality: fecal coliform bacteria, dissolved oxygen, nitrate, phosphorus, and suspended sediments. A recent survey of the trends in pollution levels between 1974 and 1981 at nearly four hundred locations on major American rivers shows that there has been no improvement in water quality at more than four-fifths of the tested sites. For example, the levels of fecal coliform bacteria decreased at only fifteen per cent of the river stations, and increased at five per cent. At half the locations, the bacterial count was too high to permit swimming, according to the standard recommended by the National Technical Advisory Committee on Water Quality Criteria. Levels of dissolved oxygen, suspended sediments, and phosphorus improved at thirteen to seventeen per cent of the locations, but deteriorated at eleven to sixteen per cent of them. The most striking change—for the worse—was in nitrate levels: increases were observed at thirty per cent of the test stations and decreases at only seven per cent. Agricultural use of nitrogen fertilizer is a main source of this pollutant; in rivers that drain cropland, the number of sampling stations that report rising nitrate levels is eight times the number reporting falling levels. Another major source is nitrogen oxides emitted into the air by vehicles and power plants and deposited in rain and snow as nitrate; this accounts for increased river nitrate levels in the Northeast, despite the relative scarcity of heavily fertilized acreage in that area. The survey also shows that there was a sharp increase in the occurrence of two toxic elements, arsenic and cadmium (a cause of lung and kidney damage), in American rivers between 1974 and 1981; but, as expected from the reduced automotive emissions, the occurrence of lead declined.

An over-all assessment of the changes in these standard measures of water quality can be gained from the average trends. For the five standard pollutants, the frequency of improving trends averaged 13.2 per cent; but the frequency of deteriorating trends averaged 14.7 per cent; thus, at more than four-fifths of the test sites, over-all water quality deteriorated or remained the same. In sum, the regulations mandated by the Clean Water Act, and more than a hundred billion dollars spent to meet them, have failed to improve water quality in most rivers. The relatively few locations that have improved are more than cancelled out by the locations that have deteriorated. Moreover, the occurrence of three serious pollutants—nitrate, arsenic, and cadmium—has increased considerably.

One of the chief symptoms of the environmental crisis in the early nineteen-seventies was eutrophication, especially in lakes. Lake Erie provided a dramatic example. The lake received an enormous burden of inadequately treated sewage and phosphate-rich detergents from the cities surrounding it, and chemical plants contributed mercury and other toxic materials as well. Rivers carried nitrate and eroded soil into the lake from heavily fertilized farms. By the nineteen-sixties and seventies, especially in its western regions and along the shoreline, Lake Erie was exhibiting the classic signs of eutrophication: heavy algal overgrowths, epidemics of asphyxiated fish, and sharply declining fish catches. Because of its notoriety as a "dying lake," Lake Erie has been intensively studied in the last decade, and the results have been evaluated by elaborate statistical techniques; the most detailed data are given in a recent lengthy E.P.A. report. This report makes a telling comparison of pollution levels along various reaches of the western lakeshore, where eutrophication had been particularly troublesome. In 1972 and 1973, three of twenty-one shoreline regions were classified as entirely or partly eutrophic; in 1978 and 1979, eutrophication was more widespread, affecting twelve of twenty-one shoreline regions.

According to the E.P.A. report, the rate of oxygen depletion in the central basin of Lake Erie increased by fifteen per cent between 1970 and 1980, following a trend that went back as far as 1930. The entry of phosphates from certain city sewage systems has declined, as a result of campaigns to reduce the use of phosphate-containing detergents—probably the most successful such effort, in Detroit, reduced phosphate concentrations in the Detroit River by nearly seventy per cent between 1971 and 1981—but the acquisition of phosphates from all the rivers entering the lake was reduced much less; only four of twelve test sites showed any improvement. Over all, phosphates entering Lake Erie decreased by about a third between 1972 and 1982. The same E.P.A. report also records the catch of commercial fish from 1920 to 1980. The once valuable catch of herring and whitefish dropped off sharply after 1950, and by 1960 it was close to zero. The E.P.A. report showed that the catch had not recovered between 1960 and 1980.

In 1970, Lake Erie was widely mourned as a dying lake, and serious efforts were made to revive it. Yet nearly two decades after our environmental reawakening Lake Erie, despite some limited improvements, remains a flagrant example of environmental pollution. The condition of less famous lakes is just as bad. This is particularly true of lakes in heavily farmed areas, where nitrogen and phosphorus fertilizers leach from the soil into rivers and lakes. A 1982 survey found that of a hundred and seven lakes in Iowa all were eutrophic, and so were more than eighty per cent of the lakes in Ohio and Pennsylvania. A national survey of changes in water quality between 1972 and 1982 showed almost no progress in lakes. Only 2.4 per cent of the total lake acreage improved; 10.1 per cent became more degraded; 62.1 per cent was unchanged; no reports were available for the remainder.

About fifty per cent of the population of the United States depends on underground sources—groundwater—for its drinking water. The United States Geological Survey and state agencies monitor the quality of groundwater by testing wells throughout the country. The results, based on readings from more than a hundred thousand wells, show that in the past twenty-five years these sources have become increasingly polluted by nitrates and toxic chemicals. Fertilizer was chiefly responsible for the rising nitrate levels. In Nebraska, a 1983 survey showed that eighty-two per cent of the wells over the nitrate limit established by health authorities (ten milligrams per litre of nitrogen in the form of nitrate) were contaminated by fertilizer nitrogen. In California's Sacramento Valley, a very heavily cropped area, nitrate contamination of wells has been monitored for a long time. In the fifty-year period following 1912, the percentage of wells with excessive nitrates (defined as five and a half milligrams per litre) approximately doubled. More recently, the percentage of wells with excessive nitrates doubled again—this time in only a four-year period, between 1974 and 1978. The major source of the nitrates is nitrogen fertilizer leaching from irrigation water. A similar trend has been observed in Iowa. In 1984, the Geological Survey summarized the situation: "Current trends suggest that nitrate accumulations in groundwater of the United States will continue to increase in the future."

Fifteen years ago, public-opinion polls on environmental issues showed that most people were worried about water and air pollution—especially smog. Now, even though these problems remain largely unsolved, polls show that as a public concern air and water pollution runs behind a new environmental threat—toxic chemicals. In the early nineteen-seventies, this problem was due largely to agricultural products—insecticides, herbicides, and fungicides. DDT and similar chlorinated insecticides were the most notorious examples. In 1972, the use of DDT and related insecticides was banned in the United States because they were shown to promote cancers and also to be a hazard to wildlife. One of the most noticeable effects of DDT was the decline in bird populations; DDT interferes with the biochemistry of reproduction, making eggs thin-shelled and thus easily destroyed before they hatch. Banning the use of DDT has been very effective. For example, between 1969 and 1975 the average DDT content of brown pelicans in South Carolina decreased by seventy-seven per cent, and by 1976 the number of fledglings more than tripled. People have benefitted as well: between 1970 and 1983, average DDT levels in body fat in the American population decreased by seventy-nine per cent. The banning of polychlorinated biphenyl, another notorious chemical pollutant—it increases the incidence of cancer and birth defects—has had a similar effect. Between 1970 and 1980, the body burden of PCB in freshwater fish decreased by fifty-six per cent, and in birds (starlings) by eighty-six per cent. In people, the percentage of Americans with relatively high levels of PCB (above three parts per million) in their fatty tissue decreased by about seventy-five per cent.

Since 1950, however, the roster of serious chemical pollutants has steadily expanded. Hundreds of toxic chemicals, many of them carcinogenic, have been detected in water supplies, air, and food. For the first time in the three-and-a-half-billion-year history of life on this planet, living things are burdened with a host of man-made poisonous substances. According to a recent E.P.A. survey, members of the general American population now carry several dozen man-made chemicals, many of them carcinogenic, in their body fat (and generally in the fat of mothers' milk as well). Toxic chemicals now seriously pollute important segments of the food chain. In the Great Lakes, for example, the toxic-chemical levels of salmon, trout, and walleye often exceed Food and Drug Administration standards for human consumption. Tumors are found on the fish with increasing frequency.

The total toxic-chemical problem is huge. The American petrochemical industry produces about two hundred and sixty-five million metric tons of hazardous waste annually; toxic chemicals generally make up about one per cent of this material, and the rest is made up of water and other non-toxic carriers. About a third of this waste is emitted, uncontrolled, into the environment. Moreover, most of the controlled, or "managed," waste is injected underground, sometimes into water systems, and thus becomes a long-term threat to the environment. Only about one per cent of the industry's toxic waste is actually destroyed. The chemical industry has, largely unrestrained, become the major threat to environmental quality.

Environmental pollution from radioactive materials is in a class by itself; it originates from a single sector of production—the manipulation of nuclear energy for peaceful or military purposes. Radiation exposure due to the normal operation of the nuclear power industry appears to be quite small compared with exposure to natural sources of radioactivity such as radon and cosmic rays; it is less than one one-hundredth of one per cent of the natural exposure. But this is a national average; near power plants, exposures are certainly higher.

There is no widely disseminated accounting of the radioactivity that enters the environment from minor nuclear-power-plant malfunctions. At most, there are only reports that an accidental emission of radioactive material has occurred—generally with no information about the actual radiation exposure but only the statement that "the amount of radiation released was harmless." (Such statements are wrong. Radiation, no matter how weak, always involves the risk of some harm, and the risk is proportional to the dose received. A very small exposure from a dental X-ray, say, has a correspondingly small risk, which is presumably worth taking in view of the expected benefit.) A partial measure of the radioactivity released by nuclear power plants is available from E.P.A. studies of krypton-85, a radioactive gas uniquely associated with the operation of such plants. The average annual concentration of krypton-85 in the air increased by eighty per cent between 1970 and 1983, thus increasing the environmental hazard.

Accidents that disrupt the containment structures protecting the environment from the huge amount of radioactive material in an operating nuclear reactor present a far larger hazard than is presented by typical malfunctions. Until 1979, this was an abstract concern, for some abstruse— and considerably disputed—statistical computations concluded that the probability of a serious accident might be as low as one in a million per year per reactor. The accident at the Three Mile Island nuclear power plant, in 1979, brought the abstract discussions down to earth. While the outcome of the accident was far less serious than it might have been—the reactor's core partially melted and extensively contaminated the interior of the reactor building and released some radioactivity into the environment—it suggested that serious mechanical failures were far more probable than the calculations had indicated.

In April of 1986, of course, a second failure occurred—at the Soviet Union's Chernobyl nuclear power plant—which led to a radioactive disaster.

At least thirty-one people have died and more than two hundred have suffered acute radiation sickness; estimates of future cancer deaths from the radioactive fallout over a wide area of Europe range above a hundred thousand; more than a hundred thousand people have been evacuated from their homes; some hundreds of square miles of agricultural land have become useless; radioactive fallout disrupted milk and vegetable production throughout most of Europe.

The hazardous consequence of one aspect of nuclear technology—fallout from test explosions of nuclear weapons in the atmosphere—has been considerably reduced by the straightforward procedure of simply stopping the process that creates it. As a result of the 1963 treaty signed by the United States and the Soviet Union, atmospheric tests have halted (except for a few conducted by China and France), and fallout radioactivity, in keeping with natural decay processes, has declined. For example, a national survey of milk showed that it contained 23.8 picocuries of strontium 90 per litre in 1964, 7.3 in 1970, and 2.0 in 1984.

Finally, we need to consider the American contribution to global environmental problems. One of these problems is the progressive depletion of ozone in the stratosphere, which is due largely to the increased use of chlorofluorocarbons (petrochemical products widely used in refrigerators and air-conditioners). The stratospheric ozone layer protects the earth from solar ultraviolet radiation; if it is sufficiently depleted, people will be exposed to an intensity of radiation capable of significantly increasing the incidence of skin cancer. Recent studies in Antarctica indicate that the ozone layer is continuing to thin out. Despite an international agreement to reduce the production of chlorofluorocarbons, and some progress in the United States, little has been done thus far to stop this chemical assault on the stratosphere. Another problem is the progressive warming of the earth's surface because of the accumulation of carbon dioxide and other gases in the upper atmosphere. Sunlight falling on the earth is sooner or later converted into heat, which radiates outward, so the planet's temperature is determined by the balance between the sunlight falling on the earth and the heat leaving it. The concentration of carbon dioxide in the atmosphere governs the re-radiation process, for the gas acts like an energy valve, allowing sunlight through but tending to hold heat back. Since 1850, the increased use of fuel that produces carbon dioxide when it is burned has gradually increased the atmospheric-carbon-dioxide concentration, and the earth's average temperature has steadily risen; an additional three or four degrees Fahrenheit in average temperature is expected by the middle of the twenty-first century. This may cause drastic changes in climate—for example, flooding of coastal areas (including many cities), and severe drought in North America, Europe, and Asia. In recent years, other gases, such as the chlorofluorocarbons, have added to the problem. As a result, the latest projections predict severe climatic changes by 2030.

This "greenhouse effect" (glass resembles carbon dioxide in its effect on sunlight and heat, a property that helps to keep a greenhouse warm in the winter) can be slowed down only if there is a sharp reduction in the use of combustible fuel, but nothing has been done thus far to deal with this problem, and it continues to carry the world toward a climatic catastrophe. . . .

[E]very aspect of human society depends on the ecosystem—for the natural resources that support production, for the air we breathe, for the green plants that feed us and other animals. Moreover, the environment is governed by stubborn, largely unalterable natural forces, while the system of production is subject to human choice. Logically, therefore, the decisions that determine the choice of production technology ought to be governed by the constraints inherent in nature. But in fact the actual direction of governance is reversed. The design of the man-made system of production is not governed by the nicely balanced attributes of the natural system; instead, as we have seen, the state of the environment is determined by the production technologies that have been chosen to support industry, agriculture, and transportation.

So the environmentalist who wishes to grapple with this illogical arrangement needs to turn from the fairly rigid but harmonious pattern of nature to the more flexible but chaotic realm of human decisions. And this realm necessarily includes not only the choice of production technologies but also the closely related economic decisions. Logic tells us that the economic system—the processes that mediate the flow of wealth—is contingent on the system of production, which is, after all, the source of the goods and services that generate economic wealth. In a logical arrangement, therefore, just as environmental constraints ought to govern the design of the production system, that design should, in turn, specify appropriate features of the economic system. For example, if the importance of eliminating smog ought to specify the design of automobile engines, then the need to build such engines ought to govern the automobile industry's investment decisions—in part, at least. But here, too, the logical direction of governance is reversed: the decisions that determine the design of the system of production—what is produced and by what technological means—are determined largely by economic considerations that are quite independent of the product's environmental impact, the chief consideration being the profitability of the enterprise.

In sum, the decisions that govern environmental quality originate in the economic realm, and are translated into the design of productive technology, which—as now constituted—in turn visits upon the environment the evils of pollution. This relationship becomes clear when we consider the origins of the major environmental problems. Smog, for example, is the end result of the economic motivation that led the auto industry to decide to manufacture large, powerful cars, for, as John DeLorean, a former General Motors executive, has said, "when we should have been planning switches to smaller, more fuel-efficient, lighter cars in the late 1960s in response to a growing demand in the marketplace, G.M. management refused because 'we make money on big cars.' "

Recent changes in the technology of electric-power production which have seriously affected environmental quality have also been economically motivated. When the utilities were persuaded that nuclear power would be "too cheap to meter," they hastened to build nuclear power plants, thereby creating the monumental hazards of nuclear accidents and the still unresolved problem of radioactive waste. Then, when this hope turned into an illusion, there was a rapid switch to coal-fired plants, because they produce cheaper electricity than oil-powered or nuclear-powered plants—but they also produce much more sulfur dioxide. In the same way, the steel industry's response to the demand for plants that would be less polluting—closing rather than improving them—is motivated by the higher profits obtainable from alternative investments in oil and chemicals. Similarly, the postwar history of American agricultural chemicals was motivated by the increased economic returns on investment that they engendered. Finally, the production of petrochemicals is more profitable than the manufacture of the product that they replace; for example, profits on detergent production are significantly higher than profits on soap production.

It is economic motivation, then, that has impelled the sweeping anti-ecological changes in the technology of production that have occurred since the Second World War. These changes have turned the nation's factories, farms, vehicles, and shops into seedbeds of pollution: nitrates from fertilizer; phosphates from detergents; toxic residues from pesticides; smog and carcinogenic exhaust from vehicles; the growing list of toxic chemicals and the mounds of undegradable plastic containers, wrappings, and gewgaws from the petrochemical industry.

The decisions to make these technological changes have been short-sighted not only because of their impact on the environment but also because they often generate serious economic problems. For example, the intensive use of agricultural chemicals has harmed not only the environment but, in recent years, the agricultural economy as well. As increasing amounts of fertilizer are applied to the soil, crop growth reaches a limit, and thereafter the yield produced per unit of fertilizer falls, and economic productivity is reduced. At the same time, excess, unassimilated fertilizer leaches through the soil into surface water and intensifies pollution. Similarly, the continued use of pesticides breeds resistance in the pests, so that more and more of the chemicals must be used to achieve the same effect. For these reasons, the economic productivity of agricultural chemicals—that is, the crop output per unit of chemical input—has decreased by fifty per cent since 1960, and it is still falling. Thus, both increased stress on the environment and falling economic efficiency are inherent in the present system of agricultural production. In the past few years, American farming has been undergoing a deepening economic crisis, marked by numerous bankruptcies, especially of family farms. Each year, as agricultural chemicals become more expensive and less efficient in improving crop production, farmers must incur a higher debt to buy the chemicals, and thereby become more vulnerable to bankruptcy. The heavy dependence of agricultural technology on chemicals has hurt not only the quality of the environment but the farmers' livelihood as well.

Economics also explains the reluctance of the petrochemical industry to deal effectively with its toxic waste. The only practical, though far from satisfactory, way to keep toxic chemicals out of the environment is to destroy them—in specially designed incinerators, for example. This process, however, is so expensive—as much as two thousand dollars per metric ton—that if it were to be applied to the total annual tonnage of toxic chemicals (an estimated two million six hundred and fifty thousand tons) it might cost about five and a half billion dollars, an amount larger than the annual profit of the thirty largest American chemical companies, which include most of the nation's petrochemical industry. Proper treatment of its waste would thus force the industry to raise prices and face serious competition from the natural products that it has replaced.

In the end, the decisions that have so gravely affected the environment have also had serious economic effects, because they govern a factor that is closely linked to both the environment and the economy—the system of production. In a free-market economy, capital tends to be invested in those production enterprises which promise to yield the greatest return in the shortest time. Since the social interest in environmental quality or long term economic efficiency is not represented in such investment decisions, neither of these desirable results is likely to be achieved by them.

There seems to be a paradox embedded in the conclusion that most, if not all, environmental pollution is the outcome of decisions guided by free-market forces. It is often argued, after all, that the market operates—automatically, in the best of circumstances—to seek out those decisions which make the most efficient use of the available resources. And one of the well-justified claims for ecological processes is that *they* are characteristically efficient: there are, after all, no "wastes" in the ecosystem. If the present system of production is counter-ecological, it must be wasteful; if this is so, new systems of production, more closely guided by ecological principles, ought to be more efficient than those devised by the present market-guided system. Why then haven't they attracted investors and entered into successful competition with the present system?

The over-all economic efficiency of the new technologies that have transformed production since the Second World War—and have polluted the country—is unmistakable. Considerably more profitable than the technologies they have replaced, the new ones have generated a more than fourfold increase in total production (as measured by the gross national product) since 1950. However, the improvement in efficiency responsible for this achievement has been unbalanced. While the efficiency with which labor is used—that is, the value of the product yielded per hour of a person's labor—has increased a great deal, the corresponding productivity of capital and natural resources such as energy has declined. For example, the postwar substitution of plastics for leather has displaced an industry characterized by low labor productivity and high capital productivity with an industry characterized by high labor productivity and low capital productivity. To generate the same value of product, the plastics industry uses about a fourth as much labor but ten times as much capital as the leather industry. The disparity between the two industries' energy productivity—the amount of energy used to produce a given value of product—is even greater: the plastics industry uses about thirty times as much energy as the leather industry.

However, if one takes a more fundamental approach to the problem of environmental quality by recognizing that it is inherently linked to the technology of production, one can find ways of improving both the economy and the environment. The electric-power industry provides an informative example. The power industry is a notorious source of pollution: responsible for a great deal of environmental dust, sulfur dioxide, and nitrogen oxide; contributing considerably to acid rain; and generating the threat of nuclear disasters. In the United States, the industry is also in a precarious economic condition: the utilities' heavy investment in huge power plants—especially nuclear plants—has driven the cost of producing electricity sharply upward and has threatened some of the companies with bankruptcy. (A *Business Week* cover story has asked the question "Are Utilities Obsolete?") A major reason for these economic difficulties is that the present technology of electric-power production is highly centralized. Typically, each new plant is very large and requires a huge capital investment—billions of dollars. The plant is so large because it represents an investment in the capacity needed well into the future. Consequently, when a new plant begins to operate, the system inevitably has an excess capacity, and for a time part of the capital investment yields little or no return. Moreover, the transmission system that distributes electricity from central stations is costly and consumes a significant fraction of the power. Finally, centralized power plants are inherently inefficient, because, for inescapable thermodynamic reasons, two-thirds of the energy available from the fuel is dispersed into the environment. This means that the industry wastes two-thirds of the fuel that it uses, and causes three times as much pollution per unit of useful energy produced as it would if the wasted energy could be recaptured for use.

The heat discarded by a central power station could readily be recaptured and used—to heat homes, for example. But large centralized plants cannot be used for this process—cogeneration—because heat can be transmitted effectively only over short distances. No one wants to live such a short distance from a power plant, especially if it is nuclear. (Some people are in this unhappy position. For example, a nuclear power plant in Gorki, in the Soviet Union, provides heat for that city; its presence must have been causing a good deal of concern since the Chernobyl disaster.) By redesigning the technology of electrical production in keeping with sensible ecological principles, both environmental and economic improvement can be achieved. What is needed is to decentralize the production of electricity and install cogenerator plants just large enough to meet the local demand for heat and electricity. With the cogenerator operating at a much higher level of both economic and thermodynamic efficiency than a conventional power plant, fuel consumption is reduced, and the environmental impact and the cost of energy are decreased.

Similar environmental and economic gains could be achieved by reorganizing agricultural production along ecological lines. For example, it has been found that the net economic returns of large-scale Midwestern organic farms, which use no fertilizer or pesticides, are equal to the returns of otherwise similar conventional farms, which use a great deal of these agricultural chemicals. This represents an economic gain for the organic farmers, since with lower production costs they are less dependent on bank loans and therefore less vulnerable to bankruptcy. Similarly, if the crop system were properly redesigned to produce both food and ethanol (a solar fuel, and thus renewable) the farmers' income could be diversified and national energy production enhanced.

These gains can be achieved only if the social need for both environmental quality and economic growth is allowed to govern the choice of production technology. Typically, measures designed to meet such a need require a relatively large initial investment. This is a serious hurdle, which people who would benefit most—the poor—have difficulty in overcoming. Another hurdle is the relatively slow rate of return on some of the necessary investments. If such an investment—for example, the relatively slow restoration of impoverished soil through a transition to organic farming—must compete with an existing investment that yields quick profits, it is certain to be ignored. However valuable to society, the investment is not likely to be made if it must compete in the free market, which favors large-scale investments over decentralized ones, and short-term over long-term returns.

Perhaps the most profound question raised by environmental issues is to what extent the choice of production technologies should be determined by private economic considerations and to what extent by social concerns like environmental quality. These values are in sharp conflict. There appears to be a broad consensus that it is in the national interest to restore the quality of the environment, and the resultant legislation confirms the general impression that achieving this goal is a social, governmental responsibility. And, as we have seen, significant environmental improvement requires the proper choice of technologies and systems of production, so that this choice, too, becomes a social responsibility. Yet in our free-market economy the right to make such a choice is in private, not public, hands, and this is a right that very few Americans would challenge. . . .

Because the effort to improve the environment is so closely linked to the decisions that govern the technology of production, it is inevitably drawn into the realm of politics. Though technological choices are often thought of as being outside the realm of public policy or politics, and driven instead by "objective" scientific considerations, the evidence contradicts this view. That high-compression automobile engines are particularly powerful and generate smog is certainly an objective scientific fact. The decision to manufacture such an engine rather than one that is less powerful but does not produce smog is, however, not a scientific necessity but a human choice. When the auto companies decided to build high-compression engines, the choice, as we know, was motivated by a private interest—higher profits. But their decision created a social problem—smog. When the decision was made, no questions were asked about the environmental effect of the new engines, and their social impact was revealed, too late, by the blanket of smog that covers the cities.

It is, of course, quite possible to choose a technology on the basis of its social consequences. When environmentalists speak of "appropriate technology," they have in mind production methods that not only enhance environmental quality but fulfill such other social purposes as conservation of energy and material resources and humane conditions of work. The social significance of a technological decision is much wider than its impact on environmental quality. The series of decisions that substituted plastics for leather, for example, aggravated not only environmental pollution but unemployment as well, for the plastics industry uses more capital and less labor than the leather industry did. In this sense, social guidance of technological decisions is vital not only for environmental quality but for nearly everything else that determines how people live: employment; working conditions; the cost of transportation, energy, food and other necessities of life; and economic growth. And so there is an unbreakable link between the environmental issue and all the other troublesome political issues. . . .

In the United States, environmental politics has followed a distinctive course. Here the environmental movement is part of the phenomenon that since the Second World War has given rise to wave after wave of popular, issue-oriented movements: for civil rights; against nuclear-weapons testing; for women's rights; for gay and lesbian rights; against the war in Vietnam; for the environment; against nuclear power and for solar energy; for world peace. These movements have a good deal in common. All of them have arisen outside the arena of conventional politics, sparked by outsiders like Martin Luther King, Jr., and Rachel Carson rather than by established political figures. Their level of public support has typically gone through successive cycles of enthusiasm and apathy. At their height, some of these movements have achieved notable successes—the civil-rights and environmental laws, the nuclear-test-ban treaty, the new employment opportunities for women—all of them accomplished by nonelectoral means: marches, demonstrations, lobbies. Yet, as the record of the Reagan Administration shows, these successes can be quickly eroded when officials hostile to them are elected to power. Indeed, the movements' greatest failure is their inability to translate the millions of votes that their combined adherents represent into significant electoral power, and put people in office who will protect their gains and expand them.

A major reason for the tenuous connection between the movements and politics is that their issues have been consigned to the political ghetto that is reserved for "special interests." In a sense, this isolation is self-imposed, for the varied concerns are usually manifested—in a legislator's office, for example—as single-minded constituents, one pleading for peace, another for sexual equality, a third for environmentalism, on down the list. Each special pleading demands a special response, at best unrelated to the other issues, and often in actual conflict with them. Each of the issues is regarded as a possible modifier of national policy but not as a creator of it—a correction in the course of the ship of state but not a motive force. Yet the issues that the movements represent, taken together, and added to those of the much older labor movement, constitute not only the major aspects of public policy but its most profound expression: human rights; the quality of life; health; jobs; peace; survival. What can unite these movements to enable them to exert an effect on national policy that expresses the profound political meaning of their collective issues?

The environmental experience suggests an answer. As we have seen, the obvious manifestations of the environmental problem—smog, toxic dumps, nuclear catastrophes—that set it apart as a "special interest" are but perceptible expressions of a deeper, underlying issue: how the choice of production technologies is to be determined. Here environmentalism reaches a common ground with all the other movements, for each of them also bears a fundamental relation to the choice of production technologies. Discrimination, for example, resembles pollution in that one of its major features—paying women and racial minorities less than white men—originates in decisions made by the managers of productive enterprises. Of course, other factors, social, cultural, and psychological, are involved, but the end result—wage discrimination—is, after all, an effective way of reducing production costs. Or, to look at this relationship from the other direction, if it were to be determined through some system of social governance that all the employees in an enterprise who do comparable work should receive equal pay, regardless of sex or race, a major effect of the social, cultural, and psychological forces that engender discrimination would be nullified. The connection between this common ground and the issues of peace and foreign policy is less direct but nevertheless substantial. It explains, for example, the apparent justification for the Administration's military belligerence—the insistence that force must be used wherever it is needed to support governments and political groups that, like the Administration, favor free-market principles of economic governance. In particular, it would be difficult to explain the Administration's deep-seated antagonism to the Soviet Union—which engenders the monstrous threat of global nuclear destruction—if it were not for the opposite views of the two governments on the stewardship of economic enterprises.

Perhaps the most useful outcome of the environmental experience is that it illuminates the relationship between the outward manifestations of the ills that trouble modern society and the common origin of those ills. But there are risks in expounding this relationship. Calling attention to their source may appear to minimize the importance of the immediate problems that initially attracted adherents to the cause, and so risk their ire. At the same time, an effort to transform the "special interest" into a critique of basic and even more troubling faults in the social structure is likely to intensify opposition to it. The path taken by Martin Luther King, Jr., in the last few years of his life is a cautionary example. At the height of his influence, King had won major victories and had acquired a broad following as the leader of a powerful attack on outward expressions of legally enforced racial discrimination: segregated schools and public facilities. Then, a few years before he was assassinated, he began to link racial discrimination to its origins and, thereby, to other social issues. He sensed, it seems, that blacks could not break out of their persistent social ghetto if they remained trapped, as a "special interest," in a political ghetto. And so he declared his opposition to the war in Vietnam, led a march of poor people (black and white) on Washington, and championed the cause of striking black garbagemen in Memphis. In this new role, King quickly became more controversial. He was out of his depth, it was said—taken in by political radicals and diverted from his true mission. But he died believing, it seems, that this new course had brought him closer to the heart of the problem he had set out to resolve: that beneath the legal basis of racial discrimination lay the deeper problems of poverty and violence; that the root of racial discrimination is also the root of poverty and war.

Neither the environmental movement nor any of the other issue-oriented movements have yet attempted to follow the road that Dr. King began to travel before he died. But the environmental experience powerfully illuminates that road—a historic passage toward a democracy that can exert its force on the germinal decisions that determine whether we and the place we inhabit will thrive.

₩ *F U R T H E R   R E A D I N G*

Craig Allin, *The Politics of Wilderness Preservation* (1982)
Nicholas A. Ashford, *Crisis in the Workplace* (1977)
William Ashworth, *Hell's Canyon* (1977)
Daniel M. Berman, *Death on the Job* (1978)
Paul Brodeur, *Expendable Americans* (1978)
Robert Van Den Bosch, *The Pesticide Conspiracy* (1978)
Rachel Carson, *Silent Spring* (1962)
William U. Chandler, *Investing in Children* (1985)
Gerard H. Clarfield and William M. Wiecek, *Nuclear America: Military and Civilian Nuclear Power in the United States, 1940–1980* (1984)
Joan Claybrook, *Retreat from Safety: Reagan's Attack on America's Health* (1984)
Barry Commoner, *The Closing Circle* (1971)
Continental Group, Inc., *Toward Responsible Growth: Economic and Environmental Concern in the Balance* (1982)
Thomas H. Corbett, *Cancer and Chemicals* (1977)
Thomas Dunlap, *DDT, Scientists, Citizens and Public Policy* (1981)
Edith Efron, *The Apocalyptics* (1984)
Paul R. Ehrlich, Anne H. Ehrlich, and John P. Holdren, *Ecoscience: Population, Environment, and People* (1971)
————, *Extinction* (1981)
Samuel S. Epstein, *The Politics of Cancer* (1978)
Daniel F. Ford, *Three Mile Island* (1982)
Michael Frome, *Battle for the Wilderness* (1974)
A. Y. Gunter, *The Big Ticket: A Challenge for Conservation* (1971)
Samuel P. Hays, *Beauty, Health, and Permanence: Environmental Politics in the United States, 1955–1985* (1987)
Craig R. Humphrey and Frederick R. Buttel, *Environment, Energy and Society* (1982)
Charles O. Jones, *Clean Air: The Policies and Politics of Pollution Control* (1975)
Wallace Kaufman and Orrin Pilkey, *The Beaches Are Moving: The Drowning of America's Shoreline* (1979)

Richard Kazis and Richard L. Grossman, *Fear at Work: Job Blackmail, Labor and the Environment* (1982)

Stephen R. Kellert, *American Attitudes, Knowledge and Behaviors Toward Wildlife and Natural Habitats* (1979–1981)

Jonathan Lash, *A Season of Spoils: The Story of the Reagan Administration's Attack on the Environment* (1984)

Adeline Gordon Levine, *Love Canal* (1982)

Donella H. Meadows et al., *The Limits to Growth* (1972)

Martin V. Melosi, *Coping with Abundance: Energy and Environment in Industrial America* (1985)

Lester Milbrath, *Environmentalists: Vanguard for a New Society* (1984)

Robert C. Mitchell, *Environmental Policy in the 1980's: Reagan's New Agenda* (1984)

Ralph W. Moss, *The Cancer Syndrome* (1980)

Hugh Nash, ed., *The Energy Controversy: Soft Path Questions and Answers by Amory Lovins and His Critics* (1979)

Roderick Nash, *Wilderness and the American Mind* (1967)

Rice Odell, *Environmental Awakening: The New Revolution to Protect the Earth* (1980)

Michael Parfit, *Last Stand at Rosebud Creek: Coal, Power and People* (1981)

John Perkins, *Insects, Experts, and the Insecticide Crisis* (1982)

Elmo Richardson, *Dams, Parks and Politics: Resource Development and Preservation in the Truman-Eisenhower Era* (1973)

Theodore Roszak, *Where the Wasteland Ends* (1973)

Alfred Runte, *National Parks: The American Experience* (1979)

Thomas J. Schoenbaum, *The New River Controversy* (1979)

Sam H. Schurr, ed., *Energy, Economic Growth, and the Environment* (1972)

Irving J. Selikoff and Douglas H. K. Lee, *Asbestos and Disease* (1978)

Julian Simon, *Interaction* (1983)

Allan R. Talbot, *Power Along the Hudson: The Storm King Case and the Birth of Environmentalism* (1972)

William Tucker, *Progress and Privilege* (1982)

Kimon Valaskakis et al., *The Conserver Society* (1979)

Richard H. K. Vietor, *Energy Policy in America Since 1945: A Study of Business-Government Relations* (1984)

Thomas Whiteside, *The Pendulum and the Toxic Cloud: The Course of Dioxin Contamination* (1979)

——, *The Withering Rain* (1971)

Langdon Winner, *The Whale and the Reactor: A Search for Limits in an Age of High Technology* (1986)

Conrad L. Wirth, *Parks, Politics and the People* (1980)

Donald Worster, *River of Empire: Water, Aridity and the Growth of the American West* (1985)

CHAPTER
14

Politics and Society

in the Reagan Era

XX

The presidency of Ronald Reagan frequently has been termed a revolution, not only by Reagan and his supporters but increasingly by critics as well. Yet if there is seemingly widespread consensus that the Reagan years somehow constituted a revolution, there has been far less agreement as to that revolution's extent and character, the degree of its success or failure, whether or not it was truly Reagan's, or what it may bode for the future. To begin with, any revolution that may have taken place was relatively modest by most historical standards. Few fundamental changes occurred in the nation's economy, its social relations, or its political system. Yet if the "Reagan Revolution" pales in comparison with the profound upheavals of the French Revolution of 1789 or the Russian Revolution of 1917, it has nevertheless produced major changes in the country's leadership, its public policy, and its political agenda. These changes are at the very least comparable with those associated with the Democratic presidencies of John F. Kennedy and Lyndon B. Johnson during the 1960s, and, in the view of some, approach even the transformation in politics and public life wrought during the New Deal and Cold War presidencies of Franklin D. Roosevelt and Harry S Truman.

As journalists and political scientists have noted, the Reagan years were marked by the continued decomposition of the old New Deal Democratic coalition forged by Roosevelt during the 1930s and by the growing ascendancy of the Republican party at the national level. Despite Democratic control of the House of Representatives (and the Senate, too, after 1986), Reagan secured passage of a series of major legislative initiatives. Through his power of appointment, moreover, he reshaped the nation's courts. He became the first president since Dwight D. Eisenhower to complete two terms in office successfully. Perhaps most important, he exercised a profound influence over the country's political agenda, molding the issues and terms of political debate throughout the decade. The succession of Vice President George Bush to the White House in 1988 confirmed the Republican party's national strength, although the Democrats retained control of both houses of Congress and indeed increased their margins in the 1990 off-year elections.

The economic changes of the Reagan era have been no less dramatic. Reagan entered the White House pledged to stem inflation, lower taxes, reduce government spending, and cut federal regulation of the economy. He succeeded in many of these efforts, although not always in ways that he and his supporters had predicted and not necessarily in ways that produced all the benefits that they claimed would follow. He halted inflation not through the new and widely publicized "supply side" economics of the far Right but through the classic Republican strategy of high interest rates and the cold bath of a major recession. He lowered taxes, especially on the well-to-do, although it is unclear whether this reduction spurred increased investment or only fueled an orgy of conspicuous consumption by the rich. He presided over a wave of deregulation during which regulatory structures in place for decades were eliminated or radically revised. Whether deregulation has heightened competition and lowered prices as its proponents predicted remains unclear. The most striking failure of deregulation, however, the crisis in the savings-and-loan industry, will saddle the federal government with a staggering load of debt that Americans will be compelled to pay off through their taxes for decades to come. Finally, and perhaps ironically, Reagan conspicuously failed to reduce government spending. Indeed, steep increases in defense costs, coupled with lower taxes, contributed to the largest annual deficits in American history. Elected as a conservative, Reagan pursued a form of Keynesian economics that would have had older conservatives such as Robert Taft and Herbert Hoover spinning in their graves. In the short run, these policies paid rich political dividends: a huge military buildup without cuts in entitlements such as Social Security and Medicare, combined with a tax cut that left many Americans with more money for private consumption. In the long run, Reagan's programs spawned an enormous increase in the nation's indebtedness that, like the savings-and-loan scandal, will be paid for by Americans for generations to come.

Reagan's success as president must also be understood, however, in light of the powerful tensions coursing through American society and culture during the 1970s and 1980s: the polarizing impact of race, the rise of religious fundamentalism, and the ambivalent revolt against modernity. Race was perhaps the single most important force driving political realignment, as white southern Democratic conservatives and blue-collar ethnics continued to shift their allegiances from the Democratic to the Republican party. Reagan also succeeded in appealing to the revival of religious fundamentalism, which swept the nation in the late 1970s and early 1980s. Indeed, much of his success as a national leader seemed to derive from a paradox: on the one hand, Reagan was himself the product a of technologically progressive, corporate, and media-driven modern culture; on the other hand, he continually evoked the images of an earlier, premodern America of individualism and traditional values. There can be no doubt that in doing so he deftly captured the ambivalence felt by many Americans, or that this was in part the secret of his great and continuing popularity.

✖ D O C U M E N T S

By 1979 the Democratic administration of President Jimmy Carter was beset by a host of problems, many of which he had inherited but few of which he had successfully resolved. Chief among them were an economy wracked by inflation and high unemployment, and an energy crisis that was in part the product of the explosive politics of the Middle East and that signaled the end of an era of cheap energy. In Washington political gridlock had set in, virtually paralyzing the efforts of either Congress or the administration to act decisively. In his July 15, 1979, speech to the nation (the first document), Carter addressed not only the problems of economics and energy but also the larger crisis of confidence that he believed pervaded the nation. Republican presidential candidate Ronald Reagan skillfully capitalized on the economic and political failures of the Carter administration, as is clear from his September 9, 1980, campaign speech before the International Business Council (the second document). Although Carter and Reagan alike invoked traditional American values, Carter, reflecting the chastened mood of the seventies, had emphasized sacrifice and restraint, while Reagan, in what would become the dominant theme of the 1980s, stressed economic growth and renewal.

Reagan's electoral victory in 1980 was the product of many forces: deep divisions in the Democratic party over civil rights, the rise of religious fundamentalism and other signs of a revolt against modernity, and a powerful campaign by business leaders to overturn the policies of the Kennedy and Johnson years. These impulses were mobilized, however, by a loose group of conservative activists who styled themselves "the New Right." In the third document, excerpted from his book *The New Right: We're Ready to Lead* (1980), New Right leader Richard A. Viguerie discusses the reasons for conservative victories. The revival of religious fundamentalism played a key role in Reagan's success. Although Reagan's legislative agenda consistently favored economic and defense issues over the cultural politics of the religious Right, he skillfully appealed for the support of fundamentalists, as in his March 8, 1983, address to the National Association of Evangelicals (the fourth document). A strikingly different vision of America was invoked by the Reverend Jesse Jackson, who in his 1988 address to the Democratic National Convention (the fifth document) compared America to a patchwork quilt representing people of diverse colors and creeds, from many different walks of life.

One measure of Ronald Reagan's success was the 1988 election of Vice President George Herbert Walker Bush as his successor. In his inaugural address, excerpts from which compose the sixth document, Bush celebrated the Republican triumph with a promise to create a "kinder" and "gentler" America.

President Jimmy Carter and the Crisis of the American Spirit, 1979

It's clear that the true problems of our Nation are much deeper—deeper than gasoline lines or energy shortages, deeper even than inflation or recession. And I realize more than ever that as President I need your help. So, I decided to reach out and listen to the voices of America.

I invited to Camp David people from almost every segment of our society—business and labor, teachers and preachers, Governors, mayors, and private citizens. And then I left Camp David to listen to other Americans, men and women like you. It has been an extraordinary 10 days, and I want to share with you what I've heard.

First of all, I got a lot of personal advice. Let me quote a few of the typical comments that I wrote down.

This from a southern Governor: "Mr. President, you are not leading this Nation—you're just managing the Government."

"You don't see the people enough any more."

"Some of your Cabinet members don't seem loyal. There is not enough discipline among your disciples."

"Don't talk to us about politics or the mechanics of government, but about an understanding of our common good."

"Mr. President, we're in trouble. Talk to us about blood and sweat and tears."

"If you lead, Mr. President, we will follow."

Many people talked about themselves and about the condition of our Nation. This from a young woman in Pennsylvania: "I feel so far from government. I feel like ordinary people are excluded from political power."

And this from a young Chicano: "Some of us have suffered from recession all our lives."

"Some people have wasted energy, but others haven't had anything to waste."

And this from a religious leader: "No material shortage can touch the important things like God's love for us or our love for one another."

And I like this one particularly from a black woman who happens to be the mayor of a small Mississippi town: "The big-shots are not the only ones who are important. Remember, you can't sell anything on Wall Street unless someone digs it up somewhere else first."

This kind of summarized a lot of other statements: "Mr. President, we are confronted with a moral and a spiritual crisis."

Several of our discussions were on energy, and I have a notebook full of comments and advice. I'll read just a few.

"We can't go on consuming 40 percent more energy than we produce. When we import oil we are also importing inflation plus unemployment."

"We've got to use what we have. The Middle East has only 5 percent of the world's energy, but the United States has 24 percent."

And this is one of the most vivid statements: "Our neck is stretched over the fence and OPEC has a knife."

"There will be other cartels and other shortages. American wisdom and courage right now can set a path to follow in the future."

This was a good one: "Be bold, Mr. President. We may make mistakes, but we are ready to experiment."

And this one from a labor leader got to the heart of it: "The real issue is freedom. We must deal with the energy problem on a war footing."

And the last that I'll read: "When we enter the moral equivalent of war, Mr. President, don't issue us BB guns."

These 10 days confirmed my belief in the decency and the strength and the wisdom of the American people, but it also bore out some of my long-standing concerns about our Nation's underlying problems.

I know, of course, being President, that government actions and legislation can be very important. That's why I've worked hard to put my campaign promises into law—and I have to admit, with just mixed success. But after listening to the American people I have been reminded again that all the legislation in the world can't fix what's wrong with America. So, I want to speak to you first tonight about a subject even more serious than energy or inflation. I want to talk to you right now about a fundamental threat to American democracy.

I do not mean our political and civil liberties. They will endure. And I do not refer to the outward strength of America, a nation that is at peace tonight everywhere in the world, with unmatched economic power and military might.

The threat is nearly invisible in ordinary ways. It is a crisis of confidence. It is a crisis that strikes at the very heart and soul and spirit of our national will. We can see this crisis in the growing doubt about the meaning of our own lives and in the loss of a unity of purpose for our Nation.

The erosion of our confidence in the future is threatening to destroy the social and the political fabric of America.

The confidence that we have always had as a people is not simply some romantic dream or a proverb in a dusty book that we read just on the Fourth of July. It is the idea which founded our Nation and has guided our development as a people. Confidence in the future has supported everything else—public institutions and private enterprise, our own families, and the very Constitution of the United States. Confidence has defined our course and has served as a link between generations. We've always believed in something called progress. We've always had a faith that the days of our children would be better than our own.

Our people are losing that faith, not only in government itself but in the ability as citizens to serve as the ultimate rulers and shapers of our democracy. As a people we know our past and we are proud of it. Our progress has been part of the living history of America, even the world. We always believed that we were part of a great movement of humanity itself called democracy, involved in the search for freedom and that belief has always strengthened us in our purpose. But just as we are losing our confidence in the future, we are also beginning to close the door on our past.

In a nation that was proud of hard work, strong families, close-knit communities, and our faith in God, too many of us now tend to worship self-indulgence and consumption. Human identity is no longer defined by what one does, but by what one owns. But we've discovered that owning things and consuming things does not satisfy our longing for meaning. We've learned that piling up material goods cannot fill the emptiness of lives which have no confidence or purpose.

The symptoms of this crisis of the American spirit are all around us. For the first time in the history of our country a majority of our people believe that the next 5 years will be worse than the past 5 years. Two-thirds of our people do not even vote. The productivity of American workers is actually dropping, and the willingness of Americans to save for the future has fallen below that of all other people in the Western world.

As you know, there is a growing disrespect for government and for churches and for schools, the news media, and other institutions. This is not a message of happiness or reassurance, but it is the truth and it is a warning.

These changes did not happen overnight. They've come upon us gradually over the last generation, years that were filled with shocks and tragedy.

We were sure that ours was a nation of the ballot, not the bullet, until the murders of John Kennedy and Robert Kennedy and Martin Luther King, Jr. We were taught that our armies were always invincible and our causes were always just, only to suffer the agony of Vietnam. We respected the Presidency as a place of honor until the shock of Watergate.

We remember when the phrase "sound as a dollar" was an expression of absolute dependability, until 10 years of inflation began to shrink our dollar and our savings. We believed that our Nation's resources were limitless until 1973 when we had to face a growing dependence on foreign oil.

These wounds are still very deep. They have never been healed.

Looking for a way out of this crisis, our people have turned to the Federal Government and found it isolated from the mainstream of our Nation's life. Washington, D.C., has become an island. The gap between our citizens and our Government has never been so wide. The people are looking for honest answers, not easy answers; clear leadership, not false claims and evasiveness and politics as usual.

What you see too often in Washington and elsewhere around the country is a system of government that seems incapable of action. You see a Congress twisted and pulled in every direction by hundreds of well-financed and powerful special interests.

You see every extreme position defended to the last vote, almost to the last breath by one unyielding group or another. You often see a balanced and a fair approach that demands sacrifice, a little sacrifice from everyone, abandoned like an orphan without support and without friends.

Often you see paralysis and stagnation and drift. You don't like it, and neither do I. What can we do?

First of all, we must face the truth, and then we can change our course. We simply must have faith in each other, faith in our ability to govern ourselves, and faith in the future of this Nation. Restoring that faith and that confidence to America is now the most important task we face. It is a true challenge of this generation of Americans. . . .

All the traditions of our past, all the lessons of our heritage, all the promises of our future point to another path, the path of common purpose and the restoration of American values. That path leads to true freedom for our Nation and ourselves.

Presidential Candidate Ronald Reagan Calls for New Economic Policies, 1980

Almost two months ago, in accepting the Presidential nomination of my party, I spoke of the historically unique crisis facing the United States. At that time I said:

> "Never before in our history have Americans been called upon to face three grave threats to our very existence, any one of which could destroy us. We face a disintegrating economy, a weakened defense and an energy policy based on the sharing of scarcity." . . .

Speech delivered before the International Business Council (Chicago, Illinois, September 9, 1980). In *Vital Speeches of the Day*, Vol. XLVI, no. 24 (October 1, 1980), 738–741 (excerpts).

I'd like to speak to you today about a new concept of leadership, one that has both the words and the music. One based on faith in the American people, confidence in the American economy, and a firm commitment to see to it that the Federal Government is once more responsive to the people.

That concept is rooted in a strategy for growth, a program that sees the American economic system as it is—a huge, complex, dynamic system which demands not piecemeal Federal packages, or pious hopes wrapped in soothing words, but the hard work and concerted programs necessary for real growth.

We must first recognize that the problem with the U.S. economy is swollen, inefficient government, needless regulation, too much taxation, too much printing-press money. We don't need any more doses of Carter's eight- or 10-point programs to "fix" or fine tune the economy. For three and one-half years these ill-thought-out initiatives have constantly sapped the healthy vitality of the most productive economic system the world has ever known.

Our country is in a downward cycle of progressive economic deterioration that must be broken if the economy is to recover and move into a vigorous growth cycle in the 1980's.

We must move boldly, decisively and quickly to control the runaway growth of Federal spending, to remove the tax disincentives that are throttling the economy, and to reform the regulatory web that is smothering it.

We must have and I am proposing a new strategy for the 1980's.

Only a series of well-planned economic actions, taken so that they complement and reinforce one another, can move our economy forward again.

We must keep the rate of growth of government spending at reasonable and prudent levels.

We must reduce personal income tax rates and accelerate and simplify depreciation schedules in an orderly, systematic way to remove disincentives to work, savings, investment and productivity.

We must review regulations that affect the economy and change them to encourage economic growth.

We must establish a stable, sound and predictable monetary policy.

And we must restore confidence by following a consistent national economic policy that does not change from month to month.

I am asked: 'Can we do it all at once?' My answer is: 'We must.'

I am asked: 'Can we do it immediately?' Well, my answer is: 'No, it took Mr. Carter three and one-half years of hard work to get us into this economic mess. It will take time to get us out.'

I am asked: 'Is it easy?' Again, my answer is: 'No. It is going to require the most dedicated and concerted peacetime action ever taken by the American people for their country.'

But we can do it, we must do it, and I intend that we will do it.

We must balance the budget, reduce tax rates and restore our defenses.

These are the challenges. Mr. Carter says he can't meet these challenges; that he can't do it. I believe him. He can't. But, I refuse to accept his defeatist and pessimistic view of America. I know we can do these things, and I know we will.

But don't just take my word for it. I have discussed this with any number of distinguished economists and businessmen, including such men as George Shultz, William Simon, Alan Greenspan, Charles Walker and James Lynn. The strategy is based on solid economic principles and basic experience in both government and the marketplace. It has worked before and will work again.

Let us look at how we can meet this challenge.

One of the most critical elements of my economic program is the control of government spending. Waste, extravagance, abuse and outright fraud in Federal agencies and programs must be stopped. The billions of the tax-payers' dollars that are wasted every year throughout hundreds of Federal programs, and it will take a major, sustained effort over time to effectively counter this.

Federal spending is now projected to increase to over $900 billion a year by fiscal year 1985. But, through a comprehensive assault on waste and inefficiency, I am confident that we can squeeze and trim 2 percent out of the budget in fiscal year 1981, and that we will be able to increase this gradually to 7 percent of what otherwise would have been spent in fiscal year 1985.

Now this is based on projections that have been made by groups in the government. Actually I believe we can do even better. My goal will be to bring about spending reductions of 10 percent by fiscal year 1984. . . .

This strategy for growth does not require altering or taking back necessary entitlements already granted to the American people. The integrity of the Social Security System will be defended by my administration and its benefits will once again be made meaningful.

This strategy does require restraining the Congressional desire to "add-on" to every old program and to create new programs funded by deficits.

This strategy does require that the way Federal programs are administered will be changed so that we can benefit from the savings that will come about when, in some instances, administrative authority can be moved back to the states.

The second major element of my economic program is a tax rate reduction plan. This plan calls for an across-the-board, three-year reduction in personal income tax rates—10 percent in 1981, 10 percent in 1982 and 10 percent in 1983. My goal is to implement three reductions in a systematic and planned manner.

More than any single thing, high rates of taxation destroy incentive to earn, to save, to invest. And they cripple productivity, lead to deficit financing and inflation, and create unemployment.

We can go a long way toward restoring the economic health of this country by establishing reasonable, fair levels of taxation.

But even the extended tax rate cuts which I am recommending still leave too high a tax burden on the American people. In the second half of the decade ahead we are going to need, and we must have, additional tax rate reductions. . . .

Another vital part of this strategy concerns government regulation. The subject is so important and so complex that it deserves a speech in itself—and I plan to make one soon. For the moment, however, let me say this:

Government regulation, like fire, makes a good servant but a bad master. No one can argue with the intent of this regulation—to improve health and safety and to give us cleaner air and water—but too often regulations work against rather than for the interests of the people. When the real take-home pay of the average American worker is declining steadily, and 8 million Americans are out of work, we must carefully re-examine our regulatory structure to assess to what degree regulations have contributed to this situation. In my administration there should and will be a thorough and systematic review of the thousands of Federal regulations that affect the economy.

Along with spending control, tax reform and deregulation, a sound, stable and predictable monetary policy is essential to restoring economic health. The Federal Reserve Board is, and should remain, independent of the Executive Branch of government. But the President must nominate those who serve on the Federal Reserve Board. My appointees will share my commitment to restoring the value and stability of the American dollar.

A fundamental part of my strategy for economic growth is the restoration of confidence. If our business community is going to invest and build and create new, well-paying jobs, they must have a future free from arbitrary, government action. They must have confidence that the economic "rules-of-the-game" won't be changed suddenly or capriciously.

In my administration, a national economic policy will be established, and we will begin to implement it, within the first 90 days.

Thus, I envision a strategy encompassing many elements—none of which can do the job alone, but all of which together can get it done. This strategy depends for its success more than anything else on the will of the people to regain control of their government. . . .

The time has come for the American people to reclaim their dream. Things don't have to be this way. We can change them. We must change them. Mr. Carter's American tragedy must and can be transcended by the spirit of the American people, working together.

Let's get America working again.

The time is now.

A New Right Activist
Explains Conservative Successes, 1980

Our success is built on four elements—single issue groups, multi-issue conservative groups, coalition politics and direct mail.

Conservative single issue groups have been accused of not only fragmenting American politics but threatening the very existence of our two-party system. Congressman David Obey of Wisconsin, a liberal Democrat, has even charged that government has nearly been brought to a standstill by single issue organizations.

Nonsense!

From *The New Right: We're Ready to Lead* by Richard A. Viguerie. Copyright 1980. Reprinted by permission of Richard A. Viguerie.

In the first place, all the New Right has done is copy the success of the old left.

Liberal single issue groups were around long before we were, and the liberals still have as many or more than we do.

Civil rights was a single issue that Hubert Humphrey used to rise to national office. The Vietnam War was a single issue that George McGovern used to rise to national prominence. The environment, consumerism, anti-nuclear power—these are all single issues around which liberals have organized and exercised power and influence.

In the area of public interest law, liberal groups such as the Environmental Defense Fund, the National Prison Project, the Mexican-American Legal Defense and Education Fund, the Southern Poverty Law Center, the National Veterans Law Center, the Women's Legal Defense Fund have drastically changed the direction of the Federal government.

Ralph Nader is nothing if not a collection of single issues. The liberals who are upset now about conservative single issue groups were not upset about the groups pushing for legalization of marijuana . . . homosexual rights . . . or ERA. . . .

Single issue groups naturally emerge because the political parties run away from issues. Single issue groups are the result *of* not the reason *for* the decline of political parties.

If one of the two major political parties had concerned itself more with issues like right to life, high taxes, the growth of the federal government, the right to keep and bear arms, a strong national defense, prayer in the schools, strengthening the family, sex on TV and in the movies, there probably would not have been an explosion of conservative single issue groups. . . .

The second key to our success is the multi-issue group which is part of the conservative movement and makes no bones about it. Such a group is conservative first, last and always. It takes strong positions on every important conservative vs. liberal issue.

The multi-issue conservative movement group also takes a broad overview of where we are going and the best way to get there.

It usually does not have as many members or supporters as single issue groups because its ranks are made up of individuals who are solidly conservative across the board.

The National Right to Work Committee can find over a million people who strongly oppose compulsory unionism.

The National Rifle Association can find nearly two million people who oppose federal gun registration.

Right to Life groups can find over a million people who oppose abortion.

But a conservative group which is pro-Right to Work, pro-Right to Life and pro-gun simply can't find a million contributors who agree on 20 different conservative issues.

For example, a local union leader may dislike the National Right to Work Committee but also oppose additional gun controls.

A pro-life supporter may not care one way or the other about compulsory unionism. And so forth.

But it is a sign of conservative strength that several of our broad spectrum groups do have, if not a million members, several hundred thousand.

Multi-issue broad spectrum groups such as The Conservative Caucus, the American Conservative Union, the Committee for the Survival of a Free Congress, the Heritage Foundation and the National Conservative Political Action Committee, to name but a few, are trying and succeeding in covering all the bases and all the issues for the conservative movement. . . .

Which brings me to the third part of the New Right's success—coalition politics.

Coalition politics is as old as the United States of America. You could call the original Thirteen Colonies a collection of issue groups who banded together to fight and defeat a common enemy—Great Britain.

The Republican Party was originally a coalition of issue groups—Free-Soil party members, pro-business northern Whigs, and some Democrats opposed to slavery.

FDR's New Deal was basically a coalition of groups—Southern farmers, blacks, Jews, organized labor, big city Democrats and the unemployed.

In fact, a liberal coalition based on the New Deal, the Fair Deal and the Great Society has dominated the nation for almost five decades.

But in the last 12 years, since Hubert Humphrey lost the Presidency to Richard Nixon in 1968, that coalition has begun to unravel. Conservatives didn't have the institutions to fill the gap then, but we do now. . . .

Coalition politics includes working within the Republican and Democratic parties to nominate conservative candidates, promote conservative positions and create conservative majorities in both parties. . . .

I want to talk now about the fourth reason for the New Right's success—direct mail.

Like all successful political movements, we must have a method of communicating with each other, and for conservatives in the 1970's it was direct mail.

Frankly, the conservative movement is where it is today because of direct mail. Without direct mail, there would be no effective counterforce to liberalism, and certainly there would be no New Right. . . .

We sell our magazines, our books, and our candidates through the mail. We fight our legislative battles through the mail. We alert our supporters to upcoming battles through the mail. We find new recruits for the conservative movement through the mail.

Without the mail, most conservative activity would wither and die.

Most political observers agree that liberals have effective control of the mass media—a virtual monopoly on TV, radio, newspapers and magazines. . . .

However, there is one method of mass commercial communication that the liberals do not control—direct mail. In fact, conservatives excel at direct mail. . . .

Raising money is only one of several purposes of direct-mail advertising letters. A letter may ask you to vote for a candidate, volunteer for campaign work, circulate a petition among your neighbors, write letters and postcards to your Senators and Congressmen, urging them to pass or defeat legislation and also ask you for money to pay for the direct mail advertising campaign. . . .

Where would conservatives be without direct mail? We would be where we were 20 years ago, on the defensive, isolated, fighting losing battles. . . .

There is another key to New Right success—our positive attitude toward the news media.

From the time I started in politics in the mid 1950's until the early 1970's, most conservatives and the national media were like cats and dogs, or oil and water—they just didn't mix.

Then in the early 1970's some of the national media began to notice our political activities.

I have to be honest and say that I shared the traditional conservatives' position on the press. Which was avoid them, recognize that they are all liberals, and be convinced that their basic purpose is to attack conservatives.

I remember one day a fairly well known writer for a major newspaper called and wanted an appointment to come and talk to me.

I was a little short of terrified. I told my secretary that we'd get back to him.

I then called some of my conservative associates and asked what I should do. Almost all advised me to avoid the reporter.

The advice went something like this—that newspaper is no friend of the conservative movement, that reporter will try to do you in, etc., etc.

But then I got to thinking. I and my conservative friends are not playing in the big leagues—but we want to.

We're not having a major influence on national policies—but we want to.

We're not close to our goal of governing America—but we want to.

I called the reporter back and said, "Why don't you come over and, if you've got time, why don't we go to lunch?"

Well, I spent an enjoyable three hours with the reporter. He wrote a basically fair and accurate story (although it wasn't as fair and objective as my mother would have written.)

And from that day forward, I felt that I and other conservatives had to change our view of the press.

I can think of no better example of the difference between the New Right and the old right.

We realize that reporters and editors are not monsters, or even hopeless ideologues.

The vast majority are good, decent men and women who are trying to do a professional job and are looking for the kind of news which will put their stories on the front page or the nightly TV newscasts.

During the next few years, the New Right's relationship with the press improved. We felt comfortable with the press and they began to cover our activities.

However, in the spring of 1977 I realized that my associates in the New Right and I needed a more professional approach to the media.

We were dealing with the media in a casual, almost accidental way. We needed someone to introduce us to the major media, to teach us how to call and conduct a press conference, how to have a press breakfast, how to get our thoughts across in a few seconds on TV, how to hold activities that the press would be interested in covering. . . .

Single issue groups—multi-issue groups—coalition politics—direct mail—these have been the four cornerstones of conservative growth and success in the 1970's. They will help us build a new majority in America in the 1980's.

As Congressman Newt Gingrich of Georgia has put it: "The way you build a majority in this country is you go out and put together everybody who's against the guy who's in. And instead of asking the question, What divides us?, you ask the question, What unites us?"

And what unites most conservatives, Republican, Democratic and Independent, is a desire for less government and more freedom for every American.

President Reagan on America's Spiritual Reawakening, 1983

Reverend clergy all, Senator Hawkins, distinguished members of the Florida congressional delegation, and all of you:

I can't tell you how you have warmed my heart with your welcome. I'm delighted to be here today.

Those of you in the National Association of Evangelicals are known for your spiritual and humanitarian work. And I would be especially remiss if I didn't discharge right now one personal debt of gratitude. Thank you for your prayers. Nancy and I have felt their presence many times in many ways. And believe me, for us they've made all the difference. . . .

So, I tell you there are a great many God-fearing, dedicated, noble men and women in public life, present company included. And, yes, we need your help to keep us ever mindful of the ideas and the principles that brought us into the public arena in the first place. The basis of those ideals and principles is a commitment to freedom and personal liberty that, itself, is grounded in the much deeper realization that freedom prospers only where the blessings of God are avidly sought and humbly accepted.

The American experiment in democracy rests on this insight. Its discovery was the great triumph of our Founding Fathers, voiced by William Penn when he said: "If we will not be governed by God, we must be governed by tyrants." Explaining the inalienable rights of men, Jefferson said, "The God who gave us life, gave us liberty at the same time." And it was George Washington who said that "of all the dispositions and habits which lead to political prosperity, religion and morality are indispensable supports."

And finally, that shrewdest of all observers of American democracy, Alexis de Tocqueville, put it eloquently after he had gone on a search for the secret of America's greatness and genius—and he said: "Not until I went into the churches of America and heard her pulpits aflame with righteousness did I understand the greatness and the genius of America. . . .

America is good. And if America ever ceases to be good, America will cease to be great."

Well, I'm pleased to be here today with you who are keeping America great by keeping her good. Only through your work and prayers and those of millions of others can we hope to survive this perilous century and keep alive this experiment in liberty, this last, best hope of man.

I want you to know that this administration is motivated by a political philosophy that sees the greatness of America in you, her people, and in your families, churches, neighborhoods, communities—the institutions that foster and nourish values like concern for others and respect for the rule of law under God.

Now, I don't have to tell you that this puts us in opposition to, or at least out of step with, a prevailing attitude of many who have turned to a modern-day secularism, discarding the tried and time-tested values upon which our very civilization is based. No matter how well intentioned, their value system is radically different from that of most Americans. And while they proclaim that they're freeing us from superstitions of the past, they've taken upon themselves the job of superintending us by government rule and regulation. Sometimes their voices are louder than ours, but they are not yet a majority.

An example of that vocal superiority is evident in a controversy now going on in Washington. And since I'm involved, I've been waiting to hear from the parents of young America. How far are they willing to go in giving to government their prerogatives as parents?

Let me state the case as briefly and simply as I can. An organization of citizens, sincerely motivated and deeply concerned about the increase in illegitimate births and abortions involving girls well below the age of consent, sometime ago established a nationwide network of clinics to offer help to these girls and, hopefully, alleviate this situation. Now, again, let me say, I do not fault their intent. However, in their well-intentioned effort, these clinics have decided to provide advice and birth control drugs and devices to underage girls without the knowledge of their parents.

For some years now, the Federal Government has helped with funds to subsidize these clinics. In providing for this, the Congress decreed that every effort would be made to maximize parental participation. Nevertheless, the drugs and devices are prescribed without getting parental consent or giving notification after they've done so. Girls termed "sexually active"—and that has replaced the word "promiscuous"—are given this help in order to prevent illegitimate birth or abortion.

Well, we have ordered clinics receiving Federal funds to notify the parents such help has been given. One of the Nation's leading newspapers has created the term "squeal rule" in editorializing against us for doing this, and we're being criticized for violating the privacy of young people. A judge has recently granted an injunction against an enforcement of our rule. I've watched TV panel shows discuss this issue, seen columnists pontificating on our error, but no one seems to mention morality as playing a part in the subject of sex.

Is all of Judeo-Christian tradition wrong? Are we to believe that something so sacred can be looked upon as a purely physical thing with no potential for emotional and psychological harm? And isn't it the parents' right to give counsel and advice to keep their children from making mistakes that may affect their entire lives?

Many of us in government would like to know what parents think about this intrusion in their family by government. We're going to fight in the courts. The right of parents and the rights of family take precedence over those of Washington-based bureaucrats and social engineers.

But the fight against parental notification is really only one example of many attempts to water down traditional values and even abrogate the original terms of American democracy. Freedom prospers when religion is vibrant and the rule of law under God is acknowledged. When our Founding Fathers passed the first amendment, they sought to protect churches from government interference. They never intended to construct a wall of hostility between government and the concept of religious belief itself.

The evidence of this permeates our history and our government. The Declaration of Independence mentions the Supreme Being no less than four times. "In God We Trust" is engraved on our coinage. The Supreme Court opens its proceedings with a religious invocation. And the Members of Congress open their sessions with a prayer. I just happen to believe the schoolchildren of the United States are entitled to the same privileges as Supreme Court Justices and Congressmen.

Last year, I sent the Congress a constitutional amendment to restore prayer to public schools. Already this session, there's growing bipartisan support for the amendment, and I am calling on the Congress to act speedily to pass it and to let our children pray.

Perhaps some of you read recently about the Lubbock school case, where a judge actually ruled that it was unconstitutional for a school district to give equal treatment to religious and nonreligious student groups, even when the group meetings were being held during the students' own time. The first amendment never intended to require government to discriminate against religious speech.

Senators Denton and Hatfield have proposed legislation in the Congress on the whole question of prohibiting discrimination against religious forms of student speech. Such legislation could go far to restore freedom of religious speech for public school students. And I hope the Congress considers these bills quickly. And with your help, I think it's possible we could also get the constitutional amendment through the Congress this year.

More than a decade ago, a Supreme Court decision literally wiped off the books of 50 States statutes protecting the rights of unborn children. Abortion on demand now takes the lives of up to 1-½ million unborn children a year. Human life legislation ending this tragedy will some day pass the Congress, and you and I must never rest until it does. Unless and until it can be proven that the unborn child is not a living entity, then its right to life, liberty, and the pursuit of happiness must be protected.

You may remember that when abortion on demand began, many, and, indeed, I'm sure many of you, warned that the practice would lead to a decline in respect for human life, that the philosophical premises used to justify abortion on demand would ultimately be used to justify other attacks on the sacredness of human life—infanticide or mercy killing. Tragically enough, those warnings proved all too true. Only last year a court permitted the death by starvation of a handicapped infant.

I have directed the Health and Human Services Department to make clear to every health care facility in the United States that the Rehabilitation Act of 1973 protects all handicapped persons against discrimination based on handicaps, including infants. And we have taken the further step of requiring that each and every recipient of Federal funds who provides health care services to infants must post and keep posted in a conspicuous place a notice stating that "discriminatory failure to feed and care for handicapped infants in this facility is prohibited by Federal law." It also lists a 24-hour, toll-free number so that nurses and others may report violations in time to save the infant's life.

In addition, recent legislation introduced in the Congress by Representative Henry Hyde of Illinois not only increases restrictions on publicly financed abortions, it also addresses this whole problem of infanticide. I urge the Congress to begin hearings and to adopt legislation that will protect the right of life to all children, including the disabled or handicapped.

Now, I'm sure that you must get discouraged at times, but you've done better than you know, perhaps. There's a great spiritual awakening in America, a renewal of the traditional values that have been the bedrock of America's goodness and greatness.

One recent survey by a Washington-based research council concluded that Americans were far more religious than the people of other nations; 95 percent of those surveyed expressed a belief in God and a huge majority believed the Ten Commandments had real meaning in their lives. And another study has found that an overwhelming majority of Americans disapprove of adultery, teenage sex, pornography, abortion, and hard drugs. And this same study showed a deep reverence for the importance of family ties and religious belief.

I think the items that we've discussed here today must be a key part of the Nation's political agenda. For the first time the Congress is openly and seriously debating and dealing with the prayer and abortion issues—and that's enormous progress right there. I repeat: America is in the midst of a spiritual awakening and a moral renewal. And with your Biblical keynote, I say today, "Yes, let justice roll on like a river, righteousness like a never-failing stream."

Now, obviously, much of this new political and social consensus I've talked about is based on a positive view of American history, one that takes pride in our country's accomplishments and record. But we must never forget that no government schemes are going to perfect man. We know that living in this world means dealing with what philosophers would call the phenomenology of evil or, as theologians would put it, the doctrine of sin.

There is sin and evil in the world, and we're enjoined by Scripture and the Lord Jesus to oppose it with all our might. Our nation, too, has a legacy of evil with which it must deal. The glory of this land has been its capacity for transcending the moral evils of our past. For example, the long struggle of minority citizens for equal rights, once a source of disunity and civil war, is now a point of pride for all Americans. We must never go back. There is no room for racism, anti-Semitism, or other forms of ethnic and racial hatred in this country.

I know that you've been horrified, as have I, by the resurgence of some hate groups preaching bigotry and prejudice. Use the mighty voice of your pulpits and the powerful standing of your churches to denounce and isolate these hate groups in our midst. The commandment given us is clear and simple: "Thou shalt love thy neighbor as thyself."

But whatever sad episodes exist in our past, any objective observer must hold a positive view of American history, a history that has been the story of hopes fulfilled and dreams made into reality. Especially in this century, America has kept alight the torch of freedom, but not just for ourselves but for millions of others around the world.

Jesse Jackson Celebrates Common Ground and the Rainbow Coalition, 1988

When I look out at this convention, I see the face of America, red, yellow, brown, black and white, we're all precious in God's sight—the real rainbow coalition. . . .

Dr. Martin Luther King Jr. lies only a few miles from us tonight.

Tonight he must feel good as he looks down upon us. We sit here together, a rainbow, a coalition—the sons and daughters of slave masters and the sons and daughters of slaves sitting together around a common table, to decide the direction of our party and our country. His heart would be full tonight. . . .

Tonight there is a sense of celebration because we are moved, fundamentally moved, from racial battlegrounds by law, to economic common ground, tomorrow we will challenge to move to higher ground.

Common ground!

Think of Jerusalem—the intersection where many trails met. A small village that became the birthplace for three great religions—Judaism, Christianity and Islam.

Why was this village so blessed? Because it provided a crossroads where different people met, different cultures, and different civilizations could meet and find common ground.

When people come together, flowers always flourish and the air is rich with the aroma of a new spring.

Take New York, the dynamic metropolis. What makes New York so special?

It is the invitation of the Statue of Liberty—give me your tired, your poor, your huddled masses who yearn to breathe free.

Not restricted to English only.

Many people, many cultures, many languages—with one thing in common, the yearn[ing] to breathe free.

Common ground! . . . .

We find common ground at the plant gate that closes on workers without notice. We find common ground at the farm auction where a good farmer loses his or her land to bad loans or diminishing markets. Common ground at the schoolyard where teachers cannot get adequate pay, and students cannot get a scholarship and can't make a loan. Common ground, at the hospital admitting room where somebody tonight is dying because they cannot afford to go upstairs to a bed that's empty, waiting for someone with insurance to get sick. We are a better nation than that. We must do better.

Common ground. What is leadership if not present help in a time of crisis? And so I met you at the point of challenge in Jay, Maine, where paper workers were striking for fair wages; in Greenfield, Iowa, where family farmers struggle for a fair price; in Cleveland, Ohio, where working women seek comparable worth; in McFarland, Calif., where the children of Hispanic farm workers may be dying from poison land, dying in clusters with Cancer; in the AIDS hospice in Houston, Texas, where the sick support one another, 12 are rejected by their own parents and friends.

Common ground.

America's not a blanket woven from one thread, one color, one cloth. When I was a child growing up in Greenville, S.C., and grandmother could not afford a blanket, she didn't complain and we did not freeze. Instead, she took pieces of old cloth—patches, wool, silk, gabardine, crockersack on the patches—barely good enough to wipe off your shoes with.

But they didn't stay that way very long. With sturdy hands and a strong cord, she sewed them together into a quilt, a thing of beauty and power and culture.

Now, Democrats, we must build such a quilt. Farmers, you seek fair prices and you are right, but you cannot stand alone. Your patch is not big enough. Workers, you fight for fair wages. You are right. But your patch labor is not big enough. Women, you seek comparable worth and pay equity. You are right. But your patch is not big enough. Women, mothers, who seek Head Start and day care and pre-natal care on the front side of life, rather than jail care and welfare on the back side of life, you're right, but your patch is not big enough.

Students, you seek scholarships. You are right. But your patch is not big enough. Blacks and Hispanics, when we fight for civil rights, we are right, but our patch is not big enough. Gays and lesbians, when you fight against discrimination and a cure for AIDS, you are right, but your patch is not big enough. Conservatives and progressives, when you fight for what you believe, right-wing, left-wing, hawk, dove—you are right, from your point of view, but your point of view is not enough.

But don't despair. Be as wise as my grandmama. Pool the patches and the pieces together, bound by a common thread. When we form a great quilt of unity and common ground we'll have the power to bring about health care and housing and jobs and education and hope to our nation.

I have a story. I wasn't always on television. Writers were not always outside my door. When I was born late one afternoon, October 8th, in Greenville, S.C., no writers asked my mother her name. Nobody chose to write down our address. My mama was not supposed to make it. And I was not supposed to make it. You see, I was born to a teen-age mother who was born to a teen-age mother.

I understand. I know abandonment and people being mean to you, and saying you're nothing and nobody, and can never be anything. I understand. Jesse Jackson is my third name. I'm adopted. When I had no name, my grandmother gave me her name. My name was Jesse Burns until I was 12. So I wouldn't have a blank space, she gave me a name to hold me over. I understand when nobody knows your name. I understand when you have no name. I understand.

I wasn't born in the hospital. Mama didn't have insurance. I was born in the bed at home. I really do understand. Born in a three-room house, bathroom in the backyard, slop jar by the bed, no hot and cold running water. I understand. Wallpaper used for decoration? No. For a windbreaker. I understand. I'm a working person's person, that's why I understand you whether you're black or white.

I understand work. I was not born with a silver spoon in my mouth. I had a shovel programmed for my hand. My mother, a working woman. So many days she went to work early with runs in her stockings. She knew better, but she wore runs in her stockings so that my brother and I could have matching socks and not be laughed at at school.

I understand. At 3 o'clock on Thanksgiving Day we couldn't eat turkey because mama was preparing someone else's turkey at 3 o'clock. We had to play football to entertain ourselves and then around 6 o'clock she would get off the Alta Vista bus; then we would bring up the leftovers and eat our turkey—leftovers, the carcass, the cranberries around 8 o'clock at night. I really do understand.

Every one of these funny labels they put on you, those of you who are watching this broadcast tonight in the projects, on the corners, I understand. Call you outcast, low down, you can't make it, you're nothing, you're from nobody, subclass, underclass—when you see Jesse Jackson, when my name goes in nomination, your name goes in nomination.

I was born in the slum, but the slum was not born in me. And it wasn't born in you, and you can make it. Wherever you are tonight you can make it. Hold your head high, stick your chest out. You can make it. It gets dark sometimes, but the morning comes. Don't you surrender. Suffering breeds character. Character breeds faith. In the end faith will not disappoint.

You must not surrender. You may or may not get there, but just know that you're qualified and you hold on and hold out. We must never surrender. America will get better and better. Keep hope alive. Keep hope alive. Keep hope alive.

President George Bush Seeks a Kinder, Gentler Nation, 1989

I come before you and assume the Presidency at a moment rich with promise. We live in a peaceful, prosperous time, but we can make it better. For a new breeze is blowing, and a world refreshed by freedom seems reborn.

For in man's heart, if not in fact, the day of the dictator is over. The totalitarian era is passing, its old ideas blown away like leaves from an ancient, lifeless tree. A new breeze is blowing, and a nation refreshed by freedom stands ready to push on. There is new ground to be broken and new action to be taken. There are times when the future seems thick as a fog; you sit and wait, hoping the mists will lift and reveal the right path. But this is a time when the future seems a door you can walk right through into a room called tomorrow.

Great nations of the world are moving toward democracy through the door to freedom. Men and women of the world move toward free markets through the door to prosperity. The people of the world agitate for free expression and free thought through the door to the moral and intellectual satisfactions that only liberty allows.

We know what works: Freedom works. We know what's right: Freedom is right. We know how to secure a more just and prosperous life for man on Earth: through free markets, free speech, free elections, and the exercise of free will unhampered by the state. . . .

America is never wholly herself unless she is engaged in high moral principle. We as a people have such a purpose today. It is to make kinder the face of the Nation and gentler the face of the world. My friends, we have work to do. There are the homeless, lost and roaming. There are the children who have nothing, no love and no normalcy. There are those who cannot free themselves of enslavement to whatever addiction—drugs, welfare, the demoralization that rules the slums. There is crime to be conquered, the rough crime of the streets. There are young women to be helped who are about to become mothers of children they can't care for and might not love. They need our care, our guidance, and our education, though we bless them for choosing life.

The old solution, the old way, was to think that public money alone could end these problems. But we have learned that that is not so. And in any case, our funds are low. We have a deficit to bring down. We have more will than wallet, but will is what we need. We will make the hard choices, looking at what we have and perhaps allocating it differently, making our decisions based on honest need and prudent safety. And then we will do the wisest thing of all: We will turn to the only resource we have that in times of need always grows: the goodness and the courage of the American people.

And I am speaking of a new engagement in the lives of others, a new activism, hands-on and involved, that gets the job done. We must bring in the generations, harnessing the unused talent of the elderly and the unfocused energy of the young. For not only leadership is passed from generation to generation but so is stewardship. And the generation born after the Second World War has come of age.

I have spoken of a thousand points of light, of all the community organizations that are spread like stars throughout the Nation, doing good. We will work hand in hand, encouraging, sometimes leading, sometimes being led, rewarding. We will work on this in the White House, in the

Cabinet agencies. I will go to the people and the programs that are the brighter points of light, and I'll ask every member of my government to become involved. The old ideas are new again because they're not old, they are timeless: duty, sacrifice, commitment, and a patriotism that finds its expression in taking part and pitching in.

We need a new engagement, too, between the Executive and the Congress. The challenges before us will be thrashed out with the House and the Senate. And we must bring the Federal budget into balance. And we must ensure that America stands before the world united, strong, at peace and fiscally sound. But of course things may be difficult. We need to compromise; we've had dissension. We need harmony; we've had a chorus of discordant voices.

For Congress, too, has changed in our time. There has grown a certain divisiveness. We have seen the hard looks and heard the statements in which not each other's ideas are challenged but each other's motives. And our great parties have too often been far apart and untrusting of each other. It's been this way since Vietnam. That war cleaves us still. But, friends, that war began in earnest a quarter of a century ago, and surely the statu[t]e of limitation has been reached. This is a fact: The final lesson of Vietnam is that no great nation can long afford to be sundered by a memory. A new breeze is blowing, and the old bipartisanship must be made new again. . . .

A President is neither prince nor pope, and I don't seek a window on men's souls. In fact, I yearn for a greater tolerance, and easy-goingness about each other's attitudes and way of life. . . .

Some see leadership as high drama and the sound of trumpets calling, and sometimes it is that. But I see history as a book with many pages, and each day we fill a page with acts of hopefulness and meaning. The new breeze blows, a page turns, the story unfolds. And so, today a chapter begins, a small and stately story of unity, diversity, and generosity—shared, and written, together. . . .

✖ *E S S A Y S*

The following essays offer three different, although not necessarily contradictory, assessments of the Reagan presidency. (Other aspects of the Reagan years have been touched on in the chapters on welfare, civil rights, the new feminism, and the environment.) In the first essay, political journalist Thomas Byrne Edsall places the Reagan presidency in the context of the continuing decline of the old New Deal coalition (with its popular base of less wealthy Americans) and the growing ascendancy of a new politics centered on television, campaign financing, political-action committees, and lobbyists. The "Reagan Revolution," he concludes, was "a revolution led by the affluent." In the second essay, liberal economists Bennett Harrison of MIT and Barry Bluestone of the University of Massachusetts, Boston, place the economic policies of the Reagan years in the context of a broad transformation of both U.S. and world economies. Much of their analysis would seem to be strengthened by the economic downturn that began in 1989.

The "Reagan Revolution" as a Revolution from Above

THOMAS BYRNE EDSALL

The past twenty years in America have been marked by two central political developments. The first is the continuing erosion of the political representation of the economic interests of those in the bottom half of the income distribution. The second is the growing dominance of the political process by a network of elites that includes fund-raisers, the leadership of interest groups, specialists in the technology and manipulation of elections, and an army of Washington lobbyists and law firms—elites that augment and often overshadow political officeholders and the candidates for office themselves.

This shift in the balance of power has not been accompanied by realignment of the electorate, although the shape and relative strength of the Republican and Democratic parties have changed dramatically.

Twice during the past twenty years, the Republican party has had the opportunity to gain majority status: in the early 1970s, and again after the 1980 election. The first opportunity emerged when the fragile Democratic coalition was fractured by the independent presidential bid of Alabama governor George C. Wallace in 1968. The Democratic party then amplified its own vulnerability four years later with the nomination of Sen. George S. McGovern, Democrat of South Dakota, whose candidacy alienated a spectrum of traditional Democrats from Detroit to Atlanta. This potential Republican opportunity crumbled, however, when the web of scandals known as Watergate produced across-the-board setbacks for the GOP in campaigns ranging from city council contests to the presidency in the elections of 1974 and 1976.

The period from 1978 to 1981 offered even more fertile terrain for the Republican party. Not only had Democratic loyalties dating back to the depression of the 1930s been further weakened during the presidency of Jimmy Carter, with the emergence of simultaneous inflation and high unemployment, but the candidacy of Ronald Reagan provided the Republican party with its first substantial opportunity to heal the fissures that had relegated the GOP to minority status for two generations. In Reagan, the party long identified with the rich found a leader equipped to bridge divisions between the country club and the fundamentalist church, between the executives of the Fortune 500 and the membership of the National Rifle Association. Just as Watergate halted Republican momentum in the early 1970s, however, the severe recession of 1981–82 put the brakes on what had the earmarks of a potential Republican takeover, for the first time since 1954, of both branches of Congress. In the first two years of the Reagan administration, the Republican party captured the Senate by a six-vote margin and, with a gain of thirty-two House seats, acquired de facto control of the House in an alliance with southern Democratic conservatives. The recession, however, resulted in the return of twenty-six House seats to the Democrats in 1982, and with those seats went the chance to establish Republican dominance of the federal government.

As the two parties have gained and lost strength, the underlying alteration of the balance of political power over the past decade has continued in a shift of power among the rich, the poor, and the middle class; among blacks and whites; among regions in the country; and among such major competitors for the federal dollar as the defense and social services sectors.

The past twenty years have, in effect, produced a policy realignment in the absence of a political realignment. The major beneficiaries of this policy realignment are the affluent, while those in the bottom half of the income distribution, particularly those whose lives are the most economically marginal, have reaped the fewest rewards or have experienced declines in their standard of living.

A major factor contributing to this development is the decline of political parties: In the United States, as well as in most democratic countries, parties perform the function of representing major interests and classes. As parties erode, the groups that suffer most are those with the fewest resources to protect themselves. In other words, the continued collapse of the broad representation role of political parties in the United States has direct consequences for the distribution of income.

As the role of parties in mobilizing voters has declined, much of the control over both election strategy and issue selection—key functions in defining the national agenda—has shifted to a small, often interlocking, network of campaign specialists, fund-raisers, and lobbyists. While this element of politics is among the most difficult to quantify, there are some rough measures. For example, there are approximately thirty Republican and Democratic consultants and pollsters, almost all based in Washington, who at this writing are the principal strategists in almost every presidential and competitive Senate race, in addition to playing significant roles in gubernatorial, House, and local referenda contests.

At another level, the years from 1974 to 1984 show a steady growth in the financial dependence of House and Senate candidates on political action committees (PACs), vehicles through which money is transferred from organized interest groups to elected officeholders. In that decade, the PAC share of the total cost of House campaigns went from 17 percent to 36 percent, while individual contributions fell from 73 percent to 47 percent, with the remainder coming from parties, loans, and other sources. For House Democratic incumbents, 1984 marked the first year in which PACs were the single most important source of cash; they provided 47 percent of the total, compared with 45 percent from individuals.

This shift has, in turn, magnified the influence of a group of lobbyists who organize Washington fund-raisers for House and Senate incumbents, among whom are Thomas Hale Boggs, Jr., whose clients include the Trial Lawyers Association, the Chicago Board of Options Exchange, and Chrysler; Edward H. Forgotson, whose clients include Enserch Corp., the Hospital Corp. of America, and the Texas Oil and Gas Corp.; Robert J. Keefe, whose clients include Westinghouse and the American Medical Association; and

J. D. Williams, whose clients include General Electric Co. and the National Realty Committee. The Washington consulting-lobbying firm of Black, Manafort, Stone, Kelly and Atwater provides perhaps the best example of the range of political and special interests one firm can represent. In 1987, one partner, Charles Black, managed the presidential bid of Rep. Jack Kemp (R-N.Y.); another, Lee Atwater, managed the campaign of Vice-President George Bush; and a third, Peter Kelly, was a principal fund-raiser for the campaign of Sen. Albert Gore (D-Tenn.). At the same time, the firm's clients have included the Dominican Republic, the anti-Communist insurgency in Angola run by Jonas Savimbi, Salomon Brothers, the government of Barbados, the Natural Gas Supply Association, and, briefly, the Marcos government in the Philippines. In addition, the firm has served as principal political consultant to the Senate campaigns of Phil Gramm (R-Tex.), Jesse Helms (R-N.C.), and Paula Hawkins (formerly R-Fla.).

A few general indicators of the scope of lobbying and political party bureaucracies point to the sizable influence small elites can exercise over public policy. In 1986, there were almost 10,000 people employed as registered Washington lobbyists, with 3,500 of these serving as officers of 1,800 trade and professional organizations, including labor unions; another 1,300 were employed by individual corporations, and approximately 1,000 represented organizations ranging from the National Right to Life Association to the Sierra Club. The six major political party committees headquartered in Washington now employ roughly 1,200 people. The creation and expansion of such ideological think tanks as the Heritage Foundation, the Center for National Policy, the Urban Institute, the American Enterprise Institute, the Cato Institute, and the Hoover Institution have established whole networks of influential public policy entrepreneurs specializing in media relations and in targeted position papers. Within a general framework of increasingly monopolized American mass media—both print and electronic—the growth of the Gannett and Los Angeles Times–Mirror chains are examples of an ever greater concentration of power within the media, just as the acquisition of NBC by General Electric has functioned to submerge a major network within the larger goals of the nation's sixth biggest corporation. Staffers acquiring expertise and influence on Capitol Hill, in the executive branch, and throughout the regulatory apparatus routinely travel to the private sector—and sometimes back again—through the so-called revolving door. In effect, an entire class of public and private specialists in the determination of government policy and political strategy has been created—a process replicated in miniature at the state level.

The rise to authority of elites independent of the electorate at large, empowered to make decisions without taking into direct account the economic interests of voters, is part of a much larger shift in the balance of power involving changed voting patterns, the decline of organized labor, a restructuring of the employment marketplace, and a transformed system of political competition. This power shift, in turn, has produced a policy realignment most apparent in the alteration of both the *pre-tax* distribution of income and the *after-tax* distribution of income. In both cases, the distribution has become increasingly regressive. The alteration of the pretax distribution of income is the subject of a broad debate in which there are those, particularly critics on the left, who argue that growing regressivity emerges from government policies encouraging weakened union representation and a proliferation of low-wage service industry jobs. On the other side, more conservative analysts contend that changes in the pre-tax distribution result from natural alterations of the marketplace and the workplace, as the United States adjusts to a changing economic and demographic environment. The figures in table 1, derived from Census Bureau data, indicate changes in the distribution of pretax household income from 1980 through 1985, the most recent year for which data from the census is available.

The data clearly show a growing disparity in the distribution of income. Of the five quintiles, all but those in the top 20 percent have seen their share of household income decline. In addition, most of the gains of the top 20 percent have, in fact, been concentrated in the top 5 percent of the income distribution. The gain of 1.1 percent for the top 5 percent translates into a total of $38.8 billion (in 1987 dollars) more for this segment of the population than if the income distribution had remained constant after 1980. These regressive trends were, moreover, intensified by the tax policies enacted between 1980 and 1985, as demonstrated in table 2, based on Census Bureau data.

What had been a $38.8 billion improvement in the status of the top 5 percent in pre-tax income over these six years becomes a $49.5 billion gain in after-tax income, while the bottom 80 percent of the population saw larger losses in its share of after-tax income between 1980 and 1985 than it had seen in the case of pre-tax income. These findings are even more sharply

Table 1   Shares of Pre-tax Household Income, by Income Distribution

	YEAR	
INCOME GROUP	1980 (%)	1985 (%)
Quintile[a]		
Bottom	4.1	3.9
Second	10.2	9.7
Third	16.8	16.3
Fourth	24.8	24.4
Top	44.2	45.7
Top 5%	16.5	17.6

Sources: Bureau of the Census, *Estimating After-Tax Money Income Distribution,* Series P-23, no. 126, issued August 1983; and ibid., *Household After-Tax Income: 1985,* Series P-23, no. 151, issued June 1987.
[a] A quintile is a block of 20% of the population.

Table 2   Shares of After-Tax Household Income, by Income Distribution

	YEAR	
INCOME GROUP	1980 (%)	1985 (%)
Quintile[a]		
Bottom	4.9	4.6
Second	11.6	11.0
Third	17.9	17.2
Fourth	25.1	24.7
Top	40.6	42.6
Top 5%	14.1	15.5

Sources: Bureau of the Census, *Estimating After-Tax Money Income Distribution.* Series P-23, no. 126, issued August 1983; and ibid., *Household After-Tax Income: 1985,* Series P-23, no. 151, issued June 1987.
[a] A quintile is a block of 20% of the population.

delineated in a November 1987 study by the Congressional Budget Office showing that from 1977 to 1988, 70 percent of the population experienced very modest increases in after-tax income or, for those in the bottom 40 percent, net drops, when changes over that period in the federal income tax, the Social Security tax, corporate tax, and excise taxes are taken into account. In contrast, those in the seventy-first to ninetieth percentiles experienced a modest improvement, and those in the top 10 percent significantly improved their standard of living. For those at the very top, the gains have been enormous. Table 3, developed from Congressional Budget Office data, shows that distribution.

What these tables point to is a major redistribution of economic power in the private marketplace and of political power in the public sector, which, in turn, has been reflected in very concrete terms in family income patterns. One of the major characteristics, then, of the post–New Deal period in American politics has been a reversal of the progressive redistribution of income that underlay the policies of the administrations of Franklin Roosevelt and Harry Truman.

In the competition between the defense and social welfare sectors, the outcome of a parallel, although more recent, shift in the balance of power can be seen in the years from 1980 through 1987. During this period, the share of the federal budget going to national defense grew from 22.7 percent in 1980 to 28.4 percent in 1987. At the same time, the share of federal dollars collectively going to education, training, employment, social services, health, income security, and housing dropped from 25.5 percent in 1980 to 18.3 percent in 1987.

In many respects, these policy changes reflect the rising strength of the Republican party. In terms of tax policy and the balance of spending between defense and social programs, the Republican party under Ronald Reagan

Table 3 Changes in Estimated Average After-Tax Family Income, by Income Distribution (in 1987 dollars)

INCOME GROUP	1977 AVERAGE INCOME ($)	1988 AVERAGE INCOME ($)	PERCENTAGE CHANGE (+ OR −)	DOLLAR CHANGE (+ OR −)
Decile[a]				
First (poor)	3,528	3,157	− 10.5	− 371
Second	7,084	6,990	− 1.3	− 94
Third	10,740	10,614	− 1.2	− 126
Fourth	14,323	14,266	− 0.4	− 57
Fifth	18,043	18,076	+ 0.2	+ 33
Sixth	22,009	22,259	+ 1.1	+ 250
Seventh	26,240	27,038	+ 3.0	+ 798
Eighth	31,568	33,282	+ 5.4	+ 1,718
Ninth	39,236	42,323	+ 7.9	+ 3,087
Tenth (rich)	70,459	89,783	+ 27.4	+ 19,324
Top 5%	90,756	124,651	+ 37.3	+ 33,895
Top 1%	174,498	303,900	+ 74.2	+ 129,402
All groups	22,184	26,494	+ 9.6	+ 2,310

Source: Congressional Budget Offices, *The Changing Distribution of Federal Taxes: 1975–1990,* October 1987.
[a] A decile is a block of 10% of the population.

has been the driving force pushing the country to the right. During the past ten years, the Republican party has made substantial gains in the competition for the allegiance of voters, gaining near parity by 1987, reducing what had been a 20- to 25-point Democratic advantage in terms of self-identification to a six- or seven-point edge.

The income distribution trends and the shifts in budget priorities began, however, before the Republican party took over the presidency and the U.S. Senate in 1980. The emergence of a vital, competitive Republican party is less a cause of the changed balance of power in the country than a reflection of the underlying forces at work in the post–New Deal phase of American politics.

Together, these forces—which include the deterioration of organized labor, the continued presence of divisive racial conflict, the shift from manufacturing to service industries, the slowing rates of economic growth, the threat of international competition to domestic production, the replacement of political organization with political technology, and the growing class-skew of voter turnout—have severely undermined the capacity of those in the bottom half of the income distribution to form an effective political coalition.

In tracing the erosion of the left wing of the Democratic party in the United States, it is difficult to overestimate the importance of the collapse of the labor movement. In 1970, the continuing growth in the number of labor union members came to a halt. Unions represented 20.7 million workers that year, or 27.9 percent of the non-agricultural work force. Through 1980, the number of workers represented by unions remained roughly the same, dropping slightly to 20.1 million employees by 1980. At the same time, however, the total work force had grown, so that the percentage of workers who were represented by unions fell to 23 percent in 1980. With the election of Ronald Reagan, however, the decline of organized labor began to accelerate sharply, a process encouraged by Reagan's firing of 11,500 striking PATCO air traffic controllers, and by the appointment of promanagement officials to the National Labor Relations Board and to the Department of Labor. From 1980 to 1986, not only did the share of the work force represented by unions drop from 23 percent to 17.5 percent, but the number of workers in unions began to fall precipitously for the first time in fifty years, dropping by 3.1 million men and women, from 20.1 million to 17 million, in 1986. During the first half of the 1980s, almost all the decline in union membership was among whites employed in private industry.

The decline of organized labor dovetailed with a continuing shift from traditional manufacturing, mining, and construction employment to work in the technology and service industries. From 1970 to 1986, the number of jobs in goods-producing industries, which lend themselves to unionization, grew only from 23.8 million to 24.9 million, while employment in the service industries, which are much more resistant to labor organizing, shot up from 47.3 million to 75.2 million.

The difficulties of organized labor were compounded by the unexpected decision on the part of many of the major corporations in the early 1970s to abandon what had been a form of tacit détente between labor and management, in which Fortune 500 companies kept labor peace through agreements amounting to a form of profit sharing by means of automatic cost-of-living pay hikes. Faced with growing competition from foreign producers—in 1968, car imports exceeded exports for the first time in the nation's history, an unmistakable signal that domestic producers of all goods faced serious foreign competition—major American companies dropped the fundamentally cordial relations that had characterized the largest part of postwar union negotiations. Catching the leaders of organized labor entirely unprepared, these corporations adopted a tough, adversarial approach regarding both pay and fringe benefits, willing to break union shops and to relocate facilities either abroad or in nonunion communities in the South and Southwest.

The decline of organized labor was particularly damaging to the Democratic party because unions represent one of the few remaining institutional links between working-class voters and the Democratic party. The decline of political parties has resulted in the end of the clubhouse tie between the party of Franklin Delano Roosevelt and the blue-collar voters of row- and tract-house neighborhoods throughout the Northeast and Midwest. In addition, it is among these white, blue-collar workers that the racial conflicts within the Democratic party have been the most divisive. Interviews with whites in Dearborn, Michigan, the west-side suburbs of Birmingham, Chicago, Atlanta, and New Orleans—all communities that have suffered major industrial layoffs and that are either part of or adjoin cities now run by Democratic black mayors—reveal voters who are disenchanted with the unions that failed to protect their jobs, and with a local Democratic party no longer controlled by whites. Race, which previously severed the tie between the white South and the Democratic party, has, in cities with black mayors, served to produce white Republican voting, not only for president but for local offices that once were unchallenged Democratic bastions.

These developments, in the 1970s, contributed significantly to the creation of a vacuum of power within the Democratic party, allowing the party to be taken over, in part, by its most articulate and procedurally sophisticated wing: affluent, liberal reformers. This faction capitalized first on the public outcry against police violence at the Chicago presidential convention in 1968, and then on the Watergate scandals in the mid-1970s, to force priority consideration of a series of reforms involving campaign finance, the presidential nominating process, the congressional seniority system, the congressional code of ethics—and an expansion of the federal role in regulating the environment, through creation of the Environmental Protection Agency and new water- and air-pollution standards. The strength of this wing of the Democratic party subsided during the 1980s, although its leverage within the party has been institutionalized through the creation of a host of primaries and caucuses in the presidential selection process, giving disproportionate influence to middle- and upper-middle-class voters and interests in a party that claims to represent the nation's working and lower-middle classes. The turnout in primaries and in caucuses is skewed in favor of the affluent and upper-middle class. In addition, these delegate selection processes have been contributing factors in the acceleration of the decline of political organizations in working-class communities.

The Democratic agenda set in the 1970s by the reform wing of the party was, however, more important for what it omitted and neglected than for what was included. The ascendancy of the reformers took place just when the fissures within the Democratic party had become most apparent. In 1968, 9.9 million mostly Democratic voters turned to George C. Wallace, the segregationist-populist governor of Alabama, and they strayed off the Democratic reservation in 1972 when Nixon beat McGovern by a margin of 47.2 million votes to 29.2 million. The cultural and ideological gulf that had steadily widened between these voters and the wings of the Democratic party supporting the antiwar movement, gay rights, women's rights, and civil rights had reached such proportions in the early and mid 1970s that rapprochement between warring factions was difficult, if not impossible.

The rise to prominence within the Democratic party of a well-to-do liberal-reform wing worked in other ways to compound the divisions in the party. Relatively comfortable in their own lives, reformers failed to recognize the growing pressure of marginal tax rates on working- and lower-middle-class voters. The progressive rate system of the federal income tax remained effectively unchanged from the early 1950s through the 1970s, so that the series of sharply rising marginal tax rates that had originally been designed to affect only the upper-middle class and rich, began to directly impinge on regular Democratic voters whose wages had been forced up by inflation. By neglecting to adjust the marginal rate system to account for inflation, in combination with repeated raising of the highly regressive Social Security tax, Democrats effectively encouraged the tax revolt of the 1970s which, in turn, provided a critically important source of support to the conservative movement and to the rise of the Republican party.

The pressures of the tax system on traditional Democratic voting blocks were aggravated by the sudden halt in 1973 of what had been steadily rising median family incomes since the end of World War II. Family income in 1981 dollars rose from $12,341 in 1947, to $17,259 in 1960, to $23,111 in 1970, and it topped out at $24,663 in 1973—a level that was not exceeded at least through 1986. Of all the blows to the Democratic coalition in the 1960s and 1970s, the stagnation of family income had the potential to inflict the most severe long-range damage. It undermined the party's basic claim that the system of government established in the years following the New Deal promised continued growth and the prospect for a better life for each new generation.

On the Republican side, the same developments that debilitated the Democratic coalition served to strengthen ascendant constituencies of the Right. For a brief period in the late 1970s and early 1980s, the constituencies and interests underpinning the Republican party had the potential to establish a new conservative majority in the electorate. The tax revolt, the rise of the religious right, the mobilization of much of the business community in support of the Republican party, renewed public support for defense spending, the political-financial mobilization of the affluent, and the development of a conservative economic theory promising growth through lower taxes—all combined to empower the political right to a degree unprecedented since the 1920s.

Proposed tax cuts provided an essential common ground for the right-of-center coalition that provided the core of the Reagan revolution. The combination of corporate tax reductions and individual tax cuts embodied in the 1981 tax bill served to unify a divided business community by providing a shared legislative goal, to strengthen the commitment of the affluent to the Republican party, and to attract white working- and lower-middle-class former Democrats who had seen their paychecks eaten away by inflation-driven higher marginal rates. The tax cut theme was adopted as a central element of the speeches of such religious-right figures as the Rev. Jerry Falwell of the Moral Majority, Ed McAteer of the Religious Roundtable, and the Rev. Marion G. (Pat) Robertson of the Christian Broadcast Network.

The sustained attacks by Democratic reformers on traditional political organizations, and their demands for changes in the financing of campaigns, meshed perfectly with the techniques developed by the Right in the acquisition of power. The deterioration of old-guard organizations, which were effectively taken out of the presidential nomination process by the reforms of the early 1970s, accelerated the shift toward a political system dominated by technology—a highly sophisticated mix of detailed polling, focus groups, targeted direct mail, and television and radio commercials precisely tailored in response to the flood of information concerning public attitudes.

The shift to expensive technology, in turn, elevated fund-raising from a critically important factor in campaigns, to the dominant factor. The sharp escalation of the importance of money gave the Republican party a decided advantage over the Democratic party. Campaign contributors are overwhelmingly concentrated among the upper-middle class and the rich, just the groups among whom Republican allegiance is strongest. The key institutions in the development of campaign technology, and in transferring such technology to candidates, are the six national party committees—the Democratic and Republican National, Senatorial, and Congressional campaign committees. It is at this level that the disparity between the parties has been most apparent. As shown in table 4, in the decade between the 1977–78 and 1985–86 election cycles, the Republican party maintained a decisive edge over the Democratic party.

The Republican party fund-raising advantage was, in many ways, encouraged by the campaign finance reforms enacted by a Democratic Congress in 1974. These reforms placed a $1,000 limit on individual contributions to any candidate for federal office, while allowing contributions of up to $20,000 to political party committees. For the Democratic party, which had depended on large contributions in excess of the new legal limits, the 1974 law became a tourniquet, stemming the flow of vital cash resources. For the Republican party, in contrast, the campaign reforms of the mid-1970s served as an invitation to capitalize on the new technology of direct mail, in order to convert the pro-Republican tilt of the affluent into a full-fledged commitment of money from literally millions of donors. By 1984, the Republican National Committee had built a donor base of 1.6 million people, a number almost matched by the National Republican Congressional Committee. In effect, the combination of the rise of regulated money in campaigns and the decline in the role of traditional neighborhood-based clubs and organizations was functioning to reduce the participation of working- and lower-middle-class voters in the political process, while encouraging the direct-mail mobilization of the affluent.

This growing political tilt in favor of the affluent is further reflected in voting turnout patterns over the past twenty years. During this period, the class-skewing of voting in favor of the affluent has grown significantly. In the presidential election year of 1964, the self-reported turnout among mem-

Table 4 Amount of Money Raised by the Three Major Committees of the Republican and Democratic Parties (in millions of dollars)

	ELECTION CYCLE				
	1985–86	1983–84	1981–82	1979–80	1977–78
Democrats raised	61.8	98.5	39.3	37.2	26.4
Republicans raised	252.4	297.9	215.0	169.5	84.5

Source: Federal Election Commission report issued May 31, 1987.

bers of professions associated with the middle and upper classes was 83.2 percent, compared with 66.1 percent among those employed in manual jobs, including skilled crafts, a difference of 17.1 points; by 1980, the spread between the two had grown to 25 points, 73 percent to 48 percent. In the off-year election of 1966, the percentage-point spread in terms of voter turnout between middle-to-upper-class job holders and those employed in manual jobs was 18.1 percent; by 1978, this had grown to a 23.8-percent spread. While overall turnout has been declining, the drop has been most severe among those in the bottom third of the income distribution.

For the Republican party, these turnout trends were a political bonanza, accentuated by trends in the correlation between income and both voting and partisan commitment. Through the 1950s, 1960s, and into the early 1970s, the sharp class divisions that characterized the depression-era New Deal coalition structure gave way to diffuse voting patterns with relatively little correlation between income and allegiance to the Democratic or Republican party. By 1980 and 1982, with the election of Reagan and then the enactment of the budget and tax bills of 1981, the correlation between income and voting began to reemerge with a vengeance. By 1982, the single most important determinant of probable voting, aside from membership in either the Republican or Democratic party, became income, with the Democratic margin steadily declining as one moved up the ladder. The changes in partisan allegiance are shown in table 5. The numbers in the table are the percentage-point Democratic advantage in the income group (+) or the Democratic disadvantage (−). Thus, for example, the very poor were 18 points more Democratic than Republican in 1956, and 36 points more Democratic than Republican in 1984.

In other words, the Reagan years polarized the electorate along sharp income lines. While income made almost no difference in the partisan loyalties of 90 percent of the population in 1956, by 1984 income became one of the sharpest dividing lines between Democrats and Republicans. In 1956, the very poor were only 5 percentage points more likely to be Democratic

Table 5   Democratic Party Allegiance, by Income, 1956 and 1984

INCOME GROUP	PERCENTAGE-POINT ADVANTAGE (+) OR DISADVANTAGE (−)	
	1956	1984
Very poor (bottom 10%)	+ 18	+ 36
Working and lower-middle class (11–30%)	+ 22	+ 29
Middle class (31–60%)	+ 17	+ 6
Upper-middle class (61–90%)	+ 13	0
Affluent (91–100%)	− 22	− 33

Source: Martin B. Wattenberg, "The Hollow Realignment: Partisan Change in a Candidate-Centered Era" (Paper delivered at the 1985 annual meeting of the American Political Science Association, based on data from the National Election Studies).

than the upper-middle class, and 40 points more likely than the affluent top 10 percent of the income distribution. By 1984, however, the spread between the poor and the upper-middle-class reached 36 points, and between the poor and the affluent, 69 points. These income correlations with partisan allegiance were replicated, in part, by actual voting patterns, as shown in table 6.

These figures accurately describe an electorate polarized by income, but what they mask are the effects of black and white voter participation on the figures. The civil rights movement, and civil rights legislation enacted in the 1960s, enfranchised millions of blacks who, in 1956, were barred from voting. During the twenty-eight years from 1956 to 1984, roughly 4.2 million blacks entered the electorate. During the same period, blacks' allegiance to the Democratic party, which in 1956 held their loyalty by a 34-percentage-point edge, increased to provide an overwhelming 72-percentage-point Democratic edge in 1984. This infusion of black Democratic support sharply increased the low-income tilt of the party: in 1984, the median family income for whites was $28,674, while for blacks it was $15,982.

The Reagan revolution was, at its core, a revolution led by the affluent. The class polarization of voters reflected in tables 10.5 and 10.6 cut across the country, but nowhere were the trends stronger than in the South, where a realignment in miniature took place among the white elite. In the 1950s, Democratic allegiance in the South was strongest among the most well-to-do whites, for whom the Democratic party was the vehicle for maintaining the pre–civil rights social structure of the Confederate states. These voters gave the Democratic party their support by a 5 to 1 margin, higher than that of any other income group in the South. By the 1980s, in the aftermath of a civil rights movement supported by the Democratic party, these same voters had become the most Republican in the South. "The class cleavage had reversed itself," John R. Petrocik, of UCLA, noted. Whites, particularly white men, have become increasingly Republican as blacks have become the most consistent source of Democratic votes. In the five presidential elections from 1968 to 1984, only one Democrat, Jimmy Carter, received

Table 6   Republican Percentage of Presidential Vote, by Income, 1956 and 1984

INCOME GROUP	EISENHOWER, 1956 (%)	REAGAN, 1984 (%)
Very poor (bottom 10%)	59	36
Working and lower-middle class (11–30%)	56	43
Middle class (31–60%)	58	57
Upper-middle class (61–90%)	57	64
Affluent (91–100%)	75	75

Source: Martin P. Wattenberg, "The Hollow Realignment: Partisan Change in a Candidate-Centered Era" (Paper delivered at the 1985 annual meeting of the American Political Science Association, based on data from the National Election Studies).

more than 40 percent of the white vote, and by 1984, white, male Protestants voted for Reagan over Mondale by a margin of 74 to 26.

The Reagan revolution would, however, have been a political failure if it had not gained extensive support from voters outside the upper-middle class. In addition to the deep inroads made in previously Democratic working-class communities in northern urban areas, perhaps the single most important source of new support for the Republican party has been the religious Right.

In a far shorter period, voters identifying themselves as born-again Christians radically shifted their voting in presidential elections. Between 1976 and 1984, these voters went from casting a 56-to-44 margin for the Democratic candidate, Jimmy Carter, to one of the highest levels of support of any group for the reelection of President Reagan in 1984: 81 to 19, according to *New York Times*/CBS exit polls. This shift represents, in effect, a gain of eight million voters for the GOP.

As a political resource, support among born-again Christians represents not only a loyal core of voters, but a growing core. In contrast with such mainline churches as the United Methodist Church, the United Church of Christ, and the United Presbyterians, which experienced membership losses from 1970 to 1980, the fundamentalist, evangelical, and charismatic churches have seen their congregations grow at an explosive rate: the Southern Baptist Convention by 16 percent, the Assemblies of God by 70 percent, and Seventh Day Adventists by 36 percent.

The Republican party has, in turn, been the major beneficiary of an internal power struggle taking place within the Southern Baptist Convention, now the largest Protestant denomination. During a ten-year fight, the denomination has been taken over by its conservative wing, believers in the "absolute inerrancy" of the Bible. This wing of the denomination, in turn, has been a leading force within the broader religious Right, as such pastors as Adrian Rogers, James T. Draper, Jr., and Charles F. Stanley—all outspoken conservatives—have won the denomination's presidency. The move to the right has been reflected in the ranks of the denomination, producing what amounts to a realignment of the ministry of the Southern Baptist Convention. James L. Guth, of Furman University, found that in just three years, surveys of Southern Baptist ministers showed a remarkable shift from a strong majority in 1981 favoring the Democratic party, 41 to 29, to nearly 70 percent in 1984 favoring the GOP, 66 to 26.

The growth of Republican strength is not, however, confined to evangelical and charismatic Christians, and the party appears to be developing a much broader religious base as part of its core constituency. In one of the most interesting recent analyses of voting trends, Frederick T. Steeper, of Market Opinion Research, and John Petrocik, of UCLA, have found that since 1976, one of the sharpest partisan cleavages emerging among white voters in the electorate is between those who attend church regularly and those who never go to church. This represents a major change from past findings. In the period from 1952 to 1960, there was no statistical difference between the Democratic and Republican loyalties of white churchgoers and nonchurchgoers. By the elections of 1972 and 1976, a modest difference began to appear, with nonchurchgoers 7 percentage points more likely to be Democrats than regular churchgoers. By 1986, however, the spread had grown to a striking 35-point difference, with regular churchgoers identifying themselves as Republicans by a 22-point margin, and with nonchurchgoers identifying themselves as Democrats by a 13-point edge. The partisan spread between churchgoers and nonchurchgoers was most extreme among white Northern Protestants (51 points) and Catholics (52 points). These findings dovetail with studies showing that the memberships of such Establishment, nonevangelical denominations as the Methodists, Episcopalians, Lutherans, and Presbyterians were significantly more supportive of the election of Ronald Reagan than the electorate at large.

The changing shape of the electorate has provided the Republican party with a base of support that has not proved adequate to produce a realignment. It has, however, proven sufficient to establish the GOP as the favored party in presidential elections, and as a full-fledged competitor in any Senate or gubernatorial contest in the nation, despite the erosion of some support. Since the election of 1980, many of the constituencies that provided vitality and strength to the Republican party have floundered or split. The right-wing PACs—the National Conservative Political Action Committee, the Free-Congress PAC, the Conservative Victory Fund, the Christian Voice Moral Government Fund—had all fallen on hard times by the end of 1987, and were no longer significant participants in the political process. In addition, after the 1986 election, when the GOP lost the Senate, the flow of cash to the major Republican committees began to slow significantly, lessening the financial advantage of the GOP over the Democratic party. The business community, which had been unified behind the 1981 budget and tax bills, splintered into warring factions over the 1986 Tax Reform Act, over monetary policy in the wake of the October 1987 stock market debacle, and over the continuing debate concerning protectionist trade legislation. Perhaps most important, after successfully polarizing the two parties along issues of taxation, defense, and domestic spending, the Reagan administration failed to expand its agenda in the mid-1980s to produce the kind of issues that divide the electorate, and separate the parties one from the other in ways essential to genuine realignment. This failure to maintain a polarizing agenda was in sharp contrast with the Conservative party in England, where Prime Minister Margaret Thatcher vowed, "Our third election victory was only a staging post on a much longer journey. . . . Whose blood would run faster at the prospect of five years of consolidation?" as she outlined initiatives on education, property taxation, and home ownership designed to strengthen the grip of the Conservative party on Britain immediately upon winning a third term. Furthermore, the coalition of the Right in the United States faces the prospect of divisive struggles on foreign policy, particularly conflicts over arms control policies that pit Republican centrists against the deeply anti-Communist conservative wing of the party; and it faces as well continuing conflicts over party policy on "social issues," between GOP party regulars and the growing political army of fundamentalist Christians—in addition to conflicts between these two factions over the control of local party structures. Perhaps most important, however, is the inherent difficulty for a party that receives its strongest levels of support from the affluent in directing effective economic appeals to the lower-middle class and the working class.

Despite conflicts and a certain loss of ideological and programmatic vitality, the development of a Republican party whose core supporters are concentrated among the affluent and among the religious gives the party a continuing advantage in low-turnout elections in which money plays a central role. Not only do the affluent vote in the highest percentages, and provide the best target for fund-raising solicitations; in a political universe where the strength of such Democratic institutions as the union hall and the political clubhouse are steadily declining, the neighborhood church provides one of the few remaining means—outside of television—of contacting and mobilizing voters.

Cumulatively, developments over the past twenty years—the deterioration of the labor movement; economically polarized partisanship; the skewing of turnout patterns by income; stagnation of the median family income; the rising importance of political money; the emergence of a Republican core composed of the well-to-do and the religious; the globalization of the economy; and competition from foreign producers—have combined to disperse constituencies and groups seeking to push the country to the left, and to consolidate those on the right. The consequences of that shift are most readily seen in the figures in table 3, which show that 80 percent of the population has experienced a net loss in after-tax income between 1977 and 1988, while the top 5 percent has seen average family income grow by $26,134, and the top 1 percent, by $117,222.

In the long run the prospects are for the maintenance of a strong, conservative Republican party, continuing to set the national agenda on basic distributional issues, no matter which party holds the White House. Barring a major economic catastrophe, or a large-scale international conflict, the basic shift from manufacturing to service industry jobs is likely to continue to undermine the political left in this country, not only for the reasons outlined earlier in this essay, but also by weakening economically—and therefore politically—those in the bottom 40 percent of the income distribution.

In the thirty-year period spanning 1949 to 1979, the number of manufacturing jobs grew by an average of three million a decade, from 17.6 million in 1949, to 20.4 million in 1959, to 24.4 million in 1969, and finally to a high of 26.5 million in 1979. This growth in no way kept pace with the increase in service industry jobs, which shot up from 26.2 million in 1949 to 63.4 million in 1979, but the continuing, if modest, manufacturing expansion provided a partial cushion in an economy going through a major restructuring—a restructuring involving the loss of 950,000 jobs in steel and other metals industries, automobiles, food production, and textiles from 1972 to 1986. From 1979 to 1986, however, the absolute number of manufacturing jobs began to decline, dropping from 26.5 million to 24.9 million, a loss of 1.6 million jobs.

These employment shifts have been particularly damaging to blacks and Hispanics. From 1970 to 1984, in major northern cities, there has been a massive decline in the number of jobs requiring relatively little education— the kind of jobs that provide entry into the employment marketplace for the poor—and a sharp increase in the number of jobs requiring at least some higher education. "Demographic and employment trends have produced a serious mismatch between the skills of inner-city blacks and the opportunities available to them . . . substantial job losses have occurred in the very industries in which urban minorities have the greatest access, and substantial employment gains have occurred in the higher-education-requisite industries that are beyond the reach of most minority workers," according to William Julius Wilson, of the University of Chicago (see table 7).

While blacks and Hispanics will, at least for the time being, disproportionately bear the burden of this shift in job requirements, the altered structure of the marketplace will work to the disadvantage of the poorly educated of all races. In 1985, there were 30.6 million whites over the age of twenty-five without a high school education—five times the number of blacks without high school degrees (5.9 million) and seven times the number of poorly educated Hispanics (4.4 million). These job market trends will intensify throughout the rest of this century. According to estimates by the Department of Labor, 21.4 million jobs will be created between 1986 and the year 2000, all of which will be in service industries or government, as losses in traditional goods manufacturing industries are unlikely to be fully offset by gains in the technology manufacturing sector. In terms of educational requirements, there will be a significant increase in the proportion of jobs requiring at least one year of college education, no change in the proportion of jobs requiring a high school degree, and a sharp decline in the percentage of jobs requiring no high school education.

In effect, trends in the job market through the next ten years will in all likelihood exacerbate the regressive distribution of income that has taken

Table 7   Changes in the Combined Number of Jobs, by Employee Education Level, in New York, Philadelphia, Boston, Baltimore, St. Louis, Atlanta, Houston, Denver, and San Francisco, 1970 and 1984

	NUMBER OF JOBS		
MEAN LEVEL OF EMPLOYEE EDUCATION	1970	1984	CHANGE, 1970–84
Less than high school	3,068,000	2,385,000	−683,000
Some higher education	2,023,000	2,745,000	+722,000

Source: Computed from William Julius Wilson, *The Truly Disadvantaged: The Inner City, the Underclass, and Public Policy* (Chicago: University of Chicago Press, 1987), table 2.6, p. 40. The table, in turn, is taken from John D. Kasarda, "The Regional and Urban Redistribution of People and Jobs in the U.S." (Paper presented to the National Research Council Committee on National Urban Policy, National Academy of Sciences, 1986).

place over the past decade. Under American democracy, those who are unemployed or marginally employed are weakest politically. The decline of traditional political organizations and unions has made significantly more difficult the political mobilization of the working poor, the working class, and the legions of white-collar workers making from $10,000 to $25,000 a year—a universe roughly containing 24.6 million white households, 3.4 million black households, and 2 million Hispanic households. Within this group, providing a political voice becomes even more difficult for those workers with poor educations who have been dispersed from manufacturing employment into cycles of marginal work. While most of those who have lost manufacturing jobs have found full-time employment, such workers have, in the main, seen wages fall and fringe benefits, often including medical coverage, decline or disappear, leaving them even further outside of the American mainstream and even less well equipped to ensure adequate educational levels for their children. When combined with the declining voter turnout rates associated with falling income, these workers have fallen into what amounts to a new political underclass.

The major forces at work in the last two decades of the post–New Deal period are, then, cumulatively functioning to weaken the influence and power of those in the bottom half of the income distribution, while strengthening the authority of those in the upper half, and particularly the authority of those at elite levels. Trends in political competition and pressures in the private marketplace have combined to create a whipsaw action, reversing New Deal policies that empowered the labor movement and reduced disparities between rich and poor. Recent forces, both in the marketplace and in the political arena, have not produced a realignment of the electorate, but, in terms of outcomes, there has been a realignment in public policy—with few forces, short of a downturn in the business cycle, working against the continuing development of a political and economic system in which the dominant pressures will be toward increased regressivity in the distribution of money and in the ability to influence the outcome of political decisions.

Reaganomics and the Great U-Turn

BENNETT HARRISON AND BARRY BLUESTONE

The standard of living of American workers—and a growing number of their families—is in serious trouble. For every affluent "yuppie" in an expensive big-city condominium, working as a white-collar professional for a high-flying high-technology concern or a multibillion dollar insurance company, there are many more people whose wages have been falling and whose families are finding it more and more difficult to make ends meet.

For more than a decade, the United States has been evolving as an increasingly unequal society. This development has been hidden by the ability of consumers, government, and businesses to maintain their accustomed spending by accumulating more and more debt. Now, on the eve of the 1990s, the underlying weaknesses of the economy are finally becoming apparent, while the assurance of a new era of stable economic growth and vitality is being challenged by debt and global competition. The time has come for a serious reappraisal of just how poorly the economy has performed under the conservative business and government policies of the last decade, and how the prospects for average American workers and their families have actually worsened.

The story is one of a series of changes in direction—reversals in course, great U-turns if you will—in the strategic policies of both business and the government, and as a consequence, a great U-turn in our material well-being. Between the end of World War II and a watershed that dates to a time between the late 1960s and the mid-1970s, the standard of living of the average American worker rose steadily. Adjusted for inflation, average family incomes were on the rise. Hourly, weekly, and annual wages and salaries were trending upward. The share of the work force whose wages were at or below the poverty level fell sharply. The numbers earning high wages rose rapidly. More and more workers could count on such basic benefits as unemployment and health insurance, paid vacations, and sick leave. This was especially true in the goods-producing industries, but even in the burgeoning service sector, the trend was toward a higher standard of living.

Perhaps no one has captured the spirit of that age better than David Halberstam in his epic work, *The Reckoning*. The symbol for the Ford Motor Company and for the nation during those days was the sporty Mustang.

> It came out in 1964, at what would prove to be the highwater mark of the American century, when the country was rich, the dollar strong, and inflation low. It was almost twenty years since the end of World War II, and it was more than a decade since the end of the Korean War. The Vietnam War was still a guerrilla action involving relatively small numbers of American advisers. The bitter and costly part of that war, which was to take more than fifty-one thousand lives, divide the country, start a runaway inflation, and completely divert the nation's attention, was still ahead. The economy was expanding. Though many of the forces that would afflict American industry were already beginning to form, they were not yet visible, and the domestic economy had never seemed so strong. . . . There was enough for everyone; the country was enjoying unparalleled prosperity, and the pie was bigger than ever. The pie would turn out to have its limits after all, but at the halcyon moment, the future seemed unbounded.

Not only was the pie growing, but especially during the 1960s, the shares were becoming more equally distributed among working people and their families. At the same time, greater income equality itself contributed to the more rapid economic growth out of which public expenditures (and even further redistribution, for example, through the War on Poverty) could be financed. Most important of all, more and more parents could realistically expect that their children would eventually be better off financially and less insecure than they had been. That belief in the future in turn brought about a greater commitment to work, saving, and investment in the present.

After about 1973, the direction changed. Wages, adjusted for inflation, began a long downward trend (fig. 1). Median annual family income stopped growing, even though more family members were working than ever before (fig. 2). And, by the latter half of the decade, even the most stable "core" workers in the economy—the roughly three-fifths of the labor force working year round and full time (YRFT)—were becoming more and more likely to earn low wages. In particular, between 1973 and 1979 one out of every five net additional YRFT workers earned less than $11,000 a year (in 1986 prices). But since 1979, fully 36 percent of such employees have earned wages and salaries below that threshold. After 1980, at the other extreme of the job distribution, the number of elite earning high wages rose as well, leaving a declining proportion of employees receiving middle-level incomes. Inequality was again rising, in the labor market and at the level of family income (fig. 3). The distribution of wealth—income from property, such as stocks, bonds, and real estate—was also becoming increasingly unequal. Worst of all, no longer could parents assume that their children would do better than they had at the same stage of their own careers.

What caused this dramatic reversal in the fortunes and expectations of American workers and their families—this great U-turn in the structure of economic opportunity in the United States?

The explanation lies not in bad luck or in something out of our control.

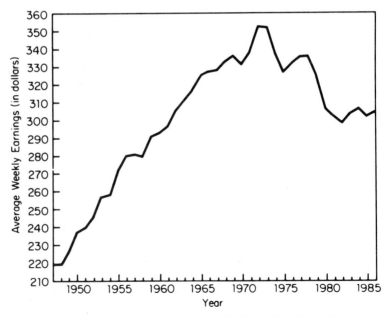

Figure 1   Real Average Weekly Earnings, 1947–1986 (in 1986 dollars)

Source: Council of Economic Advisers, *Economic Report of the President, 1987* (Washington, D.C.: Government Printing Office, 1987).

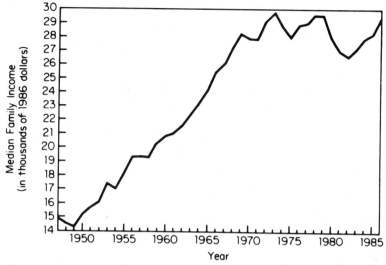

Figure 2 Real Median Family Income, 1947–1986 (in 1986 dollars)

Source: Council of Economic Advisers, *Economic Report of the President, 1987* (Washington, D.C.: Government Printing Office, 1987).

It cannot be blamed on the Japanese or the Europeans, or on unions, or on the "social welfare state." The real explanation, we believe, lies in a more fundamental set of dramatic shifts in direction, taken first by the leaders of American business in the early 1970s and then ratified by policies of the government, beginning in the latter half of that decade, even before the election of Ronald Reagan. What ultimately motivated these shifts, which add up to an across-the-board U-turn in managerial, economic, and social policy, was what happened to corporate profits—private enterprise's bottom line. While wages and family incomes continued to grow for another eight years after the midpoint of the decade of the '60s, corporate profits did not.

The Profit Squeeze

Whether measured as business owners' share of the total national income or by the conventional rate of return on investment, profits peaked in the mid-1960s and continued to fall or stagnate for the next fifteen years. From a peak of nearly 10 percent in 1965, the average net after tax profit rate of domestic nonfinancial corporations plunged to less than 6 percent during the second half of the 1970s—a decline of more than a third (fig. 4).

What caused the profit squeeze was mainly the sudden emergence of heightened international economic competition—a competition to which U.S. business leaders were initially blind. At the beginning, one could perhaps forgive the corporations their myopia. For the longest time, foreign competition was hardly a concern. Indeed, even as late as 1969, imports were no greater a share of gross national product (GNP) than before the

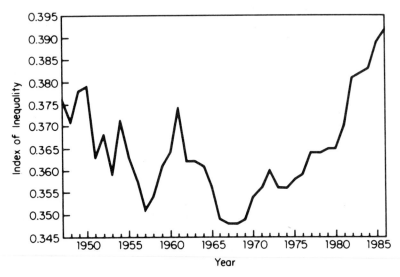

Figure 3   Family Income Inequality, 1947–1986 (GINI Index)

Source: U.S. Department of Commerce, Bureau of the Census, "Money Income of Households, Families, and Persons in the United States: 1984" (Washington, D.C.: Government Printing Office, 1986) and unpublished tabulations provided by the U.S. Census Bureau.

Great Depression in 1929. Forty years had passed and U.S. industry was no more burdened by imports than before jet transports crisscrossed the globe or geosynchronous orbiting satellites provided instantaneous worldwide communications.

But in the course of the single decade between 1969 and 1979, the value of imports practically doubled. In the manufacturing sector, a trickle of imports turned into a torrent. The value of manufactured imports relative to domestic production skyrocketed—from less than 14 percent in 1969 to nearly triple that, 38 percent, only ten years later. By 1986, for every $100 spent on goods produced in the United States, families and businesses were buying $45 worth of imports (table 1). In one industry after another—shoes, textiles, apparel, autos, steel, machine tools, consumer electronics, and eventually even computers and semiconductors—imports from Germany, Japan, Scandinavia, Italy, and the newly industrialized countries (the so-called NICs) such as South Korea, Taiwan, and Brazil made major inroads into the domestic markets of U.S. corporations.

For the first time in modern economic history, all of the major industrialized countries (as well as the NICs) were producing very much the same collection of products and were engaged in "intraindustry trade"—the trading back and forth of essentially the same products. The United States now both buys steel from *and* sells it to the United Kingdom, while Mexico both imports and exports auto parts. Along with the two-way movement of commodities came two-way investment in factories and equipment, and the composition of both inward and outward foreign direct investments became increasingly similar. The United States once built auto plants in Germany,

Figure 4   U.S. Corporate Profitability, 1963–1980 Net After-Tax Rate of Return

Source: Samuel Bowles, David Gordon, and Thomas Weisskopf, "Power and Profits: The Social Structure of Accumulation and the Profitability of the Postwar U.S. Economy," *Review of Radical Political Economics* 18, nos. 1, 2, (Spring–Summer 1986), as revised and reported to the authors by Weisskopf in December 1987 to reflect new government capital stock series.

France, England, and Mexico; now the Koreans and Japanese build them here. This complementarity led to the emergence on a global scale of chronic excess capacity in one mass-production industry after another. With every country attempting to supply its neighbors with computers, let alone shoes, each country found its corporations operating their own plants at well below full capacity. This necessarily eroded productivity and raised the unit cost of production. Nowhere was this more true than in the United States. And to make matters worse, while foreign competition raised unit costs, it simultaneously made it more difficult for firms in any one country to pass these higher costs onto their own citizens in the form of inflated prices. As a result, profits were squeezed—on the one side by rising costs; on the other by constrained prices.

Charles Sabel, a political scientist at M.I.T., summarizes the U-Turn in international economic development this way:

A fundamental cause of the slowdown of the 1970s was the saturation of domestic markets for consumer durables and hence exhaustion of new investment opportunities in the business lines that had been the mainstay of the post-war expansion. In the United States, for example, there was one car for every two residents in 1979, as against a ratio of one to four in the early 1950s. By 1970, 99 percent of American homes had refrigerators, electric irons, and radios; more than 90 percent had automatic clothes

Table 1   The Import Surge into the United States

	TOTAL IMPORTS AS A PERCENTAGE OF GNP	IMPORTED MERCHANDISE AS A PERCENTAGE OF GNP ORIGINATING IN THE U.S. MANUFACTURING SECTOR
1929	5.7	—
1939	3.7	—
1949	3.8	9.5
1959	4.7	10.8
1969	5.7	13.9
1979	10.9	37.8
1986	11.4	44.7

Sources: Council of Economic Advisers, *Economic Report of the President, 1986* (Washington, D.C.: Government Printing Office, 1986); Council of Economic Advisers, "Economic Indicators" (September 1986); and U.S. Department of Commerce, Bureau of Economic Analysis, *Survey of Current Business* 67, no. 4 (April 1987).

washes, vacuum cleaners, and toasters. Statistics from other advanced capitalist countries tell a similar story.

Saturation in one market led to saturation in others as producers looked abroad when the possibilities for domestic expansion were exhausted. The results were simultaneous export drives by companies in all the advanced countries, with similar, technologically sophisticated products going into one another's markets. . . . Increasing exports . . . from developing countries such as Taiwan, Korea, Mexico, and Brazil further increased the congestion of mass markets in the advanced economies.

In the short run, the squeezing profit margins may have been exacerbated by continued popular demands for a higher and more widely shared standard of living, especially through an expansion of the welfare state. Larger tax contributions from businesses and expanded wage-and-benefit packages for hitherto excluded groups added to the cost of doing business and reduced short-term profits still further. In America, these demands reached a crescendo during the late 1960s when, under the twin engines of accelerating consumer spending and burgeoning expenditures for the war in Vietnam, unemployment rates fell to levels not seen since 1945. With the supply of labor that tight, wages had to be bid up, and the bargaining power of labor as a whole improved. Broader unemployment insurance, as well as larger payments, also appreciably reduced what Harvard economist Juliet Schor has named "the cost of job loss," further contributing to the willingness of workers to stand up to their bosses. All of these developments contributed to the reduction of corporate profits.

As always, when the distribution of income between capital and labor arouses political and economic conflict, and both sides try to protect their share of national income, the result is growing inflation. Together with other unexpected market shocks, such as increases in the price of oil by OPEC and increases in wage, tax, and governmental regulatory pressures, the inflation of the 1970s made the squeeze on profits intolerable. Corporate managers ultimately felt impelled to develop new long-run plans. Stockholders would tolerate a dip in profits for a year or two perhaps, but the red ink that began to spill from corporate balance sheets in the late 1960s screamed out for remedy.

The Response of Business to the Crisis

And what were the new strategies? How did American business respond to these new competitive pressures? At least a few industry leaders undertook a variety of experiments in the organization of work and in labor-management relations, designed to increase productivity and thus allow their firms to cope with higher costs. Others, facing greater increases in costs and greater uncertainties in their markets, searched for more "flexible" arrangements with employees, subcontractors, customers, and governments. Some scholars believe that these corporate experiments will eventually culminate in the emergence of entirely new forms of business enterprise. In this scenario, "flexibly specialized," small-scale enterprises will continually prowl the marketplace for new niches. Already, entrepreneurs pursuing this strategy are said to be clustering together into tightly knit regional complexes or "industrial districts." Ironically, using state-of-the-art, microelectronics-based technologies, they are actually reintegrating work in a way that invokes images of the most old-fashioned, traditional, craftlike forms of production.

There is no doubt that such creative experiments in the reorganization of work are occurring in some companies and in some locations. Evidence of the vitality of at least a small number of industrial districts organized according to the flexible specialization model seems compelling. But the much more prevalent response to the crisis in profitability, particularly in the United States, has been to change little in the nature of the product or even the production process, and instead to launch what former United Auto Workers President Douglas Fraser has termed a "one-sided class war." In the words of a recent pamphlet printed jointly by the Service Employees International Union and 9 to 5, the organization of office workers:

> With the widespread image of a more "hostile" environment, U.S.-based corporations were confronted by two very different choices: (1) Improve product quality and productivity by investment and innovation while looking to public policy to "manage" trade; or (2) turn back the clock on U.S. job standards to attempt to make U.S. products "cheaper" rather than better. In the 1970s and 1980s, U.S. corporate and government leaders chose the second route—to lower job standards in order "to compete."

Specifically, the vast majority of American businesses have undertaken a series of experiments in what can best be described as *corporate restructuring*.

[T]his restructuring [consists] of three broad movements: qualitative changes amounting almost to a 180-degree U-Turn in the prevailing relationship between business and its workforce; financial restructuring, both within and among companies; and a profound alteration in the posture of the federal government, which moved to support the short-term interests of private business in direct opposition to the needs of working people and their families.

Consider the restructuring of the organization of work and of the deployment of finances. Managers have increasingly reallocated the capital at their disposal, directing it into different industries, different regions of the country, and different nations. In doing so, corporate leaders have introduced new technologies—especially in transportation and communications—to facilitate the coordination and control of the far-flung activities of their home offices. At the same time, corporations began a dramatic restructuring of their internal hierarchies. They moved toward "vertical disintegration" of their large, highly centralized industrial organizations, with their characteristic "internal labor markets." In doing so, they removed many of the career ladders that had provided well-defined paths of upward mobility for a significant fraction of the work force.

While such changes in work organization may provide "flexibility" for management, they tend to bring with them increased instability and insecurity for employees. In the course of this restructuring, managers have pared employment and increased their use of "contingent" labor, leasing more of their employees from agencies that supply temporary employees and putting more of their own workers on part-time schedules—increasingly, against their wishes. Much more blatantly, more and more managers have simply "frozen" wages, imposed outright reductions in pay, or unilaterally introduced two tiered pay systems to reduce the cost of labor by paying different wages for essentially the same work. With the threat of layoffs and plant closings all around them, labor unions found it difficult, if not impossible, to contest these actions. Lee Iacocc[a]'s famous remark during the Chrysler crisis—"It's freeze time, boys. I've got plenty of jobs at seventeen dollars an hour; I don't have any at twenty"—haunted labor in virtually every industry.

In the financial sphere, investors—especially those responsible for managing pension funds and other large pools of finance capital—accelerated the shift from productive investment to investment, often overtly speculative, primarily for short-term financial gain, while free-wheeling and well-heeled "entrepreneurs" pursued "hostile takeovers" and "forced mergers." In the colorful language of British political economist Susan Strange, language later popularized by *Business Week,* America became a "casino society." One indicator of this trend—the volume of futures trading in stocks and bonds—rose ninefold between 1973 and 1985 in contrast to only a threefold increase in the nation's total output.

Government to the Rescue

For a short period between the mid-1970s and the early 1980s, there was intense debate about whether the government should play a more constructive role in mediating the relationship between business and labor. Various corporate, labor, and academic circles called for the federal government to adopt a domestic industrial policy and intervene more actively in foreign trade. Guaranteed federal loans that saved both Lockheed and Chrysler from bankruptcy were the two best-known instances of an industrial policy in actual practice.

But beginning in 1978, and increasingly after the election of President Ronald Reagan, the administration and the Congress intervened in a very different way. Washington began to adopt policies that effectively forced workers to accept wage concessions, discredited the trade-union movement, and reduced the cost to business of complying with government regulations. Social programs were either restricted to their present levels or, like publicly assisted housing, actually cut back. A restrictive monetary regime introduced in 1979 by Paul Volcker, chair of the Federal Reserve Board, was indeed successful in curtailing inflation, but only by creating the worst recession since the 1930s. With more than one out of ten Americans unemployed by 1982, the government supported management's demand for a docile work force that would swallow wage concessions without a major fight.

The deep recessions of 1980 and 1981–82 were, by their nature, two-edged swords for the corporate sector. The drastic drop in consumer demand obviously cut into short-term profits. But at the same time, the recessions established the foundation for greater long-term returns by undercutting organized labor and by forcing workers to choose between a modicum of job security and higher wages. In the end, the recessions contributed handsomely to the corporations' bottom line.

The federal government's curtailment of its regulation of business also promoted corporate restructuring. Responding to deregulation, leaders in the airlines, trucking, and telecommunications industries were forced to devise strategies for responding to more intense competition. Virtually all of them turned to their work forces to bail them out. Management demanded wholesale wage concessions from their employees and increased pressure on the job to squeeze out more productivity from them. In some industries, especially the airlines, the quality of the deregulated service seems to have deteriorated, often dangerously, in the face of heightened competition. At the same time, government entered into more contracts with ununionized outside companies—so-called "privatization"—eroding civil-service wage standards. The growing inclination of the government to sell off what had previously been publicly owned and operated services (Conrail, for example) had the same effect.

For the first time since the 1920s, direct attacks on labor emanated from the White House. The assault began with the disbanding of the air traffic controllers' union and the appointment of conservative members to the National Labor Relations Board (NLRB). These highly publicized acts of the president contributed to shifting the balance of power between labor and management toward business, implicitly legitimating "union avoidance" as a socially acceptable posture for even the most "liberal" of managements. Unions were deliberately made the scapegoat of an economy that increasingly seemed unable to perform acceptably at home or abroad.

Lurking not far below the surface of all of these particular policies was the growing dominance of a conservative ideology that pinned the blame for the profit squeeze on "big government" itself. It followed that the most appropriate public policy for the 1980s was, to quote Reagan's campaign rhetoric, to "get the government off the backs of the people." Translated into budgetary terms, this meant cuts in social legislation, but not in the size or influence of government per se. In fact, after eight years of "Reaganomics," the public sector's influence on the economy on the eve of the 1990s is greater than ever, as evidenced by the explosive growth of military spending and the stubbornly mushrooming budget deficit. The federal government takes a larger share of the gross national product (GNP) today than when Reagan took office in 1981. Nevertheless, even middle-of-the-road Democrats and Republicans have accepted the new conventional wisdom that government spending, regulation, and redistribution of income are somehow "bad for business." What could not be sold at any price to the voters by presidential candidate Barry Goldwater in the go-go days of 1964 became the coin of the realm a mere twenty years later.

These public policies of government-induced deflation, deregulation, regressive tax reform, privatization, and out-right union-bashing have contributed directly to corporate strategies that single-mindedly concentrate on cost containment, especially the cost of labor, as the principal basis for meeting the global economic challenge. They have created a new civil war among firms and among regions of the country competing for job-creating investments, and they have pitted worker against worker. This, we believe, is what is mainly responsible for reducing both the standard of living and the economic security of the average family. It is the main reason for the great U-turn in the distribution of income since the 1970s—what Lester Thurow has aptly called the "surge in inequality"—and what we see as the growing polarization of our society.

The Failed Promise of the New Economic Era

There are those who argue that the wage cuts and inequality that we have experienced have been absolutely necessary for U.S. industry to regain its competitive edge. "No pain, no gain," they say. After all, profits rebounded smartly after the recession of 1982. Moreover, sheer job-creation between the mid-1970s and the late 1980s was substantial enough to earn the United States the sobriquet of "the great jobs machine," especially among European planners and policy makers who seemed totally incapable of stimulating any new growth in employment whatsoever during these years. But as we now know, these gains benefited a few at the expense of a great many. And in the end, it is unclear whether the high price we paid bought us much of lasting value.

To be sure, some social scientists think they see a brave new postindustrial world already emerging from the wreckage of the old. Perhaps they will turn out to be right. But on the eve of the final decade of the twentieth century, after the longest "peacetime" economic recovery on record, a new round of stable economic growth has demonstrably *not* yet emerged. The rate of personal savings has actually fallen to less than before Reagan's election. The production of non-military capital goods—business plant and equipment—has been lethargic since the end of 1984. The long-run growth in productivity remains just under 1 percent, where it has been since the late 1960s. And the overall ability of the economy to produce goods and services—the GNP—continues to grow at a pace far slower than in the two decades following World War II, and generally less than in the countries with which we are engaged in the most intense economic competition.

Worse still, what growth we *have* been able to muster—at the cost of declining average living standards and growing inequality—has been achieved almost entirely by two manifestly undesirable means. One is a boom in military spending which has aggravated the federal deficit and distorted the long-term development of civilian research and development. The other is the piling up of incredible levels of debt. In the face of falling incomes, consumers have attempted to maintain their living standards by borrowing unprecedented amounts of revolving credit. In 1986, the average family was carrying more than $11,000 worth of outstanding consumer credit, and was spending a fifth of its monthly disposable income to pay it off. At the same time, the federal government had amassed more than $1.5 trillion of new debt. In the short span of four years, the United States had transformed itself from the world's leading creditor to the nation most in hock to the rest of the world. The consolidated burden of the debts of households, government, and Third World countries could bring the entire world trading system down in a crisis unprecedented since the Great Depression of the 1930s.

▨ F U R T H E R   R E A D I N G

Martin Anderson, *Revolution* (1988)

Richard J. Barnet, *The Lean Years: Politics in the Age of Scarcity* (1980)

Laurence I. Barret, *Gambling with History: Reagan in the White House* (1983)

Barry Bluestone and Bennett Harrison, *The Deindustrialization of America* (1982)

Sidney Blumenthal, *Our Long National Daydream: A Political Pageant of the Reagan Era* (1988)

———and Thomas Byrne Edsall, eds., *The Reagan Legacy* (1988)

———, *The Rise of the Counter-Establishment: From Conservative Ideology to Political Power* (1986)

Michael J. Boskin, *Reagan and the Economy* (1987)

Samuel Bowles, David M. Gordon, and Thomas E. Weisskopf, *Beyond the Waste Land: A Democratic Alternative to Economic Decline* (1983)

Paul Boyer, ed., *Reagan as President* (1990)

David S. Broder, *Changing of the Guard* (1980, 1981)

Lou Cannon, *Reagan* (1982)

Hodding Carter, *The Reagan Years* (1988)

Jimmy Carter, *Keeping Faith* (1982)

John E. Chubb and Paul E. Peterson, eds., *The New Directions in American Politics* (1985)

Alan Crawford, *Thunder on the Right: The "New Right" and the Politics of Resentment* (1980)

Robert Dallek, *Ronald Reagan and the Politics of Symbolism* (1984)

Ronnie Dugger, *On Reagan: The Man and His Presidency* (1983)

Paul Duke, *Beyond Reagan: The Politics of Upheaval* (1986)

Thomas Byrne Edsall, *The New Politics of Inequality* (1984)

Anne Edwards, *Early Reagan* (1987)

Barbara Ehrenreich, *Fear of Falling: The Inner Life of the Middle Class* (1989)

————, *The Worst Years of Our Lives* (1990)

Thomas Ferguson and Joel Rogers, eds., *The Hidden Election: Politics and Economics in the 1980 Presidential Campaign* (1981)

————, *Right Turn: The Decline of the Democrats and the Future of American Politics* (1986)

Steve Fraser and Gary Gerstle, eds., *The Rise and Fall of the New Deal Order, 1930–1980* (1989)

William F. Grover, *The President as Prisoner: A Structural Critique of the Carter and Reagan Years* (1990)

Jerry Hagstrom, *Beyond Reagan: The New Landscape of American Politics* (1988)

Bennett Harrison and Barry Bluestone, *The Great U-Turn: Corporate Restructuring and the Polarizing of America* (1988)

Dilys Hill et al., *The Reagan Presidency: An Incomplete Revolution?* (1990)

Joseph Hogan, ed., *The Reagan Years: The Record in Presidential Leadership* (1990)

James J. Horgan and Joseph A. Cernik, eds., *The Reagan Years: Perspectives and Assessments* (1988)

Charles O. Jones, ed., *The Reagan Legacy: Promise and Performance* (1988)

————, *The Trusteeship Presidency* (1988)

Hamilton Jordan, *Crisis: The Last Year of the Carter Presidency* (1982)

Robert Kuttner, *The Economic Illusion: False Choices Between Prosperity and Social Justice* (1984)

Robert Lekachman, *Visions and Nightmares: America After Reagan* (1987)

Frank Levy, *Dollars and Dreams: The Changing American Income Distribution* (1987)

Jane Mayer, *Landslide: The Unmaking of the President, 1984–1988* (1988)

David Mervin, *Ronald Reagan and the American Presidency* (1990)

Nicolaus Mills, *Culture in an Age of Money: The Legacy of the 1980s in America* (1990)

Clark Mollenhoff, *The President Who Failed: Carter out of Control* (1980)

Gillian Peele, *Revival and Reaction: The Right in Contemporary America* (1984)

Kevin Phillips, *The Politics of Rich and Poor* (1990)

————, *Post-Conservative America* (1982)

Ronald Reagan, *An American Life* (1990)

Michael P. Rogin, *Ronald Reagan: The Movie and Other Episodes in Political Demonology* (1987)

Herbert Stein, *Presidential Economics: The Making of Economic Policy from Roosevelt to Reagan and Beyond* (1984)

Lester C. Thurow, *The Zero Sum Society* (1980)

Susan J. Tolchin and Martin Tolchin, *Dismantling America: The Rush to Deregulate* (1983)

Martin P. Wattenberg, *The Decline of American Political Parties, 1952–1980* (1984)

Garry Wills, *Reagan's America: Innocents at Home* (1987)

Elder Witt, *Reagan and the Supreme Court* (1986)

James Wooten, *Dasher: The Roots and the Rising of Jimmy Carter* (1978)

Beyond the Cold War: American Foreign Policy in the Reagan-Bush Era

✕✕

In the wake of the U.S. experience in Vietnam, Richard Nixon and Jimmy Carter alike sought to engineer what some have called America's "retreat from empire"—a scaling-back of the rampant globalism of the Kennedy and Johnson years, and the beginnings of détente with the Soviet Union and China. In contrast, Ronald Reagan campaigned for the White House on a platform that promised to restore American leadership in world affairs. Reagan and his supporters initially denounced the Soviet Union in vintage Cold War terms as an "evil empire" and pledged to rebuild U.S. military strength. Under Reagan the United States embarked on a massive military buildup, first in more or less conventional weapons and then through "Star Wars," the highly controversial Strategic Defense Initiative (SDI), which proposed to defend the United States with a high-tech "umbrella" of costly and sophisticated electronic weapons. The United States also pursued a new interventionism, especially in the Caribbean, where the Reagan administration invaded the tiny island of Grenada and launched a "covert" campaign to overthrow the left-wing Sandinista government of Nicaragua. Reagan's revival of Cold War patriotism touched a popular nerve, perhaps best symbolized by the flag waving and chants of "We're Number One" by Americans at the 1984 summer Olympic games in Los Angeles. By 1986, nevertheless, the administration was in deep trouble. Massive military spending, coupled with reduced taxes, sent the nation's indebtedness skyrocketing. The Iran-contra scandal, meanwhile, revealed that the president and his top advisers were clearly implicated in a foolish and illegal attempt to trade arms for hostages and divert the proceeds to the U.S.-sponsored "contras"—an anti-Sandinista guerrilla army—in Nicaragua.

The administration abruptly changed course during the final two years of Reagan's term. The president abandoned Cold War confrontation for a new pragmatism that included the Intermediate-range Nuclear Forces (INF) Treaty with the Russians and progress toward a more comprehensive reduction of all nuclear weapons. Much of the change owed to developments that neither Reagan nor most Americans could have anticipated—the growing economic paralysis of the Soviet Union, the rapid dismantling of much of its empire in Eastern Europe, and the rise of Mikhail Gorbachev and a new leadership dedicated to sweeping political and economic reforms. Some saw in these developments a vindication of Reagan's policies. The United States, they claimed, had won the Cold War. Others viewed the shift as a happy coincidence. Ronald Reagan, the "teflon president," had lucked out again. Still others saw in recent developments an end not only to the Cold War but to an entire era in world history.

Yet if the Cold War had ended, the many conflicting interests and impulses on which it had for a time imposed an order of a sort remained and in fact began to reassert themselves. In the Middle East, the euphoria of the new post–Cold War era was quickly shattered by the Iraqi invasion of Kuwait in August 1990 and by the Persian Gulf war in which U.S.–led forces easily crushed the Iraqis. Although President George Bush proclaimed his commitment to the establishment of a new world order, neither the character of that new order nor America's role in it were at all clear. Indeed, even as the president called for the use of force to defend "our jobs, our way of life, our own freedom, and the freedom of friendly countries around the world," liberals and conservatives alike scrambled to reconstruct their understanding of American foreign policy.

☒ D O C U M E N T S

In a March 8, 1983, speech to the National Association of Evangelicals, excerpts from which are reprinted in the first document, President Reagan invoked the image of the U.S.S.R. as a threatening "evil empire" and called for expanded U.S. military power. The second document, a graph drawn from public sources, traces the rise in military spending during the Reagan administration. The third selection, excerpted from the 1987 report of the congressional committees investigating the Iran-contra affair, describes the covert and illegal activities of Oliver North and other White House officials who sought to sell arms to Iran in return for money and the release of hostages, and then to divert the proceeds to support the U.S.–backed contra rebels in Nicaragua. In a December 1988 speech to the United Nations, Soviet president Mikhail Gorbachev outlined a new and peaceful course for relations between the Soviet Union and the United States (the fourth document). In the fifth document, the editors of *The New York Times,* summarizing nearly two months of discussion and debate on the paper's op-ed page, announced on April 2, 1989, that the Cold War was over. As the Cold War ended, however, debate focused increasingly on the future of the postwar era. In the sixth document, excerpted from a joint address to Congress following the Iraqi invasion of Kuwait, President Bush announced his administration's goal of establishing a new world order.

President Ronald Reagan on Russia as an "Evil Empire," 1983

During my first press conference as President, in answer to a direct question, I pointed out that, as good Marxist-Leninists, the Soviet leaders have openly and publicly declared that the only morality they recognize is that which will further their cause, which is world revolution. I think I should point out I was only quoting Lenin, their guiding spirit, who said in 1920 that they repudiate all morality that proceeds from supernatural ideas—that's their name for religion—or ideas that are outside class conceptions. Morality is entirely subordinate to the interests of class war. And everything is moral that is necessary for the annihilation of the old, exploiting social order and for uniting the proletariat.

Well, I think the refusal of many influential people to accept this elementary fact of Soviet doctrine illustrates an historical reluctance to see totalitarian powers for what they are. We saw this phenomenon in the 1930's. We see it too often today.

This doesn't mean we should isolate ourselves and refuse to seek an understanding with them. I intend to do everything I can to persuade them of our peaceful intent, to remind them that it was the West that refused to use its nuclear monopoly in the forties and fifties for territorial gain and which now proposes 50-percent cut in strategic ballistic missiles and the elimination of an entire class of land-based, intermediate-range nuclear missiles.

At the same time, however, they must be made to understand we will never compromise our principles and standards. We will never give away our freedom. We will never abandon our belief in God. And we will never stop searching for a genuine peace. But we can assure none of these things America stands for through the so-called nuclear freeze solutions proposed by some.

The truth is that a freeze now would be a very dangerous fraud, for that is merely the illusion of peace. The reality is that we must find peace through strength.

I would agree to a freeze if only we could freeze the Soviets' global desires. A freeze at current levels of weapons would remove any incentive for the Soviets to negotiate seriously in Geneva and virtually end our chances to achieve the major arms reductions which we have proposed. Instead, they would achieve their objectives through the freeze.

A freeze would reward the Soviet Union for its enormous and unparalleled military buildup. It would prevent the essential and long overdue modernization of United States and allied defenses and would leave our aging forces increasingly vulnerable. And an honest freeze would require extensive prior negotiations on the systems and numbers to be limited and on the measures to ensure effective verification and compliance. And the kind of a freeze that has been suggested would be virtually impossible to verify. Such a major effort would divert us completely from our current negotiations on achieving substantial reductions.

A number of years ago, I heard a young father, a very prominent young man in the entertainment world, addressing a tremendous gathering in California. It was during the time of the cold war, and communism and our own way of life were very much on people's minds. And he was speaking to that subject. And suddenly, though, I heard him saying, "I love my little girls more than anything—" And I said to myself, "Oh, no, don't. You can't—don't say that." But I had underestimated him. He went on: "I would rather see my little girls die now, still believing in God, than have them grow up under communism and one day die no longer believing in God."

There were thousands of young people in that audience. They came to their feet with shouts of joy. They had instantly recognized the profound truth in what he had said, with regard to the physical and the soul and what was truly important.

Yes, let us pray for the salvation of all of those who live in that total-itarian darkness—pray they will discover the joy of knowing God. But until they do, let us be aware that while they preach the supremacy of the state, declare its omnipotence over individual man, and predict its eventual dom-ination of all peoples on the Earth, they are the focus of evil in the modern world.

It was C. S. Lewis who, in his unforgettable "Screwtape Letters," wrote: "The greatest evil is not done now in those sordid 'dens of crime' that Dickens loved to paint. It is not even done in concentration camps and labor camps. In those we see its final result. But it is conceived and ordered (moved, seconded, carried and minuted) in clear, carpeted, warmed, and well-lighted offices, by quiet men with white collars and cut fingernails and smooth-shaven cheeks who do not need to raise their voice."

Well, because these "quiet men" do not "raise their voices," because they sometimes speak in soothing tones of brotherhood and peace, because, like other dictators before them, they're always making "their final territorial demand," some would have us accept them at their word and accommodate ourselves to their aggressive impulses. But if history teaches anything, it teaches that simple-minded appeasement or wishful thinking about our ad-versaries is folly. It means the betrayal of our past, the squandering of our freedom.

So, I urge you to speak out against those who would place the United States in a position of military and moral inferiority. You know, I've always believed that old Screwtape reserved his best efforts for those of you in the church. So, in your discussions of the nuclear freeze proposals, I urge you to beware the temptation of pride—the temptation of blithely declaring yourselves above it all and label both sides equally at fault, to ignore the facts of history and the aggressive impulses of an evil empire, to simply call the arms race a giant misunderstanding and thereby remove yourself from the struggle between right and wrong and good and evil.

I ask you to resist the attempts of those who would have you withhold your support for our efforts, this administration's efforts, to keep America strong and free, while we negotiate real and verifiable reductions in the world's nuclear arsenals and one day, with God's help, their total elimination.

While America's military strength is important, let me add here that I've always maintained that the struggle now going on for the world will never be decided by bombs or rockets, by armies or military might. The real crisis we face today is a spiritual one; at root, it is a test of moral will and faith.

Whittaker Chambers, the man whose own religious conversion made him a witness to one of the terrible traumas of our time, the Hiss-Chambers case, wrote that the crisis of the Western World exists to the degree in which the West is indifferent to God, the degree to which it collaborates in communism's attempt to make man stand alone without God. And then he said, for Marxism-Leninism is actually the second oldest faith, first proclaimed in the Garden of Eden with the words of temptation, "Ye shall be as gods."

The Western World can answer this challenge, he wrote, "but only provided that its faith in God and the freedom He enjoins is as great as communism's faith in Man."

I believe we shall rise to the challenge. I believe that communism is another sad, bizarre chapter in human history whose last pages even now are being written. I believe this because the source of our strength in the quest for human freedom is not material, but spiritual. And because it knows no limitation, it must terrify and ultimately triumph over those who would enslave their fellow man. For in the words of Isaiah: "He giveth power to the faint; and to them that have no might He increased strength. . . . But they that wait upon the Lord shall renew their strength; they shall mount up with wings as eagles; they shall run, and not be weary. . . ."

Yes, change your world. One of our Founding Fathers, Thomas Paine, said, "We have it within our power to begin the world over again." We can do it, doing together what no one church could do by itself.

God bless you, and thank you very much.

A Congressional Committee
Reports on "Irangate," 1987

The full story of the Iran-Contra Affair is complicated, and, for this Nation, profoundly sad. In the narrative portion of this Report, the Committees present a comprehensive account of the facts, based on 10 months of investigation, including 11 weeks of hearings.

But the facts alone do not explain how or why the events occurred. In this Executive Summary, the Committees focus on the key issues and offer their conclusions. Minority, supplemental, and additional views are printed in Section II and Section III.

Summary of the Facts

The Iran-Contra Affair had its origin in two unrelated revolutions in Iran and Nicaragua.

In Nicaragua, the long-time President, General Anastasio Somoza Debayle, was overthrown in 1979 and replaced by a Government controlled by Sandinista leftists.

In Iran, the pro-Western Government of the Shah Mohammed Riza Pahlavi was overthrown in 1979 by Islamic fundamentalists led by the Ayatollah Khomeini. The Khomeini Government, stridently anti-American, became a supporter of terrorism against American citizens.

U.S. Military Spending, 1980–1990: A Graphic

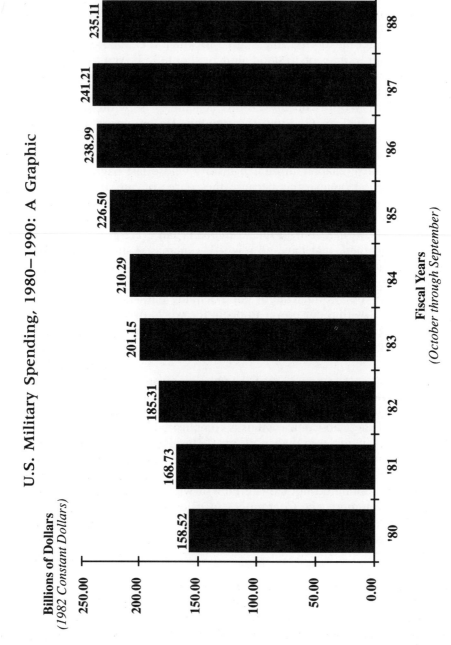

Billions of Dollars
(1982 Constant Dollars)

Fiscal Years
(October through September)

Statistics compiled by David Murphy, University of Maryland, College Park, from government statistics.

United States policy following the revolution in Nicaragua was to encourage the Sandinista Government to keep its pledges of pluralism and democracy. However, the Sandinista regime became increasingly anti-American and autocratic; began to aid a leftist insurgency in El Salvador; and turned toward Cuba and the Soviet Union for political, military, and economic assistance. By December 1981, the United States had begun supporting the Nicaraguan Contras, armed opponents of the Sandinista regime.

The Central Intelligence Agency (CIA) was the U.S. Government agency that assisted the Contras. In accordance with Presidential decisions, known as Findings, and with funds appropriated by Congress, the CIA armed, clothed, fed, and supervised the Contras. Despite this assistance, the Contras failed to win widespread popular support or military victories within Nicaragua.

Although the President continued to favor support of the Contras, opinion polls indicated that a majority of the public was not supportive. Opponents of the Administration's policy feared that U.S. involvement with the Contras would embroil the United States in another Vietnam. Supporters of the policy feared that, without U.S. support for the Contras, the Soviets would gain a dangerous toehold in Central America.

Congress prohibited Contra aid for the purpose of overthrowing the Sandinista Government in fiscal year 1983, and limited all aid to the Contras in fiscal year 1984 to $24 million. Following disclosure in March and April 1984 that the CIA had a role in connection with the mining of the Nicaraguan harbors without adequate notification to Congress, public criticism mounted and the Administration's Contra policy lost much of its support within Congress. After further vigorous debate, Congress exercised its Constitutional power over appropriations and cut off all funds for the Contras' military and paramilitary operations. The statutory provision cutting off funds, known as the Boland Amendment, was part of a fiscal year 1985 omnibus appropriations bill, and was signed into law by the President on October 12, 1984.

Still, the President felt strongly about the Contras, and he ordered his staff, in the words of his National Security Adviser, to find a way to keep the Contras "body and soul together." Thus began the story of how the staff of a White House advisory body, the NSC, became an operational entity that secretly ran the Contra assistance effort, and later the Iran initiative. The action officer placed in charge of both operations was Lt. Col. Oliver L. North.

Denied funding by Congress, the President turned to third countries and private sources. Between June 1984 and the beginning of 1986, the President, his National Security Adviser, and the NSC staff secretly raised $34 million for the Contras from other countries. An additional $2.7 million was provided for the Contras during 1985 and 1986 from private contributors, who were addressed by North and occasionally granted photo opportunities with the President. In the middle of this period, Assistant Secretary of State A. Langhorne Motley—from whom these contributions were concealed—gave his assurance to Congress that the Administration was not "soliciting and/or encouraging third countries" to give funds to the Contras because, as he conceded, the Boland Amendment prohibited such solicitation.

The first contributions were sent by the donors to bank accounts controlled and used by the Contras. However, in July 1985, North took control of the funds and—with the support of two National Security Advisers (Robert McFarlane and John Poindexter) and, according to North, [CIA] Director [William] Casey—used those funds to run the covert operation to support the Contras.

At the suggestion of Director Casey, North recruited Richard V. Secord, a retired Air Force Major General with experience in special operations. Secord set up Swiss bank accounts, and North steered future donations into these accounts. Using these funds, and funds later generated by the Iran arms sales, Secord and his associate, Albert Hakim, created what they called "the Enterprise," a private organization designed to engage in covert activities on behalf of the United States.

The Enterprise, functioning largely at North's direction, had its own airplanes, pilots, airfield, operatives, ship, secure communications devices, and secret Swiss bank accounts. For 16 months, it served as the secret arm of the NSC staff, carrying out with private and non-appropriated money, and without the accountability or restrictions imposed by law on the CIA, a covert Contra aid program that Congress thought it had prohibited.

Although the CIA and other agencies involved in intelligence activities knew that the Boland Amendment barred their involvement in covert support for the Contras, North's Contra support operation received logistical and tactical support from various personnel in the CIA and other agencies. Certain CIA personnel in Central America gave their assistance. The U.S. Ambassador in Costa Rica, Lewis Tambs, provided his active assistance. North also enlisted the aid of Defense Department personnel in Central America, and obtained secure communications equipment from the National Security Agency. The Assistant Secretary of State with responsibility for the region, Elliott Abrams, professed ignorance of this support. He later stated that he had been "careful not to ask North lots of questions."

By Executive Order and National Security Decision Directive issued by President Reagan, all covert operations must be approved by the President personally and in writing. By statute, Congress must be notified about each covert action. The funds used for such actions, like all government funds, must be strictly accounted for.

The covert action directed by North, however, was not approved by the President in writing. Congress was not notified about it. And the funds to support it were never accounted for. In short, the operation functioned without any of the accountability required of Government activities. It was an evasion of the Constitution's most basic check on Executive action—the power of the Congress to grant or deny funding for Government programs.

Moreover, the covert action to support the Contras was concealed from Congress and the public. When the press reported in the summer of 1985 that the NSC staff was engaged in raising money and furnishing military support to the Contras, the President assured the public that the law was being followed. His National Security Adviser, Robert C. McFarlane, assured Committees of Congress, both in person and in writing, that the NSC staff was obeying both the spirit and the letter of the law, and was neither soliciting money nor coordinating military support for the Contras. . . .

The NSC staff was [thus] already engaged in covert operations through Secord when, in the summer of 1985, the Government of Israel proposed that missiles be sold to Iran in return for the release of seven American hostages held in Lebanon and the prospect of improved relations with Iran. The Secretaries of State and Defense repeatedly opposed such sales to a government designated by the United States as a supporter of international terrorism. They called it a straight arms-for-hostages deal that was contrary to U.S. public policy. They also argued that these sales would violate the Arms Export Control Act, as well as the U.S. arms embargo against Iran. The embargo had been imposed after the taking of hostages at the U.S. Embassy in Tehran on November 4, 1979, and was continued because of the Iran-Iraq war.

Nevertheless, in the summer of 1985 the President authorized Israel to proceed with the sales. The NSC staff conducting the Contra covert action also took operational control of implementing the President's decision on arms sales to Iran. The President did not sign a Finding for this covert operation, nor did he notify the Congress.

Israel shipped 504 TOW anti-tank missiles to Iran in August and September 1985. Although the Iranians had promised to release most of the American hostages in return, only one, Reverend Benjamin Weir, was freed. The President persisted. In November, he authorized Israel to ship 80 HAWK anti-aircraft missiles in return for all the hostages, with a promise of prompt replenishment by the United States, and 40 more HAWKs to be sent directly by the United States to Iran. Eighteen HAWK missiles were actually shipped from Israel in November 1985, but no hostages were released.

In early December 1985, the President signed a retroactive Finding purporting to authorize the November HAWK transaction. That Finding contained no reference to improved relations with Iran. It was a straight arms-for-hostages Finding. National Security Adviser Poindexter destroyed this Finding a year later because, he testified, its disclosure would have been politically embarrassing to the President.

The November HAWK transaction had additional significance. The Enterprise received a $1 million advance from the Israelis. North and Secord testified this was for transportation expenses in connection with the 120 HAWK missiles. Since only 18 missiles were shipped, the Enterprise was left with more than $800,000 in spare cash. North directed the Enterprise to retain the money and spend it for the Contras. The "diversion" had begun.

North realized that the sale of missiles to Iran could be used to support the Contras. He told Israeli Defense Ministry officials on December 6, 1985, one day after the President signed the Finding, that he planned to generate profits on future arms sales for activities in Nicaragua. . . .

In February 1986, the United States, acting through the Enterprise, sold 1,000 TOWs to the Iranians. The U.S. also provided the Iranians with military intelligence about Iraq. All of the remaining American hostages were supposed to be released upon Iran's receipt of the first 500 TOWs. None was. But the transaction was productive in one respect. The difference between what the Enterprise paid the United States for the missiles and what it received from Iran was more than $6 million. North directed part of this profit for the Contras and for other covert operations. Poindexter testified that he authorized this "diversion."

The diversion, for the Contras and other covert activities, was not an isolated act by the NSC staff. Poindexter saw it as "implementing" the President's secret policy that had been in effect since 1984 of using non-appropriated funds following passage of the Boland Amendment.

According to North, CIA Director Casey saw the "diversion" as part of a more grandiose plan to use the Enterprise as a "stand-alone," "off-the-shelf," covert capacity that would act throughout the world while evading Congressional review. To Casey, Poindexter, and North, the diversion was an integral part of selling arms to Iran and just one of the intended uses of the proceeds.

In May 1986, the President again tried to sell weapons to get the hostages back. This time, the President agreed to ship parts for HAWK missiles but only on condition that all the American hostages in Lebanon be released first. A mission headed by Robert McFarlane, the former National Security Adviser, traveled to Tehran with the first installment of the HAWK parts. When the mission arrived, McFarlane learned that the Iranians claimed they had never promised to do anything more than try to obtain the hostages' release. The trip ended amid misunderstanding and failure, although the first installment of HAWK parts was delivered.

The Enterprise was paid, however, for all of the HAWK parts, and realized more than an $8 million profit, part of which was applied, at North's direction, to the Contras. Another portion of the profit was used by North for other covert operations, including the operation of a ship for a secret mission. The idea of an off-the-shelf, stand-alone covert capacity had become operational. . . .

The sale of arms to Iran was a "significant anticipated intelligence activity." By law, such an activity must be reported to Congress "in a timely fashion" pursuant to Section 501 of the National Security Act. If the proposal to sell arms to Iran had been reported, the Senate and House Intelligence Committees would likely have joined Secretaries Shultz and Weinberger in objecting to this initiative. But Poindexter recommended—and the President decided—not to report the Iran initiative to Congress.

Indeed, the Administration went to considerable lengths to avoid notifying Congress. The CIA General Counsel wrote on January 15, 1986, "the key issue in this entire matter revolves around whether or not there will be reports made to Congress." Shortly thereafter, the transaction was restructured to avoid the pre-shipment reporting requirements of the Arms Export Control Act, and place it within the more limited reporting requirements of the National Security Act. But even these reporting requirements were ignored. The President failed to notify the group of eight (the leaders of each party in the House and Senate, and the Chairmen and Ranking Minority Members of the Intelligence Committees) specified by law for unusually sensitive operations.

After the disclosure of the Iran arms sales on November 3, 1986, the American public was still not told the facts. The President sought to avoid any comment on the ground that it might jeopardize the chance of securing the remaining hostages' release. But it was impossible to remain silent, and inaccurate statements followed. . . .

While the President was denying any illegality, his subordinates were engaging in a coverup. Several of his advisers had expressed concern that the 1985 sales violated the Arms Export Control Act, and a "cover story" had been agreed on if these arms sales were ever exposed. After North had three conversations on November 18, 1986, about the legal problems with the 1985 Israeli shipments, he, Poindexter, Casey, and McFarlane all told conforming false stories about U.S. involvement in these shipments. . . .

In light of the destruction of material evidence by Poindexter and North and the death of Casey, all of the facts may never be known. The Committees cannot even be sure whether they heard the whole truth. . . . But enough is clear to demonstrate beyond doubt that fundamental processes of governance were disregarded and the rule of law was subverted.

The common ingredients of the Iran and Contra policies were secrecy, deception, and disdain for the law. A small group of senior officials believed that they alone knew what was right. They viewed knowledge of their actions by others in the Government as a threat to their objectives. They told neither the Secretary of State, the Congress nor the American people of their actions. When exposure was threatened, they destroyed official documents and lied to Cabinet officials, to the public, and to elected representatives in Congress. They testified that they even withheld key facts from the President.

The United States Constitution specifies the process by which laws and policy are to be made and executed. Constitutional process is the essence of our democracy and our democratic form of Government is the basis of our strength. Time and again we have learned that a flawed process leads to bad results, and that a lawless process leads to worse.

Soviet Leader Mikhail Gorbachev Charts a New Direction for the U.S.S.R., 1988

The Soviet Union's role in world affairs is well known. In view of the revolutionary restructuring that is taking place in our country—perestroika—which has a tremendous potential for promoting peace and international cooperation, we are particularly interested today in being understood correctly. . . .

What will humanity be like as it enters the 21st century? Thoughts about this already very near future are engaging people's minds. While we look forward to the future with the anticipation of change for the better, we also view it with alarm.

Today, the world is a very different place from what it was at the beginning of this century, and even in the middle of it. And the world and all of its components keep changing.

The emergence of nuclear weapons was a tragic way of stressing the fundamental nature of these changes. Being the material symbol and the bearer of the ultimate military force, nuclear weapons at the same time laid bare the absolute limits to this force.

Humankind is faced with the problem of survival, of self-protection, in all its magnitude.

Profound social changes are taking place.

In the East and in the South, in the West and in the North, hundreds of millions of people, new nations and states, new public movements and ideologies have advanced to the foreground of history.

The striving for independence, democracy and social justice manifests itself, in all its diversity and with all its contradictions, in broad and frequently turbulent popular movements. The idea of democratizing the entire world order has grown into a powerful social and political force.

At the same time, the revolution in science and technology has turned economic, food, energy, ecological, information and demographic problems, which only recently were of a national or regional character, into global problems.

The newest techniques of communications, mass information and transport have made the world more visible and more tangible to everyone. International communication is easier now than ever before.

Nowadays, it is virtually impossible for any society to be "closed." That is why we need a radical revision of the views on the totality of problems of international cooperation, which is the most essential component of universal security.

The world economy is becoming a single entity, outside of which no state can develop normally, regardless of its social system or economic level.

All this calls for creating an altogether new mechanism for the functioning of the world economy, a new structure of the international division of labour.

World economic growth, however, is revealing the contradictions of the traditional type of industrial development and its limitations. The expansion and deepening of industrialization is leading to an ecological catastrophe.

But there are many countries with insufficiently developed industry and some that are not yet industrialized. Whether these countries will follow the old technological patterns in their economic development or be able to join the search for ecologically clean industries is one of the biggest problems.

Another problem is the growing gap between the industrialized nations and most of the developing countries, which is presenting an increasingly serious threat on a global scale.

All these factors make it necessary to look for a fundamentally new type of industrial progress that would be in accordance with the interests of all peoples and states. . . .

In thinking all this over, it becomes clear that we have to look for ways together to improve the international situation, to build a new world—that is, if we are going to take into consideration the lessons of the past, the realities of the present, and the objective logic of world development.

If this is really true, it would be worthwhile to reach an understanding on the basic and genuinely universal principles of this search, and the prerequisites for it.

It is evident, in particular, that force or the threat of force neither can nor should be instruments of foreign policy. This mainly refers to nuclear arsenals, but not to them alone. All of us, and first of all the strongest of us, have to practice self-restraint and renounce the use of force in the international arena. . . .

The *New York Times* Announces the End of the Cold War, 1989

The cold war of poisonous Soviet-American feelings, of domestic political hysteria, of events enlarged and distorted by East-West confrontation, of almost perpetual diplomatic deadlock is over.

The we-they world that emerged after 1945 is giving way to the more traditional struggles of great powers. That contest is more manageable. It permits serious negotiations. It creates new possibilities—for cooperation in combating terrorism, the spread of chemical weapons and common threats to the environment, and for shaping a less violent world.

True, Europe remains torn in two; but the place where four decades of hostility began is mending and changing in complicated patterns. True, two enormous military machines still face each other around the world; but both sides are searching for ways to reduce the burdens and risks. Values continue to clash, but less profoundly as Soviet citizens start to partake in freedoms.

The experts who contributed to a two-month series on the Op-Ed page called "Is the Cold War Over?" agreed, with variations in emphasis and definition, that Soviet-American relations are entering a new era. They differed over whether Mikhail Gorbachev can last and whether his policies can outlast him, and over how much the West can or should do to help him and what to ask in return. But these questions are the stuff of genuine policy debate, not grist for old ideological diatribes.

In his four years of power, what has Mikhail Gorbachev done to bring about this reconsideration of the cold war?

A great deal, as Jeremy Stone of the Federation of American Sciences rightly pointed out. Mr. Gorbachev has pushed Yasir Arafat toward renouncing terrorism and accepting Israel, supported political settlements in Angola and Cambodia, pulled out Soviet troops from Afghanistan, agreed to vastly disproportionate cuts in medium-range missiles and pledged significant unilateral reductions in Soviet forces in Central Europe.

At home, Mr. Stone said properly, the Soviet leader is introducing economic decentralization, allowing Soviet nationalities to assert their separate identities, encouraging free speech and experimenting with elections. These measures give hope for a more open Soviet society and Government. And, as Graham Allison of Harvard's Kennedy School pointed out, this has been the very goal of America's containment policy.

But what if Mr. Gorbachev is ousted? Couldn't his successors readily reverse his actions?

Frank Carlucci argued that it's too early to foretell Mr. Gorbachev's fate or judge whether he or his successors might not simply change policies. The former Defense Secretary argued that Soviet policy is in a transitional phase.

Dimitri Simes of the Carnegie Endowment for International Peace, on the other hand, convincingly made the case that the changes occurring in the Soviet Union are of a more fundamental nature. Whoever leads the Soviet Union, he argued, would have little choice but to respond to Moscow's current economic and political weaknesses and follow the Gorbachev path.

Mr. Simes rightly argued that the debate in the Soviet Union revolves around the scope and pace of change, not the need for change. And there is little evidence that Mr. Gorbachev's foreign and military policies are under attack. Moscow simply does not have the resources for costly global challenges.

If the Soviet Union is in such bad shape, why not squeeze hard for concessions?

William Luers, a former U.S. diplomat, offered one reason. He warned against humiliating Mr. Gorbachev in ways that would unite a proud nation against the West. Ed Hewitt of the Brookings Institution provided another: Soviet leaders still have sufficient economic strength and foreign policy options to make life easier or harder for the West.

These cautions have to be kept in mind. But the West should not shy away from driving hard bargains. That can be done, as Ronald Reagan demonstrated, without destroying relations.

What should Western policy be?

Zbigniew Brzezinski correctly argued that the West needs a strategy to deal with "the gravity of the challenge and the magnitude of the opportunity." But the West would tie itself in knots if it followed his advice to "insist that any substantial assistance be reciprocated by reforms that institutionalize economic and political pluralism."

On the contrary, the West cannot manage Soviet reforms any more than it can "save" Mr. Gorbachev. It can reinforce and encourage reforms when Western interests are also at stake—by providing credits and technology on a modest and safe scale and by easing restrictions on trade. The point is for the West to rid itself of self-made restraints on expanding economic relations so that decisions can be made on a case-by-case basis.

The prospect of such economic openings and the diminishing Soviet threat are likely to give freer play to conflicts among Western industrialized powers, according to Edward Luttwak of the Center for Strategic and International Studies. He was exactly right in urging Western leaders to "act now to construct a new system of economic cooperation that would stand on its own and not lean on the imperatives of resisting" Moscow.

No one seems to have a good answer about the division of Europe, always the most dangerous East-West question. Michael Mandelbaum of the Council on Foreign Relations offered as good a prescription as anyone. He looked toward superpower talks to bring about sovereign nations in Eastern Europe and special arrangements for the two Germanys.

The Bush Administration seems less attentive to these issues and more preoccupied with Mr. Gorbachev's seizing headlines worldwide. It would do better to think of him as part of the solution, not the problem, as Richard Ullman of Princeton University counseled. "Who takes the initiative," he wrote, "matters less than the result."

The Administration now nears the completion of its East-West policy review. Hints dribble out about senior officials worrying that Mr. Reagan was too friendly with Mr. Gorbachev and too eager for arms control. That's self-defeating talk. The treaty eliminating medium-range missiles in Europe represents a substantial victory for the West. Similarly, Mr. Bush and the country would gain by early completion of a treaty to cut intercontinental-range missiles and bombers.

None of the contributors recommended cosmic disarmament agreements, and Mr. Bush would be right to avoid them. But he would be flat wrong not to exploit Moscow's willingness to compromise on cutting troops in Europe and otherwise reduce the costs and risks of security.

It would also be unfortunate if the Bush team worried too much about its right flank and tried to prove that it can out-tough Mr. Reagan. That would drain them of the imagination and boldness necessary to go beyond the cold war. Presidents Bush and Gorbachev have the opportunity of the century to refocus energies and resources from sterile conflicts onto common threats to mankind.

President George Bush Proclaims a New World Order, 1990

We gather tonight, witness to events in the Persian Gulf as significant as they are tragic. In the early morning hours of August 2nd, following negotiations and promises by Iraq's dictator Saddam Hussein not to use force, a powerful Iraqi army invaded its trusting and much weaker neighbor, Kuwait. Within 3 days, 120,000 Iraqi troops with 850 tanks had poured into Kuwait and moved south to threaten Saudi Arabia. It was then that I decided to check that aggression.

At this moment, our brave servicemen and women stand watch in that distant desert and on distant seas, side-by-side with the forces of more than 20 other nations.

Tonight, I want to talk to you about what's at stake—what we must do together to defend civilized values around the world and maintain our economic strength at home.

The Objectives and Goals

Our objectives in the Persian Gulf are clear; our goals defined and familiar.

- Iraq must withdraw from Kuwait completely, immediately, and without condition.
- Kuwait's legitimate government must be restored.
- The security and stability of the Persian Gulf must be assured.
- American citizens abroad must be protected.

These goals are not ours alone. They have been endorsed by the UN Security Council five times in as many weeks. Most countries share our concern for principle, and many have a stake in the stability of the Persian Gulf. This is not, as Saddam Hussein would have it, the United States against Iraq. It is Iraq against the world.

We stand today at a unique and extraordinary moment. The crisis in the Persian Gulf, as grave as it is, also offers a rare opportunity to move toward a historic period of cooperation. Out of these troubled times, our fifth objective—a new world order—can emerge; a new era—freer from the threat of terror, stronger in the pursuit of justice, and more secure in the quest for peace, an era in which the nations of the world, East and West, North and South, can prosper and live in harmony.

A hundred generations have searched for this elusive path to peace, while a thousand wars raged across the span of human endeavor. Today, that new world is struggling to be born, a world quite different from the one we have known, a world where the rule of law supplants the rule of the jungle, a world in which nations recognize the shared responsibility for freedom and justice, a world where the strong respect the rights of the weak.

This is the vision that I shared with President Gorbachev in Helsinki. He and other leaders from Europe, the gulf, and around the world understand that how we manage this crisis today could shape the future for generations to come.

The test we face is great—and so are the stakes. This is the first assault on the new world that we seek, the first test of our mettle. Had we not responded to this first provocation with clarity of purpose, if we do not continue to demonstrate our determination, it would be a signal to actual and potential despots around the world.

America and the world must defend common vital interests. And we will. America and the world must support the rule of law. And we will. America and the world must stand up to aggression. And we will. And one thing more; in the pursuit of these goals, America will not be intimidated.

Vital issues of principle are at stake. Saddam Hussein is literally trying to wipe a country off the face of the earth. We do not exaggerate. Nor do we exaggerate when we say Saddam Hussein will fail.

Vital economic interests are at risk as well. Iraq itself controls some 10% of the world's proven oil reserves. Iraq plus Kuwait controls twice that. An Iraq permitted to swallow Kuwait would have the economic and military power, as well as the arrogance, to intimidate and coerce its neighbors—neighbors that control the lion's share of the world's remaining oil reserves. We cannot permit a resource so vital to be dominated by one so ruthless. And we won't.

Recent events have surely proven that there is no substitute for American leadership. In the face of tyranny, let no one doubt American credibility and reliability. Let no one doubt our staying power. We will stand by our friends. One way or another, the leader of Iraq must learn this fundamental truth.

Our interest, our involvement in the gulf is not transitory. It predated Saddam Hussein's aggression and will survive it. Long after all our troops come home—and we all hope it is soon, very soon—there will be a lasting role for the United States in assisting the nations of the Persian Gulf. Our role then—to deter future aggression. Our role is to help our friends in their own self-defense, and, something else, to curb the proliferation of chemical, biological, ballistic missile, and, above all, nuclear technologies.

Let me also make clear that the United States has no quarrel with the Iraqi people. Our quarrel is with Iraq's dictator and with his aggression. Iraq will not be permitted to annex Kuwait. That is not a threat; that is not a boast; that is just the way it is going to be.

✂ E S S A Y S

As the Cold War gave way to a new and uncertain era in international affairs, historians and other foreign-policy experts hastened to explain the legacy of the Reagan era and to map out the future course of U.S. foreign relations. In the first essay, diplomatic historian John Lewis Gaddis of Ohio University offers a favorable assessment of Ronald Reagan's policies, praising the former president for "hanging tough" and for helping to bring about "the most dramatic improvement in U.S.-Soviet relations . . . since the Cold War began." In the second essay, Richard J. Barnet of the Institute for Policy Studies presents a far more critical assessment of both Reagan and George Bush and of the powerful inertial momentum of America's Cold War institutions. Note that both essays were published before the Iraqi invasion of Kuwait, the Persian Gulf war, and George Bush's call for "a new world order."

Ronald Reagan's Cold War Victory

JOHN LEWIS GADDIS

The time has come to acknowledge an astonishing development: during his eight years as president, Ronald Reagan has presided over the most dramatic

"Ronald Reagan's Cold War Victory" by John Lewis Gaddis from the *Bulletin of the Atomic Scientists*. Copyright © 1989 by the Educational Foundation for Nuclear Science, 6042 South Kimbark, Chicago, IL 60637, USA.

improvement in U.S.-Soviet relations—and the most solid progress in arms control—since the Cold War began. History has often produced unexpected results, but this one surely sets some kind of record.

Reagan was not an enthusiast for arms control before entering the White House: indeed his 1976 and 1980 campaigns appeared to reject that enterprise altogether in favor of a simpler search for national security through military superiority over the Soviet Union. That arms control has not only survived but prospered under his leadership ought to make us take a fresh look, both at the administration he headed and at the arms control process itself as it has traditionally been understood.

That process had taken on several distinctive characteristics by the end of the 1970s:

Pessimism. It is now almost forgotten (perhaps even by themselves) that Richard Nixon and Henry Kissinger had originally portrayed the SALT [Strategic Arms Limitation Treaty] I negotiations as a way to reduce the effects of America's military decline, stemming from a Soviet strategic buildup in the mid-1960s, to which the United States, because of the Vietnam War, had at first been too distracted and then too divided to respond. Arms control carried with it the tacit assumption that, in this situation, SALT was, at best, a way of minimizing the damage. Coincident but unrelated events had reinforced, by the end of the 1970s, the association of arms control with visions of U.S. military inferiority. These developments included the energy crisis and ensuing double-digit inflation; the erosion of presidential authority that began with Watergate and continued under Ford and Carter; the collapse of old allies in Iran and Nicaragua; and, most dramatically, the juxtaposition of American ineffectiveness in the Tehran hostage crisis with apparent Soviet purposefulness in invading Afghanistan.

Complexity. The Partial Test Ban Treaty of 1963 took 10 days to negotiate and fills just over two pages in the Arms Control and Disarmament Agency's published version. SALT I took two-and-a-half years to negotiate; the text is 18 pages. The unratified SALT II Treaty required almost seven years to negotiate; the resulting text and accompanying statements fill 31 pages of text. With arms control agreements becoming so complex that the experts themselves—to say nothing of average citizens—were finding them difficult to understand, it was reasonable to begin to wonder by the end of the 1970s how one would actually know whether they coincided with the national interest, or how to be sure that the Soviets understood them in precisely the same way.

Insularity. As the SALT process became more complex it appeared to take on a life of its own, insulated from outside events. Despite increasingly detailed provisions for verification, arms control still depended to a considerable extent upon trusting the Soviets. But that was becoming harder to do. After 1975 Moscow openly violated the Helsinki Agreement's human rights provisions; indirect military intervention in Angola, Somalia, and

Ethiopia suggested at a minimum an unwillingness to cooperate with the West in managing regional conflicts; the Kremlin appeared determined to push the limits of SALT I as far as possible as it continued its buildup of strategic weapons. Yet the SALT II negotiations proceeded, apparently unaffected by these less than reassuring signs.

Illogic.   The SALT process seemed to be based on two propositions generally accepted within the arms control community, but that laymen found less and less plausible when tested against the simpler standards of common sense. One was implied in the very term "arms control"; why not "arms reduction"? And why did "strategic arms limitation" agreements seem to do so little actual "limiting"? The other had to do with the assertion that safety could come only through vulnerability, and that defense, therefore, at least in the nuclear realm, was bad. However rational the experts may have found these precepts, they did not appear rational to the average citizen, and as the nuclear standoff showed signs of stretching endlessly into the future, people became uncomfortable with them.

Whether these criticisms of arms control were fair is not the point. What is important is the skill with which Ronald Reagan focused on them during his campaigns for the presidency. And even more important was the way he incorporated them, after January 1981, into a new approach to arms control that would in time, and against conventional wisdom, produce impressive results. The principal means by which he accomplished this were as follows:

Rebuilding Self-Confidence.   There are rare moments in history when public moods reverse themselves almost overnight. One occurred in March 1933, when Franklin Roosevelt replaced Herbert Hoover in the White House; another took place in Great Britain in May 1940, when Winston Churchill became prime minister; still another occurred in Western Europe in June 1947, when Secretary of State George C. Marshall announced the economic recovery plan that came to bear his name. The mood reversal that followed Reagan's January 1981 inauguration was by no means as dramatic as these, but it occurred: long before the new administration had completed its military buildup, before Paul Volcker and the Federal Reserve Board had checked inflation, and before OPEC's [Organization of Petroleum Exporting Countries] disarray had turned the energy crisis into an oil glut, the *perception* had become widespread that events were beginning to break Washington's way. And that made a big difference.

It has since become commonplace to criticize Reagan for having placed greater emphasis on imagery than on substance during his years as president. But leadership begins with the creation of self-confidence, and that—as Roosevelt, Churchill, and Marshall all knew—is a psychological process depending less upon the rational calculation of tangible gains than upon the ability to convince people that however bad things may be at the moment, time is on their side. Reagan managed during his first months in office to project—and therefore to instill—a degree of self-confidence that went well beyond anything his predecessor had achieved. Without that shift from pessimism to optimism, much of what followed could hardly have taken place.

Spooking the Soviets. The second element in the Reagan strategy proceeded logically from the first—to persuade the Kremlin that time was working against it. Nor was it so difficult to do, because events were beginning to demonstrate precisely this: Afghanistan was revealing the costs of what Paul Kennedy has called "strategic overstretch;" "Solidarity" had brought Poland to the edge of open rebellion; economic stagnation was becoming a serious problem inside the Soviet Union; and an increasingly sclerotic Kremlin leadership was responding to these difficulties with near catatonic immobility. In one sense, Reagan was lucky to have come into office at a trough in American fortunes and a peak in those of the Soviets. Things could not get much worse, and were likely to get better. But more than luck is involved in the ability to recognize that such trends are under way, and to capitalize upon them. Reagan's leadership proved decidedly superior to Carter's in that respect.

Several subsequent Reagan administration actions sought to reinforce the idea that time no longer favored Moscow. The U.S. military buildup was launched with the intention of so straining an already inefficient economy that the Soviet leadership would have little choice but to make substantial concessions on arms control. Similar intentions lay behind the Strategic Defense Initiative [SDI]. The vision of a shift from deterrence to a defense based on American technological superiority would, it was thought, shock the Soviets into contemplating for the first time significant reductions in their own long-range strategic forces.

At the same time, the administration was skillfully defusing both the U.S. nuclear freeze movement and opposition to the deployment of Pershing II and cruise missiles in Western Europe by calling for actual *reductions* in nuclear weapons, and by holding out, through SDI, the prospect of ultimately making them obsolete altogether. To the extent that the Soviets had counted on such groups to constrain administration freedom of action—and they almost certainly had—the effect again was to demonstrate that time was no longer on Moscow's side.

Negotiation from Strength. A third element in the Reagan strategy was the principle that negotiations should take place only from a position of strength. The idea dates from the Truman administration's military buildup following the outbreak of the Korean War. Over the years it had come to be understood as a way of evading negotiations altogether, since "strength" was so relative a concept that one might never actually attain it and since adversaries would presumably never negotiate from "weakness." There was reason to believe, at the outset of the Reagan years, that this devious approach was alive and well. Presidential subordinates gleefully put forward "killer" proposals for arms control talks, while the Pentagon swallowed huge military appropriations without any indication that "strength" was about to be achieved.

An important characteristic of Reagan's leadership, however, was that he was *not* devious; when he spoke of the possibility that a military buildup might actually lead to reductions in strategic weapons, he appears to have meant precisely what he said. He also understood, perhaps instinctively, a point George Kennan had been arguing: that the arms control process had become too complex while producing too little, and that the only way to rebuild a domestic consensus in support of it was to hold out clear, simple, and sweeping objectives, such as a 50 percent cut in strategic weapons on both sides.

With the 1984 elections coming up and with indications that Congress would resist further defense budget increases, it could be argued that the administration had little choice but to appear to seek negotiations with the Soviets. Certainly some Reagan advisers felt that negotiations so protracted as to produce no results were almost as desirable as having no negotiations at all. But what many of Reagan's subordinates did not understand—and what those who seek to explain what subsequently happened will have to comprehend—is that while the president may have shared their conservatism, he did not share their cynicism. For him the only question was with whom to negotiate.

Responding to Gorbachev.   It is difficult to see that much could have been accomplished in this respect until a functional Soviet leadership had been established. That happened in March 1985, and a fourth element in the Reagan strategy soon emerged, which was to acknowledge Mikhail Gorbachev as a new kind of Soviet leader whose chief priority was internal reform, and with whom one could, in the realm of external affairs, find common interests.

The White House was therefore ready to respond when Gorbachev began modifying long-standing Soviet positions on arms control in a way quite consistent with what the Reagan strategy had anticipated. Neither critics on the left, who had favored negotiations for their own sake, nor those on the right, who had sought negotiation from strength, were in any position to object. The long-stalemated arms control process suddenly accelerated, producing by the final year of the Reagan administration not only an Intermediate-range Nuclear Forces (INF) Treaty that contained unprecedented Soviet concessions on asymmetrical reductions and on-site verification, but substantial progress as well toward agreement on deep cuts in long-range strategic systems, and at least the possibility of a grand compromise that would delay if not defer altogether the deployment of SDI.

There were, to be sure, deficiencies in the Reagan strategy. Characteristically, the president found it easier to think of SDI as he had advertised it—as a first step toward abolishing nuclear weapons altogether—than as the successful bargaining chip it turned out to be. This created an opportunity for Gorbachev to endorse nuclear abolition by the year 2000 and thus to align himself with the president against Reagan's own skeptical advisers. There were few signs of progress toward conventional arms limitation, or toward restricting nuclear testing. Little thought had been given to how the United States might respond if the relaxation of controls that perestroika required were to produce actual rebellions among Soviet nationality groups, or within Eastern Europe. And almost no thought appeared to have been given to the relationship between national security and national solvency—an issue to which Gorbachev himself seemed keenly attuned.

Still, the clock on the front cover of the *Bulletin* was set back, a year ago, for the first time since 1972. That symbolic act ought to make us think critically—and without preconceptions—about how we got to that point. It was not by means of arms control as traditionally practiced: the old SALT process would never have survived the Reagan administration's insistence on asymmetrical reductions instead of symmetrical limitations, on intrusive rather than remote verification, and on the virtues of strategic defense as opposed to mutual vulnerability. Strength this time did lead to negotiations, bargaining chips did produce bargains, and "hanging tough" did eventually pay off.

The Soviets deserve much of the credit for what happened. They made most of the concessions, a pattern not likely to be repeated often in the future. It was the Reagan administration, however, that assessed correctly the potential for Soviet concessions. And because of the way it came about, this new approach to arms control has won firmer domestic support within the United States than the SALT process ever did; witness the caution both sides showed in not making it an issue during the otherwise hotly contested 1988 presidential election. How valid the approach will be in years to come remains to be seen, but as Reagan leaves office it would be uncharitable—and historically irresponsible—to begrudge the strategic vision of an administration once thought by many of us to have had none at all.

After the Cold War

RICHARD J. BARNET

As the decade draws to a close, the globe seems to be spinning faster than at any time in forty years, blurring long-familiar landscapes. The surprises of the past two years have been breathtaking: The Soviet Union, dropping its elaborate mask, displays the weakness and discontent of seventy years of rule under the Communist Party, withdraws its troops from Afghanistan, and opens up an exciting but perilous process of debate and reform. Poland has a free election, and a leader of Solidarity becomes Prime Minister. Hungary announces that it is a People's Republic no more, stops calling its ruling party Communist, and proclaims Imre Nagy, the symbol of the struggle against Soviet tanks in Budapest in 1956, a national hero. Todor Zhivkov, the Stalinist leader of Bulgaria for thirty-five years, is ousted. In one long weekend in November, East German soldiers bulldoze parts of the Berlin Wall and announce that everybody is free to go to the West. The hard-liners

Excerpted from "After the Cold War" by Richard J. Barnet, *The New Yorker*, January 1, 1990. Reprinted by permission; © 1990 Richard J. Barnet.

in Czechoslovakia capitulate to a week of massive demonstrations, and the Czech Communist Party gives up its claim to play "the leading role." Alexander Dubček, who twenty-one years ago tried to create "socialism with a human face" and was crushed by Soviet tanks, returns in triumph. Even within the Soviet Union itself Mikhail Gorbachev's uncertain strategy for maintaining control of the non-Russian republics encounters defiance in Lithuania and results in bloody clashes in Georgia, Azerbaijan, and Uzbekistan. In the heady atmosphere of *glasnost,* the failures and disappointments of *perestroika* are undisguised. Officials and pundits in the West, unable to comprehend, much less to predict, the speed and magnitude of these changes, routinely assert that Gorbachev will fall. Some assume that the breakup of the Soviet Union is inevitable.

The nations of Western Europe agree to open a highly integrated regional super-market and trading bloc in 1992—an event no less stunning than the dissolution of Communism in Eastern Europe. The leaders of the Soviet Union and China meet and announce a rapprochement, but the massacre in Tiananmen Square is a sober reminder that dramatic changes can be dramatically reversed. Japan becomes the world's most successful trading nation, the world's greatest exporter of capital, the leading supplier of foreign aid, and the financier of the United States budget deficit. As pressures build on both sides of the Atlantic for withdrawals of American troops from Europe, the United States and West Germany artfully downplay their deepening split over the future of nuclear weapons on the Continent. But within half a year the dispute over whether to have a new generation of short-range nuclear missiles in West Germany aimed at East Germany is overwhelmed by the dramatic events in the German Democratic Republic. Suddenly, an issue that most non-Germans and many Germans would like to avoid—the reunification of the two Germanys—is on the table.

Thus, many of the long-declared aims of Cold War policies over more than forty years—a "mellowing" of the Soviet system, a tempering of revolutionary zeal, support of United Nations peacekeeping efforts, improvements in human rights, greater respect for religion in the Soviet Union, a willingness to negotiate a less threatening military posture, reductions in Soviet military spending, encouragement of greater democracy and diversity in Eastern Europe—are, to a remarkable extent, moving toward realization. The conversion of the Soviet Union from a revolutionary power seeking to replace the world capitalist system into a traditional nation-state seeking membership in that system is proceeding with great rapidity.

For almost forty-five years, the Cold War has served as the organizing principle of United States strategy. Virtually every foreign relationship has been viewed as an aspect of the global struggle with Communism. The Cold War has defined American priorities and American purposes, and its approaching end offers a historic opportunity for the United States to take stock of what has happened, to reëxamine its foreign-policy goals and strategies, and to redefine its role in world affairs. For the first time since 1946, this country is being forced by events to rethink the meaning of national security in a basic way. It is a time, like the end of the Second World War, for Americans to revive old dreams of a world at peace, stabilized not by military force and hostile alliances but by political, economic, and legal institutions that respond to the cry for democracy now heard around the world. Prudence, pragmatism, and caution are admirable watchwords for confronting a time of upheaval, but if there is no larger American vision of a new world order Americans will have little choice but to accommodate or to resist the visions of others. It may now be possible to transcend the politics of the past, and to marshal resources in new ways to face the very different sorts of security problems of the future. The United States has a major role to play in the great transformations that lie ahead, but a different role, surely, from the one it played two generations ago.

So far, however, this country, the prime architect of the postwar world, is moving slowly in response to the end of the Cold War, content to let the nations of Europe take the initiative. After the months of tumultuous change that have taken place in his first year in office, President Bush has adopted a rhetoric that has begun to acknowledge the waning of the Cold War, but the impact on United States policy is as yet far from clear. The President presents the astonishing events of recent weeks as a well-earned reward for maintaining "steady" Cold War policies all these years. He sounds as though the ideas, institutional arrangements, and spending priorities that won the long war needed only to be modified to serve equally well in a post-Cold War world. Such a response to the rush of unanticipated events could have been predicted. The United States, like all the other players, was unprepared for this moment. There are file drawers of contingency plans in the Pentagon for fighting all kinds of wars that can never be fought, but the White House clearly had no contingency plans for what to do in the face of Cold War victory. President Bush was curiously low-key in his first reactions to the dramatic developments in Germany last November, giving the impression that he didn't know quite what to do but was determined to do it prudently. The contours of the new world in the making are murky, and there are no maps. As the new decade begins, the Administration seems elated by its sense of Cold War victory, careful not to press its advantage in Eastern Europe too far, and anxious about venturing into the uncharted waters of the post-Cold War world.

The United States of the early postwar years, rich beyond measure and invulnerable to attack, entered the era of its supreme power with both euphoria and apprehension. The men around President Truman, though aware of the power of the United States and the weakness of the Soviet Union, wondered whether public opinion in the United States would support a permanent global mission or whether the economy could sustain it. Fears of a revived Depression were widespread. The choices then seemed clear, and stark. Stalin's despotism, secrecy, and cruelty gave credibility to "worst case" thinking. The fateful underestimation of Hitler in the nineteen-thirties made the most pessimistic assumptions about Stalin's expansionist plans seem nothing more than elementary good sense.

The atmosphere of fear generated by the atomic bomb and by the spread of Soviet influence in Europe served American leaders as a license—even an obligation—to organize the non-Communist world under American leadership and to prepare for nuclear war. The obvious course was to adapt the strategies that had been used against Hitler to defeat the next totalitarian threat. The United States stepped easily into Britain's role of leadership as the exhausted British Empire dropped its mantle, and within months the traditionally isolationist continental nation had become the world's first truly global power. In the world of 1945, ideology offered a clear benchmark for distinguishing friend from foe: on the creed of anti-Communism and the "lessons" of Munich, Pearl Harbor, and Hiroshima, a global strategy was built.

Of all the perquisites of office, the one that bureaucracies are most reluctant to give up is the world view on which their existence depends. Political rhetoric is more easily changed than the unstated assumptions on which national-security establishments operate. If, as John Maynard Keynes lamented, modern society is in the grip of defunct economists, it is equally in the thrall of early-twentieth-century geopoliticians. In the prism of geopolitics, the Soviet Union, however profound its reforms, remains a permanent enemy of the United States by virtue of its size, its history, its huge military potential, and, above all, its geographical position. All these factors give it the opportunity—which has never been realized—to dominate the heartland of Europe. The United States fought two world wars to prevent another aspiring power from achieving such a goal. Those who look at the world through the traditional geopolitical prism view with considerable apprehension the conversion of the Soviet Union from an enemy of West Germany into an economic collaborator.

It was thus hardly surprising that the initial policy review of the Bush Administration came up with a clarion call for "the status quo plus." But the pressure of events—Gorbachev's steady stream of intriguing offers and beguiling statements, the collapse of Communism in Eastern Europe, and the domestic pressures to cut the United States military budget—has impelled the Administration toward a complex and comprehensive negotiation with the Soviet Union over the direction of the arms race, the future of Europe, and the redefinition of United States–Soviet relations. Such negotiations, as Ronald Reagan discovered, have a momentum of their own, and without a clearly articulated set of goals the United States will find it hard to keep control of the process. The Soviet Union today is a far more tractable negotiating partner than it was in the late nineteen-forties, when the pillars of United States postwar foreign policy were implanted, but the United States no longer enjoys the overwhelming power it had then to convert other nations to the American view of reality. Some of President Bush's caution reflects an awareness that whatever new American vision is proclaimed will not be easily sold. . . .

By contrast, Gorbachev's grand strategy has become clearer. He is undertaking the risks of a thoroughgoing reconstruction of the Soviet system and a reshaping of the Soviet role in the world because nothing less will rescue the Soviet Union from decline and decay. Domestic reform requires a major shift in energy and resources. The recapitalization of the Soviet economy can be accomplished, he believes, only by a significantly greater integration of it into the world economy, and that cannot be achieved without radical changes in foreign policy. Contrary to the prevailing assumptions from Lenin to Chernenko, neither the ideological mission of spreading socialism nor the game of great-power politics is useful either for rebuilding Soviet society or for achieving national security. Neither is affordable. Almost seventy-five years after the Bolshevik Revolution, the Soviet people are impatient with making endless sacrifices for the class struggle, "internationalist duty," and the building of socialism in faraway places. "Now we have parity with the United States," goes a bitter remark currently making the rounds in Moscow, "and you can see the results in the shops." Gorbachev has spelled out a long-term vision of "common security" which is mostly borrowed from intellectuals and critics in the West. He articulates it with a knowledge and a passion unmatched by any other world leader. At the heart of Gorbachev's world view is the conviction that war in Europe is implausible, and permanent mobilization for such a war weakens the Soviet Union. Stalin seized Eastern Europe as a buffer zone, to keep any future European war from Soviet territory, but Gorbachev understands that trying to hold on to it by force would doom *perestroika* and preclude advantageous political and economic relations which the West. . . .

The contrast between the intellectual ferment of the new thinking in Moscow and the sober, cautious reshuffling of old thoughts in Washington over the past year is striking. The differences in approach reflect differences in outlook. The crisis of the Soviet system is too profound to ignore, and Gorbachev's *glasnost* has stimulated an astonishing process of self-examination and self-criticism. The United States, on the other hand, is in a relatively buoyant mood. Inflation is down. Employment is up. The stock market has been booming. It is widely believed in official circles that the spurt of military spending in the nineteen-eighties increased the respect of other nations for the United States, and despite the evidence that public opinion imposes sharp limits on the actual use of military power, the national-security establishment of the United States feels vindicated by events and shows no enthusiasm for making major reductions in force levels and expenditures.

The second major difference between the superpowers flows from the first. There is a great disparity in the importance each attaches to its relationship with the other. Both the United States and the Soviet Union, judged by their recent histories, their problems, and their rhetoric, are in decline, but, just as they were never equal in power or reach during the brief "American Century," their declines differ from each other sharply. The word "superpower" has always had a hyperbolic ring to it, as if large stockpiles of nuclear weapons could be translated into world hegemony. The history of the last forty-five years suggests that this was never the case—not even when the United States had a monopoly on nuclear weapons, for those were the years of Soviet expansion in Eastern Europe and maximum Soviet influence in Western Europe. As the weapons stockpiles of the superpowers mounted, both the United States and the Soviet Union lost much of the extraordinary power they had briefly wielded over their allies and clients. The phenomenal influence that the United States exerted all over the world in the early postwar years was due primarily to its undamaged economy, its reputation as a successful democracy, its brilliantly conceived foreign-assistance programs in Europe, its economic dynamism and political stability, and, most important, the unique circumstances of that historic moment. The United States was the *only* nation with a global vision and the economic and military means to bring it into being. The Soviet Union under Stalin had to content itself with the consolidation of its dominion over Eastern Europe.

Under Khrushchev, the Soviet Union sought recognition as a superpower through boasts, threats, and promises. It also discovered the Third World, which Stalin had largely dismissed, and the worldwide battles for decolonization and independence became the arena for United States–Soviet confrontations. Under Brezhnev, the Soviet Union asserted a "parity" built upon a large increase of nuclear missiles and an unprecedented investment in an oceangoing Navy. The Politburo tried to dramatize its new status by actively aiding struggling revolutionary movements around the world, fourteen of which came to power in the latter half of the nineteen-seventies.

A central feature of Gorbachev's "new thinking" is that the Soviet Union is not a "superpower," either in the sense that it can afford to install, buy, or prop up governments around the world or in the sense that it has the resources to maintain military and naval forces with a global reach. Numerous articles in Soviet journals and statements of Soviet diplomats and academics make the point that supporting regimes and revolutionary movements is expensive, that client governments not only drain resources needed in the domestic economy but contribute little to Soviet power or prestige. Gorbachev knows that he must alter the relationship with the United States if he is to break free of failed Cold War policies. Unless the United States cooperates, he cannot cut the military budget below a certain figure or stabilize a more heterogeneous and independent Eastern Europe—a state of affairs he has done much to encourage. Nor can he court the Federal Republic of Germany without creating dangerous tensions. Above all, the United States, as President Bush noted last May, holds the Soviet Union's ticket of admission to the "community of nations," symbolized by membership in the General Agreement on Tariffs and Trade (GATT), the World Bank, and the International Monetary Fund.

The leaders of the United States, on the other hand, see the Cold War with the Soviet Union, despite its risks and costs, as a success on many levels. For the West, the Cold War years have been a period of phenomenal growth, prosperity, and commanding power. The Cold War prism has served to simplify and explain world events, to set limits on undesired domestic social spending—especially in the nineteen-eighties—and to shift the domestic political consensus to the right. The preoccupation with the United States–Soviet relationship has provided the justification for investing in the arms race rather than in the solution of urgent global economic and ecological problems—the latter a course that involves hard decisions and prickly deal-ings with banks, industry, and foreign governments. Serious attention to the world-debt crisis has been little and late. During the nineteen-eighties, more dollars have been sucked from poor countries through interest payments and flights of capital than have flowed into them. Despite all the infusions by private investors, the International Monetary Fund, and the World Bank, and from various national aid programs, the world has been witnessing a Marshall Plan in reverse.

Other critical "north-south problems," relating to trade and develop-ment, were swept from the agenda in the Reagan years. The accumulating hazards to the earth's atmosphere which threaten the continuation of human life itself were given the barest fraction of White House attention, which was reserved for Soviet missile production and tank maneuvers. Even as aging military alliances have crumbled and economic competition has inten-sified, little has actually been done to restructure relationships within the industrial world or to address in a fundamental way either the transformation of United States–European relations or the worsening of United States–Japanese relations or the crisis of underdevelopment. Instead, progress is asserted in upbeat communiqués after largely inconclusive high-level meet-ings. The Soviet Union is showing a new interest in using the United Nations as an instrument of diplomacy, rather than just a propaganda forum, but the United States, after a decade and a half of U.N.-bashing, has yet to design a strategy for developing international organizations as practical ve-hicles of coöperation in a radically new world, where global institutions are indispensable. . . .

As old enemies are transformed, new enemies float into view. National-security bureaucrats, no less than generals, tend to prepare for the last war, and so it is not surprising that they view the post-Cold War world through the Cold War prism. Old assumptions, old war plans, and old force structures remain essentially undisturbed as politicians and strategists around the globe turn their attention to new threats. Welcome though the peaceful rhetoric emanating from so many world leaders may be, peace is not yet breaking out. . . .

Leading military officers argue that the major challenges to the armed forces of the United States in the coming century are revolutionary strife, random violence, nuclear terrorism, and drug-running—all of them primarily in the Third World, which has been the only actual theatre of combat over the last forty years. As the Cold War mold breaks, nations, tribes, and religious sects take up centuries-old battles once more, free at last to be full participants in their own histories. And as these newly emerging or re-emerging forces in world politics jockey for position, jump at new oppor-tunities, and rethink their security needs, the world as it is seen from Wash-ington and Moscow in some ways looks more dangerous: high-technology weaponry is being distributed at an ever faster pace as more and more nations seek to profit from the arms trade, and nuclear proliferation, an issue that has been largely ignored over the last twenty years, is now a reality. With the shadow of nuclear weapons hovering over the conflicts of the Middle East, the Indian subcontinent, and Southern Africa, the case for increasing deterrent forces, covert operations, and actual military intervention can be made to sound plausible in the absence of more sensible approaches. Military forces are being drawn into "the war on drugs," and "narco-terrorists" are replacing the Marxist variety. Both the United States and the Soviet Union are well aware that political struggles in faraway places can be contagious. The rise of Islamic consciousness in the Middle East has contributed to the unrest in the Muslim republics of the U.S.S.R. War and brutality in Indo-China, the regional war in Central America, and the deepening crisis in Mexico have triggered a huge migration, which has already transformed the demography of the United States and will have a steadily increasing impact on its politics and its culture.

In the nineteen-eighties, the United States stepped up its military intervention in the Third World. It introduced the concept of "low-intensity conflict"—a global approach to what war planners call "ambiguous" military activities in the Third World, which range from drug-running to revolutionary guerrilla wars. "Low-intensity conflict" is a curiously callous description of what is a most intense experience for those caught in the cross fire—fifty thousand of whom have been killed in Nicaragua over the last dozen years, and more than seventy thousand in El Salvador. "Ambiguous warfare has exposed a chink in our armor," Secretary of State George Shultz declared at the National Defense University in 1986. Low-intensity conflict borrows heavily from the counter-insurgency doctrines of the early Vietnam War era. Conflict is protracted. The hope is not quick victory but the avoidance of defeat through wars of attrition. Defeat means either that undesirable—usually leftist—guerrillas come to power or, if they are already in power, that they succeed in establishing a viable government. Low-intensity conflict is fought with political, economic, and cultural weapons as well as specially designed military technology.

In the plans developed by the Reagan Administration for fighting low-intensity conflicts, there were two critical new elements, and they have achieved certain successes. The first has been the "covert" but highly publicized support of insurgents against target governments designated "Marxist-Leninist." Thus, the supplying of Stinger missiles to the Mujahideen in Afghanistan raised the cost of Soviet intervention and helped persuade the Soviet Union to withdraw its troops. As the late C.I.A. director William Casey put it, "whereas in the nineteen-sixties and nineteen-seventies anti-western causes attracted recruits throughout the third world, this decade has emerged as the decade of freedom fighters resisting communist regimes."

The second innovation of the Reagan years was "public diplomacy"—greatly increased attention to the mobilization of domestic support for foreign intervention. The mobilization was carried out by using on the American people sophisticated propaganda techniques that had hitherto been reserved for foreign countries. United States public opinion continues to oppose a military operation of the size and duration needed to overthrow the government of Nicaragua, and no evidence has come to light that the Reagan Administration ever intended to undertake such an operation, for the opposition of the Joint Chiefs of Staff was implacable. But the American people acquiesced in a large-scale war of harassment, which continues to this day.

The end of the Cold War offers a unique moment for rethinking the meaning of national security in the light of two closely related historic developments. One is the growing global consciousness that nonmilitary concerns now affect the freedom, well-being, and physical safety of people more profoundly and more dramatically tha[n] any military development in any nation. The threat to human life posed by man's destruction of the environment far surpasses any threat posed by increases in the weapons stockpiles. For inner-city Americans and suburban families, the narcotics economy poses an immediate threat to physical security for which no adequate system of deterrence, let alone defense, exists. It is increasingly evident that this nation's future is more imperilled by its own improvident economic decisions, by its permissiveness with respect to environmental destruction, and by its neglect of health and education than by the warmaking power of any other nations.

The second development is the transformation of consciousness about war. Since the early years of the century, a long process of rethinking has been under way about the uses of military power to advance national political and economic interests. Gorbachev's "new thinking" is grounded in some of the obvious lessons of the twentieth century. The First World War nearly obliterated the distinction between victor and vanquished; Britain and France suffered such grievous casualties and economic costs that they could sustain neither their empires nor stable economies and robust democracies at home. The Second World War made it clear that high-technology "conventional warfare," however noble the cause, could not be repeated without reducing whole continents to rubble. It was immediately apparent that the atomic bomb was not a weapon in the strict sense, because it could be effectively used only by *not* using it. Today, there is a growing consensus that a large-scale nuclear war would destroy all that was to be defended. Even smaller wars produce few triumphs. The long, bitter war between Iran and Iraq exacted a heavy price from both societies and resulted in victory for neither. The United States, despite its huge investment in the military, has not had a clear-cut tactical victory since General Douglas MacArthur's triumphant landing at Inchon in the summer of 1950, during the Korean War, and, that victory notwithstanding, the war ended in stalemate. The pressures of public opinion now exact political costs on adventurous, desperate leaders, even in the Soviet Union. The anger and disillusionment of Soviet citizens over the Afghanistan invasion was a significant factor in Gorbachev's decision to end it. In the Reagan Administration, the Secretary of Defense, speaking for the uniformed military, proclaimed the "Weinberger Doctrine": the armed forces will not willingly fight wars that the political leaders cannot induce the American people to support. Since Americans quickly sour on wars, even when they are successful, the doctrine is a recognition that public opinion now sets real limits on United States military operations.

But, as the United States' Panama operation shows, war has not become obsolete. All that can be said is that the nature, the function, and the scope of war have radically changed. The only politically successful wars are limited operations, short in duration, against small and weak nations. Britain's war for the Falkland Islands and the United States invasion of Grenada are prime examples. Politicians are still tempted to use a splendid little war as a piece of political theatre, provided the risks appear minor. Whenever public frustration runs high about a challenge to public order and individual security, as in the case of terrorism or drug-running, there is a strong temptation to find a military solution. The involvement of the United States military in the "war on drugs" is increasing, even though there is no prospect of victory. . . .

The degree and kind of military power required to protect United States security in this world of new and decentralized threats is not easily measured. Such old benchmarks as the missile tally and the conventional-arms "balance" seem beside the point. Unlike old-fashioned strategies for fighting wars, the new strategies for deterring conflicts and challenges are seldom put to the test. Victory is easily proclaimed whenever the fearful contingencies in the war plans do not materialize. The irrelevance of the forces to most of the wars, violence, dissolutions of nations, and acts of terrorism that do occur is not a matter for discussion.

There are, to be sure, certain short-term economic and political interests to be served by the production of weapons and the maintenance of large military forces. As every nation becomes more and more integrated into the world economy and hence more dependent on exports, many feel increasing pressure to participate in the global arms trade to earn hard currency. The Soviet Union, for example, which was the world's largest supplier of arms in 1987, the most recent year for which figures are available, is reëxamining the *political* benefits of spreading high-technology arms around the planet, but the *economic* pressures to export weapons to finance needed imports of civilian technology are stronger than ever.

While some national-security thinkers triumphantly proclaim the impending death of Communism as America's supreme Cold War victory, a better case can be made that the real winners in this long struggle are the defeated enemies of the Second World War, Germany and Japan. Both contestants in the superpower arms race have been losers. After spending more than four trillion dollars on its global security system, the United States is much less secure and much less in command than it was in 1945. The most serious national-security problems facing the country are economic, and the source of the problems is capitalist nations, not the Communist world. Like the Soviet Union but unlike Japan and Germany, the United States has systematically sacrificed economic strength to the accumulation and projection of military power. In the process, the sinews of nationhood have become frayed. Neither the neglected education system of the United States nor the country's weakened industrial base can support the global role to which our national-security élites have aspired. However, Germany and Japan, thanks in large part to their catastrophic experience in the Second

World War, and the disarmament imposed upon them at its end, have built their recovery on economic power and subtle diplomacy rather than on military aspirations. Both now have impressive military establishments, more than capable of deterring any plausible military threat, but their growing influence in the world rests on an understanding of technological development, a skill in managing the character and pace of the integration of their economies into the world economy, and a discipline in husbanding resources for long-term investment which surpasses anything demonstrated in recent years by the United States.

Ironically, Japan and, to a lesser extent, the Federal Republic of Germany have become formidable economic competitors by willingly taking the path to which the early postwar leaders of the United States beckoned them. Both have denounced their militarist pasts and have become successful trading nations. The irony is a source of bitterness. The Japanese feel victimized when they catch glimpses of Japan-bashing in the United States. They are delivering a blunt message, in words that have lost some of the tact for which their nation is famous: "You made the rules. We did as you wished. What right do you have to be angry that we are beating you at your own game?" But people in the United States feel victimized as well. "We rebuilt your country," they say. "We fed you at the end of the war more generously than we did the surrounding peoples of Asia, whom you ravaged. For forty years we have defended you, and in the process of fighting in Korea and Indo-China in behalf of the free world to which we have admitted you, we made you rich." Japan was the staging area in both wars, and the huge inflow of dollars was an important contributor to the Japanese economic miracle. "We sacrificed our own economy to carry your defense burden, and you repaid us by closing your markets to us and by creating Japan, Inc., an ingenious capitalist mutation that turns the huge Japanese trading corporations into weapons of economic warfare."

The end of the Cold War greatly increases the risks of serious confrontation between the United States and its Pacific ally. The two nations are locked in a potentially dangerous embrace: each is now extremely dependent on the other. The United States market is crucial for Japan, and the United States finances its government deficit in significant part with Japanese capital. This sort of interdependence does not augur good relations. To resolve the growing economic confrontation requires major changes in cultural habits in both countries. The United States needs to husband resources for tomorrow, and Japan is under growing pressure to raise consumption levels today.

Both societies are beset by problems of national identity as each finds itself increasingly integrated into a world system that is new and in many ways mysterious. The very concept of nationhood is changing radically, and the confused response is nationalist nostalgia. The manifest revival of nationalism in both societies is evidenced in a variety of ways, but none is more disconcerting than the reappearance in Japan of militaristic textbooks that gloss over Japanese responsibility for the war in Asia. The United States has recently been caught up in flag hysteria, the trampling of cloth calling forth more passions than can be aroused by the trampling of lives.

United States–Japanese relations are at a turning point. The United States has overemphasized the military relationship with Japan and underestimated the seriousness of the economic and technological competition. Japan plays a critical role in United States plans for fighting a future war in the Pacific against the Soviet Union. For years, the United States has been urging Japan to shoulder more of the "burden" of defense, on the ground that it was unfair for Japan to use its "free ride" under the nuclear umbrella to surge ahead of the United States in the competition over exports and finance. The world awoke not so long ago to the realization that Japan, long famous in the West for producing junk, had become the master of advanced technology, and now the Japanese are handing the world another surprise: not only is Japan the third-largest military power in the world, as measured by military budget, but it has become evident in recent years that Japan's edge in such civilian technologies as semiconductors, data processing, and telecommunications has important military implications. Even as United States–Japanese economic friction has intensified over the past decade, the United States has grown more dependent on access to Japanese technology for military purposes. Former Secretary of Defense Harold Brown has predicted that Japanese achievements in high-temperature ceramics could be "the stepping stone to a Japanese lead in military aircraft engine design and development." In 1987, the Reagan Administration blocked the Japanese computer firm Fujitsu from acquiring Fairchild Semiconductor, a firm that produces both nuclear-missile components and superconductors, on the ground of national security.

The Japanese are in a position to be major players in the high-technology-arms trade. The only restraints are the vestiges of the political culture imposed upon the Japanese under General MacArthur's "peace constitution." For more than thirty years, American leaders have been pushing the Japanese to play a larger military role, and, with United States encouragement, the Japanese government has been chipping away at the spirit of the postwar constitution. Japan's impatience at not having a political role commensurate with its economic might appears to be increasing along with its historic feelings of vulnerability and isolation.

In the United States, verbal attacks on Japan make good politics. In Japan, America-bashing is at least as popular, especially after clips of United States congressmen taking sledgehammers to a Toshiba cassette player were relentlessly rerun on Japanese television. "While one can always find an American voice of reason to counter every act of Japan-bashing in Washington," the Washington correspondent for the Japan *Times* Ayako Doi writes, "it is hard to find a Japanese who would publicly counter America-bashing in Japan." The new focus on the United States–Japanese relationship is feeding hostility in both countries, because the problems underlying the relationship are not being adequately addressed. A prominent United States business leader, a Democrat of liberal persuasion, recently observed that the United States could not afford to take Gorbachev up on his offer to demilitarize the Pacific, because it would mean abandoning the region to the Japanese. Some public-opinion polls already show that popular sentiment in the United States is more concerned with the economic threat posed by Japan than with the military threat posed by the Soviet Union.

There is a danger that the United States and Japan will slip into a new sort of Cold War. The original Cold War was a global ideological and geopolitical contest with a powerful emotional appeal, but, for all the thundering rhetoric that has continued ever since, the great issues that gave rise to the Cold War were settled by the late nineteen-forties, and the de-facto division of Europe was accepted by both the United States and the Soviet Union. All during that period, despite two Asian wars and frightening moments like the Cuban missile crisis and the crises over Berlin, the Cold War was remote from the day-to-day experience of most Americans. The wars in Korea and Indo-China and the back-alley duels of the rival intelligence agencies were fought in the name of that great crusade, but the wars were unpopular in the United States and the duels were largely unknown. (Curiously, the high point of United States–Soviet relations before Gorbachev was 1974, when Soviet arms were pouring into Vietnam to assure the final defeat of the United States in Indo-China.) The bilateral disputes between the United States and the Soviet Union were trivial. The Cold War rested on the implicit premise that there were no life-or-death issues dividing the superpowers, and thus each could take its victories and defeats in stride. For the overwhelming majority of the American people, the Cold War was a spectator's contest that generated jobs and money but required little sacrifice. On the other hand, the economic, technological, and psychological issues dividing the United States and Japan and—depending on what happens in the next few years—dividing the United States and Europe, too, affect the fundamental development strategies of the advanced industrial nations. These disputes could well touch the populations of the contending nations more deeply than the Cold War did because settling them, or even managing them, might require painful domestic changes. The current drift in United States–Japanese relations is dangerous.

Despite these shadows, the possibilities for making hopeful changes in the international system are greater than they have been at any time since 1945. The Soviet Union under Gorbachev appears eager to call off the ideological Holy War. The common security concerns of all humanity, and not class struggle, are the moving force of history, the Soviet President says. . . .

The muting of the Holy War offers a historic opportunity for curbing the numbers and mitigating the destructiveness of wars in the Third World, which have so often been encouraged and supplied by both the United States and the Soviet Union. The primary rationale for the United States policy of engaging in counter-guerrilla warfare has been that the fall of governments to "Marxism-Leninism" strengthens the hand of the Soviet Union as a global power. It would be difficult to see how Nicaragua, a desperately poor country of under four million people, could otherwise pose a threat to the United States, however it organized its economy and whatever rhetoric it chose to adopt. The arguments for military interventions will now be harder to make, but this in itself does not mean that they will cease. There can be no real development in poor countries, however, until the superpowers stop using them as Cold War battlefields. Beleaguered landowners in Central America who face armed political movements for redistribution and social justice have a strong interest in keeping the Cold War going, for United States aid offers them their only chance of survival, but the real interest of the United States is to negotiate an end to the warfare that is reducing a neighboring region to a shambles.

The idea that human progress can be achieved by ideological warfare is a dangerous reactionary notion. Perhaps more than any other factor, the dogmatic faith that military power can be used to fight, defend, or establish ideas created the conditions under which nuclear war could actually happen. (It is difficult to explain the 1962 Cuban missile crisis in any other terms.) All over Latin America, political élites, having experimented with socialism, military dictatorship, and faltering efforts to reëstablish viable democracies, are deeply pessimistic about their societies' ever evolving into stable political communities under any of the old formulas. The realization that the nostrums of both the right and the left work badly leads, on the one hand, to extremist movements such as the Shining Path, in Peru, and, on the other, to a strong desire for compromise, pragmatism, and moderation. Of all the nations of the hemisphere, Cuba and the United States seem the most inextricably caught in the time warp of the Cold War.

It is ironic and disturbing that as the Soviet Union mutes the cries of ideological warfare and tries to come to terms with the failures of socialism, the United States finds itself in a complacent—even congratulatory—mood. (That the United States ever felt deeply threatened by revolutionary ideology and experiments in the Soviet Union and other underdeveloped countries reflected a failure of confidence rather than a realistic assessment of the competition.) There is in fact no ideological victory to celebrate. The revival of unfettered free enterprise in Great Britain and the United States seems to have run its course, and the pressures to deal with the wreckage of the new capitalist prosperity—the ravaging of the environment; the abuse, waste, and neglect of what we now call human resources, principally our children; the potentially explosive increase in inequality—will eventually force another swing of the pendulum in market economies. The influence and leadership of the United States are measured not by Soviet failure but by American success.

The Cold War was about many things, but, despite the extravagant claims on both sides, it was never "a clash of two systems." Both United States-style "capitalism" and Soviet-style "socialism" are the legacies of nineteenth-century dogmas, and both are in continuous, profound transformation. The differences between "capitalism" in Japan and "capitalism" in the United States are as significant as the similarities. For the past forty years, there has been only one "system" that has expanded throughout the world, not two. (The Soviet Union was unable to permanently impose its "system" even on Eastern Europe, despite military occupation.) That system is the product of a process of global integration which exerts unrelenting pressure on every country. The product of a series of mutations in early-twentieth-century capitalism, it is fuelled by profits and the accumulation of private property. But it borrows heavily from socialism—indeed, from one of its most discredited features, which is to say, highly centralized planning by anonymous bureaucrats. The bureaucrats are servants of global corporations and banks, which by convention we call "private," and of international financial institutions such as the World Bank and the International Monetary Fund, which we call "public." These planners operate largely beyond the reach of the electorate in any nation, and mostly out of the public view.

This system is not controlled by the United States, and indeed the United States finds its own options narrowed by an increasingly integrated world economy, over which it exercises less and less control. Everywhere on the planet, the same twin processes appear to be at work—rapid economic integration accompanied by accelerating social and political disintegration. For some farmers, workers, regions, and city blocks all around the world, there is unparalleled prosperity, and for many others there is crushing poverty. This growing disparity at every level—neighborhoods, cities, continents—is promoting the dissolution of political communities, and especially of nation-states.

These same processes of change—what the economist Joseph Schumpeter called "a gale of creative destruction"—are also at work in developed countries, including the United States, where the gap between rich and poor, between cities or regions with a future and those with memories of a once prosperous past, has widened dramatically in the nineteen-eighties. It was such wrenching effects of technological and economic change that gave rise to the political, economic, and spiritual impulses out of which socialism was born. Running nations by dictatorship, whether of the left or the right, offers no way out of poverty, but the yearning for a decent society in which people can build communities without gross exploitation, without worshipping money and defiling nature, and without creating walls between a few rich and many poor is as powerful a human impulse as it ever was. Nineteenth- and early-twentieth-century road maps to the good society, however, are not much help.

The highly publicized failures of socialism in underdeveloped countries and the extraordinary prosperity within the United States in recent years make the idea of an American *perestroika* seem preposterous. Yet the United States is squandering capital to maintain an ephemeral prosperity that is politically unstable, because it is based on increasing inequality. Consider the cumulative consequences of these conditions, which the United States finds itself facing: a unique dependence on foreign financing of its debt; the paucity of long-term investment in industrial production, the modernization of services, or public infrastructure; the lack of a coherent policy on technological development, which puts the country at a serious competitive disadvantage; a frenzied, "get rich quick" economy, in the grip of takeovers, leveraged buyouts, and other manifestations of what Keynes called the "casino" economy; the descent into poverty of almost a fifth of the nation's children; the growing disparity between cities and regions with rising prospects and the large areas of the nation that are being abandoned by both government and industry; and a seeming inability to reduce significantly a military establishment much of which is increasingly irrelevant to real security needs. Still used to thinking of ourselves as "the No. 1 nation," as President Lyndon Johnson did twenty-two years ago, the people of the United States have actually fallen behind the people in other leading industrial countries with respect to maternal health, literacy, infant mortality, drug dependence, and education. We are five per cent of the world's population, and it appears that we consume more than half the hard drugs on the global market. By these crucial measures, the security of the United States is eroding.

A truce in the ideological war between mythic systems may now make it possible to redirect energy from crusades and propaganda wars to the resolution of urgent problems. Instead of mindless attacks on "government"—the rhetoric of Thatcherism and Reaganism—it may now be possible to ask, What are the proper functions of the nation-state in the world waiting to be born, and how can they be performed most efficiently and humanely? Instead of celebrating "the market," it may now be possible to ask how it could be made to work better in the service of social goals, and what should be done when it does not work. Instead of talking about "incentives" as if they were a sort of miracle drug, we may be able to look at how incentives actually operate under our system, and to strengthen those that produce desirable results, and seek to change those that produce perverse results.

A global understanding of national security is now essential, for the United States is organically connected to societies across the planet which are in a position to export considerable misery to our shores. In the nineteen-nineties, the revenge of the poor, unintended though it may be, is likely to be far more devastating than either the fiery rhetoric of the guerrilla movements of the nineteen-sixties or the challenge of the abortive oil cartel of the nineteen-seventies. Communist regimes export refugees, but military dictatorship, poverty, and war in Central America have been responsible for many more immigrants into the United States, most of them unwelcome. The effects of the worldwide boom in the narcotics industry, the spread of ozone-depleting agriculture, and the public-health crises in distant, poor countries cannot be kept from American shores by military means or, it seems, by any other—except the building of stable economies and a more equitable social order within those societies.

During the decades of the Cold War, domestic political, economic, and technological decisions made by the United States have had such an impact on other countries that foreign leaders sometimes facetiously suggest that they should have a vote in United States elections. Now it is becoming clear that the choices of underdeveloped countries can have a profound impact on life in the United States. Brazil's decisions on the rain forest affect the air quality in Chicago. Public-health policies in Zaire may have been responsible for the most serious epidemic in the history of the United States. The real security problems are global in character, and the solutions are global.

The long joust we call the Cold War no longer serves the interest of either the United States or the Soviet Union. But both societies have organized themselves on the basis of the Cold War and remain heavily dependent on the mind-set and the structures of the Cold War—large military forces, espionage, secrecy, and military production. The institutions of the Cold War will survive the normalization of relations between the United States and the Soviet Union and will set limits on the process unless the transformation of domestic institutions in both countries becomes the central focus of the process. The great challenge of the next decades is to make the domestic institutions of nations reflect the political, economic, and ecological realities of the post-Cold War world.

✖ *F U R T H E R   R E A D I N G*

George W. Ball, *Error and Betrayal in Lebanon* (1984)
Richard J. Barnet, *The Alliance* (1983)
Seweryn Bialer and Michael Mandelbaum, eds., *Gorbachev's Russia and American Foreign Policy* (1988)
John A. Booth and Thomas W. Walker, *Understanding Central America* (1990)
Terry Boswell and Albert Bergesen, eds., *America's Changing Role in the World System* (1987)
David P. Calleo, *Beyond American Hegemony* (1987)
Noam Chomsky, *Towards a New Cold War* (1982)
Kenneth M. Coleman and George C. Herring, eds., *The Central American Crises* (1985)
Robert Dallek, *Ronald Reagan and the Politics of Symbolism* (1984)
Christopher C. Demuth, *The Reagan Doctrine and Beyond* (1988)
I. M. Destler et al., *Our Own Worst Enemy* (1984)
John Lewis Gaddis, *The Long Peace* (1987)
Raymond Garthoff, *Détente and Confrontation: American-Soviet Relations from Nixon to Reagan* (1985)
Alexander George et al., eds., *U.S.-Soviet Security Cooperation* (1988)
Marvin E. Gettleman et al., eds., *El Salvador: Central America in the New Cold War* (1981)
Robert Gilpin, *The Political Economy of International Relations* (1987)
Betty Glad, *Jimmy Carter* (1980)
Roy Gutman, *Banana Diplomacy* (1988)
Fred Halliday, *The Making of the Second Cold War* (1983, 1986)
Jerry F. Hough, *Russia and the West* (1988)
William Hyland, ed., *The Reagan Foreign Policy* (1987)
Michale T. Klare, *Beyond the "Vietnam Syndrome": U.S. Interventionism in the 1980s* (1981)
———and Peter Kornbluh, eds., *Low Intensity Warfare: Counterinsurgency, Proinsurgency, and Antiterrorism in the Eighties* (1988)
Jonathan Kwitny, *Endless Enemies* (1986)
Walter LaFeber, *Inevitable Revolutions: The United States in Central America* (1983)
Robert S. Leiken and Barry M. Rubin, eds., *The Central American Crisis Reader* (1987)

David McLellan, *Cyrus Vance* (1985)

Jeff McMahan, *Reagan and the World: Imperial Policy in the New Cold War* (1985)

Michael Mandelbaum, *Reagan and Gorbachev* (1987)

Walter R. Mead, *Mortal Splendor: The American Empire in Transition* (1987)

Morris H. Morley, *Crisis and Confrontation: Ronald Reagan's Foreign Policy* (1988)

Robert Nisbet, *The Present Age* (1987)

Joseph S. Nye, *Bound to Lead: The Changing Nature of American Power* (1990)

Thomas G. Paterson, *Meeting the Communist Threat: Truman to Reagan* (1988)

William B. Quandt, *Camp David: Peacemaking and Politics* (1986)

Barry M. Rubin, *Paved with Good Intentions: The American Experience and Iran* (1980)

Jerry W. Sanders, *Peddlers of Crisis: The Committee on the Present Danger and the Politics of Containment* (1983)

Lars Schoultz, *National Security and United States Policy Toward Latin America* (1987)

Gaddis Smith, *Morality, Reason, and Power: American Diplomacy in the Carter Years* (1986)

Strobe Talbot, *Deadly Gambits* (1984)

———, *Endgame: The Inside Story of SALT-II* (1979)

———, *The Master of the Game: Paul Nitze and the Nuclear Peace* (1988)

———, *The Russians and Reagan* (1984)

Thomas W. Walker, *Reagan Versus the Sandinistas: The Undeclared War on Nicaragua* (1987)

Thomas W. Wolfe, *The SALT Experience* (1979)

Bob Woodward, *Veil: The Secret Wars of the CIA, 1981–1987* (1987)